A Comprehensive Approach

Office XP

Core

Deborah Hinkle

Margaret Marple

Kathleen Stewart

Glencoe McGraw-Hill

New York, New York Columbus, Ohio Chicago, Illinois Peoria, Illinois Woodland Hills, California

This program has been prepared with the assistance of Gleason Group, Inc., Norwalk, CT.

Editorial Director: Pamela Ross

Developmental Editors: Pamela Ross, Thomas Cain, Michele Ruschhaupt, Betsy Stern Hill

Assistant Editor: Christopher Robinson

Copy Editors: Malinda McCain, Sharon Wilkey

Composition: PDS Associates; The Format Group LLC; Creative Ink, Inc.

Design: Leggitt Associates, Creative Ink, Inc.

Screens were captured using FullShot V6 For Windows from Inbit Incorporated, Mountain View, CA.

Glencoe/McGraw-Hill

A Division of The ***McGraw·Hill*** *Companies*

Office XP: A Comprehensive Approach, Core
Student Edition
ISBN 0-07-825299-7

1 2 3 4 5 6 7 8 9 10 003/003 06 05 04 03 02 01

Between the time that Web site information is gathered and published, it is not unusual for some sites to have closed. URLs will be updated in reprints when possible.

Visit the Professional Approach Series Web site www.cas.glencoe.com

Contents

UNIT 5

EXCEL

UNIT 1

ACCESS

APPROVED COURSEWARE

What does this logo mean?

It means this courseware has been approved by the Microsoft® Office User Specialist Program to be among the finest available for learning Office XP. It also means that upon completion of this courseware, you may be prepared to become a Microsoft Office User Specialist.

What is a Microsoft Office User Specialist?

A Microsoft Office User Specialist is an individual who has certified his or her skills in one or more of the Microsoft Office desktop applications of Microsoft Word, Microsoft Excel, Microsoft PowerPoint®, Microsoft Outlook® or Microsoft Access, or in Microsoft Project. The Microsoft Office User Specialist Program typically offers certification exams at the "Core" and "Expert" skill levels. * The Microsoft Office User Specialist Program is the only Microsoft approved program in the world for certifying proficiency in Microsoft Office desktop applications and Microsoft Project. This certification can be a valuable asset in any job search or career advancement.

More Information:

To learn more about becoming a Microsoft Office User Specialist, visit www.mous.net

To purchase a Microsoft Office User Specialist certification exam, visit www.DesktopIQ.com

To learn about other Microsoft Office User Specialist approved courseware from Glencoe/McGraw-Hill, visit www.cas.glencoe.com

* The availability of Microsoft Office User Specialist certification exams varies by application, application version and language. Visit www.mous.net for exam availability.

Preface

Office XP: Core is written to help you master Microsoft Office XP. The text takes you step-by-step through the basic Office features that you're likely to use in both your personal and business life.

Organization of the Text

The text includes four *sections*—Word, Excel, PowerPoint, and Access. Each section is divided into *units* and each unit is divided into *lessons*. Each lesson builds on previously learned procedures. This building block approach, together with the Case Study and the other features listed below, enable you to maximize the learning process.

Case Study

Learning about the features of Office is one thing, but applying what you learn is another. That's why a Case Study begins every section of the text. A Case Study offers the opportunity to learn Office in a realistic business context. The files in each section relate to the section's Case Study.

Features of the Text

- *Objectives* are listed for each lesson
- Required skills for the *Microsoft Office User Specialist (MOUS) Certification Program* are listed for each lesson
- The *estimated time* required to complete each lesson (up to the "Using Help") is stated
- Within a lesson, each *heading* corresponds to an objective
- Easy-to-follow *exercises* emphasize "learning by doing"
- *Key terms* are italicized and defined as they are encountered
- Extensive *graphics* display screen contents
- *Toolbar buttons* and *keyboard keys* are shown in the text when used
- *Large toolbar buttons in the margins* provide easy-to-see references
- Lessons contain important *Notes,* useful *Tips,* and helpful *Reviews*
- *Using Help* introduces you to a Help topic related to lesson content
- A *Lesson Summary* reviews the important concepts taught in the lesson.
- A *Command Summary* lists the commands learned in the lesson
- *Concepts Review* includes true/false, short answer, and critical thinking questions that focus on lesson content
- *Lesson Applications* ask you to apply your skills in a more challenging way
- *On Your Own exercises* let you apply your skills creatively.
- Appendices, Glossary, and Index

MOUS Certification Program

For a complete listing of the MOUS skills for Office XP Core (and a correlation to the lessons in the text), see Appendix E: "MOUS Certification."

Professional Approach Web Site

Check out the Professional Approach Web site at www.cas.glencoe. A helpful Task Reference List—handy for remembering how to perform many Office tasks—is available for downloading.

Conventions Used in the Text

This text uses a number of conventions to help you learn the program and save your work.

- Text to key appears either in **boldface** or as a separate figure.
- Filenames appear in **boldface**.
- Options that you choose from menus and dialog boxes appear in a font that is similar to the on-screen font; for example, "Choose Print from the File menu." (The underline means you can press Alt and key the letter to choose the option.) Some options that you choose from a task pane or Help window appear in blue text, as they appear on-screen; for example, "Click Font in the Reveal Formatting task pane."
- You're asked to save each file with your initials, followed by the exercise name. For example, an exercise may end with this instruction: "Save the document as ***[your initials]*5-12**."

Organizing Folders

To keep organized, it's a good idea to save your work for each section in a separate folder. (For example, save all your Word documents in a Word folder, all your Excel worksheets in an Excel folder, and so on.) Within the Word, Excel, and PowerPoint sections, the text instructs you to save your files by lesson (within each section's folder). Thus, you would save Word Lesson 4 files in a "Lesson 4" folder within your Word folder. You would save Excel Lesson 4 files in a "Lesson 4" folder within your Excel folder, and so on.

If You Are Unfamiliar with Windows

If you're unfamiliar with Windows, review *Appendix A: "Windows Tutorial"* before beginning Lesson 1. This tutorial provides a basic overview of the program and shows you how to use the mouse. You might also want to review *Appendix B: "File Management"* to get more comfortable with files and folders.

Screen Differences

As you practice each concept, illustrations of the screens help you follow the instructions. Don't worry if your screen is different from the illustration. These differences are due to variations in system and computer configurations.

Acknowledgments

We want to thank the many teachers and students who have provided us with guidance over the years. We would particularly like to thank the reviewers of this text: Kathleen Anderson, Empire College, Santa Rosa, CA; Kenneth Andrews, Computer Tech, Pittsburgh, PA; Nicholas Bock, College View Academy, Lincoln, NE; Mary Davey, Computer Learning Network, Camp Hill, PA; Eric Ecklund, Cambria Rowe Business College, Johnstown, PA; Cassandra Georgetti, International Academy of Design Technology, Fairmont, WV; Debi Griggs, Bellevue Community College, Bellevue, WA; Suzanne Kidwell, Mendocino College, Willits, CA; Mary Logan, Delgado Community College, New Orleans, LA; Susan Olson, Northwest Technical College, East Grand Forks, MN; Jeffrey Strunk, Tri-State Business Institute, Erie, PA; John Walker, Doña Ana Community College (New Mexico State University), NM; Melissa Wertz, Pittsburgh Technical Institute, Oakdale, PA; Jennifer Zbozny, ICM School of Business, Pittsburgh, PA.

Installation Requirements

You'll need Microsoft Office XP to work through this textbook. Office XP needs to be installed on the computer's hard drive (or on a network). Use the following checklist to evaluate installation requirements.

Hardware

- ☑ Pentium computer with between 32 MB and 72 MB of RAM depending on the version of Windows installed
- ☑ 3.5-inch high-density disk drive and CD-ROM drive
- ☑ 245 MB or more of hard disk space for a "Typical" Office installation
- ☑ Super VGA or higher-resolution video monitor
- ☑ Printer (laser or ink-jet recommended)
- ☑ Mouse
- ☑ *Optional:* Modem

Software

- ☑ Microsoft Office XP
- ☑ Windows 98 (or later) or Microsoft Windows NT 4.0 with Service Pack 6 installed
- ☑ *Optional:* Browser (and Internet Service Provider)

Installing New Features

Some Lessons take advantage of Office features that might require installation (features not installed during a "Typical" installation). The following tables list those features and explain how to install them.

Office Features to Install

LESSON	FEATURE	HOW TO INSTALL
Ppt 4	Text converter to import an outline from Word	1. Load the Microsoft Office XP Professional CD-ROM. 2. Double-click the Setup icon. 3. Choose Add or Remove Features and click Next. 4. Click the down arrow to the left of Office Shared Features and choose Run all from My Computer. 5. Click Update.
Appendix C	Speech Recognition	

Media Content to Install

LESSON	FEATURE	HOW TO INSTALL
Ppt 5	Additional picture bullets	1. Load the Microsoft Office XP Media Content CD-ROM. 2. Click the box to accept the term of the license agreement and click Next. 3. Click Install (choose Complete to install everything on the disk).
Word 11 Ppt 6	Additional clip art	
Ppt 11	Additional sound and movie clips	

Excel Prerequisites

Excel Lesson 7 (Objective 6) requires e-mail capability. Excel Lesson 9 (Objective 7) requires that Excel's Comment feature is turned on. Excel Lesson 9 (Objective 8) requires a browser and a discussion server.

PowerPoint Features to Install

LESSON	FEATURE	HOW TO INSTALL
Ppt 2	Additional wizards	1. Load the Microsoft Office XP Professional CD-ROM. 2. Double-click the Setup icon. 3. Choose Add or Remove Features and click Next. 4. Click the down arrow to the left of Microsoft PowerPoint for Windows and choose Run all from My Computer. 5. Click Update.
Ppt 3	Additional design templates	

Word Core

2002

Word Core

CASE STUDY

Duke City Gateway Travel Agency

2002

CASE STUDY

Duke City Gateway Travel Agency

There's more to learning a word processing program like Microsoft Word than simply pressing keys. You need to know how to use Word in a real-world situation. That's why all the lessons in this book relate to everyday business tasks.

As you work through the lessons, imagine yourself working as an intern for Duke City Gateway Travel, a fictional travel agency located in Albuquerque, New Mexico.

Duke City Gateway Travel

It was 1977. Jimmy Carter was president. The first "Star Wars" was showing in movie theaters. People were buying vinyl albums like the Eagle's "Hotel California." And, Duke City Travel began doing business.

Based in Albuquerque, New Mexico, Duke City Travel took its name from Albuquerque's nickname, "Duke City." (The city was named after the Duke of Alburquerque. The first "r" was dropped in the 1880's.) Originally, Duke City Travel was just a small one-person travel agency, but it was an immediate success and began to grow.

Within a few years the company joined with six other agencies from the United States, Canada, England, and France. They formed the "Gateway Travel Group." (See Figure CS-1 for these Gateway Travel "Flagship Offices.").

The goal of each of the agencies within the Gateway Travel Group is to offer "one-stop shopping" for travelers. However, every company can interpret this goal in its own way. Duke City Gateway Travel has chosen to create four "Specialty Areas." This has the added advantage of increasing the efficiency of the individual travel agents. The four Specialty Areas are:

- International Travel
- Corporate Travel
- Group Travel
- Family Travel

FIGURE CS-1
Gateway Travel Flagship Offices

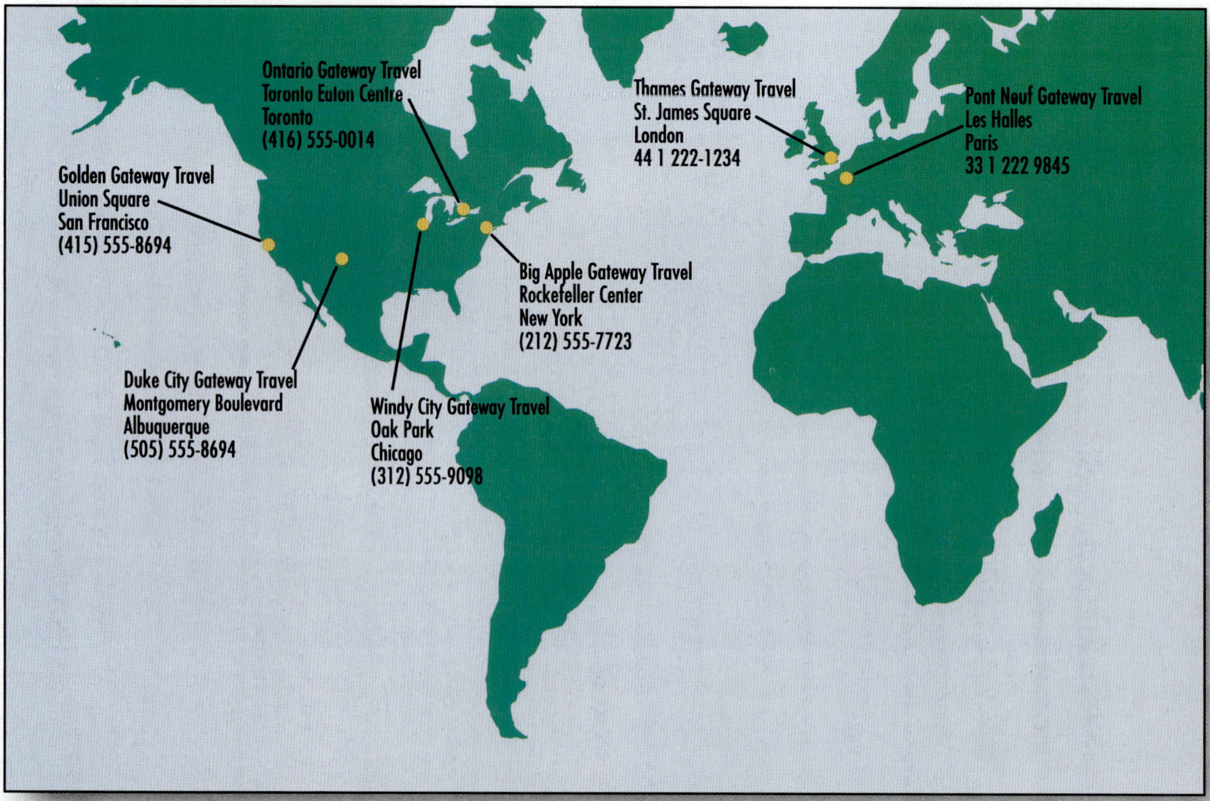

Currently, Duke City Gateway Travel has 12 employees, ranging from Susan Allen, the President/Owner, to Valerie Grier, the Office Manager. You can see a picture of each of the staff members on the next page. It might be helpful to associate the picture of the employee with their name as you work in the course. Also notice that Duke City Gateway Travel refers to travel agents as "Travel Counselors."

To understand the organization of Duke City Gateway Travel, take a look at Figure CS-2. Notice that each of the Specialty Areas is headed by a Senior Travel Counselor. A Travel Counselor or an Associate Travel Counselor works for each of the Senior Travel counselors.

All of the documents you will use in this text relate to Duke City Gateway Travel. As you work through the documents in the text, take the time to notice the following things:

- How the employees interact and how they respond to customers' queries.
- The format and tone of the business correspondence (if you are unfamiliar with the standard formats for business documents, refer to Appendix F).
- References to *The Gregg Reference Manual*, a standard reference manual for business writing and correspondence.
- The content of the correspondence (and its relation to Duke City Gateway's business).

As you use this text and become experienced with Microsoft Word, you will also gain experience in creating, editing, and formatting the sort of documents that are generated in a real-life business environment.

FIGURE CS-2
Organization Chart

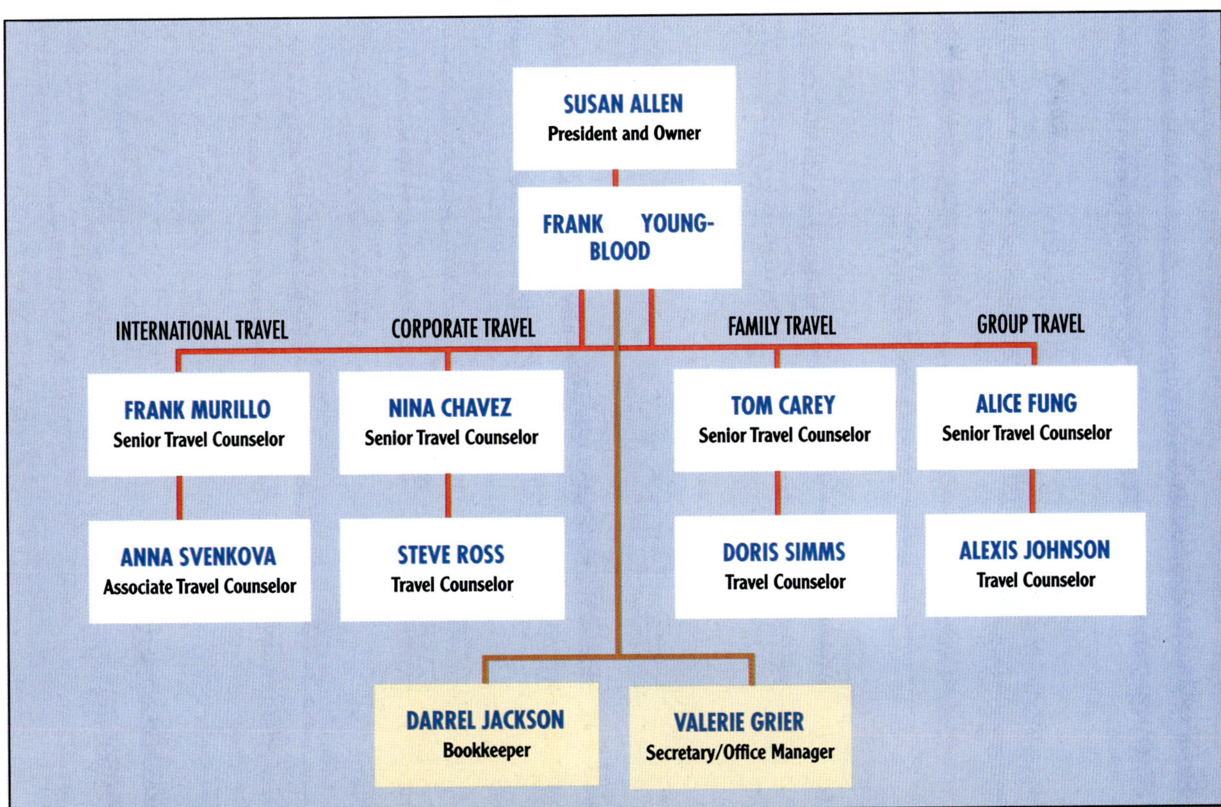

Duke City Gateway Travel

The Staff

SUSAN ALLEN
President and Owner

FRANK YOUNGBLOOD
Manager

FRANK MURILLO
Senior Travel Counselor, International Travel Specialist

NINA CHAVEZ
Senior Travel Counselor, Corporate Travel Specialist

TOM CAREY
Senior Travel Counselor, Family Travel Specialist

ALICE FUNG
Senior Travel Counselor, Group Travel Specialist

DORIS SIMMS
Travel Counselor

ALEXIS JOHNSON
Travel Counselor

STEVE ROSS
Travel Counselor

ANNA SVENKOVA
Associate Travel Counselor

DARREL JACKSON
Bookkeeper

VALERIE GRIER
Secretary/
Office Manager

UNIT 1

Basic Skills

LESSON

1

Creating a Document

OBJECTIVES

MOUS ACTIVITIES

In this lesson:

W2002 1-1
W2002 1-3
W2002 4-3

See Appendix E.

After completing this lesson, you will be able to:

1. Start Word.
2. Identify parts of the Word screen.
3. Key text into a document.
4. Perform basic text editing.
5. Name and save a document.
6. Print a document.
7. Close a document and exit Word.

Estimated Time: 1 hour

Microsoft Word is a versatile, easy-to-use word processing program that helps you create letters, memos, reports, and other types of documents. This lesson begins with an overview of the Word screen. Then you learn how to create, edit, name, save, print, and close a document.

Starting Word

There are several ways to start Word, depending on your system setup and personal preferences. For example, you can use the Start button on the Windows taskbar or double-click a Word shortcut icon that might be on your desktop.

NOTE: Windows provides many ways to start applications. If you have problems, ask your instructor for help. If you are unfamiliar with Windows, see Appendix A: "Windows Tutorial."

FIGURE 1-1
Starting Word from the Windows taskbar

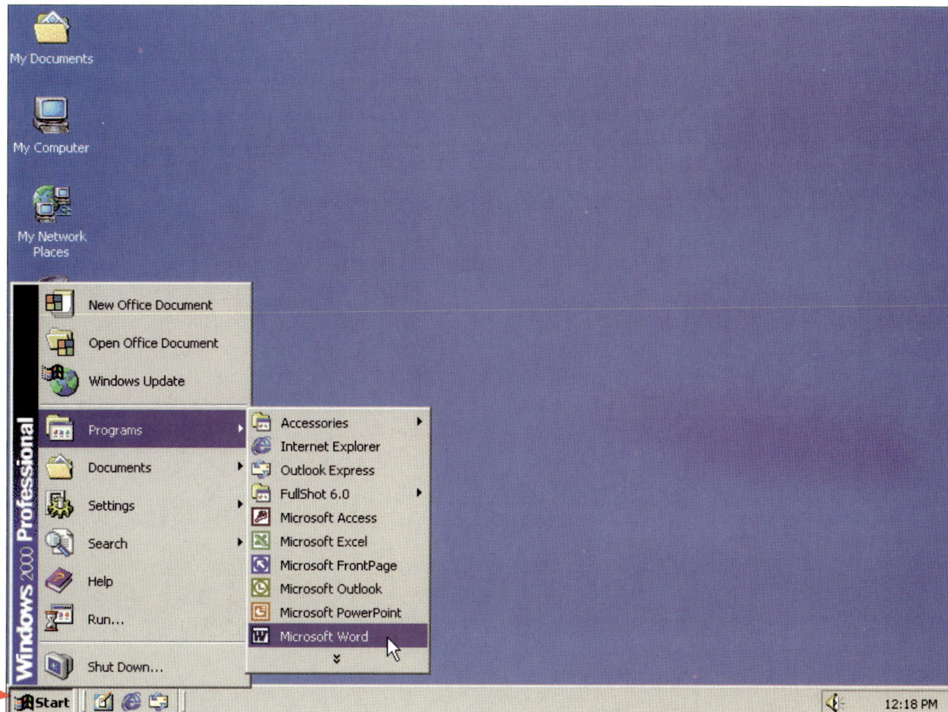

Start button

NOTE: Your screen will differ from the screen shown in Figure 1-1 depending on the programs installed on your computer.

EXERCISE 1-1 Start Word

1. Turn on your computer. Windows loads.
2. Click the Start button Start on the Windows taskbar and point to Programs.
3. On the Programs menu, click Microsoft Word. In a few seconds, the program is loaded and the Word screen appears. (See Figure 1-2 on the next page.)

NOTE: Make sure you are in Normal view. If you're not, click the Normal View button in the lower left corner of your screen.

FIGURE 1-2
Word screen

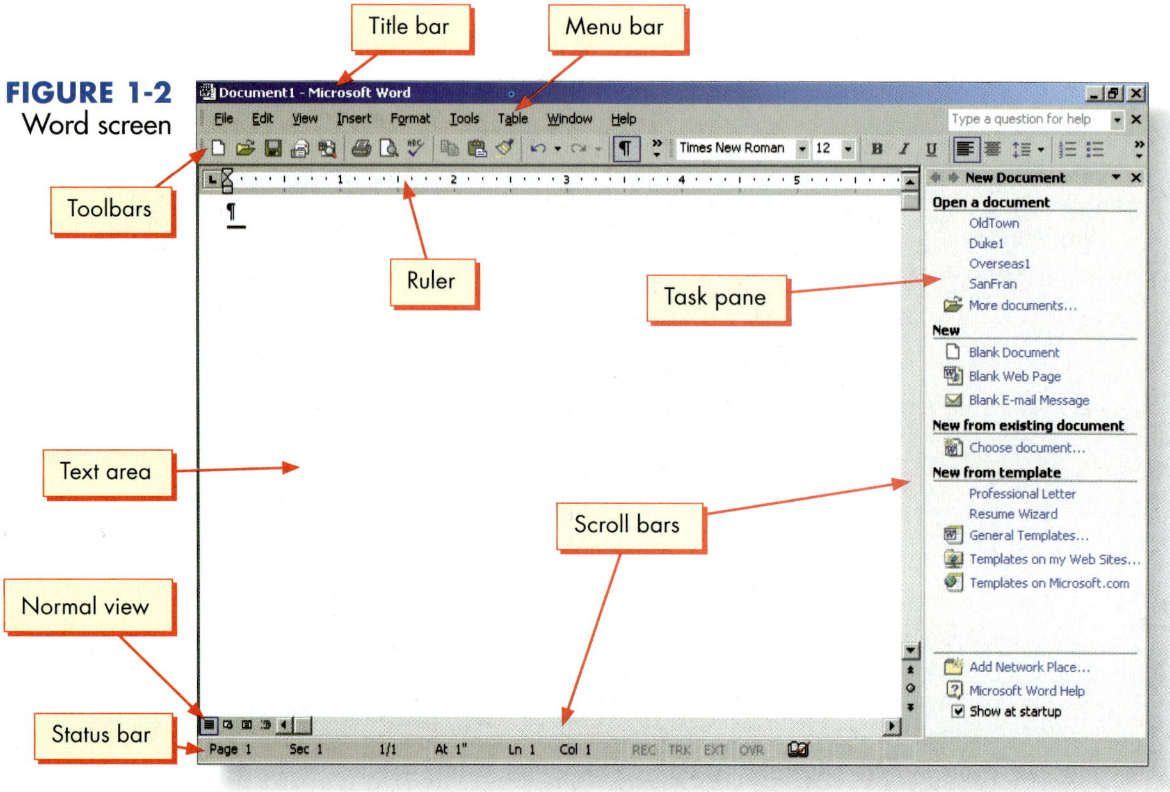

TABLE 1-1 Parts of the Word Screen

PART OF SCREEN	PURPOSE
Title bar	Displays the name of the current document. The opening Word screen is always named "Document1."
Menu bar	Contains the menus you use to perform various tasks. You can open menus by using the mouse or the keyboard.
Toolbars	Contain buttons you click to initiate a wide range of commands. Each button is represented by an icon. Word opens with the Standard and Formatting toolbars displayed in abbreviated form on one row.
Ruler	Shows placement of indents, margins, and tabs.
Text area	Displays the text and graphics in the document.
Scroll bars	Used with the mouse to move right or left and up or down within a document. To the left of the horizontal scroll bar are buttons to change the way you view a document.

continues

TABLE 1-1 Parts of the Word Screen *continued*

PART OF SCREEN	PURPOSE
Status bar	Displays information about the task you are performing, shows the position of the insertion point, and shows the current mode of operation.
New Document task pane	Displays options for opening recently used documents and creating new documents. This task pane appears when you start Word.

Identifying Parts of the Word Screen

To become familiar with Word, start by identifying the parts of the screen you'll work with extensively in this course, such as menus and toolbar buttons.

EXERCISE 1-2 Identify Menus and Menu Commands

Each of the items on the menu bar is the name of a menu that contains a list of commands.

1. Move the mouse pointer to Edit on the menu bar. Click the left mouse button to open the menu. Word displays a short version of the Edit menu with the most commonly used Edit menu commands.
2. With the Edit menu open, wait 5 seconds and Word displays the expanded Edit menu with additional commands. You can also click the arrows at the bottom of the short menu to expand the menu.

NOTE: Word's short menus are adaptive—they change as you work, listing the commands you use most frequently.

3. Without clicking the mouse button, move the pointer to View on the menu bar. Continue moving the pointer slowly across the menu bar until you display the Help menu.
4. Click Help on the menu bar to close the menu. You can also close a menu by clicking within the text area of the screen or by pressing Esc.

TIP: The menus show commands with corresponding toolbar buttons and keyboard shortcuts. For example, you can save a document by choosing Save from the File menu, by clicking the Save button on the Standard toolbar, or by pressing Ctrl+S.

5. Double-click View on the menu bar to open the View menu. Double-clicking a menu name opens the expanded menu.
6. Without clicking the mouse button, move the pointer to the Toolbars command. The right-pointing arrow indicates a submenu that shows which toolbars are currently displayed. The submenu also indicates whether the task pane is displayed.

FIGURE 1-3
Displaying menu options

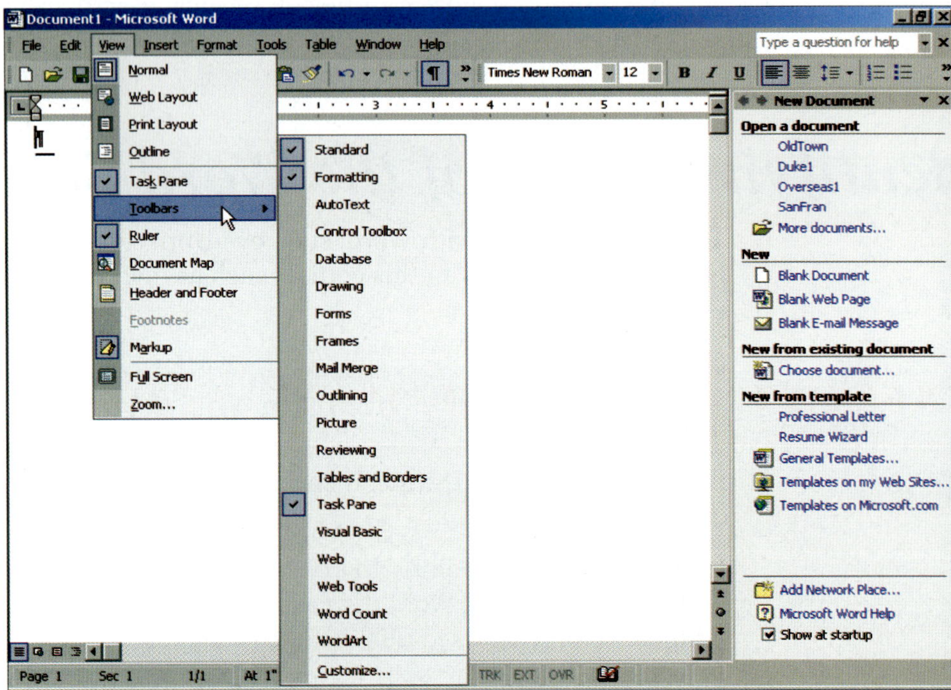

7. Make sure Task Pane is checked on the View menu (it will also appear on the Toolbars submenu).
8. Click outside the menu in a blank area of the screen to close the menu. Be careful not to click a menu option or toolbar button.

EXERCISE 1-3 Identify Buttons

When you start Word, the Standard and Formatting toolbars appear side by side below the menu bar. Only the basic buttons and those that were used most recently are displayed. To see more buttons for either toolbar, click the Toolbar Options button at the end of the toolbar. To identify a toolbar button or any other onscreen button by name, point to it with the mouse and Word will display a *ScreenTip*—a box with the button name.

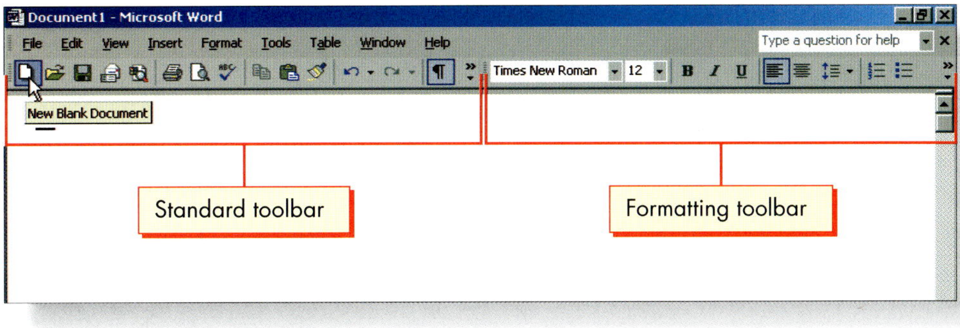

FIGURE 1-4
Identifying a toolbar button

1. Position the pointer over the New Blank Document icon on the Standard toolbar. The icon appears as a button when you point to it and a ScreenTip appears below the button with the button name. You click this button to start a new blank document.

2. Click the Toolbar Options button at the end of the Standard toolbar to see additional toolbar buttons. Move the mouse pointer over any button to identify it.

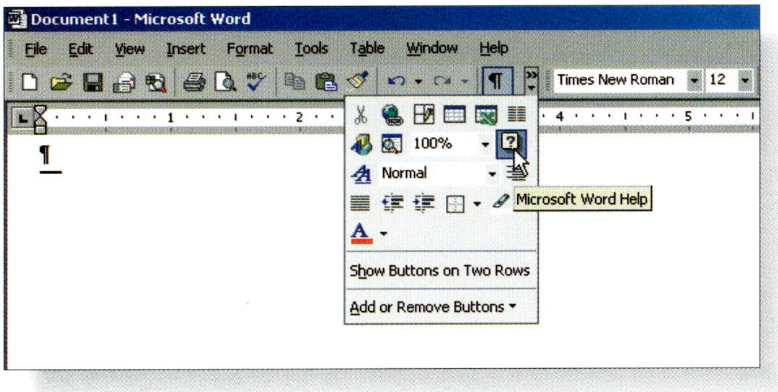

FIGURE 1-5
Displaying additional toolbar buttons

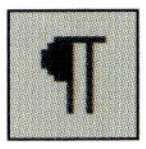

3. Click the Show/Hide ¶ button on the Standard toolbar. Click it again. Notice that when you click (or "press") a button, it appears outlined and shaded blue-gray. (If you had to click Toolbar Options to locate the Show/Hide ¶ button, notice that it now appears on your Standard toolbar.)

NOTE: Any toolbar button with a light gray icon is currently not available. However, you can still identify the button by pointing to it with the mouse.

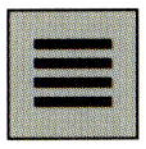

4. At the bottom left of the screen, point to the various buttons above the status bar. You use these buttons to choose various ways to view a document. Check that the Normal View button is selected.

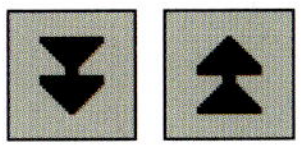

5. Point to the Next Page button at the bottom right of the screen. You use this button, along with the Previous Page button to scroll forward and backward in a document.

NOTE: You might notice the floating Language toolbar on your screen. This toolbar may be used for *speech recognition* if your computer is set up with a microphone. You can use speech recognition for menu commands, toolbar buttons, and text entry. For more information, see Appendix C.

EXERCISE 1-4 Identify Task Panes

The task pane is a screen area that makes many functions easier to access. You can display different task panes, depending on the task at hand, or hide the task pane to make more room for your document.

1. In the New Document task pane, point to the down arrow, which is the Other Task Panes button.

FIGURE 1-6
Task pane buttons

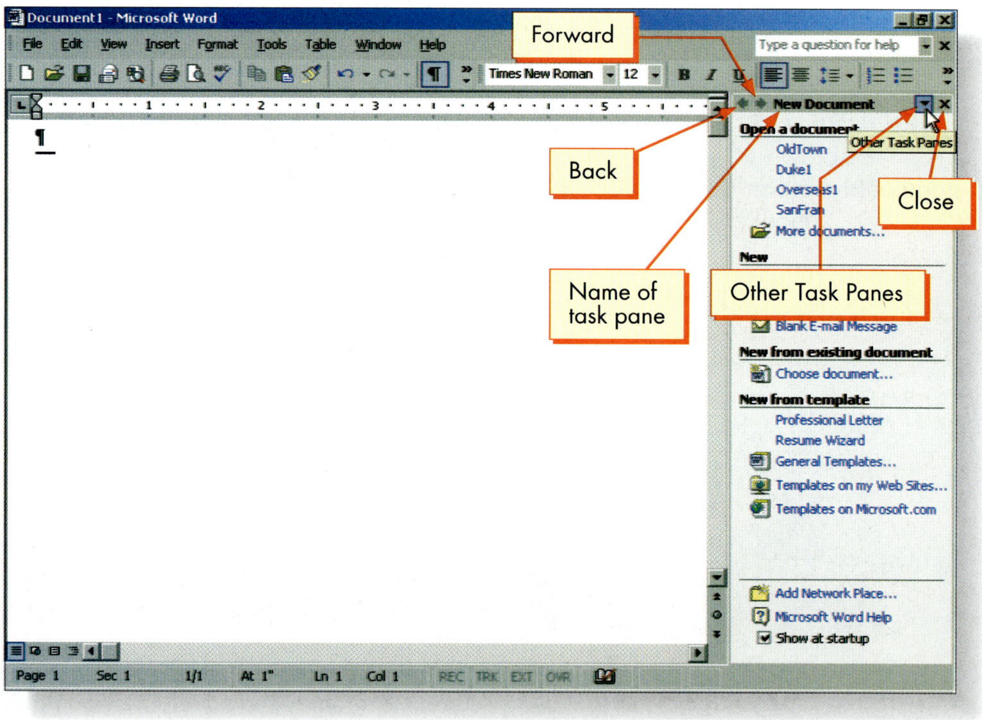

2. Click the button to display a list of the other available task panes; then open one of the other panes.

3. Click the Back button in the new task pane to return to the New Document task pane.

4. Click the Close button in the task pane to hide the pane.

NOTE: To redisplay the task pane, open the View menu and choose Task Pane. Task panes will have more meaning as you become more familiar with Word.

Keying Text

When keying text, you'll notice various shapes and symbols in the text area. For example:

- The *insertion point* is the vertical blinking line that marks the position of the next character to be entered.
- The *end mark* is a short horizontal line that moves as you key text and indicates the end of the document.
- The mouse pointer takes the shape of an *I-beam* when it's in the text area. It changes to an arrow when you point to a toolbar button or menu outside the text area.
- The *paragraph mark* ¶ marks the end of a paragraph.

EXERCISE 1-5 Key Text and Move the Insertion Point

1. Before you begin, make sure the Show/Hide ¶ button on the Standard toolbar is selected. When this feature is "turned on," you can see paragraph marks and spacing between words and sentences more easily.
2. Key the words **Duke City Gateway** (don't worry about keying mistakes now—you can correct them later). Notice how the insertion point and paragraph mark move as you key text. Notice also how a space between words is indicated by a dot.

FIGURE 1-7
The insertion point marks the place where you begin keying.

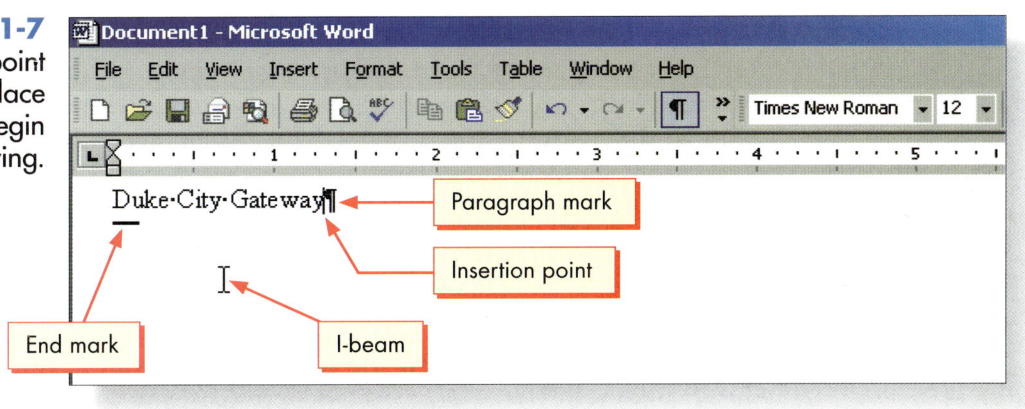

3. Move the insertion point to the left of the word "Duke" by positioning the I-beam and clicking the left mouse button.

4. Move the insertion point back to the right of "Gateway" to continue keying.

NOTE: The documents you create in this course relate to the Case Study about Duke City Gateway Travel, a fictional travel agency (see pages 3 through 6).

EXERCISE 1-6 Wrap Text and Correct Spelling

As you key more text, you'll notice Word performs several tasks automatically. For example, Word does the following by default:

- Wraps text from the end of one line to the beginning of the next line
- Alerts you to spelling and grammatical errors
- Corrects common misspellings, such as "teh" for "the" and "adn" for "and"
- Suggests the completed word when you key the current date, day, or month

NOTE: Word's ability to correct spelling and grammar and to complete words for you is discussed thoroughly in Lesson 4: "Writing Tools."

1. Continue the sentence you started in Exercise 1-5, this time keying a misspelled word. Press Spacebar and then key **is New Mexico's leeding travel agency** (don't key a period). Word recognizes that "leeding" is misspelled and applies a red, wavy underline to the word.

TIP: The Spelling and Grammar Status icon at the right side of the status bar displays an "x" instead of a check mark when it detects an error.

2. To correct the misspelling, use the mouse to position the I-beam anywhere in the underlined word and click the *right* mouse button. A shortcut menu appears with suggested spellings. Click "leading" with the *left* mouse button and Word makes the correction. Notice the change in the Spelling and Grammar Status icon on the status bar. (See Figure 1-8 on the next page.)
3. Move the insertion point to the right of "agency" and press Spacebar. Continue the sentence with another misspelled word by keying **adn** and press Spacebar. Notice that "adn" is automatically corrected to "and" when you press Spacebar.
4. Complete the sentence by keying **is located in Albuquerque on Montgomery Boulevard.** Notice how the text automatically wraps from the end of the line to the beginning of the next line. (If you spell "Albuquerque" incorrectly, right-click it and apply the correct spelling.)

FIGURE 1-8
Choose the correct spelling from the shortcut menu.

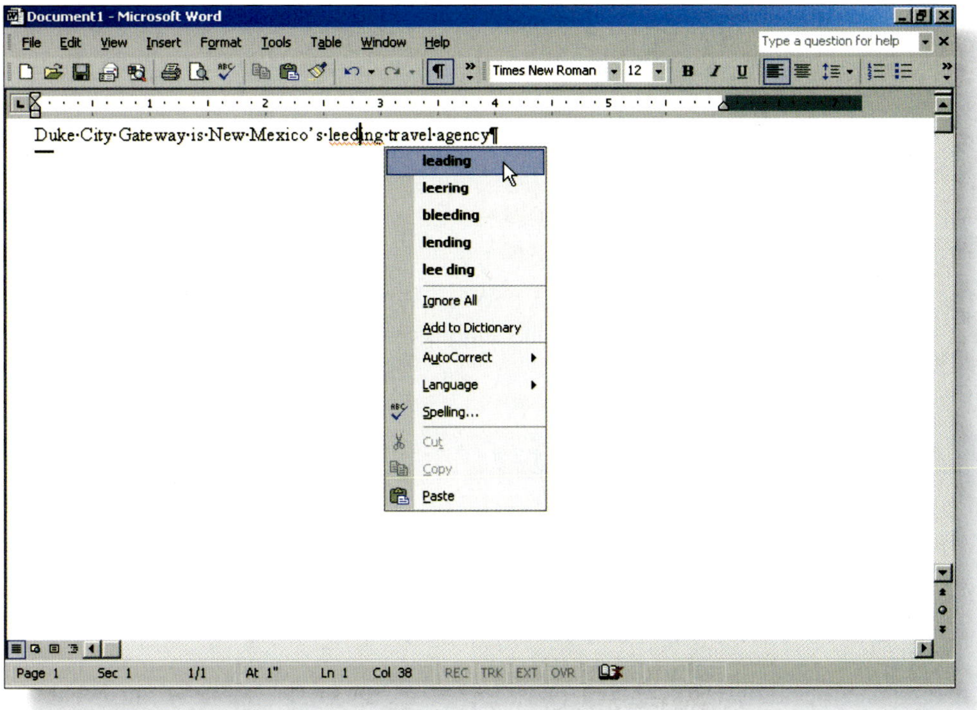

NOTE: The text "Montgomery Boulevard" may appear with a purple, dotted underline. This is called a smart tag, which Word applies to data such as dates and addresses.

5. Press Spacebar once and key the following text:

   It is a franchise division of Gateway Travel, an international travel agency with 49 offices throughout the United States, Canada, and Europe.

NOTE: Throughout this text, one space is used after a period to separate sentences. This is the standard format for word processing and desktop publishing.

6. Press Enter once to start a new line. Press Enter again to leave a blank line between paragraphs.
7. Key the second paragraph shown in Figure 1-9 (on the next page). When you key the first four letters of "Monday" in the first sentence, Word suggests the completed word in a small box. Press Enter to insert the suggested word, and then press Spacebar before you key the next word. Follow the same procedure for "Saturday."

WORD

FIGURE 1-9

```
For more information about Duke City Gateway, stop by our office Monday
through Saturday, or visit our Web site anytime. Our travel counselors will
be happy to help you plan your next trip.
```

NOTE: When Word suggests a completed word as you key text, you can ignore the suggested word and continue keying or insert it by pressing Enter.

Basic Text Editing

The keyboard offers many options for basic text editing. For example, you can press Backspace to delete a single character or Ctrl + Delete to delete an entire word.

TABLE 1-2 Basic Text Editing

KEY	RESULT
Backspace	Deletes characters to the left of the insertion point.
Ctrl + Backspace	Deletes the word to the left of the insertion point.
Delete	Deletes characters to the right of the insertion point.
Ctrl + Delete	Deletes the word to the right of the insertion point.

EXERCISE 1-7 Delete Text

1. Move the insertion point to the right of the word "It" in the second sentence of the first paragraph. (Use the mouse to position the I-beam and click the left mouse button.)
2. Press Backspace twice to delete both characters and key **Duke City Gateway**
3. In the same sentence, move the insertion point to the left of the number "49."
4. Press Delete twice and key **50**
5. Move the insertion point to the left of the word "information" in the second paragraph.
6. Hold down Ctrl and press Backspace. The word "more" is deleted.

NOTE: When keyboard combinations (such as Ctrl+Backspace) are shown in this text, hold down the first key as you press the second key. Release the second key and then release the first key. An example of the entire sequence is: Hold down Ctrl, press Backspace, release Backspace, release Ctrl. With practice, this sequence becomes easy.

7. Move the insertion point to the right of "Albuquerque" in the first sentence of the first paragraph.
8. Hold down Ctrl and press Delete to delete the word "on." Press Ctrl+Delete two more times to delete the words "Montgomery Boulevard."

EXERCISE 1-8 Insert Text

When editing a document, you can insert text or key over existing text. When you insert text, Word is in regular *Insert mode*. To key over existing text, you switch to *Overtype mode*. Double-click the status bar indicator OVR to turn Overtype mode on and off, or press Insert on the keyboard.

1. In the first sentence of the first paragraph, move the insertion point to the left of the "A" in "Albuquerque." Key **downtown** and press Spacebar once to leave a space between the two words.
2. Move the insertion point to the beginning of the document, to the left of "Duke."
3. Point to OVR on the status bar and double-click. You know you're in Overtype mode when OVR appears in black. (You're in regular Insert mode when OVR is dimmed.)
4. Press CapsLock. When you key text in Caps Lock mode, the keyed text appears in all uppercase letters.

TIP: Most keyboards have a light indicator to show when Caps Lock is turned on.

5. Key **duke city gateway** over the old text. Repeat the process for "Duke City Gateway" in the second sentence.
6. Press CapsLock to turn off Caps Lock mode. Double-click OVR (or press Insert) to turn off Overtype mode. (See Figure 1-10 on the next page.)

TIP: Always remember to turn off Overtype mode as soon as you are done editing to avoid accidentally keying over text.

FIGURE 1-10
Edited document

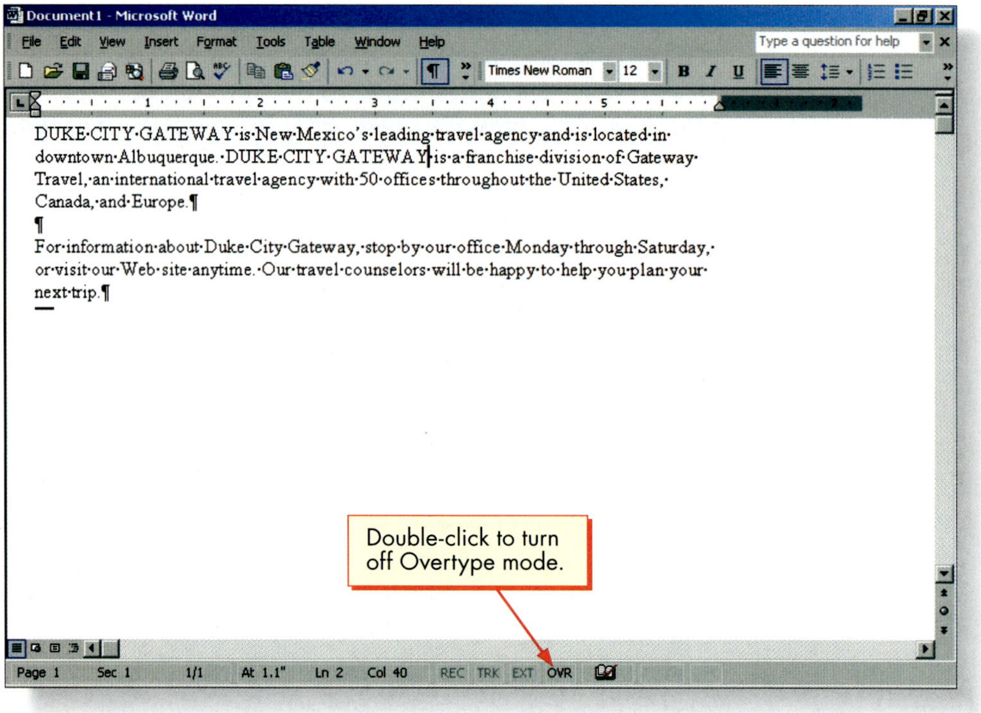

EXERCISE 1-9 Combine and Split Paragraphs

1. At the end of the first paragraph, position the insertion point to the left of the paragraph mark (after the period following "Europe").
2. Press Delete twice—once to delete the end-of-paragraph mark and once to delete the blank line between paragraphs. The two paragraphs are now combined, or merged, into one.
3. Press Spacebar once to insert a space between the sentences.
4. With the insertion point to the left of "For" in the combined paragraph, press Enter twice to split the paragraphs again.

Naming and Saving a Document

Your document, called "Document1," is stored in your computer's temporary memory. Until you name it and save it to disk, it can be lost if you have a power failure or computer hardware problem. It's always a good idea to save your work frequently.

The first step in saving a document for future use is to give it a *filename*. Here are some rules about naming documents:

- Filenames can be up to 255 characters long, including the drive letter and the folder name. The following characters cannot be used in a filename: **/ \ > < * ? " : ;**
- Filenames can include uppercase letters, lowercase letters, or a combination of both. They can also include spaces. For example, a file can be named "Business Plan."
- Throughout this course, document filenames will consist of ***[your initials]*** (which might be your initials or the identifier your instructor asks you to use, such as **rst**), followed by the number of the exercise, such as **4-1**. The filename would therefore be **rst4-1**.

You can use either the Save command or the Save As command to save a document. Here are some guidelines about saving documents:

- Use Save As when you name and save a document the first time.
- Use Save As when you save an existing document under a new name. Save As creates an entirely new file and leaves the original document unchanged.
- Use Save to update an existing document.
- Before you save a new document, decide where you want to save it. Word saves documents in the current drive and folder unless you specify otherwise. For example, to save a document to a floppy disk, you need to change the drive to A: or B:, whichever is appropriate for your computer.

NOTE: Your instructor will advise you on the proper drive and folder to use for this course. For more information about working with document files in Windows, see Appendix B: "File Management."

EXERCISE 1-10 Name and Save a Document

1. Click File to open the File menu and choose Save As. The Save As dialog box appears.
2. In the File name text box, a suggested filename is highlighted. Replace this filename by keying ***[your initials]*****1-10**.
3. At the top of the dialog box, click the down arrow in the Save in box and choose the appropriate drive for your data disk (3 1/2 Floppy (A:), for example). Make sure you have a formatted disk in the drive. (See Figure 1-11 on the next page.)
4. Click Save. Your document is named and saved for future use.

FIGURE 1-11
Save As dialog box

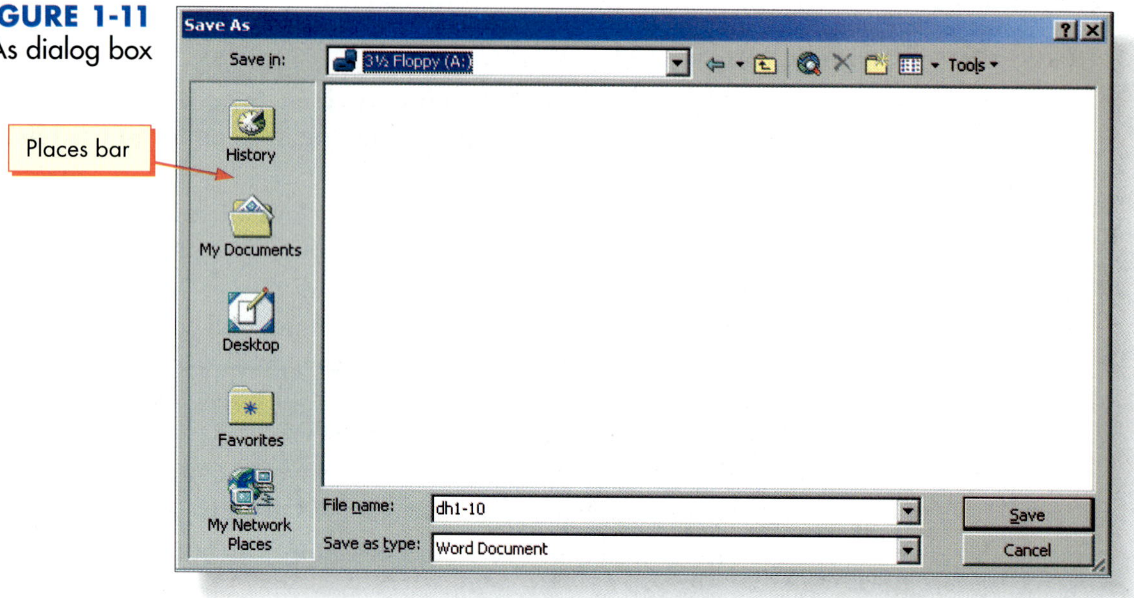

NOTE: If you were working at home and saving files to your computer's hard drive, you might use the *Places bar* on the left side of the Save As dialog box. For example, "My Documents" is a folder created by Windows to help you organize your files. Click "History" to list the most recently opened files and folders. Use "Desktop" to save a file on your desktop for easy access. "Favorites" contains shortcuts to files or folders you add to this category for easy access.

Printing a Document

After you create a document, printing it is easy. You can use any of the following methods:

- Click the Print button on the Standard toolbar.
- Choose Print from the File menu.
- Press Ctrl+P.

The menu and keyboard methods open the Print dialog box, where you can select printing options. Clicking the Print button sends the document directly to the printer, using Word's default settings.

NOTE: If you share a printer with your classmates, your instructor might ask you to key your name on all documents before printing.

EXERCISE 1-11 Print a Document

1. Choose Print from the File menu to open the Print dialog box. The dialog box displays Word's default settings and shows your designated printer.

FIGURE 1-12
Print dialog box

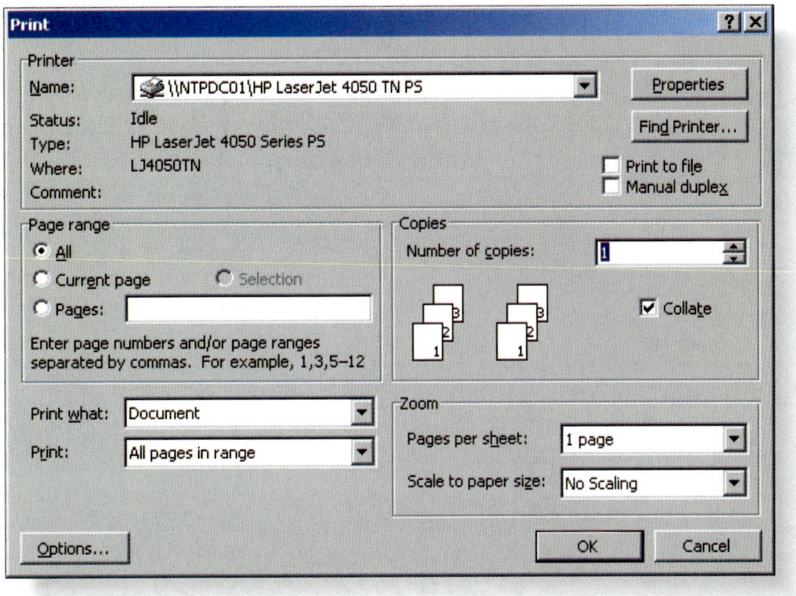

2. Click OK or press Enter to accept the settings. A printer icon appears on the taskbar as the document is sent to the printer.

Closing a Document and Exiting Word

When you finish working on a document and save it, you can close it and open another document or you can exit Word.

The easiest ways to close a document and exit Word include using:

- The Close buttons ☒ in the upper right corner of the window

FIGURE 1-13
Close buttons

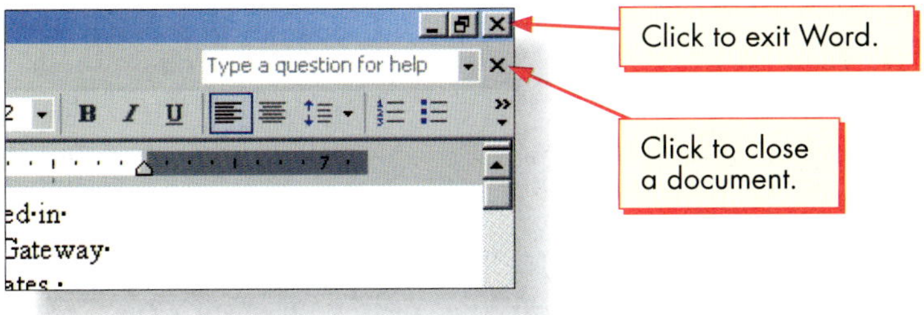

- The Close command from the File menu
- Keyboard shortcuts: Ctrl+W closes a document and Alt+F4 exits Word

EXERCISE 1-12 Close a Document and Exit Word

1. Choose Close from the File menu to close the document.

NOTE: When no document is open, the document window is gray. If you want to start a new document, click the New Blank Document button.

2. Click the Close button in the upper right corner of the screen to exit Word and display the Windows desktop.

USING HELP

On-line Help is available to you as you work in Word. Just type a question in the Ask a Question box at the top right of the screen and you'll access Word's Help system.

Find out more about using Help:

1. Start Word.

2. Locate the Ask a Question box in the upper right corner of the screen. Click the box to activate it; then key **get help**

3. Press Enter. A list of Help topics appears. Click See more at the bottom of the list to see additional topics. Notice the mouse pointer is shaped like a hand.

FIGURE 1-14
Using the Ask a Question box

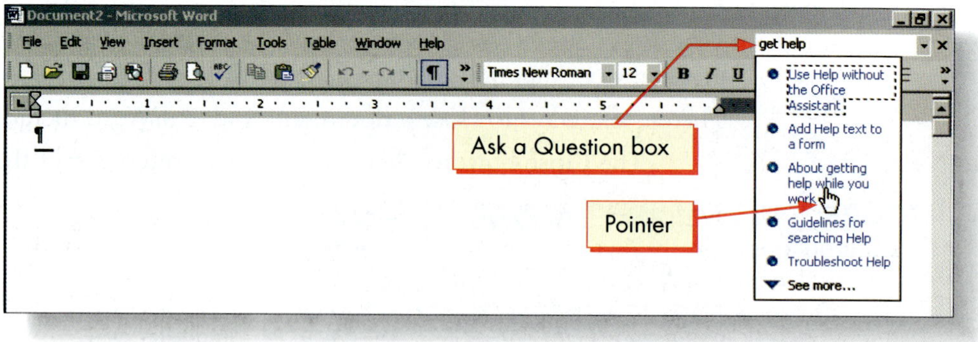

4. Click See previous to return to the first group of topics.

5. Click the topic About getting help while you work. The Help dialog box opens.

6. Click each of the topics listed in blue text (or click Show All in the upper right corner of the Help screen). Review the information.
7. Close Help by clicking the Help window's Close button.

LESSON 1 Summary

- To start Microsoft Word, click the Start button on the Windows taskbar, point to Programs, and click Microsoft Word.
- The title bar is at the top of the Word screen and displays the current document name.
- The menu bar appears below the title bar. Each menu name, when clicked, displays a list of commands to perform various tasks.
- To open a menu, point to the menu name and click. To display all options on a menu, click the arrows at the bottom of the menu.
- The Standard and Formatting toolbars appear below the menu bar. The toolbars contain buttons you click to initiate commands. Each button is represented by an icon.
- Identify a button by name by pointing to it with the mouse. Word displays a ScreenTip with the button name. Display hidden buttons by clicking the Toolbar Options button at the end of either the Standard or Formatting toolbar.
- The ruler appears below the Standard and Formatting toolbars.
- Scroll bars appear as gray shaded bars to the right and bottom of the text area. They are used to view different portions of a document. The buttons to the left of the horizontal scroll bar are used to change the way you view a document.
- The status bar is a gray bar below the horizontal scroll bar. It displays such information as the current position of the insertion point and whether certain modes are active.
- The New Document task pane appears when you start Word. It displays options for recently used documents and for creating new documents.
- To close the task pane, click its Close button. To display the task pane, choose Task Pane from the View menu.
- The blinking vertical line is called the insertion point. It marks the position of the next character to be entered. The end mark is a short horizontal line that moves as you key text and indicates the end of the document.

- The mouse pointer displays on the screen as an I-beam when it's in the text area and as an arrow when you point to a toolbar button or menu outside the text area.
- When the Show/Hide ¶ button ¶ is turned on, a paragraph mark symbol appears at the end of every paragraph.
- If your computer is appropriately equipped, speech recognition is available for menu commands, toolbar buttons, and text entry.
- Word automatically wraps text to the next line as you key text. Press Enter to start a new paragraph or to insert a blank line.
- Word flags spelling errors as you key text by inserting a red, wavy line under the misspelled word. To correct the spelling, point to the underlined word, click the right mouse button, and choose the correct spelling.
- Word automatically corrects commonly misspelled words for you as you key text. Word can automatically complete a word for you, such as the name of a month or day—Word suggests the completed word and you press Enter to insert it.
- Delete a single character by using Backspace or Delete. Ctrl+Backspace deletes the word to the left of the insertion point. Ctrl+Delete deletes the word to the right of the insertion point.
- To insert text, click to position the insertion point and key the text.
- To enter text over existing text, turn on Overtype mode by double-clicking OVR on the status bar or pressing Insert on the keyboard.
- Insert one space between words and between sentences.
- Document names, or filenames, can contain 255 characters, including the drive letter and folder name, and can contain spaces. The following characters cannot be used in a filename: / \ > < * ? " : ;
- Save a new document by using the Save As command and giving the document a filename. Use the Save command to update an existing document.
- To start a new blank document, click the New Blank Document button on the Standard toolbar or in the New Document task pane.
- To use Word Help, key a question or subject in the Ask a Question box, press Enter, and then choose a topic.

LESSON 1 Command Summary

FEATURE	BUTTON	MENU	KEYBOARD	SPEECH?
Save As		File, Save As	F12	✓
Print		File, Print	Ctrl + P	✓
Close a document	 (Menu bar)	File, Close	Ctrl + W or Ctrl + F4	✓
Exit Word	 (Title bar)	File, Exit	Alt + F4	✓

NOTE: Word provides many ways to accomplish a particular task. As you become more familiar with Word, you'll find the methods you prefer.

Concepts Review

TRUE/FALSE QUESTIONS

Each of the following statements is either true or false. Indicate your choice by circling T or F.

T F *1.* You can use the Standard toolbar to start or exit Word.

T F *2.* You can double-click OVR on the status bar to turn Overtype mode on or off.

T F *3.* You can click on the Standard toolbar to see more buttons.

T F *4.* The mouse pointer takes the shape of an arrow when it appears in the menu bar.

T F *5.* A red, wavy line appears under words that are misspelled.

T F *6.* Pressing Delete deletes characters to the left of the insertion point.

T F *7.* Ctrl+Delete deletes the word to the right of the insertion point.

T F *8.* You can save a document by choosing Save from the Edit menu.

SHORT ANSWER QUESTIONS

Write the correct answer in the space provided.

1. What menu and menu option open the Print dialog box?

____

2. Which toolbar contains the Show/Hide ¶ button?

____

3. If you begin keying a word such as "January" or "Thursday," how can you have Word complete the word for you automatically?

____

4. What area of the Word screen shows the position of the insertion point and displays indicators that show the current mode of operation?

____

5. Which toolbar contains the Print button?

____

6. What shape is the pointer when it appears in the text area of the screen?

____

7. Which command is used to save a document under a different filename?

8. What happens when you point to the down arrows at the bottom of a menu?

CRITICAL THINKING

Answer these questions on a separate page. There are no right or wrong answers. Support your answers with examples from your own experience, if possible.

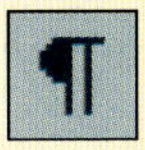

1. You can use the Show/Hide ¶ button ¶ to hide paragraph marks and space characters. When might it be useful to show these characters? When would you want to hide them?
2. Word allows great flexibility when naming files. Many businesses and individuals establish their own rules for naming files. What kinds of rules would you recommend for naming files in a business? For personal use?

Lesson Applications

EXERCISE 1-13

Key, edit, and print a document.

1. Start a new document. Turn on Caps Lock mode and key **TO THE STAFF:**
2. Turn off Caps Lock and press Enter twice to start a new paragraph.
3. Key the text shown in Figure 1-15, including the corrections. Refer to Appendix D: "Proofreaders' Marks," if necessary. *Proofreaders' marks* are handwritten corrections to text, often using specialized symbols.

TIP: When Word suggests the completed word for "September," "November," and "Saturday," you can press Enter to insert the word. Remember to press Spacebar after the completed word.

FIGURE 1-15

The lower airfares are good for travel between ~~June~~ September 15 and ~~September~~ November 15 only. Travelers must stay over one Saturday night to qualify. The reservation policy#^is first come^, first served.¶Remember: Groups booked on these low fare flights will not neccessarily be booked on the same carrier and will not necessarily arrive at the same time.

NOTE: When starting a new paragraph, remember to press Enter twice to insert a blank line between paragraphs.

4. In the first sentence, key **new** to the left of the word "lower." Add a comma after "new." Then delete the word "lower" and key **reduced**
5. Insert a hyphen between "low" and "fare" in the last sentence. No spaces should appear before or after the hyphen.
6. In the same sentence, delete the colon after "Remember," key **that**, and make the "G" in "Groups" lowercase.
7. Save the document as ***[your initials]*****1-13** on your data disk.
8. Print the document and then close it.

EXERCISE 1-14

Key, edit, and print a document.

1. Start a new document and key the two paragraphs shown in Figure 1-16 (be sure to leave a blank line between the paragraphs).

FIGURE 1-16

```
As its slogan says, Duke City Gateway truly is the gateway to the
Southwest, offering the greatest number of specialized tours to New Mexico,
Arizona, and Colorado.

The agency's tour planners and tour guides are considered experts in the
history and culture of this area.
```

2. In the first paragraph, key **Travel** after "Gateway."
3. Switch to Overtype mode and key **Colorado, and Arizona** over the text "Arizona, and Colorado."
4. Turn off Overtype mode and move the insertion point immediately after the "s" in the word "agency's" in the second paragraph.
5. Use Ctrl+Backspace to delete "The agency's" and key **Duke City Gateway's** in its place.
6. Before "area" (the last word in the last paragraph), key **remarkable**
7. Save the document as ***[your initials]*1-14** on your data disk.
8. Print and then close the document.

EXERCISE 1-15

Key, edit, and print a document.

1. Start a new document. Key the text shown in Figure 1-17. Use single spacing and key each sentence on a new line.

FIGURE 1-17

```
Reminder
Will the last one to leave the office:
Turn off all computers.
Turn down the thermostat.
Turn off the coffee machine.
Turn off the lights.
Thank you!
```

2. In the third line, change "computers" to **computer equipment**

3. In the next-to-last line, change "the lights" to **all lighting fixtures**
4. Before the "Thank you!" line, insert another line by keying **And don't forget to turn on the alarm and lock the door.**
5. Use CapsLock and Overtype mode to change "Reminder" and "Thank you!" to all uppercase letters.
6. Insert a blank line after every line of text by pressing Enter once.
7. Save the document as ***[your initials]*1-15** on your data disk.
8. Print and then close the document.

EXERCISE 1-16 Challenge Yourself

Key, edit, and print a document.

1. Start a new document and key the two paragraphs shown in Figure 1-18, including the corrections. Refer to Appendix D: "Proofreaders' Marks," if necessary.

FIGURE 1-18

```
                                        Gateway
Group travel is an imprtant part of the travel business. Tours have
                      o
been organized thru the mountains, over the seas, and across the world.
Groups have traveled on buses, ships, planes, trains and 4-wheel-drive
vehicles.
         tours are
Group travel is arranged for families, students, singles, senior citizens,
disabled people, and any group with individual needs.
                stet
```

2. Correct the spelling of "thru" in the second sentence to **through**
3. In the last sentence, key **type of** after "and any." Delete "individual" and key **special** in its place.
4. Save the document as ***[your initials]*1-16** on your data disk.
5. Print and then close the document
6. Exit Word.

On Your Own

In these exercises you work on your own, as you would in a real-life work environment. Use the skills you've learned to accomplish the task—and be creative.

EXERCISE 1-17

Write a simple paragraph about yourself that includes your first and last name. Switch to Overtype mode, turn on Caps Lock, and then key over your name in uppercase letters. Save the document as ***[your initials]*1-17** and print it.

EXERCISE 1-18

Browse menu options and toolbar buttons until you find something that looks intriguing; then find out more about it by using the Ask a Question box. In a new blank document, write a brief paragraph about your findings. Save the document as ***[your initials]*1-18** and print it.

EXERCISE 1-19

Log onto the Internet and search for sites that relate to a particular interest of yours. Jot down a few Web addresses and then key the addresses into a blank document, under an appropriate heading. Save the document as ***[your initials]*1-19** and print it.

LESSON

2

Selecting and Editing Text

OBJECTIVES

MOUS ACTIVITIES
In this lesson:
W2002 1-1
W2002 4-1
W2002 4-3

See Appendix E.

After completing this lesson, you will be able to:

1. Open an existing document.
2. Insert nonprinting characters.
3. Move within a document.
4. Undo and Redo actions.
5. Repeat actions.
6. Select text.
7. Save a revised document.
8. Work with document properties.

Estimated Time: 1¼ hours

To edit documents efficiently, you need to learn to select text and move quickly within a document. In this lesson you learn those skills, as well as how to open and save an existing document.

Opening an Existing Document

Instead of creating a new document, you start this lesson by opening an existing document. There are several ways to open a document:

- Click the Open button on the Standard toolbar.
- Choose Open from the File menu.

- Press Ctrl + O.
- Use the document links on the New Document task pane.

EXERCISE 2-1 Open an Existing File

1. On the menu bar, click File to open the File menu. Expand the menu (click the arrows at the bottom of the menu). The filenames listed at the bottom of the menu are the last four files opened from this computer. If the file you want is listed, you can click its name to open it from this list.
2. Click Open to display the Open dialog box. You're going to open a student file called **Duke1**, but first you must locate the appropriate drive on your computer.
3. Click the down arrow to the right of the Look in box and choose the appropriate drive according to your instructor's directions.

NOTE: If your instructor tells you to open a specific folder, double-click the folder in the list box under the Look in box.

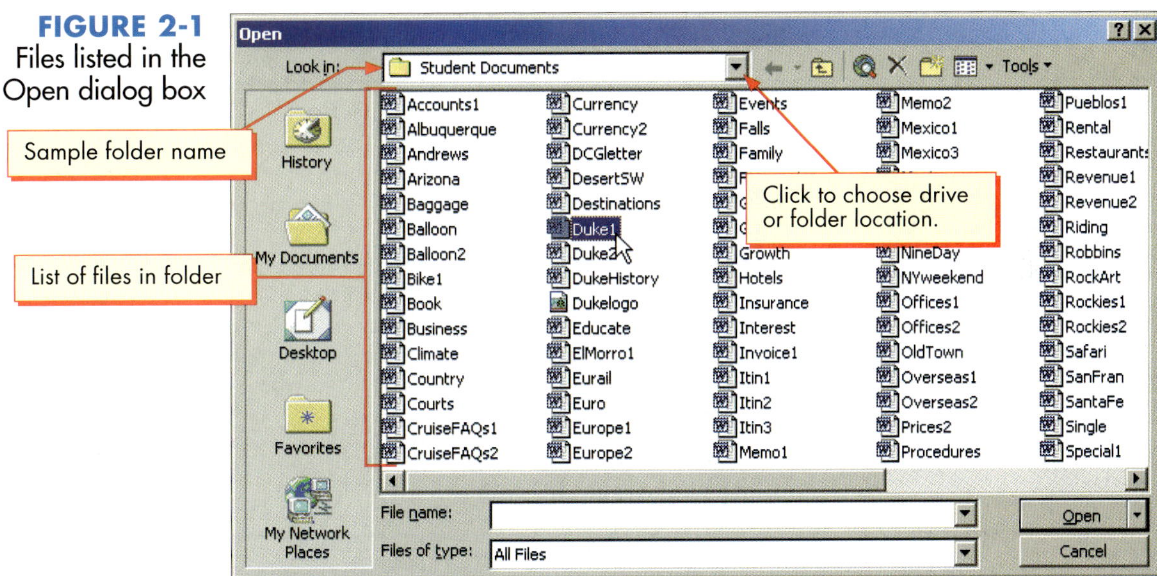

FIGURE 2-1 Files listed in the Open dialog box

4. After you locate the student files, click the arrow next to the Views button in the Open dialog box to display a menu of view options.
5. Make sure List is selected so the files are listed by filename.
6. Click the arrow next to the Views button again and choose Preview. This view provides a quick look at a document before you open it.

FIGURE 2-2
Views menu in the Open dialog box

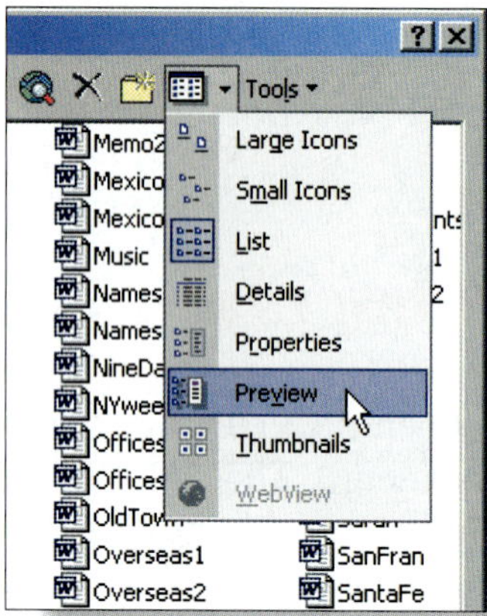

7. From the list of filenames, locate the filename **Duke1** and click it once to select it.
8. Click Open.

TIP: You can also double-click a filename to open a file.

TABLE 2-1 Open Dialog Box Buttons

BUTTON	PURPOSE
History	Lists the most recently opened files and folders.
My Documents	Opens a folder Windows provides to help you organize your document files.
Desktop	Lists items on your computer's desktop.
Favorites	Lists folders and files you have designated as "favorites" by using the Add to Favorites command on the Tools menu.
My Network Places	Lists folders and files you can access on shared network drives and on Web servers.
Up One Level	Moves up one level in the hierarchy of folders or drives on your computer or on computers connected to your network.
Search the Web	Opens the Search page of your Internet browser so you can search the Web for information.
Delete	Deletes a selected file or folder.
Create New Folder	Lets you create a new folder to organize your files.
Views	Opens a menu of view options for displaying drives, folders, files, and their icons.
Tools Tools	Opens a menu of other file functions, such as finding a file, renaming a file, and adding a file to the Favorites folder.

NOTE: The buttons in the Open dialog box also appear in the Save As dialog box.

EXERCISE 2-2 Search for a File

It can be hard to remember a file's location if you haven't used the file in a long time, and especially if you have access to many folders or network drives. When you can't remember where a file is, you can tell Word to search for it.

1. With the file **Duke1** still open in the document window, click the Search button on the Standard toolbar. The Search task pane appears.

REVIEW: You might need to first click the Toolbar Options button at the end of the Standard toolbar to locate the Search button.

2. If your task pane doesn't resemble the one shown in Figure 2-3 on the next page, click Basic Search at the bottom of the task pane.
3. Click in the Search text box and key the word **Euro** without any spaces or punctuation. In this exercise, assume that you need to check conversion rates so you are searching for a document that contains information about Euro currency.
4. Click the down arrow to the right of the Search in box. Word will search in locations that are preceded by a box with a check mark. You can click an empty box to add a check mark or check Everywhere if you're not sure where a file is located. Click the down arrow again to close the list.

NOTE: The file you're searching for is in the same location where you found **Duke1**. Check with your instructor about where to search.

5. Click the down arrow to the right of the Results should be box and make sure the Word Files check box is selected. Click any other checked box to clear the check mark. Click the down arrow again to close the list. (See Figure 2-3.)
6. Click Search. After a few seconds, the Results box displays the names of files that contain the word "Euro."
7. In the Results box, click the file named **Currency**. The file opens in a new document window. Review the document to locate "Euro" and then close it without making any changes to it or saving it. The file **Duke1** should remain open.

8. Close the Search task pane by clicking its Close button or by clicking the Search button on the Standard toolbar.

WORD

FIGURE 2-3
Searching for a file in the Search task pane

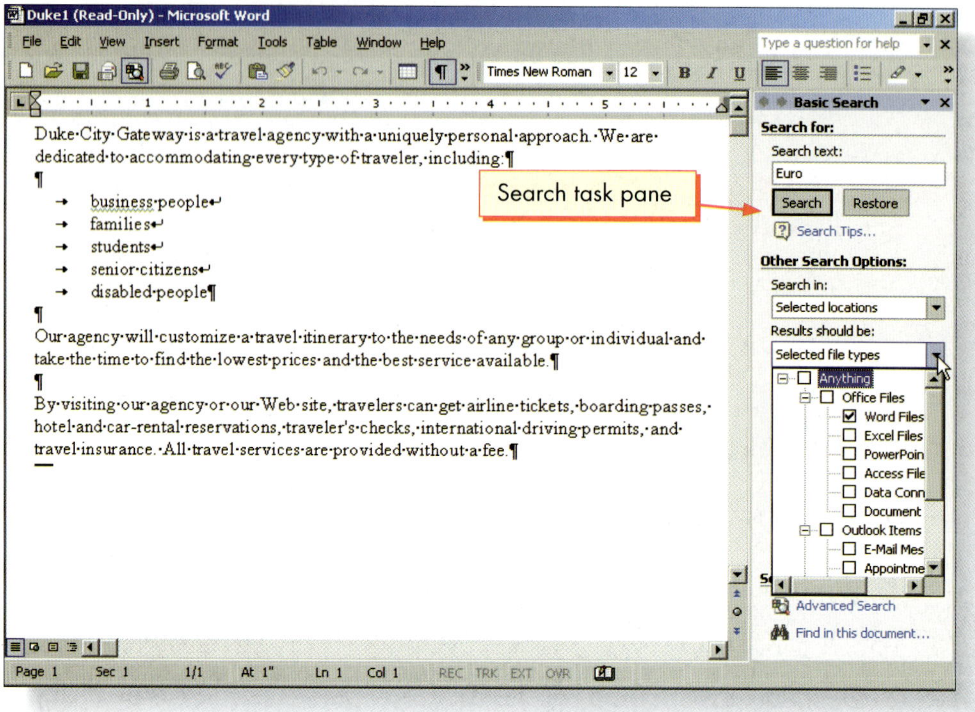

EXERCISE 2-3 Create a New Folder

Document files are typically stored in folders that are part of a hierarchal structure similar to a family tree. At the top of the tree is a disk drive letter (such as C: or A:) that represents your computer, network, floppy drive, or CD-ROM drive. Under the disk drive letter you can create folders to organize your files. These folders can also contain additional folders.

Here's a scenario: You store your files on the C: drive of your office computer. You create a folder on this drive named "Word Documents." Within this folder you create folders named "Letters," "Memos," and "Reports," each containing different types of documents.

For this course, you'll create a new folder for each lesson. You'll store your completed exercise documents in these folders.

1. From the File menu, choose Save As. You're going to save **Duke1** under a new filename, in a new folder that will contain all the files you save in this lesson.
2. Choose the appropriate drive and folder from the Save in drop-down list (for example, to save your files to a floppy disk, put a disk in the drive and make sure Save in indicates drive A:).

NOTE: Ask your instructor where to create the new folder.

3. Click the Create New Folder button. The New Folder dialog box appears.
4. In the Name box, key the folder name ***[your initials]*Lesson2** and click OK. Now your new folder's name appears in the Save in box. Word is ready to save the file in the new folder.
5. In the File name box, double-click the file's original name (**Duke1**) if it is not already selected.
6. Key the filename ***[your initials]*2-3** and click Save.

Nonprinting Characters

Lesson 1 introduced the Show/Hide ¶ button on the Standard toolbar, which shows or hides paragraph marks and other *nonprinting characters.* These characters appear on the screen but not in the printed document. Nonprinting characters are included as part of words, sentences, and paragraphs in a document. Some examples:

- A word includes the space character that follows it.
- A sentence includes the end-of-sentence punctuation and at least one space.
- A paragraph is any amount of text followed by a paragraph mark.

The document you opened contains two additional nonprinting characters: *tab characters,* which you use to indent text, and *line-break characters,* which you use to start a new line within the same paragraph. Line-break characters are useful when you want to create a paragraph of short lines, such as an address.

A *nonbreaking space* prevents two words from being divided between two lines, and a *nonbreaking hyphen* prevents hyphenated words from being divided between two lines. For example, insert a nonbreaking space between "Mr." and "Smith" to keep the name "Mr. Smith" undivided on one line, and insert nonbreaking hyphens in "up-to-date" to keep the words undivided on one line.

TABLE 2-2 **Nonprinting Characters**

CHARACTER	TO INSERT, PRESS
Tab (→)	Tab
Space (·)	Spacebar
Nonbreaking space (°)	Ctrl + Shift + Spacebar
Nonbreaking hyphen (–)	Ctrl + Shift + hyphen
Paragraph mark (¶)	Enter
Line-break character (↵)	Shift + Enter

WORD

EXERCISE 2-4 Insert Nonprinting Characters

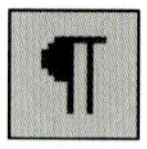

1. Click the Show/Hide ¶ button ¶ if the nonprinting characters in the document are hidden.
2. Move the insertion point to the end of the last paragraph (after "without a fee.").
3. Press Enter twice to begin a new paragraph and key **Duke City Gateway Travel has been a member in good standing of the IATA for 25** (Do not press Spacebar.)
4. Insert a nonbreaking space after "25" by pressing Ctrl + Shift + Spacebar. Then key **years.** (including the period). Word treats "25 years" as a single unit.
5. Press Spacebar and continue the paragraph by keying **For more information about our services, feel free to telephone us at (505)**
6. Insert a nonbreaking space after the area code and then key **555-1234**. Notice that the telephone number splits at the hyphen.
7. Position the insertion point to the right of the hyphen and press Backspace to delete it. Press Ctrl + Shift + hyphen to insert a nonbreaking hyphen. Now the telephone number and area code appear as a single unit.

FIGURE 2-4
Nonprinting characters

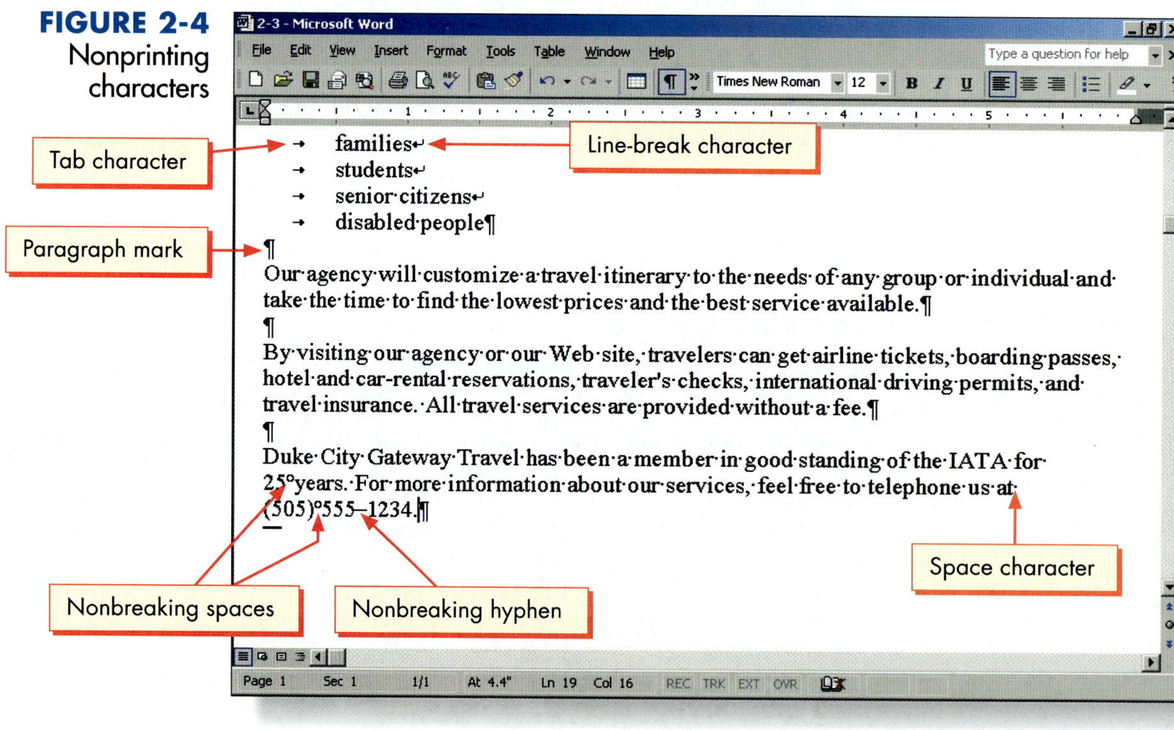

NOTE: The nonbreaking hyphen character appears longer than the regular hyphen in "car-rental" in the previous paragraph. The nonbreaking hyphen will, however, print like a regular hyphen.

8. At the end of the paragraph, press Enter twice.

9. Key the following text as one paragraph by using the line-break feature—press Shift + Enter at the end of the first and second lines.

Duke City Gateway
15 Montgomery Boulevard
Albuquerque, NM 87111

NOTE: As explained in Lesson 1, Word applies smart tags (nonprinting purple dotted underlines) to address text. Smart tags are discussed later in the course.

10. Click the Show/Hide ¶ button ¶ to hide the nonprinting characters and click it again to redisplay them.

Moving Within a Document

You already know how to move around a short document by positioning the I-beam pointer with the mouse and clicking. This is the easiest way to move around a document that fits in the document window. If a document is too long or wide to fit in the window, you need to use a different method.

Word offers two additional methods for moving within a document:

- Using the keyboard
  You can press certain keys on the keyboard to move the insertion point. The Arrow keys, for example, move the insertion point up or down one line or one character to the left or right. Key combinations quickly move the insertion point to specified locations in the document.
- Using the scroll bars
  Use the vertical scroll bar at the right edge of the document window to move through a document. The position of the scroll box indicates the approximate location in the document, which is particularly helpful in long documents. To view and move through a document that's wider than the document window, use the horizontal scroll bar at the bottom of the document window.

NOTE: Scrolling through a document does not move the insertion point. It moves only the portion of the document you are viewing in the document window. When you use the keyboard to move within a document, the insertion point always moves to a new location.

EXERCISE 2-5 Use the Keyboard to Move the Insertion Point

1. Press Ctrl+Home to move to the beginning of the document. Press End to move to the end of the first line.
2. Press Ctrl+↓ several times to move the insertion point down one paragraph at a time. Notice how the text with the line-break characters is treated as a single paragraph.
3. When you reach the end of the document, press PgUp until you return to the beginning of the document.

TABLE 2-3 Keys to Move the Insertion Point

TO MOVE	PRESS
One word to the left	Ctrl+←
One word to the right	Ctrl+→
Beginning of the line	Home
End of the line	End
One paragraph up	Ctrl+↑
One paragraph down	Ctrl+↓
Up one window	PgUp
Down one window	PgDn
Top of the window	Alt+Ctrl+PgUp
Bottom of the window	Alt+Ctrl+PgDn
Beginning of the document	Ctrl+Home
End of the document	Ctrl+End

TIP: Word remembers the last three locations in the document where you edited or keyed text. You can press Shift+F5 to return the insertion point to these locations. For example, when you open a document you worked on earlier, you can press Shift+F5 to return to the place where you were last working before you saved and closed the document.

EXERCISE 2-6 Scroll Through a Document

Using the mouse and the scroll bars, you can scroll up, down, left, and right. You can also set the Previous and Next buttons on the vertical scroll bar to scroll through a document by a specific object, such as tables or headings. For example, these buttons let you jump from one heading to the next, going forward or backward.

1. In the vertical scroll bar, click below the scroll box to move down one window.

FIGURE 2-5
Using the scroll bars

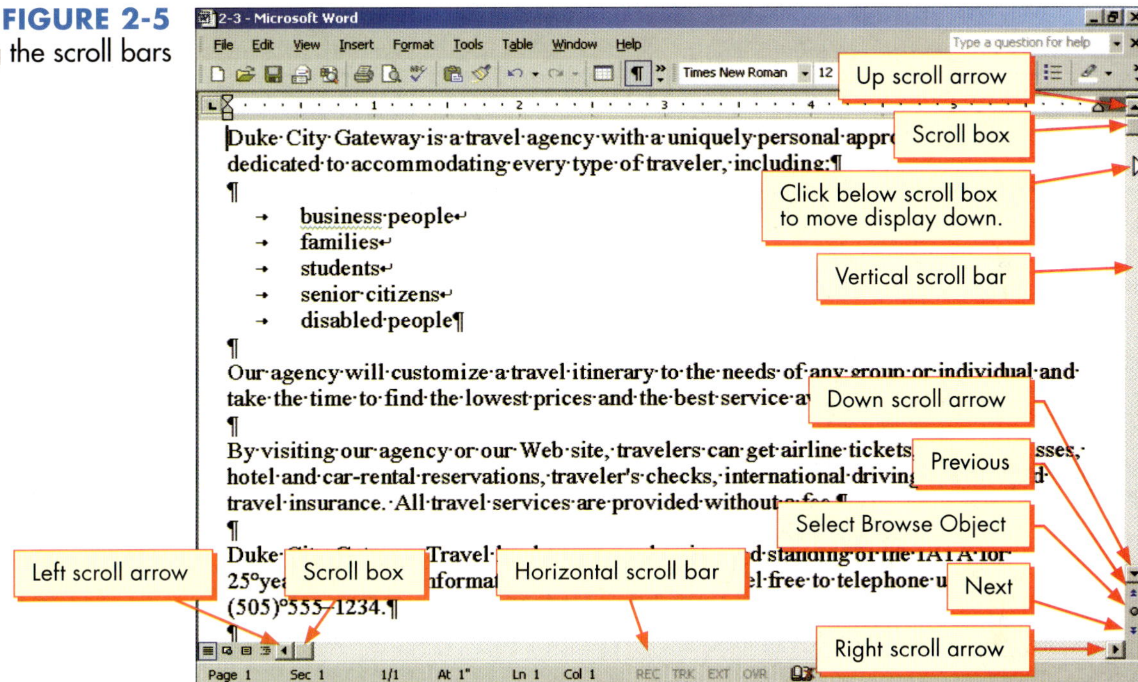

2. Drag the scroll box to the top of the scroll bar.

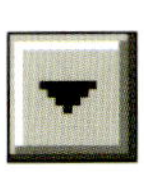

3. Click the down scroll arrow on the scroll bar three times. The document moves three lines.

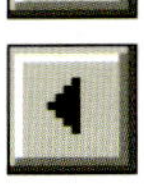

4. Click the right scroll arrow on the horizontal scroll bar once and then click the left scroll arrow once to return to the correct horizontal position.

5. Click the up scroll arrow on the vertical scroll bar three times to bring the document back into full view.

   Notice that as you scroll through the document, the insertion point remains at the top of the document.

6. Click the Select Browse Object button, located toward the bottom of the vertical scroll bar. A menu of icons appears.

7. Move the pointer over each icon to identify it. These browse options become significant as your documents become more complex. Click outside the menu to close it.

TABLE 2-4 Scrolling Through a Document

TO MOVE	DO THIS
Up one line	Click the up scroll arrow.
Down one line	Click the down scroll arrow.
Up one window	Click the scroll bar above the scroll box.
Down one window	Click the scroll bar below the scroll box.
To any relative position	Drag the scroll box up or down.
To the right	Click the right scroll arrow.
To the left	Click the left scroll arrow.
Into the left margin	Hold down Shift and click the left scroll arrow.
Up or down one page	Click Select Browse Object, click Browse by Page, and then click Next or Previous.

TIP: If you're using a mouse with a wheel, additional navigating options are available. For example, you can roll the wheel forward or backward instead of using the vertical scroll bars, hold down the wheel and drag in any direction to pan the document, or hold down Ctrl as you roll the wheel to change the magnification.

Undo and Redo Commands

Word remembers the changes you make in a document and lets you undo or redo these changes. For example, if you accidentally delete some text, you can use the Undo command to reverse the action and restore the text. If you change your mind and decide to keep the deletion, you can use the Redo command to reverse the canceled action.

There are three ways to undo or redo an action:

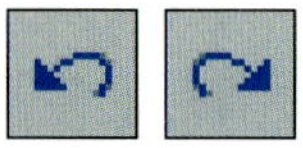

- Click the Undo button or the Redo button on the Standard toolbar.
- From the Edit menu, choose Undo or Redo.
- Press Ctrl+Z to undo or Ctrl+Y to redo.

EXERCISE 2-7 Undo and Redo Actions

1. Delete the first word in the document, "Duke," by moving the insertion point to the right of the space after the word and pressing Ctrl+Backspace. (Remember that a word includes the space that follows it.)

2. Click the Undo button to restore the word.
3. In the paragraph that begins "By visiting our," move the insertion point to the left of the word "airline" (in the first sentence).
4. Key **their** and press Spacebar once. The text now reads "can get their airline tickets."
5. From the Edit menu, choose Undo Typing. (Notice the reminder that the keyboard command Ctrl+Z exists for the same action.) The word "their" is deleted.

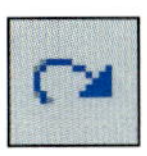

6. Click the Redo button to restore the word "their." (You might need to click the Toolbar Options button on the Standard toolbar to locate the Redo button.)
7. Click the down arrow to the right of the Undo button. Word displays a drop-down list of the last few actions, with the most recent action at the top. You can use this feature to choose several actions to undo rather than just the last action. Click the down arrow again to close the list.

FIGURE 2-6
Undo drop-down list

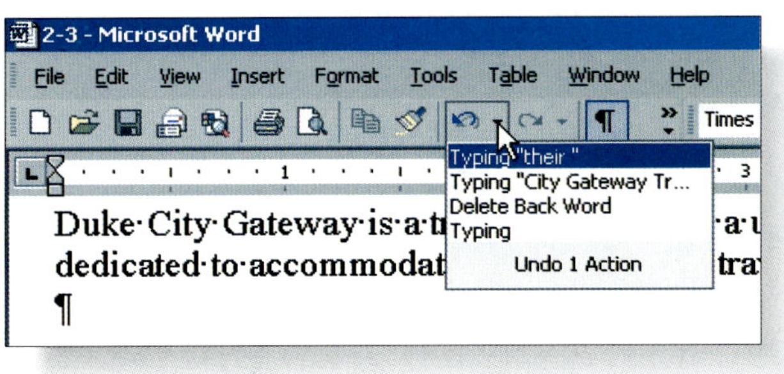

Repeat Command

Suppose you key text you want to add to other areas of a document. Instead of rekeying the same text, you can use the Repeat command to duplicate the text.

There are two ways to use the Repeat command:

- Press F4 or Ctrl+Y.
- Choose Repeat from the Edit menu.

EXERCISE 2-8 Repeat Actions

1. In the paragraph that begins "Our agency will," position the insertion point to the left of "agency."
2. Key **travel** and press Spacebar. The sentence now begins "Our travel agency will."
3. In the beginning of the next paragraph, move the insertion point to the left of the word "agency" and press F4. The word "travel" is repeated.
4. Where the agency name and address appear at the bottom of the document, position the insertion point to the right of "Gateway" and press F4. Add a space before the repeated word "travel" and change it to uppercase "T."

NOTE: When you want to undo, redo, or repeat your last action, do so before you press another key.

Selecting Text

Selecting text is a basic technique that makes revising documents easy. When you select text, that area of the document is called the *selection*, and it appears as a highlighted block of text. A selection can be a character, group of characters, word, sentence, or paragraph or the whole document. In this lesson, you delete and replace selected text. Future lessons show you how to format, move, copy, delete, and print selected text.

You can select text several ways, depending on the size of the area you want to select.

TABLE 2-5 Mouse Selection

TO SELECT	USE THE MOUSE TO
Series of characters	Click and drag, or click one end of the text block and then hold down Shift and click the other end.
Word	Double-click the word.
Sentence	Hold down Ctrl and click anywhere in the sentence.
Line of text	Move the pointer to the left of the line until it changes to a right-pointing arrow and then click. To select multiple lines, drag up or down.
Paragraph	Move the pointer to the left of the paragraph and double-click. To select multiple paragraphs, drag up or down.
Entire document	Move the pointer to the left of any document text until it changes to a right-pointing arrow and then triple-click (or hold down Ctrl and click).

EXERCISE 2-9 Select Text with the Mouse

1. Select the first word of the document by double-clicking it. Notice that the space following the word is also selected.

FIGURE 2-7
Selecting a word

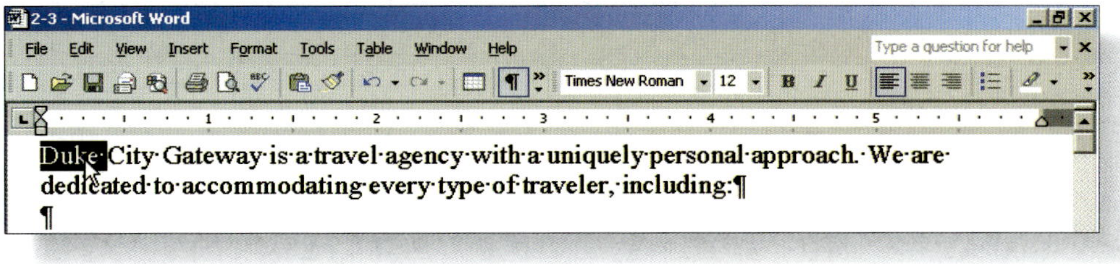

2. Cancel the selection by clicking anywhere in the document. Selected text remains highlighted until you cancel the selection.
3. Select the first sentence by holding down Ctrl and clicking anywhere within the sentence. Notice that the period and space following the sentence are part of the selection. Cancel the selection.
4. Locate the paragraph that begins "By visiting our."
5. To select the text "traveler's checks," click to the left of "traveler's." Hold down the left mouse button and slowly drag through the text, including the comma and space after "checks." Release the mouse button. Cancel the selection.

TIP: When selecting more than one word, you can click anywhere within the first word and then drag to select additional text. Word will "smart select" the entire first word.

6. To select the entire paragraph by dragging the mouse, click to position the insertion point to the left of "By." Hold down the mouse button and drag across and down until all the text and the paragraph mark are selected. Cancel the selection.
7. Select the same paragraph by moving the pointer into the blank area to the left of the text. (This is the margin area.) When the I-beam pointer changes to a right-pointing arrow, double-click. Notice that the first click selects the first line and the second click selects the paragraph, including the paragraph mark. Cancel the selection. (See Figure 2-8 on the next page.)

TIP: You can also triple-click within a paragraph to select it.

FIGURE 2-8
Selecting text

Point and double-click to select paragraph

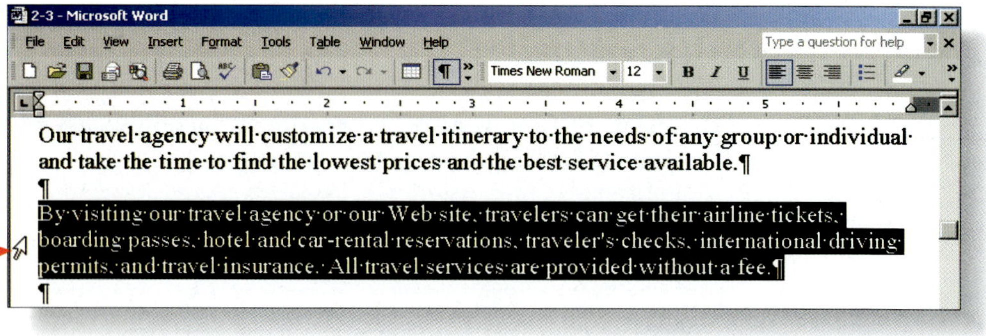

EXERCISE 2-10 Select Noncontiguous Text

In the previous exercise you learned how to select *contiguous text,* where the selected characters, words, sentences, or paragraphs follow one another. You can also select *noncontiguous text,* such as the first and last items in a list or the third and fifth word in a paragraph. To select noncontiguous text, use Ctrl and the mouse.

1. Select the first line of the list ("business people").
2. Hold down Ctrl and select the third line of the list ("students"). With these two separate lines selected, you can delete them, format them, or move them without affecting the rest of the list.
3. Cancel the selection and go to the paragraph that begins "By visiting our."
4. In the first sentence, double-click the word "our" before "Web site." With the word now selected, hold down Ctrl as you double-click the word "their" in the same sentence and "travel" in the next sentence. (See Figure 2-9.) All three words are highlighted.

FIGURE 2-9
Selecting noncontiguous words

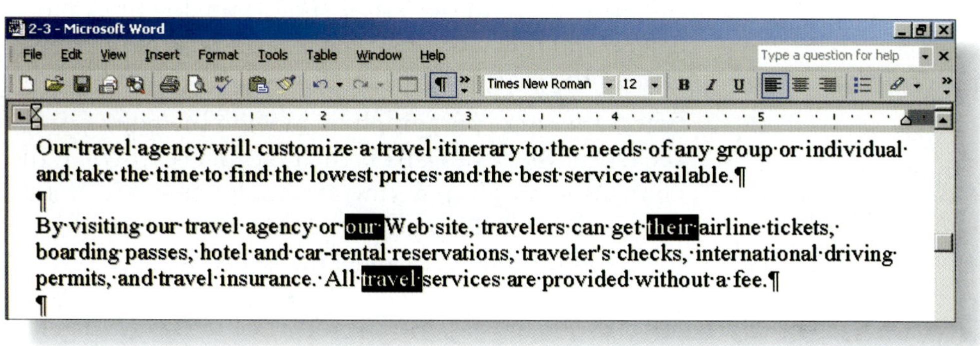

5. Press Delete to delete the selected words.

EXERCISE 2-11 Adjust a Selection Using the Mouse and the Keyboard

1. Select the paragraph beginning "By visiting our travel agency."
2. Hold down Shift and press ← until the last sentence is no longer highlighted. Release Shift.
3. Increase the selection to include the last sentence by holding down Shift and pressing End. Release Shift.
4. Increase the selection to include all the text below it by holding down Shift and clicking at the end of the document (after the ZIP Code).
5. Select the entire document by pressing Ctrl+A. Cancel the selection.

TABLE 2-6

Keyboard Selection

TO SELECT	PRESS
One character to the right	Shift+→
One character to the left	Shift+←
One word to the right	Ctrl+Shift+→
One word to the left	Ctrl+Shift+←
To the end of a line	Shift+End
To the beginning of a line	Shift+Home
One line up	Shift+↑
One line down	Shift+↓
One window up	Shift+PgUp
One window down	Shift+PgDn
To the end of a document	Ctrl+Shift+End
To the beginning of a document	Ctrl+Shift+Home
An entire document	Ctrl+A

EXERCISE 2-12 Edit Text by Replacing a Selection

You can edit a document by selecting text and then deleting or replacing the selection.

1. In the paragraph that begins "By visiting," select the words "travel agency" using the Shift+Click method: click to the left of the word "travel," hold down Shift, and click to the right of the word "agency."
2. Key **office** to replace the selected text.
3. In the paragraph that begins "Duke City Gateway Travel has been," select "IATA" and key **International Air Travel Association**. Notice that, unlike using Overtype mode, when you key over selected text, the new text can be longer or shorter than the selection.

NOTE: Although keying over selected text is an excellent editing feature, it sometimes leads to accidental deletions. Remember, when text is selected in a document (or even in a dialog box) and you begin keying text, Word deletes all the selected text with your first keystroke. If you key text without realizing a portion of the document is selected, use the Undo command to restore the text.

Saving a Revised Document

You already used the Save As command to rename the document you loaded at the beginning of this lesson. Now that you have made some additional revisions, you can save a final version of the document by using the Save command. The document is saved with all the changes, replacing the old file with the revised file.

NOTE: If you wanted to save the current document with a different filename, you would use the Save As command.

EXERCISE 2-13 Save a Revised Document

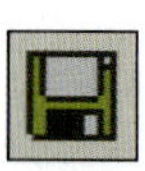

1. Click the Save button on the Standard toolbar. This action does not open the Save As dialog box. Instead, the Save icon flashes quickly at the right end of the status bar, indicating that Word is saving the document.

2. Click the Print button to print the document.
3. Close the document and exit Word. If you forget to save a document before you close it, Word reminds you to save when you try to close the application.

EXERCISE 2-14 Check Word's AutoRecover Settings

Word's *AutoRecover* feature can automatically save open documents at an interval you specify. However, this isn't the same as saving a file yourself, as you did in the preceding exercise. AutoRecover's purpose is to save open documents "in the background" so a recently saved version is always on disk. Then, if the power fails or your system crashes, the AutoRecover version of the document opens automatically the next time you launch Word. In other words, AutoRecover ensures you always have a recently saved version of your document.

Even with AutoRecover working, you need to manually save a document (by using the Save command) before closing it. AutoRecover documents are not always available; if you save and close your file normally, the AutoRecover version is deleted when you exit Word. Still, a good idea is to make sure AutoRecover is working on your system, and set it to save recovery files frequently.

1. Start Word. Open the Tools menu and click Options.
2. In the Options dialog box, click the Save tab.
3. Make sure the Save AutoRecover info every box is checked. If it is not checked, click the box.
4. Click the up or down arrow buttons to set the minutes to 5. Click OK.

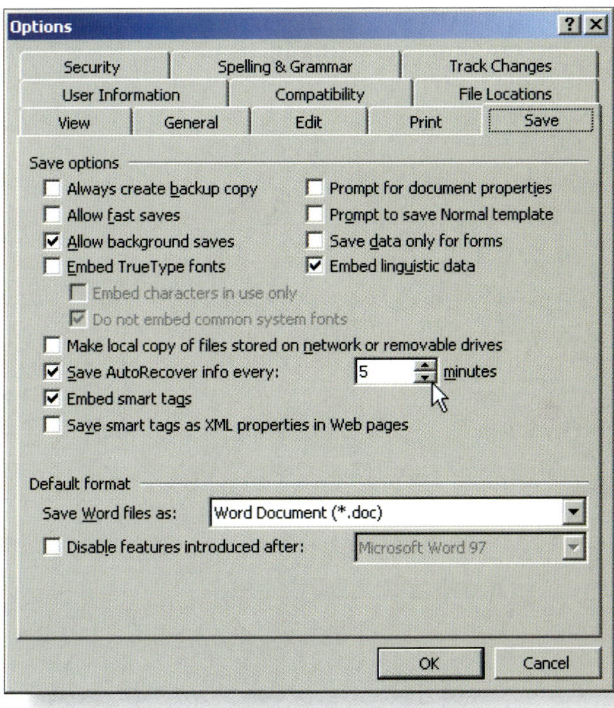

FIGURE 2-10 Setting AutoRecover options

Working with Document Properties

Information that describes your document is called a *property*. Word automatically saves your document with certain properties, such as the filename, the date created, and the file size. You can add other properties to a document, such as the title, subject, author's name, and keywords. This information can help you organize and identify documents.

NOTE: You can also search for documents based on document properties by using the Search task pane.

EXERCISE 2-15 Review and Edit Document Properties

1. Open the file ***[your initials]*2-3**. Open the File menu and choose Properties.
2. In the Properties dialog box, click the General tab. This tab displays basic information about the file, such as filename, file type, location, size, and creation date.
3. Click the Statistics tab. This tab shows the exact breakdown of the document in number of paragraphs, lines, words, and so on.
4. Click the Summary tab. Here you can enter specific document property information or change existing information. Notice that Word assigned a temporary title using the document's first sentence.

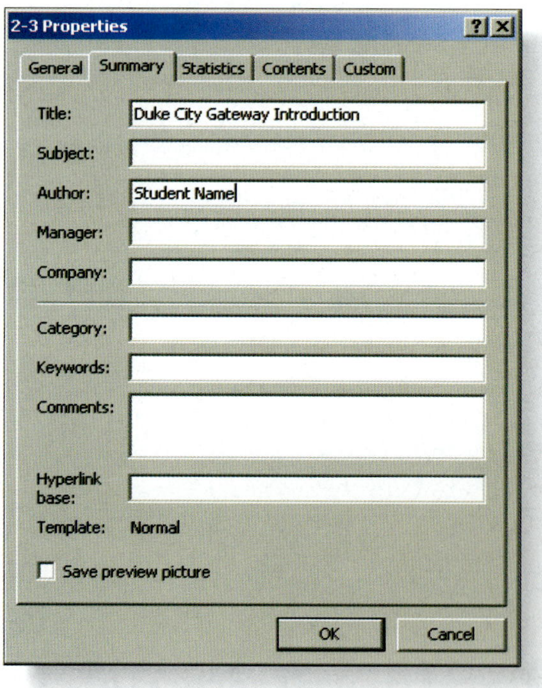

FIGURE 2-11 Entering Summary information

5. Edit the title to read **Duke City Gateway Introduction**
6. Enter your name as author. Click OK.
7. Save and close the document.

USING HELP

You have already learned how to display ScreenTips to identify on-screen items. You can also display ScreenTips that describe items. Descriptive ScreenTips are available for menu commands, dialog box options, and parts of the Word screen.

Display descriptive ScreenTips:

1. Open a new, blank document.
2. From the Help menu, choose What's This? Notice that you can also press Shift + F1. The pointer now has a question mark attached.

FIGURE 2-12
Help menu

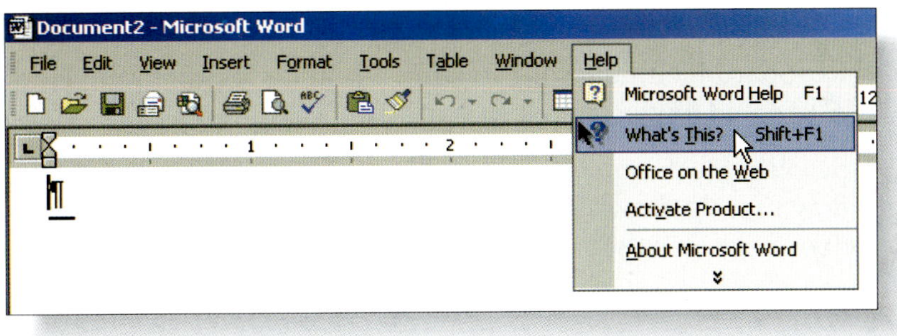

3. Click the Select Browse Object button on the vertical scroll bar. Review the description and click the description box to close it.
4. Press Shift + F1 to display the question mark pointer again. Open the File menu and choose Save As. Review the description of this command and click to close it.

5. Choose Properties from the File menu and display the Summary tab. In the upper right corner of the dialog box, click the Help button ? to display the question mark pointer. Click Subject (the word or the blank text box), review the description, and close it. You can repeat this process to see as many descriptions as you like.
6. Close the dialog box and close the document without saving.

LESSON 2 Summary

- ➤ Use the Open dialog box to open an existing file. Use the Views button in the dialog box to change the way files are listed.
- ➤ If you forget a file's name or location, use the search tools in the Search task pane to find the file.

- Create folders to organize your files. You can do this in the Save As dialog box, using the Create New Folder button.
- Nonprinting characters—such as blank spaces or paragraph marks—appear on-screen but not in the printed document. Insert a line-break character to start a new line within the same paragraph. Insert a nonbreaking space between two words or a nonbreaking hyphen in hyphenated words to keep the words together on one line.
- Use the Show/Hide ¶ button ¶ to turn the display of nonprinting characters on and off.
- When a document is larger than the document window, use the keyboard or the vertical scroll bar to view different parts of the document. Keyboard methods for moving within a document also move the insertion point.
- Keyboard techniques for moving within a document include single keys (such as PgUp and Home) and keyboard combinations (such as Ctrl+↑). See Table 2-3.
- Scrolling techniques for moving within a document include clicking the up or down scroll arrows on the vertical scroll bar or dragging the scroll box. Scrolling does not move the insertion point. See Table 2-4.
- If you make a change in a document that you want to reverse, use the Undo command. Use the Redo command to reverse the results of an Undo command.
- If you perform an action, such as keying text in a document, and you want to repeat that action elsewhere in the document, use the Repeat command.
- Selecting text is a basic technique for revising documents. A selection is a highlighted block of text you can format, move, copy, delete, or print.
- There are many different techniques for selecting text, using the mouse, the keyboard, or a combination of both. Mouse techniques involve dragging or clicking. See Table 2-5. Keyboard techniques are listed in Table 2-6.
- You can select any amount of contiguous text (characters, words, sentences, or paragraphs that follow one another) or noncontiguous text (such as words that appear in different parts of a document). Use Ctrl along with the mouse to select noncontiguous blocks of text.
- When text is selected, Word replaces it with any new text you type, or deletes the selection if you press Delete.
- Use the Save command to save any revisions you make to a document.
- Word's AutoRecover feature periodically saves open documents in the background so you can recover a file in the event of a power failure or system crash.
- Document properties are details about a file that help identify it. Properties include the filename, file size, and date created, which Word updates

automatically. Other properties you can add or change include title, subject, author's name, and keywords.

LESSON 2 Command Summary

FEATURE	BUTTON	MENU	KEYBOARD	SPEECH?
Open		File, Open	Ctrl + O or Ctrl + F12	✓
Undo		Edit, Undo	Ctrl + Z or Alt + Backspace	✓
Redo		Edit, Redo	Ctrl + Y or Alt + Shift + Backspace	✓
Repeat		Edit, Repeat	Ctrl + Y or F4	✓
Select entire document		Edit, Select All	Ctrl + A	✓
Save		File, Save	Ctrl + S or Shift + F12	✓
Document properties		File, Properties		✓

WORD

Concepts Review

TRUE/FALSE QUESTIONS

Each of the following statements is either true or false. Indicate your choice by circling T or F.

T F **1.** You can preview a file in the Open dialog box.

T F **2.** A line-break character is used to begin a new paragraph.

T F **3.** A tab mark is a nonprinting character.

T F **4.** The function of the Next button changes according to the selection you make with the Select Browse Object button.

T F **5.** Noncontiguous text does not appear consecutively in a document.

T F **6.** You can undo the last change made to a document.

T F **7.** You can double-click within a sentence to select it.

T F **8.** You can increase a selection by using Shift+End.

SHORT ANSWER QUESTIONS

Write the correct answer in the space provided.

1. Which menu contains a list of the last four files opened?

____

2. Which nonprinting character would you insert between two words to keep them together in a sentence?

____

3. Which keyboard shortcut moves the insertion point to the beginning of a document?

____

4. Where does Home move the insertion point?

____

5. What portion of the vertical scroll bar can you drag up or down?

____

6. Which keyboard shortcut repeats the text you just keyed?

____

7. How do you preview a file in the Open dialog box?

____

8. Which mouse action selects a word without dragging?

____

CRITICAL THINKING

Answer these questions on a separate page. There are no right or wrong answers. Support your answers with examples from your own experience, if possible.

1. You can use a nonbreaking space to prevent a line break between two words. Give some examples of word combinations and word-and-number combinations in which you would use a nonbreaking space.
2. Word provides many ways to select text by using the mouse. For example, you can use just the mouse, the mouse in combination with the keyboard, or just the keyboard. Which method do you prefer, and why?

Lesson Applications

EXERCISE 2-16

Select and edit text and insert a nonprinting character.

1. Open the file **SanFran**. Make the corrections shown in Figure 2-13 by selecting and then keying over the selected text.

FIGURE 2-13

```
Both tourists and native Californians frequent the ~~San Francisco office~~ [Bay Area location] of Gateway Travel. The office is in ~~a~~ bustling downtown ~~location~~ [San Francisco] and is well known for its wine-tasting tours in Sonoma and Napa Valley. Drop in ~~when~~ [the next time] you're ~~visiting~~ [in] the area.
```

2. Press Ctrl+End to move to the end of the document. Press Enter twice to start a new paragraph. Then key:

   For information about monthly travel specials, or for directions to the office, call Rebecca Lee at Golden Gateway Travel. You can also visit us on the Web at www.gwaytravel.com.

3. Insert a nonbreaking space between "Rebecca" and "Lee" in the second paragraph. (Replace the regular space with a nonbreaking space.)
4. Save the document as ***[your initials]*2-16** in your Lesson 2 folder.
5. Print and close the document.

EXERCISE 2-17

Select and repeat text and create a paragraph using line breaks.

1. Open the file **Videos**.
2. In the first sentence, replace "our agency" with **Duke City Gateway**.
3. Use the Repeat command to repeat the keyed text to the left of the word "Customers" in the last sentence. Enter a space after "Gateway" and change the "C" in "Customers" to lowercase.
4. In the second sentence, replace "any video" with **these travelogues** and replace "the agency" with **any of our offices**
5. Move to the end of the document and press Enter twice.
6. Key the text shown in Figure 2-14 as a single paragraph, using a line break for each new line.

FIGURE 2-14

Our most popular travelogues are:
The Grand Canyon
Aloha Hawaii
Paris, City of Light

7. Save the document as ***[your initials]*2-17** in your Lesson 2 folder.
8. Print and close the document.

EXERCISE 2-18

Select and edit text and insert nonprinting characters.

1. Open the file **OldTown**.
2. Split the first paragraph at the sentence that begins "For shoppers." Be sure to insert a blank line before the new paragraph.
3. Merge the second paragraph with the third paragraph. Be sure to insert a space between sentences.
4. In the second paragraph, spell out "it's" and "You'll." Replace "the best of" with **superb**.
5. At the end of the second paragraph, key the following sentence. Use a nonbreaking hyphen in "T-shirts."

   Choose from the multicolored array of turquoise, Navajo wool rugs, T-shirts, Apache baskets, and much more.
6. In the last paragraph, change "278 years" to **284** years and add a nonbreaking space between "284" and "years."
7. Between the first and second sentences of the last paragraph, insert this sentence:

   The church sits at the northern edge of Old Town Plaza and is the scene for such events as the Blessing of the Animals in May and the Old Town Fiesta in June.
8. Save the document as ***[your initials]*2-18** in your Lesson 2 folder.
9. Print and close the document.

EXERCISE 2-19 *Challenge Yourself*

Select and edit text, use nonprinting characters, and enter summary information.

1. Open the file **Summer**.

2. Revise the document as shown in Figure 2-15.

FIGURE 2-15

Summer is a great time to visit Albuquerque. ~~In June, there's~~ the New Mexico Arts & Crafts Fair~~, featuring~~ in June features more than 150 artists and craftspeople. Visitors can ~~E~~enjoy free working exhibitions, live entertainment, and wonderful ethnic food.

The Fourth of July ~~4th~~ fireworks in Albuquerque are a special treat. Dozens of fantastic aerial ~~displays~~ and ~~fantastic~~ ground displays are all part of the American Legion Fireworks Spectacular at University Stadium.

In August, the Cowboy Classic Art Show comes to the New Mexico State Fairgrounds. Also in August, the Inter-Tribal Ceremonial presents 50 tribes in a dazzling display of parades and dances at Red Rock State Park.

3. In the second sentence of the first paragraph, change the ending to **more than 200 New Mexican craftspeople and artists**

4. In the third sentence, replace "wonderful" with **a wide variety of**

5. Change the last paragraph so it becomes three lines of text as follows (use line breaks to start new lines):

Coming in August:
The Cowboy Classic Art Show at the State Fairgrounds
The Inter-Tribal Ceremonial at Red Rock State Park

6. Select the three-line paragraph you just created.

7. Press Delete, and then undo the deletion.

8. At the end of the first paragraph, change "food" to **foods**

9. Save the document as ***[your initials]*2-19** in your Lesson 2 folder.

10. Open the Properties dialog box. Key **Summer in Albuquerque** as the title, key your name as author, and key **summer tourist attractions** in the Comments box.

11. Save, print, and close the document.

On Your Own

In these exercises you work on your own, as you would in a real-life work environment. Use the skills you've learned to accomplish the task—and be creative.

EXERCISE 2-20

Write a short paragraph about a nearby town or city. Print the document. Edit the document, using the skills you learned in this lesson and changing the information to reflect the town or city you live in. Use nonbreaking spaces and nonbreaking hyphens, if needed. Save the document as ***[your initials]*****2-20** and print it.

EXERCISE 2-21

Open the file **Business**. Use your editing skills to shorten each paragraph, making the document more concise. Save the document as ***[your initials]*****2-21** and print it.

EXERCISE 2-22

Key a short portion of a historical text or novel (written before the 20th century) so you have about one-half page of document text. Edit the text to make the language more contemporary. On the Summary tab of the Document Properties dialog box, show the original author under Author. Under Comments, key **Modified by *[your name]***. Save the document as ***[your initials]*****2-22** and print it.

LESSON

3 Formatting Characters

OBJECTIVES

MOUS ACTIVITIES
In this lesson:
W2002 1-2
W2002 1-4
W2002 1-6

See Appendix E.

After completing this lesson, you will be able to:

1. Apply basic character formatting.
2. Change font types and font sizes.
3. Choose character formats from the Font dialog box.
4. Repeat and copy character formatting.
5. Change case.
6. Highlight text.
7. Use task panes to apply and remove character formatting.

Estimated Time: 1 hour

Character formatting is used to emphasize text. You can change character formatting by making text bold or italic, for example, or by changing the style of the type. Word also provides special features to copy formats and highlight text.

Basic Character Formatting

The basic character formats are bold, italic, and underline. Text can have one or more character formats.

TABLE 3-1 Character Formatting

ATTRIBUTE	EXAMPLE
Normal	This is a sample.
Bold	**This is a sample.**
Italic	*This is a sample.*
Underline	<u>This is a sample</u>.
Bold and italic	***This is a sample.***

The simplest ways to apply basic character formatting are to use:

- Buttons on the Formatting toolbar
- Keyboard shortcuts

You can apply character formatting to existing text. You can also turn on a character format before you key new text and turn it off after you key the text. For example, you can click the Bold button **B**, key a few words in bold, and click the button again to turn off the format and continue keying regular text.

EXERCISE 3-1 Apply Basic Character Formatting Using the Formatting Toolbar

1. Open the file **Music**.
2. Click the Show/Hide ¶ button ¶ to display paragraph marks and space characters, if they are not already showing.
3. In the paragraph that begins "July 1," select "The Marriage of Figaro."
4. Click the Bold button **B** on the Formatting toolbar to make the text bold. (If necessary, click the Toolbar Options button » to display the Bold button.)
5. With the text still selected, click the Italic button *I* on the Formatting toolbar to make the text bold and italic.
6. Click the Bold button **B** again to turn off the bold format and make the text italic only. Click the Bold button **B** again to restore the bold italic formatting.

NOTE: If the Bold and Italic buttons did not appear previously on the Formatting toolbar, they do now. Word changes the toolbar display according to your use. To display both the Standard and Formatting toolbars in their entirety, open the View menu and choose Toolbars, Customize. On the Options tab, check Show Standard and Formatting toolbars on two rows. Click Close.

FIGURE 3-1
Using the Formatting toolbar to apply character formatting

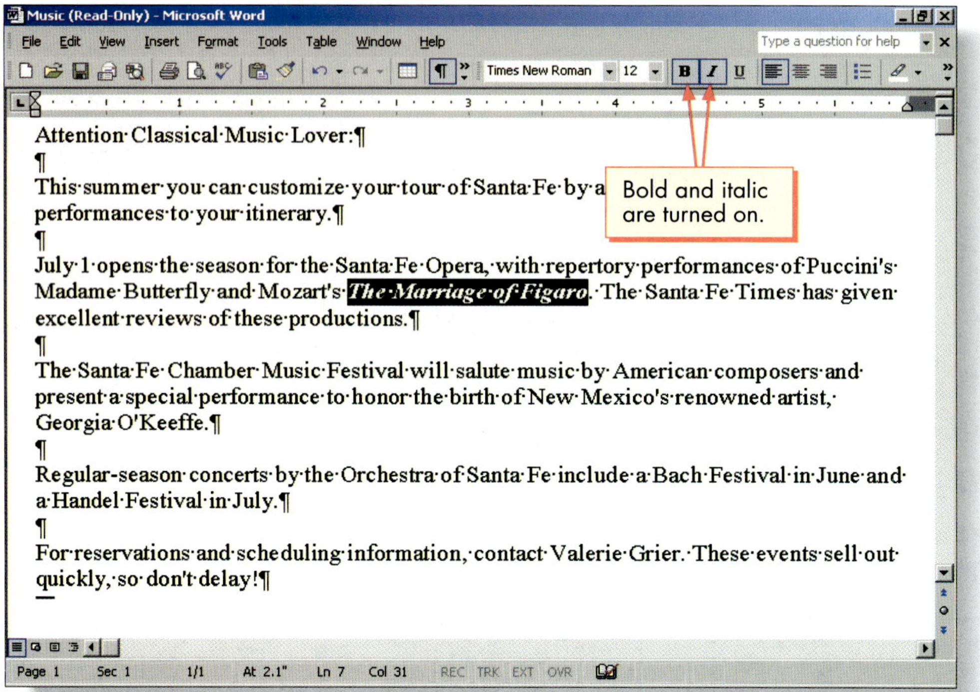

7. Move the insertion point to the end of the same paragraph and press Spacebar once.
8. Key **Its production of** and press Spacebar once.
9. Click the Bold button **B** and the Italic button *I* and key **The Magic Flute** in bold italic.
10. Click both buttons to turn the formatting off, press Spacebar, and complete the sentence by keying **won a rave review from Opera News magazine.**
11. Select the bold italic text "The Marriage of Figaro" again.
12. Press Ctrl and select the bold italic text "The Magic Flute" as well.
13. Click the Underline button U on the Formatting toolbar to underline the noncontiguous selections.
14. Click the Undo button to remove the underlines.

EXERCISE 3-2 Apply and Remove Basic Character Formatting Using Keyboard Shortcuts

If you like to keep your hands on the keyboard instead of using the mouse, you can use keyboard shortcuts to turn basic character formatting on and off. Press Ctrl+B for bold, Ctrl+I for italic, and Ctrl+U for underline. To remove character formatting from selected text, press Ctrl+Spacebar.

1. In the same paragraph, select the text "Madame Butterfly."
2. Press Ctrl+B to make the selected text bold and press Ctrl+I to add italic.
3. Move the insertion point to the end of the document and press Enter twice to start a new paragraph. (Remember, press Ctrl+End to go to the end of a document.)
4. Press CapsLock, press Ctrl+B to turn on the bold option, and key **jazz fans note:** in bold capital letters.
5. Press CapsLock to turn it off, press Spacebar, and continue keying in bold **The first annual Desert Bloom Jazz Festival, featuring some of the world's greatest musicians, will be held in Tucson next May 1-15.**
6. Select the entire new paragraph you just keyed and press Ctrl+Spacebar to remove the character formatting, which in this case is bold.

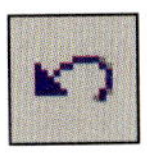

7. Click the Undo button to restore the bold formatting.

Working with Fonts

A *font* is a type design applied to an entire set of characters, including all letters of the alphabet, numerals, punctuation marks, and other keyboard symbols.

FIGURE 3-2
Examples of fonts

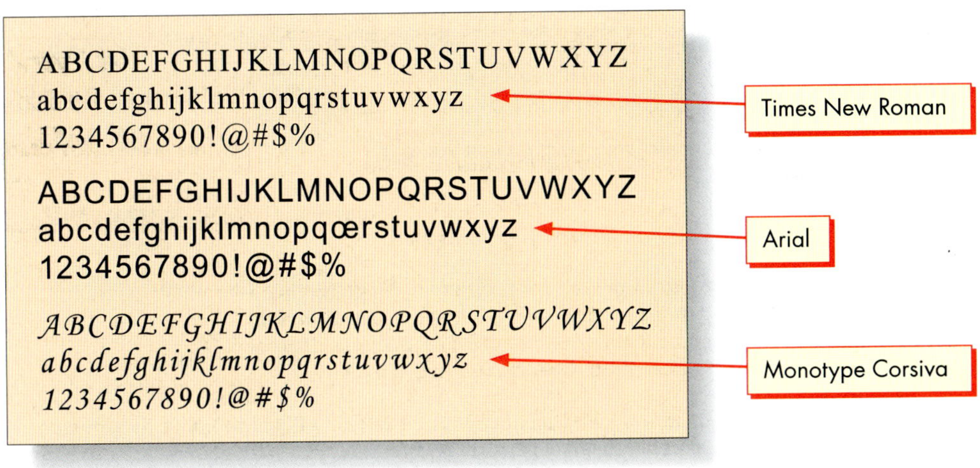

Arial is an example of a plain font; Times New Roman (Word's default font) is more ornate; and Monotype Corsiva is a more stylized font. Arial is a *sans serif* font because it has no decorative lines, or serifs, projecting from its characters. Times New Roman and Monotype Corsiva are *serif* fonts because they have decorative lines. Fonts are also available in a variety of sizes, measured in *points*. There are 72 points to an inch. Like other character formatting, you can use different fonts and font sizes in the same document.

FIGURE 3-3
Examples of different point sizes

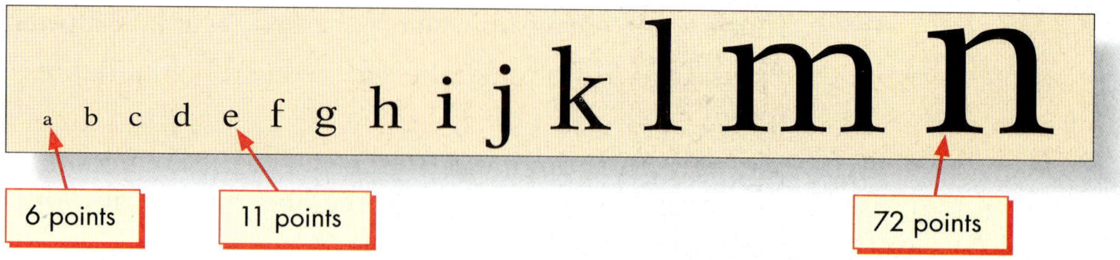

EXERCISE 3-3 Change Fonts and Font Sizes Using the Formatting Toolbar

The easiest way to choose fonts and font sizes is with the Formatting toolbar.

1. Move to the beginning of the document and select the first line, which begins "Attention." (Remember, press Ctrl + Home to move to the beginning of a document.)
2. Click the down arrow in the Font box on the Formatting toolbar to open the drop-down list. Fonts are listed alphabetically by name and are displayed graphically.

NOTE: The fonts used most recently appear at the top of the Font drop-down list. A divider line separates this list from the alphabetical list.

FIGURE 3-4
Choosing a font

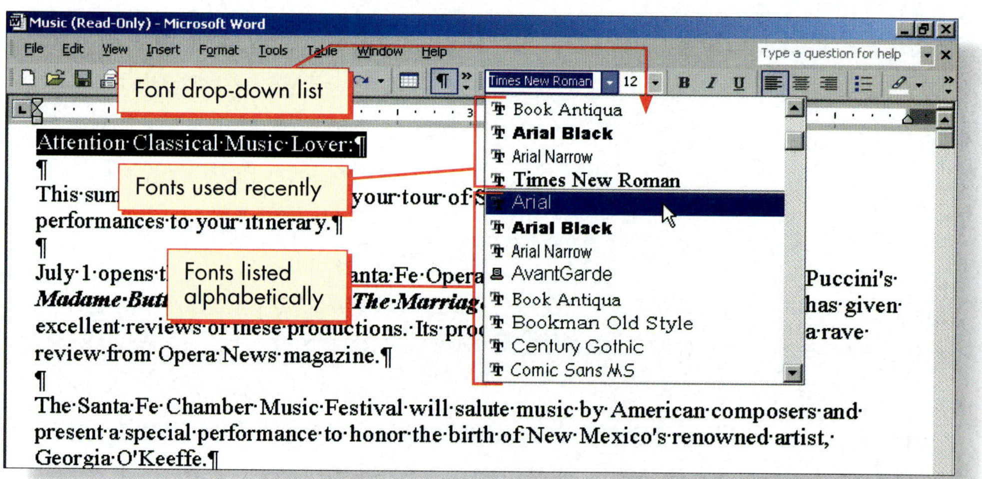

3. Using the up or down arrow or scroll box on the list's scroll bar, choose the Arial font.
4. With the text still selected, click the down arrow to open the Font Size drop-down list and choose 16 point. Now the first line stands out as a headline.

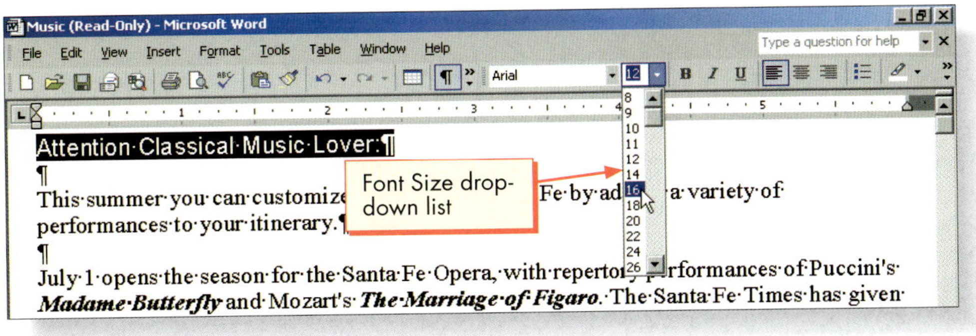

FIGURE 3-5
Choosing a font size

EXERCISE 3-4 Change Font Size Using Keyboard Shortcuts

If you prefer to use keyboard shortcuts, you can press Ctrl + Shift + > to increase font size or Ctrl + Shift + < to decrease font size. Text is increased or decreased to the next size listed in the Font Size list.

1. Move the insertion point to the end of the paragraph that begins "For reservations" and press Enter twice to start a new paragraph.
2. Press Ctrl + Shift + > and key **Call Valerie at 555-1234.** The new sentence appears in 14-point type.

NOTE: Sometimes text might appear bold on your screen when it is simply a larger font size.

3. Press Enter twice to begin another paragraph. Press Ctrl + Shift + < to reduce the font size to 12 point and key **Credit card payments are accepted**.

Using the Font Dialog Box

The Font dialog box offers a wider variety of options than those available on the Formatting toolbar. You can conveniently choose several options at one time.

There are several ways to open the Font dialog box:

- Open the Format menu and choose Font.
- Right-click (use the right mouse button) selected text to display a short-cut menu, then choose Font. A *shortcut menu* shows a list of commands relevant to a particular item that you click.
- Display the Reveal Formatting task pane and click Font.

EXERCISE 3-5 Choose Fonts and Font Styles Using the Font Dialog Box

1. Select the first line of text, which is currently 16-point Arial.
2. Open the Format menu and choose Font. In the Font dialog box, display the Font tab.
3. Choose Impact from the Font list, Italic from the Font style list, and 18 from the Size list. Preview your choices in the Preview box and click OK.

FIGURE 3-6
Using the Font dialog box

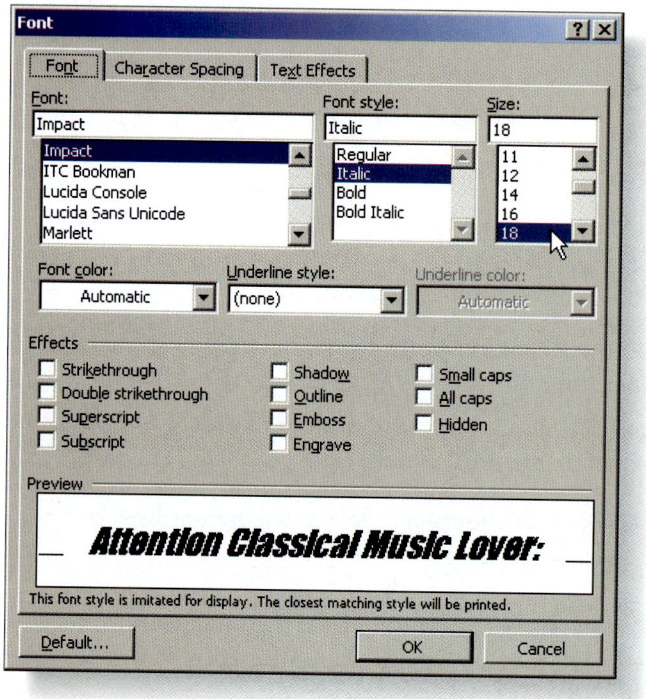

NOTE: Font availability varies depending on the type of printer you're using and the installed software. Ask your instructor to recommend a substitute font if the specified one is unavailable.

EXERCISE 3-6 Apply Underline Options and Character Effects

In addition to choosing font, font size, and font style, you can choose font color, a variety of underlining options, and special character effects from the Font dialog box.

1. Select the text "JAZZ FANS NOTE" in the last paragraph (do not select the colon).

2. Click the selected text with the right mouse button to display the shortcut menu.

FIGURE 3-7
Shortcut menu

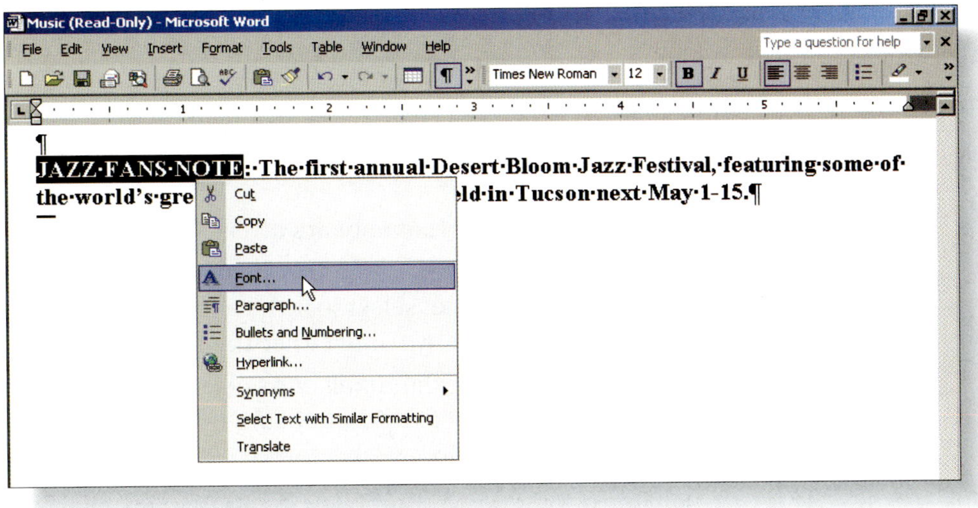

3. Choose Font to open the Font dialog box.
4. Click the down arrow to open the Underline style drop-down list. Drag the scroll box down to see all the available underline styles. Choose one of the dotted line styles.
5. Click the down arrow to the right of the Font color box and choose Blue. Both the text and the underline are now blue in the Preview box.

FIGURE 3-8
Font color options in the Font dialog box

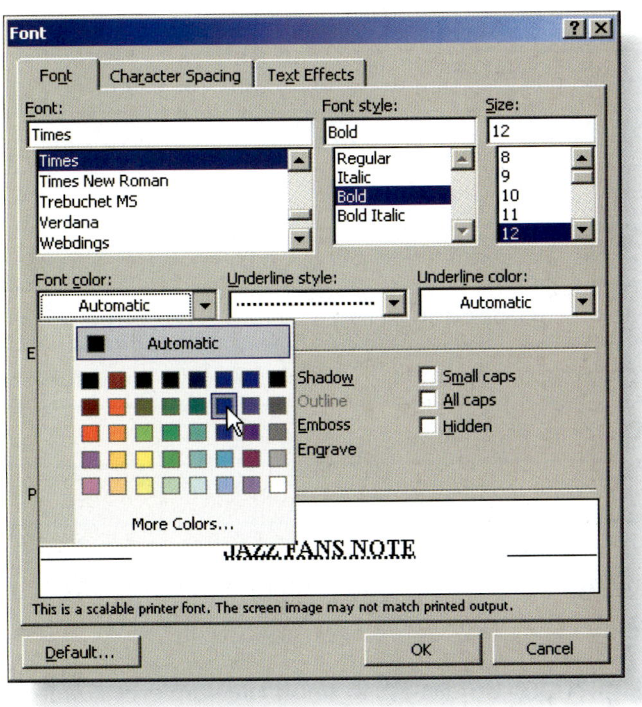

6. Click the down arrow to the right of the Underline color box and choose Red. Click OK.
7. Click anywhere in the document to deselect the text, which is now blue with a red dotted underline.

NOTE: As a rule, punctuation such as colons and periods should not be underlined.

8. Select the sentence that appears after "JAZZ FANS NOTE:" and remove the bold formatting.
9. In the same sentence, select just the text "Desert Bloom Jazz Festival." Open the Font dialog box by using either the Format menu or the shortcut menu.
10. Under Effects, click the Small caps check box and click OK. The text that was formerly lowercase now appears in small capital letters.
11. Select the sentence that begins "Call Valerie."
12. Open the Font dialog box, click the Strikethrough check box, and click OK. The text appears with a horizontal line running through it.

TABLE 3-2 Font Effects in the Font Dialog Box

EFFECT	DESCRIPTION AND EXAMPLE
Strikethrough	Applies a ~~horizontal line~~ through text.
Double strikethrough	Applies a ~~double horizontal line~~ through text.
Superscript	Raises text ^{above} other characters on the same line.
Subscript	Places text $_{\text{below}}$ other characters on the same line.
Shadow	Applies a **shadow**.
Outline	Displays the inner and outer border of text.
Emboss	Makes text appear raised off the page.
Engrave	Makes text appear imprinted on the page.
Small Caps	Makes lowercase text SMALL CAPS.
All Caps	Makes all text UPPERCASE.
Hidden	Hidden text does not print and appears on-screen only if Word's View options are set to display hidden text. See Tools, Options, View.

13. Click the Undo button to undo the strikethrough effect.

14. Select the first line of text, which begins "Attention."
15. Open the Font dialog box and click the Text Effects tab. These effects are intended for screen display, including online use.
16. Click each of the text effect options in the Animations list, noticing the effect in the Preview box. Choose one of the text effects and click OK. (You can only choose one effect at a time.)
17. Open the Save As dialog box (File, Save As) and create a new folder for your Lesson 3 files. Save the document as ***[your initials]*3-6**.
18. Print the document. Notice that the text effect does not print.

TIP: Animated text appears as regular text in a printed document. To remove a text effect, click (none) in the Font dialog box on the Text Effects tab.

EXERCISE 3-7 Use Keyboard Shortcuts for Underline Options and Font Effects

Word provides keyboard shortcuts for some underlining options and font effects as an alternative to opening the Font dialog box.

1. Start a new sentence at the end of the last paragraph by keying **To beat the heat, bring plenty of H2O.**
2. Select the "2."
3. Press Ctrl+= to make it subscript.
4. Select the blue, dotted-underlined text "JAZZ FANS NOTE." Press Ctrl+Shift+W to change the dotted underlining to words-only underlining.

TABLE 3-3 Keyboard Shortcuts for Underlining and Character Effects

KEYBOARD SHORTCUT	ACTION
Ctrl+Shift+W	Turn on or off words-only underlining.
Ctrl+Shift+D	Turn on or off double underlining.
Ctrl+Shift+=	Turn on or off superscript.
Ctrl+=	Turn on or off subscript.
Ctrl+Shift+K	Turn on or off small capitals.
Ctrl+Shift+A	Turn on or off all capitals.
Ctrl+Shift+H	Turn on or off hidden text.

EXERCISE 3-8 Change Character Spacing

The Character Spacing tab in the Font dialog box offers options for changing the space between characters or the position of text in relation to the baseline. Character spacing can be expanded or condensed horizontally, as well as raised or lowered vertically. Text can also be scaled—stretched or condensed horizontally at a percentage of its original size.

1. Select the first line of text, which begins "Attention."
2. Open the Font dialog box. Click the Text Effects tab and choose (none) to remove the animation effect.
3. Click the Character Spacing tab.
4. Click the down arrow to open the Scale drop-down list. Click 150% and notice the change in the Preview box. Change the scale back to 100%.
5. Click the down arrow to display the Spacing options. Click Expanded, and then click OK. The text appears with more space between characters.

TIP: You can increase the space between characters even more by increasing the number in the By box (click the arrows or key a specific number). Experiment with the Expanded, Condensed, and Scaling options on your own to see how they change the appearance of text.

Repeating and Copying Formatting

Just as you repeated text using F4 in the last lesson, you can use the same method to repeat character formatting. You can also copy character formatting with a special tool on the Standard toolbar—the Format Painter button.

EXERCISE 3-9 Repeat Character Formatting

Before trying to repeat character formatting, keep in mind that you must use the Repeat command immediately after applying the format. In addition, the Repeat command repeats only the last character format applied. (If you apply multiple character formats from the Font dialog box, the Repeat command applies all formatting.)

1. In the paragraph that begins "July 1," select "repertory" and click the Italic button *I* to make it italic.
2. Move the insertion point into the next paragraph, before the word "special."
3. Press F4 to repeat your last action (turning on the Italic button *I*). Key **very** and press Spacebar once. The word "very" appears in italic.

4. Select the sentence that begins "Call Valerie."
5. Open the Font dialog box. Click the Font tab and choose another font, such as Impact. Make the font style italic, change the font size to 12 points, and change the font color to red. Click **OK**. The text appears with the new formatting.
6. Select the text "JAZZ FANS NOTE:" (including the colon) and press F4. Word repeats all formatting you chose in the Font dialog box. If you apply each character format separately, using the Formatting toolbar, the Repeat command applies only the last format you chose.

FIGURE 3-9
Repeating character formatting

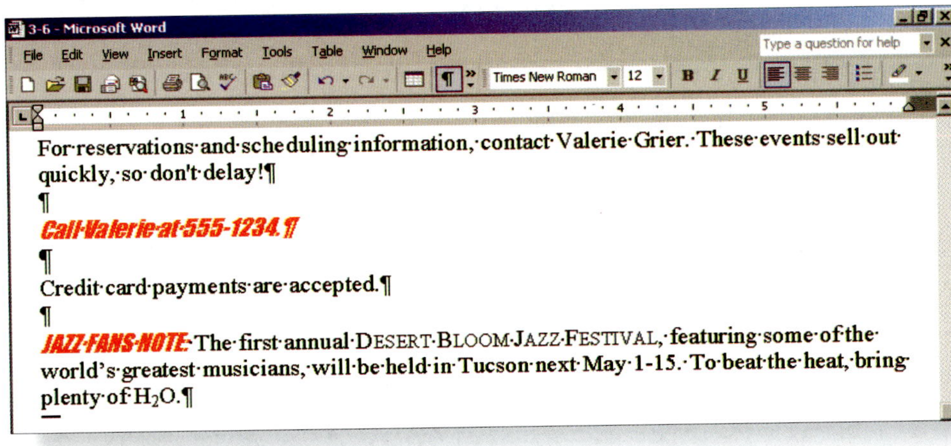

EXERCISE 3-10 Copy Character Formatting

The Format Painter button makes it easy to copy a character format. This is particularly helpful when you copy text with multiple formats, such as bold italic small caps.

To use Format Painter to copy character formatting, first select the text with the formatting you want to copy and then click the Format Painter button. The mouse pointer changes to a paintbrush with an I-beam pointer. Use this pointer to select the text to which you want to apply the copied formatting.

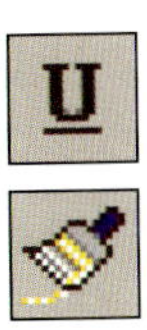

1. In the paragraph that begins "July 1," select "The Santa Fe Times" and click the Underline button to underline the publication name.
2. With the text still selected, click the Format Painter button on the Standard toolbar. When you move the pointer back into the text area, notice the new shape of the pointer.
3. Use the paintbrush pointer to select "Opera News" in the next sentence. This copies the underlining to the selected text and the pointer returns to its normal shape. (See Figure 3-10 on the next page.)

FIGURE 3-10
Copying character formatting

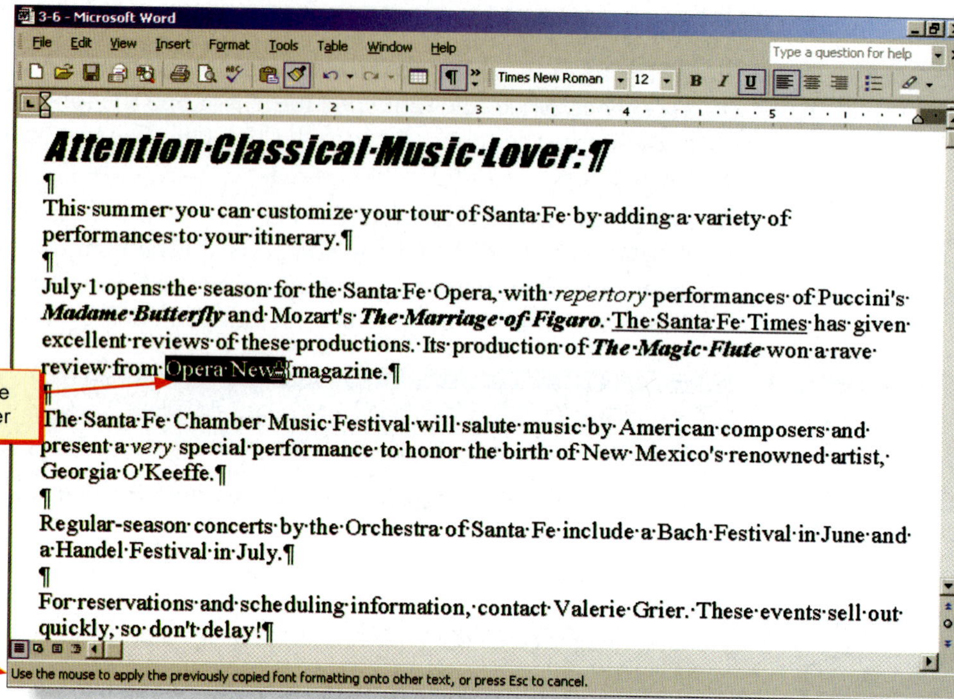

Selecting text with the Format Painter pointer

Status bar explains action

TIP: Notice the status bar at the bottom of the Word screen as you perform different tasks. It often explains the task and provides information.

4. Select the small caps word "Desert" in the last paragraph.
5. Double-click the Format Painter button. Double-clicking the button lets you copy formatting repeatedly.
6. Scroll to the top of the document. Notice that the paintbrush pointer becomes an arrow when you move out of the text area to use the scroll bars.
7. Select the sentence that begins "This summer." The small caps formatting is applied to the sentence and the pointer remains the paintbrush pointer.
8. Scroll down to the line that begins "Call Valerie at" and select the sentence. The paintbrush pointer copies the new formatting over the old formatting.
9. Press Esc or click the Format Painter to stop copying and restore the regular pointer.
10. Save the document as ***[your initials]*3-10** in your Lesson 3 folder.

NOTE: Remember to use this folder for all the exercise documents you create in this lesson.

11. Print the document and leave it open for the next exercise.

Changing Case

You've used [CapsLock] to change case and you've seen the Small Caps and All Caps options in the Font dialog box. You can also change the case of characters by using keyboard shortcuts and the Change Case dialog box.

EXERCISE 3-11 Change Case

1. Select the sentence that begins "Credit card payments." Press [Shift]+[F3]. This keyboard shortcut changes cases. Now the text appears in all uppercase letters.
2. With the sentence still selected, press [Shift]+[F3] again. Now the sentence appears in all lowercase letters.
3. Press [Shift]+[F3] again and the original case is restored.

FIGURE 3-11
Change Case dialog box

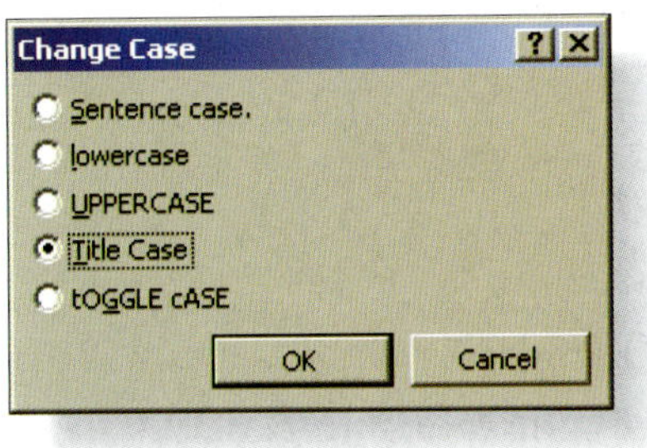

4. With the sentence still selected, open the Format menu and choose Change Case.
5. In the Change Case dialog box, click Title Case and click OK. This option changes the first letter of each word to uppercase, which is the common format for titles.
6. Click the Undo button to undo the change of case. Deselect the text.

Highlighting Text

To emphasize parts of a document, you can mark text with a color highlighter by using the Highlight button on the Formatting toolbar. As with the Format Painter button, when you click the Highlight button, the pointer changes shape. You then use the highlight pointer to select the text you want to highlight. In addition, you can choose from several highlighting colors.

EXERCISE 3-12 Highlight Text

1. Make sure no text is selected. On the Formatting toolbar, click the down arrow to the right of the Highlight button to display the color choices. Click yellow to choose it as the highlight color. This turns on the Highlight button and the color indicator box on the button appears yellow.

FIGURE 3-12
Highlighting text

Highlighted text

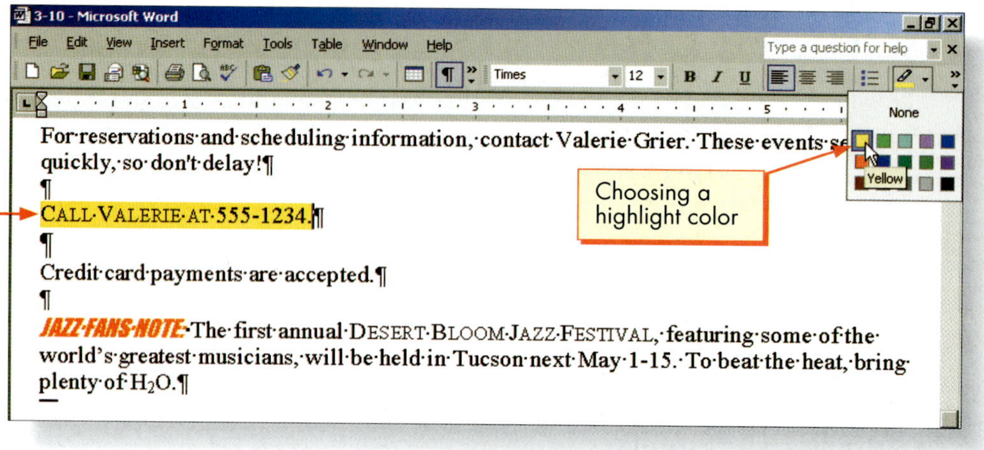

2. Move the highlight pointer into the text area.
3. Drag the pointer over the entire sentence that begins "Call Valerie."
4. Press Esc to turn off the highlighter and restore the normal pointer.
5. Select the first line of text, which begins "Attention."
6. Click the Highlight button to highlight the selection. This is another way to use the highlighter—by selecting the text and then clicking the Highlight button.
7. Select the first line of text again. Remove the highlight by clicking the down arrow to display the highlight color choices and choosing None.
8. Select the remaining highlighted text and click the Highlight button. Because None was last chosen (as shown in the color indicator box on the button), this action removes the highlight from the selected text.

NOTE: You can use highlighting to mark text as you work on a document or to point out text for others who might open the same document later. It is not meant for printed documents, because the colors might print too dark. You can use shading, which is discussed in Lesson 4, to emphasize text in a printed document.

Using Task Panes to Apply and Remove Character Formatting

The Reveal Formatting and the Styles and Formatting task panes offer convenient ways to apply, reuse, and remove character formatting. They also show descriptions of the formatting you've applied. Using these task panes reminds you of the formatting you've used in the document and helps to make sure your use of formatting is consistent.

EXERCISE 3-13 Use the Reveal Formatting Task Pane

1. From the Format menu, choose Reveal Formatting. The Reveal Formatting task pane appears, showing the formatting of the selected text.

REVIEW: To open any task pane, you can choose Task Pane from the View menu and click the Other Task Panes button ▼ to choose from the list of available task panes.

2. Click within any of the formatted text in the document. Notice the description of the text in the Font section of the task pane.
3. Click the box to the left of Paragraph in the task pane to collapse that section, because this lesson is focused on character formatting.
4. Click within, or select, the word "***Butterfly***." The task pane describes the formatting you've applied to the text.
5. In the Reveal Formatting task pane, move the mouse pointer to the box that contains the word "***Butterfly***." A down arrow appears in the box.

FIGURE 3-13 Using the Reveal Formatting task pane

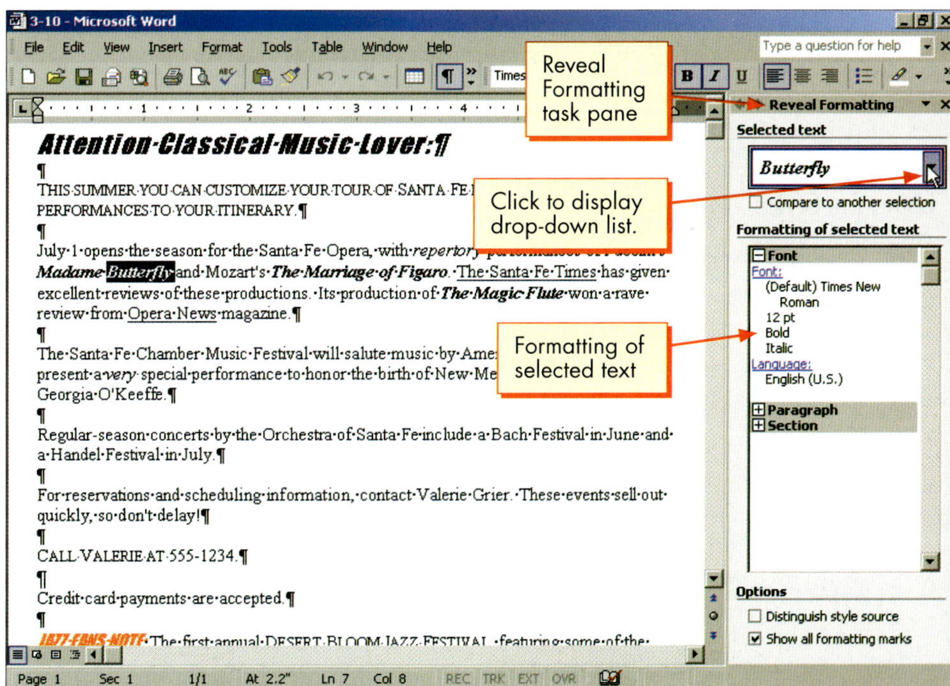

6. Click the down arrow to open a drop-down list. Notice the available options.
7. Choose Select All Text With Similar Formatting from the drop-down list. Word selects all the bold italic text in the document. At this point, you can

use the Formatting toolbar or the Font dialog box to change the formatting for the selected text.

8. Move the mouse pointer to the blue underlined word Font in the Reveal Formatting task pane. This text is a *hyperlink*, which you click to go to another location—in this case, a dialog box.
9. When the pointer becomes a hand pointer, click to open the Font dialog box.
10. Change the font style to bold and the font color to dark blue. Click OK.

EXERCISE 3-14 Use the Styles and Formatting Task Pane

1. At the top of the Reveal Formatting task pane, click the Other Task Panes button and choose Styles and Formatting.

NOTE: You can also display the Styles and Formatting task pane by choosing Styles and Formatting from the Format menu.

2. Open the Show drop-down list at the bottom of the task pane to display Formatting in use. The task pane lists the formats currently in use. These are the character formats you've used in the document. By seeing the formatting currently in use, you can reapply the same formatting to make your document consistent.

FIGURE 3-14 Using the Styles and Formatting task pane

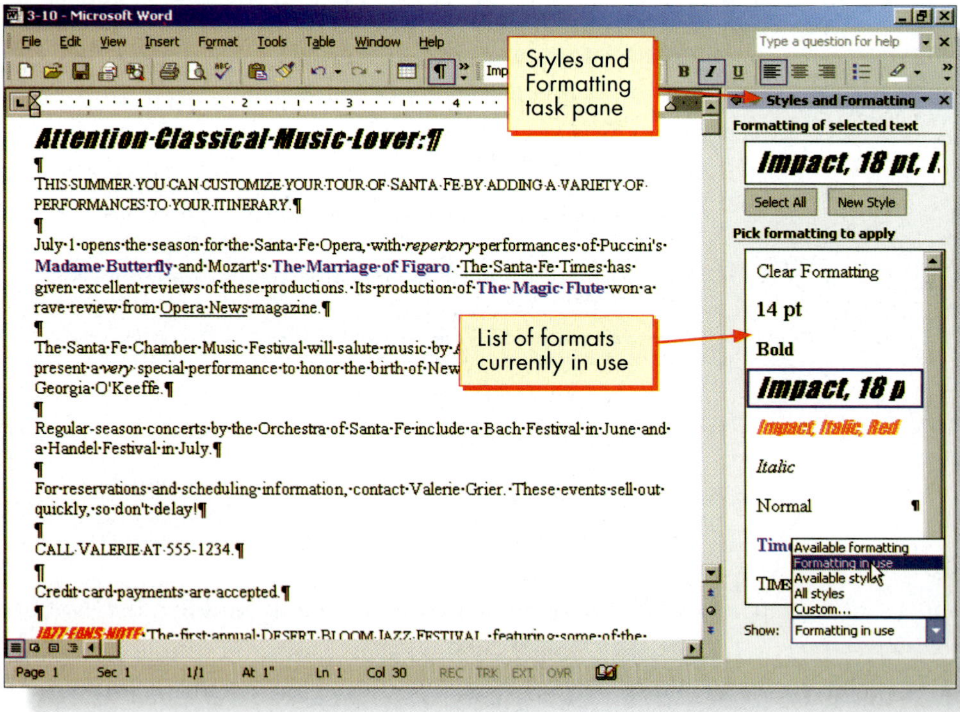

3. Point to any of the formats listed in the pane and a box will appear to describe the formatting.
4. Point to the small caps formatting listed in the task pane. Click the drop-down arrow and choose Select All 3 Instance(s). In this easy way, the task pane selects the small caps text that appears in three locations in the document. You can now change the formatting or apply one of the other formats listed in the task pane.
5. Choose Clear Formatting from the task pane list. Word restores the small caps text to Normal text. Normal means the default font, 12-point Times New Roman, with no additional formatting.
6. Use the task pane to select all underlined text and change it to italic.
7. Change the italic words "*repertory*" (in the paragraph that begins "July 1") and "*very*" (in the next paragraph) to normal text.

EXERCISE 3-15 Apply a Character Style

You can apply your own character formats, as you've done so far, or use predefined character formats called character styles. A *character style* is a named format that uses specific font and character formatting options. Some of Word's predefined character styles are called: Emphasis (which is Times New Roman italic), Strong (which is Times New Roman bold), and Hyperlink (Times New Roman, underlined, blue font color).

1. Delete the paragraph that begins "Call Valerie" and the blank paragraph mark below it.
2. In the paragraph that begins "For reservations," position the insertion point at the end of the first sentence (after "Grier" and before the period). Key **at valeriegrier@gwaytravel.com**
3. Select the e-mail address you just keyed.
4. At the bottom of the task pane, open the Show drop-down list and choose All styles. Now the task pane lists all the predefined character and paragraph styles.

NOTE: You'll learn about paragraph styles in the next lesson.

5. Scroll down the list. Character styles are indicated by an underlined small "a" to the right of the style name.
6. Choose the character style Hyperlink. Word applies the style to the selected text.

NOTE: Generally, the Hyperlink style is used for e-mails or Web addresses so you can click the hyperlink and go to that location (if your computer has the Internet capability). This particular e-mail address is fictional and not activated as a hyperlink.

7. Open the Show drop-down list and change it back to Formatting in use. Notice that the Hyperlink character style is added to the list.

TIP: If you key an e-mail or Web address in a document and press Spacebar after it (or a comma or period and then Spacebar), Word automatically formats the address as hyperlink style.

8. Save the document as ***[your initials]*****3-15** in your Lesson 3 folder.
9. Print and close the document.

LESSON 3 Summary

- Use the Formatting toolbar to apply basic character formatting (for example, bold **B**, italic *I*, and underline U) to selected contiguous text and noncontiguous text (text that is not adjacent).
- Use keyboard shortcuts to apply and remove basic character formatting. See the Command Summary.
- A font is a type design applied to an entire set of characters, including all letters of the alphabet, numerals, punctuation marks, and other keyboard symbols.
- A font can be serif (with decorative lines) or sans serif (with no decorative lines). Fonts are available in a variety of sizes, which are measured in points.
- Use the Formatting toolbar to change fonts and font sizes.
- Use keyboard shortcuts to change font sizes: Ctrl+Shift+> increases text by one font size and Ctrl+Shift+< decreases text by one font size.
- Use the Font dialog box to change fonts, font sizes, and font styles. The Font dialog box also has settings for underline styles, font and underline colors, effects such as small caps and shadow, animated character effects, and character spacing.
- Keyboard shortcuts are available for some underline styles and font effects. See Table 3-3.
- A shortcut menu shows a list of commands relevant to a particular item. To display a shortcut menu, point to the item and right-click the mouse.
- Use F4 to repeat character formatting.

- Use the Format Painter button to copy character formatting. Double-click the button to apply formatting to more than one selection.
- Use the Highlight button to apply a color highlight to selected text that you want to emphasize onscreen.
- A hyperlink often appears as blue underlined text you click to open a software feature (such as a dialog box or a Help topic) or go to an e-mail or Web address.
- Use the Reveal Formatting task pane to see how selected text is formatted, to select similarly formatted text, to clear formatting, and to access the Font dialog box (as well as other formatting dialog boxes).
- Use the Styles and Formatting task pane to see and apply formatting used in the document, to select similarly formatted text, to clear formatting, and to choose other formatting styles, including character styles. Switch between task panes by using the Other Task Panes button .

LESSON 3 Command Summary

FEATURE	BUTTON	MENU	KEYBOARD	SPEECH?
Bold	B	Format, Font	Ctrl + B	✓
Italic	I	Format, Font	Ctrl + I	✓
Continuous, single underlining	U	Format, Font	Ctrl + U	✓
Increase font size	12	Format, Font	Ctrl + Shift + >	✓
Decrease font size	12	Format, Font	Ctrl + Shift + <	✓
Open Font dialog box		Format, Font	Ctrl + D	✓
Remove character formatting		Format, Font	Ctrl + Spacebar	✓
Repeat character formatting		Edit, Repeat	F4 or Ctrl + Y	✓
Change case		Format, Change Case	Shift + F3	✓
Reveal Formatting task pane		Format, Reveal Formatting		✓
Styles and Formatting task pane	A	Format, Styles and Formatting		✓

Concepts Review

TRUE/FALSE QUESTIONS

Each of the following statements is either true or false. Indicate your choice by circling T or F.

T F **1.** You can apply single underlining from the Formatting toolbar.

T F **2.** To remove character formatting, press Ctrl + Delete.

T F **3.** Small Caps is an example of a font.

T F **4.** Times New Roman is an example of a sans serif font.

T F **5.** You can use F4 to repeat text or to repeat character formatting.

T F **6.** After clicking the Format Painter button, you can press Esc to restore the regular pointer.

T F **7.** You can use the Font dialog box to change character spacing.

T F **8.** You must use the Font tab in the Font dialog box to apply the shadow effect.

SHORT ANSWER QUESTIONS

Write the correct answer in the space provided.

1. Which toolbar contains a button to highlight text?

____

2. From which task pane can you open the Font dialog box?

____

3. What unit of measurement is used to measure fonts?

____

4. What keyboard shortcut increases the font size of selected text to the next available size?

____

5. What character effect places a horizontal line through text?

____

6. Which button do you use to copy character formatting?

____

7. What keyboard shortcut do you use to change the case of selected text?

____

8. What character spacing setting inserts more space between characters?

____

CRITICAL THINKING

Answer these questions on a separate page. There are no right or wrong answers. Support your answers with examples from your own experience, if possible.

1. Select three examples of effective character formatting in magazine advertisements, articles, or other publications. Describe why you think the character formatting was particularly effective.

2. Using a large font size, key **Fonts & styles** 10 times on 10 separate lines (you can use the Repeat Typing command). Use a different font for each line. Describe the differences you see among the fonts.

Lesson Applications

EXERCISE 3-16

Apply and copy character formatting; change font size, case, and character spacing.

1. Start a new document by keying the text shown in Figure 3-15, including the corrections. Use 12-point Arial type. Refer to Appendix D: "Proofreaders' Marks," if necessary.

FIGURE 3-15

In hotel classificatoin, Tourist/Budget is geared to those seeking the lowest possible prices. This type of property has limited ~~services~~ amenities, yet offers funct^i^onal accommodations. Moderate means the hotel is suitable for cost-conscious clients. The rooms are simple and comfortable. First Class hotels offer a selective variety of facilities ~~and services~~ (stet) that will please a majority of travellers. Deluxe hotels are outstanding properties with fine rooms, public areas, and services. They are the better hotels in the area and will satisfy most discriminating travellers. Luxury hotels are ~~the~~ exceptional hotels, offering the highest standard of service and facilities. They are classified as the world's finest.

2. In the first line, change the case of the text "Tourist/Budget" to all capitals.
3. Copy or repeat the all-capitals formatting to the following words in the paragraph that describe hotel classifications: "Moderate," "First Class," "Deluxe," and "Luxury."
4. Create a new paragraph for each hotel classification, beginning with "MODERATE." (You should have four new paragraphs.) Be sure to include a blank line after each paragraph.
5. At the beginning of the document, insert three blank lines (press Enter three times). Key the title **Guide to Hotel Classification** at the first paragraph mark.
6. Change the text you just keyed to bold, orange, small caps in 16-point type.
7. Make the text "the lowest possible prices" (in the paragraph under the title) and the text "the world's finest" (in the last paragraph) bold at the same time.
8. Select the entire document and make it italic.
9. Save the document as ***[your initials]*3-16** in your Lesson 3 folder.
10. Print and close the document.

EXERCISE 3-17

Apply and copy character formatting and change font size.

1. Open the file **Memo1**.
2. Make the first line ("To the staff") 14 points and change the font to Impact. (If Impact is not available, choose a bold-looking font from the Font list.)
3. Use the Format Painter button to apply the formatting of the first line to the last line.
4. Apply the shadow effect to the first line.
5. Use the Formatting toolbar to make the text "101 Reasons to Visit the Caribbean" bold. With the text still selected, make it italic as well.
6. Position the insertion point in the next paragraph, before the word "interesting." Press F4 to repeat the last selected character formatting (italic), key **very** and press Spacebar.
7. Position the insertion point at the beginning of the last line, key **This book is** and press Spacebar. Make the word "Must" lowercase.
8. Select the entire last line and format as 12-point Times New Roman. Add red double underlining to the entire sentence except the exclamation point.
9. Save the document as ***[your initials]*3-17** in your Lesson 3 folder.
10. Print and close the document.

EXERCISE 3-18

Apply and copy character formatting, highlight text, and use the task pane to select text and apply formatting.

1. Open the file **Special1**.
2. Key the text shown in Figure 3-16 at the beginning of, and as part of, the first paragraph.

FIGURE 3-16

```
Traveling alone? Want to experience the wonders of the world? Join one of
Duke City Gateway's tours, and meet others who share your special interests.
```

3. Highlight the second paragraph (which begins "Our local") in yellow.
4. Format the list of items, from "The Great Sphinx" through "The Great Wall of China," as Arial italic.
5. Copy the formatting for the second list (from "Hawaii" through "Tahiti").
6. Split the last paragraph so "For more information" starts a new paragraph. Be sure to leave a blank line between paragraphs.

7. Open the Styles and Formatting task pane. Apply the Arial italic format listed in the task pane to the last paragraph.
8. Use the task pane to select all the Arial italic text in the document. Reduce the font size of the selected text to 11 points.
9. Format the phone number in the last paragraph as bold italic with a blue underline.
10. Use the task pane to apply the bold italic blue underlined format to the first sentence ("Traveling alone?").
11. Select just the question mark of the formatted text and remove the underline.
12. Remove the highlight from the second paragraph.
13. Save the document as ***[your initials]*3-18** in your Lesson 3 folder.
14. Print and close the document.

EXERCISE 3-19 Challenge Yourself

Apply and repeat character formatting, change case, and use the task pane to select text and apply formatting.

1. Open the file **Baggage**.
2. At the end of the paragraph that begins "B. Baggage Delay," apply the strikethrough effect to the text "other than your residence."
3. Repeat the effect for "Terms" (excluding the colon) in the next paragraph.
4. Place the insertion point after the "Terms" strikethrough text and before the colon and key the word **Conditions**. Format the new word in blue text without the strikethrough effect.
5. Apply double underlining to the title of the document.
6. Change the title to all caps.
7. Make "A. Baggage Loss or Damage" and "B. Baggage Delay" small caps.
8. Key the text shown in Figure 3-17 at the end of the document. (There should be a blank line before the new text.)

FIGURE 3-17

```
If you experience baggage problems:
1st Notify airline personnel at the airport.
2nd Call us at 555-1234 or send an e-mail to valeriegrier@gwaytravel.com.
```

9. Use the Styles and Formatting task pane to:
   - Apply the format of the title to the line that begins "If you experience."
   - Apply the Hyperlink character style to the e-mail address in the last line (if it is not already applied).
   - Select all instances of bold double-underlined text and change the font of the selected text to Arial.
10. Change the case of the line that begins "IF YOU EXPERIENCE" to sentence case.
11. Save the document as ***[your initials]*3-19** in your Lesson 3 folder.
12. Print and close the document.

On Your Own

In these exercises you work on your own, as you would in a real-life work environment. Use the skills you've learned to accomplish the task—and be creative.

EXERCISE 3-20

Create a list of ten companies in which you are interested. (They could be potential employers, local companies, companies that make products that interest you.) Include the companies' addresses. Format each of the company names differently, using character formats and effects. Save the document as ***[your initials]*3-20** and print it.

EXERCISE 3-21

Create an itinerary for a long trip you would like to take. To make the itinerary interesting, use some of the character formatting features you learned in this lesson. Copy and repeat formatting as needed. Remember, though, the itinerary must be readable. Save the document as ***[your initials]*3-21** and print it.

EXERCISE 3-22

Log onto the Internet and find an attractive Web site. Summarize the information from the site in a Word document at least a half page long. Give the document an interesting title. Using the character formatting you learned in this lesson, try to make your document look as much like the Web site as possible. Save the document as ***[your initials]*3-22** and print it.

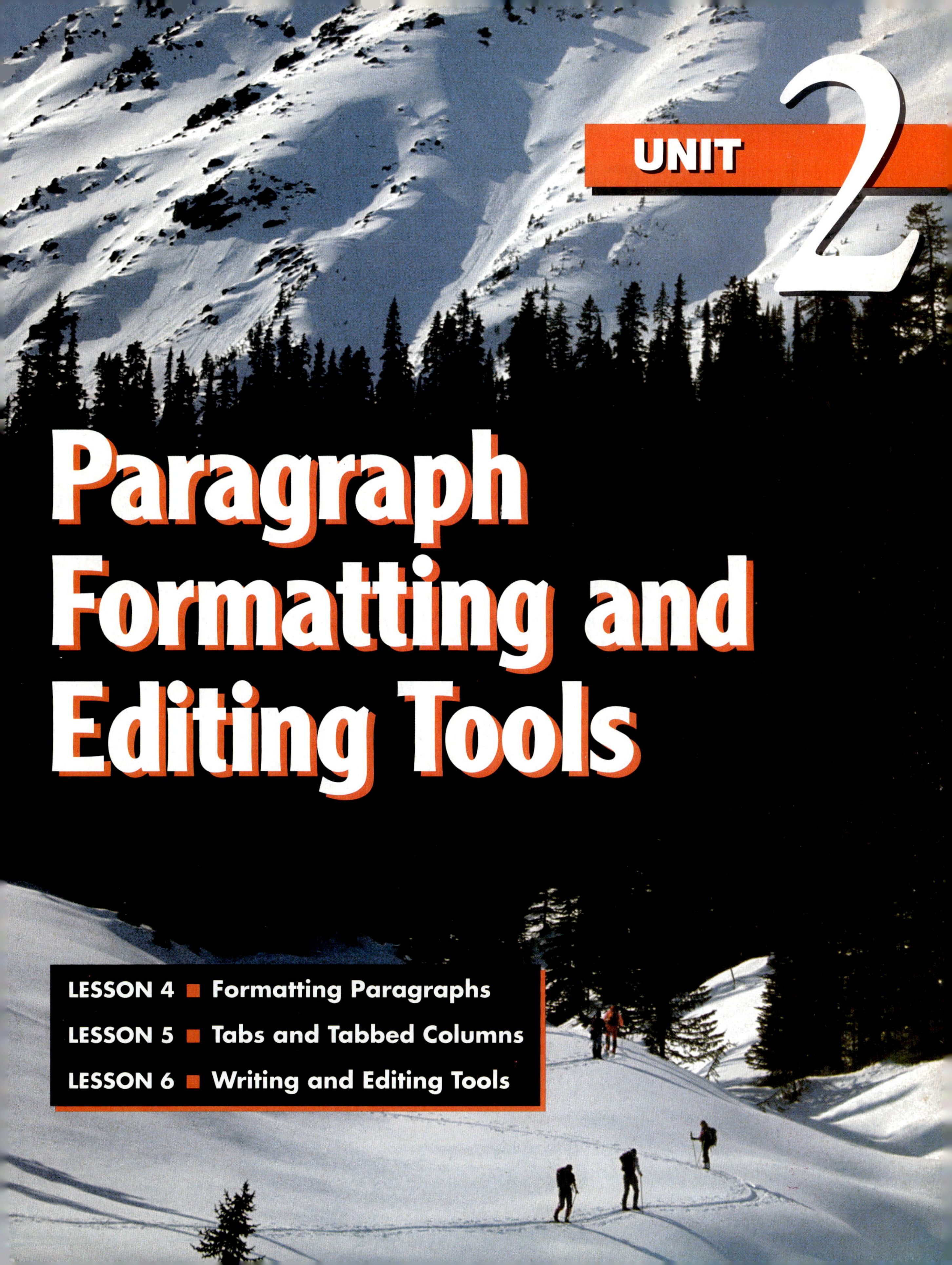

UNIT 2

Paragraph Formatting and Editing Tools

LESSON 4

Formatting Paragraphs

OBJECTIVES

MOUS ACTIVITIES
In this lesson:
W2002 1-1
W2002 2-1
W2002 2-3
W2002 2-4

See Appendix E.

After completing this lesson, you will be able to:

1. Align paragraphs.
2. Change line and paragraph spacing.
3. Set paragraph indents.
4. Apply borders and shading.
5. Repeat and copy paragraph formats and apply paragraph styles.
6. Create bulleted and numbered lists.
7. Insert symbols and special characters.

Estimated Time: 1½ hours

A paragraph in Word is any text that ends with a hard return. You insert a hard return when you press Enter. Paragraph formatting lets you control the appearance of individual paragraphs. For example, you can change the alignment of text from left to centered or the spacing between lines from single to double. You can indent paragraphs, number them, or add borders and shading to them.

Paragraph formatting is applied to an entire paragraph. All formatting for a paragraph is stored in the paragraph mark and carried to the next paragraph when you press Enter. You can copy paragraph formats from paragraph to paragraph and view formats through the task panes.

Paragraph Alignment

Paragraph alignment determines how the lines in a paragraph appear in relation to the left and right margins. A *margin* is blank space that appears from the edge of text to the edge of the paper.

There are four ways to align text, as shown in Figure 4-1. Left-alignment is Word's default setting.

FIGURE 4-1 Paragraph alignment options

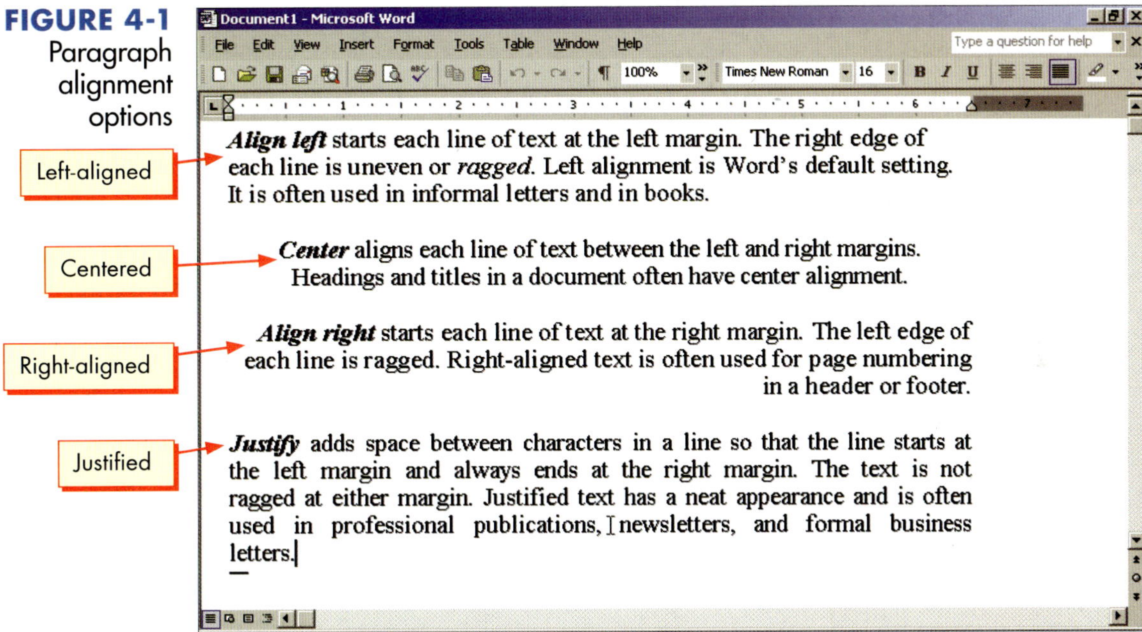

EXERCISE 4-1 Change Paragraph Alignment

The easiest way to change paragraph alignment is to use the alignment buttons on the Formatting toolbar. You can also use keyboard shortcuts: Ctrl + L left-align; Ctrl + E center; Ctrl + R right-align; Ctrl + J justify.

FIGURE 4-2 Alignment buttons on the Formatting toolbar

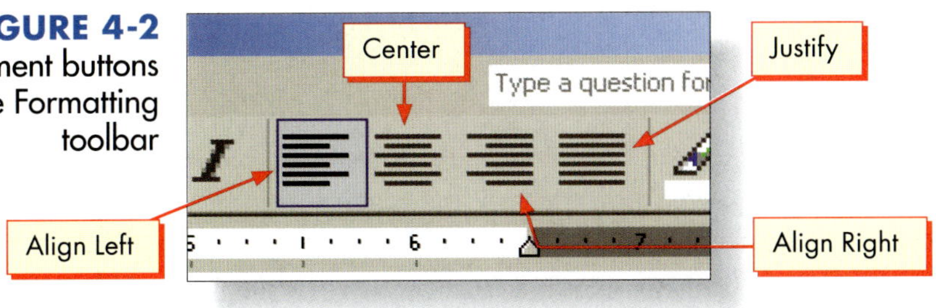

1. Open the file **Turquoise**.

WORD

NOTE: The documents you create in this course relate to the Case Study about Duke City Gateway Travel, a fictional travel agency (see pages 3 through 6).

2. Position the insertion point anywhere in the first paragraph.
3. Click the Center button on the Formatting toolbar to center the paragraph.

REVIEW: If you do not see on the toolbar any button discussed in this lesson, click the Toolbar Options button to display more buttons. Click the button you want, and it will be added to the toolbar display.

4. Continue to change the paragraph's formatting by clicking the Align Right button, the Justify button, and the Align Left button. Notice how the lines of text are repositioned with each change.
5. Position the insertion point in the second paragraph and press Ctrl+E to center the paragraph.
6. Use the keyboard shortcut Ctrl+R to right-align the third paragraph.
7. Combine the fourth and fifth paragraphs, and then use the keyboard shortcut Ctrl+J to justify the merged paragraph. When you *justify* a paragraph, Word adds horizontal space that aligns text evenly along the left and right margins, creating a smooth edge on both sides.

NOTE: When applying paragraph formatting, move the insertion point within the paragraph or just before the paragraph mark. You do not need to select the entire paragraph.

Line and Paragraph Spacing

Line space is the amount of vertical space between lines of text in a paragraph. Line spacing is typically based on the height of the characters, but you can change it to a specific value. For example, some paragraphs may be single-spaced and some double-spaced. Single-spacing is Word's default setting.

Paragraph space is the amount of space above or below a paragraph. Instead of pressing Enter multiple times to increase space between paragraphs, you can set a specific amount of space before or after paragraphs.

EXERCISE 4-2 Change Line Spacing

You can apply the most common types of line spacing—single, 1.5 lines, or double—by using keyboard shortcuts (single space, Ctrl+1; 1.5 line space, Ctrl+5; double space, Ctrl+2). Additional spacing options, as well as other paragraph formatting options, are available in the Paragraph dialog box or from the Line Spacing button.

1. Position the insertion point in the first paragraph.
2. Press Ctrl+2 to double-space the paragraph.
3. With the insertion point in the same paragraph, press Ctrl+5 to change the spacing to 1.5 lines. Press Ctrl+1 to restore the paragraph to single spacing.
4. With the insertion point in the same paragraph, click the down arrow to the right of the Line Spacing button on the Formatting toolbar. Choose 2.0 to change the line spacing to double. Choose 1.0 to restore the paragraph to single spacing.

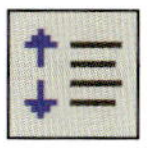

FIGURE 4-3
Using the Line Spacing button

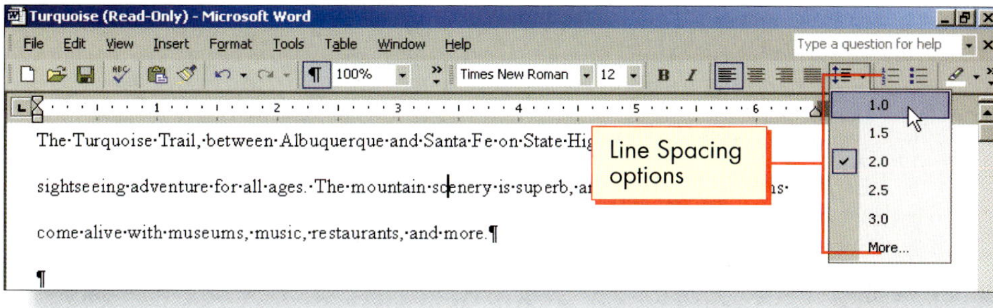

5. Right-click the first paragraph and choose Paragraph from the shortcut menu. (You can also open the Paragraph dialog box by choosing Paragraph from the Format menu.)
6. Click the down arrow to open the Line spacing drop-down list and choose Double. The change is reflected in the Preview box.

FIGURE 4-4
Paragraph dialog box

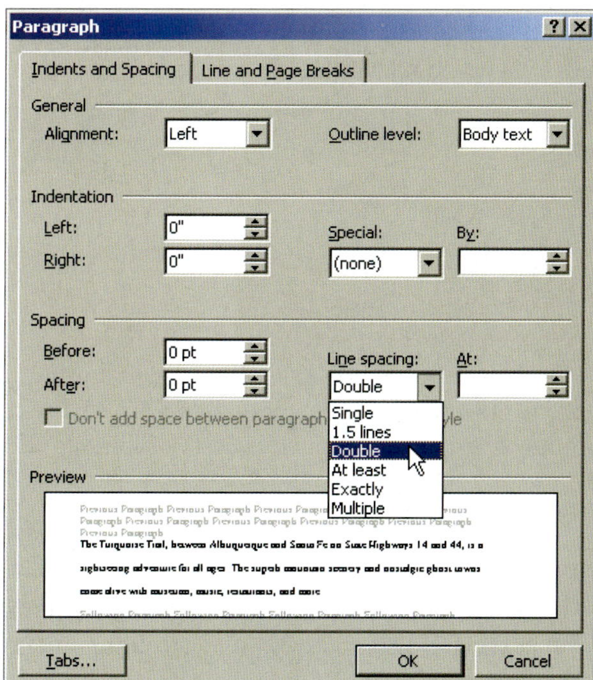

7. With the dialog box still open, choose Single from the Line spacing drop-down list. The Preview box shows the change.
8. Choose Multiple from the Line spacing drop-down list. In the At box, key **1.25**. (Select the text that appears in the box and key over it.) Press Tab to see the change displayed in the Preview box.
9. Click OK. Word adds an extra quarter-line of space between lines in the paragraph.

FIGURE 4-5
Paragraph line-spacing options

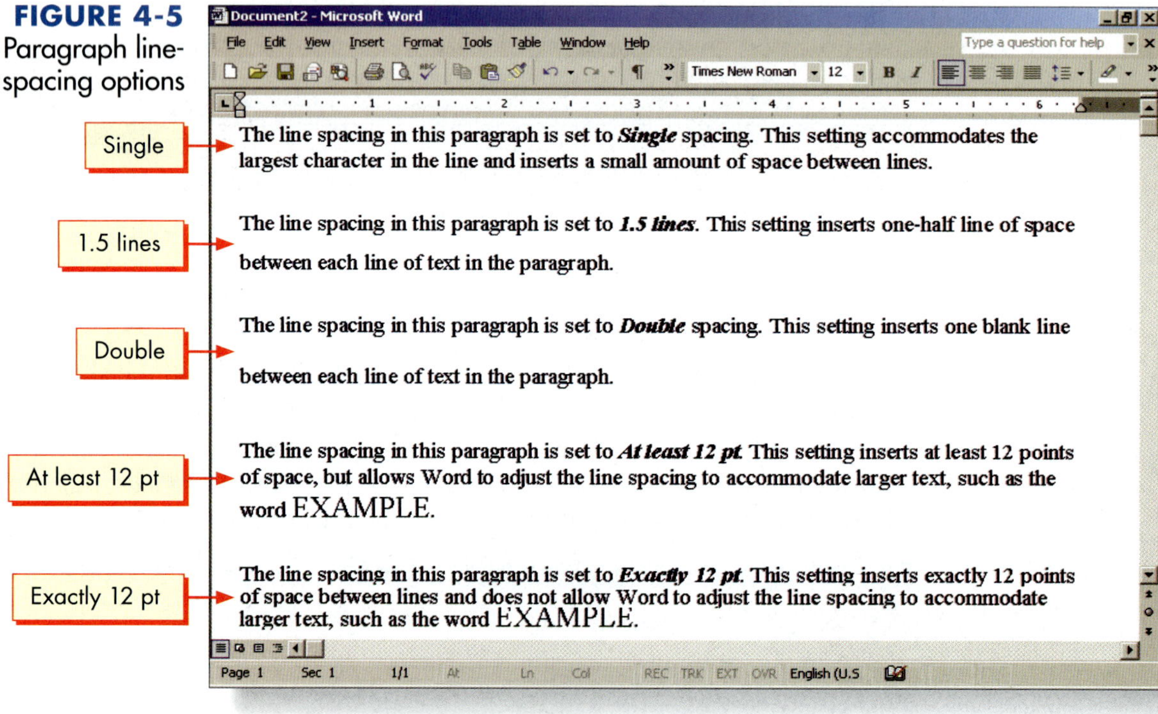

EXERCISE 4-3 Change Paragraph Spacing

You use the Paragraph dialog box to set the space between paragraphs. Paragraph spacing is set in points. If a document has 12-point text, then one line space equals 12 points, one-half line space equals 6 points and two line spaces equal 24 points.

1. Select the whole document by pressing Ctrl+A. Press Ctrl+L to left-align all paragraphs.
2. Move the insertion point to the beginning of the document (Ctrl+Home) and use the keyboard shortcut Ctrl+1 to change the first paragraph back to single spacing.

3. Click the Bold button to turn on bold, key **The Turquoise Trail** in all capitals, and press Enter.
4. Move the insertion point into the heading you just keyed. Although this heading includes only three words, it is also a paragraph. Any text followed by a paragraph mark is considered a paragraph.
5. Open the Paragraph dialog box. You use the text boxes labeled Before and After to choose an amount of space for Word to insert before or after a paragraph.
6. Set the Before text box to 72 points (select the "0" and key **72**). Because 72 points equal one inch, this adds one inch to the existing one-inch top margin, placing the title two inches from the top of the page.
7. Press Tab, set the After text box to 24 points, and click OK. The heading now starts at two inches (check on the status bar that the insertion point is positioned At 2") and is followed by two line spaces.
8. Click the Center button to center the heading.

TIP: The keyboard shortcut Ctrl+0 (zero) adds 12 points of space before a paragraph (pressing it again removes the space), and Ctrl+Shift+N removes all paragraph and character formatting, restoring the text to default formatting.

Paragraph Indents

An *indent* increases the distance between the side of a paragraph and the left or right margin. Indented paragraphs appear to have different margin settings. Word provides a variety of indents to emphasize paragraphs in a document, as shown in Figure 4-6.

FIGURE 4-6
Paragraph indents

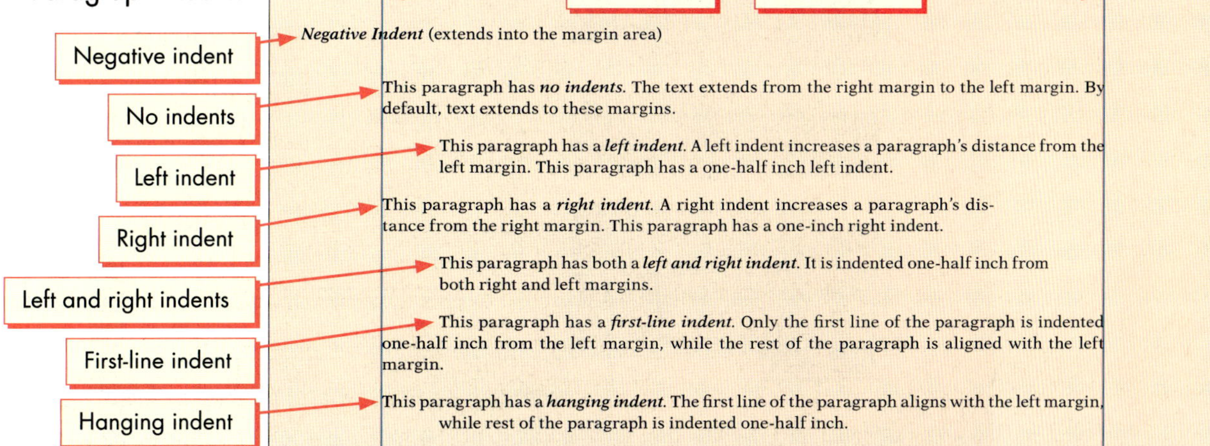

To set paragraph indents, you can use one of these methods:

- Indent buttons on the Formatting toolbar
- Paragraph dialog box
- Keyboard
- Ruler

EXERCISE 4-4 Set Indents Using Indent Buttons and the Paragraph Dialog Box

1. Select from the paragraph that begins "From Albuquerque" through the end of the document.

2. Click the Increase Indent button on the Formatting toolbar. The selected text is indented 0.5 inch from the left side.
3. Click the Increase Indent button again. Now the text is indented 1 inch.

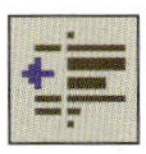

4. Click the Decrease Indent button twice to return the text to the left margin.
5. With the text still selected, open the Paragraph dialog box.
6. Under Indentation, change the Left setting to 0.75 inch and the Right setting to 0.75 inch.
7. Click to open the Special drop-down list in the Paragraph dialog box and choose First line. Word sets the By box to 0.5" by default. Notice the change in the Preview box.

FIGURE 4-7
Setting indents with the Paragraph dialog box

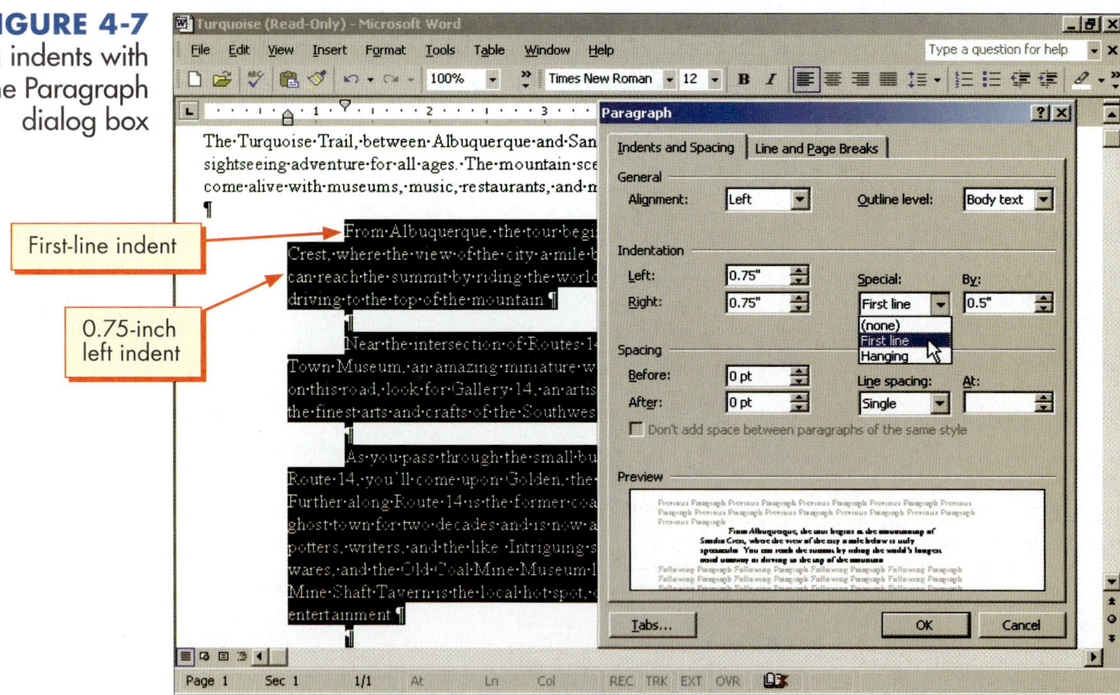

NOTE: To set a *negative indent*, which extends a paragraph into the left or right margin areas, enter a negative number in the Left or Right text boxes. Any indent that occurs between the left and right margins is known as a *positive indent*.

8. Click OK. Now each paragraph is indented from the left and right margins by 0.75 inch and the first line of each paragraph is indented another 0.5 inch.

TIP: The keyboard shortcut Ctrl+M increases an indent, Ctrl+Shift+M decreases an indent, Ctrl+T creates a hanging indent, and Ctrl+Shift+T removes a hanging indent.

EXERCISE 4-5 Set Indents Using the Ruler

You can set indents by dragging the *indent markers* that appear at the left and right of the horizontal ruler. There are four indent markers:

- The *first-line indent* marker is the top triangle that appears at the left of the ruler. Drag it to the right to indent the first line of a paragraph.
- The *hanging indent* marker is the bottom triangle. Drag it to the right to indent the remaining lines of a paragraph.
- The *left indent* marker is the small rectangle. Drag it to move the first-line indent marker and the hanging indent marker at the same time.
- The *right indent* marker appears at the right margin on the ruler. Drag it to the left to create a right indent.

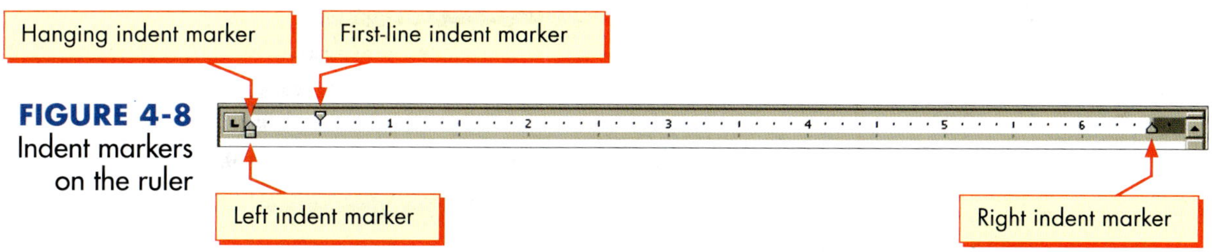

FIGURE 4-8 Indent markers on the ruler

1. Position the insertion point in the first paragraph below the title.
2. Point to the first-line indent marker on the ruler. A ScreenTip confirms that you are pointing to the correct marker.
3. Drag the first-line indent marker 0.5 inches to the right. The first line of the paragraph is indented by 0.5 inch.
4. Drag the first-line indent marker back to the zero position. Point to the hanging indent marker and drag it 0.5 inches to the right. The lines below the first line are indented 0.5 inch, creating a hanging indent.

5. Drag the hanging indent marker back to the zero position. Drag the left indent marker (the small rectangle) 1 inch to the right. The entire paragraph is indented by 1 inch.
6. Select the first two paragraphs below the title and press Ctrl + Shift + N to remove all formatting from the paragraphs.
7. Position the insertion point in the second paragraph, which begins "From Albuquerque," and re-create the indents using the ruler:
   - Drag the left indent marker 0.75 inch to the right to indent the entire paragraph.
   - Drag the first-line indent marker to the 1.25-inch mark on the ruler.
   - Drag the right indent marker 0.75 to the left (to the 5.75-inch mark on the ruler). Now the paragraph is indented like the paragraphs below it.
8. Use the Format menu to display the Styles and Formatting task pane.
9. In the list of available formats, point to the formats you created for the title and the indented text and notice the description that appears.
10. Use the task pane to select all instances of the indented format (which is listed as Left: 0.75″).
11. Use the ruler to drag the first-line indent marker to the 1-inch mark. Now the opening line of each paragraph is indented only 0.25 inch.
12. Switch to the Reveal Formatting task pane. Notice the description of the paragraph formatting of the selected text.

FIGURE 4-9
Indenting text

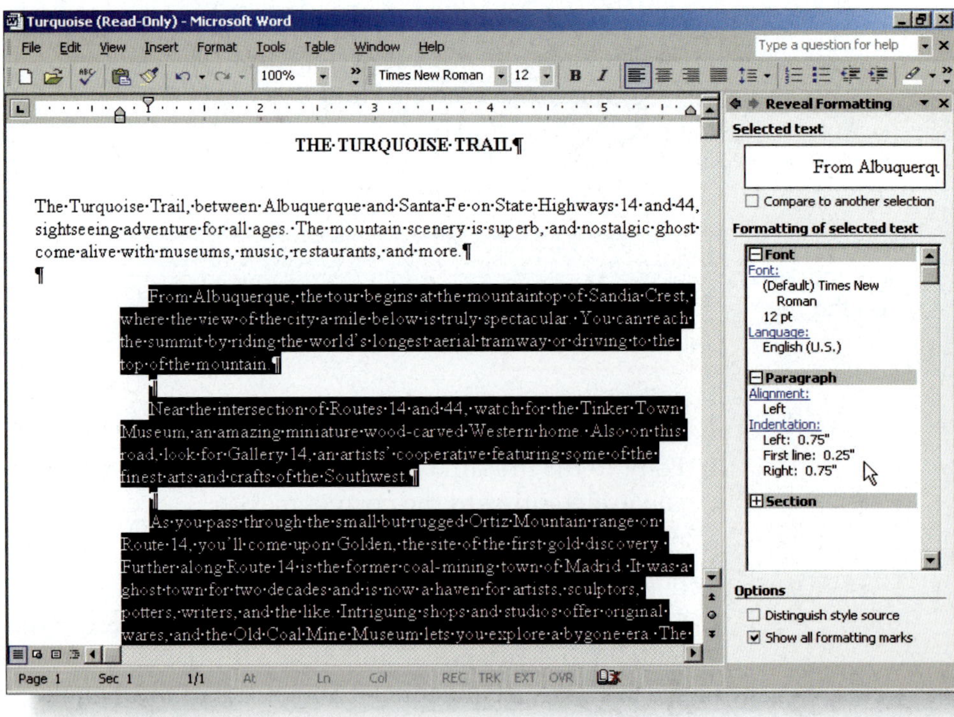

TIP: You can click the Alignment or Indentation links in the task pane to open the Paragraph dialog box.

13. Save the document as ***[your initials]*4-5** in a new folder for Lesson 4.
14. Print the document. Do not close it.

Borders and Shading

To add visual interest to paragraphs—or to an entire page—you can add a *border,* such as a line or a box. You can also use *shading* to fill in the background behind the text of a paragraph. Shading can appear as a shade of gray, as a pattern, or as a color. Borders can appear in a variety of line styles and colors.

This lesson explains how to use the Borders and Shading dialog box to set border and shading options and how to use the Borders button on the Formatting toolbar (which applies the most recently selected border style).

EXERCISE 4-6 Add Borders to Paragraphs

1. With the file ***[your initials]*4-5** open, go to the end of the document. Press Enter twice to start a new paragraph

NOTE: Remember that paragraph formatting is contained in the paragraph mark. When you press Enter to start a new paragraph, the formatting (indents, line spacing, paragraph spacing) is applied to the new paragraph.

2. Press Ctrl + Q to remove the formatting carried over from the previous paragraph (or choose Clear Formatting from the Styles and Formatting task pane).
3. Key the text shown in Figure 4-10.

FIGURE 4-10

```
Let Duke City Gateway be your trail guide! We can provide you with a
colorful printed guide of a trail you can follow at your leisure and in
your own vehicle. Or we can lead the way with an escorted tour. Call us
today at 555-1234 for more information.
```

4. Make sure the insertion point is to the left of the current paragraph mark or within the paragraph.

5. Choose Borders and Shading from the Format menu. The Borders and Shading dialog box appears. Click the Borders tab, if necessary.
6. Scroll to see the options in the Style box and choose the first border style (the solid line).
7. Open the Color drop-down list and choose Blue.
8. Open the Width drop-down list and choose 2 ¼ pt.
9. Under Setting, click the Box style. The Preview box shows the Box setting. Each button around the Preview box indicates a selected border.

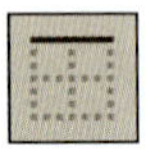

10. Click the top line of the box border in the Preview box. The top line is deleted and the corresponding button is no longer selected. Click the Top Border button or the top border area in the diagram to restore the top line border.

FIGURE 4-11
Borders and Shading dialog box

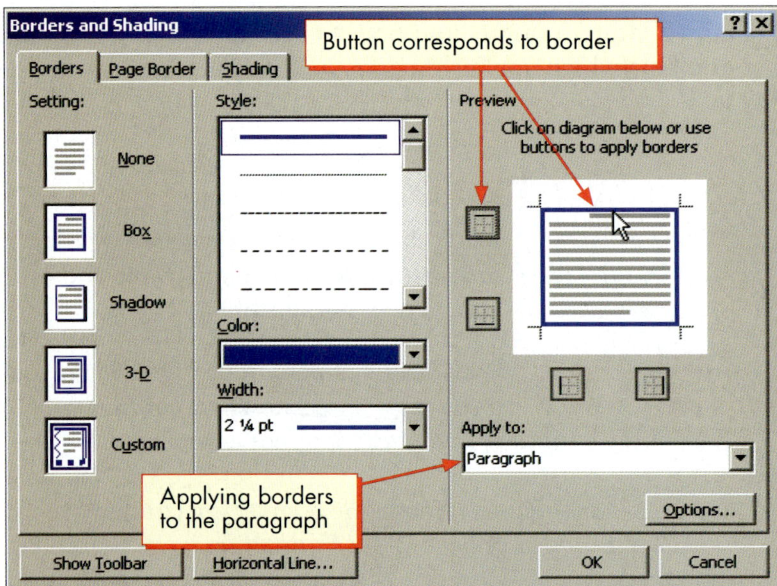

11. Click the Options button. In the Border and Shading Options dialog box, change the top, bottom, left, and right settings to 5 points to increase the space between the text and the border. Click OK.
12. Change the Box setting to Shadow. This setting applies a black shadow to the blue border. Notice that the Apply to box is set to Paragraph. Click OK. The shadow border is applied to the paragraph.
13. Click anywhere within the title “THE TURQUOISE TRAIL.”
14. Click the down arrow next to the Borders button on the Formatting toolbar. A menu of border options appears.

FIGURE 4-12
Border options on the Formatting toolbar

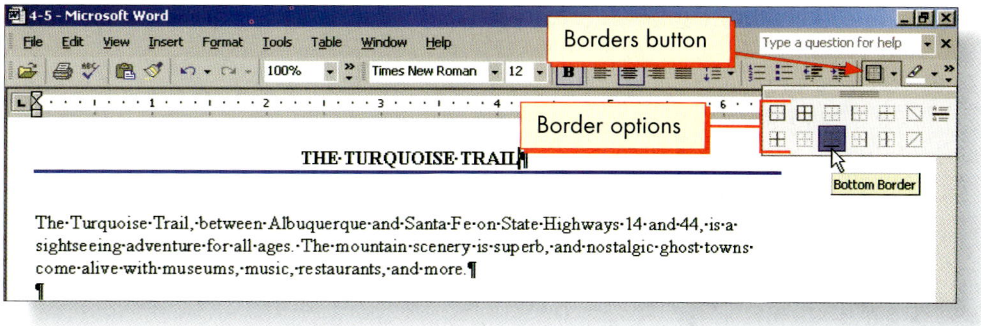

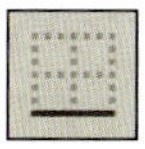

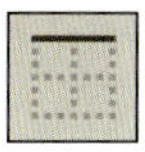

15. Click the Bottom Border button. A bottom border with the options previously set in the Borders and Shading dialog box (solid line, 2¼ points wide, blue) is applied to the title.
16. Click the No Border button to delete the border.
17. Reapply the bottom border and click the Top Border button to add a top border as well.

NOTE: Borders and shading, when applied to a paragraph, extend from the left margin to the right margin or, if indents are set, from the left indent to the right indent.

EXERCISE 4-7 Apply Borders to Selected Text and a Page

In addition to paragraphs, you can apply borders to selected text or to an entire page.

1. In the third paragraph below the title (which begins "Near the"), select the text "Gallery 14." Open the Borders and Shading dialog box.
2. From the Style box, scroll to choose the fifth line style from the bottom. Word automatically applies the Box setting.
3. Change the Color to red. Notice that the Apply to box indicates Text.

NOTE: When the Apply to box indicates Text, the borders are applied only to the selected text and not to the paragraph. If you include a paragraph mark in your selection, the borders are applied to the paragraph unless you change the Apply to setting to Text. It's important to notice the Apply to setting when applying borders and shading, or you might not get the results you intended.

4. Click the Page Border tab. Choose the third-to-last line style (a band of three shades of gray) and click the 3-D setting. The width should be 3 points.
5. Click OK. Notice the text border added to "Gallery 14" and the page border. Word changes the document display to Print Layout view so you can see the page border.

FIGURE 4-13
Applying borders to selected text and to the page

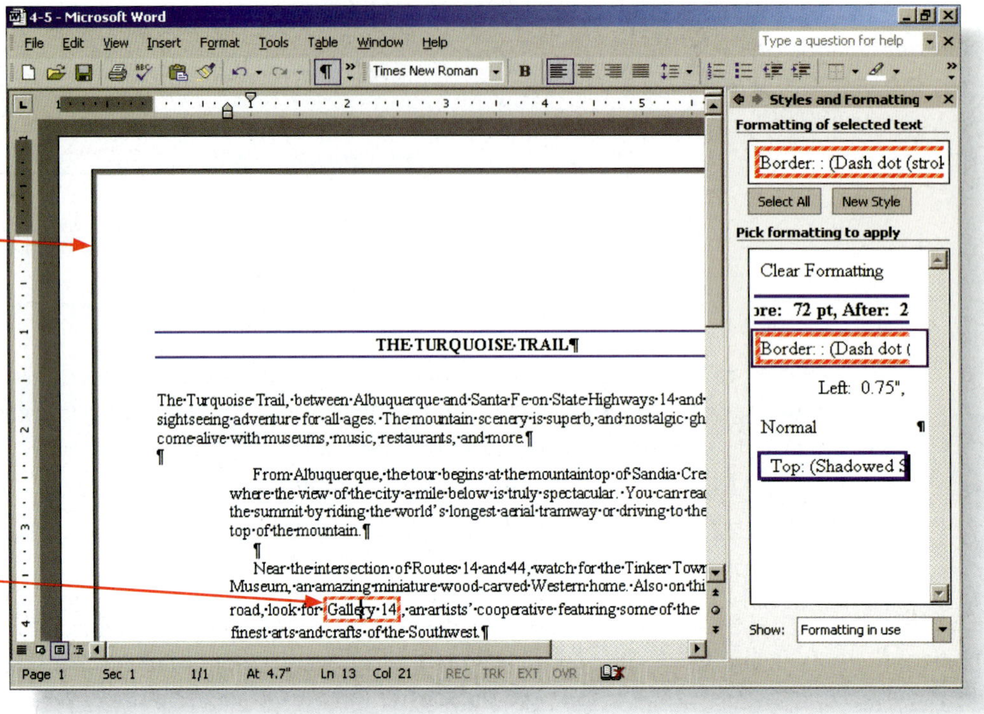

6. Display the Styles and Formatting task pane. Open the **Show** drop-down list at the bottom of the task pane and choose **Formatting in use**. Notice the new border styles.

7. Click the Normal View button located at the bottom left of the status bar to return to Normal view. The page border is not visible in this view.

EXERCISE 4-8 Apply Shading to a Paragraph

1. Click anywhere in the last paragraph and open the Borders and Shading dialog box.
2. Click the **Borders** tab. Remove the current border setting by choosing **None**.
3. Click the **Shading** tab. Under **Fill**, choose the third box in the first row of the color palette, which is 10% gray. (See Figure 4-14 on the next page.)
4. Open the **Style** drop-down list and scroll to view other shading options. Notice that you can apply a pattern, such as vertical lines or a grid. Close the **Style** drop-down list without choosing a style.
5. Click **OK** to apply the gray shading to the paragraph.

NOTE: Shading can affect the readability of text. When using dark colors or patterns, it's a good idea to choose a larger type size and bold text.

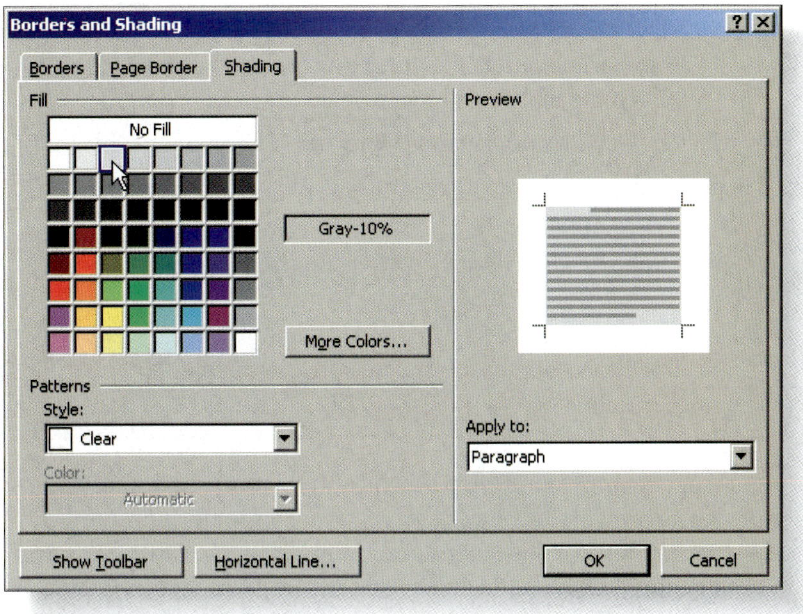

FIGURE 4-14 Shading options in the Borders and Shading dialog box

6. Save the document as ***[your initials]*****4-8** in your Lesson 4 folder.
7. Print the document. Do not close it.

Repeating and Copying Formats

You can quickly repeat, copy, or remove paragraph formatting using many of the techniques you learned in Lesson 3 for character formatting. For example, use F4 to repeat paragraph formatting, use the Format Painter button to copy paragraph formatting, and use the task panes to apply formatting you or Word have already created.

EXERCISE 4-9 Repeat, Copy, and Remove Paragraph Formats

1. Click anywhere in the first paragraph under the title (which begins "The Turquoise Trail") and change the paragraph alignment to justified.

NOTE: You can click in a paragraph when repeating, copying, or removing formatting. You do not have to select the entire paragraph.

2. Click within the next paragraph and press F4 to repeat the formatting. Do the same for the rest of the paragraphs in the document.
3. Click anywhere in the last paragraph with the shading.

4. Click the Format Painter button and then click within the paragraph above the shaded paragraph to copy the paragraph formatting (both the shading and the indents).
5. Click the Undo button to undo the paragraph formatting.
6. Click anywhere in the shaded paragraph and press Ctrl+Q to remove the formatting.
7. Click the Undo button to restore the formatting.

EXERCISE 4-10 Apply a Paragraph Style from the Task Pane

You can apply your own paragraph formats, as you've done so far, or use predefined paragraph styles. A *paragraph style* is a format created by Word that uses specific paragraph formatting, such as spacing, indentation, and alignment; and often includes specific character formatting. You can use Word's predefined paragraph styles for document titles and headings as well as longer paragraphs (often called body text).

1. Make sure the Styles and Formatting task pane is displayed. Select the text with the red text border ("Gallery 14") and choose Clear Formatting from the task pane.
2. Select all the text below the title, including the shaded paragraph.
3. Choose All styles from the Show drop-down list to see all the predefined paragraph and character styles in the task pane.
4. Point to the paragraph style Body Text in the list. This style uses the "Normal" style (which is 12-point Times New Roman, left-aligned, single-spaced) with 6-point spacing after paragraphs.
5. Click the Body Text style to apply it to the selected paragraphs.

NOTE: Typically, you would format a long document using a combination of Word's body text styles (such as Body Text and Body Text Indent) and heading styles (such as Heading 1 and Heading 2). This helps give your document a unified look.

6. Make sure paragraph marks are showing (click the Show/Hide ¶ button if necessary). Delete the paragraph marks between paragraphs. These aren't needed, because the Body Text style includes spacing after paragraphs.
7. Select the paragraphs below the title again and apply the Body Text First Indent paragraph style. This style adds a 0.15-inch first-line indent to the paragraphs.

FIGURE 4-15
Applying a paragraph style

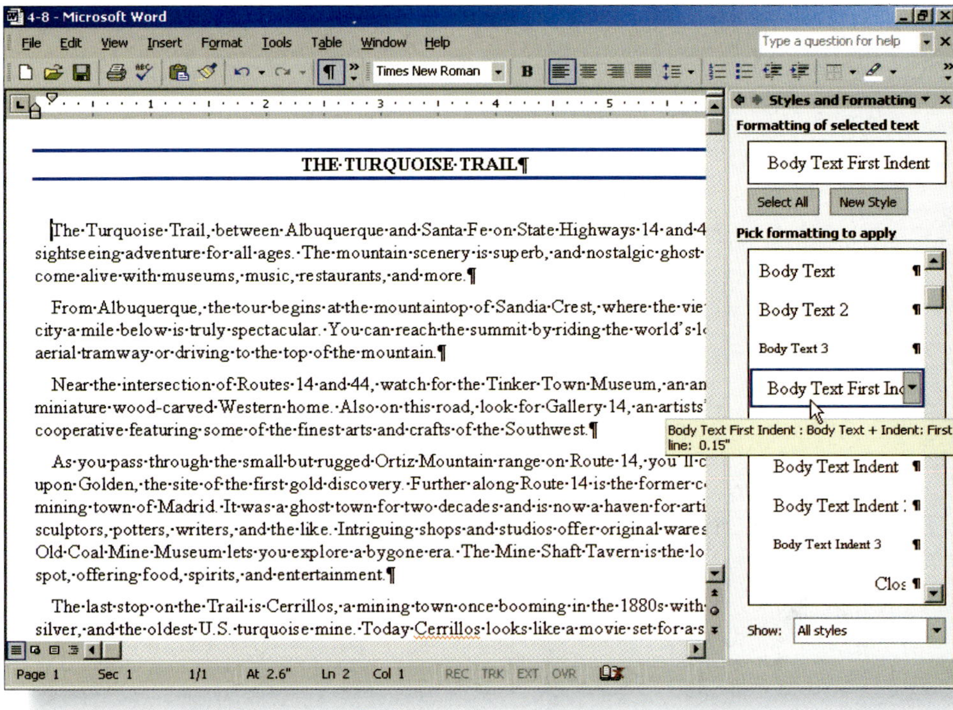

8. Scroll the style list to view some of the other available paragraph styles (each has a paragraph mark to the right of the style name).
9. Click within the document title and then scroll to the Title style at the bottom of the list. Point to the style to see its characteristics; then click the style name to apply it to the document title. Notice that the Title style includes character formatting (16-point Arial).
10. Use the Paragraph dialog box to change the spacing for the title back to 72 points before and 24 points after.
11. Use the Borders and Shading dialog box to remove the page border (click the Page Border tab and choose None).
12. Save the document as ***[your initials]*4-10** in your Lesson 4 folder.
13. Print and close the document.

Bulleted and Numbered Lists

Bulleted lists and *numbered lists* are types of hanging indents you can use to organize important details in a document. In a bulleted list, each paragraph is preceded by a character known as a bullet (•). In a numbered list, each paragraph is preceded by a sequential number or letter.

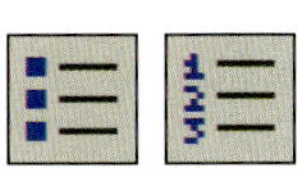

To create bulleted lists or numbered lists, you can use the Bullets and Numbering dialog box or the Bullets button or Numbering button on the Formatting toolbar (which apply the most recently selected bullet or numbering style).

WORD

EXERCISE 4-11 Create a Bulleted List

1. Open the file **Memo2**. This document is a two-page memo. If the task pane is displayed, you might want to close it to allow more room for the document.
2. Change the date in the date line of the memo to today's date.
3. Scroll toward the end of the document and select the list of items from "Airline tickets" to "Flight bag."
4. Choose Bullets and Numbering from the Format menu. The Bullets and Numbering dialog box appears.
5. Click the Bulleted tab if it is not showing and choose the standard round bullet shape.

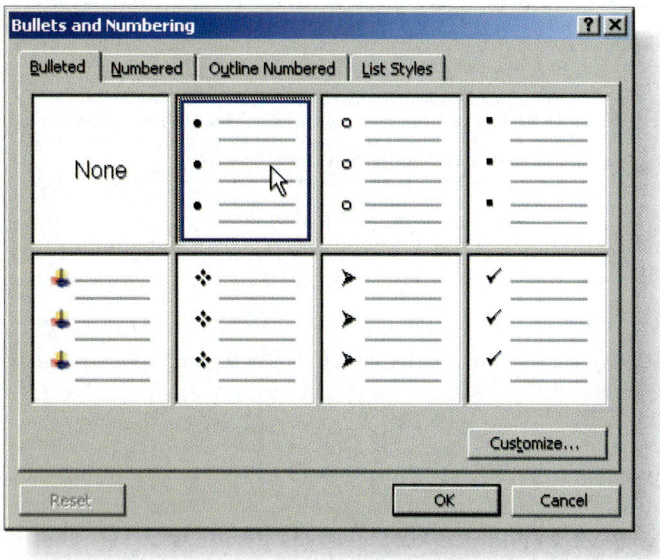

FIGURE 4-16 Bullet options in the Bullets and Numbering dialog box

6. Click the Customize button to check the settings in the Customize Bulleted List dialog box.
7. Under Bullet position, check that the Indent at setting is 0.25 inch. Under Text position, check that the Tab space after setting is 0.5 inch and the Indent at setting is 0.5 inch. These are the customary settings for bulleted lists. Adjust your settings if needed.
8. Click OK in the Customize Bulleted List dialog box and then click OK in the Bullets and Numbering dialog box. The selected text is a bulleted list. (See Figure 4-17 on the next page.)
9. Scroll up to the paragraph under the heading "Record Keeping." At the end of the paragraph, change the period after "master file" to a colon.

FIGURE 4-17
Bulleted list

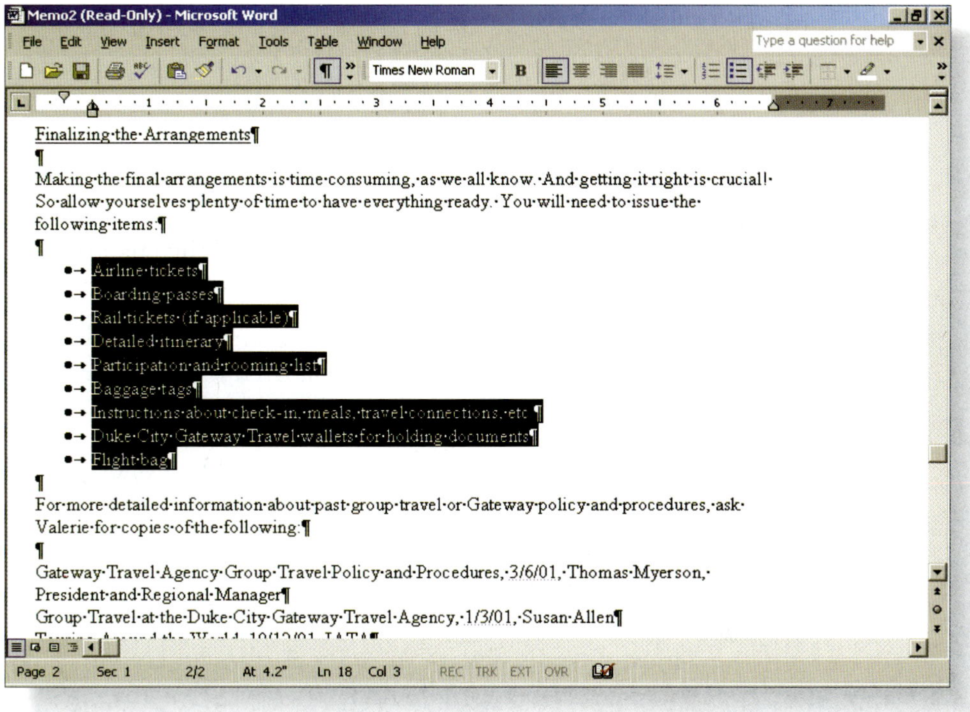

10. Press Enter twice. Key the following list, pressing Enter at the end of each line except the last line:

Name
Itinerary
Accommodations
Options bought
Money paid

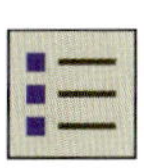

11. Select the list and then click the Bullets button on the Formatting toolbar. (You might need to click the Toolbar Options button to locate the Bullets button.) Word applies the bullet style that was most recently chosen in the Bullets and Numbering dialog box.

12. Click the Undo button to undo the bullets applied to the list.

TIP: To add color and interest to a document, you can apply a picture bullet. Click the Picture button in the Customized Bulleted List dialog box, select a picture bullet, and click OK. You can also choose a symbol character for a bullet. Symbols are discussed later in the lesson.

EXERCISE 4-12 Create a Numbered List

1. Select the list of items you just keyed (from "Name" through "Money paid").

2. Open the Bullets and Numbering dialog box and click the Numbered tab.
3. Choose one of the numbered (1, 2, 3) styles.
4. Click the Customize button to check the settings in the Customize Numbered List dialog box.
5. Under Number position, check that the Aligned at setting is 0.25 inch. Under Text position, check that the Tab space after setting is 0.5 inch and the Indent at setting is 0.5 inch. These are the customary settings for numbered lists. Adjust your settings if needed.

TIP: When a list contains 10 or more items, change the Number position setting in the Customize Numbered List dialog box to Right alignment so all the numbers right-align attractively.

6. Click OK in the Customize Numbered List dialog box. Then click OK in the Bullets and Numbering dialog box.
7. Select the last three paragraphs in the document, from "Gateway Travel Agency" through "IATA."

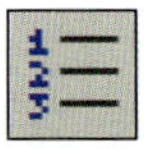

8. Click the Numbering button to format the list using the style that was most recently chosen from the Bullets and Numbering dialog box.

NOTE: If the AutoCorrect Options button appears after you apply numbering formats to the list, ignore the button. Word detects other list formats in the document and wants to offer you options to make your document consistent. AutoCorrect is taught later in this course.

9. With the list still selected, open the Bullets and Numbering dialog box and choose the uppercase Roman numeral format. Click OK.

EXERCISE 4-13 Change a Bulleted or Numbered List

Word's bulleting and numbering feature is very flexible. After a list is bulleted or numbered, you can change it in several ways. You can:

- Convert bullets to numbers or numbers to bullets in a list.
- Add or remove items in a bulleted or numbered list and have the list renumbered automatically.
- Interrupt a bulleted or numbered list to create several shorter lists.
- Turn bullets or numbering off for part of a list or the entire list.
- Customize the bulleted or numbered list by changing the symbol or font used or the position of bullets, numbers, and text.

1. Select the list that starts with "Airline tickets."
2. Open the Bullets and Numbering dialog box and click the Numbered tab.

3. Choose a numbered format and click OK to convert the bullets to numbers.
4. Select and delete the sixth item in the list, "Baggage tags." Word renumbers the list automatically.
5. Place the insertion point at the end of the last item in the numbered list (to the right of "Flight bag").
6. Press Enter and key **Baggage tags**. The formatting is carried to the new line.
7. Place the insertion point at the end of the sixth item (after "etc.") and press Enter.
8. Key in italic ***These items are optional:***

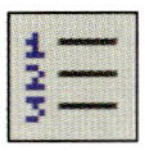

9. Click within the italic text and click the Numbering button on the Formatting toolbar to turn numbering off for this item. The numbered list still continues below the italic text.
10. Right-click the numbered item below the italic text and choose Restart Numbering from the shortcut menu. The numbering no longer continues from the previous list, but starts with "1."
11. Insert a blank line above the italic text (click to the left of "*These*" and press Enter).

EXERCISE 4-14 Create an Outline Numbered List

An *outline numbered list* has indented subparagraphs. For example, your list can start with item number "1)," followed by another level of indented items numbered "a)," "b)," and "c)." An outline numbered list can have up to nine levels and is often used for technical or legal documents.

FIGURE 4-18 Outline numbered options in the Bullets and Numbering dialog box

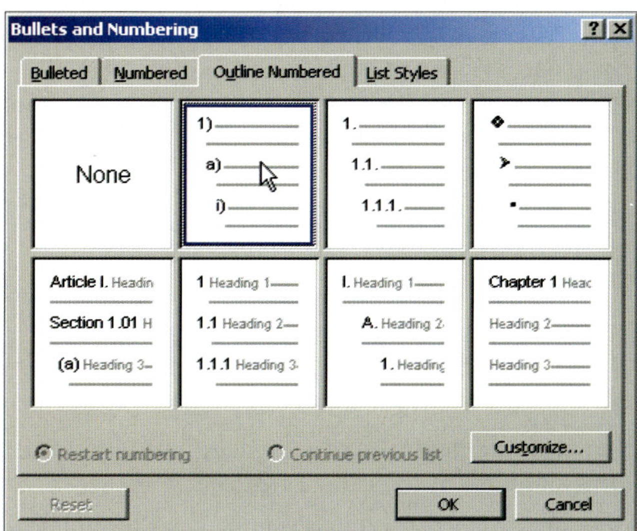

1. Select the numbered list that begins with "Name" and open the Bullets and Numbering dialog box.
2. Click the Outline Numbered tab. Notice the outline numbering styles available.
3. Click the outline numbered option that begins with 1) and click OK. The

list has the outline number format with different indent settings from the previous numbered list.

4. Position the insertion point at the end of "1) Name" and press Enter.

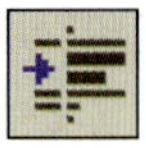

5. Click the Increase Indent button (or press Tab) and key **Group name**.
6. Press Enter and key **Participant name**. The numbered list now has two indented subparagraphs.
7. With the insertion point at the end of "b) Participant name," press Enter and click the Increase Indent button (or press Tab). You can now add a third level to your list.

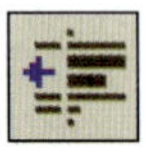

8. Click the Decrease Indent button (or press Shift+Tab) once, and then click it again. You can now add a new item numbered "2)."
9. Delete the paragraph mark in the new line numbered "2)."
10. Under "2) Itinerary," add the following three indented subparagraphs:

    Air
    Land
    Sea

11. If your document is now three pages long (the status bar will show "2/3," indicating that you are looking at page 2 of 3 pages), delete the blank paragraph marks below the four underlined headings ("Deadlines," "Record Keeping" and so on). Format each underlined heading with 3 points of paragraph spacing after it.
12. Save the document as ***[your initials]*4-14** in your Lesson 4 folder.
13. Print the document. Leave it open for the next exercise.

Symbols and Special Characters

The fonts you use with Word include *special characters* that do not appear on your keyboard, such as those used in foreign languages (for example, ç, Ö, and Ω). There are additional fonts, such as Wingdings and Symbol, that consist entirely of special characters.

To insert symbols and special characters in your documents, you can use the Symbol command on the Insert menu or use keyboard shortcuts.

EXERCISE 4-15 Insert Symbols

1. Scroll toward the beginning of the document. Position the insertion point to the immediate left of the title "Deadlines."
2. Choose Symbol from the Insert menu. The Symbol dialog box appears.

3. Make sure the Symbols tab is showing. Choose (normal text) from the Font drop-down list box.
4. Scroll through the grid of available symbol characters for normal text. You can also open the Subset drop-down list and see the list of symbol categories.
5. Open the Font drop-down list and choose Wingdings. The characters included in the Wingdings font appear in the grid.

FIGURE 4-19
Symbol dialog box

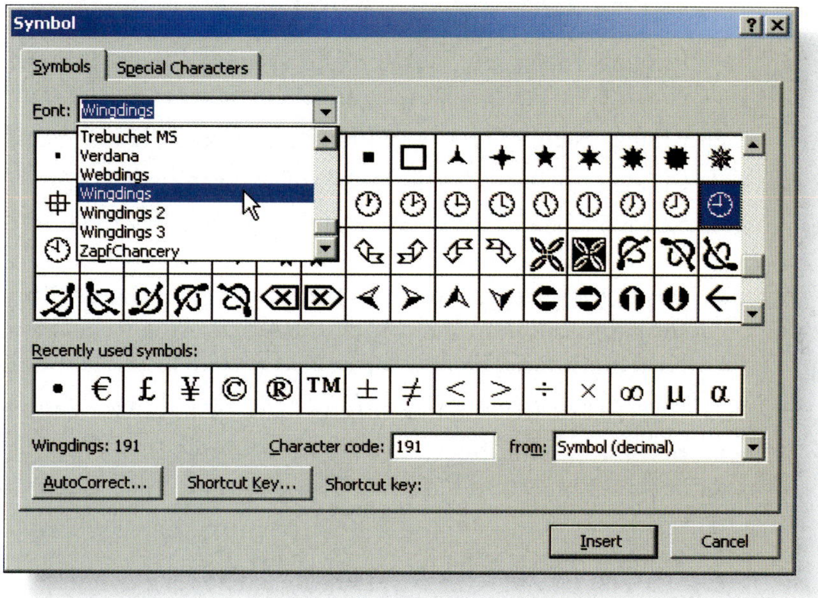

6. Scroll down the grid and click any of the clock symbols.

TIP: Notice the Recently Used Symbols shown in the Symbol dialog box. Word displays the 16 most recently used symbols.

7. Click Insert and then click Close. The symbol appears in the document.
8. Select the clock and increase its font size to 24.
9. Select the Roman numeral list at the end of the document. You're going to change the numerals to a symbol character.
10. Open the Bullets and Numbering dialog box. Display the Bulleted tab, click Customize, and then click Character.
11. Choose a symbol from either the Symbol or Wingdings font that would be appropriate for this bulleted list. Click OK and then click OK again. The Roman numerals are replaced with your chosen bullet symbol.

WORD

EXERCISE 4-16 Insert Special Characters

You can use the Symbol dialog box and shortcut keys to insert characters such as an en dash or an em dash. An *en dash* is slightly wider than a hyphen. An *em dash,* which is somewhat wider than an en dash, is used in sentences where you would normally insert two hyphens.

1. Scroll to the paragraph that begins "July 1." Position the insertion point to the immediate right of the "1," hold down Shift, and press → three times to select the space, hyphen, and space. (This technique is much easier than trying to drag to select the three characters.)
2. Choose Symbol from the Insert menu and click the Special Characters tab.
3. Choose Em Dash from the list of characters. (Notice the keyboard shortcut listed for the character.) Click Insert and then click Close. The em dash replaces the three characters.
4. Select the three characters immediately following "July 15." Press Alt + Ctrl + the minus sign on the numeric keypad. An em dash is inserted. (If you don't have a numeric keypad, press F4 to repeat the character.)
5. Insert em dashes after "July 17," "August 1," and "August 15."
6. Scroll to the numbered lists under "Finalizing the Arrangements." In the second numbered list, edit "Flight bag" to read **Easy Carry flight bag**
7. Position the insertion point to the immediate right of "Carry." Open the Symbol dialog box and insert the trademark symbol from the Special Characters list. (Note that you can also use the keyboard shortcut Ctrl + Alt + T.)

TIP: Not only can you use keyboard shortcuts to insert some special characters, but you can also key text Word will automatically convert to a special character or symbol. For example, you can key **(tm)** and Word's AutoCorrect feature will insert the trademark symbol automatically. Or you can key **:)** and Word will insert a happy face character. To review the special characters AutoCorrect can enter automatically, choose AutoCorrect Options from the Tools menu and click the AutoCorrect tab.

8. Format the first line of the memo with 72 points of paragraph spacing before it so the first line is two inches from the top of the page. (See Appendix F: "Standard Forms for Business Documents.")
9. Make the memo two pages long by selecting the entire document and reducing it by one font size (use Ctrl + Shift + <).
10. Go to the end of the document and press Enter twice. Notice that pressing Enter once starts a new bulleted item and pressing Enter again turns off the bulleted formatting, creating two new unbulleted paragraph marks.

11. Key your initials in lowercase letters. These are referred to in business documents as your reference initials

NOTE: Reference initials are the initials of the person who keys the document, when that person is not the writer of the document.

12. Save the document as ***[your initials]*4-16** in your Lesson 4 folder.

13. Print and close the document.

USING HELP

By now you might be familiar with or aware of Microsoft Office's speech recognition feature. If your computer is equipped with a microphone, you can dictate text instead of keying it, and use voice commands for menu, toolbar, and dialog box items.

Learn more about speech recognition:

1. In the Ask a Question box in the upper right corner of the screen, key **speech recognition** and press Enter.

2. Review the list of topics. Click About speech recognition

3. Review the information in the Help window. To understand the difference between dictation and voice commands, click the link at the bottom of the window, Dictating text and giving commands

FIGURE 4-20
Getting Help about speech recognition

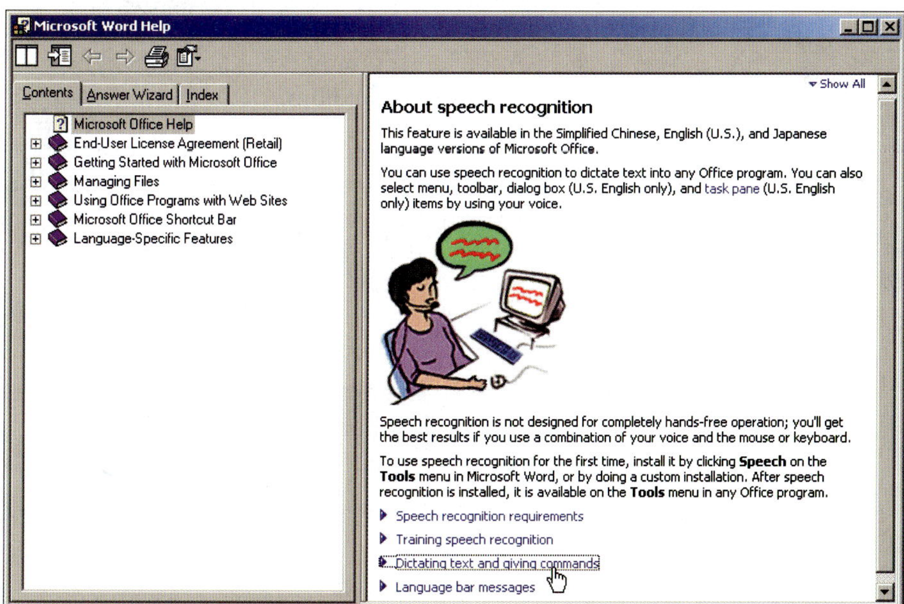

4. Click the Ask a Question box to select the text you entered and press Enter to reopen the list of topics. Choose another topic.
5. Close Help when you have finished.

LESSON 4 Summary

- Paragraph alignment is the horizontal position of paragraphs in relation to the left and right margins. Paragraphs can be left-aligned, centered, right-aligned, or justified.
- Line space is the amount of vertical space between lines of text in a paragraph. Lines can be single-spaced, 1.5-line spaced, double-spaced, or set to a specific value.
- Paragraph space is the amount of space above or below a paragraph. Paragraph space is set in points—12 points of space equals one line space for 12-point text.
- A left indent or right indent increases a paragraph's distance from the left or right margin. A first-line indent indents only the first line of a paragraph. A hanging indent indents the second and subsequent lines of a paragraph.
- To set indents by using the horizontal ruler, drag the left indent marker (small rectangle), the first-line indent marker (top triangle), or the hanging indent marker (bottom triangle), which are all on the left end of the ruler, or the right indent marker (triangle) on the right end of the ruler.
- A border is a line or box added to selected text, a paragraph, or a page. Shading fills in the background of selected text or paragraphs. Borders and shading can appear in a variety of styles and colors.
- Repeat paragraph formats by pressing F4. Copy paragraph formats by using the Format Painter button. Apply an existing formatting to selected text by using the Styles and Formatting task pane. Remove paragraph formats by pressing Ctrl + Q or choosing Clear Formatting from the task pane.
- Use the Styles and Formatting task pane to apply a paragraph style—one of Word's predefined formats, such as Heading 1 or Body Text.
- Format a list of items as a bulleted or numbered list. In a bulleted list, each item is indented and preceded by a bullet character or other symbol. In a numbered list, each item is indented and preceded by a sequential number or letter.
- Click Customize in the Bullets and Numbering dialog box to check or adjust the position of bullets or numbers, to check or adjust the position of text, and to change the symbol or font used.

- Remove a bullet or number from an item in a list by clicking the Bullets button or the Numbering button on the toolbar. Press Enter mid-list to automatically add another bulleted or numbered item. Press Enter twice in a list to turn off bullets or numbering.
- An outline numbered list has indented subparagraphs, such as paragraph "1)" followed by indented paragraph "a)" followed by indented paragraph "i)." Increase or decrease the level of numbering for each line item by clicking the Increase Indent button or Decrease Indent button.
- Insert symbols, such as foreign characters, by using the Symbols tab in the Symbol dialog box. Wingdings is an example of a font that contains all symbols.
- Insert special characters, such as an em dash (—), by using the Special Characters tab in the Symbol dialog box.

LESSON 4 Command Summary

FEATURE	BUTTON	MENU	KEYBOARD	SPEECH?
Left-align text		Format, Paragraph	Ctrl + L	✓
Center text		Format, Paragraph	Ctrl + E	✓
Right-align text		Format, Paragraph	Ctrl + R	✓
Justify text		Format, Paragraph	Ctrl + J	✓
Single space		Format, Paragraph	Ctrl + 1	✓
Double space		Format, Paragraph	Ctrl + 2	✓
1.5-line space		Format, Paragraph	Ctrl + 5	✓
Remove paragraph formatting		Format, Paragraph	Ctrl + Q	
Restore text to Normal formatting			Ctrl + Shift + N	

continues

LESSON 4 Command Summary *continued*

FEATURE	BUTTON	MENU	KEYBOARD	SPEECH?
Increase indent	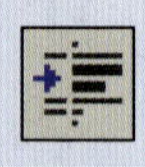	Format, Paragraph	Ctrl + M	✓
Decrease indent	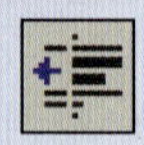	Format, Paragraph	Ctrl + Shift + M	✓
Hanging indent		Format, Paragraph	Ctrl + T	✓
Borders	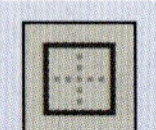	Format, Borders and Shading		✓
Shading		Format, Borders and Shading		✓
Bulleted list	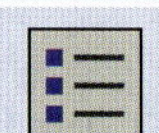	Format, Bullets and Numbering		✓
Numbered list	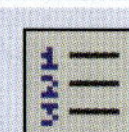	Format, Bullets and Numbering		✓
Symbols and special characters		Insert, Symbol		✓

Concepts Review

TRUE/FALSE QUESTIONS

Each of the following statements is either true or false. Indicate your choice by circling T or F.

T F *1.* You can use the toolbar to right-align paragraphs.

T F *2.* Text that is left-aligned has a ragged left edge.

T F *3.* The Reveal Formatting task pane lists all Word paragraph styles.

T F *4.* The keyboard shortcut Ctrl + 5 changes spacing to 1.5 lines between paragraphs.

T F *5.* You can use the Styles and Formatting task pane to apply an existing paragraph formatting style to text.

T F *6.* Wingdings is a font that contains symbols.

T F *7.* You use 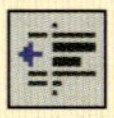 to increase a paragraph indent.

T F *8.* A hanging indent indents all lines in a paragraph except the first line.

SHORT ANSWER QUESTIONS

Write the correct answer in the space provided.

1. Which type of paragraph alignment adds horizontal space to align text evenly along the left and right margins?

____

2. What is the keyboard shortcut for centering text?

____

3. Single, 1.5, and double are examples of what type of spacing?

____

4. If a paragraph uses 12-point Times New Roman text, how many points do two lines of paragraph spacing contain?

____

5. If you click 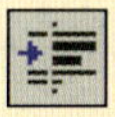 once, how far is selected text indented from the left margin?

____

6. Body Text is an example of what type of style?

____

7. What menu commands open the Bullets and Numbering dialog box?

____

8. Which indent marker is the top triangle on the left side of the ruler?

____

CRITICAL THINKING

Answer these questions on a separate page. There are no right or wrong answers. Support your answers with examples from your own experience, if possible.

1. You can use keyboard shortcuts to change paragraph alignment or you can use the alignment buttons on the Formatting toolbar. Which method do you prefer? Why? When might you use the other method?
2. Many people use bulleted lists and numbered lists interchangeably. Are there times when a bulleted list would be more appropriate than a numbered list and vice versa? Explain your answer.

Lesson Applications

EXERCISE 4-17

Change alignment, line spacing, and paragraph spacing; copy formatting; and apply shading.

1. Start a new document.
2. Key the text shown in Figure 4-21, with the formatting as specified. Use single spacing. Use line breaks (Shift + Enter) to format the text as three paragraphs.

FIGURE 4-21

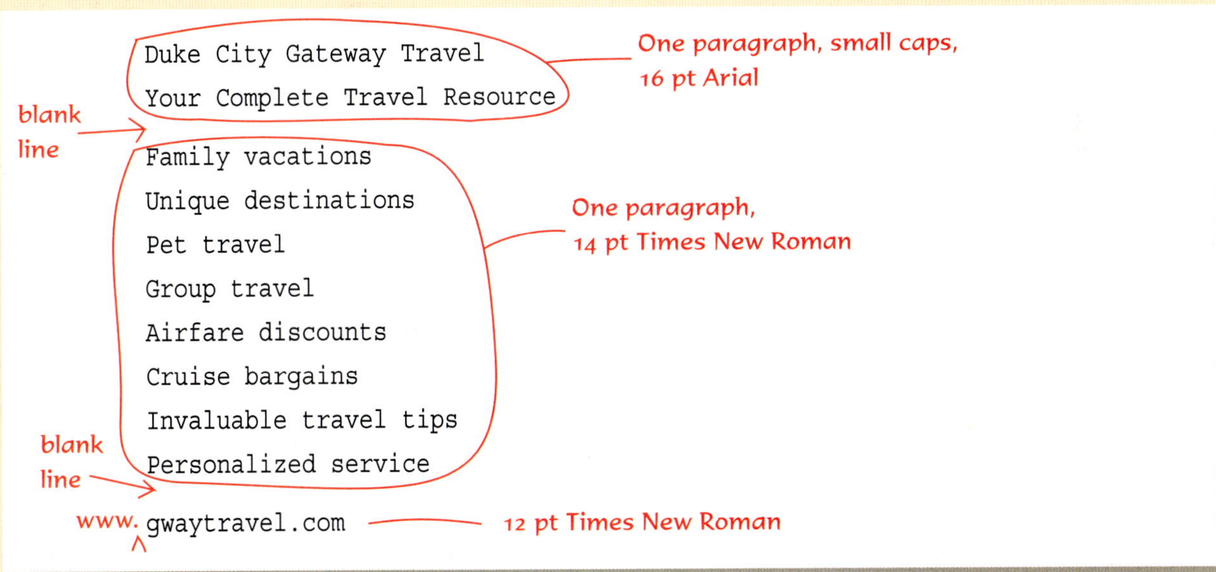

3. Center all the text.
4. Change the line spacing in only the second paragraph to 1.5 lines. Change all the text in this list to Title case (by either editing the text or using the Change Case dialog box).
5. Change the paragraph spacing for only the first paragraph to 72 points before and 24 points after.
6. Add 10% gray shading to the first paragraph. Add a page border using the box setting and the double wavy line style.
7. Apply the character and paragraph formatting of the first paragraph to the last paragraph (the Web address). Delete the extra paragraph mark above the last paragraph.

WORD

8. Save the document as ***[your initials]*****4-17** in your Lesson 4 folder.
9. Print and close the document.

EXERCISE 4-18

Change alignment, line spacing, and paragraph spacing; add a border; repeat formatting; apply a paragraph style; and add symbols.

1. Open the file **Offices1**.
2. Change the title to "East Coast Gateway Travel Offices" and delete all office locations except New York, Boston, and Washington. There should be a blank line below the title and between office locations.
3. Format the first office location with 1.5-line spacing.
4. Repeat the formatting for the remaining two locations.
5. Apply the paragraph style Heading 1 to the title. Change the paragraph spacing to 72 points before and 24 points after. Delete the blank paragraph mark after the title.
6. Add a 3/4-point, black, double-line bottom border to the title.
7. Center the second office location text and right-align the last office location text.
8. Replace the text "Tel." throughout the document with the telephone symbol of the Wingdings font (first row, eighth symbol). Leave the space between the symbol and the telephone number.
9. Save the document as ***[your initials]*****4-18** in your Lesson 4 folder.
10. Print and close the document.

EXERCISE 4-19

Indent paragraphs, create bulleted and numbered lists, and change paragraph spacing.

1. Open the file **Safari**.
2. Make corrections to the document, as shown in Figure 4-22 (on the next page). Refer to Appendix D: "Proofreaders' Marks," if necessary. When splitting the first paragraph, be sure to include a blank line between the two new paragraphs.
3. Customize the bullets to a symbol or picture bullet of your choice.
4. Format the title with paragraph spacing of 72 points before and 24 points after. Delete the blank paragraph mark below the title.

FIGURE 4-22

Gateway Travel Walking Safari in Zambia — 16-pt Arial bold centered

Congratulations on choosing our most exciting special tour: a walking safari in North Luangwa National Park, Zambia. It's one thing to experience an African safari from a Land Cruiser, but for the wildest time imaginable, there's nothing like a walking safari. The feeling of immediacy and intimacy with the landscape and its inhabitants has made the walking safari the most popular new tour in Africa. The rugged and roadless 1800-square-mile wildlife enclave between the Luangwa River and the 4600-foot Muchinga Escarpment provides the ~~optimal~~ perfect setting.

to date

12-pt Arial

You'll be thrilled at the sight of: ← 6pt spacing after

Elephants
Lions
Leopards
Buffalo
Zebras
Crocodiles
Hippos
400 species of birds

Bulleted list, 1.5 line spacing

Walking safaris here take two forms: ← 6pt spacing after

day walks from permanent rustic bush camps
point-to-point walks from one mobile tented camp to another

Numbered list, 1.5 line spacing

Either way, you'll be accompanied by experienced guides and you won't be looking through a window. (ital)

5. Add to the title a double-line bottom border in the style and color of your choice.
6. Save the document as ***[your initials]*4-19** in your Lesson 4 folder.
7. Print and close the document.

W O R D

EXERCISE 4-20 Challenge Yourself

Create an outline numbered list, apply paragraph styles, change line spacing, apply shading, and insert a symbol.

1. Start a new document. As an opening paragraph, key **The Gateway Travel Web site (gwaytravel.com), in conjunction with the Travel Outfitters Company, offers the following items for your travel convenience**:
2. After the opening paragraph, key the text shown in Figure 4-23 as an outline numbered list with the numbering style 1), a), i).

FIGURE 4-23

```
Clothing
     Waterproof outerwear
     Deerskin travel slippers
     Packable hats
          Fleece
          Gore-Tex
          Straw
Appliances and gadgets
     Travel hair dryers
     Travel pillows
     Luggage locks
     Travel clocks
     Electrical adapter kits
     Toiletries kits
```

3. At the top of the document, add the title **Online Travel Catalog**
4. Apply Heading 1 style to the title and Body Text style to the opening paragraph.
5. Apply 10% gray shading to the text "gwaytravel.com" in the opening paragraph.
6. Change the line spacing of the outline numbered list to 1.5 lines.
7. Insert an appropriate symbol to the left of the title. Add a space between the symbol and the title text.
8. Save the document as ***[your initials]*4-20** in your Lesson 4 folder.
9. Print and close the document.

On Your Own

In these exercises you work on your own, as you would in a real-life work environment. Use the skills you've learned to accomplish the task—and be creative.

EXERCISE 4-21

Create a flyer for an event, such as a meeting or concert. Use a variety of paragraph alignment settings, line spacing, and paragraph spacing. Add shading to one or more paragraphs and a page border. Include a bulleted list. Save the document as ***[your initials]*****4-21** and print it.

EXERCISE 4-22

Create a set of instructions for how to make something. Use a bulleted list for the materials needed. Use a numbered list to describe the step-by-step instructions. Use borders or shading for emphasis or for paragraphs containing special notes or tips. Save the document as ***[your initials]*****4-22** and print it.

EXERCISE 4-23

Review the foreign-language characters in the Symbols dialog box (normal text). Use a foreign-language dictionary (such as an online dictionary on the Internet) to find a few foreign words you can key in a document by inserting the appropriate foreign-language characters. Include the English translations. Save the document as ***[your initials]*****4-23** and print it.

LESSON 5

Tabs and Tabbed Columns

OBJECTIVES

MOUS ACTIVITIES
In this lesson:
W2002 2-2
See Appendix E.

After completing this lesson, you will be able to:

1. Set tabs.
2. Clear tabs.
3. Adjust tab settings.
4. Set leader tabs.

Estimated Time: 1 hour

Tabs are a paragraph-formatting feature used to align text. When you press the Tab key [Tab], Word inserts a tab character and moves the insertion point to the tab setting, called the *tab stop*. You can set custom tabs or use Word's default tab settings.

NOTE: As with other paragraph-formatting features, tab settings are stored in the paragraph mark at the end of a paragraph. Each time you press [Enter], the tab settings are copied to the next paragraph. You can set tabs before you key text or for existing text.

Setting Tabs

Tabs are set to distribute text evenly between the left and right margins. Word's default tabs are set every half-inch. These tabs are indicated at the bottom of the horizontal ruler by tiny tick marks.

FIGURE 5-1
Default tabs

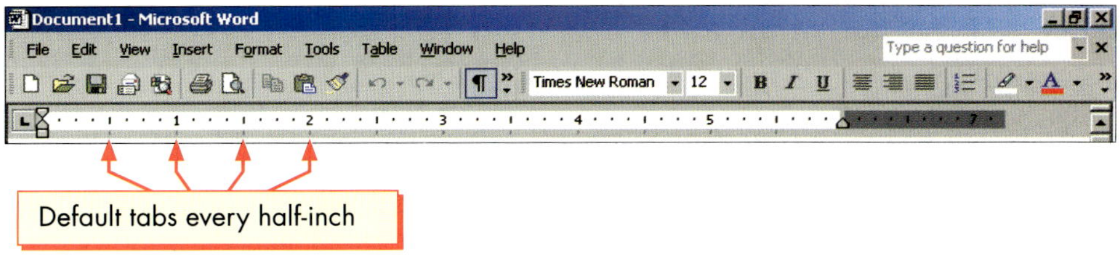

If you don't want to use the half-inch default tab settings, you have two choices:

- Change the distance between the default tab stops.
- Create custom tabs.

The four most common types of custom tabs are left-aligned, centered, right-aligned, and decimal-aligned. Custom tab settings are indicated on the horizontal ruler by *tab markers*.

FIGURE 5-2
Types of tabs

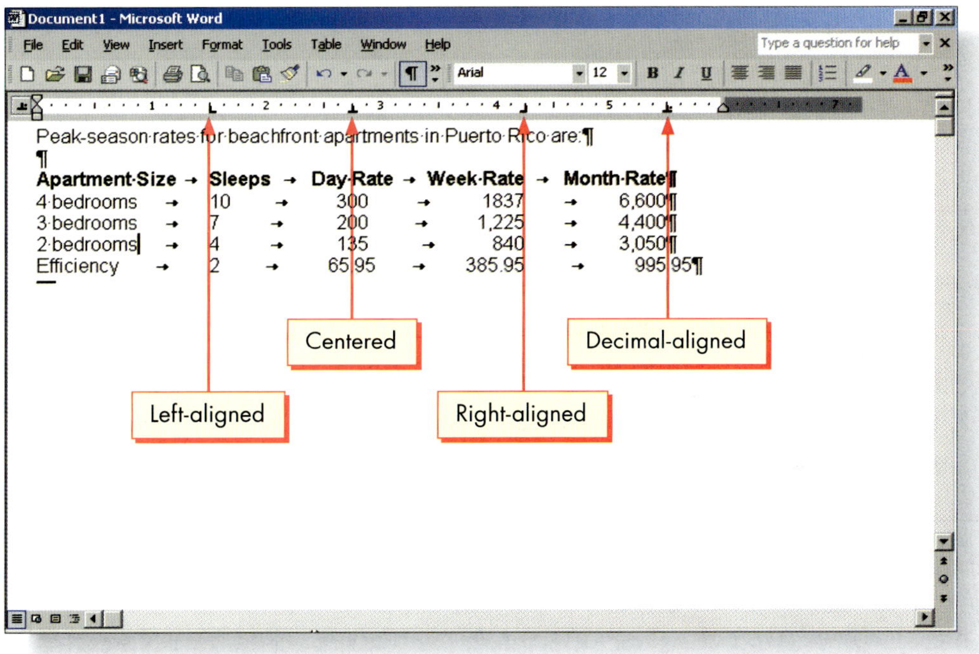

There are two ways to set tabs:

- Use the Tabs dialog box.
- Use the ruler.

TIP: You can open the Tabs dialog box by choosing Tabs from the Format menu, by clicking Tabs in the Reveal Formatting task pane, or by double-clicking on the ruler (which also inserts a tab stop).

TABLE 5-1 Types of Tabs

RULER SYMBOL	TYPE OF TAB	DESCRIPTION
└	Left-aligned	The left edge of the text aligns with the tab stop.
┴	Centered	The text is centered at the tab stop.
┘	Right-aligned	The right edge of the text aligns with the tab stop.
┴:	Decimal-aligned	The decimal point aligns with the tab stop. Use this option for columns of numbers.
|	Bar	Inserts a vertical line at the tab stop. Use to create a divider line between columns.

EXERCISE 5-1 Set Tabs Using the Tabs Dialog Box

1. Open the file **Eurail**.
2. In the second paragraph under the heading (which begins "The Eurailpass is intended"), key the following new sentence at the end of the paragraph:

   Sample costs (in U.S. dollars) are as follows:
3. Press Enter twice. Key the following text, pressing Tab once between items:

   Length   Adult   Child (age 4-11)   Youth (age 12-25)

   Notice that the text you keyed aligns with default settings on the ruler, which are positioned every half-inch. Pressing Tab and using default tab settings does not always create a professional-looking document.

¶

NOTE: Tabs are nonprinting characters that can be displayed or hidden. When working with tabs, display them by clicking the Show/Hide ¶ button ¶ on the Standard toolbar.

4. With the insertion point in the line you just keyed, open the Format menu and choose Tabs. The Tabs dialog box appears. Notice that the Default tab stops text box is set to 0.5 inches.
5. Change the Default tab stops setting to 1 inch and click OK. The distance between the tabbed settings increases and the text aligns with the new 1-inch default settings.

FIGURE 5-3
Using the Tabs dialog box to change default tab settings

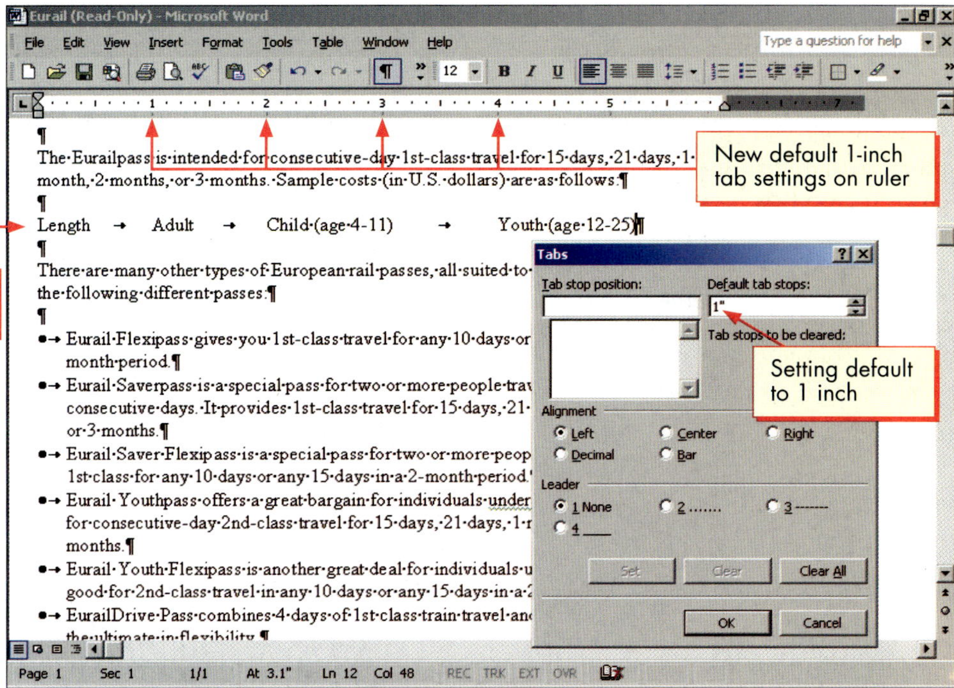

6. At the end of the line of tabbed text, press Enter and key the text shown in Figure 5-4, pressing Tab where indicated. Use single spacing.

FIGURE 5-4

```
15 days [Tab] 554 [Tab] 277 [Tab] 388
1 month [Tab] 890 [Tab] 445 [Tab] 623
2 months [Tab] 1,260 [Tab] 630 [Tab] 882
3 months [Tab] 1,558 [Tab] 779 [Tab] 1,089
```

Notice that the 1-inch default tab settings have not improved the alignment of the text, and there is a problem with the numeric text. Numeric text should be right-aligned. To format the text with custom tab settings, use the features in the Tabs dialog box.

7. Select all the tabbed text, from "Length" through "1089." Open the Tabs dialog box.
8. Key **2** in the Tab stop position text box.
9. Under Alignment, choose Right and then click Set. You've just created a 2-inch right-aligned tab setting for the "Adult" price column. Next you'll set two more right tab settings for the remaining two columns.

10. Key **4** in the Tab stop position text box and click Set. (Right alignment is already set.)

FIGURE 5-5
Right-aligned custom tabs in the Tabs dialog box

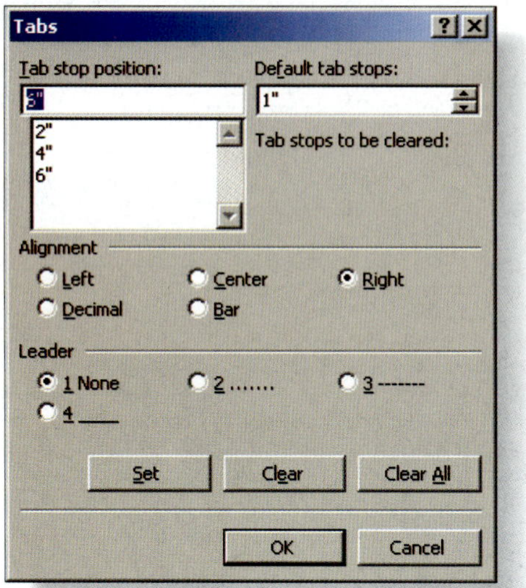

11. Create a 6-inch right-aligned tab setting. Click OK to close the dialog box. The ruler now shows three right tab markers. These symbols indicate the type and location of a tab stop. Notice how the tabbed columns are better spaced and right-aligned.

NOTE: When you set a custom tab, Word clears all default tabs to the left of the new tab marker.

12. Format the column headings (which start with "Length") as bold.

13. Display the Reveal Formatting task pane (Format menu, Reveal Formatting).

14. Select or click within the right-tabbed text. Notice the tab settings in the task pane.

FIGURE 5-6
Tabbed text

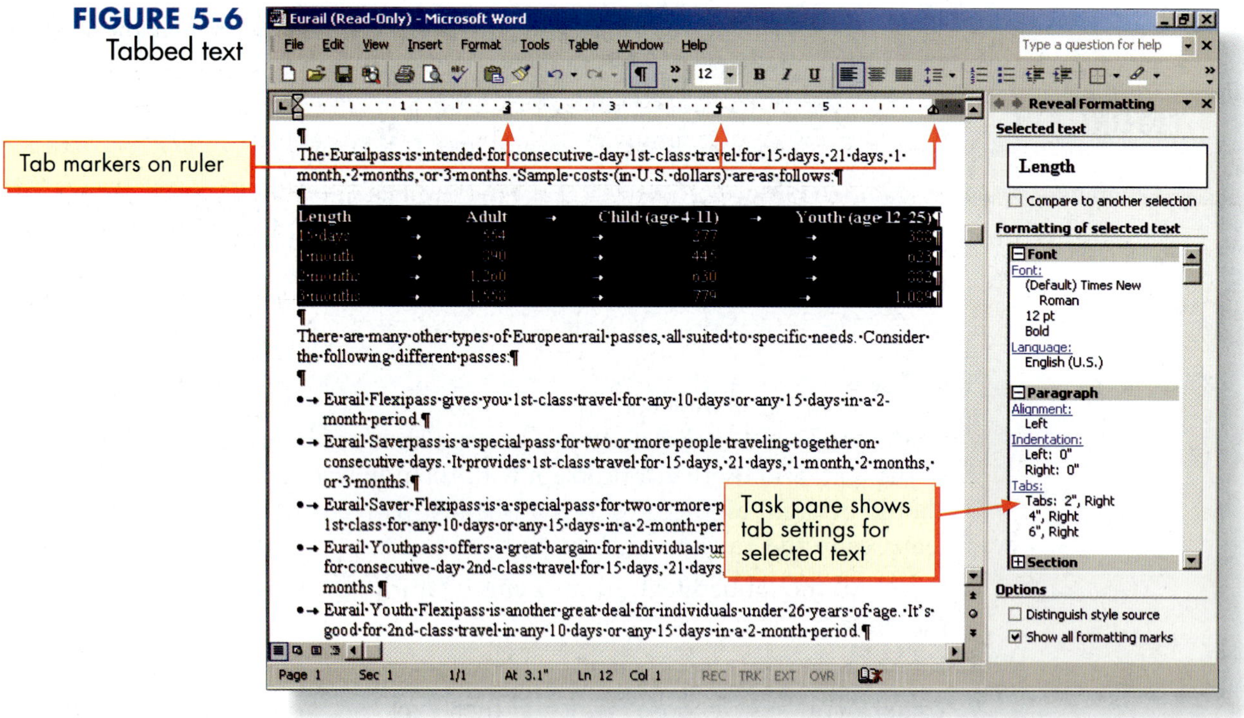

TIP: When setting tabs or applying other paragraph formatting, you need only place the insertion point within a paragraph.

EXERCISE 5-2 Set Tabs Using the Ruler

Setting tabs by using the ruler is an easy, two-step process: click the Tab Alignment button on the left of the ruler to choose the type of alignment and then click the position on the ruler to set the tab.

1. At the end of the document, insert a new paragraph mark and key the text shown in Figure 5-7, inserting tab characters as shown. You might want to close the task pane so you'll have more room.

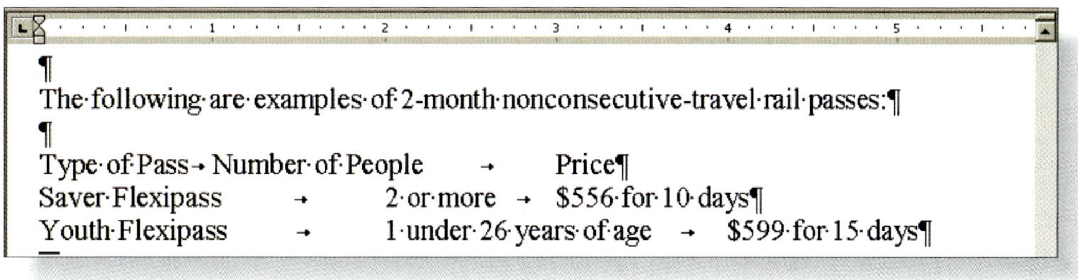

FIGURE 5-7 Text and tab characters to key

2. Select the tabbed text you just keyed.

3. Point to the Tab Alignment button on the horizontal ruler. The default setting for the button is Left Alignment, and each time you click the button, the alignment changes.
4. Click the Tab Alignment button repeatedly until it cycles through all the available tab types and returns to the Left Alignment position.

TIP: Clicking the Tab Alignment button cycles through all tab types and the first-line indent and hanging indent symbols. With an indent symbol showing, you can click on the ruler at the desired position (instead of dragging the symbol).

5. Click the Tab Alignment button until it shows center alignment.
6. Click the ruler at 3 inches. Word inserts a center-aligned tab marker at 3 inches (which is the center of the text line) and deletes the default tab markers to the left of the new tab.
7. With the Tab Alignment button still showing center alignment, click the ruler at 5.5 inches. The selected text now has two custom tab settings.

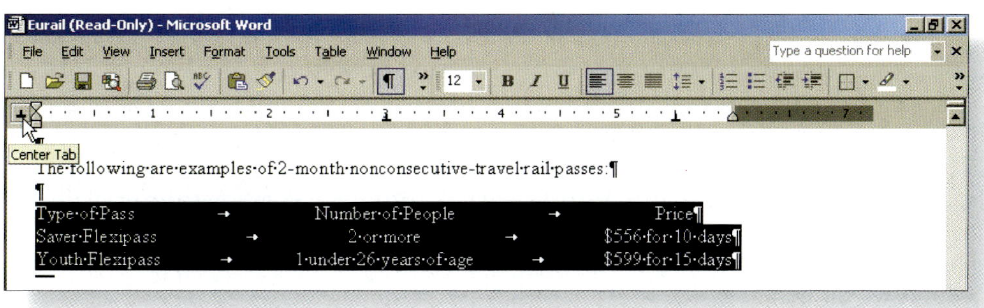

FIGURE 5-8 Setting tabs with the ruler

8. Format the column headings ("Type of Pass," "Number of People," and "Price") as bold.
9. Save the document as ***[your initials]*5-2** in a new folder for Lesson 5.
10. Print the document and close it.

EXERCISE 5-3 Use Tabs to Create a Memo from Scratch

A memo (more formally called "memorandum") is a standard business document. It consists of a heading, which you create with tabs, followed by the body of the memo. It also often ends with reference initials (the initials of the person who keyed the document). Memos are formatted with a specific amount of space before and after lines.

NOTE: Refer to Appendix F: "Standard Forms for Business Documents" for more information.

1. Start a new blank document. You are going to create a cover memo for the previous document you created.
2. Set a 1-inch left tab and then key the memo heading shown in Figure 5-9. Where indicated, press Tab and insert today's date. Leave one blank line between lines.

FIGURE 5-9

```
MEMO TO: Tab Frank Murillo

FROM: Tab Steve Ross

DATE: Tab [Today's date]

SUBJECT: Tab Information about European Train Travel
```

3. On the third blank line below the Subject line, key the following paragraph:

   In response to our meeting yesterday, the attached information is part of our new Train Travel packet. It is also available on our Web site.
4. On the second blank line below the paragraph you just keyed, add reference initials to the document by keying your initials in lowercase letters.
5. Below your reference initials, key **Attachment**. This is often referred to as the Enclosure Notation. Assume that you will attach the previous document you created to this cover memo.

TIP: There are many ways to create business documents, and each business has its own style. Some businesses might include "MEMORANDUM" specially formatted across the top, some might format the memo heading in bold, some might include a filename notation at the bottom. Some businesses might forgo written memos altogether and rely on e-mail. See *The Gregg Reference Manual* as a style guide for printed business documents.

6. Add 72 points of paragraph spacing before the first line of the memo heading. This places the heading 2 inches from the top of the page.

FIGURE 5-10
Basic memo format

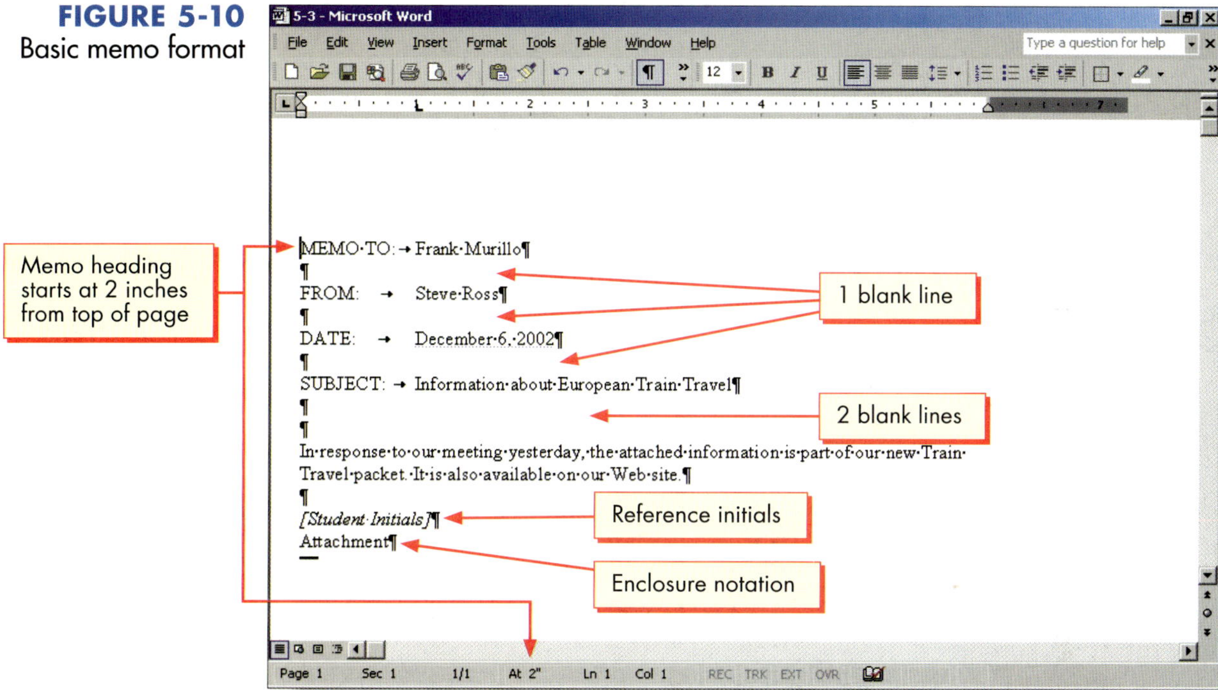

NOTE: Another way to position the memo heading is by changing the top margin. Margins are discussed in Lesson 7: "Margins, Templates, and Printing Options."

7. Save the document as ***[your initials]*5-3** in your Lesson 5 folder.
8. Print the document and close it.

Clearing Tabs

You can clear custom tabs all at once or individually. When you clear custom tabs, Word restores the default tab stops to the left of the custom tab stop.

There are three ways to clear a tab:

- Use the Tabs dialog box.
- Use the ruler.
- Press Ctrl + Q.

EXERCISE 5-4 Clear Tabs Using the Tabs Dialog Box and the Keyboard

1. Open the file **Currency2**.
2. Select the tabbed text from "Austria" through the end of the document. Notice the tab markers on the ruler for the selected text.
3. Press Ctrl + Q. All the tab settings are deleted (but the tab characters are not deleted).

4. Click the Undo button  to restore the settings.
5. With the text still selected, open the Tabs dialog box. Using the dialog box, you can clear all tab settings or individual tab settings.
6. Click the 2.5-inch tab setting in the Tab stop position box to select it. Click Clear and then click OK. The text in the third column moves to the nearest default tab stop.

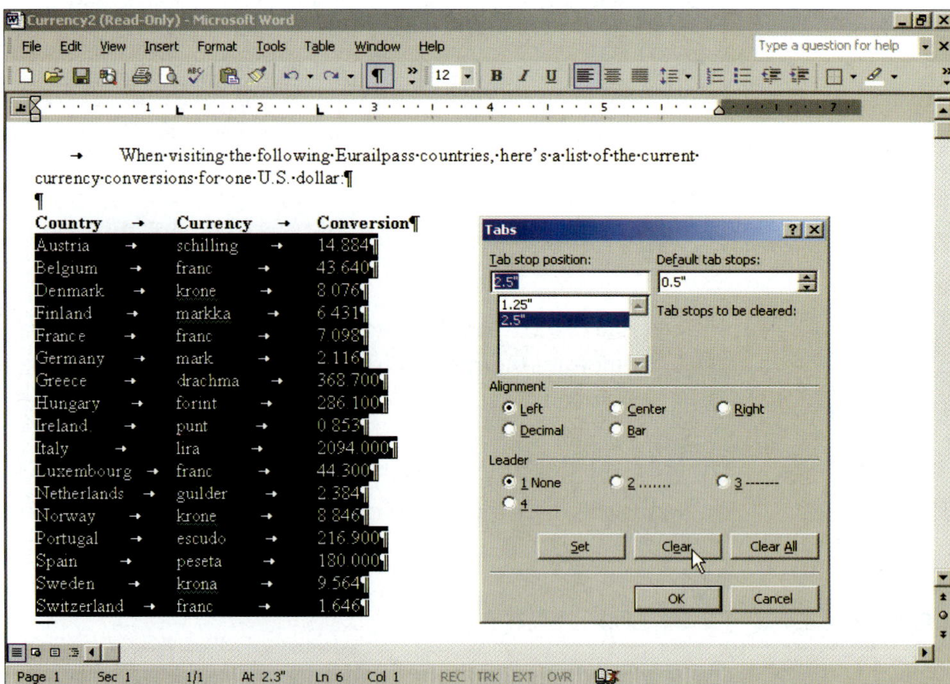

FIGURE 5-11 Using the dialog box to clear a tab setting

7. Click the Tab Alignment button until it shows decimal alignment and click the ruler at 3 inches. The decimal point in the numeric text aligns with the 3-inch tab setting.

EXERCISE 5-5 Clear Tabs Using the Ruler

1. In the paragraph below the title, position the insertion point to the left of "When" (after the tab character).
2. Point to the 0.75-inch left tab marker on the ruler. The ScreenTip "Left Tab" appears.

NOTE: When clearing or adjusting tabs using the ruler, watch for the ScreenTip to correctly identify the item you are pointing to. If no ScreenTip appears, you might inadvertently add another tab marker.

3. Drag the tab marker down and off the ruler. The 0.75-inch custom tab is cleared and Word restores the 0.5-inch default tab.
4. Press Backspace to delete the tab character to the left of "When."

NOTE: Remember, to remove tabs from text, you must delete the tab characters.

Adjusting Tab Settings

You can adjust tabs inserted in a document by using either the Tabs dialog box or the ruler.

EXERCISE 5-6 Adjust Tab Settings

1. Select all the tabbed text from "Austria" through the end of the document.
2. Open the Tabs dialog box.

TIP: You can double-click a tab marker on the ruler to open the Tabs dialog box.

3. Click the 1.25-inch tab setting in the Tab stop position box to select it. Adjust the alignment for the setting by clicking Center. Click OK. The middle column is now center-aligned at the 1.25-inch mark on the ruler. You'll improve this setting later in this exercise.

4. With the same text still selected, place the pointer on the 3-inch decimal tab marker on the ruler.
5. When the ScreenTip indicates "Decimal Tab," drag the marker to the 5.5-inch position on the ruler. The column is now decimal-aligned at 5.5 inches.

FIGURE 5-12
Using the ruler to adjust a tab setting

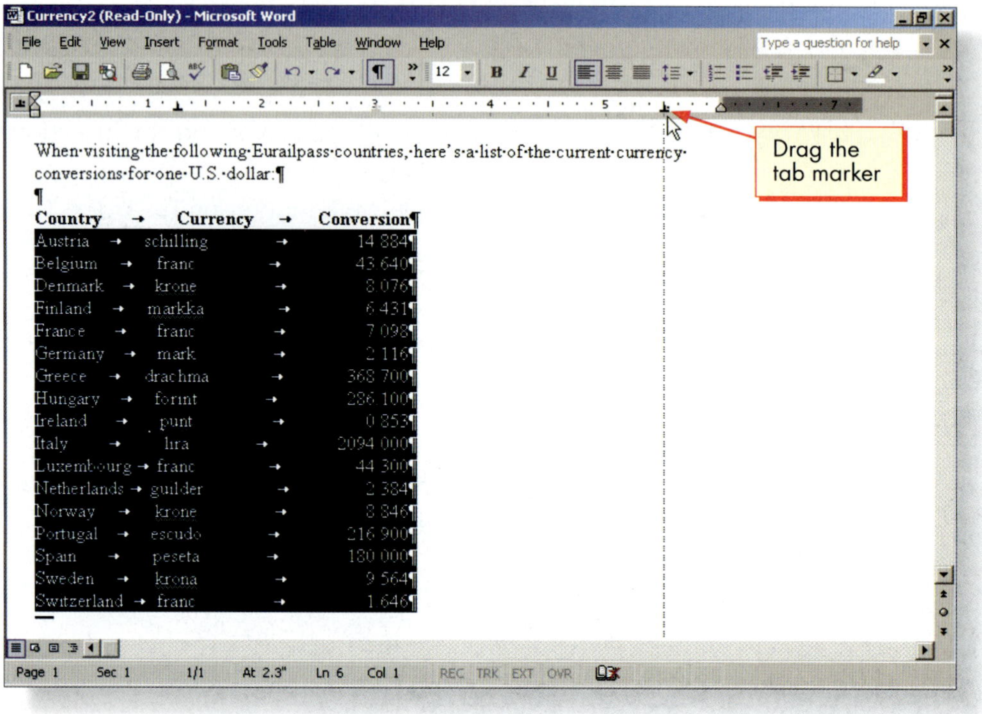

NOTE: When you change tab settings with the ruler, be careful to drag the tab marker only to the right or to the left. If you drag the tab marker up or down, you might clear it from the ruler. If you inadvertently clear a tab marker, click the Undo button to restore it.

6. With the text still selected, drag the 1.25-inch tab marker to 2.75 inches on the ruler.
7. Select the bold column headings ("Country," "Currency," "Conversion"). Use the Tabs dialog box to clear all tab settings and set a 2.75-inch center tab and a 5.8-inch right tab.

Setting Leader Tabs

A *leader tab* is used to lead the reader's eye from one tabbed column to the next. Leaders are often found in a table of contents, in which dotted lines fill the space between the headings on the left and the page numbers on the right.

You set leader tabs by choosing a dotted line, dashed line, or solid line pattern that appears to the left of the tab stop.

FIGURE 5-13
Leader patterns

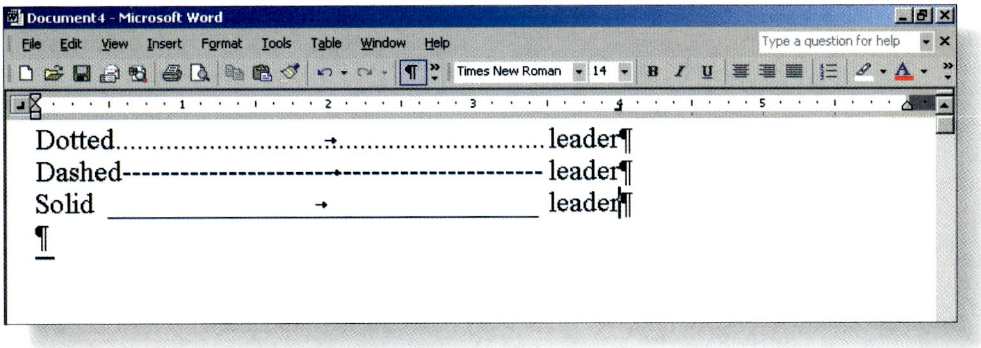

EXERCISE 5-7 Set Leader Tabs

1. Select the text from "Austria" through the end of the document.
2. Open the Tabs dialog box.
3. Click the 5.5-inch tab in the Tab stop position box to select it.
4. Under Leader, click the second leader pattern (the dotted line).
5. Click Set.
6. Select the 2.75-inch tab, click the second leader pattern, and click Set. Click OK to close the dialog box. A dotted-line leader fills the space to the left of the tab settings.

NOTE: Leader patterns always fill the space to the left of a leader tab setting.

7. Go to the end of the document and press Enter twice to start a new paragraph. Press Ctrl+Q to clear existing tab settings.
8. Key the following two lines of text, pressing Tab where indicated:

   Date: Tab
   Source: Tab

9. Select the two lines of text and open the Tabs dialog box.
10. Set a 4-inch right-aligned tab with an underline leader. Click OK. (See Figure 5-14 on the next page.)
11. Make the selected text bold. Hide nonprinting characters (click the Show/Hide ¶ button ¶) to better see your leader tabs.

W O R D

FIGURE 5-14
Creating underline leader tabs

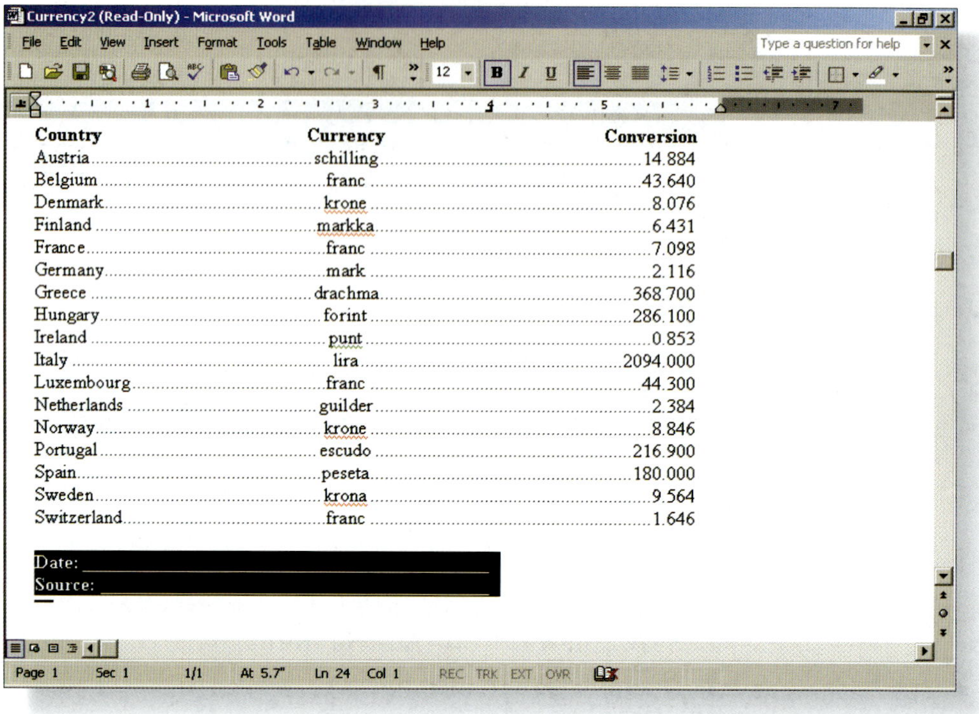

12. Make the following two formatting changes to the document:

- Add 72 points of paragraph spacing before the document title.
- Format all the tabbed text, including the last two lines of the document, with 1.5 line spacing.

13. Save the document as ***[your initials]*5-7** in your Lesson 5 folder.

14. Print and close the document.

USING HELP

You can use Word's Click and Type feature to enter text in any blank area of a page without setting tabs or pressing Enter to position the insertion point. Just double-click in a blank area, and Click and Type automatically positions the item where you double-clicked. You just need to change your view mode and become familiar with the Click and Type pointer.

Use Help to learn about the Click and Type feature:

1. Click in the Ask a Question box above the Formatting toolbar and key **click and type**. Press Enter to display a list of related Help topics.

2. Click the topic About Click and Type. This Help window provides an overview of the Click and Type feature. Notice the varying shapes of the Click and Type pointer.

FIGURE 5-15
Learning about Click and Type

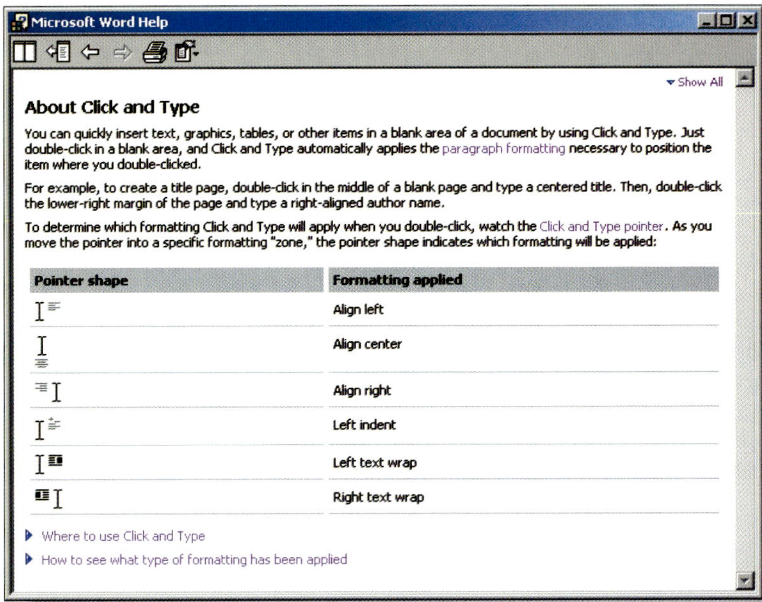

3. Click the Ask a Question box again and press Enter to redisplay the list of topics.
4. Click the topic Use Click and Type to insert text and graphics. This Help window shows you how to use the feature. Notice that you have to switch to Print Layout View or Web Layout View. You do this by clicking either of these view buttons, located at the bottom left above the status bar.
5. Close the Help window. Then start a new blank document and experiment with the Click and Type feature. Use the feature to insert a centered title. Remember to position the mouse where you want to enter the text, wait to see the appropriate Click and Type pointer shape, and then double-click. A few lines down, on one line, key a left-aligned item, a center-aligned item, and a right-aligned item. Close the document without saving it.

LESSON 5 Summary

- Tabs are used to align text and to distribute tabbed columns evenly between the left and right margins.
- You press Tab to insert a tab character and move the insertion point to a tab setting, also called a tab stop.
- Word has default tab stops every half-inch, as indicated on the bottom of the horizontal ruler. You can change the distance between default stops or create custom tab settings.

- Creating a custom tab setting means choosing the tab position and the alignment. You can use the Tabs dialog box or the ruler. To use the ruler, click the Tab Alignment button on the ruler and choose the appropriate alignment (left, right, and so on). Then click on the ruler where you want to position the tab.
- Remove tabs by using the Tabs dialog box, by dragging tab markers off the ruler, or by using the keyboard shortcut Ctrl+Q.
- Adjust tab settings by dragging tab markers to a new position on the ruler or by using the Tabs dialog box.
- A leader tab uses a series of dots, dashes, or solid underlines to fill the empty space to the left of a tab stop. Use the Tabs dialog box to set a leader tab.

Concepts Review

TRUE/FALSE QUESTIONS

Each of the following statements is either true or false. Indicate your choice by circling T or F.

T F 1. In Word, you can use Spacebar to align text.

T F 2. When you set a custom tab, Word clears all default tabs to the left of the tab stop.

T F 3. You cannot set tabs for existing text.

T F 4. You can either select a paragraph or place the insertion point within the paragraph when setting tabs for the paragraph.

T F 5. When custom tabs are cleared, you must reestablish default tabs or you will have no tabs at all.

T F 6. Tabs inserted in a document cannot be adjusted after they are set.

T F 7. The symbol for a center tab is ⊥.

T F 8. You can use the ruler to set a leader tab.

SHORT ANSWER QUESTIONS

Write the correct answer in the space provided.

1. What are the two ways to set tabs?

____

2. How do you display tab characters if they are not visible on-screen?

____

3. Which dialog box is used to set a leader?

____

4. What type of tab do you use ┘ to create?

____

5. What interval does Word use for default tabs?

____

6. How do you clear a tab by using the ruler?

____

7. Which keyboard shortcut can you use to clear tab settings for a selected paragraph?

8. Does a leader appear to the left or to the right of a leader tab setting?

CRITICAL THINKING

Answer these questions on a separate page. There are no right or wrong answers. Support your answers with examples from your own experience, if possible.

1. Some books and magazines use leader tabs in the table of contents and index. Based on representative books and magazines, create a few general guidelines on when to use leader tabs. Support your view with examples.
2. Do you find it easier to read text that is centered in a column or text that is left-aligned? What about numbers that are centered or right-aligned? Create samples to support your position.

Lesson Applications

EXERCISE 5-8

Clear tab settings, change default tab stops, and set custom tabs.

1. Open the file **Restaurants**.
2. Clear all the tab settings in the document.
3. Format the title as 14-point bold, all caps, centered, with paragraph spacing of 72 points before and 24 points after.
4. Format the line with the column headings (beginning with "Name") as bold.
5. Change the default tab stops for the document to every 2 inches.
6. For the last three lines of tabbed text, use center tabs to center the text under the headings "Cuisine" and "Average Dinner Price."
7. Change the line spacing for all the tabbed text to double-spaced.
8. Save the document as ***[your initials]*****5-8** in your Lesson 5 folder.
9. Print and close the document.

EXERCISE 5-9

Set and adjust custom tabs.

1. Start a new document. Make sure the document is in Normal view.
2. Format the paragraph mark as Arial.
3. Key the text as shown in Figure 5-16. Include the corrections and use single spacing. Be sure a blank line precedes and follows the new paragraph that begins "Highlights."

FIGURE 5-16

```
Gateway Travel Historic Tour: The Freedom Trail in Boston

Boston is a city rich in history. It's hard to turn a corner without running
into a historic site. Many of the ~~sights~~ sites are connected by the Freedom
Trail, a walk that takes you from the Colonial era through the American
Revolution.¶Highlights of the Freedom Trail include:
```

NOTE: This figure contains proofreading marks. See Appendix D: "Proofreaders' Marks."

WORD

4. Format the title as 14-point bold, small caps, and centered. Add paragraph spacing of 72 points before and 24 points after.
5. Key the text shown in Figure 5-17, with the corrections as shown. Tab between entries. Use 1.5-line spacing.

FIGURE 5-17

~~Building~~ Site	Date	Address
Paul Revere House	1680	19 North Square
Old North Church	1723	193 Salem (St)
Faneuil Hall	1742	1 Faneuil Hall Square
Old Statehouse	1748	206 Washington (St)

6. Format the tabbed text with 0.75 inch left and right indents and then create two left-aligned tab settings for the date and address columns. Adjust the tab markers on the ruler until the columns appear evenly spaced within the indented area.
7. Underline the column headings.
8. Save the document as ***[your initials]*****5-9** in your Lesson 5 folder.
9. Print and close the document.

EXERCISE 5-10

Clear tabs and set leader tabs.

1. Open the file **Glossary**.
2. Increase the title size to 14 points.
3. Three blank lines below the title, key the paragraph shown in Figure 5-18. Use single spacing. Include one blank line below the new paragraph. The text should not be bold.

FIGURE 5-18

Cruises are among the most popular vacation choices, and for good reason. Travelers enjoy luxurious accommodations and the ability to visit numerous destinations while on the open seas. To help you enjoy your adventure, our travel specialists prepared the following glossary of nautical terms. The seafaring world has a language all its own!

4. Justify the new paragraph.
5. Clear the existing tab setting for the tabbed text.
6. Set a 6-inch dotted leader tab that right-aligns the glossary definitions.
7. Change the line spacing for the tabbed text to 1.5 lines.
8. Apply a 2¼-point single-line blue shadow border to the page.
9. Save the document as ***[your initials]*5-10** in your Lesson 5 folder.
10. Print and close the document.

EXERCISE 5-11 Challenge Yourself

Create a business memo with tabbed columns.

1. Open the file **Courts**.
2. At the top of the document, add the following new paragraph:

   The group leader for our Hawaii tennis tour has asked about public tennis courts in Oahu. I have provided her with the following information:
3. Add a blank line below the new paragraph.
4. Above the new paragraph, add a standard memo heading. (See Appendix F: "Standard Forms for Business Documents.") The memo is to Nina Chavez from Steve Ross. Use today's date. The subject is **Oahu Tennis Courts**. Be sure to use the correct spacing between lines and the correct tab setting.
5. If you have not already done so, apply 72 points of paragraph spacing before the first line of the memo heading (so "MEMO TO" starts at the 2-inch mark).
6. Format the tabbed text as four tabbed columns: use a left-aligned tab setting for the second column ("Name of Court") and center-aligned tab settings for the third and fourth columns. Adjust the tab markers until the columns are evenly spaced between the left and right margins.
7. Format the column headings as bold italic.
8. In the last column, replace each "Yes" and "No" with Wingdings characters, using the box with a checkmark for "Yes" and the box with an "x" for "No." If desired, increase the font size of the symbols.
9. Format the blank line below the "SUBJECT" line with a 1-point black bottom border.
10. Add your reference initials to the bottom of the memo.
11. Save the document as ***[your initials]*5-11** in your Lesson 5 folder.
12. Print and close the document.

WORD

W O R D

On Your Own

In these exercises you work on your own, as you would in a real-life work environment. Use the skills you've learned to accomplish the task—and be creative.

EXERCISE 5-12

Create a tabbed table on any topic. Use three columns, column headings, and at least three lines of tabbed text below the headings. Format the text attractively, making sure your columns are evenly spaced between the left and right margins. Save the document as ***[your initials]*****5-12** and print it.

EXERCISE 5-13

Write a short business memo. The memo is from you, to a person and about a subject of your choosing. Use the correct spacing and tab settings for the memo heading. Save the document as ***[your initials]*****5-13** and print it.

EXERCISE 5-14

Go to the Internet. Use a search engine to locate Web sites on a particular topic. Create a document that lists five Web site names and then lists their Web addresses in a right-aligned, tabbed column with leaders. Save the document as ***[your initials]*****5-14** and print it.

LESSON 6

Writing and Editing Tools

OBJECTIVES

MOUS ACTIVITIES
In this lesson:
W2002 1-1
W2002 1-3
See Appendix E.

After completing this lesson, you will be able to:

1. **Use AutoComplete, AutoCorrect, AutoText, and smart tags.**
2. **Check spelling and grammar.**
3. **Use the Thesaurus.**
4. **Find and replace text.**
5. **Move text.**
6. **Copy text.**

Estimated Time: 1½ hours

You've seen how the intuitive features of Word recognize when you key a date or a misspelling—an automatic mechanism flags the text, corrects the text, or completes the text for you. Word provides additional tools that help keep your documents error-free and save you from having to key text. For example, there are writing tools to help you with spelling, grammar, and vocabulary and tools to help you find and replace text. There are also editing tools that enable you to move or copy a block of text easily without having to rekey it.

Using AutoComplete, AutoCorrect, AutoText, and Smart Tags

By now you are familiar with the first three automatic features listed here:

- *AutoComplete* suggests the completed word when you key the first four or more letters of a day, month, or date. If you key "Janu," for example, Word displays a box suggesting the word "January," which you can insert by pressing Enter.
- *AutoCorrect* corrects commonly misspelled words as you key text. If you key "teh" instead of "the," for example, Word automatically changes the spelling to "the." You can create AutoCorrect entries for text you frequently misspell, and you can control AutoCorrect options.
- *AutoText* can insert automatically over 40 commonly used entries, including letter salutations and closings (such as "To Whom It May Concern," or "Sincerely yours"). You can also create AutoText entries for text you frequently use.
- *Smart tags* help you save time by performing actions in Word that you'd normally open other programs (such as Outlook) to do. Word recognizes dates, addresses, and user-defined data types through the use of smart tags, which appear as purple dotted lines beneath text.

EXERCISE 6-1 See AutoComplete, AutoCorrect, and Smart Tags in Action

1. In a new document, begin keying the current day of the week in all lowercase letters. When you see the AutoComplete tip that suggests the current day, press Enter. Word completes the day and AutoCorrect capitalizes the first letter.
2. Key a comma and a space; then begin keying the month, day, and year. When you see the AutoComplete tip that suggests the current date, press Enter to insert it.
3. Press Enter to start a new paragraph. The date has a smart tag indicator (the purple dotted line). By now you've seen how Word tags dates and other data in your documents.

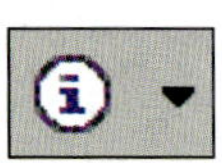

4. Move the I-beam over the date until the Smart Tag Actions button  appears.
5. Click the button to see the list of actions. You can perform Microsoft Outlook functions, such as setting up a meeting for this date or opening your Outlook calendar, without launching Outlook.

FIGURE 6-1
Smart tag list of actions

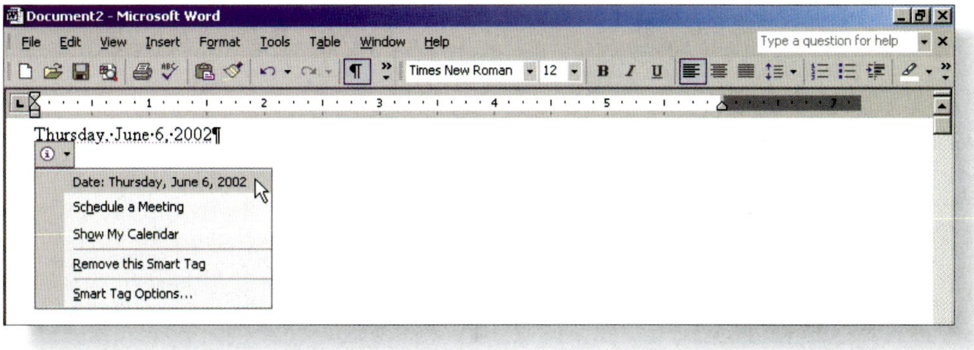

6. Click the option to remove the smart tag from the date.
7. In the line below the date, key the following sentence. Use the exact spelling and case as shown and include the period.

   TRavel insurence is importent.

   AutoCorrect corrects the capitalization and spelling automatically.

NOTE: AutoCorrect corrects your text only after you complete a word by either pressing Spacebar or keying punctuation, such as a period or comma.

8. Open the Tools menu and choose AutoCorrect Options to open the AutoCorrect dialog box. Notice the available AutoCorrect options.

FIGURE 6-2
AutoCorrect dialog box

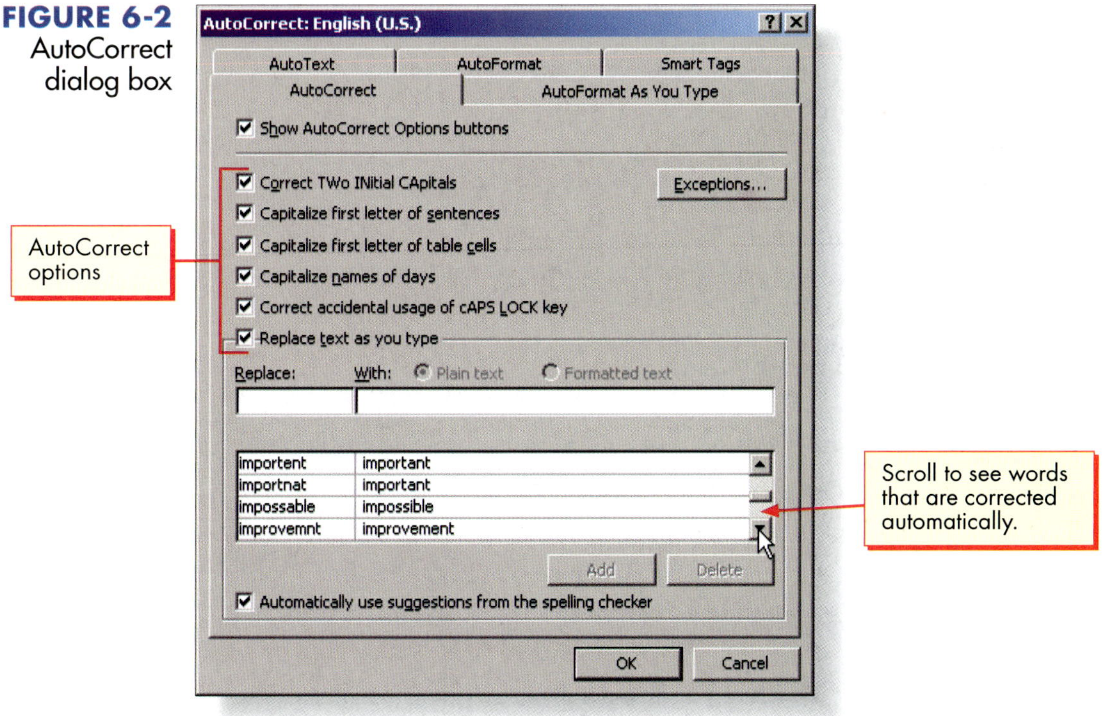

WORD

9. Scroll down the list of entries and notice the words that Word corrects automatically (assuming the Replace text as you type option is checked).
10. Click Cancel to close the dialog box.

TABLE 6-1 AutoCorrect Options

OPTIONS	DESCRIPTION
Correct TWo INitial CApitals	Corrects words keyed accidentally with two initial capital letters, such as "WOrd" or "THis."
Capitalize first letter of sentences	Corrects any word at the beginning of a sentence that is not keyed with a capital letter.
Capitalize first letter of table cells	Corrects any word at the beginning of a table cell that is not keyed with a capital letter.
Capitalize names of days	Corrects a day spelled without an initial capital letter.
Correct accidental usage of cAPS LOCK key	If you turn on CapsLock accidentally and then key "tODAY", AutoCorrect changes the word to "Today" and turns off CapsLock.
Replace text as you type	Makes all corrections automatically.

EXERCISE 6-2 Create an AutoCorrect Entry

You can create AutoCorrect entries for words you often misspell. You can also use AutoCorrect to create shortcuts for text you use repeatedly, such as names or phrases. Examples of these types of AutoCorrect entries are:

- **btw** for **by the way**
- **dc** for **Duke City Gateway Travel**

1. Open the AutoCorrect dialog box. In the Replace box, key **asap**
2. In the With box, key **as soon as possible**
3. Click the Add button to move the entry into the alphabetized list. Click OK.
4. Start a new paragraph in the current document and key the sentence **Encourage tour groups to order it asap.** Word spells out the entry, just as you specified in the AutoCorrect dialog box.

EXERCISE 6-3 Control AutoCorrect Options

At times you might not want text to be corrected. You can undo a correction or turn AutoCorrect options on or off by clicking the AutoCorrect Options button and making a selection.

1. Move the I-beam anywhere over the phrase "as soon as possible" until a small blue box appears beneath the word "as."

FIGURE 6-3
Controlling AutoCorrect options

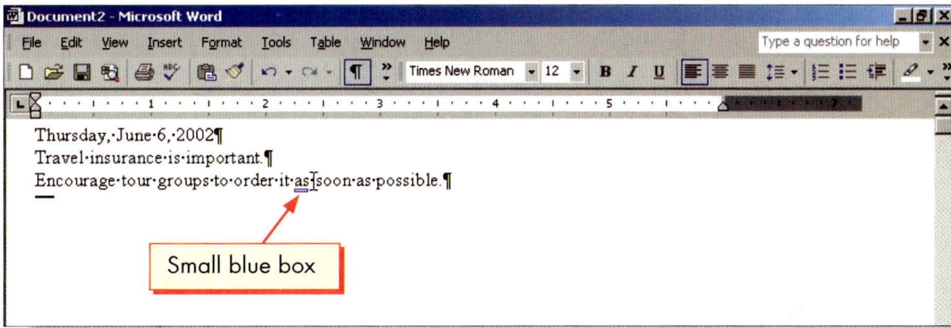

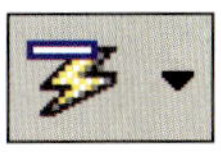

2. Slide the I-beam down over the small blue box until your mouse becomes a pointer and the box turns into the AutoCorrect Options button.
3. Click the button and choose Change back to "asap" from the menu to undo the correction.

FIGURE 6-4
Undoing automatic corrections

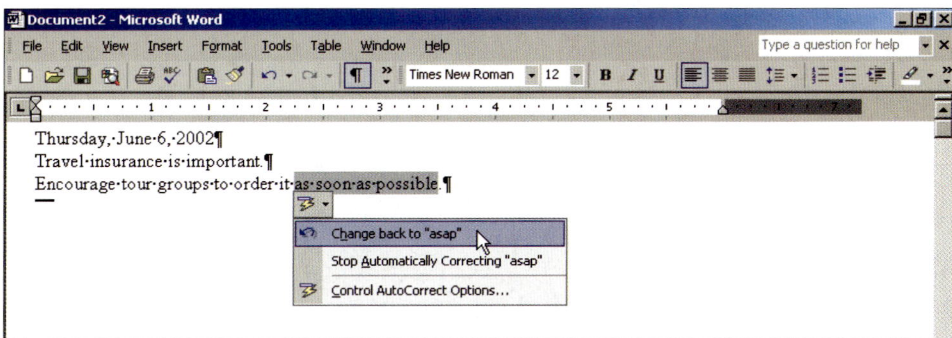

4. Click the AutoCorrect Options button again and choose Redo AutoCorrect. The words "as soon as possible" are restored.
5. Click the button again and choose Control AutoCorrect Options. The Auto-Correct dialog box opens.
6. Remove the AutoCorrect entry: Select "asap" from the list, click the Delete button, and then click OK.

W O R D

EXERCISE 6-4 Insert an AutoText Entry

AutoText is another feature you can use to insert text automatically. Word stores a group of AutoText entries that are commonly used in business documents. You can access these entries from the Insert menu, the AutoCorrect dialog box, or a special AutoText toolbar.

1. Insert a blank line after the date.
2. With the insertion point positioned in this blank line, open the Insert menu and choose AutoText. Without clicking the mouse, move the pointer slowly down the AutoText submenu to see the existing AutoText entries.
3. Position the pointer over Salutation and click To Whom It May Concern:. The text is automatically inserted in the document.
4. Click the Undo button to undo the insertion.
5. For better access to Word's AutoText entries, display the AutoText toolbar by opening the View menu and choosing Toolbars, AutoText.
6. On the AutoText toolbar, click All Entries. The same list of Word AutoText entries is displayed.
7. Point to Attention Line and click Attention:. The text is entered in the document.

FIGURE 6-5 Using the AutoText toolbar

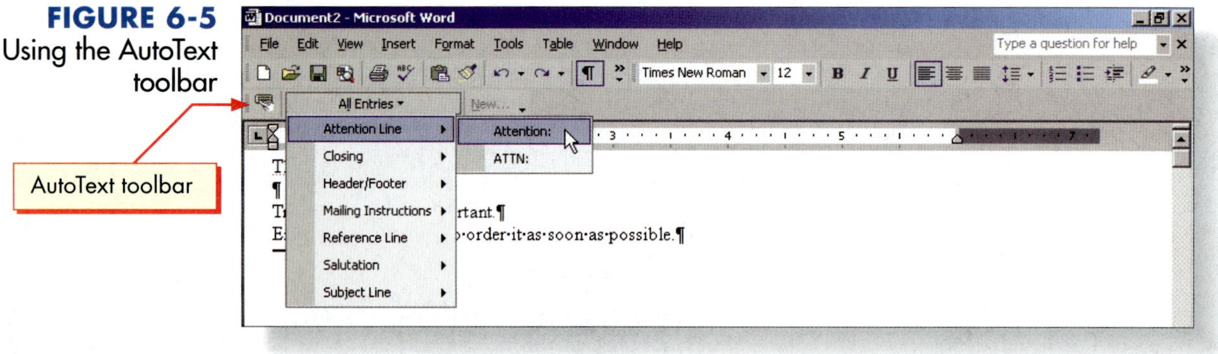

8. Insert a tab character after the AutoText entry and key **Travel Counselors**
9. Save the document as ***[your initials]*6-4** in a new folder for Lesson 6. Print the document and leave it open for the next exercise.

EXERCISE 6-5 Create and Insert New AutoText Entries

You can create AutoText entries for text you use repeatedly (including the text formatting), such as phrases, sentences, paragraphs, and logos. Once you create an entry, you can insert it with just a few keystrokes.

1. Delete the date and Attention line in the document.
2. In its place, key a standard memo heading, using the following text:

   MEMO TO:

   FROM:

   DATE:

   SUBJECT:

   Format the "MEMO TO:" line with 72 points of spacing before the paragraph, and include the correct line spacing before and after the remaining memo heading lines. (See Appendix F: "Standard Forms for Business Documents.") Include tab characters after the colons and set a 1-inch left tab.
3. Select the entire memo heading, including the blank lines below it.
4. Click New on the AutoText toolbar. The Create AutoText dialog box appears with a suggested name for the entry.

TIP: When the AutoText toolbar is not displayed, you can create an AutoText entry by choosing Insert, AutoText, New from the menu or by pressing Alt + F3.

FIGURE 6-6
Create AutoText dialog box

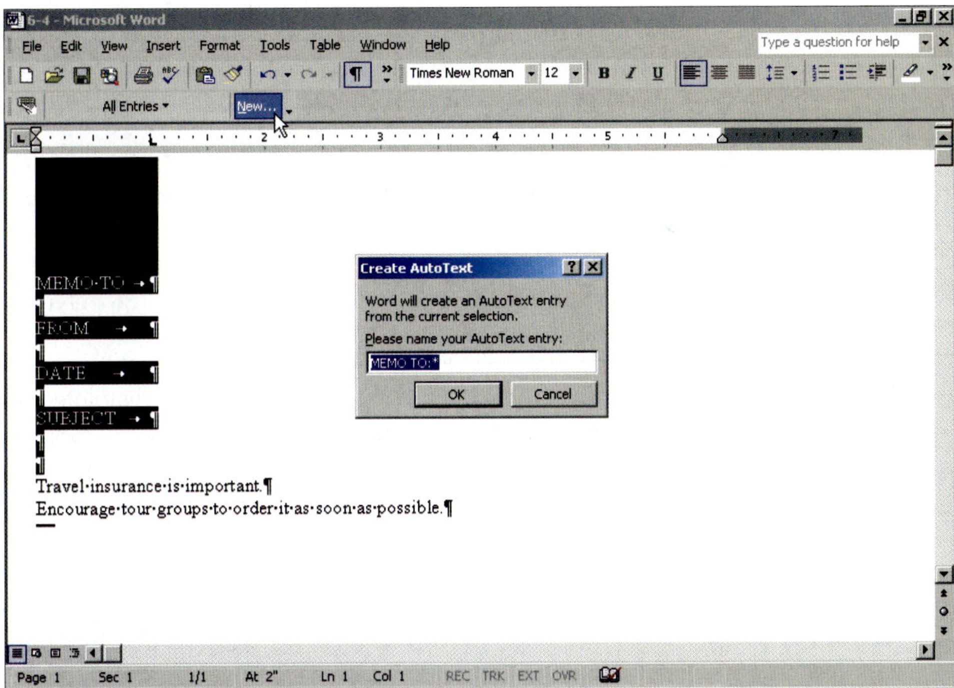

5. Replace the suggested name ("MEMO TO*") by keying ***[your initials]*** **memoheading**. Click OK.
6. Merge the two paragraphs below the heading into one paragraph.

7. Press Enter twice after "as possible." Key the following closing paragraph:

   For more information, check our Web site at www.gwaytravel.com.

8. Select the last paragraph and press Alt + F3 to open the Create AutoText dialog box.

9. Name the AutoText entry ***[your initials]*website**. Click OK.

10. Delete everything in the document except the paragraph that begins "Travel insurance." Position the insertion point to the left of "Travel."

FIGURE 6-7
Inserting an AutoText entry

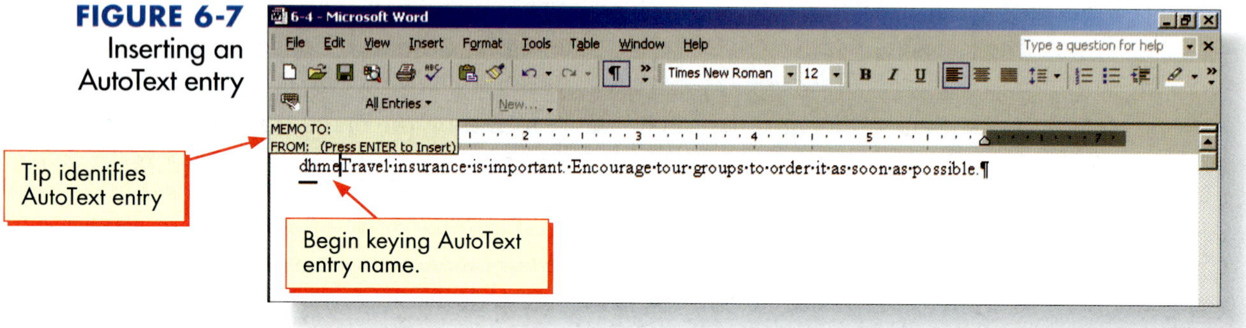

11. Begin keying the name of the letterhead AutoText entry, ***[your initials]* memoheading**. After keying the first few letters, an AutoComplete tip identifies the AutoText entry you created for the memo heading. Press Enter to insert the memo heading at the top of the document.

NOTE: To insert an AutoText entry that has a name with fewer than four letters, you must key the AutoText entry name and press F3.

12. Position the insertion point two blank lines below the last paragraph.

13. Click All Entries on the AutoText toolbar. Point to Normal in the list. The submenu shows the AutoText entries you created.

NOTE: "Normal" refers to the Normal template, on which new documents are based. The Normal template contains all AutoText entries. Templates are discussed later in the textbook.

14. Choose the "website" entry. The text is inserted in the document.

EXERCISE 6-6 Edit and Delete AutoText Entries

After you create an AutoText entry, you might need to change it. If you no longer use an entry, you can delete it.

1. Edit the last paragraph so it begins **For more information about participating insurance companies,**

2. Select the paragraph and click the AutoText button on the AutoText toolbar.
3. In the dialog box, scroll to the existing AutoText name, *[your initials]*website. Select it and click Add.
4. Click Yes to redefine the AutoText entry. The entry now includes the text you added.
5. To test the change, delete the last paragraph, click the AutoText button, choose the website entry, and click Insert.

TIP: The dialog box method for inserting AutoText is helpful if you forget the name of an entry or just need to preview an entry before inserting it.

6. Reopen the dialog box that lists the AutoText entries.
7. Click the first entry that contains your initials and click Delete.
8. Repeat the process for the second entry and click OK to close the dialog box.
9. Hide the AutoText toolbar.

REVIEW: Use the View menu or right-click any toolbar button and choose AutoText from the list of toolbars to close the toolbar.

10. Complete the memo heading—the memo is to **Travel Counselors**, from you, with today's date, and the subject is **Travel Insurance**.
11. Save the document as ***[your initials]*6-6** in your Lesson 6 folder.
12. Print and close the document.

Checking Spelling and Grammar

Correct spelling and grammar are essential to good writing. As you've seen, Word checks your spelling and grammar as you key text and alerts you to errors with these on-screen indicators:

- A red wavy line appears under misspelled words.
- A green wavy line appears under possible grammatical errors.
- The Spelling and Grammar Status icon at the right end of the status bar contains an "X."

EXERCISE 6-7 Spell- and Grammar-Check a Document

You can right-click an individual spelling or grammar error and choose a suggested correction, or run a spelling and grammar check on an entire document by clicking the Spelling and Grammar button on the Standard toolbar (or pressing F7).

1. Open the file **Educate**. This document has several errors, indicated by the red and green wavy lines. The Spelling and Grammar Status icon on the status bar contains an X—another indicator that the document has errors.
2. At the top of the document, press Enter twice and move the insertion point to the first paragraph mark.
3. Using 16-point bold type, key the title **Vacations Can Be Educational**

NOTE: You might notice that as you key text, the Spelling and Grammar Status icon shows a pencil, indicating that Word is checking as you key.

4. If your title has a misspelling, right-click the misspelled word and choose the corrected spelling from the shortcut menu.
5. Right-click the grammatical error "are the range" in the first paragraph under the title. Choose "is the range" from the shortcut menu.

NOTE: Word's spell- and grammar-check tool is not foolproof. For example, it cannot correct a word that is correctly spelled but incorrectly keyed, such as "sue" instead of "use." It might also apply a green wavy line to a type of grammatical usage, such as the passive voice, which might not be preferred but is not incorrect.

6. To run a spell- and grammar-check for the entire document, position the insertion point at the beginning of the document and click the Spelling and Grammar button on the Standard toolbar. Word locates the first misspelling, "formaal."

FIGURE 6-8
Checking spelling

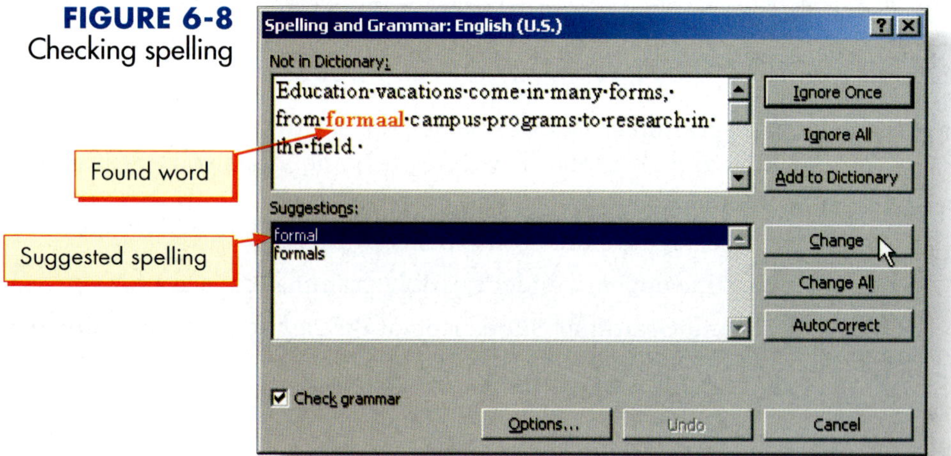

7. Click Change to correct the spelling to the first suggested spelling, "formal." Next, Word finds a repeated word, "as."

TIP: To check spelling without also checking grammar, click the Check grammar check box to clear it.

8. Click Delete to delete the repeated word. Next, Word finds a grammatical error: "Their" is used incorrectly.

9. In the dialog box, select "Their" and key **There**. Click Change to change the spelling in the document. Next, Word locates "cavate," which should be "excavate," as you can see from the text.

10. In the dialog box, delete the space between "ex" and "cavate" and click Change. Word stops on the name "Atacama."

11. Click Ignore Once, because this name is correctly spelled but is not in Word's dictionary. Next, Word flags "desert" and suggests "Desert."

12. Click Change to accept the suggestion.

13. Click OK when the check is complete. Notice that there are no more wavy lines in the document and the Spelling and Grammar Status icon shows a check mark.

TABLE 6-2 Dialog Box Options When Checking Spelling and Grammar

OPTION	DESCRIPTION
Ignore Once	Skips the word.
Ignore All	Skips all occurrences of the word in the document.
Add to Dictionary	Adds the word to the default dictionary file in Word. You can also create your own dictionary and add words to it.
Change	Changes the word to the entry in the Change To box or to the word you chose from the Suggestions list.
Change All	Same as Change, but changes the word throughout the document.
AutoCorrect	Adds the word to the list of corrections that Word makes automatically.
Options	Lets you change the Spelling and Grammar options in Word.
Undo	Changes back the most recent correction made.
Cancel	Discontinues the checking operation.

Using the Thesaurus

The *Thesaurus* is a tool that can improve your writing. Use the Thesaurus to look up a *synonym* (a word with a similar meaning) for a selected word to add variety or interest to a document.

The Thesaurus sometimes displays *antonyms* (words with the opposite meaning) and related words. You can look up synonyms for any of these words to get additional word choices.

EXERCISE 6-8 Use the Thesaurus

You can start the Thesaurus by pressing Shift+F7, by using the shortcut menu (right-clicking a word), or by choosing Tools, Language, Thesaurus from the menu.

1. In the second paragraph below the title, select the word "rigorous" or simply place the insertion point in the word. Read the paragraph to understand the use of the word.
2. Press Shift+F7. The Thesaurus dialog box appears with a list of possible meanings for "rigorous" as an adverb. It also gives you a list of synonyms, with "exact" as the recommended word.
3. Click the word "hard" in the Meanings list. A list of synonyms appears in the Synonyms list. These words are more appropriate for the sentence.

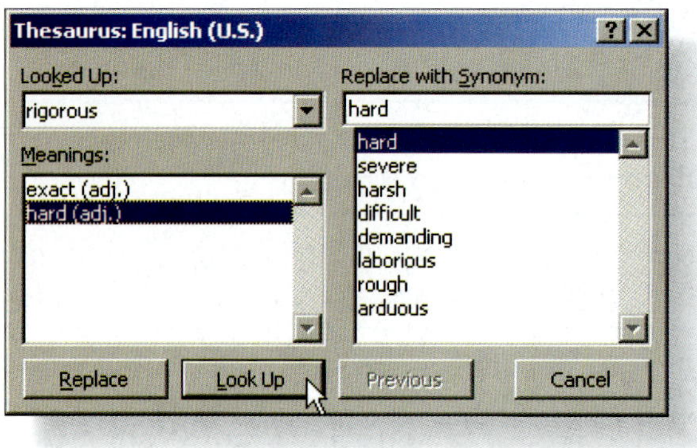

FIGURE 6-9
Using the Thesaurus

4. Click the Look Up button. A list of more meanings and synonyms appears.
5. Choose "difficult" in the Meanings list. Then choose the synonym "demanding" (or another synonym) and click the Replace button. Word replaces "rigorous" with "demanding" (or your chosen word).
6. Save the document as ***[your initials]*6-8** in your Lesson 6 folder.
7. Print the document and leave it open for the next exercise.

Finding and Replacing Text

Instead of scrolling through a document, you can use the Find command to locate text or move quickly to a specific document location. The Find command can find individual words, formatting, and special characters.

The Replace command finds your specified text or formatting and replaces it with your specified alternative. You can replace all instances of text or formatting at once or you can find and confirm each replacement.

- To use Find: Choose Find from the Edit menu or press Ctrl+F.
- To use Replace: Choose Replace from the Edit menu or press Ctrl+H.

EXERCISE 6-9 Find and Replace Text

1. Position the insertion point at the beginning of the document and choose Find from the Edit menu. The Find and Replace dialog box opens, with the Find tab selected.
2. Delete any text in the Find what text box and key **education**
3. Click the More button, if it is present, to expand the dialog box. The expanded dialog box offers more search options to help you narrow a search.

TIP: Click the Less button when you're not interested in these search options and you want to make the dialog box smaller. To see more of the document text during a search, drag the dialog box by its title bar to the bottom right corner of the screen.

4. Clear any check boxes that might be checked, and click the No Formatting button (if it is active) to remove any formatting from previous searches. The dialog box should look like the one in Figure 6-10.

FIGURE 6-10 Using the Find feature

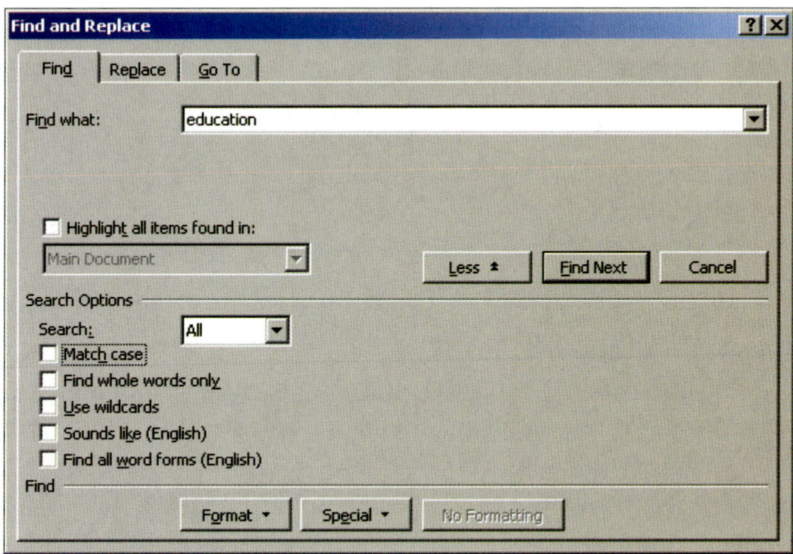

5. Click Find Next. Notice that the first occurrence of "education" occurs in the bold title word "Educational." If you continue clicking Find Next, you'll find all word forms of "education"—uppercase, lowercase, and as part of other words.
6. Click the Match case search option and then click Find Next until you reach the end of the document. Word only found the text as you entered it, in lowercase letters.

7. Click OK in the dialog box that says Word finished searching the document.

8. Clear the Match case check box. Click the Highlight all items found in check box and click Find All. Word selects all forms of the word "education." Move the dialog box to the side to see the selected text.

9. Click the Replace tab in the dialog box. Now you can replace the selected text with another word.

FIGURE 6-11
Using the Replace feature

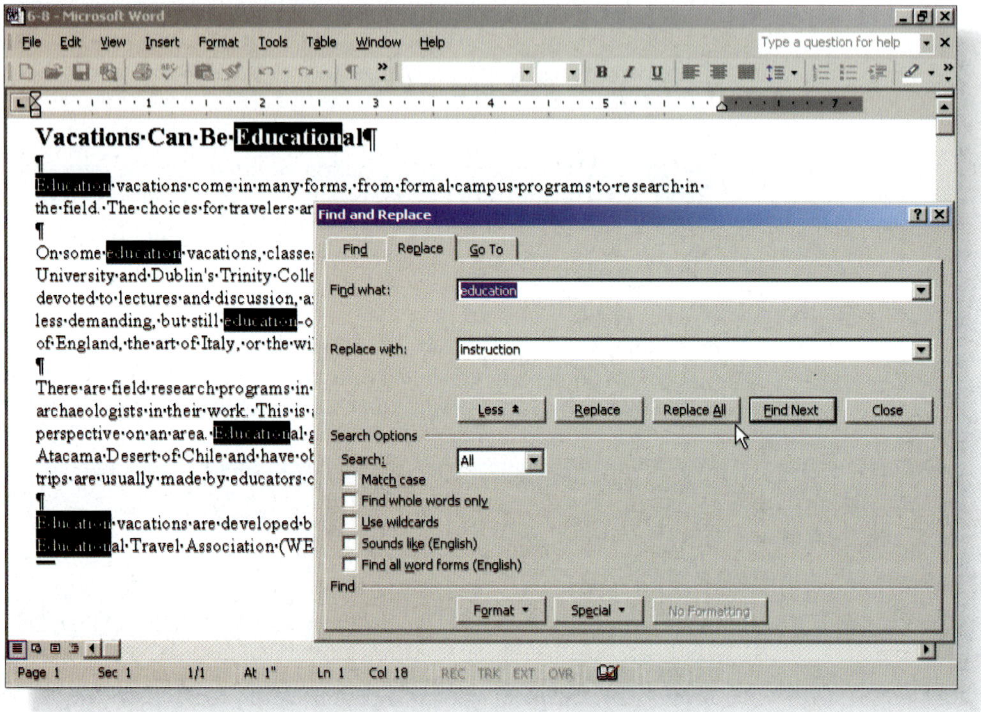

10. Key **instruction** in the Replace with text box. Because you can see all instances of the selected word in this short document, click Replace All.

NOTE: Click Replace All to perform a global replacement, which replaces all instances of the text in the entire document. To perform a selective replacement, you click Find Next to have Word locate each word, and then click Replace to confirm each replacement (as in the next exercise).

11. Click OK when Word finishes the process and close the dialog box. Word replaces all forms of "education" with the appropriate form of "instruction," using the correct case as needed.

12. Click the Undo button to undo the Replace All command.

NOTE: After replacing text, you can always undo the action. If you used Replace All, all changes are reversed at once. If you used Replace, only the last change is reversed, but you can undo the last several changes individually by selecting them from the Undo drop-down list.

EXERCISE 6-10 Replace Text Using Find Next

Replacing each occurrence of text individually by using the Find Next and Replace buttons in the Find and Replace dialog box allows you to be more selective in your replacements.

1. Position the insertion point at the beginning of the document and choose Replace from the Edit menu.
2. Key **education** in the Find what text box, if it is not already there.

NOTE: You can open the Find what (or Replace with) drop-down list and choose text that was previously entered in the text box.

3. Click the Find whole words only search option, so Word ignores "educational."
4. Click in the Replace with text box and key **college-education**. Click the No Formatting button if it is active.
5. Adjust the position and size (click Less) of the dialog box so you can see more of the document text.
6. Click Find Next. Word skips the title line and finds the first occurrence of the search word. Click Replace to replace the word.
7. Continue to click Replace until Word finds "education-oriented." Then click Find Next to keep this text as is.
8. Continue to click Replace until Word finishes searching the document. Click OK and then close the dialog box.
9. Save the document as ***[your initials]*6-10** in your Lesson 6 folder and print it.

TIP: There are other useful search options in the Find and Replace dialog box. Use wildcards lets you search for text by using special search operators. A wildcard is a symbol that stands for missing or unknown text. For example, the wildcard "?" finds any character. Search for "b?te" to find "bite" and "byte." The Sounds like search option lets you find a word that sounds like the search text but is spelled differently. For example, search for "insure" to find "insure" and "ensure."

EXERCISE 6-11 Delete Text with Replace

You can also use the Replace command to delete text automatically. Key the text to be deleted in the Find what text box and leave the Replace with text box blank. You can find and delete text with confirmation by using the Find Next option or without confirmation by using the Replace All option.

1. Position the insertion point at the beginning of the document and press Ctrl+H to open the Find and Replace dialog box with the Replace tab selected.
2. Expand the dialog box (click More) and clear any of the checked boxes. Key **-education** (including the preceding hyphen) in the Find what text box.
3. Press Tab to move to the Replace with text box and press Delete to remove the last entry.

NOTE: Remember, pressing Tab in a dialog box moves the insertion point from one text box to another and highlights existing text. Pressing Enter executes the dialog box command.

4. Click Replace All. Click OK and close the dialog box. Word deleted the text "-education" from the document. "College-education vacations" now appears as just "College vacations."
5. Save the document as ***[your initials]*****6-11** in your Lesson 6 folder.
6. Print and then close the document.

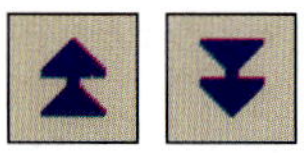

TIP: After you initiate a find using the Find and Replace dialog box, you can close the dialog box and use the Previous Find and Next Find buttons at the bottom of the vertical scroll bar to continue the search without having the dialog box in your way.

EXERCISE 6-12 Find and Replace Formatting and Special Characters

In the Find and Replace dialog box, you can use the Format button to find and replace formatting (such as fonts or indents) and the Special button to find and replace special characters (such as paragraph marks or tab characters).

1. Open the file **SantaFe**. The document contains highlighting, which you'll replace with bold formatting; and it has tab characters to indent paragraphs, which you'll delete by using the Replace command.
2. Position the insertion point at the top of the document. Open the Find and Replace dialog box with the Replace tab selected. Make sure the dialog box is expanded.
3. Delete any existing text or formatting from the Find what text box. Click the Format button. Notice the types of formatting you can search for. Choose Highlight from the list. "Highlight" appears below the text box.
4. Press Tab. Delete any existing text or formatting from the Replace with text box. Click the Format button and choose Highlight from the list. Choose Highlight again. "Not Highlight" appears below the text box.

FIGURE 6-12
Replacing formatting

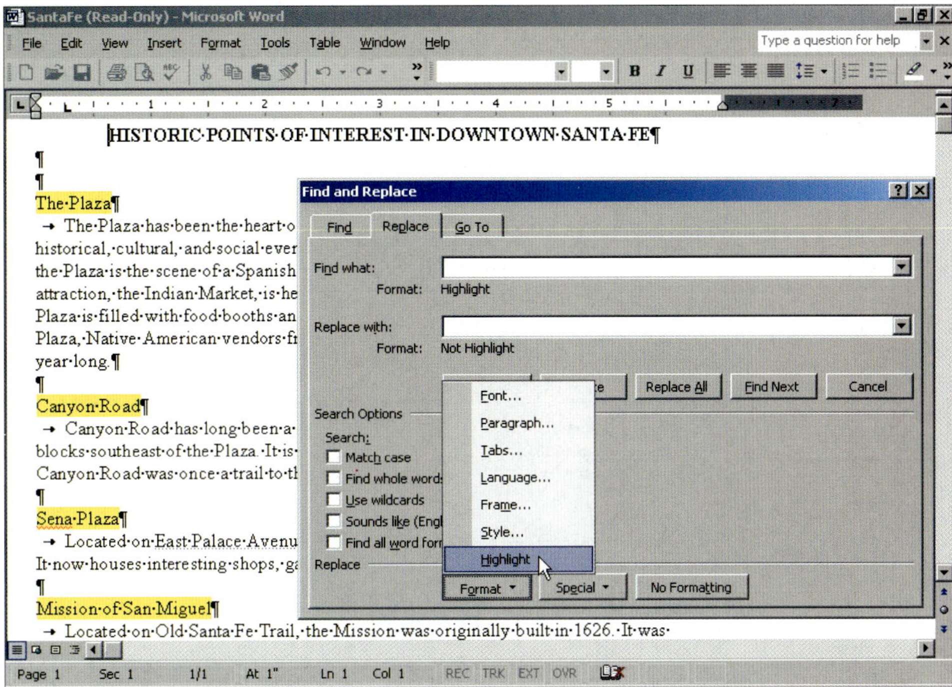

5. Click the Format button again and choose Font. The Replace Font dialog box opens.
6. Set the font to Arial and bold and then click OK. Perform a global replacement by clicking Replace All and then close the dialog box. The highlighted text is now Arial bold.
7. Format the title text as Arial to match the headings.
8. To delete the tab characters, reopen the Find and Replace dialog box with the Replace tab selected. Clear the formatting for the Find what text box. Click the Special button and choose Tab Character. A code (^t) is inserted in the Find what text box. (See Figure 6-13 on the next page.)

TIP: Instead of opening the Special list, you can key the special character code directly into the text box for certain characters or document elements. In addition to **^t** for a tab character, key **^p** for a paragraph mark, **^l** for a manual line break, or **^+** for an em dash.

9. Clear the formatting for the Replace with text box and leave it empty.
10. Perform a Replace All and then close the dialog box. The tab characters are deleted from the document.
11. Save the document as ***[your initials]*6-12** in your Lesson 6 folder.
12. Print and then close the document.

FIGURE 6-13 Replacing special characters

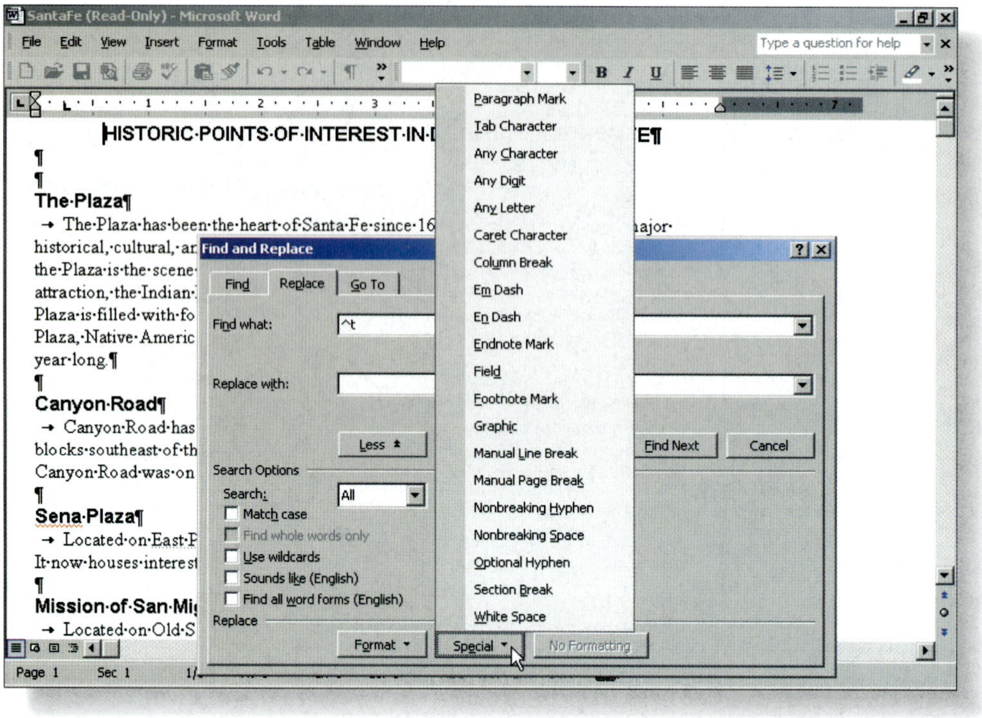

Moving Text

One of the most important features of word processing is the capability to move (or copy) a block of text from one part of a document to another, or from one document to another, without rekeying the text. The most common way to move text is by using the *cut-and-paste* method.

Moving text by the cut-and-paste method is simple: select the text you want to move, use the Cut command, move to the location where you want to place the the text, and use the Paste command.

When you cut text, Word stores the text on the *Clipboard*, a temporary storage area. Understanding the Clipboard is the first step in learning how to cut and paste text.

EXERCISE 6-13 Display the Clipboard Task Pane

There are two types of Clipboards:

- The Word Clipboard stores one item at a time. Each time you store a new item on this Clipboard, it replaces the previous item.
- The Office Clipboard is like 24 separate Clipboards and is located on the Clipboard task pane. It is used to collect items without erasing previous items. You can store items from all Office applications.

1. Open the file **NYweekend**.
2. Open the Edit menu and choose Office Clipboard. The Clipboard task pane opens, displaying the Office Clipboard. Notice the two buttons at the top of the task pane: Paste All [Paste All] and Clear All [Clear All].
3. If the box below these buttons does not say "Clipboard empty," click the Clear All button [Clear All] to remove anything stored on the Clipboard from previous editing.

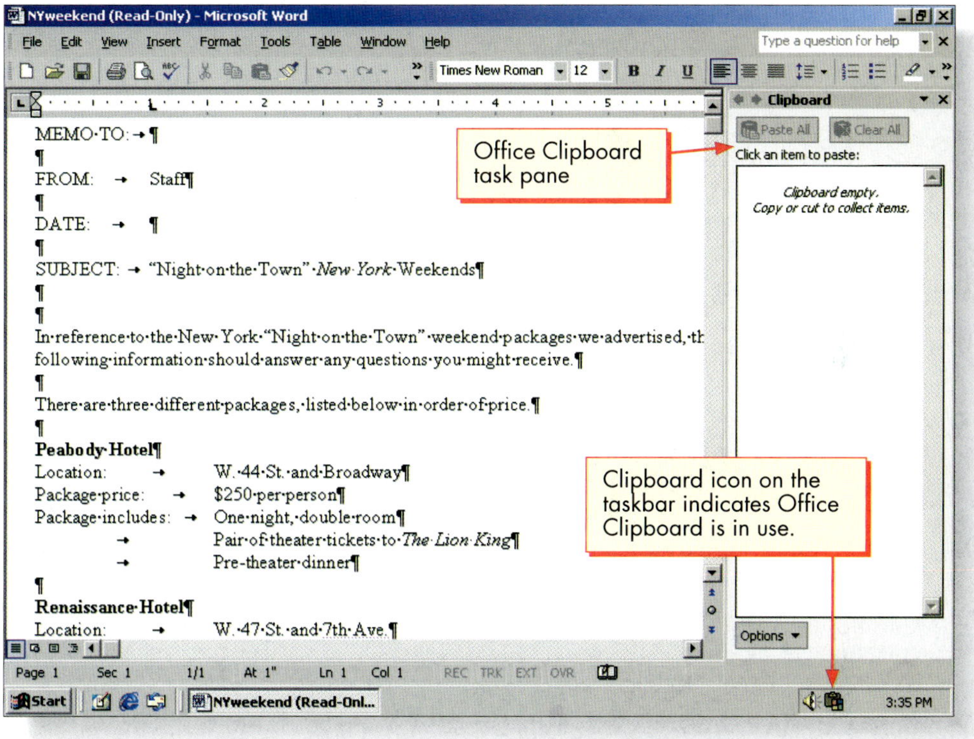

FIGURE 6-14
Clipboard task pane

4. To see all the document text within the document window, open the View menu, choose Zoom, and change the zoom to Page width. Click OK.

EXERCISE 6-14 Use Cut and Paste to Move Text

There are many ways to cut and paste text. For example, you can use the:

- Cut button and Paste button on the Standard toolbar
- Clipboard task pane (for pasting)
- Shortcut menu
- Keyboard shortcuts Ctrl+X to cut and Ctrl+V to paste

1. Select the word "Staff" in the "FROM:" line of the memo. You are going to move it to the first line of the memo.

2. Click the Cut button on the Standard toolbar to remove the text from the document and store it on the Clipboard. Notice that the text appears as an item on the Clipboard task pane.
3. Position the insertion point to the right of the tab character in the "MEMO TO:" line to indicate where you want to insert the text.
4. Click the "Staff" item on the Clipboard task pane to paste "Staff" in its new location.

NOTE: When you point to an item on the Clipboard task pane, you can just click the item to paste it or click the down arrow that appears to the right of the text. Clicking the arrow displays two options: Paste and Delete. Clicking Paste is another way to paste the item; clicking Delete deletes the item from the Clipboard task pane.

5. Click the Paste Options button that now appears below the pasted text. The available options help to make sure the text you paste has the formatting you want. In this case, the default option Keep Source Formatting is fine, so click the button again to close the menu.

FIGURE 6-15
Pasting text

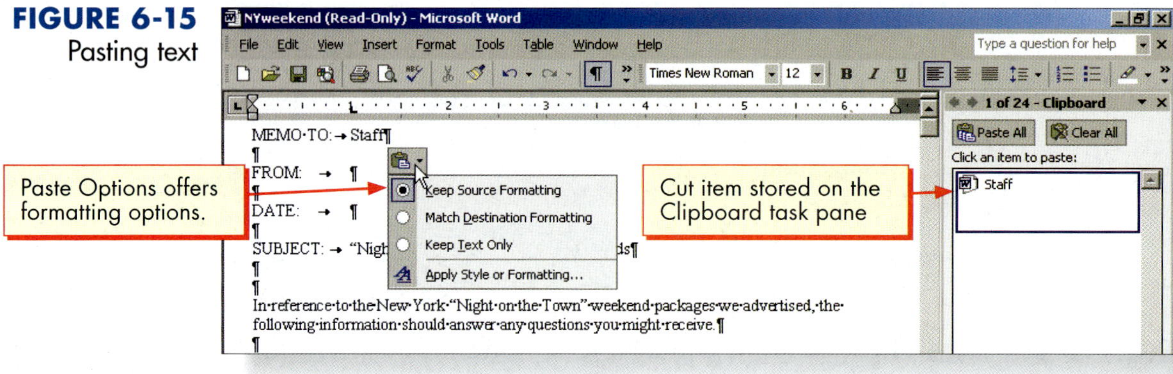

NOTE: In the list of paste options, "source" refers to the original text location and "destination" refers to the new text location. These options are very useful when the formatting of one location is different from that of the other location.

6. Select the text *"New York"* in the subject line of the memo and then click the Cut button on the Standard toolbar. The text is added to the Clipboard task pane.

NOTE: You might already have noticed that when you delete, cut, move, or paste text, Word automatically adjusts the spacing between words—this is the Smart Cut and Paste feature in action.

7. Position the insertion point to the left of "Night on the Town" in the subject line. Click the Paste button on the Standard toolbar to paste "New York" in its new location.

8. Click the Paste Options button and choose Keep Text Only to remove the italic formatting.

NOTE: You could also choose Match Destination Formatting to remove the italic formatting and match the text around the pasted text.

9. Select the paragraph near the bottom of the document that begins "All the hotels are." Include the paragraph mark on the blank line below the paragraph.

TIP: When you use the cut-and-paste method to move paragraphs, you can preserve the correct spacing between paragraphs by including the blank line below the paragraph you're moving as part of the selection.

FIGURE 6-16
Using the shortcut menu to cut

Include this blank line when moving an entire paragraph.

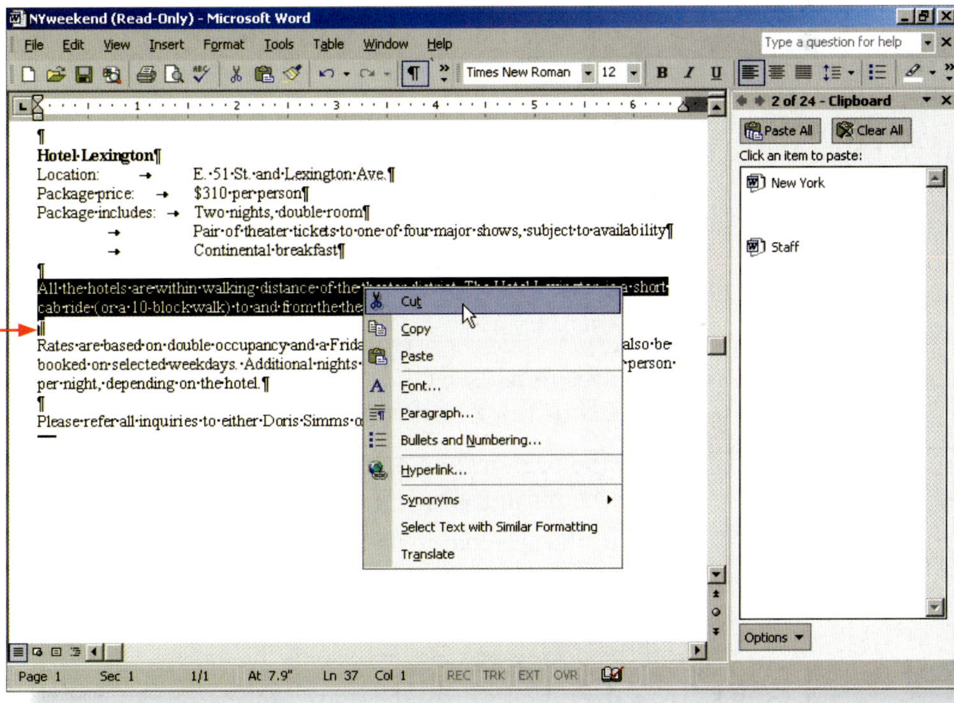

10. Point to the selected text and click the right mouse button to display the shortcut menu. Click Cut. The text appears as a new item on the Clipboard task pane.

11. Right-click the I-beam pointer to the left of "Please refer" on the last line and then choose Paste from the shortcut menu. The paragraph moves to its new location.

NOTE: You can ignore the Paste Options button when you have no need to choose a formatting option.

12. Select the first sentence in the paragraph that begins "All the hotels." Don't forget to include the period. Press Ctrl+X to cut the text. The new item appears at the top of the Clipboard task pane.
13. In the same paragraph, position the insertion point just before the paragraph mark. Press Ctrl+V to paste the text, or click the first item in the Clipboard task pane. (Notice that the first Clipboard item is the sentence you cut and the second item is the paragraph you cut.)

14. Press Ctrl+Z to undo the paste. Press Ctrl+Z again to undo the cut. (Remember, you can also click the Undo button to undo actions.) Notice that the text remains on the Clipboard.

NOTE: The Cut, Copy, Paste, and Undo commands are also available from the Edit menu.

15. Click the Clear All button to clear all Clipboard items. Close the Clipboard task pane.

NOTE: The Paste All button on the Office Clipboard is used to copy all the Clipboard items at once to the location of the insertion point.

EXERCISE 6-15 Use Drag and Drop to Move Text

You can also move selected text to a new location by using the *drag-and-drop* method. Text is not transferred to the Clipboard when you use drag and drop.

1. Select the paragraph beginning "All the hotels," including the blank line below the paragraph.
2. Point to the selected text. The I-beam changes to a left-pointing arrow.
3. Click and hold down the left mouse button. The pointer changes to the drag-and-drop pointer. Notice the dotted insertion point near the tip of the arrow and the dotted box at the base of the arrow.
4. Drag the pointer until the dotted insertion point is positioned to the left of the line beginning "Rates are based on." Release the mouse button. The paragraph moves to its new location. (See Figure 6-17 on the next page.)

TIP: Use cut and paste to move text over long distances—for example, onto another page. Use drag and drop to move text short distances where you can see both the selected text and the destination on the screen at the same time.

FIGURE 6-17
Drag-and-drop pointer

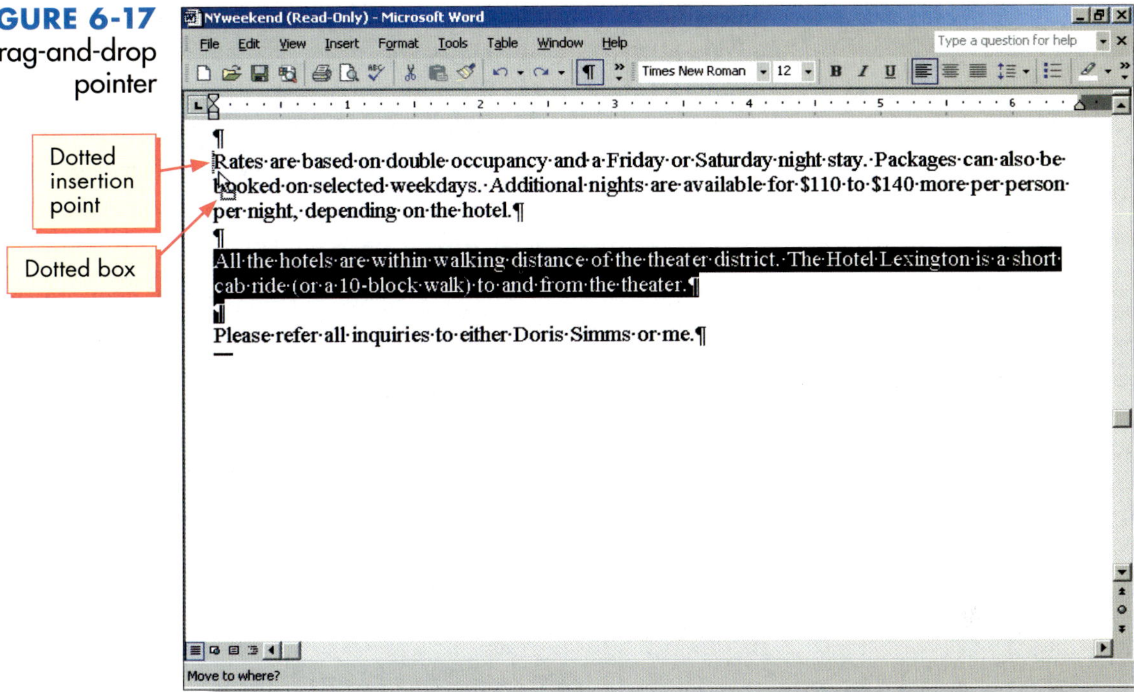

5. Add your name to the "FROM:" line of the memo heading and key today's date in the date line.
6. Save the document as ***[your initials]*6-15** in your Lesson 6 folder and print it.

Copying Text

Copying and pasting text is similar to cutting and pasting text. Instead of removing the text from the document and storing it on the Clipboard, you place a copy on the Clipboard.

EXERCISE 6-16 Use Copy and Paste

There are many ways to copy and paste text. For example, you can use the:

- Copy button and Paste button on the Standard toolbar
- Clipboard task pane (for pasting)
- Shortcut menu
- Keyboard shortcut Ctrl+C to copy and Ctrl+V to paste

1. Under "Hotel Lexington," select the entire line that contains the text "Continental breakfast." Include the tab character to the left of the text and the paragraph mark to the right of the text.

2. Click the Copy button on the Standard toolbar to transfer a copy of the text to the Word Clipboard. Notice that the selected text remains in its original position in the document.

NOTE: When the Office Clipboard is not open, the regular Word Clipboard is in operation. This Clipboard only contains the last item you cut or copied. With the Office Clipboard open, you can store up to 24 cut or copied items.

3. Right-click the I-beam pointer to the left of the blank paragraph mark above "Hotel Lexington."
4. Choose Paste from the shortcut menu. A copy of the paragraph is added to the "Renaissance Hotel" package description and the Paste Options button appears.

5. Click the Paste Options button and notice that the same options are available as for cutting and pasting text. Keep the source formatting and click in the document window.
6. Position the insertion point to the left of the blank paragraph mark above "Renaissance Hotel." Press Ctrl+V to paste the text into the "Peabody Hotel" package description.
7. Under "Renaissance Hotel," select the entire line that contains the text "$20 credit for room service." Include the tab character to the left of the text and the paragraph mark to the right of the text.
8. Press Ctrl+C to copy this text.
9. Position the insertion point to the left of the blank paragraph mark above the paragraph that begins "All the hotels are within."
10. Open the Office Clipboard task pane.
11. Click the Clipboard item that contains the text, "$20 credit for room service." The Clipboard content is pasted into the document at the location of the insertion point.

EXERCISE 6-17 Use Drag and Drop to Copy Text

To copy text by using the drag-and-drop method, press Ctrl while dragging the text. Remember, drag and drop does not store text on a Clipboard.

1. Scroll so you can see the text under "Peabody Hotel" and "Renaissance Hotel."
2. Under "Package Includes" for the Renaissance Hotel, apply italic formatting to the word "Carousel" and then select the text after *"Carousel"* from the comma through the word "availability." Do not include the paragraph mark.

3. While holding down [Ctrl], drag the selected text to the immediate right of the word *"King"* in the Peabody Hotel section. The plus sign attached to the drag-and-drop pointer indicates the text is being copied rather than moved.

FIGURE 6-18
Copying with the drag-and-drop pointer

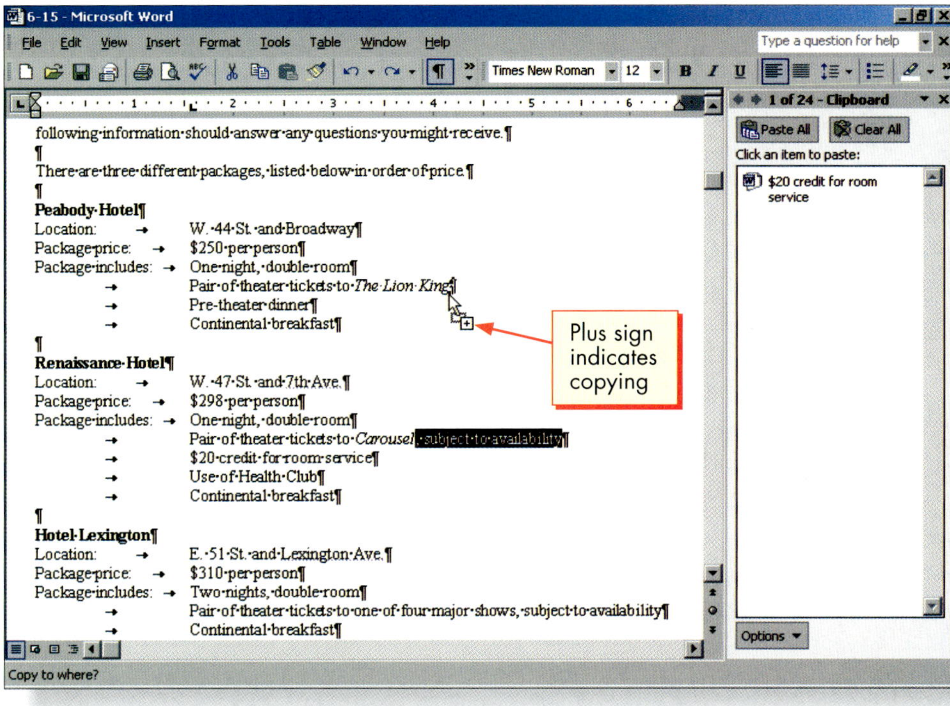

TIP: Dragging is not effective over long distances within a document. Try these alternative methods: To cut, select the text, hold down [Ctrl], scroll as needed, and right-click where you want to paste the text. To copy, select the text, hold down [Ctrl] and [Shift], scroll as needed, and right-click where you want to copy the text.

4. Clear the Office Clipboard and close the task pane.
5. If the memo does not fit on one page, reduce the font of the entire document by one size.
6. Save the document as ***[your initials]*6-17** in your Lesson 6 folder. Print and close the document.

EXERCISE 6-18 Copy Text from One Document to Another Using Copy and Paste Special

Moving or copying text from one document into another is easy. Remember that the Paste command inserts text in the format of the document from which it was cut or copied. You can use the Paste Options button [icon] to remove or change the formatting of pasted text, or you can use Paste Special to paste text without formatting.

1. Open the files **Albuquerque** and **Climate**.

TIP: To open both files at the same time, click the Albuquerque filename in the Open dialog box, hold down Ctrl, click the Climate filename, and then click Open.

2. Click the Climate button on the taskbar to make it the active document. Notice that this document text is 14-point Arial.

3. Copy the first paragraph, beginning "Albuquerque is renowned."

4. Make Albuquerque the active document.

TIP: Instead of using the taskbar to switch between open documents, you can display both documents on the screen at the same time by opening the Window menu and choosing Arrange All. Each document will appear in a separate window with its own scroll bars. You then click one of the windows to make it the active document.

5. Start a new paragraph at the end of Albuquerque and paste the text copied from Climate. Notice that the format of the new text does not match the format of the current document. Click the Undo button to remove the new text.

6. Open the Edit menu and choose Paste Special. In the Paste Special dialog box, choose Unformatted Text and click OK. Now the format of the new text takes on the format of the current document.

FIGURE 6-19
Using Paste Special

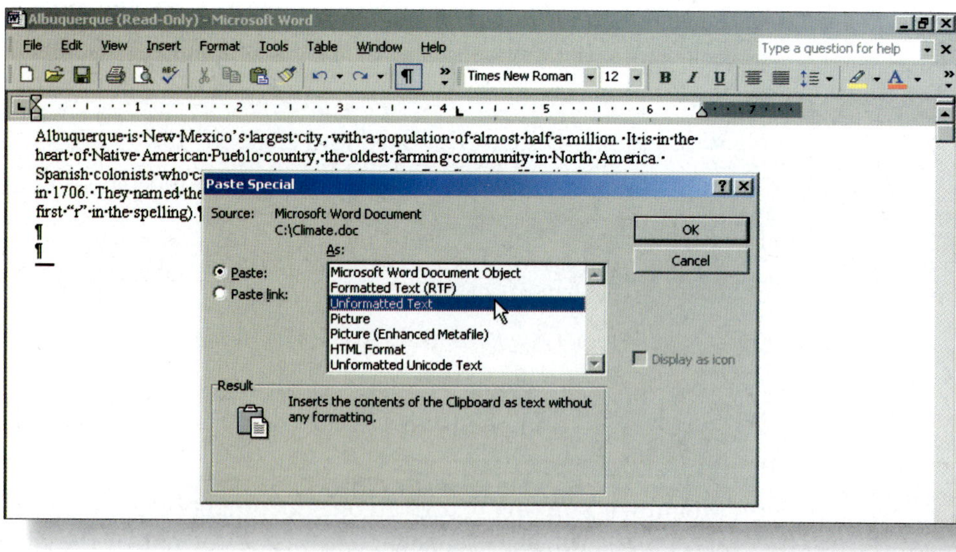

7. Save the document as ***[your initials]*6-18** in your Lesson 6 folder. Print and close the document.
8. Close the Climate document.

TIP: You can insert an entire file into the current document by using the Insert, File command. Move the insertion point to the place in the document where you want to insert the file. Then choose File from the Insert menu and double-click the filename. The text from the entire file is inserted where the insertion point is located.

USING HELP

When cutting or copying text in a long document, you can use a special Word feature to split the document into two panes. Each pane has its own scroll bar so you can clearly see two parts of the same document.

Use Help to find out how to split a document into panes:

1. Key **split a document into panes** in the Ask a Question text box and press Enter.
2. Click the first topic View two parts of a document simultaneously
3. Review the information, paying attention to the location of the split box. Then close the Help window.
4. Open any document. Locate the split box and try splitting the document screen into two panes. Scroll within each pane.
5. Close the document without saving.

LESSON 6 Summary

- Key words such as days, months, and dates and use the AutoComplete feature to complete the text for you by pressing Enter when you see the suggested text.
- Use smart tags to perform Microsoft Outlook functions, such as creating entries in Outlook's contact list, without opening Outlook.
- The AutoCorrect feature corrects some misspelled words and capitalization for you automatically as you key the text.
- Use the AutoCorrect dialog box to create entries for words you misspell often or to create shortcuts for phrases you use often.

- When you don't want Word to make an automatic correction, use the AutoCorrect Options button . (Point to the blue box under the corrected text to display the AutoCorrect Options button.)
- Word stores AutoText entries for standard business document phrases (such as "To Whom It May Concern"). Insert these entries without having to key the text by using the Insert menu or the AutoText toolbar.
- Create your own AutoText entries for words or phrases you use often by clicking New on the AutoText toolbar.
- Use the AutoText tab in the AutoCorrect dialog box to edit and delete AutoText entries.
- Use the spelling and grammar checker to check the spelling and grammar of an entire document.
- Use the Thesaurus to look up synonyms for a selected word to add variety and interest to your document.
- Use the Find and Replace dialog box, Find tab, to find text in a document. Use the Replace tab to replace text. Expand the dialog box by clicking More; make it smaller by clicking Less.
- Use different search options in the Find and Replace dialog box to narrow your search. For example, use Match case to locate words or phrases that match the case of text keyed in the Find what text box.
- To delete text by using the Replace command, key the text to be deleted in the Find what text box and leave the Replace with text box blank.
- Find words or phrases with character or paragraph formatting by using the Format button in the Find and Replace dialog box.
- Replace text selectively (one occurrence at a time) by using the Find Next and Replace buttons in the Find and Replace dialog box.
- Replace text globally (all occurrences in the document) by using the Replace All button in the Find and Replace dialog box.
- Find and replace character and paragraph formatting by using the Format button in the Find and Replace dialog box. Find and replace special characters by using the Special button in the Find and Replace dialog box.
- Display the Clipboard task pane to open the Office Clipboard, which can store up to 24 different cut or copied items.
- Use the Cut and Paste commands to move text or the Copy and Paste commands to copy text in a document or between multiple documents.
- Use toolbar buttons, the shortcut menu, or keyboard shortcuts to cut, copy, and paste. Use the Clipboard task pane to paste text.

- Use the drag-and-drop method to copy or move text from one location to another in a document or between documents.
- Use the Paste Options button or the Paste Special command to control the formatting of pasted text.

LESSON 6 Command Summary

FEATURE	BUTTON	MENU	KEYBOARD	SPEECH?
Create AutoText entry	or New... (AutoText toolbar)	Insert, AutoText, New	Alt + F3	✓
Check spelling and grammar		Tools, Spelling and Grammar	F7	✓
Thesaurus		Tools, Language, Thesaurus	Shift + F7	✓
Find		Edit, Find	Ctrl + F	✓
Replace		Edit, Replace	Ctrl + H	✓
Open Office Clipboard		Edit, Office Clipboard		✓
Cut		Edit, Cut	Ctrl + X	✓
Copy		Edit, Copy	Ctrl + C	✓
Paste		Edit, Paste	Ctrl + V	✓

WORD

Concepts Review

TRUE/FALSE QUESTIONS

Each of the following statements is either true or false. Indicate your choice by circling T or F.

T F *1.* AutoCorrect automatically changes "THis" to "This" and "monday" to "Monday."

T F *2.* Smart tags appear as green wavy lines.

T F *3.* The Thesaurus finds synonyms for words.

T F *4.* AutoComplete suggests a complete word or phrase for a date or an AutoText entry.

T F *5.* The content of the Office Clipboard is replaced each time you copy or cut text.

T F *6.* You can use the Less button in the Find and Replace dialog box to make the dialog box smaller.

T F *7.* When finding and replacing text, the Replace All button allows you to confirm each replacement.

T F *8.* You can use the Office Clipboard to paste, but not copy, text.

SHORT ANSWER QUESTIONS

Write the correct answer in the space provided.

1. Which function key starts a spell check?

___

2. Which option in the Spelling and Grammar dialog box lets you skip over an incorrectly spelled word?

___

3. To delete text with the Replace command, which text box do you leave blank?

___

4. When you click New on the AutoText toolbar, which dialog box opens?

___

5. Where is the Spelling and Grammar Status icon located?

___

6. What is the special character code used for finding a paragraph mark?

___

7. How do you remove the existing Clipboard items on the Office Clipboard?

___

8. After pasting text, what appears immediately below the pasted text?

___

CRITICAL THINKING

Answer these questions on a separate page. There are no right or wrong answers. Support your answers with examples from your own experience, if possible.

1. This lesson taught several ways to move and copy text. Which method(s) do you prefer? Explain your answer.

2. Some people consider the Replace feature to be only a way to correct misspelled words. It can be much more than that, however. Can you describe some ways to use this feature to increase your efficiency?

Lesson Applications

EXERCISE 6-19

Create an AutoText entry and check grammar and spelling.

1. In a new blank document, key the text ***[your name]*'s Good News Café** and press Enter twice. (AutoCorrect applies the accent mark over the "e" of "Café.")
2. Select the text and the paragraph marks and format them as 12-point Arial.
3. Select the text only (excluding the paragraph marks) and create an AutoText entry named ***[your initials]*cafe**.
4. At the last paragraph mark, key the text shown in Figure 6-20. Include the corrections. Wherever "gn" appears, key the AutoText entry you just created (*[your initials]*café), pressing Enter when you see the AutoComplete tip.

FIGURE 6-20

The best vegetarian restaurant in Tucson is gn. This popular choice for healthy dining is located at the [southeast] corner of Wilmot Road and East Broadway.

gn serves 3 meals a day following its own strict rules: everything is fresh, organic, and made from scratch.

The menu at gn features pages of unusual dishes, such as cashew chicken and veggie nut burgers. Natural fruit shakes, fat free brownies and fresh baked muffins make desserts agreeable.

gn is open 7 days a week. Reservations are taken for five or more people, and credit cards are not accepted.

5. Spell-check and grammar-check the document.
6. Format the title as 16-point bold small caps with a text shadow. Add another paragraph mark below the title.
7. Format the restaurant name in small capitals throughout the document. (Use the Repeat command or the Styles and Formatting task pane.)
8. Delete the AutoText entry you created.
9. Use the Thesaurus to find another word for "agreeable" in the next to last paragraph.

10. Save the document as ***[your initials]*6-19** in your Lesson 6 folder.
11. Print and close the document.

EXERCISE 6-20

Remove smart tags, replace text and character formatting, and move and copy text.

1. Open the file **Falls**.
2. Format the document as a memo to the Office Staff from Frank Youngblood. Use today's date. The subject is Montana Waterfalls. Use the appropriate spacing.
3. Remove the smart tags from the memo heading.
4. Copy the italic text *"Pine Creek Falls"* and paste it at the beginning of the paragraph directly below it. Use the Keep Text Only paste option to paste the text without italics.
5. After the pasted text, key **is** and make "A" lowercase.
6. Replace the word "falls" with **Falls** wherever it appears in the name of a particular falls. Use a selective search and choose the Find whole words only option. (Remember to clear any formatting that might exist.)
7. Replace the italic formatting of the waterfall names with not italic, bold, small caps formatting. Make sure no search options are checked before you begin replacing.

TIP: Instead of clicking the Format button in the Find and Replace dialog box, you can use keyboard shortcuts. For example, click in one of the text boxes and press Ctrl+I for italic. Press the combination again for not italic.

8. Find the word "Travel" and replace it with "Use." Make sure no formatting is specified.
9. Move "Big Timer Falls" above "Wraith Falls"; then move "Wraith Falls" to the end of the document. Correct line spacing if needed.
10. Add your reference initials to the document.
11. Save the document as ***[your initials]*6-20** in your Lesson 6 folder.
12. Print and close the document.

EXERCISE 6-21

Check spelling and grammar, replace text, and move and copy text.

1. Open the files **Special1** and **Special2**.
2. In Special1, copy the list of five items starting with "Hawaii."

3. Close the document, leaving Special2 open.
4. In Special2, paste the copied text just below the paragraph that begins "Our naturalist tours." Use the Paste Options button to match the destination formatting.
5. In the new list, move the five items into alphabetical order.
6. Format this list and the list that begins "Notre Dame Cathedral" as bulleted lists. Format the first item in each list with 6 points of spacing before the paragraph.
7. Use the Replace command to selectively replace "our" with "Duke City Gateway's" in the document. Replace uppercase and lowercase "our" but do *not* replace "our" in the following:
   - "among our most popular"
   - the last paragraph
8. Replace "tours" with "expeditions," except when the word occurs in "special-interest tours."
9. Add a title to the document by keying **Interesting Tours for Travelers with Interests** in bold.
10. Center the title and apply paragraph spacing of 72 points before and 24 points after.
11. Spell-check and grammar-check the document, using Word's suggested spelling for "Colosseum."
12. Save the document as ***[your initials]*****6-21** in your Lesson 6 folder.
13. Print and close the document.

EXERCISE 6-22 Challenge Yourself

Move text and copy text using Paste Special.

1. Open the file **Baggage**. Open the Office Clipboard and clear all copied items.
2. Cut the "Exclusions" paragraph and paste it before the "Terms" paragraph.
3. Start a new paragraph at the end of the document and key **Additional coverage can be purchased for:**
4. In the paragraph that begins "Exclusions," cut the text "household furniture or furnishings; contact lenses; money, securities, tickets, or documents;" and paste it at the end of the last paragraph.
5. Convert the pasted text to a bulleted list as shown (notice that "or" is changed to "and"):
   - **Household furniture and furnishings**
   - **Contact lenses**
   - **Money, securities, tickets, and documents**

6. Switch the information under items A and B so that A is "Baggage Delay" and B is "Baggage Loss or Damage."

7. Select the A and B paragraphs and click the Numbering button to change the paragraph formatting. Make sure these paragraphs have the same indent and tab settings as the bulleted list.
8. In the paragraph that begins "Terms," move the text "precious gems," (including the comma) before the word "watches."
9. Change both instances of "The company" to "The insurance company."
10. Open the file **Invoice1**.
11. Copy the six lines at the top of the document (the Duke City Gateway information). Close the document.
12. Use the Paste Special command to paste the text as unformatted text at the bottom of the Baggage document. Allow two blank lines before the pasted text.
13. Apply 10% gray shading to the title text only (not the paragraph).
14. Copy the formatting of the title text to the text you pasted from Invoice1. (Use Format Painter or the Styles and Formatting task pane.)
15. Change the font size of the title to 14 points and add 72 points of spacing before the paragraph. Add another blank line below it.
16. Clear and close the Office Clipboard.
17. Save the document as ***[your initials]*6-22** in your Lesson 6 folder.
18. Print and close the document.

On Your Own

In these exercises you work on your own, as you would in a real-life work environment. Use the skills you've learned to accomplish the task—and be creative.

EXERCISE 6-23

Key a popular nursery rhyme or the lyrics to a popular song. Copy the text and paste the copy below the original. Use the Thesaurus to change several words in the copied paragraph, choosing either synonyms or antonyms. Spell- and grammar-check the document, accepting Word's suggestions. Save the document as ***[your initials]*6-23** and print it.

EXERCISE 6-24

Copy some text from the Internet (use Ctrl+C). Use Paste Special to paste the text, without formatting, into a new document. Change the text by finding and replacing words. Apply your own character and paragraph formatting. Save the document as ***[your initials]*6-24** and print it.

EXERCISE 6-25

Write a short proposal for changing something in your city, neighborhood, or school. Make the proposal at least three paragraphs long. At the end of the document, create a bulleted summary of the proposal, copying and pasting text from the proposal for the bulleted items. Save the document as ***[your initials]*6-25** and print it.

UNIT 3

Page Formatting

LESSON 7 ■ **Margins, Templates, and Printing Options**

LESSON 8 ■ **Page and Section Breaks, Headers and Footers**

LESSON

7

Margins, Templates, and Printing Options

OBJECTIVES

MOUS ACTIVITIES

In this lesson:

W2002 1-5
W2002 3-3
W2002 3-5
W2002 4-2

See Appendix E.

After completing this lesson, you will be able to:

1. Change margins.
2. Use print preview.
3. Change paper size and page orientation.
4. Choose print options.
5. Print envelopes and labels.
6. Insert the date and time.
7. Send a document as e-mail.
8. Create documents using templates and wizards.

Estimated Time: 1¾ hours

In previous lessons you learned to format text and paragraphs. Now you'll learn more about the printed page, beginning with a better understanding of margins—the spaces between the edges of the text and the edges of the paper. You'll learn how to change a document's margins and preview how a document will look before printing it. Word offers many useful printing features, including changing the *orientation*—the direction (horizontal or vertical) in which a document is printed.

To create and print professional-looking memos and letters, you'll use Word's templates, and as an alternative to printing, you'll convert a Word document to an e-mail message.

Changing Margins

By default, a document's margin settings are:

- Top margin 1 inch
- Bottom margin 1 inch
- Left margin 1.25 inches
- Right margin 1.25 inches

FIGURE 7-1
Page layout showing default margin settings and standard-sized paper

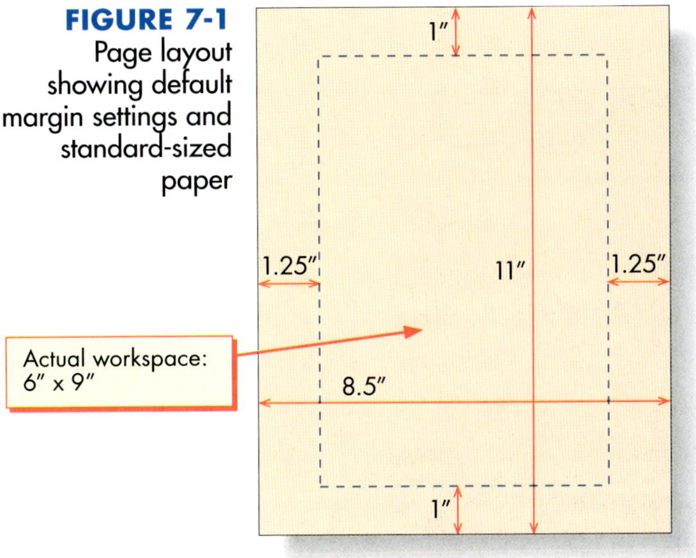

Using standard-size paper (8.5 × 11 inches) and Word's default margin settings, you have 6 × 9 inches on the page for your text. To increase or decrease this workspace, you can change margins by using the Page Setup dialog box or the rulers in Print Layout view or Print Preview.

EXERCISE 7-1 Change Margins for a Document Using the Page Setup Dialog Box

When working in Normal view, you use the Page Setup dialog box to change margin settings for a document.

1. Open the file **Rockies2**.

NOTE: The documents you create in this course relate to the Case Study about Duke City Gateway Travel, a fictional travel agency (see pages 3 through 6).

2. Choose Page Setup from the File menu. (Make sure no text is selected.)

W O R D

3. Click the Margins tab, if necessary. The dialog box shows the default margin settings.
4. Edit the margin text settings so they have the following values (or click the arrow boxes to change the settings). As you do so, notice the changes in the Preview box.

Top	1.5
Bottom	1.5
Left	2
Right	2

FIGURE 7-2
Changing margins in the Page Setup dialog box

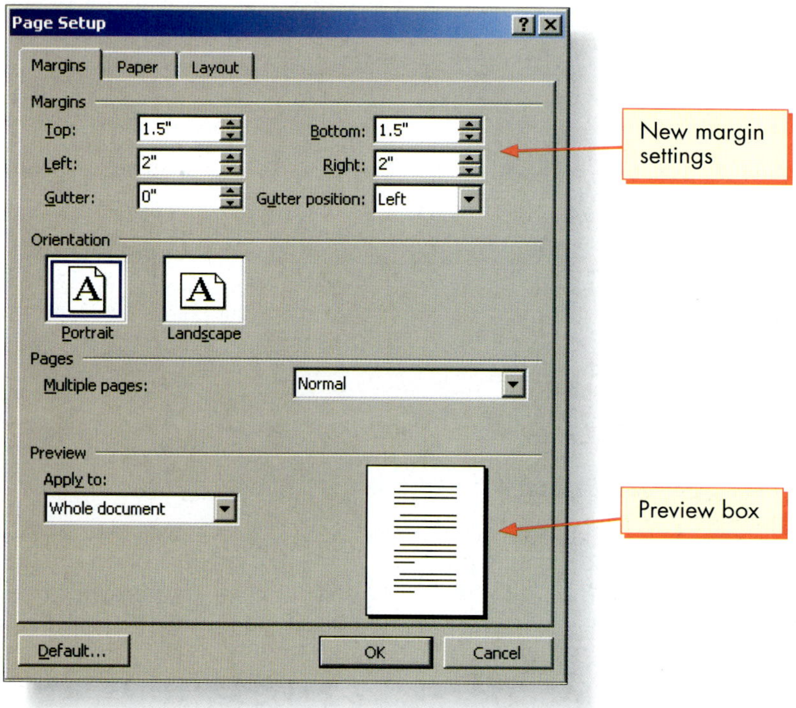

TIP: Press Tab to move from one margin text box to the next box and to see the new settings in the Preview box. Press Shift + Tab to move to the previous margin text box if necessary.

5. Click the down arrow to open the Apply to drop-down list. Notice that you can choose either Whole document or This point forward (from the insertion point forward). Choose Whole document and click OK to change the margins of the entire document.
6. Display the Reveal Formatting task pane and scroll down to Section. If Section is preceded by a plus sign (+), click the plus sign to display the current margin settings for the document.

FIGURE 7-3
Reveal Formatting task pane showing margin settings

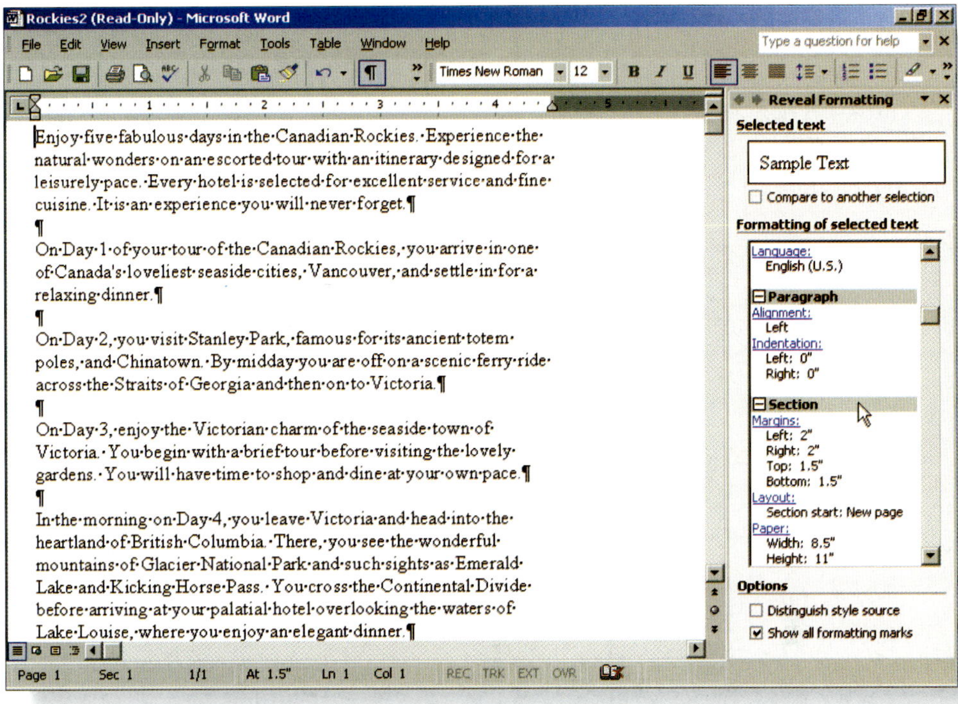

EXERCISE 7-2 Change Margins for Selected Text Using the Page Setup Dialog Box

When you change margins for selected text, you create a new *section*. Documents are often divided into sections, each of which can have its own formatting. When a document contains more than one section, you see double-dotted lines, or *section breaks*, between sections.

1. Select the text from the second paragraph to the end of the document.
2. Click the Margins link under Section in the Reveal Formatting task pane.
3. Change the margins to the following settings:

Top	**2**
Bottom	**2**
Left	**1.5**
Right	**1.5**

4. Choose Selected text from the Apply to box. Click OK.
5. Scroll to the beginning of the selection. Word applied the margin changes to the selected text and created a new section, as indicated by the section break lines. The section appears on a new page.

FIGURE 7-4
Changing margins for selected text creates a new section.

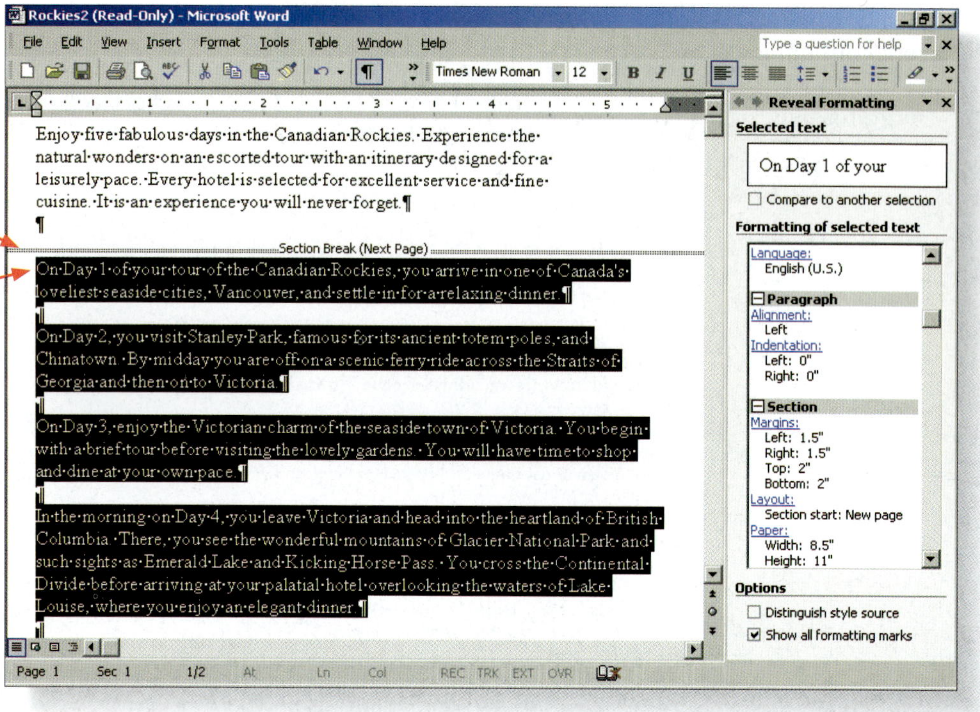

EXERCISE 7-3 Change Margins in Print Layout View

In Print Layout view you can see how text will be positioned on the printed page. Print Layout view displays headers, footers, and other page elements not visible in Normal view. You can change margins quickly and easily in Print Layout view by using the ruler.

1. Move the insertion point to the beginning of the document (Ctrl + Home). In bold uppercase letters, key **CANADIAN ROCKIES TOUR** and press Enter. Center the title and add two blank line spaces below it.
2. Switch to Print Layout view by clicking the Print Layout View button at the left of the horizontal scroll bar (or choose Print Layout from the View menu). You now see only page 1 of the document.
3. On the vertical scroll bar, drag the scroll box down (or click the down arrow button) and notice that the new section starts on a new page.

NOTE: New sections do not necessarily have to start on a new page. You'll learn how to control section breaks in the next lesson.

4. Click in the new section. The status bar shows that the document contains two pages and two sections. The new section has a larger top margin

(2 inches)—notice the extra space at the top of the page and the margin settings in the Reveal Formatting task pane.

TIP: You might want to use the horizontal scroll bar to adjust your view of the document.

5. To see more of the page, close the Reveal Formatting task pane. To see the margin areas, choose Zoom from the View menu and then choose Page width. Click OK.

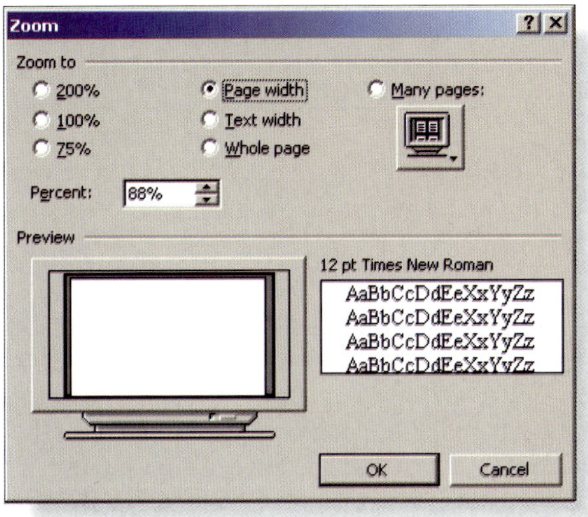

FIGURE 7-5
Zoom dialog box

6. Move the insertion point back to the top of the document (the first section). The gray area on the vertical ruler shows the 1.5-inch top margin. The gray areas on the horizontal ruler show the 2-inch left and right margins. The white area in the horizontal ruler shows the text area, which is a line length of 4.5 inches. See Figure 7-6 (on the next page).

7. To change the top margin, position the pointer over the top margin boundary on the vertical ruler. The top margin boundary is between the gray area and the white area on the ruler. The pointer changes to a two-headed arrow and a ScreenTip displays the words "Top Margin."

8. Press and hold down the left mouse button. The margin boundary appears as a dotted horizontal line.

9. Drag the margin boundary slightly up and release the mouse button. The text at the top of the document moves up to align with the new top margin. (See Figure 7-6.)

10. Click the Undo button to restore the 1.5-inch top margin.

11. Hold down Alt and drag the top margin boundary *down* until it is at 2 inches on the ruler. Release Alt and the mouse button. Holding down this key as you drag shows the exact margin and text-area measurements.

FIGURE 7-6
Changing the top margin in Print Layout view

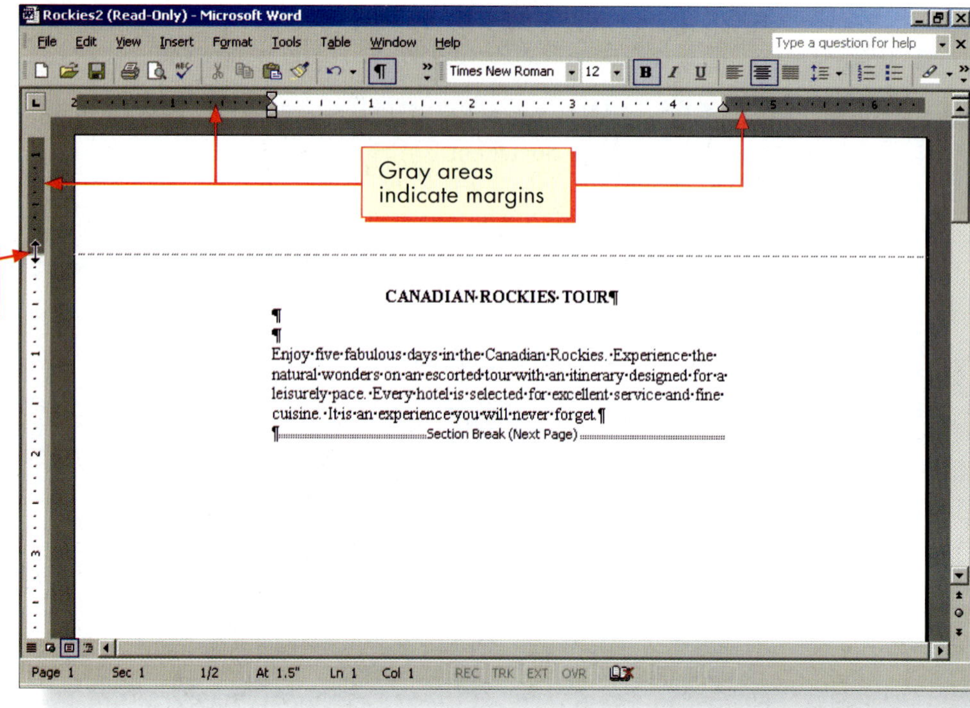

12. To adjust the left margin, position the pointer over the left margin boundary on the horizontal ruler until the ScreenTip displays "Left Margin."

NOTE: Changing left and right margins is trickier because you want to make sure you're pointing to the margin boundary and not an indent marker before you begin dragging. Just move the pointer slowly until you see the two-headed arrow and the Left Margin ScreenTip.

13. Hold down Alt and drag the margin boundary to the left to create a 1.75 inch left margin. Release Alt and the mouse button. Word shifts your text to adjust to the 1.75 left margin. (See Figure 7-7 on the next page.)

14. Using the same procedure, drag the right margin boundary until it is located 1.75 inches from the right. Be sure to watch for the two-headed arrow before dragging. The first section now has 1.75-inch left and right margins and a 2-inch top margin.

15. Scroll to the next page (section 2). Click within the text to activate this section's ruler. Change the top margin to 1.75 inches.

16. Save the document as ***[your initials]*****7-3** in a new folder for Lesson 7.

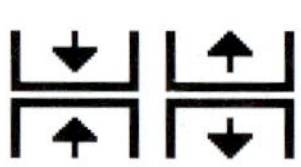

NOTE: If you move the pointer to the top of the page in Print Layout view, you'll see the Hide White Space button. Click the button to hide the white space (the margin area) at the top and bottom of each page and the gray space between pages so you can see more document text. Point to the top of the page and click the Show White Space button to restore the space.

FIGURE 7-7
Dragging the left margin while holding down Alt

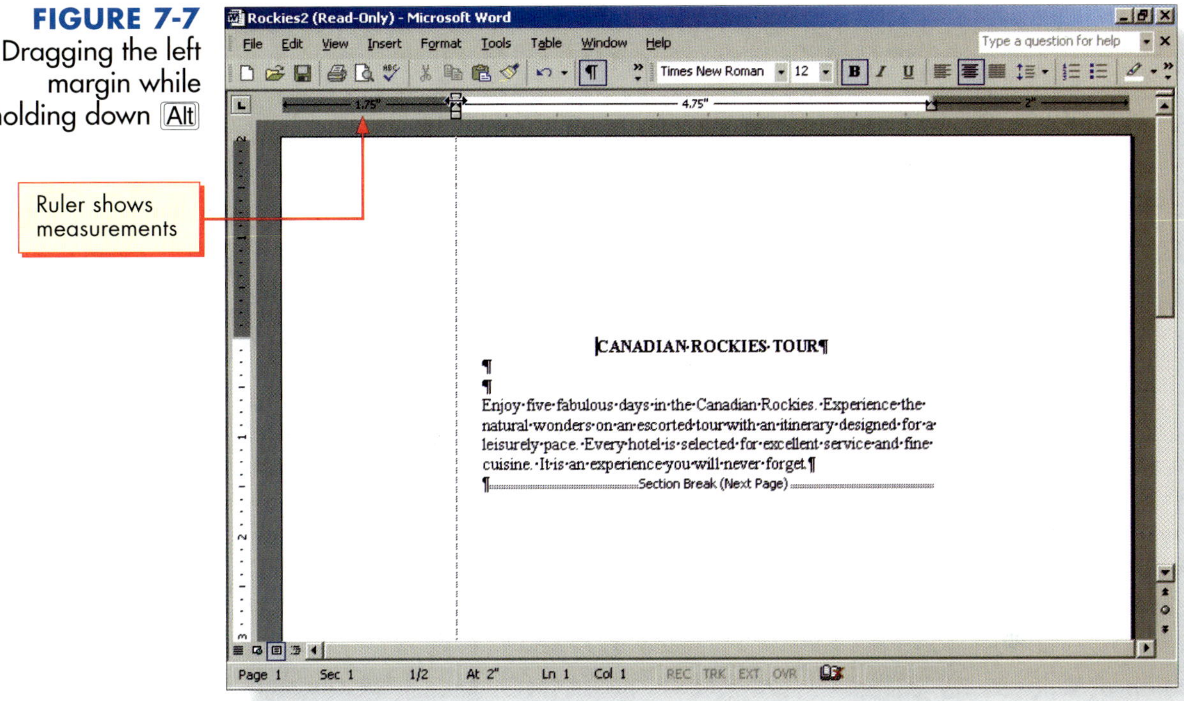

Using Print Preview

Viewing a document in Print Preview is the best way to check how a document will look when you print it. You can view multiple pages at a time, adjust margins and tabs, and edit text.

To display a document in Print Preview, click the Print Preview button on the Standard toolbar or choose Print Preview from the File menu.

EXERCISE 7-4 View a Multiple-Page Document in Print Preview

Print Preview displays entire pages of a document in reduced size. You can view one page at a time or multiple pages at a time

1. Move the insertion point to the top of the document.

2. Click the Print Preview button on the Standard toolbar to open the Print Preview window.

3. Click the One Page button on the Print Preview toolbar to display just page 1 of the document.
4. On the vertical scroll bar, click the down arrow button to display page 2.

5. On the Print Preview toolbar, click the Multiple Pages button. You use the grid that appears to choose the number of pages you want to view and

how they are configured in the window. For example, 1 × 2 pages means one row by two pages across.

6. Move the pointer across the top row of the grid to highlight the first two pages. Click the second page. You now see both pages of the document simultaneously.

FIGURE 7-8
Viewing multiple pages in Print Preview

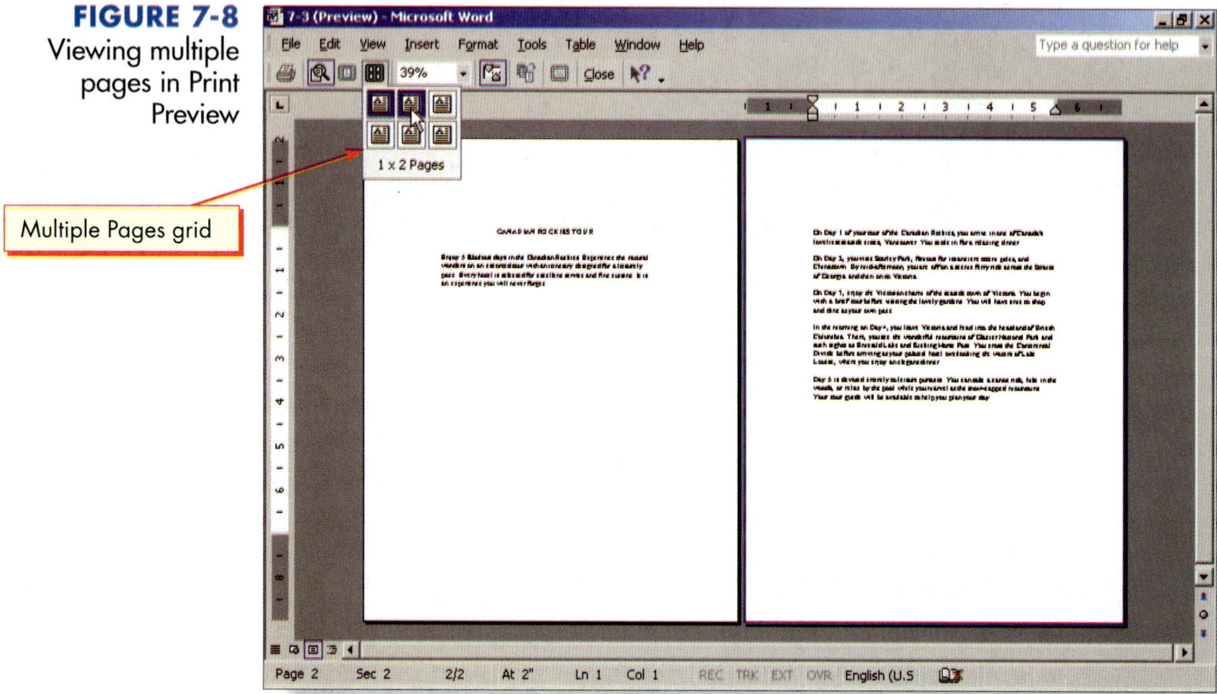

7. Click the Print button on the Print Preview toolbar to print the document.
8. Click Close on the Print Preview toolbar to close the Preview window and return to Print Layout view.
9. Close the document.

TABLE 7-1 Print Preview Toolbar Buttons

BUTTON	FUNCTION
Print	Prints the document in the Print Preview window.
Magnifier	Changes the I-beam pointer to a magnifying glass and vice versa. With the magnifying glass pointer, click in the document to zoom in and out. With the I-beam pointer, edit document text.

continues

TABLE 7-1 Print Preview Toolbar Buttons *continued*

BUTTON	FUNCTION
One Page	Displays one page at a time.
Multiple Pages	Displays the number of pages you select from a grid.
38% Zoom	Use to choose a magnification to reduce or enlarge the page or pages displayed.
View Ruler	Displays or hides the Print Preview ruler, which you can use to change margins, tabs, and indents.
Shrink to Fit	Shrinks a document to fit on one less page when the last page contains only a few lines of text.
Full Screen	Hides most screen elements to show more of the document. Click again to restore the previous view.
Close Close Preview	Closes the Print Preview window and returns to the previous view.
Context Sensitive Help	Use to identify or get information about an item in the Print Preview window.

EXERCISE 7-5 Change Margins in Print Preview

When you view a page in Print Preview you can see all four margins at once. The page has its own horizontal and vertical ruler you can use to adjust margins, or you can open the Page Setup dialog box within the Print Preview window to change margin settings. When you change a margin in Print Preview, you see the effect on the whole page and on the entire document.

NOTE: You can also change tabs in Print Preview by dragging the tab markers on the ruler, just as you do in Normal view.

1. Open the file **Mexico1**. Switch to Print Preview. If the rulers are not displayed, click the View Ruler button.
2. Click the Multiple Pages button and highlight the top three pages. Click the third page. You now see the entire document in a 1 × 3 page configuration, which is one row by three pages across.
3. Use the File menu to open the Page Setup dialog box.

TIP: Notice that the menu bar is accessible in the Print Preview window so you don't have to close Print Preview to choose various menu options.

4. Change the left and right margins to 1 inch and click OK. The document should now fit on two pages.

NOTE: As in Print Layout view, you can also use the vertical and horizontal rulers in Print Preview to drag margin boundaries, pressing Alt to see the exact measurements.

EXERCISE 7-6 Edit Text in Print Preview

To edit text you magnify a page to the desired size and then switch to edit mode.

1. Click the One Page button and display page 1.
2. If the magnifying glass pointer is not visible, click the Magnifier button on the Print Preview toolbar.
3. Click the top of the title area of page 1. The view of the document is enlarged to 100% as shown in the Zoom box on the Print Preview toolbar.

NOTE: When the magnifier pointer shows a plus sign, it will enlarge the page you click. When it shows a minus sign, it will reduce the page you click.

4. Click the Magnifier button to change the pointer to the regular I-beam you use for editing text.
5. Select the italic text "*Riviera Princess*" in the first paragraph and use the keyboard shortcut Ctrl + B to make the text bold.
6. Click within the title on the first line. Use the menu to open the Paragraph dialog box and apply 72-point spacing before the title. Notice that the status bar shows "1/3," indicating that the document is again three pages long.
7. Click the Magnifier button to cancel edit mode. Click page 1 to reduce it. Then display all 3 pages.
8. Click the Shrink to Fit button to reduce the document from 3 pages to 2. This reduces the font size of the document text.
9. Click the View Ruler button to hide the rulers and make more room to view the document.
10. To enlarge the document without full magnification, click the down arrow next to the Zoom box and choose Two Pages.

FIGURE 7-9
Changing magnification of edited document

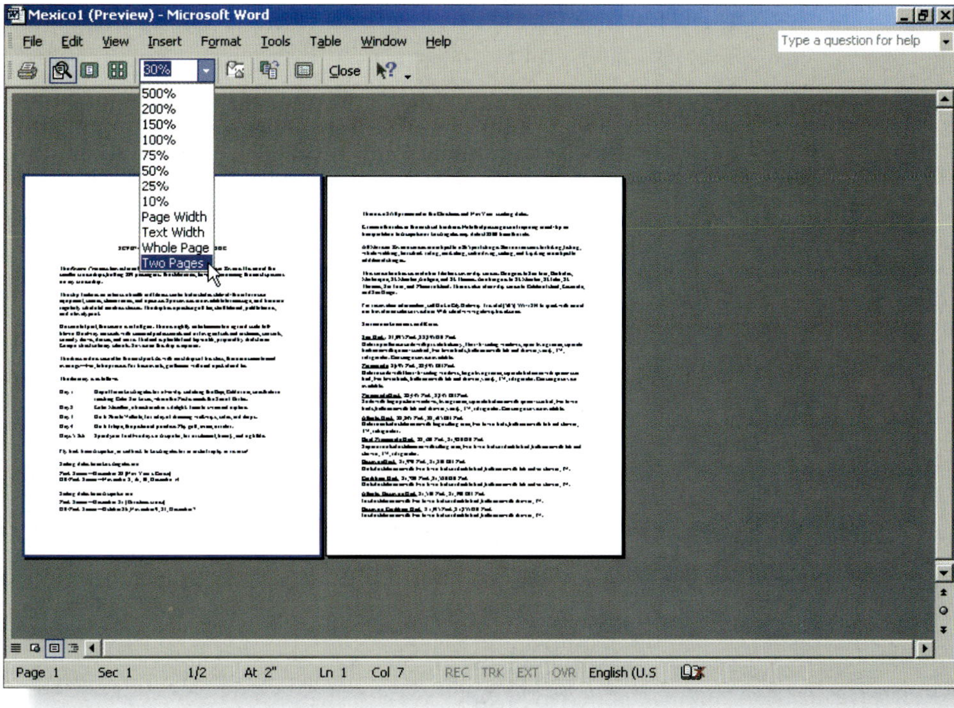

11. Close the Print Preview window.

12. Save the document as ***[your initials]*7-6** in your Lesson 7 folder.

13. Print the document. Leave it open for the next exercise.

Changing Paper Size and Page Orientation

When you open a new document, the default paper size is 8.5 × 11 inches. Using the Page Setup dialog box, you can change the paper size to print a document on legal paper or a custom-size paper.

The Page Setup dialog box also gives you a choice between two page-orientation settings: Portrait and Landscape. A *portrait* page is taller than it is wide. For example, an 8.5 × 11 inch portrait page is 8.5 inches wide and 11 inches tall. This orientation is the default in new Word documents. A *landscape* page is wider than it is tall. For example, using the same paper size, a landscape page is 11 inches wide and 8.5 inches tall. You can apply page-orientation changes to sections of a document or to the entire document.

EXERCISE 7-7 Change Paper Size and Page Orientation

1. Make sure no text is selected. Open the Page Setup dialog box.

2. Click the Paper tab. Notice the default paper size settings: Letter, 8.5″ in width, 11″ in height.
3. Click the arrow to open the Paper size drop-down list. Choose Legal. Notice the change in the page height and the change in the Preview box.
4. Change the paper size back to Letter.
5. Click the Margins tab. Notice the two orientation choices, Portrait and Landscape.
6. Click Landscape. Now the width is 11″ and the height is 8.5″. The change in orientation is reflected in the Preview box.
7. Click OK to change the document to landscape orientation. Switch to Print Preview to see the change more clearly and view all three pages.
8. While still in Print Preview, press Ctrl + Z to undo the change in orientation.
9. Magnify page 2 to 100%, and then position the insertion point to the left of the bold heading "**Stateroom Locations and Rates**."
10. Open the Page Setup dialog box again and choose Landscape. Open the Apply to drop-down list and choose This point forward. Click OK. Word applies landscape orientation from just the insertion point to the end of the document, creating a separate section on a new page.
11. View all pages of the document in Print Preview; then close the Print Preview window.

FIGURE 7-10
Changing page orientation

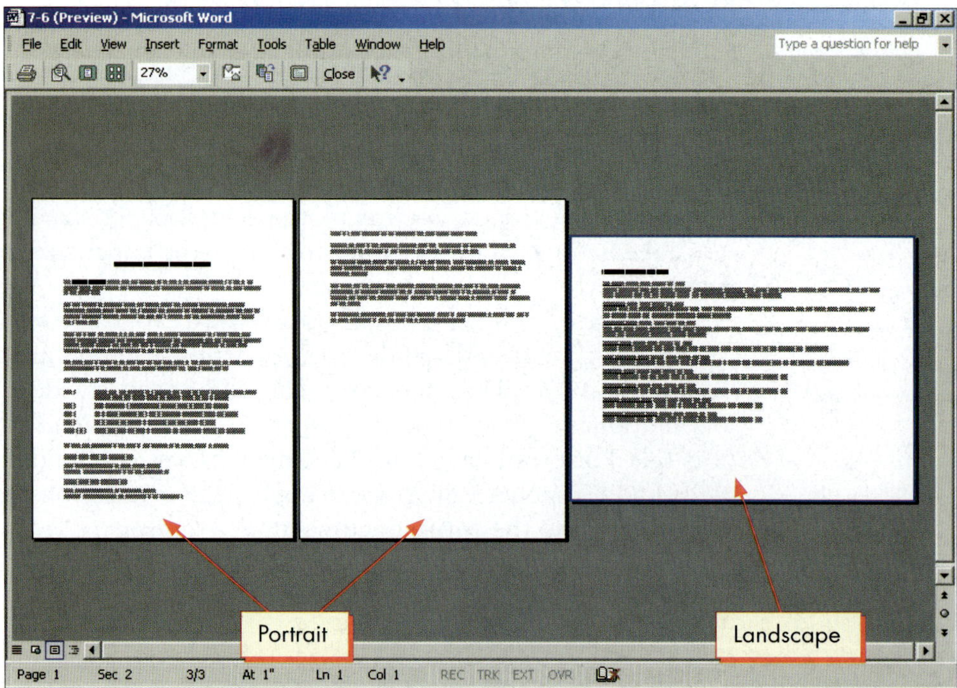

12. Save the document as ***[your initials]*7-7** in your Lesson 7 folder. Leave it open for the next exercise.

Choosing Print Options

When you click the Print button to print a document, Word prints the entire document. If you open the Print dialog box, however, you can choose to print only part of a document. You can also select other print options from the dialog box, including collating copies of a multi-page document, printing selected text, or printing multiple document pages on one sheet of paper.

EXERCISE 7-8 Choose Print Options from the Print Dialog Box

1. With the document *[your initials]*7-7 open, click anywhere on the first page.
2. Choose Print from the File menu to open the Print dialog box.
3. Click Current page and click OK. Word prints page 1 of the document.

FIGURE 7-11
Print dialog box

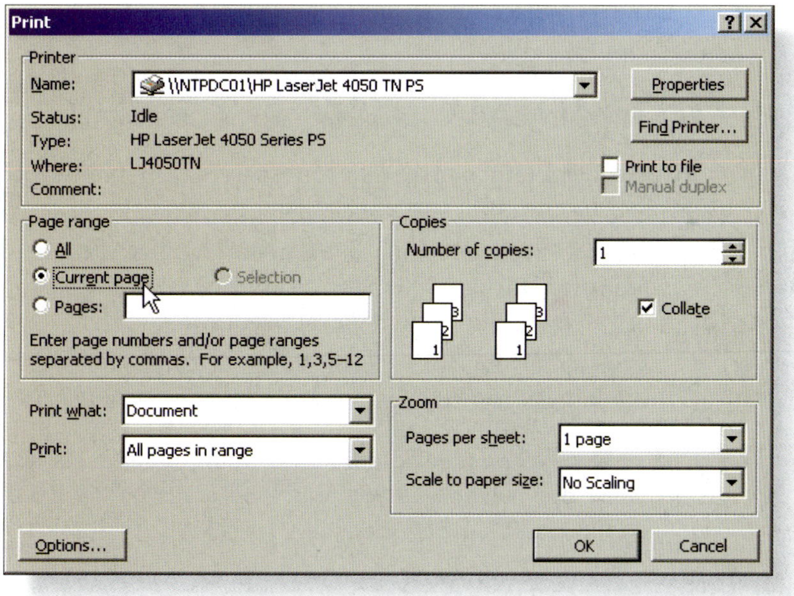

4. Open the Print dialog box again. Notice that you can also enter specific page numbers or page ranges. Key **1-2** in the Pages text box.
5. In the Number of copies text box, use the up arrow to change the number of copies to 2. Notice that the Collate box is checked by default.
6. Click the Collate box to uncheck it. With this box not checked, Word will print two copies of page 1 and then two copies of page 2.

7. Click the down arrow to open the Print what drop-down list. It shows the various elements you can print in addition to the entire document. Click again to close the list.

8. Click the down arrow to open the Print drop-down list, which gives you the option to print even or odd pages. Click again to close the list.

9. Click the down arrow to open the Pages per sheet drop-down list, which gives you the option to print your selection over a specified number of sheets. Choose the 2 pages setting. This allows you to print two pages on one sheet of 8.5 × 11-inch paper, with each page reduced to fit on the sheet.

10. Open the Scale to paper size drop-down list, which gives you the option to print on a different paper or envelope size (Word adjusts the scaling of the fonts, tables, and other elements to fit the new size). Close the drop-down list.

11. Change the number of copies back to 1 and then click OK. Word prints reduced versions of pages 1 and 2 on one sheet of paper.

12. On page 3 of the document, select the title and the first 3 paragraphs below it. Open the Print dialog box again.

13. Click Selection and then click OK. Word prints just the selected text.

14. Close the document without saving.

Printing Envelopes and Labels

Word provides a tool to print different size envelopes and labels. Using the Envelopes and Labels command, you can:

- Print a single envelope without saving it or attach an envelope to a document for future printing. The attached envelope is added to the beginning of the document as a separate section.
- Print labels without saving them, or create a new document that contains the labels. You can print a single label or a full page of the same label.

TIP: When printing envelopes, your printer might require you to feed the envelope manually. If you print labels on other than 8.5 x 11-inch sheets, you might need to feed the labels manually.

EXERCISE 7-9 Print an Envelope

1. Open the file **Andrews**. This document is a one-page letter.

2. Open the Tools menu. Choose Letters and Mailings, Envelopes and Labels.

3. Click the Envelopes tab if it is not displayed. Notice that Word detected the address in the document and placed this text in the Delivery address text box. You can edit this text as needed.

FIGURE 7-12
Envelopes and Labels dialog box

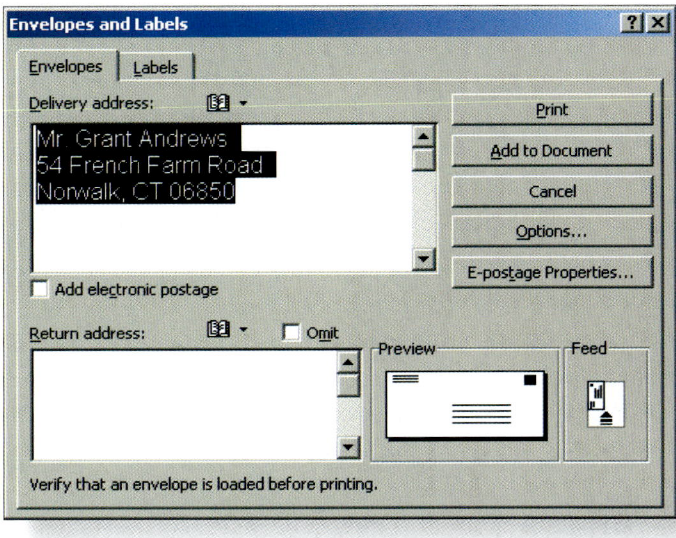

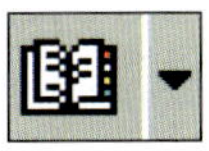

TIP: You can use addresses from a Microsoft Outlook contact list by clicking the Insert Address button in the Envelopes and Labels dialog box.

4. In the Delivery address text box, enter the full ZIP+4 code by keying a hyphen followed by **1129** after "06850."
5. Make sure the Omit box is not checked. Select and delete any text in the Return address text box and then key the following return address, starting with your name:

   [your name]
   Duke City Gateway Travel
   15 Montgomery Boulevard
   Albuquerque, NM 87111-2307

6. Select the return address again and copy it to the Clipboard (use Ctrl + C). You'll need it again for the next exercise.
7. Place a standard business-size envelope in your printer. The Feed box illustrates the feeding method accepted by your printer.

NOTE: If you don't have an envelope, you can use a blank sheet of paper to test the placement of the addresses. Ask your instructor how to proceed. You might have to feed the envelope or blank sheet manually.

8. Click Print. When Word asks if you want to save the return address as the default return address, click No. Word prints the envelope with the default font and text placement settings.

NOTE: Check your printer to see what you need to do to complete a manual envelope feed. If the printer is flashing or displaying a message, you might have to press a button.

EXERCISE 7-10 Choose Envelope Options

Before printing an envelope, you can choose additional envelope options. For example, you can add the envelope content to the document for future use. You can also click the Options button in the Envelopes and Labels dialog box to:

- Change the envelope size. The default size is Size 10, which is a standard business envelope.
- Print codes for automated handling by the U.S. Postal Service. For example, you can print a bar code that represents the ZIP code for the delivery address or print a FIM-A code that identifies the front of an envelope (used on preprinted courtesy reply envelopes). To print these codes, your printer must be able to print graphics.
- Change the font and other character formatting of the delivery address or return address.

NOTE: If your computer is equipped with electronic postage software, you can choose options to apply postage to the envelope.

1. Open the Envelopes and Labels dialog box again.

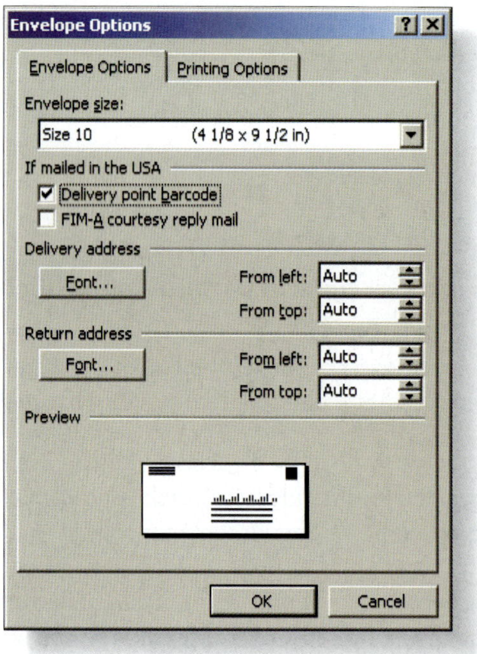

FIGURE 7-13 Envelope Options dialog box

2. Paste the Duke City Gateway Travel address from the Clipboard into the Return address box.
3. Click the Options button in the Envelopes and Labels dialog box to open the Envelope Options dialog box. Click the Envelope Options tab if it is not displayed.
4. Under Envelope size, click the down arrow to look at the different size options. Click the arrow again to close the list.
5. Click the Delivery point barcode box to select it. Notice the change in the Preview box.
6. Click the Font button for the Delivery address. The Envelope Address dialog box for the delivery address opens.

7. Make the text bold and all caps and change the font size to 10. Click OK. Click OK to close the Envelope Options dialog box.

8. Delete the punctuation from the delivery address and add **–1129** to the ZIP code.

NOTE: The delivery address format preferred by the U.S. Postal Service is all caps with no punctuation.

9. Click Add to Document to add the envelope information to the top of the document as a separate section. Don't save the return address as the default address.

NOTE: When the envelope is added to the document, you can also format or edit the envelope text just as you would any document text. The default font for envelope addresses is Arial.

FIGURE 7-14
Envelope added to the document

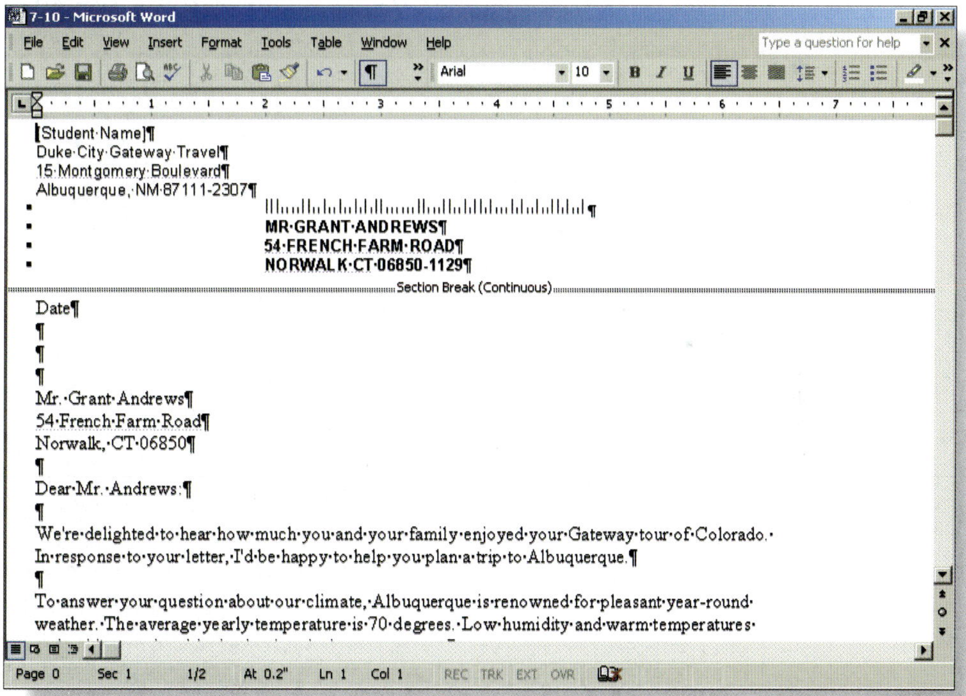

10. View the letter and envelope in Print Preview.

11. Close the Print Preview window and save the document as ***[your initials]*****7-10** in your Lesson 7 folder. You'll apply finishing touches to the letter and print both the letter and envelope later in the lesson.

WORD

EXERCISE 7-11 Print Labels

The Labels tab in the Envelopes and Labels dialog box makes it easy to print different size labels for either a return address or a delivery address.

1. Position the insertion point in the envelope section of the document. Open the Envelopes and Labels dialog box and click the Labels tab.
2. Click the Use return address check box to create labels for the letter sender.
3. Select the address text and press Ctrl+Shift+A to turn on all caps. Delete the comma after the city.
4. Click the option Full page of the same label to create an entire page of return address labels.
5. Click the Options button to choose a label size.
6. Scroll the Product number list to see the various label options and choose 5160, the product number for a standard Avery address label.

FIGURE 7-15 Choosing label options

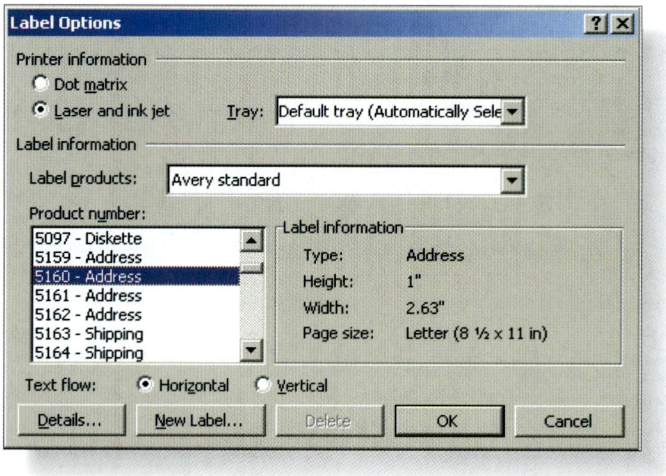

7. Click OK and click New Document to save the labels as a separate document. (If you click Print, you can print the labels without saving them.) Do not save the return address.
8. Select all the label text and format it as 11-point Arial Narrow.
9. Save the document as ***[your initials]*7-11** in your Lesson 7 folder.
10. Switch to Print Preview to view the labels on the page.
11. Prepare the printer for a sheet of 5160-size labels or feed a blank sheet of paper into the printer.
12. Print the labels and then close the document.

Inserting the Date and Time

You've seen that when you begin keying a month, AutoComplete displays the suggested date and you press Enter to insert the date as regular text. You can also:

- Insert the date or time in a variety of formats using the Date and Time dialog box.
- Insert the date or time as a *field*, which means Word automatically updates it each time you print the document. A field is a set of hidden codes that tells Word to insert specific text.

EXERCISE 7-12 Insert and Modify Date and Time Formats

1. In the document *[your initials]*7-10, delete the word "Date" (but not its paragraph mark) at the top of the letter.
2. With the insertion point in the same position, press Alt + Shift + D. Word inserts the date in the default date format (month/day/year).

TIP: The keyboard shortcut for inserting the time is Alt + Shift + T.

3. Undo the insertion, because this isn't the correct date format for a business letter.
4. Open the Insert menu and choose Date and Time.

FIGURE 7-16 Date and Time dialog box

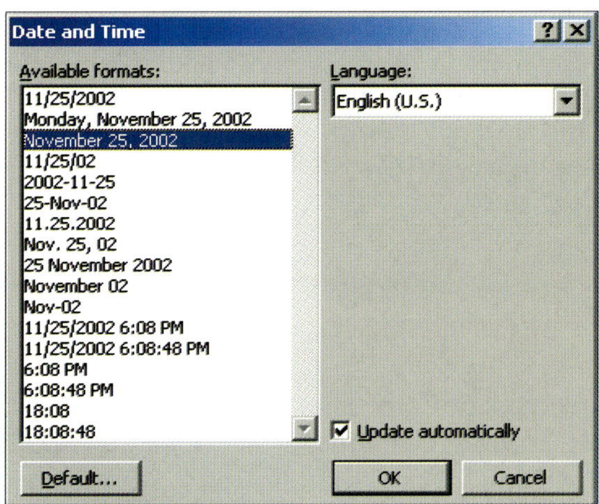

5. From the list of available date and time formats, choose the third format (the standard date format for business documents). Check the Update automatically box and click OK.

TIP: The Update Automatically option is usually not used in business correspondence when you want a record of when a document was written. It's more appropriate in a form letter you use repeatedly and want the date updated with each use.

6. Click the date field. The gray shading identifies the text as a field.

7. At the end of the paragraph that begins "To answer your question," start a new sentence by keying **Right now (**
8. Open the Date and Time dialog box and insert the first format that includes both the date and time. Continue the sentence by keying **) it's sunny and 68 degrees.** Add a comma between the date and time.

NOTE: You can also use this dialog box to insert the date and time in a particular text format and not insert it as an updateable field.

9. Add 72 points of spacing before the date at the top of the letter. Add your reference initials, followed by **Enclosures** at the bottom of the letter. To make sure the letter follows the correct format, see Appendix F: "Standard Forms for Business Documents."
10. Save the document as ***[your initials]*7-12** in your Lesson 7 folder.

11. Prepare the printer for a standard business envelope. Click the Print button to print the envelope and the letter, and then close the document.

TIP: When an envelope is added to a document as a separate section, you can print only the envelope by opening the Print dialog box and keying **s1** (for Section 1) or **0** in the Pages text box. Word prints only the envelope (Section 1). You can also print just the envelope by clicking anywhere in the envelope text and choosing the Current Page option in the Print dialog box.

Sending a Document as E-Mail

Instead of printing a document, you can send it as e-mail directly from Word. In this case, the document *is* the e-mail message. You can also send a document as an attachment. As an added bonus, you can include hyperlinks in the e-mail message to direct recipients to another Internet location.

When you send a document as e-mail, Word sends the document in HTML format so recipients can easily read it.

EXERCISE 7-13 Send a Document as E-Mail and Insert a Hyperlink

To send a document as the body of an e-mail message or as an e-mail attachment, choose File, Send To, and then either Mail Recipient or Mail Recipient (as Attachment). You can also click the E-mail button on the Standard toolbar to send a document as the body of an e-mail message.

1. Open the file **Balloon1**.

2. Click the E-mail button on the Standard toolbar. An e-mail header appears above the document text, along with e-mail toolbar buttons.

FIGURE 7-17
Sending a document as e-mail

E-mail toolbar

E-mail header

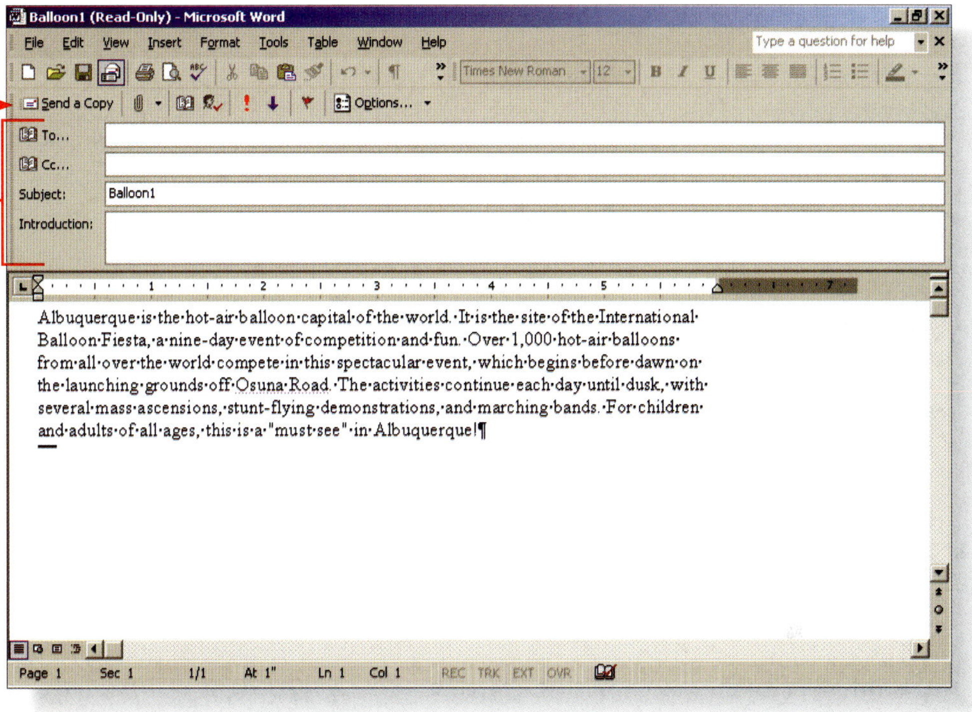

NOTE: To hide the e-mail header and toolbar, you click the E-mail button button again.

3. In the To text box of the e-mail header, key an e-mail address.
4. In the Subject line, edit the existing text to read **Balloon Fiesta Coming October 6!**
5. At the end of the document, press Enter twice and key the following new paragraph:

   For more information about Albuquerque and the Balloon Fiesta, go to www.abqcvb.org, the Web site for the Albuquerque Convention and Visitors Bureau.

   Word converts the Web address to a hyperlink.
6. Hold down Ctrl and point to the hyperlink you just keyed. When the pointer becomes a hand with a pointing finger, click the hyperlink. You should see an Internet browser window for the home page of the Albuquerque Convention and Visitors Bureau.
7. Close the browser.
8. Send the e-mail by clicking Send a Copy. Word sends the e-mail to the specified address and then closes the e-mail header.
9. Save the document as ***[your initials]*7-13**. Print and close the document.

TABLE 7-2 E-Mail Toolbar Buttons

BUTTON	FUNCTION
Send a Copy	Sends a copy of the document to the e-mail address specified.
Insert File	Opens the Insert File dialog box from which you can choose a file to attach.
Address Book	Displays the Address Book entries added to Outlook.
Check Names	Checks the recipient name against the e-mail address listed in the Address Book.
Importance: High	Sets the importance level of the e-mail as high priority.
Importance: Low	Sets the importance level of the e-mail as low priority.
Message Flag	Creates a follow-up reminder for you in Outlook.
Options...	Opens the Message Options dialog box from which you can specify delivery options.

Creating Documents Using Templates and Wizards

So far, you've created your own memos and letters, using the standard format for business documents. To save time and create a professional-looking document, you can use a Word template. A *template* is a file that contains formatting information, styles, and sometimes text for a particular type of document. Word provides many different categories of templates, including letters and faxes, memos, reports, publications, and Web pages.

EXERCISE 7-14 Create a Document Using a Template

1. Choose File, New from the menu to display the New Document task pane.
2. Under New from template, click General Templates to open the Templates dialog box. The tabs in the dialog box show the categories of available templates.

3. Just above **Preview** in the dialog box, make sure the Large Icons button is pressed. Click the various tabs to see the available templates. Click any icon shown on a tab to see a preview of the template design.

NOTE: Some templates might not be installed on your computer.

4. Display the **Letters & Faxes** tab and click the Professional Letter icon. Under **Create New**, make sure **Document** is selected. You will create a new document based on the Professional Letter template.

FIGURE 7-18
Choosing a template

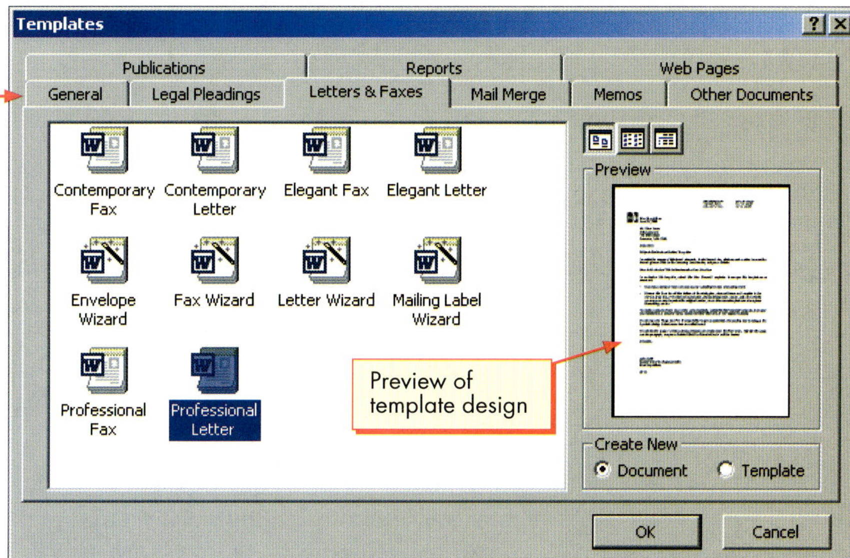

TIP: If you choose Template under Create New, you create a new template using the Word template styles and formatting. You could customize that template with your own company information, save it, and then reuse it for future correspondence.

5. Click **OK**. Word opens a new document using Word's uniquely formatted "professional" style. *Placeholder text*—formatted text you replace with your own information—appears throughout the letter.
6. In the upper right corner, click to select the placeholder text that reads "[Click here and type return address]." Key **15 Montgomery Boulevard**, press Enter, and key **Albuquerque, NM 87111**
7. Use the I-beam to drag and select the placeholder text that reads "Company Name Here" (you cannot click to select this text) and key **Duke City Gateway Travel**

8. Select the company name and make it one font size smaller so it fits on one line.
9. Click to select the placeholder text that reads "[Click **here** and type recipient's address]." Key **Ms. Marla Bienstock**, press Enter, key **63 Elk Ridge Road**, press Enter, and key **Las Cruces, NM 88005**
10. In the salutation line, select the text "Sir or Madam," and key **Ms. Bienstock**
11. Select the placeholder paragraph that begins "Type your letter here" and key the three paragraphs shown in Figure 7-19. Paragraph formatting for spacing is included in the template, so you don't have to insert a blank line between paragraphs.

FIGURE 7-19

Enclosed are the tickets for your business trip to Chicago. Your seats are in business class, as you requested.

Also enclosed is a list of some of Chicago's best restaurants, all located within minutes of your hotel.

Have a pleasant trip and thank you for choosing Duke City Gateway Travel. We look forward to helping you again.

12. In the letter closing, click the first line of placeholder text and key **Steve Ross**. Click the second line of placeholder text and key **Travel Counselor**.
13. On the next line, add your reference initials, followed by an enclosures notation. Open the Styles and Formatting task pane. From the list of available formatting, apply the Reference Initials style and the Enclosure style to the new lines.
14. Increase the font size for all text below the company name to 12 points.
15. Change the paragraph spacing for the date to 12 points before and 36 points after.
16. Save the document as ***[your initials]*7-14** in your Lesson 7 folder.
17. Print the document.

EXERCISE 7-15 Create a Document Using a Wizard

A *wizard* is an automated and interactive template. It walks you through the creation of a particular type of document and prompts you to choose formatting options and enter text through a series of dialog boxes. Like other Word templates, wizards are included in the Templates dialog box and organized by category.

1. Choose File, New from the menu to display the New Document task pane. Click the General Templates link to open the Templates dialog box.
2. Display the Letters & Faxes tab. Double-click the Letter Wizard icon. The Office Assistant displays the first message as it walks you through the process.
3. Click the Send one letter option. The Letter Wizard – Step 1 of 4 dialog box appears.

FIGURE 7-20
Letter Wizard – Step 1 of 4 dialog box

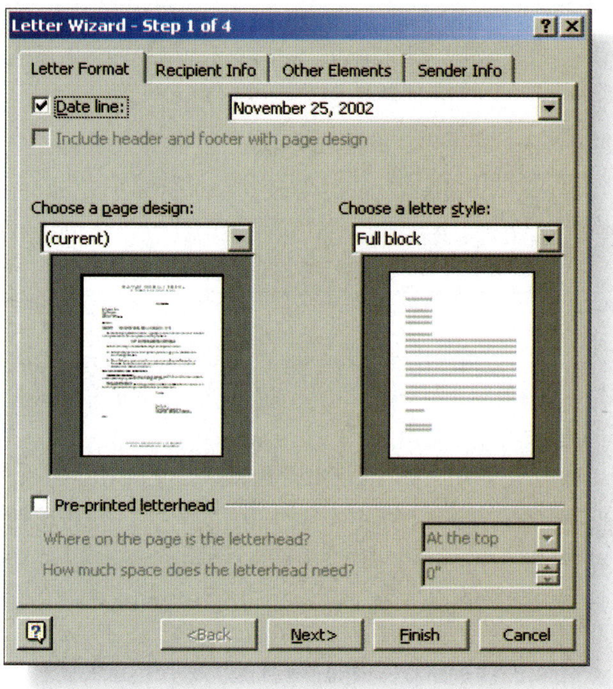

4. Choose a page design, such as Contemporary Letter. (Do not choose a merge letter style.) Choose a letter style, such as Modified Block. Click Next.
5. In the next dialog box, enter the name and address information from the previous letter you created to Ms. Marla Bienstock. The Office Assistant guides you through the steps. Change the salutation style to Business, which uses a colon instead of a comma. Click Next.
6. In the Other Elements dialog box, add the mailing instruction VIA OVERNIGHT MAIL. Click Next.
7. In the Sender Info dialog box, enter the information shown in Figure 7-21. Click Finish when you complete the information.

WORD

FIGURE 7-21
Letter Wizard – Step 4 of 4 dialog box

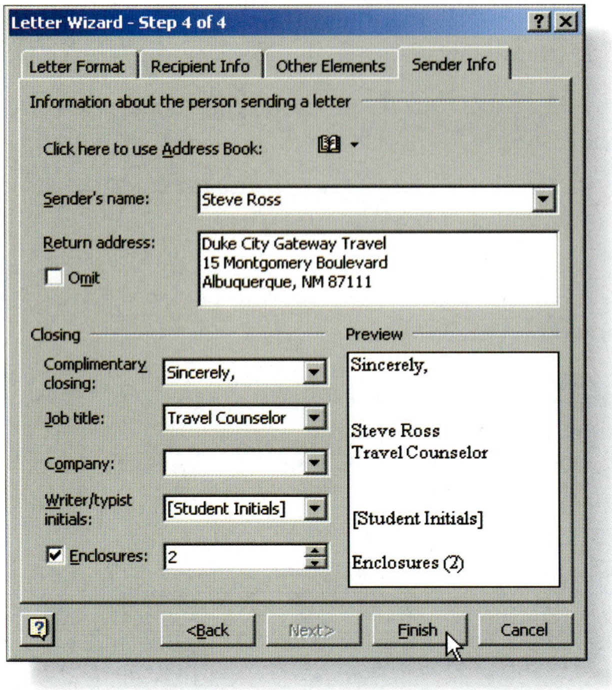

8. For the body text of the letter, copy the three paragraphs in *[your initials]*7-14 and paste them into the new letter, matching the destination formatting.
9. Cancel the Office Assistant. Then make any adjustments to the letter formatting to improve its appearance, such as changing the font size to 12 points.
10. Save the document as ***[your initials]*7-15** in your Lesson 7 folder.
11. Print the document. Close all open documents.

NOTE: The formatting stored in templates is often complex and highly stylized. Templates for business documents often do not follow the traditional standard business style with regard to spacing.

USING HELP

Now that you worked in Print Layout view and Print Preview, learn all the ways you can view a document. Let the Office Assistant locate the appropriate Help screen.

Use Help to learn about document views:

1. Press F1 to display the Office Assistant.

2. Key **view document** in the Office Assistant text box and press Enter.
3. Click the first suggested topic, About ways to view a Word document.
4. In the right pane of the Help window, click to read about the different document views.
5. Close the Help window when you finish.

LESSON 7 Summary

- Change the actual space for text on a page by changing margins (left, right, top, and bottom). You can key new margin settings in the Page Setup dialog box.
- Changing margins for selected text results in a new section for the selected text.
- Print Layout view shows how text is positioned on the printed page. Use the view buttons on the horizontal scroll bar to switch between Print Layout view and Normal view.
- Print Preview shows how an entire document looks before printing. Use the Multiple Pages button, the One Page button, and the scroll bar to view all or part of the document. Change the Zoom as needed.
- Change margins in Print Layout View or in Print Preview by positioning the pointer over a margin boundary on a ruler and dragging. Press Alt to see the exact ruler measurement as you drag.
- Edit a document in Print Preview by clicking the Magnifier button to change the magnifier pointer to the I-beam pointer.
- A document can print in either landscape (11″ × 8.5″) or portrait (8.5″ × 11″) orientation. Choose an orientation in the Page Setup dialog box, Margins tab.
- A document can be scaled to fit a particular paper size. Choose paper size options in the Page Setup dialog box, Paper tab.
- Choose print options such as printing only the current page, specified pages, selected text, collated copies of pages, and reduced pages by opening the Print dialog box.
- Use Word to print different size envelopes. You can print delivery codes, change address formatting, and make the envelope part of the document for future printing. Use Word to print different size address labels—either a single label or a sheet of the same label.
- Insert the date and time in a document as an automatically updated field. Use the Date and Time dialog box to choose different date and time formats.

➤ Send a document as an e-mail message or as an attachment to an e-mail message. Include a hyperlink in the message, if desired. Word automatically formats a Web or e-mail address as a hyperlink. To use a hyperlink, press Ctrl and click the link.

LESSON 7 Command Summary

FEATURE	BUTTON	MENU	KEYBOARD	SPEECH?
Change margins, paper size, orientation		File, Page Setup		✓
Print Layout view		View, Print Layout	Alt + Ctrl + P	✓
Print Preview		File, Print Preview	Ctrl + F2	✓
Normal view		View, Normal	Alt + Ctrl + N	✓
Choose print options		File, Print	Ctrl + P	✓
Print envelopes and labels		Tools, Letters and Mailings, Envelopes and Labels		✓
Insert date		Insert, Date and Time	Alt + Shift + D	✓
Insert time		Insert, Date and Time	Alt + Shift + T	✓
Send document as e-mail		File, Send to, Mail Recipient		✓

Concepts Review

TRUE/FALSE QUESTIONS

Each of the following statements is either true or false. Indicate your choice by circling T or F.

T F ***1.*** Word has default settings for margins that are automatically set for each new document.

T F ***2.*** You can change the top and bottom margins by using the ruler in either Normal view or Print Layout view.

T F ***3.*** You can edit a document in Print Preview.

T F ***4.*** The Page Setup dialog box provides horizontal and vertical rulers to drag margins to the desired position.

T F ***5.*** A Word template can contain placeholder text that you replace with your own information.

T F ***6.*** The Multiple Pages button in Print Preview displays a long document one page at a time.

T F ***7.*** In landscape orientation, text runs across the wider part of the page.

T F ***8.*** Printing a two-page document on one sheet of paper is an option available in the Print dialog box.

SHORT ANSWER QUESTIONS

Write the correct answer in the space provided.

1. Which view is displayed when you click  ?

____

2. What does the pointer look like when it is located over the margin boundary in Print Layout view?

____

3. Which toolbar button enables you to turn a Word document into the body of an e-mail message?

____

4. Which button do you click in a wizard dialog box to accept the default settings?

____

5. Which tab, in which dialog box, do you use to change page orientation?

____

6. What are the menu commands to add an envelope to a document?

____

7. How do you switch to edit mode in Print Preview?

____

8. Which keyboard combination inserts the date?

____

CRITICAL THINKING

Answer these questions on a separate page. There are no right or wrong answers. Support your answers with examples from your own experience, if possible.

1. Collect samples of printed documents with interesting treatments of margins (books, magazines, and advertisements). How does the margin treatment contribute to the overall feeling of the document?
2. What might you notice about a document in Print Preview that you wouldn't notice in Normal view?

Lesson Applications

EXERCISE 7-16

Set margins, use Print Preview, and change page orientation.

1. Open the file **Insurance**.
2. At the end of the paragraph that begins "We strongly recommend," add the text **Consider the following:**
3. Key the text shown in Figure 7-22, including the corrections. Use single spacing.

FIGURE 7-22

International Travel Medical Insurance with up to $1,000,000 in medical coverage

Travel Protection Plans for trip cancellations, lost baggage, basic medical coverage~~, and other essentials~~ [stet]

Multi-trip Plans for all trips taken during a given year

Annual Renewable ^International^ Insurance for families, individuals, and groups

[ital] (marked for the underlined plan names); "families," and "individuals," marked to be switched

4. Format the text you just keyed as a bulleted list with 6 points of spacing before paragraphs.
5. Change the page orientation for the document to landscape.
6. Switch to Print Preview. Choose Text Width from the Zoom box so you can read the text.
7. Switch to edit mode. Insert one blank line after the first line (the title) and before the last line (the agency name). Change the title to all capitals.
8. While still in Print Preview, open the Font dialog box and change the font for the entire document to 22-point Arial Black.
9. View both pages of the document at the same time. Using the Print Preview toolbar, shrink the document to fit on one page.
10. Change the top margin to 1.5 inches.
11. Increase the document title and the agency name by one font size.
12. Save the document as ***[your initials]*****7-16** in your Lesson 7 folder.
13. Print and close the document.

W O R D

EXERCISE 7-17

Change margins, insert the date, use Print Preview, and print an envelope.

1. Open the file **DCGletter**.
2. Format the document as a business letter by adding the letter heading and spacing shown in Figure 7-23. See Appendix F: "Standard Forms for Business Documents" to check the formatting.

FIGURE 7-23

Set 2" top margin

[insert today's date] ← Use correct date format

Insert 3 blank lines

Ms. Barbara Almy
Almy-Price, Inc.
4200 Constance Place NE
Albuquerque, NM 87104

Insert 1 blank line

Dear Ms. Almy:

3. At the end of the document, press Enter twice and key **Sincerely,**
4. Press Enter four times and key **Anna Svenkova**. On the next line, key her title, **Associate Travel Counselor**. Press Enter twice and key your reference initials.
5. Switch to Print Preview and view both pages of the document at the same time.
6. View only page 2 of the document in 100% magnification and edit the paragraph that begins "Our staff of 12," as shown in Figure 7-24.

FIGURE 7-24

The 15 members of our staff ~~Our staff of 12~~ all have expertise in different areas of the travel business. You will be dealing primarily with me and with ~~the agency's manager, Frank Youngblood. Should you need to make overseas travel arrangements for yourself, your staff, or your family,~~ Frank Murillo, ~~will help you. He is~~ the agency's international counselor. You also will be speaking with ~~on the phone to~~ Valerie Grier, our secretary/office manager, and most probably to our bookkeeper, Darrell Jackson. We're all here to ensure that your travel needs are handled ~~taken care of~~ efficiently.

7. Delete the paragraph that begins "As an added service" along with the paragraph that follows it and extra blank lines.
8. View both pages of the document again and view page 1 in 100% magnification. Delete the paragraph that begins "For local-area residents" and the paragraph that follows it. (Delete extra blank lines.)
9. Shrink the document to fit on a single page.
10. Switch to Normal view to spell-check the document.
11. Add an envelope to the document. For document identification purposes, include just your name for the return address. Do not include bar codes. In the delivery address, do not change the case formatting or remove punctuation. Modify the zip code, however, so it contains the ZIP+4 code **–3009**.

NOTE: When formatting an address in the traditional style (using upper and lower case instead of all caps), include punctuation marks (such as a comma between the city and state) so postal service OCR (optical character recognition) software interprets the information correctly.

12. Save the document as ***[your initials]*7-17** in your Lesson 7 folder.
13. Print the envelope and the letter, and then close the document.

EXERCISE 7-18

Change margins, create an envelope, choose print options, and send a document as an e-mail message.

1. Open the file **ElMorro1**.
2. Change the left and right margins to 1.25 inches.
3. Format the title as 14-point bold with a shadow effect. Add 72 points of paragraph spacing before the title.
4. Justify all text below the title.
5. Add an envelope to the document, using the El Morro National Monument address that appears at the end of the document. (Tip: Select the address before opening the Envelopes and Labels dialog box.) For the return address, use your name, followed by the Duke City Gateway agency name and address (see step 5 of Exercise 7-9). Do not save this return address as the default return address.
6. At the end of the document, format the text from "For more information" through the phone number with 1.75-inch left and right indents, a 1-point box border, and 10% gray shading.
7. Send the document as an e-mail message to your instructor or yourself, if an e-mail address is available; otherwise, do not send the message and close the e-mail header.

NOTE: If you send the e-mail message, ask your instructor how to get into your mail program to print the sent message. The message will print with the e-mail header.

8. Save the document as ***[your initials]*7-18** in your Lesson 7 folder.
9. Print the envelope and then print the two pages of the document on one sheet. (Reminder: The envelope is page 0, and the document is pages 1–2.)
10. Close the document.

EXERCISE 7-19 Challenge Yourself

Use a wizard to create a document, use Print Preview, and change margins.

1. Start a new document using the Memo Wizard. Choose the Professional style.
2. Choose the following options in the wizard dialog boxes:
   - Title: Include the suggested title "Interoffice Memo"
   - Heading Fields: Include the date, your name, and the subject **New Insurance Plan**
   - Recipient: The memo is to Frank Youngblood with copies ("CC:") to Susan Allen and Valerie Grier
   - Closing Fields: Include your initials as the typist initials
   - Header/Footer: Clear all check boxes
3. For the body of the memo, key the text shown in Figure 7-25.

FIGURE 7-25

```
Our new employee health insurance plan is now in effect. Tomorrow each of
us will receive a kit that includes the following items:

Claim forms
ID cards
Member handbook
Provider directory

The administration kit is in Valerie's office.
```

4. Format the list of four items as a bulleted list, using one of the List Bullet styles in the Styles and Formatting task pane.

5. Delete any blank paragraph marks in the memo. Add 11-point paragraph spacing before the paragraph that begins "The administration."
6. Reduce the memo title by one font size so it fits on one line.
7. Change the date format in the date line to the third format in the Date and Time dialog box.
8. View the document in Print Preview and increase the top margin to 1.5 inches.
9. Save the document as ***[your initials]*7-19** in your Lesson 7 folder.
10. Print and close the document.

On Your Own

In these exercises you work on your own, as you would in a real-life work environment. Use the skills you've learned to accomplish the task—and be creative.

EXERCISE 7-20

Use the Resume Wizard or a resume template to create your resume. Include as much detail about yourself as possible. Save the document as ***[your initials]*7-20** and print it.

EXERCISE 7-21

Create a cover letter for your resume, using a matching template style. Address the cover letter to a prospective employer. Print an envelope for the letter. Save the document as ***[your initials]*7-21** and print it.

EXERCISE 7-22

Using the New Document task pane, go to the Microsoft.com templates site on the Web and choose a template from any category. Preview the template on the Web site, and then edit it in Word, using your own information. Save the document as ***[your initials]*7-22** and print it.

LESSON

8

Page and Section Breaks, Headers, and Footers

OBJECTIVES

MOUS ACTIVITIES

In this lesson:

W2002 3-1
W2002 3-3

See Appendix E.

After completing this lesson, you will be able to:

1. Use soft and hard page breaks.
2. Control line and page breaks.
3. Control section breaks.
4. Use the Go To feature.
5. Add page numbers.
6. Add headers and footers.
7. Add a continuation page header.

Estimated Time: 1½ hours

Just as text wraps automatically from the end of one line to the beginning of the next line, text flows automatically from the end of one page to the beginning of the next page. This process is called *pagination*, and there are techniques for controlling where pages break, particularly in long documents.

Long documents commonly include sections, which were introduced in Lesson 7. Sections have a significant impact on pagination, and are discussed in this lesson in greater detail. Page numbers, headers, and footers are useful additions to long documents. A *header* is text that appears in the top margin; a *footer* is text that appears in the bottom margin. Headers and footers can contain descriptive information about a document, such as the date, title, and author's name.

Using Soft and Hard Page Breaks

As you work on a document, Word is constantly calculating the amount of space available on the page. Page length is determined by the size of the paper and the top and bottom margins. For example, using standard-size paper and default margins, page length is nine inches. When a document exceeds this length, Word creates a *soft page break*. Word adjusts this automatic page break as you add or delete text. A soft page break appears as a horizontal dotted line on the screen in Normal view. In Print Layout view, you see the actual page break—the bottom of one page and the top of the next.

EXERCISE 8-1 Adjust a Soft Page Break Automatically

1. Open the file **CruiseFAQs1**.
2. Scroll to the bottom of page 1. Notice the soft page break that splits the paragraph beginning "A cruise is ideal for."
3. In the fourth line of the paragraph, position the insertion point to the left of the sentence beginning "You can also meet" and press Enter twice to split the paragraph. Notice the adjustment of the soft page break.

FIGURE 8-1
Adjusting the position of a soft page break

Soft page break

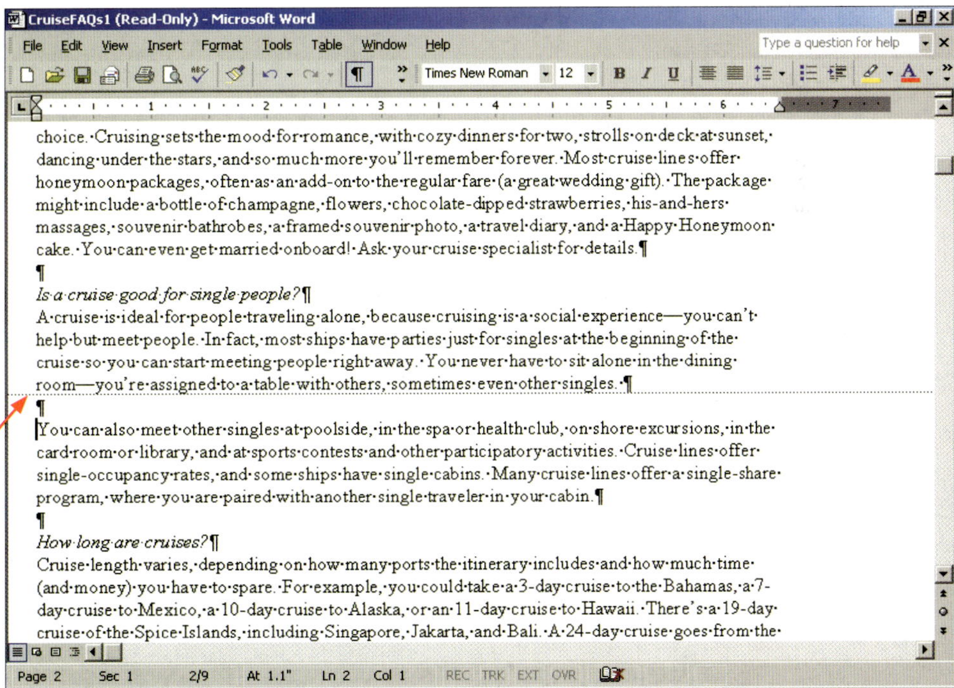

4. Press Backspace twice to restore the original soft page break.
5. Change the document's left and right margins to 1.25 inches. This changes the soft page breaks throughout the document.

EXERCISE 8-2 Insert a Hard Page Break

When you want a page break to occur at a specific point, you can insert a *hard page break*. In Normal View, a hard page break appears on the screen as a dotted line with the words "Page Break."

There are two ways to insert a hard page break:

- Use the keyboard shortcut Ctrl + Enter.
- Choose Insert, Break from the menu.

1. Working with the same paragraph, move the insertion point to the left of the italic line above the paragraph (*"Is a cruise good for single people?"*)
2. Press Ctrl + Enter. Word inserts a hard page break so the italicized paragraph and the entire paragraph that follows are not divided between two pages.
3. Switch to Print Layout view and scroll until you can see the bottom of page 1 and the top of page 2. (You might need to change the zoom setting to Page Width.)

FIGURE 8-2
Inserting a hard page break

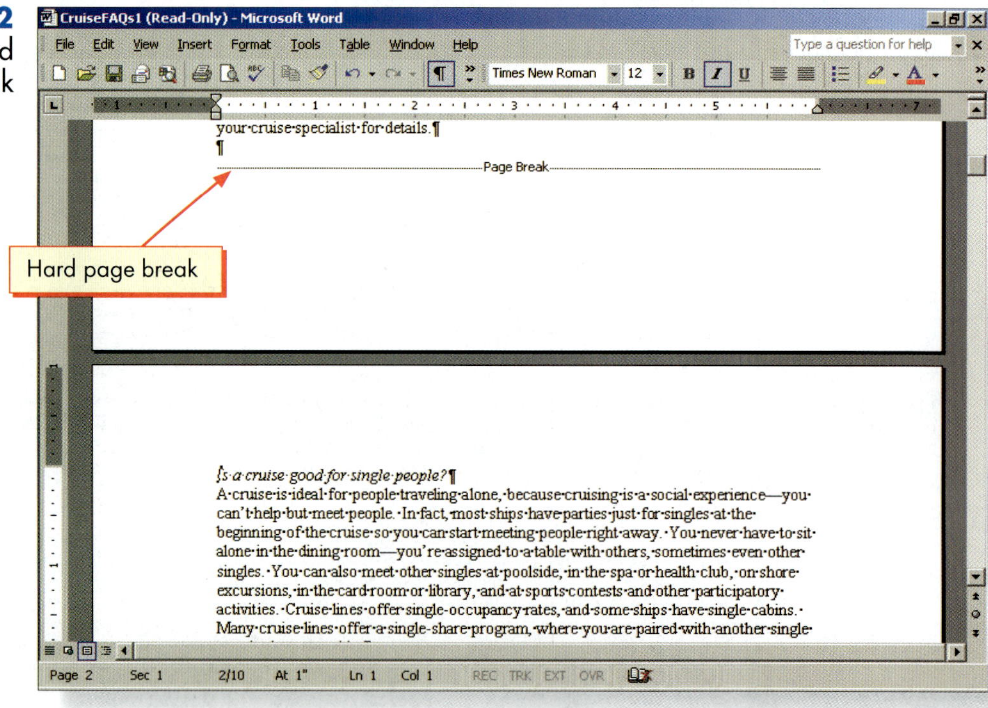

4. Scroll to the bottom of page 2. If the italic *"Do I need insurance?"* is by itself at the bottom of the page, you'll want to keep it with the paragraph that follows it.

NOTE: Printer drivers sometimes affect pagination. Your page breaks might differ from those shown in this lesson.

5. Position the insertion point before *"Do"* and choose Break from the Insert menu.

FIGURE 8-3
Break dialog box

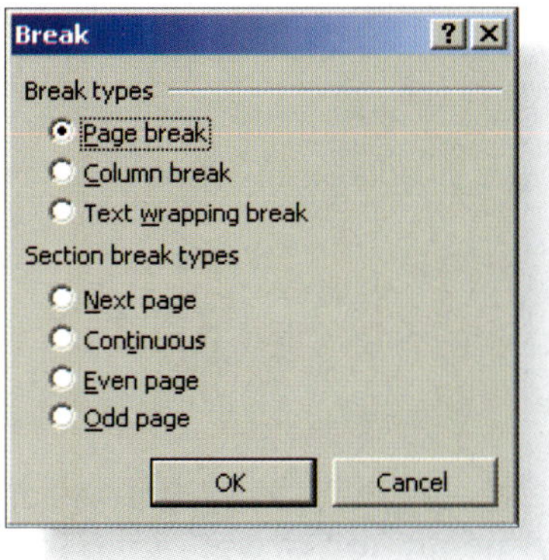

6. In the Break dialog box, make sure Page break is selected and click OK. This is another way to insert a hard page break. Notice that this dialog box is used for other types of breaks, as you'll see later in the lesson.

7. Scroll to the bottom of page 3. If the paragraph *"Is there laundry service onboard?"* is by itself at the bottom of the page, insert a hard page break before it.

EXERCISE 8-3 Delete a Hard Page Break

You cannot delete a soft page break, but you can delete a hard page break by clicking the page break and pressing Backspace or Delete.

1. Move the insertion point to the page break you just inserted by positioning the I-beam over the page break and clicking.
2. Press Delete to delete the page break.
3. Scroll back to the hard page break you inserted at the bottom of page 2. Place the insertion point to the left of *"Do I need insurance"* and press Backspace. The page break is deleted.

Controlling Line and Page Breaks

To control the way Word breaks paragraphs, choose one of four line and page break options from the Paragraph dialog box.

- Widow/Orphan control
  A *widow* is the last line of a paragraph and appears by itself at the top of a page. An *orphan* is the first line of a paragraph and appears at the bottom of a page. By default, this option is turned on to prevent

widows and orphans. Word moves an orphan forward to the next page and moves a widow back to the previous page.

- Keep lines together
  This option keeps all lines of a paragraph together on the same page rather than splitting the paragraph between two pages.
- Keep with next
  If two paragraphs need to appear on the same page, no matter where page breaks occur, use this option. This option is most commonly applied to titles that should not be separated from the first paragraph following the title.
- Page break before
  Use this option to place a paragraph at the top of a new page.

EXERCISE 8-4 Apply Line and Page Break Options to Paragraphs

1. At the bottom of page 2, right-click within the paragraph *"Do I need insurance?"* to open the shortcut menu. You are going to format the paragraph so it will not be separated from the paragraph that follows it.
2. Choose Paragraph from the shortcut menu to open the Paragraph dialog box and click the Line and Page Breaks tab.

FIGURE 8-4
Line and Page Break options in the Paragraph dialog box

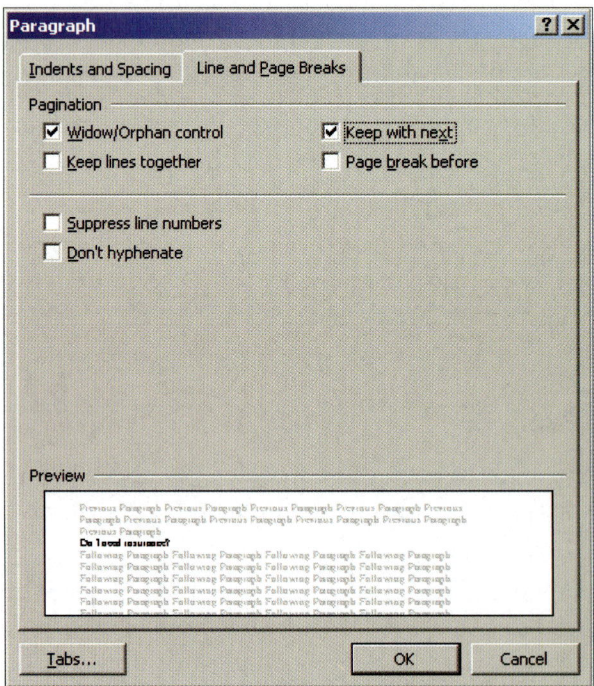

3. Click Keep with next to select it and then click OK. Word moves the soft page break, keeping the two paragraphs together. Notice that a small black bullet appears to the left of the italic paragraph, indicating that the paragraph is formatted with a line or page break option.

NOTE: The small square bullet is a nonprinting character that appears only if the Show/Hide ¶ button is turned on.

4. Change to Normal view to see the soft page break. Display the Reveal Formatting task pane. Notice that the **Keep with next** option appears in the task pane as an applied paragraph format.

FIGURE 8-5
Applying the Keep With Next option

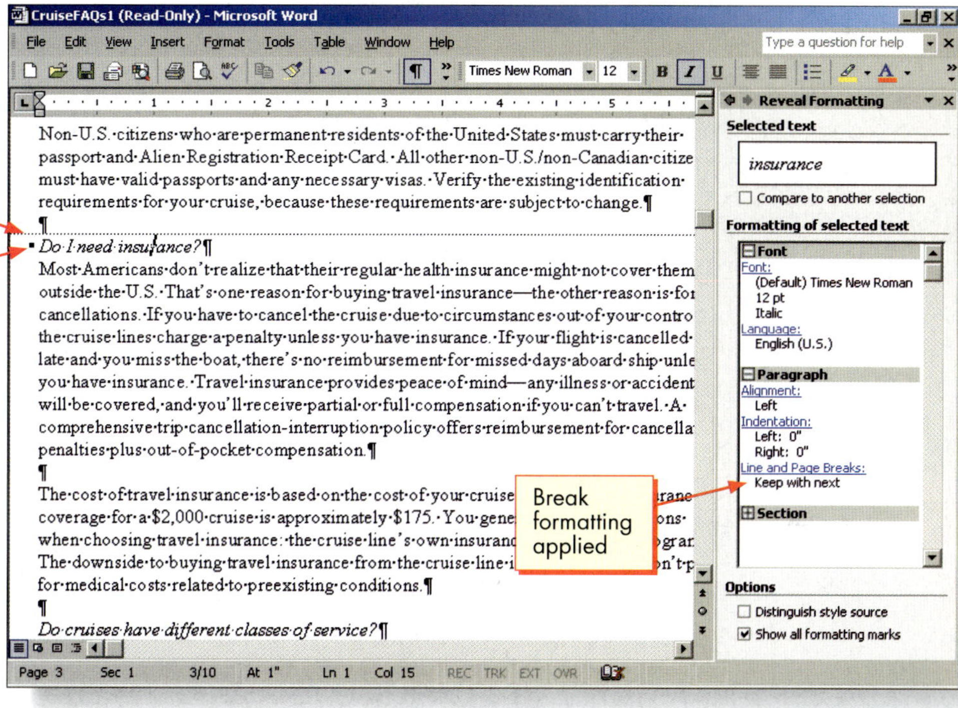

TIP: You can click the Line and Page Breaks link in the task pane to open the Paragraph dialog box, Line and Breaks tab, if you want to adjust the formatting.

5. Apply the **Keep with next** paragraph option to the italic paragraph *"Is there laundry service onboard?"* at the bottom of page 3.

6. Locate the long paragraph at the bottom of page 4 that starts "Dining on a cruise ship." (You might want to close the task pane to make more room for the document text.)

7. Toward the end of the paragraph, split the paragraph at the sentence that starts "Most ships offer health-conscious" (insert a blank line before the new paragraph). The new paragraph is divided by a soft page break.

8. With the insertion point in or at the beginning of the new paragraph, open the Paragraph dialog box (**Line and Page Breaks** tab), choose **Keep lines together**, and click **OK**. The soft page break moves above the paragraph to keep the lines of text together.

NOTE: Keep lines together is used for lines of text within one paragraph. Keep with next requires a minimum of two paragraphs but can be applied to more than two paragraphs.

FIGURE 8-6
Applying the Keep Lines Together option

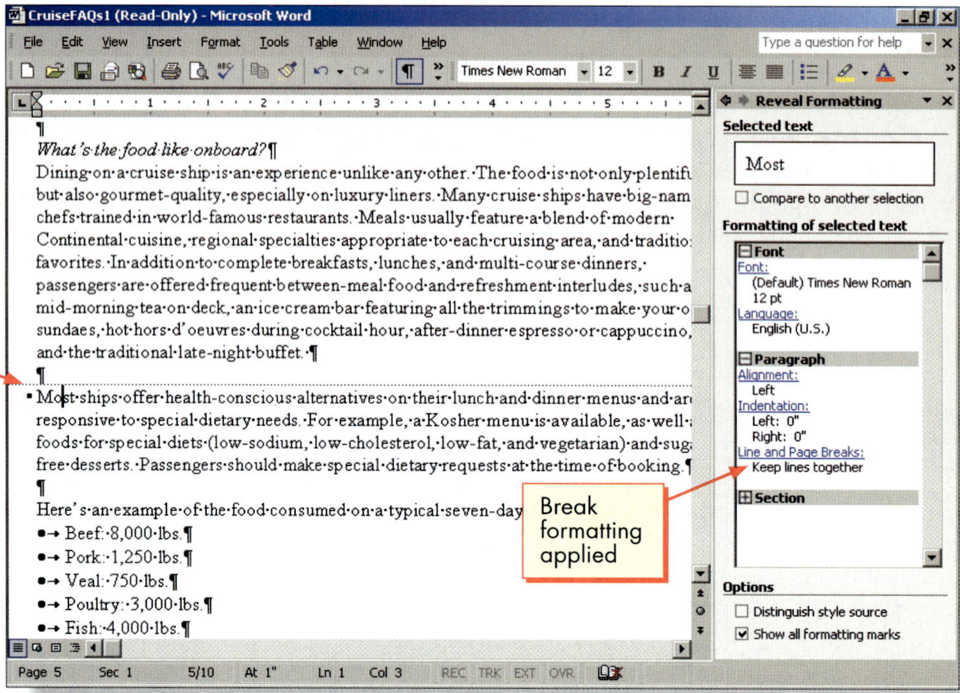

9. Scroll to the italic paragraph *"What are theme cruises?"* on page 7. Position the insertion point in this italic paragraph, which you will format so it begins at the top of the page.
10. Open the Paragraph dialog box, click **Page break before**, and click **OK**. Word starts the paragraph at the top of page 8 with a soft page break before it.
11. Save the document as ***[your initials]*8-4** in a new folder for Lesson 8.

TIP: Remember the various methods for moving within a long document. For example, you can drag the scroll box on the vertical scroll bar and use the scroll arrows to adjust the view. You can also use keyboard shortcuts: Ctrl+↑ or ↓ to move up or down one paragraph, PgUp or PgDn to move up or down one window, and Ctrl+Home or Ctrl+End to move to the beginning or end of a document.

Controlling Section Breaks

Section breaks separate parts of a document that have formatting different from the rest of the document. You saw in the previous lesson how formatting selected text resulted in a new section. For better control in creating sections, you can insert a section break directly into a document at a specific location using the Break dialog box. You can also choose from one of three types of section breaks:

- Next page
  This default option starts a section on a new page.

- **Continuous**
  With this type of section break, the section follows the text before it without a page break.
- **Even page or Odd page**
  Use to start a section on the next even- or odd-numbered page. This feature is useful for reports in which chapters must begin on either odd-numbered or even-numbered pages.

EXERCISE 8-5 Insert Section Breaks Using the Break Dialog Box

1. On pages 9 and 10, select the text *"What do I need to know about ship terminology?"* and the list below it. Move the selection to the end of the document. (Be sure to leave a blank line before the moved text.)
2. With the insertion point to the left of *"What do I need,"* choose Break from the Insert menu.
3. Under Section break types, choose Continuous and click OK. Word begins a new section on the same page, from the position of the insertion point.
4. Click above and below the section mark. Notice that the section number changes on the status bar, but the page number stays the same.

FIGURE 8-7 Inserting a continuous section break

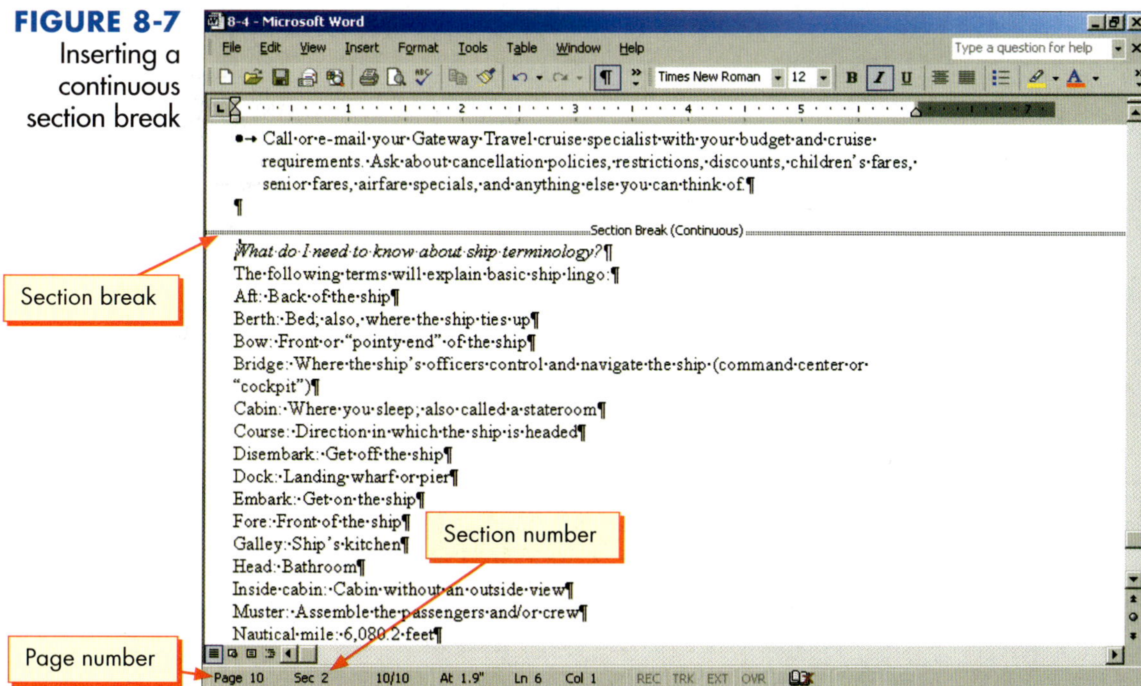

WORD

EXERCISE 8-6 Apply Formatting to Sections

After you create a new section, you can change its formatting or specify a different type of section break. This is often useful for long documents, which might contain many sections that require different page formatting, such as different margin settings or page orientation. For example, you can change a Next page section break to a Continuous section break or you can change the page orientation of a section, without affecting the rest of the document.

NOTE: The formatting you apply to the section is stored in the section break. If you delete a section break, you also delete the formatting for the text above the section break. For example, if you have a two-section document and you delete the section break at the end of section 1, the document becomes one section with the formatting of section 2.

1. With the insertion point in the new section, choose Page Setup from the File menu.
2. Click the Layout tab and click to open the Section start drop-down list. From this list, you can change the section break from Continuous to another type.

FIGURE 8-8 Using the Page Setup dialog box to modify the section

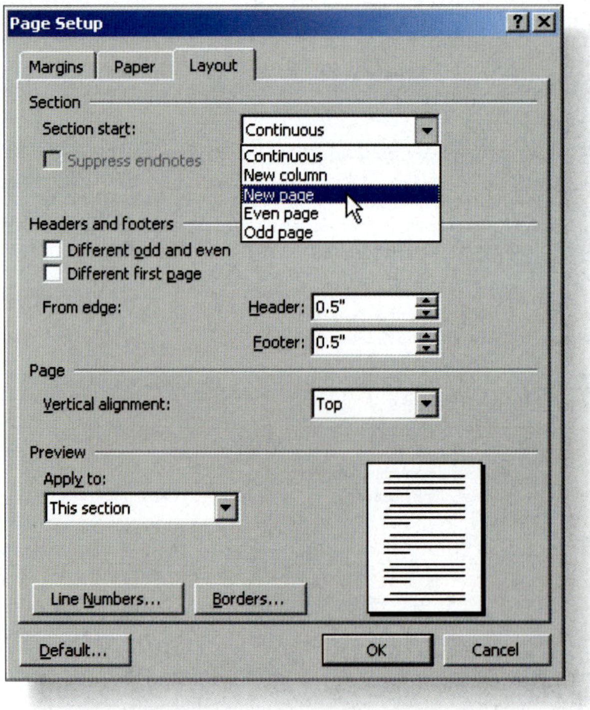

3. Choose New page to start this section on a new page.

4. Click the Margins tab and change the left and right margins to 1.5 inches. Click OK. Notice that the new section now starts on a new page with a Next Page section break.
5. Click within section 1 and open the Page Setup dialog box. Change the left and right margins for this section back to 1 inch. (Make sure the Apply to box says This section.) Click OK.
6. View the document in Print Layout view.

EXERCISE 8-7 Change the Vertical Alignment of a Section

Another way to format a section is to specify the vertical alignment of the section on the page. For example, you can align a title page so the text is centered between the top and bottom margins. Vertical alignment is a Layout option available in the Page Setup dialog box.

1. Click within section 2.
2. Open the Page Setup dialog box and click the Layout tab.
3. Open the Vertical alignment drop-down list and choose Center. Click OK. The text is centered vertically on the page.

4. Switch to Print Preview. Use the Multiple Pages button to view the document two pages at a time.
5. With the last page of the document in the Print Preview window, open the Page Setup dialog box. Change the vertical alignment of section 2 to Justified. Click OK. Word justifies the last page of the document so the text extends from the top to the bottom margin.

TABLE 8-1 Vertical Alignment Options

OPTIONS	DESCRIPTION
Top	Aligns the top line of the page with the top margin (default setting).
Center	Centers the page between the top and bottom margins with equal space above and below the text.
Justified	Aligns the top line of the page with the top margin and the bottom line with the bottom margin with equal spacing between the lines of text (similar in principle to the way Word justifies text between the left and right margins).
Bottom	Aligns the bottom line of a partial page along the bottom margin.

FIGURE 8-9
Changing vertical alignment for section 2

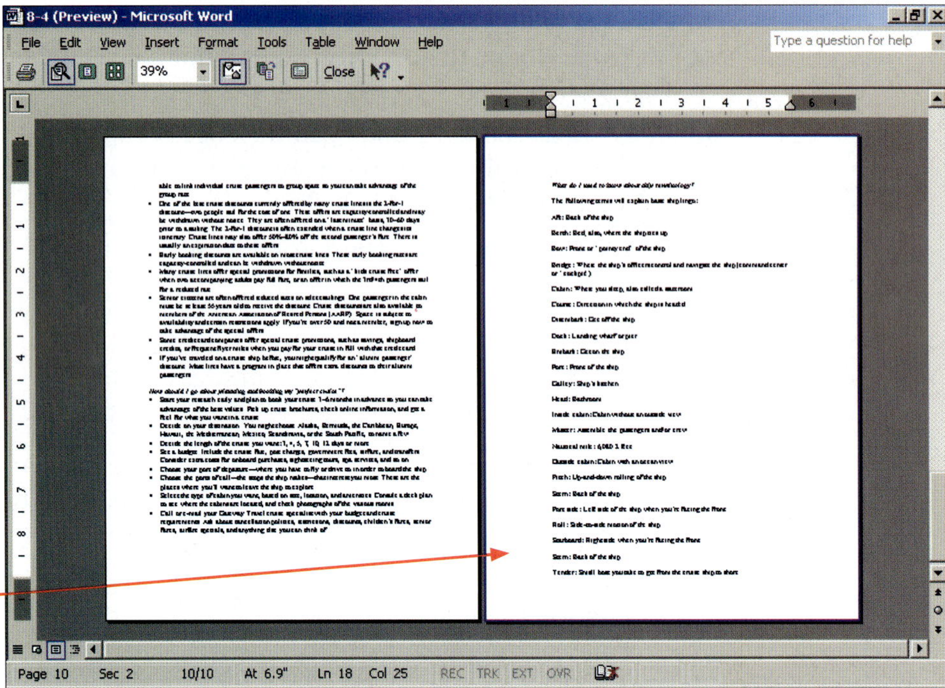

Section 2 with justified vertical alignment

6. In either Print Preview or Print Layout view, change the paragraph at the top of page 8 (*"What are theme cruises?"*) so it does not start on a new page (clear the Page break before check box in the Paragraph dialog box).

REVIEW: To edit a document in Print Preview, click the Magnifier button to switch to edit mode, position the I-beam, and use the menu to open a dialog box.

7. At the top of the document, add another line below the title. Then format the title as 14 points, centered, with 48 points of spacing before the paragraph.
8. Save the document as ***[your initials]*8-7** in your Lesson 8 folder.
9. Print the document two pages per sheet.

Using the Go To Feature

The Go To feature enables you to move through a document quickly. For example, you can go to a specific section, page number, comment, or bookmark. (Comments and bookmarks are discussed later in this course.) Go To is a convenient feature for long documents—it's faster than scrolling and it moves the insertion point to the specified location.

Go To is a tab in the Find and Replace dialog box. There are three ways to initiate the Go To command:

- Choose Edit, Go To from the menu.
- Press Ctrl + G or F5.
- Double-click on the status bar (anywhere to the left of "REC").

EXERCISE 8-8 Go To a Specific Page or Section

1. Switch to Normal view and press F5. Word displays the Go To tab, located in the Find and Replace dialog box.

FIGURE 8-10 Using the Go To feature

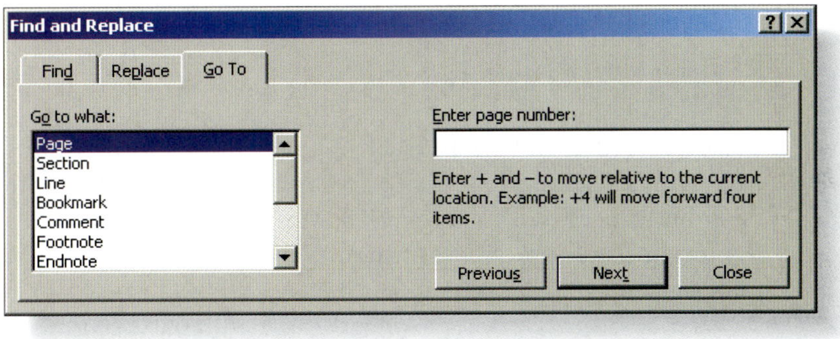

2. Scroll through the Go to what list to review the options. Choose Section from the list and click Next to move to section 2.

3. Choose Page from the Go to what list and click Previous. The insertion point moves to the top of the previous page.

4. Key **2** in the Enter page number text box and click Go To. The insertion point moves to the top of page 2.

5. Close the dialog box.

EXERCISE 8-9 Go To a Relative Destination

You can use Go To to move to a location relative to the insertion point. For example, with Page selected in the Go to what list, you can enter **+2** in the text box to move forward two pages from the insertion point. You can move in increments of pages, lines, sections, and so on. Another option is to move by a certain percentage within the document, such as 50%—the document's midpoint.

1. Double-click the word "Page" on the status bar to reopen the dialog box.

2. Choose Line from the Go to what list and enter **1** in the text box. Click Go To. The insertion point moves to the first line in the document.
3. Enter **+40** in the text box and click Go To. The insertion point moves forward 40 lines from the previous location.
4. Enter **-40** in the text box and click Go To. The insertion point moves back to the previous location.
5. Click Page in the Go to what list, enter **50%** in the text box, and click Go To. The insertion point moves to the midpoint of the document.

NOTE: You must select Page in the Go to what list to use a percentage.

6. Close the dialog box.

Adding Page Numbers

Word automatically keeps track of page numbers—the status bar shows the current page and the total number of pages in a document. But it's important to add printed page numbers to a multi-page document. The easiest way to add page numbers is to choose Page Numbers from the Insert menu to open the Page Numbers dialog box.

EXERCISE 8-10 Add Page Numbers

1. In the current document (*[your initials]*8-7), position the insertion point at the top of the document.
2. Choose Page Numbers from the Insert menu. Word displays the Page Numbers dialog box. Notice that the default setting for page number placement is the bottom of the page, right-aligned. Also, by default, Word prints page numbers on the first page.

FIGURE 8-11
Page Numbers dialog box

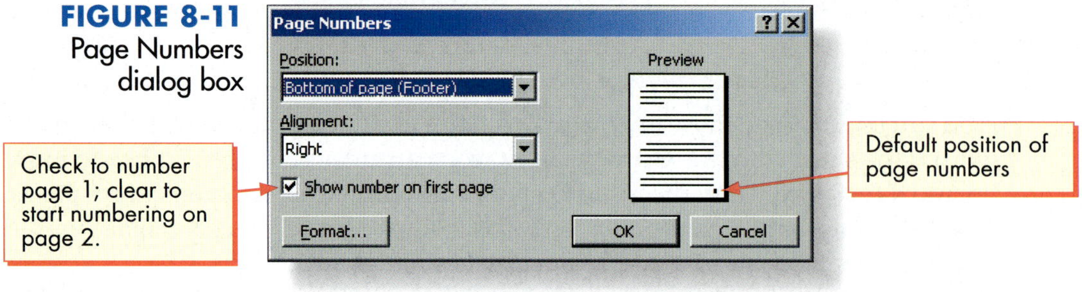

3. Click the down arrow to open the Position drop-down list. Choose Top of page (Header). Notice the change in the Preview box.

4. Open the Alignment drop-down list and choose Center. The Preview box reflects the change.

5. Click OK; then switch to Print Preview to view the page numbers.

NOTE: You can see page numbers only in Print Preview, Print Layout view, or on the printed page.

6. Click the View Ruler button to display the rulers. The page numbers appear within the 1-inch top margin. Specifically, page numbers are positioned 0.5 inch from the top edge of the page.

FIGURE 8-12
Viewing page numbers in Print Preview

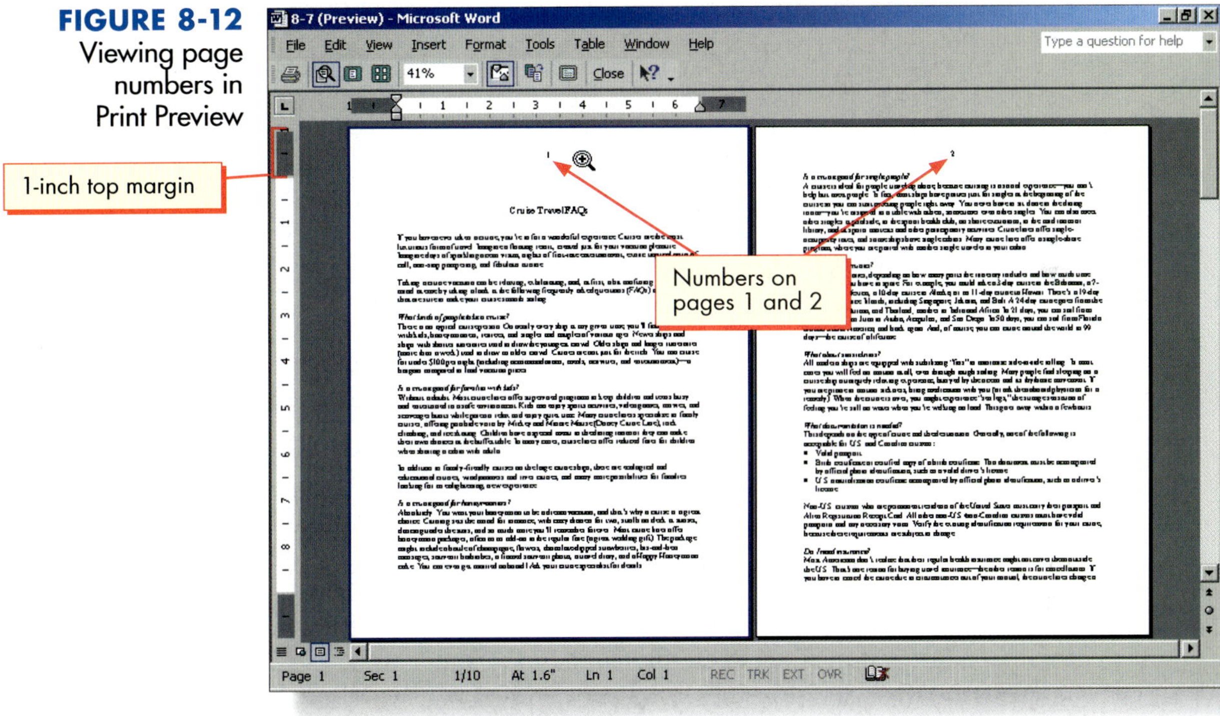

7. Use the Magnifier pointer for a closer view of the numbers. Scroll to see the page numbers throughout the document.

EXERCISE 8-11 Modify the Page Number Format

Not only can you change the placement of page numbers and decide if you want to number the first page, but you can also change the format of page numbers. For example, instead of using numerals such as 1, 2, and 3, you can use Roman numerals (i, ii, iii) or letters (a, b, c). You can also use different page number formats for different sections.

1. While still in Print Preview, choose Page Numbers from the Insert menu.
2. Change the alignment to right. Clear the Show number on first page check box so page 1 does not display a page number.
3. Click the Format button. In the Page Number Format dialog box, open the Number format drop-down list, scroll to the bottom, and choose uppercase Roman numerals (I, II, III…).

FIGURE 8-13
Page Number Format dialog box

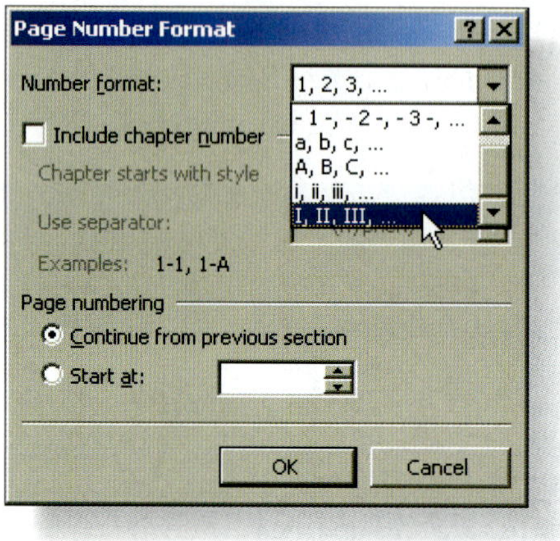

4. Click OK in the Page Number Format dialog box and then click OK in the Page Numbers dialog box. The numbers are now right-aligned, starting with Roman numeral II, and page 1 is not numbered.

EXERCISE 8-12 Vary Page Numbers in Print Layout View

In addition to using the Page Numbers dialog box, you can also vary page numbers in Print Layout view. For example, you can:

- Apply character formatting such as bold or italic to page numbers.
- Add the word “Page” before the page number.

1. Display the document in Print Layout view.
2. Reopen the Page Numbers dialog box and change the number format back to the 1, 2, 3 format.
3. Scroll to the top of page 2. The page number appears in gray on your screen at the right margin.
4. Double-click the page number. This activates the dotted header pane (the area at the top of the page that contains the page number), displays the Header and Footer toolbar, and dims the document text.

NOTE: Notice that the header pane is titled “Section 1.” That’s because this is a two-section document.

5. In the header pane, position the I-beam just before the number 2. If the I-beam changes to a four-headed arrow, continue to move the mouse until the I-beam is just before the number. Click to position the insertion point. A shaded frame appears around the number.

FIGURE 8-14
Working with page numbers in Print Layout view

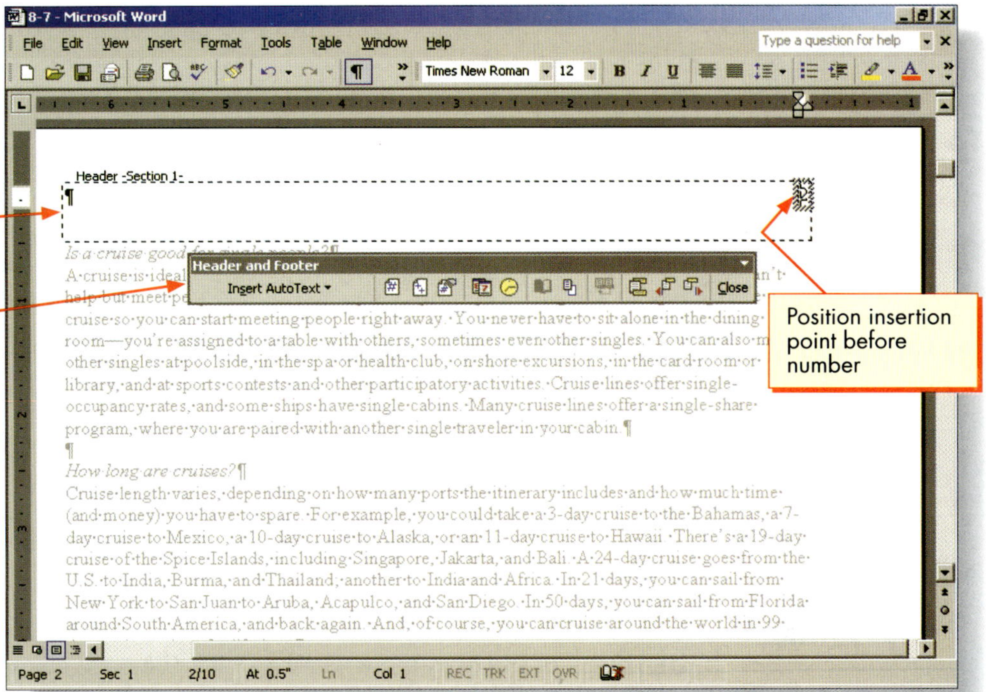

6. Key **Page** and press [Spacebar] once.
7. Scroll to the header pane on page 3 to view the revised header text.

NOTE: Changing one page number affects all page numbers.

8. To apply character formatting to the page number, drag the I-beam pointer (not the four-headed arrow pointer) over the word "Page" and the number 3 to select both.
9. Using the Formatting toolbar, change the text to Arial italic.

FIGURE 8-15
Formatted page number with "Page" added

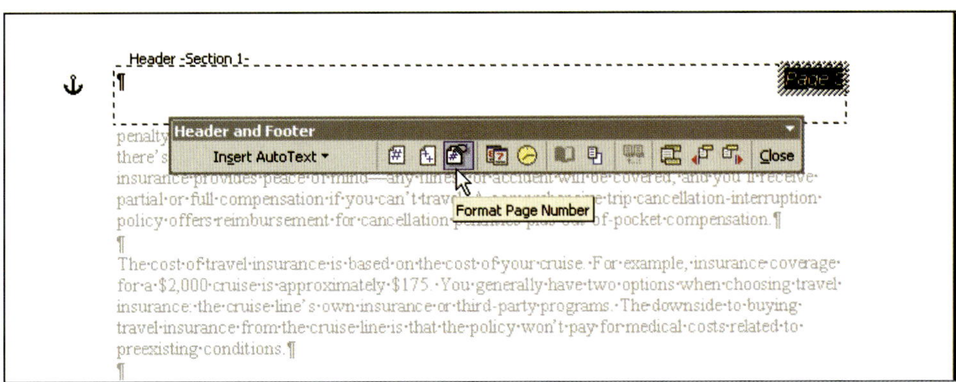

10. Click the Format Page Number button on the Header and Footer toolbar. This is another way to open the Page Number Format dialog box and change the number format.

11. Close the dialog box without making changes.

TIP: The page number doesn't have to be selected in the pane before you use the Format Page Number button.

12. Double-click outside the header pane to return to Print Layout view.

13. Save the document as ***[your initials]*8-12** in your Lesson 8 folder.

14. Print only pages 1–2 of the document.

EXERCISE 8-13 Remove Page Numbers in Print Layout View

To remove page numbers, delete the text in the header or footer area.

1. On page 2 of the document, double-click the page number text to activate the header pane.

2. Select the text ("Page 2") and press Delete.

3. Scroll to the header area of page 3. The page number is deleted on that page as well.

4. Close the Header and Footer toolbar.

5. Close the document without saving.

Adding Headers and Footers

Headers and footers are typically used in multiple-page documents to display descriptive information. In addition to page numbers, a header or footer can contain such things as:

- The document name
- The date and/or the time you created or revised the document
- An author name
- A graphic, such as a company logo
- A draft or revision number

This descriptive information can appear in many different combinations. For example, the second page of a business letter typically contains a header with the name of the addressee, the page number, and the date. A report can contain a footer with the report name and a header with the page number and chapter name. A newsletter can contain a header with a title and logo on the first page and a footer with the title and page number on the pages that follow.

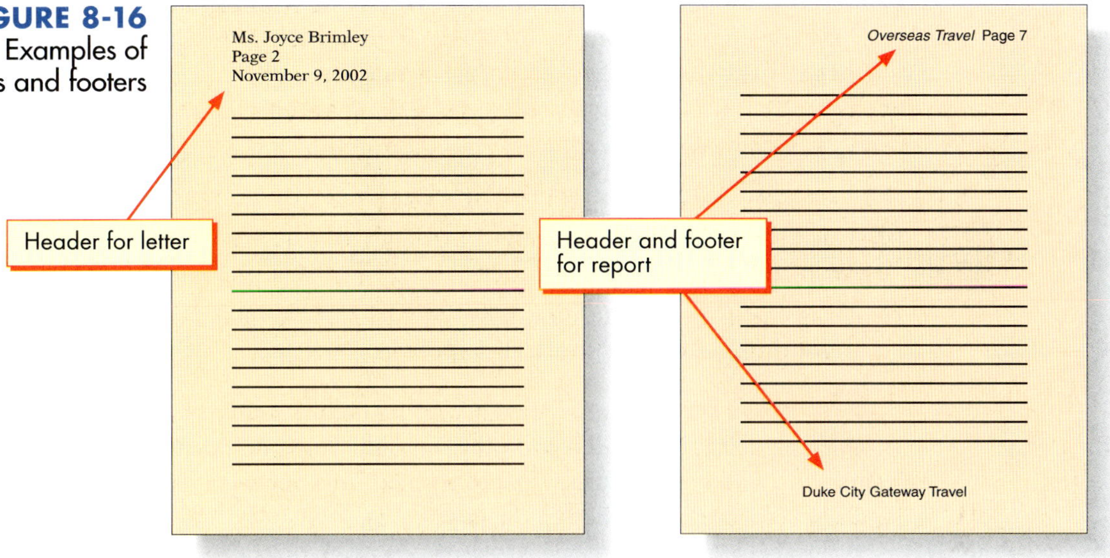

FIGURE 8-16 Examples of headers and footers

EXERCISE 8-14 Add a Header to a Document

1. Open the file **CruiseFAQs1**. This is the original one-section document.
2. Copy the title "Cruise Travel FAQs" (copy just the text, not the paragraph mark). You're going to use this text to create a header.
3. Choose Header and Footer from the View menu. Word switches temporarily to Print Layout view and displays the Header and Footer toolbar. The header pane is also visible.
4. Click the Page Setup button on the Header and Footer toolbar. The Layout tab in the Page Setup dialog box appears.
5. Check the Different first page check box and click OK. This option will allow you to create a different header and footer on page 1 than you'll use for the rest of the document.

NOTE: The Different first page option is often used when a document contains a title page and you want to create a different header/footer for the remaining pages.

6. Click the Show Next button on the Header and Footer toolbar to move to the next header pane. The document contains two header panes. The first

header pane is labeled First Page Header and the second header pane is labeled Header.

7. Paste the Clipboard contents into the page 2 header pane. Use the Keep Text Only paste option to turn off the bold format. The text now appears on every page of the document except the first page.

8. Insert a tab character before the copied text. Notice that there are two preset tab settings on the ruler: 3-inch centered and 6-inch right-aligned.

9. Press Tab after the title text. Key **Page** and press Spacebar.

10. Click the Insert Page Number button on the Header and Footer toolbar. Word inserts the page number.

11. Drag the 3-inch centered tab marker to 3.25 inches and drag the 6-inch right-aligned tab marker to 6.5 inches.

NOTE: The preset tab settings are default settings for a document with the default 1.25-inch left and right margins. In such a document, the 3-inch tab centers text and the 6-inch tab right-aligns text. This document, however, has 1-inch left and right margins, so it's best to adjust the tabs.

12. Click the Show Previous button and notice that the first-page header pane is still blank. Click the Show Next button to return to the header you created.

TABLE 8-2 Buttons on the Header and Footer Toolbar

BUTTON	PURPOSE
Insert AutoText	Insert common header or footer items, such as running total page numbers (Page 1 of 10), the filename, or the author's name.
Insert Page Number	Insert the page number.
Insert Number of Pages	Insert the total number of pages in the document.
Format Page Number	Open the Format Page Number dialog box.
Insert Date	Insert the current date.
Insert Time	Insert the current time.

continues

TABLE 8-2 Buttons on the Header and Footer Toolbar *continued*

BUTTON	PURPOSE
Page Setup	Open the Page Setup dialog box.
Show/Hide Document Text	Display or hide the document text.
Same as Previous	Link or unlink the header or footer in one section to or from the header or footer in the previous section.
Switch Between Header and Footer	Move between the header and footer.
Show Previous	Show the header or footer of the previous section.
Show Next	Show the header or footer of the next section.

EXERCISE 8-15 Add a Footer to a Document

1. With the header on page 2 displayed, click the Switch Between Header and Footer button to display the footer pane.
2. Key your name and press Tab.
3. With the insertion point at the center of the footer, click Insert AutoText on the Header and Footer toolbar. Notice the types of AutoText entries you can insert into a header or footer.
4. Choose Created on from the AutoText list. This AutoText entry inserts a field that displays the text "Created on" plus the date and time the document was created. For example, if you created and saved the document for the first time on June 5, 2002, at 10:00 in the morning, the text "Created on 6/5/02 10:00 AM" would be inserted.
5. Press Tab, open the AutoText list again, and choose Filename. The document's name is inserted. This footer information prints at the bottom of each page except the first. (See Figure 8-17 on the next page.)
6. Adjust the tab positions by dragging the center tab marker to 3.25 inches and the right tab marker to 6.5 inches.
7. Click the Show Previous button to display the first-page footer pane.
8. Key **Duke City Gateway Travel—Cruise Specialists** in italic and center-align the text. Leave the first-page header pane blank.

FIGURE 8-17
Inserting AutoText in a footer

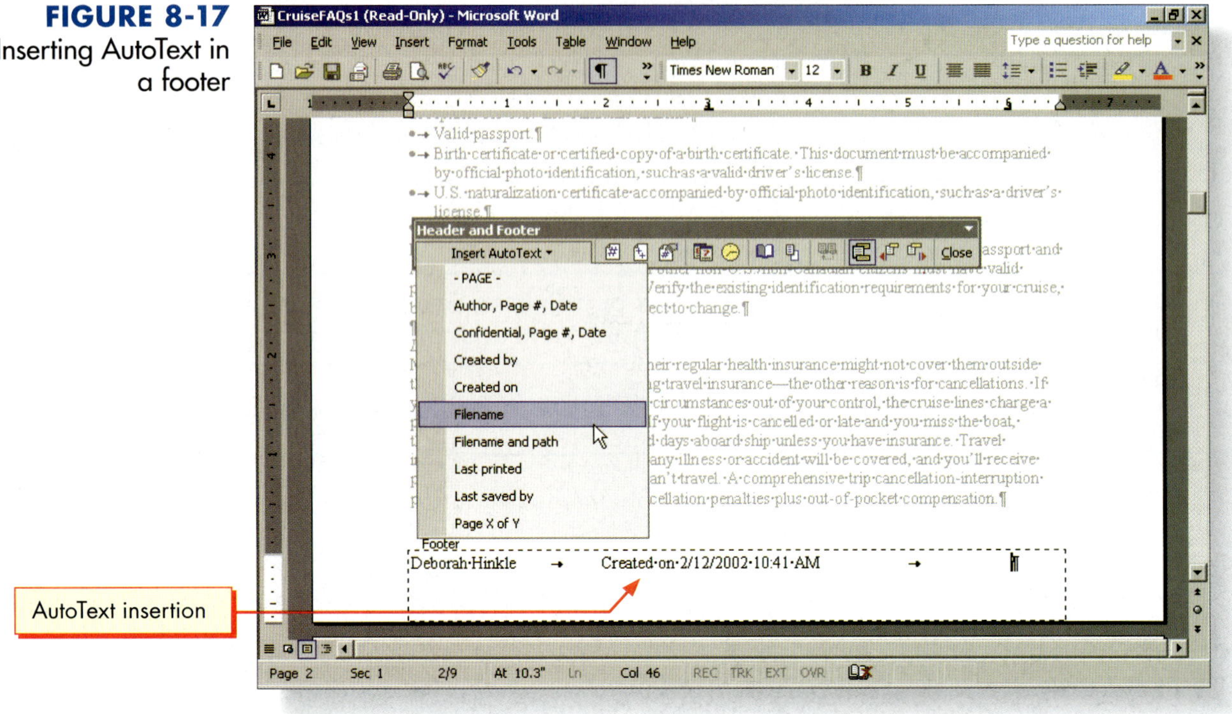

TIP: If you wanted to use the same footer text in section 2 that you used in section 1, you would open the section 2 footer pane and click the Same as Previous button. This links the section 2 footer to the section 1 footer, so the same text appears in both footer panes.

9. Click Close to return to the document in Normal view.
10. Switch to Print Preview and view the document's headers and footers.
11. Adjust page breaks as needed (for example, if an italic question appears by itself at the bottom of a page).
12. Delete the portion of the document about ship terminology (pages 8–9). Then save the document as ***[your initials]*8-15** in your Lesson 8 folder.
13. Print the document 4 pages per sheet and then close it.

Creating Continuation Page Headers

It's customary to use a header on the second page of a business letter or memo. A *continuation page header* for a letter or memo is typically a three-line block of text that includes the addressee name, the page number, and the date.

There are three rules for letters and memos with continuation page headers:

- Page 1 must have a 2-inch top margin.

- Continuation pages must have a 1-inch top margin.
- Two blank lines must appear between the header and the continuation page text.

EXERCISE 8-16 Add a Continuation Page Header to a Letter

The easiest way to create a continuation page header using the proper business format is to apply these settings to your document:

- Top margin: 2 inches
- Header position: 1 inch from edge of page
- Page Setup Layout for Headers and Footers: Different First Page
- Additional spacing: Add two blank lines below the header text

By default, headers and footers are positioned 0.5 inch from the top or bottom edge of the page. When you change the position of a continuation page header to 1 inch, the continuation page appears to have a 1-inch top margin, beginning with the header text. The document text begins at the page's 2-inch margin and the two additional blank lines in the continuation header ensure correct spacing between the header text and the document text.

1. Open the file **DCGletter**.
2. Add the date to the top of the letter. (Key today's date or use the Insert, Date and Time command. Remember to clear the box that updates the date automatically.)
3. On the fourth line below the date, add the following inside address:

   Ms. Lisa Knapp
   Napton Semiconductors
   400 Sara Road
   Rio Rancho, NM 87124
4. On the second line below the address, add **Dear Ms. Knapp:** followed by one blank line.
5. Choose Page Setup from the File menu and click the Layout tab. Check Different first page and set the Header to 1 inch from the edge.
6. Click the Margins tab and set a 2-inch top margin and 1.25-inch left and right margins. Click OK.

7. Display the header pane. Click the Show Next button to move to the header pane on page 2.
8. Create the header in Figure 8-18 (on the next page), inserting the information as shown. Press Enter twice after the last line.

FIGURE 8-18

```
Ms. Lisa Knapp
Page [Click [#] for the page number]
[Current date]
```

TIP: If you use the Insert Date button on the Header and Footer toolbar, Word inserts an automatically updating date field in the format 12/25/2002 instead of the format December 25, 2002 used in letters and memos.

FIGURE 8-19
Continuation page header for a letter

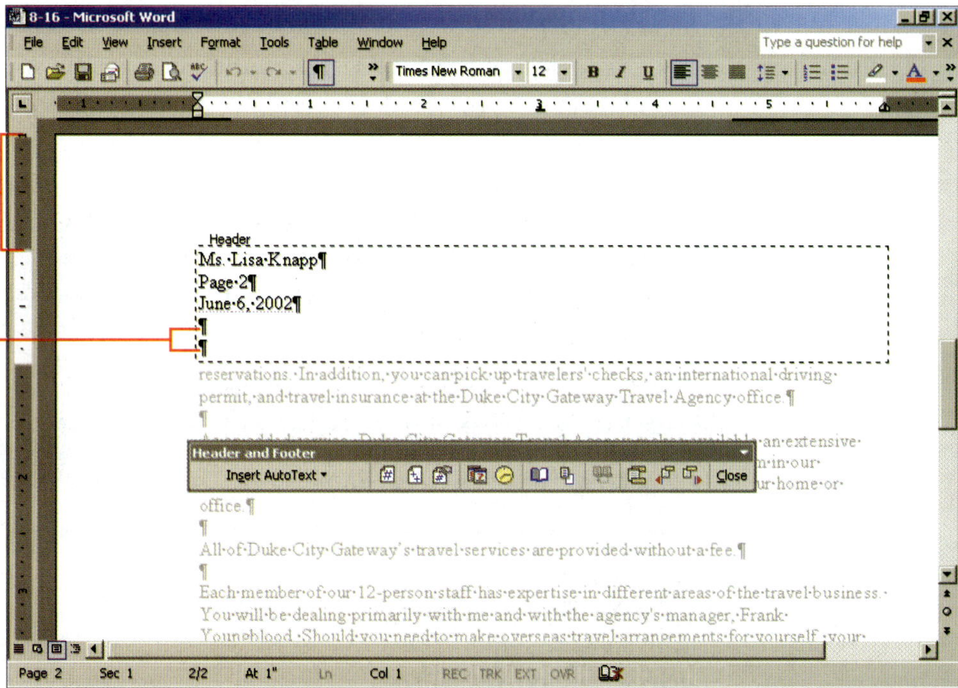

9. Close the header pane and view both pages in Print Preview.
10. Add the letter closing (the letter is from Tom Carey, Senior Travel Counselor) followed by your reference initials. Check Appendix F: "Standard Forms for Business Documents" for correct spacing.
11. Save the document as ***[your initials]*8-16** in your Lesson 8 folder.
12. Print and close the document.

LESSON 8 Summary

- Pagination is the Word process of flowing text from line to line and from page to page. Word creates a soft page break at the end of each page. When you edit text, you adjust line and page breaks. You can adjust the way a page breaks by manually inserting a hard page break (Ctrl + Enter).
- Delete a hard page break by clicking it and pressing Delete or Backspace.
- The Paragraph dialog box contains line and page break options to control pagination. To prevent lines of a paragraph from displaying on two pages, click in the paragraph and apply the Keep lines together option. To keep two paragraphs together on the same page, click in the first paragraph and apply the Keep with next option. To insert a page break before a paragraph, click in the paragraph and choose the Page break before option.
- Use section breaks to separate parts of a document that have different formatting. Apply a Next page section break to start a section on a new page or a Continuous section break to continue the new section on the same page. Apply an Even page or Odd page section break to start a section on the next even- or odd-numbered page.
- Change the vertical alignment of a section by clicking within the section and choosing File, Page Setup. On the Layout tab, under Vertical alignment, choose an alignment (Top, Center, Justified, or Bottom).
- Use the Go To command to go to a specific page or section in a document. You can also go to a relative destination, such as the midpoint of the document or the 50th line.
- A header is text that appears in the top margin; a footer is text that appears in the bottom margin. These text areas are used for page numbers, document titles, the date, and other information.
- Always add page numbers to long documents. You can choose the position of page numbers (examples: bottom centered, top right) and the format (examples: 1, 2, 3 or A, B, C). You number the first page or begin numbering on the second page (you can also begin numbering the second page with "1" instead of "2" if appropriate).
- Check page numbers in Print Preview or Print Layout view (they are not visible in Normal view). In Print Layout view, you can activate the header or footer pane that contains the page number by double-clicking the text and then modify the page number text (examples: make it bold or add the word "Page" before the number).

- To remove page numbers, activate the header or footer pane that contains the numbering, select the text, and then delete it.
- To add header or footer text to a document, choose View, Header and Footer. Use the Header/Footer toolbar buttons to insert the page number, date, and time or to insert AutoText for the filename, author, print date, or other information. You can switch between the header and footer pane and move to the next or previous pane. Sections can have different headers and footers.
- A document can have a different header or footer for the first page than for the rest of the pages. Choose the Different first page option in the Page Setup dialog box (Layout tab).
- Use the Page Setup dialog box to change the position of the header or footer text from the edge of the page. The default position is 0.5 inch.
- Memos or letters that are two pages or longer should have a continuation page header—a three-line block containing the addressee name, page number, and date. Set the header to 1 inch from the edge, add two blank lines below the header, and use a 2-inch top margin. Apply the Different first page setup option, leaving the first-page header blank.

LESSON 8 Command Summary

FEATURE	BUTTON	MENU	KEYBOARD	SPEECH?
Insert hard page break		Insert, Break	Ctrl + Enter	✓
Apply line and page break options		Format, Paragraph, Line and Page Breaks		✓
Insert section breaks		Insert, Break		✓
Apply formatting to sections		File, Page Setup		✓
Go To		Edit, Go To	Ctrl + G or F5	✓
Add page numbers		Insert, Page Numbers		✓
Add header/footer		View, Header and Footer		✓

Concepts Review

TRUE/FALSE QUESTIONS

Each of the following statements is either true or false. Indicate your choice by circling T or F.

T F 1. You can delete a soft page break by pressing Delete.

T F 2. To insert a section break, press Ctrl+Enter.

T F 3. One way to insert a page break is to choose Break from the Insert menu.

T F 4. The default position for page numbers is at the bottom right of the page.

T F 5. A nonprinting character appears to the left of any paragraph to which you apply the Keep with next option.

T F 6. Section breaks appear in the Print Preview window as double dotted lines.

T F 7. Page breaks appear in Print Layout view as single dotted lines.

T F 8. You can use the Go To feature to move the insertion point from one section to another.

SHORT ANSWER QUESTIONS

Write the correct answer in the space provided.

1. Which type of page break is automatically adjusted as you key text?

____

2. Which type of section break does not start on a new page?

____

3. What is the term for the last line of a paragraph that appears alone at the top of a page?

____

4. Which option would you apply to a paragraph so it is not divided by a page break?

____

5. Which dialog box and tab would you display to change the vertical alignment of a section?

____

6. Which type of vertical alignment spaces text so the top line aligns with the top margin and the bottom line aligns with the bottom margin?

____

7. Which layout option do you use to begin a document header on the second page and leave the first-page header blank?

____

8. On the Header and Footer toolbar, what is the purpose of the  button?

____

CRITICAL THINKING

Answer these questions on a separate page. There are no right or wrong answers. Support your answers with examples from your own experience, if possible.

1. Describe a situation where you would use a continuous section break.
2. What information do you think most businesses would include in the header or footer of a business report? Would this information differ from the information found in a business letter header or footer?

Lesson Applications

EXERCISE 8-17

Work with page breaks and add page numbers.

1. Open the file **DesertSW**.
2. Delete the page break at the end of page 1.
3. Delete the heading that followed the page break, "Desert Southwest Travel Guide."
4. Using the Format menu, display the Styles and Formatting task pane. Then apply to the following document headings the Word heading styles indicated here:

"The Region"	Heading 1
"Climate" and "History"	Heading 2
"Destinations"	Heading 1
"Parks and Monuments" and "Cities"	Heading 2
"Phoenix," "Flagstaff," "Santa Fe," and *"Albuquerque"*	Heading 3
"Events" and "Transportation/Accommodations"	Heading 1

5. Delete the blank lines before and after the styled headings.
6. Insert page breaks before all four headings styled as Heading 1.

TIP: Use the task pane to select all instances of the Heading 1 text, and then choose the option in the Paragraph dialog box to apply a page break before paragraphs. Include the Keep with next option.

7. Format the first page as follows:
   - Make the first line ("Desert Southwest Travel Guide") 20-point bold, centered, all caps, with 72 points of spacing before the paragraph.
   - Center the five lines of travel agency information.
   - Format the two paragraphs following the travel agency information as 14-point justified with 1.5-line spacing. Insert an extra line before the paragraph starting "One of the most."
8. On pages 9 and 10, make the list of events fit on one page by formatting it as a bulleted list with no blank lines between events. Delete the blank line before the first event ("*Various Dances*").
9. Insert page numbers at the top right, without numbering the first page.
10. Save the document as ***[your initials]*8-17** in your Lesson 8 folder.
11. Print the document 4 sheets per page and then close it.

WORD

EXERCISE 8-18

Work with page breaks and line and page break options, insert section breaks, format sections, and add page numbers.

1. Open the file **Mexico1**. Edit the text on page 1 as shown in Figure 8-20.

FIGURE 8-20

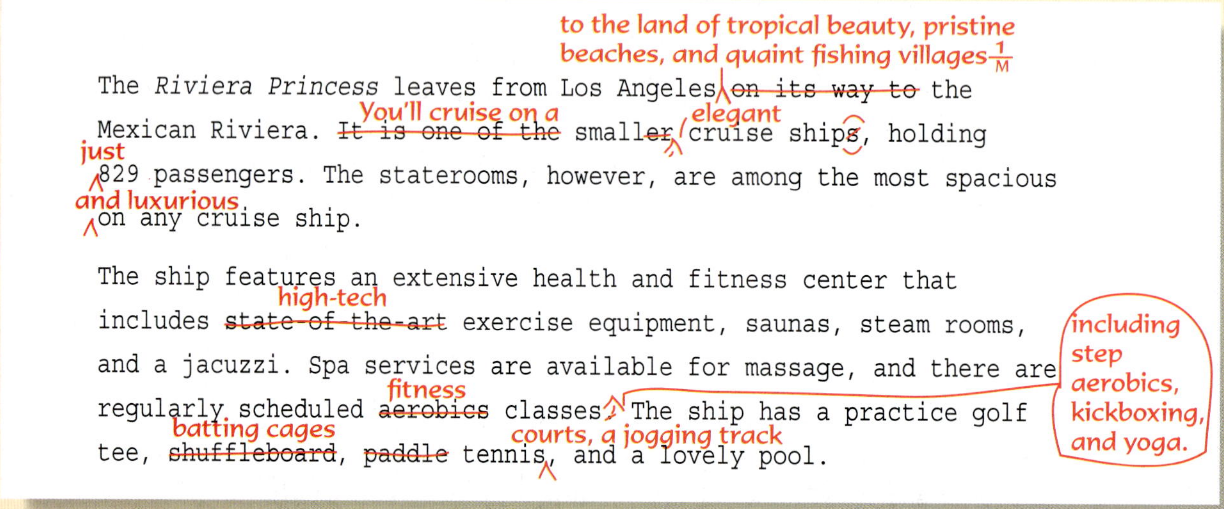
The *Riviera Princess* leaves from Los Angeles on its way to the Mexican Riviera. It is one of the smaller cruise ships, holding 829 passengers. The staterooms, however, are among the most spacious on any cruise ship.

The ship features an extensive health and fitness center that includes state-of-the-art exercise equipment, saunas, steam rooms, and a jacuzzi. Spa services are available for massage, and there are regularly scheduled aerobics classes. The ship has a practice golf tee, shuffleboard, paddle tennis, and a lovely pool.

2. Format the title with 72 points of spacing before the paragraph.

3. Format the paragraph "Sailing dates from Los Angeles are:" so it appears on the same page as the paragraph following it (if it does not already).

4. Insert a hard page break at the bold heading "**Stateroom Locations and Rates**" to start it on a new page.

5. Insert continuous section breaks before "The itinerary is as follows" on page 1 and before the paragraph that begins "Examine the rates in the enclosed brochure." (Tip: Position the insertion point to the left of the text and then insert the section break.)

6. Format this new section (section 2) with 1.75-inch left and right margins.

7. Delete the hard page break before the heading on page 3 and insert a Next Page section break.

8. Change the vertical alignment of the new section (section 4) so it is justified between the top and bottom margins. Delete the blank paragraph mark below the heading.

9. Insert page numbers at the bottom center of all pages including page 1.

10. Check page numbers in Print Layout view. If the last page is not numbered "3," double-click the page number, click the Format Page Number button on the Header and Footer toolbar, and set page numbering to start at 3.

11. View the document in Print Preview to check the pagination.

12. Save the document as ***[your initials]*****8-18** in your Lesson 8 folder.

13. Print and close the document.

EXERCISE 8-19

Work with page and section breaks and insert a footer.

1. Open the file **WestFest1**.

2. Delete the page break at the end of page 1 (the title page) and insert a Next Page section break in its place.

3. Format the title page attractively and center it vertically on the page.

4. Make the bold headings for the four music festivals described in this document ("The Aspen Music Festival," "The Santa Fe Chamber Music Festival," "The Santa Fe Opera," "The San Francisco Jazz Festival") start on a new page, but not as new sections.

5. Check the rest of the document. If a page break separates any heading from the paragraph it introduces, apply the paragraph formatting option to keep the paragraphs together.

6. Create a footer that appears on all pages of the document and contains the following three elements:

[Filename] **Created by [your name]** **Page [page number]**

Use AutoText for the first two elements (the filename and "Created by"). Center-align the second element and right-align the last element.

7. Adjust the center and right tab settings in the footer to accommodate the document's 1-inch left and right margins. (Remember, the default tab settings are designed for a document with 1.25-inch left and right margins.)

8. Format the footer text as 11 points.

9. Save the document as ***[your initials]*****8-19** in your Lesson 8 folder.

10. Print the document 4 pages per sheet and then close it.

EXERCISE 8-20 ✚ *Challenge Yourself*

Create a continuation page header for a business letter.

1. Open the files **Robbins** and **Special3**.

2. Format Robbins as a business letter to the following address. The letter will be from Tom Carey, Senior Travel Counselor.

Ms. Donna Robbins
14 Big Horn Drive NE
Albuquerque, NM 87122

3. After the paragraph that begins "Choose your," start a new paragraph by keying **You might also consider one of Duke City Gateway's special-interest tours:**
4. Switch to the Special3 window. Copy paragraphs 4 through 8 (from "Our local" through "Salzburg") and paste them below the text you just keyed in the letter document. There should be one blank line before and after the pasted text.
5. Format the copied paragraphs with bullets and a 0.5-inch right indent. Leave the blank lines between the bulleted paragraphs.
6. Adjust page setup options for a continuation page header. Change the left and right margins to 1.25 inches.
7. Create a three-line continuation page header that prints on page 2. (Use the correct date format.)
8. Check the document in Print Preview. Save the document as ***[your initials]*8-20** in your Lesson 8 folder.
9. Print the document and close both documents.

On Your Own

In these exercises you work on your own, as you would in a real-life work environment. Use the skills you've learned to accomplish the task—and be creative.

EXERCISE 8-21

Write a short report about your 10 favorite TV shows or movies. Include a document title. Each show or movie should be a separate paragraph with a heading. Adjust page breaks as needed to keep headings with their related paragraphs. Include page numbers and document information (author, filename, date) in a header and/or footer. Save the document as ***[your initials]*8-21** and print it.

EXERCISE 8-22

Write a two-page letter (to a prospective employer, a friend, or whomever). Create your letterhead in the first-page header pane and create a continuation header in the second-page header pane. Save the document as ***[your initials]*8-22** and print it.

EXERCISE 8-23

Research a topic on the Internet that interests you. Copy several paragraphs and assemble the text into a new document at least two pages long. Check pagination. Add appropriate headers and footers and include page numbering. Save the document as ***[your initials]*8-23** and print it.

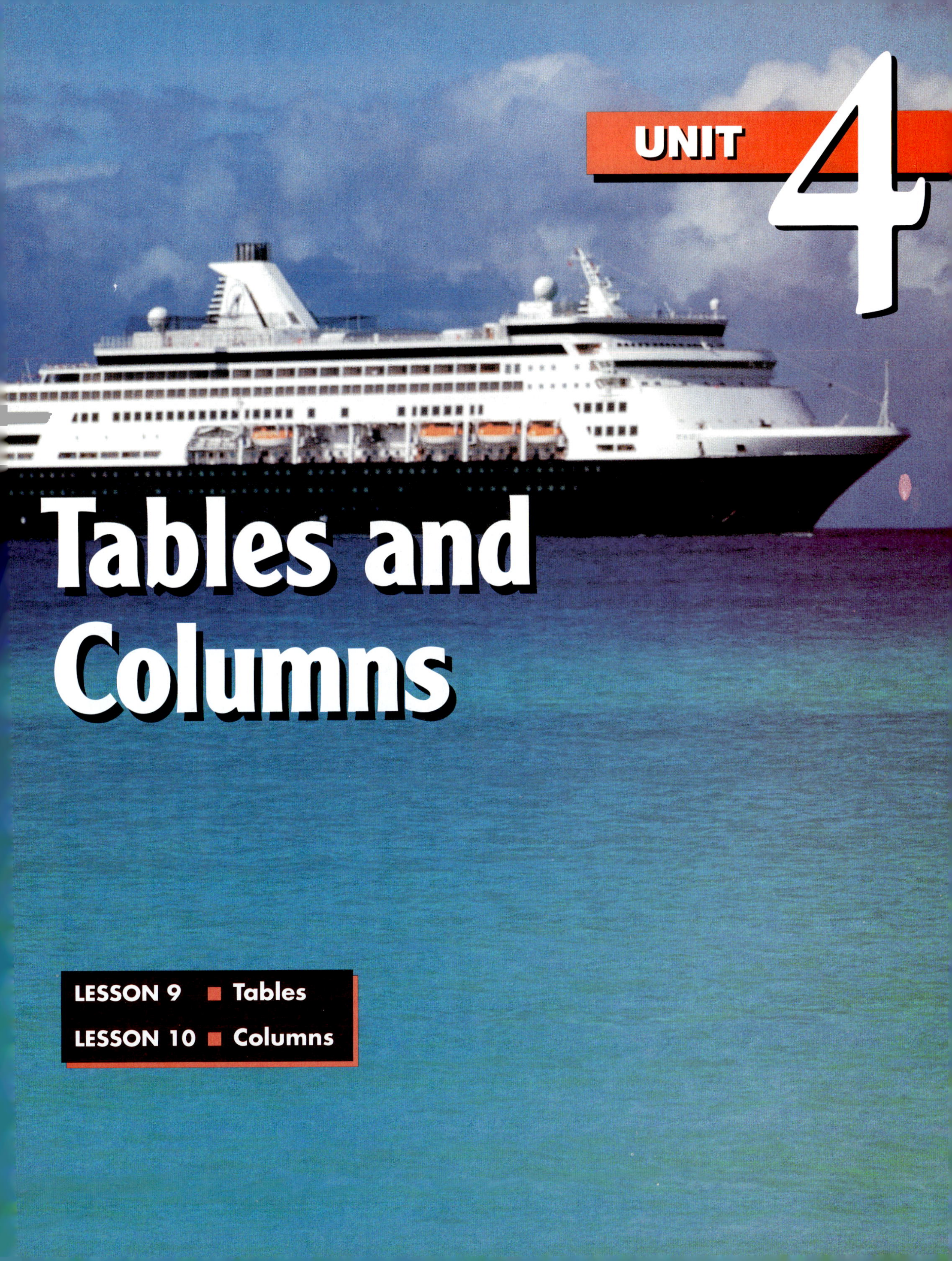

UNIT 4

Tables and Columns

LESSON

9 Tables

OBJECTIVES

MOUS ACTIVITIES
In this lesson:
W2002 3-4
See Appendix E.

After completing this lesson, you will be able to:

1. Create a table.
2. Key and edit text in tables.
3. Select cells, rows, and columns.
4. Edit table structures.
5. Format tables and cell contents.

Estimated Time: 1½ hours

A *table* is a grid of rows and columns that intersect to form *cells*. The lines that mark the cell boundaries are called *gridlines*. It's often easier to read or present information in table format than in paragraph format. Using Word's table feature, you can create a table and insert text, pictures, or another table into the table's cells.

Creating a Table

There are two ways to create a table:

- Insert a table by using the Insert Table dialog box or the Insert Table button on the Standard toolbar.
- Draw a table by using the Tables and Borders toolbar.

FIGURE 9-1
Columns, rows, and cells in a table

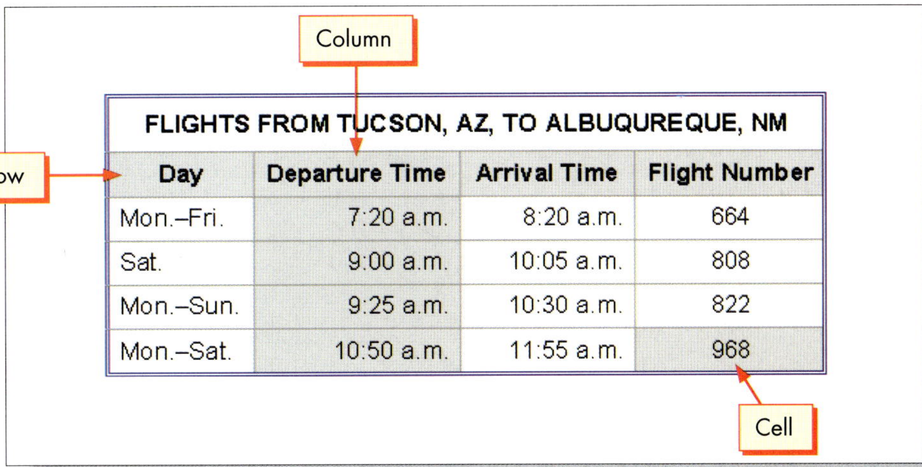

FLIGHTS FROM TUCSON, AZ, TO ALBUQUREQUE, NM			
Day	**Departure Time**	**Arrival Time**	**Flight Number**
Mon.–Fri.	7:20 a.m.	8:20 a.m.	664
Sat.	9:00 a.m.	10:05 a.m.	808
Mon.–Sun.	9:25 a.m.	10:30 a.m.	822
Mon.–Sat.	10:50 a.m.	11:55 a.m.	968

NOTE: You can apply formatting options to tables, such as borders and shading, or display a table with or without gridlines.

EXERCISE 9-1 Insert a Table

Use the Insert Table command to create a table with the number of rows and columns you specify. There are two ways to insert a table:

- Use the Insert Table button on the Standard toolbar to provide an adjustable grid.
- Use the Insert Table dialog box (accessed from the Insert Table button on the Tables and Borders toolbar or by choosing Table, Insert from the menu and Table from the submenu).

1. Open the file **Riding**. Enter today's date in the memo date line.

NOTE: The documents you create in this course relate to the Case Study about Duke City Gateway Travel, a fictional travel agency (see pages 3 through 6).

2. Position the insertion point at the second paragraph mark below the paragraph that begins "Listed below."

3. Click the Insert Table button on the Standard toolbar. A grid containing five columns and four rows appears below the button.
4. Position the pointer in the upper left cell of the grid. Hold down the left mouse button and drag the pointer across to highlight four columns. Then drag the pointer down past the bottom of the grid to highlight five rows. The table dimensions appear below the grid.

FIGURE 9-2
Specifying table dimensions with the table grid

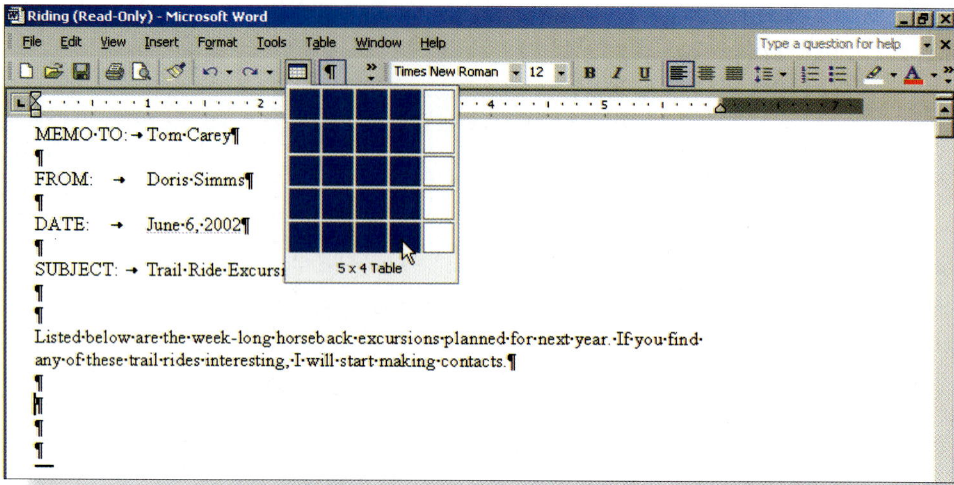

5. Release the mouse button. A 5-row by 4-column table appears, with the insertion point in the first cell. Each column is the same width and the table extends from the left to the right margin. Notice the markers on the ruler that indicate the column widths.

NOTE: When you create a table, each gridline automatically has a ½-point black border that is printed. You can remove borders by opening the Borders and Shading dialog box, displaying the Borders tab, and choosing None under Setting. Gray table gridlines appear on-screen only and not in the printed document.

6. Click the Undo button to undo the table.
7. Choose Insert, Table from the menu; then choose Table from the submenu. The Insert Table dialog box appears.

FIGURE 9-3
Insert Table dialog box

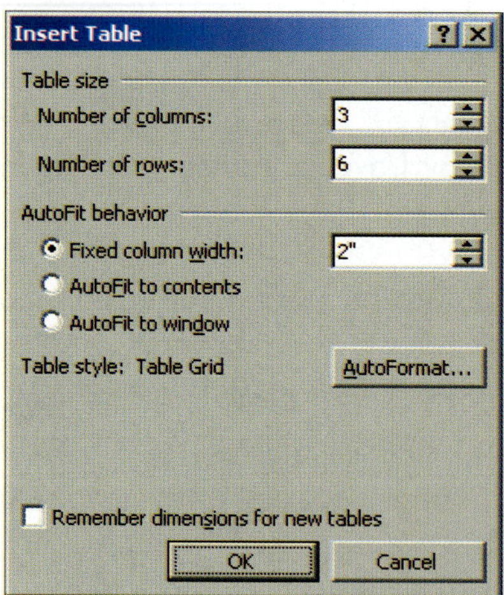

8. Key **3** in the Number of columns text box and **6** in the Number of rows text box. You can also click the up or down arrows to the right of these boxes.
9. In the Fixed column width text box, change the default (Auto) to **2** inches and click OK. Word inserts a 6-row by 3-column table with 2-inch columns. The insertion point is positioned in the first cell and the table is left-aligned.

EXERCISE 9-2 Draw a Table

You can draw a table in your document by using the Tables and Borders toolbar, which you open by using the Tables and Borders button on the Standard toolbar.

1. Click the Tables and Borders button on the Standard toolbar. Word changes to Print Layout view, displays the Tables and Borders toolbar, and changes the pointer to a pencil shape.
2. Position the pencil pointer at the third paragraph mark below the current table. Drag diagonally down to draw a rectangle about the same size as the current table. As you drag, the pointer creates a dotted rectangle. Release the mouse button.

NOTE: You can click the Undo button at any time to undo a drawing action.

3. After drawing the outside border of the table, draw two vertical lines in the table to create three columns (just like in the other table).

FIGURE 9-4
Drawing a table

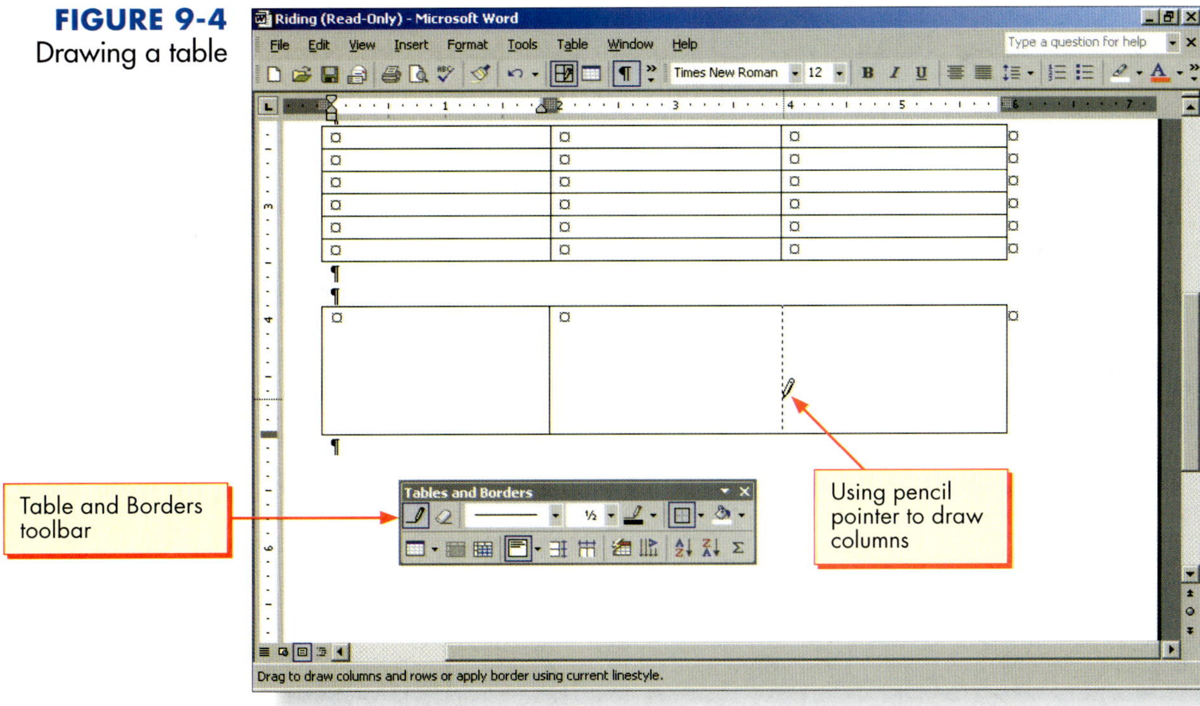

4. Draw two horizontal lines, creating three rows. Don't worry about creating perfectly spaced rows or columns—you'll space them evenly later in the lesson.

FIGURE 9-5
Adding rows

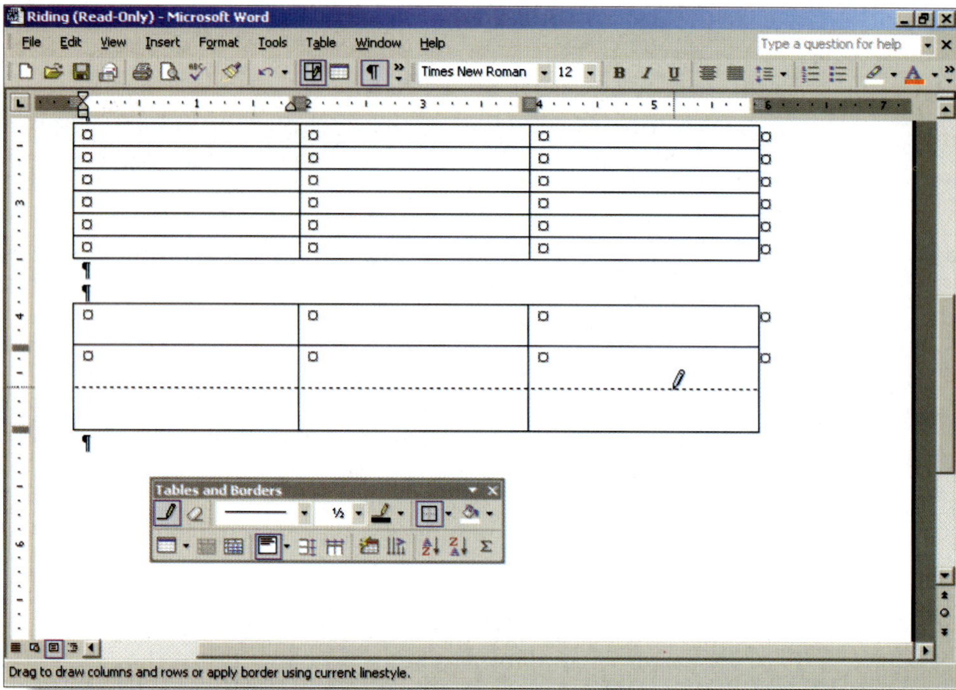

5. Click the Eraser button on the Tables and Borders toolbar and drag the eraser pointer along one of the row or column lines you drew. Release the mouse button.
6. Click the Draw Table button and redraw the line.
7. Press Esc or click the Draw Table button again to restore the normal pointer.
8. Close the Tables and Borders toolbar and switch back to Normal view.

TABLE 9-1 Tables and Borders Toolbar Buttons

BUTTON	PURPOSE
Draw Table	Draw a freehand table
Eraser	Erase table lines
Line Style	Choose a border style

continues

TABLE 9-1 Tables and Borders Toolbar Buttons *continued*

BUTTON	PURPOSE
Line Weight	Choose a border weight
Border Color	Choose a border color
Outside Border	Choose or remove a border
Shading Color	Choose a shading color
Insert Table	Choose to insert a cell, row, column, or table
Merge Cells	Merge two or more cells
Split Cells	Split cells
Align Top Left	Choose to align cell text left, right, top, bottom, and/or centered
Distribute Rows Evenly	Make rows the same height
Distribute Columns Evenly	Make columns the same width
Table AutoFormat	Choose a predefined table format
Change Text Direction	Orient text vertically
Sort Ascending	Sort in ascending order
Sort Descending	Sort in descending order
AutoSum	Calculate the sum of values in cells

NOTE: The Insert Table button functions differently on the Tables and Borders toolbar than on the Standard toolbar. The button on the Tables and Borders toolbar opens the Insert Table dialog box. The button on the Standard toolbar displays the table grid.

Keying and Editing Text in Tables

Keying and editing text in tables is similar to working with text in paragraphs. The Insert and Delete keys work the same way. But if you key text in a cell and press Enter, a new paragraph is created within the same cell.

To move the insertion point to different cells in a table, use the mouse, the Arrow keys, or the following keyboard shortcuts:

TABLE 9-2 Shortcuts for Moving Between Cells

TO MOVE TO	PRESS
Next cell	Tab
Previous cell	Shift + Tab
First cell in the current row	Alt + Home
Last cell in the current row	Alt + End
Top cell in the current column	Alt + PgUp
Last cell in the current column	Alt + PgDn

EXERCISE 9-3 Key and Edit Text in a Table

The first row of a table is often the *header row,* in which each cell contains a heading for the column of text below it.

1. In the first table, position the insertion point in the first cell and key **Name**
2. Press Tab and key **Location** in the next cell. Press Tab and key **Cost (US)**. This is the header row for the table.
3. Press Tab to go to the first cell of the second row and key **Autumn Colored Trails**
4. Press Tab or → to go to the next cell and key **Woodbury Riding Camp**. Go to the next cell and key **1450**

5. Key the text shown in Figure 9-6 in the remaining rows of the table, inserting each phrase or number into a different cell. Remember not to press Enter.

FIGURE 9-6

Spring on the Range	Portland Dude Ranch	1850
Bareback in Winter	Arizona Desert Trails	2100
Texas Summer Trails	Bandera State Park	980
Cowgirls in Saddles	Blanco River Trails	1500

6. Press Alt + Home to move to the first cell in the last row and Shift + Tab to move to the third cell in the previous row. Change "980" to **995**.
7. In the third cell in the first row, key **$** after "US" inside the parentheses.
8. Save the document as ***[your initials]*9-3** in a new folder for Lesson 9. Leave the document open for the next exercise.

Selecting Cells, Rows, and Columns

There are several ways to select the contents of cells, rows, and columns. After you select the contents, you can delete, copy, or move them or change the format.

To help with selection, *end-of-cell markers* (¤) indicate the end of each cell. In addition, *end-of-row markers* (¤) to the right of the gridline of each row indicate the end of each row.

EXERCISE 9-4 Select Cells

¶

1. If your end-of-cell markers are not displayed, click the Show/Hide ¶ button ¶.
2. To select the first cell in the first table, position the pointer just inside the left edge of the cell (between the cell's left border and the letter "N"). When the pointer becomes a solid black right-pointing arrow ➚ , click it to select the cell. (See Figure 9-7 on the next page.)
3. Using the I-beam pointer, drag over the text "1850" in the third row. Notice that the text is highlighted, but the end-of-cell marker is not.
4. Press Tab to move to the next cell. Again, the text in the cell is highlighted, but the end-of-cell marker is not.

FIGURE 9-7
Selecting a cell

Black right-pointing arrow

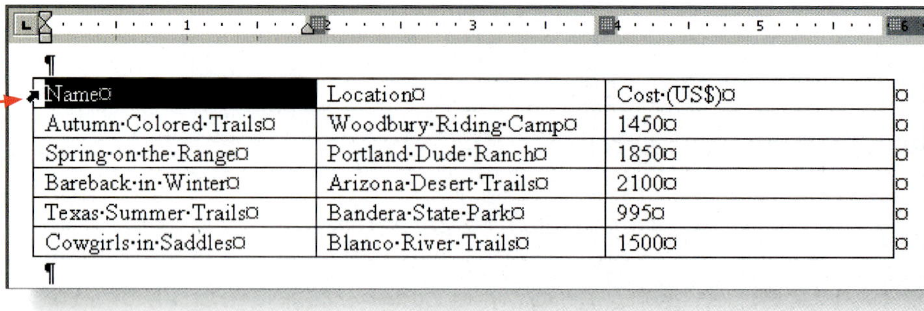

Name¤	Location¤	Cost·(US$)¤
Autumn·Colored·Trails¤	Woodbury·Riding·Camp¤	1450¤
Spring·on·the·Range¤	Portland·Dude·Ranch¤	1850¤
Bareback·in·Winter¤	Arizona·Desert·Trails¤	2100¤
Texas·Summer·Trails¤	Bandera·State·Park¤	995¤
Cowgirls·in·Saddles¤	Blanco·River·Trails¤	1500¤

5. Using the I-beam pointer, triple-click within any cell to select the entire cell (including the end-of-cell marker).

EXERCISE 9-5 Select Rows, Columns, and Tables

1. In the first table, point to the left of the third row. When you see the white right-pointing arrow, click to select the row.

FIGURE 9-8
Selecting a row

White right-pointing arrow

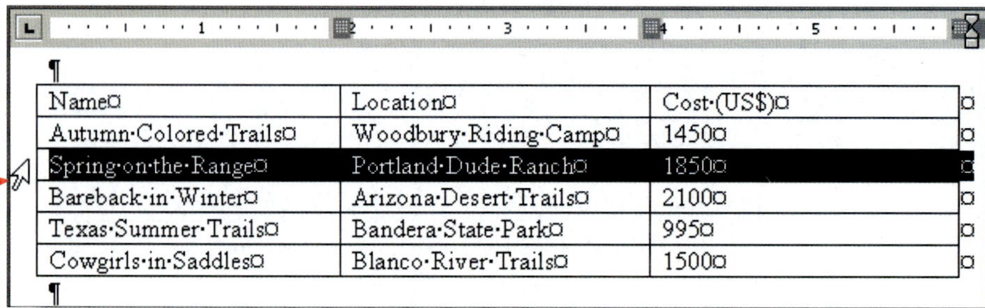

Name¤	Location¤	Cost·(US$)¤
Autumn·Colored·Trails¤	Woodbury·Riding·Camp¤	1450¤
Spring·on·the·Range¤	Portland·Dude·Ranch¤	1850¤
Bareback·in·Winter¤	Arizona·Desert·Trails¤	2100¤
Texas·Summer·Trails¤	Bandera·State·Park¤	995¤
Cowgirls·in·Saddles¤	Blanco·River·Trails¤	1500¤

2. Point just inside the left border of any cell in the previous row and double-click. That row is selected.
3. Position the insertion point anywhere in "Arizona" (in the fourth row). Choose Table, Select, Row from the menu. The fourth row is selected.
4. Point to the left of the third row and drag the pointer down one row to select both the third and fourth rows.
5. Point to the top border of the third column. When the pointer changes to a solid black down arrow ⬇, click to select the column. (See Figure 9-9 on the next page.)
6. Position the insertion point before "Location" in the second column. Drag down through "Blanco River Trails" to select column two.
7. Press and hold down Alt while you click in column 1. The column is selected.

FIGURE 9-9
Selecting a column

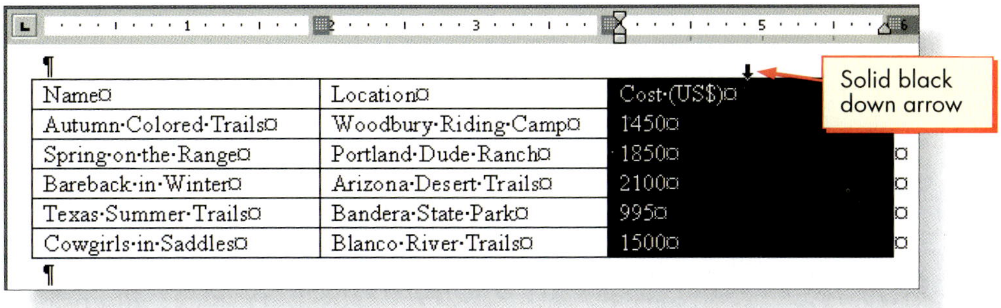

8. Point to the top of column two and drag the black arrow pointer across to select columns two and three. Deselect the columns.
9. Position the insertion point anywhere in the table. Choose Table, Select, Table from the menu to select the entire table. Click anywhere in the table to deselect it.
10. Switch to Print Layout view. Scroll until you can see the top of the first table.
11. Move the I-beam over the table until the table move handle appears at the top left of the table.
12. Move the I-beam over the handle. When the I-beam changes to a four-headed arrow pointer, click to select the table.
13. Click anywhere in the table to deselect it. Return to Normal view.

NOTE: Another way to select a table is to position the insertion point anywhere in the table, turn off Num Lock on the keyboard, and press Alt + 5 on the numeric keypad.

TABLE 9-3 Selecting Table Elements

TO SELECT	MOUSE	MENU	KEYBOARD
Cell	Click left inside edge of cell	Table, Select, Cell	Shift + End
Row	Click to the left of the row *or* double-click left inside edge of a cell	Table, Select, Row	
Column	Click column's top border	Table, Select, Column	Alt + click in column
Table	Click table move handle in Print Layout view	Table, Select, Table	Alt + 5 (numeric keypad)

TIP: To extend a selection in a table (row, column, or cell), hold down Shift while pressing an arrow key. You can also hold down Shift while clicking another location in the table.

Editing Table Structures

In addition to editing the contents of a table, you can edit a table's structure to add, delete, move, and copy cells, rows, and columns. You can also merge and split cells or change a table's position or dimensions.

To modify tables, use the Standard toolbar, the Tables and Borders toolbar, or the shortcut menu.

EXERCISE 9-6 Insert Cells, Rows, and Columns

1. Display the Tables and Borders toolbar by opening the View menu and choosing Toolbars, Tables and Borders. Notice that Word remains in Normal view when you open the toolbar this way.

2. Position the insertion point anywhere in the first table. Notice that both toolbars show the Insert Table button.
3. In the first table, select the first cell in the first row. Notice that the Insert Table button on the Standard toolbar changes to the Insert Cells button.

NOTE: The Insert Table button on the Standard toolbar changes to an Insert button for cells, rows, or columns, depending on what you select in the table.

4. On the Tables and Borders toolbar, click the down arrow to the right of the Insert Table button and choose Insert Cells from the drop-down list. The Insert Cells dialog box opens.

FIGURE 9-10
Insert Cells dialog box

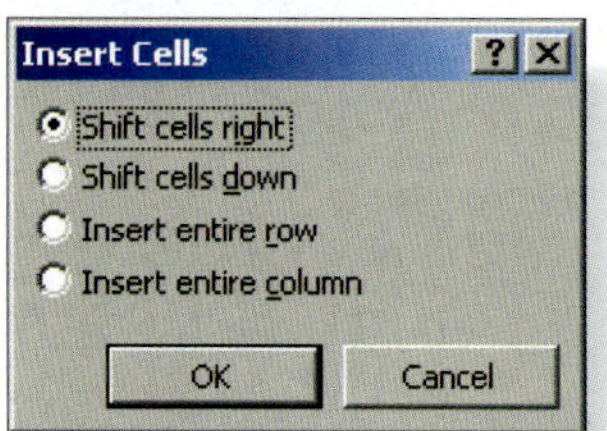

5. Click Shift cells right and click OK. Word inserts a new cell and shifts the other cells in row one to the right. Notice that the Insert Cells button replaced the Insert Table button on the Tables and Borders toolbar.
6. Click the Undo button to delete the new cell.

NOTE: The Insert Table button on the Tables and Borders toolbar changes to reflect the last item you inserted from the button's drop-down list.

7. Drag the insertion point from "Autumn Colored Trails" through "Portland Dude Ranch" in the second column. Click the Insert Cells button on the Standard toolbar.

8. Click Shift cells down and then click OK. Four new cells appear above these cells.

NOTE: The number of selected cells (or rows or columns) determines the number of cells (or rows or columns) inserted.

9. Select the first row. Click the Insert Rows button on the Standard toolbar. A new row appears at the top of the table.

10. Select the second row. Click the down arrow to the right of the Insert Cells button on the Tables and Borders toolbar and choose Insert Rows Below from the drop-down list. A new row appears below the selected row.

11. Click the Undo button to delete the new row.

NOTE: When you use the Insert Rows button on the Standard toolbar, the new row is automatically placed above the selected row. You can choose where you want your row inserted (above or below the selected row) by choosing Insert Rows Above or Insert Rows Below from the Tables and Borders toolbar (or by choosing Table, Insert from the menu).

12. Move the insertion point to the left of the paragraph mark below the first table. Click the Insert Rows button on the Standard toolbar.

13. In the Insert Rows dialog box, key **2** in the Number of rows text box and click OK. Two more rows are added to the table.

TIP: When the insertion point is in the last cell of the last row, pressing Tab inserts a row below the current last row.

14. Select the second column of the first table. Click the Insert Columns button on the Standard toolbar. The new column appears to the left of the selected column.

15. Select the third column. Click the down arrow to the right of the Insert Rows Below button on the Tables and Borders toolbar. Choose Insert Columns to the Right from the drop-down list. A new column appears to the right of the selected column.

16. Click the Undo button to delete the new column.

NOTE: When you use the Insert Columns button on the Standard toolbar, the new column is automatically placed to the left of the selected column. You can insert a column to the right by choosing Insert Columns to the Right from the Tables and Borders toolbar (or by choosing Table, Insert from the menu).

17. Close the Tables and Borders toolbar.

TIP: When just the end-of-row markers are selected, you can click the Insert Columns button to extend the table to the right.

EXERCISE 9-7 Delete Cells, Rows, and Columns

1. In the first table, select the blank cells in the third and fourth rows. Open the Table menu and choose Delete, Cells. The Delete Cells dialog box opens.
2. Click Shift cells up. Click OK and the cells disappear.

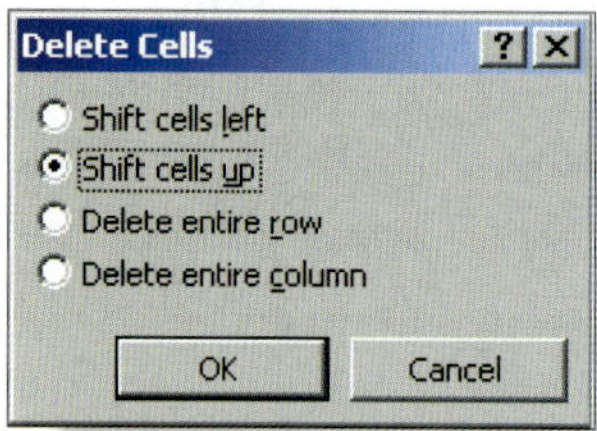

FIGURE 9-11 Delete Cells dialog box

3. Select the blank rows at the bottom of the first table. Open the Table menu and choose Delete, Rows. The rows are deleted.
4. Select the second column (which should be blank). Right-click the column and choose Delete Columns from the shortcut menu. Your table should now have only the top row blank.
5. Save the document as ***[your initials]*9-7** in your Lesson 9 folder.

NOTE: Earlier the columns were resized automatically to fit in the table and some of the text wrapped. The columns do not automatically resize when the blank column is deleted, so some text remains wrapped.

EXERCISE 9-8 Move and Copy Cells, Rows, and Columns

In addition to using toolbar buttons and the shortcut menu, you can also use keyboard shortcuts to cut, copy, or paste.

1. Select the row that begins "Name."
2. Point to the first selected cell in the row. When you see a left-pointing arrow, drag and drop the selection into the empty row above. The text now appears in the first row.
3. Select the row that begins "Spring on the Range," but not its end-of-row marker.

4. Click the Cut button. The text is deleted, but the empty row remains.
5. Position the insertion point in the first cell of the second row. Press Ctrl+V to paste the text.
6. Select the bottom three cells in the third column and copy them to the Clipboard.
7. Click within the cell containing "Arizona Desert Trails" and paste the text. The pasted cells overwrite the previous text.

8. Undo the paste.
9. Select only the text in the first three rows (not the end-of-row markers) and cut the text.
10. Click in the first cell in the second row and paste the text. Your table should have the top row blank with the "Autumn Colored Trails" row below the "Spring on the Range" row.

NOTE: If you paste text somewhere on the table where there is not enough room for all the cells, Word adds additional columns or rows to accommodate the text.

EXERCISE 9-9 Merge and Split Cells

1. Select the first row. Open the Table menu and choose Merge Cells. Deselect the row. The cells in the row are merged into a single cell.
2. In the first row, key the table title **Trail Ride Excursions**
3. With the insertion point in the merged cell, right-click the first row and choose Split Cells from the shortcut menu. The Split Cells dialog box appears.
4. Key **3** in the Number of columns text box and click OK. The row is split into three cells again and the title text wraps in the first cell.

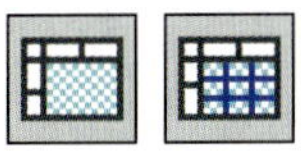

TIP: You can also merge and split cells by using the Merge Cells button and the Split Cells button on the Tables and Borders toolbar.

5. Display the Tables and Borders toolbar by using the button on the Standard toolbar. Change to Normal view.
6. With the first row selected in the table, click the Merge Cells button on the toolbar to merge back to a single cell.

EXERCISE 9-10 Change Table Dimensions and Position Tables

You can adjust and position a table in the following ways:

- Change the width of columns, the space between columns, and the height of rows.
- Use AutoFit to change the width of a column to fit the longest text.
- Indent a table or center it horizontally on the page.

1. Select the second table (position the insertion point in any cell and then, with Num Lock turned off, press Alt + 5 on the numeric keypad).

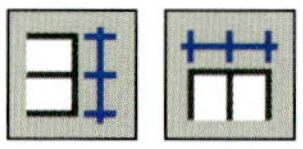

2. Using the Tables and Borders toolbar, click the Distribute Rows Evenly button; then click the Distribute Columns Evenly button. The hand-drawn rows and columns are now evenly spaced.
3. Select the first table. Open the Table menu and choose Table Properties. Click the Row tab.
4. Click Specify height and set the text box to **0.4** inches. Make sure the Row height is box is set to At least.

NOTE: You can use the Column tab in the Table Properties dialog box to specify column width and the Cell tab to specify cell width.

FIGURE 9-12
Table Properties dialog box

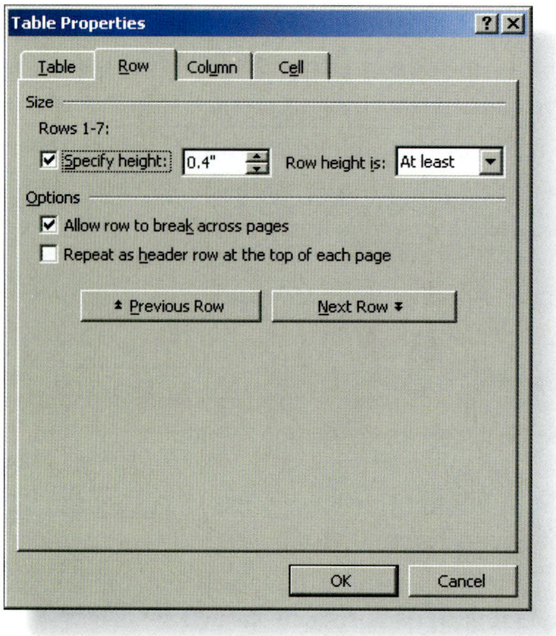

5. Click the Table tab in the Table Properties dialog box. Under Alignment, choose Center and click OK. The table is centered horizontally on the page and the row heights are taller.

TIP: When a table appears on a page by itself, center it vertically and horizontally. Use the Layout tab in the Page Setup dialog box to choose vertical alignment.

6. Deselect the table. Make sure the ruler is displayed.
7. Position the pointer on the right border of the last column until it changes to a vertical double bar for resizing ◂||▸.

FIGURE 9-13
Dragging a table border

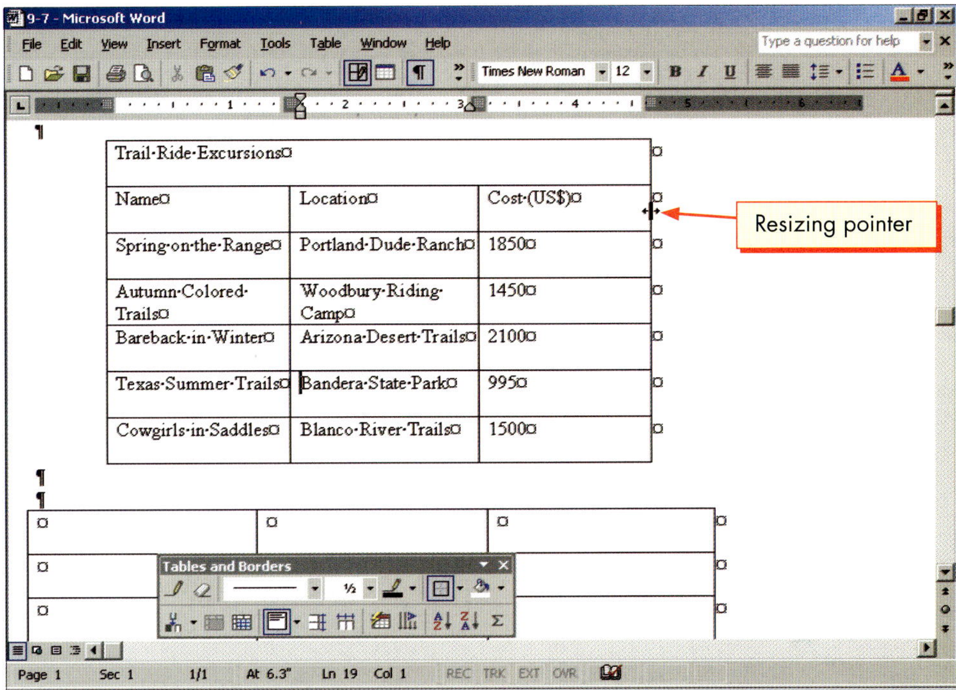

8. Drag the border one-half inch to the right to widen the column. (Hold down Alt as you drag to see the exact ruler measurements.)
9. Click the Undo button and position the pointer on the right border of the cell containing "Woodbury Riding Camp." Drag one-half inch to the right. The second column is wider but the last column is now narrower.

NOTE: As long as the cell is not selected, dragging the right border adjusts the entire column width, not just the cell width.

10. Click the Undo button. Hold down Shift and drag the second column border one-half inch to the right again. The second column is now wider and the last column remains the same width.
11. Click the Undo button. Double-click the right border of the second column (making sure the pointer is the vertical double-bar resizing pointer ✢). The column is adjusted to the width of the widest cell entry.

TIP: You can simultaneously adjust all the columns to fit the width of each column's widest cell entry by choosing AutoFit from the Table menu and AutoFit to Contents from the submenu.

12. Click anywhere in the first table except in the first row. If the Tables and Borders toolbar is obscuring the table, move it to the bottom of the screen.

13. On the ruler, point to the right column marker for the second column. When you see the ScreenTip "Move Table Column," drag the marker a short distance to the right. Release the mouse button.

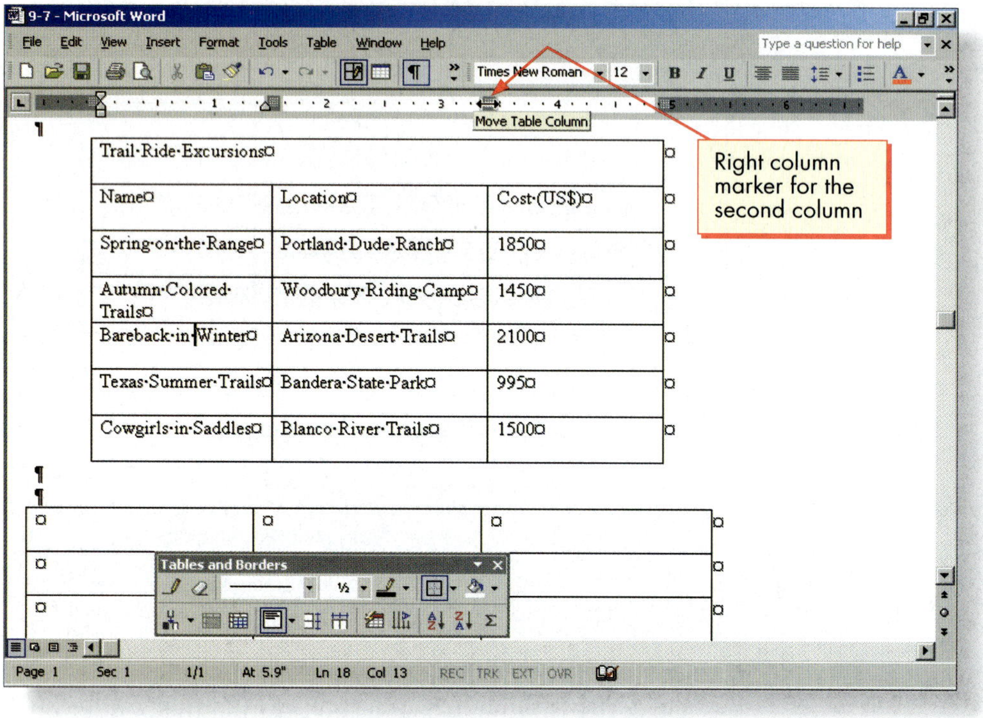

FIGURE 9-14
Dragging a column marker

14. Hold down Alt and drag the marker until the ruler measurement for the second column is 1.75 inches.

NOTE: This technique is similar to dragging margin borders in Print Layout view or Print Preview.

15. Use the same technique to adjust the first column width to 1.75 inches and the third column width to 1 inch. The merged row adjusts to the new table width.

16. Save the document as ***[your initials]*9-10** in your Lesson 9 folder.

17. Select the first table and print the selection. Leave the document open.

NOTE: The ruler measures column width by the actual space for text within the cells. The Table Properties dialog box (Preferred width text box) includes the left and right cell margins, which are .08 inch by default. Thus, 1-inch wide columns set by using the ruler appear as 1.16-inch wide in the dialog box.

Formatting Tables and Cell Contents

There are many ways to make a table more attractive and easier to read. For example, you can:

- Format table text.
- Align text within columns horizontally and align text within cells or rows vertically.
- Apply borders and shading.
- Use Table AutoFormat to apply a predesigned table style.
- Change the direction of text from horizontal to vertical.
- Sort table text.

EXERCISE 9-11 Align and Sort Table Text

The default alignment of text in a table is the upper left of a cell. You can change the vertical alignment (top, center, or bottom) and the horizontal alignment (left, center, or right) by using the alignment buttons on the Tables and Borders toolbar.

Sorting is another important table feature. You can sort a single column, selected rows, or an entire table in either ascending order (A–Z or lowest to highest number) or descending order (Z–A or highest to lowest number).

1. Select the table title in the first row of the first table and format it as bold, 14-point, all caps.
2. Select row 2 and make the text bold.
3. Select "Location" and the cells below it. Click the down arrow next to the Align Top Left button on the Tables and Borders toolbar to display a menu of alignment buttons.
4. Click the Align Center Left button to left-align and center the text vertically in the selected cells. Notice the Align Center Left button now appears on the Tables and Borders toolbar.
5. Click within the title in the first row. Click the down arrow next to the Align Center Left button and then click the Align Center button to center the text horizontally and vertically.
6. Select "Cost (US$)" and the cells below it. Click the down arrow next to the Align Center button.
7. Click the Align Center Right button to right-align the text and vertically center it within the selected cells.
8. Select "Name" and the cells below it. Click the down arrow next to the Align Center Right button.

W O R D

9. Click the Align Center Left button to left-align the text and vertically center it within the selected cells.

TIP: To change the vertical alignment of a large group of cells without affecting the horizontal alignments (left, right, and center) in each cell, choose Table Properties from the Table menu. Click the Cell tab. Under Vertical alignment, click the Center button to vertically center the text in every cell.

10. Select rows 3 (the text below the header row) through 7 of the first table.
11. Choose Table, Sort from the menu. Choose Column 1 from the Sort by drop-down list, choose Text from the Type drop-down list, and click Ascending.
12. Click OK. The rows are sorted alphabetically in ascending order by the column 1 text.

TIP: You can use the Table, Sort menu command to sort selected text that is not in a table, such as a bulleted list.

EXERCISE 9-12 Apply Borders and Shading

1. Select the first row (the title). On the Tables and Borders toolbar, click the arrow next to the Shading Color button and choose Pale Blue from the drop-down palette (the sixth color in the last row).
2. Select the entire table.
3. Use the Line Style and the Line Weight drop-down lists on the Tables and Borders toolbar to set a 1½-point single-line border.
4. Click the Outside Border button to make the line changes to the outside border. Click within the table to deselect it and view the borders. Notice that Word has changed to Print Layout view.
5. Click the arrow beside the Border Color button and choose Blue from the palette.
6. With the pencil pointer activated, drag it over each outside border of the table one at a time and then over the bottom border of the first row. (See Figure 9-15 on the next page.)
7. Click the Draw Table button or press Esc to restore the normal pointer.

NOTE: You can apply formats to tables by using the Borders and Shading dialog box. (From the Format menu, choose Borders and Shading.) You can apply the changes to a cell or to the entire table.

FIGURE 9-15
Drawing a border

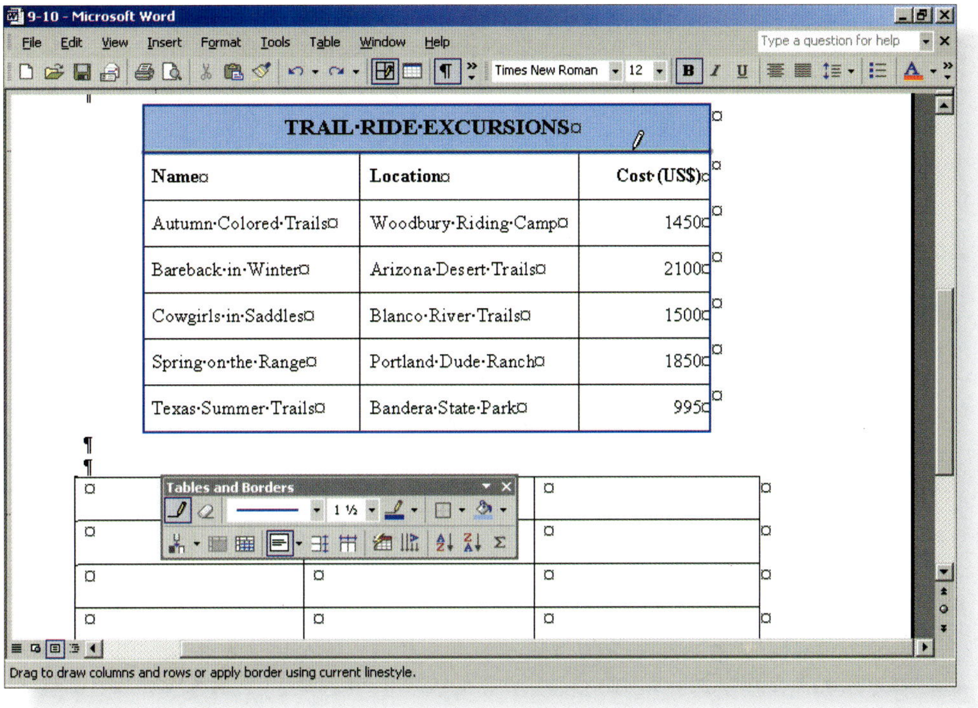

EXERCISE 9-13 Use Table AutoFormat

The Table AutoFormat feature enables you to quickly apply a professional design to a table by using one of Word's built-in table formats.

1. Select the text in rows 2 through 4 (from "Name" through "2100") but not the end-of-row markers. Copy the selected text to the Clipboard.
2. Click the first cell in the blank table and paste the copied text.

3. On the Tables and Borders toolbar, click the Table AutoFormat button.
4. Click the various AutoFormats in the Table styles list box and view the effect in the Preview box. (See Figure 9-16 on the next page.)
5. Choose the Table Grid 8 format and click Heading rows under Apply special formats to.
6. Click Apply to apply the format.
7. Select the second table, including the blank paragraph marks above and below it, and press Delete.

NOTE: You can use Delete to delete a table if you include other text or paragraph marks in the selection. If you select just a table, you can delete it with Backspace or the menu command Table, Delete, Table.

FIGURE 9-16
Applying a Table AutoFormat

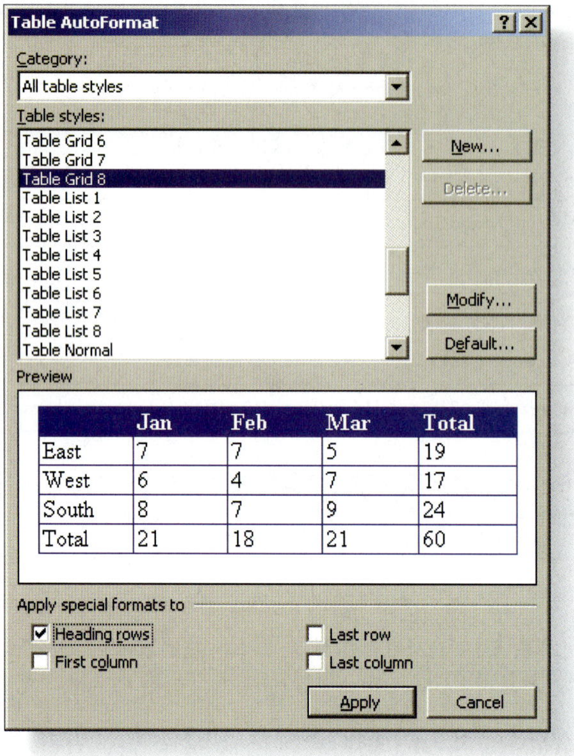

8. Add your reference initials on a second blank line below the table.
9. Save the document as ***[your initials]*9-13** in a new Lesson 9 folder.
10. Print and close the document.

EXERCISE 9-14 Change Text Direction

In addition to changing the alignment of text in a table cell, you can also change the text orientation so the text is displayed vertically or horizontally.

1. Start a new document. Use the Insert Table button to insert a table with 2 columns and 8 rows.
2. In the first cell of the first row, key **Hotel Rates (US$)**. Press Tab and key **Converted Rates (Marks)**. Format both headings as bold.
3. Key **100** in the first cell of the second row. Press Tab and key **211.60**. Key the data shown in Figure 9-17 (on the next page) into the remaining table cells.

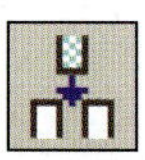

4. Select the first column and click the Insert Columns button on the Standard toolbar.

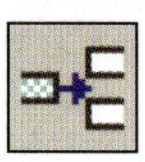

5. Select the first row and click the Insert Rows button on the Standard toolbar.

FIGURE 9-17

150	317.40
200	423.20
600	1,269.60
800	1,692.80
1,000	2,116.00
1,500	3,174.00

6. Position the insertion point in the first cell of the second row. Key **Nightly** in bold. Position the insertion point in the first cell of the sixth row. Key **Weekly** and format it as bold.

7. Select the table and format all text as 14 points. Make sure the Tables and Borders toolbar is displayed.

8. Select the cell containing "Nightly" and the three blank cells below it. Merge the cells by clicking the Merge Cells button  on the Table and Borders toolbar.

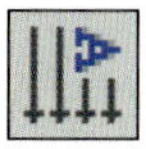

9. With the insertion point in the merged cell, click the Change Text Direction button  on the Tables and Borders toolbar to rotate "Nightly" until it reads from top to bottom. Click the button again so "Nightly" reads from bottom to top.

NOTE: If you are in Normal view when you rotate text, Word changes to Print Layout view.

10. Select the cell containing "Weekly" through the last cell of the first column. Merge the cells.

11. With the merged cell selected, rotate the text until "Weekly" reads from bottom to top.

12. Merge the cells in the first row and key the title **German Hotel Rates** in the merged row. Format the title as 16-point bold, all caps.

13. Select the entire table. Use the Table menu to open the Table Properties dialog box. Click the Row tab and set the row height to **0.5** inch Exactly.

14. Click the Table tab and choose Center alignment to horizontally center the table on the document page. Click OK.

15. With the table still selected, choose Table, AutoFit, AutoFit to Contents from the menu to change all column widths to be as wide as the longest text in the column.

NOTE: When a table has a title, AutoFit changes the title's column to fit the length of the title. Columns under a title might not AutoFit to the width of the widest text in those cells because of the width of the title.

16. With the table still selected, click the down arrow next to the Align button on the Tables and Borders toolbar. Click the Align Center button to vertically and horizontally center all text.

17. Select only the cells containing numbers and right-align them, using the Formatting toolbar.

18. Apply a shading color to the first row and to the cells that contain "Hotel Rates (US$)," "Converted Rates (Marks)," "Nightly," and "Weekly."

19. Select the table again. Using the Tables and Borders toolbar, change the line style to double, choose a border color, and set the line weight to 3/4 point. Apply the border to the outside of the table.

20. Draw the same style border to separate the Weekly and Nightly sections of the table.

FIGURE 9-18
Table with rotated text

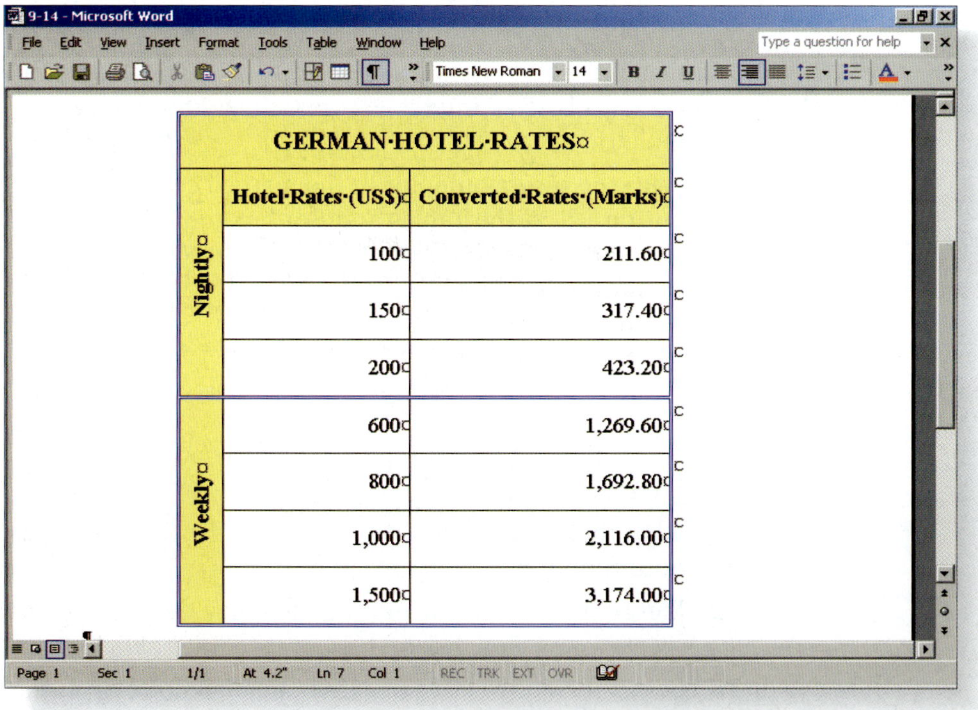

GERMAN HOTEL RATES		
	Hotel Rates (US$)	Converted Rates (Marks)
Nightly	100	211.60
	150	317.40
	200	423.20
Weekly	600	1,269.60
	800	1,692.80
	1,000	2,116.00
	1,500	3,174.00

21. Open the Page Setup dialog box, Layout tab. Center-align the document vertically and click OK.

22. Save the document as ***[your initials]*****9-14** in your Lesson 9 folder. Print and close the document.

LESSON 9 Summary

- Word tables help to present information in an easy-to-read format. Rows and columns intersect to form cells; gridlines mark cell boundaries.
- Insert a table by using the Insert Table dialog box or by drawing the table with the pencil pointer.
- The Tables and Borders toolbar offers a wide variety of options for formatting table text and modifying table structures. See Table 9-1.
- Navigate between table cells for keying or editing text by using keyboard shortcuts. See Table 9-2.
- Use one of several methods for selecting cells, rows, columns, and tables. See Table 9-3.
- Modify the structure of a table by inserting or deleting cells, rows, or columns. Move and copy cells, rows, and columns by using cut and paste, copy and paste, and drag and drop.
- Merge two or more cells into one cell; split a merged cell into multiple cells.
- Change table dimensions and table position by using the Table Properties dialog box. Drag column borders to change column width or double-click a column border to AutoFit text.
- Format table text by changing the vertical or horizontal alignment within a cell. Use the Align buttons on the Tables and Borders toolbar.
- Sort the table text in ascending or descending order. For example, alphabetize the rows below the table heading by the first column.
- Make tables more attractive by applying border and shading options from the Tables and Borders toolbar.
- Apply one of Word's built-in table formats by using the Table AutoFormat feature from the Tables and Borders toolbar.
- Change the text orientation of a table cell so the text is displayed vertically or horizontally.

LESSON 9 Command Summary

FEATURE	BUTTON	MENU	KEYBOARD	SPEECH?
Insert table		Table, Insert, Table		✓
Draw table		Table, Draw Table		✓
Insert cells		Table, Insert, Cells		✓
Insert rows above		Table, Insert, Rows Above		✓
Insert rows below		Table, Insert, Rows Below		✓
Insert columns to left		Table, Insert, Columns to the Left		✓
Insert columns to right		Table, Insert, Columns to the Right		✓
Delete cells		Table, Delete, Cells		✓
Delete rows		Table, Delete, Rows		✓
Delete columns		Table, Delete, Columns		✓
Delete table		Table, Delete, Table	Backspace	✓
Merge cells		Table, Merge Cells		✓
Split cells		Table, Split Cells		✓
Distribute rows evenly		Table, AutoFit, Distribute Rows Evenly		✓
Distribute columns evenly		Table, AutoFit, Distribute Columns Evenly		✓
Sort text	or	Table, Sort		✓
Table AutoFormat		Table, Table AutoFormat		✓
Change text direction				✓

Concepts Review

TRUE/FALSE QUESTIONS

Each of the following statements is either true or false. Indicate your choice by circling T or F.

T F **1.** To split a merged cell, delete all text in the merged cell.

T F **2.** To move to the top cell in the current column, press Alt + PgDn.

T F **3.** You can use the Table AutoFormat dialog box to apply formats to existing tables.

T F **4.** You can apply shading from the Tables and Borders toolbar.

T F **5.** After inserting a cell, row, or column in a table, the Insert Table button  on the Tables and Borders toolbar becomes a button for the last inserted item.

T F **6.** You can insert a table from the Standard toolbar.

T F **7.** By default, when you insert a table, it has borders that will be printed.

T F **8.** You press Alt + 7 to select a table.

SHORT ANSWER QUESTIONS

Write the correct answer in the space provided.

1. What would the button  do to selected cells in a table?

____

2. Which keyboard shortcut moves the insertion point to the previous cell?

____

3. Which nonprinting character marks the end of a cell?

____

4. What is the button  used for?

____

5. What are the nonprinting lines called that mark the boundaries of cells?

____

6. Which button on the Tables and Borders toolbar do you use to delete a line you drew?

____

7. Which table element can you select when the pointer appears as  ?

____

8. Which dialog box do you use to change column width?

____

CRITICAL THINKING

Answer these questions on a separate page. There are no right or wrong answers. Support your answers with examples from your own experience, if possible.

1. Review the table formats in the Table AutoFormat dialog box. Which table formats would you be most likely to use on a day-to-day basis? Which seem more useful in a business setting?
2. You learned how to insert a table automatically and draw a table manually. What are the benefits of each method? Which do you prefer?

Lesson Applications

EXERCISE 9-15

Create a table, enter text in the table, and edit and format the table.

1. Start a new document.
2. Create a table with nine rows and four columns.
3. Key the text shown in Figure 9-19 in the table, leaving the first cell blank. For convenience, after you key the first set of months, copy the text to the cells at the bottom of the column.

FIGURE 9-19

	Month	High	Low
Santa Fe	January	40	18
	April	59	35
	July	82	56
	October	62	38
Taos	January	40	10
	April	53	21
	July	87	50
	October	67	32

4. Merge the cell that contains "Santa Fe" with the three blank cells below it. Do the same for the cell that contains "Taos" and the blank cells below it.
5. Change the entire table to 16-point Arial and the row height to at least 0.45 inch.
6. Center the table text vertically within the cells.
7. Use the column markers or column borders to adjust the second column to 1.25 inches wide, and the third and fourth columns to 1 inch wide.
8. Change the text direction of "Santa Fe" so it reads from the bottom to the top of the cell. Format the text as 26-point bold. Format "Taos" the same way.
9. Change the first column to 0.75 inch wide.

10. Center-align the text in columns one, three, and four.
11. Insert a new row at the top of the table, merge the cells, and key the title **Average Temperatures** in 24-point bold small caps.
12. Change the font color of the second row to white. Apply black shading to the row.
13. Apply 20% gray shading to the first row.
14. Add a ½-point, double-line black outside border to the table.
15. Center the table vertically and horizontally on the page.
16. Save the document as ***[your initials]*9-15** in your Lesson 9 folder.
17. Print and close the document.

EXERCISE 9-16

Edit and format a table.

1. Open the file **Itin3**.
2. On page 1 in the one-column table, set the column width to 3 inches.
3. Insert a 0.75-inch-wide column to the left of the column.
4. Move the text "Day 1" to the first cell in the new column. Move all the remaining day numbers to the appropriate cell in the new column.
5. Delete all the text below the table. Above the table, delete the text from "Travel to the Southwest via bus" through "Las Vegas."
6. Insert a new row at the top of the table and merge the cells in the row.
7. Cut the bold title (but not its paragraph mark) that is just above the table and paste it into the first row. There should be a total of two blank lines above the table.
8. Apply the AutoFormat Table Grid 4 to the table, removing the special formats for the last row and the last column.
9. Adjust the second column to 5.25 inches wide.
10. Format the text in each cell in column 2 as a bulleted list, using the standard bullet character. Customize the bulleted text by changing the bullet position to 0 inch and changing the text position (tab space after and indent) to 0.15 inch.
11. In each bulleted paragraph, make each sentence a separate bulleted item.
12. Format the table title with 6 points of spacing before and after it.
13. Set a 2-inch top margin and 1.25-inch left and right margins.
14. Format the document title as 14-point bold small caps and centered.
15. Save the document as ***[your initials]*9-16** in your Lesson 9 folder.
16. Print and close the document.

EXERCISE 9-17

Create a table, and edit and format the table.

1. Start a new document and change the page to landscape orientation.
2. Insert a table with five rows and six columns, and key the text shown in Figure 9-20 into the cells. Note that "3/4" should not appear as a fraction, but as two regular numbers with a slash between them.

FIGURE 9-20

Monday	Tuesday	Wednesday	Thursday	Friday	Sat./Sun.
			1	2	3/4
5	6	7	8	9	10/11
12	13	14	15	16	17/18
19	20	21	22	23	24/25

3. Add a sixth row to the table and key **26**, **27**, **28**, **29**, and **30**, beginning with the first cell.
4. Change each column to 1.2 inches wide.
5. Change the weekday headings in the top row to 16-point bold italic. Change the top row height to at least 0.4 inch, and center the text horizontally and vertically.
6. In the cell for the 6th, key **RSVP for Red Rock Ranch Trip** as a new paragraph below the date.
7. In the cell for the 1st, key **Mail travel documents for Vegas** as a new paragraph below the date.
8. In the cell for the 19th, key **Noon visit with regional managers** as a new paragraph below the date.
9. Key **Staff meeting** below the date in the cells for the 16th and the 30th.
10. Change the row height for rows 2 through 6 to exactly 0.9 inch.
11. Insert a new first column, merge the cells in the column, and key **JUNE**
12. Change the text direction of "JUNE" so it reads from the bottom to the top of the column. Change the font size to 72 points and the column width to 1 inch. The text should be bold but not italic.
13. Center the text in column 1 horizontally and vertically.
14. Change the zoom to Page Width to view the entire table.
15. Apply a ½-point triple-line outside border to columns 2 through 7.

16. Apply a 3-point solid-line outside border and 20% gray shading to the first column.
17. Draw a ½-point double-line border at the bottom of row one.
18. Center the table horizontally and vertically on the page.
19. Save the document as ***[your initials]*9-17** in your Lesson 9 folder.
20. Print and close the document.

EXERCISE 9-18 Challenge Yourself

Draw a table, enter text in the table, edit and format the table.

1. Start a new document and change the page orientation to landscape.
2. Using the Draw Table feature and the default ½-point single-line style, draw a rectangle large enough to fit the page (in Print Layout view), leaving about 1-inch left and right margins. (The exact dimensions are unimportant; just draw a rectangle you can see clearly on the page.)
3. Draw four vertical lines to create five columns. The lines don't have to be evenly spaced.
4. Draw four horizontal lines to create five rows.
5. Merge the cells in row one.
6. Select the table and use the Tables and Borders toolbar to distribute the columns and rows evenly.
7. Key the text shown in Figure 9-21 into the table.

FIGURE 9-21

3-Year Computer-Related Office Expenditures				
Year	Paper	Toner	Machines	Maintenance
2001	288.50	468.00	9,767.00	108.00
2002	367.00	389.00	3,568.00	127.50
2003	402.00	332.75	850.00	235.00

8. Apply the Table Contemporary AutoFormat.
9. Format the title row as 26-point small caps, centered and bold.
10. Format the text in row 2 as 20-point bold. Increase the font size for the remaining rows to 18 points.
11. Change the row height for all rows to 1 inch.

12. Horizontally center the column headers from "Paper" through "Maintenance." Right-align the numeric text under these headers.
13. Horizontally center the text in column 1 (from "Year" through "2003").
14. Center all text vertically within the cells.
15. Center the table vertically and horizontally on the page.
16. Sort the bottom three rows in descending order by column 1.
17. Add a dollar sign to each of the amounts in the 2003 row.
18. Apply a 2¼-point solid-line outside border to the table.
19. Check the document in Print Preview. Save it as ***[your initials]*****9-18** in your Lesson 9 folder.
20. Print and close the document. Close the Tables and Borders toolbar.

On Your Own

In these exercises you work on your own, as you would in a real-life work environment. Use the skills you've learned to accomplish the task—and be creative.

EXERCISE 9-19

In landscape orientation, create a table that lists five local restaurants. Create column headings to include such information as the restaurant name, location, best dish, and worst dish. Include a final column that contains your rating (use Wingding characters to display the rating more visually). Save the document as ***[your initials]*****9-19** and print it.

EXERCISE 9-20

Create a table that shows your current course schedule. Include all relevant information as well as a column (or row) for personal comments or notes. Format the table attractively. Copy the table and paste it a few lines below the original. Apply a different formatting treatment to the copied table. Save the document as ***[your initials]*****9-20** and print it.

EXERCISE 9-21

Create a table that rates Internet sites. Include in the table the site name, address, any other pertinent information, and your review. Add additional commentary in paragraph form below the table. Save the document as ***[your initials]*****9-21** and print it.

LESSON 10

Columns

OBJECTIVES

MOUS ACTIVITIES
In this lesson:
W2002 **3-2**
See Appendix E.

After completing this lesson, you will be able to:

1. **Create multiple-column layouts.**
2. **Key and edit text in columns.**
3. **Format columns and column text.**
4. **Control column breaks.**

Estimated Time: 1 hour

Word can arrange document text in newsletter-style columns. The continuous flow of text from one column to another can make a document more attractive or easier to read.

Documents commonly have one to three columns. A document can also have a multiple-column layout; for example, it can have one section with a standard one-column layout and another section with a three-column layout.

Creating Multiple-Column Layouts

There are two ways to create multiple-column layouts:

- Use the Columns button on the Standard toolbar.
- Use the Columns dialog box.

You can change the column format for a whole document, a section, or selected text.

EXERCISE 10-1 Use the Toolbar to Create Columns

1. Open the file **WestFest2** and switch to Print Layout view. If necessary, click the Show/Hide ¶ button ¶ to display nonprinting characters.

NOTE: Normal view displays column text in a single, continuous, narrow column. Use Print Layout view or Print Preview to see how columns are arranged on a page.

2. On page 2, locate the paragraph that begins "This is just a taste."
3. Position the insertion point to the left of "This" and insert a continuous section break.
4. With the insertion point still in the new section, click the Columns button on the Standard toolbar. A box containing four columns appears below the button.

FIGURE 10-1
Choosing a column layout

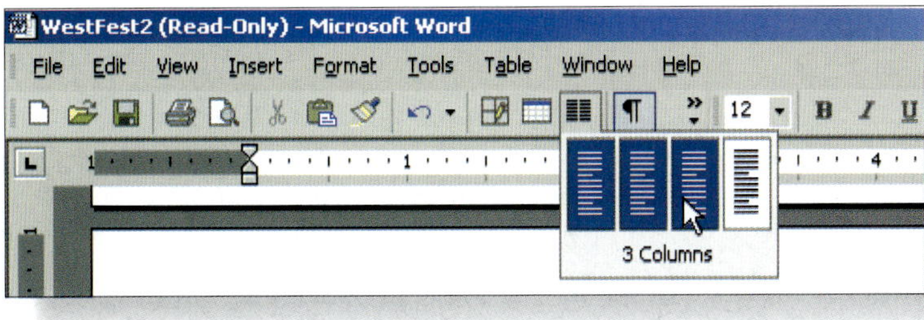

5. Move the pointer to the right, across three of the columns, and click. The new section is now in three columns.

FIGURE 10-2
One- and three-column layouts in Print Layout view

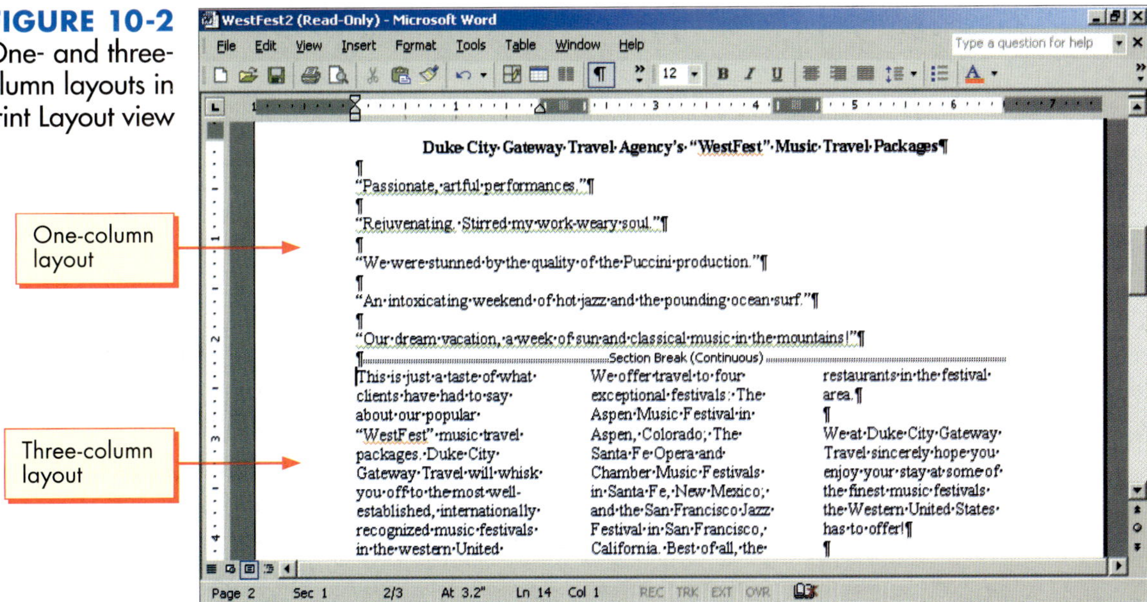

EXERCISE 10-2 Use the Columns Dialog Box to Set Up Columns

The Columns button creates columns with default settings—for example, columns of equal width with 0.5 inch of space between them. The Columns dialog box lets you choose your own settings, such as column width, the amount of space between columns, and the option to insert a line between columns.

1. While still in Print Layout view, go to the last page and position the insertion point at the beginning of the paragraph that starts *"Contact your."*
2. Open the Format menu and choose Columns.
3. In the Columns dialog box, key **1** in the Number of columns text box or click the One preset box.

FIGURE 10-3
Columns dialog box

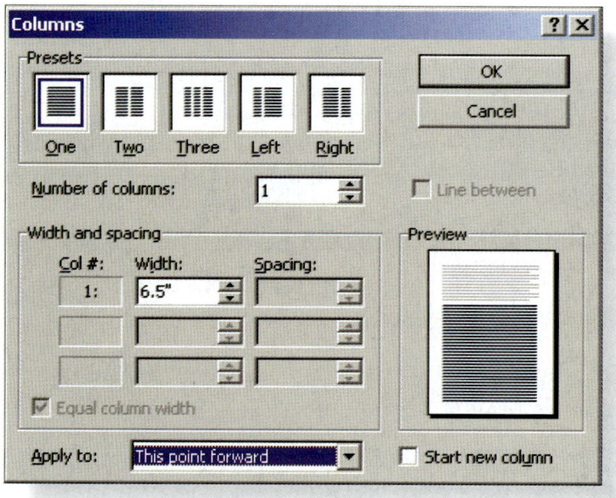

4. Choose This point forward from the Apply to drop-down list. The Preview box reflects the options you specify.

NOTE: To control how column formatting is applied in a document, it's very important to first position the insertion point correctly and then check the setting of the Apply to box in the Columns dialog box.

5. Click OK. A continuous section break is automatically inserted at the location of the insertion point and the new section is formatted as one column.
6. Press Enter to insert an extra blank line between the sections.
7. Position the insertion point at the beginning of the paragraph "This is just a taste" on the second page and open the Columns dialog box.
8. Set the Spacing text box for Col #1 to **0.25** inches to specify spacing between columns. Click the Equal column width check box to make all the columns equal in width.

9. Choose This section from the Apply to drop-down list to apply these settings to only this section. Click the Line between check box. Notice that the Preview box reflects these options.

10. Click OK. The columns in this section are spaced 0.25 inches apart with a line between them.

NOTE: You can manually adjust the Width and Spacing settings for individual columns if you clear the Equal column width check box. Key a number in the appropriate Width and Spacing box or click the up and down arrows.

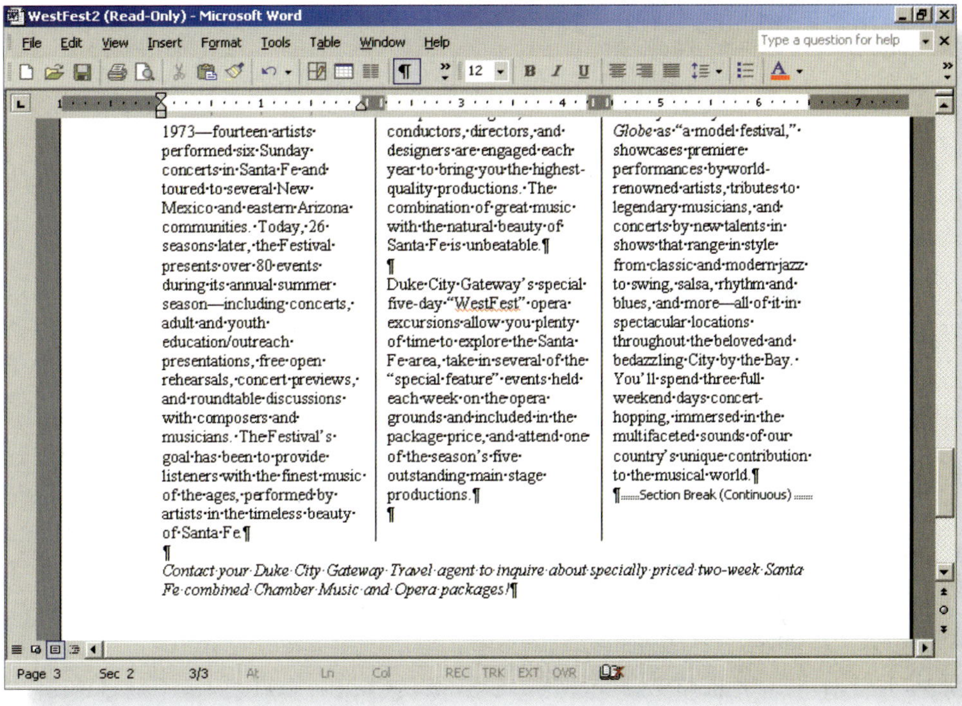

FIGURE 10-4 Document with modified column settings and new section

Keying and Editing Text in Columns

You can key and edit text in multiple-column layouts the same way you do in standard one-column layouts. Moving the insertion point around is a little different, however.

To move the insertion point from the bottom of a column to the top of the next column, you press [→]. You press [←] to move from the top of a column to the bottom of the previous column. To move from the bottom line of a column to the first line of the same column on the next page, press [↓].

TIP: If a document has a page that contains blank lines between the end of the text in a column and the page break, press [↓] more than once to move to the top line of the column on the next page.

EXERCISE 10-3 Key and Edit Column Text

1. On page 2, column 3, scroll to the paragraph above the heading "**The Santa Fe Chamber Music Festival**." Position the insertion point at the end of the paragraph, after "love of music."
2. Press Enter twice and key the text shown in Figure 10-5. Use single spacing. Notice that the text is inserted into the document just as it would be if the format were one column.

FIGURE 10-5

```
The Festival offers over 250 musical events, including orchestral perfor-
mances, chamber music, lavish operas, provocative contemporary music
concerts, lectures, master classes, and children's concerts.
```

3. On the same page, position the insertion point at the end of the text in column 3 and press →. The insertion point moves to the first column at the top of the next page.
4. Press ← to return to the previous location.
5. On the same page, position the insertion point at the end of column 1 and press → again. The insertion point moves to the top of column 2.
6. Press ← to return to the previous location. Position the insertion point anywhere in the last line of column 1.
7. Press ↓ and the insertion point moves to the same position in the same column at the top of the next page.
8. Move the insertion point to the end of the paragraph above the heading "**The San Francisco Jazz Festival**" (after "stage productions."). Key the text shown in Figure 10-6.

FIGURE 10-6

```
Your package also includes lodging at the world-famous Hotel Santa Fe and
the use of a rental car for five days.
```

9. Save the document as ***[your initials]*10-3** in a new folder for Lesson 10. Leave it open for the next exercise.

Formatting Columns and Column Text

You can create and change font and paragraph formats for text in columns the same way you create and change them for standard layouts.

After you format columns, you can change column width and the amount of space between columns two ways:

- Use the ruler.
- Use the Columns dialog box.

EXERCISE 10-4 Format Column Text

1. On page 2, column 3, select the heading "**The Aspen Music Festival**."
2. Format the text as bold italic, with 6 points of spacing after, and delete the blank line below it.
3. Apply the same formatting to the remaining three headings in the column text and delete the blank line below each heading.
4. Position the insertion point in the paragraph below the last heading on page 3.

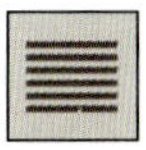

5. Click the Justify button on the Formatting toolbar to justify the text. Notice that in this case, justified text doesn't create evenly spaced lines.

6. Click the Undo button.

EXERCISE 10-5 Use the Ruler to Change Column Width and Spacing

1. Make sure the ruler is displayed.
2. On page 2, position the insertion point at the bottom of column 1. Notice on the horizontal ruler that the column has its own indent markers and margins.
3. Point to the column's right margin on the ruler. A ScreenTip displays "Right Margin." (See Figure 10-7 on the next page.)
4. Using the two-headed arrow pointer ↔, drag the right margin 0.5 inch to the left until the column is 1.5 inches wide. Hold down Alt while dragging to see the exact measurement.
5. Release the mouse button. Because these columns were set to be equal in width, they all become narrower and the spacing between them increases. Notice the page breaks change because the text re-flows.

FIGURE 10-7
Using the ruler to adjust column width

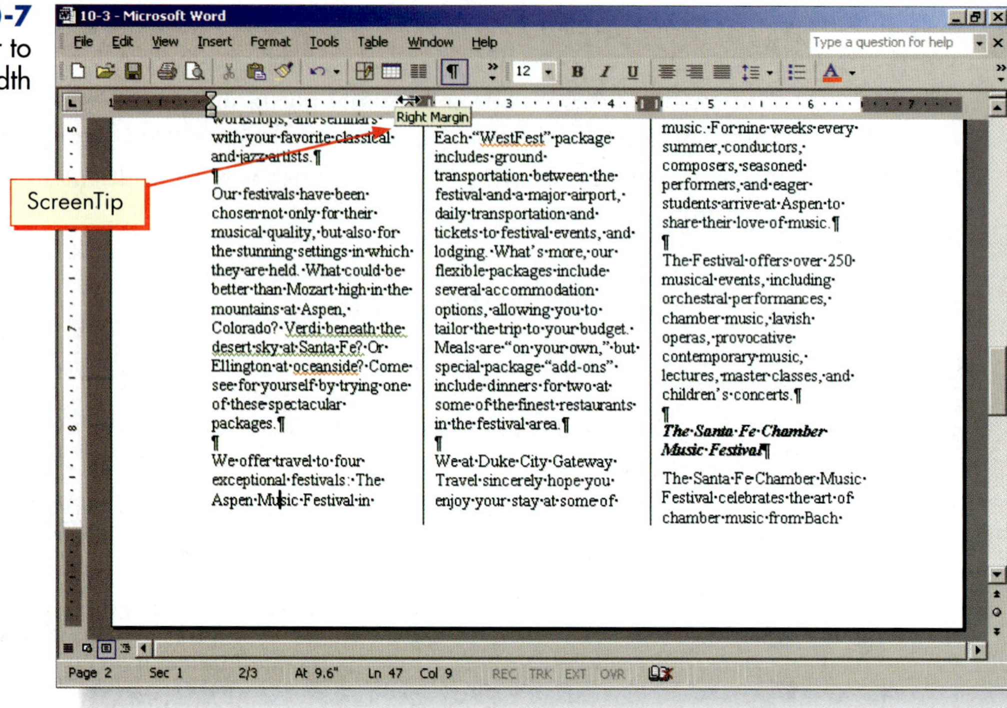

NOTE: When adjusting columns of unequal width, only the width of the adjusted column changes.

6. Open the Columns dialog box. Click Equal column width to deselect this option.
7. Click OK. The ruler now contains column markers in the gray areas. You can drag these markers to adjust the width of individual columns.
8. Make sure the insertion point is in column 1. Position the pointer over the first column marker. A ScreenTip displays "Move Column."

FIGURE 10-8
Dragging a column marker

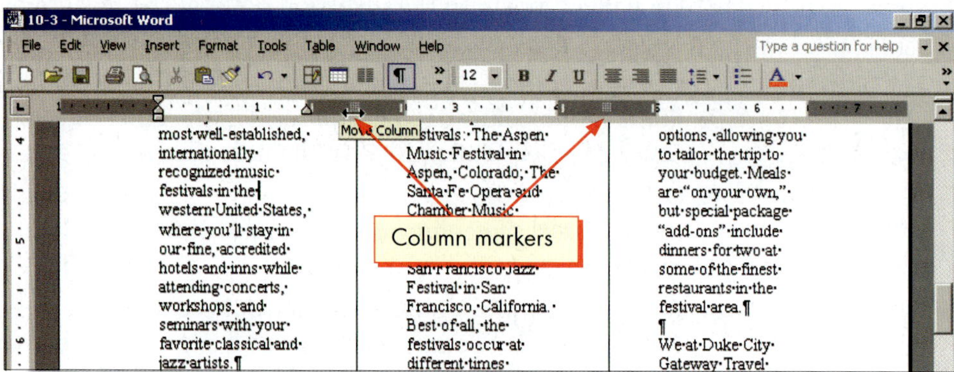

9. Drag the column marker 0.5 inch to the right. The width of column 1 increases as it makes column 2 narrower.
10. Move the pointer a little farther to the right, to the left margin area of column 2, until the ScreenTip "Left Margin" appears.
11. Use the two-headed arrow pointer ↔ to move the left margin 0.5 inch to the left. This decreases the space between the first two columns.
12. Open the Columns dialog box. Notice the different settings for columns 1 and 2.
13. Set the spacing for column 1 to **0.4** inch and check Equal column width. Click OK. Word changes the width for all three columns to 1.9 inches and the space between columns to 0.4 inch.

Controlling Column Breaks

Word automatically breaks columns at the end of the page or section. However, you can insert a column break manually so the columns end where you want them to end.

EXERCISE 10-6 Insert Column Breaks

You can insert a column break by using the Break dialog box, the Columns dialog box, or the keyboard shortcut Ctrl + Shift + Enter.

1. On page 3 of the document, position the insertion point before "***The Santa Fe Opera***."
2. Choose Insert, Break from the menu to open the Break dialog box.
3. Choose Column break and click OK. A column break is inserted and "***The Santa Fe Opera***" appears at the top of the column.
4. Press Backspace to delete the column break.
5. At the bottom of page 2, position the insertion point before "***The Santa Fe Chamber Music Festival***."
6. Press Ctrl + Shift + Enter to insert a column break.
7. Press Backspace to remove it.
8. With the insertion point in the same position, open the Columns dialog box.
9. Choose This point forward from the Apply to drop-down list, click Start new column and click OK. A new section is inserted. Notice that the section break has the same effect as the previous column break.
10. Click the Undo button.

WORD

TIP: You can also use the Paragraph dialog box to control column breaks. For example, if a column break separates a paragraph from its heading, you can use the Keep with next pagination option.

EXERCISE 10-7 Balance the Length of Columns

Column lengths are often unequal at the ends of sections or pages. You can balance the columns by inserting a continuous section break.

1. On page 3, at the bottom of column 3, select the paragraph mark after "to the musical world" and all of the text following it, up to but not including the last paragraph mark in section 3.
2. Press Delete and section 2 becomes one column again. (The formatting in the last paragraph mark applies to the remaining section.)
3. Format the first line on page 2 (the title) as Arial bold, small caps, with 72 points of paragraph spacing before the title. Two blank lines should separate the title from the text.
4. Click within section 2 and open the Columns dialog box. Set the formatting to three columns of equal column width, 0.25-inch spacing between columns, and a vertical line between columns. Click OK.
5. Switch to Print Preview to see the unbalanced columns; then return to Print Layout view.
6. Position the insertion point at the end of the document, after "musical world."
7. Insert a Continuous section break. Word creates columns of equal length on the last page.
8. Format the text on page 1 (the title page) as 14-point Arial bold, centered, with 1.5-line spacing. Format the first line as small caps with 144 points of spacing before the paragraph.
9. Insert page numbers that are centered at the bottom of the page. Start numbering at 0 (so page 2 is numbered "1"). Do not include the page number on the first page.

REVIEW: Use the Insert, Page Numbers command and then click the Format button to change the starting page number.

10. Preview all pages of the document, and then save it as ***[your initials]*10-7** in your Lesson 10 folder.
11. Print and close the document. (See Figure 10-9 on the next page.)

FIGURE 10-9
Final document with balanced columns

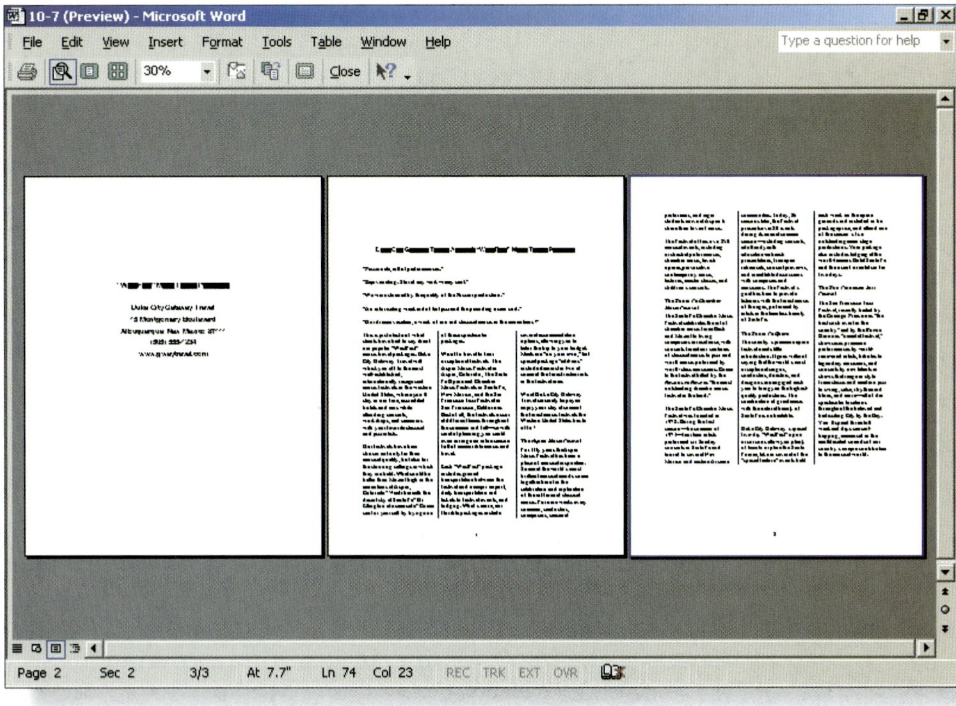

USING HELP

You learned how to create columns in this lesson, and you even changed the number of columns from three to one. Now let Word show you another simple way to remove columns by using the Standard toolbar.

Explore Help topics about columns:

1. Key **remove columns** in the Ask a Question text box and press Enter.
2. Click Remove newsletter-style columns.
3. Review the information in the Help window.
4. Click the Contents tab and review other column topics. Explore the topic Troubleshoot newsletter-style columns.
5. Close the Help window when you finish.

LESSON 10 Summary

- The Columns feature creates a continuous flow of text from one column to another, as in a newsletter layout. You can change an entire document, a section, or a selection to column format.
- The Columns button on the Standard toolbar applies Word's default column settings. The Columns dialog box enables you to choose a variety of options, such as changing column width or the space between columns.
- Adjust column width and spacing by dragging column markers and column margins on the ruler or by using the Columns dialog box. Create equal column widths by choosing that option in the Columns dialog box.
- Use the Break dialog box or press Ctrl + Shift + Enter to control column breaks. The Columns dialog box also has a Start new column option for controlling column breaks.
- Balance the length of columns by inserting a continuous section break at the end of the column text.

LESSON 10 Command Summary

FEATURE	BUTTON	MENU	KEYBOARD	SPEECH?
Insert columns		Format, Columns		✓
Insert column break		Insert, Break	Ctrl + Shift + Enter	✓

Concepts Review

TRUE/FALSE QUESTIONS

Each of the following statements is either true or false. Indicate your choice by circling T or F.

T F *1.* When working with columns, use Normal view to see the columns as they are arranged on the page.

T F *2.* You can use the ruler to change column width.

T F *3.* Formatting text in multiple columns is very different from formatting text in standard layout.

T F *4.* Pressing  at the end of any column moves the insertion point to the top of the next column.

T F *5.* The default setting for spacing between columns is 1 inch.

T F *6.* A continuous section break is used to balance columns.

T F *7.* To quickly choose a column layout for the current section, click 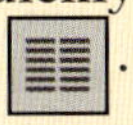.

T F *8.* You can open the Columns dialog box by using the Insert menu.

SHORT ANSWER QUESTIONS

Write the correct answer in the space provided.

1. What type of line can you apply from the Columns dialog box?

____

2. Which toolbar includes the Columns button ?

____

3. Which arrow do you press to move from the top of any column to the bottom of the previous column?

____

4. Which dialog box do you use to add a vertical line between columns?

____

5. Which key do you press while adjusting column widths on the ruler to see an exact measurement display?

____

6. What shape is the pointer when you use the ruler to adjust column widths?

____

7. What is the keyboard shortcut to insert a column break?

____

8. What option in the Columns dialog box do you select to make all columns the same width?

____

CRITICAL THINKING

Answer these questions on a separate page. There are no right or wrong answers. Support your answers with examples from your own experience, if possible.

1. Imagine a newspaper that doesn't use columns. Then, imagine an 8.5 × 11-inch newsletter, also without columns. What problems would these publications present to readers?
2. Find examples in magazines, newspapers, and newsletters of columns of different widths. Which width do you feel is most readable?

Lesson Applications

EXERCISE 10-8

Create a three-column layout, key text in columns, and balance the columns.

1. Open the file **Destinations** and switch to Print Layout view.
2. Use the Columns dialog box to create a three-column layout for the list of countries, with 1 inch of spacing between columns. Keep the introductory paragraph in one-column format.
3. Insert the following countries at the end of the list:

   Estonia
   Romania
   Bulgaria
   Lithuania
   Norway
   Latvia
4. Select the entire list of countries and sort by paragraphs in ascending order. (Use the Table, Sort menu command.)
5. Balance the columns on the page.
6. Two inches from the top of the page, key the title **Foreign Tourist Offices in the United States** in 14-point bold, all caps, and centered.
7. Insert two blank lines below the title.
8. Save the document as ***[your initials]*10-8** in your Lesson 10 folder.
9. Print and close the document.

EXERCISE 10-9

Create a two-column layout, key text in columns, and format and balance the columns.

1. Open the file **Turquoise**.
2. Change the page orientation to landscape.
3. Format the entire document as two columns.
4. At the top of the first column, key the heading **New Mexico/Santa Fe Sightseeing: The Turquoise Trail Scenic and Historic Area**
5. Insert two blank lines after the new heading.
6. Format the heading as 24-point italic.

7. At the end of the document, key the new paragraph shown in Figure 10-10. Use single spacing and insert a blank line before the paragraph.

FIGURE 10-10

```
No tour of New Mexico is complete without a visit to one of the 18 timeless
pueblos. Circle off Route 14 going toward Interstate 25 and visit the Santo
Domingo Pueblo. The pueblo was settled about 700 years ago and today is
the home of 3,500 Native Americans. Don't miss Trader Fred's Trading Post,
world famous for its rugs, jewelry, and crafts for over 100 years. But keep
a lookout along the way because there are many beautiful sights to see and
other places to stop for local goods.
```

8. Change the space between columns to 1 inch and keep the columns equal width.
9. At the beginning of the text under the heading, insert a continuous section break.
10. Format the heading section as one column.
11. In the heading, delete the colon and start the heading text beginning *"The Turquoise Trail"* on a new line.
12. Change the text in the new line to small caps and center both lines of the heading. Make sure there are two blank lines after the heading.
13. Balance the length of the columns in section 2.
14. Center the entire document vertically on the page.
15. Preview the document, and then save it as ***[your initials]*****10-9** in your Lesson 10 folder.
16. Print and close the document.

EXERCISE 10-10

Create a three-column layout, key text in columns, change column spacing, and balance columns.

1. Open the files **Offices2** and **Gateway**.
2. Copy the second heading of **Gateway** ("**Gateway Travel—Your Gateway to the World**") and the paragraph that follows it.
3. Paste the selected text at the beginning of **Offices2**, and insert two blank lines after the pasted text.
4. Insert a continuous section break before "Golden Gateway Travel."

5. Use the Columns button [Columns] to create a three-column layout for the list of travel offices.
6. Change the spacing between columns to 0.2 inch, but keep the columns equal width (with no line between columns).
7. Add the Duke City Gateway Travel office (shown here) as the first listing in section 2. Include a blank line below the new listing.

   Duke City Gateway Travel
   15 Montgomery Boulevard
   Albuquerque, NM 87111
   Tel. (505) 555-1234
   Fax (505) 555-1244

8. Insert a column break at the start of the listing for "New England Gateway Travel" in the first column by using Ctrl+Shift+Enter.
9. Insert a column break at the start of the listing for "Ontario Gateway Travel" by using the Break dialog box.
10. Insert two blank lines below the document title and format the title as all caps, 14-point bold italic, centered.
11. Format the heading "Gateway Travel Offices" as small caps, centered.
12. Change the top margin to 2 inches.
13. Save the document as ***[your initials]*****10-10** in your Lesson 10 folder.
14. Print the document. Close both documents.

EXERCISE 10-11 *Challenge Yourself*

Create a three-column layout, format columns and column text, and balance columns.

1. Open the file **CruiseFAQs2**.
2. Insert another blank line below the title (there should be two), and then format the title as 20-point Arial bold, centered, with 72 points of spacing before the paragraph.
3. Format the document from the first italic question ("*What kinds of people take a cruise?*) through the end of the document as three columns of equal width.
4. Balance the columns at the end of the document.
5. Change the font for the entire document to Arial. Change the font size for section 2 to 10 points.
6. In section 2, add 3-point spacing after all the italic questions and before the first bullet ("Valid passport") on page 2.

7. Change the space between columns to 0.2 inch and make sure there's a line between columns.
8. Add a box page border using a 1½-point double-line style.
9. Add a page number centered at the bottom of page 2.
10. Save the document as ***[your initials]*10-11** in your Lesson 10 folder.
11. Print and close the document.

On Your Own

In these exercises you work on your own, as you would in a real-life work environment. Use the skills you've learned to accomplish the task—and be creative.

EXERCISE 10-12

Convert a document you've written (or any existing document) to a multiple-column layout in landscape orientation. Use a one-column format for the document title and a two- or three-column format for the remaining text. Balance the columns and insert column breaks where needed. Save the document as ***[your initials]*10-12** and print it.

EXERCISE 10-13

Copy a news article from a news source on the Internet. Use the text to create a multi-column document that looks like a newspaper article. Include a heading and a line between columns, and justify the column text. Save the document as ***[your initials]*10-13** and print it.

EXERCISE 10-14

Create a one-page personal newsletter. Design an attractive title and use a multi-column layout with the appropriate number of columns and space between columns. Save the document as ***[your initials]*10-14** and print it.

UNIT 5

Advanced Topics

LESSON

11 Graphics and Charts

OBJECTIVES

MOUS ACTIVITIES
In this lesson:
W2002 **5-1**
W2002 **5-2**

See Appendix E.

After completing this lesson, you will be able to:

1. **Insert clip art.**
2. **Move and format clip art.**
3. **Create WordArt.**
4. **Create diagrams.**
5. **Create charts.**
6. **Edit chart data.**
7. **Modify charts.**

Estimated Time: 1¼ hours

A picture is worth a thousand words, even in word processing. Word provides ready-to-use pictures, called *clip art,* to add impact to your documents. Word also provides additional graphics tools: WordArt, used to make a dramatic statement with text, and charts and diagrams, used to display information visually. These exciting tools enable you to add attention-grabbing images to a text document.

Inserting Clip Art

Microsoft Office provides access to a wide variety of drawings, photographs, sound effects, music, videos, and other media files, called *clips.* This lesson focuses mainly on clip art, which are drawings.

When you want to insert clips in a document, you can use one of two search methods:

- Open the Insert Clip Art task pane and search for pictures by keyword.
- Open the Microsoft Clip Organizer window and view collections of clips organized by category (such as Business, People, and Transportation).

EXERCISE 11-1 Find Clips by Using Keywords

Each clip in the Microsoft Office collection has keywords associated with it. Using a keyword is an easy way to narrow down your search for an appropriate clip.

1. Open the file **Balloon2**.

NOTE: The documents you create in this course relate to the Case Study about Duke City Gateway Travel, a fictional travel agency (see pages 3 through 6).

2. Position the insertion point at the second paragraph mark below the title.
3. Open the Insert menu and choose Picture; then choose Clip Art from the submenu. The Clip Art task pane opens.

TIP: You can also click the Insert Clip Art button on the Drawing toolbar to insert clip art. To display the Drawing toolbar, choose Toolbars from the View menu and click Drawing.

4. In the Search text box in the task pane, key **balloon**. The task pane has two search option boxes, one for searching specific collections of clips and the other for searching for specific types of clip files. You would use these boxes to narrow your search.
5. Make sure the Search in text box is set for All collections. If it is not, click the down arrow and check the Everywhere box. Make sure the Results should be text box is set for All media file types. If it is not, click the down arrow and check the All media types box. (See Figure 11-1 on the next page.)
6. Click the Search button. The task pane displays clips containing a balloon.

NOTE: If you're currently connected to the Internet, the search results will include clips from the Microsoft Web collection. These clips are identified by a tiny globe at the bottom left corner of the picture.

7. Point to the clip of the balloons and light bulb. A ScreenTip displays the image size, file format (WMF), and some of the keywords associated with the clip.

FIGURE 11-1
Using a keyword to find clips

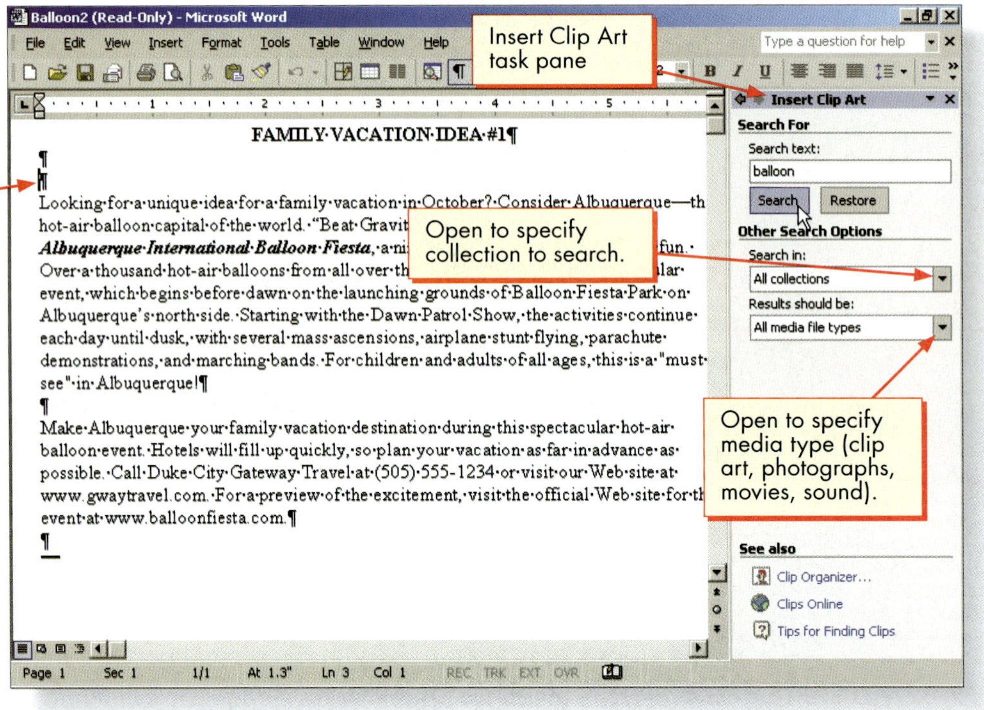

8. Click the clip to insert it into the document.

FIGURE 11-2
Inserting a clip from the task pane

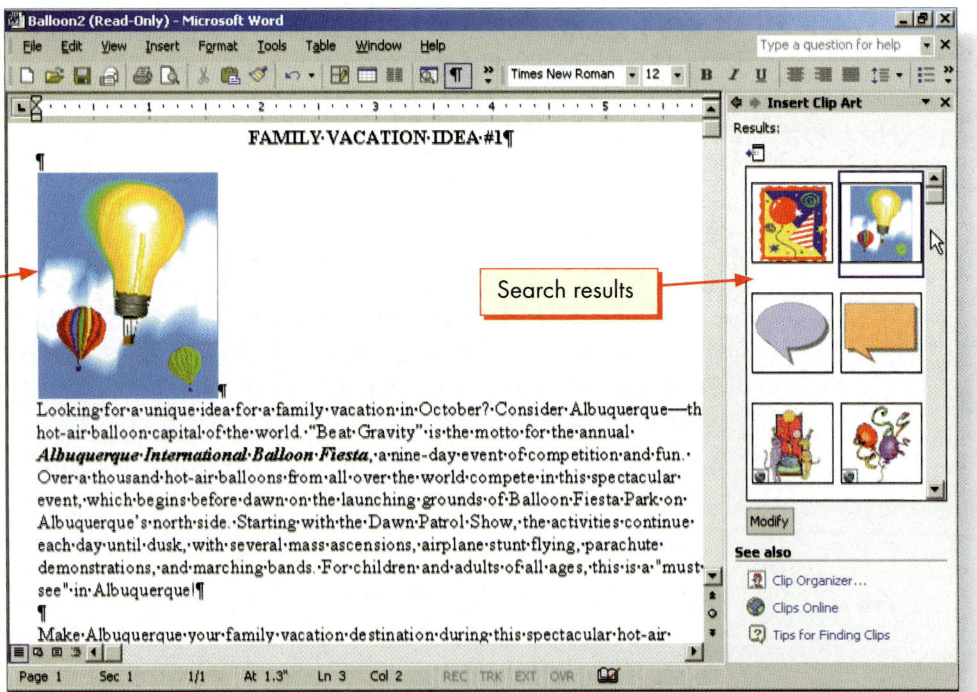

9. In the task pane, click the Modify button. You can now enter another keyword to search for more clips.

EXERCISE 11-2 Find Clips by Browsing Categories

All clips in the Microsoft Office collection are organized by category. You can browse clips by category in the Microsoft Clip Organizer window.

1. Click Clip Organizer at the bottom of the task pane. The Microsoft Clip Organizer window appears.
2. Under Collection List, click the plus sign next to Office Collections to expand the list of categories.
3. Click various category names to display the available clips. Expand a category, if necessary, to display subcategories.
4. To locate a computer picture, scroll to the Technology category. Click the plus sign to expand the category, and then click Computing.
5. Point to the computer picture selected in Figure 11-3. Click the down arrow that appears to the right of the picture. A pop-up menu appears with several options. For example, you can copy the clip, find clips of similar style, or preview a larger version of the clip.

FIGURE 11-3
Inserting a clip from the Microsoft Clip Organizer window

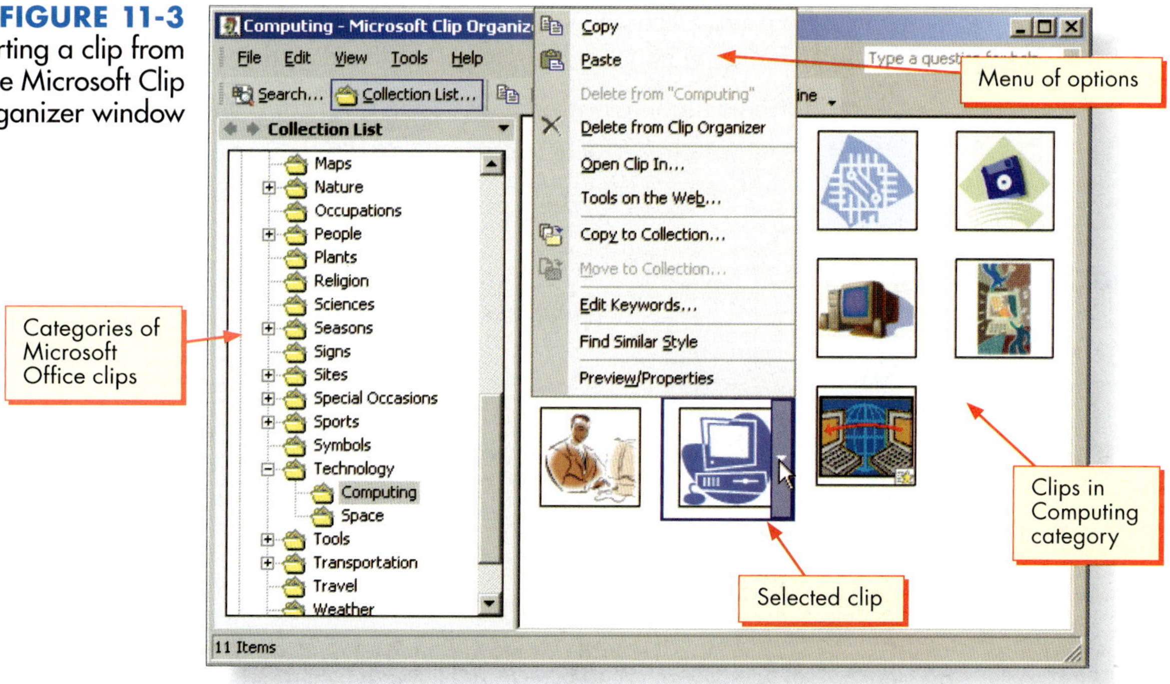

6. Click Copy to copy the clip to the Clipboard.

7. Click within the document and position the insertion point at the last paragraph mark. Paste the clip.

REVIEW: Right-click where you want to paste the clip and then choose Paste from the shortcut menu, or use the Paste button or Ctrl + V.

8. Save the document as ***[your initials]*11-2** in a new folder for Lesson 11.
9. Close the Insert Clip Art task pane. Right-click the Microsoft Clip Organizer on the Windows task bar and close it. Click No when asked if you want the clip to remain on the Clipboard.

Moving and Formatting Clip Art

After you insert a clip in a Word document, there are many ways to manipulate it. You can change its size, trim it, change its position, and apply formatting options. To manipulate any graphic, you must select it first.

EXERCISE 11-3 Select Clip Art

To select clip art, you click it. A selected graphic has a *selection rectangle* around it, formed by eight small squares at each side and corner of the object. These squares are *sizing handles,* which you drag to resize the graphic.

1. Scroll to the balloon picture near the top of the document.
2. Click the picture to select it. Notice the selection rectangle and the sizing handles. Also notice that the Picture toolbar appears when a picture is selected.

FIGURE 11-4 Clicking a picture to select it

NOTE: If the Picture toolbar does not appear, open the View menu and choose Toolbars, Picture.

3. Click outside the borders of the picture to deselect it. The Picture toolbar disappears.

FIGURE 11-5
Picture toolbar

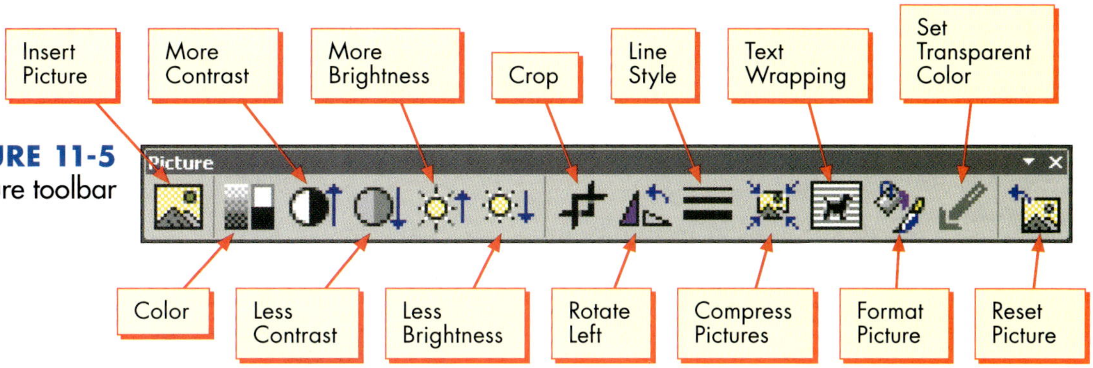

EXERCISE 11-4 Size Clip Art

When you *size* a picture, you reduce or enlarge it. You can *scale* a picture to be a percentage of its original size. *Proportional sizing* resizes a picture while maintaining its relative height and width.

1. Click the balloon picture to select it.
2. Move the pointer to the sizing handle in the top right corner until the pointer looks like this: ⤢
3. Drag the sizing handle toward the center of the picture and notice that a dotted-line box appears. The box represents the new size.

FIGURE 11-6
Sizing a picture

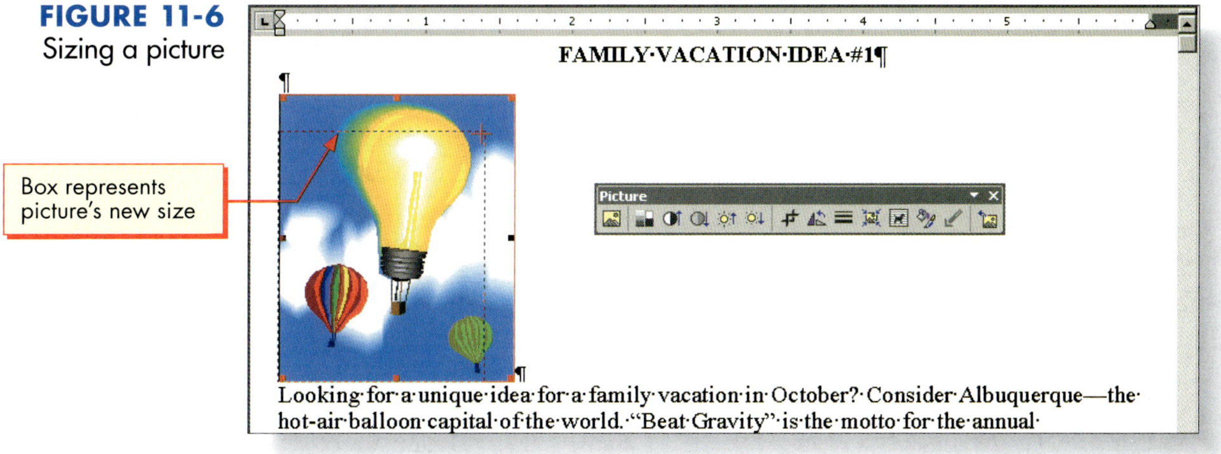

W O R D

4. Release the mouse button and notice that the picture size changes proportionately.
5. Drag the top center sizing handle down and release the mouse button. Notice that the picture size changes disproportionately.

NOTE: The four corner sizing handles resize the image proportionately. The top center, bottom center, and side center handles distort the image's original proportions as the size changes.

FIGURE 11-7
Picture sized proportionately and disproportionately

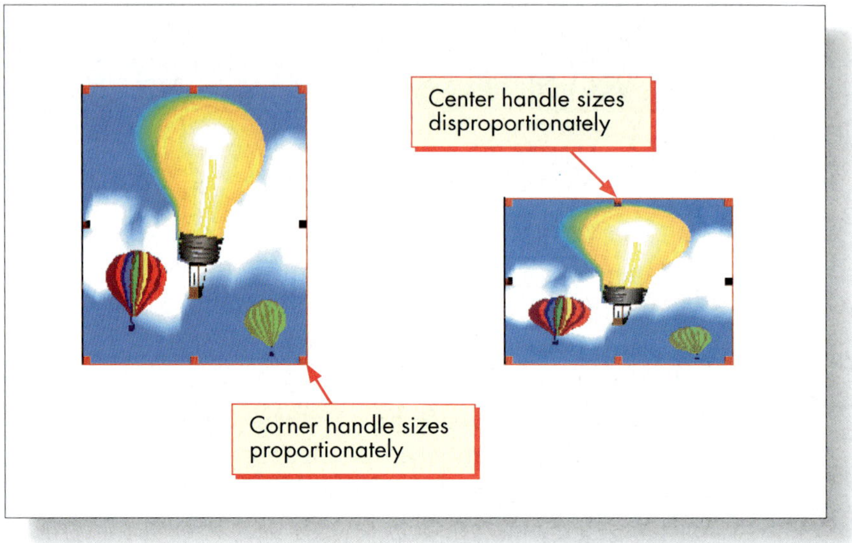

6. Click the Undo button to undo the disproportionate resizing.
7. Select the computer picture. Instead of using the sizing handles to size it, click the Format Picture button on the Picture toolbar.
8. In the Format Picture dialog box, click the Size tab. Under Scale, change the Height to 50%. Press Tab. The Width automatically changes to 50% because you are scaling proportionately. (See Figure 11-8 on the next page.)

NOTE: In the Format Picture dialog box, when the Lock aspect ratio box is checked, Word scales a picture proportionately, and when the Relative to original picture size box is checked, Word scales the picture from its original size.

9. Click OK. The computer picture is half its original size.

TIP: You can use the Size tab of the Format Picture dialog box to size a picture. Simply enter the desired measurements in the appropriate text boxes.

FIGURE 11-8
Format Picture dialog box, Size tab

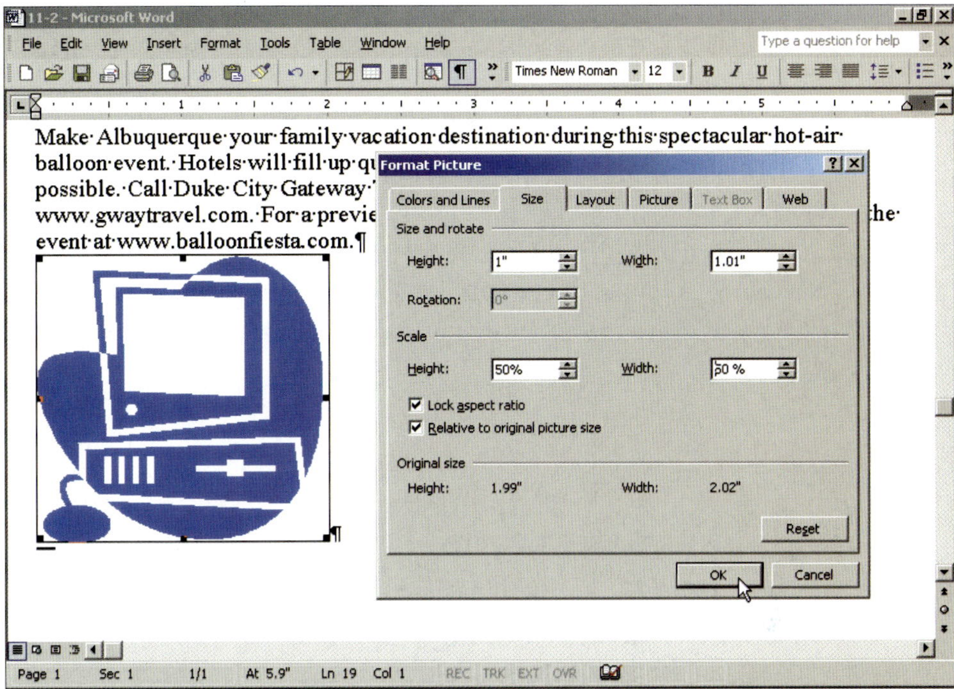

EXERCISE 11-5 Crop Clip Art

When you trim or *crop* a picture, you hide part of the picture. For example, if you have a picture of a person standing next to a computer, you can crop either the person or the computer out of the picture. What you crop is neither displayed on screen nor printed, but remains part of the original image.

1. Select the computer picture.
2. Click the Crop button on the Picture toolbar. Word switches to Print Layout view.
3. Place the cropping tool over the bottom middle sizing handle and drag toward the top of the picture until you have only the monitor showing.
4. Release the mouse button and notice that the graphic is cropped from the bottom.
5. Click the Undo button to undo the cropping.

NOTE: The top, bottom, and side sizing handles crop those sides, respectively. The four corner sizing handles crop a picture from each respective corner.

EXERCISE 11-6 Restore Clip Art to Its Original Size

1. Select the balloon picture.
2. Click the Reset Picture button on the Picture toolbar. The picture changes back to its original size, as it appeared when you first inserted it.
3. Select the computer picture. Reset the picture to its original size.
4. Change the picture back to the 50% size.
5. Save the document as ***[your initials]*11-6** in your Lesson 11 folder.

EXERCISE 11-7 Move Clip Art

You can move a picture by cutting and pasting or by using drag-and-drop.

1. Select the computer picture and cut it, placing it on the Clipboard.
2. Paste the picture at the paragraph mark above the paragraph beginning "Make Albuquerque."
3. Select the picture, point to it with the arrow pointer, hold down the mouse, and drag the picture back to the last paragraph mark. The pointer changes to the drag-and-drop shape, the pointer you use for dragging and dropping text.

FIGURE 11-9
Dragging a picture

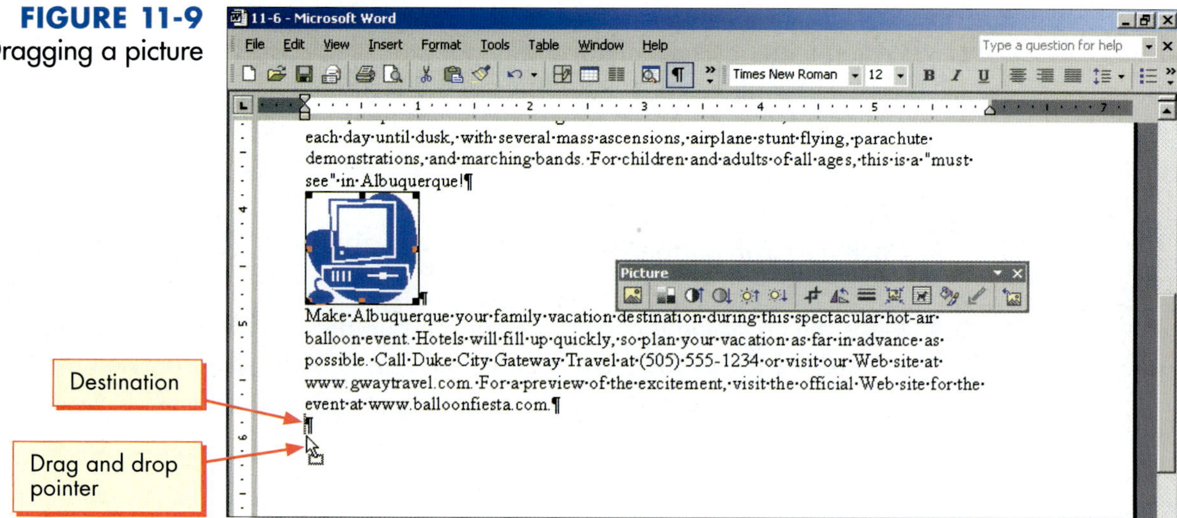

4. Release the mouse button. The picture is positioned at the last paragraph mark. If it is not, click the Undo button and drag it again.

NOTE: To delete a picture, select it and press Delete or Backspace.

EXERCISE 11-8 Change Wrapping Style

When you insert a graphic, it appears in the document as an *inline graphic*, by default. An inline graphic is treated like a character and aligns with the current paragraph. You can change an inline graphic to a *floating graphic*. A floating graphic is placed on the drawing layer of the Word document. You can move the floating graphic freely and layer it behind or in front of text or other objects, changing how text wraps around the graphic. This feature is called *text wrapping*.

1. Select the balloon picture. The picture is an inline graphic, treated by Word like any text object. It is left-aligned with its own paragraph mark.

2. Click the Text Wrapping button on the Picture toolbar. Notice the wrapping options available.
3. Choose Square. Text now wraps around the picture. Notice the anchor symbol and the different selection handles around the picture (now circles instead of solid squares). These are characteristics of a selected floating picture.

FIGURE 11-10 Changing the wrapping style

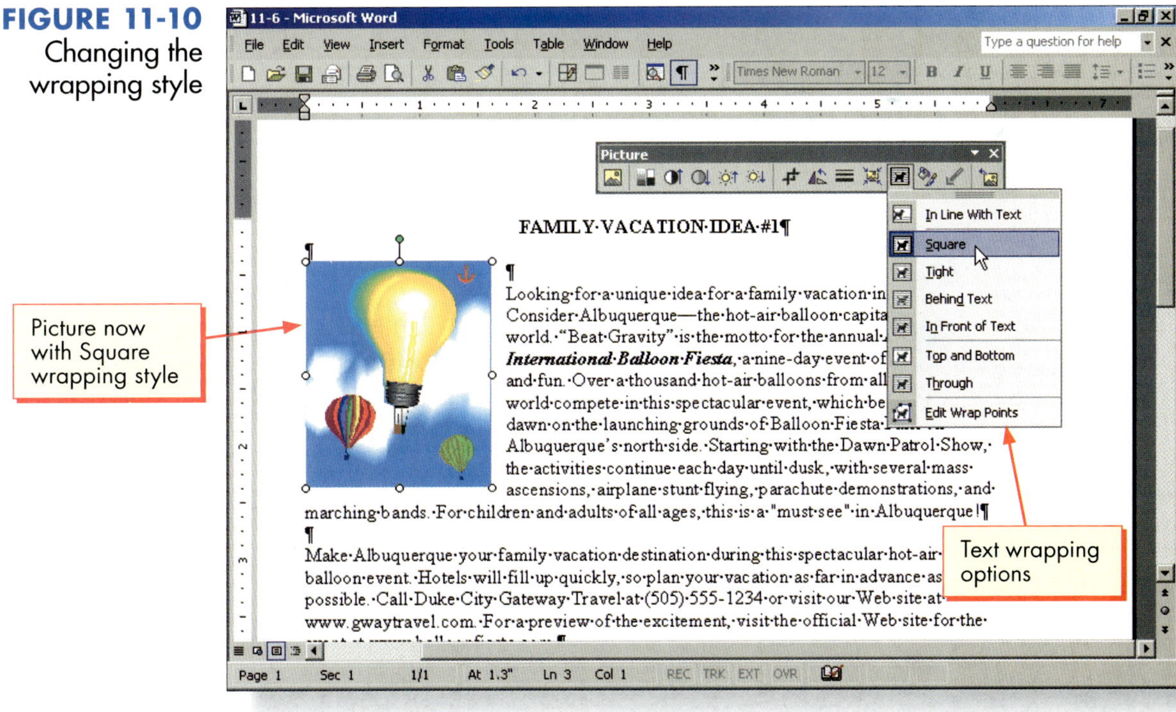

NOTE: The green circle above the picture is the rotation handle. You can drag this handle to rotate the picture either left or right.

4. Move the pointer over the picture. The pointer is now a four-headed arrow. You use this pointer to drag the floating picture freely on the page.
5. Using the four-headed arrow, drag the picture to different locations in the document. Notice how the text wraps squarely around the picture.

TIP: As you drag a floating picture, Word displays a dotted-line outline of the picture. You can use the top edge of the outline as a positioning guide.

6. Change the picture back to an inline graphic by choosing the In-Line With Text wrapping style. The picture returns to the area where it was first inserted. If it appears on the same line as the first paragraph, click before "Looking" and press Enter twice, leaving a blank line below the picture.
7. Select the picture and click the Center button on the Formatting toolbar to center-align the picture.

TIP: To align an inline picture, use the Alignment buttons on the Formatting toolbar. To align a floating picture, open the Format Picture dialog box and select the Layout tab.

8. Select the computer picture and change the wrapping style to Top and Bottom.
9. Move the picture around. Notice how text wraps only around the top and bottom and not the sides of the picture.
10. Change the wrapping style to Tight. This style is like Square, but the text wraps more closely around the contours of the picture.
11. Position the picture to the left of the last paragraph.

TIP: To fine-tune the position of a floating graphic, use the Arrow keys. To move a graphic by very small increments, hold down Ctrl as you move the Arrow keys.

12. Increase the balloon picture size by 25% (key **125%** in the Height text box).
13. Format the document title as 16 points with 72 points of spacing before the paragraph.
14. Save the file as ***[your initials]*11-8** in your Lesson 11 folder and print it. Leave it open for the next exercise. (See the final document in Figure 11-11 on the next page.)

FIGURE 11-11
Preview of final document

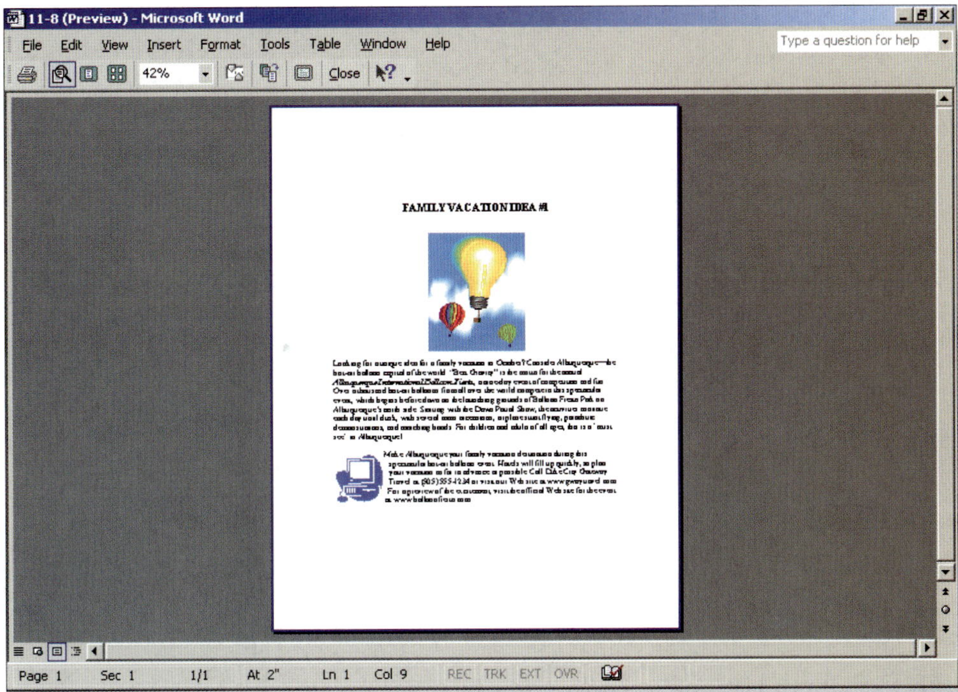

Creating WordArt

WordArt is a drawing tool you can use to create special effects with text. You can choose from a variety of WordArt styles, and then modify the object by editing the text or changing the shape, wrapping style, size, color, position, and so on.

EXERCISE 11-9 Create WordArt

1. Select the title text "FAMILY VACATION IDEA #1" up to, but not including, the paragraph mark. Click the Cut button to place the text on the Clipboard. (Because you'll be creating WordArt from this text, not including the paragraph mark will retain the spacing before the title.)
2. Open the Insert menu and choose Picture, WordArt. The WordArt Gallery dialog box appears, displaying a number of WordArt styles. (See Figure 11-12 on the next page.)

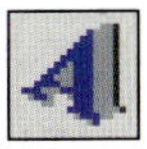

TIP: You can also click the Insert WordArt button on the Drawing toolbar to open the WordArt Gallery dialog box.

FIGURE 11-12
WordArt Gallery dialog box

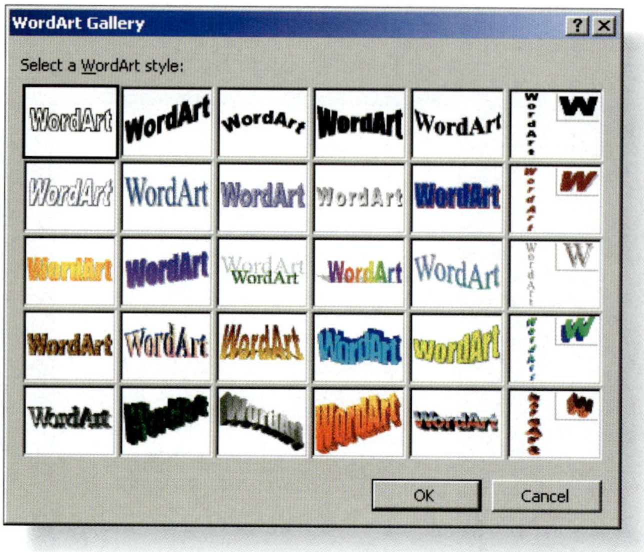

3. Choose one of the styles and click **OK**. The Edit WordArt Text dialog box appears. You can key or paste text in the **Text** box when creating WordArt.

FIGURE 11-13
Edit WordArt Text dialog box

4. Use Ctrl+V to paste the title text in the **Text** box. Click **OK**. The WordArt object is inserted in the document as an inline graphic.
5. Click the WordArt object to select it. The WordArt toolbar appears. (See Figure 11-14 on the next page.)

6. Click the WordArt Gallery button on the WordArt toolbar and choose another style. Some styles are more readable than others, particularly for all uppercase text. Experiment until you find the style you like best; then close the WordArt Gallery dialog box.

FIGURE 11-14
WordArt toolbar

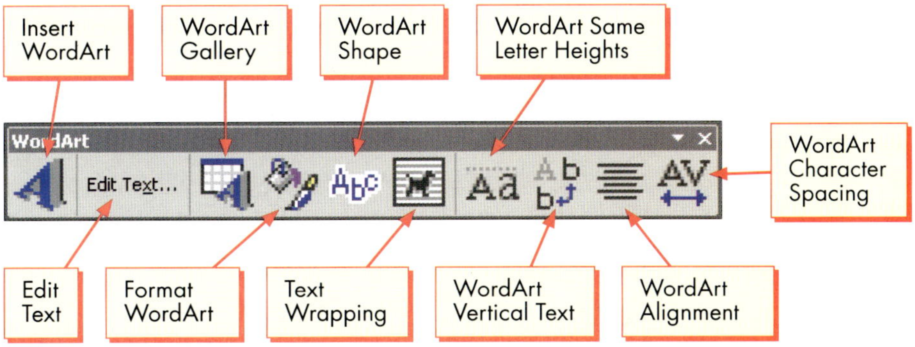

7. Click the WordArt Shape button and choose another shape. If you don't like the results, click the Undo button.

NOTE: As with any graphic object, there are many options for modifying a WordArt object. Several options appear on the WordArt toolbar, and you can use the toolbar to open the Format WordArt dialog box, where you can change the color, size, and position.

FIGURE 11-15
Title text using a simple WordArt style

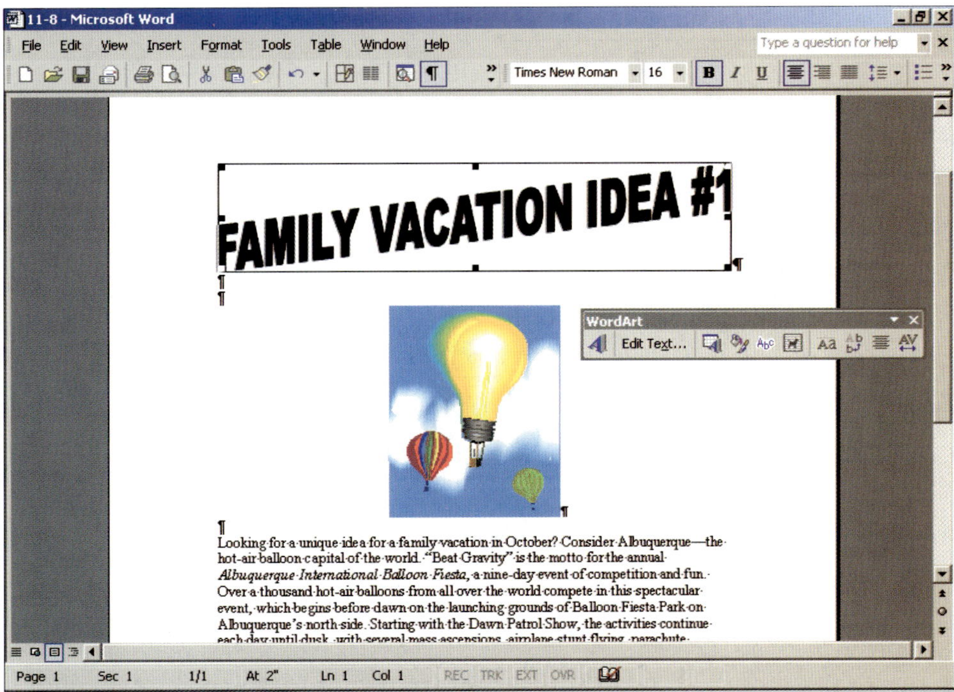

8. Save the document as ***[your initials]*11-9** in your Lesson 11 folder.
9. Print and close the document.

Creating Diagrams

Using Word's diagram tools, you can insert six types of diagrams:

- *Organizational,* sometimes called *org chart,* illustrates the top-down relationship of members of an organization
- *Cycle,* illustrates a process that has a continuous cycle
- *Target,* illustrates steps towards a goal
- *Radial,* illustrates relationships of objects to a main object
- *Venn,* illustrates where areas overlap between objects
- *Pyramid,* illustrates foundation-based relationships

EXERCISE 11-10 Create a Diagram

To insert a diagram, choose Diagram from the Insert menu or click the Insert Diagram or Organization Chart button on the Drawing toolbar. Choose a diagram type from the Diagram Gallery dialog box.

1. Start a new document and key the title **Gateway Travel Offices in the U.S.** Center the text and change it to 14-point Arial Black. Press Enter twice.
2. Choose Diagram from the Insert menu to open the Diagram Gallery dialog box.

FIGURE 11-16
Diagram Gallery dialog box

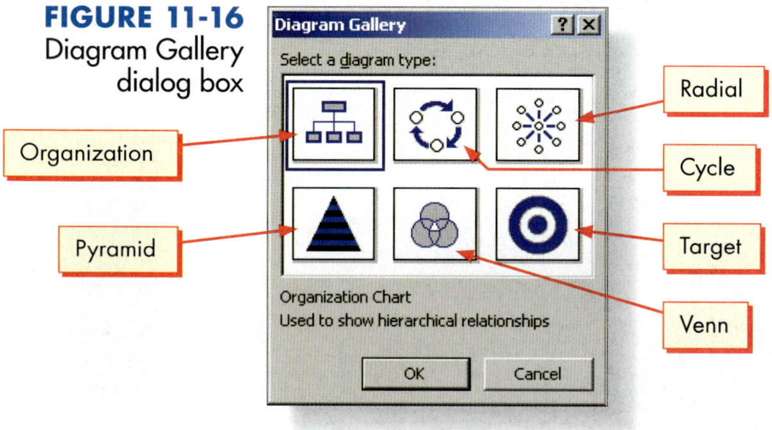

3. Click the Radial diagram (third diagram in first row) and click OK. The radial diagram is inserted in the document. The diagram displays with a drawing space and a nonprinting border. Inside the border are sizing handles. The Radial Diagram toolbar also appears.
4. Select the innermost circle in the Radial diagram, if it is not already selected. To select a circle, point to the circle's edge and click when you see the four-headed arrow pointer. The selected circle has round selection handles. (See Figure 11-17 on the next page.)
5. With the innermost circle selected, click the Insert Shape button on the Diagram toolbar four times. The Radial diagram should now have seven outer circles.

FIGURE 11-17
Inserting a radial diagram

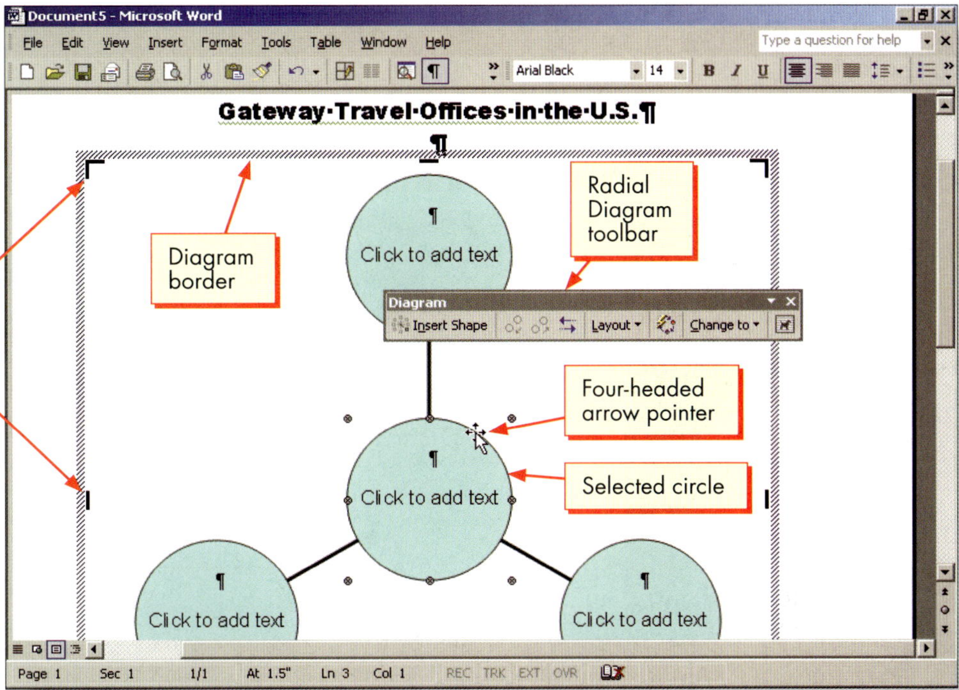

EXERCISE 11-11 Add Text to a Diagram

1. Click inside the center circle and key **Albuquerque**. Don't worry if the text doesn't fit on one line—you'll resize the diagram later in this exercise.
2. Click in the topmost circle and key **San Francisco**
3. Moving clockwise, key the following cities, one per circle, in each of the remaining circles: **Chicago**, **New York**, **Boston**, **Atlanta**, **Washington, D.C.**, **Honolulu**
4. Click a blank area inside the chart border.
5. On the Radial Diagram toolbar, click Layout and then choose Scale Diagram. The diagram now has round sizing handles along its border.
6. Point to the middle right sizing handle. The two-headed arrow pointer appears. (See Figure 11-18 on the next page.)
7. Use the pointer to drag the sizing handle slightly to the right. Release the mouse button. "Albuquerque" should fit on one line. If it doesn't, drag the sizing handle a little more to the right.

8. Click the AutoFormat button on the Radial Diagram toolbar. In the Diagram Style Gallery dialog box, click to preview some of the styles. Then choose 3-D Color and click Apply.

FIGURE 11-18
Scaling the radial diagram

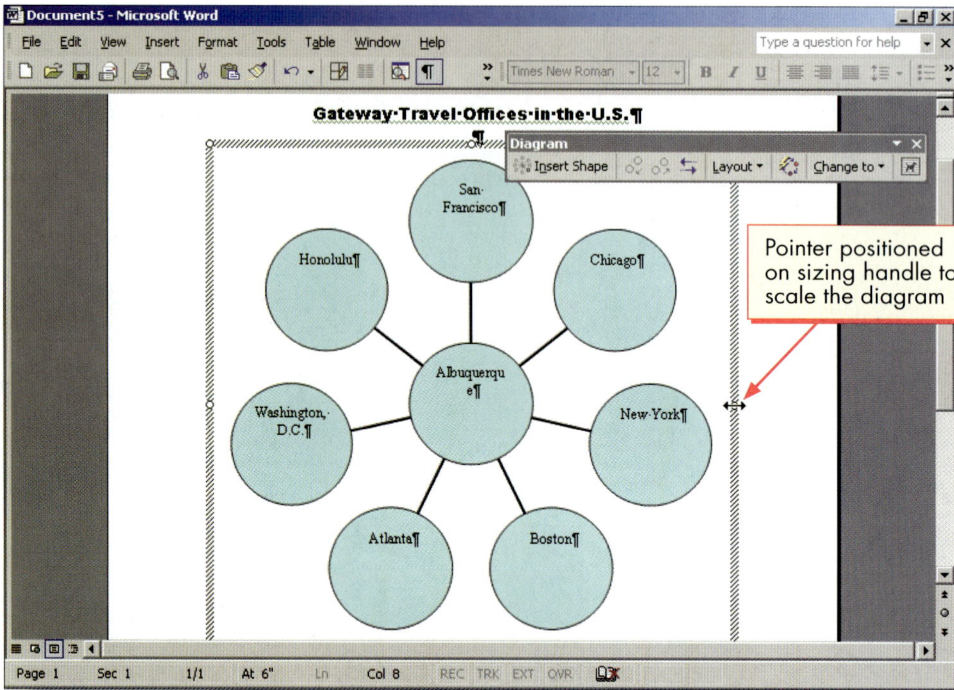

9. Add an extra blank line below the document title, and then center the document vertically on the page (Page Setup, Layout tab).

FIGURE 11-19
Completed radial diagram

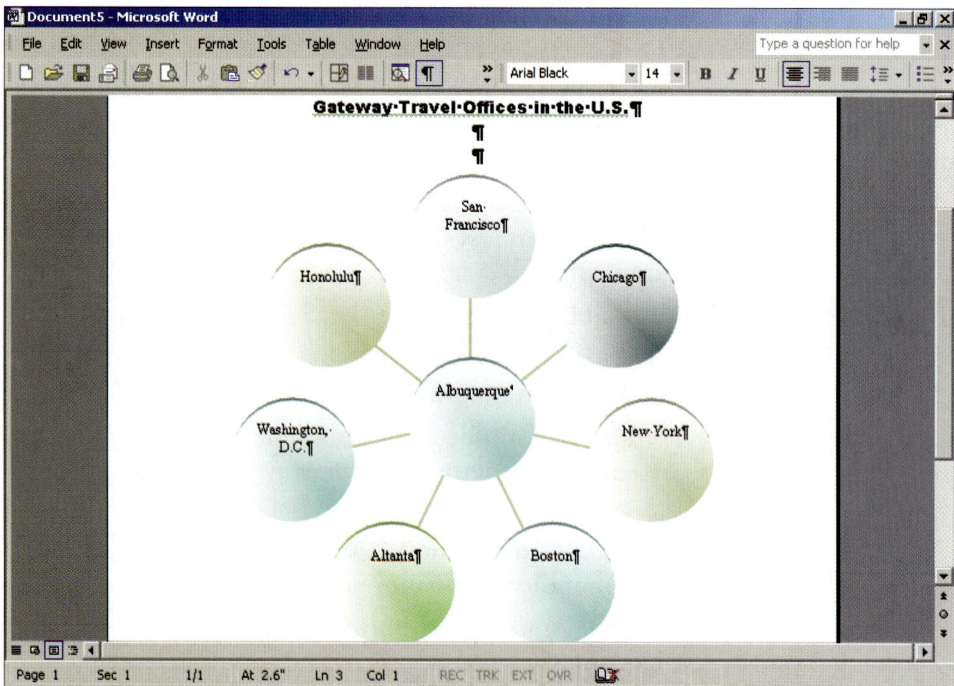

10. Save the file as ***[your initials[*****11-11** in your Lesson 11 folder.

11. Print and close the document.

Creating Charts

A chart is a visual representation of numeric data. Charts often make values in a table easier to understand. You can usually look at a chart and quickly grasp the meaning of the numbers.

You create a chart in a Word document by inserting a generic chart as an object. Word uses Microsoft Graph to create and edit the chart. You enter the chart data in a table called a *datasheet*. The datasheet is similar to an Excel worksheet. When you first create the chart, the datasheet contains sample data, and the chart is displayed in a 3-D column graph format. You replace the sample data with your own numbers and column labels.

EXERCISE 11-12 Insert a Chart in a Document

1. Open the file **Growth**. Add the date and make the letter from Doris Simms, Travel Counselor. Include your reference initials and an enclosure notation.

2. Position the insertion point in the blank line below the paragraph that begins "As you requested."

3. Open the Insert menu and choose Picture, Chart. A sample chart is inserted in the document between the second and third paragraphs. Word displays the graph editing screen, which includes the Microsoft Graph menu and toolbars and the datasheet. The chart is based on sample data in the datasheet. You'll replace this data with your own labels and numbers in the next exercise. (See Figure 11-20 on the next page.)

4. Click the Toolbar Options button on the Graph toolbar to see the available Standard and Formatting chart toolbar buttons.

5. Click anywhere in the document. The datasheet disappears and the Word menu and toolbars reappear.

6. Click the chart once to select it. Notice the selection handles. Word treats the chart as an inline graphic object. You can move or resize it. To edit the chart, you must redisplay the graph editing screen and the datasheet.

FIGURE 11-20 Inserting a chart

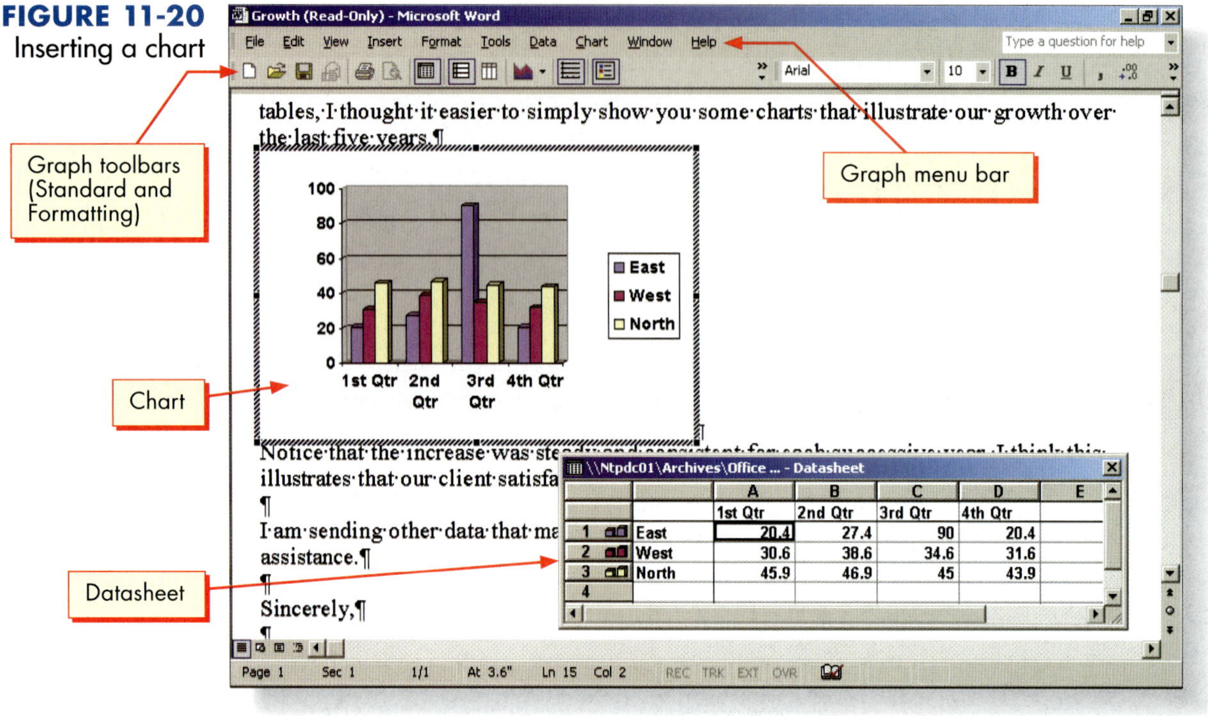

EXERCISE 11-13 Key Data in the Graph Datasheet

1. Double-click the chart to open the graph editing screen.
2. If necessary, drag the datasheet by its title bar to another location so you can see more of the underlying graph.
3. Click the upper left gray box of the datasheet to select the entire datasheet (or press Ctrl+A).
4. Press Delete. This deletes the sample data. The entire datasheet is now blank and ready for you to key new data. Notice that the chart disappears when you erase the sample data.

NOTE: Although you can perform multiple Undo actions elsewhere in Word, in Microsoft Graph you can only undo your last action. Be careful when making changes!

5. Key the data and headings shown in Figure 11-21 (on the next page). The chart grows as you key the data. Notice that you can't see the entire row 1 label "Total Revenues" after you enter the value in the adjacent column—this doesn't affect how the label is displayed on the chart.

6. If necessary, press Enter after keying the last figure to make sure it is entered in the chart. Data is not entered until you move to another cell.

FIGURE 11-21 Datasheet with new data

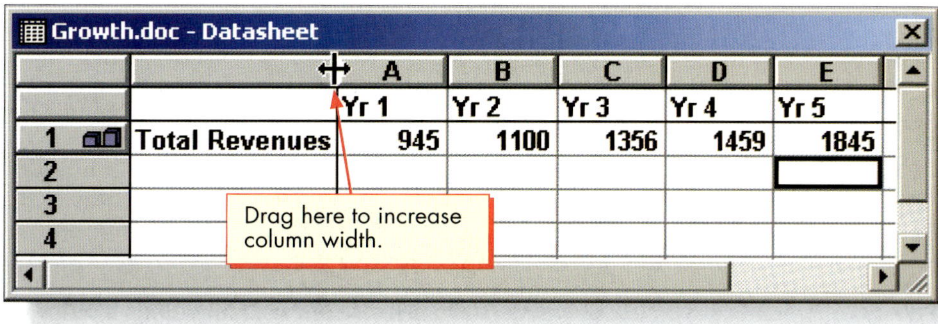

TIP: You can change the width of datasheet columns to display text that might be hidden. Move the pointer to the divider line between the columns until the two-headed arrow appears; then hold down the mouse button and drag to the desired width (or double-click the divider line). If the datasheet is too small to show all the data, point to the side or bottom border of the datasheet window and then use the two-headed arrow pointer to drag to a larger size.

7. While still in the graph editing screen, choose Datasheet from the View menu or click the View Datasheet button on the Graph toolbar. The datasheet disappears. Notice that you are still in the graph editing screen, but you can see more of your document.
8. Click the View Datasheet button to display the datasheet again.
9. Click anywhere in the document to redisplay the Word menu and toolbars.
10. Save the document as ***[your initials]*****11-13** in your Lesson 11 folder. Leave it open for the next exercise.

TABLE 11-1 Microsoft Graph Standard and Formatting Toolbar Buttons

BUTTON	FUNCTION
Import File	Imports files or data from another application
View Datasheet	Shows or hides the datasheet window
By Row	Plots data series by rows
By Column	Plots data series by columns

continues

TABLE 11-1 Microsoft Graph Standard and Formatting Toolbar Buttons *continued*

BUTTON	FUNCTION
Data Table	Displays the values for each data series in a grid below the chart
Chart Type	Changes the chart type for an individual data series, chart group, or entire chart
Category Axis Gridlines	Shows or hides category axis gridlines
Value Axis Gridlines	Shows or hides value axis gridlines
Legend	Adds or deletes a chart legend
Drawing	Displays or hides the Drawing toolbar
Fill Color	Applies a color to the selected chart element
Microsoft Graph Help	Starts Microsoft Graph Help
Currency Style	Applies the Currency style ($100.00) to selected cells
Percent Style	Applies the Percent style (100%) to selected cells
Comma Style	Applies the Comma style (1,100.00) to selected cells
Increase Decimal	Increases the number of digits displayed after the insertion point for selected cells
Decrease Decimal	Decreases the number of digits displayed after the insertion point for selected cells
Angle Clockwise	Rotates selected text down at a 45-degree angle
Angle Counterclockwise	Rotates selected text up at a 45-degree angle

EXERCISE 11-14 Create a Chart from a Word Table

You can create a chart by selecting data in a Word table and then choosing Insert, Picture, Chart. The selected data will appear automatically in the chart's datasheet.

1. In the document *[your initials]*11-13, select the chart and press Delete. (Remember, click a chart once to select it or double-click a chart to activate the chart editing window and display the datasheet.)
2. Open the file **Revenue1**. The table in this file has more up-to-date revenue figures for the travel agency and displays the data differently (showing the data in decimal figures representing millions).
3. Select the table. Open the Insert menu and choose Picture, Chart. Word inserts a chart, using the table data, and displays the chart's datasheet.

NOTE: You can also copy the data from a Word table and then paste it into an empty datasheet.

FIGURE 11-22 Charting data from a Word table

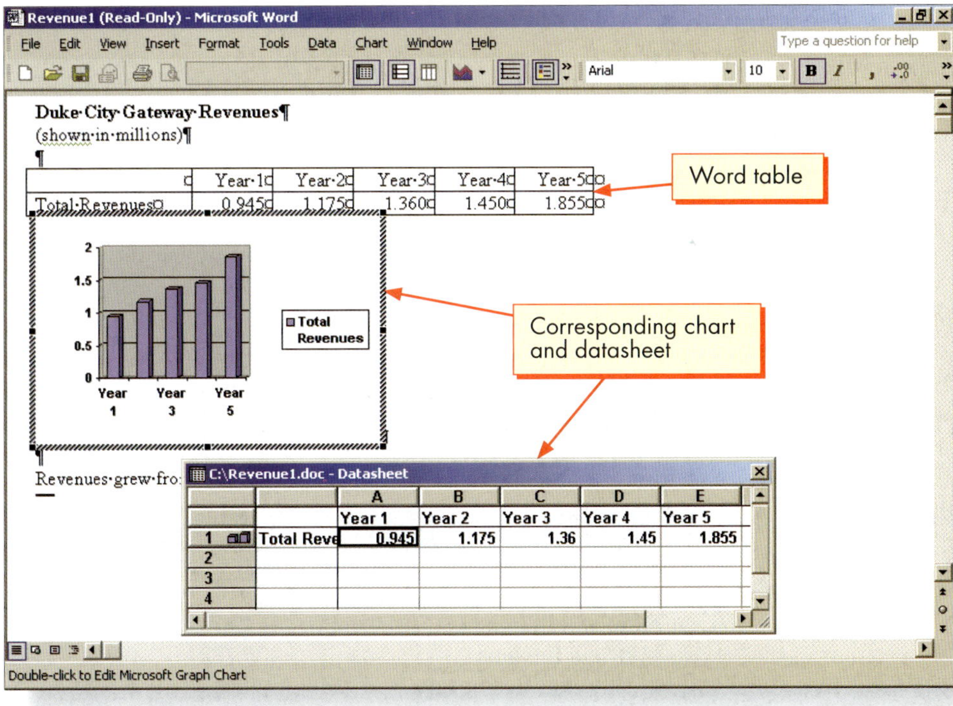

4. Click outside the chart to deactivate the chart editing window.
5. Click the chart to select it. Drag the chart's middle right sizing handle to the right until you can see all five of the year labels, with the text all on one line.

6. Copy the chart to the Clipboard.
7. Paste the chart into the document *[your initials]*11-13, at the same paragraph mark as the previous chart (above "Notice that").
8. Close the file **Revenue1** without saving.

Editing Chart Data

After you create a chart, you might need to edit the data. Numbers in a chart can be changed only on the datasheet.

EXERCISE 11-15 Edit Chart Data

1. In the document *[your initials]*11-13, double-click the chart to open the graph editing screen.
2. Click the View Datasheet button if the datasheet is not displayed.
3. Resize the datasheet so you can see all columns at once (drag the right edge).
4. Change the Year 5 total revenue to **2.155** (press Enter after keying the text to enter the value). Notice that the chart changes with the new value.

NOTE: If you inadvertently key a value in the wrong cell of the datasheet, Microsoft Graph might add another column or row to your chart. To delete the additional column or row, click the gray box at the beginning of the column or row that contains the erroneous data.

5. Add two new rows of data to the datasheet for New Business and Repeat Business, as shown in Figure 11-23. (You don't have to type the zero before each decimal point; they'll be entered automatically.) Adjust the width of the first column to accommodate "Repeat Business."

FIGURE 11-23 Datasheet with two new rows

11-13.doc - Datasheet

		A	B	C	D	E
		Year 1	Year 2	Year 3	Year 4	Year 5
1	Total Revenues	0.945	1.175	1.36	1.45	2.155
2	New Business	0.661	0.762	0.816	0.799	0.742
3	Repeat Business	0.284	0.413	0.544	0.651	1.413
4						

EXERCISE 11-16 Switch Data Series from Rows to Columns

Data is plotted in a chart in groups of *data series*, which are collections of related data points. These values are usually found within the same column or row in the datasheet. Each data series is distinguished by a unique color. Sometimes it's hard to know in advance if it's better to arrange your data in rows or in columns on the datasheet. Microsoft Graph lets you enter it either way and switch back and forth.

1. Double-click the chart if it is not activated.
2. Click the By Column button on the Graph toolbar. The graph columns are grouped by column data instead of row data. Notice that the data is now grouped into three categories, showing the yearly changes within each of the three categories.

TIP: Depending on the type of data in your chart, switching data series between row and column orientations is often a good idea. Sometimes a different view can emphasize and improve chart data in a way you didn't anticipate.

3. Click the By Row button to change the data series groupings back to a row orientation.

TIP: You can also change data series by choosing Series in Rows or Series in Columns from the Data menu.

4. Click anywhere in the document to redisplay the Word document.
5. Click the chart once to select it. You might need to resize the chart again to display the year labels on one line.
6. Click the Center button on the Formatting toolbar to center the chart horizontally.
7. Create a letterhead for the document by keying the following information in the header pane, formatted as 10-point Arial, right-aligned.

   Duke City Gateway Travel
   15 Montgomery Boulevard
   Albuquerque, NM 87111
   (505) 555-1234
   www.gwaytravel.com

8. Change the top margin to 2 inches.
9. Preview the document; then save it as ***[your initials]*****11-16** in your Lesson 11 folder. (See the final document in Figure 11-24 on the next page.)

FIGURE 11-24
Document with modified chart and letterhead

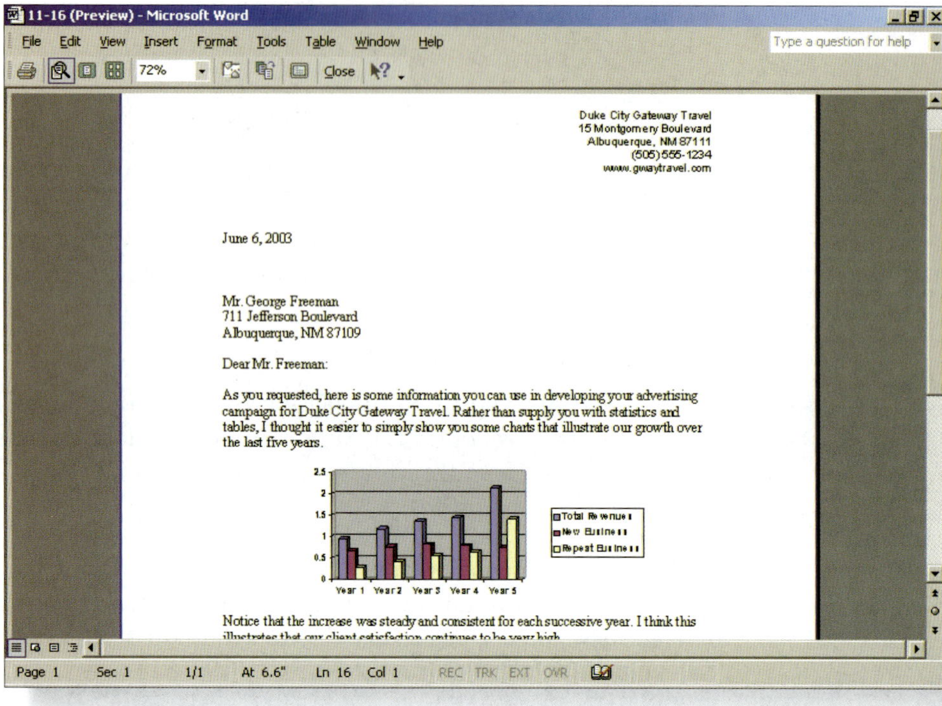

10. Print the document. Leave it open for the next exercise.

Changing Chart Types and Adding Options

When selecting a chart type, the data you are charting generally determines the choices you can use. Although you might like the look of a certain chart type, it might not be appropriate for the numbers or the message you are trying to communicate.

Microsoft Graph offers you a variety of chart types, including column, bar, and line charts. For charts with a single data series, the pie chart is a popular choice. Many charts can be displayed using a 3-D visual effect. You can also combine different types within a single chart, such as column and line.

EXERCISE 11-17 Change Chart Types

There are 14 different chart types, and each type has 2 or more sub-types.

1. Double-click the chart to open the graph editing screen. Hide the datasheet.

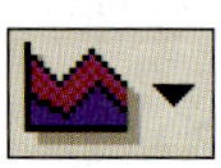

2. Click the arrow next to the Chart Type button 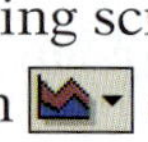 on the Graph toolbar. A pop-up menu displays some basic chart types.

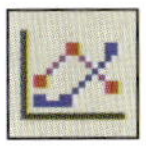

3. Choose Bar Chart, the first option on the second row. The chart changes to a one-dimensional bar chart.
4. Click the Chart Type button arrow again, and choose Line Chart, the first option on the fourth row.
5. Choose some of the other chart options, to see how they display your data.
6. Choose **Chart Type** from the **Chart** menu. In the **Chart Type** dialog box, look at the **Standard Types** tab. This dialog box provides many more chart types and chart sub-types than the Chart Type button offers.
7. Under **Chart type**, choose **Column**. Seven sub-types are available for column charts.

FIGURE 11-25
Chart Type dialog box

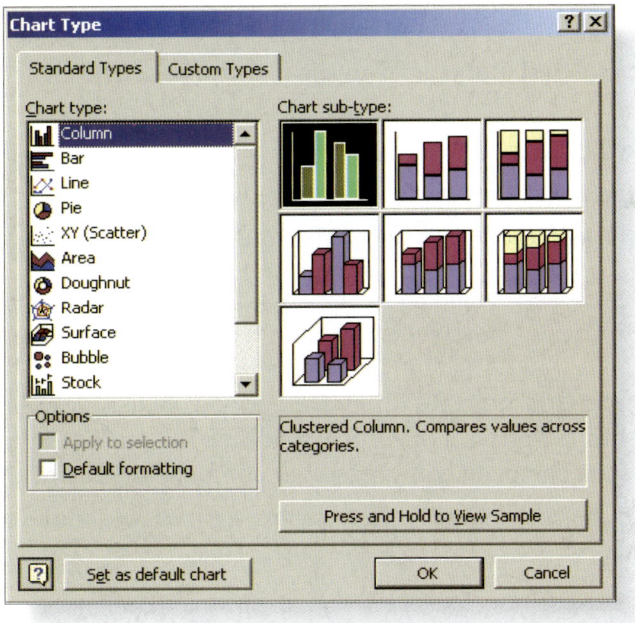

8. Under **Chart sub-type**, click the first sub-type on the second line, which is the clustered column with a 3-D visual effect. This is the default chart type you started with.
9. Use the **Press and Hold to View Sample** button to see a preview of the chart. The Chart Sub-type window is replaced by a **Sample** window, displaying the selected sub-type as it will appear. Release the button.
10. Select the second sub-type on the first row—the **Stacked Column**—and use the **Press and Hold to View Sample** button to preview the sub-type.
11. Select the first sub-type—**Clustered Column**—and click **OK**. The chart type is changed to a simple one-dimensional column chart.
12. Click anywhere in the document to return to Word. Notice that removing the 3-D effect makes the chart easier to read.

WORD

EXERCISE 11-18 Add Chart Options

Charts are very versatile. You can add, remove, or modify chart elements (such as a chart title or gridlines), change colors, and format chart data.

1. Double-click the chart to open the graph editing screen. Hide the datasheet.
2. Position the pointer over various parts and areas of the chart. A ScreenTip will identify the parts by name.

NOTE: You can format any part of a chart by right-clicking the part and then opening the Format dialog box for that part. Depending on the part, the dialog box might provide color, pattern, line, placement, and font options.

3. Choose Chart Options from the Chart menu. The Chart Options dialog box appears.
4. Click the Titles tab.
5. For the Chart title, key **Growth at Duke City Gateway Travel**
6. For the Value (Y) axis, key **(Millions)**

NOTE: In this chart, the Value (Y) axis is the vertical axis, listing the revenue amounts. The Category (X) axis is the horizontal axis, showing the years.

7. Click the Gridlines tab. Under Category (X) axis, click Major gridlines. Click OK. Chart titles and a set of vertical gridlines are added to the chart. Notice that the plot area has been compressed to compensate for the additional text.
8. Make the chart wider and taller, as desired, but make sure the letter fits on one page.

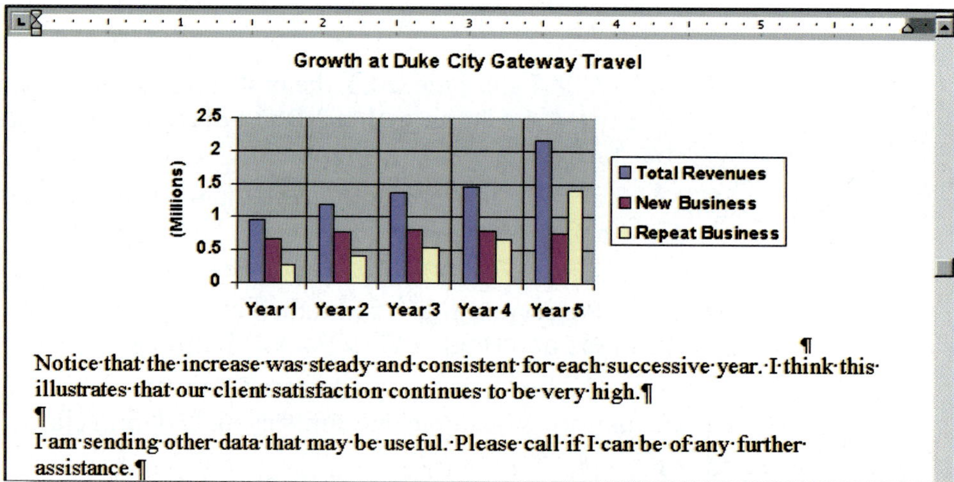

FIGURE 11-26
Chart with title and vertical gridlines

9. Save the file as ***[your initials]*****11-18** in your Lesson 11 folder.
10. Print and close the file.

LESSON 11 Summary

- Add ready-to-use pictures to your document in the form of drawings (clip art) or photographs. You can also add sound effect, music, and video clips.
- Search for clips by keyword, using the Insert Clip Art task pane, or view collections of clips by category from the Microsoft Clip Organizer window (click the link at the bottom of the task pane).
- Click a clip to select it. You can copy, paste, resize, crop, and format a selected clip.
- A selected clip is surrounded by a selection rectangle with sizing handles at each side and corner. Drag a corner sizing handle to make a clip larger or smaller while keeping the original proportions of the clip. Use the Format Picture dialog box (Size tab) to resize a clip to exact measurements or a percentage of the original size.
- Crop a clip to hide part of it from view. Click the Crop button on the Picture toolbar, position the crop tool on a sizing handle, and drag until you have hidden the part of the picture you want cropped.
- You can undo any action applied to a clip. You can also restore a clip to its original size by clicking the Reset Picture button on the Picture toolbar.
- By default, a clip is inserted in a document as an inline graphic and treated like a character or word. To move a clip that is an inline graphic, cut and paste the clip or drag and drop it. You can use the alignment buttons on the Formatting toolbar to change the horizontal alignment of a clip.
- To move a clip freely on the page, change it from an inline graphic to a floating graphic by changing its wrapping style. Use the Text Wrapping button on the Picture toolbar. You can drag a floating graphic to position it anywhere on the page, and have the document text wrap around the graphic. The Square wrapping style wraps text around all sides of a graphic.
- Use the WordArt feature to create special effects with text. Choose from a variety of WordArt styles and modify the WordArt object by using the WordArt toolbar buttons (to change shape, size, color, wrapping style, alignment, and so on).
- Use Word's diagram feature to insert six different types of diagrams, including an organization chart or a target or radial diagram. Add text to a diagram by clicking in each box or circle in the diagram and keying the text.

- Use a chart to represent numeric data visually. Charts are created in Microsoft Graph. When you first insert a chart, it appears in the default chart style (3-D bar) with sample data. Chart data is contained in a table called a datasheet. You enter your own data in the datasheet and then click outside the chart to deactivate Microsoft Graph and return to Word.
- Click a chart to select it (for deleting, moving, or resizing). Double-click a chart to activate Microsoft Graph (for editing the datasheet, changing the chart type, or changing other chart options).
- To navigate in the datasheet, use Enter, Tab, or the arrow keys. To select all data in the datasheet, press Ctrl+A.
- To enter new data in the datasheet, delete the sample data. In the first row under "A," "B," "C," and so on, key your column headings (the category axis of the chart). In the first column to the right of "1," "2," "3," and so on, key your row headings (the value axis of the chart). Key the corresponding numeric values in the datasheet.
- Edit chart data by clicking a datasheet cell and keying the new data.
- Create a chart from a Word table by selecting the data in the table and then using the Insert, Picture, Chart command. Edit the datasheet as necessary.
- Microsoft Graph has its own Standard and Formatting toolbars for modifying a chart. For example, switch data series from rows to columns by clicking the By Column button. Reverse this procedure by clicking the By Row button. See Table 11-1.
- There are 14 different types of charts, and each type has 2 or more sub-types. Use the Chart Type button on the toolbar to choose from a group of chart types, or open the Chart Type dialog box (open the Chart menu and choose Chart Type) to see all types and sub-types.
- Add options such as a chart title or gridlines by selecting the chart, choosing Chart Options from the Chart menu, and clicking the appropriate tab in the Chart Options dialog box.
- Change the chart position in the Word document by clicking to select the chart and then using the alignment buttons on the Formatting toolbar. Resize a selected chart by dragging a sizing handle to increase or decrease the chart size.

LESSON 11 Command Summary

FEATURE	BUTTON	MENU	KEYBOARD	SPEECH?
Insert clip art		Insert, Picture, Clip Art		✓
Format picture		Format, Picture		✓
Crop picture		Format, Picture, Picture		✓
Resize picture		Format, Picture, Size		✓
Reset picture		Format, Picture, Size		✓
Change wrapping style		Format, Picture, Layout		✓
Insert WordArt		Insert, Picture, WordArt		✓
Insert Diagram		Insert, Diagram		✓
Insert Chart		Insert, Picture, Chart		✓
View Datasheet		View, Datasheet		✓
Chart Type		Chart, Chart Type		✓
Plot data series by rows	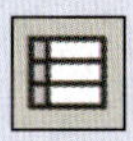	Data, Series in Rows		✓
Plot data series by columns		Data, Series in Columns		✓
Add/delete chart options		Chart, Chart Options		✓

Concepts Review

TRUE/FALSE QUESTIONS

Each of the following statements is either true or false. Indicate your choice by circling T or F.

T F 1. You can search for clip art by keyword in the Insert Clip Art task pane.

T F 2. Clips are organized alphabetically in the Microsoft Clip Organizer window.

T F 3. The terms "size" and "crop" are used interchangeably in Word.

T F 4. After you size or crop a picture, you can easily reset it to its original size.

T F 5. The organization chart option is included in the Diagram Gallery dialog box.

T F 6. To select a WordArt object, point to the object and click.

T F 7. You right-click a chart to open the graph editing screen.

T F 8. You can edit chart data without changing a chart's datasheet.

SHORT ANSWER QUESTIONS

Write the correct answer in the space provided.

1. Which toolbar appears on the screen when you insert clip art?

____

2. How do you open the Microsoft Clip Organizer window?

____

3. When you insert a picture, what is its default wrapping style?

____

4. Name one way to insert WordArt.

____

5. What is the table called in Microsoft Graph where a chart's values are entered?

____

6. What is the purpose of ?

7. After a chart is inserted in Word, how do you activate Microsoft Graph to make changes to the chart?

8. How do you use the Microsoft Graph toolbar to display or hide a datasheet?

CRITICAL THINKING

Answer these questions on a separate page. There are no right or wrong answers. Support your answers with examples from your own experience, if possible.

1. Find three examples of clip art in newsletters, advertisements, letters, or other publications. Explain how the clip art helps to communicate the message of the text.
2. When would you use charts rather than tables in a document? Create a few sample charts and explain their potential use.

W O R D

Lesson Applications

EXERCISE 11-19

Insert, size, position, and format clip art and WordArt.

1. Open the file **Special3**. Set a 1.75-inch top margin and 1-25-inch left and right margins.
2. Add two blank lines at the top of the document. At the first blank line, insert a WordArt object. Choose the third style in the third row of the WordArt Gallery dialog box. Use the text **Gateway Travel Tours**
3. Format the text below the WordArt object (from "Some of our" through the end of the document) as two columns with 0.25 inch between the columns. Balance the length of the columns.
4. In the paragraph that begins "Our local area," change the last words "student tours" to **golf tours**. At the end of the paragraph, insert clip art of a golfer. Search for the clip art by using the keyword "golf." Scale the picture proportionately to 60% and apply square text wrapping. Adjust the picture position to place it attractively to the right of the "Our local area" paragraph.
5. Locate the paragraph that begins "Our naturalist." At the beginning of the paragraph, insert clip art of a backpacker. Size the picture to 1.2 inches high (make sure Lock aspect ratio is checked) and apply square text wrapping. Place the picture attractively to the left of the paragraph.
6. Add a page border to the document. Readjust picture positions after the border is added, if needed.
7. Save the document as ***[your initials]*11-19** in your Lesson 11 folder.
8. Print and close the document.

EXERCISE 11-20

Insert a diagram and insert a chart with added options.

1. Start a new document. Create a memo to Staff from Alexis Johnson. The subject is **Sales Analysis**. For the body of the memo, key the following text:

   An analysis of our customer base over a two-year period shows that repeat business and referrals are the foundation of our business. Additional sources of new business are the Internet, advertising (print ads and direct mail), and walk-in traffic to the office. See the attached chart.
2. Two lines below this paragraph, insert a pyramid diagram. Use the Insert Shape button twice so you have a total of 5 layers. Add the following text,

one per layer, from top to bottom. You'll have to reduce the font size for the top text item to fit.

Walk-ins
Advertising
Internet
Referrals
Repeat Business

3. To make the diagram fit on page 1 of the memo, right-click the diagram border, open the Format Diagram dialog box, and scale the diagram to 85% of its original size.
4. Use the AutoFormat button on the Diagram toolbar to choose another style. Make the diagram text bold.
5. Deselect the diagram and insert a page break at the end of the page.
6. On page 2, insert a standard column chart (clustered column sub-type) with the data shown in Figure 11-27.

FIGURE 11-27

	2002	2003
Repeat Business	.93	1.41
Referrals	.38	.4
Internet	.24	.26
Advertising	.2	.22
Walk-ins	.11	.07

7. Add the chart title **Sales Analysis** and the value axis title **Millions of Dollars**.
8. Resize the chart to the width of the document text area (6 inches)—use the ruler as a guide. Make the chart taller, as well.
9. Add a continuation page header to page 2.
10. Change the diagram font to Arial to match the text in the chart.
11. Save the document as ***[your initials]*11-20** in your Lesson 11 folder.
12. Print and close the document.

EXERCISE 11-21

Insert, size, wrap, and position clip art; insert and modify a diagram.

1. Start a new document using the Professional Letter template.

2. In the Company Name box, key **Duke City Gateway Travel**. Select the text and change it to 14 points.
3. In the return address box, key the following four lines of text:

   15 Montgomery Boulevard
   Albuquerque, NM 87111
   (505) 555-1234
   www.gwaytravel.com
4. After the address, insert a clip art image by using the keyword **travel**. Change the clip art to square text wrapping, resize it appropriately, and position it to the right of the address text.
5. Address the letter to the following recipient. The letter should be from Frank Youngblood, Manager.

   Mr. Paul Saunders
   Mesquite Software Consulting
   234 Valencia Court
   Santa Fe, NM 87505
6. Key the text shown in Figure 11-28 for the body of the letter.

FIGURE 11-28

Thank you for letting us plan your company's recent trip to Japan. We're glad you found it easy to work with us and communicate your needs.

We're available for all your employee travel needs, both business and personal, as described in the enclosed brochure. We look forward to working with you again in the near future.

7. Add your reference initials and an enclosure notation, using the appropriate styles (choose the styles from the Styles and Formatting task pane).
8. On a new line between the two paragraphs (before "We're available"), insert a radial diagram with the text **Duke City Gateway Travel** in the center and the following four text items around the center:

   International Travel
   Corporate Travel
   Family Travel
   Group Travel
9. Apply a style you like and then use the Layout button on the Diagram toolbar to scale the diagram so the letter fits on one page (drag the right middle sizing handle).
10. Format the text in the center shape of the diagram as bold.

11. Save it as *[your initials]***11-21** in your Lesson 11 folder.
12. Print and close the document.

EXERCISE 11-22 Challenge Yourself

Insert WordArt, insert charts, edit chart data, change chart type, and add chart options.

1. In a new document, key the title **International Tour Revenues**. Assume this is a page in a report and apply Heading 1 style to the title.
2. Insert two blank lines below the title.
3. Open the file **Revenue2**. Insert a chart based on the Word table. If the chart's datasheet has a blank first row, delete the entire blank row. (Right-click a cell in the blank row and choose Delete, Entire row.)
4. Copy the chart to the Clipboard. (Tip: Deactivate Microsoft Graph and select the chart object in Word.) Close Revenue2 without saving.
5. Paste the chart object at the second paragraph mark in the new document.
6. Expand the width of the chart until its right border is even with the right margin. Change the data series groupings so they are grouped by column (there should be four groups of columns).
7. Edit the datasheet, changing the years to **2001**, **2002**, and **2003**. Change "Castles" to **Bavarian Castles**
8. Add the chart title **Third Quarter Revenues**. Resize the chart as needed to display the value axis figures in 5,000 units (40,000, 35,000, 30,000 and so on).
9. Above the chart, write a brief paragraph that starts "The following chart compares" and explains the data shown.
10. Copy the modified chart to the Clipboard. Three paragraph marks below the chart, paste a copy of the chart.
11. Activate the copied chart. In the datasheet, delete the columns for the first two years, leaving only 2003.
12. Delete the chart title. Change the chart type to a pie chart (first sub-type). Use the Data Labels tab in the Chart Options dialog box to show percentages for each slice of the pie.
13. At the blank paragraph mark above the pie chart, key a brief paragraph explaining this 2003 chart data. Mention the actual dollar values for each tour (get this data from the datasheet).
14. Add a cover page to the document. Use the following title text:

    Tour Revenues
    Duke City Gateway Travel
    Prepared by *[your name]* on *[today's date]*

15. Create WordArt from the first line of the title. Format and position all title text attractively.
16. Save the document as ***[your initials]*****11-22** in your Lesson 11 folder.
17. Print and close the document.

On Your Own

In these exercises you work on your own, as you would in a real-life work environment. Use the skills you've learned to accomplish the task—and be creative.

EXERCISE 11-23

Log onto the Internet and use Word's Insert Clip Art task pane to search only for photographs with the keyword **sports**. Insert one of the photographs into a blank document, add some accompanying text, and then save the document as ***[your initials]*****11-23**. Print the document.

EXERCISE 11-24

Insert a target diagram into a blank document. Add text appropriate for this type of diagram. (A target diagram shows steps toward achieving a goal, the goal being the "bull's eye.") Save the document as ***[your initials]*****11-24** and print it.

EXERCISE 11-25

Create a simple column chart, using your own data. Copy the chart twice in the same document, and apply different chart types or sub-types for the same data (such as 3-D Cone or Pyramid). Save the document as ***[your initials]*****11-25** and print it.

LESSON 12

Sharing Your Work

OBJECTIVES

After completing this lesson, you will be able to:

1. **Create comments.**
2. **Compare and merge documents.**
3. **Convert documents into Web pages.**

Estimated Time: 1 hour

MOUS ACTIVITIES

In this lesson:

W2002 6-1
W2002 6-2
W2002 6-3

See Appendix E.

In most offices, more than one person works on a document. A document might have a primary author and several editors. Word provides tools that make it easy to collaborate with others—on your computer instead of on paper—to produce a finished document. After you have a finished document, you might take it one step further—sharing it with others on the World Wide Web.

Creating Comments

Comments are notes or annotations you add to a document. Each person who adds a comment is called a *reviewer.* Comments are color-coded by reviewer.

Word refers to comments and any other type of document revision marks as *markup.* You can display, hide, or print markup.

In Normal view, you insert, edit, and view comments in the *Reviewing pane*—a narrow horizontal pane that opens at the bottom of the screen. In Print Layout view, you can enter, edit, and view comments in *markup balloons* that appear in the document margin with a line leading to where the comment was inserted.

EXERCISE 12-1 Add Comments to a Document

The easiest way to add a comment to a document is to use the Reviewing toolbar. You can also use the keyboard shortcut Alt+Ctrl+M or choose Comment from the Insert menu.

1. Open the file **CruiseFAQs2**. Make sure the document is in Normal view.
2. Display the Reviewing toolbar by right-clicking any toolbar button and then choosing Reviewing.

NOTE: If the toolbar appears in the document text area, drag it above the ruler to dock it.

3. Choose Options from the Tools menu and click the User Information tab.
4. Enter your name and initials in the appropriate data fields. Click OK.

TIP: If you review a document by using another person's computer, your comments will be attributed to the person whose name appears in the User Information tab. Make sure to change the name in the User Information tab to your name when you insert comments, and then back to the original user's name when you are finished.

5. Position the insertion point at the beginning of the document.

6. Click the New Comment button on the Reviewing toolbar. The Reviewing pane opens, showing your name, followed by the date and time you are inserting the comment. The entry in the Reviewing pane is color-coded to the reviewer. A vertical line, called a *comment reference mark*, also appears in the document where you inserted the comment. The line is color-coded to the reviewer.
7. In the Reviewing pane, at the insertion point, key:

   This is a shortened version of the longer CruiseFAQs document. Make sure Frank Youngblood reviews both documents.

8. Scroll within the document to the paragraph below "*What kinds of people take a cruise?*" Select "$100" and click the New Comment button to insert another comment.

NOTE: When you comment on a selected word, sentence, or paragraph, the text is enclosed by two comment reference marks. You can also just position the insertion point at a particular location and insert a comment.

9. In the Reviewing pane, key **Check to see if this figure is still valid.** Notice the comment reference marks around "$100" in the document. (See Figure 12-1 on the next page.)

FIGURE 12-1
Inserting a comment

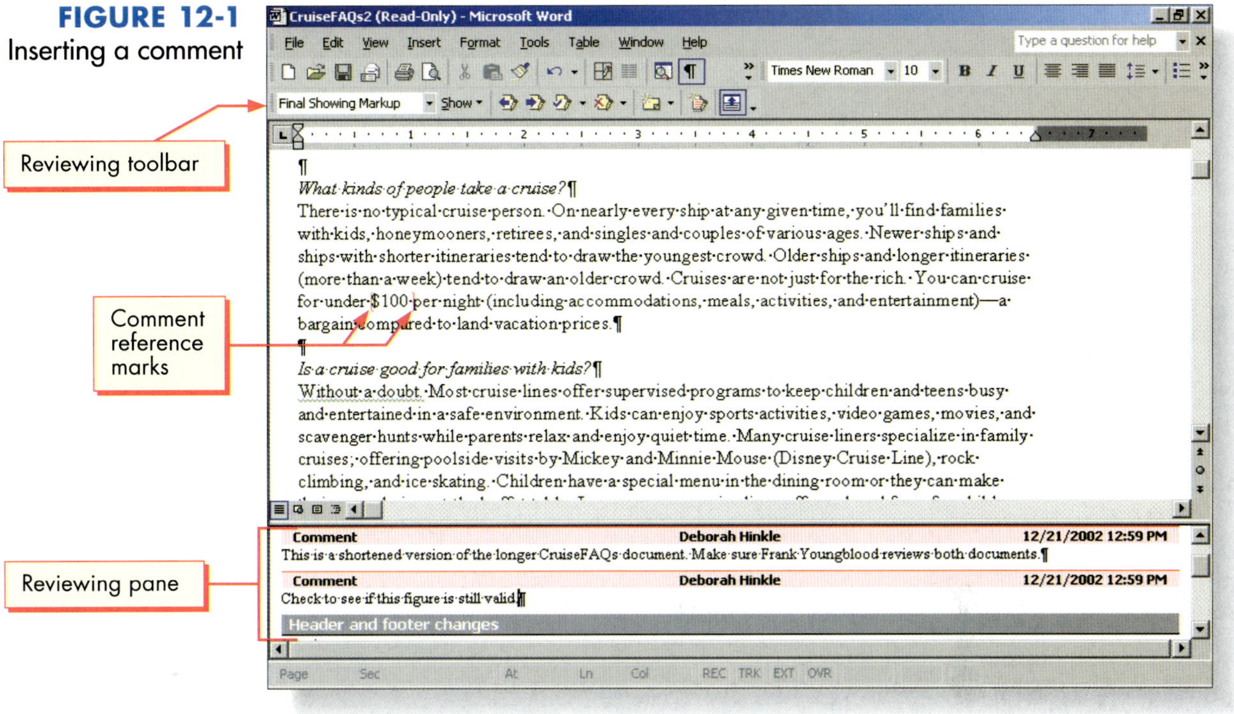

10. Click the Reviewing Pane button on the Reviewing toolbar to close the Reviewing pane.

TIP: The Reviewing Pane button opens and closes the Reviewing pane.

11. Switch to Print Layout view.

12. Use the View menu to change the zoom to 75%. Notice that your comments appear as balloons, with lines leading to where the comments were inserted.

13. Move the insertion point over a balloon. A ScreenTip displays the name of the reviewer and the time and date when the reviewer entered the comment. (See Figure 12-2 on the next page.)

14. Increase the zoom back to 100%. On the second page, locate the paragraph below the text *"How long are cruises?"* Select the entire paragraph (which starts "Cruise length varies.")

15. Press Alt + Ctrl + M to insert a new comment. Word inserts a balloon in the right margin area.

16. Use the horizontal scrollbar to see the entire balloon, and then key the comment **Check the number of days for each cruise mentioned here.** The document now has three comments.

FIGURE 12-2
Comments displayed as balloons in Print Layout view

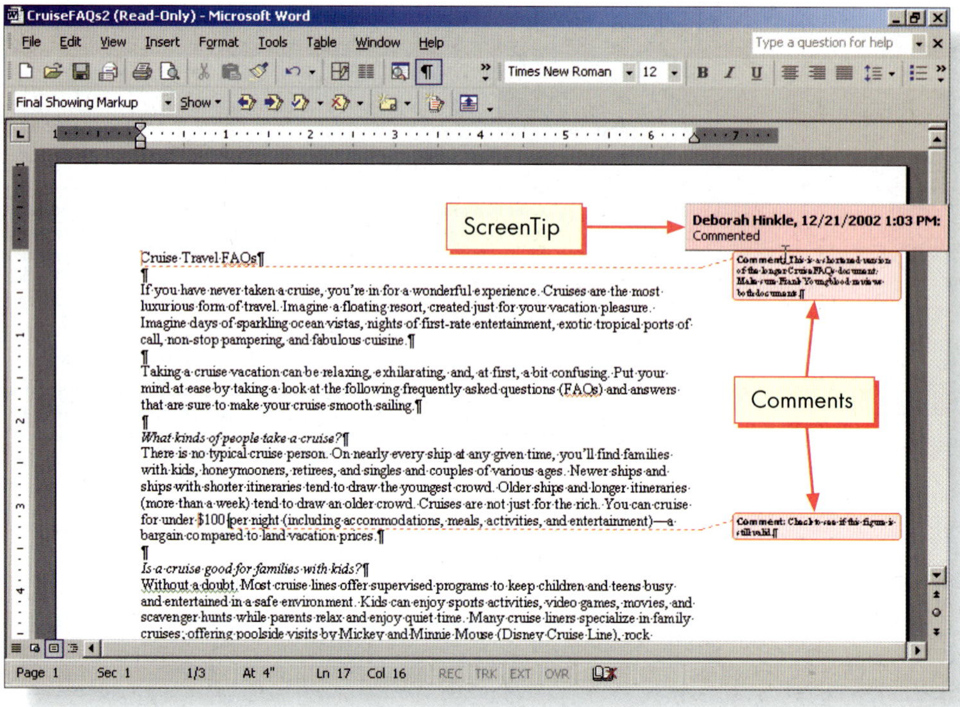

TABLE 12-1 Reviewing Toolbar Buttons

BUTTON	DESCRIPTION
Show	Displays a menu to control which reviewer corrections or comments are displayed.
Previous	Goes to the previous comment.
Next	Goes to the next comment.
Accept Change	Accepts selected change and removes highlighting.
Reject Change/Delete Comment	Rejects selected change and removes highlighting; deletes one or all comments
New Comment	Inserts a comment at the insertion point.

continues

TABLE 12-1 Reviewing Toolbar Buttons *continued*

BUTTON	DESCRIPTION
Track Changes	Marks changes in the document and keeps track of all changes by reviewer name.
Reviewing Pane	Displays or hides the Reviewing pane

NOTE: The Display for Review drop-down list appears at the left of the Reviewing toolbar. Use this list box to view the document before and after reviewer changes.

EXERCISE 12-2 Edit and Delete Comments

You can edit and delete comments by working directly with the balloon text in Print Layout view or by using the Reviewing pane in Normal view.

1. Click the comment in the first balloon. The comment appears highlighted (the balloon's background color darkens and the dotted connector line becomes solid).
2. Select the name "Frank Youngblood" and change it to **Susan Allen**
3. Click the Next button on the Reviewing toolbar. The second comment mark is highlighted.

TIP: The Next and Previous buttons are helpful for jumping from one comment to another, particularly in a long document. The insertion point moves to the next or previous comment.

4. Click the Reject Change/Delete Comment button on the Reviewing toolbar. The comment is removed from the document.

NOTE: You can also delete a comment by right-clicking the comment balloon and choosing Delete Comment from the shortcut menu. To delete all comments, click the arrow to the right of the Reject Change/Delete Comment button and choose Delete All Comments in Document.

5. Switch to Normal view and click the Reviewing Pane button to display the Reviewing pane. The two remaining comments are listed.
6. In the Reviewing pane, change the word "here" in the second comment to **in this paragraph**

WORD

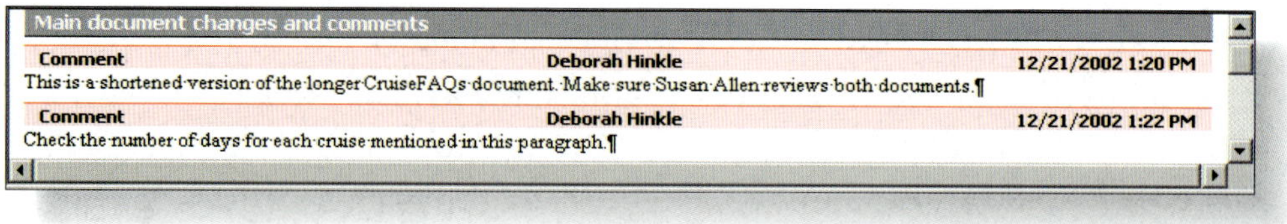

FIGURE 12-3 Edited text of two remaining comments

7. Close the Reviewing pane.
8. Save the document as ***[your initials]*12-2** in a new folder for Lesson 12.

TIP: You can set the Select Browse Object button on the vertical scroll bar to browse by comments. Then the double-arrow scroll buttons become the Previous Comment and Next Comment buttons.

EXERCISE 12-3 Print Comments

You can print a document with its balloon comments, as they appear in Print Layout view, or you can print just a list of a document's comments. You can also print a document without comments.

1. Switch to Print Layout view and then to Print Preview. Notice that comments appear in Print Preview. (Scroll to view the two comments, or use the Multiple Pages button to display all pages in the document.)
2. Click the Print button. The document prints with comments.

NOTE: Word sets the zoom level and page orientation to best display the comment balloons in your printed document.

3. Open the Print dialog box. Notice that Print what is automatically set to Document showing markup. This setting will appear when you print from any view that displays balloon comments. Click Cancel.
4. Close the Print Preview window and switch to Normal view. Notice that balloon comments are not displayed.
5. Open the Print dialog box. Notice that Print what is set to Document. With this setting, the document would print without comments.

TIP: From the Print what drop-down list in the Print dialog box, choose Document to print a document without comments, choose Document showing markup to print a document with its comments in balloons, or choose List of markup to print the document's comments only.

6. Open the Print what drop-down list box and choose List of markup. Click OK. Word prints your comments as a list, similar to how comments appear in the Reviewing pane.
7. Close the document.

Comparing and Merging Documents

Suppose you have two similar documents—an edited copy of a document and the original document. You can use the Compare and Merge feature to compare the edited document with the original. Word will show the differences as tracked changes. *Tracked changes* are revision marks that show where an insertion, deletion, or other editing change occurred.

When comparing two documents, use the *legal blackline* feature, which compares the documents and creates a third document that shows the changes. Law firms use this feature to maintain records of all document revisions and versions.

EXERCISE 12-4 Compare and Merge Documents

1. Open the file **Turquoise**. This is a revised version of a document called **Trail**. You're going to compare both files to see how they are different.
2. Before comparing documents, make your own revisions to this document. Key **in Cibola National Forest** after the text "the tour begins" in the second paragraph. In the same paragraph, delete the second sentence (which begins "You can reach").
3. Choose Compare and Merge Documents from the Tools menu.
4. In the Compare and Merge dialog box, click the Legal blackline check box to select it.

FIGURE 12-4
Compare and Merge dialog box

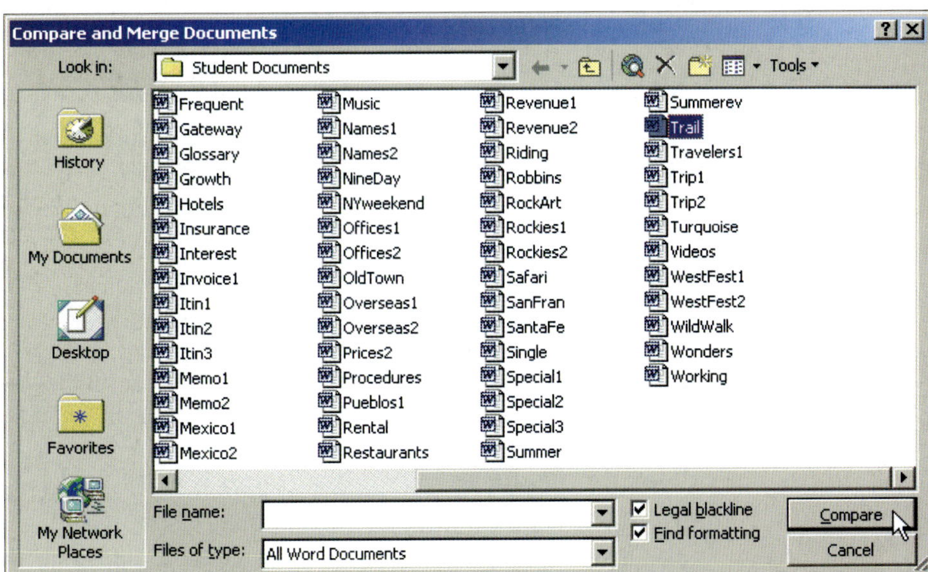

NOTE: The Legal blackline feature compares the two documents and opens a new document to display the changes. When comparing more than two documents, do not check this box. Instead, click Merge or open the Merge drop-down list and choose one of the Merge options.

5. Select the file **Trail** and then click Compare. Word opens a new document that compares the edited file, Turquoise, with the original file, Trail. All these changes appear as revision marks. Deleted text appears as strike-through text; new text is underlined. Revisions are color coded by reviewer. A black vertical line, called a *revision bar,* appears to the left of each line with a revision.

FIGURE 12-5
Merged documents showing revision marks

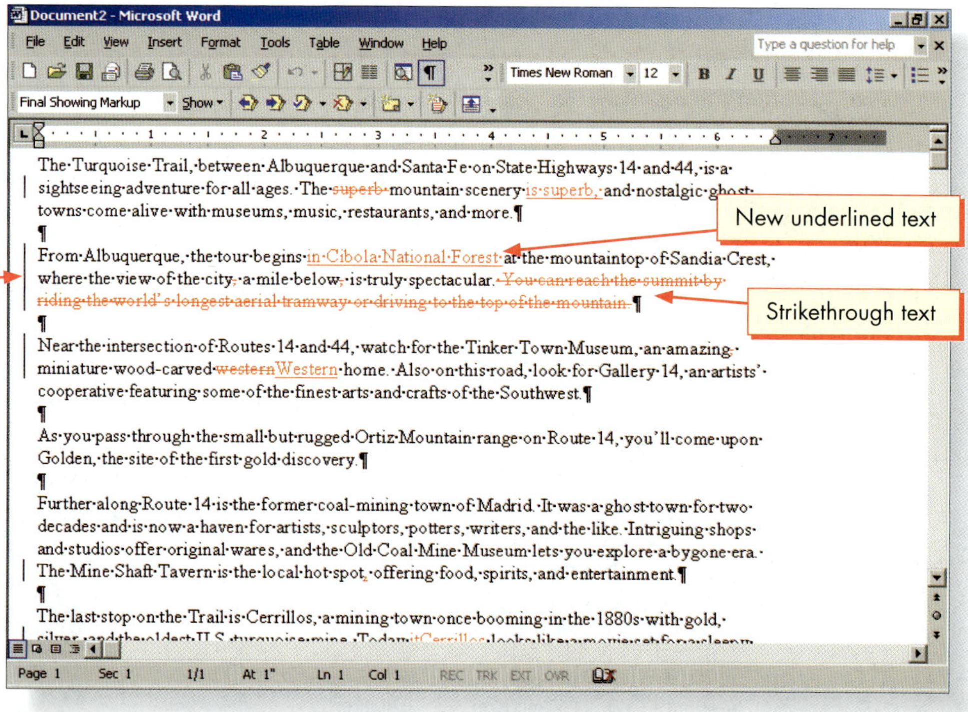

6. Switch to Print Layout view. This is another way to view revision marks—the deleted text appears in balloons in the margin.

TIP: In Normal view, revisions also appear in the Reviewing pane.

7. Save the document as ***[your initials]*12-4** in your Lesson 12 folder.
8. Print the document. Word prints the document with the revisions, changing the zoom level to best display the revision balloons.

NOTE: Printing a document with revision marks is a good way to keep a record of changes made to a document.

EXERCISE 12-5 Accept and Reject Revisions

Now that you have a new revised document, you can decide which revisions you want to accept or reject. When you accept a deletion, the text is removed from the document. When you accept an insertion, the new text is no longer underlined and color-coded. You can accept or reject revisions individually or all at once. To accept or reject revisions:

- Use the Reviewing toolbar.
- Right-click the revision mark or balloon and use the shortcut menu.

1. Switch to Normal view and examine the first paragraph. The second sentence was edited to begin "The mountain scenery is superb," splitting the sentence into two parts. To accept this change, right-click the deleted text "~~superb~~" and choose Accept Deletion from the shortcut menu. Right-click the inserted text "is superb," and choose Accept Insertion from the shortcut menu.
2. Click the Next button on the Reviewing toolbar. Word selects the next revision, the text you inserted.
3. To accept this correction, click the Accept Change button on the Reviewing toolbar. The text is no longer underlined and color-coded.
4. Using the left mouse button, click the sentence you deleted in this paragraph.
5. Assume you decided to keep this sentence and click the Reject Change/Delete Comment button on the Reviewing toolbar. The sentence no longer has a line through it.
6. Review the remaining revisions in the document. Notice the deletion of commas in the second paragraph, the correction of "western" to "Western" in the third paragraph, and the addition of a comma in the fifth paragraph. Notice that the quotation marks around "Casa Grande" were deleted in the last paragraph.
7. To accept all the remaining revisions, click the arrow to the right of the Accept Change button and choose Accept All Changes in Document. (You can also open the Display for Review drop-down list at the left end of the Reviewing toolbar and choose Final.)

NOTE: To reject all changes in a document, click the arrow to the right of the Reject Change/Delete Comment button and choose Reject All Changes in Document.

8. Save the document as ***[your initials]*12-5** in your Lesson 12 folder.
9. Print the document and then close it. Close **Turquoise** without saving changes.

WORD

Converting Documents into Web Pages

After a document is revised and finalized, you can convert it to the Web Page file format. Web pages use the *HTML* (Hypertext Markup Language) file format. The HTML file format makes a document readable in a browser, on an intranet, or on the World Wide Web. Anyone with a browser can open a document saved in this file format instead of opening the document in Word.

NOTE: Although HTML file format is commonly used to create the kind of Web pages you might see on the Internet, you can save any document in this format just to make it more accessible.

EXERCISE 12-6 Preview a Document as a Web Page

1. Open the file **Balloon2**. Close the Reviewing toolbar.
2. To make the document more suitable for a Web page, apply the Hyperlink style to the two Web addresses in the last paragraph.

REVIEW: To automatically apply the style, insert a space character after each Web address and then select and delete the space character. Or, open the Styles and Formatting task pane and apply the Hyperlink style.

3. To see how this document would look in a browser, open the File menu and choose Web Page Preview. Word opens your browser automatically and displays the document.
4. Scroll through the document in the browser window, and then close the browser window.

EXERCISE 12-7 Save a Document as a Web Page

You can save any document in Web Page file format. To make the document look more like a Web page, you can apply a Web theme. Similar to a template, a *Web theme* formats the document with a color scheme, background, bullets, and other design elements.

1. Open the File menu and choose Save as Web Page (you might have to expand the menu). At the bottom of the Save As dialog box, notice that Web Page is indicated as the file format in the Save as type box.
2. In the File name box, change the name to ***[your initials]*12-7**.

3. Locate your Lesson 12 folder from the **Save in** drop-down list box and click **Save**. The file is saved in Web Page format and Word changes the view to Web Layout view.
4. If the task pane is open, close it to get a better view of the document in Web Layout view.

NOTE: In Web Layout view, text is wrapped to fit the window, you can see any backgrounds you might have applied, and graphics are positioned just as they would be in a Web browser.

5. Format the last two sentences in the document as two bulleted paragraphs.
6. Open the **Format** menu and choose **Theme**. Choose a theme from the list. (Themes might not all be installed on your computer—try **Blends** or **Cascade**.) Click **OK**.

FIGURE 12-6
Theme dialog box

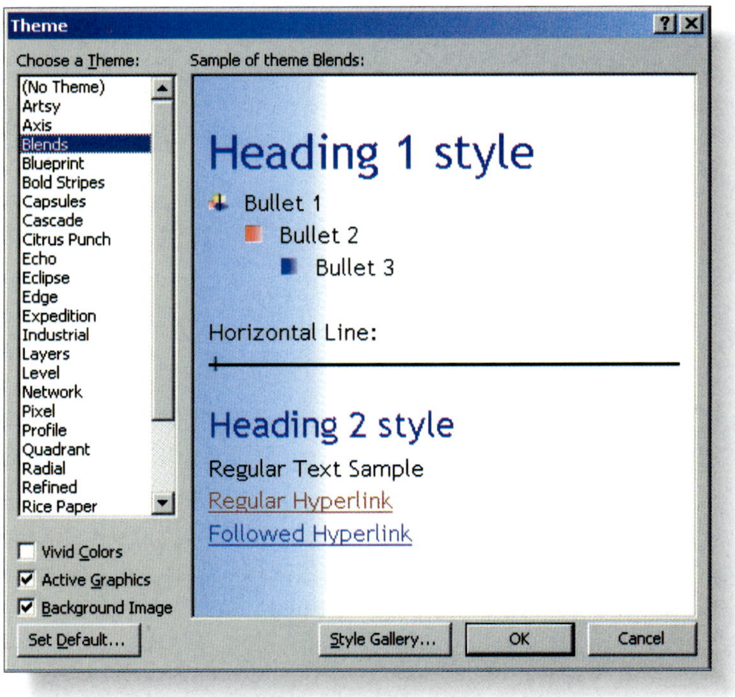

7. Use the Styles and Formatting task pane to apply the Heading 1 style to the document title. Delete the blank lines below the title.
8. Preview the Web page in your browser; then close the browser window.
9. Save the document, print it, and close it.

W O R D

USING HELP

Comments and tracked changes are both important collaboration features in Word. In addition to what this lesson taught, you can also track your own changes as you edit a document and change the way tracked changes and comments appear in a document.

Use Help for more information about comments and tracked changes:

1. Key **track changes** in the Ask a Question box.
2. Click the topic About tracked changes and comments.
3. Review the information in the Help window.
4. If the Contents tab of the Help window displays other Markup topics, explore topics such as "Track changes while you edit," and "Change the way tracked changes and comments look." Or, display the Answer Wizard tab, key **track changes**, press Enter, and explore the topics displayed.
5. Close Help when you finish.

LESSON 12 Summary

- Use comments to insert notes in a document. Comments are color-coded by reviewer. Make sure your name and initials appear in the Options dialog box on the User Information tab before inserting your comments.
- In Normal view, comments appear in the Reviewing pane (open the pane by first displaying the Reviewing toolbar). In Print Layout view and Print Preview, comments appear as balloons in the margins.
- Edit comment text in either the comment balloon or the Reviewing pane. Use the Next button and the Previous button on the Reviewing toolbar to move from comment to comment. See Table 12-1.
- To delete a comment, click within the comment text and click the Reject Change/Delete Comment button, or right-click the comment text and choose Delete Comment from the shortcut menu.
- To print comments with a document, use the Print command from Print Layout view or Print Preview. Or, open the Print dialog box and choose Document showing markup from the Print what drop-down list. Word scales the document text of the printed document to make room for the comment balloons.
- To print comments separate from a document, open the Print dialog box and choose List of markup from the Print what drop-down list.

- You can compare two documents, such as an edited copy of a document and the original document. Open the edited file, open the Compare and Merge dialog box, check Legal blackline, and then click Compare. Word opens a new document that shows the differences as color-coded revision marks.
- In Normal view, revision marks appear as underlines for inserted text, strike-throughs for deleted text, and revision bars to the left of each revised line. In Print Layout view or Print Preview, revision marks appear in the text and in balloons in the margin.
- You can accept or reject revisions in a revised document. Use the Reviewing toolbar buttons to go to the next revision and to accept or reject a revision. You can also right-click a revision and use the shortcut menu to accept or reject it.
- To accept all revisions at once, click the arrow to the right of the Accept Change button and choose Accept All Changes in Document, or open the Display for Review drop-down list on the Reviewing toolbar and choose Final.
- Save a document in Web Page file format, known as HTML, as an alternative to Word Document file format. HTML format makes the document readable in a browser, on an intranet, or on the Internet.
- To see how a document would look as a Web page, view it in your browser by choosing Web Page Preview from the File menu.
- After you save a document as a Web page, Word displays the document in Web Layout view. Apply a Web theme to a document to make it more attractive.

LESSON 12 Command Summary

FEATURE	BUTTON	MENU	KEYBOARD	SPEECH?
Comments		Insert, Comment	Alt + Ctrl + M	✓
Comments, print		File, Print, Print what		✓
Compare and Merge Documents		Tools, Compare and Merge Documents		✓
Web Page Preview		File, Web Page Preview		✓
Web Theme		Format, Theme		✓
Save as Web Page		File, Save as Web Page		✓

Concepts Review

TRUE/FALSE QUESTIONS

Each of the following statements is either true or false. Indicate your choice by circling T or F.

T F ***1.*** In Normal view, comments appear in balloons.

T F ***2.*** You can access the Reviewing pane from the Formatting toolbar.

T F ***3.*** You can print a document with or without revision marks.

T F ***4.*** Comments and revision marks both appear in Print Preview.

T F ***5.*** You must number each comment you add to a document.

T F ***6.*** If you use someone else's computer to enter comments or revisions, you do not have to change the user name.

T F ***7.*** You can switch to Web Layout view to preview a document in your browser.

T F ***8.*** HTML is the file format for Web pages.

SHORT ANSWER QUESTIONS

Write the correct answer in the space provided.

1. When you're checking revisions, what does the button  do?

____

2. When you compare and merge two documents by using the legal blackline feature, how does Word display the differences between the two documents?

____

3. When you point to a comment balloon in Print Layout view, what does the ScreenTip display?

____

4. Where are comments displayed if you want to view them in Normal view?

____

5. How do you use the shortcut menu to delete a comment in Print Layout view?

____

6. After you save a document in Web Page format, in what view does Word display the document?

7. What appears to the left of a line that contains a revision mark?

8. Which toolbar do you use for comments and tracked changes?

CRITICAL THINKING

Answer these questions on a separate page. There are no right or wrong answers. Support your answers with examples from your own experience, if possible.

1. Think of a scenario in which the Compare Documents feature could be helpful.
2. Saving a document in Web Page format is easy, but designing a Web page can be very complex. Think of some of your favorite Web sites. What constitutes good Web page design? What helps make Web content readable? How would you design a Web page for a company?

W O R D

Lesson Applications

EXERCISE 12-8

Insert and delete comments.

1. Open the file **Educate**.
2. Review the spelling and grammar errors in the document, as identified by Word's wavy underlines. Insert comments to describe each error in the document. You should have a total of six comments. (Note that the name "Atacama" is spelled correctly.)
3. Save the document as ***[your initials]*12-8a** in your Lesson 12 folder.
4. Print the document with the comments showing.
5. Make all corrections in the document, and then delete all the comments.
6. At the top of the document, add the title **Education Vacations**. Format the title attractively and set a 2-inch top margin.
7. Add to the document an appropriate clip that is sized and positioned attractively.
8. Save the document as ***[your initials]*12-8b** in your Lesson 12 folder.
9. Print and close the document.

EXERCISE 12-9

Compare two documents, work with comments, rewrite part of a document, and accept revisions.

1. Open the file **Rockies2**.
2. Compare the document to **Rockies1**.
3. View changes in Print Layout view.
4. At the top of the document, add the following comment:

   Rockies1 contains spelling errors. Rockies2 lists each day of the itinerary as a separate paragraph.
5. In the first paragraph, select the last sentence, "It is an experience you will never forget." Insert a comment with the text **This is a cliché.**
6. Save the document as ***[your initials]*12-9a** in your Lesson 12 folder.
7. Print the document, showing revision marks.
8. Delete the first comment. Delete the second comment and rewrite the sentence it referred to so the sentence does not sound like a cliché—use more original language, avoid overused expressions, and do not start the sentence with "It."

9. Accept all changes in the document.
10. At the top of the document, create a WordArt title using the following text:

    Canadian Rockies
    Five-Day Escorted Tour
11. Format the text from "On Day 1" through the end as two balanced columns of equal width. Center the document vertically on the page, and add a page border. If desired, change the font of the document text.
12. Save the document as ***[your initials]*12-9b** in your Lesson 12 folder.
13. Print and close the document. Close Rockies2.

EXERCISE 12-10 Challenge Yourself

Convert a document into a Web page.

1. Open the file **Safari**.
2. Format all the text as 12-point and then apply the Expedition theme.
3. Format the document title as Heading 1 style.
4. Format the list below "You'll be thrilled" as a bulleted list. Format the two lines below "Walking safaris here" as a bulleted list, with each bulleted item starting with a capital letter.
5. Search the document for two consecutive hyphens and replace with an em dash.
6. Insert a clip that relates to the document. If possible, search for a clip online. Size the clip appropriately and position it below the title, left-aligned, or wrapping to the left of the first paragraph.
7. Preview the document as a Web page.
8. Close the Web page window; then save the document in Web Page format as ***[your initials]*12-10** in your Lesson 12 folder.
9. Print and close the document.

On Your Own

In these exercises you work on your own, as you would in a real-life work environment. Use the skills you've learned to accomplish the task—and be creative.

EXERCISE 12-11

Key a page of text from a book or magazine you find interesting. Insert at least five comments. They can be humorous or insightful, or they can simply describe how you feel about the text. Save the document as ***[your initials]*****12-11**. Print the document with comments displayed.

EXERCISE 12-12

Compare any two similar documents. Insert a comment describing your results. Save the new document as ***[your initials]*****12-12** and print it with revision marks displayed.

EXERCISE 12-13

Imagine creating a Web page for yourself or an employer. Create a short document that would welcome people to this new Web page. Apply a Web theme and/or insert clip art. Preview the document in your browser, save it in Web Page format as ***[your initials]*****12-13**, and then print it.

Excel Core

2002

Excel

Core

2002

CASE STUDY

Klassy Kow Ice Cream, Inc.

UNIT 1

Introduction to Excel

UNIT 2

Working With Formulas and Functions

UNIT 3

Improving Uses of Worksheet Information

CASE STUDY

There's more to learning a spreadsheet program like Microsoft Excel than simply keying data. You need to know how to use Excel in a real-world situation. That's why all the lessons in this book relate to everyday business tasks.

As you work through the lessons, imagine yourself working as an intern for Klassy Kow Ice Cream, Inc., a fictional San Francisco business that manufactures and sells ice cream.

Klassy Kow Ice Cream, Inc.

Klassy Kow Ice Cream, Inc., was formed in 1985 by Conrad Steele shortly after the death of his father. Since 1967, Conrad's father and mother had been dairy farmers in Klamath Falls, Oregon. As an addition to their farm, Archibald and Henrietta Steele opened a small ice cream shop. They made their own ice cream from fresh cream, eggs, and butter—starting simply with vanilla, chocolate, and strawberry flavors. They also sold cones, sundaes, shakes, and malts.

As word spread about their delicious ice cream, Archie and Henrietta's business blossomed from a seasonal shop to a year-round one. Eventually, the Steeles' expanded the number of flavors and started to offer hand-packed ice cream pies and cakes. They also started to sell to small supermarkets in southern Oregon under the "Klassy Kow" name, allowing their many customers to buy half-gallons at their favorite supermarket.

The business continued to expand and soon reached into supermarkets in the Pacific Northwest. Archibald and Henrietta opened new ice cream shops in Medford, Oregon, and in Eureka and Red Bluff, California.

After Archibald Steele died, Conrad and his mother sold the dairy farm but kept the ice cream shops. They continue to buy ice cream from the new owners (the Klamath Farm) and have expanded the ice cream business to include 33 franchised ice cream shops in the West.

In 1998, with Klassy Kow continuing to grow steadily, Conrad decided to move the corporate headquarters to San Francisco, California. His mother, Henrietta, is retired and still lives in Klamath Falls. She continues to help create and test new flavors for the Klamath Farm.

The company now has over 170 employees, but the number of employees in the San

FIGURE CS-1
Sales area for Klassy Kow Ice Cream, Inc.

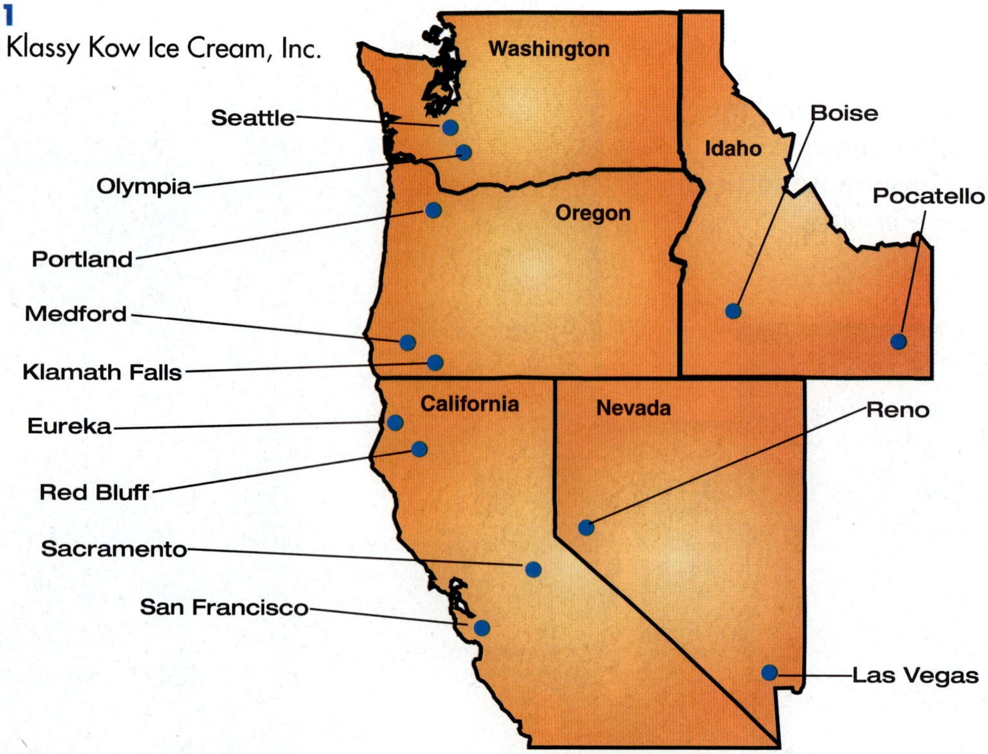

Francisco office is surprisingly small. Most of the employees work in the ice cream shops scattered across Washington, Idaho, Oregon, Nevada, and northern California. Figure CS-1 shows the general area in which Klassy Kow Ice Cream Shops are located. Some of the more important employees from the San Francisco office are shown in Figure CS-2. It might be helpful to associate the pictures of the employees with their names as you work in the course. Pay particular attention to each person's area of responsibility.

Conrad Steele, who is now president and chief executive officer of Klassy Kow, is responsible for the general operation of the company. He says, "I love to see the big smiles on the customer's face after the first lick. It makes it all worth it."

Conrad visits many of the ice cream shops and likes to keep in touch with customers. He visits Klamath Farms at least four times a year to keep in contact with his major supplier.

All the worksheets, documents, and graphics you will use in this course relate to Klassy Kow Ice Cream, Inc. As you work with the worksheets in the text, take the time to notice the following things:

- The types of worksheets needed in a small business to carry on day-to-day business.
- The formatting of worksheets. Real businesses don't always pay much attention to formatting internal worksheets. However, they do focus on formatting worksheets that the customer will see.
- The types of business activities required by a company such as Klassy Kow. For example, it must deal with employees, internal accounting, and suppliers.

As you use this text and become more experienced with Microsoft Excel, you will also gain expertise in creating, editing, and formatting the sort of worksheets generated in a real-life business environment.

FIGURE CS-2
Key Employees

CONRAD STEELE
President and Chief Executive Officer

JUAN SANTE
Vice President, Financial Operations

KEIKO SUMARA
Sales and Marketing Manager

ROBIN MCDONALD
Director of Human Resources

Klassy Kow Ice Cream, Inc.

Products

Sugar Cones	Waffle Cones
Ice Cream	Frozen Yogurt
Shakes	Malteds
Ice Cream Sodas	Ice Cream Sundaes
Ice Cream Cakes	Ice Cream Pies

Ice Cream Sandwiches

Coffee Soda

Klassy Kow Klassics

Klassy Kowabunga
(An ice cream freeze, in several shapes)

KowOwow
(A cow-shaped ice cream bar)

UNIT 1

Introduction to Excel

LESSON

1

Getting Started with Excel

OBJECTIVES

MOUS ACTIVITIES

In this lesson:

Ex2002 1-2
Ex2002 1-4
Ex2002 2-1
Ex2002 2-3
Ex2002 3-7
Ex2002 4-2

See Appendix E.

After completing this lesson, you will be able to:

1. Start Excel.
2. Navigate in a workbook.
3. Open an existing workbook.
4. Edit a worksheet.
5. Manage files.
6. Print Excel files.

Estimated Time: 1 hour

Microsoft Excel is *electronic spreadsheet software*. You can use Excel to produce professional reports that perform simple business or personal calculations, financial or scientific calculations, or database management and even let you create charts. Excel is powerful but easy to use. You'll become a productive Excel user as soon as you learn the basics.

Starting Excel

There are several ways to start Excel, depending on how your computer is installed. For example, you can use the Start button on the Windows taskbar, My Computer, or Windows Explorer. If your desktop has an Excel shortcut icon, you can double-click it to start Excel.

NOTE: Windows provides many ways to start applications. If you have problems, ask your instructor for help. If you are unfamiliar with Windows, see Appendix A: "Windows Tutorial."

EXERCISE 1-1 Start Excel

When the instructions tell you to "click" a menu option or a toolbar button, use the left mouse button. Use the left mouse button to carry out commands unless you are told explicitly to use the right mouse button.

1. Turn on your computer. Windows loads.

2. Click the Start button Start on the Windows taskbar and point to Programs.

3. On the Programs submenu, click Microsoft Excel. In a few seconds, the program is loaded and a blank Excel workbook opens.

FIGURE 1-1
Starting Excel from the Windows taskbar

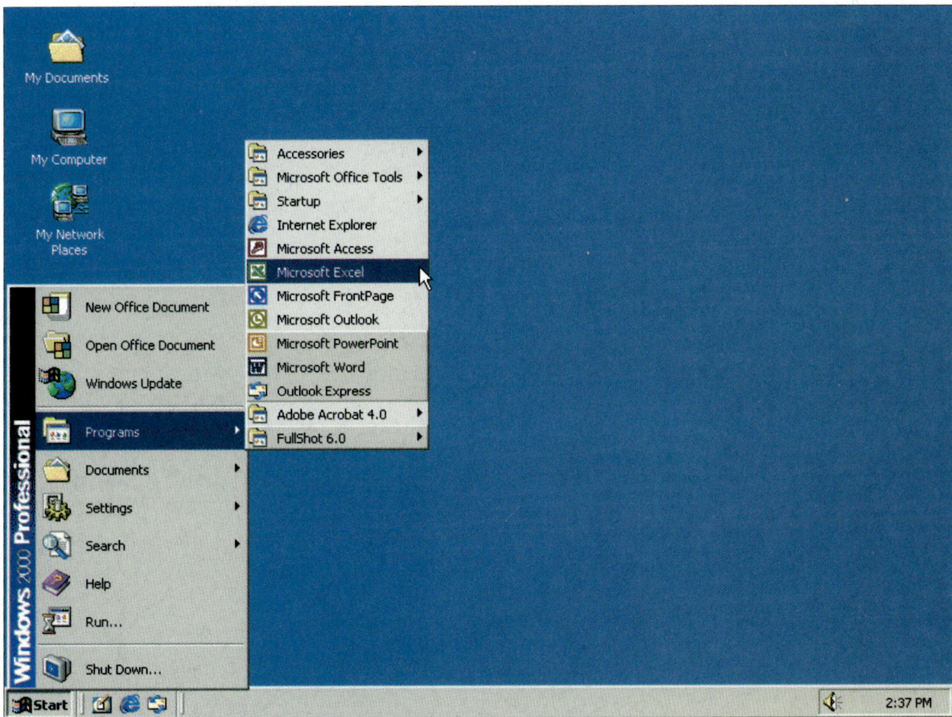

EXERCISE 1-2 Identify Parts of the Excel Screen

Excel opens showing a blank workbook, the menu bar, the Standard toolbar, the Formatting toolbar, and the New Workbook task pane (see Figure 1-2). New workbooks are numbered and named Book1, Book2, and so on during each work session.

Depending on your screen, the Standard and Formatting toolbars appear on one or two rows.

NOTE: If you do not see the New Workbook task pane, choose Task Pane from the View menu. The filenames in your task pane are the most recently used documents at your computer.

FIGURE 1-2
Excel screen

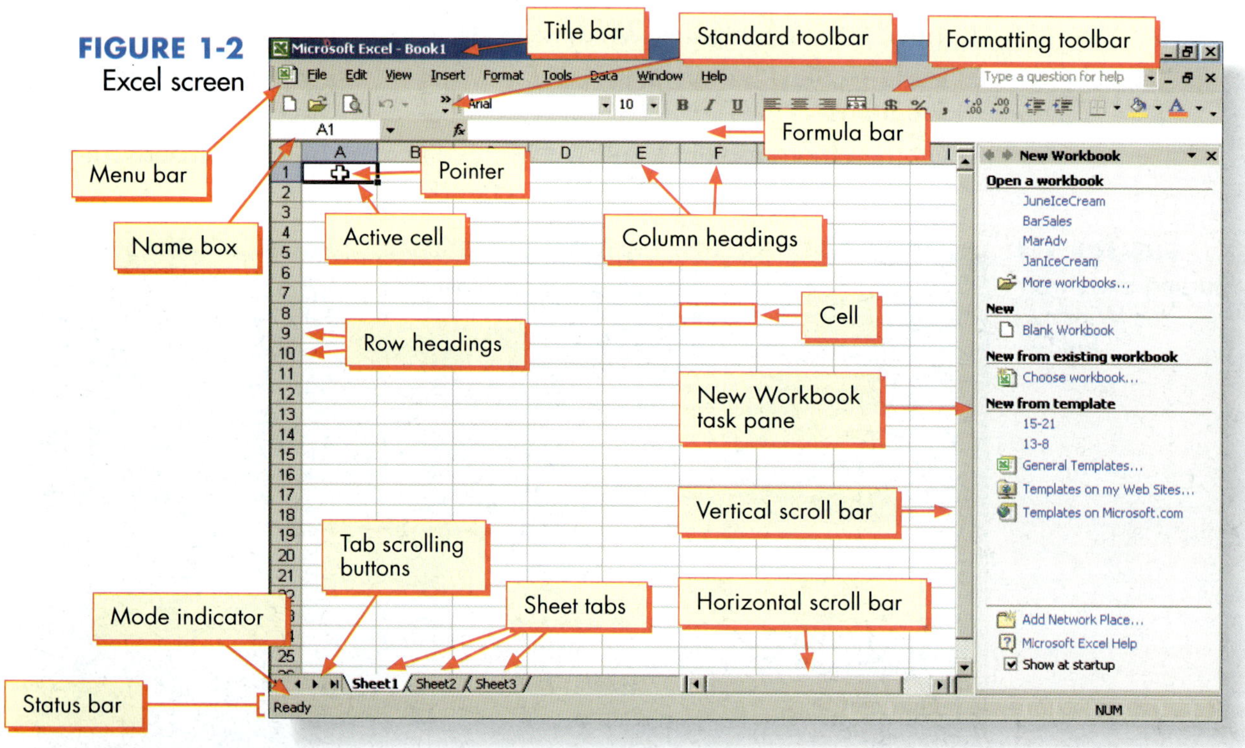

TABLE 1-1 Parts of the Excel Screen

PART OF SCREEN	PURPOSE
Title bar	Contains the program name ("Microsoft Excel") and the name of the workbook.
Menu bar	Displays the names of menus used to perform various tasks.
Standard toolbar	A row of buttons used to execute commands with the mouse.

continues

TABLE 1-1 Parts of the Excel Screen *continued*

PART OF SCREEN	PURPOSE
Formatting toolbar	A row of buttons used to apply font, size, style, color, and number formats with the mouse.
Name box	A drop-down list that shows the address of the active cell. You can also use it to move the pointer to a specific location.
Formula bar	Displays the contents of the active cell. You can also enter text, numbers, or formulas in the formula bar.
Column headings	Alphabetic characters across the top of the worksheet that identify columns.
Row headings	Numbers down the left side of the worksheet that identify rows.
Active cell	The cell outlined in a heavy black border. It is ready to accept new data, a formula, or for you to edit its current contents.
Status bar	Displays information about the current task and shows the current mode of operation.
Scroll bars	Used to move different parts of the screen into view.
Sheet tabs	Indicators at the bottom of the worksheet to identify sheets in the workbook.
Tab scrolling buttons	Navigation buttons to scroll through worksheet tabs.

NOTE: The first two steps in this exercise organize the Standard and Formatting toolbars on separate rows. If your toolbars are already in two rows (as shown in Figure 1-4), you do not need to perform steps 1 and 2, so start with step 3.

1. Click the Toolbar Options button on either the Standard or Formatting toolbar. The shortcut menu shows Show Buttons on Two Rows if your toolbars are on one row. (See Figure 1-3 on the next page.)
2. Click Show Buttons on Two Rows. The toolbars are rearranged, one on top of the other, so you can see more buttons at once.
3. Click View on the menu bar. If the menu is not expanded to show all the choices, move the pointer down to the bottom of the menu and click the down-pointing arrows. These are the More arrows. The menu expands.

FIGURE 1-3
Showing toolbars on two rows

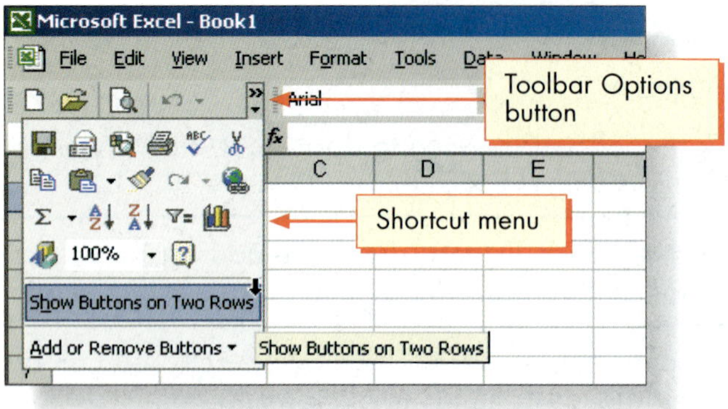

4. Move the pointer to Full Screen and click. The Full Screen view shows the menu bar, the worksheet tabs, and the Full Screen floating toolbar.
5. Click Close Full Screen on the floating toolbar.

6. Position the pointer over the New button  on the Standard toolbar, but do not click. A *ScreenTip* (a box with the button name) appears below the button.

NOTE: You might notice a floating Language toolbar on your screen. This toolbar, which appears only if your computer is set up with a microphone, can be used for speech recognition. You can use speech recognition for menu commands, toolbar buttons, and text entry. For more information, see Appendix C.

Navigating in a Workbook

A *workbook* is the file Excel creates to store your data. When you look at the screen, you are viewing a worksheet. A *worksheet* is an individual page or tab in the workbook. A new workbook opens with three blank worksheets. You can insert or delete worksheets in the workbook. A workbook can have from 1 to 255 worksheets.

A worksheet has a grid that defines *rows* and *columns*. The rows are numbered and reach row 65,536. There are 256 columns, lettered from A to Z, then AA to AZ, BA to BZ, and so on, up to column IV.

The intersection of a row and a column forms a rectangle known as a *cell*. You enter a piece of information (text, a number, or a formula) in a cell. Cells have *cell addresses* or *cell references*, which identify where the cell is located on the worksheet. Cell B2, for example, is the cell in column B, row 2.

NOTE: When you give a cell address, the column letter always comes first.

The *active cell* is the cell that appears outlined with a thick border on the worksheet. It is ready to accept data or a formula or, if it already contains data or a formula, it is ready to be modified. It is the cell in which you are currently working. When you open a new workbook, the active cell is cell A1, the top left cell in the worksheet. Cell A1 is referred to as *"Home."*

The mouse pointer is a thick white cross when you move it across cells in the worksheet. When you point at one of the worksheet tabs or a menu or toolbar item, it is a white arrow.

TABLE 1-2 Navigation Commands in a Workbook

PRESS	TO DO THIS
Ctrl + Home	Move to the beginning of the worksheet
Ctrl + End	Move to the last used cell on the worksheet
Home	Move to the beginning of the current row
PgUp	Move up one screen
PgDn	Move down one screen
Alt + PgUp	Move one screen to the left
Alt + PgDn	Move one screen to the right
↑, ↓, ←, →	Move one cell up, down, left, or right
Ctrl +Arrow key	Move to the edge of a group of cells with data
F5 or Ctrl + G	Open the Go To dialog box
Click	Move to the cell that is clicked
Tab	Move to the next cell in a left-to-right sequence
Shift + Tab	Move to the previous cell in a right-to-left sequence
Ctrl + Backspace	Move to the active cell when it has scrolled out of view
Ctrl + PgUp	Move to the previous worksheet
Ctrl + PgDn	Move to the next worksheet

EXERCISE 1-3 Move Between Worksheets

A new workbook has three worksheets named Sheet1, Sheet2, and Sheet3. The Sheet1 worksheet is displayed when a new workbook is opened.

1. Click the Sheet2 tab. You can tell which sheet is active, because it is white. The others are gray.

NOTE: Cell A1 is the active cell on all three worksheets in a new workbook.

2. Click the Sheet3 tab. All three sheets are empty.
3. Press Ctrl + PgUp. This shortcut moves to the previous worksheet, Sheet2, in this case.

NOTE: When keyboard combinations (such as Ctrl + PgUp) are shown in this text, hold down the first key without releasing it and press the second key. Release the second key and then release the first key.

4. Press Ctrl + PgDn. This command moves to the next worksheet, Sheet3.
5. Click the Sheet1 tab to return to Sheet1.

EXERCISE 1-4 Go to a Specific Cell

When you move the mouse pointer to a cell and click, the cell you clicked on becomes the active cell. It is outlined with a black border, and you can see the cell address in the *Name box*. The Name box is the text box with a drop-down arrow at the left edge of the formula bar. You can use it to view the address of the cell that is currently active. You can also use it to move the location of the active cell.

1. Move the mouse pointer to cell D4 and click. Cell D4 is now the active cell, and the cell address appears in the Name box.

FIGURE 1-4
Active cell shows a thick border

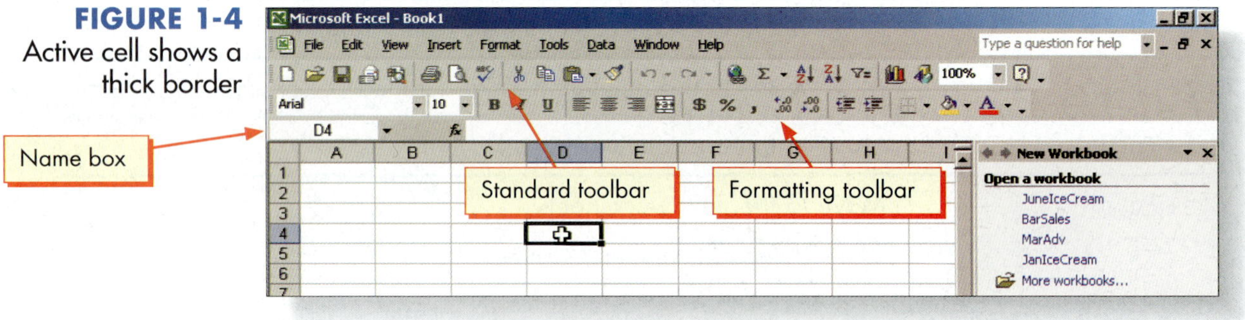

2. Press Ctrl + Home. This shortcut makes cell A1 the active cell.
3. Press Ctrl + G to open the Go To dialog box.

TIP: An alternative way to open the Go To dialog box is to use the Go To command on the Edit menu.

4. Key **b19** in the Reference box and press Enter. B19 becomes the active cell, and its address is shown in the Name box.

FIGURE 1-5
Go To dialog box

5. Press F5. This is another shortcut for the Go To command. Recently used cell addresses are listed in the Go to list in the Go To dialog box.
6. Key **c2** and click OK.
7. Click the arrow next to the Name box. The current cell address is highlighted.
8. Key **a8** and press Enter.

FIGURE 1-6
Using the Name box

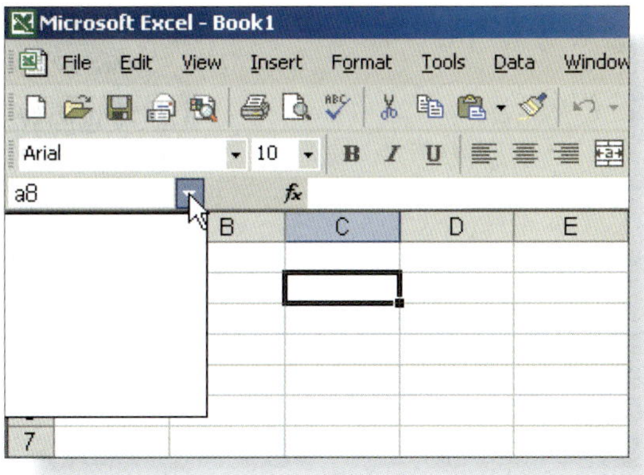

9. Press Ctrl + Home to return to cell A1.

EXERCISE 1-5 Scroll Through a Worksheet

When you scroll through a worksheet, the location of the active cell does not change. Instead the worksheet moves on the screen so you can see different columns or rows. On most screens you will see about 20 to 24 rows at a time and about 9 to 12 columns for a new workbook with no data.

FIGURE 1-7
Using scroll bars

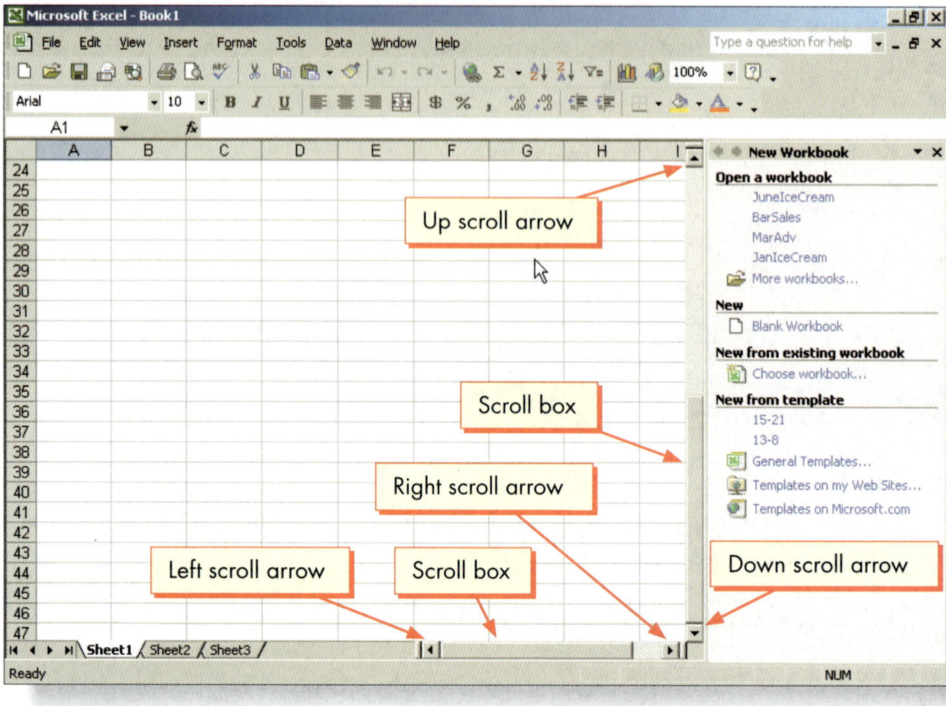

TABLE 1-3

Scrolling Through a Worksheet

TO MOVE THE VIEW	DO THIS
Up one line	Click the up scroll arrow.
Down one line	Click the down scroll arrow.
Up one screen	Click the scroll bar above the scroll box.
Down one screen	Click the scroll bar below the scroll box.
To any relative position	Drag the scroll bar up or down.
To the right	Click the right scroll arrow.
To the left	Click the left scroll arrow.

1. On the vertical scroll bar, click below the scroll box. The worksheet has been repositioned so you see the next group of about 20 rows.
2. Click above the vertical scroll box. The worksheet has scrolled up to the top row.

3. Click the right scroll arrow on the horizontal scroll bar once. The worksheet scrolls to the right.
4. Click the left scroll arrow once to return to the original horizontal position.
5. Click the down scroll arrow on the vertical scroll bar twice.

NOTE: You cannot see the active cell (cell A1) during your scrolling.

6. Drag the scroll box to the top of the vertical scroll bar. Notice that in all this scrolling, the active cell has not changed from cell A1.

EXERCISE 1-6 Change the Zoom Size

The *Zoom size* controls how much of the worksheet you see on the screen. You can set the Zoom size to see more or less on screen so you won't need to scroll as much. The 100% Zoom size shows the data close to print size.

1. Click the down arrow next to the Zoom button. The Zoom submenu opens.
2. Click 75%. The worksheet is reduced so you can see more columns and rows.

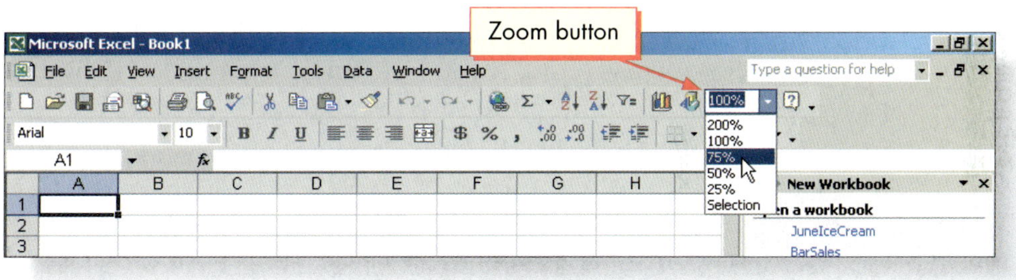

FIGURE 1-8
Changing the Zoom size

3. From the View menu, choose Zoom. The Zoom dialog box opens.
4. Click the 200% Magnification button in the Zoom dialog box. Click OK. The worksheet is made larger, but you see less.

TIP: It is faster for most people to change views by using the Zoom button than by using the Zoom dialog box.

5. Click the arrow next to the Zoom button. Key **85**. You do not need to key the percent sign.
6. Press Enter. You can enter any Zoom size or choose from the list.
7. Click the arrow next to the Zoom button. Choose 100%.

EXERCISE 1-7 Close a Workbook

After you finish working with a workbook, you usually would save your work and close the workbook. You can close a workbook in several ways.

- Use the Close Window button [X] on the right side of the menu bar.

FIGURE 1-9
Close Window button

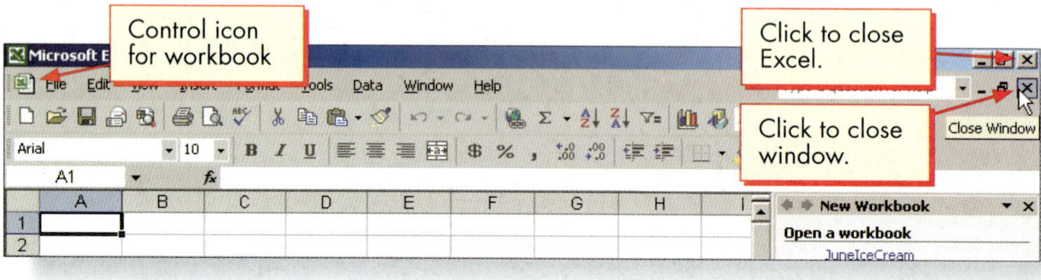

- Use the Control icon for the workbook. The Control icon for the workbook is to the left of the word File on the menu bar. Choose Close from the Control menu.
- Use the File menu.
- Use keyboard shortcuts. Ctrl + W or Ctrl + F4 closes a workbook.

1. From the File menu, choose Close. The workbook closes, and a blank gray screen appears. If you have made a change to the workbook, a dialog box asks if you want to save the changes.
2. Click No if this dialog box opens.

Opening an Existing Workbook

In addition to starting a new workbook, you will often open workbooks that have already been created. There are several ways to open an existing workbook.

- Click the Open button on the Standard toolbar.
- From the File menu, choose the Open command.
- Use the keyboard shortcut Ctrl + O.
- Click the filename (or More workbooks to display the filename) in the Open a workbook section of the New Workbook task pane.
- Double-click the workbook filename in Windows Explorer or My Computer.

EXERCISE 1-8 Open a Workbook

1. Click the Open button. The Look in text box shows the most recently used folder.
2. Click the down arrow next to the Look in box. Choose the appropriate drive according to your instructor's directions. The workbooks for this text appear in the list box.

NOTE: Your instructor will advise you on the proper drive and folder to use for this course. For more information about working with files in Windows, see Appendix B: "File Management."

3. Click the arrow next to the Views button. A list of View options appears.
4. Choose List to see a list of the filenames.
5. Click the arrow next to the Views button again. This time, choose Preview to see a preview of the workbook.

NOTE: Not all workbooks have a preview; it depends on computer settings at the time they are saved.

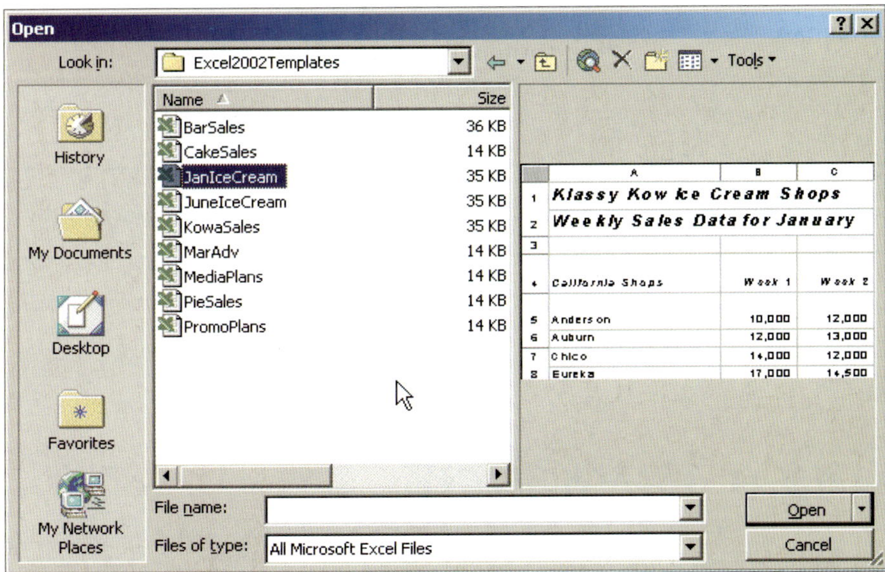

FIGURE 1-10
Open dialog box

6. Find **JanIceCream**. Double-click the filename. The workbook opens and the New Workbook task pane closes.

NOTE: The workbooks in this course relate to the Case Study about Klassy Kow Ice Cream, Inc., a fictional manufacturer of ice cream (see pages 357 through 360).

TABLE 1-4 Open Dialog Box Buttons

BUTTON	ACTION
History	Lists the most recently opened files and folders.
My Documents	Opens a Windows folder for storing your documents.
Desktop	Lists items on your computer's desktop.
Favorites	Lists folders and files you have designated as "favorite" by using the Add to Favorites command on the Tools menu.
My Network Places	Lists folders and files you can use on network drives and Web servers.
Back	Moves to the last most recently used folder.
Up One Level	Moves up one level in the hierarchy of folders or drives on your computer or other computers in your network.
Search the Web	Opens the Search page of your Internet browser so you can start a Web search for information.
Delete	Deletes the selected files or folders.
Create New Folder	Creates a new folder for storing your work.
Views	Lists options for showing file information in the dialog box.

Editing a Worksheet

The JanIceCream workbook has three worksheets. The sheets have been renamed WeeklySales, Owners, and Chart to better indicate what is on the sheet. For instance, the WeeklySales sheet shows sales for each city in each of the four weeks in January.

Worksheet cells contain text, numbers, or formulas. A simple formula calculates an arithmetic result, so simply by viewing the worksheet itself you might not know if the cell contains a number or a formula. However, you can determine a cell's content by using the formula bar. You can use the formula bar to change the contents of cells by retyping or editing the current contents of the cell.

EXERCISE 1-9 View Worksheets and Cell Contents

1. Click the Owners tab. The Owners worksheet shows the name of the shop owner.

TIP: If you do not see column F and row 19, set your Zoom size to **85%** or smaller so you can see columns A through F and up to row 19.

2. Click the Chart tab. The Chart tab has a bar chart showing January sales data for each store.
3. Press Ctrl+PgUp. This moves to the Owners worksheet.
4. Press Ctrl+PgDn. The active tab is the Chart sheet.
5. Click the WeeklySales tab.
6. Press F5 to open the Go To dialog box.
7. Key **a5** and press Enter. The active cell is changed to cell A5. This cell contains the name of a city ("Anderson") which you can see in the formula bar and on the worksheet.

FIGURE 1-11 Cell contents and the formula bar

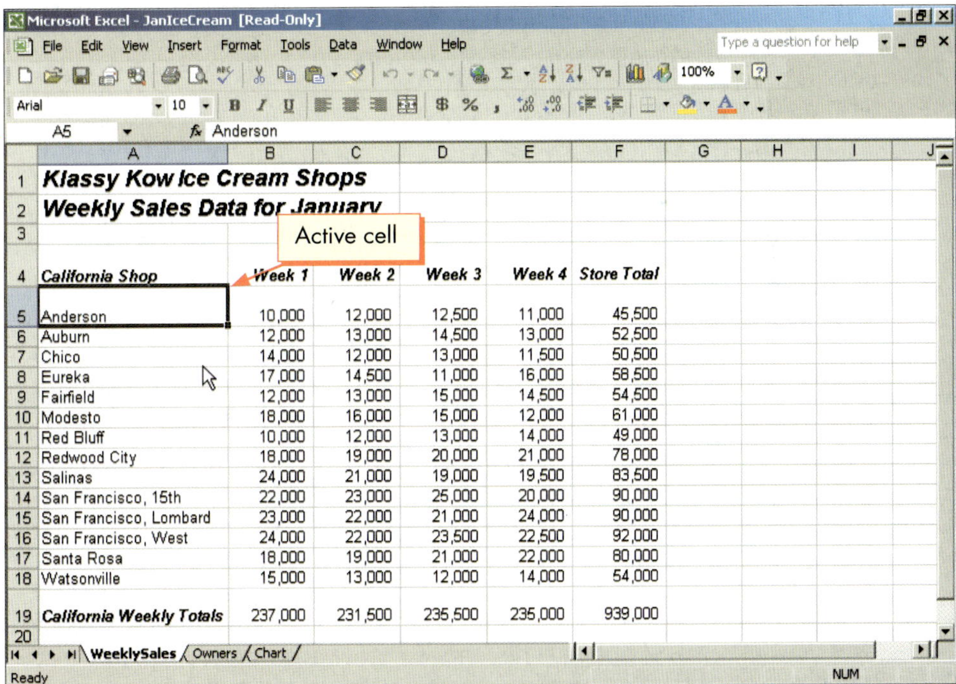

	A	B	C	D	E	F
1	Klassy Kow Ice Cream Shops					
2	Weekly Sales Data for January					
3						
4	California Shop	Week 1	Week 2	Week 3	Week 4	Store Total
5	Anderson	10,000	12,000	12,500	11,000	45,500
6	Auburn	12,000	13,000	14,500	13,000	52,500
7	Chico	14,000	12,000	13,000	11,500	50,500
8	Eureka	17,000	14,500	11,000	16,000	58,500
9	Fairfield	12,000	13,000	15,000	14,500	54,500
10	Modesto	18,000	16,000	15,000	12,000	61,000
11	Red Bluff	10,000	12,000	13,000	14,000	49,000
12	Redwood City	18,000	19,000	20,000	21,000	78,000
13	Salinas	24,000	21,000	19,000	19,500	83,500
14	San Francisco, 15th	22,000	23,000	25,000	20,000	90,000
15	San Francisco, Lombard	23,000	22,000	21,000	24,000	90,000
16	San Francisco, West	24,000	22,000	23,500	22,500	92,000
17	Santa Rosa	18,000	19,000	21,000	22,000	80,000
18	Watsonville	15,000	13,000	12,000	14,000	54,000
19	California Weekly Totals	237,000	231,500	235,500	235,000	939,000
20						

8. Press F5, key **c10**, and press Enter. Cell C10 contains a number. In the formula bar, the number does not show the comma.
9. Press F5, key **f17**, and press Enter. Cell F17 contains a formula, which you can see in the formula bar. Formulas calculate a number.

EXERCISE 1-10 Replace Cell Contents

When the workbook is in Ready mode, you can edit or replace the contents of a cell. To replace a cell's contents, you make it the active cell, key the new data, and press Enter. You can also click the Enter button ✓ in the formula bar or press any arrow key on the keyboard to complete the replacement.

If you replace a number used in a formula, the result of the formula changes because Excel automatically recalculates it when you complete your change.

1. Click cell B5 to make it the active cell.
2. Key **20000** without a comma. As you key the number, it appears in the cell and in the formula bar. The status bar shows Enter to indicate that you are in the Enter mode.

FIGURE 1-12
Replace cell contents

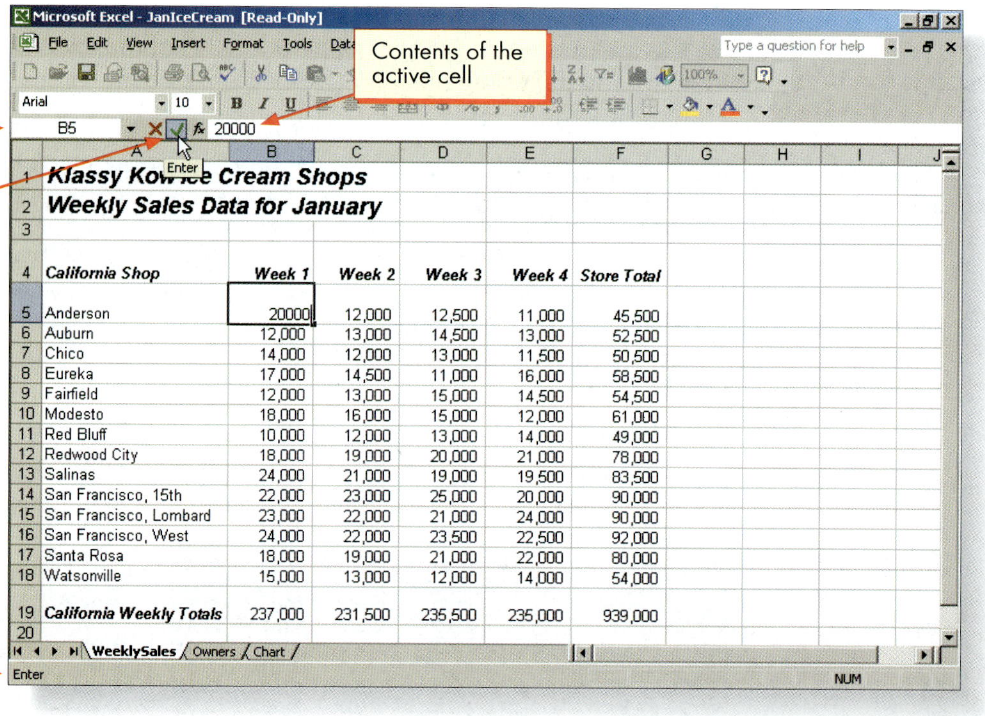

3. Press Enter. Excel adds a comma automatically, and the next cell in column B is active. The "Store Total" amount (cell F5) and the "California Weekly Totals" amounts (in cells B19 and F19) are automatically recalculated. The worksheet returns to Ready mode.

4. Press ↑ to move to cell B5. Key **10000** without a comma. Click the Enter button ✓ in the formula bar. Notice that when you use the Enter button ✓, the pointer stays in cell B5.

TIP: The commas are part of the cell format. Excel adds them automatically.

5. Click the Chart tab. Notice the length of the Anderson bar, showing sales between $40,000 and $50,000.
6. Click the WeeklySales tab.
7. In cell B5, key **0**, and press ↓. A zero appears as a short dash in this worksheet.
8. Click the Chart tab. The chart on this worksheet is based on the data in the WeeklySales worksheet. Now that you have reduced the sales in the WeeklySales, notice that the Anderson bar is shorter to show fewer sales.
9. Click the WeeklySales tab and key **10000** in cell B5. Press →.

EXERCISE 1-11 Edit Cell Contents

If a cell contains a long or complicated entry, you can edit it rather than rekeying the entire entry. When you edit a cell's contents, the worksheet changes to Edit mode. Edit mode starts if you:

- Double-click the cell.
- Click the cell and press F2.
- Click the cell and then click anywhere in the formula bar.

TABLE 1-5 Keyboard Shortcuts in Edit Mode

KEY	TO DO THIS
Enter	Completes the edit and returns to Ready mode.
Esc	Cancels the edit and restores the existing data.
Home	Moves the insertion point to the beginning of the data.
End	Moves the insertion point to the end of the data.
Delete	Deletes one character to the right of the insertion point.
Ctrl + Delete	Deletes everything from the insertion point to the end of the line.
Backspace	Deletes one character to the left of the insertion point.
← or →	Moves the insertion point one character left or right.
Ctrl + ←	Moves the insertion point one word left.
Ctrl + →	Moves the insertion point one word right.

1. Click cell A2. The text in cell A2 is long, and it runs into columns B and C.
2. Press F2. Edit mode is shown in the status bar. An insertion point appears in the cell at the end of the text.
3. Double-click "Data" in the cell.

TIP: Double-clicking highlights or selects a word in all of the Office applications.

4. Key **Information**. It replaces the word "Data."

FIGURE 1-13
Using Edit mode

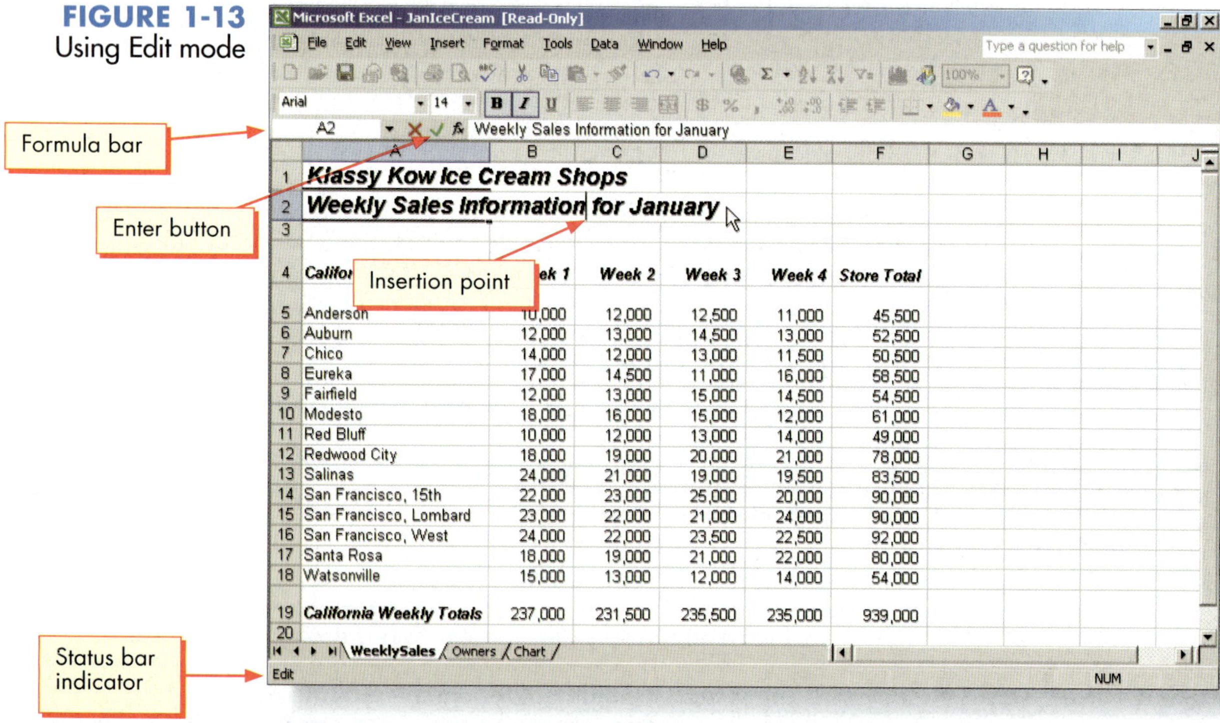

5. Press Enter to complete the edit. Pressing Enter does not start a new line in the cell when the worksheet is in Edit mode.
6. Double-click cell A4. This starts Edit mode, and an insertion point appears in the cell.
7. Click to the left of the "S" in "Shop."
8. Key **Retail** and press Spacebar. Press Enter.
9. Click cell F1. There is nothing in this cell.
10. Key your first name, a space, and your last name in the cell. Press Enter. If your name is longer than column F, part of it might run into column G and even into column H.

E X C E L

EXERCISE 1-12 Clear Cell Contents

When you clear the contents of a cell, you delete the text, number, or formula in that cell.

1. Click cell B5. Press Delete. The number is deleted, and Excel recalculates the formula results in cells F5, B19, and F19.

NOTE: A green triangle might appear in the upper left corner of F5 and B19 to indicate that a formula error has occurred.

2. Press → to move the pointer to cell C5.
3. From the Edit menu, choose Clear and then Contents. The number is deleted, and the formula is recalculated again. A green triangle might appear in cell C19 to indicate that this formula now has a problem.

EXERCISE 1-13 Use Undo and Redo

The Undo and Redo commands enable you to quickly recover from errors. The Undo command reverses the last action you performed in the worksheet. For example, if you delete the contents of a cell, the Undo command restores what you deleted. The Redo command reverses the action of the Undo command. It "undoes" your Undo.

To use the Undo command, you can:

- Click the Undo button on the Standard toolbar.
- Press Ctrl+Z.
- From the Edit menu, choose Undo.

To use the Redo command, you can:

- Click the Redo button on the Standard toolbar.
- Press Ctrl+Y.
- From the Edit menu, choose Redo.

Excel keeps a history or list of your editing commands, and you can undo or redo several at once.

1. Click the Undo button. The number in cell C5 is restored.
2. Click the Redo button. The number is cleared again.
3. Click cell A8 and key **Gotham**. Press Enter.
4. In cell A9 key **Los Angeles** and press Enter.
5. Click the arrow next to the Undo button to display the history list.

6. Move the mouse to highlight the top two actions and click. The last two changes are undone, and the original city names are restored.

FIGURE 1-14
Undoing multiple edits

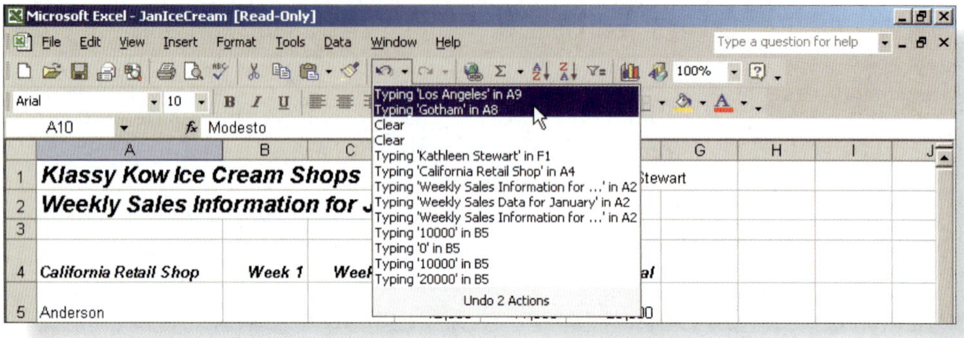

NOTE: Depending on the actions that have been undone and redone on your computer, your list might be different from the one shown in Figure 1-14.

7. Click the arrow next to the Redo button to display the history list.
8. Move the mouse to highlight the top two actions and click. The names you keyed are restored.
9. Press Ctrl + Home to place the pointer in cell A1.

TIP: If you place the pointer in cell A1 when you save a workbook, that's where the pointer is the next time you open the workbook.

Managing Files

Workbook files are usually stored in folders. A *folder* is a location on your disk drive, network, floppy, or CD drive. Folders are organized in a structure like a family tree. The top is a disk drive letter such as A, B, or C to represent your disk drive, other disk drives, or other storage devices. Under each disk drive letter, you can create folders to help you organize and manage your work. A folder can also contain additional folders.

For your work in this text, you will save your files in a folder you create for each lesson.

EXERCISE 1-14 Create a New Folder and Use Save As

1. Open the File menu and choose Save As. You will save **JanIceCream** with a new filename in a lesson folder you will create.

NOTE: Ask your instructor where to save lesson folders for this course.

2. Choose the appropriate drive and folder location from the Save in drop-down list.

3. Click the Create New Folder button. The New Folder dialog box opens.
4. In the Name box, key ***[your initials]*Lesson1**. Click OK. Your new folder's name now appears in the Save in box.
5. In the File name box, make sure the filename **Copy of JanIceCream** is highlighted or selected. If it is not highlighted, triple-click it.

NOTE: JanIceCream is a "read-only file." This means you cannot change it and save it under its current filename. To save the file, Excel automatically gives it a new name that includes the original filename preceded by "Copy of."

FIGURE 1-15
Save As dialog box

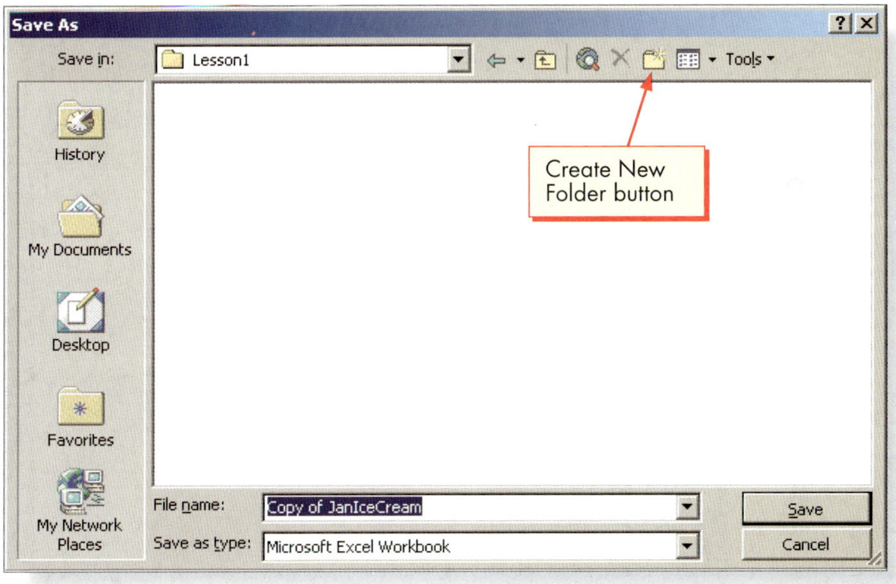

NOTE: Excel automatically assigns the **.xls** extension to files you save, but if your computer uses the standard Windows settings you will not see the filename extensions.

6. Key ***[your initials]*1-14** and click Save. Your new filename now appears in the title bar of the workbook.

Printing Excel Files

When the worksheet is finished, printing it is easy. You can use any of these methods to print a worksheet:

- Click the Print button on the Standard toolbar.
- Click Print while in Print Preview.

- From the File menu, choose Print.
- Press Ctrl + P.

Clicking the Print button on the Standard toolbar sends the worksheet directly to the printer, using Excel's default print settings. The other methods open the Print dialog box, where you can change printing options.

EXERCISE 1-15 Preview a Worksheet

The Print Preview command enables you to see the worksheet as it will print. You should always preview your work before sending it to the printer.

1. Click the Print Preview button . The worksheet is shown in a reduced size so you can see the entire page.

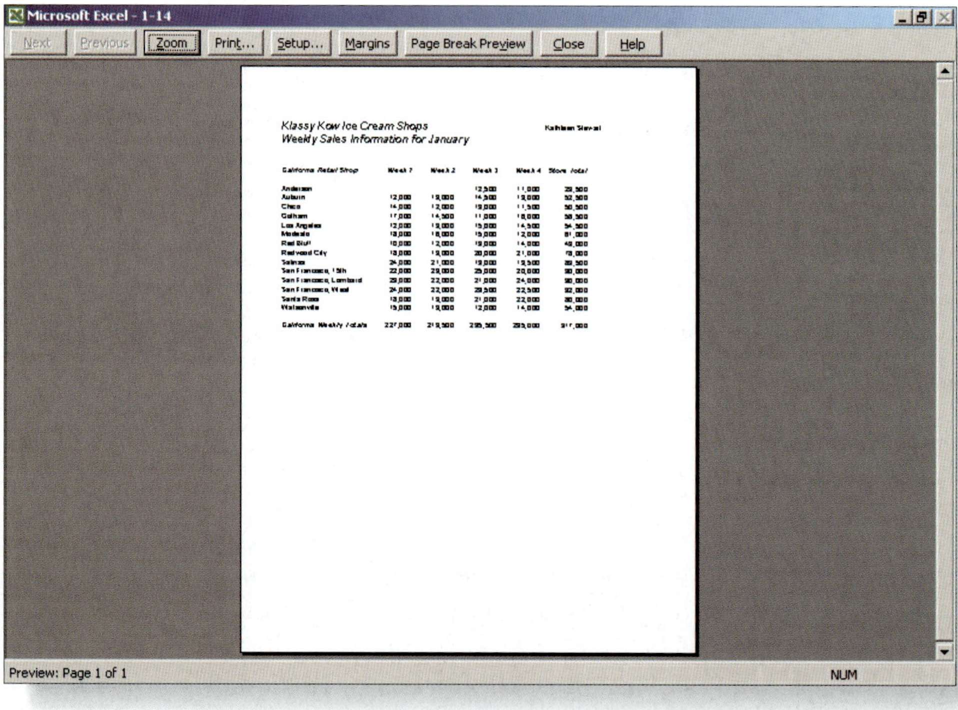

FIGURE 1-16 Worksheet in Print Preview

2. Move the mouse pointer near the main title. The mouse pointer appears as a small magnifying glass icon.
3. Click the mouse button while pointing at the main title. The worksheet changes to a larger size, close to the actual print size.
4. Move the mouse pointer near any number in the "Week 2" column. The mouse pointer appears as a white solid arrow.
5. Click anywhere to return to a reduced size.

NOTE: Changing the size in the Print Preview window is called zooming in and out.

6. Zoom in on the "California Weekly Totals" row. Click anywhere to zoom out.
7. Click Print. The preview window closes, and the Print dialog box displays your workstation's default printer and settings.
8. Click OK. A printer icon appears on the taskbar as the worksheet is sent to the printer. Only the WeeklySales worksheet is printed.

EXERCISE 1-16 Print a Workbook

You can print all three sheets in the workbook with one command. To print the entire workbook, you must use the Print dialog box. You can print a workbook by using either of these methods:

- From the File menu, choose Print.
- Press Ctrl + P.

1. From the File menu, choose Print. The Print dialog box opens with your default settings.

FIGURE 1-17
Print dialog box

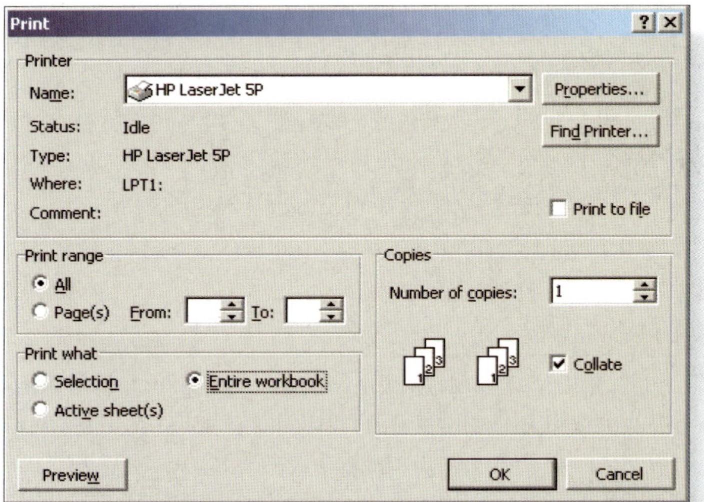

Print choice here

2. In the Print what section, click the option button for Entire workbook.
3. Click Preview. The reduced size shows the first page, the WeeklySales sheet. The status bar shows that this is page 1 of 3.
4. Press PgDn. This is the second sheet, the Owners worksheet.
5. Press PgDn. This is the Chart sheet. It is set to print in a landscape orientation.
6. Click Previous two times to return to the first sheet.

7. Click Print. All three sheets are sent to the printer.

EXERCISE 1-17 Exit Excel

You can exit Excel and close the workbook at the same time. If you give the command to exit Excel, you will see a reminder to save the workbook if you have not yet done so.

There are four ways to close a workbook and exit Excel:

FIGURE 1-18
Control menus

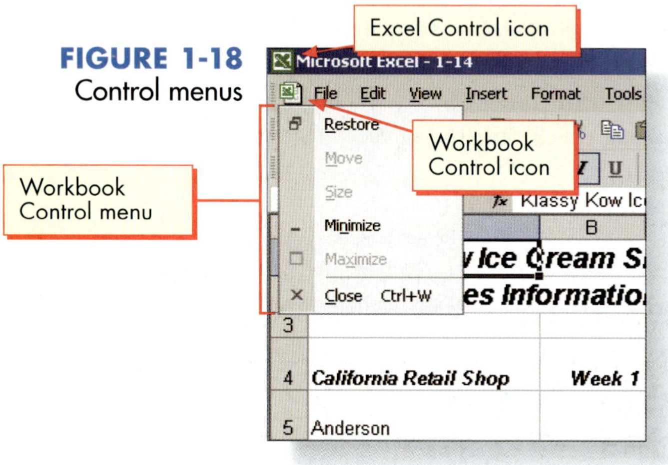

- Use the Close Window button ☒ to close the workbook or the Close button ☒ to close Excel. (The close buttons are in the upper right corner of the windows.)
- From the File menu, choose Close (to close the workbook) or Exit (to close Excel).
- Use the Control icons in the upper left corner. The Excel Control icon is next to the application name in the title bar.
- Use the keyboard shortcuts Alt+F4 to exit Excel.

1. Click the Close Window button ☒ to close the workbook. Do not save changes if asked.
2. Click the Close button ☒ to exit Excel.

USING HELP

Online Help is available when you work in Excel. You can type a question in the Ask a Question box at the top right of the screen to start Excel's Help system.

Get acquainted with using Help:

1. Start Excel.
2. Locate the Ask a Question box in the upper right corner of the screen. Click the box to activate it. Key **get help**
3. Press Enter. A list of Help topics appears.
4. Click See more at the bottom of the list to display additional topics. Notice the mouse pointer is shaped like a hand.
5. Click See previous to return to the first list of topics.
6. Click the topic About getting help while you work. The Help dialog box opens.

7. Click each of the topics listed in blue text (or click Show All in the upper right corner of the Help screen). Review the information.

FIGURE 1-19
Getting Help while you work

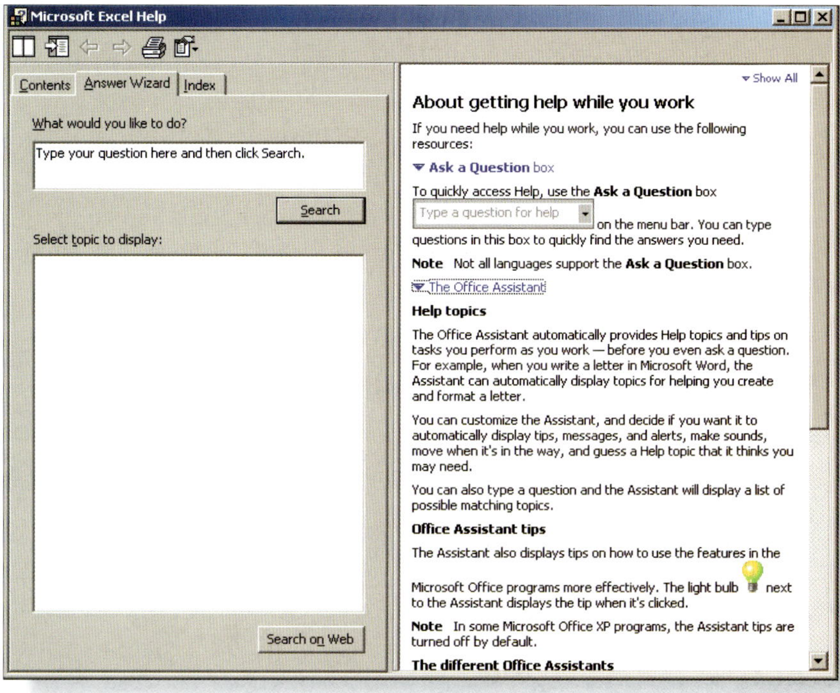

8. Click the Help window's Close button [X].

LESSON 1 Summary

- There are different ways to start Excel, depending on your computer and its settings.
- Excel opens with a blank workbook. The menu bar is across the top. When you click a menu name, a list of commands is displayed.
- The Standard and Formatting toolbars can be set to show on one or two rows.
- A new workbook opens with three worksheets. A worksheet is an individual tab in the workbook.
- Press Ctrl + PgUp and Ctrl + PgDn to move between worksheets in a workbook.
- Worksheets are divided into cells, which are the intersections of rows and columns. The location of the cell is its address (also called its cell reference).
- Move the pointer to a specific cell with the Go To command or by clicking the cell.
- The active cell is outlined with a black border. It is ready to accept new data or a formula or be edited.
- The Name box shows the address of the active cell. You can also use it to change the active cell.

- If you use the scroll box or arrows to reposition the worksheet on the screen, the active cell does not change.
- The Zoom size controls how much of the worksheet you can see at once.
- Replace any entry in a cell by clicking the cell and keying new data. Edit long or complicated cell data rather than rekeying it.
- The Undo button and the Redo button both have history arrows so you can undo or redo multiple commands at once.
- Preview your worksheet or the entire workbook before printing it. To print and preview all the worksheets in a workbook, choose File, Print. Then choose Entire workbook.

LESSON 1 Command Summary

FEATURE	BUTTON	MENU	KEYBOARD	SPEECH
Clear Cell Contents		Edit, Clear, Contents	Delete	✓
Close a document	(Menu bar)	File, Close	Ctrl + W or Ctrl + F4	✓
Exit Excel	(Title bar)	File, Exit	Alt + F4	✓
Full Screen		View, Full Screen		✓
Go To		Edit, Go To	F5 or Ctrl + G	✓
Open a workbook		File, Open	Ctrl + O	✓
Print		File, Print	Ctrl + P	✓
Print Preview		File, Print Preview		✓
Redo		Edit, Redo	Ctrl + Y	✓
Save As		File, Save As	F12	✓
Undo		Edit, Undo	Ctrl + Z	✓
Zoom	38%	View, Zoom		✓

Concepts Review

TRUE/FALSE QUESTIONS

Each of the following statements is either true or false. Indicate your choice by circling T or F.

T F **1.** A worksheet contains at least one workbook.

T F **2.** The Name box shows the address of the active cell.

T F **3.** The Zoom size for a particular screen is permanent.

T F **4.** You can use the scroll bars to move the pointer to a specific cell.

T F **5.** You can replace a cell's contents by clicking the cell and keying new data.

T F **6.** You must use Windows Explorer to create a new folder.

T F **7.** Edit mode starts when you press F2.

T F **8.** If you click the Print button, all worksheets are printed.

SHORT ANSWER QUESTIONS

Write the correct answer in the space provided.

1. What is the name for the cell with the heavy black border that is ready to accept new data, a formula, or for you to edit?

____

2. Give an example of a cell address for a title somewhere in the first column of a worksheet.

____

3. What is one keyboard shortcut for the Go To command?

____

4. What command enables you to use a different filename for a workbook?

____

5. What is the keyboard shortcut to move the pointer to cell A1?

____

6. Which part of the Excel screen shows the contents of the active cell?

____

7. How do you print all three sheets in a workbook with one command?

8. What do you use to reposition the worksheet on the screen without changing the location of the active cell?

CRITICAL THINKING

Answer these questions on a separate page. There are no right or wrong answers. Support your answers with examples from your own experience, if possible.

1. You can replace or edit cell contents. Discuss when you might use each procedure.
2. The Go To command moves to a specific cell. How is that different from the scroll bars? When would you use scroll bars?

Lesson Applications

EXERCISE 1-18

Open a workbook. Edit and print a worksheet.

1. Open **JanIceCream**.

REVIEW: Set the Zoom size so you can see as much of the data as possible.

2. Edit cell A2 to show the current month.

TIP: You do not need to key the commas. Excel does this automatically for you.

3. Change the first week total for Modesto to **15500**.
4. Key your first and last name in cell A20. Press Ctrl+Home.
5. Save the workbook as ***[your initials]*1-18** in your Lesson 1 folder.
6. Preview the worksheet and print it.
7. Close the workbook.

EXERCISE 1-19

Open a workbook. Edit a worksheet. Print a worksheet.

1. Open **BarSales**.
2. Change cell A3 to show **2001-2003**.
3. Change the fourth quarter amount for 2001 to **55000**.

NOTE: Numbers align at the right edge of a cell; text aligns at the left edge unless you change its alignment.

4. Key your first and your last name in cell A12. Press Ctrl+Home.

TIP: The keyboard shortcut for the Save As command is F12 in most Windows applications.

5. Save the workbook as ***[your initials]*1-19** in your Lesson 1 folder.
6. Preview the worksheet and print it.
7. Close the workbook.

EXERCISE 1-20

Open and edit a workbook. Print a workbook.

1. Open **JuneIceCream**.
2. In cell F1 on the WeeklySales sheet, key your first and last name. Press Ctrl+Home.

TIP: It is good practice to position the pointer at cell A1 before saving so the worksheet opens with that cell as the active cell.

3. In cell B16 on the Owners sheet, key your first and last names. Press Ctrl+Home.
4. Press Ctrl+P and select the option to print the entire workbook.
5. Preview the workbook before printing it. Print all the sheets.
6. Save the workbook as ***[your initials]*****1-20** in your Lesson 1 folder.
7. Close the workbook.

EXERCISE 1-21 Challenge Yourself

Open a workbook. Edit worksheets. Print a workbook.

1. Open **JanIceCream**.
2. On the WeeklySales sheet, change the values for the first week as shown here.

TIP: Start in cell B5 and press Enter to key the values down a column.

FIGURE 1-20

	A	B
5	Anderson	12000
6	Auburn	14000
7	Chico	12000
8	Eureka	18000
9	Fairfield	15000

continues

FIGURE 1-20 *continued*

	A	B
10	Modesto	16000
11	Red Bluff	11000
12	Redwood City	16000
13	Salinas	26000
14	San Fransicso, 15th	24000
15	San Fransicso, Lombard	24000
16	San Fransicso, West	*[Skip this cell.]*
17	Santa Rosa	19000
18	Watsonville	16000

3. In cell E1, key **Prepared by *[your first and last name]***. Press Ctrl+Home.
4. On the Owners sheet, key your first and last name in cell C1. Press Ctrl+Home.
5. Save the workbook as ***[your initials]*1-21** in your Lesson 1 folder.

REVIEW: Choose File, Print to print the entire workbook.

6. Preview and print the entire workbook, including the chart.

NOTE: If you use a black and white printer, the chart uses shades of gray for the bars.

7. Close the workbook.

On Your Own

In these exercises you work on your own, as you would in a real-life work environment. Use the skills you've learned to accomplish the task—and be creative.

EXERCISE 1-22

Open **JuneIceCream**. On the WeeklySales sheet, practice each of the navigation shortcuts in Table 1-2. On the Owners sheet, change each owner's name to someone you know. Include your own name as one of the owners. Print this worksheet. Save the workbook as ***[your initials]*1-22** in your Lesson 1 folder. Close the workbook.

EXERCISE 1-23

Open **MarAdv**. Change the month to this month. Using the Internet or a map, change each city to a different city in your state. Change the titles to specify your state, too. Key your first and last name in cell A14. Save the workbook as ***[your initials]*1-23** in your Lesson 1 folder and print it.

EXERCISE 1-24

In the Open dialog box, select and highlight the filename of each of the workbooks you used in this lesson (**JanIceCream**, **MarAdv**, **JuneIceCream**, and **BarSales**). Which of these files does not have a preview? In the Excel Help system, look up how to save a file with a preview. On a piece of paper, write in your own words what you should do to save a file with a preview. Include your first and last name, the exercise number, and the date.

LESSON 2

Creating a Workbook

OBJECTIVES

MOUS ACTIVITIES

In this lesson:

Ex2002 1-2
Ex2002 3-1
Ex2002 3-3
Ex2002 4-2
Ex2002 5-1
Ex2002 5-2

See Appendix E.

After completing this lesson, you will be able to:

1. Enter labels.
2. Change the font.
3. Select cell ranges.
4. Modify column width and row height.
5. Enter values and dates.
6. Save a workbook.
7. Enter basic formulas.

Estimated Time: 1½ hours

When you create a new workbook, you always start with three blank worksheets. You can key text, numbers, or formulas in any cell in any of these worksheets. Although Excel applies some automatic styles or formats as you enter information in a worksheet, you can change the font and font size, adjust the width and height of columns, or add colors.

Entering Labels

If you key data that begins with a letter in a blank cell, Excel recognizes it as a *label*. Labels are aligned at the left edge of the cell and are not used in calculations.

EXERCISE 2-1 Enter Labels in a Worksheet

As you key data, it appears in the active cell and in the formula bar. If you change your mind, you can press Esc to start over. You can also press Backspace to edit the entry.

There are several ways you can complete an entry.

TABLE 2-1 Ways to Complete a Cell Entry

KEY OR BUTTON	RESULT
Press Enter	Completes entry and moves the pointer to the cell below.
Press Tab	Completes entry and moves the pointer to the cell to the right.
Press Shift + Tab	Completes entry and moves the pointer to the cell to the left.
Press an arrow key	Completes entry and moves the pointer one cell in the direction of the arrow.
Click another cell	Completes the entry and moves the pointer to the clicked cell.
Click the Enter button	Completes the entry, and the current cell remains active.

1. Start Excel. A blank workbook opens with the New Workbook task pane at the right. Cell A1 on Sheet1 is active.

NOTE: The first new workbook in a work session is named Book1 until you save it with another name. The next new workbook is Book2, and so on.

2. If the Office Assistant starts, hide it. (Choose Hide the Office Assistant from the Help menu.)

3. Click the Close button in the New Workbook task pane. This gives you more room to work on the sheet.

REVIEW: You can reopen the task pane by choosing View, Task Pane.

4. If the Standard and Formatting toolbars are shown on one row, show them on two rows.

REVIEW: To show the Standard and Formatting toolbars on two rows, click the Toolbar Options button and click Show Buttons on Two Rows.

5. In cell A1, key **Klassy Kow Sa** to start a label. The worksheet is in Enter mode, shown in the status bar. The label appears in the formula bar and in the cell.
6. Press Backspace to delete **Sa**.

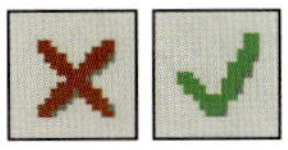

7. Key **Promotions**. Notice that an Enter button and a Cancel button appear in the formula bar when you are in Enter mode.

FIGURE 2-1
Label appears in the formula bar and the cell

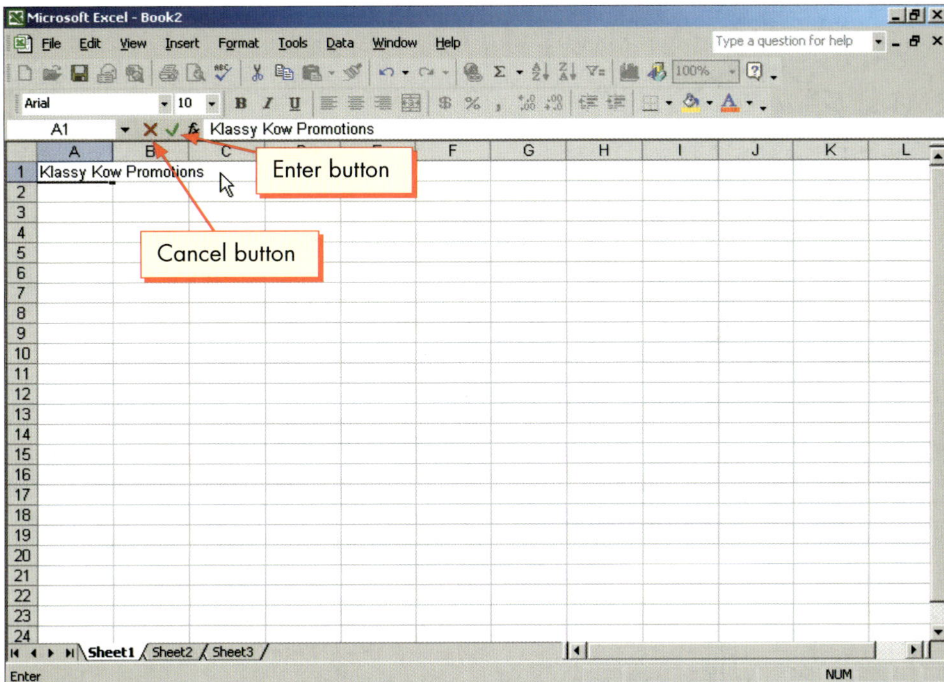

8. Press Enter. The label is completed in cell A1, and the pointer moves to cell A2. The label is longer than column A, so it spills into columns B and C.
9. In cell A2, key **Market** to start a label. Let's say this is a mistake. Press Esc to delete your entry. You can always use Esc to delete an entry if you haven't yet pressed Enter or moved away from the cell.

REVIEW: If you have pressed Enter or moved away from the cell and you need to delete your entry, click in the cell to make it active. Key the new data and press Enter or move the pointer away from the cell.

10. Key **Company Plan** and click the Enter button in the formula bar. The entry is completed. The formula bar shows the entire label, but it spills into cell B2.
11. Click cell A3 to make it active, if it is not already.
12. Key **Name** and press →. The pointer is now in cell B3.

13. Key **Starting Date** and press [→]. The label is too long for column B and spills into column C.

14. Key **Ending Date** in cell C3 and press [→]. The new label cuts off the label from column B and spills into cell D3. You will fix these problems soon.

NOTE: Text can spill into adjacent cells only if they are empty.

15. Key **Price** and press [→]. Key **Special Price** in cell E3 and press [Enter]. This label is not cut off, because there is nothing in the cell to the right.

16. Key the following labels, starting in cell A4. Press [Enter] after each.

Berry Kowabunga

Easter Bunny Pie

Triple-Scoop Cone

24 oz. Malted

Changing the Font

The default font for data keyed in a new workbook is 10-point Arial. You can change the font style and the font size by using the Formatting toolbar or by using the Format Cells dialog box. If you choose a larger font size, the height of the row is automatically made taller to fit the font.

EXERCISE 2-2 Change the Font, Font Size, and Style

1. Click cell A1. The formula bar shows the entire title.

2. Click the down arrow next to the Font box on the Formatting toolbar. A drop-down list appears, showing font names for your computer.

FIGURE 2-2
Choosing a font

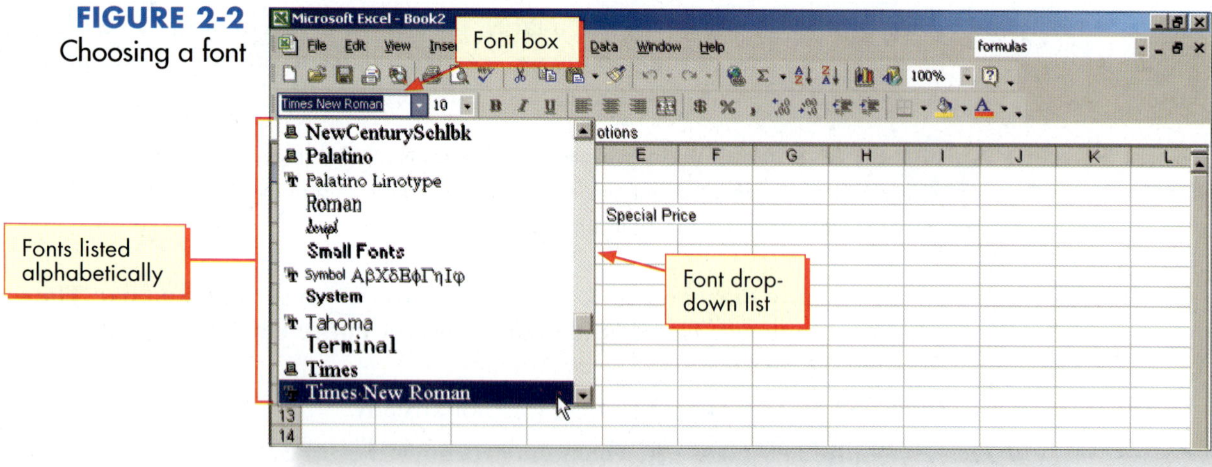

3. Key **t** to move to the font names starting with "T."
4. Choose Times New Roman.

NOTE: You also could have scrolled in the Font drop-down list to the new font.

5. Click the drop-down arrow next to the Font Size box on the Formatting toolbar. Choose 16. The label spills into column D. Notice that row 1 is now taller than the other rows to accommodate the larger font size.

TIP: You can choose a font size or you can key a size that is not in the list.

FIGURE 2-3
Choosing a font size

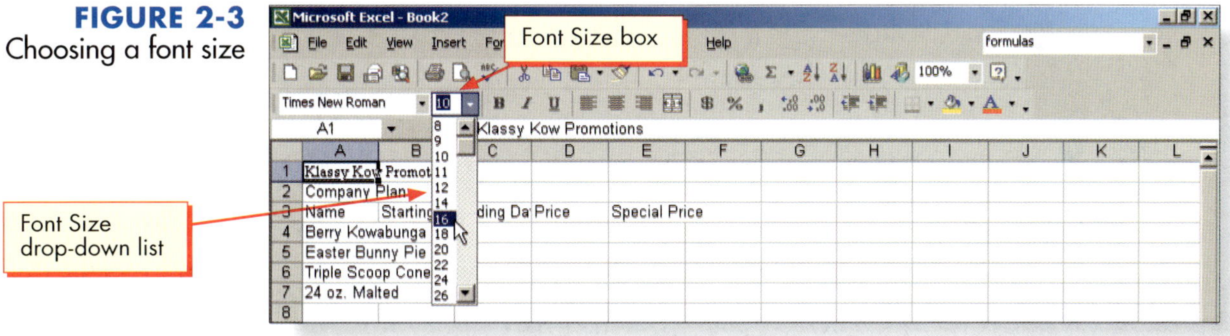

EXERCISE 2-3 Use the Format Painter

With the Format Painter, you can copy cell formats from one cell to another. This is often faster than applying formats individually to a cell that is unformatted.

To use the Format Painter, make the cell with formatting the active cell. Then click the Format Painter button. While the pointer is a white cross with a small paintbrush, click the cell to be formatted.

1. Make sure cell A1 is the active cell.

2. Click the Format Painter button. Cell A1 shows a moving marquee, and the pointer is a thick white cross with a paintbrush. (See Figure 2-4 on the next page.)
3. Click cell A2. The font and size are copied, and row 2 is made taller. The Format Painter command is canceled.
4. Make sure cell A2 is now the active cell.
5. Double-click the Format Painter button. This locks the painter on so you can format more than one cell.

FIGURE 2-4
Using the Format Painter

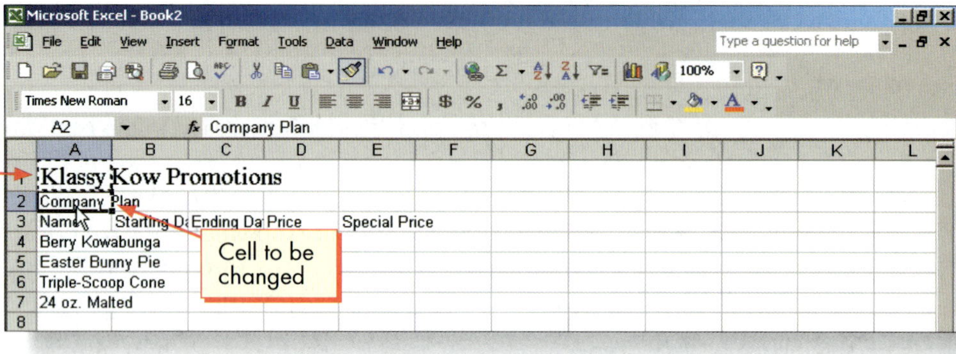

6. Click cell A3 to copy the format. Then click cell B3 to copy the format again.

7. Click the Format Painter button to cancel the command.

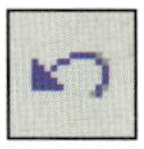

8. Click the arrow next to the Undo button .

NOTE: In this case, Excel regards the use of the Format Painter as a type of Paste command (it shows the use of the Format Painter as a "Paste Special" in the Undo button's history list. You will learn about copying and pasting later in the course.

9. Undo the last two **Paste Special** commands. These are your last two uses of the Format Painter. The labels in row 3 return to the default font and font size (10-point Arial).

10. Press Esc to cancel the marquee.

Selecting Cell Ranges

In many cases, you will find it helpful to work with a range of cells. A *range* is a group of cells that form a rectangle on the screen. For example, you might need to format all the cells in rows 3 through 7 of a worksheet.

When a range is active, it is highlighted on the screen. Like an individual cell, a range has an address. A *range address* shows the upper left cell address and the lower right cell address, separated by a colon.

TABLE 2-2

Examples of Range Addresses

RANGE ADDRESS	CELLS IN THE RANGE
A1:B3	6 cells on 3 rows and in 2 columns
B1:B100	100 cells, all in column B
C3:C13	11 cells, starting at cell C3, all in row 3

continues

TABLE 2-2 **Examples of Range Addresses** *continued*

RANGE ADDRESS	CELLS IN THE RANGE
D4:F12	27 cells on 9 rows and in 3 columns
E1:IV1	256 cells, or the entire row 1

EXERCISE 2-4 Select Ranges with the Mouse

When you start to select a range of cells, you will see a thick white, cross-shaped pointer. This is called the *selection pointer* because it is used to select ranges of cells on the worksheet.

There are several ways to select a range of cells by using the mouse:

- Drag across adjacent cells to select the range.
- Hold down Shift and click a cell to identify a range that extends from the active cell to the cell in which you pressed Shift+click.
- Click the Select All button (see Figure 2-5) to select the entire worksheet.
- Click a column heading letter to select a column or click a row heading number to select a row.
- Drag across adjacent column heading letters or row heading numbers to select multiple columns or rows.

REVIEW: The column headings are the cells at the top of a worksheet labeled A, B, C, and so on. The row headings are the cells at the left side of a worksheet labeled 1, 2, 3, and so on.

1. Click cell A3 to make it active.
2. While you see the thick white, cross-shaped pointer, click and drag to the right to cell E3.

TIP: If you do not select the correct cells, click cell A3 and try again.

3. Release the mouse button. Cells A3 through E3 are selected. The Name box shows the first cell in the range. The first cell appears white, and the remaining cells are light blue-gray or purple. (See Figure 2-5 on the next page.)
4. Click the Bold button **B**. All the cells in the selected range are now bold.

FIGURE 2-5
Selecting a range of cells

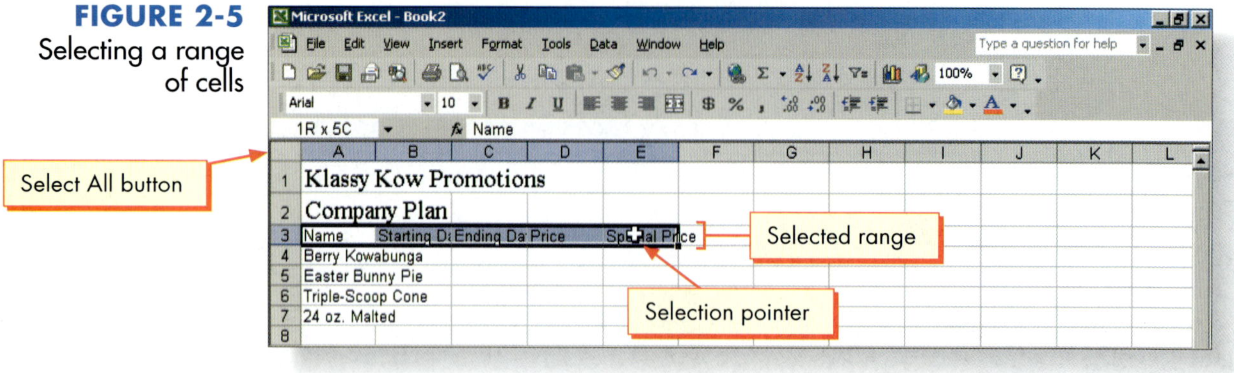

TIP: You can also apply bold by using the keystroke combination Ctrl + B. You can apply italic by using Ctrl + I.

5. Click cell A1. This makes cell A1 active and deselects the range. The range is no longer highlighted.
6. Click cell A1 and drag to cell F1. Do not release the mouse button.
7. Drag down to cell F3 and then release the mouse button. The selected range is A1:F3.

TIP: If you select the wrong range of cells, click cell A1 and try again.

8. Click cell A1 to deselect the range and make cell A1 active again.
9. Point to the row 1 heading. The pointer changes shape and is a solid black arrow. The pointer shows a different shape when you are about to select an entire row or column.
10. Click the row 1 heading to select the row.
11. Click cell B2. The range is deselected. You can click any cell to deselect a range.
12. Point to the row 1 heading. Click and drag down through the row headings from the row 1 heading to the row 5 heading.
13. Release the mouse button. Five rows are now selected.
14. Click any cell to deselect the rows.
15. Click the column A heading. This selects the column.
16. Click any cell to deselect the column.
17. Click the column B heading and drag to the column G heading. This selects a range that includes all the cells in columns B through G.
18. Click cell B5. Hold down Shift and click cell E18. This is another way to select a range. This range is B5:E18.

EXERCISE 2-5 Select Ranges with Keyboard Shortcuts

You can select a range of cells by using keyboard shortcuts. These shortcuts work in many other Windows programs (and particularly Office programs) for selecting data.

TABLE 2-3 Keyboard Shortcuts to Select Cell Ranges

KEYSTROKE	TO DO THIS
Shift +arrow key	Selects from the active cell, moving in the direction of the arrow.
Ctrl + Spacebar	Selects the current column.
Shift + Spacebar	Selects the current row.
F8	Starts Extend Selection mode.
Esc	Ends Extend Selection mode.
F8 +arrow key	Extends selection from active cell in the direction of the arrow.
Shift + PgUp	Extends selection from active cell up one screen.
Shift + PgDn	Extends selection from active cell down one screen.
Ctrl + Shift + Home	Extends selection from active cell to beginning of data.
Ctrl + Shift + End	Extends selection from active cell to end of data.

NOTE: Ctrl + A selects every available cell on a worksheet—all 65,536 rows and all 256 columns.

1. Click cell A3. Hold down Shift and press → four times. The range is A3:E3.
2. Click the down arrow next to the Font box. Key **t** and choose Times New Roman (or scroll to the font).
3. Click the down arrow next to the Font Size box. Choose 12.
4. Hold down Shift and press ↓ to reach row 15. The range is extended to A3:E15.
5. Click cell A3 to deselect the range.
6. Press F8. This starts Extend Selection mode. Notice that EXT appears in the status bar.
7. Press → four times. Press ↓ to reach row 15. The range A2:E15 is selected again.

TIP: If you go too far, press [↑] to reach row 15.

8. Press [Esc] to cancel Extend Selection mode.
9. Click cell A4. Hold down [Shift] and click E15. This is another way to select the range.
10. Hold down [Ctrl]. Click cell A17 and drag across to cell E17. Now two different-sized ranges that are not next to each other are selected at the same time.

FIGURE 2-6
Selecting two ranges

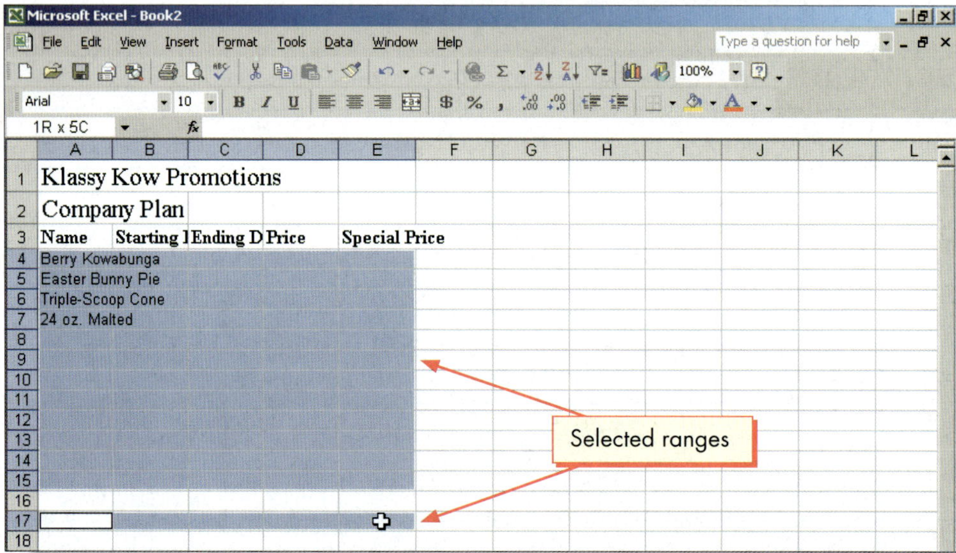

11. Click cell A4. Hold down [Shift] and click cell A7.
12. Change the font to 12-point Times New Roman.
13. Press [Ctrl]+[Home].

Modifying Column Width and Row Height

Excel makes all columns 8.43 spaces wide in a new workbook. Many labels do not fit in a column this wide. So, as you've seen, if the column on the right is empty, the label spills into it so you can still see the label on the screen. However, if the column on the right is not empty, you need to widen the column so the label is not cut off.

Rows in a new workbook are 12.75 points high to fit the default 10-point Arial font. Although Excel resizes the height of the row for some changes you make, there are times when Excel might not resize the row height and you will need to do it.

Here are the ways you can resize column widths and row heights:

- Drag a column or row border to a different size.
- Double-click a column's right border to AutoFit the column. *AutoFit* means the column is widened to fit the longest entry in the column.
- Double-click a row's bottom border to AutoFit the row height. A row is AutoFitted to fit the largest font size.
- Open the Format menu, and choose Row and then Height or Column and then Width.

When you use the mouse to change the row height or column width, you will see the size in a ScreenTip. For rows, the height is shown in points (like fonts) as well as in pixels. For columns, the width is shown in character space and in pixels. A *pixel* is a screen dot, a single point of color on the screen. A *character space* is the average width of a numeric character in the standard font used in the worksheet.

If you use the menu to change the column width or row height, you must key the entry by using points or character spaces, not pixels.

EXERCISE 2-6 Modify Column Width

In this exercise you use every method we've described to modify column width.

1. Place the pointer on the vertical border between the column headings for columns A and B. Notice the pointer changes to a two-headed arrow with a wide vertical bar.

FIGURE 2-7
Resizing columns

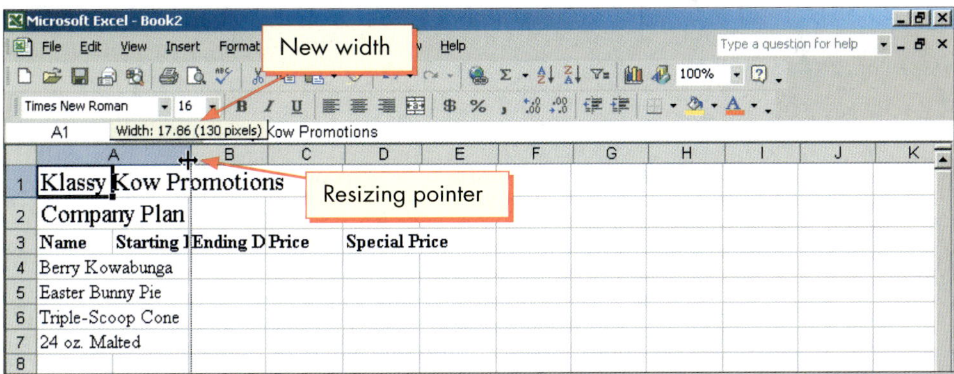

2. Drag the pointer to the right until the ScreenTip shows 17.86 (130 pixels). At this width, the column should be wide enough for the longest promotion item.

TIP: Be careful about AutoFitting columns that include worksheet titles in rows 1 and 2. Excel will AutoFit the column to include the long worksheet titles.

3. Place the pointer between the column headings for columns B and C. Double-click. Excel AutoFits Column B to fit the label.
4. Double-click the border between the column headings for columns C and D. Excel AutoFits column C.

NOTE: If you change information in a column to which you've applied AutoFit, the column does not automatically widen to fit the new entry. You must AutoFit the column again.

5. Click anywhere in column D.
6. Open the Format menu. Choose Column and then Width. The Column Width dialog box opens.
7. Key **10** and press Enter. The column width is changed to 10 spaces.
8. Double-click the border between the column headings for columns E and F to AutoFit column E.

EXERCISE 2-7 Modify Row Height

Now you will use different methods for modifying row height.

1. Place the pointer on the horizontal border between the headings for rows 3 and 4. The pointer turns into a two-headed arrow.
2. Drag down until the ScreenTip shows 22.50 (30 pixels).

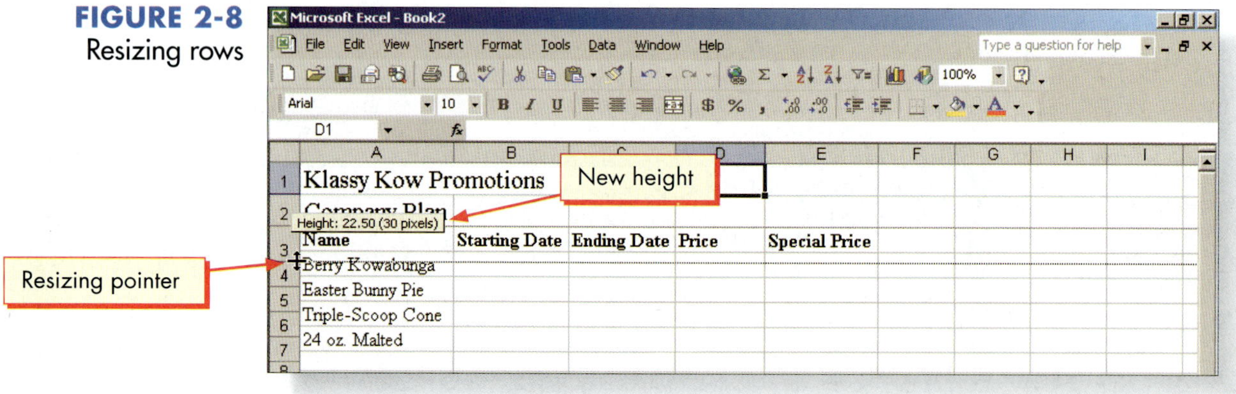

FIGURE 2-8
Resizing rows

3. Click anywhere in row 4.
4. Open the Format menu and choose Row and then Height. The Row Height dialog box opens.
5. Key **22.5** and press Enter. The row is 22.5 points high.

Entering Values and Dates

When you key an entry that starts with a number or an arithmetic symbol, Excel assumes it is a *value*. A value is right-aligned in the cell and is included in calculations. Arithmetic symbols include =, –, and +.

TIP: You can format a number as a label by keying an apostrophe before the number. The number is then not used in calculations.

EXERCISE 2-8 Enter Dates and Values

Excel recognizes dates if you key them in a typical date style. For example, if you key "1/1/03," Excel formats it as a date. Dates have special formats and can be used in date arithmetic.

1. Click cell B4.
2. Key **12/1/02** and press Enter. Excel recognizes a date and shows either two or four digits for the year (depending on how your computer is configured to show dates).
3. Continue keying the following dates in column B. Press Enter after each one.
   3/15/02
   8/01/02
   10/15/02
4. Key these dates in cells C4:C7.
   12/31/02
   4/15/02
   8/31/02
   11/15/02
5. Key the following prices in the "Price" and "Special Price" columns. Figure 2-10 on the next page shows the worksheet thus far.

FIGURE 2-9

	D	E
4	2.59	2.19
5	12.99	10.99
6	2.39	2.09
7	2.69	2.29

FIGURE 2-10
Worksheet data entry completed

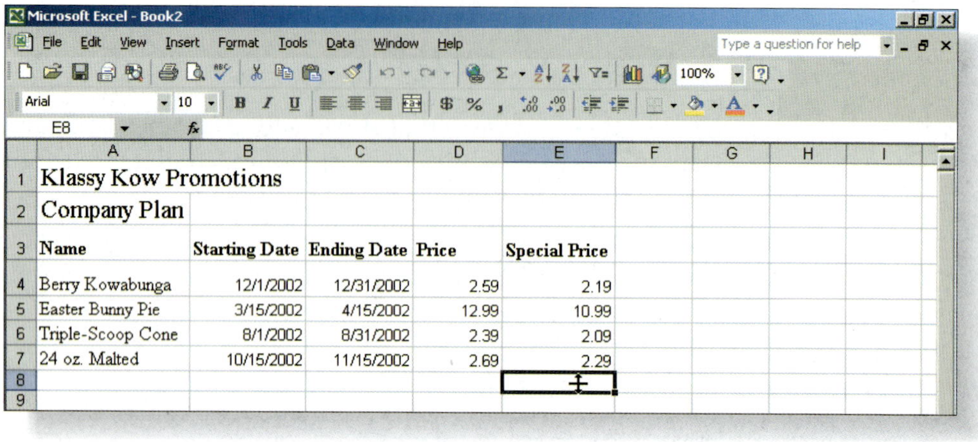

EXERCISE 2-9 Apply Number Formats from the Toolbar

When you first key a value, it is formatted in a "General" style. This style shows only the digits in the number and no commas. If the value has a decimal point, it is shown with as many places after the decimal point as you key.

To increase the readability of your worksheet, you can apply common formats by using the Formatting toolbar. Generally, to apply a format from the Formatting toolbar, you first select the range of cells to be formatted and then click a button from the toolbar.

1. Click cell D4. Drag to select cells D4:E7.
2. Click the Currency Style button [$] from the Formatting toolbar. The cells in the range are reformatted to show a dollar sign and two decimal places.

EXERCISE 2-10 Apply Date Formats from the Dialog Box

When you key a date, Excel applies a standard format that shows two digits for the month, two digits for the day, and either two or four digits for the year. Excel includes many date formats in the Format Cells dialog box. You can open the Format Cells dialog box for the active cell or the active range by:

- Opening the Format menu and choosing Cells.
- Pressing Ctrl+1.
- Right-clicking the cell or range and choosing Format Cells from the shortcut menu.

1. Click cell B4. Notice that the year is shown as 2002 in the formula bar.
2. Click and drag to select cells B4:C7.

3. Point at any of the selected cells and right-click. A shortcut menu opens.
4. Choose Format Cells. The Format Cells dialog box opens.
5. Click the Number tab.
6. Click Date in the Category list on the left. Many preset date formats are displayed in the Type box on the right.
7. Click a Type that shows the date first, a hyphen, an abbreviation for the month, another hyphen, and a two-digit year (example "14-Mar-01") and click OK. All of the dates are reformatted, using this new date format.

FIGURE 2-11 Choosing a date format

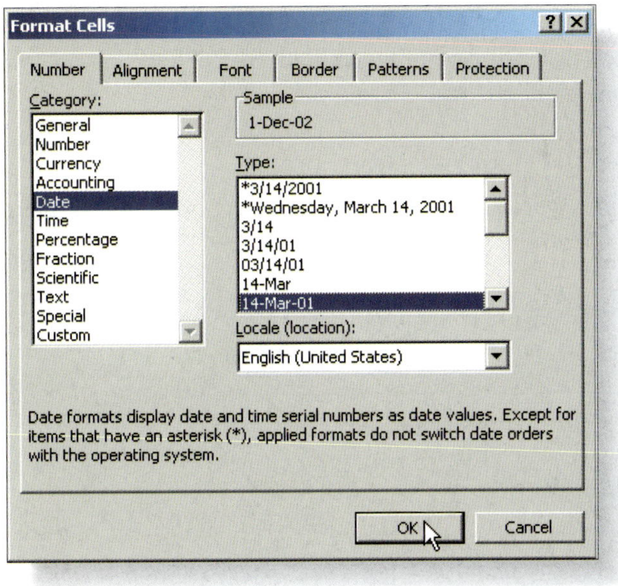

NOTE: Two-digit years between 00 and 29 are shown as the 21st century (2000, 2001, 2015). Two-digit years between 30 and 99 are shown as the 20th century (examples 1930, 1950, and 1999).

EXERCISE 2-11 Change the Font Color

In addition to changing the font, size, and style, you can set a new color for data in a workbook. You can change the font color for a selected cell or range by:

- Clicking the Font Color button in the Formatting toolbar.
- Opening the Format Cells dialog box and choosing the Font tab.

1. Select cells E4:E7 (this is the column with the special prices).
2. Click the Font Color button. The color shown on the button is applied to the selected range.

3. Click the arrow next to the Font Color button [A]. A color palette opens, showing color swatches for the available colors.

TIP: The color swatches in the palette have ScreenTips indicating the color's name.

4. Click "Green" in the fourth column. The palette closes, and the color is applied to the selected range.
5. Select cells A1:A2.

TIP: After you change the color of a selected range, deselecting the range or selecting another column enables you to see the color you applied without any highlighting.

6. Press Ctrl + 1 and click the Font tab.
7. Click the drop-down arrow for Color. Choose Dark Purple (in the second row from bottom) and click OK.

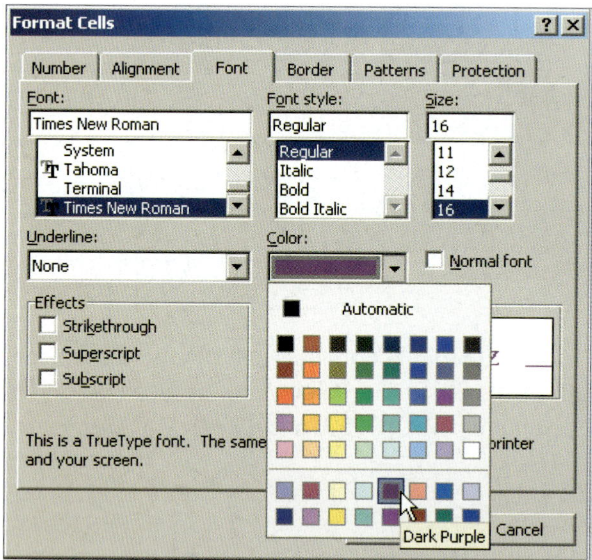

FIGURE 2-12
Changing the color from the Format Cells dialog box

EXERCISE 2-12 Rename a Worksheet and Change the Tab Color

As you have learned, each new workbook opens with three sheets named Sheet1 through Sheet3. You can rename a worksheet with a more descriptive name, which is often a good idea. It helps you remember a worksheet's purpose. If others are using the worksheet, renaming also helps them identify the worksheet's purpose.

Worksheet names can be up to 31 characters. You can use spaces in the name of a worksheet tab.

1. Double-click the worksheet tab for Sheet1. The tab name is selected.
2. Key **Promos** and press Enter.
3. Double-click Sheet2 and name it **Plans**. The Plans sheet is empty.

TIP: Another way to rename a worksheet tab is to right-click the tab and choose Rename.

4. Right-click the Promos tab and choose Tab Color. The Format Tab Color dialog box opens with a palette of colors.
5. Choose the color in the third column, fifth row—a medium yellow—as the tab color. Click OK. Notice that it is difficult to see the color when the tab is selected.

FIGURE 2-13
Changing the tab color

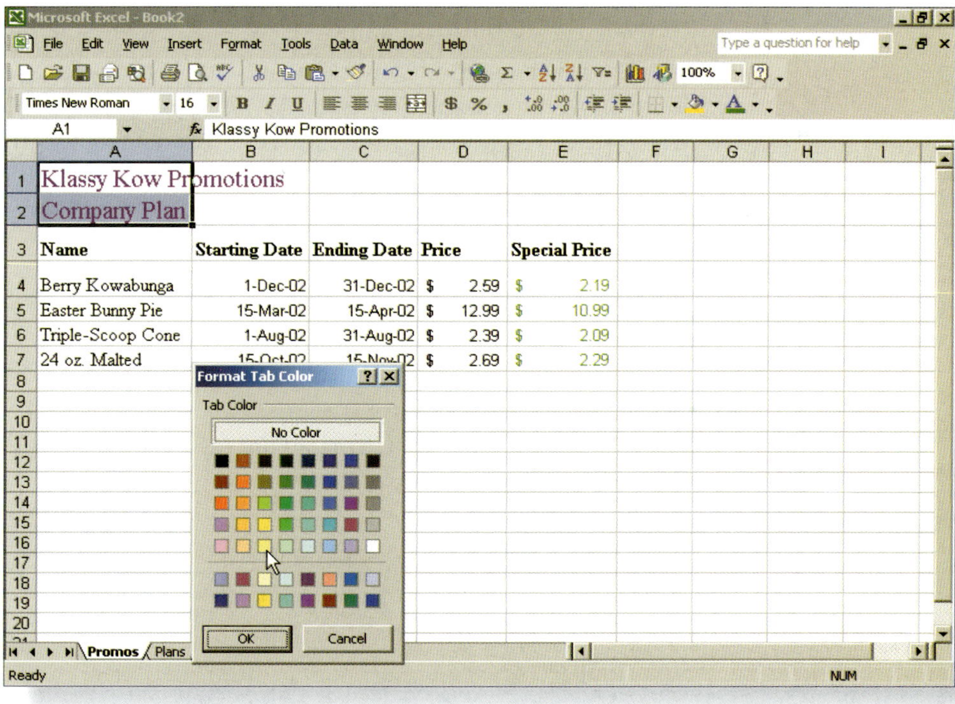

6. Click the Plans tab. Now you can see the color of the Promos tab better, because it's no longer selected.
7. Click the Promos tab again to make it the active sheet.

Saving a Workbook

When you create a new workbook or make changes to an existing one, you must save the workbook to keep your changes. Until you save your changes, your work can be lost if there is a power failure or computer problem.

To save a workbook, you must first give it a filename. A *filename* is the file identifier you see in the Open dialog box, My Computer, or Windows Explorer. When you name a file in Windows, you can use up to 255 characters. (Included in those 255 characters are the drive and folder names, so the actual filename is typically limited to around 230 to 240 characters.) Generally, it is a good idea to keep filenames as short as possible.

You can use uppercase or lowercase letters, or a combination of both, for filenames. Windows does not distinguish between uppercase and lowercase. You can use spaces in a filename, too. You cannot use the following characters in a filename: \ ? : * " < > |

Filenames are followed by a period and three-letter extension, usually supplied automatically by the software. Excel workbooks, for example, have the extension ".xls," and Word documents have the extension ".doc." Extensions identify the type of file.

For a new workbook, you can use either the Save or the Save As command to name the workbook. When you make changes to an existing workbook and want to save it with the same filename, use Save. When you want to save a workbook with a different filename, use Save As.

Excel saves workbooks in the current drive or folder unless you specify a different location. For example, to save a workbook to a floppy disk, you need to change the drive to A: or B:, whichever is appropriate for your computer.

Throughout the exercises in this book, filenames consist of two parts:

- ***[your initials]***, which might be your initials or an identifier your instructor asks you to use, such as **kms**
- The number of the exercise, such as **2-13**

NOTE: You might or might not see filename extensions, depending on how your computer is set.

EXERCISE 2-13 Save a Workbook

Saving a file after you've been working on it for a while is always a good idea. Depending on how difficult it would be to re-do the work, you should probably save your file every fifteen minutes to a half hour.

1. Click cell A1.

TIP: Wherever the pointer is when you save a workbook is where it appears the next time you open the workbook. Many people prefer to make A1 the active cell before closing the workbook. If you do that, A1 will be active when you next open the workbook.

2. Click the Save button.
3. Choose the appropriate drive and folder location from the Save in drop-down list.

NOTE: Your instructor will tell you what drive to use to save your workbooks.

4. Click the Create New Folder button.
5. In the Name box, key ***[your initials]*Lesson 2**. Click OK.
6. In the File name box, key ***[your initials]*2-13**
7. Click Save. The title bar shows the new filename.

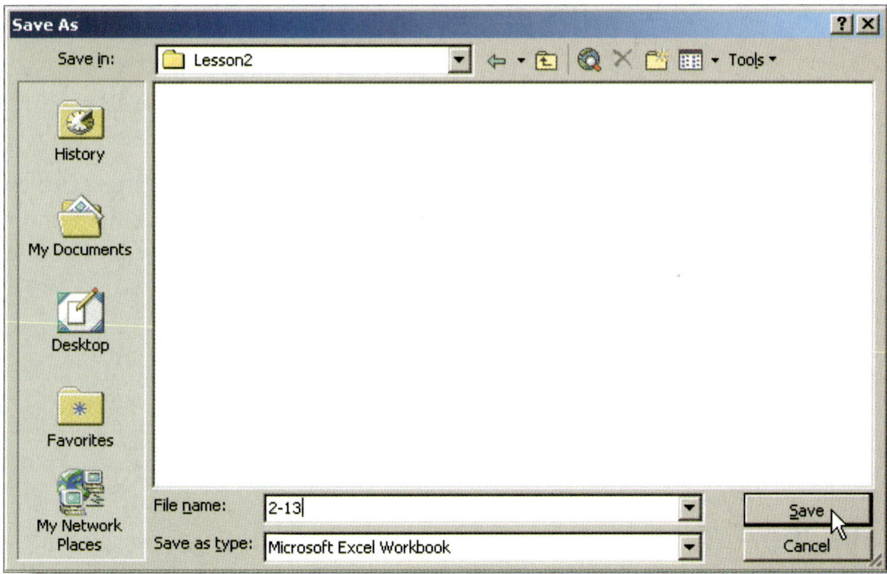

FIGURE 2-14
Saving a new workbook

Entering Basic Formulas

A *formula* is a series of instructions that performs a calculation and displays an answer. You key a formula in a cell. After you press a completion key, the formula results appear in the cell. The formula itself is visible in the formula bar.

Formulas are one of the main reasons for using Excel, because a formula performs calculations for you. If you later change any of the numbers used for the calculations, Excel can easily recalculate the formula to show a revised answer.

Formulas always begin with an = sign as an identifier. After the = sign, you enter the address of the cells you want to add, subtract, multiply, or divide. Then you use *arithmetic operators* in the ten-key pad or across the top of the keyboard to complete the calculation. You probably recognize all of the arithmetic operators shown in Table 2-4, with the possible exception of "exponentiation." The *exponentiation* operator raises a number to a power. For example, 3^2 represents 3 to the second power, or 32, which means 3 x 3 or 9.

TABLE 2-4 **Arithmetic Operators**

KEY OR SYMBOL	OPERATION
^	Exponentiation
*	Multiplication
/	Division
+	Addition
-	Subtraction

NOTE: When combined arithmetic operators are calculated in a specific order: first, exponentiation; second, multiplication and division; and finally addition and subtraction. You will learn about this order in Lesson 5.

EXERCISE 2-14 Key a Basic Formula

In your workbook, you can calculate the difference between the regular price and a special promotion price. This is a simple subtraction formula. You will be working in column F. If you cannot see column F, set your Zoom size to a smaller size so you can see it.

1. Click cell F3. Key **Difference** and press Enter. The label is automatically formatted with the same style as the other labels in the row.

NOTE: If three or more columns to the immediate left of the cell in which you enter data are already formatted, Excel applies the same format to the cell in which you are entering data.

2. Double-click the border between the column headings for columns F and G to AutoFit column F.
3. Key **=d4-e4** in cell F4. The formula appears in the cell and in the formula bar. The cells used in the formula are outlined in colors that match the colors of the formula in the cell. (See Figure 2-15 on the next page.)
4. Press Enter. The difference in price is 40 cents. It is shown in the same format ("Currency") as the cells used in the formula.

FIGURE 2-15
Keying a formula

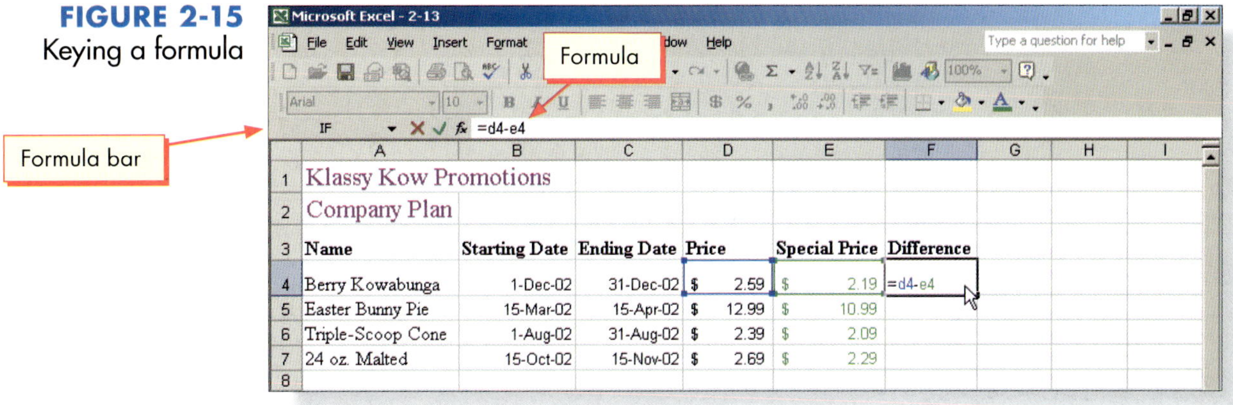

5. Press [↑] to return to cell F4. Notice that the formula bar shows the formula, but the cell shows the result of the formula.

NOTE: When you enter a formula, Excel capitalizes cell references, even if you did not capitalize them when you keyed them.

EXERCISE 2-15 Enter a Basic Formula by Pointing

You can use the mouse to point to cells used in the formula. This increases accuracy because you don't have to worry about keying the wrong cell address.

1. Click cell F5. Key = to start the formula.
2. Click cell D5. The address appears in cell F5 and in the formula bar. Cell D5 has a moving marquee.
3. Key – to subtract the next cell.
4. Click cell E5. It is placed in the formula after the minus sign and now has the moving marquee.

FIGURE 2-16
Enter a formula by pointing

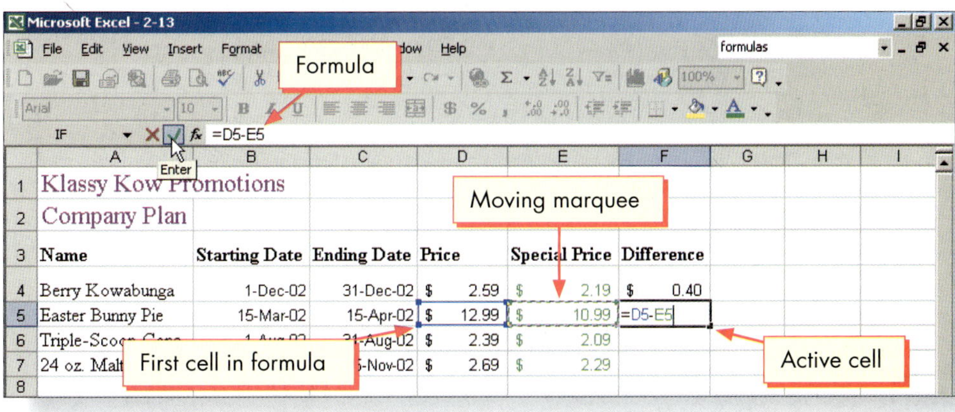

5. Click the Enter button ✓ in the formula bar. The difference of $2 is calculated.

EXERCISE 2-16 Copy a Basic Formula by Using the Copy and Paste Buttons

The formula in cell F5 is the same as the one in cell F4 except for the row references. The formula is relative to its location on the worksheet. When you copy a formula with row or cell references, Excel usually makes this adjustment automatically.

1. Click cell F5. Click the Copy button. The cell now has a moving marquee. The status bar tells you to select the destination for the copy.
2. Click cell F6 and drag to select the range F6:F7.
3. Click the Paste button. The formula is copied to both cells in the range. The Paste Options button appears just below the pasted data.
4. Place the pointer on the Paste Options button. A down arrow appears next to the button. Click the down arrow; options for copying the data are listed.
5. Click Keep Source Formatting to format the copied results in the same style as the original.

FIGURE 2-17
Copying a formula

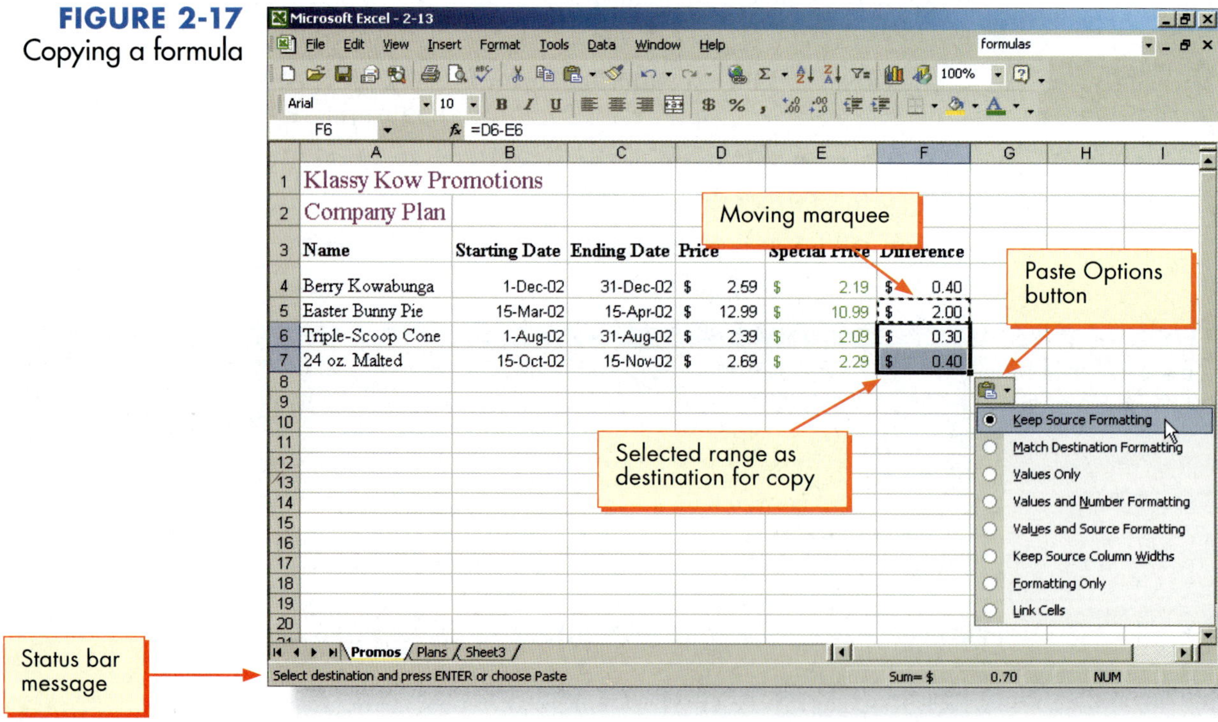

6. Press Esc to cancel the moving marquee and finish the Paste command.

NOTE: You can press Enter to complete a Copy or Paste command. This automatically cancels the moving marquee.

7. Click cell F6 and review the formula in the cell. Notice that Excel has automatically adjusted the formula to take into account the relative position of the cell.
8. Click cell F7. Review the formula. Excel has adjusted it as well.

EXERCISE 2-17 Use AutoSum, Average, and Max

Some calculations are so common in business and personal use that Excel includes them as functions. A *function* is a built-in mathematical formula included in Excel. An example of a function is "SUM," in which Excel automatically totals a column or row. The formula for a function always starts with =, just like a formula.

1. Click cell F8. Click the AutoSum button Σ in the Standard toolbar. A formula is placed in the cell, with the word "SUM" followed by the range that will be summed. A moving marquee surrounds cells that will be summed.

FIGURE 2-18
Using AutoSum

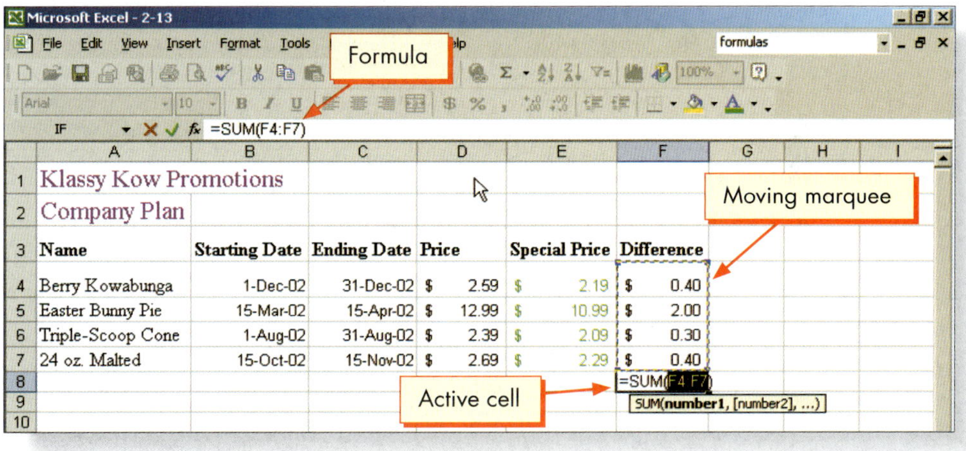

2. Press Enter. The formula is completed.
3. Click cell F8. Notice that the formula includes the function name SUM and the range in parentheses.
4. Click cell D8.
5. Click the down arrow next to the AutoSum button Σ on the standard toolbar.

6. Choose Average. The AVERAGE function now appears in the formula bar and in the active cell. A moving marquee surrounds the cells in the range.
7. Press Enter to complete the function. Then click cell D8 again. Notice that now the formula includes the function name AVERAGE and the range of cells that is averaged.

NOTE: The SUM function simply adds the values in the cells. The AVERAGE function adds the values in the range and then divides by the number of cells in the range, thus calculating the average of the values in the range.

8. Click cell D9. Click the arrow next to the AutoSum button Σ.
9. This time, choose Max. A moving marquee surrounds the cells that will be used by the MAX function. The MAX function is used to determine the largest value in a range.

NOTE: Excel functions ignore titles in a column/row because they are not values; they are labels, which are not used in calculations.

10. Click cell D4 and drag to select the range D4:D7. Don't include cell D8 in this function, because it is the average you just calculated.
11. Press Enter.
12. Click cell D9 again. The result of the formula shows the highest price in the column.

EXERCISE 2-18 Check Results with AutoCalculate

Excel has an easy-to-use feature called *AutoCalculate* that displays formula results for a selected range in the status bar. AutoCalculate can display sums, averages, counts, maximums, or minimums. You can set the AutoCalculate feature by right-clicking in the status bar.

1. Right-click the status bar. Choose Sum from the shortcut menu.
2. Select the range F4:F7. AutoCalculate shows the sum in the status bar. (See Figure 2-19 on the next page.)
3. Right-click the status bar and choose Average. The average of the cells in the range appears in the status bar.
4. Select the range D4:D7. AutoCalculate shows the average of these cells (the same result as from your formula in cell D8).
5. Select the range E4:E7.
6. Right-click the status bar and choose Max. The highest price is shown in the status bar.

FIGURE 2-19
Using AutoCalculate

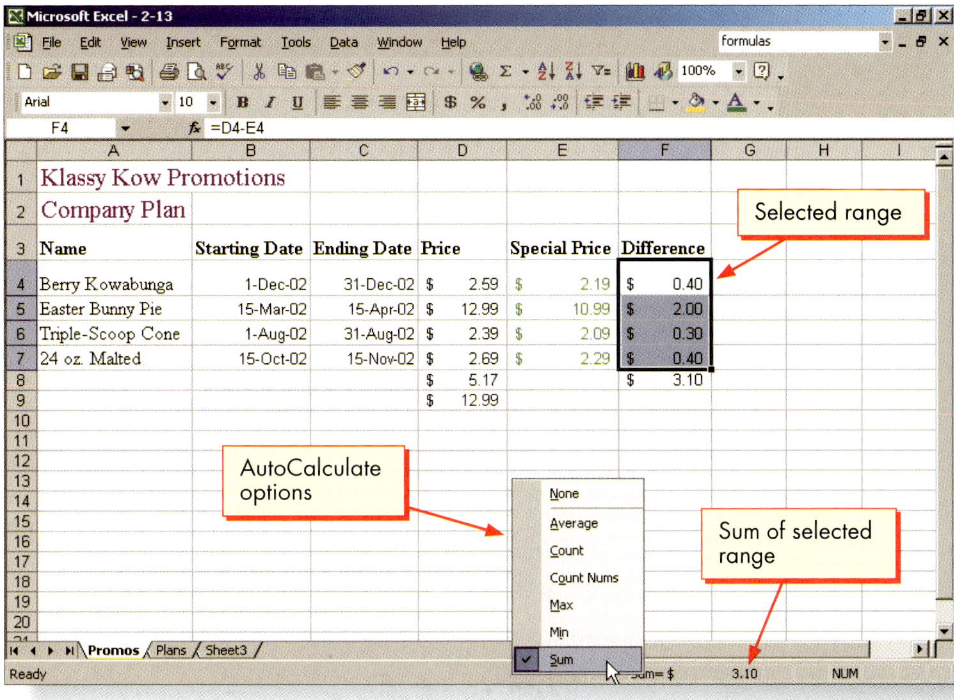

7. Select cells A4:A7. Right-click the status bar and choose Count. The COUNT function counts how many cells contain data.
8. Key your first and last name in cell A9.
9. Press F12 and save the workbook as ***[your initials]*2-18** in your Lesson 2 folder.
10. Preview and print your worksheet.

NOTE: If you print to a black and white printer, the colors will appear as shades of gray.

11. Click the Close Window button ☒ to close the workbook.

USING HELP

Building basic formulas is an important skill. You will use it as the basis for becoming a proficient Excel user. Read more about Excel formulas by asking a question.

Look up formulas by asking a question:

1. Start Excel if it's not open, and close the New Workbook task pane.
2. Click in the Ask a Question box in the upper right corner.
3. Key **formulas** and press Enter. Click See more.

4. Click the topic Create a formula.
5. Click Show All at the top right of the window. Read the Help information about all the different types of formulas.
6. When you finish investigating formulas, close the Help window.

LESSON 2 Summary

- In a blank workbook, you can key values, labels, dates, or formulas. Excel recognizes data by the first character you key in the cell.
- Labels are aligned at the left edge of a cell. If they are longer than the column width, they spill into the next column if it is empty. Otherwise, they appear cut off on the screen.
- To complete a cell entry, press Enter, Tab, or any arrow key or click another cell. You can also click the Enter button ✓ in the formula bar.
- The default font for data is 10-point Arial. You can change the font, the font size, the color, and the style.
- Use the Format Painter to copy formats from one cell to other cells.
- Many commands require that you first select a range of cells. You select a range of cells by using the mouse or keyboard shortcuts.
- The default row height matches the default font size. The row height adjusts if you choose a larger font. The default column width is 8.43 character spaces. It does not adjust when you use a larger font or if you key long data.
- Common formats, such as "Currency," can be applied to cells from the Formatting toolbar. Many other formats are available in the Format Cells dialog box.
- It's usually a good idea to change the default worksheet tab name to a more descriptive name. You can also change the worksheet tab color for visual cues.
- You must save a new workbook to keep your work. For a new workbook, you can use the Save or the Save As command.
- To create a formula in a cell, you can key it or you can construct it by pointing to the cells used in the formula. All formulas begin with the = symbol.
- When you copy a formula, Excel adjusts it to match the row or column where the copy is located.
- Excel has functions for common calculations such as Sum, Average, Max, Min, and Count.
- You can see results for some functions without keying a formula if you use AutoCalculate.

LESSON 2 Command Summary

FEATURE	BUTTON	MENU	KEYBOARD	SPEECH
AutoSum	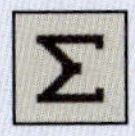			✓
Column Width		Format, Column, Width		✓
Copy		Edit, Copy	Ctrl + C	✓
Currency Style		Format, Cells		✓
Font Color		Format, Cells		✓
Font	Font box Formatting toolbar	Format, Cells		✓
Font Size	Font Size box Formatting toolbar	Format, Cells		✓
Format Painter		Edit, Paste Special		✓
New Workbook		File, New, Blank Workbook	Ctrl + N	✓
Paste		Edit, Paste	Ctrl + V	✓
Rename sheet		Format, Sheet, Rename		✓
Row Height		Format, Row, Height		✓
Save		File, Save	Ctrl + S	✓
Tab color		Format, Sheet, Tab Color		✓

Concepts Review

TRUE/FALSE QUESTIONS

Each of the following statements is either true or false. Indicate your choice by circling T or F.

T F *1.* If you key ABC Company in a cell, Excel will recognize it as a label.

T F *2.* When text is too long for the column, it spills to the next row.

T F *3.* A range is a rectangular group of cells.

T F *4.* Formulas must be keyed in the formula bar.

T F *5.* Common format styles are shown as buttons on the Standard toolbar.

T F *6.* The AutoSum button uses the SUM function.

T F *7.* AutoCalculate and AutoSum both display the results in a worksheet cell.

T F *8.* If you copy a formula from one cell to another, Excel changes it to match the new row and column.

SHORT ANSWER QUESTIONS

Write the correct answer in the space provided.

1. What symbol is used to start a formula?

____

2. Describe how to rename a worksheet tab.

____

3. What keyboard shortcut opens the Format Cells dialog box?

____

4. If the pointer is in cell B3 as you key a label and you want to key a label in cell C3, what key can you press to go directly to cell C3?

____

5. Give an example of a range address.

____

6. What function key starts Extend Selection mode?

____

7. How can you AutoFit a column to the longest text in it?

____

8. List three arithmetic operators that might be used in a formula.

____

CRITICAL THINKING

Answer these questions on a separate page. There are no right or wrong answers. Support your answers with examples from your own experience, if possible.

1. When you copy a formula, Excel changes the cell address to match where the copied formula is located. Give an example of when this is helpful. Think of a situation when you might not want Excel to do this.
2. Why does Excel have different data types such as values, labels, and dates? What are some of the differences among these types?

Lesson Applications

EXERCISE 2-19

Enter and format labels and values. Enter and copy a formula.

1. Create a new workbook. Save it as ***[your initials]*2-19** in your Lesson 2 folder.
2. Key the following labels in the specified cells:
   - **A1** **Klassy Kow Ice Cream**
   - **A2** **Ice Cream Pie Sales**
   - **A3** **March 31,** *[and the current year]*
3. Select all three cells and make them 16-point Times New Roman.
4. Format the date to show the month spelled out, the date, a comma, and four digits for the year.

REVIEW: Press Ctrl+1 to format the date.

5. Make column A 20.71(150 pixels) wide.
6. Key the labels and values shown in Figure 2-20.

FIGURE 2-20

	A	B	C	D	E	F
4		Week 1	Week 2	Week 3	Week 4	Total
5	Turtle Candy	10	3	5	8	
6	Rainbow	4	7	6	2	
7	Neapolitan	2	0	3	0	
8	Cookie Crunch	3	5	2	0	

7. Make the labels in row 4 bold.
8. Change the height of row 4 to 22.50 (30 pixels).
9. Click cell F5 and use AutoSum.
10. Copy the formula in cell F5 to cells F6:F8.
11. Change the height of row 5 to 22.50 (30 pixels).

12. Key your first and last name in cell A10.
13. Return the pointer to cell A1.
14. Preview and print the worksheet. Save and close the workbook.

EXERCISE 2-20

Format and key a label. Enter and copy a formula. Use AutoSum. Rename a worksheet.

1. Open **PieSales**. In cell A9, set the font to 12-point Times New Roman, bold. Then key **Quarter Total**
2. In cell B9, key =
3. Create a formula that adds cells B5 through B8. Use the mouse to construct the formula.

NOTE: If you accidentally key an addition symbol (+) at the end of a formula, Excel notes the error and can correct it. Read the message box and click Yes.

4. Copy the formula to the range C9:E9.
5. Change the font for cells B9:E9 to 12-point Times New Roman, bold.

NOTE: When you select more than one cell and use AutoSum, there is no moving marquee and you do not need to press Enter.

6. Use AutoSum to add the values in cells F5:F9.
7. Use the Format Painter to copy the format from cell A9 to the range F5:F9.
8. Use the Format Cells dialog box to format the range B5:F9 to use a Number format with no decimals and the thousands separator.
9. In cell F4, key **Year Totals**. Excel formats this automatically.
10. Rename the worksheet **Pies**.
11. Key your first and last name in cell A10.
12. Preview and print the worksheet.
13. Make A1 the active cell, save the workbook as ***[your initials]*2-20** in your Lesson 2 folder, and close it.

EXERCISE 2-21

Change the font. Modify column width and row height. Enter and copy a formula. Rename a worksheet.

1. Open **MediaPlans**. Save it in your Lesson 2 folder as ***[your initials]*2-21**.

2. Make the labels in row 2 bold.
3. Widen column A to show the data.
4. In cell E3, create a formula that multiplies "# of Times Run" by "Individual Cost." Copy the formula to all appropriate cells.

TIP: If you copy a formula to the wrong cell, delete the cell contents.

5. Make sure the font for the formula's results matches the font of the other values in the worksheet.
6. Set a row height of 18.75 (25 pixels) for rows 3 through 8.
7. Rename the sheet **MediaPlans**.
8. Key your first and last name in cell A10.
9. Preview and print the worksheet.
10. Return the pointer to cell A1. Save and close the workbook.

EXERCISE 2-22 *Challenge Yourself*

Create a workbook. Enter and format labels and values. Enter formulas.

1. Create a new workbook.
2. Rename Sheet1 as **DailySales**.
3. Save the workbook as ***[your initials]*2-22** in your Lesson 2 folder.
4. Format the range A1:A2 as 16-point Times New Roman.
5. Key the following labels in the specified cells:
   - A1 **Klassy Kow Ice Cream Shops**
   - A2 **Daily Double Scoop Sales in *[your home city]***
   - B3 **Friday**
   - C3 **Saturday**
   - D3 **Sunday**
6. Make all the labels in row 3 12-point Times New Roman, bold.
7. Change the height of row 3 to 36 pixels.
8. Format the range A4:D8 as 12-point Times New Roman.
9. In cells A4 through A8, key the names of five different flavors of ice cream, one in each cell. Manually size the column to fit the longest flavor.

NOTE: If you type a flavor name that begins with a "k," "d," or the same letter as one of your other flavors, you might see an AutoComplete ScreenTip. Ignore it and continue typing.

10. In cells B4:D8, key values to indicate how many double-scoop cones were sold on each day.
11. Format the values so they appear without decimals and with a thousands separator (a comma).
12. Add the label **Flavor Totals** in cell E3.
13. Add the label **Totals** in cell A9. Use the same format for this label as was used in row 3. Set the row height for row 9 to 24 pixels. Check that all values use the same font and size.
14. Use AutoSum to add the values for each flavor and for each day. Format the results so they appear without decimals and a thousands separator (comma).
15. Key your first and last name in cell A12.
16. Return the pointer to cell A1. Preview and print the worksheet.
17. Save the workbook and close it.

On Your Own

In these exercises you work on your own, as you would in a real-life work environment. Use the skills you've learned to accomplish the task—and be creative.

EXERCISE 2-23

Open **MediaPlans**. Change the names in column A to the names of radio stations, TV stations, newspapers, or magazines in your city. Call each medium and ask the cost of a popular ad. Change the costs in the worksheet. Add your name and the exercise number to the worksheet. Save it as ***[your initials]*2-23** in your Lesson 2 folder. Print the worksheet and close it.

EXERCISE 2-24

Sketch on paper a workbook that shows the names of five people in your class or with whom you work. List each person's city, phone number (with area code in parentheses), and birthday. Include a main title and titles for the columns.

Create a workbook based on your sketch. Format it attractively. Add your name and the exercise number to the worksheet. Save it as ***[your initials]*2-24** in your Lesson 2 folder. Print the worksheet and close it.

EXERCISE 2-25

Look through a print or Internet catalog and list five products you would like to purchase. Make sure one of the products is small enough that you will want to purchase several of them.

In a new workbook, list the product name, the store or Web site, and the price for each product. Add a quantity column to show how many of each item you would purchase. Create a formula to show what it would cost to buy your items (do not include such things as sales tax or shipping charges). Add your name and the exercise number to the worksheet. Save it as ***[your initials]*2-25** in your Lesson 2 folder. Print the worksheet and close it.

LESSON 3

Using Editing and Formatting Tools

OBJECTIVES

MOUS ACTIVITIES

In this lesson:

Ex2002 1-2
Ex2002 1-3
Ex2002 1-4
Ex2002 3-5
Ex2002 3-6
Ex2002 3-7

See Appendix E.

After completing this lesson, you will be able to:

1. Use AutoCorrect.
2. Look at Trace Error options.
3. Use Spelling.
4. Use Find and Replace.
5. Use AutoFill and series.
6. Apply an AutoFormat.
7. Change the page setup.

Estimated Time: 1½ hour

Keying labels and values is the first step in creating a workbook. You must also make your workbooks accurate and easy to use. Excel has several tools that can help you. It has electronic dictionaries that can correct common spelling errors as you type. You can check the spelling of the entire workbook with Excel's Spelling command. Other tools enable you to quickly find and replace data and to fill in information automatically.

Using AutoCorrect

The *AutoCorrect* feature makes spelling corrections for you as you type. It recognizes common errors such as "teh" and corrects it to "the." It capitalizes the days of the week and the months and corrects some capitalization errors, such as THis. You can also set it to help you enter routine data more efficiently.

EXERCISE 3-1 Use AutoCorrect to Correct Errors

The **KowaSales** worksheet compares sales of Kowabunga ice cream, which is available in several flavors, over a period of three years. For the years 2001 and 2002, a percentage increase is computed.

NOTE: As you key the labels for this exercise, make sure to key the errors that are shown. Excel will automatically correct some of them for you. You'll correct the other errors later.

1. Open **KowaSales**.
2. In cell A1, key **KLassy KOw** and press Spacebar. The two incorrect uppercase letters are corrected automatically. Notice that the font and size were already set for cell A1.
3. Key **Ice Cream Shops** to complete the label. Press Enter.
4. Key **saturday** and press Enter. As you can see, AutoCorrect capitalizes the days of the week.
5. In cell A3, change the font to 9-point Arial.
6. Key **teh shop tracked olny saturday sales.** Press Enter. Many common errors are corrected as soon as you press Spacebar, but not all errors are found by AutoCorrect. The word "only" has not been corrected, nor was "the" capitalized. Leave these errors for now.

EXERCISE 3-2 Set AutoCorrect Options

If AutoCorrect is correcting work you do not want corrected, you can change what AutoCorrect corrects. For example, if you type "acn," AutoCorrect automatically changes your typing to "can." If "ACN" were the initials of an employee or a company you want to show as a label, you would want to delete this type of correction from AutoCorrect. You can also add new types of corrections to AutoCorrect.

1. Choose Tools, and then choose AutoCorrect Options. The errors and corrections in AutoCorrect are listed in alphabetical order.
2. In the Replace box, key **kk**. Press Tab.

NOTE: AutoCorrect is a shared component of all Office applications (Access, Excel, PowerPoint, and Word). Each of these programs uses the same AutoCorrect.

3. In the With box, key **Klassy Kow**. Click Add to add this entry to the AutoCorrect list. Click OK.

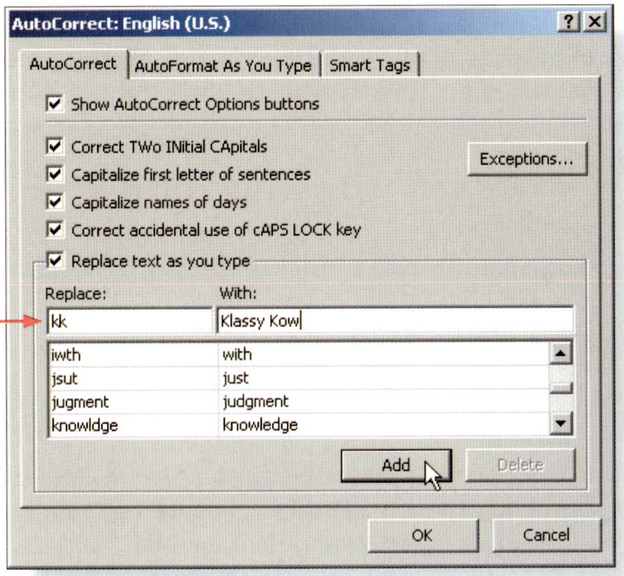

FIGURE 3-1 AutoCorrect dialog box

4. Click cell F3, key **kk**, and press Spacebar. The initials are changed to "Klassy Kow."
5. Key **Marketing Department** to finish the label. Press Enter.
6. Choose Tools, and then choose AutoCorrect Options.
7. In the Replace box, key **kk** to move to the "Klassy Kow" entry in the list.
8. Click Delete to remove the entry. Click OK.
9. Click cell F4, key **kk**, and press Enter. The initials are not changed because the entry has now been removed from AutoCorrect.
10. Delete the characters in cell F4.
11. Press Ctrl + Home to return to cell A1.

NOTE: You have been instructed to delete the "Klassy Kow" AutoCorrect entry so other students in other classes can use your computer without having this entry already listed among the AutoCorrect entries.

Looking at Trace Error Options

Excel automatically alerts you to problems with formulas by displaying the Error Checking Options button. This button appears on the worksheet as a small exclamation point within a diamond. It is located next to a cell that has a formula error. Excel also displays a small green triangle in the top left corner of the cell. When an Error Checking Options button pops up to warn of a potential error, you can review the type of error, fix it, or ignore the error.

NOTE: The Error Checking Options button might also be called the Trace Error button, depending on the type of error Excel discovers.

EXERCISE 3-3 Review Error Checking Options

Cells B12:D12 display a small triangle in the top left corner, signaling a potential error.

1. Click cell B12. The Trace Error button appears to the left of the cell.
2. Position the mouse pointer on the Trace Error button to see a ScreenTip message.
3. Click the down arrow next to the button. Its shortcut menu opens. The first line in the menu explains the error, that the formula omits adjacent cells. Excel assumes that a SUM formula in cell B12 would sum the cells directly above, B7:B11. However, the formula is currently correct in its present state. It correctly sums the cells B7 through B10.

FIGURE 3-2
Trace Error button

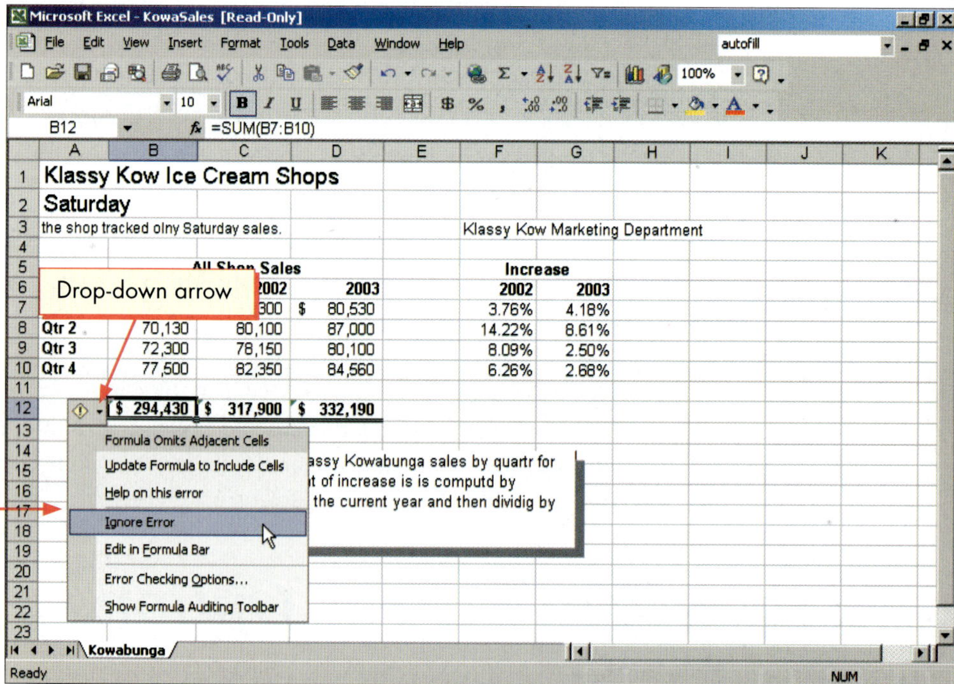

TIP: It is good practice in a worksheet not to leave blank rows that will interfere with calculations.

4. Choose Ignore Error. The small triangle is removed.
5. Click cell C12 and drag to select the range C12:D12.
6. Position the mouse pointer on the Trace Error button and click the down arrow.
7. Choose Ignore Error. The formulas in these cells are also correct. Excel now will ignore this "error."
8. Press Ctrl + Home to return to cell A1.

Using Spelling

AutoCorrect does not find all errors, only those that are considered common typographical mistakes. Excel's Spelling feature does a more thorough job of scanning the worksheet and finding words that do not match entries in its dictionaries. It also finds repeated words. The Spelling dialog box provides options for handling errors. These options are described in Table 3-1.

TABLE 3-1 Spell-Check Dialog Box Options

BUTTON	ACTION
Ignore Once	Do not change the spelling of this occurrence of the word. If it is a repeated word, do not delete one of the words.
Ignore All	Do not change the spelling for any occurrences of the word. If it is a repeated word, do not delete the double word.
Add to Dictionary	Add this word to the dictionary so Excel will not regard it as misspelled.
Change	Replace the current spelling with the highlighted alternative in the Change To box.
Delete	Appears only for repeated words. Click to delete one occurrence of the word.
Change All	Replace the current spelling with the highlighted alternative every time this misspelling occurs.
AutoCorrect	Add the misspelled word with its correction to the AutoCorrect list.
Undo Last	Reverse/undo the last spelling correction.
Options	Offers choices for changing the dictionary language, ignoring uppercase and words with numbers, and ignoring Internet addresses.

EXERCISE 3-4 Spell-Check a Worksheet

Excel starts spell-checking at the active cell and checks to the end of the worksheet. When the spell-checker reaches the end of the worksheet, a dialog box opens, asking if you want to continue spell-checking from the beginning of the worksheet.

The **KowaSales** worksheet has a text box that starts near row 14 with several spelling errors. (A text box is used for special text displays and notations. You will learn how to create them in a later lesson. If you accidentally click the text box in this lesson, click any cell away from the box to continue working.)

TIP: You can select a range of cells and then click the Spelling button to spell-check only that range.

1. Click the Spelling button. Excel finds "workshet" in the text box. It offers two suggestions for the correct spelling.

2. Click worksheet in the Suggestions list.

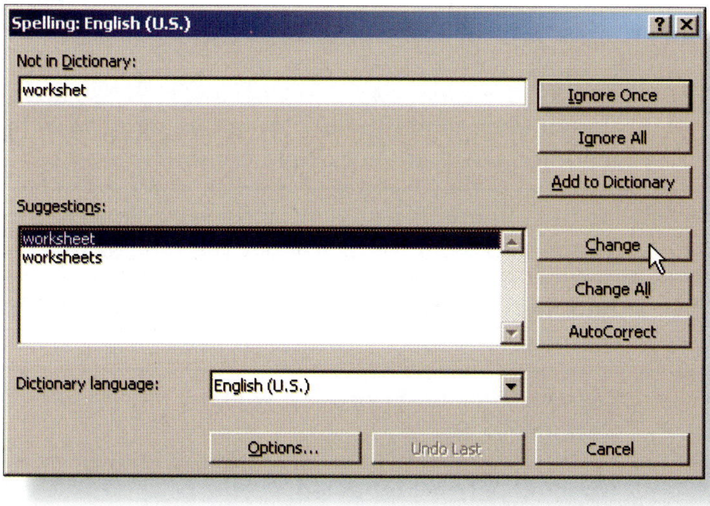

FIGURE 3-3
Spelling dialog box

3. Click Change. The correction is made but you will not see it until you close the Spelling dialog box. Notice that the next error that is found is "Klassy." This spelling is not an error; it is correct.

TIP: You can move the Spelling dialog box by dragging its title bar.

4. Click Ignore All. Excel will ignore any more occurrences of "Klassy." The next word is "Kowabunga," because it does not match any words in the dictionary. Again, this is the correct spelling.

5. Click Ignore All. The word "quartr" appears next in the text box.

6. Double-click quarter in the Suggestions list. A double-click is the same as clicking the word and then clicking Change. The next error is a Repeated Word, two occurrences of the word "is."
7. Click Delete to remove one occurrence of the word.
8. Choose the correct alternative for "computd" and click Change.
9. Correct "dividng."
10. "Kow" is correct, so ignore all occurrences of it.
11. Correct any other errors Excel finds. When all errors have been corrected or ignored, a message box tells you that the spell check is complete.
12. Click OK.
13. Click cell A3. Notice that Excel did not find the capitalization error in cell A3.
14. Start the Edit mode. Then position the insertion point at the beginning of the entry in the cell.

REVIEW: F2 starts Edit mode. Home positions the insertion point at the beginning of the entry.

15. Change "the" to "The." Press Enter.

Using Find and Replace

You can use the Find command to locate words, a sequence of characters, or even formats. Typically, you would use the Find command to locate a *character string*, a sequence of letters, numbers, or symbols. A character string can be alphabetic or numeric. However, you can also use the Find command to locate formats, such as everything in the worksheet that is bold.

You can use wildcards in a Find command when you are not sure about spelling or want to find a group of data. A *wildcard* is a character that represents one or more numbers or letters. Excel recognizes two common wildcard characters. They are:

- * Represents any number of characters
- ? Represents a single character

The character string "mar*" would find everything in the worksheet that includes the characters "mar" followed by any number of letters or values. This would include "March," "Mar2003," and "Marketing." The character string "?n" would locate all entries that start with a single character followed by an "n." Examples are "in," "2n," and "on."

There are two ways to start the Find command:

- Press Ctrl+F.
- Open the Edit menu and choose Find.

The Replace command typically locates occurrences of a character string and substitutes a replacement string. A *replacement string* is a sequence of characters that is exchanged for existing data. The Replace command can also search for a format, replacing it with another format.

There are two ways to start the Replace command:

- Press Ctrl+H.
- Open the Edit menu and choose Replace.

Find and Replace share a dialog box, so you can actually use any of these four methods to start either command.

EXERCISE 3-5 Find Data

In the Find and Replace dialog box, you can choose whether to search the worksheet or the workbook. You can search by column or row. If you know, for example, that the name you are looking for is in either column A or B, it is faster to search by column. You can also choose to search formulas or values, in addition to labels. Other options let you match the capitalization or the entire cell contents. The Find command searches only worksheet cells. It does not search objects that might be embedded within a worksheet (such as the text box in **KowaSales**).

In Find and Replace character strings, do not include format symbols such as the dollar sign and the comma. These are inserted as part of the formatting of a worksheet and are not really worksheet data.

1. Press Ctrl+Home to make sell A1 active.
2. Press Ctrl+F. The Find and Replace dialog box opens. Notice that each command has a separate tab.
3. Key **2002** in the Find what box.
4. Click Find All. The dialog box expands to list information about two cells that include this string of numbers. The first occurrence is highlighted in the worksheet and the list. (See Figure 3-4 on the next page.)

TIP: You can expand the Find dialog box by dragging its corners.

5. Click the second cell identifier in the Find tab. The pointer moves to that cell in the worksheet.
6. Double-click "2002" in the Find what box and key **qtr**. Character strings you key in the Find what box are not case-sensitive unless you turn on the Match case option.
7. Click the Options button. The dialog box expands to show you additional settings.

FIGURE 3-4
Find and Replace dialog box, Find tab

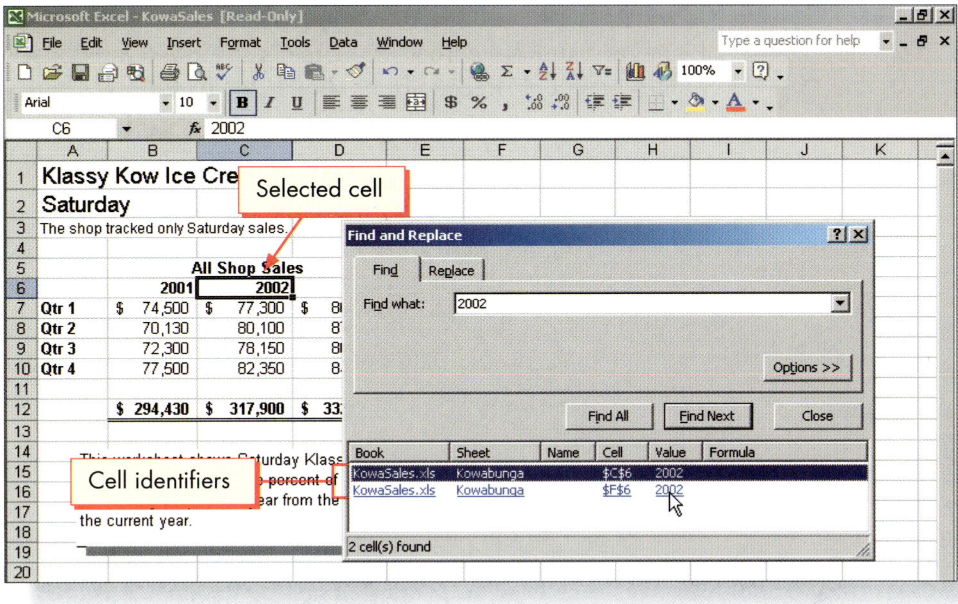

8. Click the arrow next to the Within box. You can find data within the active sheet or the entire workbook.

9. Choose Sheet, if it is not already selected.

10. Click the arrow next to the Search box. For many worksheets, you might not see much difference in speed if you search by columns or by rows.

11. Choose By Rows, if it is not already selected.

12. Click the arrow next to the Look in box. Excel ignores character strings within values and comments unless you specify that these should be included in the search. (A comment is a message you can insert in a worksheet.)

13. Choose Formulas, if it is not already selected.

14. Click Find All. Four cells include this character string.

EXERCISE 3-6 Use Wildcards

Now you will use wildcards with the Find and Replace commands.

1. Double-click "qtr" in the Find what box and key ***500**. This character string is used to find all cells with an entry that ends in "500" preceded by any amount of letters or numbers.

2. Click Find All. Two values in the worksheet match this character string.

3. Double-click "*500" in the Find what box and key **o***(lowercase letter "O," not zero, and an asterisk). This character string is used to find all cells with an entry that includes the letter "o" followed by any amount of other characters.
4. Click Find All. There are several cells with such entries.
5. Double-click "*o" in the Find what box and key **????0** (four question marks and a zero). This character string is used to find cell contents that end in 0, preceded by characters.
6. Click Find All. There are 17 cells in the list.
7. Click Close to close the Find and Replace dialog box.

EXERCISE 3-7 Replace Data

You can replace a character string one occurrence at a time or all at once. Sometimes replacing them all at once can be a problem because you might locate some character strings you didn't anticipate.

1. Press Ctrl + Home to make cell A1 active.
2. Press Ctrl + H. The same Find and Replace dialog box opens, this time with the Replace tab active. Excel remembers your most recent Find character string.
3. Double-click "????0" in the Find what box and key **2003.**
4. Click in the Replace with box and key **2004**. This will change occurrences of "2003" to "2004."
5. Click Find Next to locate the first occurrence of "2003."

FIGURE 3-5 Find and Replace dialog box, Replace tab

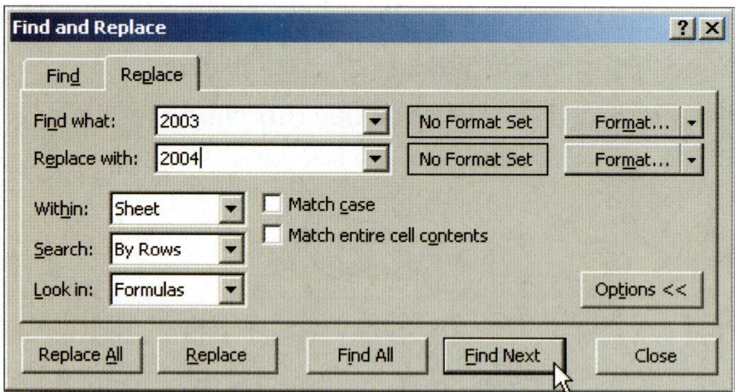

6. Click Replace to change "2003" to "2004." Excel locates the next occurrence.
7. Click Replace. Excel doesn't locate any additional occurrences of "2003."

EXERCISE 3-8 Replace a Function in a Formula

1. Double-click "2003" in the Find what box and key **sum**.
2. Click Find All. Excel locates three cells with the SUM function.
3. Double-click "2004" in the Replace with box and key **avg**. Let's say you wanted to change the function in those three cells from SUM to AVERAGE, but you incorrectly key in this abbreviation rather than the entire word.
4. Click Replace. The first occurrence is replaced. Excel notifies you that this is incorrect spelling for the AVERAGE function. The cell shows #NAME?, a type of error.
5. Click Replace All. Two more replacements are made. This is an example of what could happen if you replace all instances with a new character string that contains an error.
6. Click OK. Because you misspelled "average," all the cells affected by the replacement show an error message.
7. Click Close to close the Find and Replace dialog box. You will correct the errors in the next exercise.

EXERCISE 3-9 Correct Errors with Replace

Now you can use Find and Replace to correct the spelling of "average."

1. Click cell B12. Position the pointer on the Trace Error button.
2. Click the arrow next to the button. This is an "Invalid Name Error." The name of the function is "average," not "avg." (See Figure 3-6 on the next page.)
3. Click cell B12 to close the shortcut menu.
4. Press Ctrl + H.
5. Double-click in the Find what box and key **avg**.
6. Press Tab. In the Replace with box, key **average**.
7. Click Find All. All the cells with the misspelled function are listed.
8. Click Replace All. The replacements are made.
9. Click OK and then click Close. Another Trace Error button has appeared. The AVERAGE function assumes that all the cells immediately above the cell containing the function are included in the range. That's not true in this case.
10. Click cell B12 and drag to select the range B12:D12.
11. Position the mouse pointer on the Trace Error button. A down arrow appears next to the button. Click the arrow next to the button.

FIGURE 3-6
Error messages

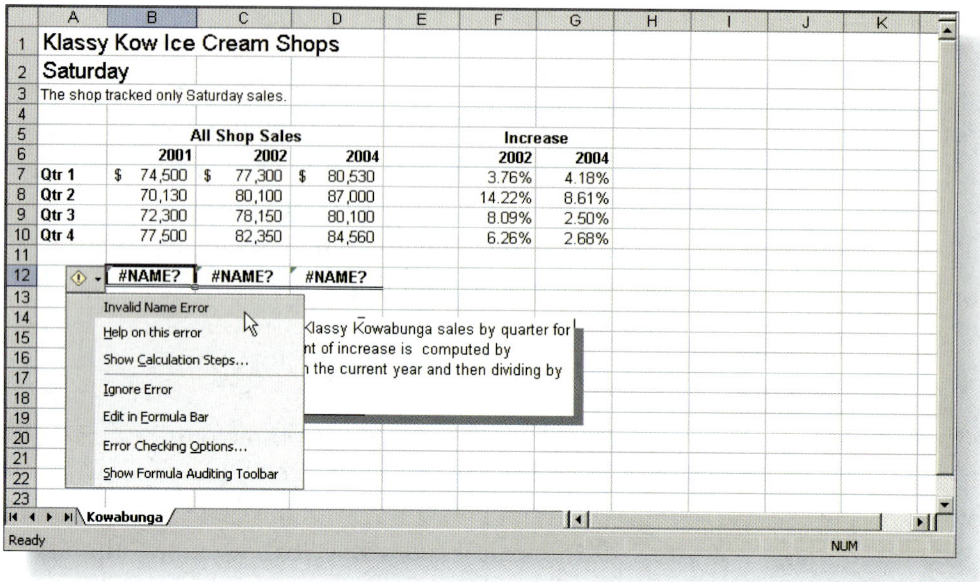

12. Choose Ignore Error because you know why it is occurring.

EXERCISE 3-10 Find and Replace Formats

In addition to finding or replacing characters, you can locate formats and change them. For example, you can find the labels and values that are bold 10-point Arial and change them to bold italic. When you replace formats, you should not show any text or numbers in the Find what or Replace with boxes.

1. Press Ctrl + Home to make A1 active.
2. Press Ctrl + H.
3. Double-click in the Find what box and press Delete. The box is empty.
4. Double-click in the Replace with box and press Delete.
5. Click the arrow next to Format to the right of the Find what box.
6. Click Choose Format From Cell. The dialog box closes, and the pointer shows the selection pointer with an eyedropper.
7. Click cell B6. The dialog box expands. The format from cell B6 is shown in the Preview area for Find what.
8. Click the arrow next to Format to the right of the Replace with box.
9. Choose Format. The Replace Format dialog box opens.
10. Click the Font tab. In the Font list, choose Arial.
11. In the Font style list, choose Bold Italic. In the Size list, choose 10.
12. Click OK. The previews show what will be found and how it will be replaced. (See Figure 3-7 on the next page.)

FIGURE 3-7
Replacing formats

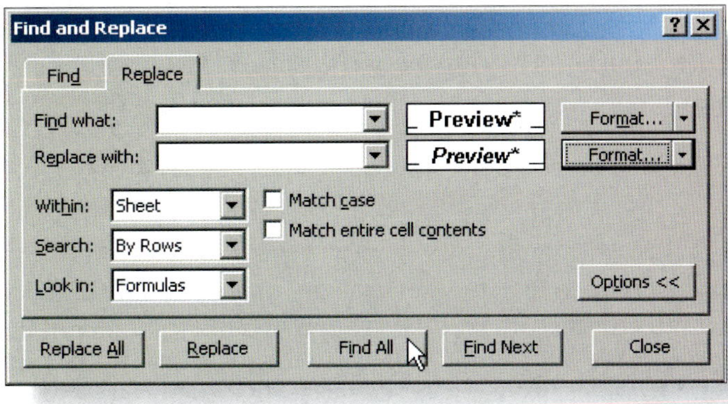

13. Click Find All. The cells with 10-point Arial bold are listed.

14. Click Replace All. The replacements are made.

15. Click OK and then click Close. Two labels were not replaced (cells C5 and F5), because they include more formatting than just 10-point Arial bold. Notice also that no values were changed.

NOTE: You can click the Close button to close the Find and Replace dialog box.

16. Save the workbook as ***[your initials]*3-10** in a new folder for Lesson 3.

EXERCISE 3-11 Reset the Find and Replace Formats

After replacing formats, it is usually a good idea to remove all your settings. If you don't, they are still in effect the next time you use Find and Replace and could affect your results.

1. Press Ctrl + H.

2. Click the arrow next to Format for the Find what box.

3. Click Clear Find Format. The area shows No Format Set.

4. Click the arrow next to Format for the Replace with box.

5. Click Clear Replace Format.

6. Click Close.

Using Series and AutoFill

A *series* is a list of labels, numbers, dates, or times that follows a pattern. The days of the week are a series that repeats every seven days. Months repeat their pattern every twelve months. These are common series that Excel recognizes if you key a label in the series.

You can create your own series by keying two values or labels to set an interval. The *interval* is the number of steps between numbers or labels. For example, the series “1, 3, 5, 7” uses an interval of two because each number is increased by 2 to determine the next number. The series “Qtr 1, Qtr 2, Qtr 3” uses an interval of one.

EXERCISE 3-12 Create Month and Week Series

The easiest way to create a series is by using the *AutoFill command,* which copies and extends data from a cell or range of cells to adjacent cells. The AutoFill command uses the *Fill handle,* a small rectangle at the lower right corner of a cell or range.

1. Press Ctrl+G. The Go To dialog box opens.
2. Key **a25** and press Enter. The insertion point is in cell A25.
3. Key **January** and press Enter.

TIP: AutoFill works only if you spell the first entry correctly.

4. Click cell A25. Click the Down scroll arrow on the vertical scroll bar several times until you can see rows 25 through 36 on your worksheet.
5. Place the pointer on the Fill handle for cell A25. The pointer changes to a solid black cross.
6. Drag down to cell A36. As you drag, a ScreenTip shows each month as it is filled in.

FIGURE 3-8 Creating a month series

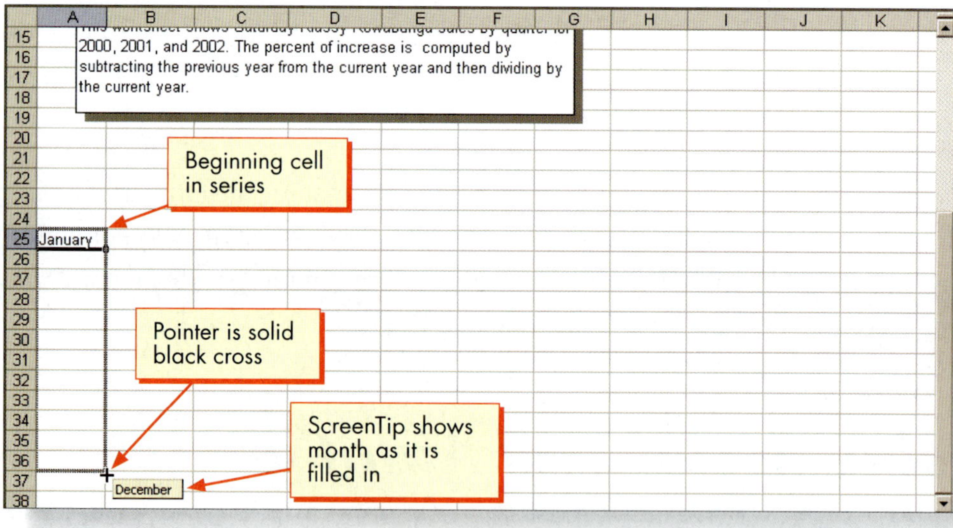

7. Release the mouse button. The series is filled with the remaining months. The AutoFill Options button also appears just below your filled selection. It includes additional options for filling the data.
8. Click cell B24. Key **Week 1** and press Enter.

9. Click cell B24 and place the mouse pointer on its Fill handle.
10. Drag right to cell E24. Release the mouse button. The series is filled with additional weeks.

EXERCISE 3-13 Create a Number Series

You can quickly fill in values on a worksheet by using a series. To establish a value series, first key two values in the series. Then select both cells and drag the Fill handle. If you drag the Fill handle too far, just drag it back to where you wanted to finish.

1. Click cell B25. Key **5** and then press Enter.
2. Key **10** in cell B26. This sets a pattern with an interval of 5, increasing each value by 5.
3. Click cell B25 and drag to select cell B26. There is one Fill handle for the range.
4. Place the pointer on the Fill handle for cell B26.
5. Drag down to B36 and release the mouse button. The series is filled in, and the range is selected.
6. Make the column 10.71 (80 pixels) wide.

EXERCISE 3-14 Copy Data with AutoFill

When there is no apparent pattern in the range, the Fill handle just copies data rather than creating a series.

1. The series you just filled in should still be selected. The Fill handle for the range is located in cell B36. Place the mouse pointer on the Fill handle.
2. Drag right to column E and release the mouse button. The range is copied because no pattern was set for going from one column to the next.

FIGURE 3-9
Using the Fill pointer to copy

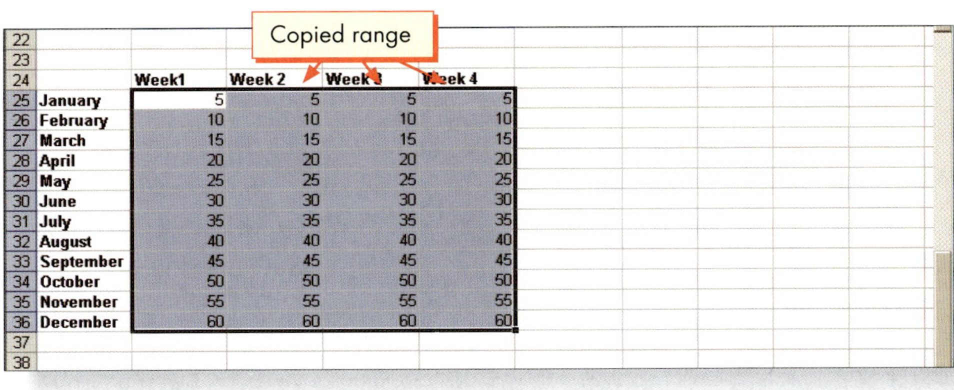

EXERCISE 3-15 Copy a Formula with AutoFill

You can also use AutoFill to copy a formula.

1. Click cell F25.
2. Click the AutoSum button [Σ]. The SUM function is displayed, with the range to be summed shown as B25:E25.
3. Press [Enter]. The formula is completed.
4. Click cell F25 and look at the formula bar. You can copy this formula to the rest of the rows by using the Fill handle.
5. Place the pointer on the Fill handle.
6. Drag down to cell F36 and release the mouse. Excel copies the formula, and the AutoFill Options button appears.
7. Move the mouse pointer to the arrow next to the button and click. The options determine how AutoFill completes the task. You do not need to make a change.
8. Click cell F26. The copied formula is relative to where it is on the worksheet, just as when you use Copy and Paste.

Applying AutoFormats

An *AutoFormat* is a built-in set of formatting instructions that applies fonts, colors, borders, and other formatting features to a range of cells. It enables you to quickly change the appearance of your work.

EXERCISE 3-16 Apply an AutoFormat

If you place the pointer anywhere in a range of cells, an AutoFormat is applied to that entire range.

1. Click cell B24.
2. From the Format menu, choose AutoFormat. The AutoFormat dialog box shows a sample of several Excel AutoFormats. Notice that the range A24:F36 is selected on your worksheet.
3. Scroll to find Colorful 2 in the AutoFormat list and click the sample. It is outlined with a dark border to indicate that it is the active AutoFormat. (See Figure 3-10 on the next page.)
4. Click OK. Excel applies the “Colorful 2” AutoFormat to the selected range. The colors, fonts, borders, and shading for the range are reformatted.

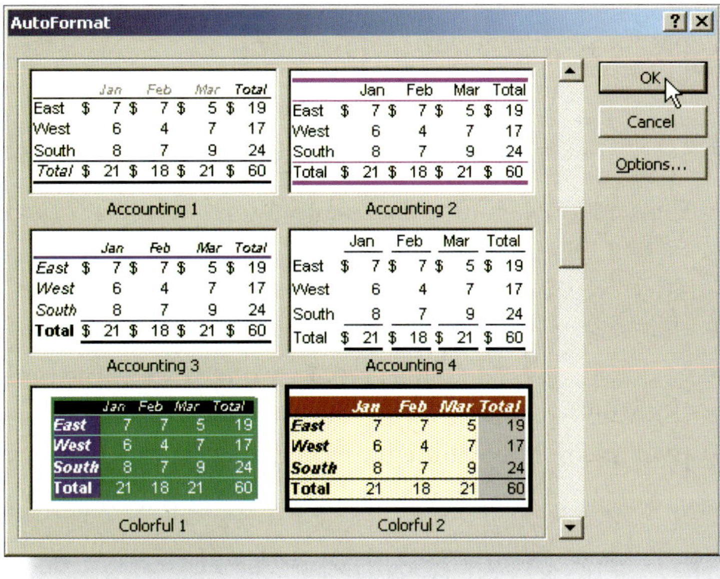

FIGURE 3-10
AutoFormat dialog box

5. Press Ctrl + Home to make cell A1 active. In reformatting the bottom part of your worksheet, you now have a problem with the top part.
6. Click cell B7. This cell and others show several # symbols; however, the formula bar still shows the correct value for cell B7. The "Colorful 2" AutoFormat adjusted the column widths, making them too narrow for the top of the worksheet. The # symbol indicates that the value in the cell is too wide for the column.

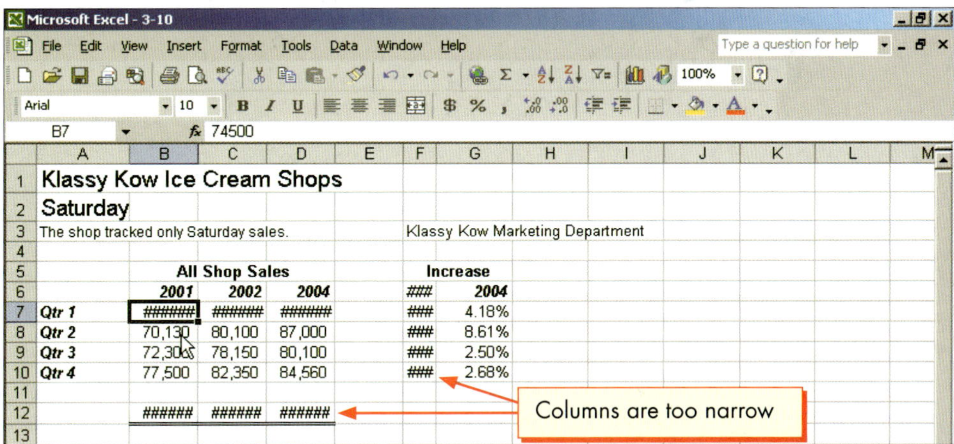

FIGURE 3-11
Columns not wide enough for existing values

7. AutoFit column B.
8. AutoFit all the columns that show the # symbol. Notice that column F AutoFits to the label in F3. This is much wider than necessary.
9. Change the width of column F to 13.57 (100 pixels).

EXERCISE 3-17 Change AutoFormat Options

You can change AutoFormat options. For example, you can keep your own formatting selections for the font, colors, column width, row heights, and more.

1. Click cell B24. Notice that the font for the labels is bold italic. This is the setting for the "Colorful 2" AutoFormat.
2. Click cell A5 and drag to select cells A5:D12.
3. Choose Format and then AutoFormat. Click Colorful 2.
4. Click Options. The dialog box expands to show the options you can set for this AutoFormat.
5. Click the Font box to remove the check mark.

FIGURE 3-12
AutoFormat Options

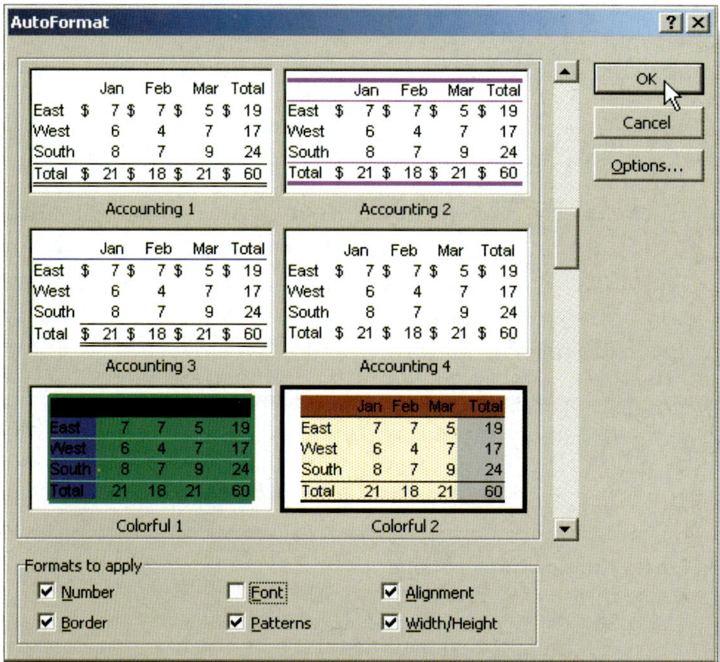

6. Click OK. "Colorful 2" is applied, but now without the bold italic font.
7. Press Ctrl+Home to make cell A1 active.

EXERCISE 3-18 Print a Selection

If you include multiple sections on a single worksheet, you might want to print a section separately. In the current worksheet, for example, you might want to print only the monthly data at the bottom.

To print a portion of a worksheet, select the range of cells you want to print. Open the Print dialog box, and choose Selection.

1. Go to cell A23 and key your first and last name. Press Enter.
2. Select the range A23:F36 as the range to be printed.
3. Choose File and then Print.
4. Choose Selection in the Print what area.
5. Click Preview. The print preview shows the selected range that will be printed.
6. Click Print. Only the range you specified is printed.

Changing the Page Setup

In addition to printing a portion of a worksheet, you have many other options for setting how Excel prints your worksheet. From the Page Setup dialog box, you can:

- Create headers and footers
- Change margins or center the worksheet
- Change the page orientation
- Scale the worksheet to fit the page or print larger than the page
- Print gridlines and row or column headings
- Change the page order

In this lesson, you will create a header and a footer, display row and column headings, and change the margins. You will use the other print options in other lessons.

EXERCISE 3-19 Set Headers and Footers

A *header* prints at the top of each page in a worksheet. A *footer* prints at the bottom of each page. Headers and footers can be used to display a company name, a department, the date, or even a company's logo. Excel has preset headers and footers, but you can also create your own.

A header or footer can have up to three sections. The left section prints at the left margin. The center section prints at the horizontal center of the page. The right section aligns at the right margin.

You can open the Page Setup dialog box by:

- Clicking Setup in the Print Preview window.
- Opening the File menu and choosing Page Setup.

1. Press Ctrl + Home to make cell A1 the active cell.

2. Click the Print Preview button.
3. Click Setup (at the top of the Print Preview window). The Page Setup dialog box opens.
4. Click the Header/Footer tab. You create a header, a footer, or both, using this dialog box.
5. Click the arrow at the right of the Header box. Several preset headers are listed. Sections are separated by comas. If you choose a single item, it prints in the center section. Two items print in the center and at the right margin. Three items print at the left margin, in the center, and at the right margin.

NOTE: The same preset items are available for footers and headers.

6. Find and click the first occurrence of your filename. The Header preview box shows the new header.

FIGURE 3-13
Page Setup dialog box

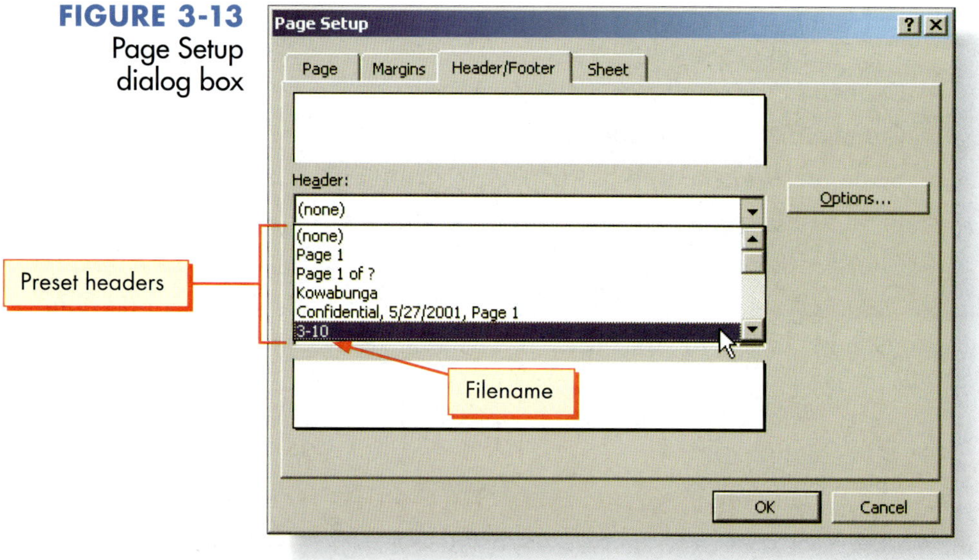

7. Click Custom Footer. The Footer dialog box shows the three sections and buttons for preset items. The insertion point is in the Left section.

NOTE: The buttons in the Custom Footer dialog box offer the same information you saw listed in the preset Footer text box list.

8. Key your first and last name.
9. Click in the Center section. The insertion point is now in the Center section.

10. Click the Filename button. The code for displaying the filename is &[File]. (See Figure 3-14 on the next page.)

FIGURE 3-14
Adding a custom footer

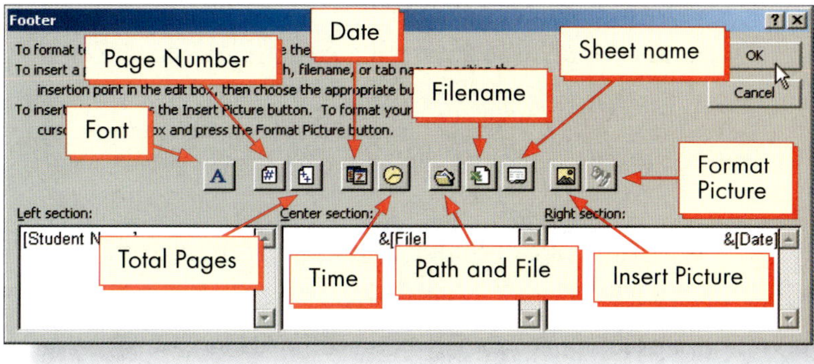

11. Press Tab. The insertion point is at the right edge of the Right section.

12. Click the Date button. The code for displaying the current date is &[Date].

13. Click OK in the Footer dialog box. Your custom footer appears in the Footer box.

EXERCISE 3-20 Print Gridlines and Row and Column Headings

Gridlines and row and column headings are visible while you work on a worksheet; however, they do not print as a default. You can turn them on to print. Printing a worksheet with the gridlines and row and column headings makes it easy to locate data or to re-create a worksheet, if needed.

1. With the Page Setup dialog box open, click the Sheet tab.

2. In the Print section, click to place a check mark in the Gridlines box.

3. Click to place a check mark in the Row and column headings box.

4. Click OK. Excel returns you to the Print Preview window.

EXERCISE 3-21 Change Page Margins and Column Widths in Print Preview

Excel has default left and right margins of .75 inch for a new worksheet. The top and bottom margins are both 1 inch. The header and footer are preset to print .5 inch from the top and bottom of the page.

You can see the margins in the Print Preview window. You can also change the margins and the column widths in the Print Preview window by dragging a marker. A *marker* is a small black rectangle at the location for the margin or the right edge of a column. As you drag a marker, the margin setting or column width is shown in inches or character spaces in the status bar.

1. Click Margins (at the top of the Print Preview window). Margin and column markers appear as small black rectangles at the edges of the page.

NOTE: If Excel already displays your margin and column markers, do not click Margins.

2. Place the mouse pointer over the left margin marker. It changes to a two-headed arrow.
3. Click and drag right to set a left margin of about 1.00. Watch the status bar for the setting as you drag. Your margin setting does not need to be exact.

FIGURE 3-15
Changing page margins in Print Preview

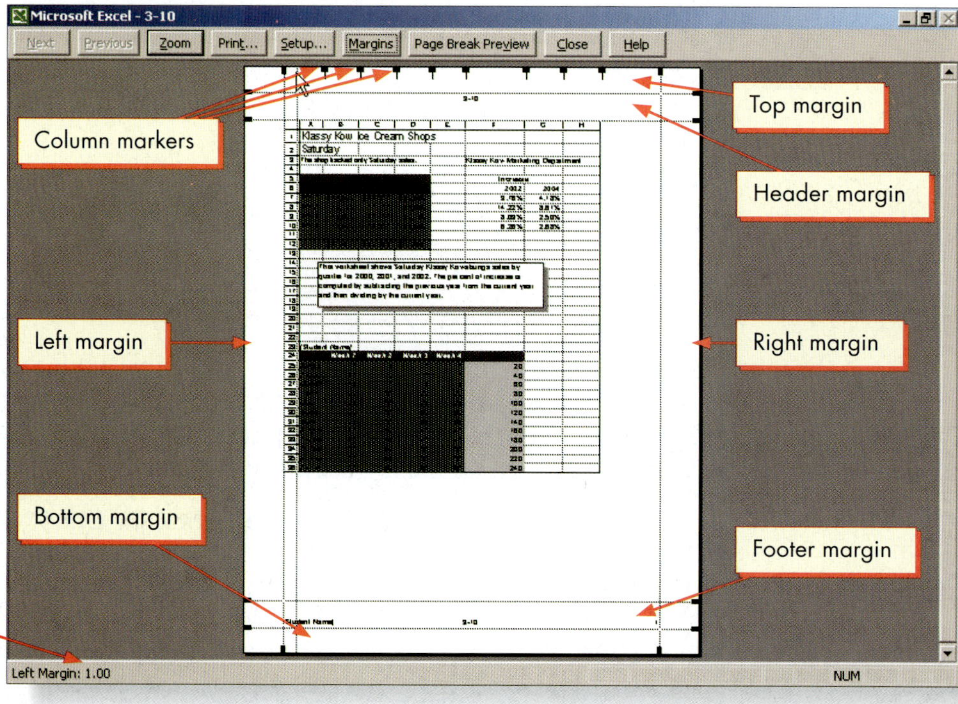

4. Place the mouse pointer over the right margin marker. Click and drag left to reach about 1.00.
5. Place the pointer on the column marker between columns A and B. Drag right to make column A wider, about 10. The width is shown in the status bar.
6. Make column F slightly less wide.
7. Click Close to close the Print Preview window.

8. Click the Print button.
9. Save the workbook as ***[your initials]*3-21** in your Lesson 3 folder and close it.

USING HELP

Series and AutoFill are time-saving features of Excel. They enable you to work more quickly and more accurately. Read more about series and the AutoFill command by asking a question.

Look up AutoFill and series by asking a question:

1. Start Excel and close the New Workbook task pane.
2. Click in the Ask a Question box in the upper right corner.
3. Key **autofill** and press Enter.
4. Click See more.
5. Click the topic About filling in data based on adjacent cells. Read the information.

FIGURE 3-16
Viewing Help about AutoFill

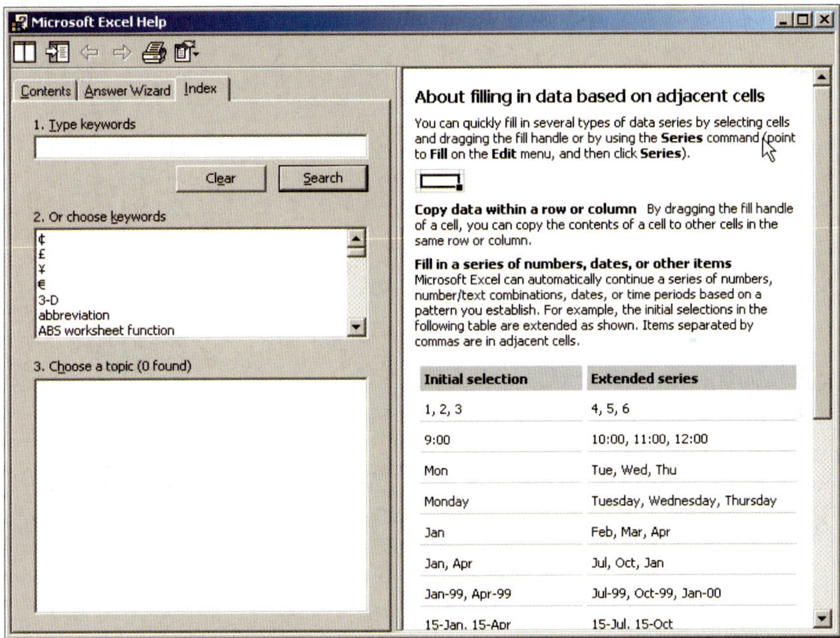

6. Close the Help window.

LESSON 3 Summary

➤ AutoCorrect corrects common typing errors as you work. You can add your own entries or delete existing ones.

- The Spelling command spell-checks a worksheet by comparing labels to dictionary entries. Options let you decide if and how to make the correction.
- The Find command locates and lists all occurrences of data that match your Find what character string. You can use wildcards in the character string.
- The Replace command locates and substitutes new data for existing data. You can complete the changes one at a time or all at once.
- Excel displays options buttons for some commands and formula errors. You can look at the message for the button, make a change, or ignore it.
- All cells have a Fill handle that can be used for filling in a series or for copying data.
- Excel recognizes common series for the days of the week, the months of the week, and patterns such as "Week 1," "Week 2," and so on.
- You can create your own series with any interval by keying at least two cells that define the pattern.
- AutoFormats apply colors, fonts, and other formatting options to a range.
- The Page Setup dialog box includes many options for controlling how your worksheet prints.

LESSON 3 Command Summary

FEATURE	BUTTON	MENU	KEYBOARD	SPEECH
Spelling		Tools, Spelling	F7	✓
Find		Edit, Find	Ctrl + F	✓
Replace		Edit, Replace	Ctrl + H	✓
AutoFormat		Format, AutoFormat		✓
Page Setup		File, Page Setup		✓
Margins		File, Page Setup		✓
Gridlines		File, Page Setup		✓
Row/column headings		File, Page Setup		✓

continues

LESSON 3 Command Summary *continued*

FEATURE	BUTTON	MENU	KEYBOARD	SPEECH
Column width		Format, Column, Width		✓
Header/Footer		View, Header/Footer		✓
AutoFill/series		Edit, Fill, Series		✓
Print selection		File, Print		✓

Concepts Review

TRUE/FALSE QUESTIONS

Each of the following statements is either true or false. Indicate your choice by circling T or F.

T F **1.** If you key THe as part of a label, AutoCorrect will automatically fix the capitalization error.

T F **2.** The Spelling command completes columns of month or day names.

T F **3.** You can use a wildcard character in the Find command.

T F **4.** The Replace command can be used to locate and change the font or the font style.

T F **5.** Options buttons are screen messages that tell you what command to choose next.

T F **6.** The Fill handle displays a small hollow circle.

T F **7.** A series is a list with a recognizable pattern.

T F **8.** The option to print a selected range is in the Page Setup dialog box.

SHORT ANSWER QUESTIONS

Write the correct answer in the space provided.

1. What wildcards does Excel use?

---

2. What feature enables you to automatically complete a list of twelve months after you key one month?

---

3. What keyboard shortcut opens the Replace dialog box?

---

4. How can you use part of the formatting choices from an AutoFormat?

---

5. Name the three sections available for a footer.

---

6. In Print Preview, how can you tell Excel to print row and column headings?

____

7. In the Print Preview window, what do you use to display markers on-screen for the margins and columns?

____

8. What is the name for screen messages Excel displays for commands and errors?

____

CRITICAL THINKING

Answer these questions on a separate page. There are no right or wrong answers. Support your answers with examples from your own experience, if possible.

1. Find and Replace are powerful commands. Give an example of when they could be timesavers. Think of times when they might create problems.

2. You can copy a formula with the Copy and Paste buttons (as you did in Lesson 2) or with the Fill handle. Which do you prefer and why? When wouldn't it be a good idea to used AutoFill to copy a formula?

Lesson Applications

EXERCISE 3-22

Use Find and Replace. Create a footer. Change the left margin.

1. Open **MayPromo**. Save it as ***[your initials]*3-22** in your Lesson 3 folder.
2. Replace all occurrences of "california" with **Washington**.

NOTE: You do not need to key uppercase characters in a Find character string, but you should key them in the Replace character string.

3. Change the worksheet tab name to **MayExpense**
4. Change the height of row 12 to 18.75 (25 pixels) and the width of column A to 24.29 (175 pixels).
5. Create a footer that shows your name in the left section.
6. In the footer's center section, click the Tab Name button. Add the date to the right section.
7. Change the left margin to 1.25 in print preview.

TIP: You can drag the left margin marker at the top or the bottom of the Print Preview window.

8. Preview and print the worksheet, and then save and close the workbook.

EXERCISE 3-23

Create series. Apply an AutoFormat. Set AutoFormat options.

1. Create a new workbook. Save it as ***[your initials]*3-23** in your Lesson 3 folder.
2. Key **Klassy Kow Specials** in cell A1. In cell A2, key **Price Promotions**
3. In cell B3, key **Regular Price**. In cell C3, key **Special Price**. In cell D3, key **Savings**. AutoFit each column to show the label.
4. In cell A4, key **Ice Cream Cakes**

REVIEW: Press Ctrl+1 to format the date.

5. In cell A5, key **January 1, 200x** (using next year in place of the "x"). Key **February 1, 200x** in cell A6, with the same year. Select both cells and format the date to spell out the month and show the date, a comma, and a four-digit year.

6. Select cells A5:A6 if they are not already selected and use the Fill handle for the range to extend the dates to May 1 of the same year.
7. Select cells B5:D9 and format them for Currency Style.
8. Key **12.5** in cell B5. Use AutoFill to copy this value to the range B6:B9.
9. Key the following special prices:
   - **January** **9.99**
   - **February** **11.25**
   - **March** **10.50**
   - **April** **10.99**
   - **May** **9.99**
10. In cell D5, key **=**. Click cell B5 and then key **–** for subtraction. Click cell C5 and press Enter. This formula computes the difference between the regular price and the special price.
11. Use AutoFill for cell D5 to copy the formula to cells D6:D9.
12. Press Ctrl+Home to make cell A1 active.
13. Rename the worksheet tab as **Cakes**
14. Use the Accounting 2 AutoFormat, but turn off the option for Number.

TIP: If you don't turn off the Number option, you will need to format the date and currency numbers again.

15. Add a custom header to show your name at the left, the tab name in the center, and the filename at the right.
16. Preview and print the worksheet, and then save and close the workbook.

EXERCISE 3-24

Spell-check a worksheet.

1. Open **OrderSheet**. Spell-check the worksheet and correct all misspelled words.

NOTE: The correct spelling of Klassy Kow's flavor is "Bubble Gum Goo."

2. In cell F3, key today's date in this format: mm/dd/yy.
3. In cell F4, key ***[your last name]'s*** **Supermarket**
4. Key the following quantities for each ice cream flavor. Not all flavors are being ordered. No quantity appears for flavors that are not being ordered.
   - **Vanilla** **25**
   - **Chocolate** **25**

- Strawberry 20
- Butter Pecan 10
- French Vanilla 10
- Chocolate Chip 10
- Chocolate Mint Melody 10
- Peppermint Candy 10
- Raspberry Swirl 15
- Purple Kow 12

The flavors in Rows 17-24 are not being ordered.

- Apple Pie 5
- Rum Raisin 5
- Blueberry 5
- New York Cherry 5

5. Paint the format from cell E28 to cell E32.
6. Press Ctrl + Home to make cell A1 active.
7. Save the workbook as ***[your initials]*3-24** in your Lesson 3 folder.
8. Preview and print the worksheet, and then close the workbook.

EXERCISE 3-25 Challenge Yourself

Use AutoCorrect. Create day series. AutoFill values. Apply an AutoFormat. Create a footer. Change the margins.

1. Create a new workbook. Rename Sheet1 as **ShakeSales**. Save the workbook as ***[your initials]*3-25** in your Lesson 3 folder.
2. Key **Klassy Kow Ice Cream Shops** in cell A1. Key **Daily Shake Sales in *[your home city]*** in cell A2.
3. In cell B3, key **Chocolate**. In cell C3, key **Vanilla**
4. In cell A4, key **monday**. Fill in the days of the week up to and including "Sunday" in column A.
5. In cell B4, key **4**. In cell B5, key **8**. Extend this series down column B to reach "Sunday." Copy the entire range to the "Vanilla" column.
6. Use AutoSum to total the values for each flavor.
7. Apply the Classic 1 AutoFormat.
8. Change the width of column A to 16.43 (120 pixels).
9. Change the left and top margins to 2.00 (or as close to 2 inches as you can get on your computer).

EXCEL

10. Add a custom footer with your name at the left, the filename in the center, and the date at the right.
11. Press Ctrl+Home to make cell A1 active.
12. Preview, print, and save the worksheet, and then close the workbook.

On Your Own

In these exercises you work on your own, as you would in a real-life work environment. Use the skills you've learned to accomplish the task—and be creative.

EXERCISE 3-26

Open **PieSales**. Change the date in cell A3 to today's date. One at a time, apply six of the AutoFormats to the worksheet. Record which one you like best, and then apply it again. Create a custom footer with your name in the left section, the name of the AutoFormat in the center, and the date at the right. Save the worksheet as ***[your initials]*3-26** in your Lesson 3 folder. Preview and print it, and then close the workbook.

EXERCISE 3-27

Create a new workbook and save it as ***[your initials]*3-27** in your Lesson 3 folder. In cell A1, key the label **Using AutoFill and Series**. Format it with an 18-point font.

Build a 15-month series in column A, using a 3-month interval. Build a 15-day series in column B, using an every-other-day interval. In row 20, build a 10-year series, using a 4-year interval. In row 22, build a 10-value series starting at 2 and using an interval of 2. In cell A24, key today's date. In cell A25, key the date one week from today. Build a 12-date series in column A, using cells A24:A25 to start the series.

Add your name, the filename, and the date in a custom header. Preview and print the worksheet, and then close the workbook.

EXERCISE 3-28

Use the Internet or printed maps to determine the approximate mileage between your city and five major cities in your part of the country. Also include approximate driving time to drive to each city. Create a workbook that shows this information in an easy-to-read layout. Include a main title and column titles. Apply an AutoFormat to your worksheet and spell-check it. Add your name, the filename, and the date in a custom header. Save the workbook as ***[your initials]*3-28** in your Lesson 3 folder. Preview and print the worksheet, and then close the workbook.

LESSON 4

Working with Cells, Columns, Rows, and Sheets

OBJECTIVES

MOUS ACTIVITIES

In this lesson:

Ex2002 1-1
Ex2002 1-2
Ex2002 3-1
Ex2002 3-2
Ex2002 3-3
Ex2002 4-1

See Appendix E.

After completing this lesson, you will be able to:

1. **Insert and delete worksheets.**
2. **Insert and delete cells.**
3. **Add labels by using AutoComplete and Pick From List.**
4. **Copy, move, and paste cell contents.**
5. **Work with columns and rows.**
6. **Work with cell alignment.**
7. **Use Merge and Center.**
8. **Apply borders and shading.**

Estimated Time: 1¼ hours

Excel provides many ways to modify a workbook or worksheet. You can add or delete worksheets if you realize you need more or fewer sheets than the usual three. You might have to insert or delete cells, columns, or rows in a worksheet if you find you forgot data and need to make room for it. This lesson focuses on modifying workbooks and worksheets and on enhancing worksheets with additional formatting.

Inserting and Deleting Worksheets

A new workbook opens with three sheets, enabling you to separate parts of your work. For example, if you decide to keep invoices for each month on a separate sheet, you would need more than three worksheets in the workbook.

EXERCISE 4-1 Insert Worksheets

When you insert a new worksheet, it is placed in front of the currently active sheet. Excel names new sheets starting with the next number in sequence, based on what is already in your workbook. For example, if the worksheet currently includes Sheet1, Sheet2, and Sheet 3, a new sheet would be named Sheet4.

1. Open **AcctRec**. This workbook has one worksheet named AR for "Accounts Receivable." Notice that there is no Sheet1.
2. Press Shift+F11. A new worksheet named Sheet1 is placed in front of the AR sheet.
3. Double-click Sheet1 on the worksheet tab.
4. Key **SalesReps** and press Enter. The worksheet tab is renamed.
5. Right-click the SalesReps tab. A shortcut menu opens.
6. Choose Insert. The Insert dialog box opens.
7. Click the General tab, if it is not already open. This tab indicates the types of objects you can insert in your workbook.

FIGURE 4-1
Insert dialog box

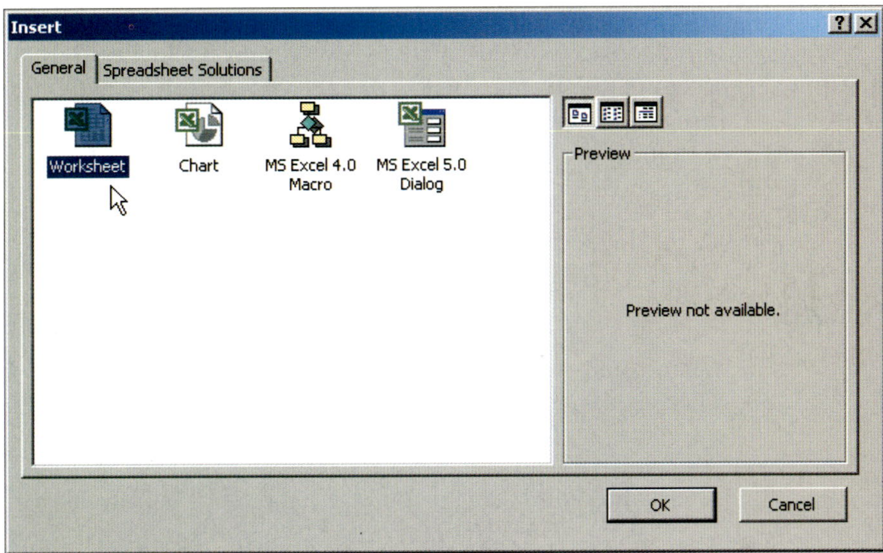

8. Click Worksheet and then click OK. A new Sheet2 is placed before the SalesReps worksheet.

EXERCISE 4-2 Move and Delete Worksheets

You can rearrange worksheet tabs to place them in a different order. Additionally, if you don't need all the sheets in a workbook, you should delete them so they don't take unnecessary file space.

1. Click the AR tab. It becomes active and appears on top of the other sheets.
2. Point at the tab to display a white arrow pointer.
3. Click and drag the tab to the left of Sheet2. As you drag, you see a small sheet icon and a triangle that marks the new position of the sheet.
4. Release the mouse button. The AR sheet is now the leftmost tab.
5. Right-click the Sheet2 tab. The sheet becomes the active sheet and a shortcut menu opens.
6. Choose Delete. The sheet is deleted, and the SalesReps worksheet is active.

TIP: You can also move a sheet by using the shortcut menu.

7. Click the AR tab.

Inserting and Deleting Cells

If you have accidentally forgotten a column or row entry, you can insert a cell to make room for the missing information. There might also be times when you discover you have extra entries in a column and need to delete cells. When you insert or delete cells, you decide if the existing cells should move up, down, left, or right.

EXERCISE 4-3 Insert Cells

When you insert or delete a cell, you affect the entire worksheet, not just the range where you are working. The insertion or deletion can sometimes rearrange data you did not want to change.

1. Set the Zoom size so you can see part of columns A through most of column H on the screen. Try a size of 75% or 85%.
2. Click cell B8.
3. Press Ctrl++ in the numeric keypad. (The *numeric keypad* is the set of number and symbol keys at the right side of the keyboard. It is sometimes called the "ten-key pad"). An Insert dialog box opens with choices about what happens after the cell is inserted. (See Figure 4-2 on the next page.)

NOTE: If you use a laptop computer that does not have a numeric keypad, press Ctrl+Shift++, using the + in the top row of keys.

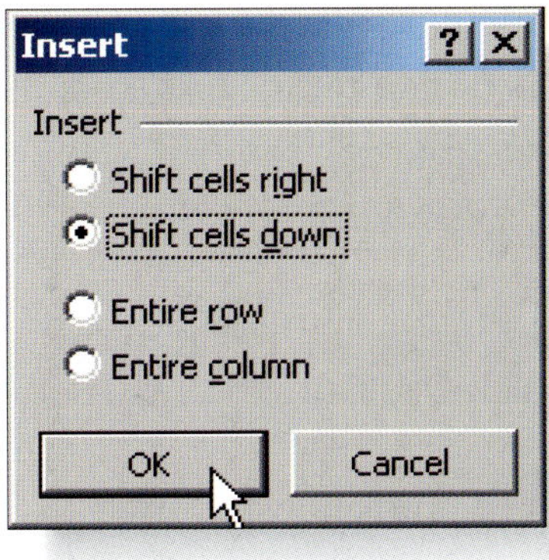

FIGURE 4-2
Insert dialog box

4. Choose Shift cells down if it's not already selected and click OK. A blank cell is inserted. The cells originally in cells B8:B15 have moved down to cells B9:B16. The data in the other columns did not shift.
5. Click cell C12. The reference number and date are in the wrong columns and you would like to fix the problem.
6. Right-click cell C12 and choose Insert.
7. Choose Shift cells right and click OK. All the cells in the worksheet shift to the right, including those in column H and beyond.

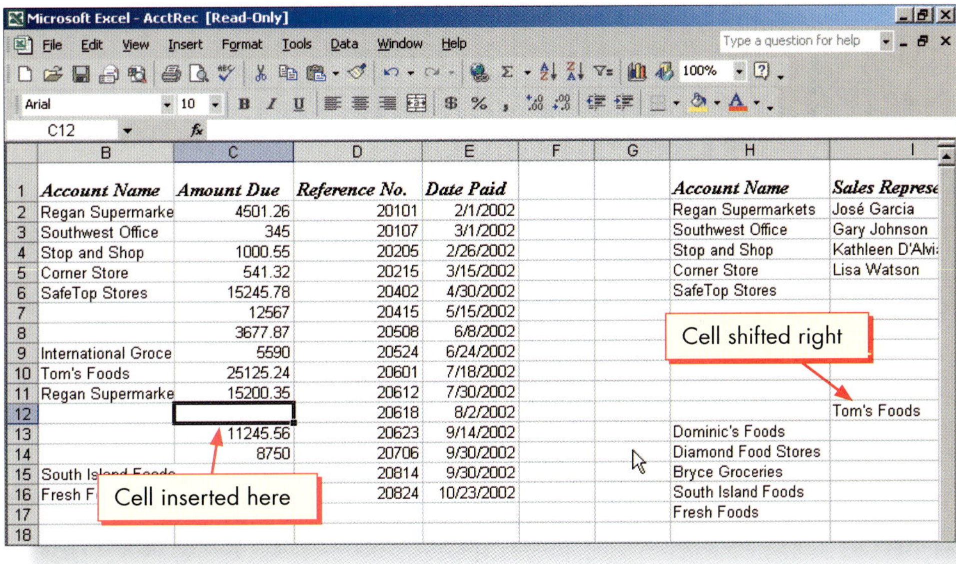

FIGURE 4-3
One cell inserted, with other cells shifted right

EXERCISE 4-4 Delete Cells

When you delete cells, just as when you insert cells, you need to watch the entire worksheet to make sure data elsewhere on the sheet is not affected.

1. Scroll the worksheet so you can see columns D through I. Adjust your Zoom size if you can't see all the columns at the same time.
2. Click cell H7.
3. Press Ctrl + -. The Delete dialog box opens.

4. Choose Shift cells up, if it's not already selected, and click OK. As you can see, this won't work. There is no room for "Tom's Foods" in column H where it belongs.

5. Click the Undo button. Before you can delete H7, you need to delete the extra cell in H12.
6. Click cell H12. Press Ctrl + - on the numeric keypad.
7. Choose Shift cells left and click OK. Only the cells in columns H and beyond are shifted.
8. Now you can right-click cell H7 and choose Delete.
9. Choose Shift cells up, if it's not already selected, and click OK.
10. Select cells H8:H10. Right-click any cell in the range.
11. Choose Delete and Shift cells up. Click OK.
12. Press Ctrl + Home.

Adding Labels with AutoComplete and Pick From List

Labels in a column often are repeated. For example, frequent customers, standard suppliers, or cities might be repeated many times in a column. Excel has two features that make it easy to enter duplicate labels in a column. Both features use text already in the column.

- *AutoComplete* displays a suggested label after you key the first character in a cell. This method is most helpful when most labels don't start with the same characters.
- *Pick From List* displays a list of all the labels already in the column. You can then choose a label from the list. This method is most helpful when you are not sure how to spell the label or when several labels start with the same characters.

EXERCISE 4-5 Use AutoComplete

When you key a new label, Excel scans the column for the same initial characters. In the cell, it displays a suggested entry that starts with the same letter. If the suggestion is correct, you can simply press Enter. If the suggested label is not what you want, ignore it and continue to key the correct label.

Many times you need to key a few characters before Excel makes the correct suggestion.

1. Click cell B7.

TIP: AutoComplete is not case-sensitive. You can key lower- or uppercase letters to see a suggested label.

2. Key **r** to see an AutoComplete suggestion. In this case, Excel's suggestion is correct.

FIGURE 4-4
An AutoComplete suggestion

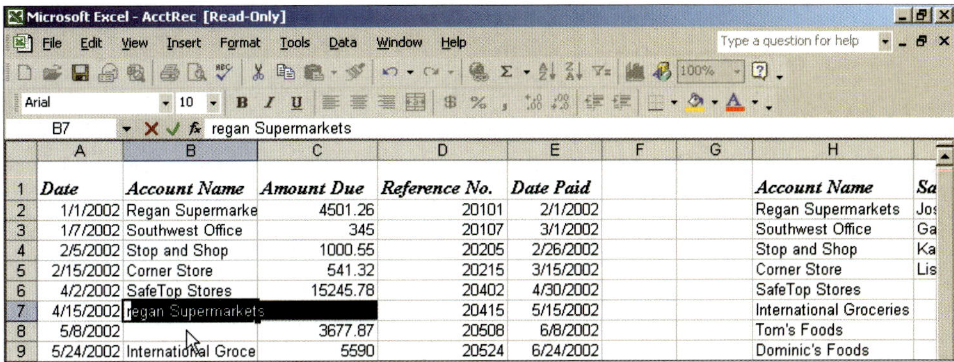

3. Press Enter. The label is entered.
4. Key **s** in cell B8. No suggestion is made, because several labels in the column start with "s." Excel needs more information.
5. Key **t** to see a suggestion for "Stop and Shop."
6. Press Enter.
7. Click cell B12 and key **south**. Excel has still not found a match.
8. Press Spacebar. It now suggests "South Island Foods." That's the correct choice.
9. Press Enter.
10. Key **PDQ Shop** in cell B13 and press Enter. No suggestion is made, because no existing label starts with "p."
11. Click cell C15 and key **87**. Excel does not make AutoComplete suggestions for values.
12. Press Esc.

EXERCISE 4-6 Use Pick From List

The Pick From List option appears on the shortcut menu when you right-click a cell in a column containing labels.

1. Right-click cell I6. A shortcut menu appears.

2. Choose Pick From List from the shortcut menu. Excel displays a list of labels already in column I.
3. Click José Garcia.

FIGURE 4-5
Using Pick From List

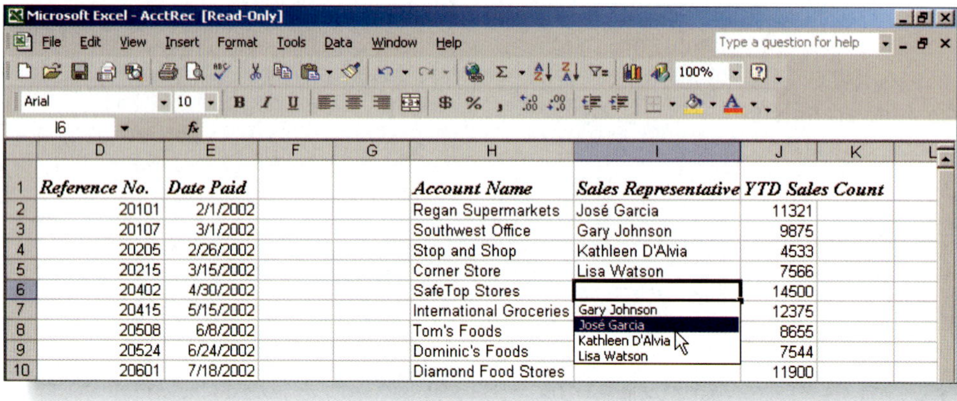

4. Right-click cell I7. Choose Pick From List.
5. Click Lisa Watson.
6. Right-click cell B14. Choose Pick From List. The list is longer and includes a scroll bar.
7. Find and click Tom's Foods.
8. Right-click cell C15. Choose Pick From List. Excel does not display a list for values.
9. Press Esc.

Copying, Moving, and Pasting Cell Contents

You can copy, move, or cut and paste cell contents to speed data entry or to make changes in a worksheet. When you copy or cut a cell or range of cells, a duplicate of the data is placed on the *Windows Clipboard*. This is a temporary memory area used to keep data you have copied or cut.

Data that is cut can be pasted once. Data that is copied can be pasted many times and in many locations. Copied data stays on the Windows Clipboard until you copy or cut another cell or range. Then that data replaces the data on the Clipboard.

The Cut command and the Paste command are used to move labels and values from one cell to another. To use cut and paste, you first select the cells you want to cut, and then you can:

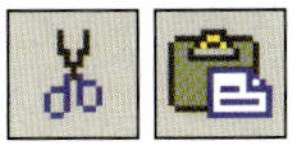

- Click the Cut button. Position the pointer at the new location and then click the Paste button or press Enter.
- Press Ctrl+X. Position the pointer at the new location and press Ctrl+V.
- From the Edit menu, choose Cut. Position the pointer at the new location, open the Edit menu, and choose Paste.
- Right-click the selected cells. Choose Cut from the shortcut menu. Position the pointer at the new location, right-click, and choose Paste from the shortcut menu.
- Select the cell or range. Drag it to a new location.

The Copy and Paste commands make a duplicate of the data in another location. To use copy and paste, you first select the cells you want to copy, and then you can:

- Click the Copy button. Position the pointer at the new location and then click the Paste button or press Enter.
- Press Ctrl+C. Position the pointer at the new location and press Ctrl+V.
- From the Edit menu, choose Copy. Position the pointer at the new location, open the Edit menu, and choose Paste.
- Right-click the selected cells. Choose Copy from the shortcut menu. Position the pointer at the new location, right-click, and choose Paste.
- Select the cell or range. While holding down the Ctrl key, drag it to a new location.

Cut, Copy, and Paste commands are similar in most Windows programs. If you learn the basics in one program, you should be able to use these commands in most programs.

EXERCISE 4-7 Cut and Paste Cell Contents

When you paste cells that have been cut, the cut data replaces any existing data unless you tell Excel to insert the cut data.

1. Click cell C14. Click the Cut button. A moving marquee surrounds the cell.
2. Click cell C12 and then click the Paste button. The data is removed from cell C14 and pasted in C12. The marquee is canceled.
3. Select cells B15:B16. Press Ctrl+X. The range displays the moving marquee, and the Office Clipboard task pane opens. (You will work with the Office Clipboard task pane later in this lesson.) (See Figure 4-6 on the next page.)

FIGURE 4-6
Cutting cell contents

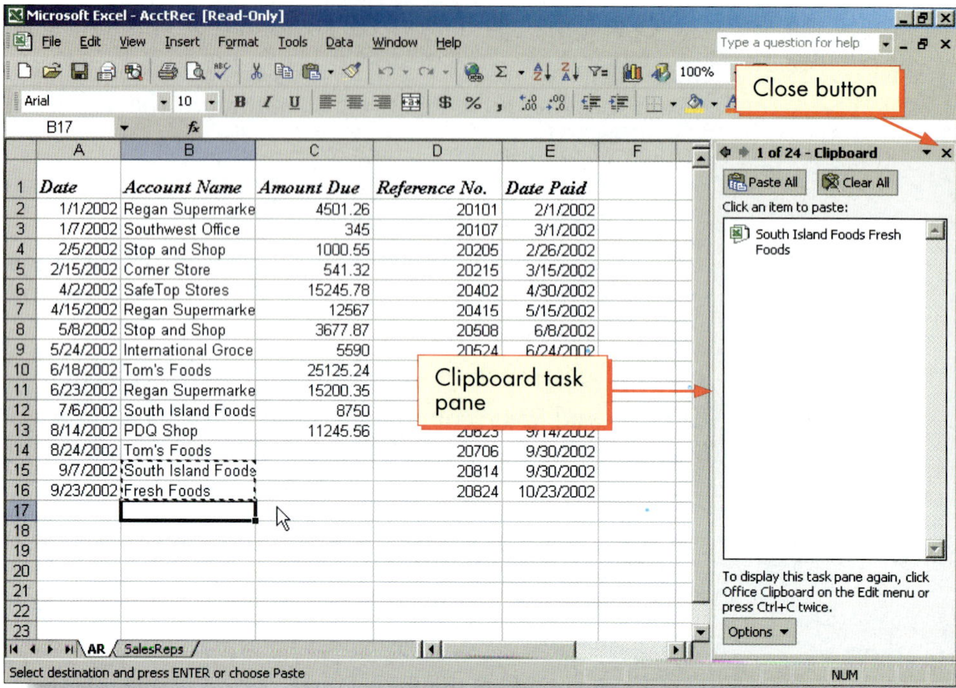

4. Click cell B17 and press Enter.
5. Click the Cut button. The range displays a moving marquee.
6. Right-click cell B14. A regular Paste would replace the existing entry.
7. Choose Insert Cut Cells. The cells that had been cut are inserted into the column.

8. Click the Close button on the Clipboard task pane.

EXERCISE 4-8 Copy and Paste Cell Contents

The Paste Options button appears just below a pasted selection. When you click it, you see a list of options that establish how the selection is pasted.

1. Click cell B9 and click the Copy button. The cell is surrounded by the moving marquee.

2. Click Cell B13 and click the Paste button. The label is pasted, the original data is removed, and the Paste Options button appears.
3. Rest the mouse pointer on the Paste Options button. Click its arrow.
4. Choose Formatting Only. This option copies only the formatting; it does not copy the actual label. (See Figure 4-7 on the next page.)

FIGURE 4-7
Pasting over existing data

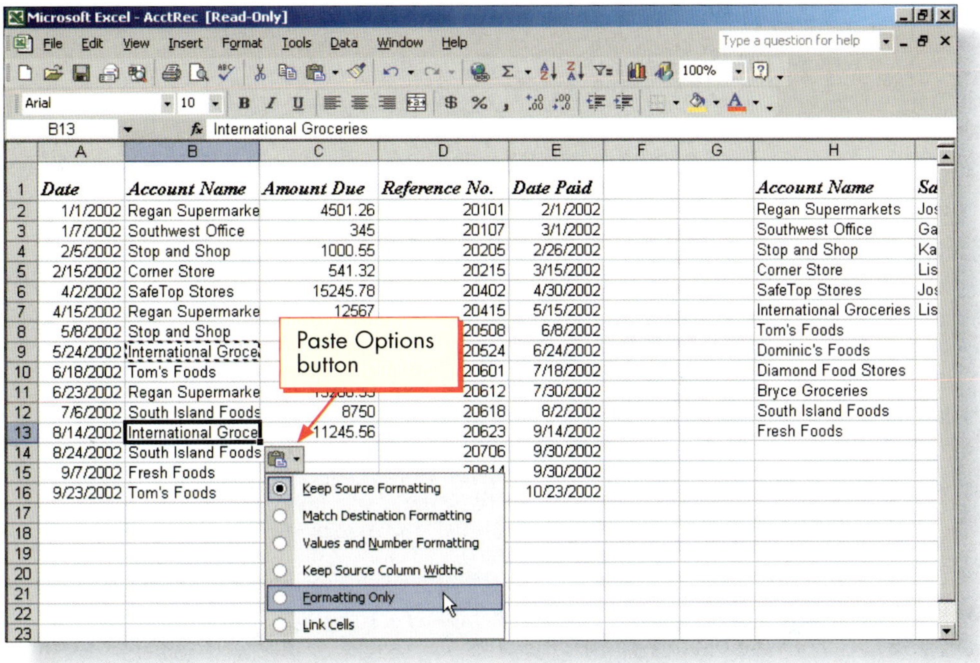

TIP: The marquee is not automatically canceled after you click the Paste button. This enables you to paste the data again in a different location.

5. Press Esc. The marquee is canceled.
6. Click cell I2 and drag to select the range I2:I7.
7. Press Ctrl+C. Excel displays a marquee around the range.
8. Click cell I8. You only need to click in the first cell for the copy.
9. Press Ctrl+V. The range of names is duplicated, and the marquee is still shown. The Paste Options button appears again.
10. Click cell I14. Press Ctrl+V to paste the data again.
11. Press Esc to cancel the marquee.
12. Select the range C8:C10 and press Ctrl+C to copy the range.

REVIEW: Copied cells replace existing data unless you choose the option to insert them.

13. Right-click cell C11.
14. Choose Insert Copied Cells. The Insert Paste dialog box opens.
15. Choose Shift cells down, if it's not already selected. Click OK. The copied cells are inserted and the existing cells are shifted down in the column.
16. Press Esc to cancel the marquee.

EXERCISE 4-9 Use Drag and Drop

Use the drag-and-drop method to cut or copy data when you can see the original copy and where you want to paste the data at the same time. The *drag-and-drop pointer* is a four-headed arrow that is visible when you point at the edge of a cell or range.

1. Select cell C16. Place the pointer at the edge of the cell. The drag-and-drop pointer appears.
2. Hold down the mouse button and drag to cell C17. A ScreenTip identifies the cell. You can also see a ghost highlight that shows where the cell will be placed.

FIGURE 4-8 Using drag and drop to cut and paste

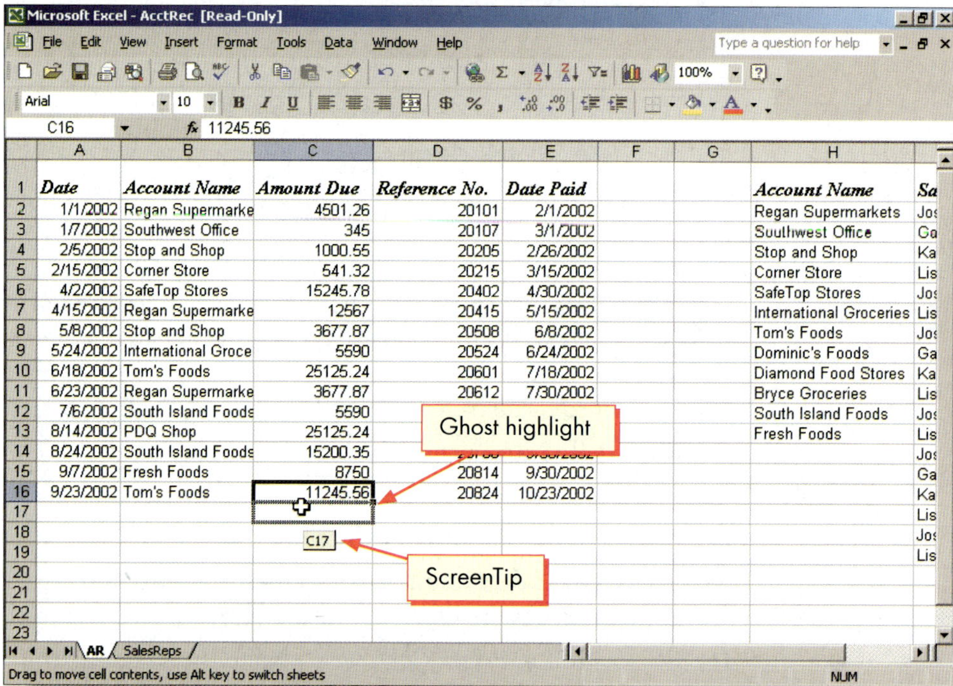

3. Release the mouse button. You have used the drag-and-drop method to perform a cut and paste.
4. Place the pointer at the edge of cell C17 to display the drag-and-drop pointer.
5. Hold down Ctrl. You will see a tiny plus sign (+) next to the drag-and-drop pointer to signify this will be a copy and paste. Do not release Ctrl.
6. Click and drag to cell C16. Release the mouse button first and then release Ctrl. You have used the drag-and-drop method to perform a copy and paste.
7. Select cells B6:B7. Place the pointer at the edge of the range to display the drag-and-drop pointer.
8. Hold down the Ctrl key to display the plus sign (+). Do not release the Ctrl key.

9. Click and drag down to cells B17:B18. Release the mouse button and then Ctrl. Both labels are copied.

EXERCISE 4-10 Use the Office Clipboard

The *Office Clipboard* is a temporary memory area that can hold up to 24 copied items. It is separate from the Windows Clipboard. The Office Clipboard is available when any of the Office applications (Excel, Access, Word, or PowerPoint) is running. It is shared among all these programs so something you copy in Excel can be pasted in Word.

1. Choose View, Task Pane. The Clipboard task pane opens.

NOTE: If your Clear All button is grayed out or dimmed, you have nothing on the Clipboard and can continue.

2. Click the Clear All button in the task pane.
3. Select the range A4:E4 and click the Copy button. An icon appears in the task pane, as well as a copy of the data.
4. Select the range A6:A7 and click the Copy button. Another icon appears in the pane, above the first icon.
5. Select the range A8:E8 and click the Copy button. A third icon appears. Three items have been copied.
6. Press Esc.
7. Click cell A17. Click the second item in the task pane to paste the two dates to the active cell.

FIGURE 4-9 Using the Clipboard Task Pane

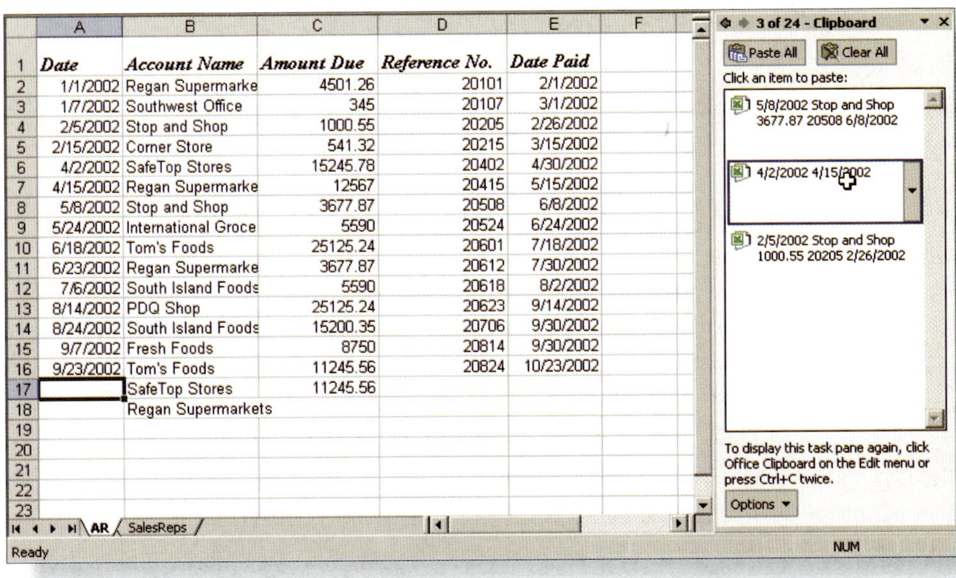

8. Click cell A19. Click the third item in the task pane to paste it.
9. Repeat these steps to paste the first item, beginning in cell A20.
10. Click the Clear All button [Clear All] in the task pane and then close it.

Working with Columns and Rows

You can insert columns and rows in a worksheet, as well as deleting them. The important thing to remember about inserting or deleting rows and columns is that the insertion or deletion extends across the entire worksheet. If you have used different parts of the worksheet for various types of data, for instance, you could be interrupting data somewhere on the sheet that is not immediately visible.

EXERCISE 4-11 Insert Rows

If you insert a column or row, check for formulas that might be affected by the insertion. Excel updates formulas to include an inserted row or column if it falls within the original range used in the formula.

1. Click cell C18 and key **345.7** to fill in the cell.

2. Click cell C21, click the AutoSum button [Σ], and then press [Enter]. The SUM function sums the range C2:C20.

3. Click cell J20 and click the AutoSum button [Σ]. A Trace Error button [◇] opens to tell you several cells used in the formula are empty.
4. Press [Enter].

NOTE: You can include empty cells in a formula range if a value might be added later. The Trace Error button will identify this as an error.

5. Click cell A12. Press [Ctrl]+[+] in the numeric keypad. The Insert dialog box opens.
6. Choose Entire row and click OK. A new row is inserted, and the existing rows shift down. Notice that the new row spans the worksheet and interrupts the names and counts in columns H and J. (See Figure 4-10 on the next page.)
7. Click cell C22. The formula has been updated to include rows 2 through 21. Another Trace Error button [◇] refers to the empty cells.
8. Position the mouse pointer on the Trace Error button [◇]. Click its arrow.

FIGURE 4-10
Row inserted

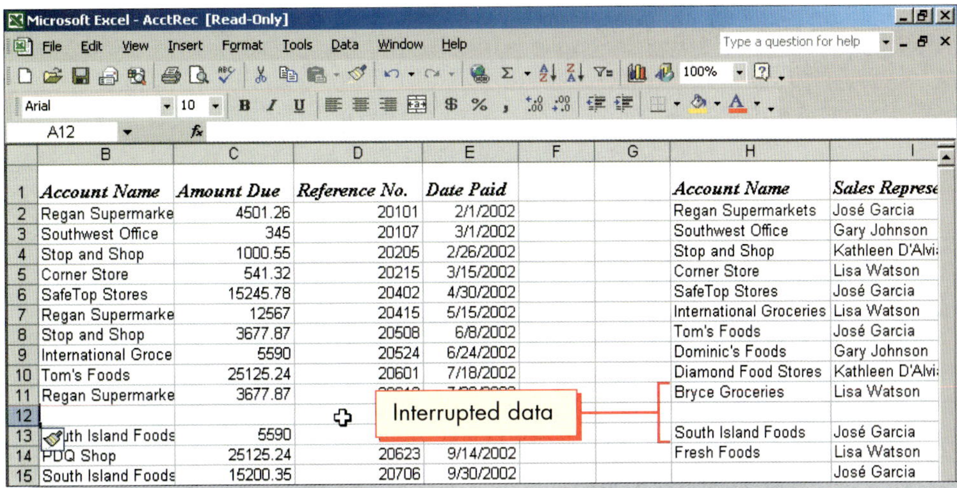

9. Press Esc after you view the cause of the error.
10. Click the row heading for row 15.
11. With the black down-arrow pointer, drag to select the row headings for rows 15 through 17. Three rows are selected or highlighted.
12. Right-click any of the selected row headings. The shortcut menu opens.
13. Choose Insert. Three rows are inserted, because you selected three rows before giving the Insert command.

FIGURE 4-11
Inserting three rows at once

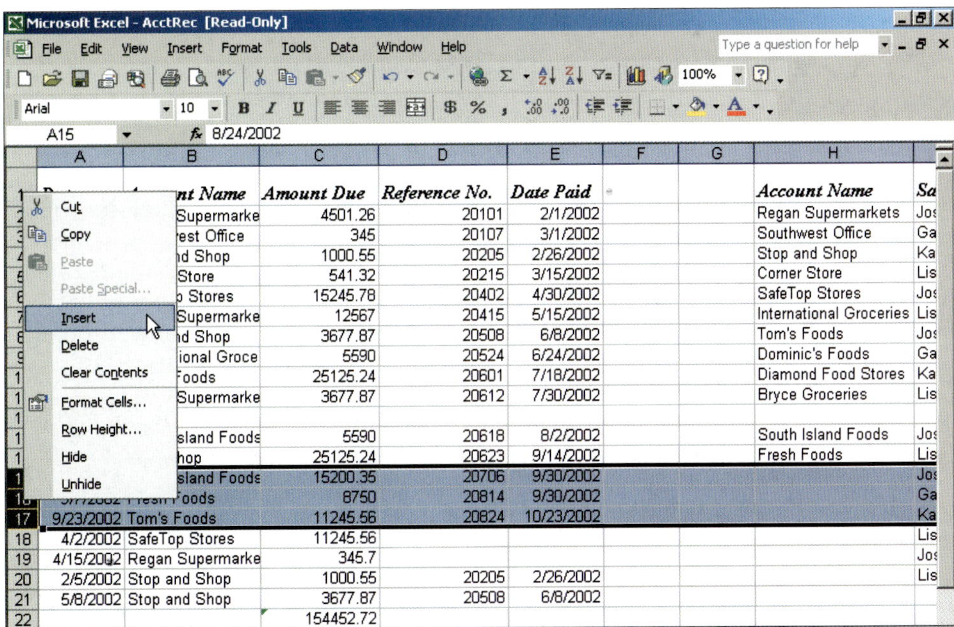

EXERCISE 4-12 Delete Rows

1. Click cell A12 and press Ctrl+- (you can use the - in the numeric keypad or in the top row of keys). The Delete dialog box opens.
2. Choose Entire row and click OK. The row is deleted.
3. Select the range A6:E7.
4. Drag the range to the location A14:E15 and drop it.
5. Click the row heading for row 6. Drag to select the row headings for rows 6 and 7.
6. Right-click one of the selected row headings. Choose Delete. Two rows are deleted. Notice that some of the account names are now missing from column H.
7. Click anywhere in row 14. Choose Delete from the Edit menu.
8. Choose Entire row and click OK.
9. Click cell C21. Through all the adjusting, the formula has been updated to sum the correct rows.

EXERCISE 4-13 Insert and Delete Columns

When you insert a column, it could interrupt separate data that is in another part of the worksheet. (After all, any new column goes all the way down to row 65,536.)

1. Right-click the column D heading. The column is selected and the shortcut menu opens.
2. Choose Insert. One column is inserted, and the existing columns move right.

NOTE: When you choose Insert or Delete from the shortcut menu, the dialog box does not open.

3. Key **Discount** in cell D1 and press Enter. Excel uses the same format in this column as in the three columns with formatted labels that precede it.
4. Click anywhere in column G. Press Ctrl+-.
5. Choose Entire column and click OK. Column G is deleted, and the other columns move left to fill the space.

EXERCISE 4-14 Hide and Unhide Columns and Rows

You can hide a column or a row if you do not need to see it until another time. For example, if you have a Discount column in your worksheet but have not yet filled-in the discount amounts, you might want to hide the column until it is filled in. You might want to hide a column so it doesn't take up space on the screen. You might want to hide columns or rows that include information you need for your file but don't really need to see or print. Even though a row or column is hidden, its values are used in calculations.

You can see when columns or rows are hidden, because their column or row headings are also hidden.

1. Right-click the column heading for column D to select the column.
2. Choose Hide from the shortcut menu. Column D is hidden.
3. Drag across the row headings for rows 12 through 14.
4. Open the Format menu and choose Row and Hide.
5. Click cell C21. Notice that the formula still sums all the rows, even though three are hidden from view.
6. Drag across the column headings for columns C through E. Column D is hidden between these two columns.
7. Point at the column heading for either column and right-click. Choose Unhide from the shortcut menu.

NOTE: To unhide a column or row, select the rows or columns on both sides of the hidden rows or columns.

8. Drag across the headings for rows 11 through 15. Rows 12 through 14 are hidden between these rows.
9. From the Format menu, choose Row and Unhide. Rows 12 through 14 are now visible.
10. Press Ctrl + Home to make cell A1 active.

EXERCISE 4-15 Freeze and Unfreeze Rows and Columns

In large worksheets, seeing two related columns or rows on-screen at the same time is sometimes impossible. You can keep data in view on-screen by freezing one of the columns or rows.

1. Click the arrow next to the Zoom button.
2. Key **110** and press Enter. This enlarges the display. Now you aren't able to see all the rows.
3. Click cell A2.
4. From the Window menu, choose Freeze Panes. A solid horizontal line identifies where the row(s) are locked in position, between rows 1 and 2.

5. Press the Down arrow to reach Row 25. The labels in row 1 do not scroll out of view.
6. Press Ctrl+Home. The pointer returns to the first unfrozen cell (cell A2).
7. From the Window menu, choose Unfreeze Panes.
8. Click cell C1. From the Window menu, choose Freeze Panes. The solid line is vertical to show that columns A and B are frozen.
9. Press → to reach column K. Columns A and B do not scroll.
10. Press Ctrl+Home. The pointer returns to the first unfrozen cell.

TIP: To freeze an entire column, click anywhere in the first row of that column. To freeze an entire row, click in the first column of that row.

11. From the Window, choose Unfreeze Panes.
12. Click the arrow next to the Zoom button. Choose 100%.
13. Save the workbook as ***[your initials]*****4-15** in a new folder for Lesson 4.

Working with Cell Alignment

Cell alignment establishes how the contents of a cell are positioned in the cell. Cell contents can be aligned both horizontally and vertically.

NOTE: What you see when you align content in a cell depends on the width and height of the cell. For example, if you change vertical alignment of the contents of a row that is already so short that the contents can't be repositioned, you won't see any difference. The row is not tall enough to show any adjustment.

TABLE 4-1 Horizontal Alignment Options

SETTING	RESULT
General	Aligns numbers and dates on right, text on left, and centers errors and logical values.
Left (Indent)	Aligns cell contents on the left side of the cell or indented by the number of spaces entered in the Indent box. If a label is wider than the cell, it spills into the cell to the right if it is empty. If the adjacent cell is not empty, the label is partially visible.
Center	Aligns contents in the middle of the cell. If the entry is wider than the cell, it spills into the cells on the left and right if they are empty. If the adjacent cells are not empty, the label is partially visible.

continues

TABLE 4-1 Horizontal Alignment Options *continued*

SETTING	RESULT
Right (Indent)	Aligns cell contents on the right side of the cell or indented by the number of spaces entered in the Indent box. If a label is wider than the cell, it spills into the cell on the left if it is empty. If the cell on the left is not empty, the label is partially visible.
Fill	Repeats the cell contents until the cell's width is filled.
Justify	Spreads the text to the left and right edges of the cell. This works only for wrapped text that is more than one line.
Center across selection	Places the text in the middle of a selected range of columns.

TABLE 4-2 Vertical Alignment Options

SETTING	RESULT
Top	Aligns cell contents at the top of the cell.
Center	Aligns cell contents in the vertical middle of the cell.
Bottom	Aligns cell contents at the bottom of the cell.
Justify	Spreads text to fill to the top and bottom edges of the cell. This works only for wrapped text that is more than one line.
Distributed	Positions text at an equal distance from the top and bottom edges.

EXERCISE 4-16 Change the Horizontal Alignment

The Formatting toolbar contains three Alignment buttons: the Align Left button, the Center button, and the Align Right button.

1. Click cell A1. This label is left-aligned, but the dates in the column are right-aligned for a slightly off-balance look.

2. Click the Align Right button. The label is now aligned at the right edge of the cell and balances the dates better.
3. Double-click the border between the column headings for columns B and C. The column title and the entries are left-aligned labels.

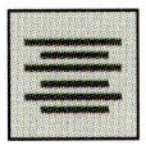

4. Click cell B1 and click the Center button. Column titles are often centered over labels.

5. Click cell C1. Click the Align Right button. Now the label better aligns with the values in the column.

EXERCISE 4-17 Use Center Across Selection

1. Right-click the row 1 heading and choose Insert.
2. Key **Klassy Kow Accounts Receivable** and press Enter.
3. Format cell A1 as 16-point Times New Roman.
4. Select the range A1:F1. You want to center the title over this part of the worksheet.
5. Right-click a cell in the range and choose Format Cells. The Format Cells dialog box opens.
6. Click the Alignment tab.
7. Click the arrow for the Horizontal box to display the options.

FIGURE 4-12 Alignment tab in the Format Cells dialog box

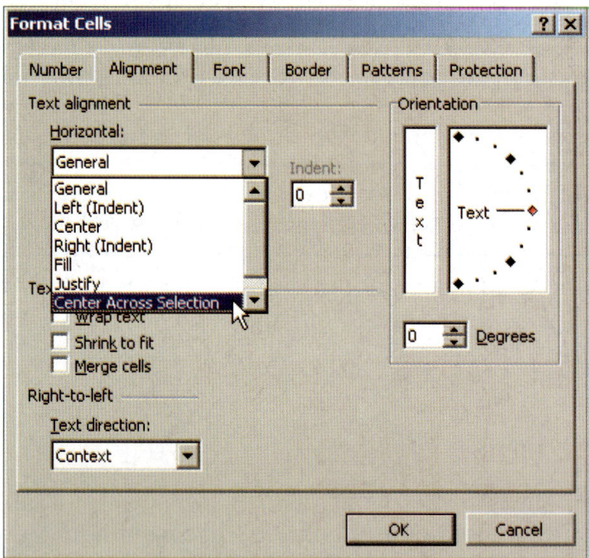

8. Choose Center Across Selection. Click OK. The label is now centered over the columns you selected.

EXERCISE 4-18 Change the Vertical Alignment

1. Change row 1 to 37.50 (50 pixels) high. You can see that the label is at the bottom of the cells.

2. Press Ctrl+1 to open the Format Cells dialog box.
3. On the Alignment tab, click the arrow for the Vertical box.
4. Choose Center and then Click OK. The label is now centered within the row.

EXERCISE 4-19 Wrap Text and Change Indents

If a label has more than one word and is rather long, you can turn on the Wrap Text setting. This allows the label to split into more than one line in the cell so the column doesn't have to be so wide. (It will, of course, take up more vertical space.)

Another way to improve the appearance of your worksheets is by adding an indent to labels. This moves them away from the left edge of the cell.

1. Change column E to 10.71 (80 pixels) wide. Notice that this is wide enough for the data, but not wide enough for the label.
2. Click cell E2 and press Ctrl+1.
3. On the Alignment tab, click to place a check mark for Wrap text in the Text control section.
4. Click OK. The label splits into two lines, but now the row isn't high enough.
5. Change row 2 to 30.00 (40 pixels) high.
6. Click the Center button. The wrapped label looks better centered.
7. Click cell B3.
8. Press F8 to start Extend Selection mode.
9. Press Ctrl+↓. This selects the cells with data.
10. Press Ctrl+1.
11. On the Alignment tab, click the arrow for the Horizontal box.
12. Choose Left (Indent).
13. Click the up arrow for Indent to change it to 1.
14. Click OK. The labels are now indented one space from the left edge of the cell, leaving some space between them and the right-aligned dates in column A.
15. Double-click the border between the column headings for columns B and C.

Using Merge and Center

You can merge cells to combine a range of cells into one cell that occupies the same amount of space. You can merge any number of columns and rows to create special effects and alignment settings. The range of cells you want to merge should be empty except for the top left cell.

EXERCISE 4-20 Use Merge and Center

1. Select the range H1:J21 and click the Cut button.
2. Click the SalesReps worksheet tab and then press Enter to paste the data. This data is now on its own sheet.
3. Double-click the border between each set of columns to AutoFit each one.
4. Select the range B15:C21 and press Delete.
5. Click cell A1 and key **Supermarket Sales Associates**. Press Enter.
6. Click cell A1 and drag to select the range A1:C1.

7. Click the Merge and Center button. The three cells are now one, and the label is centered.

NOTE: You can unmerge cells by clicking the Merge and Center button to turn off the command.

8. Click cell C2 and point at an edge to show the drag-and-drop pointer.
9. Click and drag the cell to cell D3.
10. Click cell D3 and drag to select cells D3:D12.
11. Click the Merge and Center button. The cells are one, and the label is horizontally centered at the bottom.

EXERCISE 4-21 Change Cell Orientation

The label in the new cell D3 is displayed horizontally like the rest of your worksheet data. Because the cells are merged vertically, you want to change the text's rotation to match.

1. Right-click cell D3 and choose Format Cells.
2. On the Alignment tab, click the red diamond in the Orientation box.
3. Drag the red diamond down to show –90 degrees (that's "minus 90 degrees"). Click OK. The text is rotated –90 degrees. Notice that you will need to change the vertical centering as well. (See Figure 4-13 on the next page.)

TIP: You can also key the degree of rotation in the text box below the graphic.

4. Press Ctrl + 1. You are going to adjust the vertical centering now.
5. On the Alignment tab, click the arrow next to the Vertical box.

FIGURE 4-13
Rotating text –90 degrees

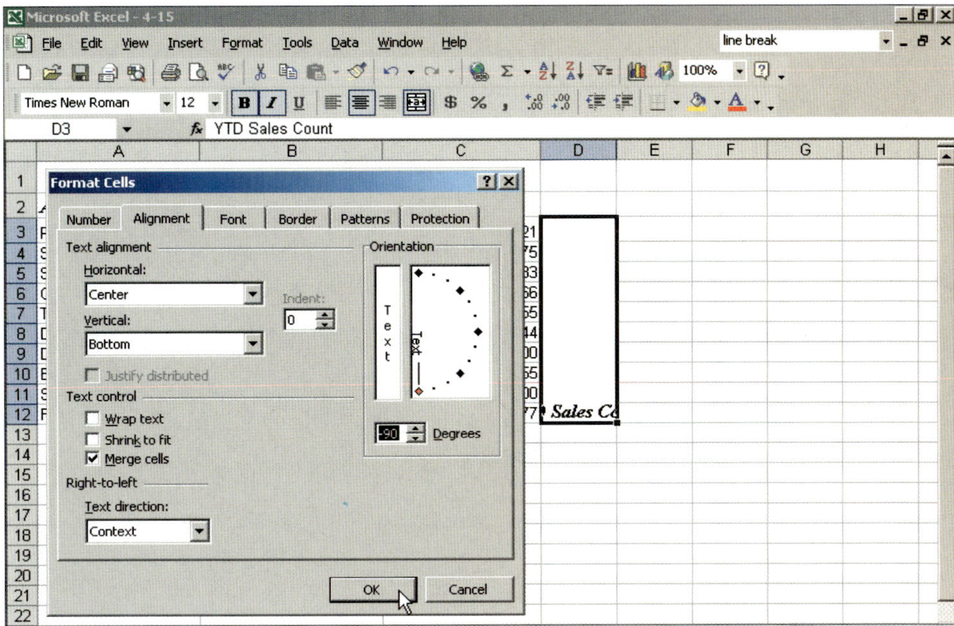

6. Choose Center and click OK.

7. Change column C to 11.43 (85 pixels) wide.

Applying Borders and Shading

A *border* is a line drawn around a cell or a range of cells. You can use borders to draw attention to a part of a worksheet, to show totals, or simply to group information in your worksheet.

Shading is the background pattern or color for a cell or a range of cells. You can use shading in much the same way as a border—to group information on the worksheet, to add emphasis, or to make your worksheet easier to read and more attractive.

EXERCISE 4-22 Apply Cell Borders Using the Borders Button

It's important to remember that cells share borders, so adding a border to the bottom of cell A1 has the same effect as adding a border to the top of cell A2.

Excel provides two methods to apply a border to a cell or a range of cells:

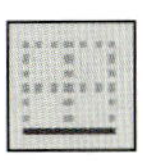

- Use the Borders button.
- Use the Format Cells dialog box.

1. Click cell C12.

2. Click the Borders button. Notice that the current border style (a single-line bottom border) is shown on the button. This is the current border style that Excel applies to cell C12.
3. Click cell C14 to see the border better. Notice that the border fills the width of the cell.
4. Select cell C13 and click the AutoSum button Σ. Press Enter.
5. Click cell C13 and then click the arrow next to the Borders button. Excel shows 12 border styles, each with a descriptive ScreenTip.

FIGURE 4-14
Borders palette

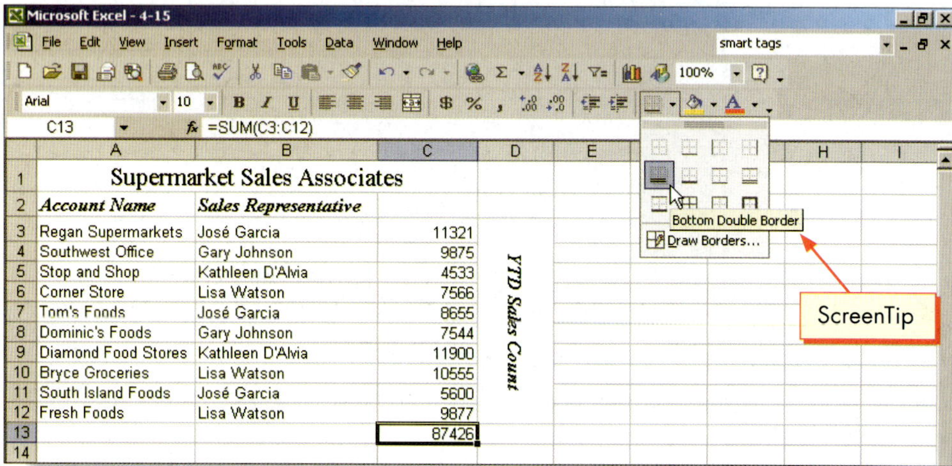

6. Click Bottom Double Border.

TIP: Totals in accounting and other financial reports are often shown with a single border above and a double border below.

7. Click cell B13 to see the border. Notice that the Borders button shows the last-used style.

EXERCISE 4-23 Apply Borders Using the Dialog Box

You can also use the Format Cells dialog box to apply borders. This method provides a bit more flexibility in defining borders.

1. Click the AR worksheet tab and then press F5. Key **c22** and press Enter.
2. Press Ctrl + 1.
3. Click the Border tab. There are presets for None, an Outline, or Inside.

TIP: Inside borders can be applied only to multiple cells, not to a single cell.

4. Click Outline. The Border buttons around the preview show which borders are available for an outline border.
5. Click None to remove the border.
6. Click the down arrow for the Color box. Choose "Red" in the first column, third row.

NOTE: You must choose the Color and Style of a line before choosing the style of border in the Format Cells dialog box.

7. In the Style box, choose a single line (first column, last line).
8. In the Text preview area, click where the top border will be located. A preview of the red single-line border is shown.

FIGURE 4-15 Border tab in the Format Cells dialog box

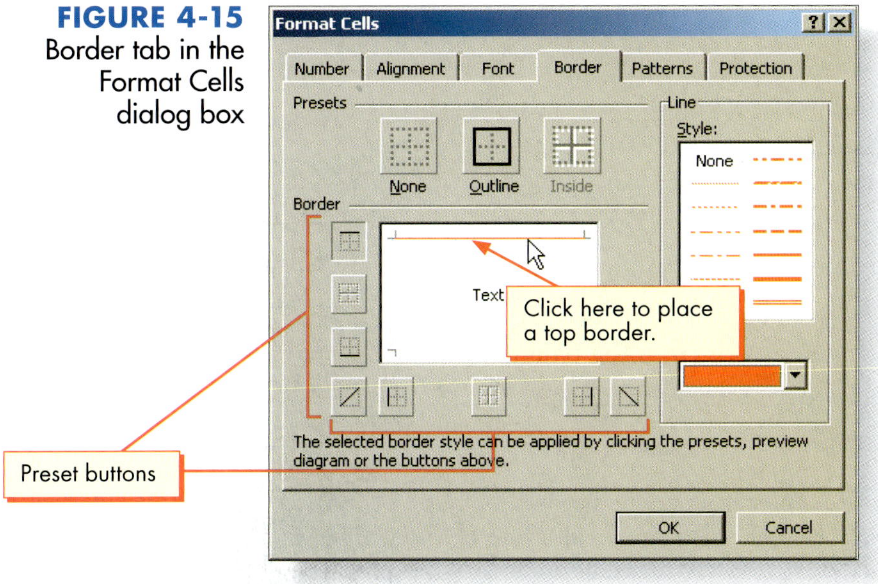

9. In the Style box, choose a double line (second column, last line).

NOTE: Click in the Text preview to turn the borders on and off.

10. In the Text preview area, click where the bottom border will be located.
11. Click OK.
12. Deselect the cell in the worksheet so you can see the borders you have created.

EXERCISE 4-24 Draw Cell Borders

You can draw your own borders around a cell or range of cells without first selecting the cells. Excel follows the cell edges so your lines are straight. If you are accustomed to drawing in other programs, this can be quicker than selecting cells and using the buttons or the dialog box.

1. Click the down arrow next to the Borders button.
2. Choose Draw Borders. The Borders toolbar opens. The pointer is a pencil shape.

FIGURE 4-16
Borders toolbar

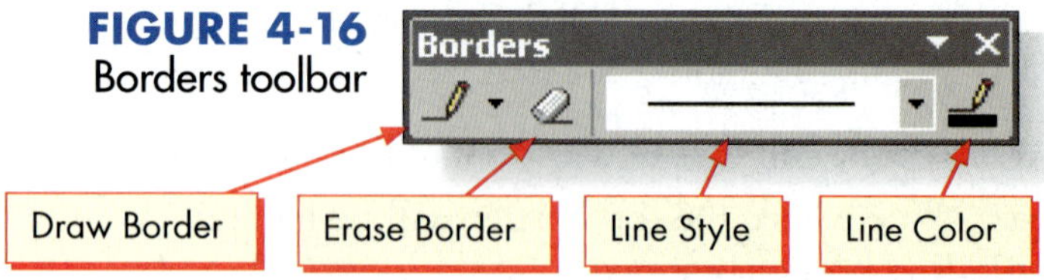

3. Click the top left corner of cell A2 with the Pencil pointer. Drag to the bottom right corner of cell F2.
4. Release the mouse button. The border is completed.

5. Click the Erase Border button. The pointer changes to an eraser shape.
6. Click cell A2, drag to cell F2, and then release the mouse button. The border is removed.

7. Click the Draw Border button.

8. Click the arrow next to the Line Style button. A palette of line styles opens.
9. Choose one of the dashed or dotted styles.

10. Click the Line Color button.
11. Choose a dark color from the palette.
12. Draw a border around the range A2:F2.
13. Click the Close button on the Borders toolbar.

TIP: You can open the Borders toolbar by choosing View, Toolbars. You can also right-click any toolbar and turn it on from the shortcut menu.

EXERCISE 4-25 Apply Shading

The background of a cell or a range of cells can be filled or shaded with a solid color or a pattern. Light solid colors are best for cells with data.

Excel provides two methods for applying shading to a cell or a range of cells:

- Use the Fill Color button
- Use the Format Cells dialog box

1. Click the SalesReps worksheet tab.

2. Select the range A3:C3. Click the Fill Color button. Excel applies to the range the color shown beneath the paint bucket icon.
3. Click in row 5 to see the shading.

4. Click the Undo button. The shading is removed, and the range is still selected.
5. Click the arrow next to the Fill Color button. The color palette opens.
6. Choose **Gray-25%** in the last column, in the second row from the bottom.
7. Select the range A5:C5. Press Ctrl+1 and click the **Patterns** tab.
8. For the **Cell shading Color**, choose **Gray-25%** in the last column, in the second row from the bottom. Click **OK**. The pattern is solid.

9. Double-click the Format Painter button. This locks the painter on.
10. Select the ranges A7:C7, A9:C9, and A11:C11. Each range you select receives the shading.
11. Click the Format Painter button to turn it off.

EXERCISE 4-26 Use a Pattern

A pattern might be dots or crisscrossed lines. Patterns are acceptable for cells that do not contain data or for cells with minimal data.

1. Click cell D3 and press Ctrl+1.
2. Click the **Patterns** tab. For the **Cell shading Color**, choose **Gray-25%** in the second row from the bottom.
3. Click the arrow for the **Pattern** box. The patterns include dots, stripes, and crosshatches.
4. Choose **12.5% Gray** in the first row of pattern tiles, the second from the right. This is a dotted pattern.

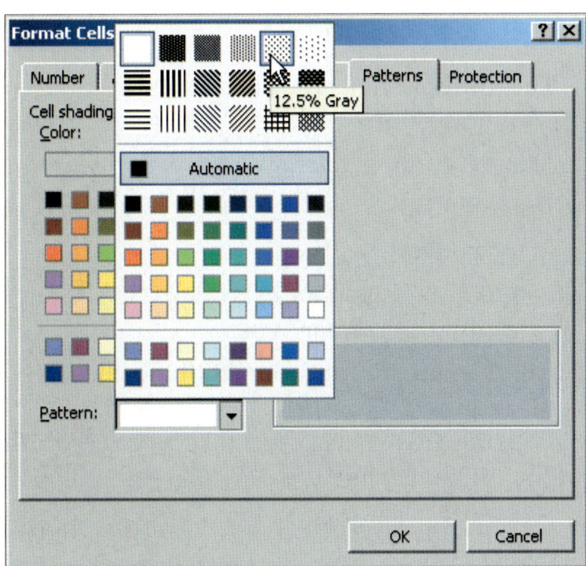

FIGURE 4-17
Changing the pattern

5. Click OK.

TIP: Many patterns make it difficult to read data in the cell.

EXERCISE 4-27 Complete the Number Formatting

To complete this worksheet, you want to format the numbers in a more readable style. The Comma Style button inserts commas and two decimal places. If you want one or no decimal places, you can use the Decrease Decimal button to remove positions one at a time.

You can build your own formats by using the Format Cells dialog box. For example, you can create a format that shows a *leading zero,* which is a zero (0) as the first digit in a number, typically a decimal number (example "0.59"). Normally, Excel does not show a leading zero because it has no value.

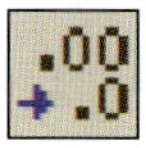

1. Select the range C3:C13. Click the Comma Style button. Commas and two decimal places are added to the values.
2. Click the Decrease Decimal button. One decimal position is removed.
3. Click the Decrease Decimal button again. The values still have the commas, but no decimals.
4. Click the AR worksheet tab.
5. Click cell C3. Hold down Ctrl and click cell C22.
6. Press Ctrl+1. Click the Number tab.
7. Choose Accounting in the Category list. A sample is displayed in the dialog box.
8. Click OK. This format aligns the currency symbol at the left edge of the cell.
9. Select the range C4:C21. Click the Comma Style button.
10. Select the range E3:E21.
11. Press Ctrl+1 and click the Number tab.
12. Choose Custom in the Category list. Click 0 in the Type list. The zero appears in the entry box under Type.
13. Click after the 0 in the box and key **00000** to show six zeros. Zero **(0)** means that a digit is required. This format requires that the entry be six digits. If the value uses only five digits, Excel inserts a zero in the first position. (See Figure 4-18 on the next page.)
14. Click OK.

15. Key your first and last name in cell A23. Print the worksheet.
16. Key your first and last name in cell A14 on the SalesReps worksheet. Print the worksheet.

FIGURE 4-18
Custom format for the Reference numbers

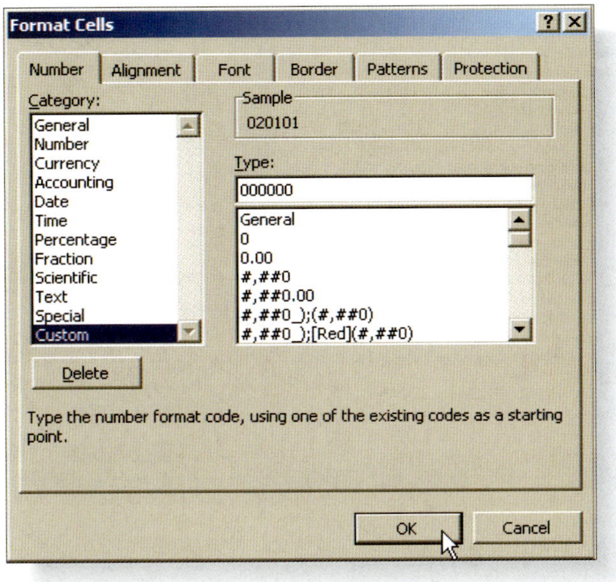

17. Press Ctrl + Home to make cell A1 active.
18. Save the workbook as ***[your initials]*4-27** in your Lesson 4 folder and then close it.

USING HELP

In addition to freezing parts of the worksheet on the screen, you can split the worksheet into more than one window or pane.

Explore how to split panes:

1. Start Excel and close the New Workbook task pane.
2. Click in the Ask a Question box in the upper right corner.
3. Key **split panes** and press Enter.
4. Click the topic View two parts of a sheet by splitting or freezing panes.
5. Click Show All in the top right corner. Read the information. (See Figure 4-19 on the next page.)

FIGURE 4-19
Using Help to learn about split panes

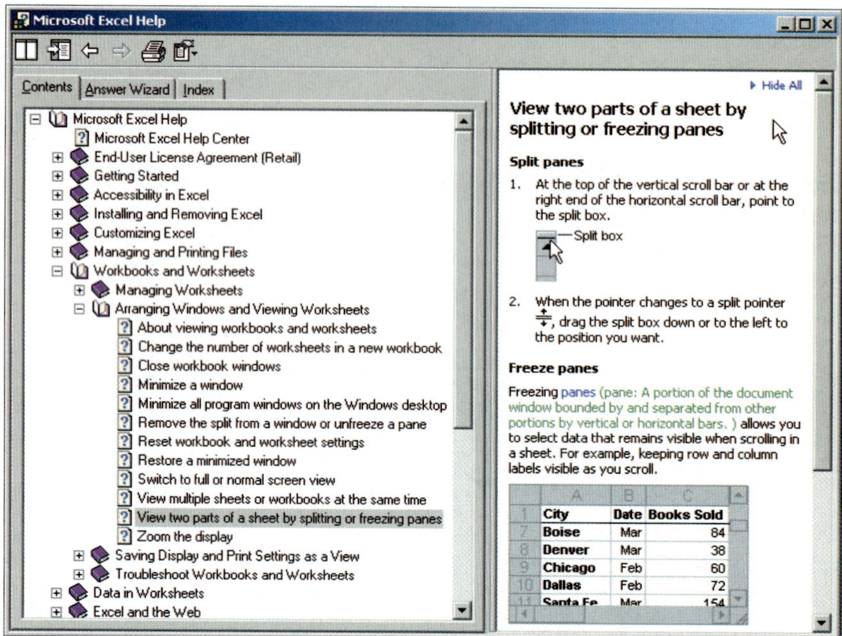

6. Close the Help window.

LESSON 4 Summary

- You can insert, delete, move, and rename worksheets in a workbook.
- Insert or delete cells when you need more space for missing data or have blank rows or columns in a worksheet.
- The AutoComplete feature makes suggestions when you key a label in a column that begins with the same characters as labels that are already in the column.
- The Pick From List feature displays a list of all labels already in the current column.
- When you cut or copy data, it is placed on the Windows Clipboard. Copied data can be pasted more than once.
- The Office Clipboard stores up to 24 copied elements. It is shared among Word, Excel, Access, and PowerPoint.
- When you delete or insert a row or column, it is inserted across the entire worksheet. Be careful about data that is elsewhere on the sheet but out of view.

- Change the cell alignment of data to make it easy to read and more professional. There are several horizontal and vertical alignment choices.
- Text can be wrapped, indented, or rotated.
- The Merge and Center command combines a range of cells into one cell.
- Borders outline a cell or range of cells with a variety of line styles and colors.
- Shading is the background pattern or color for a cell or range of cells.

LESSON 4 Command Summary

FEATURE	BUTTON	MENU	KEYBOARD	SPEECH
Align Left	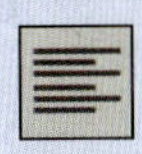	Format, Cells	Ctrl + 1	✓
Align Right		Format, Cells	Ctrl + 1	✓
Border	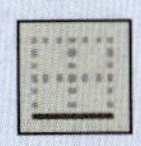	Format, Cells	Ctrl + 1	✓
Center	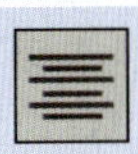	Format, Cells	Ctrl + 1	✓
Comma Style	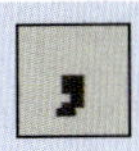	Format, Cells	Ctrl + 1	✓
Copy		Edit, Copy	Ctrl + C	✓
Cut		Edit, Cut	Ctrl + X	✓
Decrease Decimal	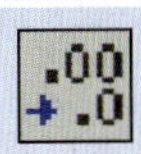	Format, Cells	Ctrl + 1	✓
Delete cell, row, column		Edit, Delete	Ctrl + -	✓
Freeze rows/columns		Window, Freeze Panes		✓
Hide/unhide column		Format, Column, Hide/Unhide		✓
Hide/unhide row		Format, Row, Hide/Unhide		✓

continues

LESSON 4 Command Summary *continued*

FEATURE	BUTTON	MENU	KEYBOARD	SPEECH
Indent text	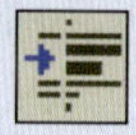	Format, Cells	Ctrl + 1	✓
Insert cell, row, column		Insert, Cells	Ctrl + +	✓
Merge and Center		Format, Cells	Ctrl + 1	✓
Text orientation		Format, Cells	Ctrl + 1	✓
Paste		Edit, Paste	Ctrl + V	✓
Shading		Format, Cells	Ctrl + 1	✓
Unfreeze rows/columns		Window, Unfreeze Panes		✓
Wrap text		Format, Cells	Ctrl + 1	✓

Concepts Review

TRUE/FALSE QUESTIONS

Each of the following statements is either true or false. Indicate your choice by circling T or F.

T F **1.** Inserted cells do not affect the position of existing cells.

T F **2.** A column is hidden when it is frozen.

T F **3.** Freezing rows and columns locks them in position on the screen.

T F **4.** AutoComplete fills in formulas and cell addresses.

T F **5.** You can set both horizontal and vertical cell alignment.

T F **6.** Shading creates a shadow effect around the cell.

T F **7.** The Merge and Center command works for only one row or one column at a time.

T F **8.** The Windows Clipboard and the Office Clipboard both store 12 items of cut or copied data.

SHORT ANSWER QUESTIONS

Write the correct answer in the space provided.

1. What two commands help you enter labels in columns that already have many labels?

____

2. If you want to repeat a lengthy label several times throughout a worksheet, would you cut it or copy it?

____

3. What does the term "drag and drop" mean?

____

4. What is the default alignment for values and dates in a cell?

____

5. What command will lock rows or columns in position on the screen?

____

6. What command combines several cells into one cell occupying the same screen space?

____

7. How can you format a number to show leading zeros?

____

8. What alignment option allows a label to split within a cell?

____

CRITICAL THINKING

Answer these questions on a separate page. There are no right or wrong answers. Support your answers with examples from your own experience, if possible.

1. If you delete a row or column, it is deleted across the entire worksheet. What problems could result from this?

2. AutoComplete and Pick From List are handy and easy to use. What are the advantages of each? What are the disadvantages of each?

Lesson Applications

EXERCISE 4-28

Cut and paste rows. Copy and paste labels.

1. Open **KowOwow** and save it as ***[your initials]*****4-28** in your Lesson 4 folder.
2. On the Oregon sheet, cut the "Ashland" row. Right-click the "Eugene" row and choose Insert Cut Cells.
3. Cut the "Medford" row and insert it at the "Roseburg" row.
4. Select the range A5:A10. Display the drag-and-drop pointer and hold down the Ctrl key. Drag a copy to the range A13:A18.
5. Key the following values for 2003:

FIGURE 4-20

	Chocolate	Vanilla
2003		
Ashland	22000	21000
Eugene	27000	28000
Klamath Falls	20000	18000
Medford	18000	16000
Roseburg	17000	15000

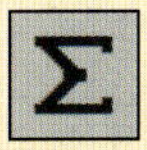

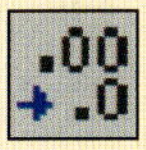

6. Select the range D5:D9 and click the AutoSum button Σ. Do the same for the range B10:D10.
7. Select the range B5:D10. Click the Comma Style button ,. Click the Decrease Decimal button .00 +.0 two times.
8. On the California sheet, copy the range A5:A19 to A22:A36.
9. Use AutoSum to determine the totals for 2003.
10. Format the range B5:D19 to show commas, no decimals, and no currency symbols.
11. Preview the entire workbook. Add a custom footer with your first and last name at the left, the filename in the center, and the date at the right on both sheets.

REVIEW: You must open the Print dialog box to print/preview the entire workbook. Press PgDn or PgUp to move between pages.

12. Print the entire workbook. Save and close it.

EXERCISE 4-29

Insert worksheets. Move worksheets. Copy labels.

1. Open **EstKowO** and save it as ***[your initials]*4-29** in your Lesson 4 folder.
2. Insert two new worksheets and name them **Nevada** and **Washington**.
3. Arrange the worksheets so they are in alphabetical order, going from left to right.
4. Select the range A1:D4 on the California sheet. Click the Copy button. Go to the Nevada sheet and paste the cells. Go to the Washington sheet and paste the cells again. Cancel the Paste command.
5. On the Nevada sheet, change column A to 21.57 (156 pixels) wide. Change columns B, C, and D each to 10.00 (75 pixels) wide. Make the same changes on the Washington sheet. Check the column widths on the California and Oregon sheet. Make sure the column widths in these sheets are the same as the others.
6. Preview the Nevada sheet. Add a custom footer with your first and last name at the left, the tab name in the center, and the date at the right. Print the sheet.
7. Preview the Washington sheet and add the same custom footer. Print the sheet.
8. Save and close the workbook.

EXERCISE 4-30

Work with cell alignment options. Cut and paste cells. Apply borders.

1. Open **EstKowO** and save it as ***[your initials]*4-30** in your Lesson 4 folder.
2. Select the range B5:D5. Hold down Ctrl and select the range B10:D10. While holding down the Ctrl key, add the ranges B13:D13 and B18:D18. Click the Currency Style button.
3. Click the Decrease Decimal button two times.

TIP: A column filled with # symbols simply means the column is not wide enough. Removing the decimal positions makes values fit in the column better.

4. Cut row 4 and insert it at row 3. Select the range A3:D3 and open the Format Cells dialog box. Choose Center Across Selection from the Horizontal align-

ment choices. Center cells A12:D12 across the selection also. Do the same for cells A1:D2.

5. Select the range B4:D4 and click the Center button.
6. Select the ranges B10:D10 and B18:D18. Apply a single top and double bottom border.
7. Preview the worksheet. Change the left margin to 2.00 inches.
8. Add a custom footer with your first and last name at the left, the filename in the center, and the date at the right. Print the sheet.
9. Save and close the workbook.

EXERCISE 4-31 Challenge Yourself

Cut and paste rows. Change cell alignment.

1. Open **CakeSales** and save it as ***[your initials]*4-31** in your Lesson 4 folder.
2. Cut and insert the rows to arrange the flavors in alphabetical order.
3. Apply the Accounting 1 AutoFormat. Change the alignment for cells A1:A2 to left and then center the cells across the range A1:E2.
4. AutoSum the values in row 8.
5. Add a custom footer with your first and last name at the left, the filename in the center, and the date at the right. Turn off the gridlines and row and column headings.
6. Print the worksheet. Save and close the workbook.

On Your Own

In these exercises you work on your own, as you would in a real-life work environment. Use the skills you've learned to accomplish the task—and be creative.

EXERCISE 4-32

NOTE: This exercise requires the use of ***[your initials]*2-28**, the file saved in an "On Your Own" exercise in Lesson 2.

Open ***[your initials]*2-28**. Add three more names to the list and use AutoComplete to enter cities for the new people. Use Pick From List to give one of the new people the same birthday as someone already in the list. Merge and center the main title. Apply shading to the worksheet to enhance its readability. Delete the cell with your name and the exercise number. Add the usual custom footer (be sure to include your name). Save the workbook as ***[your initials]*4-32** in your Lesson 4 folder. Print the worksheet, save the book, and close it.

EXERCISE 4-33

Create a new workbook and save it as ***[your initials]*4-33** in your Lesson 4 folder. In cell A1, key **Restaurants and Fast Food Shops**. Enter three column titles to list the names of restaurants or fast food shops in your city, their phone numbers, and their cuisine ("Italian," "Seafood," and so on.). Key the names of ten restaurants or fast food shops (use the phone book or Internet to find names, if you need to). Use AutoComplete for the cuisine type when possible. Apply borders and shading or use Merge and Center to format your work. Add the usual footer (make sure to include your name). Print the worksheet. Save and close the workbook.

EXERCISE 4-34

Create a new workbook with a variety of labels and values to experiment with alignment options. For example, you might key **This is wrapped text** and then apply that setting to the cell to illustrate it. Experiment with the settings you did not use in this lesson. Add the usual footer (be sure to include your name). Save the worksheet as ***[your initials]*4-34** in your Lesson 4 folder. Print and close it.

UNIT 2

Working with Formulas and Functions

LESSON 5

Using Simple Formulas and Functions

OBJECTIVES

MOUS ACTIVITIES
In this lesson:
Ex2002 1-2
Ex2002 2-2
Ex2002 3-1
Ex2002 3-6
Ex2002 3-7
Ex2002 5-1
Ex2002 5-2

See Appendix E.

After completing this lesson, you will be able to:

1. **Use a template to create a workbook.**
2. **Build addition and subtraction formulas.**
3. **Build multiplication and division formulas.**
4. **Use order of precedence in a formula.**
5. **Use math and statistical functions.**
6. **Use relative, absolute, and mixed references.**
7. **Refine format and print options.**

Estimated Time: 2 hours

In this lesson, you spend more time building formulas, using each of the common business arithmetic operations (addition, subtraction, multiplication, and division). In the process of learning more about formulas, you will review the mathematical order of precedence. This determines how Excel completes a series of calculations.

Previous lessons have introduced you to the concept of *relative reference* in Excel. You have seen how Excel updates a reference in a formula relative to its position when it is copied to a new location. In this lesson you explore other types of references.

Using a Template to Create a Workbook

A *template* is a model or sample workbook that can include font types and styles, alignment settings, borders, labels, values, and formulas. A template is useful as the basis for a workbook that is the same each week or month but with different data. For example, you might key an income statement every month that is the same except for the amounts.

You can use a template as the model for a workbook by:

- Choosing General Templates in the New from template section of the New Workbook task pane.
- Choosing the template name in the New from template section of the New Workbook task pane.

Templates are automatically saved with an .xlt filename extension. This is different from a workbook's .xls extension. Templates are also automatically saved in a Templates folder. (Templates must be in the Templates folder if you want the templates to be listed in the Templates dialog box.)

NOTE: Check with your instructor if you need help locating the templates used in this lesson.

EXERCISE 5-1 Create a Workbook from a Template

When you create a new workbook from a template, a copy of the template opens as a new workbook. The workbook has the same name as the template, followed by a number.

1. If the New Workbook task pane is not open, choose View, Task Pane.

NOTE: You can also open the New Workbook task pane by choosing File, New.

2. Click General Templates in the New from template section of the task pane. The Templates dialog box appears. It has tabs for the different groups of templates on your computer.

NOTE: Ask your instructor which tab has the template for this lesson.

3. Find the template **KlassyKow**. (See Figure 5-1 on the next page.)

FIGURE 5-1
Templates dialog box

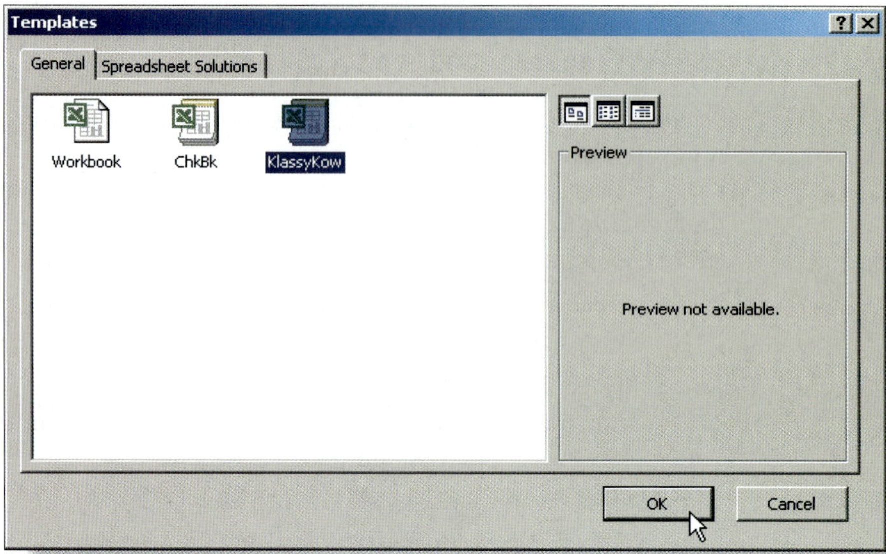

4. Click **KlassyKow** and then click OK. A new workbook opens with labels, values, and a picture. The title bar shows the template name with a number, probably 1.

NOTE: The workbooks in this course relate to the Case Study about Klassy Kow Ice Cream, Inc., a fictional manufacturer of ice cream (see pages 357 through 360).

5. Press F12 and save the workbook as ***[your initials]*5-1** in a new folder for Lesson 5. The title bar now shows your filename.

Building Addition and Subtraction Formulas

Simple addition formulas total or sum cells using the plus sign (+). Subtraction formulas compute the difference between cells using the minus sign (–).

TIP: When cells are next to each other in a row or a column, it is usually faster to use AutoSum than to key a formula for addition.

EXERCISE 5-2 Create and Copy Addition Formulas

This worksheet tracks monthly expenses of sales representatives. The budgeted amounts for each week need to be added, as well as the expenses for each week. (The expenses are entered each week because they change from week to week.)

You start by keying a formula to determine the total budgeted amount for the month for each salesperson.

1. Scroll down the worksheet and click cell B28.
2. Press [=] to start a formula.
3. Scroll up and click cell B9, the budget amount for the first week for Kim Tomasaki. A marquee appears around the cell and it is outlined in a color.
4. Key + and click cell B14, the second week budget amount.

TIP: You can use [+] on the numeric keypad or at the top of the keyboard to key the plus symbol in a formula.

5. Key + and click cell B19, the third week.
6. Key + and click cell B24, the fourth week. This is the addition formula to determine the total budgeted amount for the month for this salesperson.

FIGURE 5-2
Entering an addition formula

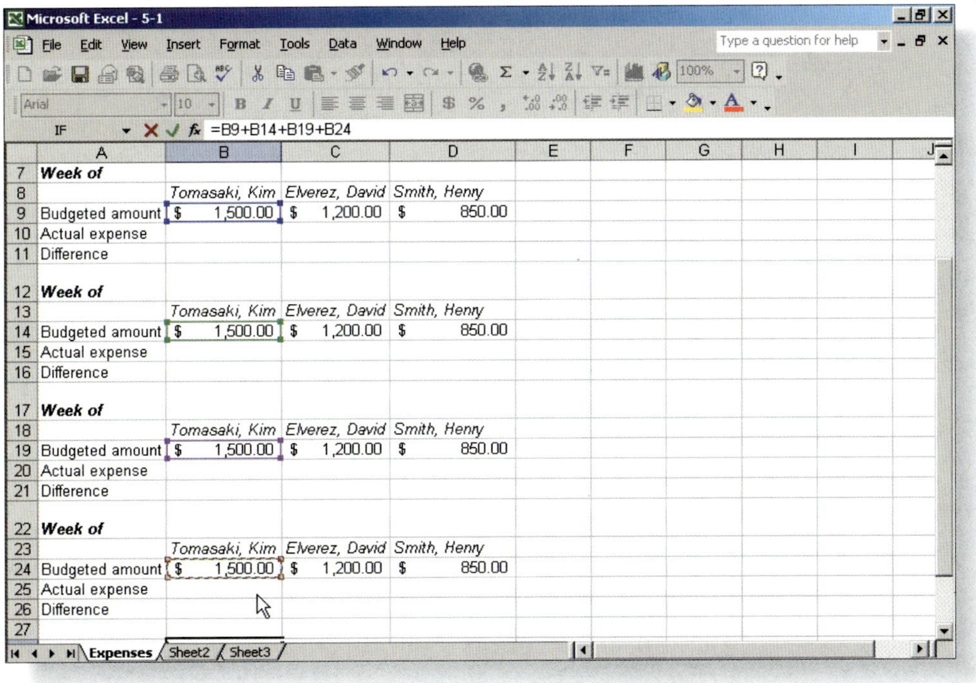

7. Press [Enter].

REVIEW: You can click the Enter button [✓] in the formula bar to finish a formula.

8. In cell B29, key = to start the formula.
9. Click cell B10, the cell where the first week's actual amount will be keyed.

REVIEW: You can include empty cells in a formula.

10. Key **+** and click cell B15, the second week.
11. Key **+** and click cell B20, and then key **+** and click cell B25.
12. Key **+** again to make a deliberate error.
13. Press Enter. The last plus sign is not necessary, and Excel proposes a correction, eliminating the extra + sign.

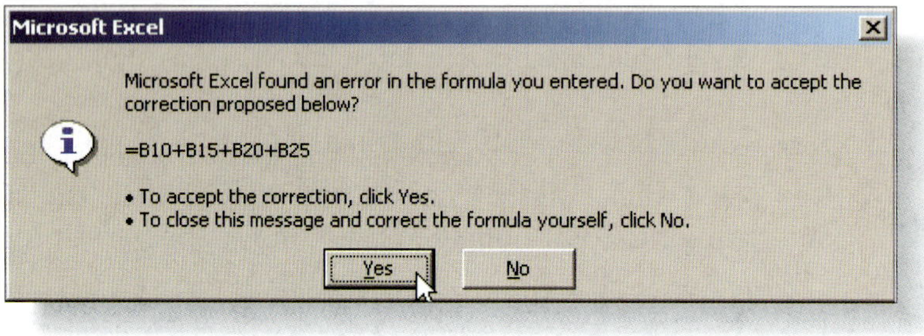

FIGURE 5-3 Error message box about incorrect formula

14. Choose Yes. This worksheet displays a single dash to indicate zero, and the cell shows a small green triangle indicating an error.
15. Click cell B29 and position the mouse pointer on the Trace Error button.
16. Click the arrow next to the Trace Error button. You are told that the formula refers to empty cells.
17. Choose Ignore Error.
18. Select cells B28:B29. Position the mouse pointer on the Fill handle for the range.

REVIEW: The Fill handle pointer is a black cross when you point to the bottom right corner of the cell.

19. Drag the Fill handle to cell D29 to copy the formulas. The AutoFill Options button appears just below the filled range and more green triangles appear.
20. Click cell C29.
21. Individually select each cell with an error, click the arrow next to the Trace Error button, and ignore the error.

EXERCISE 5-3 Create and Copy Subtraction Formulas

This worksheet computes by subtracting the actual amount from the budgeted amount. You can use - on the numeric keypad or at the top of the keyboard.

1. Click cell B30 and press = to start a formula.

2. Click cell B28, the budgeted total.

NOTE: Because there are no actual values, the difference is the same as the budget total.

3. Key – and click cell B29, the actual total. Press Enter.
4. Use the Fill handle to copy cell B30 to cells C30:D30.
5. Click cell B11. Key = and click cell B9, the budgeted amount for the week.
6. Key – and click cell B10, the actual amount for the week. Press Enter.
7. Use the Fill handle to copy cell B11 to cells C11:D11. The AutoFill options button appears, as well as green triangles to mark errors.

NOTE: Error triangles do not print and have no other effect on your worksheet, so you can ignore them when you know that nothing is wrong.

8. Click the Copy button.

REVIEW: You can paste data on the Windows Clipboard multiple times.

9. Click cell B16 and click the Paste button.
10. Click cell B21 and click the Paste button. Paste again in cell B26.
11. Press Esc to cancel the marquee. The differences are the same as the budget amounts, because no actual expenses are shown yet.

Building Multiplication and Division Formulas

Multiplication formulas use an asterisk (*). You might use a multiplication formula to determine an employee's weekly wages by multiplying hours worked by the rate of pay.

A division formula uses a slash (/). Division formulas can be used to determine percentages, averages, individual prices, and so on.

The result of a multiplication or division formula might be formatted with decimals if the result is not a whole number. A *whole number* is a value without a fraction or decimal.

EXERCISE 5-4 Create Multiplication Formulas

Klassy Kow projects that its salespeople will spend 10% more money next year than this year. You can multiply the current total amounts by 10% to determine next year's increases. When you multiply by a percent, you can key the actual percent with the percent sign (%). If you do not key the percent sign, you must key the decimal equivalent of the percent value.

TIP: Convert a percent to its decimal equivalent by dividing the percent amount by 100. For example, 89% is 89/100 or .89.

1. Select cells A28:A29. Display the drag-and-drop pointer, hold down Ctrl, and drag the cells to cell A32.

REVIEW: Display the drag-and-drop pointer by pointing at the top or bottom edge of a selection.

2. Click cell A32 and press F2.
3. Press Home and key **Increased**
4. Delete **Total** and press Enter.
5. Edit cell A33 to show **Increased Actual**
6. Widen column A to fit these labels.
7. Click cell B32 and key =
8. Click cell B28, key * and then key **10%**. Press Enter. This amount is the increase in dollars, not a new total amount.

EXERCISE 5-5 Edit a Formula in the Formula Bar

A percent of increase determines how much more money will be needed. To determine what the new total will be, you need to multiply by 110%, because 110% is the current amount (100%) plus the expected increase (10%).

1. Click cell B32 and click in the formula bar. A text insertion point appears, and the cell used in the formula is outlined in color.
2. Click between the 1 and the 0 in the formula bar.
3. Key **1** to change the percent to 110%.
4. Press Enter. The new total is calculated. (See Figure 5-4 on the next page.)
5. Copy cell B32 to cells C32:D32.
6. Copy cells B32:D32 to cells B33:D33.

EXCEL

FIGURE 5-4
Editing a formula in the formula bar

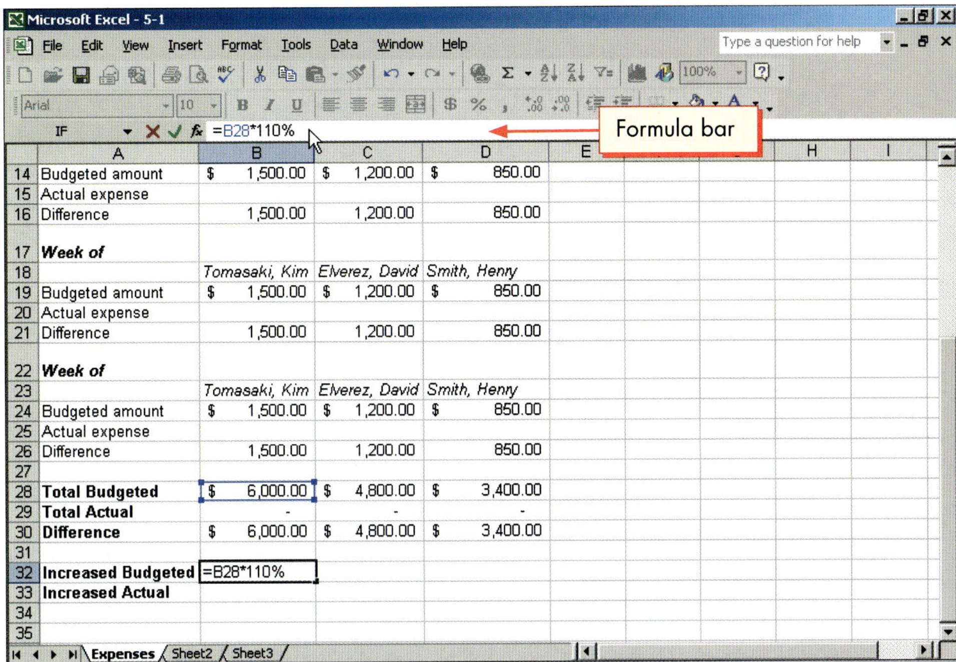

EXERCISE 5-6 Create Division Formulas

1. Select cells B10:D10. These expenses are keyed each month after the sales reps submit their reports.

NOTE: The template includes formatting for cells B10:D10.

2. Key **1000** and press Enter.
3. Key **950** and press Enter.
4. Key **725** and press Enter. As you fill in the amounts, the difference is calculated.
5. In cells B15:D15, key these values:

   1300 **1250** **925**

6. Key these values in cells B20:D20 and cells B25:C25. The totals are calculated in rows 28 and 29 as you key the values.

   900 **850** **625**

   1000 **750** **575**

7. Click cell B31 and key **=** to start a formula.

8. Click cell B29 and key / for division. Dividing the actual amount by the budget amount determines the percent of actual expenses in relation to the budget amount.
9. Click cell B28 and press Enter. The result is formatted as a decimal, not a percent.

EXERCISE 5-7 Apply the Percent Style and Increase Decimal Positions

Excel converts a decimal to a percent when you apply the Percent Style. It does this by multiplying the decimal value by 100. For example, .7 is .7*100 or 70%.

You can apply the Percent Style by:

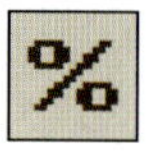

- Clicking the Percent Style button on the Formatting toolbar.
- Choosing **Percentage** from the **Category** list in the Format Cells dialog box.

After a percent style is applied, you can choose to show more or fewer decimal positions.

1. Click cell B31 and click the Percent Style button. The percent symbol is added, and the value is converted.

2. Click the Increase Decimal button two times. A decimal position is added with each click.
3. Use the Fill handle to copy the formula in cell B31 to cells C31:D31.
4. In cell A31, key **Actual as % of Budget**. Because three rows precede this row, the format of those rows is applied.
5. Widen column A to show this label. Press Ctrl + Home.
6. Save the workbook as ***[your initials]*5-7** in your Lesson 5 folder.
7. Print the worksheet. Close the workbook.

Using Order of Precedence in a Formula

Excel follows basic mathematical rules when it calculates a formula. These rules include an *order of precedence*, sometimes called *order of operation* or *math hierarchy*. The order of precedence determines what portion of a formula is calculated first. Generally, a formula is calculated from left to right, but some arithmetic operators take priority over others. For example, if you key a formula with both a multiplication symbol (*) and an addition symbol (+), Excel calculates the multiplication operation first even if it is the second symbol as you move from left to right. You can override the order of precedence by enclosing parts of the formula within parentheses.

When two operators have the same order of precedence—for example, multiplication and division—you perform the operations from left to right (see Table 5-1).

Figure 5-5 shows three formulas with the same values and the same operators. The results differ, depending on the placement of the parentheses.

FIGURE 5-5 Parentheses change the order of operations

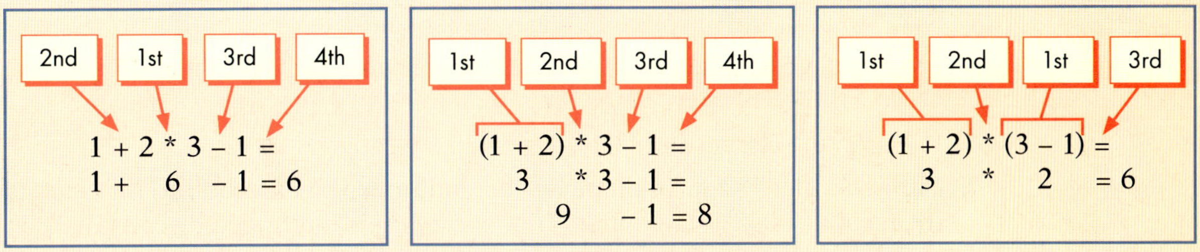

TABLE 5-1 Operator Precedence in Excel

OPERATOR	PRECEDENCE	DESCRIPTION
^	1st	Exponentiation
*	2nd	Multiplication
/	2nd	Division
+	3rd	Addition
-	3rd	Subtraction
&	4th	Concatenation (symbol used to join text strings)
=	5th	Equal to
<	5th	Less than
>	5th	Greater than

TIP: Using the first letter for each description in the table, you can memorize this saying to recall the order of precedence for parentheses and the first five operators: "Please excuse my dear Aunt Sally" (parentheses, exponentiation, multiplication, division, addition, and subtraction).

EXERCISE 5-8 Compare Formulas

In this worksheet, you calculate the dollar value of all beverages sold. You need to total the counts for each state and multiply by the price. As part of the learning process, you first key the formula with an error and then fix it.

1. Open **DrinkSize**. Save the workbook as ***[your initials]*5-8** in your folder for Lesson 5.
2. Click cell B11 and key =
3. Click cell B5, the price for a 16 oz. soda.
4. Key * to multiply the price by the number sold.
5. Select cell C5 and key **+**. Click cell D5 and key **+**. Click cell E5 and key **+**. Click cell F5. This part of the formula adds the count from each state.
6. Press Enter. The result looks OK, but it is wrong.
7. Click cell B11. The formula includes a multiplication symbol, so that part of the formula is calculated first. That is, cell B5 is multiplied by cell C5. Then the other cells are added to the result of that multiplication.
8. Right-click the AutoCalculate area and choose Sum.

REVIEW: AutoCalculate is visible in the status bar.

9. Select cells C5:F5. The total quantity sold is 30,000. You can use an empty cell to calculate the correct amount.
10. Click cell D11 and key = to start a formula.
11. Click cell B5, key ***30000**, and press Enter. This is the correct amount—the total number sold (30,000) multiplied by the price.

EXERCISE 5-9 Revise a Formula in the Worksheet

1. Double-click cell B11 to start Edit mode. The formula is in the cell and in the formula bar. The referenced cells are outlined in color.

REVIEW: The mode indicator is in the status bar.

2. In the worksheet cell, click in front or to the left of C5.
3. Key a left parenthesis **(** in front of C5.
4. Press End. The insertion point in the cell moves to the end of the formula.
5. Key a right parenthesis **)**.
6. Press Enter. These parentheses force the additions to be calculated first. Then the result of the additions is multiplied by cell B5. (See Figure 5-5 on the next page.)
7. Copy the formula in cell B11 to cells B12:B15.
8. Click cell B12. Notice that the formula multiplies the price in cell B6 by the counts in row 6 for 32 oz. soda. This is correct.

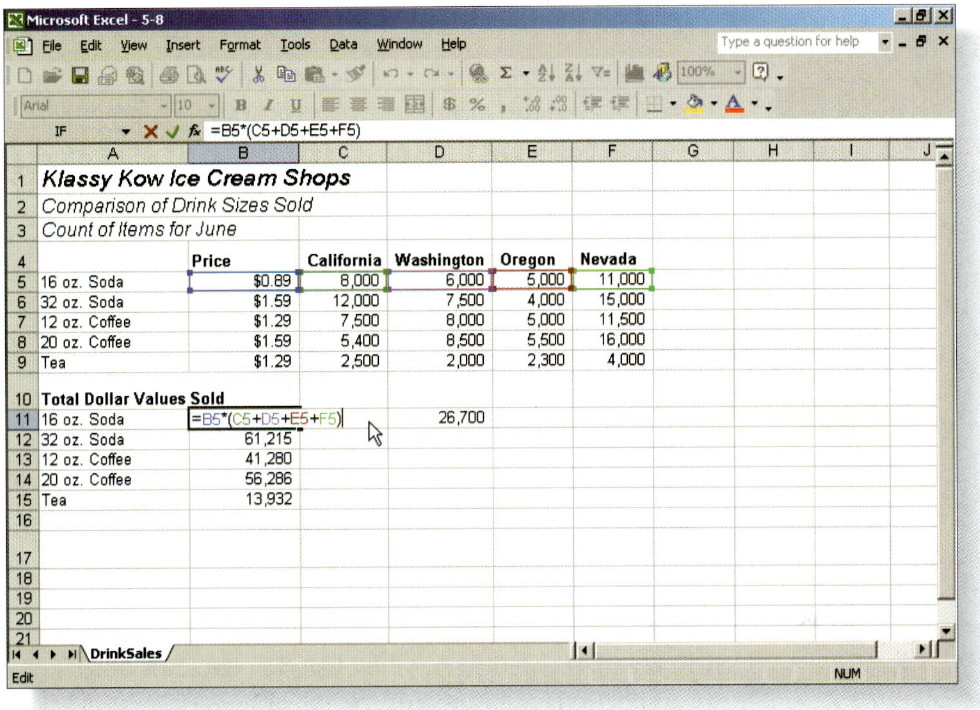

FIGURE 5-5
Changing the order of precedence

9. Delete the contents of cell D11 and press Ctrl + Home.
10. Save the workbook as ***[your initials]*5-9** in your Lesson 5 folder.
11. Print the worksheet. Close the workbook.

Using Math and Statistical Functions

Excel has many categories of functions that perform common mathematical, statistical, financial, and other calculations. A *function* is a built-in formula.

Many functions do things automatically that would be difficult or impossible for you to do manually. Suppose you have a list of two million numbers in random order and need to know which one is the largest number. Excel has a function that will do this for you much more quickly than you could if you had to search the entire list.

Functions have a *syntax*, which defines the necessary parts of the function and the order of those parts. Most functions follow a similar syntax, which includes an equal sign and the name of the function, followed by parentheses. Inside the parentheses, you place arguments.

An *argument* is what the function needs to complete its calculation, usually one or more values or cell ranges. A few functions do not have arguments, but most have at least one argument. If a function has more than one argument, the arguments are separated by commas. A function's arguments can consist of:

- Cell references (individual cells or ranges)
- Constants (a number keyed in the formula)
- Another function (known as a nested function)
- Range names

FIGURE 5-6 Syntax for the SUM function

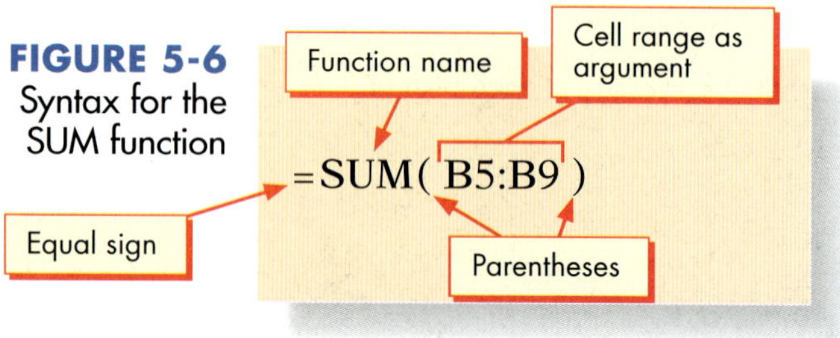

EXERCISE 5-10 Use SUM and the Formula Bar

SUM is a mathematical function listed in Excel's Math&Trig category. It is a practical way to add long columns or rows of values so you don't need to key individual cell references in an addition formula. The SUM function ignores cells with:

- Text
- Error values such as #NAME?

NOTE: Excel inserts the SUM function when you use the AutoSum button Σ.

TABLE 5-2 Examples of the SUM Function

FUNCTION(ARGUMENT/S)	CELL DATA	RESULT
=SUM(A1:A3)	A1=10, A2=20, A3=30	60
=SUM(50,60)	None	110
=SUM(A1,250)	A1=25	275
=SUM(A1,B2,C1:C2)	A1=10, B2=20, C1=10, C2=30	70
=SUM(A1, B2)	A1=25, B2="Ice Cream"	25
=SUM (A1, B2)	A1=25, B2=#NAME?	25

1. Open **DownTime**. Save the workbook as ***[your initials]*5-10** in your Lesson 5 folder.

2. Click cell B10.
3. Key **=sum(** to start the SUM function. An Argument ScreenTip opens to show you the syntax for the function.

FIGURE 5-7
SUM function and Argument ScreenTip

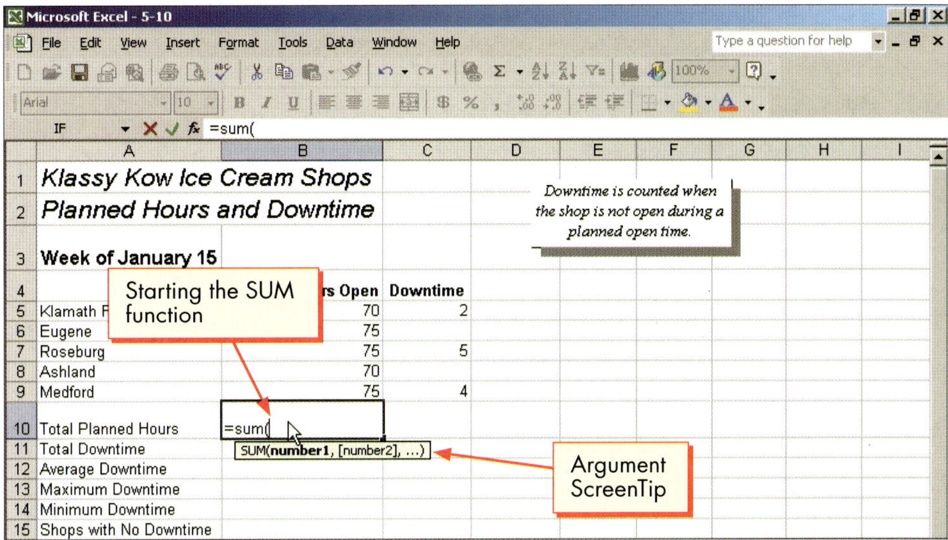

4. Click cell B5 and drag to select cells B5:B9. The function will sum the range B5:B9.
5. Press Enter.
6. Click cell B10 and look in the formula bar. For the SUM function, Excel adds the closing parenthesis for you. This formula is the same as keying =b5+b6+b7+b8+b9.

EXERCISE 5-11 Use the Insert Function Dialog Box

Although you can key functions in a cell, you can also use the Insert Function dialog box to choose the function. When you do, Excel opens a *Functions Arguments dialog box* to help you complete the function. This is helpful when you are just learning how to use a function, because each argument is described in the dialog box. It also helps you learn how to build formulas properly.

1. Click cell B11. You want to place the sum of the values from column C into cell B11.
2. Click the Insert Function button *fx*. The Insert Function dialog box opens. (See Figure 5-8 on the next page.)
3. Click the arrow next to the Or select a category list. Choose Math & Trig.

TIP: Functions are listed in alphabetical order.

FIGURE 5-8
Insert Function dialog box

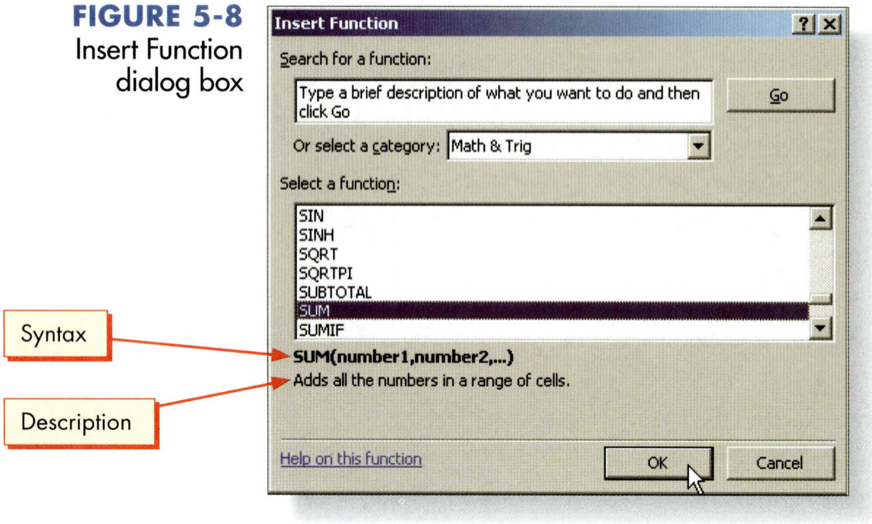

4. In the Select a function list, scroll to find SUM.
5. Click SUM to see its syntax and a description in the dialog box.
6. Click OK. The Function Arguments dialog box opens. In the Number1 box, Excel assumes that you want to sum the range just above cell B11.
7. Click and drag the dialog box down and to the right until you can see more of columns B and C (see Figure 5-9).

FIGURE 5-9
Function Arguments dialog box

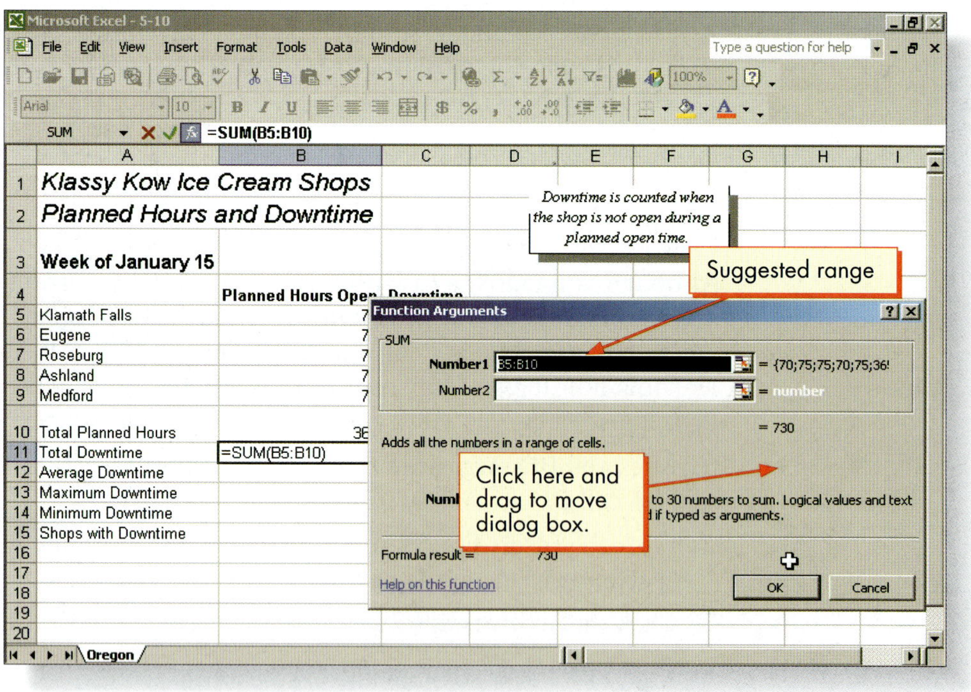

8. Click cell C5. A marquee appears around the cell, and its address is entered in the Number1 box in the Function Arguments dialog box.

NOTE: If you click in the wrong cell or number box, reposition the pointer and click again in the correct location.

9. Click in the Number2 box and click cell C6. A marquee appears around the cell and the cell's address is shown. Notice that the formula appears in both the formula bar and the cell. When cells are not in a range, they are separated by commas in the SUM function.
10. Click in the Number3 box and click cell C7.
11. Click in the Number4 box and click cell C8.
12. Click in the Number5 box and click cell C9.

FIGURE 5-10
Function Arguments dialog box with cells entered separately

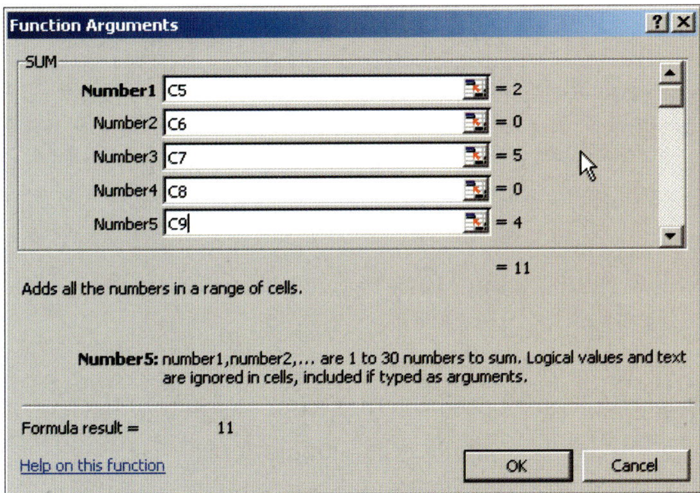

13. Press Enter. The dialog box closes, and the result is displayed in the cell. For now, ignore the green triangle.

EXERCISE 5-12 Use the AVERAGE Function

The AVERAGE function calculates the arithmetic mean of a range of cells. The *arithmetic mean* adds the values in the cells and then divides by the number of values. The AVERAGE function ignores:

- Text
- Blank or empty cells (but not zeros)
- Error values such as #NAME?
- Logical values

NOTE: A logical value is "True," "False," "Yes," or "No."

TABLE 5-3 Examples of the AVERAGE Function

FUNCTION(ARGUMENT/S)	CELL DATA	RESULT
=AVERAGE(A1:A3)	A1=10, A2=20, A3=30	20
=AVERAGE(50,60)	None	55
=AVERAGE(A1,250)	A1=25	137.5
=AVERAGE(A1,B2,C1:C2)	A1=10, B2=20, C1=10, C2=30	17.5
=AVERAGE(A1, B2)	A1=25, B2="Ice Cream"	25
=AVERAGE(A1, B2)	A1=25, B2=#NAME?	25
=AVERAGE(A1:A3)	A1=20, A2=0, A3=40	20
=AVERAGE(A1:A3)	A1=20, A2=Empty, A3=40	30

1. Click cell B12. You want to place the average of the values from column C into cell B12.
2. Click the Insert Function button fx.
3. Choose Statistical in the Or select a category list.
4. In the Select a function list, locate AVERAGE.
5. Click AVERAGE to see its syntax and description. Click OK.
6. Drag the dialog box until you can see column C. The Number1 box shows the range directly above cell B12.
7. Click cell C5 and drag to select cells C5:C9. As you drag, the Function Arguments dialog box collapses so you can see your work better.
8. Release the mouse button. The dialog box expands, and the range you selected is entered in the Number1 box.
9. Click OK. The result is formatted as a General number. Ignore the error triangle for now.
10. Press Ctrl+1 and click the Number tab.
11. Choose Number in the Category list.
12. Click the Down button to set 0 decimals.
13. Click OK. The value is rounded up to the next whole number.

TIP: When you round a decimal to a whole number, any decimal value that is .5 or greater is rounded up to the next whole number. For example, 3.6 is rounded up to 4.

EXERCISE 5-13 Use the MIN and MAX Functions

The MIN and MAX functions are statistical functions that show the minimum (smallest) value and the maximum (largest) value in a range. The MIN and MAX functions ignore:

- Text
- Blank or empty cells (but not zeros)
- Error values such as #NAME?
- Logical values

TABLE 5-4 Examples of the MIN and MAX Functions

FUNCTION(ARGUMENT/S)	CELL DATA	RESULT
=MAX(A1:A3)	A1=10, A2=20, A3=30	30
=MAX(50,60)	None	60
=MIN(A1,250)	A1=25	25
=MIN(A1,B2,C1:C2)	A1=10, B2=20, C1=10, C2=30	10
=MAX(A1, B2)	A1=25, B2="Ice Cream"	25
=MAX(A1, B2)	A1=25, B2=#NAME?	25
=MIN(A1:A3)	A1=20, A2=0, A3=40	0
=MIN(A1:A3)	A1=20, A2=Empty, A3=40	20

1. Click cell B13. You want to place the largest value from column C into cell B13.
2. Click the Insert Function button [fx].
3. Choose Statistical in the Or select a category list.
4. In the Select a function list, double-click MAX. The dialog box opens and the Number1 box automatically shows the address of the cell directly above.
5. Arrange the Function Arguments dialog box so you can see column C.
6. Click cell C5 and drag to select cells C5:C9. The dialog box collapses.

7. Release the mouse button. The range is shown as Number1.
8. Click OK. Ignore the error triangle.
9. Click cell B14 and click the Insert Function button [fx].
10. Choose Statistical in the Or select a category list. In the Select a function list, double-click MIN.
11. Arrange the Function Arguments dialog box and select cells C5:C9.
12. Click OK. Ignore the error triangle.

EXERCISE 5-14 Use the COUNT Function

The COUNT function tallies the number of values in a range. The COUNT function ignores:

- Text
- Blank or empty cells (but not zeros)
- Error values such as #NAME?
- Logical values

TABLE 5-5 Examples of the COUNT Function

FUNCTION(ARGUMENT/S)	CELL DATA	RESULT
=COUNT(A1:A3)	A1=Empty, A2=20, A3=30	2
=COUNT(A1:A3)	A1=30, A2=Empty, A3=#NAME?	1
=COUNT(A1:A3)	A1=25, A2="Ice Cream," A3=3	2
=COUNT(13, 21, 111)	None	3
=COUNT(A1, B2, C1:C2)	A1=25, B2=0, C1="Hello," C2=4	3

1. Double-click cell A15. Edit mode starts.
2. Double-click No and press Delete. Delete the extra space and press Enter. The label now indicates shops with downtime.
3. Click cell B15 and click the Insert Function button [fx].
4. Choose Statistical. In the Select a function list, double-click COUNT.
5. Select cells C5:C9. Click OK. Ignore the error.

EXERCISE 5-15 Use the COUNTA Function

A similar function COUNTA tallies values as well as labels in a range. The COUNTA function ignores:

- Blank or empty cells (but not zeros)
- Error values such as #NAME?
- Logical values

TABLE 5-6 Examples of the COUNTA Function

FUNCTION(ARGUMENT/S)	CELL DATA	RESULT
=COUNTA(A1:A3)	A1=Empty, A2=20, A3=30	2
=COUNTA(A1:A3)	A1=30, A2=Empty, A3=#NAME?	1
=COUNTA(A1:A3)	A1=25, A2="Ice Cream," A3=3	3
=COUNTA(13, 21, 111)	None	3
=COUNTA(A1, B2, C1:C2)	A1=25, B2=0, C1="Hello," C2=4	4

NOTE: The Count option in AutoCalculate shows the same results as the COUNTA function. AutoCalculate's Count Nums option shows the same results as the COUNT function.

1. In cell A16, key **Number of Oregon Shops**
2. Click cell B15 and drag the Fill handle to cell B16. Excel copies the COUNT function, and the argument range is moved down a row.
3. Double-click cell B16. Edit mode starts.
4. In cell B16, drag to select C6:C10 in the formula.
5. Click cell A5 in the worksheet and drag to select cells A5:A9. Your selected range replaces the range in the formula. (See Figure 5-11 on the next page.)
6. Press Enter. The result is 0, because the Count function ignores text.
7. Double-click cell B16.
8. Position the insertion point and key **a** after COUNT.
9. Press Enter. The new function COUNTA includes labels; there are five Oregon shops.
10. Click cell B16 and look in the formula bar.

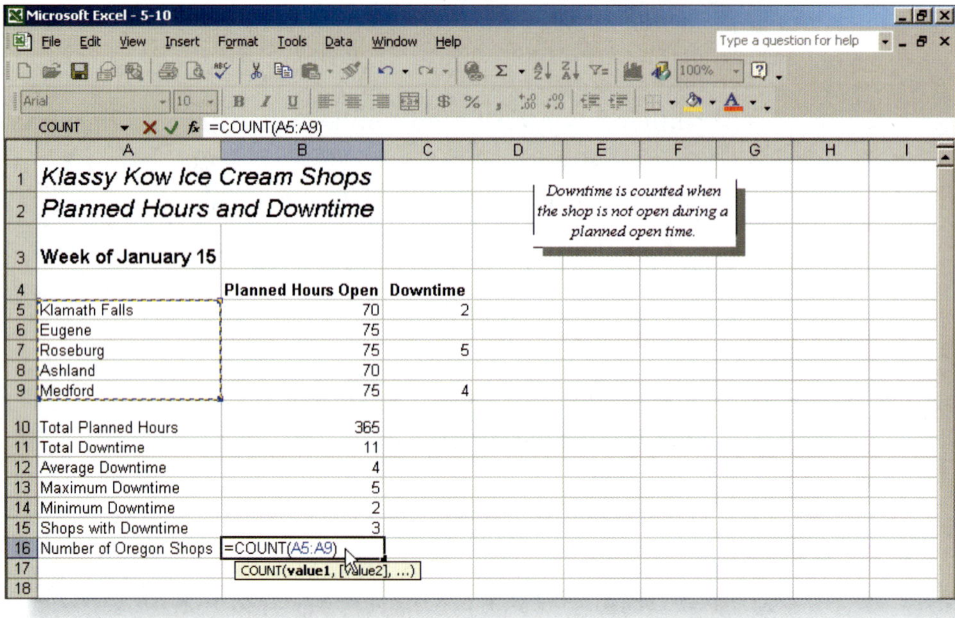

FIGURE 5-11 Editing the COUNT function

Using Relative, Absolute, and Mixed References

When you copy a formula, Excel does not make an exact duplicate of the formula. It adjusts the formula relative to the row or column where the copy is located. This is known as a *relative reference* and is often exactly what you want Excel to do.

There are situations, however, when you don't want Excel to use a relative reference. Instead, you want Excel to copy the formula exactly. A cell with an *absolute reference* does not change when a formula is copied. An absolute reference uses two dollar signs ($) in its address, one in front of the column reference and one in front of the row reference. For example, B5 is an absolute reference to cell B5.

Excel can also use a *mixed reference,* in which a dollar sign is placed in front of the reference for either the row or the column. In a mixed reference, part of the cell reference is adjusted when a formula is copied, and the other part of the cell reference is not changed. For example, $B5 is a mixed reference with an absolute reference to column B but a relative reference to row 5.

Dollar signs used in a cell address do not signify currency. They are a reserved symbol used to mark the type of cell reference.

TABLE 5-7 Cell References

ADDRESS	TYPE OF REFERENCE
B1	Relative
B1	Absolute
$B1	Mixed (Column letter is absolute; row number is relative.)
B$1	Mixed (Row number is absolute; column letter is relative.)

EXCEL

EXERCISE 5-16 Copy a Formula with a Relative Reference

1. In cell A17, key **Cost per Down Hour**. In cell B17, key **25**
2. Format cell B17 as currency with no decimals.
3. In cell D4, key **Cost**
4. Key **3** in both cell C6 and cell C8.
5. Click cell D5. Key **=** to start the formula.
6. Click cell C5, key * and then click cell B17. This formula uses relative references.
7. Press Enter. The result is $50.
8. Drag the Fill handle for cell D5 to copy the formula to cell D9. The copied formulas show a dash for zero and an error triangle.
9. Click each cell in column D and look in the formula bar. The column did not change as you copied, because you copied to the same column. But each time you went down a row in column D, the row reference increased in the formula. As a result, the copied formulas multiply by an empty cell.

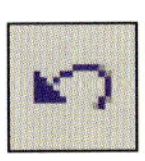

10. Click the Undo button. Only your copy is undone.

EXERCISE 5-17 Create a Formula with an Absolute Reference

Because absolute references are common to many calculations, Excel has a quick way of adding dollar signs to a cell reference. You simply press F4 while the formula bar is open to cycle through each reference option.

1. Click cell D5 and press F2.

REVIEW: F2 starts Edit mode, the same as double-clicking the cell.

2. Click between B and 1 in the worksheet cell.
3. Press F4. Two dollar signs are inserted, one before B and one before 1.

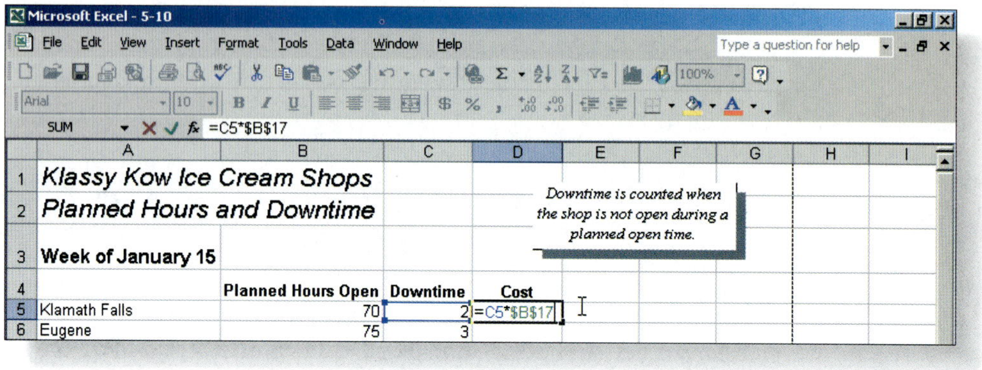

FIGURE 5-12 Making a cell reference absolute

4. Press F4. The dollar sign appears only with 17.
5. Press F4 again. The dollar sign appears only with B.
6. Press F4 again. The dollar signs are removed.
7. Press F4 once more. The absolute reference appears again.
8. Press Enter. Click cell D5 and look in the formula bar.
9. Use the Fill handle for cell D5 and copy the formula down to cell D9.
10. Click each copied cell and look in the formula bar.
11. Press Ctrl + Home.
12. Save the workbook as ***[your initials]*5-17** in your Lesson 5 folder.
13. Print the worksheet. Close the workbook.

EXERCISE 5-18 Use Mixed References

As one of its school-time promotions, Klassy Kow Ice Cream Shops plans to give out free multiplication tables, reduced in size and printed on cards. You will create the multiplication table using mixed references.

1. Open **MultTable**. Save it as ***[your initials]*5-18** in your Lesson 5 folder.
2. Set the Zoom percent to 75% (or any size that lets you see the entire worksheet on your monitor).
3. Click cell B4. You want to show the result of multiplying 1 by 1 in cell B4.

4. Key = and click cell A4. This will be a mixed reference.
5. Press [F4] three times to show $A4. This part of the formula will always use column A, but the row will change.
6. Press * and click cell B2.
7. Press [F4] two times to show B$2. This part of the formula will always use row 2, but the column will change.

FIGURE 5-13 Mixed reference formula

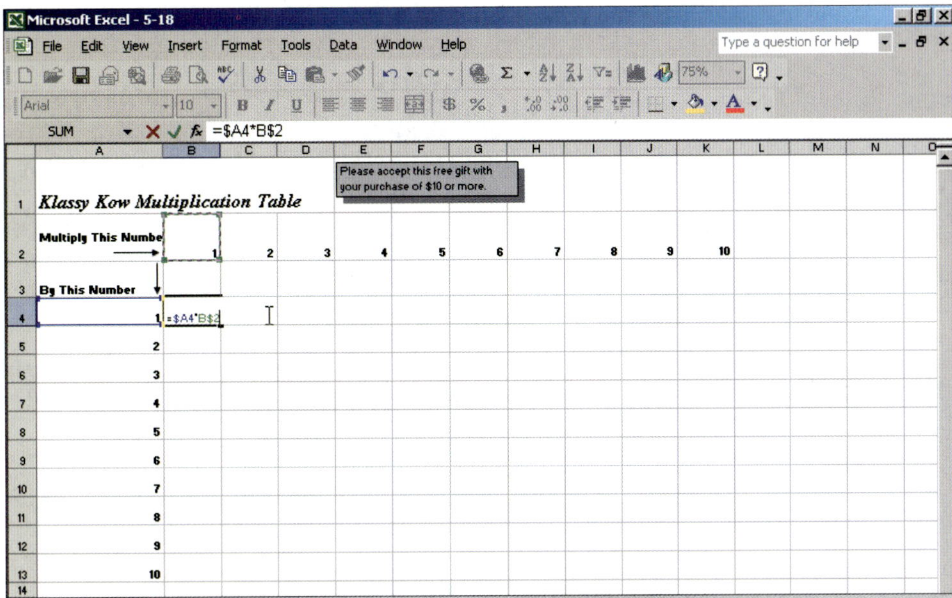

8. Press [Enter].
9. Use the Fill handle to copy cell B4 to cell K4.
10. Use the range Fill handle to copy cells B4:K4 down to row 13.

Refining Format and Print Options

This worksheet has many numbers and is too wide to print on a single page. Before printing, you can make some adjustments so it is easy to follow and prints on one page.

EXERCISE 5-19 Add Borders and Shading

Borders and shading will make it easier to follow numbers across the wide page.

1. If you can't see the complete label in cell A2, widen column A.

2. Select cells A2:K13 and press Ctrl + 1.
3. Click the Border tab.
4. In the Border preset group, click the Top Border button.
5. Click the Middle Border and then the Bottom Border buttons. Click OK.

FIGURE 5-14
Setting top, middle, and bottom borders

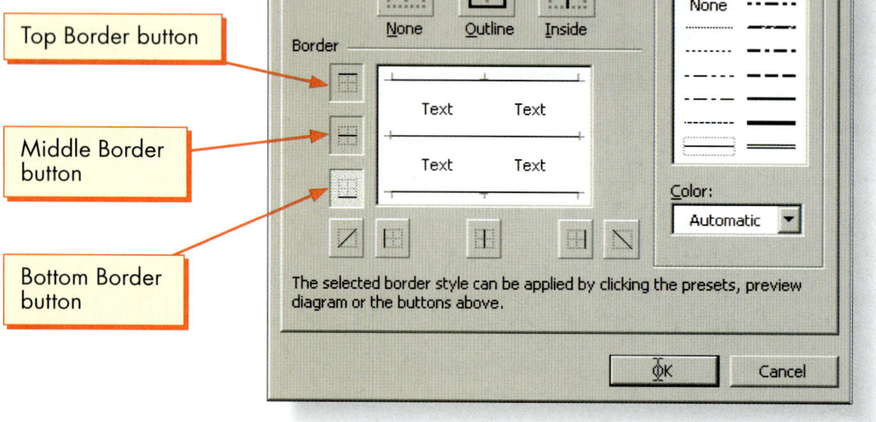

6. Select cells A2:K2 and cells A3:A13.

7. Click the arrow next to the Fill Color button.
8. Choose Gray-25% in the last column, the second row from the bottom.
9. Press Ctrl + Home.

EXERCISE 5-20 Change Page Orientation

Page orientation is a print setting that determines if the worksheet prints in a landscape or portrait orientation. The default is a *portrait* orientation, one that is taller than it is wide.

Many worksheets are too wide to fit in a portrait orientation. You can then try a landscape orientation. A *landscape* orientation is horizontal—the page is wider than it is tall.

1. Click the Print Preview button. The worksheet does not fit on a single page in a portrait orientation. You can see in the status bar that it requires more than one page.

2. Press PgDn. The part of the worksheet that does not fit appears on a second page.

TIP: Excel splits the worksheet between columns, based on the page margins.

3. Press PgUp to return to page 1.
4. Click Setup.
5. Click the Page tab.
6. Click the Landscape button in the Orientation group.
7. Click OK. The worksheet now fits on a single page with a landscape orientation.

EXERCISE 5-21 Change Scaling and Page Margins

In addition to changing the page orientation, Excel has a Scaling command that enables you to set a size percentage for the printed page. For example, you can set a worksheet to print at 50% of its size or 150% of its size. You might need to do this if you want to print the worksheet on a 5- by 7-inch card, for example, or if you want to enlarge it for a special display. When you enlarge a worksheet, your printer will split the pages between columns so you can tape the parts together.

You have seen that you can change margins by dragging the margin markers. If you need to set a precise margin and have difficulty dragging a marker, you can use the Margins tab to key a specific setting.

1. Click Setup.
2. Click the Page tab.
3. In the Scaling section, click the Adjust to button.
4. Double-click 100 and key **75**
5. Click OK. The worksheet is reduced to 75% of its normal size. This is only a print adjustment and does not affect the font sizes specified in the worksheet.
6. Click Setup. Click the Margins tab.
7. Double-click in the Left box and key **1**
8. Double-click in the Right box and key **1**. (See Figure 5-15 on the next page.)
9. Add your standard footer and print the worksheet. Click Close to exit from Print Preview.

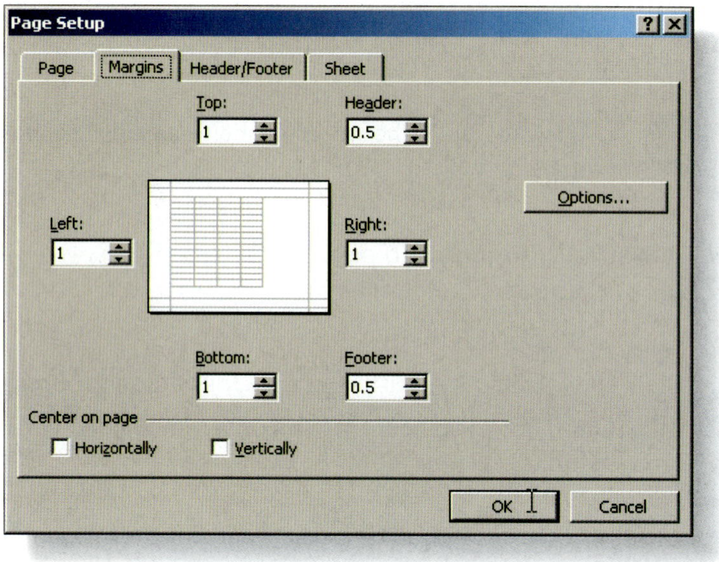

FIGURE 5-15 Margins tab for Page Setup

EXERCISE 5-22 Print Formulas

You can view the formulas within your worksheet all at once instead of checking the formula bar cell-by-cell. This enables you to troubleshoot problems more easily. It is also helpful to print a worksheet with the formulas visible to provide documentation for your work.

1. Press Ctrl + ~. The formulas in each cell are visible.

NOTE: You can turn the display of formulas on and off by choosing Tools, Options. Click the View tab and turn Formulas on or off.

2. Click the column A heading.
3. Scroll the worksheet to the right and hold down Shift while clicking the column K heading. All the columns are selected.
4. From the Format menu, choose Column and AutoFit Selection. Excel autofits each column to its longest entry.
5. Click the Print Preview button.
6. Click Setup and click the Page tab.
7. Double-click 75 in the Adjust to box and key **100**. Click OK. At its normal size, the worksheet occupies two pages, because printed formulas require more space than values.
8. Click Setup and click the Margins tab.
9. Double-click in the Left box and key **.5**. Double-click in the Right box and key **.5**.

TIP: You can either set a scaling percentage or choose the Fit to option.

10. Click the Page tab. In the Scaling section, click the Fit to button.

11. Choose **1** page(s) wide by **1** tall.

12. Click OK. Excel does its own scaling so the worksheet fits on a single landscape page with .5-inch left and right margins.

13. Click Print and click OK.

14. Press Ctrl+~ to hide the formulas. Press Ctrl+Home.

15. Save the workbook as ***[your initials]*****5-22** in your Lesson 5 folder.

16. Print the worksheet. Close the workbook.

USING HELP

You learned about basic math and statistical functions in this lesson. Use the Ask a Question box to obtain additional information about using and building functions.

Use Help to view additional information about functions:

1. Click in the Ask a Question box and key **functions**. Press Enter.

2. Click the topic About functions.

3. Click Show All in the top right corner. Scroll and read the information.

FIGURE 5-16
Learning about functions

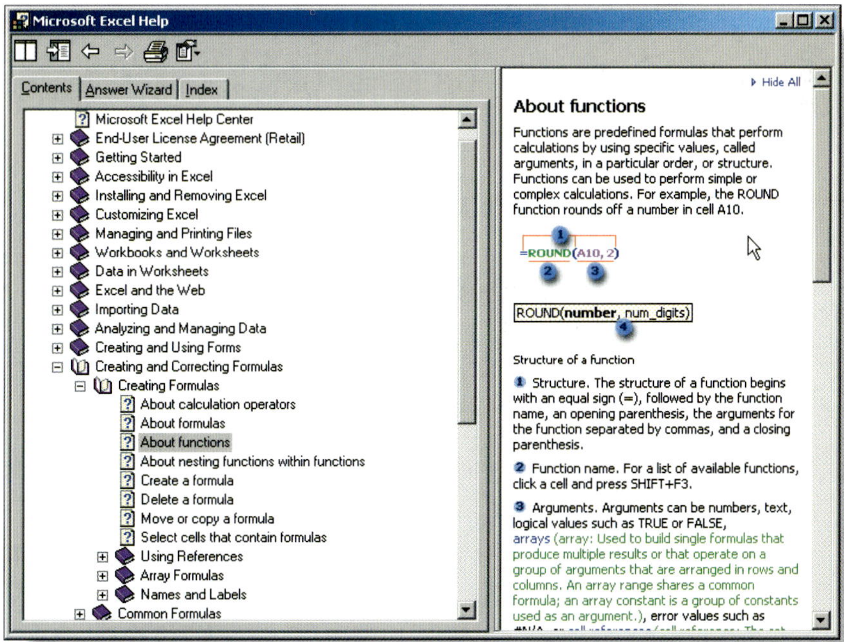

4. Close the Help window when you have finished reading about functions.

LESSON 2 Summary

- Use a template to create workbooks that use the same labels and other basic information on a routine basis.
- Templates can include such elements as labels, values, formatting, formulas, and pictures.
- You can edit a formula in the formula bar and within the cell in Edit mode.
- The Percent Style converts a decimal value to its percent equivalent.
- In calculating formulas, Excel follows mathematical order of precedence.
- You can establish a different order of precedence in a formula by keying parentheses around the calculations that you want performed first.
- Excel has several categories of business, mathematical, and statistical functions. You can key them in the cell or use the Insert Function button *fx*.
- Functions have a syntax that must be followed. For most functions, this includes an equal sign, the name of the function, and parentheses. Inside the parentheses, you show the function's arguments.
- The SUM function adds the cells or values indicated in its argument.
- The AVERAGE function calculates the arithmetic mean.
- The MIN function displays the smallest value in a range. The MAX function displays the largest value in a range.
- The COUNT function counts the number of values in a range. The COUNTA function does the same thing as the COUNT function, but includes labels.
- Excel has relative, absolute, and mixed references. These references determine what happens when the formula is copied.
- A portrait orientation prints a vertical page. A landscape page prints a horizontal page.
- The Scaling section of the Page tab enables you to print the worksheet in a reduced or enlarged size. You can also choose to have Excel fit the worksheet on a page.
- To set a precise margin, use the Margins tab in the Page Setup dialog box.
- You can print a worksheet with formulas displayed for documentation or help in locating problems.

LESSON 5 Command Summary

FEATURE	BUTTON	MENU	KEYBOARD	SPEECH
Absolute/ mixed reference			F4	
Display/ hide formulas		Tools, Options	Ctrl + ~	✓
Edit mode			F2	✓
Fit to page		File, Page Setup		✓
Increase Decimal	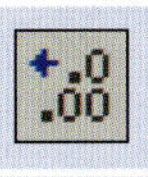	Format, Cells	Ctrl + F1	✓
Insert Function		Insert, Function		
New, from template		File, New	Ctrl + N	✓
Page margins	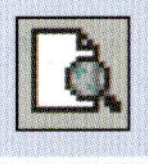	File, Page Setup		✓
Page orientation		File, Page Setup		✓
Percent Style	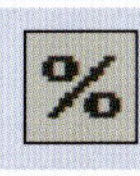	Format, Cells	Ctrl + F1	✓
Scaling		File, Page Setup		✓

Concepts Review

TRUE/FALSE QUESTIONS

Each of the following statements is either true or false. Indicate your choice by circling T or F.

T F *1.* A template opens as a new worksheet with the template name and a letter.

T F *2.* You must use the plus symbol on the numeric keypad in a formula.

T F *3.* The multiplication symbol in a formula is /.

T F *4.* To multiply by a percent, you must key the decimal equivalent of the percent.

T F *5.* You can control the order of precedence in a formula with parentheses.

T F *6.* Division is calculated before addition in a formula without parentheses.

T F *7.* AutoSum uses the SUM function.

T F *8.* An absolute reference does not adjust when the formula is copied to another cell.

SHORT ANSWER QUESTIONS

Write the correct answer in the space provided.

1. What is the keyboard shortcut to display or hide formulas?

____

2. Which page orientation is taller than it is wide?

____

3. How would the cell reference F3 be described?

____

4. What function displays the arithmetic mean of a range of cells?

____

5. What type of operation is being performed in the formula =A4*B4?

____

6. What term is used to describe the information between parentheses in a function?

____

7. What button displays a list of function categories and names?

____

8. What function would display the highest sales amount in a column?

____

CRITICAL THINKING

Answer these questions on a separate page. There are no right or wrong answers. Support your answers with examples from your own experience, if possible.

1. Why is it helpful to set the Zoom percentage while working? Is this different from scaling the worksheet?
2. Why is it necessary to have an absolute cell reference in some formulas? Why can't all formulas use relative references?

Lesson Applications

EXERCISE 5-23

Create a workbook from a template. Build addition and subtraction formulas.

1. Use the **KlassyKow** template to create a workbook. Save it as ***[your initials]*5-23**.

TIP: Look for recently used templates in the New from Template section of the New Workbook task pane.

2. Edit the label in cell C3 to show the current month.
3. Edit cells A7, A12, A17, and A22 to show the date of each Friday in the current month. If the current month has a fifth Friday, do not include it.
4. In cells B10:D10, key the following actual expenses:

   1300 1000 895

5. Add actual expenses for the weeks as follows:

FIGURE 5-17

Second week	1600	900	750
Third week	1000	1300	850
Fourth week	1200	2000	500

6. In cell B11, use a formula to subtract the actual expense from the budgeted amount. Copy the formula to cells C11:D11.
7. Select cells B11:D11 and click the Copy button.
8. Click cell B16 and click the Paste button. Paste again in cells B21 and B26. Press Esc when you finish.

NOTE: Negative numbers are shown in parentheses in this workbook. A negative number means the sales rep spent more money than budgeted.

9. In cell B28, add the budget amounts for Kim Tomasaki. Copy the formula for the other salespeople.
10. In cell B29, add the actual amounts for Kim Tomasaki. Copy the formula for the other salespeople.

11. In cell B30, subtract the total actual expense from the total budgeted amount. Copy the formula.
12. Select cells E28:E30 and click the AutoSum button Σ. Widen the column to show the data.
13. Add your standard footer with this addition: In the center section, show the filename as usual. Press Spacebar and add the worksheet tab name.

TIP: You can place more than one item in a footer/header section.

14. Print the worksheet. Save and close the workbook.

EXERCISE 5-24

Use Statistical functions. Use relative references. Change the page orientation. Adjust the scaling percentage.

1. Open **ShopPart** and save it as ***[your initials]*5-24** in your Lesson 5 folder.
2. In cell A21, key **Number of Shops**. Make the row 22.50 (30 pixels) high.
3. In cell B21, click the Insert Function button *fx*. Find and choose COUNTA. Select cells B7:B20 as its argument.
4. Copy the formula to cells C21:D21. The formula does not distinguish between Yes and No.
5. Click cell A7 and press Ctrl+H. In the Find what entry box, key **no** and press Tab. In the Replace with box, do not key anything. This will replace "No" with nothing, creating empty cells.
6. Click Find Next. Click Replace. The first occurrence of No is now an empty cell.

TIP: For multiple Find and Replace tasks, look at the first Find and Replace to make sure it is what you want. If it is, you can then click Replace All.

7. Click Replace All. Click OK and close the Find and Replace dialog box. The counts are updated.
8. Center cells B21:D21.
9. Change the page orientation to landscape. Set the scaling to print the worksheet at 110% of normal size.
10. Add your standard footer and print the worksheet.
11. Save and close the workbook.

EXERCISE 5-25

Use Math functions. Use absolute references.

1. Open **ORSundaes** and save it as ***[your initials]*5-25** in your Lesson 5 folder.
2. Key the following values in cells C4:C13.

FIGURE 5-18

	Location	Sundaes Sold
4	Ashland	1000
5	Eugene	1500
6	Klamath Falls	2250
7	Medford	1540
8	Roseburg	1250
9	Ashland	1200
10	Eugene	1650
11	Klamath Falls	2100
12	Medford	1020
13	Roseburg	950

3. Key the following values in cells C15:C19.

FIGURE 5-19

15	Ashland	900
16	Eugene	650
17	Klamath Falls	800
18	Medford	620
19	Roseburg	550

4. In cell H6, click the Insert Function button fx. Choose AVERAGE and use cells C4:C8 as Number1.
5. Display the Trace Error button menu and ignore the error.
6. Compute the average sales for medium and large sundaes in cells H7 and H8. Remove all Trace Error buttons.
7. In cell H9, key **=sum(** to start the formula. Select cells C4:C8 and press Enter.
8. Edit the formula in cell H9 to multiply the sum by the price in cell A5. Use an absolute reference for the price.
9. Repeat these steps to determine revenue for medium and large sundaes.

TIP: You can copy the formula in cell H9 and then edit the cell addresses for SUM as well as for the price.

10. In cell H13, add the three revenues to find a total.
11. Delete row 14. It is an unnecessary blank row.
12. Format the values in column C and cells H6:H8 as 12-point Times New Roman, Comma Style, with no decimal places.
13. Format cells H9:H11 and H13 as 12-point Times New Roman and Currency, with two decimal places.
14. Size all columns so all the data is visible.
15. Add your standard footer. Change the left margin to 1.25 inches.
16. Print the worksheet. Save and close the workbook.

EXERCISE 5-26 Challenge Yourself

Use parentheses and order of precedence.

1. Open **ICOrder**. Save it as ***[your initials]*5-26** in your Lesson 5 folder.
2. For three different items, key a value of your choice indicating how many of the items were purchased on this order. Use values less than 10.
3. In cell C14, determine the amount due. The formula should multiply the quantity by the price for each item. Then multiply that total by 1 + the tax rate. (You can use the tax rate that would apply in your state or you can use a 4.5% tax rate.)

TIP: A 4.5% tax rate makes the final cost 104.5% of the pre-tax total.

4. Add your standard footer and print the worksheet. Save the workbook.
5. Display and print the formulas on one landscape page.
6. Close the workbook without saving it.

On Your Own

In these exercises you work on your own, as you would in a real-life work environment. Use the skills you've learned to accomplish the task—and be creative.

EXERCISE 5-27

Create a new workbook that is a division table similar to the multiplication table you completed in this lesson. Apply borders and shading to make the worksheet easy to read. Print it in a landscape orientation that fits on one page. Add your standard footer. Save the workbook as ***[your initials]*5-27** in your Lesson 5 folder. Print the worksheet, save the workbook, and close it.

EXERCISE 5-28

Open ***[your initials]*4-33** from your Lesson 4 folder. Add a column at the right for **Average Cost per Meal**. Key a value for each restaurant and format the cells as currency with two decimals. In a cell in column A, two rows below your data, key **Tip Percentage**. Find out what an acceptable tip percentage is in your city and key it in column B. Add another column to your data for **Meal with Tip**. Then multiply your cost by the percentage (it's an absolute reference). Apply formatting, borders, and shading so your worksheet is consistent in its appearance. Save the workbook as ***[your initials]*5-28** in your Lesson 5 folder. Print the worksheet, save the workbook, and close it.

EXERCISE 5-29

Develop a worksheet based on one of your interests or hobbies. Make sure it contains at least 10 values. Use formulas that add, subtract, multiply, and divide the values in meaningful ways. Use all the functions introduced in this lesson. Then use absolute and mixed references and change the order of precedence by using parentheses in formulas. Make sure that all the formulas are labeled appropriately. Display the formulas. Add your standard footer. Save the worksheet as ***[your initials]*5-29** in your Lesson 5 folder. Print the worksheet and close the workbook.

LESSON 6

Using Logical and Financial Functions

OBJECTIVES

After completing this lesson, you will be able to:

1. **Use the IF function.**
2. **Use AND, OR, and NOT functions.**
3. **Work with styles.**
4. **Work with page breaks.**
5. **Use the PMT and FV functions.**

MOUS ACTIVITIES

In this lesson:

Ex2002 3-1
Ex2002 3-4
Ex2002 3-6
Ex2002 5-2

See Appendix E.

Estimated Time: 1½ hours

In addition to the mathematical and statistical functions you have used, Excel has many other categories of built-in functions. You will work with two new types of functions in this lesson–logical functions and financial functions.

A *logical function* involves a formula that determines whether something is true. There are only six logical functions: IF, AND, OR, NOT, TRUE, and FALSE. Except for the IF function, a formula with a logical function shows the word "TRUE" or "FALSE" as a result.

A *financial function* performs a common business calculation that involves money. These include how to determine depreciation and how to figure loan payments.

Using the IF Function

The IF function gives your worksheet decision-making capabilities. For example, if a bill is more than 30 days past due, you can decide if a late fee is added and how much the late fee will be. The IF function follows the form "If X, then Y; otherwise Z." X, Y, and Z represent the three arguments for the IF function.

The syntax for the IF function is:

=IF(logical_test, value_if_true, value_if_false)

Example: =IF(C5>50,C5*2,"None")

- Logical_test is the first argument, the condition. It's a statement or expression that is either true or false. For example, the expression C5>50 is either true or false.
- Value_if_true, the second argument, is what the formula shows if the condition is true. In the example, if C5 is greater than 50, it is multiplied by 2. The value_if_true can be a formula, a value, some text, or a cell reference.
- Value_if_false, the third argument, is what the formula shows if the condition is not true. The value_if_false can be a formula, a value, some text, or a cell reference. In the example, if C5 is not greater than 50, the result is the word "None."

EXERCISE 6-1 Use IF to Show Text

You can create an IF function to display text depending on whether the condition is true or false. For example, you could display "Delinquent Account" if the account is more than 30 days overdue. If you key an IF function, you must enclose the text to be displayed in quotation marks. If you use the Function Arguments dialog box, Excel inserts the quotation marks for you.

IF functions use relational or comparison operators as well as the usual arithmetic operators.

TABLE 6-1 Relational (Comparison) Operators

OPERATOR	DESCRIPTION
=	Equal to
<>	Not equal to
>	Greater than
<	Less than
>=	Greater than or equal to
<=	Less than or equal to

1. Open **BonusPay**. Press F12 and save the workbook as ***[your initials]*6-1** in a folder for Lesson 6.
2. Click cell C4.

3. Click the Insert Function button. In the Or select a category list, choose Logical.
4. Choose IF in the Select a function list. Click OK.
5. Click cell B4. The address appears in the Logical_test box.

REVIEW: Move the Function Arguments dialog box so you can see the cells you want to click.

6. Key > in the Logical_test box after B4.
7. Key **60000** in the Logical_test box after >. This test will determine if cell B4 is greater than 60000.
8. Click in the Value_if_true box.
9. Key **Yes**. If cell B4 is greater than 60000, cell C4 will display the word "Yes."
10. Click in the Value_if_false box.
11. Key **No**. If cell B4 is not greater than 60000, cell C4 will display the word "No."

FIGURE 6-1
Function Arguments dialog box for IF

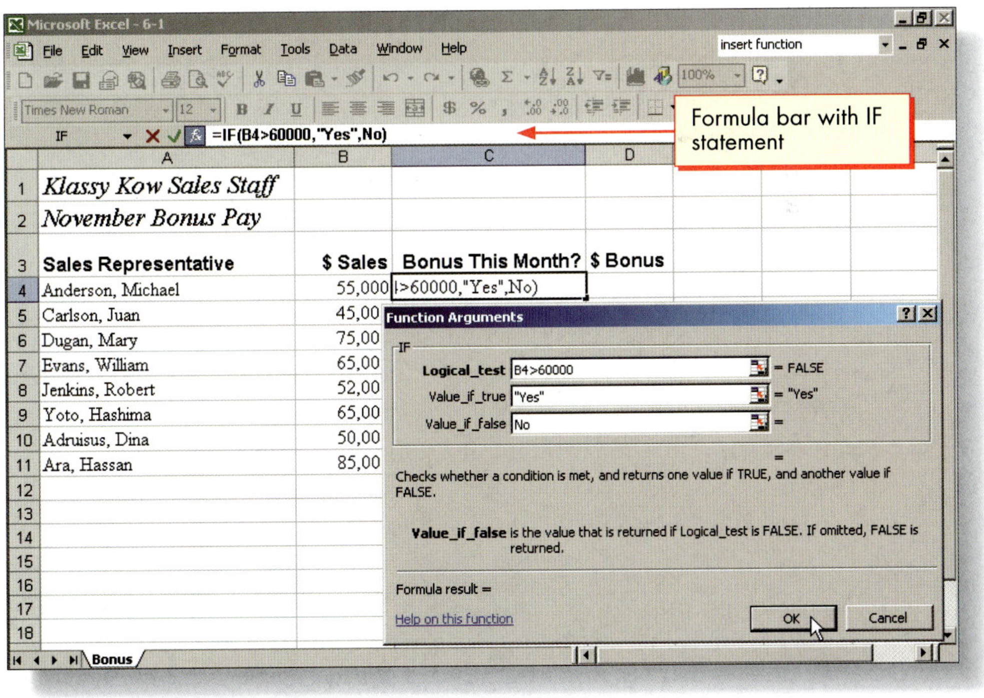

12. Click OK. The result of this IF formula for cell C4 is No.

13. Look at the formula in the formula bar. When you use the Function Arguments dialog box, quotation marks are inserted around the text for you.
14. Click the Center button and use the Fill handle to copy the formula to cell C11.

NOTE: The AutoFill Options button opens after you use the Fill handle. Just ignore it.

EXERCISE 6-2 Use IF to Calculate a Value

The result of an IF condition can show the value in a cell, or it can compute a result. Here's an example of how an IF statement might be used: Excel could determine if a salesperson fulfills the conditions to receive a bonus, and, if the conditions are met, could then calculate the bonus.

1. Click cell D4. Key **=if(** to start an IF formula. The ScreenTip displays the syntax for the function.
2. Click cell C4. A marquee appears around the cell, and the address appears after the left parenthesis. This starts the Logical_test.
3. Key **="yes"** after C4. This logical test will determine if cell C4 shows "Yes." Text in a logical test is not case sensitive.

NOTE: When you key text as part of the Logical_test, you must include quotation marks.

4. Key a comma after "yes" to separate the logical test from the value_if_true.
5. Click cell B4. A marquee appears around the cell and the address appears after the comma.
6. Key ***2.5%** after B4. The formula multiplies the sales amount by 2.5% if cell C4 shows "Yes."
7. Key a comma after "2.5%" to separate the value_if_true from the value_if_false.
8. Key **""** (two quotation marks with nothing between them). This represents no text, or nothing. If cell C4 does not show "Yes," cell D4 will show nothing. It will be blank. (See Figure 6-2 on the next page.)
9. Press Enter. Excel added the closing right parenthesis for you. Cell D4 shows nothing, because this sales rep does not receive a bonus.
10. Click cell D4 and click the Comma Style button.
11. Use the Fill handle to copy the formula to cell D11.
12. Click the Decrease Decimal button two times.

FIGURE 6-2 Keying an IF statement

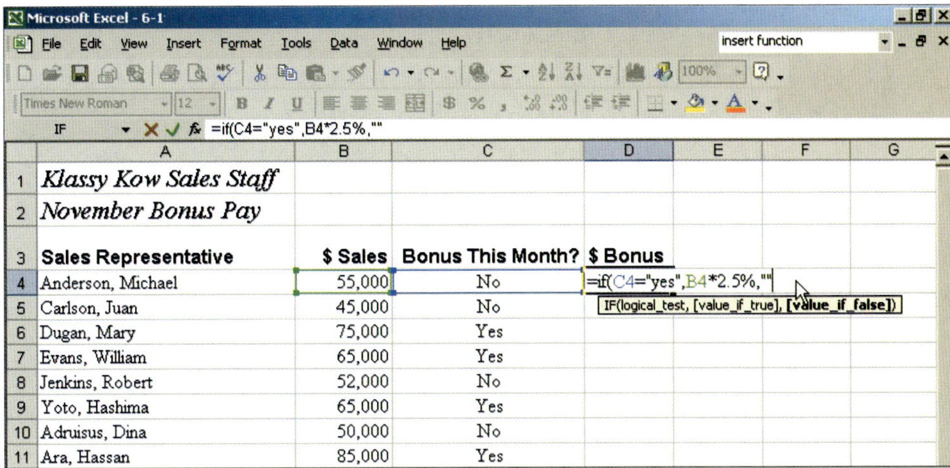

13. Add your standard footer and print the worksheet.
14. Save the workbook ***[your initials]*6-2** in your Lesson 6 folder.
15. Close the workbook.

Using AND, OR, and NOT Functions

The AND, OR, and NOT functions are logical functions that show either "TRUE" or "FALSE" in the cell. These functions ignore labels and empty cells, so you use them only with values (numbers).

EXERCISE 6-3 Use the AND Function

In an AND function, you can use several logical tests. All tests or expressions must be true for the result cell to show TRUE. Otherwise, it shows FALSE.

TABLE 6-2 Examples of the AND Function

EXPRESSION	RESULT IS
AND(C4>10, D4>10)	TRUE if both C4 and D4 are greater than 10; FALSE if either C4 or D4 is 10 or less.
AND(C4>10, C4<100)	TRUE if C4 is greater than 10 but less than 100; FALSE if C4 is 10 or less than 10 or 100 or greater than 100.
AND(C4>10, D4>10	FALSE if C4 is greater than 10 but D4 is 10 or less than 10; TRUE if both C4 and D4 are greater than 10.
AND(C4>10, C4<100)	FALSE if C4 is greater than or equal to 100 or less than 10; TRUE if C4 is between 10 and 100.

1. Open **CustCount**.
2. Use AutoFill for cell D3 to fill in the days of the week up to column I.
3. In cell J3, key **Over 150 on Weekend?**
4. Click cell J4.
5. Click the Insert Function button *fx*. In the Or select a category list, choose Logical.
6. Choose AND and click OK.
7. Click cell G4. The address appears in the Logical1 box.
8. Key **>** in the Logical1 box after G4.
9. Key **150**, but don't press Enter yet. This test will determine if cell G4 is greater than 150.

NOTE: Don't click OK or press Enter until you have entered all arguments in the Function Arguments dialog box.

10. Click in the Logical2 box. Click cell H4 and key **>150**. The second condition is that cell H4 also is greater than 150.
11. Click in the Logical3 box. Click cell I4 and key **>150**. The third condition is that cell I4 is greater than 150.

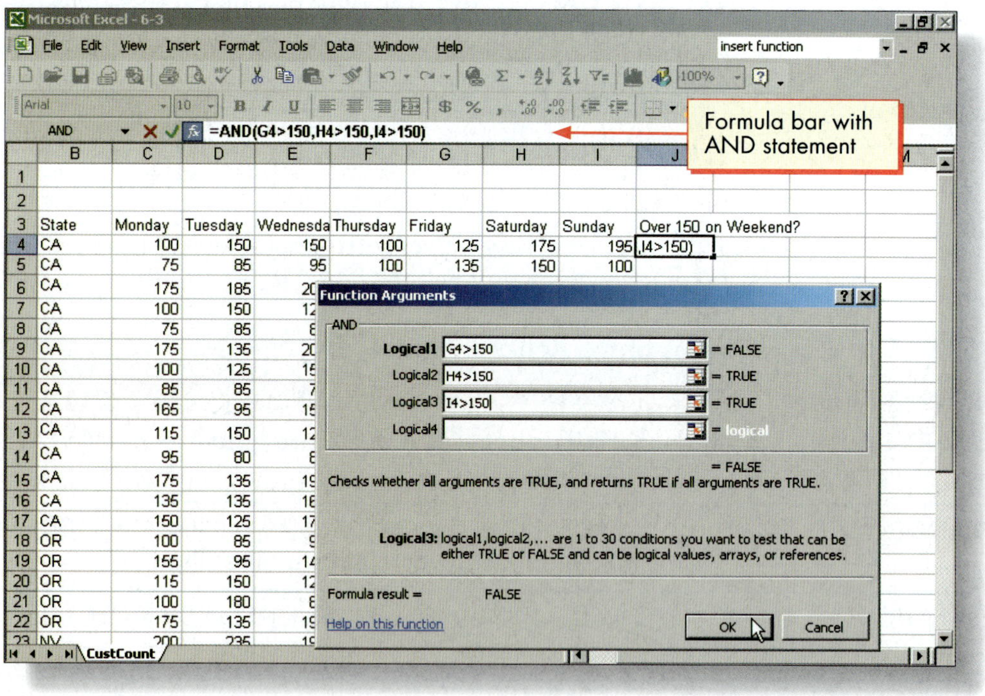

FIGURE 6-3
Function Arguments dialog box for AND

12. Click OK. The customer count must be greater than 150 each weekend day to show TRUE. Look at the formula in the formula bar.

13. Copy the formula to cell J35. Only weekends in which all three days were greater than 150 show TRUE. A day's count that is equal to 150 is not greater than 150.
14. Turn on Wrap text for cell J3. Format row 3 as 37.50 (50 pixels) high. Autofit column J.

EXERCISE 6-4 Use the OR Function

In an OR function, any one of your logical tests can be true for the result cell to show TRUE. If they are all false, the result is FALSE.

TABLE 6-3 Examples of the OR Function

EXPRESSION	RESULT IS
OR(C4>10, D4>10)	TRUE if either C4 or D4 are greater than 10; FALSE only if both C4 and D4 are less than or equal to 10.
OR(C4>10, D4<100)	TRUE if C4 is greater than 10 or if D4 is less than 100; FALSE only if C4 is equal to or less than 10 and D4 is equal to or greater than 100.
OR(C4>10, D4>10)	TRUE if either C4 or D4 is greater than 10; FALSE only if C4 is equal to or less than 10 and D4 is equal to or less than 10.

1. Display the drag-and-drop pointer for cell J3.

REVIEW: Point at any edge of the cell to display the drag-and-drop pointer.

2. Hold down Ctrl. Drag a copy of the label to cell K3.
3. Press F2 and edit the copied label to read **Over 175 On Weekend?** Autofit column K.
4. In cell K4, key **=or(** to start the function.
5. Click cell G4. A marquee appears around the cell, and the address appears in the formula.
6. Key **>** after G4. Key **175** after >. This logical test will determine if cell G4 is greater than 175.
7. Key a comma after 175.
8. Click cell H4. Key **>175**. The second condition will test if cell H4 is greater than 175.

9. Key a comma and click cell I4. Key **>175**

FIGURE 6-4
Keying an OR function

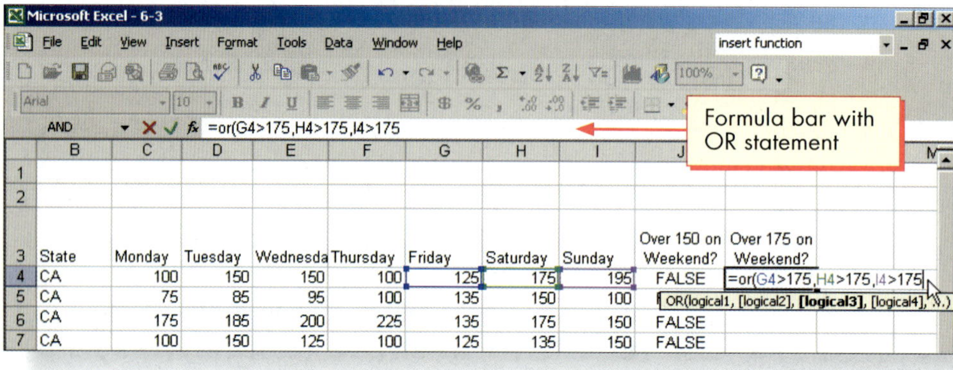

REVIEW: You can click the Enter button in the formula bar to complete a formula.

10. Press Enter. If the customer count is greater than 175 on any weekend day, the result is TRUE. Look at the formula in the formula bar.

11. Use AutoFill to copy the formula to cell K35.

EXERCISE 6-5 Use the NOT Function

In the NOT function, the reverse or opposite of your condition must be true for the result cell to show TRUE. The NOT function has one argument.

TABLE 6-4

Examples of the NOT Function

EXPRESSION	RESULT IS
NOT(C4>10)	TRUE if C4 is 10 or less than 10; FALSE if C4 is 11 or greater.
NOT(C4=10)	TRUE if C4 contains any value other than 10; FALSE if C4 is 10.

1. Click cell L3. Key **Sunday>100?**

2. Click cell L4. Key **=not(** and click cell I4.

3. Key **<100**. The formula tests if cell I4 is less than 100. If cell I4 contains 100 or a number greater than 100, cell L4 will show TRUE. (See Figure 6-5 on the next page.)

4. Press Enter.

5. Copy the formula to L35. All stores had at least 100 customers on Sunday.

FIGURE 6-5
Keying a NOT function

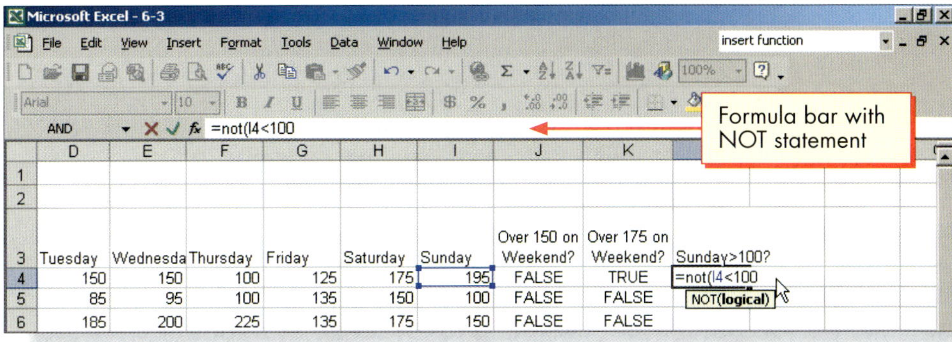

6. Save the workbook as ***[your initials]*6-5** in your folder for Lesson 6.

Working with Styles

A *style* is a set of formatting specifications for labels or values. You have already used some of Excel's default styles when you clicked the Currency Style button, the Comma Style button, or the Percent Style button. There are six possible predefined styles for a new workbook: Comma, Comma [0], Currency, Currency [0], Normal, and Percent. The default style for new data keyed in a new workbook is Normal. Comma, Currency, and Percent styles are available as buttons on the Formatting toolbar.

EXERCISE 6-6 Apply a Style

1. Select cells C36:I36 and click the AutoSum button.
2. From the Format menu choose Style. The Style dialog box shows that the Normal style is used for these values. The settings for the Normal style are also shown.
3. Click the arrow next to the Style name list. The six default styles are listed.

FIGURE 6-6
Style dialog box

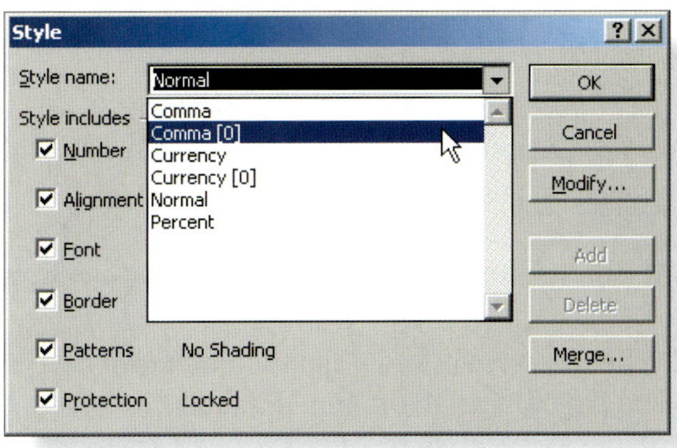

4. Choose Comma [0]. This is the comma style with no decimal places.
5. Click OK. Notice that these cells are now not properly aligned with the rest of the values in the columns. You will fix that in the next exercise.

EXERCISE 6-7 Clear Cell Formats and Reapply a Style

You can remove a style as well as your own formatting from a cell or a range. The cell(s) then return to the default Normal style.

1. From the Edit menu, choose Clear and then Formats. The cells in row 36 are returned to the Normal style.
2. Click cell C4 and press [F8] to start Extend Selection mode.
3. Press [→] six times to select up to column I.
4. Hold down [Ctrl] and press [↓].
5. From the Format menu, choose Style.
6. Click the arrow next to the Style name list. Choose Comma [0].
7. Click OK. The new style is applied and all the values are properly aligned.
8. Press [Ctrl]+[Home].

Working with Page Breaks

A *page break* is a code that tells the printer to start a new page. When a worksheet is too wide or too tall to fit on the default paper size for your printer, Excel inserts an automatic page break. This page break appears as a dashed line on the screen. You can accept Excel's location for page breaks, or you can move the break to a new location.

EXERCISE 6-8 Preview and Change Page Breaks

1. Click the Print Preview button. You can see that the worksheet is too wide to print in a portrait orientation.
2. Press [PgDn]. The part of the worksheet that does not fit on the first page is shown on page 2.

NOTE: In Print Preview, [PgDn] moves to the next page only if your screen is showing a reduced view of the worksheet. If you don't see the second page, click the Zoom button to zoom out.

3. Click Page Break Preview. A message box explains how you can adjust page breaks.
4. Click OK. The pages are shown next to each other with a background page number. The page break is the blue dashed line.

NOTE: The background page number does not print.

FIGURE 6-7
Page Break Preview

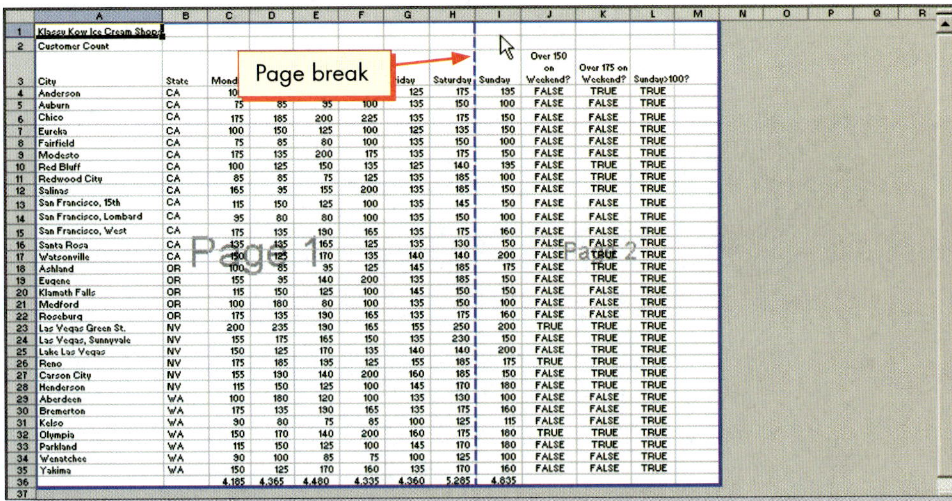

5. Place the pointer on the blue dashed line to display a two-headed arrow.
6. Click and drag the dashed blue line to the left so it is between columns F and G.
7. Release the mouse button. The page break line is now solid blue. It turns solid blue whenever you manually set or adjust it.
8. Widen any column in which the label in row 3 is not visible.

TIP: You can autofit columns while in Page Break Preview.

9. Click the Print Preview button again. The screen shows the normal Print Preview.
10. Click Normal View to return to the worksheet. You can see dashed lines for page breaks in Normal View.

EXERCISE 6-9 Insert a Page Break

If, for example, you decided you want only three columns to print per page, you could insert your own page breaks to create the look you want. You can also delete page breaks if you decide to change the page orientation and fit more columns per page. When you insert a page break, it is placed to the left of the active cell.

1. Click the Print Preview button .

2. Click Page Break Preview. Click OK in the message box.
3. Click cell J1. If you insert a page break here, it will be between columns I and J.
4. From the Insert menu, choose Page Break. The page break is solid blue because you inserted it manually.

FIGURE 6-8
Inserting a page break

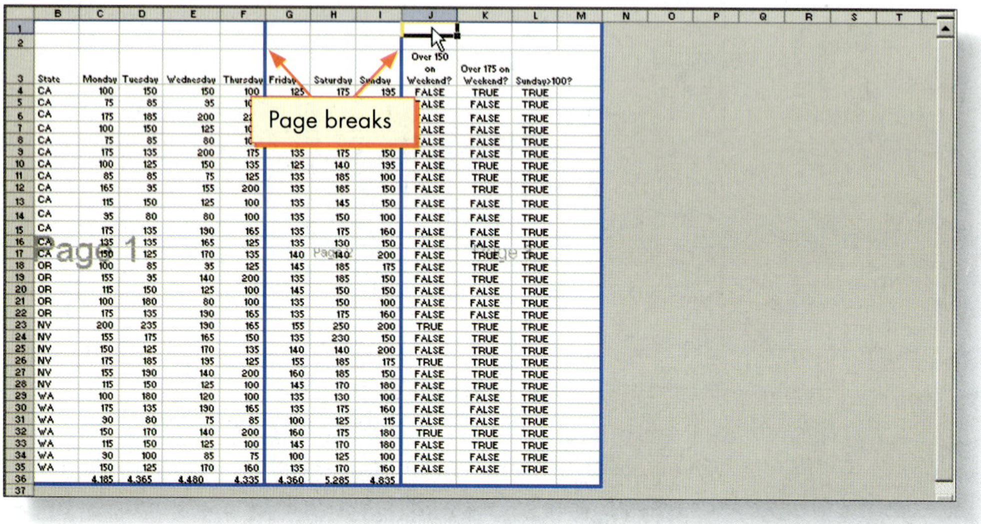

5. Click the Print Preview button.
6. Press PgDn to view the pages.

EXERCISE 6-10 Set Print Titles

To make this three-page worksheet easier to follow, you can repeat the labels in column A on each printed page. Then you will see the city name on each page so it is easy to determine which values belong with each city.

1. Click Setup.
2. Click the Sheet tab.
3. Click to place a check mark for Gridlines. Notice that the Print titles section is dimmed because you cannot set these titles from Print Preview.
4. Click OK. Click Normal View.
5. From the File menu, choose Page Setup.
6. Click the Sheet tab. This is the same dialog box you see from Print Preview, but the Print titles section is now available.
7. Click to place an insertion point in the Columns to repeat at left text box.

8. Click anywhere in column A.

FIGURE 6-9
Setting print titles

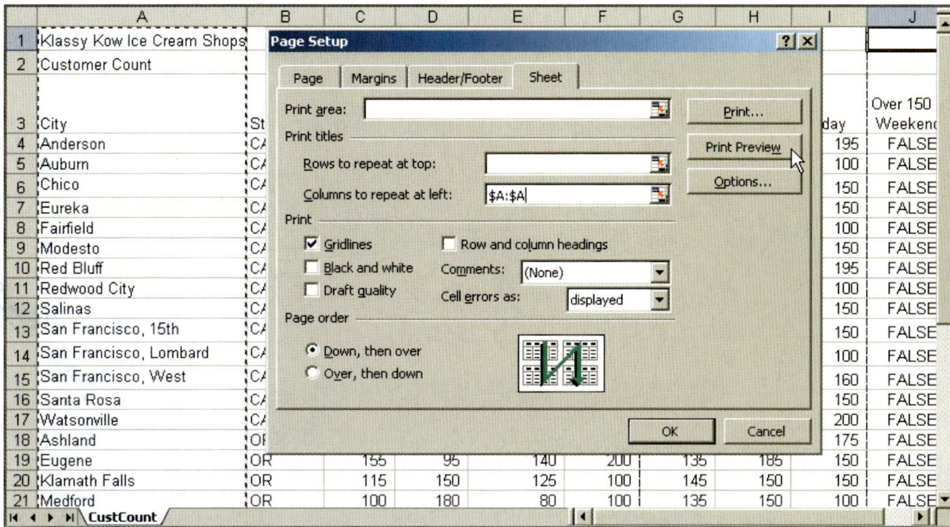

9. Click Print Preview.

10. Press PgDn and PgUp to view the pages.

EXERCISE 6-11 Center a Page Horizontally

Although you can change the left and right margins to make a page appear centered, Excel can automatically center a worksheet horizontally or vertically on the printed page.

1. Click Setup.
2. Click the Margins tab.
3. In the Center on page section, choose Horizontally.
4. Click OK. All pages are horizontally centered.

EXERCISE 6-12 Change the Footer Font and Print Page Numbers

The default font for data in headers and footers is 10-point Arial. You can change any section in the footer to any font and size available on your computer.

1. Click Setup and the Header/Footer tab. Click Custom Footer.
2. In the Left section, click the Font button A.
3. Choose 8 as the Size and click OK.

4. Key ***[your first and last name]***. The font is applied as you type.
5. Click in the Center section.

6. Click the Page Number button. The code is &[Page], and it is 10-point Arial.
7. Press Spacebar to insert a space after &[Page].
8. Key **of** and press Spacebar.

9. Click the Pages button. The code is &[Pages]. This footer will display Page 1 of 3 on the first page.
10. Drag across &[Page] of &[Pages] to select all of it.
11. Click the Font button. Choose 8 as the Size and click OK.

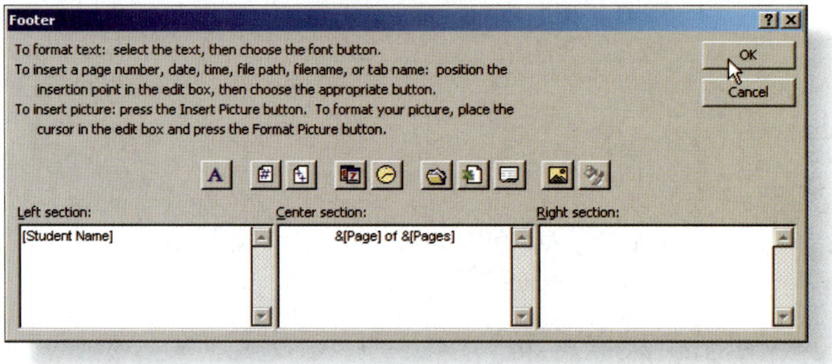

FIGURE 6-10 Printing page numbers

12. Click in the Right section and click the Font button.
13. Choose 8 as the Size and click OK. Insert the filename.
14. Close the Footer and Page Setup dialog boxes and then close Print Preview.
15. Print the worksheet.

EXERCISE 6-13 Remove a Page Break

You can remove a manual page break and let Excel insert its own page breaks if they are needed.

1. Click the Print Preview button.
2. Click Page Break Preview and click OK.
3. Click cell J1. The page break is to the left of this column.
4. From the Insert menu, choose Remove Page Break.
5. From the View menu, choose Normal.
6. Save the workbook as ***[your initials]*6-13** in your Lesson 6 folder.
7. Close the workbook.

Using the PMT and FV Functions

Financial functions analyze money transactions such as loans and savings or investment plans. The PMT and FV functions use the idea of an annuity. An *annuity* is a series of equal payments made at regular intervals for a specified period of time.

Many of Excel's financial functions use the same or similar arguments:

- *Rate* is the interest for the period. If you make monthly payments, you must divide the rate by 12 to find the monthly interest rate.
- *Nper* is the total number of periods during which a payment is made. Another way to look at this argument is that it is the total number of payments. For example, a five-year loan with monthly payments would use an Nper of 60 (12 months a year * 5 years).
- *PV* is present value or the amount of the loan. It is the current cash value of the money transaction.
- *FV* is future value or the cash balance at the end of the total time period. For a loan, the FV is 0 because you must pay back every penny. For an investment, FV is how much you will have at the end of your savings or investment time.
- *Type* specifies whether payments are made at the beginning or the end of the period.

EXERCISE 6-14 Use the PMT Function

The PMT ("Payments") function can be used to determine how much your monthly payments are if you borrow money to buy a computer, a car, or a house.

When constructing these formulas you will notice that the various values for the arguments required by the function are often placed in individual cells. This lets you use the cell reference as the argument for the function. If you want to test different scenarios, you can simply change the values in the cells and the function will recalculate, using the new values.

1. Open **CU**.
2. In cell B4, key **4** to plan a four-year loan.
3. In cell B5, key **=** to use a formula to compute the number of payments.
4. Click cell B4 and key ***12**. Press Enter. You will make a total of 48 payments (4 years * 12 months in a year).

TIP: By using a formula to determine the number of payments, you only need to change the number of years to test different loan lengths. That's why the number of years is placed in a cell by itself. The formula will refer to cell B5 for the Nper.

5. In cell B6, key **20000**, the amount of money borrowed.
6. In cell B7, key **4.9%** as the interest rate.
7. Click cell B9.
8. Click the Insert Function button.
9. In the Or select a category list, choose Financial.
10. Click PMT (you might have to scroll down the list). Click OK.
11. Click cell B7. The cell address appears in the Rate box, the first argument.
12. Key **/12** in the Rate box after B7. An annual interest rate must be divided by 12 to figure a monthly payment.
13. Click in the Nper box. This argument is the total number of payments.
14. Click cell B5 for the number of payments.
15. Click in the Pv box and click cell B6. The present value is the cash for the loan now.
16. Click in the Fv box. The future value is what you will owe at the end of the loan, 0. You do not need to enter anything in this box.
17. Click in the Type box and key **1** for a payment at the beginning of the month.

TIP: Most loans use Type 1 because it costs less to pay at the beginning of the month than at the end.

FIGURE 6-11
Function Arguments dialog box for PMT

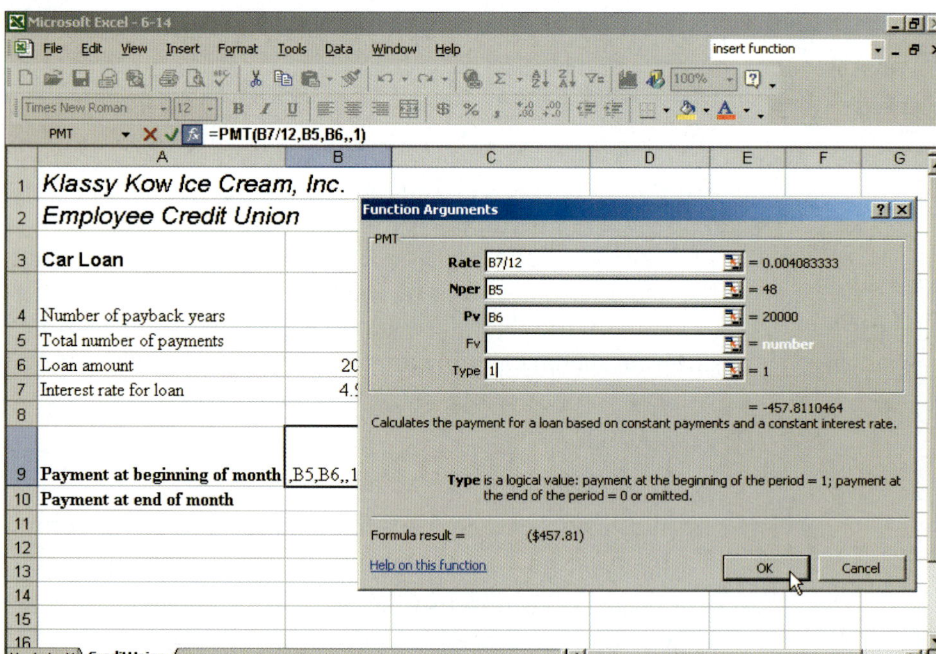

18. Click OK. The result is a negative number, because it is money that you have to pay. It is money out of your pocket.

EXERCISE 6-15 Key a PMT Function

Rather than using the Insert Function button and the Function Arguments dialog box, you key a PMT function from scratch in this exercise.

1. Click cell B10.
2. Key **=pmt(** to start the function.
3. Click cell B7 for the Rate, the first argument in the PMT function.
4. Key **/12** to divide the rate by 12.
5. Key a comma to separate the arguments.
6. Click cell B5. The second argument is the number of payments.
7. Key another comma, and click cell B6. This is the present value or the amount of the loan.
8. Press Enter. If you do not key a future value, Excel assumes it is 0. If you do not key a type, it is assumed to be a 0 type.

FIGURE 6-12 Keying a PMT function

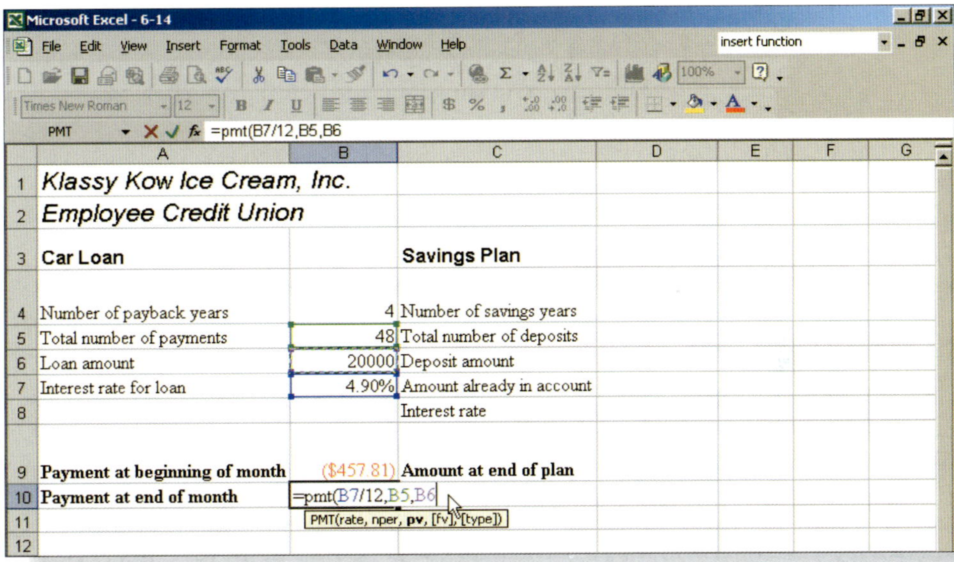

EXERCISE 6-16 Use the FV Function

The FV ("Future Value") function can be used to determine such things as how much you will have in your savings account if you make regular deposits. You could also include any money currently in the account when you start.

1. Click cell D4 and key **5** to plan a five-year savings plan.

2. In cell D5, key =
3. Click cell D4 and key ***12**. Press Enter.
4. In cell D6, key **50** as the amount saved each month.
5. In cell D7, key **1000** as the amount of money already in the account.
6. In cell D8, key **5.25%** as the interest rate.

REVIEW: If you do not key the % sign, you must key the decimal equivalent of the value.

7. In cell D9, click the Insert Function button *fx*.
8. Choose Financial and FV. Click OK.
9. Click cell D8 for the Rate. Key **/12** in the Rate box after D8.
10. Click in the Nper box and then click cell D5.

NOTE: The Function Arguments dialog box shows the syntax and a description of each argument when you click its box.

11. Click in the Pmt box and click cell D6. The payment is how much you plan to pay into your savings account each month.
12. Click the Pv box and click cell D7. The present value is what you have in the account to start.
13. Click the Type box and key **1** for a deposit at the beginning of the month.

TIP: In a savings plan, Type 1 pays more interest.

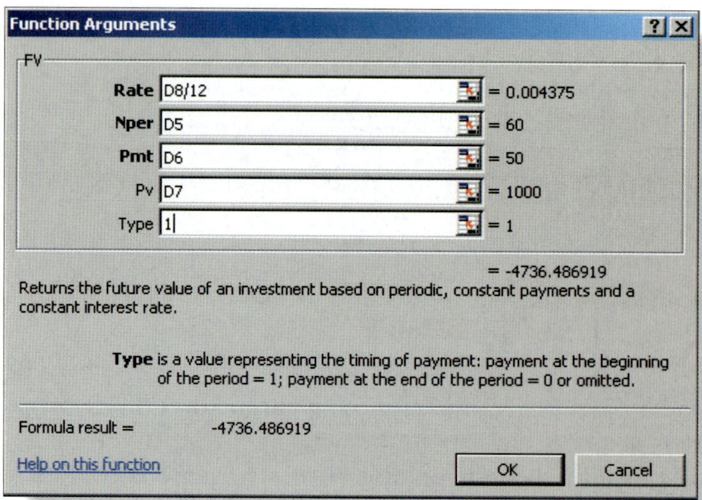

FIGURE 6-13
Function Arguments dialog box for FV

14. Click **OK**. The result is shown as a negative number, because the FV function assumes the bank's or lender's point of view. This is money that they would have to pay to you.

EXERCISE 6-17 Format Negative Numbers

Many business reports show negative numbers in red. Excel's Number and Currency formats can show negative numbers in red or black, with or without parentheses, with a leading minus sign, or simply in parentheses. The Accounting style shows negative numbers in parentheses.

TIP: If you print to a black-ink printer, don't show negative numbers in red.

1. Select cells B9:B10 and cell D9.
2. Press Ctrl+1.
3. Click the **Number** tab and choose **Currency**.
4. In the **Negative numbers** list, choose the non-red **($1,234.10)**.
5. Click **OK**.
6. Click the Bold button **B** while the cells are selected.
7. Add your standard footer.
8. Save the workbook as ***[your initials]*6-17** in your Lesson 6 folder.
9. Print the worksheet and close the workbook.

LESSON 6 Summary

- The IF function enables you to create formulas that test whether a condition is true. If it is true, you specify what should be shown or done. You also set what appears or is done if the condition is false.
- The IF function can show text in its result, it can calculate a value, or it can show a cell reference.
- AND, OR, and NOT are logical functions that show either TRUE or FALSE as a result.
- Logical functions use relational or comparison operators.
- A style is a set of formatting specifications for labels and values.

- You can remove all formatting from a cell and return to the default Normal Style.
- Page breaks determine where a new page starts. Excel inserts page breaks based on the paper size and the margins.
- You can insert and delete your own page breaks.
- Page Break Preview shows the page breaks as solid or dashed blue lines.
- If a worksheet requires more than one page, you can repeat column or row headings from page to page to make it easier to read the worksheet.
- The Margins tab in the Page Setup dialog box includes options to center a page horizontally or vertically.
- The Font button in the Custom Header/Footer dialog box opens the Font dialog box for regular font changes.
- You can print each page number as well as the total number of pages in a worksheet as a header or a footer.
- Financial functions include PMT ("Payment") and FV ("Future Value") and other common business calculations.
- The PMT function calculates a regular payment for a loan, using an interest rate.
- The FV function calculates how much an amount (including any added payments) will be worth in the future at a given interest rate.
- Negative numbers can be shown in red, within parentheses, or with a leading minus (–) sign.

LESSON 6 Command Summary

FEATURE	BUTTON	MENU	KEYBOARD	SPEECH
Apply style		Format, Style		✓
Center page		File, Page Setup		✓
Delete page break		Insert, Remove Page Break		✓
Insert page break		Insert, Page Break		✓
Page break preview		View, Page Break Preview		✓
Print titles		File, Page Setup		✓

Concepts Review

TRUE/FALSE QUESTIONS

Each of the following statements is either true or false. Indicate your choice by circling T or F.

T F 1. An IF function has three arguments.

T F 2. You must key quotation marks around text in the Function Arguments dialog box.

T F 3. The AND and OR functions usually show the same results.

T F 4. Excel has a preset style for each Number category in the Format Cells dialog box.

T F 5. Arguments in a function are separated by commas.

T F 6. Most of Excel's styles have a button on the Standard toolbar.

T F 7. The PMT function determines how much your money will grow over a period of time.

T F 8. The Print Titles option can repeat rows or columns on each page of a worksheet.

SHORT ANSWER QUESTIONS

Write the correct answer in the space provided.

1. What dialog box helps you complete built-in functions?

____

2. Which argument in a financial function refers to the total number of periods (also the total number of payments or deposits)?

____

3. Which logical function shows the opposite of the condition?

____

4. What Excel feature describes a set of formatting specifications?

____

5. What menu and menu option do you use to manually place a page break?

____

6. How can you distinguish between an automatic page break and one that you placed?

____

7. Which financial function would help you determine how much money will be in your account at the end of a year if you make regular deposits?

____

8. What is the purpose of the Type argument in financial functions?

____

CRITICAL THINKING

Answer these questions on a separate page. There are no right or wrong answers. Support your answers with examples from your own experience, if possible.

1. Why are there separate logical operators for greater than (>) and greater than or equal to (>=)?

2. What other functions do you recognize from the Insert Function dialog box? How would you test them?

Lesson Applications

EXERCISE 6-18

Use the IF function.

1. Use the **KlassyBirth** template to create a workbook. Save it as ***[your initials]*6-18** in your Lesson 6 folder.

TIP: Look for recently used templates in the New from Template section of the New Workbook task pane.

2. Change the label in cell C3 to show **Favorite Flavor**
3. In cells A4:D9, key the following information:

FIGURE 6-14

	Name	Shop	Favorite Flavor	Male/Female
4	Marian Most	Las Vegas, Green	Chocolate	F
5	Tommy Dunne	Lake Las Vegas	Bubble Gum Goo	M
6	Luella Orr	Carson City	Chocolate	F
7	Patrick Adams	Reno	Vanilla	M
8	Asata Akai	Henderson	Strawberry	F
9	Efren Aldo	Las Vegas, Sunnyvale	Chocolate	M

4. Widen column B to fit the longest item. Left-align the flavors in column C.
5. Key **Chocolate?** as the label in cell E3. Copy the format from one of the other labels and adjust the column width to fit the label.
6. Use the IF function in cell E4 with C4="chocolate" as the Logical_test. Show **Yes** if the customer's favorite flavor is chocolate. Show **Other** if chocolate is not the favorite. Copy the formula for the rest of the column, and center the results.
7. Change the page orientation to landscape. Add your standard footer and print the worksheet.
8. Save the workbook.

NOTE: If the Picture toolbar pops up, click its Close button [X].

9. Press Ctrl+~. Adjust the width of each column manually to fit its longest entry, but don't fit the width to the main titles or the image.
10. Print the formulas to fit on one landscape page.
11. Close the workbook without saving.

EXERCISE 6-19

Work with page breaks.

The financial staff keeps track of the retirement accounts managed by Klassy Kow for its employees. The worksheet needs to be printed with each year on a separate page. Each year shows five funds and a total. There are a few more formatting changes and you will need to check for errors, as well.

1. Open **RetireAcct** and save it as ***[your initials]*6-19** in your Lesson 6 folder.

TIP: Set the Zoom percentage to 75% to see more on the screen.

2. Autofit each column that is not wide enough.
3. Select cells A7:A8 and A12:A16. Press Ctrl+1. Set a horizontal left indent of 1. Set a left indent of 2 for cells A9:A10.
4. Select cells B3:G3 and center the range across the selection. Repeat these steps for years 2001 and 2000.
5. Change the page orientation to landscape.
6. In Page Break Preview, drag the first page break so it is between columns G and H, if it is not already there. The second page break should be between columns M and N.

7. Click the Print Preview button [Print Preview] and view all three pages.

NOTE: If Excel inserts an automatic page break as you switch views, just drag the new dashed line on top of your solid line.

8. Close print preview. From the File menu, choose Page Setup. Repeat rows 1:2 and column A:A as print titles.
9. Add the standard custom footer and show the page number after your name. Print the worksheet.
10. Locate any cells that display green error triangles. Display the error message. On a separate sheet of paper, write an explanation of what is wrong.

NOTE: Make sure to include your name, the date, the exercise number, and the exercise step on your piece of paper.

11. Save and close the workbook.

EXERCISE 6-20

Use AND and OR functions.

1. Open **SerAwards**. Save it as ***[your initials]*6-20** in your Lesson 6 folder.
2. In cell E4, use an AND function to show TRUE if the employee has greater than 2 years of service and a performance rating equal to 4. Copy the formula to rows E5:E16.
3. In cell F4, use an OR function to show TRUE if the employee has greater than 4 years of service or a performance rating equal to 4. Copy the formula to cells F5:F16.
4. Set the page to be horizontally centered. Add your standard footer, using a 9-point font, and print the worksheet.
5. Save and close the workbook.

EXERCISE 6-21 Challenge Yourself

Use the PMT function to calculate mortgage payments at different interest rates.

Klassy Kow Ice Cream, Inc., is in the process of choosing a construction loan to finance expansion at the headquarters building. They have compiled information from four lenders. You are now ready to build a worksheet to analyze the results. The loan will be for 10 years with payments made at the beginning of each month. The company wants to borrow $500,000.

1. Create a new workbook and save it as ***[your initials]*6-21** in your folder for Lesson 6.
2. Key **Construction Loan Comparison** in cell A1 and choose a large font size. In cell A2, key **As of mm/dd/yy** (use today's date). Make this cell 2 points smaller than the font size you used in cell A1.
3. Key the following in cells B3:C5 (don't key anything in cell C5 yet):

Loan Amount	**-$500,000**
Years to Repay	**15**
Number of Payments	

TIP: If you key a dollar sign with a value, the value is formatted as Currency.

4. Key a formula in cell C5 to determine the total number of payments.
5. Widen column B to show the label in cell B5, and format row 3 as 22.50 (30 pixels) high.
6. Select cells A3:D6 and apply Outside Borders.
7. Key the information shown in Figure 6-15.

FIGURE 6-15

	B	C	D	E
9	Lender Name	Rate	Monthly Payment	Total Cost
10	Freedom Financial	11%		
11	Southwest Lenders	10.75%		
12	East-West Bank	11.25%		
13	State Investment Trust	10.65%		

8. Make the labels in row 9 bold and centered. Turn on Wrap text for cells D9:E9.
9. Use the PMT function in cell D10 to determine the monthly payment for the first lender. Because you will copy the formula for the other lenders, use absolute references where appropriate. Copy the formula.

NOTE: If you make the loan amount a negative number, the payment amounts will be positive values.

10. In cell E10, key a formula to multiply the monthly payment by the total number of payments. Use an absolute reference where appropriate so you can copy this formula, too. Copy the formula.
11. Make any formatting changes so your worksheet is attractive and easy to read.
12. Add your standard footer and print the worksheet. Save the workbook.
13. Display and print the formulas on one landscape page.
14. Close the workbook without saving.

On Your Own

In these exercises you work on your own, as you would in a real-life work environment. Use the skills you've learned to accomplish the task—and be creative.

EXERCISE 6-22

You can use the PV function to calculate how much money you would lend to somebody today based on an interest rate and a period of time. For example, if you are a banker and expect a 6% return on money you lend, you can determine how much to lend a customer who can afford to pay $200 a month for five years.

Create a new workbook that illustrates this idea as if you were the banker. Use Help to learn about the PV function. Then use PV in the new workbook to determine what you can lend this customer in the described circumstances. Add your standard footer. Save the workbook as ***[your initials]*6-22** in your Lesson 6 folder. Print the worksheet, save the workbook, and close it.

EXERCISE 6-23

Use Excel's Help system to learn more about styles. Then create a new workbook and key two meaningful labels and two values. Create two different styles for the labels, each using different fonts, colors, and perhaps borders or shading. Create two different styles for values that are different from what you have already seen in Excel's styles. Apply these styles to your data. Add your standard footer. Save the workbook as ***[your initials]*6-23** in your Lesson 6 folder. Print the worksheet, save the workbook, and close it.

EXERCISE 6-24

Open **AcctRec** and save it as ***[your initials]*6-24** in your Lesson 6 folder. Select and copy cells A2:E16 to cell A17. Paste again in cells A32 and A47. Add a custom footer that shows your name at the left and the page number in the center. Look at the worksheet in regular Print Preview and then in Page Break Preview. (Note that Excel prints the pages down and then across on a worksheet like this.) On the Sheet tab of the Page Setup dialog box, change the page order and print the worksheet with this new setting. Save and close the workbook.

LESSON

7

Using Advanced Functions and Hyperlinks

OBJECTIVES

After completing this lesson, you will be able to:

1. Use the INT function.
2. Use the ROUND function.
3. Use date and time arithmetic.
4. Create nested functions.
5. Use Text functions.
6. Create a hyperlink.

MOUS ACTIVITIES

In this lesson:

Ex2002 1-2
Ex2002 2-3
Ex2002 3-1
Ex2002 5-2
Ex2002 7-2

See Appendix E.

Estimated Time: 1¼ hours

In this lesson, you learn about the INT and ROUND functions, which can be used with your own formulas and with many of the other categories of functions. You learn how to use Date and Time functions to perform date or time calculations. You also see how to nest one function inside another, which can produce useful formulas that are specifically created to solve complex problems.

You're also introduced to Excel's Text functions that enable you to edit and display labels, as well as to use labels in calculations. Finally, you learn how to create hyperlinks within Excel worksheets.

Using the INT Function

Sometimes the value you see on the screen is not the same value shown in the formula bar. This occurs because Excel stores the full number of decimals that are keyed or calculated in a cell, even if the cell is formatted to show fewer decimal places. For example, if you key 1.2345 in a cell but format the cell for two decimal places, Excel displays 1.23 in the cell. In a calculation, however, Excel uses the full value, 1.2345.

If you want Excel to use the value as shown in the cell, you can use the INT or ROUND functions.

INT stands for "Integer." An *integer* is a whole number (that is, a number with no decimal or fractional parts). The INT function (in the Math & Trig category) shows only the non-decimal portion of a number. To do this, it truncates or cuts off all digits after the decimal point. The INT function has one argument, the value or cell to be adjusted.

TABLE 7-1 **Examples of the INT Function**

EXPRESSION	CELL DATA	RESULT
INT(C4)	C4=9.7	9
INT(9.792)	None	9
INT(A1)	A1=-9.7	-9

EXERCISE 7-1 Use INT with a Value

1. Create a new workbook and save it as ***[your initials]*****7-1** in a new folder for Lesson 7.

TIP: Close the New Workbook task pane for more screen space.

2. In cell A1, key **Integer and Round Training**. In cell A2, key **Human Resources Department**. Select both cells and make them 17-point Arial.
3. In cell A3, key **Integer Samples**. Format it as 10-point bold Arial. Format row 3 as 27.00 (36 pixels) high.
4. Key the following values in cells A4:A8:

   1.2

   3.4

   5.6

   7.8

   9.0

NOTE: The General number format shows only significant digits after the decimal point, so 0 after the decimal point is not displayed.

5. In cell B4, key **=int(** and click cell A4.

REVIEW: You will see an Argument ScreenTip for the INT function.

6. Press [Enter]. The integer value of 1.2 is 1.
7. Copy the formula in cell B4 to cells B5:B8.
8. Select cells A9:B9.
9. Click the AutoSum button [Σ]. The integer values are used in column B.

EXERCISE 7-2 Compare Formula Results Using INT

1. In cell A10, press [Ctrl]+[B] to start bold.
2. Key **Multiplication Sample** and press [Enter].
3. In cell A11, key **10.2** and press [Enter].
4. Key **5.8** in cell A12 and press [Enter].
5. Key = in cell A13 and click cell A11.
6. Key * and click cell A12. Press [Enter]. This is a simple multiplication formula.
7. Select cells A11:A13 and drag-and-drop a copy to cells B11:B13.

REVIEW: Hold down the [Ctrl] key to copy with drag-and-drop.

8. Click cell B13 and press [F2].
9. Position the pointer after the equal sign. Key **int(** and press [Enter]. The result is formatted as an integer. (See Figure 7-1 on the next page.)
10. In cell C11, key **=int(** and click cell B11. Press [Enter].
11. In cell C12, key **=int(** and click cell B12. Press [Enter]. Both cells show integer values now.
12. Key = in cell C13. Click cell C11, key * and then click cell C12. Press [Enter]. This result is different because it uses the integer values, not the full values in the cells in column B.

FIGURE 7-1
Changing a formula to an integer result

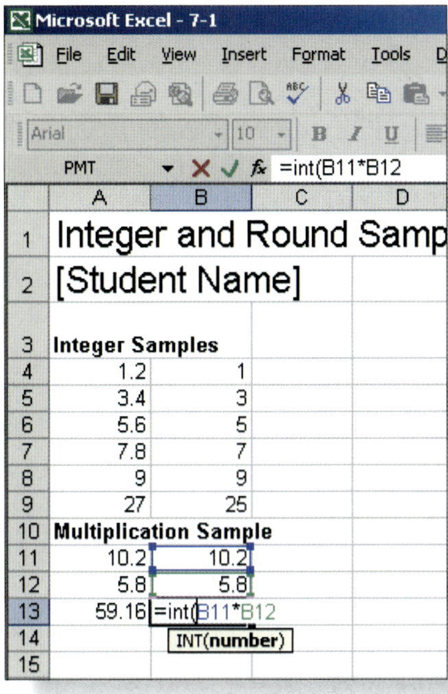

13. Click cell B13 and display the Trace Error button shortcut menu. The formula is inconsistent because it is different from those in cells A13 and C13.

14. Choose Ignore Error.

Using the ROUND Function

The ROUND function "rounds" a value to a specified digit to the left or right of the decimal point. *Rounding* a number means that it is made larger or smaller, a greater or lesser value. The ROUND function uses two arguments: the value to be rounded and the number of digits used for rounding. If the second argument is a negative number, the rounding occurs to the left of the decimal point.

TABLE 7-2
Examples of the ROUND Function

EXPRESSION	CELL DATA	RESULT
ROUND(C4, 1)	C4=9.736	9.7
ROUND(C4, 2)	C4=9.736	9.74
ROUND(C4, 0)	C4=9.736	10
ROUND(C4, -1)	C4=9.736	10
ROUND(C4, -2)	C4=9.736	0

TIP: Rounding is often used in financial calculations to round to the nearest dollar.

EXERCISE 7-3 Use Insert Function for ROUND

1. Select cells A3:C13 and drag and drop a copy to cells E3:G13.
2. Edit cell E3 to show **Round Samples**. Delete cells F4:F8.
3. In cell F4, click the Insert Function button fx.
4. In the Or select a category list, choose Math & Trig.
5. In the Select a function list, choose ROUND. Click OK.
6. In the Number box, click cell E4.
7. In the Num_digits box, key **0**.

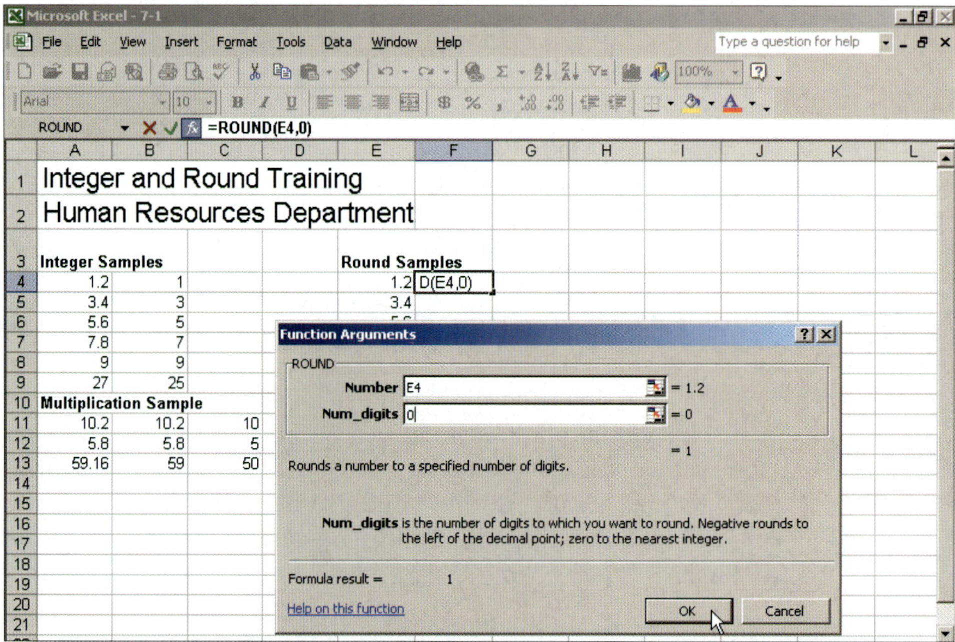

FIGURE 7-2
Using ROUND

8. Click OK. The value 1.2 is rounded to 1 with no decimal positions. It rounds down because the value after the decimal point is less than 5.
9. Display the Fill handle for cell F4 and copy the formula down to cell F8.
10. Edit cells E4:E8 to show the following values. As you do, notice how the values in column F are rounded up or down.

1.3

3.5

5.4

7.7

9.2

EXERCISE 7-4 Key a ROUND Formula

1. Click cell E13. Note that the result is 59.16.
2. Press Delete.
3. Key **=round(** and click cell E11. Key * and click cell E12.
4. Key a comma and key **1**
5. Press Enter. This rounds the result to one decimal position.

FIGURE 7-3 Keying a ROUND formula

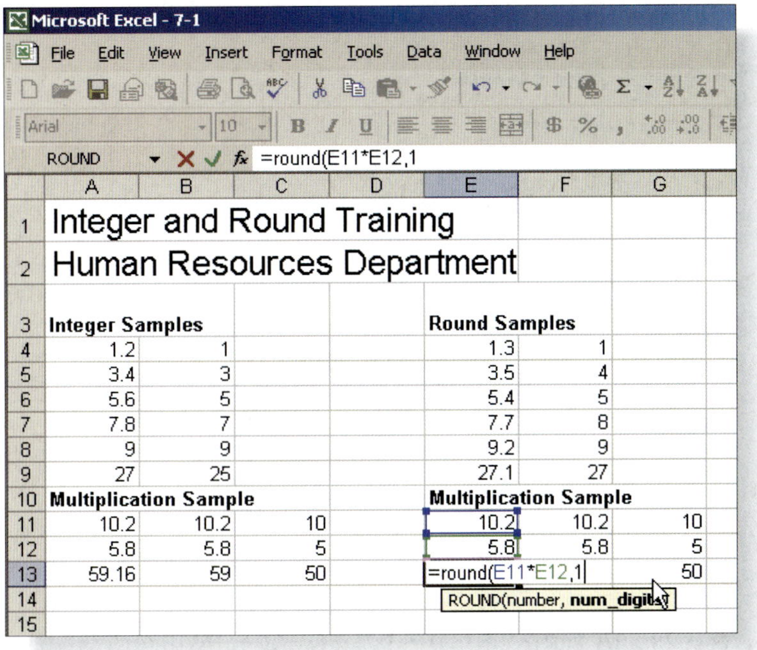

6. Click cell G11 and press Delete.
7. Key **=round(** and click cell F11.
8. Key a comma and then key **0**

NOTE: Ignore error triangles as you work.

9. Press Enter. Notice the result in cell G13.
10. Click cell G12 and press Delete.
11. Key **=round(** and click cell F12. Key a comma and key **0**
12. Press Enter. Notice the result in cell G13.

Using Date and Time Arithmetic

Excel's Date & Time functions can be used to calculate ages, hours worked, days passed, and future dates. When you work with dates and times, you need to understand how Excel uses a serial number system. A *serial number* is a date shown as a value. Excel's date system sets January 1, 1900 as 1; January 2, 1900 as 2; and counts the days from that point all the way to December 31, 9999.

You can key dates in a variety of ways. As you do, Excel assigns the closest matching date format to the date you key. The format on screen might not match exactly what you key, depending on whether your format matches a built-in date format.

TABLE 7-3 Sample Date Formats

KEYED CHARACTERS	FORMULA BAR	SCREEN DISPLAY
1-1-02	01/01/2002	01/01/02
1/1/02	01/01/2002	01/01/02
1-Jan-02	01/01/2002	01-Jan-02
January 1, 2002	01/01/2002	01-Jan-02
Jan 1, 2002	01/01/2002	01-Jan

EXERCISE 7-5 Key Dates and Use TODAY

Excel has a TODAY function that automatically displays the current date by using the computer's internal clock. This function has no arguments. When you use the TODAY function, Excel formats the result in a standard date style. The TODAY function is described as *volatile,* which means its results change depending on the current day or time.

1. Format row 14 as 33.75 (45 pixels) high. Then format cell A14 as bold and key **Determining a Person's Age**
2. In cell A15, key your first name. Widen column A to see your name.
3. In cell B15, key your birthday in the format **mm/dd/yy**
4. Press Enter. Your birthday is formatted in a default date format.
5. Click cell G14, key **=today()**, and press Enter.
6. Click cell G14 and press Ctrl+1.
7. In the Number tab, choose General.
8. Click OK. The serial number that represents today's date is shown.

9. Click the Undo button.

EXERCISE 7-6 Create a Custom Date Format

1. Click cell B15 and press Ctrl + 1.
2. Click the Number tab and choose Date in the Category list.
3. Scroll through the Type list. There is no preset format to show the date, the month spelled out, and a two-digit year (1 May 03).
4. Click Custom in the Category list. The Type list shows the codes for several number formats. You can choose one as a starting point to build your own format.
5. Scroll down the Type list to find d-mmm.
6. Click the code to select it. The Sample shows your birthday with that format.
7. Click in the Type box, above the Type list.
8. Delete the hyphen and press Spacebar.
9. Edit the code to show dd mmmm y. Two **dd**'s show the date with a leading zero, if necessary. Four **mmmm**'s spell out the month. A single **y** shows a two-digit year.
10. Look at the Sample.

FIGURE 7-4
Creating a custom date format

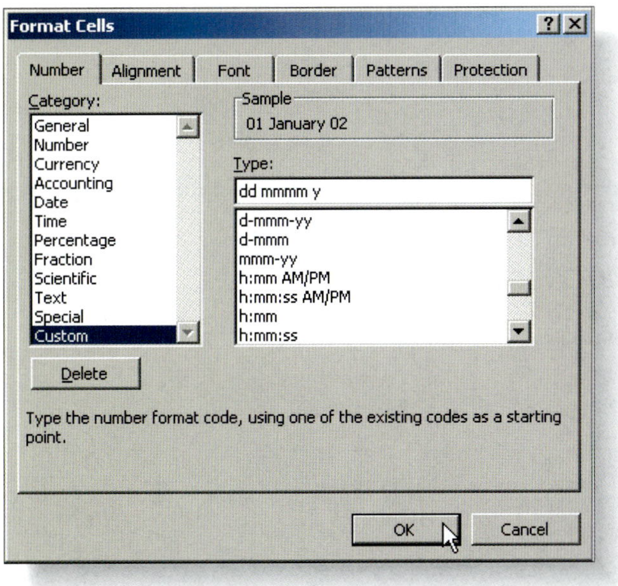

11. Click OK. Your birthday is reformatted.

12. Click the Format Painter button and click cell G14.
13. Widen column G to see the reformatted date.

EXERCISE 7-7 Determine a Person's Age

To determine a person's age, subtract the person's birthday from today. The result is a serial number that can be converted to the person's age.

1. Click cell C15. Key = and click cell G14. The first part of the formula shows today's date.
2. Press F4 and make it an absolute reference.

REVIEW: An absolute reference does not change when the formula is copied.

3. Key a minus sign and click cell B15 to subtract your birthday from today.
4. Press Enter. Your age is formatted as a date. Widen the column to see the result.
5. Click cell C15 and press Ctrl + 1.
6. Choose Number with 2 decimal places and click OK. This is your age in days.
7. Press F2. Press Home and →.
8. Key a left parenthesis after the equal sign.

REVIEW: Excel does division before subtraction based on its order of precedence.

9. Press End and key a right parenthesis after B15.

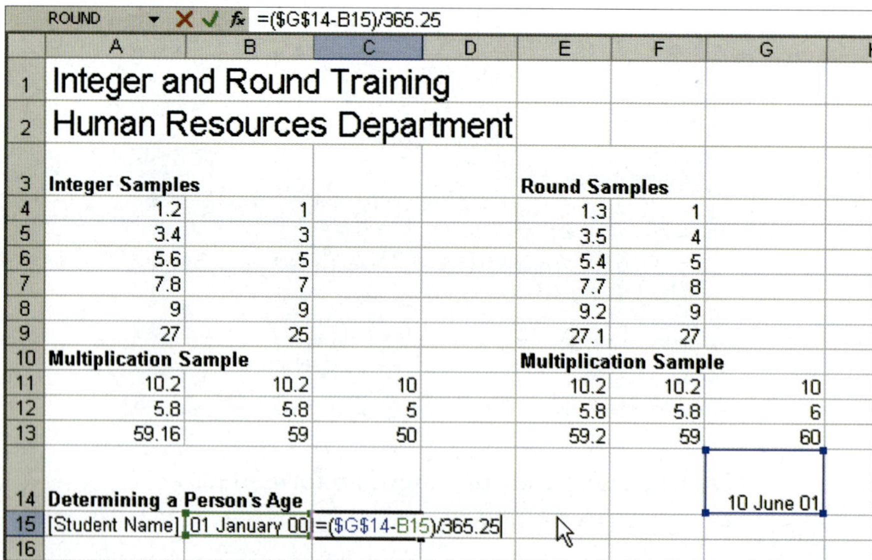

FIGURE 7-5 Converting the age formula to years

10. Key **/365.25** to divide by the number of days in a year. Press [Enter].

EXERCISE 7-8 Determine Time Worked

Figuring time worked or time passed is similar to figuring your age. You subtract the beginning time from the ending time.

1. Format row 16 as 33.75 (45 pixels) high.
2. Format cell A16 as bold and key **Determining Hours Worked**

REVIEW: Continue typing and ignore AutoComplete suggestions if they are wrong.

3. In cell A17, key **Time In**. In cell B17, key **Time Out**. Widen columns, if necessary.
4. In cell A18, key **8:30 am** and press [→]. Excel capitalizes the AM/PM reference for you.
5. In cell B18, key **4:30 pm**. Excel shows times as you key them, using a 12-hour AM/PM clock.
6. In cell C18, key **=** and click cell B18.
7. Key a minus sign and click cell A18. Press [Enter]. The result is formatted as time, because times are keyed in the two cells used in the formula.

EXERCISE 7-9 Format Time Results

1. Click cell C18 and press [Ctrl]+[1].
2. Choose Number with 2 decimal places. Click OK. Excel shows time as a fraction of a 24-hour day.
3. Press [F2] and press [Home].
4. Press [→] and key a left parenthesis after the equal sign.

REVIEW: Excel does multiplication before subtraction unless you insert parentheses.

5. Press [End] and key a right parenthesis.
6. Key ***24** to multiply by the number of hours in a day. Press [Enter].
7. Add your standard footer and print the worksheet.
8. Save the workbook as ***[your inititals]*7-9** in your Lesson 7 folder.

REVIEW: Press [Ctrl]+[~] to toggle the formulas on and off.

EXCEL

9. Display the formulas and hide column D. Print the worksheet in landscape orientation, fit to one page.
10. Close the workbook without saving.

Creating Nested Functions

A *nested* function is a function inside another function. The logical test or argument for the main function is another function. The IF function is a function that is often used in nested functions. The ROUND function is another function in which other functions can be nested.

EXERCISE 7-10 Nest SUM and ROUND

1. Open **CookieCrunch** and save it in your Lesson 7 folder as ***[your initials]*7-10**. This worksheet uses a formula to compute a 5% increase in sales for each day of the week.

NOTE: A 5% increase multiplies the previous day's sales by 105%.

2. Click cell H9. Click the Insert Function button *fx*.
3. In the Search for a function box, key **round**
4. Click Go. Click OK.
5. Move the Function Arguments dialog box to see column headings and column H.
6. In the Number box, you want the sum of Sunday's sales.

NOTE: If SUM is not in the Function Name list, click More Functions and find SUM in the Math & Trig or Most Recently Used category.

7. Click the arrow next to the Function Name box.
8. Choose SUM and click OK. The Function Arguments dialog box shows the SUM function, and it is nested in the ROUND function in the formula bar. The SUM function is bold in the formula bar, and the suggested range for its argument is highlighted. (See Figure 7-6 on the next page.)
9. Click anywhere in the word ROUND in the formula bar. The Function Arguments dialog box shows SUM(H4:H8) as the first argument.
10. Click in the Num_digits box and key **2.** Click OK.
11. Display the Fill handle for cell H9.
12. Drag the handle left to copy the formula to cells G9:B9.

FIGURE 7-6
Nesting SUM in a ROUND function

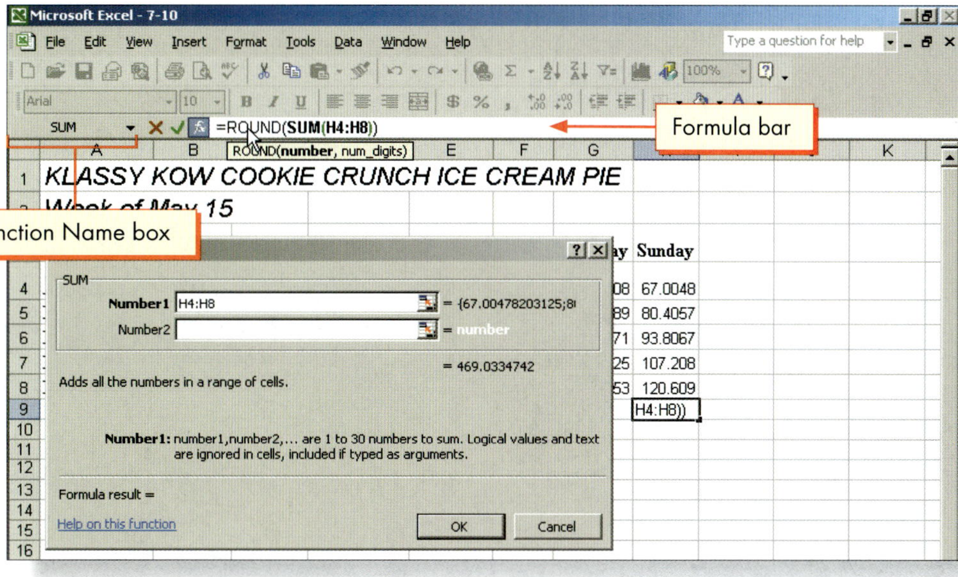

EXERCISE 7-11 Create a Nested IF Function

A nested IF function tests for more than one logical test. In your worksheet, you will now check to see if the daily total is over 400, and then if it is over 375.

1. Select cells B4:H9. Press Ctrl + 1. Use the Number format with 0 decimal places.
2. Click cell B10 and click the Insert Function button *fx*. In the Logical category, choose IF and click OK.
3. In the Logical_test box, click cell B9. Key **>400** after B9 in the box.
4. Click in the Value_if_true box. Key **Over 400**
5. Click in the Value_if_false box. If the value is not over 400, you will also test to see if it is over 375.
6. Click the arrow next to the Function Name box and choose IF. The Function Arguments dialog box updates to show another IF statement. You can see both in the formula bar. The second IF function is bold in the formula bar to show that it is the one you are now building.
7. In the Logical_test box, click cell B9. Key **>375** after B9.
8. Click in the Value_if_true box. Key **Over 375**
9. Click in the Value_if_false box. Key **Under Quota** and click OK. (See Figure 7-7 on the next page.)
10. Copy the formula to cells C10:H10 and widen columns if needed.
11. Right-align cells C10:H10.

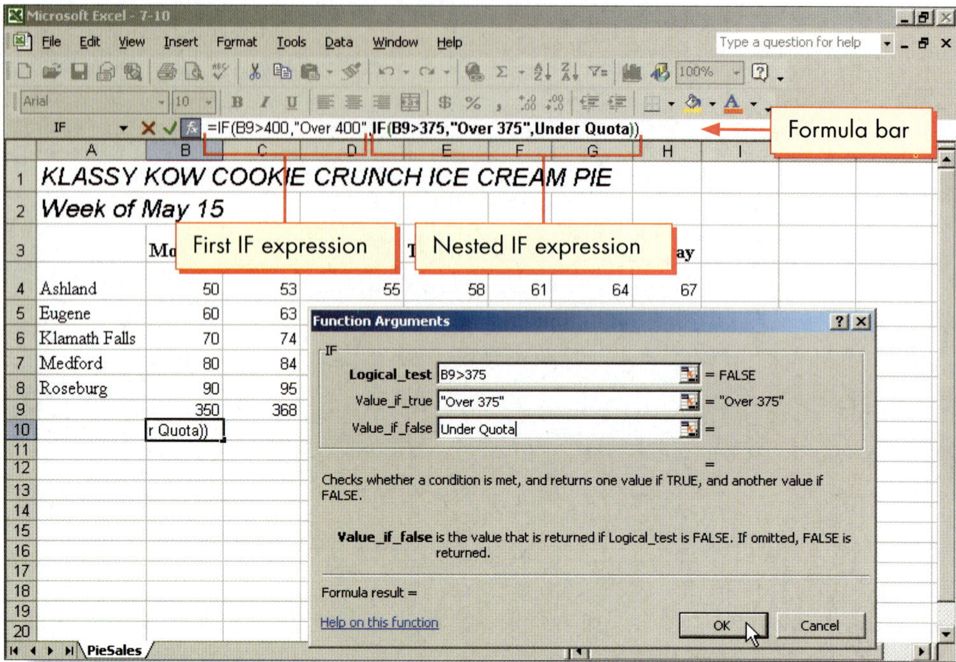

FIGURE 7-7
Nesting IF functions

Using Text Functions

Although Excel is best known for working with values and formulas, it also has several Text functions. Two easy-to-use functions are UPPER and PROPER, used to convert text to uppercase and title case.

NOTE: Excel also has a LOWER function to convert text to lowercase.

EXERCISE 7-12 Use the UPPER Function

1. Click cell A12. Click the Insert Function button *fx*.
2. In the Text category, choose UPPER and click OK.
3. In the Text box, click cell A4.
4. Click OK. The formula displays the label in cell A4 in uppercase letters.
5. Make row 12 tall enough to show the label.
6. Click cell A13 and key **=upper(** to start the function.
7. Key **"less than 375"** with the quotation marks and press Enter. The formula displays the text you keyed in uppercase letters.

REVIEW: When you key text in an argument, you must include the quotation marks.

8. Click cell A2 and press F2. Press Home.
9. Key **=upper("** to insert the UPPER function.

FIGURE 7-8
Adding the UPPER function to text

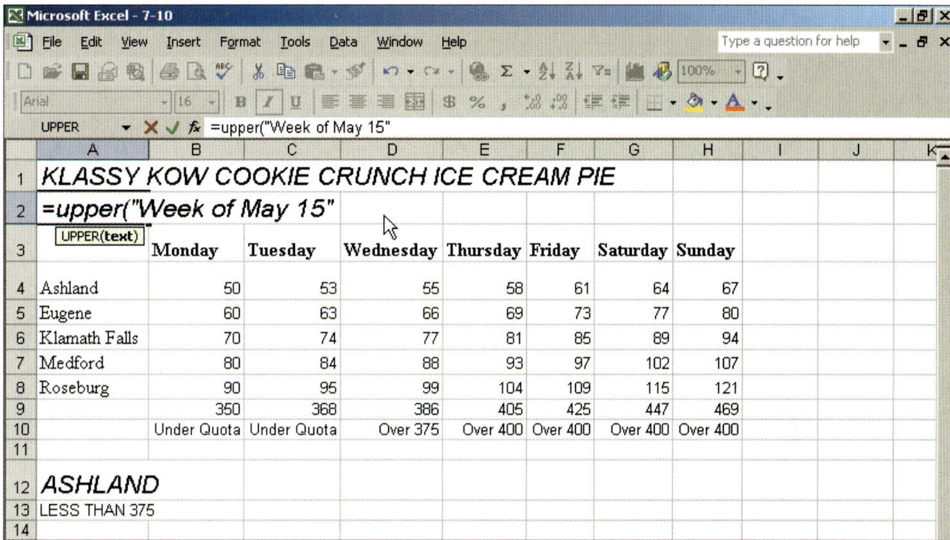

10. Press End and key " for the closing quote. Press Enter.

EXERCISE 7-13 Use the PROPER Function

1. Click cell A15. Click the Insert Function button *fx*.
2. In the Text category, choose PROPER and click OK.
3. In the Text box, click cell A1. Click OK. The formula displays the label in cell A1 with initial uppercase letters.
4. Click cell A16 and key **=proper(**
5. Key **"these results are for Oregon shops"** and press Enter.
6. Add the standard footer and print the worksheet.
7. Save your workbook as ***[your initials]*7-13** in your Lesson 7 folder.

Creating a Hyperlink

A *hyperlink* is a clickable object or text that, when clicked, displays another file, opens another program, shows a Web page, or displays an e-mail address. A hyperlink is a shortcut to files on your computer, your network, or on the World Wide Web. As you insert hyperlinks in your work, Excel keeps a list of the addresses and shows them in the Insert Hyperlink dialog box. You can key a new entry or choose an existing name from the list.

A text hyperlink is shown in a color and underlined. There are several ways to add a hyperlink to your worksheet:

- Click the Insert Hyperlink button on the Standard toolbar.
- Choose Hyperlink from the Insert menu.
- Right-click the cell and choose Hyperlink from the shortcut menu.
- Press Ctrl + K.

EXERCISE 7-14 Create a Hyperlink

1. Click cell G12.

2. Click the Insert Hyperlink button. The Insert Hyperlink dialog box opens.

3. Click the E-mail address button in the Link to bar. Key **glencoe@mcgraw-hill.com** in the E-mail address text box.

4. Select the address in the Text to display box.

5. Key **Click here to return to sender**. Click OK. Hyperlink text appears in a color and is underlined.

FIGURE 7-9
Insert Hyperlink dialog box

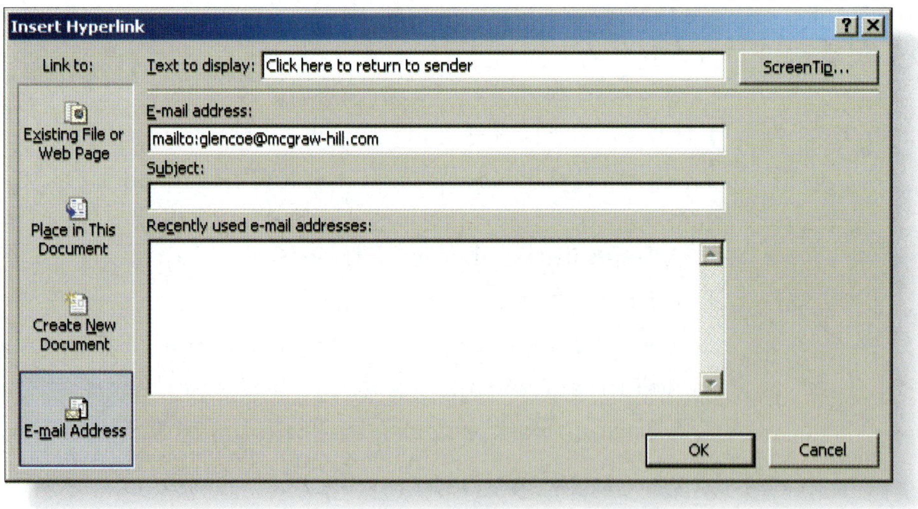

6. Position the mouse pointer on cell G12 to see the ScreenTip. (See Figure 7-10 on the next page.)

FIGURE 7-10
Hyperlink and ScreenTip

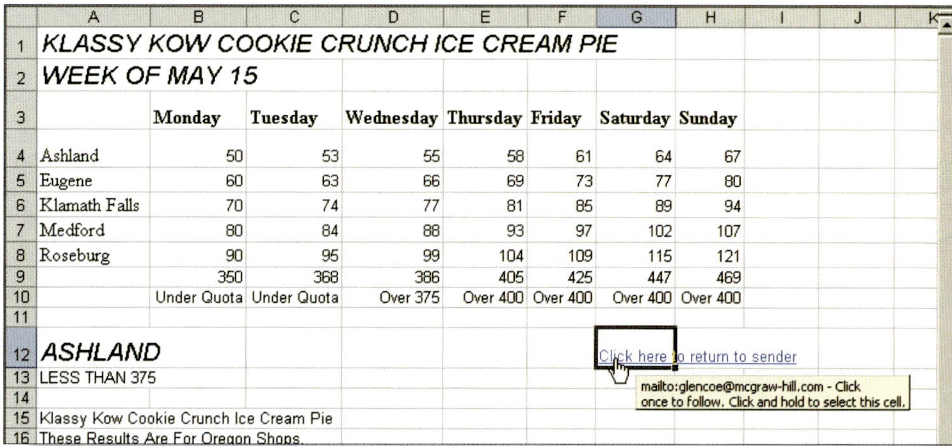

	A	B	C	D	E	F	G	H
1	KLASSY KOW COOKIE CRUNCH ICE CREAM PIE							
2	WEEK OF MAY 15							
3		Monday	Tuesday	Wednesday	Thursday	Friday	Saturday	Sunday
4	Ashland	50	53	55	58	61	64	67
5	Eugene	60	63	66	69	73	77	80
6	Klamath Falls	70	74	77	81	85	89	94
7	Medford	80	84	88	93	97	102	107
8	Roseburg	90	95	99	104	109	115	121
9		350	368	386	405	425	447	469
10		Under Quota	Under Quota	Over 375	Over 400	Over 400	Over 400	Over 400
11								
12	ASHLAND						Click here to return to sender	
13	LESS THAN 375							
14								
15	Klassy Kow Cookie Crunch Ice Cream Pie							
16	These Results Are For Oregon Shops.							

TIP: To edit or delete a hyperlink, right-click the cell and choose Edit Hyperlink or Remove Hyperlink.

EXERCISE 7-15 Save a Workbook in a Different Format

If you send a workbook to someone who uses a different version of Excel, you can save the file in the appropriate format for them. You can also send a copy of your Excel workbook to someone who uses a different electronic spreadsheet program.

1. Press F12. The Save As dialog box opens.
2. Click the Save as type arrow.

NOTE: Lotus is an electronic spreadsheet program similar to Excel. Excel can open a Lotus workbook.

3. Choose WK4(1-2-3) for a Lotus format. The filename is the same, but the workbook will have a different filename extension.
4. Click Save. A message box alerts you about possible problems in converting the file.
5. Click Yes.

FIGURE 7-11
Message box about converting file

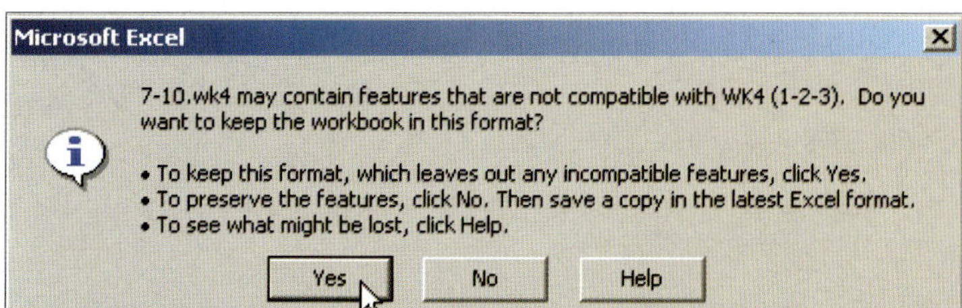

6. Close the workbook.

LESSON 7 Summary

- Use the INT function to display a value without any decimal positions. It shows only the part of the value to the left of the decimal.
- The ROUND function adjusts a value up or down based on how many digits you use for rounding. It can round to the left or right of the decimal point.
- Excel uses a serial number system for dates and times. This enables it to make date and time calculations.
- When you key a date, Excel formats it with a preset date format similar to the one you key.
- You can create your own formats by using the Custom category in the Number tab of the Format Cells dialog box.
- In most date and time calculations, you will need to convert the results to the proper format. For example, in determining a person's age, Excel initially shows the result in days. Time results are initially shown in fractions of a 24-hour day.
- A nested function is a function within a function.
- Two helpful Text functions are UPPER and PROPER.
- Hyperlinks enable you to jump to other files, e-mail addresses, or Web sites.

LESSON 7 Command Summary

FEATURE	BUTTON	MENU	KEYBOARD	SPEECH
Insert hyperlink		Insert, Hyperlink	Ctrl + K	

Concepts Review

TRUE/FALSE QUESTIONS

Each of the following statements is either true or false. Indicate your choice by circling T or F.

T F *1.* The INT and ROUND functions use the same arguments.

T F *2.* An integer is a whole number, a non-decimal number.

T F *3.* Excel uses a serial number system for dates.

T F *4.* A nested function is placed in the cell below the first formula.

T F *5.* You can convert uppercase text to title or sentence case with the PROPER function.

T F *6.* A hyperlink is a flashing cell with a formula.

T F *7.* Excel has five preset date formats.

T F *8.* To convert a fraction of a day to hours, multiply by 365.25.

SHORT ANSWER QUESTIONS

Write the correct answer in the space provided.

1. What is the term used to describe a function inside a function?

____

2. Which Text function converts text to all capital letters?

____

3. What is the keyboard shortcut for displaying the Save As dialog box?

____

4. What does a hyperlink do?

____

5. Which function inserts the current date?

____

6. What does the INT function do?

____

7. How would Excel display this value =ROUND(1.567,2)?

____

8. Name two functions that are often used in nested formulas.

CRITICAL THINKING

Answer these questions on a separate page. There are no right or wrong answers. Support your answers with examples from your own experience, if possible.

1. How would you determine the number of days until Christmas?

2. Which function do you think has more value in business use: INT or ROUND? Why?

Lesson Applications

EXERCISE 7-16

Use date arithmetic. Create a nested function.

1. Open **PastDue** and save it as ***[your initials]*7-16** in your Lesson 7 folder.
2. Select cells C4:C13. Replace all occurrences of "2000" with the current year. Individually change the current year in these cells to last year for those months that are still in the future.

TIP: You can limit a Find and Replace task to selected cells.

3. In cell D4, key a formula to compute the due date 30 days after the invoice date. Copy the formula.
4. In cell E4, use a formula to subtract cell D4 from today. Format the result with no decimal places. Copy the formula. Some customers might be very late, and some might show a negative number of days, meaning bills are not yet due.
5. Format negative numbers in column E to show in red without parentheses or a minus sign.
6. In cell F4, create an IF formula. The first logical test is that cell E4 be greater than 120 days. If this is so, the Value_if_true is **Over 120.** As the Value_if_false, nest another IF function. The logical test is that cell E4 be over 60. The Value_if_true for this IF statement is **Over 60**. The Value_if_false entry for the second IF statement is **OK**. Copy the formula and right-align the results.
7. Add your standard footer and print the worksheet.
8. Save and close the workbook.

EXERCISE 7-17

Use time arithmetic.

1. Create a new workbook and save it as ***[your initials]*7-17** in your Lesson 7 folder.
2. Format cells A1:A2 as 17-point Arial. In cell A1, key **Klassy Kow Parkland Shop**. Key **Part-Time Hours** in cell A2.
3. In cell B3:D3, key the following labels. Make them bold, turn on Wrap text, and center them.

   Starting Time **Ending Time** **Hours Worked**

4. In cell A4, key **Monday** and make it bold.

5. Key the data shown in the figure. Widen column A to fit the longest worker name.

NOTE: When the time is on the hour, you do not need to key the colon or the zeros. Excel inserts them and capitalizes AM and PM.

FIGURE 7-12

		Starting Time	Ending Time
5	Keiko Yang	11 am	8:30 pm
6	Eugene Sanchez	12 pm	10 pm
7	Millie Hanes	9:30 am	4 pm
8	Michael Bianciotto	10 am	5:30 pm
9	Aneta Monroe	2 pm	10 pm

6. In cell D5, key a formula to determine hours worked. Format the result as a Number with 2 decimal places. Copy the formula.

REVIEW: Convert a fraction of a day to hours by multiplying by 24.

7. Make sure that all data is visible. Format rows 3 and 4 as 30.00 (40 pixels) high.
8. Add your standard footer and print the worksheet.
9. Save and close the workbook.

EXERCISE 7-18

Create a nested function.

In this worksheet, you create a nested IF function. The IF statement shows the name of the state with the maximum value for each product.

1. Open **JulyDrinks**. Save it as ***[your initials]*7-18** in your Lesson 7 folder.
2. In cell G5, click the Insert Function button. Choose Logical and then IF. Click cell B5 for the Logical_test.
3. Key = after B5 and then click the arrow next to Function Name. Click More Functions, choose Statistical, MAX, and then click OK. Select cells B5:E5 as Number1 and click OK.
4. Click anywhere in the word IF in the formula bar. Click the Value_if_true box and key **California**

5. Click the Value_if_false box. Click the arrow next to Function Name and choose IF. Click cell C5 for the Logical_test. Key = after C5 and then click the arrow next to Function Name. Choose MAX and select cells B5:E5 as Number1.
6. Click anywhere in the second occurrence of IF in the formula bar. Click the Value_if_true box and key **Washington**
7. Click the Value_if_false box. Click the arrow next to Function Name and choose IF. Click cell D5 for the Logical_test. Key = after D5 and then click the arrow next to Function Name. Choose MAX and select cells B5:E5.
8. Click anywhere in the third occurrence of IF in the formula bar. Click the Value_if_true box and key **Oregon**
9. Click the Value_if_false box. Key **Nevada**. Click OK.
10. Center the results and copy the formula to row 9.
11. Set the page to be horizontally centered. Add your standard footer and print the worksheet. Save the workbook.

REVIEW: Page centering options are on the Margins tab.

12. Show the formulas and print the worksheet, fit to one landscape page, not horizontally centered.
13. Close the workbook without saving.

EXERCISE 7-19 Challenge Yourself

Use date arithmetic and the INT function.

The human resources department is responsible for maintaining records that list an employee's birthday, age, and other related data. You have been asked to create a worksheet with new employees (hired within the last two months).

1. Create a new workbook and save it as ***[your initials]*7-19** in your Lesson 7 folder.
2. Key **Klassy Kow New Employees** in cell A1. Key **Birthday and Age** in cell A2. Choose a font and size for both cells.
3. Key these labels in cells A3:C3 and make them bold:

   Name **Birthday** **Age**
4. In cells A4:A10, key the first and last names of six new employees. Use classmates' or family members' names, or create new names.
5. Key birthdays in column B for each of your employees. Format the birthdays in a date format that you like.

TIP: Key birthdays in **mm/dd/yy** format for speed, and format them later.

6. Key a formula that determines the person's age and show the result as an integer.

TIP: Nest the formula to determine an age in the INT function.

7. Adjust the height of rows 3 and 4 to show more white space. Make other adjustments to format your worksheet in a professional manner.
8. Add your standard footer and print the worksheet.
9. Save and close the workbook.

On Your Own

In these exercises you work on your own, as you would in a real-life work environment. Use the skills you've learned to accomplish the task—and be creative.

EXERCISE 7-20

In a new workbook, key your name and the names of three family members in a column. In the next column, key birthdays for each person. In the third column, calculate the number of days until the person's next birthday. Apply an AutoFormat or use your own format choices to make the worksheet attractive. Add your standard custom footer. Save the workbook as ***[your initials]*****7-20** in your Lesson 7 folder. Print the worksheet, save the workbook, and close it.

EXERCISE 7-21

Use Excel's Help system to explore information about the custom number formats and the codes that Excel uses. In a new workbook, key three dates, three values, and three labels in a column. Copy this data to another column. In the copied column, apply a custom format that you have learned about in the Help system. In the third column, key a brief description of the format. Save the workbook as ***[your initials]*****7-21** in your Lesson 7 folder. Print the worksheet, save the workbook, and close it.

EXERCISE 7-22

Create a new workbook with a list of 10 persons' first names in column A. In column B, key each person's height in inches, using heights between 60 and 75 inches. In column C, use an IF formula to show "Tall" if the person is 72 inches or more, "Average" if the person is between 64 and 71 inches, and "Short" if the person is less than 63 inches tall. Add a main title and column headings. Format the worksheet with an AutoFormat or your own formatting. Add your standard footer. Save the workbook as ***[your initials]*****7-22** in your Lesson 7 folder. Print the worksheet and close the workbook.

UNIT 3

Improving Uses of Worksheet Information

LESSON

8

Building Charts

OBJECTIVES

MOUS ACTIVITIES
In this lesson:
Ex2002 3-7
Ex2002 6-1
See Appendix E.

After completing this lesson, you will be able to:

1. Preview and print charts.
2. Edit chart objects.
3. Create charts.
4. Edit chart data.
5. Use images and patterns for a data series.
6. Create combination charts.

Estimated Time: 2 hours

A *chart* is a visual display of information in a worksheet. Charts can be prepared so you can quickly make comparisons, identify patterns, and recognize trends in data.

You can create a chart on its own sheet or within a worksheet containing data. In either case, the chart is linked to the worksheet data that is used to create that chart. Because they are linked in this way, the chart is automatically updated when you edit the worksheet data.

Previewing and Printing a Chart

An *embedded chart* is a chart that appears on the same sheet as the worksheet data. It is a graphic object and can be selected, sized, moved, and changed in various ways. An *object* is a separate element or part of a worksheet or chart.

EXERCISE 8-1 Preview a Chart

You will notice that when you select a chart, the Data menu is replaced by the Chart menu. Depending on how your computer is set, the Chart toolbar might also open when you select a chart.

1. Open **SeptChart** and save it as ***[your initials]*8-1** in a new folder for Lesson 8.

> **NOTE:** The workbooks in this course relate to the Case Study about Klassy Kow Ice Cream, Inc., a fictional manufacturer of ice cream (see pages 357 through 360).

2. Change the Zoom size to 75% so you can see more of the worksheet and the chart at the same time.

3. Click the Print Preview button. This chart shows the value from column F for each city. The chart is positioned below the worksheet data.

> **NOTE:** If you're using a black-and-white printer, Print Preview shows the chart in shades of gray.

4. Close the preview.
5. Click in the white chart background area to select the chart. It is surrounded by small black rectangles, known as *selection handles.* The data that is plotted on the chart is outlined in the worksheet. The Name box shows that the Chart Area is the active object.

FIGURE 8-1
Chart selected in the worksheet

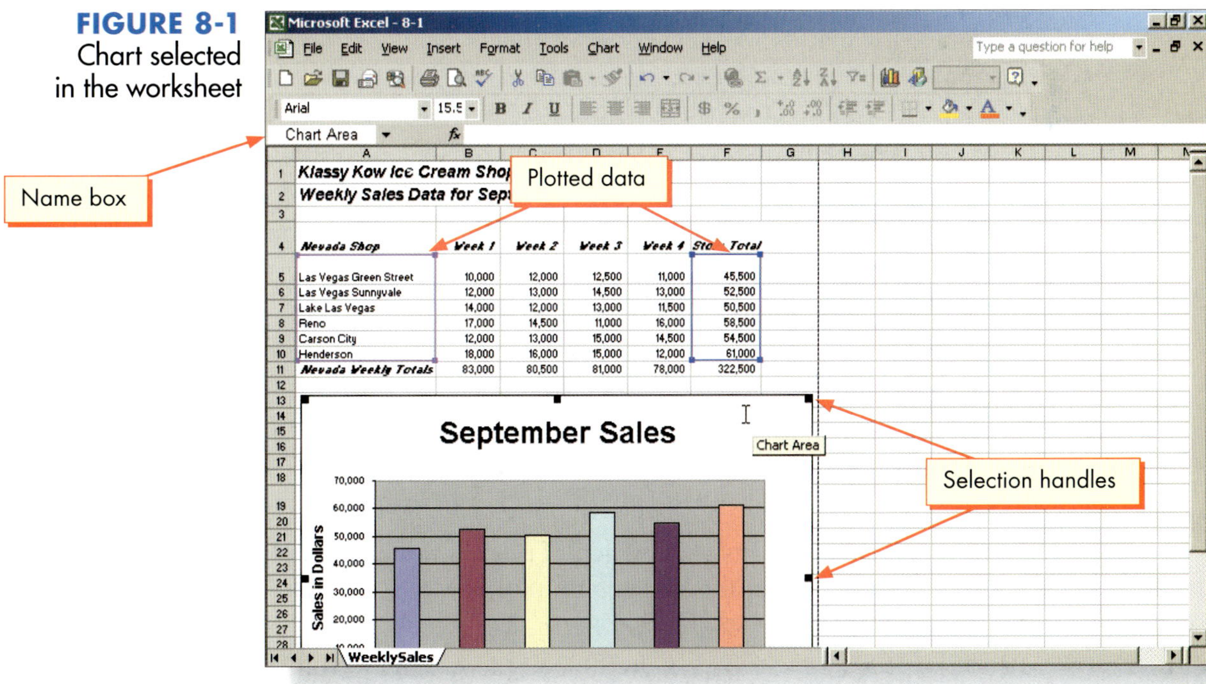

6. Click the Print Preview button. Only the chart is shown, because it is selected.

NOTE: If the Chart toolbar is open, close it for this exercise.

7. Close the preview.

EXERCISE 8-2 Print a Chart

1. Click cell D1 to deselect the chart. The selection handles are removed from the chart.
2. Click the Print Preview button. Excel displays both the worksheet and its chart.
3. Add your standard footer.
4. Click Print and click OK. The worksheet and chart print on a single page.
5. Click in the white background chart area to select the chart. The selection handles are visible.

6. Click the Print button. The selected chart prints by itself in landscape orientation. When you print a selected object, the footer is not included because the footer is a page setting.

Editing Chart Objects

A chart is made up of objects, or elements. You can format each object by using many of the same format settings that you use for a worksheet. Following are descriptions of Excel chart objects:

- The *chart area* is the background for the chart. It can be filled with a color or pattern.
- The *category axis* is created from the row or column headings in the data. A category describes what is shown in the chart.
- The *category title* is an optional title for the chart's categories.
- The *value axis* shows the values on the chart. Excel creates a range of values (the *scale*) based on the data.
- The *plot area* is the rectangular area bounded by the category and value axes.
- The *chart title* is an optional title or name for the chart.
- A *data series* is a collection of related values from the worksheet. These values are in the same column or row and translate into the columns, lines, pie slices, and so on.
- A *data point* is a single value or piece of data from the data series.

- A *data marker* is the object that represents individual values. The marker can be a bar, a column, a symbol, an image, or other symbol.
- A *legend* is an object that explains the symbols, patterns, or colors used to differentiate the series in the chart.
- A *gridline* is a horizontal or vertical line that extends across the plot area to make it easier to read and follow the values.
- A *tick mark* is a small line or marker on the category (x) and value (y) axes to help in reading the values.

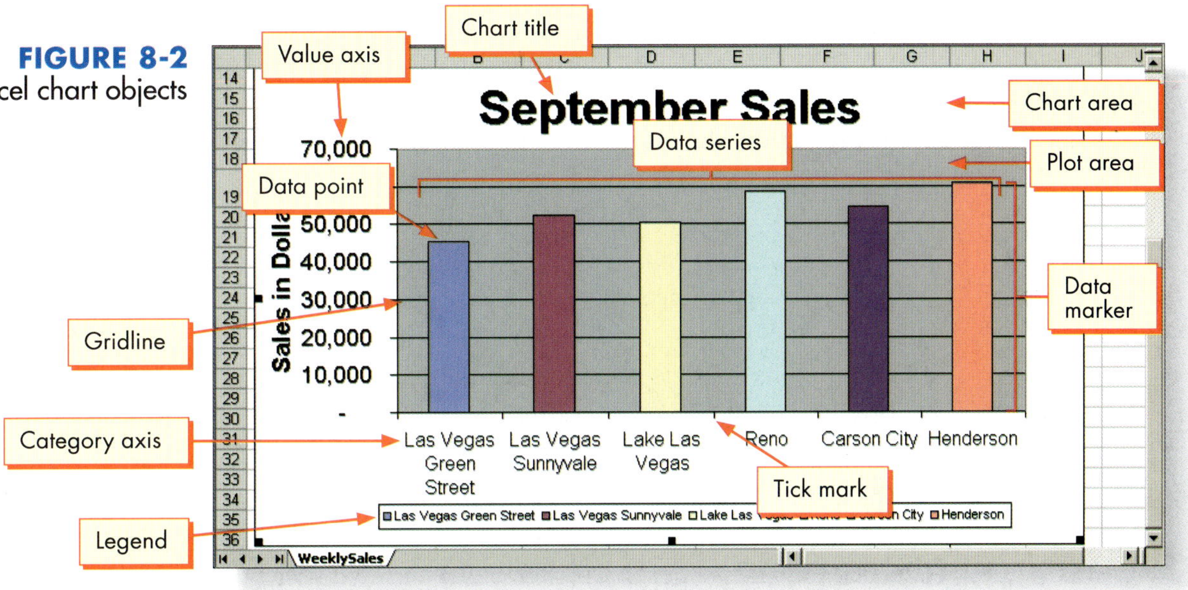

FIGURE 8-2
Excel chart objects

All chart objects show a ScreenTip when you position the mouse pointer on the object. To edit a chart object, you first select it by pointing and clicking. When an object is selected, it shows selection handles and its name appears in the Name box.

EXERCISE 8-3 Format the Chart Title

1. Position the mouse pointer on the chart title "September Sales." A ScreenTip appears showing that it is the Chart Title.
2. Click the chart title. It is selected and shows selection handles with an outline. Its name appears in the Name box.
3. Click to the left of the **S** in "September." The text insertion point is in position, and the outline and selection handles are removed.
4. Key **Nevada** and press the Spacebar. The word is inserted.
5. With the I-beam pointer, drag across the entire chart title to select it.

6. Point anywhere in the selected text and right-click. A shortcut menu opens.
7. Choose Format Chart Title. The Format Chart Title dialog box has Font and Properties tabs.
8. On the Font tab, choose Bold Italic and click OK. The title is reformatted.
9. Click the white background area of the chart to deselect the title.

EXERCISE 8-4 Format the Data Series

The series of values shown in this chart are the values in column F. The data series is represented by the height of the columns. The values are plotted against the y-axis in this chart, the column of numbers at the left. The category for this chart is the city name, shown along the bottom axis (the x-axis).

1. Scroll the window to see the city names along the chart's category axis (the x-axis).
2. Rest the mouse pointer on the Reno column to see its ScreenTip. It is one data point from the series.
3. Right-click the Reno column. The entire data series is selected, and each column has a single selection handle in its middle. The Name box shows Series 1, because this is the first (and only) series in this chart.
4. Choose Format Data Series.
5. Click the Data Labels tab. A *data label* is an optional title shown for each value. It is simply the value from column F in this case.
6. Click to place a check mark for Value in the Label Contains group.

FIGURE 8-3
Format Data Series dialog box

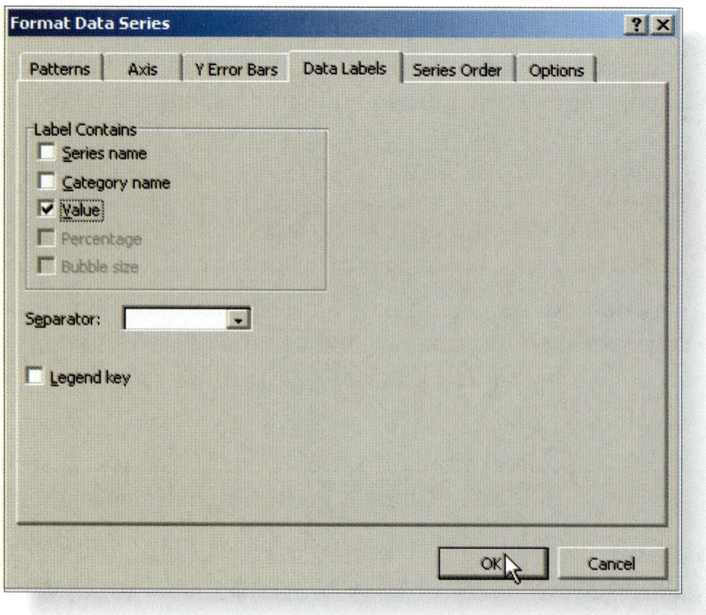

7. Click OK. The value of each data point appears above its column.
8. Rest the mouse pointer on one of the data labels to see the ScreenTip.
9. Right-click any of the labels and choose Format Data Labels. The Format Data Labels dialog box includes tabs for the colors, font, number, and alignment.
10. Click the Font tab and choose 9 points as the Size. Click OK. The data labels look better in a smaller font.

EXERCISE 8-5 Change the Data Series Colors

1. Right-click any column and choose Format Data Series.
2. Click the Options tab.
3. Click to remove the check mark for Vary colors by point. Click OK. All the columns are now the same color.
4. Right-click a column again and choose Format Data Series.
5. Click the Patterns tab. The Area group includes solid colors for the columns.
6. Click any color swatch in the Area group. Click OK. All the columns are changed to the new color.
7. Right-click a column and choose Format Data Series. Click the Options tab.
8. Click to place a check mark in the Vary colors by point box. Click OK. The colors are not varied, however, even though you just turned on that setting.

TIP: The Automatic option must be turned on for colors to be varied.

9. Right-click a column again and choose Format Data Series.
10. Click the Patterns tab again. Click the Automatic button in the Area group. Click OK.

EXERCISE 8-6 Format the Category Axes

1. Position the mouse pointer on a city name to see its ScreenTip. The Category Axis is the x-axis in this chart. It represents the city names.
2. Right-click any city name and choose Format Axis.
3. On the Font tab, choose Bold.
4. Click the Patterns tab. Notice that the Major tick mark type is Outside (that is, outside the bottom border of the chart.). Move the dialog box so you can see a tick mark clearly.

5. Choose Cross for Major tick mark type. Click OK. The tick mark now crosses the bottom border.

EXERCISE 8-7 Format the Value Axes

The Chart toolbar includes buttons for many of the same commands that are shown in the shortcut menus. To display or hide the Chart toolbar, right-click any other toolbar and click Chart. You can also display the Chart toolbar by choosing Toolbars and Chart from the View menu.

You can change the shape of the toolbar by dragging an edge to make it taller or wider. You can also position the toolbar by dragging it by its title bar.

TABLE 8-1 Chart Toolbar

BUTTON	DESCRIPTION
Chart Objects	Lists all the objects in the chart and enables you to choose an object for editing.
Format Object (varies)	Opens the format dialog box for the selected object in the chart.
Chart Type	Lists the chart types available.
Legend	Displays or hides a legend.
Data Table	Displays or hides a table showing the data series.
By Row	Plots a data series by rows.
By Column	Plots a data series by column.
Angle Clockwise	Rotates text downward.
Angle Counterclockwise	Rotates text upward.

1. Display the Chart toolbar.

2. Click one of the values along the y-axis, the sales in dollars. You can see selection handles at the top and bottom of the vertical axis that show it is selected. The **Chart Objects** box on the toolbar shows **Value Axis**; so does the **Name** box.

3. Click the Format Axis button on the Chart toolbar. The Format Axis dialog box opens.

TIP: The Format button on the Chart toolbar shows the name of the selected object. It changes, depending on what is selected.

4. Click the **Number** tab. Choose **Currency** with **0** decimals and **$** as the **Symbol**.
5. Click the **Font** tab and key **7** as the size. Click **OK**.
6. Click the title "Sales in Dollars" along the left edge of the chart. Its name, **Value Axis Title**, appears in the **Chart Objects** box, and it shows selection handles.
7. Click the Format Axis Title button on the Chart toolbar.
8. On the **Font** tab, choose 10-point italic. Click **OK**.
9. Click the arrow next to the Chart Objects button on the toolbar. The list includes all the objects in the chart.
10. Click **Plot Area**. The plot area is the background grid for the columns. It is selected, and the data is outlined in the worksheet.
11. Click the Format Plot Area button on the Chart toolbar.
12. In the **Area** section, click the **None** button. Click **OK**. The grid color is removed.
13. Click the arrow next to the Chart Objects button on the toolbar. Choose **Chart Area**. The chart's background is selected.

14. Click the Format Chart Area button on the Chart toolbar.
15. On the **Patterns** tab, click the **None** button in the **Area** section. Click **OK**. The chart background is removed.

TIP: The chart area background is white. Choosing to use no background color means your chart will print faster than with a white background color and look the same when you use white paper.

16. Click a cell in the worksheet. Press Ctrl+Home.
17. Save the workbook as ***[your initials]*8-7** in your Lesson 8 folder.
18. Print the worksheet with the chart. Close your workbook.

Creating Charts

Before you build your own chart, you must answer two questions. First, what data should you use to create the chart? Second, what type of chart is best for your data? With practice and experience, you can develop a good sense of how to identify data and choose chart types.

You can create basic chart types such as column charts, bar charts, pie charts, and line charts. You can also create specialized charts such as doughnut and radar charts. Table 8-2 describes the chart types available.

TABLE 8-2 Chart Types in Excel

TYPE	DEFINITION
Column	A column chart is the most popular chart type. Column charts show how values change over a period of time. They can also show comparisons among items and can be prepared with 3-D effects. You can stack the columns. Categories are on the horizontal axis (x) and values are on the vertical axis (y).
Bar	Bar charts illustrate comparisons among items or show individual figures at a specific time. They are similar to column charts. Bar charts can use 3-D effects and can show stacked bars. Categories are on the vertical axis (y) and labels might be easier to read than in a column chart. Values are on the horizontal axis (x).
Line	Line charts show trends in data over a period of time. They emphasize the rate of change. 3-D effects are available for line charts. Lines can be stacked and can show markers.
Pie	Pie charts show one data series and compare the sizes of each part of a whole. Pie charts usually should have less than six data points to be relatively easy to interpret. A pie chart can use 3-D effects and can show exploded slices.
Doughnut	Doughnut charts, like pie charts, compare the sizes of parts. A doughnut chart has a hole in the middle. A doughnut chart shows the relative proportion of the whole. A doughnut chart can show more than one data series, with each concentric ring representing a series.
XY (Scatter)	XY (Scatter) charts are used to show relationships between two values, such as comparing additional advertising to increased sales. Scatter charts are different because they do not have a category; both axes show numbers/values.

continues

TABLE 8-2 Chart Types in Excel *continued*

TYPE	DEFINITION
Area	Area charts look like colored-in line charts. They show the rate of change like a line chart but emphasize the magnitude of the change. 3-D effects are available.
Radar	Radar charts show the frequency of data relative to a center point and to other data points. There is a separate axis for each category, and each axis extends from the center. Lines connect the values in a series.
Surface	Surface charts are useful for finding optimum combinations of two sets of data. They show two or more series on a surface. Surface charts can use 3-D effects.
Bubble	Bubble charts compare sets of three values. They are like XY scatter charts with the third value displayed as the size of the bubble. Bubble charts can be 3-D.
Stock	Stock charts are often called "high-low-close charts." They use three series of data in high, low, close order. They can also use volume as a fourth series.
Cylinder	Cylinder charts use a cylindrical shape to show more effect for 3-D column and bar charts.
Cone	Cone charts use a conical shape for dramatic effect in 3-D column and bar charts.
Pyramid	Pyramid charts use a pyramid shape for dramatic effect in 3-D column and bar charts.

EXERCISE 8-8 Create and Edit an Automatic Chart

An automatic chart is inserted in a separate sheet at the press of a key. After you select the values and labels for the chart, just press F11 to create a column chart. You can edit an automatic chart as you would any chart.

To create a column chart, you first select the range of data to be plotted. This should include the category information as well as the values.

1. Open **MayChart** and save it as ***[your initials]*8-8** in your Lesson 8 folder.
2. Select cells A3:B7. This range includes the state category and the values.
3. Press F11. A column chart is created on its own sheet in the workbook.

4. Click the chart title and click the Format Chart Title button on the Chart toolbar.
5. Click the **Font** tab. Format the title as 18-point bold and click **OK**.
6. Click in the title to place the text insertion point.
7. Edit the title to **Number of Kowabungas Sold**

8. Click any column and then click the Format Data Series button on the toolbar.
9. Click the **Options** tab. Click to place a check mark for **Vary colors by point**. Click **OK**.
10. While all columns are selected, click the "Oregon" column. It is selected alone.

11. Click the Format Data Point button on the toolbar.
12. Click the **Patterns** tab and choose a different color in the **Area** group. Click **OK**. Only the selected column is changed.

FIGURE 8-4
Changing an individual column

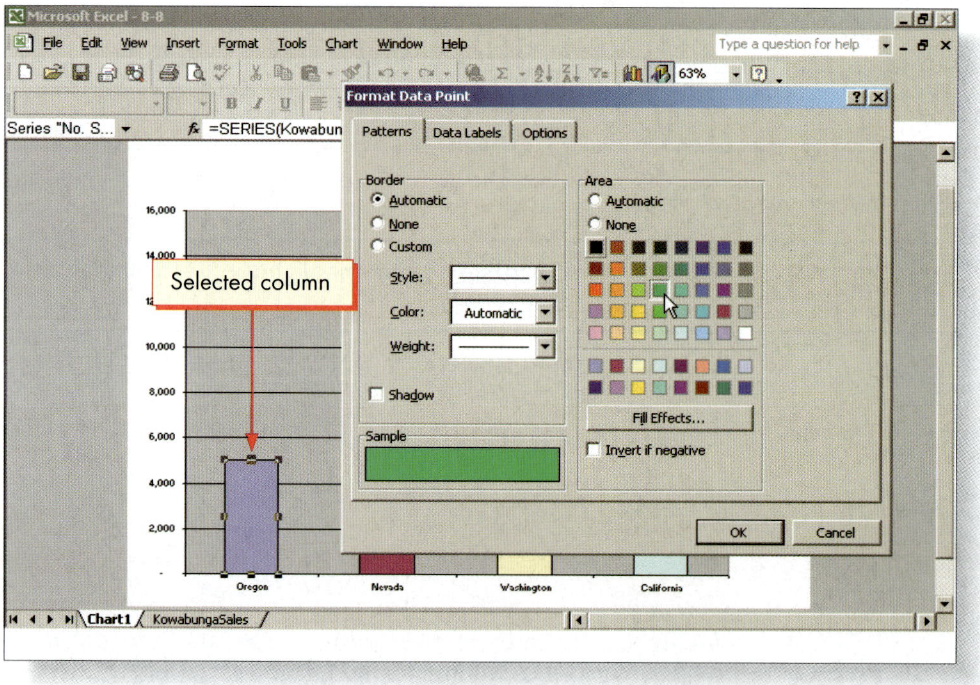

EXERCISE 8-9 Create an Embedded Chart

An embedded chart appears on the same sheet as the data. You create it by using the Chart Wizard. A *wizard* is a series of dialog boxes that lead you step-by-step through the process of creating an object or using a complex feature in Excel. You can start the Chart Wizard by:

- Clicking the Chart Wizard button on the Standard toolbar.
- From the Insert menu, choosing Chart.

1. Click the **KowabungaSales** tab. Cells A3:B7 are still selected.

2. Click the Chart Wizard button. The first Chart Wizard dialog box lists the types of charts available.

TIP: When you have time, experiment with Custom Types to see other chart types.

3. On the Standard Types tab, choose Pie in the Chart type list. Several sub-types for pie charts are shown on the right, with the first one selected. A description appears below the list.

FIGURE 8-5
Creating a pie chart by using the wizard

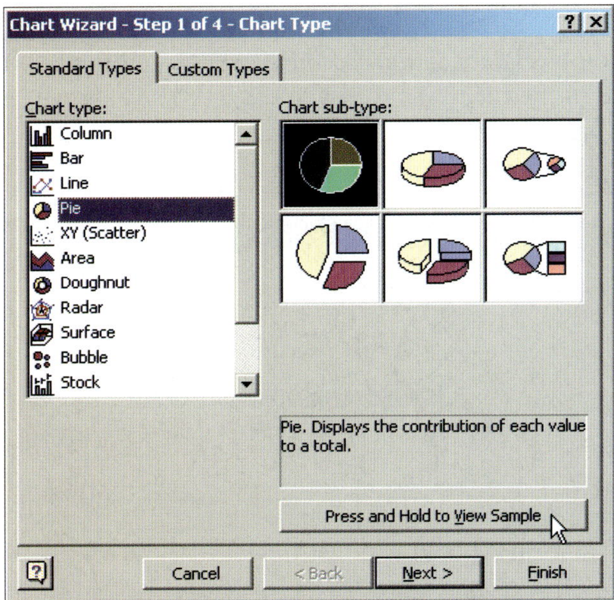

4. Click Press and Hold to View Sample and hold down the mouse button. A sample of your pie chart is shown. Release the mouse button.

5. Click Next. The second dialog box shows the Data range that you selected, A3:B7. The range is shown with absolute references as well as the worksheet tab name. Excel assumes that the series is in a column, because the values are in column B.

6. Click the Rows button. The sample changes to show what your chart looks like if the series is in rows. This pie chart does not make sense.

TIP: If you are not sure if your data is in rows or columns, click each button to see which chart seems more logical.

7. Click the Columns button.
8. Click the Series tab. There is one series or one set of values in this chart. Because the series is in a column, Excel has named the series by using the label from column B.
9. Click Next. The third Chart Wizard dialog box has three tabs of Chart Options for a pie chart.
10. On the Titles tab, drag across the current Chart title to select it.
11. Key **Comparison of State Sales** in the Chart title box. After a few seconds, the new title appears in the preview area.
12. Click the Legend tab. You can choose where to place the legend.
13. Choose Bottom. The legend is below the chart.
14. Click the Data Labels tab. For a pie chart, you can show names, labels, or percents.
15. Click to place a check mark for Percentage in the Label Contains area. The percent of the pie that each slice represents is shown.
16. Click Next. The Chart Location dialog box shows that the chart will be placed as an object in the worksheet.

FIGURE 8-6
Embedding the chart in the worksheet

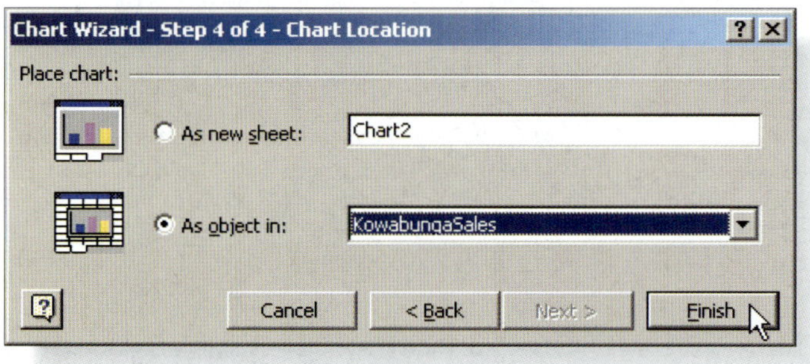

17. Click Finish. The chart is on the sheet with its data.

EXERCISE 8-10 Move and Size a Chart

1. Point at the white background chart area. Drag the chart so its top left corner aligns at cell D1.

NOTE: Move the Chart toolbar so you can see your work area.

2. Point at the bottom right selection handle. A two-headed sizing pointer appears.

NOTE: Change the Zoom size so you can see column K and row 19.

3. Click and drag the bottom right selection handle to cell K19. As you drag, the chart is made larger.
4. Click in column B to deselect the chart.

EXERCISE 8-11 Format a Legend and Pie Slices

1. Right-click the legend and choose Format Legend.
2. Click the Font tab. Change the font size to 9 points and click OK.
3. Right-click the pie and choose Format Data Series.
4. Click the Data Labels tab.
5. Click to remove the check mark for Percentage. Click OK. The pie is larger because there's more room without the data labels (percents).
6. While the pie is selected, left-click the California slice. Only that slice is selected.
7. Right-click the California slice and choose Format Data Point.

FIGURE 8-7 Pie chart with a single slice selected

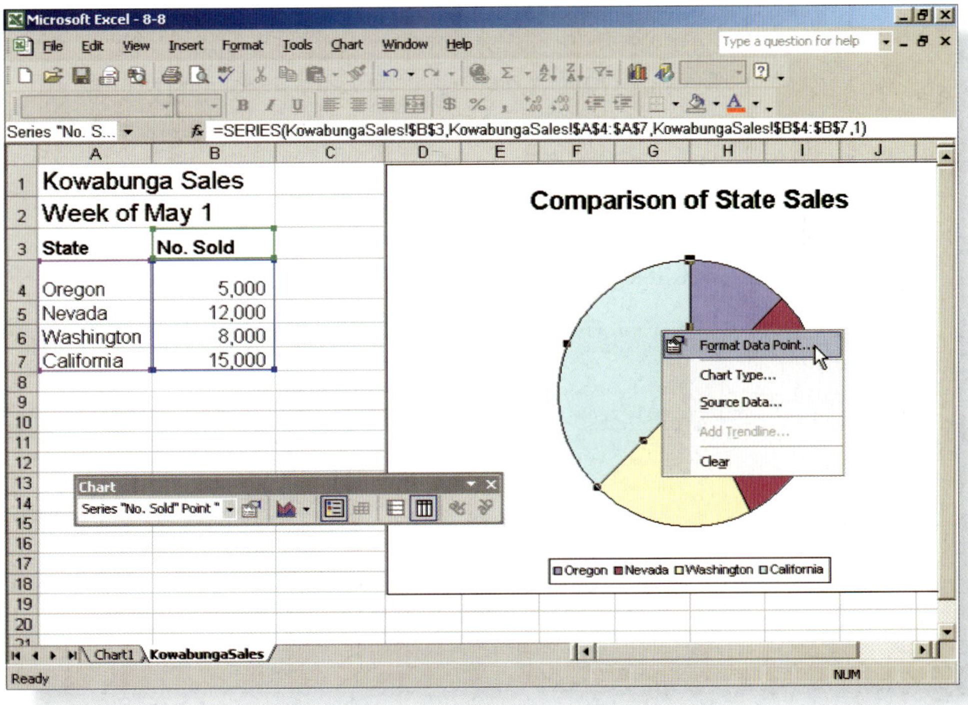

8. Click the Data Labels tab and Percentage. Click OK. The data point percentage is shown for the California slice.

9. Click any cell in the worksheet.

10. Save the workbook as ***[your initials]*8-11** in your Lesson 8 folder.

11. Click the Print Preview button. The chart and worksheet are shown.

12. Click Setup, click the Page tab, and change to Landscape orientation.

13. Add your standard footer and print the worksheet.

EXERCISE 8-12 Create a Chart Sheet

A chart sheet shows a chart by itself in a separate sheet. It is still linked to the data in the worksheet.

1. Select cells A3:B7 and click the Chart Wizard button.

2. On the Standard Types tab, choose Bar in the Chart type list.

3. In the Chart sub-type group, choose Clustered bar with a 3-D visual effect, the first sub-type in the second row.

4. Click Press and Hold to View Sample and hold down the mouse button.

5. Release the mouse button.

6. Click Next. The Data range is cells A3:B7, the states and values. In this bar chart, the category is along the left side of the chart. The values are along the bottom of the chart.

7. Click Next. A bar chart has six tabs of Chart Options.

8. On the Titles tab, key **Comparison of Weekly Sales** in the Chart title box.

NOTE: You might notice a slight delay before titles appear in the preview area.

9. Click in the Value (Z) axis box. Key **Number Sold**

FIGURE 8-8 Chart options for a bar chart

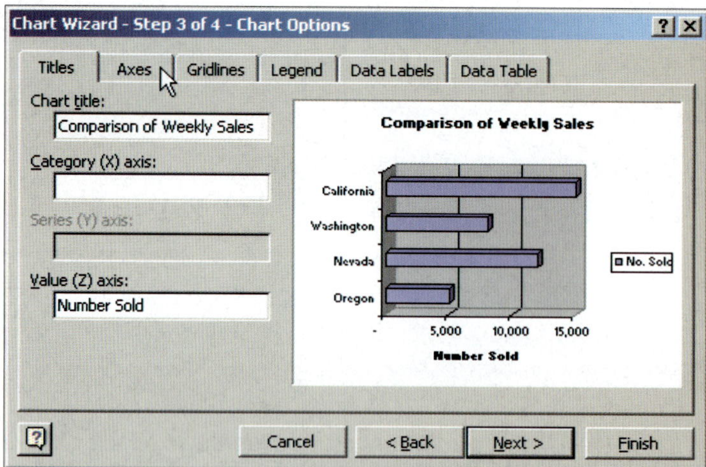

10. Click the Axes tab. The chart shows the categories and the values on the chart. Both show a check mark.

EXERCISE 8-13 Add Gridlines and a Data Table

1. Click the Gridlines tab. Only major gridlines are shown along the value axis.
2. Click to place a check mark for Minor gridlines in the Value (Z) axis group.
3. Click the Legend tab. The legend is shown on the chart.
4. Click to remove the check mark for Show legend.
5. Click the Data Labels tab. It is not necessary to show any labels on this chart.
6. Click the Data Table tab. A data table shows the values and categories below the chart.
7. Click to place a check mark for Show data table.
8. Click Next. You can place a chart in the worksheet or in a separate sheet.
9. Choose As new sheet. Key **BarChart** in the box.
10. Click Finish. The bar chart is on its own sheet.

Editing Chart Data

After you create a chart, you might find that you need to change the values in the worksheet. Because the chart is linked to the data, changes that you make in the worksheet are shown in the chart.

You might also discover that you need to add another category or data series to your chart. Both are easy to accomplish.

EXERCISE 8-14 Change Chart Data

1. Click the KowabungaSales tab. Notice the pie-slice size for Oregon and its corresponding value in the worksheet.
2. Click the BarChart tab. Note the length of the bar for Oregon.
3. Click the Chart1 tab. Note the height of the Oregon column.

REVIEW: The Chart toolbar appears when a chart is selected. You can move it out of the way if necessary.

4. Click the KowabungaSales tab.

5. Click cell B4, key **10000**, and press Enter. Notice the larger pie slice for Oregon.
6. Click the Chart1 tab. The height of the Oregon column is increased.
7. Click the BarChart tab. Note the length of the Oregon bar.

EXERCISE 8-15 Add a Data Point

If you add another state and its total to the worksheet, you add a data point. If you insert the new data point within the chart's data range, it appears automatically in all charts linked to the data. If you add new data below or above the chart's data range, you need to reset the data range for each chart.

1. On the KowabungaSales sheet, key **Idaho** in cell A8.
2. Key **5000** in cell B8. This new data point is not within the existing data range for the charts.
3. Click the white background area for the pie chart. The data range is highlighted in the worksheet.
4. Position the pointer on the bottom right handle for cell B7. A two-headed sizing arrow appears.
5. Drag the sizing arrow to include the Idaho information in the data range. The chart is updated when you release the mouse button.

FIGURE 8-9
Adding a data point (before releasing mouse button)

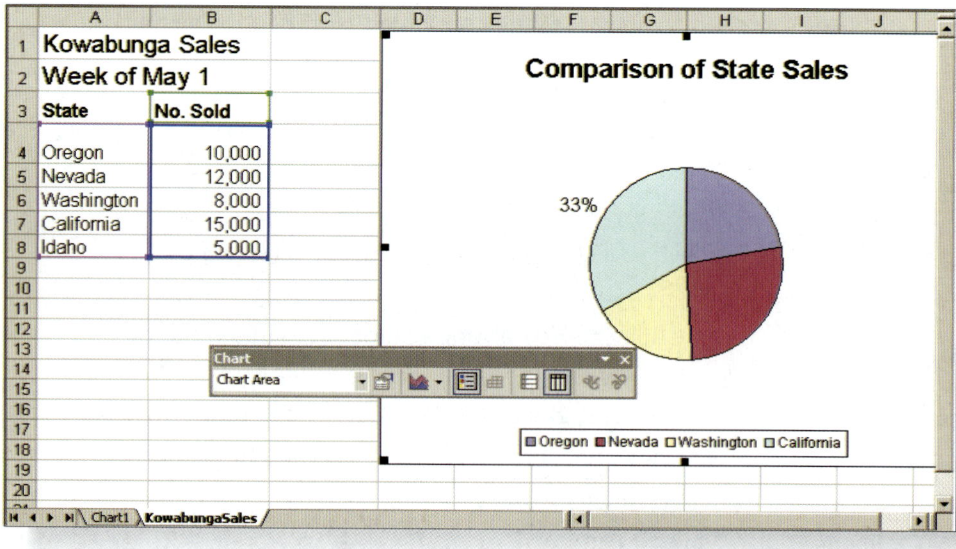

6. Click the Chart1 tab.

7. Right-click the white column-chart background. Choose Source Data. The Source Data dialog box opens on top of the KowabungaSales tab with the current data range selected.

8. In the Data range entry box, edit the address to show **B8** instead of B7. Click OK. The column chart is updated to include Idaho.

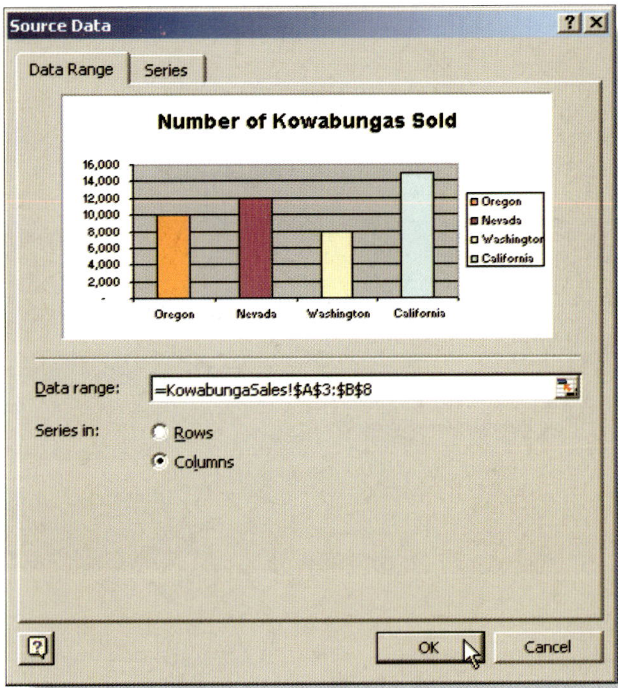

FIGURE 8-10 Source Data dialog box

9. Click the BarChart tab. Right-click the white bar-chart background.

10. Choose Source Data. The current data range is selected in the worksheet.

REVIEW: The dialog box collapses as you drag. It expands when you release the mouse button.

11. Click cell A3 and drag to select cells A3:B8. Click OK.

EXERCISE 8-16 Add a Data Series

If you add another column of values to the worksheet, listing a second product, you add another series.

NOTE: A pie chart has only one series.

1. On the KowabungaSales sheet, key the following values in cells C4:C8:

   6000

   12000

   4500

   15000

   25000

2. In cell B3, key **Kowabunga**. In cell C3, key **KowOwow**

3. Click the white background for the pie chart. Drag the chart to the right so its left edge aligns at the left side of column E.
4. Format the label in cell C3 to match the other labels in row 3.
5. Format the values in column C to match the other values in the worksheet.
6. Autofit columns B and C.
7. Click the Chart1 tab. Right-click the white chart background and choose Source Data.
8. Click cell A3 and drag to select cells A3:C8. Click OK. The column chart now shows two columns for each state, one for each product. Oregon has a different color scheme because you changed it earlier.

FIGURE 8-11
Adding a data series

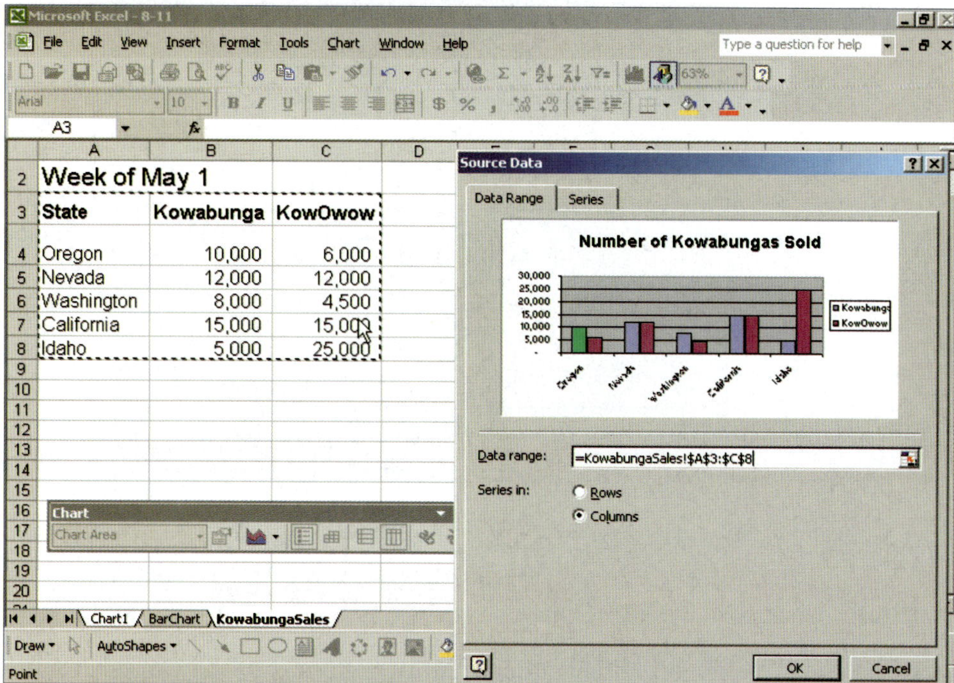

REVIEW: Look at the legend or display the ScreenTip to determine which column represents "Kowabunga."

9. Right-click any column for Kowabunga products. Choose Format Data Series.
10. Click the Patterns tab and choose a different color in the Area group. Click OK.
11. Point at the chart title and click to select it.
12. Click within the text to display a text insertion point.
13. Edit the title to **Number of Kowabungas and KowOwows Sold**
14. Click the white background.

15. Add your standard footer to the chart sheet.
16. Save the workbook as ***[your initials]*8-16** in your Lesson 8 folder. Print the chart sheet.

EXERCISE 8-17 Delete a Data Point and a Data Series

1. Click the KowabungaSales tab.
2. Right-click the row 8 heading and delete the row. The pie chart is updated.
3. Click the BarChart tab. The Idaho data is removed from all charts.
4. Click the KowabungaSales tab.

NOTE: You can delete any chart object or the entire chart by selecting it and pressing Delete.

5. Select cells C3:C7 and press Delete. This deletes the KowOwow series on the column chart.
6. Click the Chart1 tab. The second column is gone, but the legend still shows a marker for the data series.
7. Right-click the white chart background and choose Source Data.
8. In the Data range box, edit the last cell reference to show **b7**. Click OK.
9. Click the legend and press Delete.
10. Save the workbook as ***[your initials]*8-17** in your Lesson 8 folder.

Using Images and Patterns for a Data Series

Charts initially use solid colors in the columns, bars, pie slices, and other objects. You can change from a solid color to a pattern or an image. Patterns can be used to better distinguish bars, columns, or slices, if you use a black-and-white printer. Images allow you to show a picture that represents the data that you are using.

You can insert an image in a worksheet by:

- Clicking the Insert Clip Art button on the Drawing toolbar.
- From the Insert menu, choosing Picture and then Clip Art.

The Drawing toolbar usually appears at the bottom of the window. You can display the Drawing toolbar by:

- Right-clicking any toolbar and choosing Drawing.
- From the View menu, choosing Toolbars and then Drawing.

EXERCISE 8-18 Use an Image for a Data Series

In a bar or column chart, if you want to use an image, it usually looks best if you use a two-dimensional image rather than 3-D one.

1. Click the BarChart tab. Click the chart background to display the Chart toolbar (or click View, Toolbars, Chart).

2. Click the arrow next to the Chart Type button on the Chart toolbar. A palette with several chart types opens.
3. Choose Bar Chart (first icon, second row) to change the chart to a two-dimensional chart.
4. Click any bar in the chart. All the bars show selection handles.

5. Click the Insert Clip Art button on the Drawing toolbar. (If the Drawing toolbar is not open, click View, Toolbars, Drawing.) The Insert Clip Art task pane has search options for finding images in the Media Gallery.
6. In the Search text box, key **kowabunga** to find the image.

NOTE: Ask your instructor for help if you cannot find the image.

7. Click Search. An image of a Kowabunga is shown in the task pane.

FIGURE 8-12
Searching for an image

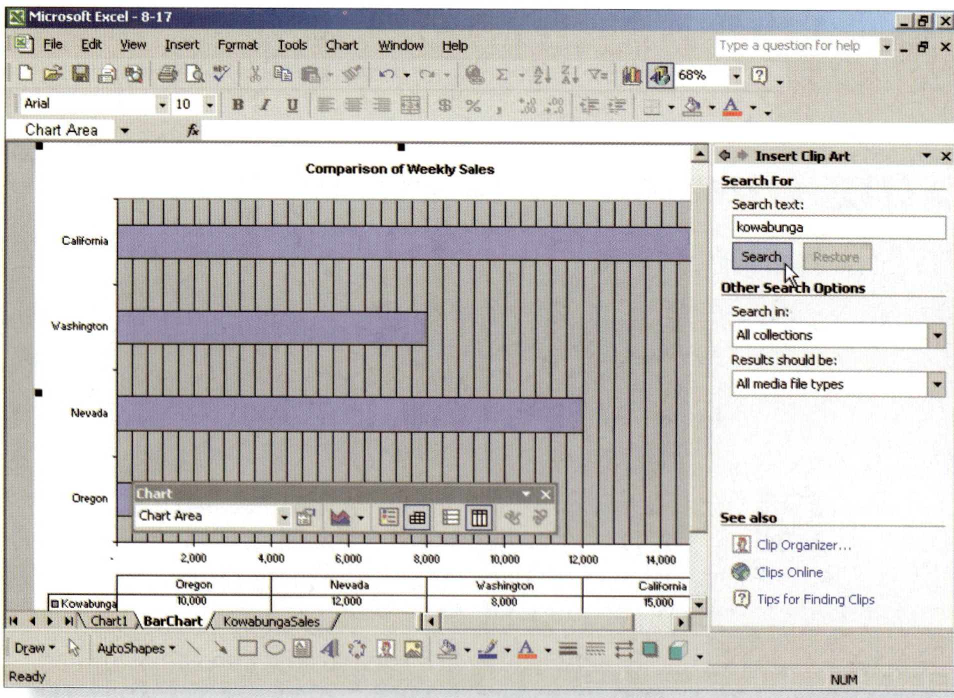

8. Click the image in the task pane. It is inserted in the selected object, the bars. The image is stretched to fit the length of the bar and is distorted.

EXERCISE 8-19 Format the Image

1. Right-click any bar and choose Format Data Series.
2. Click the Patterns tab.
3. Click Fill Effects in the Area group. You can apply gradients (blended colors), textures, patterns, and picture settings.
4. Click the Picture tab. The default for most images is a Stretch format.
5. In the Format group, choose Stack and click OK.
6. Click OK again. The image tiles (stacks) inside the length of the bar.

FIGURE 8-13
Changing the picture format setting

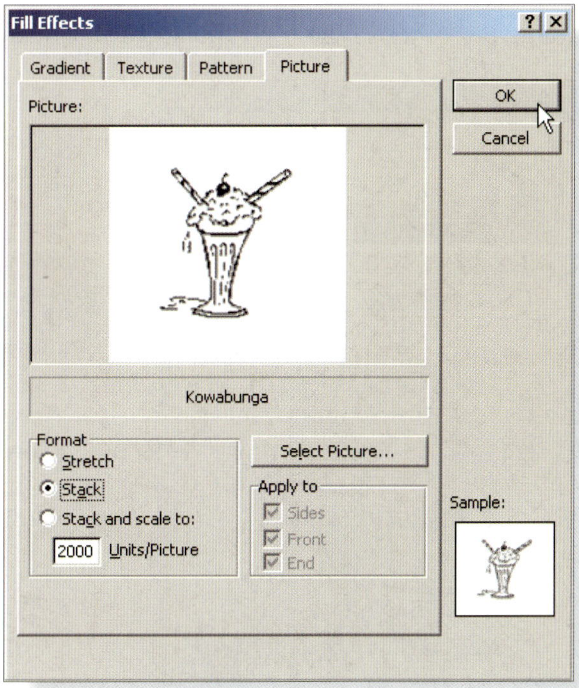

7. Save the workbook as ***[your initials]*8-19** in your Lesson 8 folder.
8. Add your standard footer and print the chart.
9. Close the Insert Clip Art task pane.

EXERCISE 8-20 Use a Gradient for a Data Series

A *gradient* is a blend of colors. In Excel, you can build color blends that use one or two colors, or you can choose from preset gradients. A gradient can give a special effect to bars, columns, or pie slices in a chart.

1. Click the Chart1 tab.

2. Right-click any column and choose Format Data Series.
3. Click the Patterns tab and Fill Effects.

TIP: A one-color gradient uses the color that you choose and blends to dark (black) or light (white).

4. Click the Gradient tab.
5. In the Colors group, choose Two colors.
6. Click the arrow for Color 1 and choose a dark color.
7. Click the arrow for Color 2 and choose a light color.
8. In the Shading styles box, choose Horizontal.

NOTE: The Variants area controls how the two colors blend, top to bottom or left to right.

9. In the Variants box, choose the top right variant. Click OK.

FIGURE 8-14 Using a gradient for fill

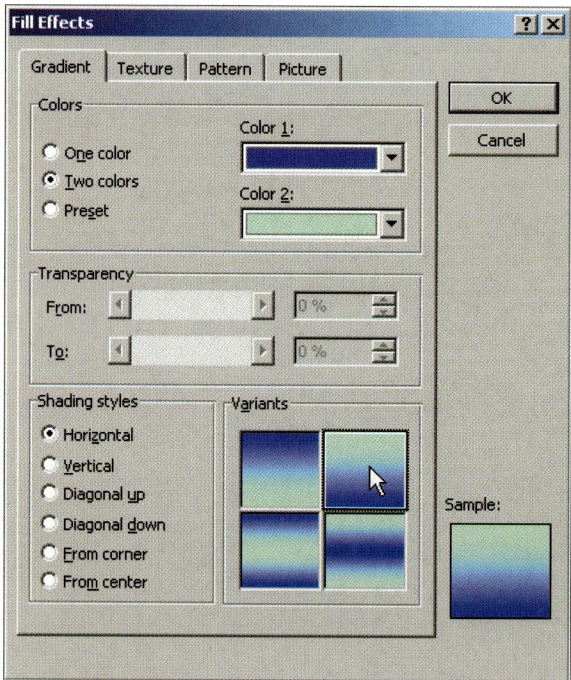

10. Click OK again. All the columns show the gradient.

NOTE: If you're using a black-and-white printer, the gradient uses shades of gray.

11. Save the workbook as ***[your initials]*8-20** in your Lesson 8 folder.
12. Print the chart.

EXERCISE 8-21 Use a Texture and a Pattern for a Data Series

A *texture* is a background that appears as a grainy, non-smooth surface. A *pattern* is a cross-hatched, dotted, dashed, or similar pattern.

1. Click the KowabungaSales tab.
2. Click the pie to select it. The Chart toolbar opens.
3. Click the California slice to select only it.
4. Click the Format Data Point button on the Chart toolbar.
5. Click the Patterns tab. Click Fill Effects.
6. Click the Texture tab. Notice that some textures look similar to marble, wood, and canvas.
7. Click any texture tile. Its description appears below the group.
8. Choose White marble. Click OK and then click OK again.
9. Click to select only the Nevada slice. Click the Format Data Point button on the Chart toolbar.
10. Click the Patterns tab. Click Fill Effects.
11. Click the Pattern tab. The patterns in the first two columns are described as percentages. They are dotted blends of the Foreground and Background colors. The other patterns have descriptive names.
12. Click several different pattern tiles and read their descriptions.
13. Click the arrow for the Foreground color. Choose Black (first tile).
14. Click the arrow for the Background color. Choose White (last column, fifth row).

FIGURE 8-15
Using a pattern as a Fill Effect

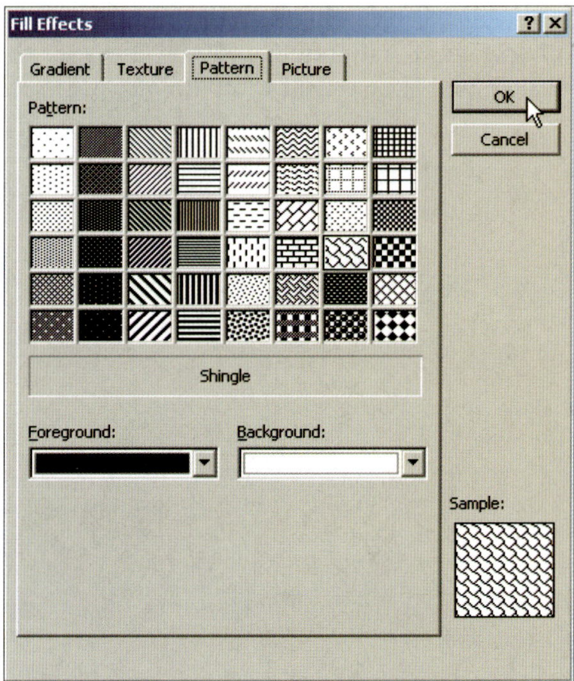

15. Choose one of the patterns, not a dotted percentage. Click OK.
16. Click OK again. Click a cell in the worksheet.
17. Save the workbook as ***[your initials]*8-21** in your Lesson 8 folder.
18. Print the worksheet.

Creating a Combination Chart

A *combination chart* is a single chart that has multiple series and chart types or number scales. A combination chart has at least two series or two sets of values. Some combination charts use the same chart type for each series, but a secondary number scale. A *secondary scale* is a set of axis values that is different from the first (primary) set.

EXERCISE 8-22 Create a Combination Chart

1. Click the white background for the pie chart.
2. Drag the chart so its top left corner aligns at cell A9. The chart will be below the data.

NOTE: The formula multiplies the price by the number sold.

3. Key the data in Figure 8-16 to add another series for the number of KowOwows sold and two series for the dollar value sold of both products.

FIGURE 8-16

	A	B	C	D	E
3	State	Kowabunga	KowOwow	$Kowabunga	$KowOwow
4	Oregon	5,000	12,000	=b4*2.39	=c4*2.19
5	Nevada	12,000	15,000		
6	Washington	8,000	10,000		
7	California	15,000	25,000		

4. Copy the formulas to row 7.
5. Format the results as Currency with no decimals and a dollar sign. Format the font size so the results match the other values.

6. Autofit columns D and E.
7. Click the Chart1 tab. Right-click the white background for the chart.
8. Choose Source Data. The chart currently plots cells A3:B7.
9. Click cell A3 and drag to select cells A3:C7. Click OK.
10. Right-click any Kowabunga bar and choose Chart Type. These are the same chart types you see in the Chart Wizard.
11. Choose Line in the Standard Types tab.
12. Choose Line with markers displayed at each data value. Click OK. The Kowabunga series is now shown as a line.
13. Save the workbook as ***[your initials]*8-22** in your Lesson 8 folder.

FIGURE 8-17
Changing the chart type for a data series

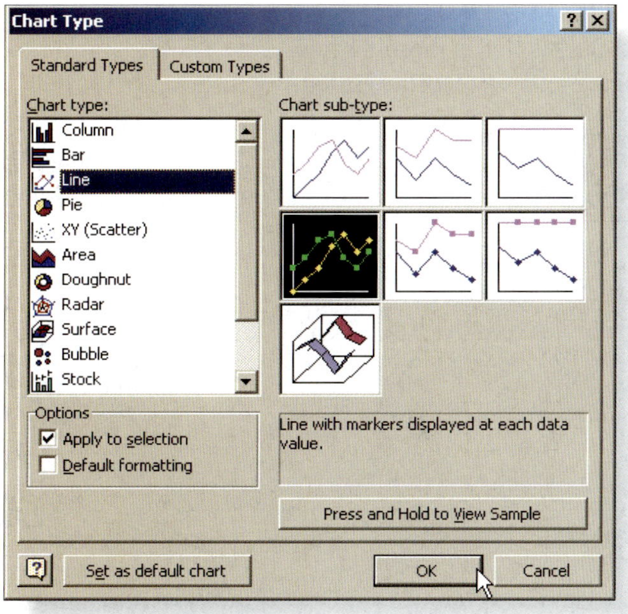

14. Print the chart.

EXERCISE 8-23 Build a Chart with Two Series

You can show the dollar sales and the number of items sold on the same chart. These values will be two different series on the chart.

1. Click the KowabungaSales tab.

REVIEW: Use Ctrl to select noncontiguous ranges. Ranges for a chart need not be contiguous.

2. Select cells A3:A7, C3:C7, and E3:E7. This includes the number of items sold and the dollar values.
3. Click the Chart Wizard button. Choose a Column chart type and a Clustered Column sub-type.
4. Click Next. The series or values are in columns, but the dollar values are disproportionately larger than the number sold.
5. Click the Series tab. There are two series, one for the product and one for the dollars. For the name of each series, Excel uses the label at the top of the column.
6. In the Series list, choose KowOwow.
7. In the Name box, drag across the reference to select it.
8. Key **Number Sold**
9. In the Series list, choose $KowOwow. In the Name box, drag across the reference and key **Dollar Sales**

FIGURE 8-18
Changing a series name

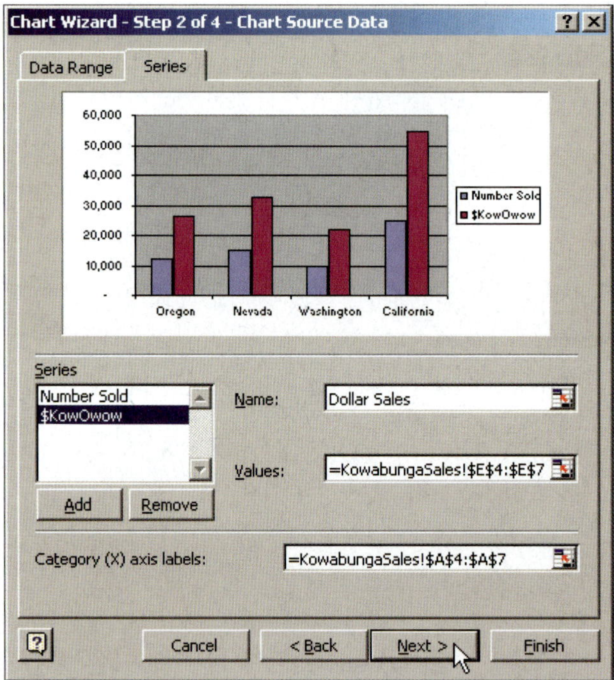

10. Click Next. The Chart Options include six tabs.
11. On the Titles tab, key **Units and Dollars** as the Chart title.
12. Click Next.
13. Choose As new sheet and name the sheet **ComboChart**
14. Click Finish. Both series use the same value axis, so the dollar column is disproportionately taller.

EXERCISE 8-24 Add a Secondary Axis

Because the values are very different, you should use two axes on the chart, one to show the number of items and one to show the dollar amounts. This makes it easier to understand the values in the chart.

1. Right-click a Dollar Sales bar and choose Chart Type.
2. Choose Line in the Standard Types tab.
3. Choose Line with markers displayed at each data value. Click OK.

NOTE: To use a secondary axis, use different chart types for each data series.

4. Right-click a Number Sold bar and choose Format Data Series.
5. Click the Axis tab.
6. Click the radio button for Secondary axis. The selected series will be plotted on a separate value axis. Click OK.
7. Right-click the Dollar Sales line. Choose Format Data Series.
8. Click the Patterns tab. In the Line group, click the arrow next to Color: and choose Black.
9. In the Marker group, click the arrow next to Style. A list of shapes for the line markers is shown.
10. Choose a style.
11. Click the arrow for the Foreground color. Choose Black.
12. Click the arrow for the Background color. Choose Black.
13. Click the up spinner button for Size to reach 10 pts.
14. Click OK. Click the white chart background to see the changes.
15. Add the standard footer to the sheet.
16. Save the workbook as ***[your initials]*8-24** in your Lesson 8 folder.
17. Print the chart sheet and then close the workbook.

LESSON 8 Summary

- Charts can be embedded within a worksheet. They can also be placed in a separate sheet.
- A chart is linked to the data that it is plotting. If the data is edited, the chart reflects the changes.
- A chart includes many individual objects that can be edited.

EXCEL

- Right-click a chart object to see its shortcut menu.
- Charts show data series, which are the chart's values. A pie chart can have only one series, but other types of charts can show multiple data series.
- You can make many chart changes directly from the Chart toolbar.
- If you select data and press F11, Excel creates an automatic column chart.
- The Chart Wizard is a series of dialog boxes in which you choose options for creating a chart.
- Excel's standard types of business charts include bar, column, line, and pie charts.
- Move a chart by selecting it and dragging it. Size a chart by dragging one of its selection handles.
- After a chart is created, you can add a data point or an entire series to it.
- Although charts typically use solid color for columns, slices, and bars, you can use images, patterns, textures, or gradients to add visual appeal to your charts.
- A combination chart typically has at least two series and uses different chart types for each series. However, some combination charts use a single chart type but a secondary axis because the values from the various series are disproportionate.

LESSON 8 Command Summary

FEATURE	BUTTON	MENU	KEYBOARD	SPEECH
Chart title, format		Chart, Chart Options		✓
Axis, format		Chart, Chart Options		
Data series, format		Chart, Chart Options		
Data labels, format		Chart, Chart Options		
Legend, format		Chart, Chart Options		
Clip art, insert		Insert, Picture, Clip Art		✓
Chart, create		Insert, Chart	F11	✓

Concepts Review

TRUE/FALSE QUESTIONS

Each of the following statements is either true or false. Indicate your choice by circling T or F.

T F **1.** A chart sheet includes the related worksheet data.

T F **2.** A selected object displays selection handles.

T F **3.** You can change the color of all or individual bars or columns in a chart.

T F **4.** Excel determines the best type of chart for your data in the Chart Wizard.

T F **5.** A data series can be in rows or columns.

T F **6.** If you insert another item in a range used in a chart, you add a data point.

T F **7.** Each slice in a pie chart represents a data series.

T F **8.** You can use a crisscrossed pattern to fill a bar or column.

SHORT ANSWER QUESTIONS

Write the correct answer in the space provided.

1. What name describes a chart that appears in the worksheet with the data?

____

2. What Chart toolbar button do you use to change a bar chart to a column chart?

____

3. What is the keyboard shortcut to create an automatic chart?

____

4. What name is used for the small black rectangles that appear around an active chart object?

____

5. What term describes a blend of colors for filling a bar or column?

____

6. What can you use when two data series have drastically different values?

____

7. What happens if you delete from the worksheet a data series used in a column chart?

____

8. What are the other common names for the x- and y-axes used in most charts?

____

CRITICAL THINKING

Answer these questions on a separate page. There are no right or wrong answers. Support your answers with examples from your own experience, if possible.

1. Discuss and determine what data and related charts might be developed for your school.

2. What are some advantages of using charts over printed data? What are some pitfalls of charts?

Lesson Applications

EXERCISE 8-25

Create a scatter chart. Edit chart objects. Preview and print a chart.

A scatter chart is commonly known as an XY scatter chart or a "scattergram." This type of chart does not have a category axis. Both axes show values instead. In this chart, you show the relationship between a price decrease and increased sales.

1. Open **Scatter** and save it as ***[your initials]*8-25** in your Lesson 8 folder.
2. Format cell A1 as 18-point Times New Roman. Delete row 2.
3. Format cells A2:B2 as 12-point Times New Roman bold. Format row 2 as 22.50 (30 pixels) high. Format column A as 16.43 (120 pixels) wide. Autofit column B.
4. Select cells A2:B8 and choose XY (Scatter chart), using data points connected by smoothed lines. Create the chart as an object in the worksheet.
5. Place the chart below the worksheet data and size it to reach cell G30.
6. Right-click a value on each axis and use a 9-point font. On the vertical axis (Y), format the numbers to show commas with no decimal places.
7. Delete the legend.
8. Edit the chart title to **Percentage Price Decrease and Increased Sales**
9. Select the Chart Area and click the arrow next to the Fill Color button. Choose No Fill.

REVIEW: The Fill Color button shows the most recently selected color.

10. Click the Plot Area and click the Fill Color button.

NOTE: A chart with no background fill color prints more quickly.

11. Add your standard footer. Print the worksheet and chart.
12. Save and close the workbook.

EXERCISE 8-26

Create a stock chart. Edit chart data. Preview and print a chart.

A stock chart plots daily stock price information. In a stock chart, you list the prices in this order: high price, low price, closing price. There are five sub-types for this chart, with some that include the volume of stocks sold.

1. Create a new workbook and save it as ***[your initials]*8-26** in your Lesson 8 folder.
2. Format cell A1 as 16-point Arial and key **Klassy Kow Stock Investments**
3. In cell B2, key **High**. In cell C2, key **Low**. In cell D2, key **Close**. Make these labels bold, and format the row as 26.25 (35 pixels) high.
4. In cell A3, key **Greenbriar Dairy Services**. This is the company whose stock prices will be shown in the chart. Format column A as 21.43 (155 pixels) wide.
5. In cell A4, key **April 1**. Use AutoFill to fill down to April 10. Delete rows 9 and 10. You will show stock prices for eight days in April.

NOTE: When preparing a stock chart, you should eliminate weekend and other non-trading days.

6. Key the values shown in Figure 8-19.

FIGURE 8-19

	High	Low	Close
April 1	28.25	22.125	24
April 2	27	21.5	24.5
April 3	26.75	20	26.75
April 4	30	27.5	29.75
April 5	28	24.25	27.15
April 8	32.75	30	32.75
April 9	35	27.5	32.125
April 10	38	34.25	34.35

TIP: Stock prices are shown as decimals on most exchanges. In the past, stock prices were stated in fractions. If you key a fraction, Excel converts it to a decimal. You can display a fraction by choosing Fraction in the Format Cells dialog box.

7. Select cells A4:D11 and create a stock chart, using the first sub-type. In the Series tab in the wizard, name Series1 **High**. Name Series2 **Low** and Series3 **Close**.

8. Key **Greenbriar Dairy Services** as the main chart title. On the Axes tab, turn off the labels along the bottom of the chart. On the Gridlines tab, show minor gridlines for the value axis.
9. Do not show a legend, but make sure to show the data table. Place the chart in a separate sheet. Click Finish.

NOTE: The chart shows markers that you might not see until you format them differently.

10. Right-click one of the lines. Choose Format High-Low Lines. Choose a heavy (thick) weight for the line.

TIP: The marker size is shown in points, like a font.

11. Right-click the top of any line and choose Format Data Series. Use a circle for the marker and make its Size 10 pts. Choose the same foreground and background color, but use a color different from the line color. This formats the high price on the line.

NOTE: Excel sets the number scale based on the values used in the chart.

12. Right-click the bottom of any line and choose Format Data Series. Use a pyramid shape for the marker and make its Size 10 pts. Choose the same foreground and background color, but use a color different from the line color and the high marker. This formats the low price.
13. Change the Zoom size to 200%. Scroll the chart to see a line, and right-click the marker between the high and low prices on any line. The marker is tiny and difficult to see. Choose Format Data Series. Use a rectangle shape for the marker and make its Size 10 pts. Choose the same foreground and background color, but use a color different from the line color, the high marker, and the low marker. This formats the close price.
14. Change the Zoom size to 65%.
15. Right-click a value along the vertical axis and choose Format Axis. Click the Scale tab. Make the minimum number **15**. Click OK.
16. Add your standard footer and print the chart.
17. Save and close the workbook.

EXERCISE 8-27

Create an exploded pie chart. Edit chart objects.

The custom charts are variations of the standard chart types. When you print to a black-and-white printer, you can choose an option to create a black-and-white chart. An exploded pie chart shows one of the slices detached from the rest of the pie to emphasize the slice.

1. Open **ExPie** and save it as ***[your initials]*8-27** in your folder for Lesson 8.

REVIEW: Because a pie chart has only one series, it does not have any category titles.

2. Create a pie chart, using the Custom Types to choose a B&W Pie Chart.
3. Key **Shake Flavor Comparison** as the chart title. Show only the category names and no legend. Place the chart in a separate sheet named **PieChart**.
4. Format the chart title to be 24 points.

TIP: You can change the font for a chart object from the Font and Size buttons on the Formatting toolbar.

5. Select the pie. Then click the Butterscotch slice.
6. Point at the slice and drag it up and away from the other slices, not dragging it too far.
7. Select the Vanilla slice and format it to show solid white.
8. Preview the chart and add your standard custom footer. Print the chart.
9. Save and close the workbook.

EXERCISE 8-28 Challenge Yourself

The Klassy Kow Credit Union maintains savings records for employees who contribute regularly to their accounts. You want to prepare a bubble chart to show employees that it is best to start saving as soon as possible. A bubble chart is similar to an XY scatter chart, but it can show an additional series.

1. Open **BubbleChart** and save it as ***[your initials]*8-28** in your Lesson 8 folder.
2. In cell D5, use the FV function to determine the value of an account with the interest rate in cell B3 and the other information as shown. The original amount is the PV, the amount in the account when the savings program starts. Assume that payments are made at the beginning of the month. Copy the formula.

REVIEW: Divide the interest rate by 12 for monthly payments. Multiply the number of years by 12 to determine the Nper. Use absolute references.

3. Select cells A4:A9, B4:B9, and D4:D9 and create a bubble chart. In the Series tab, make sure column A is the x-axis, column B is the y-axis, and column D shows the Sizes.

4. As a main chart title, key **Growth of Your Deposits**. Place the chart in a separate sheet named **Bubbles**
5. Format the bubbles to show different colors for each one.
6. Preview the entire workbook. Add the standard footer to both sheets, and print both.
7. Save and close the workbook.

On Your Own

In these exercises you work on your own, as you would in a real-life work environment. Use the skills you've learned to accomplish the task—and be creative.

EXERCISE 8-29

In a new workbook, key your city, state, and ZIP code in cell A1. Starting in cell A3, key the date and month for the past 10 days. Use the local newspaper or an Internet site to determine the high temperature for each of those days and key the values in column B. Create a line chart that plots the average daily temperature. Decide on a main title and whether or not you need axis titles, gridlines, a legend, or a data table. Embed the chart in the worksheet. Format the line chart and its markers in an attractive manner. Position the chart appropriately in relation to the worksheet data. Add a second title in cell A2 and format both titles with a larger font. Add your standard footer and print the worksheet and chart. Save the workbook as ***[your initials]*8-29** in your Lesson 8 folder and close it.

EXERCISE 8-30

Build an embedded pie chart to show your weekly expenses. Use at least four categories or types of expenses. Add a main title and decide whether to show labels or percentages on the chart. Save the workbook as ***[your initials]*8-30** in your Lesson 8 folder. Add your standard footer, print the chart sheet, and close the workbook.

EXERCISE 8-31

Open ***[your initials]*7-22** from your folder for Lesson 7. Save it as ***[your initials]*8-31** in your folder for Lesson 8. Create a column chart that shows the names on the category axis and heights in inches on the value axis. Add an appropriate title and vary the colors of the data points. Place the chart in a separate sheet. Make other formatting changes so your chart is easy to interpret. Add your standard footer and print the chart. Save and close the workbook.

LESSON

9 Adding Design Elements

OBJECTIVES

MOUS ACTIVITIES

In this lesson:

Ex2002 3-6
Ex2002 6-2
Ex2002 7-1
Ex2002 7-3

See Appendix E.

After completing this lesson, you will be able to:

1. Add callouts to a worksheet.
2. Format drawing objects.
3. Insert WordArt.
4. Insert a picture.
5. Use a background picture.
6. Add an image to a header or footer.
7. Insert a comment.
8. Save a workbook as a Web page.

Estimated Time: 1¾ hour

In addition to charts, Excel has other features to increase the visual appeal of your worksheets. These features add design objects to your worksheet that can be sized, moved, and formatted. Design objects include text boxes, lines (with or without arrows), callouts, and images.

Design objects are placed on a draw layer. The *draw layer* is an invisible layer that is separate from the worksheet data.

REVIEW: An object is a separate element (part) of a worksheet.

Adding Callouts to a Worksheet

An *AutoShape* is a common, recognized figure, shape, or outline. AutoShapes, as well as other drawing objects, are located on the Drawing toolbar. AutoShapes include common callout shapes. A *callout* is descriptive text enclosed in a shape. Callouts typically include a line or arrow that points to data or an object on the worksheet.

TABLE 9-1 Drawing Toolbar

BUTTON	FUNCTION
Draw	Displays a list of commands for adjusting drawing objects.
Select Objects	Activates a pointer for selecting objects.
AutoShapes	Displays a list of preset objects.
Line	Draws a vertical, horizontal, or diagonal line.
Arrow	Draws a line with an arrow.
Rectangle	Draws a rectangle or square. Hold down Shift to make a square.
Oval	Draws an oval (an ellipse) or circle. Hold down Shift to make a circle.
Text Box	Draws a rectangle to hold text.
Insert WordArt	Inserts an image from the WordArt Gallery.
Insert Diagram or Organization Chart	Inserts a blank organization chart, a radial diagram, a pyramid diagram, or other business diagrams.
Insert Clip Art	Inserts clip art from the Media Gallery.
Insert Picture from File	Inserts an image saved on a disk, your hard drive, or the network.

continues

TABLE 9-1 Drawing Toolbar *continued*

BUTTON	FUNCTION
Fill Color	Sets the background color for an object.
Line Color	Sets the color of a line or the outline of an object.
Font Color	Changes the color of text in an object.
Line Style	Displays a list of line thicknesses (weights) and styles (single, double, and so on.)
Dash Style	Displays a list of dash styles.
Arrow Style	Displays a list of arrow sizes, shapes, and positions.
Shadow Style	Displays a list of shadow styles and positions for drawing objects.
3-D Style	Displays a list of 3-dimensional effects for drawing objects.

EXERCISE 9-1 Add a Callout to a Worksheet

Callouts and most other AutoShapes have the following features:

- Selection handles, round white handles surrounding the shape.
- An *adjustment handle,* a yellow diamond handle on an AutoShape used to change the shape and design of the AutoShape. (The adjustment handle makes changes based on the design of the AutoShape, so each shape has its own type of adjustments.)
- A *rotation handle,* a green circle that acts as a handle to rotate an object.
- A *bounding box,* a rectangular outline around an object.

1. Create a new workbook from the **K&KSales** template. Save the workbook as ***[your initials]*9-1** in a new folder for Lesson 9.

REVIEW: Click General Templates in the New From Template group on the New Workbook task pane.

2. Add the following data to columns B and C in the worksheet. Any green error triangles will be removed as you key values in the cells used in the formulas.

FIGURE 9-1

State	Kowabunga	KowOwow
Oregon	2575	2000
Nevada	3550	3000
Washington	5600	4500
California	6500	6700

3. Display the Drawing toolbar by right-clicking any visible toolbar and choosing Drawing. The Drawing toolbar usually appears at the bottom of the screen.
4. Click AutoShapes on the Drawing toolbar. Choose Callouts.

TIP: Each callout AutoShape has a ScreenTip with its name.

5. Choose Rounded Rectangular Callout, the first row, the second shape. The pointer changes to a thin cross.

FIGURE 9-2
Choosing a callout

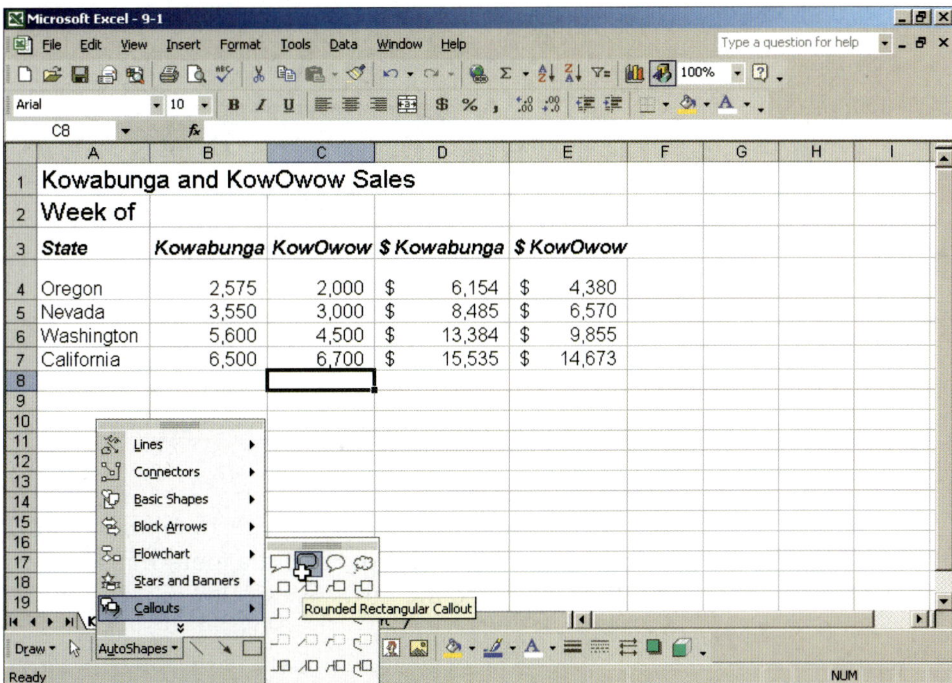

6. Click and drag to draw a rectangular shape starting at cell F3 and extending to cell G4. The shape appears with a text insertion point in the callout, round white selection handles, and diagonal lines outlining the shape.
7. Key **KowOwow prices were decreased early in the year.**

FIGURE 9-3
New callout on the worksheet

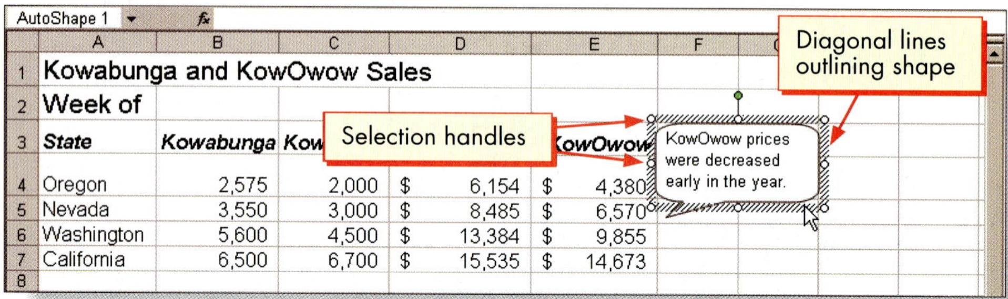

8. Click cell F7. The AutoShape is deselected.
9. Using the four-headed arrow pointer, click the outline or bounding box of the callout. It is selected and shows a dotted pattern as the outline. The dotted-pattern outline selects the entire object. You can now see its adjustment handle.

FIGURE 9-4
Selected callout

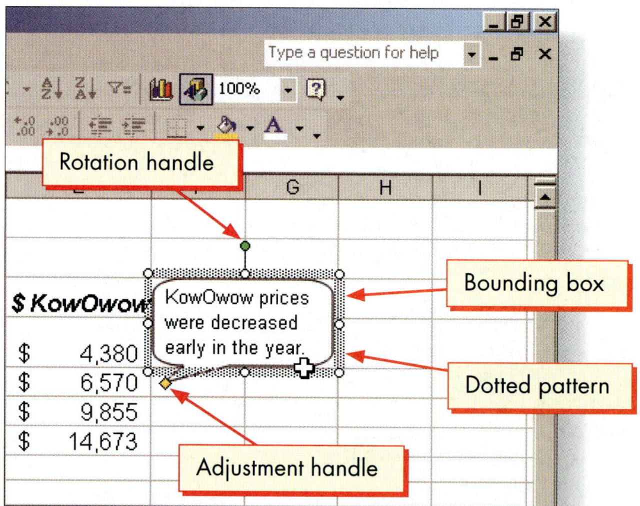

10. Click inside the callout. The text insertion point appears, and the dotted lines become diagonal lines. The diagonal-lines border means you can work with the text inside the box.
11. Click cell C7.

EXERCISE 9-2 Add a Text Box to a Worksheet

A text box is similar to a callout but it does not have connector lines or arrows. You can use a text box to display titles, comments, or notes.

1. Click the Text Box button on the Drawing toolbar. The pointer changes to an upside-down lowercase "T."
2. Placing the intersection of the lines in the "T" pointer at the top left corner of cell C11, click and drag to draw a rectangular shape that extends to cell D13. The shape appears with the diagonal-lines border and a text insertion point.

NOTE: If you draw a shape that you do not like, click to select it (it will then show the dotted pattern outline), and press Delete. Then try again.

3. Key **California shops report on Friday; others report on Monday.**
4. Click cell E9. The text box is deselected.
5. Using the four-headed arrow pointer, click the outline of the text box. When the box object is selected, it shows a dotted-pattern outline.
6. Click inside the text box. When you click inside the box, it is selected for text editing and shows diagonal lines.

NOTE: When an AutoShape, text box, or other drawing object is selected, its name appears in the Name box.

7. Click cell A11.

EXERCISE 9-3 Add a Line with an Arrow to a Worksheet

1. Click the Arrow button on the Drawing toolbar. The pointer changes to a thin cross.
2. Point near the top left corner of the text box you just drew.
3. Hold down Shift and drag to the lower right corner of cell A7. Release the mouse button and then release Shift. The arrow appears where you finish drawing. The line has two selection handles.

TIP: Holding down Shift while drawing a line keeps it straight.

4. Click cell A9. The line is deselected.
5. Using the four-headed arrow pointer, click the line. It is selected again.

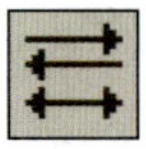

6. Click the Arrow Style button on the Drawing toolbar. A palette of lines and arrows opens.

7. Choose Arrow Style 7 for a line with arrows at both ends.

8. Click the Line Style button. A palette of weights or thickness settings opens.

9. Choose 1½ point. The line is now thicker.

Formatting Drawing Objects

Many drawing objects have a fill color, an outline or border color, a line thickness or weight, and a font style and size. You can also change the size and position of drawing objects and add special effects, such as shadows.

EXERCISE 9-4 Change the Font of Text in Drawing Objects

1. Using the four-headed arrow pointer, click the outline of the rounded rectangle callout shape. The shape displays the dotted pattern outline. This means edits will affect all the text in the shape.

TIP: If you cannot click to select an object, click the Select Objects button on the Drawing toolbar.

2. With the object selected (and showing the dotted pattern outline), choose 10-point Times New Roman from the Formatting toolbar. The text changes.

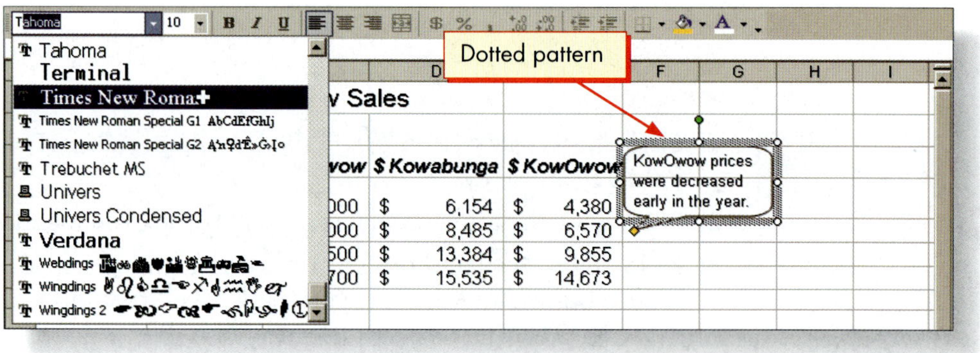

FIGURE 9-5 Entire callout selected, changing the font for all the text

3. Click inside the rounded rectangle callout to display a text insertion point. The outline displays diagonal lines with the selection handles, meaning that your edits will affect only the selected text.

4. Double-click "KowOwow" to select the word.

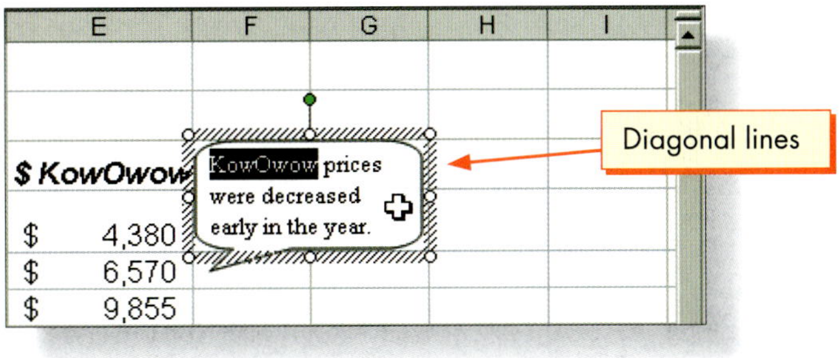

FIGURE 9-6 Changing font of selected text in a callout

5. Choose 11-point Times New Roman from the Formatting toolbar.

6. Click the Bold button. Only the selected text in the callout is changed.

EXERCISE 9-5 Change the Colors of Drawing Objects

1. Using the four-headed arrow pointer, click the line running from cell A7 to the text box. The line is selected.

2. Click the Line Color button on the Drawing toolbar. The color on the button is applied to the line.
3. Click the arrow next to the Line Color button. A palette of colors opens.
4. Choose Green (fourth swatch, second row) in the palette. The line is recolored.

TIP: The Line Color button shows the last selected color. The palette swatches have ScreenTips with the color name.

5. Using the four-headed arrow pointer, click the text box. The dotted pattern outline appears, indicating that the shape is selected.
6. Click the Line Color button. The color on the button (Green) is applied to the outline of the text box.

7. Click the Fill Color button. The color on the button is applied to the background of the text box.
8. Click the arrow next to the Fill Color button. The color palette opens.
9. Choose Light Green in the last row of the palette (fourth swatch).

EXERCISE 9-6 Move and Size Drawing Objects

1. Using the four-headed arrow pointer, click the rounded rectangle callout to show the dotted pattern outline.

2. Place the pointer on the top right selection handle to display a two-headed arrow. This is a sizing pointer.
3. Drag up slightly to reach the middle of row 2.

TIP: When an object is selected with the dotted pattern outline, you can nudge it by pressing any arrow key.

4. Place the mouse pointer on the outline of the callout. The four-headed arrow appears again.
5. Drag the callout down so its top edge is now at row 7.

6. Click the arrow next to the Font Color button and choose White. The text is invisible because it is on a white background.

NOTE: You can use the Font Color button or the Fill Color button on the Drawing or Formatting toolbar.

7. Click the arrow next to the Fill Color button and choose Black. Now you can see the text.

EXERCISE 9-7 Reshape and Rotate a Drawing Object

You can drag the adjustment handle on an AutoShape to reshape the object. The changes you can make depend on the AutoShape and vary from shape to shape. The adjustment handle is a yellow diamond.

The rotation handle enables you to rotate an object in any direction. It is a small green circle.

1. Click the adjustment handle for the callout.
2. Click and drag the adjustment handle to the right. Part of the callout adjusts.

TIP: If an object appears to be anchored to its adjustment handle, deselect the object. Then select it by clicking the bounding box.

3. Double-click the adjustment handle. It returns to its default location for the shape.
4. Click and drag the adjustment handle so it points to the label in cell E3.
5. Place the mouse pointer over the green rotation handle. A circulating arrow surrounds the handle.
6. Drag in any direction, moving the mouse in a small arc to rotate the object. The shape rotates, but the text does not.

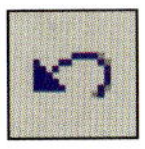

TIP: Click the Undo button to practice rotating objects until you are comfortable with the results.

FIGURE 9-7
Rotating an object

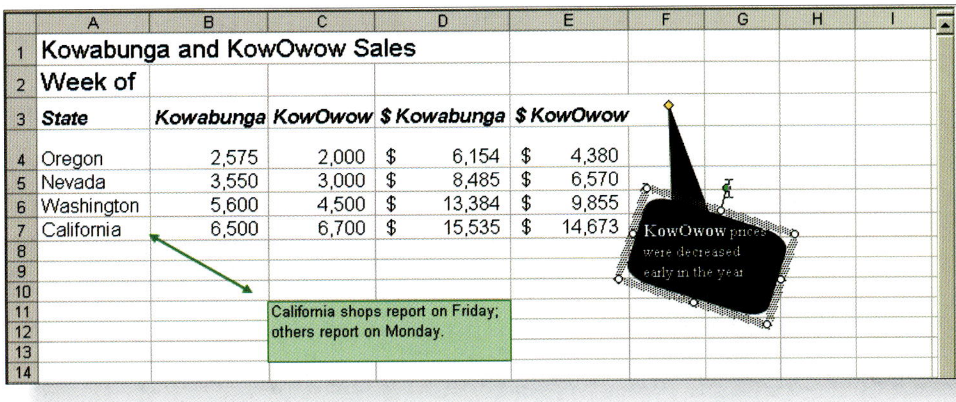

7. Reposition the adjustment handle so it points to cell E3 after you finish experimenting with rotation.

EXERCISE 9-8 Change an AutoShape

1. Select the text box. It shows the dotted pattern with the selection handles.
2. Choose Draw on the Drawing toolbar. A menu of additional commands appears.
3. Choose Change AutoShape. A list of shapes appears.
4. Choose Stars and Banners. A list of star and banner shapes appears.
5. Choose Change Shape to Double Wave (last button, last row). This shape has two adjustment handles.

FIGURE 9-8
Changing the AutoShape

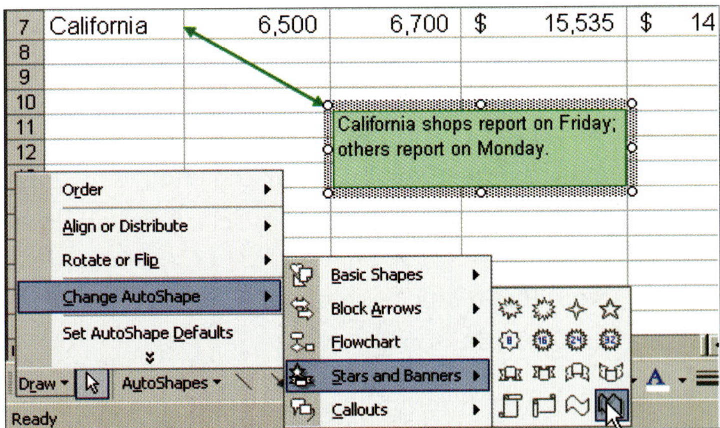

6. Click the bottom adjustment handle and drag it to the left. You are not able to drag very far. This adjusts the wave.
7. Click the left adjustment handle and drag it down. You are again not able to drag very far.
8. Place the pointer on the bottom middle selection handle to display a two-headed sizing arrow.
9. Click and drag down to row 16 to make the shape taller.
10. Place the pointer on the right middle selection handle to display a two-headed sizing arrow.
11. Drag right to the middle of column E to make the shape wider.
12. Using the four-headed arrow pointer, click the line to select it.
13. Place the mouse pointer on the lower selection handle to display a two-headed sizing arrow.
14. Hold down Shift and drag the handle to extend the line closer to the wave. Release the mouse button and then release Shift.

EXERCISE 9-9 Add Text to an AutoShape

You can add text to any shape. You would first draw the shape, then select it, and then key the text.

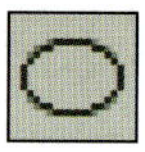

1. Click the Oval button on the Drawing toolbar. The pointer turns to a thin crosshair.
2. Click at the top left corner of cell F14 and drag down to the bottom right corner of cell H17.
3. Release the mouse button. An oval shape is displayed, with the most recently used fill color.
4. Click the arrow next to the Fill Color button.
5. Choose Tan in the bottom row, second swatch.
6. Key **This report is completed each week at corporate headquarters.**
7. Click to display the dotted pattern and change the font to 9-point Arial.
8. Place the pointer on the middle left selection handle to display a sizing pointer.
9. Drag left to the middle of column E.

10. Click the Center button.

EXERCISE 9-10 Use the Format AutoShape Dialog Box

Although you can make one change at a time to objects by using the Drawing and Formatting toolbars, you can use the Format AutoShape dialog box to make several changes at once to an AutoShape.

You can open the Format AutoShape dialog box by:

- Right-clicking the shape outline and choosing Format AutoShape from the shortcut menu.
- Selecting the shape so it displays the dotted pattern and then pressing Ctrl + 1.
- Selecting the shape so it displays the dotted pattern and choosing AutoShape from the Format menu.

1. Right-click the outline of the oval shape and choose Format AutoShape. The Format AutoShape dialog box includes several tabs for making changes to the shape.
2. Click the Colors and Lines tab.
3. In the Line group, click the arrow for Color.
4. Choose Brown in the first row, second swatch.

FIGURE 9-9
Format AutoShape dialog box

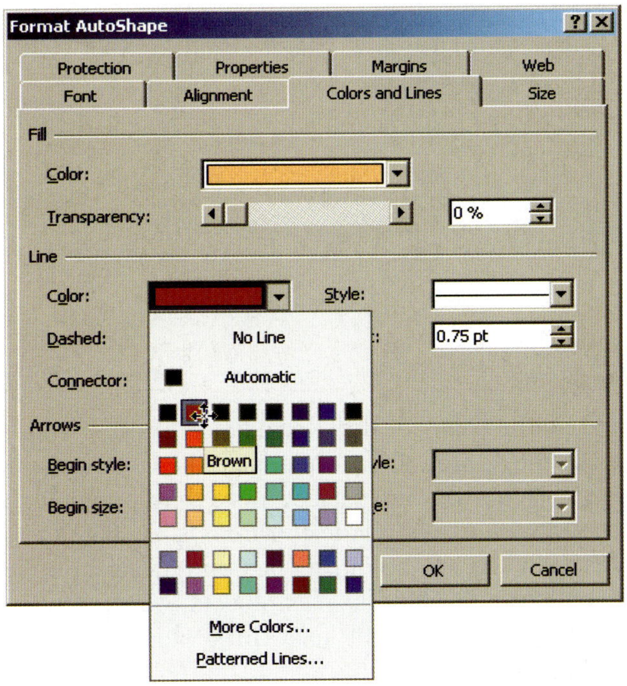

5. Click OK.

EXERCISE 9-11 Add a 3-D Effect

A *3-D effect* applies a three-dimensional look to an object so it appears to have a depth, as well as a height and width.

1. Make sure the oval shape is selected and shows the dotted pattern outline.
2. Click the 3-D Style button  on the Drawing toolbar. A palette of three-dimensional designs opens.

FIGURE 9-10
3-D options

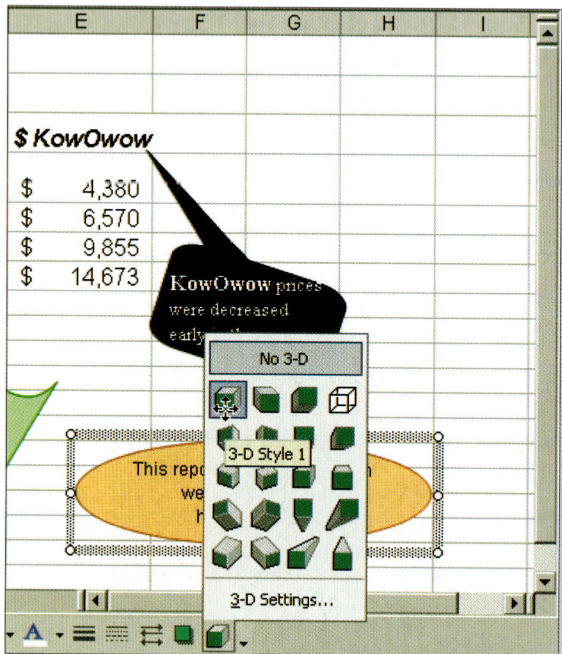

3. Click 3-D Style 1, the first button in the first row. The oval shape is changed to a three-dimensional shape with highlights and shadows.

EXERCISE 9-12 Align or Distribute Drawing Objects

When you use more than one drawing element on your worksheet, you can arrange the objects so they align at the top edges, the left edges, the right edges, and so on. To align objects, you must select more than one object. With only one object selected, the Align and Distribute commands are not available. The alignment of objects uses each object's bounding box and its selection handles.

The Distribute command spaces objects evenly across the area occupied by the objects. You must select at least three objects for the Distribute command to be available.

1. Make sure the 3-D oval is selected and shows the dotted pattern outline.
2. Drag the oval object so its bottom edge is at row 20.

3. Using the four-headed pointer, hold down Shift and click the wave object. Both objects are selected and show handles.

NOTE: The Name box is empty when more than one object is selected.

4. Click Draw on the Drawing toolbar.
5. Choose Align or Distribute. Alignment options appear in the submenu. The Distribute options are dimmed, because only two objects are selected.
6. Choose Align Bottom. The two shapes are aligned on their bottom edges relative to the object that was lowest on the screen.

FIGURE 9-11
Aligning objects

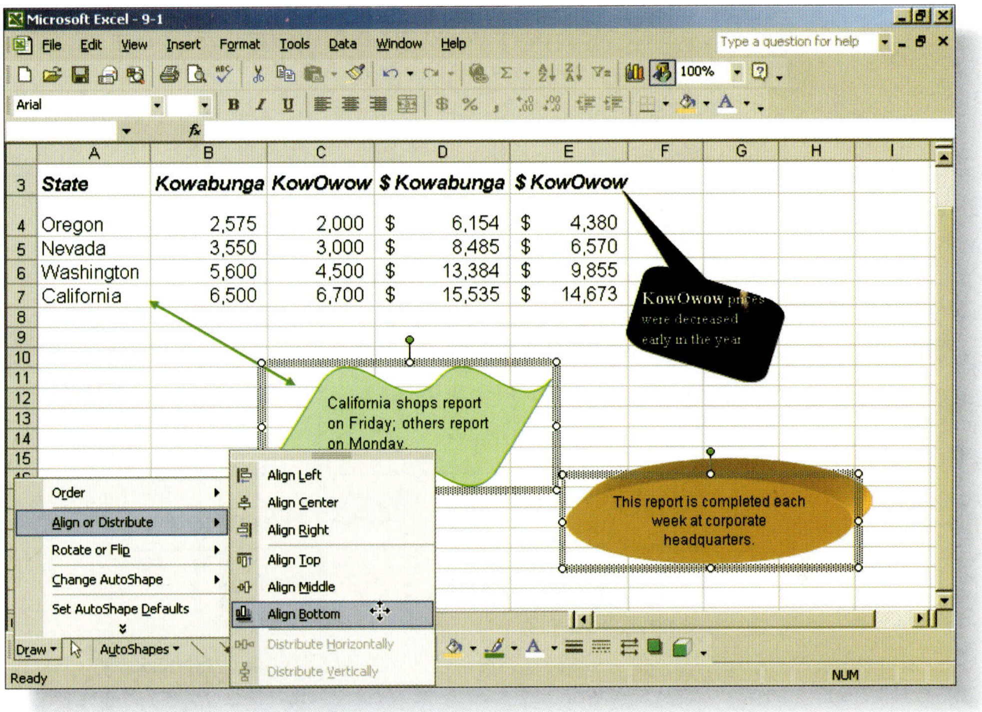

7. Using the four-headed pointer, hold down Shift and click the line object. Three objects are selected.
8. Click Draw. Choose Align or Distribute and then Distribute Vertically. The three objects are spaced evenly between the top edge of the top object and the bottom edge of the bottom object.

Inserting WordArt

WordArt is an application that is included with Microsoft Office and works in all the Office applications. A WordArt image is text that is shaped and colored. A text image from the WordArt Gallery is similar to an AutoShape: it is an object with selection handles, an adjustment handle, and a rotation handle.

You can insert WordArt by:

- Clicking the Insert WordArt button button on the Drawing toolbar.
- From the Insert menu, choosing Picture and WordArt.

EXERCISE 9-13 Insert WordArt on a Worksheet

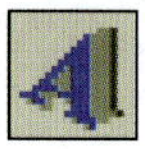

1. Click cell B18.
2. Click the Insert WordArt button on the Drawing toolbar. The WordArt Gallery displays 30 variations.
3. Click the style in the bottom row, second from the right.

FIGURE 9-12
WordArt Gallery

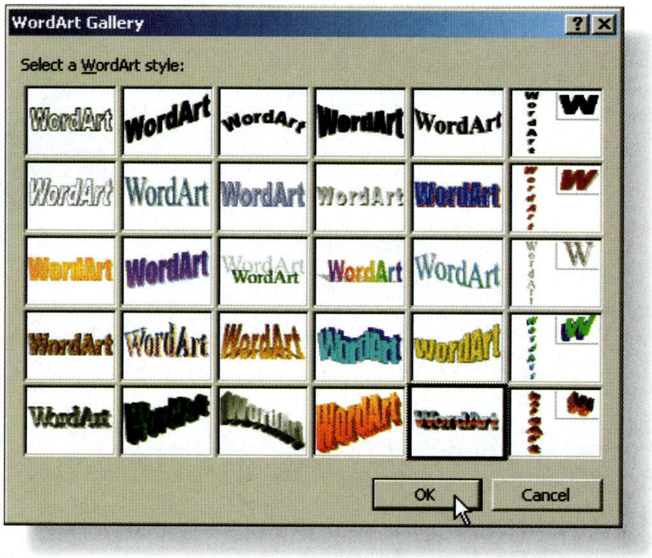

4. Click OK. The Edit WordArt Text box opens with default sample text.
5. Key **Klassy Kow**. The text you key replaces the sample text.
6. Click the arrow for the Size and choose 24.
7. Click OK. The WordArt image appears on the worksheet in a default location and the WordArt toolbar opens.
8. With the four-headed pointer, drag the WordArt object so its top left handle is at cell B18. (See Figure 9-13 on the next page.)
9. Save your workbook as ***[your initials]*9-13** in your Lesson 9 folder.
10. Add your standard footer and print the worksheet.

FIGURE 9-13
WordArt image and toolbar

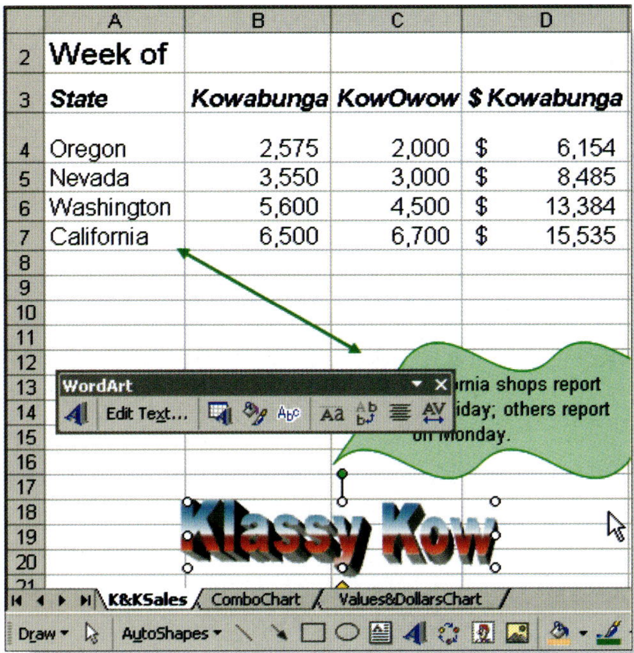

EXERCISE 9-14 Insert WordArt on a Chart

1. Click the ComboChart tab.
2. Click the Insert WordArt button.
3. Choose a style that is different from the style you used in the previous exercise and click OK.
4. Key **Klassy Kow** and click OK. The WordArt image appears on the chart.
5. With the four-headed pointer, move the WordArt image to the top left corner of the plot area.

REVIEW: The plot area is the gray background area with gridlines.

6. Click away from the WordArt image to deselect it.
7. Save the workbook as ***[your initials]*9-14** in your Lesson 9 folder.
8. Add your standard footer and print the chart sheet.

Inserting a Picture as an Object

Like shapes and WordArt, images add visual appeal to your work. You can insert any image from the Media Gallery or any of your own files on a worksheet or on a chart. When you insert an image, Excel treats it as an object (just like WordArt or an AutoShape). You can edit the size, position, and other elements of an image, depending on what type of image it is.

TIP: For the best effect, use only one or two images or objects on a worksheet or chart.

EXERCISE 9-15 Insert a Picture from a File

To insert a picture, you must have the picture in a graphics format as a file on a disk, on your hard drive, or on your network. The **KowOwow** file that is used in the following exercise is a *TIF* file (Tagged Image Format), a popular graphics format for printing images.

You can insert a picture from a file by:

- Clicking the Insert Picture from File button on the Drawing toolbar.
- From the Insert menu, choosing Picture and From File.

You can set the Insert dialog box to show previews so you see the image before inserting it.

1. Click the **Values&DollarsChart** tab.

2. Click the Insert Picture from File button on the Drawing toolbar. The Insert Picture dialog box opens.
3. Open the folder where your student files are located and click **KowOwow** to select it.

4. Click the arrow next to the Views button and choose Preview. A preview of the image is shown in the dialog box.

FIGURE 9-14
Inserting a picture from a file

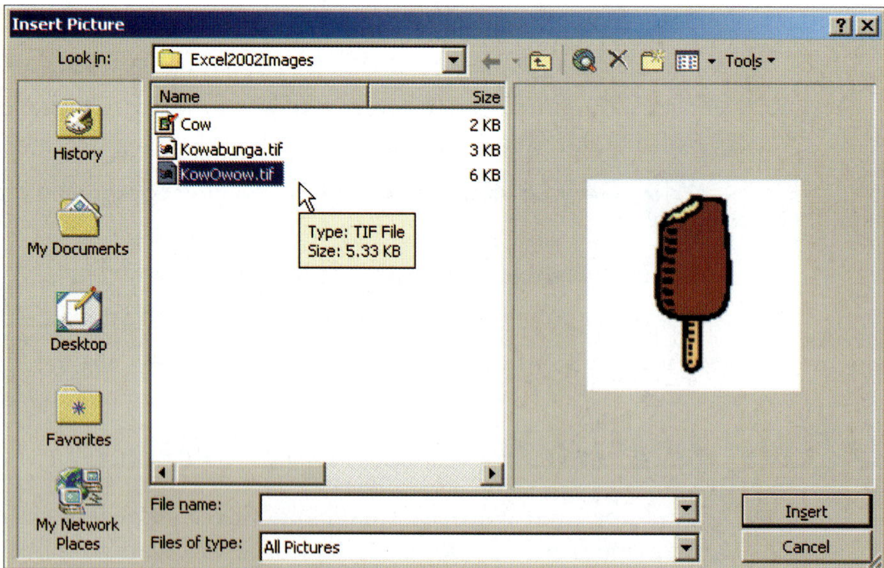

5. Double-click **KowOwow**. The image is inserted at a default size in a default position on the worksheet.

EXERCISE 9-16 Format the Picture

1. Double-click the white background for the image. The Format Picture dialog box opens.

TIP: You can double-click the background or right-click an object and choose from the shortcut menu to format a picture.

2. Click the Properties tab. There are only two settings on this tab.
3. If it's not already selected, select Do not size with chart. This will enable you to size the picture separately from the chart.
4. If it's not already selected, select Print object. You can turn this setting off if you want to print quickly without the picture.
5. Click the Size tab. The Scale group shows how the image is sized, based on its original size.
6. Under Scale, double-click the value in the Height box, key **100**, and press Tab. The Width is adjusted automatically because Lock aspect ratio is selected.

FIGURE 9-15
Format Picture dialog box

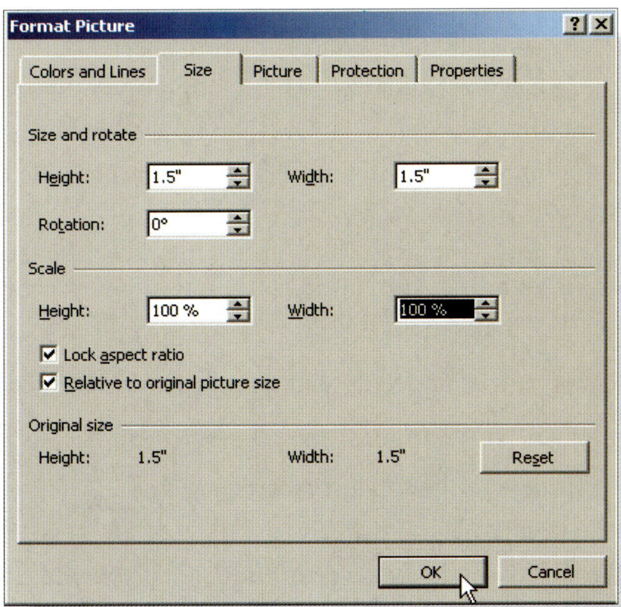

EXCEL

NOTE: The aspect ratio keeps an image proportional as you resize it.

7. Click OK.
8. Point at the white background for the image.
9. Drag the image below the legend. The white background might cover and hide the secondary axis values.
10. Place the mouse pointer on the middle left handle to display a sizing pointer.
11. Drag the handle to the left to uncover the axis values.

EXERCISE 9-17 Insert an Image from the Media Gallery

The Media Gallery includes images from Microsoft and other sources. These images are installed on your computer or network drive and have been cataloged so they appear in the Insert Clip Art task pane.

1. Click the Insert Clip Art button on the Drawing toolbar.
2. In the Search text box, key **cows**. This option searches for all images that have the word "cows" in the title or the description.
3. Click Search. An image from the gallery is shown in the task pane.
4. Click the image. It is inserted in the chart.
5. Right-click the image background and choose Format Picture.
6. Click the Colors and Lines tab.
7. Click the arrow for Color in the Fill group. A palette opens.
8. Choose a light color and click OK. The image background is filled.
9. Place the pointer on the bottom right selection handle to display the two-headed sizing arrow.
10. Hold down Shift and drag the pointer up and to the left to make the image smaller. As you drag, the Name box shows the new scale percentage. Size the image to about 100% by 100%.

NOTE: Holding Shift and dragging a corner handle keeps the size proportional.

11. Drag the image to the top left plot area.
12. Close the task pane.
13. Save the workbook as ***[your initials]*9-17** in your Lesson 9 folder.
14. Add the standard footer and print the chart sheet.

Using a Background Picture

You can choose any graphics file as a background for a worksheet. The image is *tiled,* or repeated across the worksheet. A background is for screen display and does not print. If you use a background image, you should check that it does not make your data difficult to read.

EXERCISE 9-18 Insert a Tiled Image

1. Click the **K&KSales** tab.
2. From the Format menu, choose Sheet, Background. The Sheet Background dialog box opens.

3. Click the arrow next to the Views button and choose Preview.
4. Open the folder where your student files are located and click **Kowabunga** to select it.
5. Click Insert. The image appears in the background.

6. Click the Print Preview button. Print Preview shows that the background image does not print.
7. Close the preview.

EXERCISE 9-19 Delete a Tiled Image

1. From the Format menu, choose Sheet.
2. Choose Delete Background. The background is removed.
3. Click any cell.
4. Press Ctrl + Home.

Adding an Image to a Header or Footer

You can also insert images in headers and footers. A company logo or symbol is an example of an image that might be used in a header or footer.

EXERCISE 9-20 Insert an Image in a Footer

1. Click the Print Preview button.
2. Click Setup. Click the Header/Footer tab.

3. Choose Custom Footer.
4. Click in the Right section box.
5. Select the existing text and press Delete.
6. Click the Insert Picture button. The Insert Picture dialog box opens.

7. Open the folder where your student files are located and click **Kowabunga** to select it.
8. Choose Insert. You do not see the image in the Header/Footer dialog box.

FIGURE 9-16 Inserting a picture in a footer

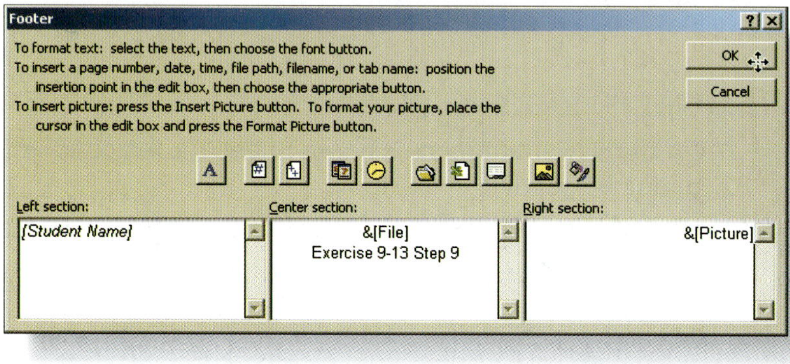

9. Click OK. Click OK again. You can see the image in Print Preview.
10. Print the sheet.

Inserting Comments

In addition to using pictures and AutoShapes, you can annotate a cell with a comment. A *comment* is explanatory text attached to a cell. Comments are a way for you to tell others who use your work what you did or what they should do.

Cells with comments display a small red triangle in the upper right corner. The comment itself appears in a text box when you move the pointer over the cell with the comment (if the comment indicator in the Options dialog box for your computer is set to display comments).

EXERCISE 9-21 Insert and Display a Comment

1. Right-click cell A2. Choose Insert Comment. The comment text box opens and displays the user name for your computer, followed by a colon.
2. Key **Edit this cell to enter the appropriate date**. (See Figure 9-17 on the next page.)
3. Click cell B5 to close the comment text box.

FIGURE 9-17
Inserting a comment

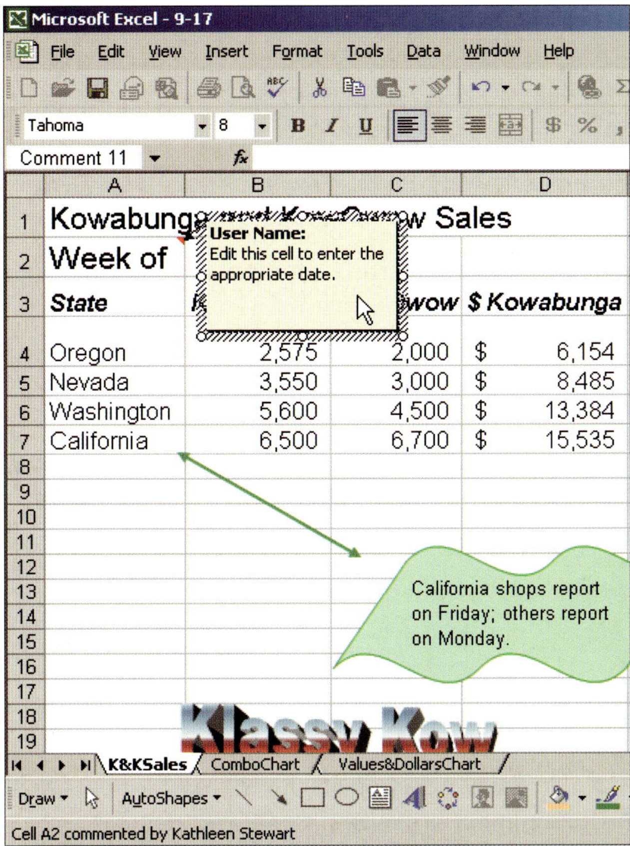

TIP: You can click any cell to close and hide the comment.

4. Move the mouse pointer over cell A2 to display the comment.

NOTE: Check with your instructor if the comment is not visible on your computer.

5. Click the Print Preview button. Comments do not print as a default.
6. Close the preview.

EXERCISE 9-22 Edit, Print, and Delete a Comment

1. Right-click cell A2 and choose Edit Comment.
2. Edit the text to read **Edit this cell each week. . .**
3. Click any cell to finish and hide the comment.

4. Move the pointer over cell A2 to see the edited comment.
5. Right-click cell A2 and choose Show Comment. The comment stays visible.
6. Click the Print Preview button. Comments do not print even when they show on-screen.
7. Close the preview.
8. Choose File, Page Setup. Click the Sheet tab.
9. In the Print group, click the Comments arrow. You must use this setting to print comments.
10. Choose As displayed on sheet. Click OK.

NOTE: You can print comments as they appear on the sheet or at the end of the data on a separate sheet.

11. Click the Print button. The comment prints as it appears on the worksheet.
12. Right-click cell A2 and choose Delete Comment.

Saving a Web Page

You can save an Excel workbook as an HTML file so it can be viewed on the World Wide Web, using most browsers. An *HTML* file uses *Hypertext Markup Language*, a widely used and recognized format for Web pages. Web pages are saved with an .htm extension.

EXERCISE 9-23 Save a Workbook as a Web Page

You can save the entire workbook or just the active worksheet as a Web page. When you save the entire workbook, the Web page shows the worksheet tabs.

1. Click cell A1.
2. From the File menu, choose Save as Web Page. The Save As dialog box shows that the Save as type is Web Page.
3. Set the Save in folder to your Lesson 9 folder.
4. In the Save area, choose Entire Workbook.
5. Click Change Title. This will be the title that appears in the title bar of the browser.
6. Key **Kowabunga and KowOwow Sales** and click OK. (See Figure 9-18 on the next page.)

FIGURE 9-18
Saving a Web page

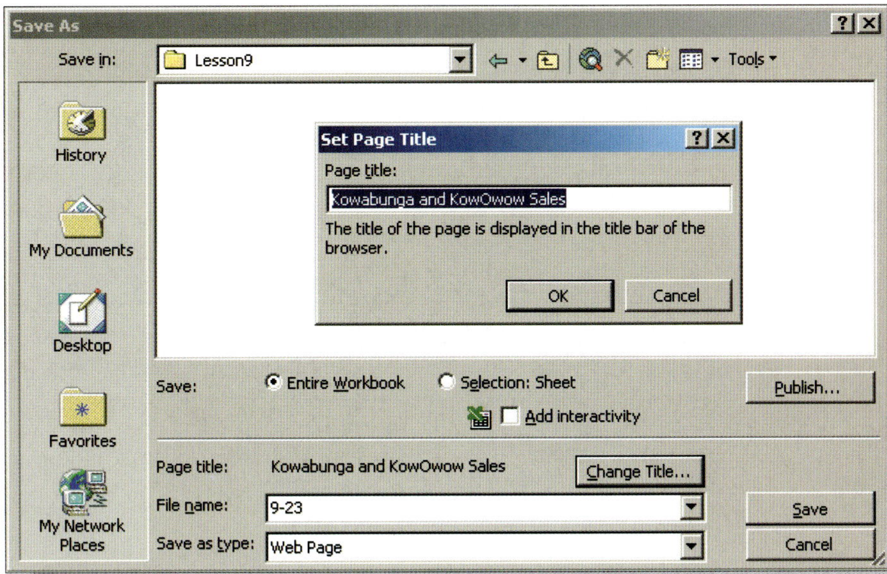

7. Name the workbook ***[your initials]*****9-23**. Click Save.

EXERCISE 9-24 Use Web Page Preview

You can use Web Page Preview before or after you save a file to see what your Web page will look like in your browser. When you choose Web Page Preview, the browser on your computer is launched and the browser displays the file.

1. From the File menu, choose Web Page Preview. The browser on your computer starts and shows your file.
2. Maximize the browser window. Look for the title of the Web page in your browser's title bar.
3. Click the worksheet tabs to see the charts.

4. Click the Close button to close the browser.
5. Close the workbook.

NOTE: You must have a workbook open to use Web Page Preview. However, the workbook does not need to be the file you want to preview.

6. Click the New button. A blank workbook opens.
7. From the File menu, choose Web Page Preview. The blank workbook opens in the browser.
8. From the File menu, choose Open.
9. Click the Browse button.

10. Find ***[your initials]*9-23** and click to select it.
11. Click Open and then click OK.
12. Close the browser and then the blank workbook.

EXERCISE 9-25 Use Discussion Comments

A *discussion comment* is a comment that is attached to a document and visible in a browser. Discussion comments appear in a window at the lower part of the screen. These comments are stored on a discussion server and can be read and responded to by anyone with access to the document.

NOTE: Check with your instructor to determine if your classroom has a discussion server for your use.

1. Open ***[your initials]*9-23** from your Lesson 9 folder.
2. From the Tools menu, choose Online Collaboration.
3. Choose Web Discussions. The Web Discussions toolbar opens.

4. Click the Insert Discussion about the Workbook button.
5. Key **This workbook is completed at corporate on Monday after all offices have reported their data.**
6. Close the Web Discussions toolbar.
7. Save and close the workbook, using the current filename.
8. Preview the workbook in your browser. Look for the discussion comments at the bottom of the window.
9. Close the browser.

LESSON 9 Summary

- An AutoShape is a common shape or form. A callout is used to attach a text description to a cell or other object.
- AutoShapes and callouts are placed on the draw layer, an invisible layer separate from the worksheet data.
- You can change the font within an AutoShape or change its size, shape, rotation angle, and colors.
- Many AutoShapes have a fill color, as well as an outline or border color. Text within an AutoShape has a color, too.
- To show text in a shape other than a rectangle, start with a text box and change its shape.

- Lines, with or without arrows, are objects that can be placed on the draw layer.
- AutoShapes can be formatted with 3-D effects and shadows. They can also be aligned and distributed for a balanced appearance on the sheet.
- You can use WordArt to create a design object that is shaped text. The WordArt Gallery includes 30 WordArt styles.
- You can place images on a sheet or a chart. Images can be taken from a disk or the Media Gallery.
- You can use images in headers and footers as well as for a background in a worksheet.
- Comments display when the mouse pointer touches a cell with the comment. Comments can be used as annotations, notes, or explanations for data on a worksheet.
- A workbook or worksheet can be saved as a Web page so it can be viewed by using a browser on the Internet.
- Discussion comments are used to attach notes and annotations to a worksheet that is viewed on the Internet.

LESSON 9 Command Summary

FEATURE	BUTTON	MENU	KEYBOARD	SPEECH
Callout	AutoShapes ▾	Insert, Picture, AutoShapes		✓
Text box		Chart, Chart Options		✓
Line	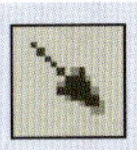			✓
Line color		Format, AutoShape		
Fill color		Format, AutoShape		
WordArt	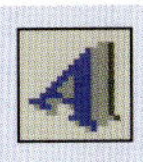	Insert, Picture, WordArt		✓
Header/ footer image		File, Page Setup		✓

continues

LESSON 9 Command Summary *continued*

FEATURE	BUTTON	MENU	KEYBOARD	SPEECH
Comment		Insert, Comment		✓
Picture/image		Insert, Picture, From File		✓
Background picture		Format, Sheet, Background		✓
Web page		File, Save as Web Page		✓

Concepts Review

TRUE/FALSE QUESTIONS

Each of the following statements is either true or false. Indicate your choice by circling T or F.

T F **1.** Drawing elements are placed on a draw layer.

T F **2.** Callouts can use various shapes to display text.

T F **3.** You can change the font and fill color of a drawing object from the Drawing toolbar.

T F **4.** AutoShapes cannot be changed, but can be deleted and redrawn.

T F **5.** WordArt is an Excel utility.

T F **6.** The Media Gallery includes images from a variety of subjects and categories.

T F **7.** A background image appears behind the worksheet data.

T F **8.** A cell with a comment displays a small red triangle.

SHORT ANSWER QUESTIONS

Write the correct answer in the space provided.

1. What name is used for the small yellow diamond that appears when a drawing object is selected?

____

2. What does the pointer look like when you move a drawing object?

____

3. What does the pointer look like if you want to size a drawing object?

____

4. What name describes an annotation that can be set to appear only when the mouse pointer passes over the cell?

____

5. What term describes an image that repeats across the page?

____

6. How do you insert an image in a header?

____

7. What can you do so others can see your worksheet on the Internet?

____

8. What name describes images available and cataloged for Office applications on your computer?

____

CRITICAL THINKING

Answer these questions on a separate page. There are no right or wrong answers. Support your answers with examples from your own experience, if possible.

1. What are the differences between comments and callouts? Why and when would you use each?

2. What kinds of images might be appropriate for a header or footer?

Lesson Applications

EXERCISE 9-26

Add a comment in an AutoShape. Format the AutoShape.

The default comment box is a rectangle shape. You can replace the shape with a callout shape from AutoShapes.

1. Create a new workbook, using the **K&KSales** template. Save the workbook as ***[your initials]*9-26** in your Lesson 9 folder.
2. Key the values shown in Figure 9-19 in the appropriate cells.

FIGURE 9-19

State	Kowabunga	KowOwow
Oregon	15000	16500
Nevada	18000	19200
Washington	17570	18050
California	19000	19500

REVIEW: The formulas are calculated and the charts are completed as you fill in the data.

3. Add a comment in cell C7. Delete the user name and colon and key this text (do not use bold type): **California's best sales this year!** Right-click the cell and show the comment.
4. Use the four-headed pointer to select the comment object. Then click Draw and choose Change AutoShape. Use the cloud callout. Size the callout so you can see the text. Position the callout below and to the right of cell C7. Use the adjustment handle to make the connector clouds angle toward the cell.
5. Choose a size and color for the text and the fill. Center the text horizontally.
6. Choose File, Page Setup to print the worksheet with the comment as displayed.

REVIEW: Comments in any shape do not print unless you turn on the option to print them.

7. Add your standard footer and print the sheet.
8. Save and close the workbook.

EXERCISE 9-27

Add and format callouts.

The Stars and Banners category has shapes that can highlight a cell in eye-catching ways.

1. Open **CASales** and save it as ***[your initials]*9-27** in your Lesson 9 folder.
2. Select rows 6 through 18 and format them as 25.50 (34 pixels) high.
3. Use Explosion 1 from the Stars and Banners AutoShapes and draw a shape around cell F16. While the shape is selected, right-click it and choose Format AutoShape. Use no fill.

NOTE: No fill means you can see the cell contents through the shape.

4. From the Basic Shapes category, draw a lightning bolt in cells D1 through F3. While the bolt is selected, choose Draw, and then choose Rotate or Flip. Flip the object horizontally so it points toward the data.
5. Apply a light yellow or orange color as fill.

6. Select the bolt and click the 3-D button. Choose 3-D Style 7 in the second row.
7. Add your standard footer and print the worksheet.
8. Save and close the workbook.

EXERCISE 9-28

Insert a picture. Link a cell to an AutoShape.

Although you can type text in many AutoShapes, you can also link an AutoShape to a cell. Then the cell's contents are displayed in the AutoShape.

1. Open **Contest**. Save the workbook as ***[your initials]*9-28** in your Lesson 9 folder.
2. Insert **Cow** (the GIF file) at the top left of the worksheet. Position the image so you can see all of it.
3. From the Stars and Banners category in the AutoShapes, draw a Curved Up Ribbon from cell D9 to E13.
4. While the shape is selected, click in the formula bar. Key **=d6** and press Enter. The value from cell D6 appears in the shape.

5. Right-click the AutoShape to format it. Use 19-point bold for the font. Center the text horizontally and vertically.

REVIEW: Use the Alignment tab to set centering options.

6. Move the AutoShape so it does not cover any of column C.
7. Format cell D6 to use white for the font so the formula result is invisible in that cell.
8. Edit cell B8 to show **25300**. This becomes the lowest difference and the new winner.
9. Add your standard footer and print the worksheet.
10. Save and close the workbook.

EXERCISE 9-29 *Challenge Yourself*

You can paste a "picture" of cells to another sheet in the same workbook. This picture is similar to an AutoShape. A cell picture can be pasted and linked on the same worksheet so that when the cells are edited, the picture updates.

1. Open **CASales** and save it as ***[your initials]*9-29** in your Lesson 9 folder.
2. Select cells F4:F18 and copy the range.

REVIEW: You can click the Copy button or right-click and choose Copy from the shortcut menu.

3. Go to the chart. Hold down Shift and open the Edit menu. Choose Paste Picture. The picture of the cells is an object with selection handles.

NOTE: You must hold down Shift to see the Paste Picture command.

4. Drag the cell picture object to the white chart background at the right, with the top of the object aligned with the "San Francisco, Lombard" bar.
5. Format the picture object to have a black line color and light gray fill.
6. Click the Shadow button. Choose Shadow Style 6 in the second row.
7. After the shadow is applied, click the Shadow Style button again. Click Shadow Settings. The Shadow toolbar opens. Change the shadow color to darker gray or black.
8. Add your standard footer and print the chart sheet.
9. Save and close the workbook.

On Your Own

In these exercises you work on your own, as you would in a real-life work environment. Use the skills you've learned to accomplish the task—and be creative.

EXERCISE 9-30

Search the Web to find sites from which you can download images. Download an image and save it in your Lesson 9 folder. In a new workbook, insert the image. Then size and format it. In cells away from the image, key an explanation of where you found the image and how you formatted it. Use two rows for your explanations. Add your standard footer and print the sheet. Save the workbook as ***[your initials]*9-30** in your Lesson 9 folder and close it.

EXERCISE 9-31

Open ***[your initials]*8-30** from your Lesson 8 folder. Delete the main title and insert rows so you can use WordArt for the main title. Select a WordArt style and choose a font size. Position the object as a title for your chart and data. Save the workbook as ***[your initials]*9-31** in your Lesson 9 folder. Print the worksheet, save the workbook, and close it.

EXERCISE 9-32

In a new workbook, draw five text boxes and key your name in each. Then change each text box to a different AutoShape. Adjust each AutoShape's handles to reshape the object. Try changing fill and line colors. Add your standard footer and print the sheet. Save your worksheet as ***[your initials]*9-32** in your Lesson 9 folder. Then preview the sheet in your browser. Save and close the workbook.

LESSON 10

Working with Multiple Worksheets and Lists

OBJECTIVES

MOUS ACTIVITIES
In this lesson:
- Ex2002 1-2
- Ex2002 1-5
- Ex2002 3-1
- Ex2002 3-7
- Ex2002 4-1
- Ex2002 4-2
- Ex2002 4-3

See Appendix E.

After completing this lesson, you will be able to:

1. Copy and group worksheets.
2. Create a 3-D reference.
3. Use functions in a 3-D reference.
4. Copy data to another workbook.
5. Sort and filter data in a list.
6. Use COUNTA in a 3-D reference.
7. Set print areas and print selections.
8. Create a custom view.

Estimated Time: 1¾ hours

An Excel workbook can have up to 255 worksheets. This enables you to separate data on different sheets for ease in building and reviewing information. Through groups and 3-D references, you can gather information from multiple sheets (and multiple workbooks) to calculate grand totals, differences, and averages.

Copying and Grouping Worksheets

If, for example, you use Excel to track monthly sales for a product line for several stores, it is good practice to keep each month's data on a separate worksheet. The sheets are basically the same except for the month and the values. You can copy the first sheet and edit it to prepare the second sheet. You can group the sheets and change the formatting in all of them in one step.

EXERCISE 10-1 Copy and Rename Worksheets

1. Open **JanKowO** and save it as ***[your initials]*10-1** in a new folder for Lesson 10.

2. Right-click the January tab. The shortcut menu opens.

3. Choose Move or Copy. The Move or Copy dialog box opens. The To book list includes the names of any open workbooks and a new book. The Before sheet list enables you to move or copy the current sheet before the current sheet or place it last in the tabs.

NOTE: Click the down arrow to see the entire To book list.

4. Click to highlight (move to end) in the Before sheet list.

5. Click to place a check mark in the Create a copy check box.

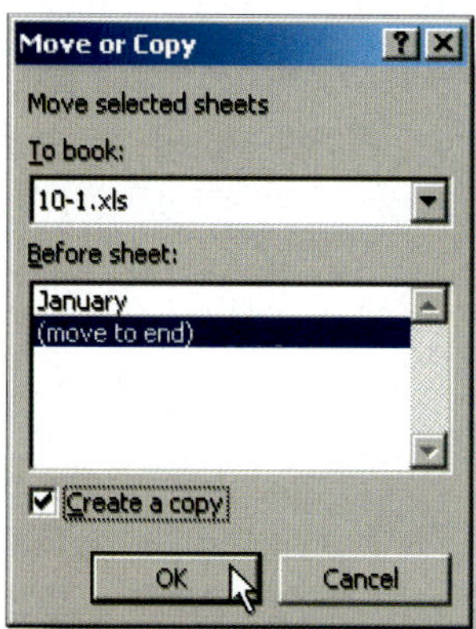

FIGURE 10-1 Copying a worksheet to the end

6. Click OK. A new worksheet named January (2) is inserted after the January sheet. It is an exact duplicate of the January sheet.

7. Click each worksheet tab to review the sheets.

8. Right-click the January (2) tab and choose Rename.

9. Key **February** and press Enter.

10. Double-click cell A2 and change "January" to **February**

11. Right-click the February tab. Choose Move or Copy.

12. Choose (move to end) in the Before sheet list.

13. Click to place a check mark in the Create a copy box.

14. Click OK. A new worksheet named February (2) is inserted after the February sheet.

15. Double-click the February (2) tab and key **March**. Press Enter.

REVIEW: You can double-click or right-click a sheet tab to rename it.

16. Double-click cell A2 and change "February" to **March**

EXERCISE 10-2 Group Worksheets and Delete Data

When worksheets are grouped, editing and formatting commands affect all sheets in the group. This is an easy way to make changes to several worksheets at once, as long as the worksheets are basically the same.

1. While the **March** worksheet is active, hold down Ctrl and click the **February** tab. Both worksheets are selected or active.

NOTE: The word [Group] appears in the title bar.

2. Click cell B4 and drag to select cells B4:C8.

FIGURE 10-2
Grouped worksheets

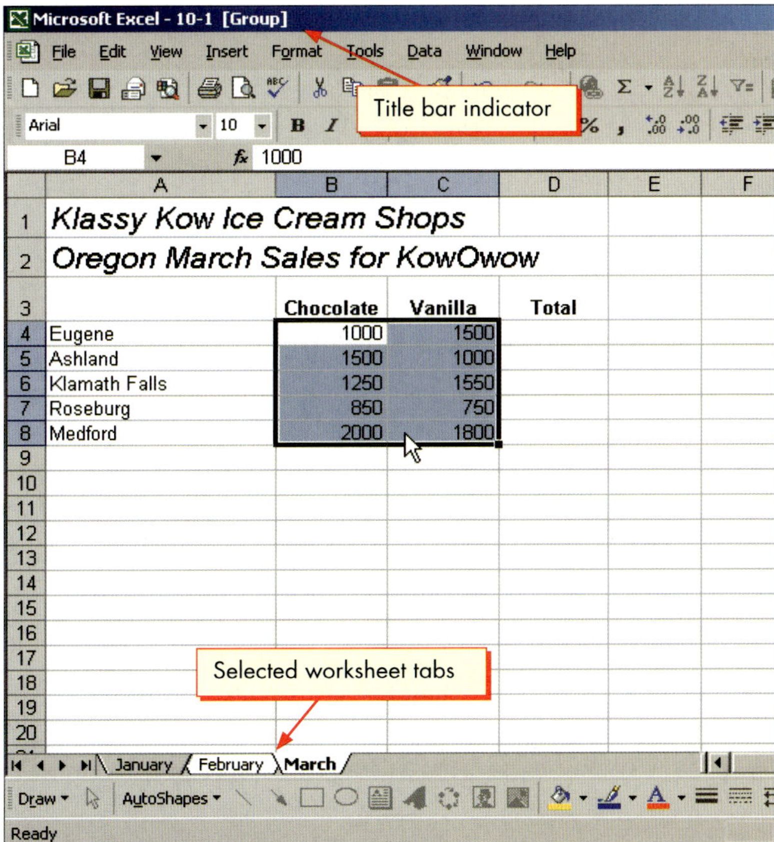

3. Press Delete. The values are cleared from both sheets.
4. Click the **January** tab. The other two worksheets are ungrouped.

TIP: You can ungroup sheets by clicking a sheet that is not in the group or by right-clicking a sheet in the group and choosing Ungroup Sheets.

5. Click the February tab to see that the cells are cleared.
6. Click the March tab.

EXERCISE 10-3 Group Worksheets and Insert Data

1. While the March worksheet is active, hold down Shift and click the January tab. All three worksheets are selected or active.
2. Click cell A3 and key **Shop**
3. Right-click any sheet tab and choose Ungroup Sheets.
4. Click the February tab and key the values in Figure 10-3 to complete the worksheet.

FIGURE 10-3

Shop	Chocolate	Vanilla
Eugene	1200	1025
Ashland	1500	1600
Klamath Falls	975	1035
Roseburg	1050	1200
Medford	1800	1560

5. Click the March tab and key the values in Figure 10-4.

FIGURE 10-4

Shop	Chocolate	Vanilla
Eugene	1300	1225
Ashland	1675	1650
Klamath Falls	1975	935
Roseburg	1450	1175
Medford	1645	1800

EXERCISE 10-4 Format Values and Insert a Function

1. While the March worksheet is active, hold down Shift and click the January tab.
2. Click cell B4 and drag to select cells B4:D8.
3. Click the Comma Style button.
4. Click the Decrease Decimal button two times.
5. Select cells D4:D8 and click the AutoSum button.
6. Right-click any sheet tab and choose Ungroup Sheets.
7. Check each sheet for its formatting and SUM function.

EXERCISE 10-5 Insert and Move a Worksheet

1. Click the January tab and press Ctrl+Home.
2. Press Shift+F11. A new worksheet is inserted in front of (to the left of) the January sheet.

REVIEW: You can also insert a sheet by choosing Insert, Worksheet or by right-clicking a worksheet tab and choosing Insert.

3. Press Shift+F11 again. Another new worksheet is inserted.

NOTE: New sheet numbers start at the next available number.

4. Right-click the Sheet2 tab and choose Delete.
5. Double-click the Sheet1 tab and rename it **FirstQuarter**
6. Right-click the FirstQuarter tab and choose Move or Copy.
7. Choose (move to end) and click OK.

REVIEW: You can also drag a worksheet tab to reposition it.

EXERCISE 10-6 Copy Data to a Worksheet

1. Click the March tab and select cells A1:A2.
2. Click the Copy button.

3. Click the FirstQuarter tab and press Enter. The labels are copied to the blank worksheet.

REVIEW: If you press Enter to complete a Copy and Paste operation the selection marquee is automatically canceled.

4. Double-click cell A2 and change "March" to **First Quarter**
5. Click the March tab and select cells A3:A8.
6. Press Ctrl + C.
7. Click the FirstQuarter tab and click cell A3.
8. Press Enter. The labels are copied, but the column width is not.
9. Format column A as 21.57 (156 pixels) wide.
10. Click the March tab and select cells B3:D3.
11. Press Ctrl + C and click the FirstQuarter tab.

NOTE: Close the Clipboard pane for more working space.

12. Click cell B3 and press Enter.

TIP: Drag across the column headings to select multiple columns and adjust the width.

13. Format columns B, C, and D each as 10.00 (75 pixels) wide.
14. Format row 3 as 22.50 (30 pixels) high.

EXERCISE 10-7 Copy Multiple Worksheets

1. While the FirstQuarter tab is active, hold down Shift and click the January tab. All four worksheets are now a group.
2. Right-click any sheet tab in the group and choose Move or Copy.
3. Choose (move to end).
4. Click to place a check mark for Create a copy.
5. Click OK. Four new worksheets are inserted, one copy of each grouped sheet.

EXERCISE 10-8 Scroll Multiple Worksheets

Now that you have eight worksheets in your workbook, you cannot see all the worksheet tabs at once. The worksheet tab scrolling buttons are at the left edge of the tab names. These buttons enable you to scroll tabs.

The tab scrolling buttons share space with the horizontal scroll bar and are separated from it by the tab split box. You can drag the tab split box to change the number of visible tabs or the size of the horizontal scroll bar.

1. Position the mouse pointer on the tab split box. The pointer is a two-headed arrow.
2. Click and drag the pointer to the right until you see all the tabs.

NOTE: Depending on your screen size, you might not be able to drag the tab split bar far enough to see all the tabs.

FIGURE 10-5
Dragging the tab split box

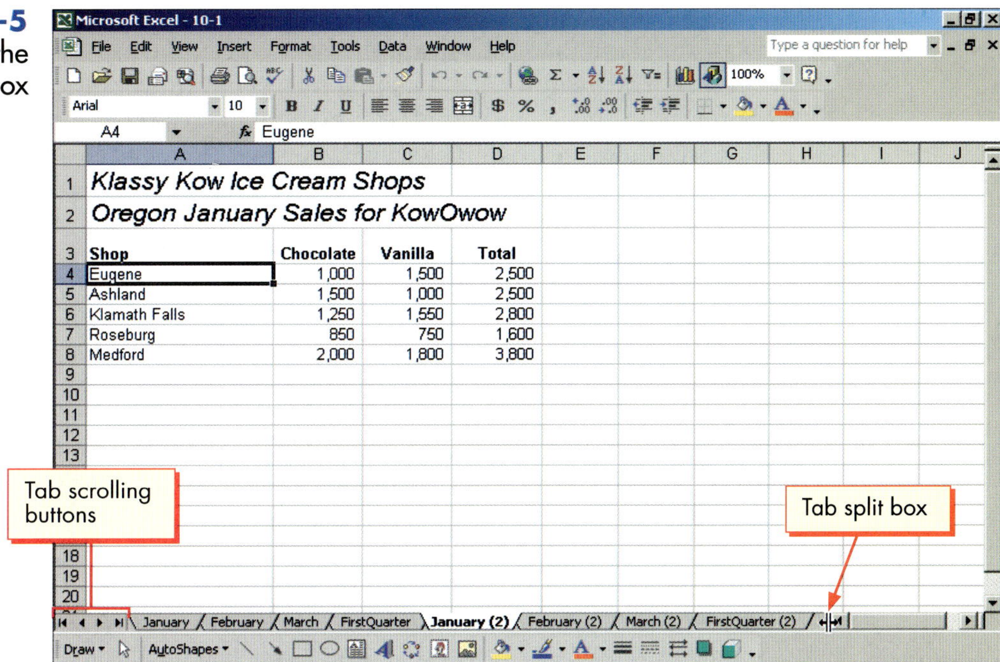

3. Rename the copied sheets as follows (in the order shown):
   April
   May
   June
   SecondQuarter
4. Position the mouse pointer on the tab split box.
5. Click and drag the pointer to the left so you see the worksheets tabs up to FirstQuarter.
6. Click each tab scrolling button to see how it moves through the tab names.
7. Right-click any of the tab scrolling buttons. A shortcut menu with a list of the tab names opens.

8. Choose April. The sheet is visible and active.
9. Double-click cell A2 and change the month to **April**
10. Click the far-right tab scrolling button. The tab names at the end are visible.
11. Change cell A2 on the May sheet to show **May** as the month. Change the month on the June sheet to **June**
12. On the SecondQuarter sheet, edit the title in cell A2 to show the correct quarter.

Creating a 3-D Reference

If a formula refers to cells in another worksheet, the formula is described as a *3-D reference*. The formula is a dynamic link between worksheets. If the value in the referenced cell is edited, the formula recalculates the result.

A 3-D reference is valuable when you want to calculate a total based on data on several sheets. In your workbook, for example, you can now use a 3-D reference to determine the first-quarter sales by adding each shop's January, February, and March values.

EXERCISE 10-9 Create a 3-D Reference

You can create a 3-D reference by pointing to the cells in the appropriate worksheet. Excel inserts the worksheet tab name followed by an exclamation point with the cell address.

1. Click the far-left tab scrolling button. Then click the FirstQuarter tab.
2. Click cell B4 and key = to start a formula.
3. Click the January tab and click cell B4. The formula bar shows =January!B4, and a marquee appears around the cell.
4. Key + to add the next reference.
5. Click the February tab and click cell B4. The worksheet tab names are followed by an exclamation point.
6. Key + to continue.
7. Click the March tab and click cell B4. (See Figure 10-6 on the next page.)
8. Press Enter. The formula is completed, and the result is shown on the FirstQuarter sheet.
9. Click cell B4 and look at the formula bar.
10. Display the Fill handle and copy the formula to cells B5:B8.

TIP: Ignore the AutoFill Options button.

FIGURE 10-6
Creating a 3-D formula

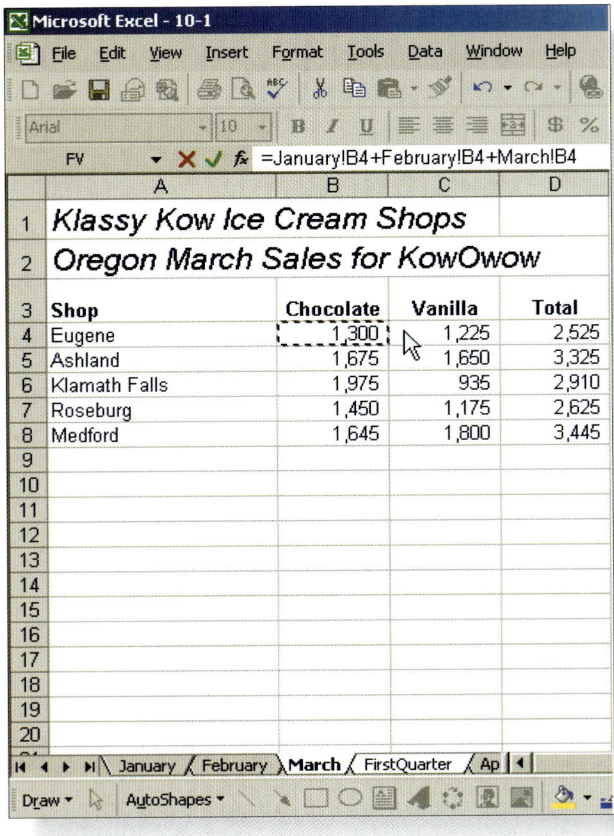

11. While the filled range is selected, display the Fill handle again and copy the formula to column C.
12. Click cell C4. The reference is adjusted to show the correct cell address and the worksheet tab name.
13. Select cells D4:D8 and click the AutoSum button.

EXERCISE 10-10 Use Paste Special

If you have created a format with several attributes on one worksheet, you can copy only the format by using the Format Painter. You can accomplish the same effect by using the Paste Special dialog box.

1. Click the March tab and click cell B4. This value is formatted with commas and no decimal positions.
2. Click the Copy button.
3. Click the FirstQuarter tab.
4. Click cell B4 and drag to select cells B4:D8.

5. From the Edit menu, choose Paste Special. The Paste Special dialog box opens. You can copy everything, only the values, only the formats, and other choices depending on your data.
6. Click the button for Formats.

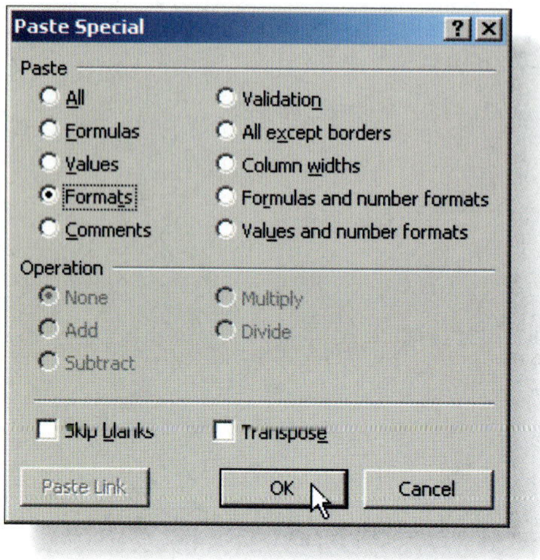

FIGURE 10-7 Paste Special dialog box

7. Click OK. The values are formatted.

EXERCISE 10-11 Edit Underlying Data

If you change the value in a cell used in a 3-D reference, the formula is automatically recalculated. Before you begin, notice that the First Quarter total for "Eugene" is currently 7,250.

1. Click the January tab.
2. Click cell B4 and key **0**
3. Click the FirstQuarter tab. The result is recalculated.
4. Click the January tab and click cell B4.
5. Key **2000** and click the FirstQuarter tab.

EXERCISE 10-12 Enter Data in Grouped Worksheets

1. Click the far-right tab scrolling button and click the April tab.
2. Hold down Shift and click the June tab. Three sheets are grouped.
3. Select cells B4:C8.
4. Key the following values and press Enter after each. These values appear in column B.

   1000

   2000

1000
2000
1000

5. Continue to key the next set of values in column C, pressing Enter after each.

   2000
   1000
   2000
   1000
   2000

6. Click the SecondQuarter tab. The sheets are ungrouped. The April, May, and June sheets all have the same values.
7. Click cell B4 and key = to start a formula.
8. Click the April tab and click cell B4. Key + to add the next reference.
9. Click the May tab and click cell B4. Key + to continue.
10. Click the June tab, click cell B4, and press Enter.
11. Copy the formula to cells B5:B8 and then to column C.
12. Select cells D4:D8 and click the AutoSum button Σ.
13. Select cells B4:D8 and format them as Comma Style, with no decimal places.

Using Functions and Formulas in a 3-D Reference

In addition to simple addition, subtraction, multiplication, and division, you can use functions in a 3-D reference. Although you can key a 3-D formula, you are less likely to make an error by pointing at the references. In addition, when you point, Excel includes the worksheet tab name and the exclamation point.

EXERCISE 10-13 Use AVERAGE in a 3-D Reference

1. With the SecondQuarter tab active, press Shift+F11.
2. Move the new sheet after the SecondQuarter sheet and name it **AverageSales**
3. Click the SecondQuarter tab and click cell A1.
4. Press Ctrl+C, click the AverageSales tab, and press Enter.
5. Key **Average Monthly Sales** in cell A2. Format the font and size to match cell A1.

6. Copy cells A3:A8 on the SecondQuarter sheet to cell A3 on the AverageSales sheet.
7. Copy cells B3:C3 on the SecondQuarter sheet to cells B3:C3 on the AverageSales sheet.
8. Format columns A:C as 13.57 (100 pixels) wide. Format row 3 as 22.50 (30 pixels) high.
9. Click and drag the tab split box so you can see all the worksheet tab names (or as many as possible). Then scroll the names to show the January tab.
10. Click cell B4 on the AverageSales sheet and key **=average(** to start the function.
11. Click the January tab and click cell B4. Its address is inserted in the formula.
12. Key a comma to separate the arguments in the function.
13. Click the February tab and click cell B4.
14. Key a comma and click the March tab.
15. Click cell B4, key a comma, and click the April tab.
16. Click cell B4, key a comma, and click the May tab.
17. Click cell B4, key a comma, and click the June tab.

FIGURE 10-8
Using AVERAGE in a 3-D reference

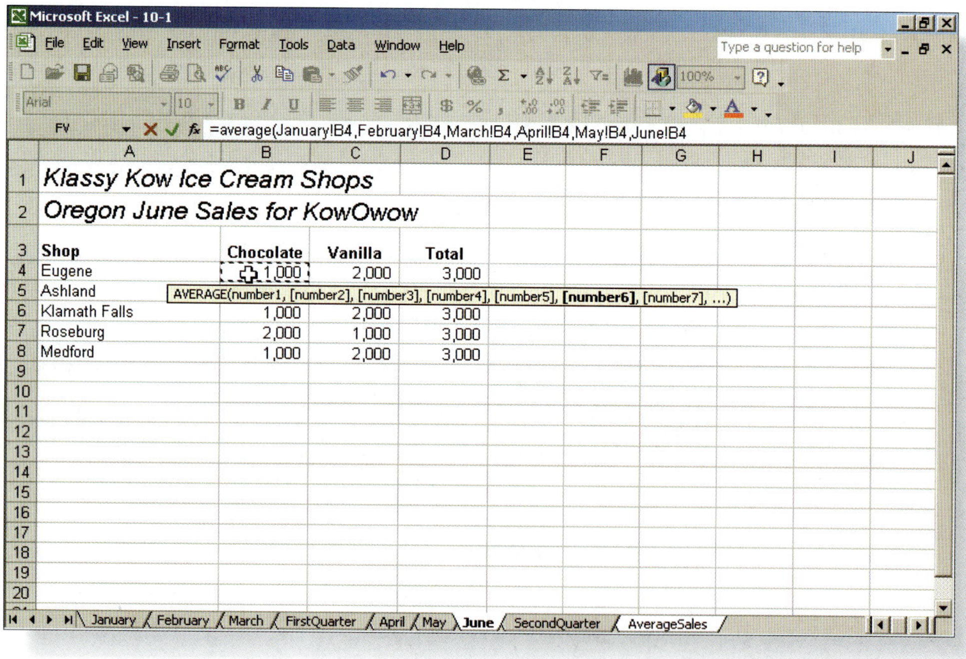

18. Click cell B4 and press Enter.
19. Click cell B4 and view the formula in the formula bar.
20. Press F2 and key **round(** after the = sign in the formula.

21. Press End and key **,0)** to round the average with no decimal places. Press Enter.
22. Copy the formula to cell B8 and then to column C.
23. Format the values to show commas with no decimal positions.

EXERCISE 10-14 Use MAX and Paste Functions in a 3-D Reference

1. On the AverageSales tab, copy cell A2 to cell A10. Copy cells B3:C3 to cell A11.
2. Format row 11 as 22.50 (30 pixels) high. Edit cell A10 to show **Maximum Monthly Sales**

3. Click cell A12 and click the Insert Function button.
4. Choose MAX and click OK. Move the Function Arguments dialog box so that you can see the cells you need to click.

REVIEW: MAX is in the Statistical category.

5. Click the January tab. Click cell B4 and drag to select cells B4:B8.
6. Click in the Number2 box in the Function Arguments dialog box.
7. Click the February tab. Click cell B4 and drag to select cells B4:B8.

FIGURE 10-9 Using the Function Arguments dialog box for a 3-D reference

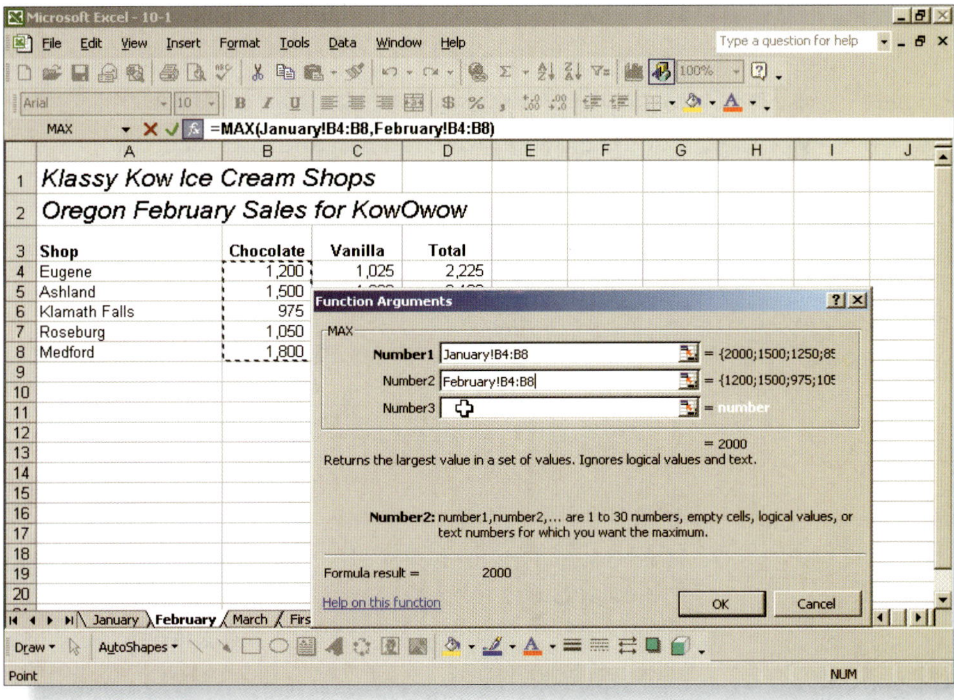

8. Click in the Number3 box and click the March tab.
9. Click cell B4 and drag to select cells B4:B8.
10. Click in the Number4 box and click the April tab.
11. Select cells B4:B8, click in the Number5 box, and click the May tab.

TIP: Scroll the number boxes in the Function Arguments dialog box if they do not automatically appear.

12. Select cells B4:B8, click in the Number6 box, and click the June tab.
13. Select cells B4:B8 and click OK.
14. Copy the formula to cell B12.
15. Click the May tab. Click cell C4 and key **12000**
16. Click the AverageSales tab and note the new maximum for "Vanilla." The "Vanilla" average for "Eugene" changes, too.

EXERCISE 10-15 Use Multiplication in a 3-D Reference

1. Right-click the SecondQuarter tab and choose Move or Copy.
2. Create a copy of the sheet at the end of the tabs. Name the copied worksheet **ProjectedSales**
3. Edit cell A2 to show **Third Quarter Projected Sales**
4. Select and delete cells B4:C8.
5. Click cell B4 and key = to start the formula.
6. Click the SecondQuarter tab and click cell B4.
7. Key ***110%** and press Enter.

NOTE: The formula multiplies second-quarter sales by 110% to determine projected sales that are 10% higher.

8. Copy the formula in cell B4 to cells B5:B8 and then to column C.

EXERCISE 10-16 Print Grouped Worksheets

1. Hold down Ctrl and click the FirstQuarter tab. It is selected with the ProjectedSales tab.
2. Hold down Ctrl and click the SecondQuarter tab. Three worksheets are selected or grouped.

3. Hold down Ctrl and click the AverageSales tab. Four worksheets are selected or grouped.

4. Click the Print Preview button. These four sheets are shown in the preview.

5. Click Setup and create your standard footer on the first sheet. In the Center section, type a comma after the filename code and click the Page Number button.
6. Close the Footer and Page Setup dialog boxes. Press PgDn to display page 4.
7. Click Setup and create your standard footer with the page number added to the Center section.
8. Click Print and click OK to print four sheets.
9. Save the workbook as ***[your initials]*10-16** in your Lesson 10 folder.

NOTE: If you save a workbook while sheets are grouped and later open it, it opens with the sheets grouped.

EXERCISE 10-17 Print Formulas for Grouped Worksheets

1. Press Ctrl+~. The formulas are displayed on each of the grouped worksheets.
2. Right-click a sheet in the group and ungroup them.
3. Group the FirstQuarter and the SecondQuarter sheets. These are the same, so you can format them for printing together.
4. Autofit each of the columns while the formulas are displayed.
5. Click the Print Preview button.
6. Click Setup. Change the first sheet to landscape orientation, fit to one page. Close the Page Setup dialog box.
7. Press PgDn and click Setup again. Change to landscape orientation, and choose the option to fit the worksheet on one page.
8. Add your standard footer to the second sheet.
9. Print both sheets.
10. Close the workbook without saving.

Copying Data to Another Workbook

In addition to copying data within a workbook, you can copy or move data from one workbook to another. You can create a new workbook from existing workbooks, eliminating the need to rekey preexisting labels and values. When you work with multiple workbooks, you can arrange them so you can see all of them on the screen at once in different layouts.

EXERCISE 10-18 Copy Data by Using Tiled Windows

The "Departments" workbook has four worksheets, each listing employees in a particular department. You can create a new workbook that lists all employees on one sheet by copying data from each of the sheets.

The "Departments" workbook was saved with the sheets grouped so when you open it, they are already grouped.

1. Open **Departments**.

2. Click the New button. A new workbook opens. It is maximized and on top of the "Departments" workbook.
3. Save the new workbook as ***[your initials]*10-18** in your Lesson 10 folder.
4. From the Window menu, choose Arrange. The Arrange dialog box opens.
5. Choose Horizontal and click OK. Both workbooks are displayed in tiled windows that are the same size. The active workbook has a colored title bar.

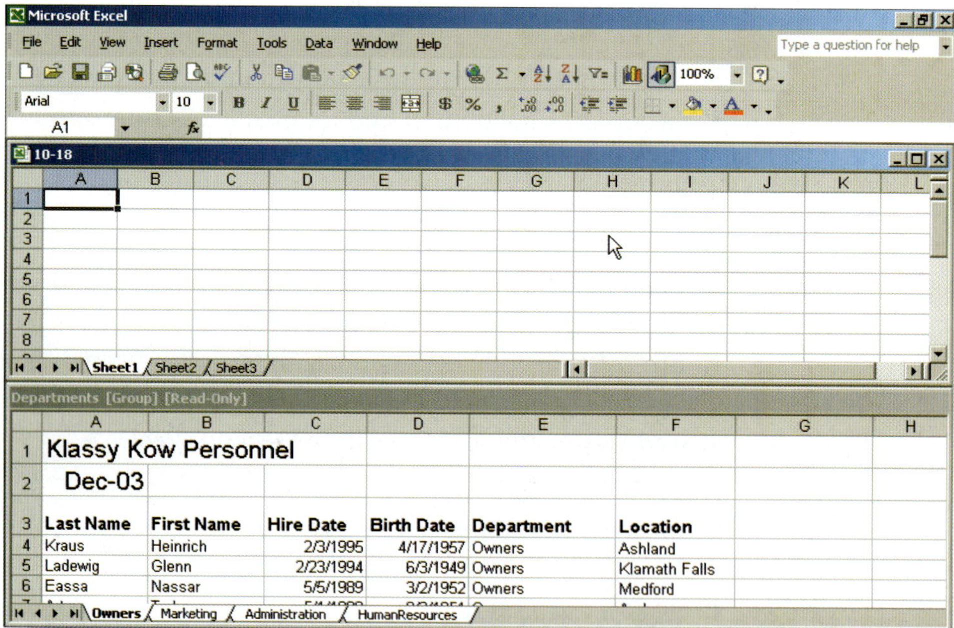

FIGURE 10-10
Tiled windows

TIP: The workbook that is active when you tile the windows horizontally appears in the top half of the screen.

6. Right-click any tab in the "Departments" workbook and ungroup the sheets.
7. Click the Owners tab and click cell A1.
8. Press F8 to start Extend Selection mode. Use → to extend the selection to column F.

REVIEW: EXT appears in the status bar when Extend Selection mode is on.

9. Use ↓ to extend the selection to row 8.
10. Click the Copy button.
11. Click cell A1 in ***[your initials]*****10-18** and press Enter. The data and cell formatting are copied, but the row heights and column widths are not.

NOTE: You can format the new workbook after copying all the data.

EXERCISE 10-19 Copy Data by Using Maximized Windows

You can copy data from one workbook to another even if both windows are maximized. You switch between workbooks by using the taskbar.

1. Maximize ***[your initials]*****10-18**.
2. Click Departments on the taskbar.
3. Click the Marketing tab. Click cell A4 and drag to select cells A4:F8.
4. Press Ctrl+C.
5. Click ***[your initials]*****10-18** on the taskbar, click cell A9, and press Enter. The second set of names is added to the list.
6. Click Departments on the taskbar and click the Administration tab.
7. Click cell A4 and drag to select cells A4:F7. Press Ctrl+C.
8. Click [your initials]10-18 on the taskbar, click cell A14, and press Enter. Another set of names is added to the list.

TIP: You can click the workbook name on the taskbar or press Ctrl+F6 to move between open workbooks.

9. Switch to the Departments workbook and click the HumanResources tab. Select cells A4:F6 and copy them to cell A18 in [your initials]10-18.
10. Switch to the Departments workbook and close it.
11. In your workbook, format column A as 13.57 (100 pixels) wide. Autofit each of the other columns.

Sorting and Filtering a List

The workbook you just created by copying data is a list. A *list* is a table of information with a row of headers (titles) followed by rows of data. Excel has several list commands that enable you to work with the data much like a database. For example, you can sort a list to arrange the rows in different orders.

You can also filter a list to display only certain rows. A *filter* is criteria or a specification for data in your list. A filter hides rows that do not meet your criteria.

EXERCISE 10-20 Sort a List

An *ascending sort* sorts rows in A-to-Z order or lowest value to highest value. A *descending sort* sorts rows in Z-to-A order or highest value to lowest. If you select a range of cells on the screen and sort them, the sort uses the first column of the range.

1. Select cells A4:F20. You should not include titles when selecting data to be sorted.
2. Click the Sort Ascending button. The rows are alphabetized according to the last name.
3. Click the Sort Descending button. The rows are alphabetized in reverse, from Z to A.
4. Click the down arrow next to the Undo button. Undo the last two actions. The rows are returned to the original order.

REVIEW: Undo keeps a history of your edits.

5. Click cell F4 to deselect the range.
6. With cell F4 selected, click the Sort Ascending button. The rows are alphabetized according to the data in column F, but the titles are included in the sort because you did not first select the data.
7. Click the Undo button.

EXERCISE 10-21 Name a List as a Range

Excel has requirements for using the various List commands effectively. One requirement is that you must name the list as a range. A named range is a descriptive label for a selection of cells. Rather than referring to the range as cells A4:F20, you could call it "Employees," for example.

REVIEW: A range is a rectangular group of cells.

If you name the range of cells in a list, you do not need to select the cells before sorting. You just need to click anywhere in the column that you want to sort. Naming the range also gives you the ability to sort easily by other columns. When you name a list as a range, you need to include the title or label row with the rows of information.

Excel recognizes the range name "Database" automatically as a list. Using this range name makes many of Excel's List commands easier and faster. "Database" is a special, reserved word in Excel.

1. Select cells A3:F20. Remember that titles are included when you name a list range.
2. Click the Name box. Key **Database** and press Enter. This names the selected cells "Database."

FIGURE 10-11 Naming a range for a list

Name box

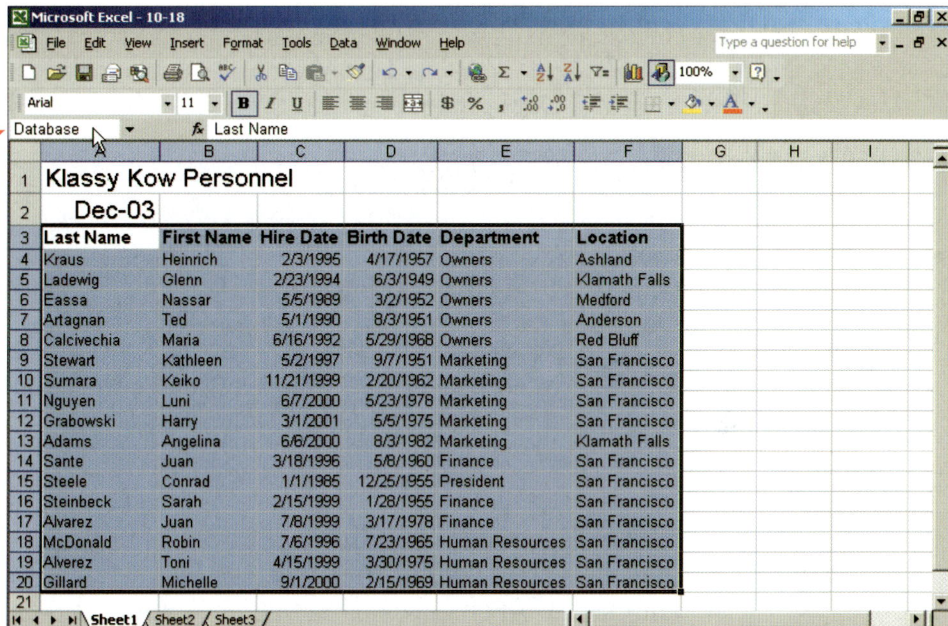

	A	B	C	D	E	F
1	Klassy Kow Personnel					
2	Dec-03					
3	Last Name	First Name	Hire Date	Birth Date	Department	Location
4	Kraus	Heinrich	2/3/1995	4/17/1957	Owners	Ashland
5	Ladewig	Glenn	2/23/1994	6/3/1949	Owners	Klamath Falls
6	Eassa	Nassar	5/5/1989	3/2/1952	Owners	Medford
7	Artagnan	Ted	5/1/1990	8/3/1951	Owners	Anderson
8	Calcivechia	Maria	6/16/1992	5/29/1968	Owners	Red Bluff
9	Stewart	Kathleen	5/2/1997	9/7/1951	Marketing	San Francisco
10	Sumara	Keiko	11/21/1999	2/20/1962	Marketing	San Francisco
11	Nguyen	Luni	6/7/2000	5/23/1978	Marketing	San Francisco
12	Grabowski	Harry	3/1/2001	5/5/1975	Marketing	San Francisco
13	Adams	Angelina	6/6/2000	8/3/1982	Marketing	Klamath Falls
14	Sante	Juan	3/18/1996	5/8/1960	Finance	San Francisco
15	Steele	Conrad	1/1/1985	12/25/1955	President	San Francisco
16	Steinbeck	Sarah	2/15/1999	1/28/1955	Finance	San Francisco
17	Alvarez	Juan	7/8/1999	3/17/1978	Finance	San Francisco
18	McDonald	Robin	7/6/1996	7/23/1965	Human Resources	San Francisco
19	Alverez	Toni	4/15/1999	3/30/1975	Human Resources	San Francisco
20	Gillard	Michelle	9/1/2000	2/15/1969	Human Resources	San Francisco
21						

3. Click cell A4 to deselect the cells.
4. Click the Sort Ascending button. The rows are arranged in alphabetical order by last name.
5. Click any department name in column E and click the Sort Descending button. The data is arranged by department in reverse alphabetical order.
6. Undo the last two sort actions to return the rows to the original order.
7. Click cell A4 to deselect the range.

EXERCISE 10-22 Filter a List

Filters enable you to keep a large list, but display only required information. For example, an employee list includes all the workers in a company. To print a report of employees in a certain department, you can filter the list to show only those workers.

When you filter a list, you display records based on some requirement that you choose. You can print your list while it is filtered so you see only the records that match your requirements.

The AutoFilter command adds drop-down arrows next to the row headings so you can choose from a list of labels or values in the list. What you choose in the list is used to display only the rows matching your choice.

1. From the Data menu, choose Filter and then AutoFilter. A down arrow appears in each of the labels in row 3.
2. Click the Department down arrow and choose Human Resources. Only the rows that match are displayed. The other rows are hidden. The row headings for the visible rows are blue to remind you that the list is filtered. The down arrow for Department is blue, too.

FIGURE 10-12 Creating an AutoFilter

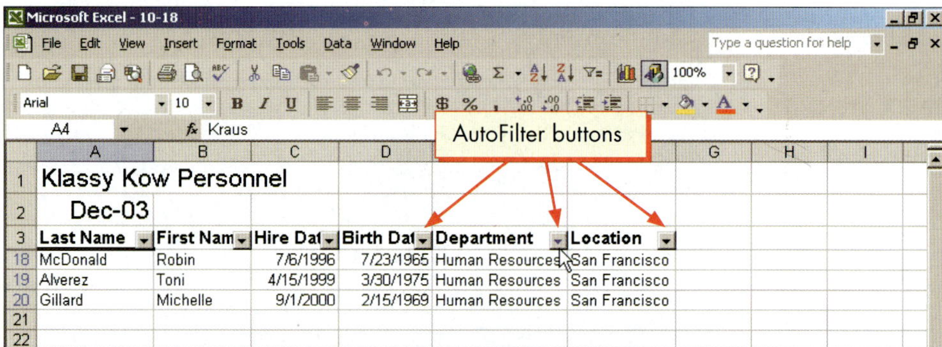

3. Click the Department down arrow and choose (All). All the rows are shown.
4. Click the Location down arrow and choose Klamath Falls. Only the employees located in that city are listed.
5. Click the Location down arrow and choose San Francisco. The list changes to show only the San Francisco employees.
6. Click the Department down arrow and choose Marketing. This adds another requirement to the list, which now shows employees in the Marketing department in San Francisco.

NOTE: A filter does not rearrange or sort the rows.

7. Choose (All) from the Department list. Choose (All) from the Location list.

EXERCISE 10-23 Create a Custom AutoFilter by Using Or

A simple AutoFilter chooses one item from the list. A Custom AutoFilter gives you the ability to filter by more than one item and to use operators such as "greater than."

1. Click the Department down arrow and choose (Custom. . .). The dialog box shows the name of the column.
2. In the first entry box, choose equals. This means the department will be equal to your next choice.
3. Click the down arrow for the entry box to the right and choose Finance. The department should be "Finance."
4. Click the Or button. This adds another option to the filter.
5. Click the down arrow for the first box below the And/Or buttons. Choose equals.
6. Click the down arrow for the entry box to the right and choose Marketing. This filter requires that the department be either "Finance" or "Marketing."

TIP: This filter is described as an "Or condition."

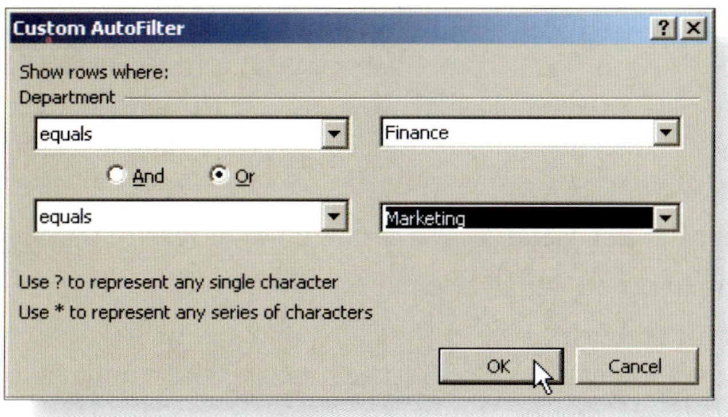

FIGURE 10-13
Creating a Custom AutoFilter with Or

7. Click OK. The employees are either in the Finance or the Marketing department.
8. Choose Data, Filter, Show All. All the rows are shown.

EXERCISE 10-24 Create a Custom AutoFilter by Using And

1. Click the Hire Date down arrow and choose (Custom. . .).
2. In the first entry box, choose is greater than.

3. Click in the entry box to the right and key **1/1/90**. The first filter is that the date be greater than January 1, 1990, which means a date later than that date.

NOTE: You can key a value in an entry box. You do not need to choose from the list

4. Click the And button.
5. Click the down arrow for the first box below the And/Or buttons.
6. Choose is less than.
7. Click in the entry box to the right and key **12/31/95**. The second filter requires that the hire date be less than December 31, 1995 (that is, it must be before that date).
8. Click OK. These employees were hired between 1990 and 1995.
9. Choose Data, Filter, Show All.

EXERCISE 10-25 Use Wildcards in a Custom AutoFilter

A *wildcard* is a keyboard character (usually * or ?) used in filters to represent characters that you do not know. For example, if you know that an employee's name ends in "ish" but you don't remember the first part of the name, you could use a wildcard to find all employees whose names end with "ish" by keying "*ish" in the entry box to be matched. You can key the wildcard characters or use Excel's operators. Excel has operators in its list that enable you to build wildcard filters by using words.

1. Click the Last Name down arrow and choose (Custom. . .).
2. In the first entry box, choose equals.
3. Click in the entry box to the right and key **s*** This entry finds last names that begin with "S." The asterisk means that any number of characters can come after the "S."

FIGURE 10-14 Keying a wildcard

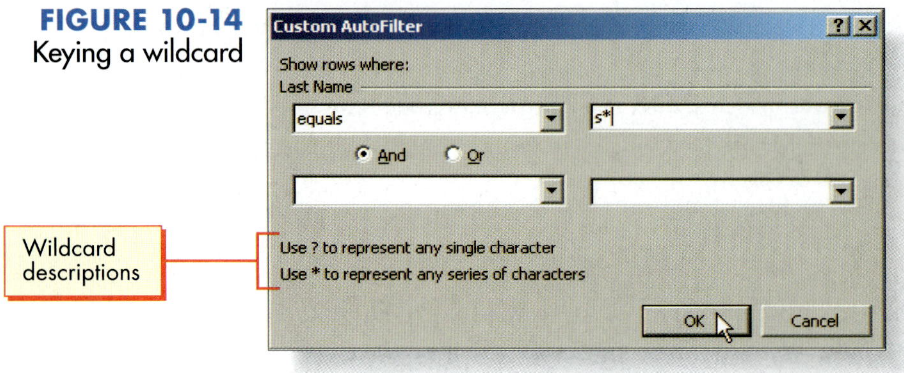

4. Click OK. The employees whose names begin with "S" are listed.
5. Click the Last Name down arrow and choose (Custom. . .). Excel replaces the asterisk with a filter from its list.
6. In the first entry box, choose equals.
7. Click in the entry box to the right and key ***ar*** to find employees whose names have "ar" anywhere in them.
8. Click OK. The last names are filtered.
9. Click the Last Name down arrow and choose (Custom. . .). Using the wildcard in this case is the same as using the "contains" filter.
10. Click Cancel. Click the Last Name arrow and choose (All).

EXERCISE 10-26 Filter Dates and Text

1. Click the Birth Date down arrow and choose (Custom. . .).
2. In the first entry box, choose ends with.
3. Click in the entry box to the right and key **1951** to find employees born in 1951.
4. Click OK. No records are filtered because "ends with" is a text filter and does not work with dates.
5. Click the Birth Date down arrow and choose (Custom. . .). In the first entry box, choose is greater than. In the entry box to the right, key **12/31/50**
6. Click the And button.

TIP: Excel recognizes the year in two- or four-digit formats.

7. In the box below the And/Or buttons, choose is less than.
8. In the entry box to the right, key **1/1/52**. Click OK. These are employees who were born in 1951.
9. Choose Data, Filter, Show All.
10. Click the First Name down arrow and choose (Custom. . .).
11. In the first entry box, choose ends with. Click in the entry box to the right and key **n** to find employees whose names end in "n."
12. Click OK. The filter works with a label.
13. Choose Data, Filter, Show All.
14. Choose Data, Filter, AutoFilter. The AutoFilter buttons are removed.

Using COUNTA in a 3-D Reference

The COUNTA function counts cells that have values or labels. You can use it to count the number of employees per department.

EXERCISE 10-27 Create a 3-D Reference with COUNTA

1. Select cells A1:A2. Copy them to cell A1 on Sheet2. Widen column A to show the date.
2. On Sheet2, key **Department** in cell A3. Key **# of Employees** in cell B3.
3. Format the labels in row 3 as bold and make the row 22.50 (30 pixels) high.
4. Key the following department names in cells A4:A7:

   Marketing

   Finance

   Human Resources

   Owners
5. Select cells A4:A7 and click the Sort Ascending button. A Sort Warning message box tells you that you might not have selected all the data.

REVIEW: Because there is no range name, you must select the cells to be sorted.

6. Choose Continue with the current selection. Click Sort.

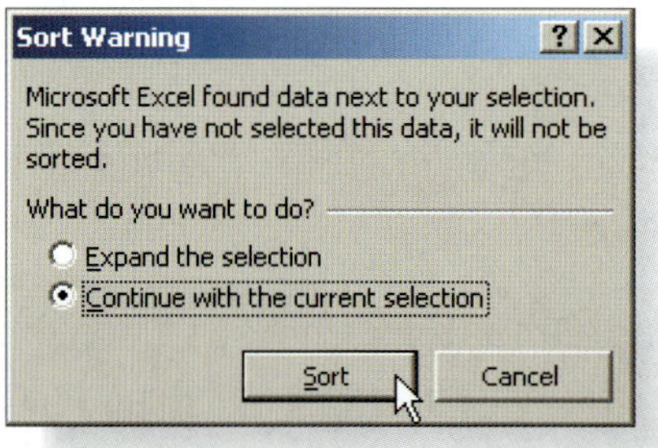

FIGURE 10-15 Sort Warning message box

7. Format column A as 15.71 (115 pixels) wide.
8. In Sheet1, click any department name and sort in an ascending order. This list has a range name, so you don't need to select any cells.
9. Click cell B4 in Sheet2 and click the Insert Function button.
10. Choose COUNTA in the Statistical category and then click OK.
11. Click Sheet1. Move the Function Arguments dialog box so you can see the department.
12. Select cells E4:E6. The reference appears in the Value1 box. (See Figure 10-16 on the next page.)
13. Click OK. There are three employees in the Finance department.
14. Repeat these steps or key the formula for each of the departments listed in Sheet2.
15. Save the workbook.

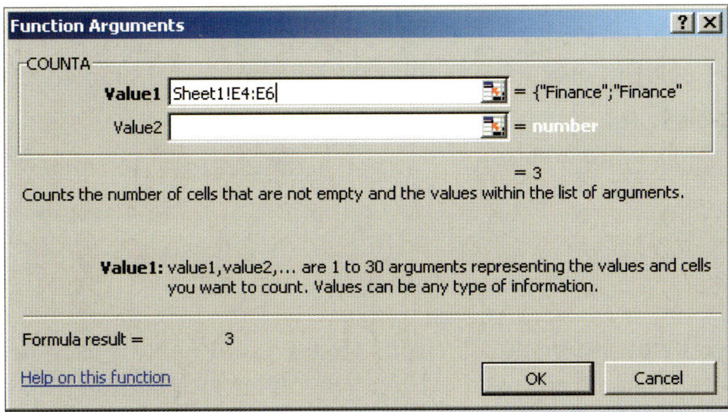

FIGURE 10-16
Using COUNTA in a 3-D reference

Using Print Areas and Print Selections

When you give a Print command, Excel prints the entire worksheet because that is the default print area. A *print area* is the range of cells to be printed. If you want to print only a portion of the worksheet, you can select the cells and define them as the print area. When you set your own print area, it is saved with the workbook.

You can select cells on the worksheet and print them by using the Selection choice in the Print what area of the Print dialog box. When you use this method, the selection is not saved with the workbook.

EXERCISE 10-28 Set and Clear a Print Area

1. On the Sheet1 tab, add the standard custom footer.
2. Click the Name box arrow and choose Database. The list range is selected.
3. From the File menu, choose Print Area, and then Set Print Area. The range is outlined by a dashed outline.
4. Click cell G1 to see the outline better.
5. Click the Print Preview button. As you can see, only the print area will be printed.
6. Print the area and close the preview.
7. From the File menu, choose Print Area and then Clear Print Area. The print selection is removed.

EXERCISE 10-29 Print a Selection

1. Click the Name box arrow and choose Database.
2. From the File menu, choose Print.

3. Click the button for **Selection** in the **Print what** group.
4. Click **Preview**. This is the same range as you printed previously.
5. Close the preview without printing.
6. Click cell G1. The print range is deselected.

EXERCISE 10-30 Print Noncontiguous Selections

If you want to print selections that are not next to each other, Excel prints each one on a separate page. Although you cannot change this feature, you can copy and paste a live link of each range to another area of the worksheet. Then you can print multiple ranges on a single page.

A *live link* is a simple formula that refers to a cell such as =A4. If you change the original data, the link is updated.

1. Select cells A4:F6 to select the employees in the Finance department.
2. Hold down Ctrl and select cells A10:F14 to include employees in the Marketing department.

E X C E L

FIGURE 10-17 Selecting two ranges for printing

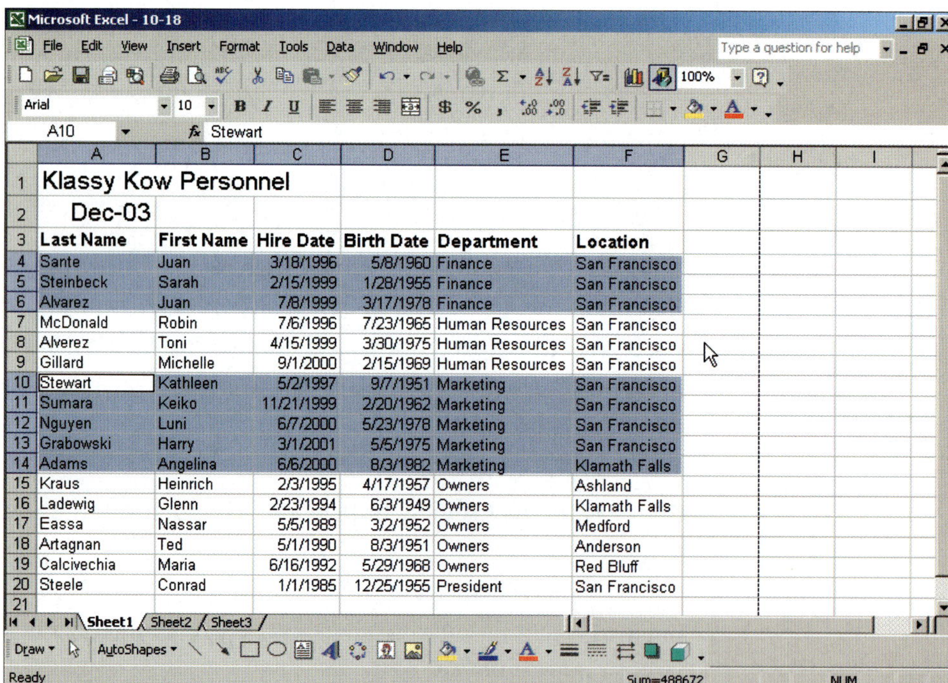

	A	B	C	D	E	F
1	Klassy Kow Personnel					
2	Dec-03					
3	Last Name	First Name	Hire Date	Birth Date	Department	Location
4	Sante	Juan	3/18/1996	5/8/1960	Finance	San Francisco
5	Steinbeck	Sarah	2/15/1999	1/28/1955	Finance	San Francisco
6	Alvarez	Juan	7/8/1999	3/17/1978	Finance	San Francisco
7	McDonald	Robin	7/6/1996	7/23/1965	Human Resources	San Francisco
8	Alverez	Toni	4/15/1999	3/30/1975	Human Resources	San Francisco
9	Gillard	Michelle	9/1/2000	2/15/1969	Human Resources	San Francisco
10	Stewart	Kathleen	5/2/1997	9/7/1951	Marketing	San Francisco
11	Sumara	Keiko	11/21/1999	2/20/1962	Marketing	San Francisco
12	Nguyen	Luni	6/7/2000	5/23/1978	Marketing	San Francisco
13	Grabowski	Harry	3/1/2001	5/5/1975	Marketing	San Francisco
14	Adams	Angelina	6/6/2000	8/3/1982	Marketing	Klamath Falls
15	Kraus	Heinrich	2/3/1995	4/17/1957	Owners	Ashland
16	Ladewig	Glenn	2/23/1994	6/3/1949	Owners	Klamath Falls
17	Eassa	Nassar	5/5/1989	3/2/1952	Owners	Medford
18	Artagnan	Ted	5/1/1990	8/3/1951	Owners	Anderson
19	Calcivechia	Maria	6/16/1992	5/29/1968	Owners	Red Bluff
20	Steele	Conrad	1/1/1985	12/25/1955	President	San Francisco
21						

3. From the **File** menu, choose **Print**. Click the button for **Selection** in the **Print what** group.
4. Click **Preview**. Each selection will be printed on its own page.
5. Press PgDn and PgUp to view the print selections.

6. Close the preview without printing.
7. Select cells A4:F6 and click the Copy button.
8. Go to cell H4.
9. From the Edit menu, choose Paste Special.
10. Click Paste Link. The range is copied to cell H4 and linked to the original range.
11. Press Esc to remove the marquee.
12. Select cells A10:F14 and click the Copy button.
13. Go to cell H7.
14. From the Edit menu, choose Paste Special. Click Paste Link.
15. Press Esc to remove the marquee.
16. Widen the columns to accommodate the longest text.
17. Select cells H4:M11. From the File menu, choose Print.
18. Click the button for Selection in the Print what group.
19. Click Preview. You can print the two ranges on one page now.
20. Print the ranges.

Creating Custom Views

A *view* is a set of display and print settings for a workbook. It includes column widths, gridlines, window size and position, the active sheet, and more. You can use a view to keep certain arrangements of your data so you do not need to keep making the same changes. For example, you can save one view of your worksheet with a particular sheet on top and no gridlines. Then you can save another view with gridlines and a different sheet active.

EXERCISE 10-31 Create Custom Views

1. Press Ctrl+Home. Save your workbook as ***[your initials]*10-31** in your Lesson 10 folder.
2. From the View menu, choose Custom Views. The Custom Views dialog box shows that there are currently no views for your workbook.
3. Click Add. The Add View dialog box opens.
4. Key **Normal** as the name for this view.
5. Make sure there is a check mark for Print settings and Hidden rows, columns and filter settings. (See Figure 10-18 on the next page.)

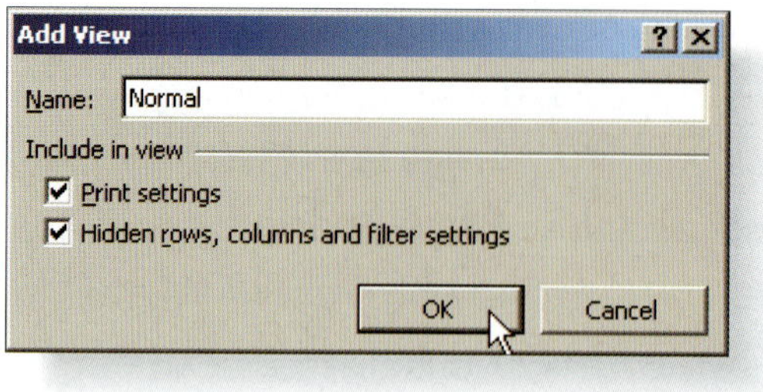

FIGURE 10-18 Adding a custom view

6. Click OK.
7. Select and delete cells H4:M11.
8. From the Tools menu, choose Options.
9. On the View tab, click to remove the check mark for Gridlines. Click OK.
10. Right-click the column D heading and hide the column.
11. Go to Sheet2.
12. From the View menu, choose Custom Views.
13. Click Add and key **Revised** as the name for this view.
14. Make sure there is a check mark for Print settings and Hidden rows, columns and filter settings. Click OK.

NOTE: Custom views are saved with the workbook.

15. Save and close the workbook.

EXERCISE 10-32 Display Views

1. Open ***[your initials]*10-31** from your Lesson 10 folder. It opens in the most recently used view with Sheet2 active.
2. Click the Sheet1 tab. This view does not show gridlines or column D.
3. From the View menu, choose Custom Views.
4. Click Normal and click Show. This is your original worksheet.
5. Close the workbook without saving.

LESSON 10 Summary

- Use grouped worksheets so you can print them with one command, format them in the same way, and delete data or key data on all of them at the same time.
- You can copy an entire worksheet and choose where to place it in the workbook. You can also move worksheet tabs to rearrange them.
- Copy data and formats from one worksheet to another one with regular Copy and Paste commands. Column widths and row heights are not copied.
- A 3-D reference is a formula that refers to cells or values in a different worksheet. A 3-D reference can use simple formulas or functions.

- Copy data from one workbook to another by opening both workbooks. Tile the windows, if desired, or use maximized windows.
- A list is a table of data with a row of labels as titles, followed by any number of rows of data. If you name the range that includes the labels and all the data, you can sort the list by clicking any column and using the Sort Ascending button and the Sort Descending button.
- Sort an unnamed list by selecting the rows to be sorted, not including titles or totals. Then specify the type of sort (ascending or descending).
- A filter enables you to display certain rows from a list. You can use AutoFilters by selecting from a list.
- Create a custom filter to use more than one requirement or to use wildcard features.
- The print area is the range of cells to be printed. You can set a print area that is different from the entire worksheet. A print area can be saved for future use.
- A print selection is not saved for future use. If you choose more than one selection, each one prints on a separate page.
- To print multiple selections on one page, paste a link to each range on an unused part of the worksheet and print that selection.
- A custom view is a set of display and print choices for a worksheet. You can save several views with the workbook.

LESSON 10 Command Summary

FEATURE	BUTTON	MENU	KEYBOARD	SPEECH
Copy sheet		Edit, Move or Copy Sheet		✓
Arrange windows		Window, Arrange		✓
Sort, ascending		Data, Sort		✓
Sort, descending		Data, Sort		✓
AutoFilter		Data, Filter, AutoFilter		
Print area, set		File, Print Area, Set Print Area		✓
Print area, clear		File, Print Area, Clear Print Area		✓
Custom view		View, Custom Views		✓
Paste Link		Edit, Paste Special		✓

Concepts Review

TRUE/FALSE QUESTIONS

Each of the following statements is either true or false. Indicate your choice by circling T or F.

T F 1. Grouped worksheets can be formatted all at once.

T F 2. Grouped worksheets are permanent.

T F 3. The Edit, Paste Special command can be used to copy and link data on the worksheet.

T F 4. You can copy data only when the windows are tiled, not maximized.

T F 5. A simple AutoFilter uses the column titles and an item from the column.

T F 6. An ascending sort arranges rows in alphabetical order.

T F 7. If you want to use more than one condition and an operator such as "greater than," use a Custom AutoFilter.

T F 8. A 3-D reference is a formula that refers to another worksheet.

SHORT ANSWER QUESTIONS

Write the correct answer in the space provided.

1. What name describes workbook settings such as sort orders and column widths that have been saved for repeated displaying as needed?

____

2. What keyboard shortcut inserts a blank worksheet?

____

3. Describe how a 3-D reference appears in the formula bar.

____

4. What does a filter do?

____

5. What type of sort would arrange rows so that the largest number is first?

____

6. How can you determine if worksheets are grouped?

____

7. What command enables you to paste formats, formulas, or links?

8. Describe one way to print only cells A5:D10?

CRITICAL THINKING

Answer these questions on a separate page. There are no right or wrong answers. Support your answers with examples from your own experience, if possible.

1. In your school or the company where you work, how could you use 3-D references? Give examples of worksheets that might be used in such a reference.
2. What kinds of uses can you think of for sorting and filtering data?

EXCEL

Lesson Applications

EXERCISE 10-33

Copy data. Create a 3-D reference.

In addition to statistical and mathematical functions and formulas, you can use most other categories of functions in a 3-D reference. The IF statement in this workbook tests whether employees have worked for five or more years.

1. Open **Personnel** and save it in your Lesson 10 folder as ***[your initials]*10-33.**
2. Change the year in each of the following cells to the current year: D3, D9, D12, and D13. This will give you some employees who were only recently hired.
3. Rename Sheet2 **Vested**. In cell A1, key **Vested Employees** and make it 16-point Arial.
4. In cell A2, key **As of** and apply the same font as cell A1. Right-align this label.
5. Key **=now()** in cell B2 and use the same font again. Left-align the date and format it to show the month spelled out, the date, a comma, and four digits for the year.
6. Copy cells A2:B15 on Sheet1 to cell A3 on the Vested sheet.

REVIEW: You can move between worksheets by pressing Ctrl+PgUp and Ctrl+PgDn.

7. Widen each column so no data is invisible. Make the labels in row 3 bold and centered. Format rows 3 and 4 as 18.75 (25 pixels) high.
8. In cell C3, key **Vested?** Format it like the other labels in row 3.
9. Click cell C4. Use an IF function. In the Logical_test box, click cell B2 and press F4 to make it an absolute reference.
10. Key – to subtract the hire date.
11. Click the Sheet1 tab and click cell D3 for the first hire date. Key **>1825** after D3 in the entry box. This subtracts 1,825 days from the employee's hire date.

NOTE: Date arithmetic uses serial numbers; five years is equal to 1825 days.

12. In the Value_if_true box, key **Yes**. In the Value_if_false box, key **No**. Click OK.
13. Copy the formula for the other employees and center the results.

REVIEW: Use the Margins tab in the Page Setup dialog box to center the worksheet.

14. Add your standard footer and print the worksheet horizontally centered.
15. Save and close the workbook.

EXERCISE 10-34

Copy worksheets. Create a 3-D reference. Group and ungroup worksheets.

1. Create a new workbook and save it as ***[your initials]*10-34** in your Lesson 10 folder.
2. Key **Klassy Kow Ice Cream Shops** in cell A1. Make it 18-point Times New Roman. Key **Ice Cream Sandwich Sales** in cell A2 and use the same font.
3. Key **Week 1** in cell B3 and make it 10-point Arial bold. Use the Fill handle to fill in to Week 4 in cell E3. Center these labels and make each column 6 pixels wider than its current size.
4. Key the following labels in cells A4:A7:

   Vanilla

   Chocolate

   Strawberry

   Chocolate Chip
5. Widen column A as needed. Format row 4 as 18.75 (25 pixels) tall. Rename Sheet1 **March**.
6. Key the data in Figure 10-19 to complete the worksheet.

FIGURE 10-19

	Week 1	Week 2	Week 3	Week 4
Vanilla	15000	14500	12500	15000
Chocolate	10000	12000	10500	12500
Strawberry	8000	7500	9000	8500
Chocolate Chip	15000	20000	16000	14000

7. Make two copies of the March sheet so you have sheets for April and May. Rename the sheets accordingly. Group Sheet2 and Sheet3 and delete them.

EXCEL

8. On the April sheet, delete the values. Key a formula in cell B4 to multiply the March value by 110% to determine the April value. Copy the formula to the other value cells.
9. On the May sheet, delete the values and key a formula to multiply the April value by 115%. Copy the formula.
10. Group the worksheets. Format the values to show commas and no decimals. Ungroup the sheets.

NOTE: You cannot draw AutoShapes or insert images when worksheets are grouped.

11. Click the March tab. From the Basic Shapes category, draw a Sun in cells E1:E2. While the sun is selected, fill it with an appropriate color.
12. Select the sun object and click the 3-D Style button. Choose 3-D Style 1.
13. Click the 3-D Style button. Choose 3-D Settings. Click the Depth button on the toolbar. Choose Custom and make the new depth half the value of its default setting. Close the 3-D Settings toolbar.
14. Select the sun object and click the Copy button. Click the April tab and click the Paste button. Drag the sun into position on the April tab.
15. Click the May tab and paste and position the sun.
16. Group the sheets, and key your name in cell A12. Print the sheets.
17. Ungroup the worksheets. Save and close the workbook.

EXERCISE 10-35

Group and ungroup worksheets. Copy data to another workbook.

When you copy data from one workbook to another, you might need to check the 3-D references. They might not be the same in different workbooks.

1. Create a new workbook and save it as ***[your initials]*10-35** in your Lesson 10 folder.
2. Rename Sheet1 **October**, Sheet2 **November**, and Sheet3 **December**. Group all three sheets.
3. Open **SandwichSales**.

REVIEW: You can switch between open windows by pressing Ctrl+F6 or by clicking the name on the taskbar.

4. Copy cells A1:A2 from **SandwichSales** to cell A1 in ***[your initials]*10-35**.
5. Key your first and last name in cell A15 in ***[your initials]*10-35**. Ungroup the sheets.

6. Copy cells A3:E8 in **SandwichSales** to cell A3 in the October sheet of ***[your initials]*10-35**.
7. Copy cells A9:E13 in **SandwichSales** to cell A3 in the November sheet. The copied cells cause a #REF error message to display, because the formula reference is now wrong.
8. Delete the cells with #REF messages. Key a formula in cell B4 that multiplies the October values by 108%. Copy the formula to cells B5:E7.
9. Copy cells A14:E18 from **SandwichSales** to the December sheet. Delete the cells with errors and key and copy a formula (to column E) that multiplies the November values by 108%.
10. Group the November and December sheets. Insert a row at row 4 and copy the labels (Week 1, etc.) from the October sheet. Adjust the column widths on the grouped sheets so all data is visible.
11. Group all sheets and add your standard footer to each sheet. Print the sheets.
12. Save and close your workbook. Close **SandwichSales** without saving.

EXCEL

EXERCISE 10-36 Challenge Yourself

Create a filter. Create and display custom views.

You can save filtered results in a custom view for display at any time. If you add records in the Normal view, the added records appear in the custom view the next time you show it.

1. Open **Personnel** and save it as ***[your initials]*10-36** in your Lesson 10 folder.
2. Select the column labels (row 2) and the data rows, and name the range **Database**
3. Add your standard footer and change the page orientation to landscape.
4. Create a custom view named **Normal**
5. Create an AutoFilter to show the employees in the Marketing department. While the records are being filtered, create another view named **Marketing**
6. While the records are being filtered, add yourself as an employee of the Marketing department in your home city. Print the filtered worksheet.
7. Show the Normal view to make sure you are listed in that view. Redefine the database range to include your name.
8. Save and close the workbook.

On Your Own

In these exercises you work on your own, as you would in a real-life work environment. Use the skills you've learned to accomplish the task—and be creative.

EXERCISE 10-37

In a new workbook, key the first and last names of students in your class or coworkers in your company. Include a label for each column. Name the range **Database**. Sort the rows alphabetically by last name. Add your standard footer and print the worksheet. Sort the rows in descending order by first name and print the worksheet. Save the workbook as ***[your initials]*10-37** in your Lesson 10 folder and close it.

EXERCISE 10-38

Open ***[your initials]*10-37** from your Lesson 10 folder. On Sheet2, create a 3-D reference for the first label to display the same label as the one on Sheet1. Copy the reference to create a "duplicate" of Sheet1 on Sheet2. Save the workbook as ***[your initials]*10-38** in your Lesson 10 folder. Display the formulas on Sheet2 and widen the columns to show the complete reference. Add your standard footer and print the worksheet. Hide the formulas and resize the columns. Save and close the workbook.

EXERCISE 10-39

Use the Office Assistant to look up "lists." Print the guidelines for reference. In a new workbook, create a list of 12 company names, retail stores, or restaurants in your city. In separate columns, list a phone number, the year they started in business, and an average hourly wage for someone who works at this establishment. Format the list attractively and name the range according to the guidelines. Save your workbook as ***[your initials]*10-39** in your Lesson 10 folder. Add your standard footer and print the worksheet. Sort the rows by year started in business, with the oldest establishment listed first. Print the worksheet in this order. Sort the rows by average hourly wage in ascending order. Print the worksheet again. Close the workbook without saving.

Cross-Curriculum Projects

Office XP is a useful tool for any of your document, worksheets, presentations, or databases. This section of the text provides suggestions for projects related to your other classes.

Types of Projects

Review the bar on this page that identifies the four types of projects. For every application and for every unit there are project suggestions involving Language Arts, Science and Math, Social Studies, and Vocational Education. The icon in front of the project identifies the type of project.

Teamwork

You may be working with other students on a project. If so, part of your project grade will typically be based on your team's performance. You will need to work together as a group to define the goals of the project and to divide the work equally. Remember to listen attentively to everyone's opinions and encourage creativity.

TYPES OF PROJECTS

Language Arts

Science & Math

Social Studies

Vocational Education

WORD

Key an article that interests you from a newspaper or magazine. Let wordwrap automatically start each new line for you and press Enter twice to begin a new paragraph. After each paragraph, correct the misspelled words that Word marked. Add a paragraph describing why you chose this article. (Unit 1)

Modify the document **Summer.doc** by adapting it to discuss your own town. (Unit 1)

Create a list of chemical formulas for common things you might find in a classroom. Use superscript and subscript text where appropriate. (Unit 1)

The document **Balloon1.doc** mentions that Albuquerque is the hot air balloon capital of the world. Prepare a report describing how hot air balloons fly. (Unit 1)

Imagine that it's 1849 and you're traveling from the east coast to the west coast for the gold rush. Describe your route and the modes of transportation you might use. (Unit 1)

Imagine time-traveling back to an ancient city anywhere in the world. Write a description of the city and its way of life. Try to persuade other time travelers to visit the city. (Unit 1)

Write a short description of the type of job you would like when you graduate. Include the following subjects: location of the job, type of business, position, expected salary. Discuss working conditions you find desirable and the kinds of benefits you hope will be offered. Save this report, and then edit it to reflect the job you'll be looking for in five years. (Unit 1)

Create a list of company names, addresses, and phone numbers for prospective employers. Use line-break characters to make each company's data one paragraph. (Unit 1)

When performing a grammar check, Word flags sentences with double negatives, passive verbs, pronoun errors, and errors of agreement between subjects and verbs. Create sentences to illustrate each of these errors (one error per sentence). Below the incorrect sentence, key the correct grammar. (Unit 2)

Open the file **Rockies2.doc** and change 12 words (verbs and nouns) to words with similar meanings. Indicate your changes in bold. (Unit 2)

Each planet has its own astronomical symbol. List the planets, beginning with the symbol, then the planet name, and a very brief description. Use tabs to separate each item. (Unit 2)

Imagine that you are in the future. Create a bulleted travel checklist of items you would need for a two-week trip to the Moon colony. Be creative in thinking of items to bring along. (Unit 2)

Now that you are familiar with character and paragraph formatting, create a one-page flyer, suitable for posting, on one or more of the following topics (be sure to include the appropriate facts, such as names, dates, and places) (Unit 2):

- A handout for Paul Revere to distribute on his ride in 1775
- An announcement of the first time the United States celebrated Martin Luther King Day
- A wanted poster for Benedict Arnold
- A wanted poster for Jesse James
- A presidential campaign poster for a candidate in an election held anytime between the 1860s and 1880s
- A promotional poster for the Seneca Falls, New York, Women's Rights Convention

Imagine you own a restaurant that serves all your favorite foods. Write a report that describes the restaurant—its name, location, menu, policies, etc. Use the Microsoft Word thesaurus to make the description sound appealing. Spell-check and grammar-check the document. (Unit 2)

Using a numbered list, write a procedure for reconciling a checkbook. (Unit 2)

Every language contains proverbs or idiomatic expressions. In a paragraph, describe a non-English proverb or idiomatic expression. In a separate section, key the proverb or expression in landscape mode using a large font, centered attractively on the page. (Unit 3)

Key a short children's story or fable. Use a 6-inch margin at the top of every page to allow space for your own illustrations. Create a footer that contains the story title and the page number. Include a cover page with an illustration but with no footer. (Unit 3)

Imagine that you are Thomas Edison. Write a letter to a bank asking for a loan to finance a new invention. Include a description of the idea on a new page that will be included with the letter. Be sure your letter includes an appropriate date and return address. (Unit 3)

Use the press release template to write about one of the following types of events (Unit 3):

- A scientific breakthrough
- An advance in health care
- The merger of two science-related companies
- The launch of a new computer, technology, or software package
- The results of a survey or poll

Create an information sheet containing biographical data about the U.S. president that you regard as the least well-known. In a separate section, using different page formatting, write a short report about the most significant event that occurred during that president's term of office. (Unit 3)

Create a list of noted political or military leaders. Divide the list into three groups: 18th Century, 19th Century, 20th Century. Each group should contain at least eight people and appear on a separate page. Add a title page as a separate section and add page numbers to section 2. (Unit 3)

- Write a letter to a manufacturing company informing it that you have an idea for a new product. Include a description of the idea using different page formatting on a new page that will be attached to the letter. (Unit 3)

- Use the Resume Wizard or one of the résumé templates to draft your résumé. (Unit 3)

- Describe an event in your life as if it were a newspaper story, complete with a headline. Run the headline across the top of the page and format the article in a three-column format. Balance the columns. (Unit 4)

- Many people experience a turning point in their lives—a point that changes their lives forever. Describe the turning point in the life of a famous person or someone you know. Use a newspaper format, complete with a headline. Run the headline across the top of the page, format the article in three-columns, and balance the columns. (Unit 4)

- Create a four-column table of 10 important inventions. Set up the table as follows: column 1, invention; column 2, year; column 3, inventor; column 4, inventor's nationality. (Unit 4)

- Create a table of 10 endangered species. List the species as row headings and use the following column headings: Species Group (for example, mammal, bird, or reptile), Scientific Name, Location(s). If the living quantity of the species is known, include that information as well. (Unit 4)

Create a four-column table of 10 explorers. Set up the table as follows: column 1, year; column 2, explorer name; column 3, nationality; column 4, discovery or area of exploration.
(Unit 4)

Create a table that describes your family (immediate or extended). For each column heading, name a family member. Use the following row headings: relationship to you, date of birth, age, interests, best quality. Add row headings if you like. (Unit 4)

Create a table of the top 10 businesses in your area. List the businesses in order of sales. Include the company name, town, gross sales, and net sales. (Note: Private companies may not publish their sales figures.) (Unit 4)

Create a table of at least five professions that interest you. Include the following information: years of education required, specialized training necessary, and starting salary. (Unit 4)

Using a two-column by five-row table, insert clip art in the left column and a foreign-language description of the clip art in the right column. Add appropriate column headings. If your school has a color printer, print the clip art in color, making sure your description includes a reference to the color(s). (Unit 5)

Create an advertisement that uses clip art and shapes. Make sure your ad copy includes at least seven adjectives. (Use the thesaurus if necessary.) (Unit 5)

Describe the discovery of the electric light. Use the clip art picture of a light bulb to illustrate the document. Include a WordArt title. (Unit 5)

Write a description of the route you would use for one of the following trips. Consult a map and be specific with your description. Include clip art in the document, modifying the art and placing it as desired. (Unit 5)

- A road trip from Bangor, Maine, to San Diego, California
- A road trip from Anchorage, Alaska, to Key West, Florida
- An imaginary trip by Norsemen to Minnesota
- Christopher Columbus's route

Write a report about a legal issue that interests you. Advocate a position on the issue. Insert appropriate clip art in the report (one possible piece of clip art would be the balanced scale clip art (representing the "scales of justice"). (Unit 5)

EXCEL

Prepare a worksheet report on the total output of 5 literary figures from the same time period, showing the total number of plays, poems, novels, short stories, and essays. These categories are the column headings; author names are row labels. Include formulas for total works by author. (Unit 1)

Prepare a worksheet report on the world's principal languages. List the 10 most widely spoken languages, showing the number of people speaking the language and the countries where it is spoken. (Unit 1)

Create a worksheet report on renewable versus non-renewable fuels in residential heating across the U.S. Show the primary fuel by geographic region, with regions (e.g., Northeast) as column headings and "Renewable" and "Non-renewable" as row labels. (Unit 1)

Imagine you're planning a trip abroad and want to compare the weather at different times of the year in 10 different countries. Build a worksheet that shows the average high temperature in each of the 4 seasons, with the seasons as column headings and the countries as row labels. (Unit 1)

Analyze your daily activities, and prepare a worksheet report showing calories consumed with each activity. Column headings would be "Activity," "Duration," "Calories Burned/Minute," and "Total Calories Burned." Row headings would be the days of the week. (Unit 1)

- Prepare a worksheet report showing the percentage of U.S. population living in urban versus rural areas in 1800, 1850, 1900, 1950, and 1990. Use the years as the column headings and "Urban," "Suburban," and "Rural" for row labels. (Unit 1)

- Create a simple worksheet showing the countries on each continent with the greatest populations and greatest population densities, with the continents as the column headings, and the 2 population categories as the row labels. (Unit 1)

- Prepare a worksheet report that shows the number of armed conflicts worldwide that have occurred in 10-year intervals, beginning in 1945. Column headings are the year intervals (e.g., 1945-1954, 1955-1964, etc.); row labels are the continents. Include formulas showing totals. (Unit 1)

- Create a worksheet showing your skills and interests, and 5 different jobs in which those abilities are important. For column headings use the job titles, and for row labels use 10 skills or interests. Then place an X in each cell for each job in which a skill or interest is important. (Unit 1)

- Research 3 companies where you'd like to work, and prepare a worksheet listing all entry-level positions and the number of new hires for each company on an annual basis. Company names are column headings; "Entry Positions" and "New Hires" are the row labels. (Unit 1)

- Create a data sheet for recording your observations on the number and type of insects found around the edge of a pond, including date, time of observation, location, and other relevant characteristics. (Unit 2)

- Demonstrate the effect of passive solar heating by recording the temperature at the same time of day in the same places for a week. Use the MIN, MAX, and AVERAGE functions to compare your findings. (Unit 2)

- Prepare a worksheet report on fuel efficiency ratings on 5 sports-utility and 5 sub-compact vehicles. Use the MIN, MAX, and AVERAGE functions to compare your findings. (Unit 2)

- You are making a trip by car from Boston to Seattle. Plot 5 different routes, with appropriate stops, and calculate the estimated driving times for each day between stops. Total the driving times. Use the MIN and MAX functions to show the slowest and fastest and the longest and shortest routes. (Unit 2)

- Prepare a worksheet report on U.S. public debt since 1940. Use 5-year intervals. List the president, the dollar amount of debt, per-capita debt, interest paid, interest payment as a percent of federal spending, and percent increase. Print on a single page, including a page showing the formulas. (Unit 2)

- You are analyzing the results of a charity sports sale. Create a sales tally with at least 20 sales, with totals ranging from $2 to $100. Create formulas showing the total amount of sales over $25 and total sales under $5. (Unit 2)

- You administer the billing for a law office. Create a time-log worksheet for an attorney for a week, showing her appointments across the day, the name of the client with whom the attorney met, and the total billable time for each day. Use time math for the last field, and appropriate time formats. (Unit 2)

- Make a list of the shop equipment in your school. Include the manufacturer, year purchased, and category. Use date math to calculate age. Add page breaks, and include headers, footers, print titles. (Unit 2)

- Research the 10 highest circulating newspapers in the U.S. Prepare a chart comparing their average daily readerships, and their increase or decrease in circulation in the last 5 years. (Unit 3)

- Research total U.S. books sales for the last calendar year. Using a chart, display data for the categories to include: adult fiction, nonfiction, science fiction, and children's books. (Unit 3)

Prepare a worksheet report on 5 Internet major on-line news Web sites. Analyze them for such characteristics as intended audience, number of links to other sites, use of graphics, and the average article length, using a separate worksheet for each magazine. Include a summary worksheet for the 5 Web sites. (Unit 3)

Demonstrate the effectiveness of the Endangered Species Act by plotting estimates of the population of the bald eagle and the osprey since 1940. Choose an appropriate chart to display your results, enhancing your chart with titles, borders, and legends. (Unit 3)

Build a pie chart of the animal kingdom, showing the best estimates of the number of species in each phylum. Title and label all components. (Unit 3)

Build a chart showing U.S. government spending by category in the last fiscal year compared to 10 years earlier. Enhance the chart with appropriate labels, titles, and legends. (Unit 3)

Prepare a worksheet showing change in the per capita income of the world's five wealthiest and poorest nations over the last ten years. Show the results of each category in a line chart. (Unit 3)

Create a line chart supporting or refuting the hypothesis that the world's average temperature is rising. Show the data in 10-year increments, starting in 1900. (Unit 3)

You are the proprietor of a property-management firm with a contract to do all repairs for a condominium association. Produce a summary bill and 6 supporting invoices for the month of March using multiple worksheets for such services as snow removal, firewood, garage service, etc. (Unit 3)

You own a specialty woodworking shop. Prepare a flyer marketing your services, using clip art, callouts, borders, and other enhancements to make your flyer more visually appealing. (Unit 3)

Visit an auto repair shop, and research the amount of work they do in the following categories: inspections, routine maintenance, engine repair work, body work, and other. Present the data in a chart form, using appropriate labels and titles. (Unit 3)

POWERPOINT

- Locate three versions of the story of King Arthur. Create a presentation that gives information about each of them: the author, the publication or movie release date, and the audience for which you think each version was intended. (Unit 1)

- Research two authors who used pen names (for example, Mark Twain and George Eliot). Create a presentation that gives four or five key facts about each author and his or her works. (Unit 1)

- Investigate the life of F. Scott Fitzgerald, and create a presentation about five key events in his life. (Unit 1)

- Create a presentation that explains how RBIs are determined in baseball. Research and present information about leading hitters. (Unit 1)

- Create a presentation that explains how RBIs are determined in baseball. Research and present information about leading hitters. (Unit 1)

- Create a presentation about three significant advances in astronomy in the past ten years. (Unit 1)

- Research the divisions of geological time, and create a presentation showing the names and typical life forms of four different eras. (Unit 1)

- Create a presentation that describes the governmental structure of Canada. (Unit 1)

- Decide which are the two most important amendments to the U.S. Constitution, and create a presentation justifying your choices. (Unit 1)
- Research the westward expansion of the United States, and create a presentation that explains the importance of steamboats and railroads. (Unit 1)
- Create a presentation explaining the importance of safety awareness for asbestos-removal workers. (Unit 1)
- Read Benjamin Franklin's *Autobiography*, and create a presentation arguing that Franklin's ideas are still valuable for business. Use Franklin's own words to support your points. (Unit 1)
- Create a presentation to be given by a manufacturing supervisor explaining why employees should choose overtime work. (Unit 1)
- Create a presentation comparing Chaucer's "Canterbury Tales" in its original Middle English with a modern version. Use passages from at least three different sections. Save the presentation as a Web page. (Unit 2)
- Create a presentation comparing R. L. Stevenson's *Treasure Island* with the cartoon version, and try to persuade your audience that the printed version is better. (Unit 2)
- Create a presentation urging a fictional movie studio to do a remake of the Tracy-Hepburn anti-computer movie "Desk Set" with a modern pro-computer theme. Explain the new plot, and offer suggestions for casting and sets. (Unit 2)
- Research the history of computers, and create a presentation explaining why binary arithmetic has been crucial to their development. Save the presentation as a Web page. (Unit 2)
- Create a presentation about Isaac Asimov's life and his contributions to modern scientific understanding. (Unit 2)
- Locate Galileo's 1615 letter to the Grand Duchess Christina, explaining his ideas about the solar system. Create a presentation explaining his ideas. Save the presentation as a Web page. (Unit 2)
- Research number theory, focusing especially on knowledge about prime numbers. Create a presentation explaining prime numbers. (Unit 2)

- Research five important Supreme Court decisions of the 20th century. Create a presentation explaining why each is important, the relevant social and legal circumstances, and the consequences of the decision. (Unit 2)

- Create a presentation describing political tensions among China, Japan, and Korea during the 20th century. Include at least one hyperlink to a relevant Web site. (Unit 2)

- Create a presentation tracing the history and growth of world communication systems, explaining how and why life has changed in the past 300 years. (Unit 2)

- Create a presentation explaining an ad campaign for a bicycle repair business. (Unit 2)

- Research how a popular fast-food chain determines locations for new restaurants. Determine what location in your neighborhood is most likely to meet their criteria, and then create a presentation to the Zoning Board asking for construction permission. Include a hyperlink to an Excel worksheet with supporting information. (Unit 2)

- Using different sizes of the arrow shape, create a presentation showing four kinds of Exit signs. (Unit 2)

- Create a presentation comparing the strengths of a filmed version of Jane Austen's *Pride and Prejudice* with the novel, focusing on how film enhances understanding. Use pictures, office art, and color where appropriate. (Unit 3)

- Create a presentation that demonstrates the importance of knowing Latin roots in building a better vocabulary. Include at least four interesting, useful words derived from each of five Latin roots. Highlight the roots by using a different color font. (Unit 3)

- Using AutoShapes, create a presentation describing a fictional student production of "Our Town." (Unit 3)

- Using the objects in PowerPoint and your own or others' poetry, create a presentation that encloses brief poems within shapes that fit their meaning. Explain the reasons for your choices. (Unit 3)

- Research the life and achievements of four famous mathematicians. Create a presentation explaining their work and contributions. Use pictures and color to add visual interest. (Unit 3)

- Create a presentation about constellations. For each of four constellations visible in the spring sky, present the shape, the stars, the name, and the myth behind the name. (Unit 3)

- Create a presentation examining the color spectrum of red, orange, yellow, green, blue, indigo, and violet and explaining why rainbows appear. (Unit 3)

- Create a presentation comparing the construction of the Brooklyn Bridge with those of the Golden Gate and Chesapeake Bay Bridges. Compare costs, time, suspension methods, and effects. Use pictures, office art, and color where appropriate. (Unit 3)

- Research 20th-century national rates of literacy and changes in Gross National Product, and create a presentation linking several countries' growth in literacy with increases in their GNP. Use pictures, office art, and color where appropriate. (Unit 3)

- Research the history of the Iditarod race in Alaska, and create a presentation explaining its rules and why it is important to the state. (Unit 3)

- Create a presentation showing essential sections in a music store. Crop a clip art object for each category — rock, classical, country, and others — and include them in the presentation. (Unit 3)

- Create a series of ads for a multiplex theater. Use the star AutoShape duplicated to emphasize the star quality of the movies shown. (Unit 3)

- Using appropriate clip art, create a presentation promoting membership in a gym. (Unit 3)

ACCESS

In tblCustomers, filter the records to show customers from Tennessee. Then edit the name of each company/store to a German, Spanish, or French equivalent. (Unit 1)

Using tblPayroll, sort descending by the amount of federal tax. Then determine the percentage of higher federal tax (the tax bracket) for salaried workers. (Unit 1)

Use tblEmployees and tblPayroll to compare salaries and hourly work rates in your city to those in the database. (Unit 1)

Add five new records using frmNewProducts for home and automotive repair products or tools. You may need to look at tblCategories and tblProducts to review and determine product categories. (Unit 1)

Using tblEmployees, tblJobCodes, and tblPayroll, find employees who work in plant operations. Determine the typical raise in your city for this year (such as 3%, 6%) and change the salaries or rates for operations personnel to show the same raise percentage. (Unit 1)

Add an advertising slogan field to tblSalesCampaign. Then create a form named frmSalesSlogans for tblSalesCampaigns using all the fields. Using the form, add a slogan for each campaign. (Unit 2)

Add a new table named tblWeather that records daily high and low temperatures indoors and outdoors, daily precipitation, and whether the precipitation was rain or snow. Include a Memo field for unusual weather conditions such as high humidity, hurricane-force winds, etc. Enter 10 records for the first 10 days of this month. (Unit 2)

- Add a new table named tblDemographics that includes the Employee ID field and fields that reveal basic demographic information about an employee. Such fields might include educational level, place of birth, height, etc. Enter records for all employees in tblEmployees. (Unit 2)

- Add a Memo field to tblJobCodes to list qualifications for each position. Qualifications might be a type of degree or certification or a certain number of years of experience. Enter basic qualifications for each code. Create a tabular landscape report named rptQualifications that shows the job code, title, and qualifications. (Unit 2)

- Add a new table named tblVehicles for all vehicles owned by the company. Assign each vehicle an ID number. Include fields for the type, vehicle identification number (if any), make and model, year, mileage-to-date, and other appropriate fields. Include a category that notes whether the vehicle is for business or maintenance. Enter 10 records that include cars, trucks, lawn maintenance vehicles, and others. (Unit 2)

PowerPoint®

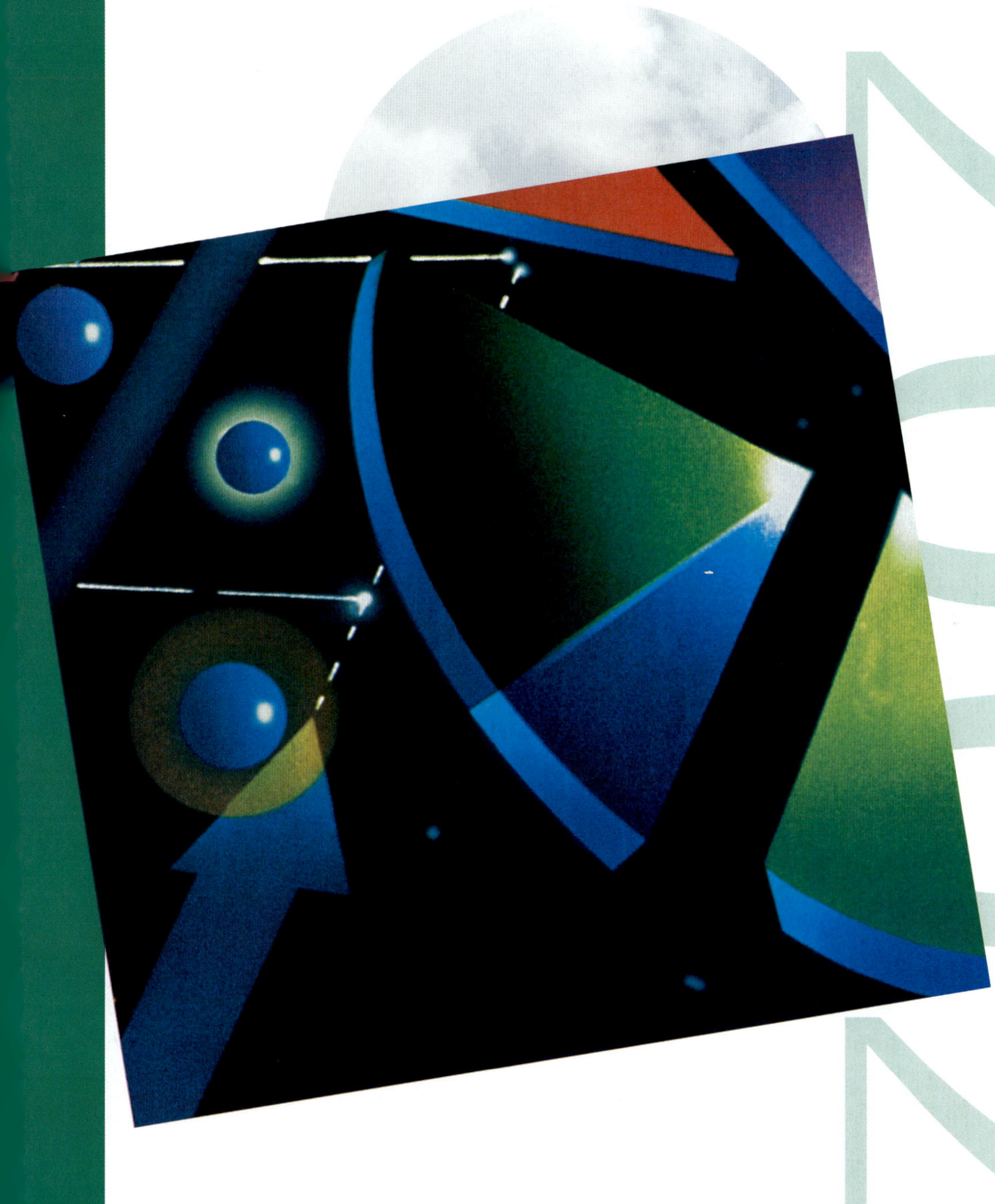

2002

PowerPoint®

2002

CASE STUDY

There's more to learning a presentation graphics program like Microsoft PowerPoint than simply keying text on colored backgrounds and calling the result a "presentation." You need to know how to use PowerPoint in a real-world situation. That's why all these lessons relate to everyday business tasks.

As you work through lessons, imagine yourself working as an intern for Good 4 U, a fictional New York restaurant.

Good 4 U

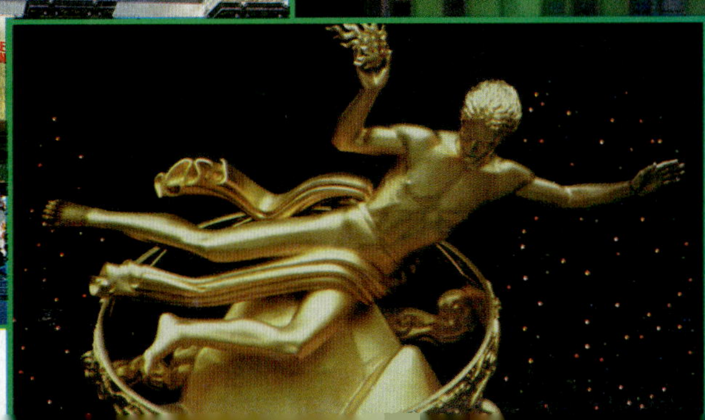

Good 4 U Restaurant

Good 4 U restaurant has been in business for only a little over three years—but it's been a success from the time it served its first veggie burger. The restaurant—which features healthy food and has a theme based on the "everyday active life"—seems to have found an award-winning recipe for success. (Figure CS-1 shows the interior of the largest dining room in the restaurant. It features plants and a wide expanse of windows looking over Central Park South, a tree-lined avenue on the south side of New York's Central Park. As you can see, there are even outside tables with umbrellas!)

The food at Good 4 U is all low fat. The menu features lots of vegetables (all organic, of course!), as well as fish and chicken. The restaurant doesn't serve alcohol, instead offering fruit juices and sparkling water. Good 4 U's theme of the "everyday active life" is reflected on the restaurant's wall's with running, tennis, and bicycling memorabilia. This theme really reflects the interests of the two co-owners. Julie Wolfe led the New York Flash to two Women's Professional Basketball Association championships in her ten years with the team. Gus Irvinelli is an avid tennis player and was selected for the U.S. Amateur team. Even the chef, Michele Jenkins, leads an everyday active life—she rides her bicycle ten miles a day in and around Central Park.

Two years ago, Roy Olafsen was a marketing manager for a large hotel chain. He was overweight and out-of-shape. In the same week that his doctor told him to eat better and exercise

FIGURE CS-1 Interior of Good 4 U Restaurant

regularly, Roy received a job offer from Good 4 U. "It was too good to pass up," he says. "It was my chance to combine work and a healthy life style." As you work in the text, you'll discover that Good 4 U is often involved in health-oriented projects, as well as events that focus on athletics.

In your work as an intern at Good 4 U Restaurant, you will have a chance to meet many of the people who work at Good 4 U. You will certainly interact with the four key people shown in Figure CS-2. In fact, you will find that you will be be doing most of your work for Roy Olafsen, the Marketing Manager.

All the presentations you will use and create in this course relate to Good 4 U restaurant. As you work with the presentations in the text, take the time to notice the following things:

- The types of presentations needed in a small business to carry on day-to-day business.
- The design of presentations. Real businesses must often focus on designing eye-catching, informative presentations for customers. The business's success often depends on developing attractive presentations that sell its services to customers.
- The "Tips for Designing Presentations" on the next page of this Case Study. Good presentations generally follow these guidelines.

As you use this text and become more experienced with Microsoft PowerPoint, you will also gain experience in creating, editing, and designing the sort of presentations generated in a real-life business environment.

FIGURE CS-2
Key Employees

MICHELE JENKINS
Head Chef

JULIE WOLFE
Co-Owner

GUS IRVINELLI
Co-Owner

ROY OLAFSEN
Marketing Manager

In your first meeting with Roy Olafsen, he gave you the following tips for designing presentations. These tips can be applied to any presentation, but can be modified, as needed.

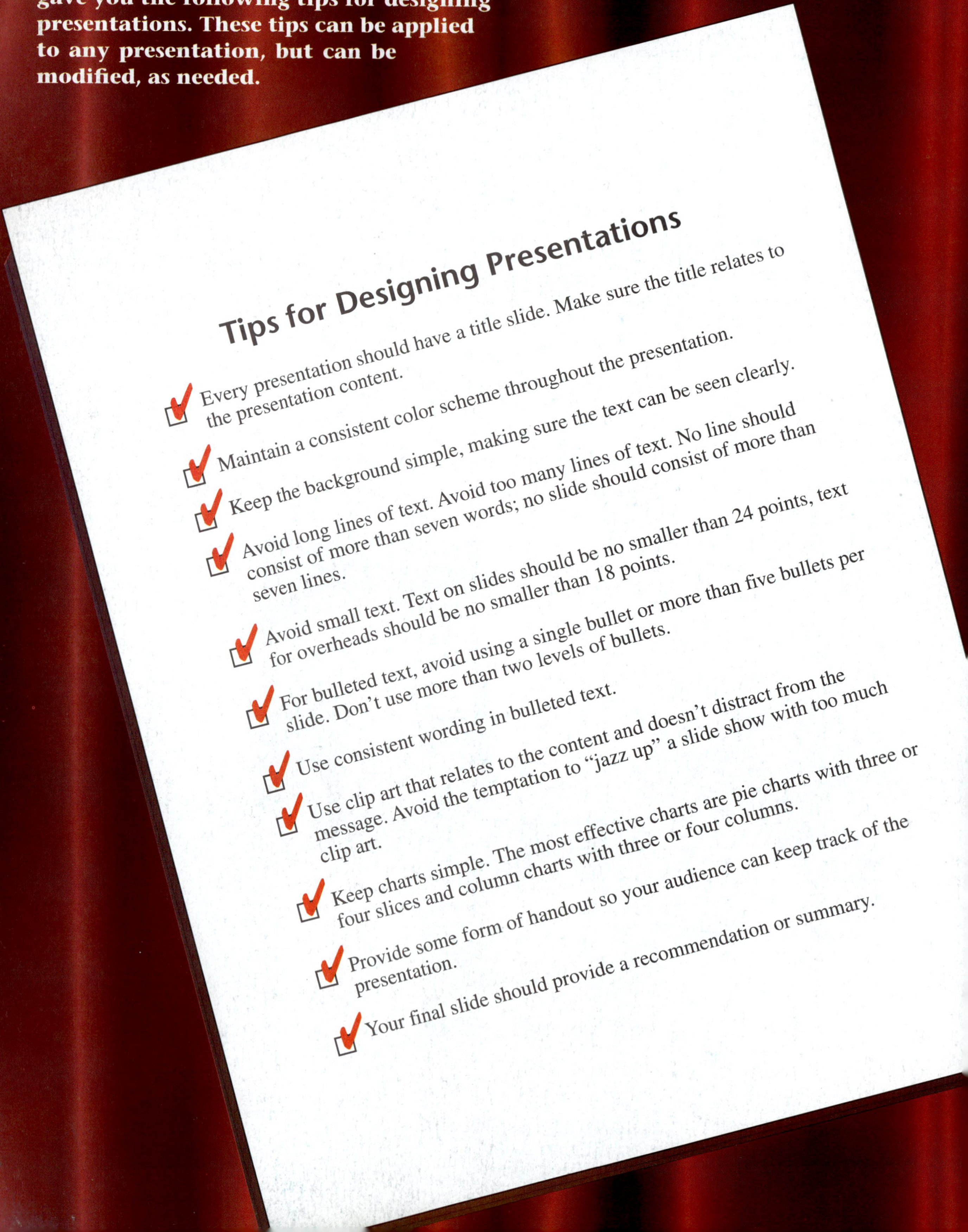

Tips for Designing Presentations

- Every presentation should have a title slide. Make sure the title relates to the presentation content.
- Maintain a consistent color scheme throughout the presentation.
- Keep the background simple, making sure the text can be seen clearly.
- Avoid long lines of text. Avoid too many lines of text. No line should consist of more than seven words; no slide should consist of more than seven lines.
- Avoid small text. Text on slides should be no smaller than 24 points, text for overheads should be no smaller than 18 points.
- For bulleted text, avoid using a single bullet or more than five bullets per slide. Don't use more than two levels of bullets.
- Use consistent wording in bulleted text.
- Use clip art that relates to the content and doesn't distract from the message. Avoid the temptation to "jazz up" a slide show with too much clip art.
- Keep charts simple. The most effective charts are pie charts with three or four slices and column charts with three or four columns.
- Provide some form of handout so your audience can keep track of the presentation.
- Your final slide should provide a recommendation or summary.

UNIT 1

Basic Skills

LESSON

1 What Is PowerPoint?

OBJECTIVES

MOUS ACTIVITIES

In this lesson:

PP2002 **1-1**
PP2002 **2-2**
PP2002 **5-1**
PP2002 **7-2**
PP2002 **7-3**

See Appendix E.

After completing this lesson, you will be able to:

1. Start PowerPoint.
2. Navigate in PowerPoint.
3. Key text on a slide.
4. Work with PowerPoint views, tabs, and task panes.
5. Run a presentation as a slide show.
6. Name and save a presentation.
7. Print slides and handouts.
8. Close a presentation and exit PowerPoint.

Estimated Time: 1½ hours

Microsoft PowerPoint is a powerful but easy-to-use presentation graphics program you can use to create professional-quality slide presentations. This lesson begins with an overview of many PowerPoint features and provides a road map of the various PowerPoint screen views, tabs, and panes.

Starting PowerPoint

Start

There are several ways to start PowerPoint, depending on your system setup and your personal preferences. For example, you can use the Start button Start on the Windows taskbar or double-click the PowerPoint shortcut icon if one appears on your Windows desktop.

EXERCISE 1-1 Start PowerPoint

When you start PowerPoint, a new blank presentation automatically appears, ready for you to start keying text.

NOTE: If you are unfamiliar with Windows, refer to Appendix A: "Windows Tutorial."

1. Turn on your computer to load Windows.
2. Click the Start button **Start** on the Windows taskbar and point to Programs.

FIGURE 1-1 Starting PowerPoint from the Windows taskbar

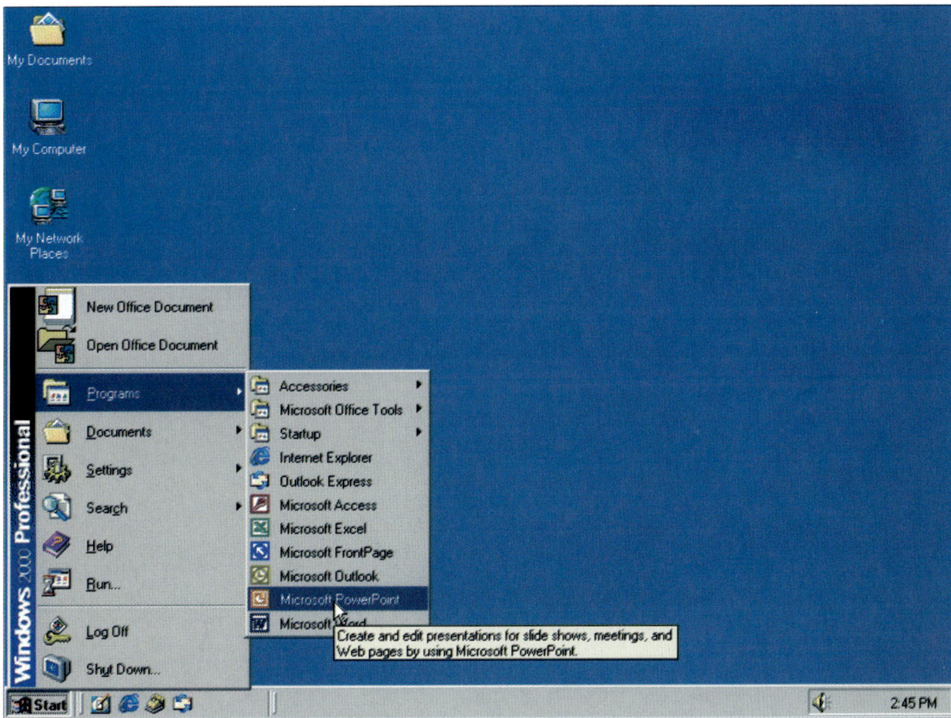

Start button

NOTE: Windows provides many ways to start applications. If you have problems, ask your instructor for help.

3. On the Programs submenu, click Microsoft PowerPoint. In a few seconds, the program is loaded and the PowerPoint window appears. (See Figure 1-2 on the next page.)

FIGURE 1-2
PowerPoint opening window

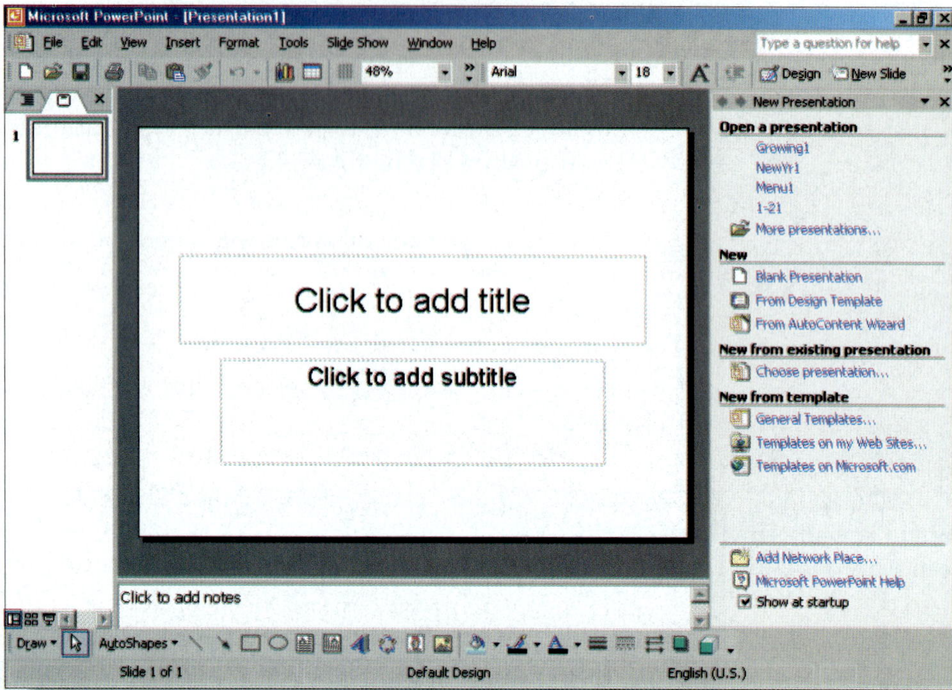

Normal View button

4. If your screen does not look like Figure 1-2, click the Normal View button in the lower left corner of the window or ask your instructor for assistance.

EXERCISE 1-2 Open an Existing Presentation

The opening PowerPoint window displays a blank slide, ready for you to add text, images, and additional slides. In Lesson 3 you will create a presentation from scratch, using this blank slide.

In this exercise you open an existing PowerPoint presentation. The presentation was created especially for this lesson to give you an overview of many of PowerPoint's features.

1. Click File on the menu bar and then choose Open to display the Open dialog box.

TABLE 1-1 **Toolbar Buttons in the Open Dialog Box**

BUTTON	NAME	PURPOSE
	Back	Enables you to return to a folder or place you previously opened while working in this dialog box.

continues

TABLE 1-1 Toolbar Buttons in the Open Dialog Box *continued*

BUTTON	NAME	PURPOSE
	Up One Level	Moves up one level in the hierarchy of folders or drives on your computer or on computers connected to your computer.
	Search the Web	Opens the Search page of your Internet browser (if you are on-line) so you can search the Web for information.
	Delete	Deletes a file or folder.
	Create New Folder	Enables you to create a new folder to organize your files.
	Views	Opens a menu of view options for displaying files and file icons.
Tools ▾	Tools	Opens a menu of other file utilities, such as finding a file, renaming a file, and adding a file or folder to the Favorites folder.

2. Click the down arrow next to the Look in box and choose the appropriate drive and folder for your student files according to your instructor's directions.

FIGURE 1-3
Files listed in the Open dialog box

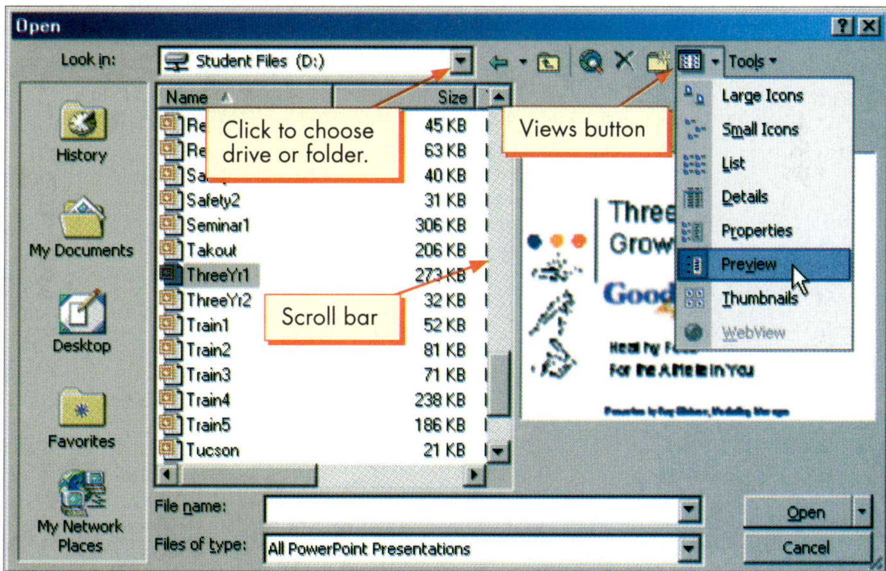

NOTE: Your instructor will advise you where to locate the files for this course. For more information about working with files, folders, and directories in Windows, see Appendix B: "File Management."

3. When you locate the student files, click the arrow next to the Views button in the Open dialog box to display a menu of view options.
4. Choose List to list all files by name.
5. Click the Views button again and this time choose Preview to get a quick look at a presentation's first slide before opening it.
6. Locate the file **ThreeYr1** (use the scroll bar if you need to) and click once to select the file.
7. Click Open. (You can also double-click the file's name to open it.) PowerPoint opens the file in Normal view.

NOTE: The presentations you create in this course relate to the Case Study about Good 4 U, a fictional restaurant (see pages 691 through 694).

Navigating in PowerPoint

If you are already familiar with other Microsoft Office programs, you'll feel right at home with PowerPoint. Although a number of new buttons appear in the PowerPoint window, it's easy to recognize similarities to Microsoft Word and Microsoft Excel.

FIGURE 1-4
Main features in PowerPoint's Normal view

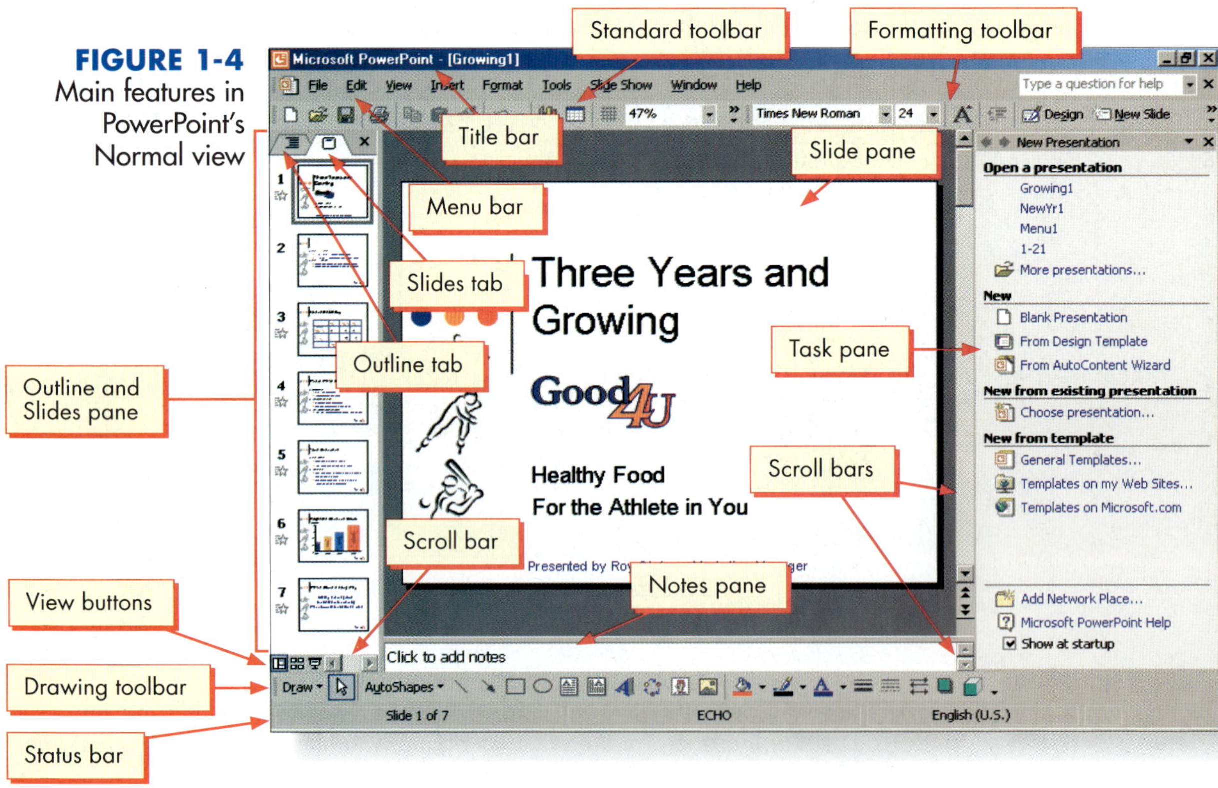

NOTE: The task pane or the Outline and Slides pane shown in Figure 1-4 might not be visible on your screen. You learn how to display these features later in this lesson.

TABLE 1-2 Main Parts of the PowerPoint Window

PART OF WINDOW	PURPOSE
Title bar	Contains the name of the presentation.
Menu bar	Displays the names of menus you use to perform various tasks. You can open menus by using the mouse or the keyboard.
Toolbars	Rows of buttons that give instant access to a wide range of commands. Each button is represented by an icon and accessed by using the mouse. PowerPoint opens with the Standard and Formatting toolbars displayed in abbreviated form on one line at the top of the window and the Drawing toolbar at the bottom of the window.
Outline and Slides pane	The area that can display either an outline of the presentation's text or thumbnails—miniature pictures—of the presentation's slides. You choose either Outline or Slides by clicking the appropriate tab.
Slide pane	The area where you create, edit, and display presentation slides.
Notes pane	The area where you can add presentation notes for either the presenter or the audience.
Task pane	An area that can appear on the right side of the PowerPoint window, displaying a list of commands that are relevant to the task on which you are currently working.
Scroll bars	Used with the mouse to move a slide view or outline text right or left and up or down. You can also use the vertical scroll bar to move from slide to slide.
View buttons	Three buttons located in the lower left corner of the window. You use these buttons to switch between Normal view (the default), Slide Sorter view, and Slide Show.
Status bar	Displays information about the presentation you're working on.

EXERCISE 1-3 Identify Parts of the PowerPoint Window

The first step to getting familiar with PowerPoint is to identify the parts of the window you'll be working with in this course, such as menus, toolbars, buttons, tabs, and panes. There are many different objects in the PowerPoint window. ScreenTips help you identify these objects. A *ScreenTip* is the box displaying an object's name that appears under a button or other object when you point to it.

1. Use the mouse to point to the Normal View button in the lower left corner of the window. PowerPoint displays the button's ScreenTip. If this button is not already selected, click it with the left mouse button.

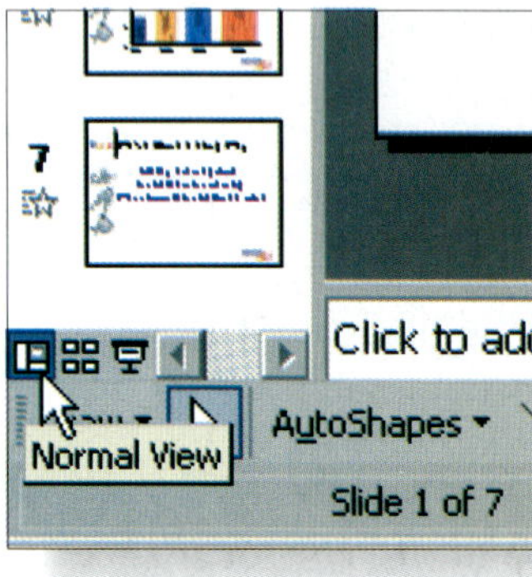

FIGURE 1-5
Identifying a button

2. Point to other buttons in the window to identify them by name.
3. If the Office Assistant is displayed, click it with the right mouse button to display a shortcut menu. Choose Hide on the shortcut menu.

TIP: If you'd prefer to display the Office Assistant, click Help on the menu bar and choose Show the Office Assistant. When the Office Assistant is displayed, you can also right-click it and use the shortcut menu to choose another animated character.

EXERCISE 1-4 Work with Menus and Toolbars

You access PowerPoint commands by choosing menus, toolbar buttons, or task pane items.

1. Move the pointer to View on the menu bar. Click the left mouse button to open the menu. PowerPoint displays a short version of the View menu with the most commonly used View menu commands.
2. Expand the menu either by keeping it open for a few seconds or by pointing to the arrows at the bottom of the menu. Notice the additional commands on the expanded menu.

NOTE: PowerPoint's short menus are adaptive—they change as you work, listing the commands you use most frequently.

3. To close the menu, click View or a blank area of the window, or press Esc.
4. Open the View menu again and point to Toolbars. On the Toolbars submenu, three toolbars should be selected: Standard, Formatting, and Drawing. If one of these does not have a check mark, click it on the Toolbars submenu to select it. (See Figure 1-6 on the next page.)

POWERPOINT

FIGURE 1-6
Displaying menu options

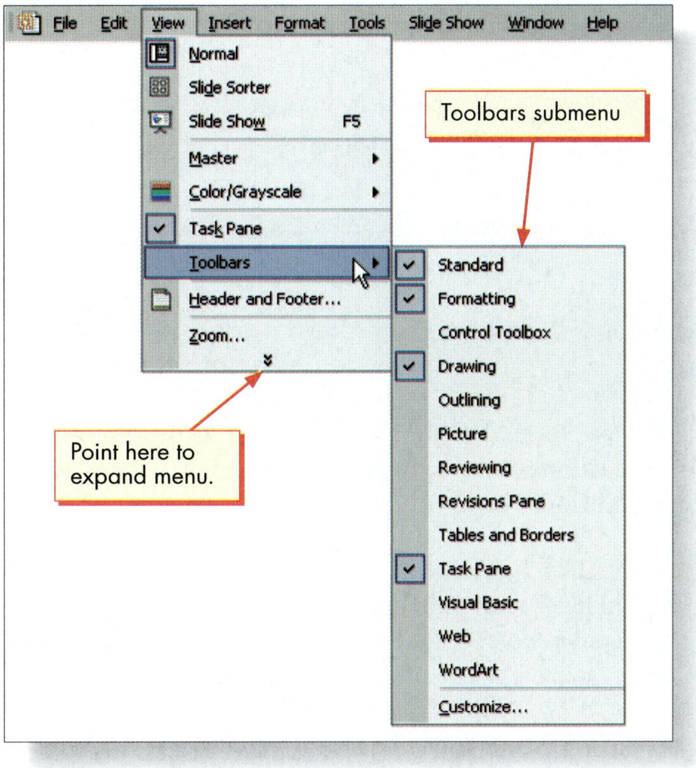

NOTE: Your Toolbars submenu might not have a check mark next to Task Pane. You learn about displaying the task pane later in this lesson.

5. Close the View menu. Open the Tools menu and expand it. Without clicking the mouse button, move the pointer left to Format on the menu bar. Continue moving the pointer left on the menu bar until you display the Edit menu. Close the Edit menu.

TIP: A menu shows which commands have corresponding toolbar buttons or keyboard shortcuts. For example, you can save a document by choosing File on the menu bar and then clicking Save, by clicking the Save button on the Standard toolbar, or by holding down Ctrl and pressing S (this is shown as Ctrl+S).

6. Point to buttons on the Standard toolbar to identify them by name.
7. Click the Toolbar Options button at the end of the Standard toolbar to see the rest of this toolbar's buttons. Move the mouse pointer over any button to identify it. (See Figure 1-7 on the next page.)

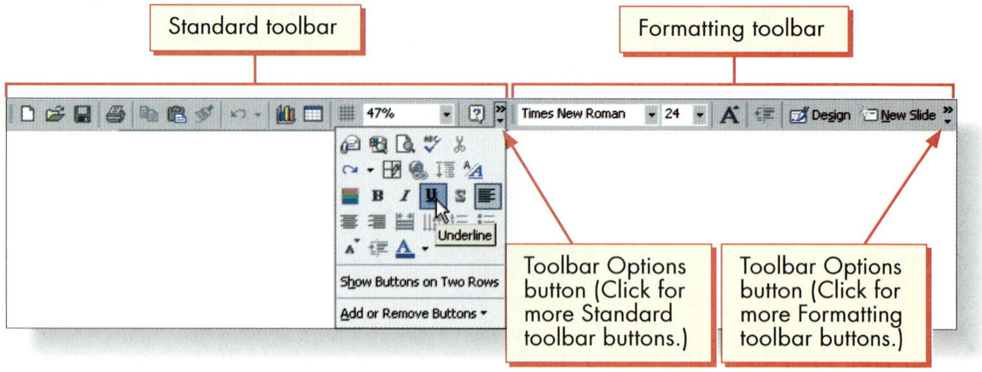

FIGURE 1-7 Side-by-side toolbars

8. Click the Toolbar Options button at the end of the Formatting toolbar to see additional toolbar buttons for the Formatting toolbar. Press Esc to hide the additional buttons.

NOTE: When you click the Toolbar Options button and use one of these "hidden" toolbar buttons, the button will move off the "More Buttons" list and onto the regular toolbar. PowerPoint's toolbars are adaptive—they change as you work, displaying the buttons you use most frequently.

EXERCISE 1-5 Work with Docked and Floating Toolbars

Sometimes it's convenient to move a toolbar to another location in the window—so you don't need to move your mouse back and forth when you're using the same tool repeatedly. Toolbars are either docked or floating. A *docked toolbar* is attached to one of the edges of the program window. A *floating toolbar* is not attached; you can drag its title bar to freely move it wherever you want. You *drag* a title bar by pointing to it and then holding down the left mouse button while you move the mouse.

1. Point to the move handle on the left end of the standard toolbar. When the four-pointed arrow appears, drag it down until the toolbar appears to be in the middle of your window. The Standard toolbar is now a floating toolbar. (See Figure 1-8 on the next page.)

2. Point to the bottom edge of the floating toolbar. When a vertical two-pointed arrow appears, drag it up or down to change the shape of the toolbar.

3. Point to the Standard toolbar's title bar and drag it to a new location on your window.

4. Double-click the Standard toolbar's title bar. The toolbar returns to its original place next to the Formatting toolbar. It is once again docked.

FIGURE 1-8
Moving a toolbar

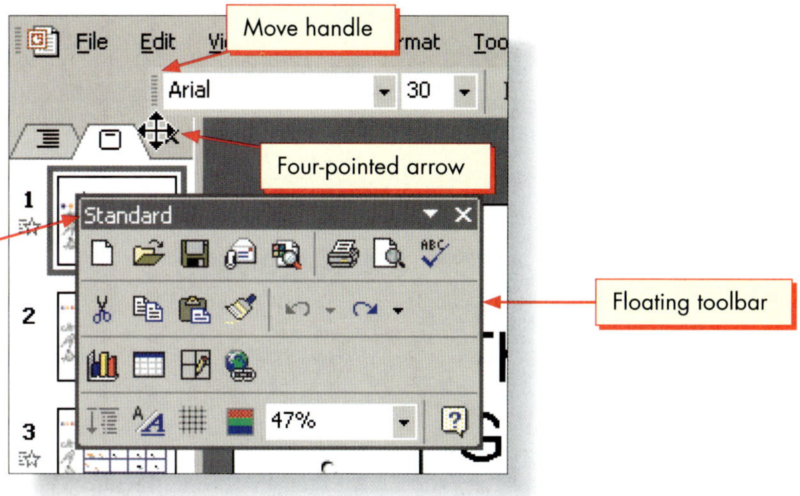

NOTE: You might notice a floating Language toolbar on your screen. This toolbar can be used for speech recognition if you computer is set up with a microphone. You can use speech recognition for menu commands, toolbar buttons, and text entry. For more information, see Appendix C.

EXERCISE 1-6 Move from Slide to Slide

PowerPoint provides several ways to move from slide to slide in a presentation, using the mouse or the keyboard.

1. Drag the vertical box on the slide pane to the bottom. Notice the box that displays slide numbers and slide titles as you drag. When you release the mouse button at the bottom of the scroll bar, slide 7 appears in your window. Notice the heavy border around the slide 7 thumbnail in the slide pane. This identifies it as the current slide. (See Figure 1-9 on the next page.)
2. Drag the scroll box up to display slide 6. Notice that the slide number is indicated on the left side of the status bar.
3. Click the Previous Slide button at the bottom of the vertical scroll bar several times to move back in the presentation. Use the Next Slide button to move forward.
4. As an alternative to clicking and , press PgDn and PgUp on your keyboard several times. Use this method to move to slide 2. Check the status bar for the slide number.

FIGURE 1-9
Moving from slide to slide

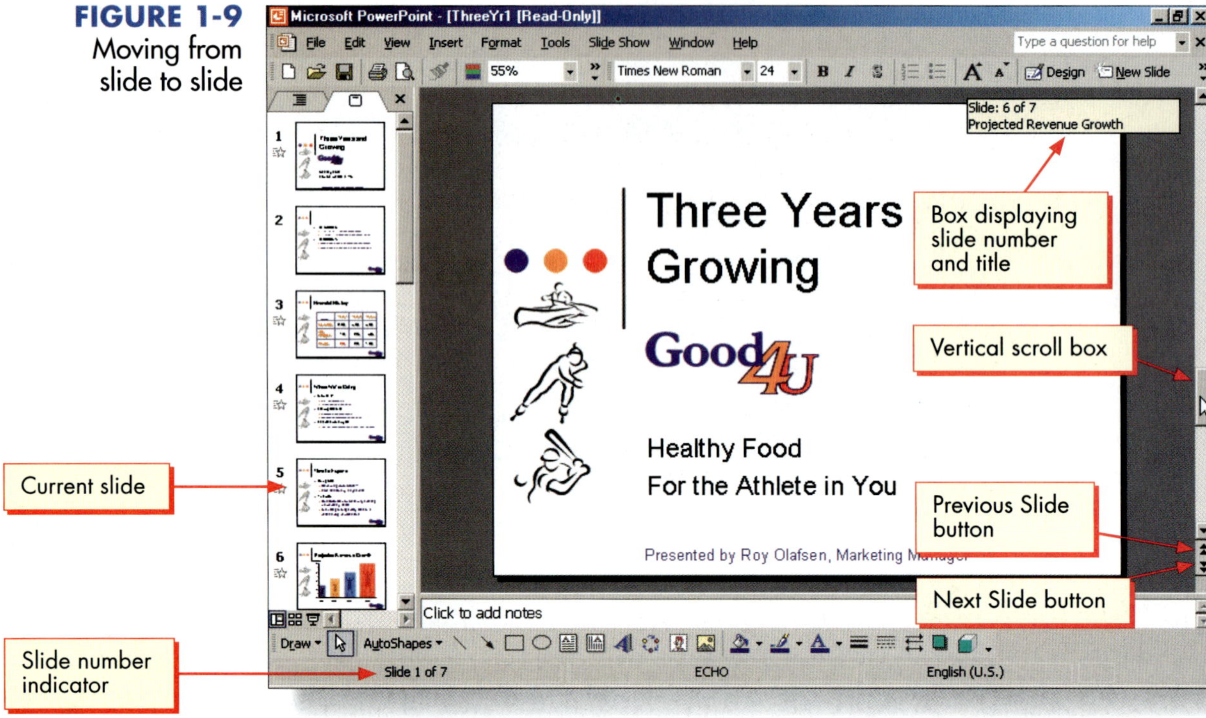

Keying Text on a Slide

Editing text in PowerPoint is very similar to editing text in a word processor. You click an *I-beam* to position the *insertion point* where you want to key new text. You can also drag the I-beam to select existing text. An I-beam is a mouse pointer in the shape of an uppercase "I". An insertion point is a vertical blinking bar indicating where text you key will be placed. The keys Enter, Delete, and Backspace work the same way as in a word processor.

It is important to understand that you *activate* a placeholder when you click the I-beam in it, making it ready to accept text.

EXERCISE 1-7 Edit Text on a Slide

Text on the slide is contained in text *placeholders*. Placeholders are used for *title text* (the text that usually appears at the top of a slide), *body text* (text in the body of a slide), and other objects, such as pictures. Placeholders help keep design layout and formatting consistent within a presentation.

Body text often contains *bullets* and is sometimes called "bulleted text." Bullets are small dots, squares, or other symbols placed to the left of each item in a list or series of paragraphs to add emphasis and readability.

1. With slide 2 displayed, click anywhere on the line of text that begins "Gus Irvinelli."

   Notice the box that surrounds the text. The wide border made up of tiny diagonal lines indicates the text box is activated and in edit mode, meaning you can edit and insert text.

2. Without clicking, move the mouse pointer outside the border to the right and then back inside.

   Notice that the pointer changes from an I-beam inside the border to an arrow pointer outside the border. When the pointer rests on top of the border, it becomes a four-pointed arrow.

3. Drag the I-beam across the text "an avid" to select it. (Click to the left of "an avid," hold down the left mouse button, drag the I-beam across the two words, and then release the mouse button.)

FIGURE 1-10
Selecting text to edit it

4. Key **a professional** to replace the selected text. (You don't need to delete selected text before keying new text.)
5. To place the insertion point, click the I-beam to the right of the words "healthy eating" near the bottom of the slide.
6. To insert a new line, press Enter. Notice that a new dimmed bullet appears at the beginning of the new line.

NOTE: Bulleted text lists the points being made in a slide presentation. This presentation uses open circle and solid dot bullets. Later in this course, you will learn how to change bullet shapes and colors.

7. On the new blank bullet line, key **Make their financial investment grow**
8. Instead of a title, slide 2 contains an empty text placeholder. Click the placeholder containing the text "Click to add title." Then key **Where We Came From**
9. Click a blank part of the slide area to deactivate the text box. To make sure you're clicking a blank area, click when the pointer is a simple arrow, not an I-beam or a four-pointed arrow.

Using Tabs, Views, and Task Panes

PowerPoint provides a selection of panes and views to help streamline your work. Using these various views, you can choose to work on presentation text in outline format, rearrange slides in Slide Sorter view, or work on an individual slide in the Slide pane. You can change the way you work by doing any of the following:

- Display or hide the Task pane or the Outline and Slides pane.
- Change the information being displayed in the Task pane or the Outline and Slides pane.
- Drag borders to change the size of panes.
- Switch between Normal and Slide Sorter view.

EXERCISE 1-8 Use the Outline and Slides Pane

1. Point to the right border of the Outline and Slides pane. When the splitter bar +||+ appears, drag it about an inch to the right. The tabs area becomes wider, and the tab labels change from icons to text. (See Figure 1-11 on the next page.)
2. Click the Outline tab. The Outline pane displays the presentation's text in outline format.
3. Drag the right border of the Outline pane area to the right so you can see more of the text. Notice that the changes you made in the Slide pane are reflected in the outline.
4. Scroll down in the outline until you see the text for slide 4.
5. Working in the Outline pane and using normal text-editing methods, change "Miami in 01" to read **Miami in 2001** and change "02" in the next bulleted item ("Los Angeles") to read **2002**

   Notice that as you work, your changes are reflected in the Slide pane.

NOTE: You can key an entire slide presentation in outline format if that's the way you like to work. You will learn more about outlines in Lesson 4.

FIGURE 1-11
Working with the Outline and Slides pane

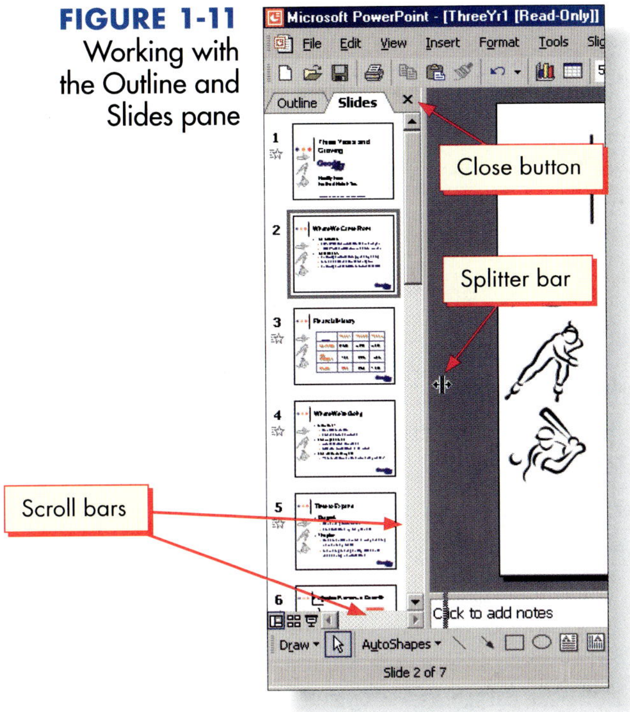

6. Click the Close button X on the Outline and Slides pane to hide it. The Slide pane expands to fill the space.
7. Click the Normal View button in the lower left corner of the window. The Outline and Slides pane is displayed again.
8. In the Outline pane, notice the wavy red underline beneath the word "frist." Like Word, PowerPoint checks your spelling as you work and uses the same red underline to indicate mistakes.
9. Position the I-beam in the Outline pane over the word "frist," click the right mouse button, and choose "first" from the shortcut menu.

FIGURE 1-12
Correcting a spelling error

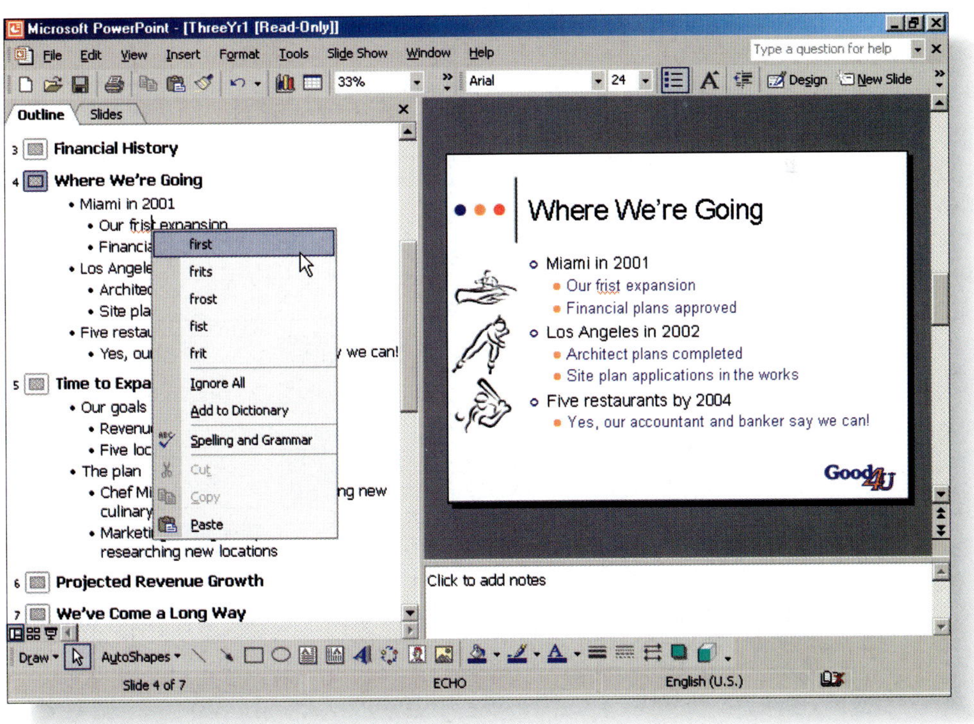

POWERPOINT

TIP: You can correct spelling in either the Outline pane or the Slide pane.

10. Click the Slides tab. The Outline and Slides pane becomes smaller and the size of the Slide pane increases.

EXERCISE 1-9 Work with Task Panes

When you choose certain commands, such as the Design command, specialized task panes appear on the right side of your window. They provide commonly used commands related to the action you are currently performing.

1. Click the Design button on the right side of the Formatting toolbar. The Slide Design task pane appears. It has commands that enable you to change the overall appearance of a presentation.

FIGURE 1-13 Working with Task Panes

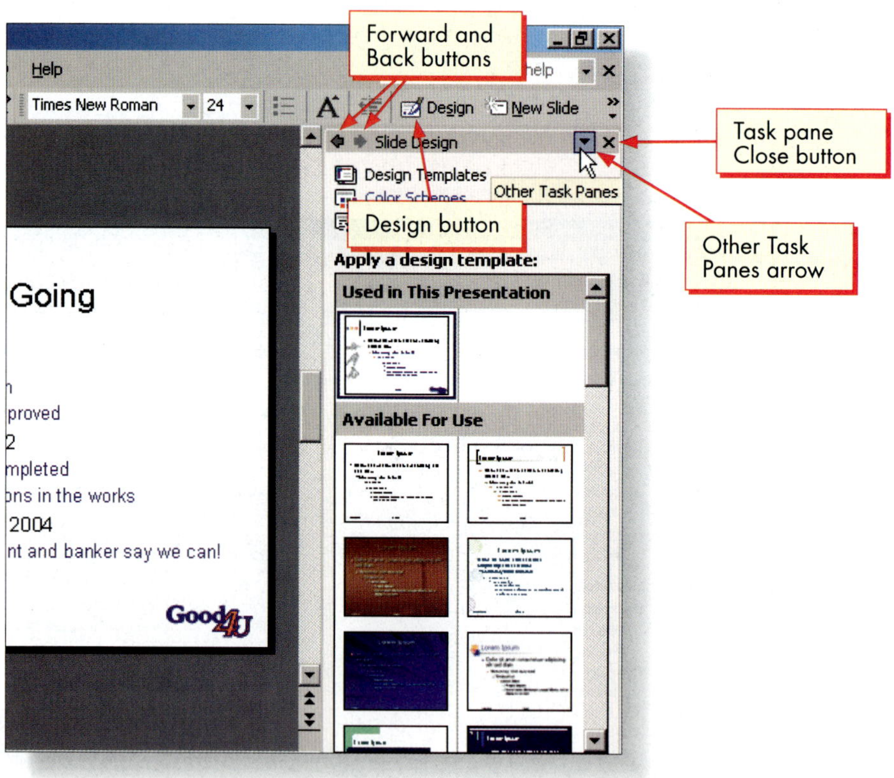

2. Click the Other Task Panes arrow. A drop-down list appears.

3. Choose Slide Design – Color Schemes. The task pane changes to show samples you can choose.

POWERPOINT

4. Click the Other Task Panes arrow ▾ again. This time choose Clipboard.

5. Click the Back button at the top of the Clipboard task pane. The Slide Design – Color Schemes task pane reappears. The Back button and Forward button enable you to return to recently used task panes.
6. Click the Task Pane's Close button ☒. This removes the task pane from the screen.
7. Click View on the menu bar, and then click Task Pane. The Slide Design task pane is displayed again.

EXERCISE 1-10 Use Slide Sorter View

Slide Sorter view displays a window of presentation slides, just as they would look if they were 35-mm slides placed on a light box. In this view you can easily rearrange slides or apply special slide show effects.

1. Click the Slide Sorter View button, located in the lower left corner of the window to the right of the Normal button. You can now see several slides in the window.

FIGURE 1-14
Slide Sorter view

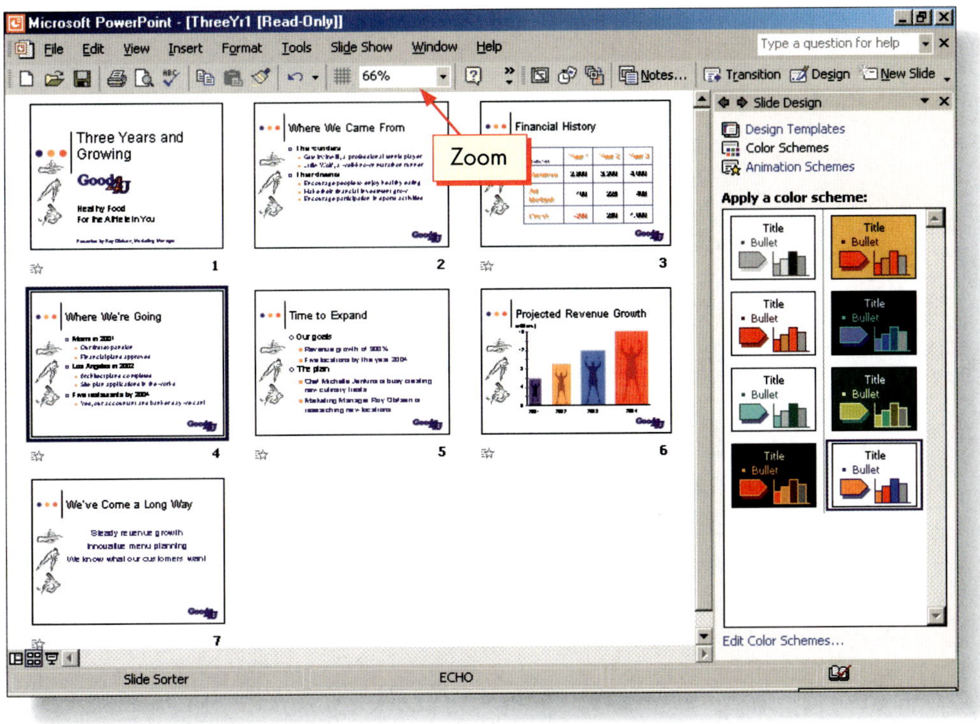

2. On the Standard toolbar, click the down arrow next to the Zoom box and choose 66%. This should enable you to see all seven slides in this presentation at the same time.

TIP: Experiment with the zoom percentage. Depending on your screen resolution, a different percentage might be needed to show all seven slides at once.

3. Double-click slide 1 to look at it in Normal view.

TIP: The Zoom box is also available in Normal view. If the slide pane is active, Zoom changes the magnification of the slide within the pane. If the Outline and Slides pane is active, Zoom changes that area instead.

Running a Slide Show

Usually the goal of creating a PowerPoint presentation is to present it as a slide show. You can present a slide show by using 35-mm slides or overhead transparencies, or you can present it directly from a computer. One of the advantages of running a slide show from your computer is that you can use special animation effects.

EXERCISE 1-11 Run a Slide Show

One way to start a slide show is to click the Slide Show button. After you begin running a slide show, PowerPoint provides navigation tools to move from slide to slide.

1. Click the Slide Show button at the bottom left of the PowerPoint window (next to the Slide Sorter View button). After a few seconds, the first slide in the presentation fills the screen.
2. Click the left mouse button to move to slide 2. The left mouse button is one of many ways to move forward in a slide presentation.
3. Press N on the keyboard to move to the next slide, slide 3.

TIP: As an alternative to clicking the left mouse button, you can press N to move forward through the slides. N means "Next" and P means "Previous." You can also use the right and left arrow keys and PgDn and PgUp to move forward and backward in a slide show.

4. Press N again to move to slide 4, which is titled "Where We're Going."
5. Using the left mouse button, click anywhere to see a sample of a PowerPoint text animation. Click twice more to see the remaining text on this slide.
6. Press Esc to end the slide show.

EXERCISE 1-12 Start a Slide Show from Any Slide

If you had to interrupt a slide show, or you only want to show specific slides, you can begin a slide show from any slide.

1. Move to slide 5 in Normal view.
2. Click the Slide Show button to resume the slide show from slide 5.
3. Click the left mouse button twice to display the text animations on this slide.

EXERCISE 1-13 Use Onscreen Navigation Tools

During a slide show, you can navigate from slide to slide or to a specific slide by using a shortcut menu. You can also highlight points for your audience by using a pen pointer to write or draw on the screen.

1. With slide 5 ("Time to Expand") still displayed, right-click anywhere on the screen to display the shortcut menu.

   The shortcut menu provides a variety of options related to the slide show. Notice that you can click Next or Previous to move forward or backward in the slide show.

FIGURE 1-15
Slide Show shortcut menu

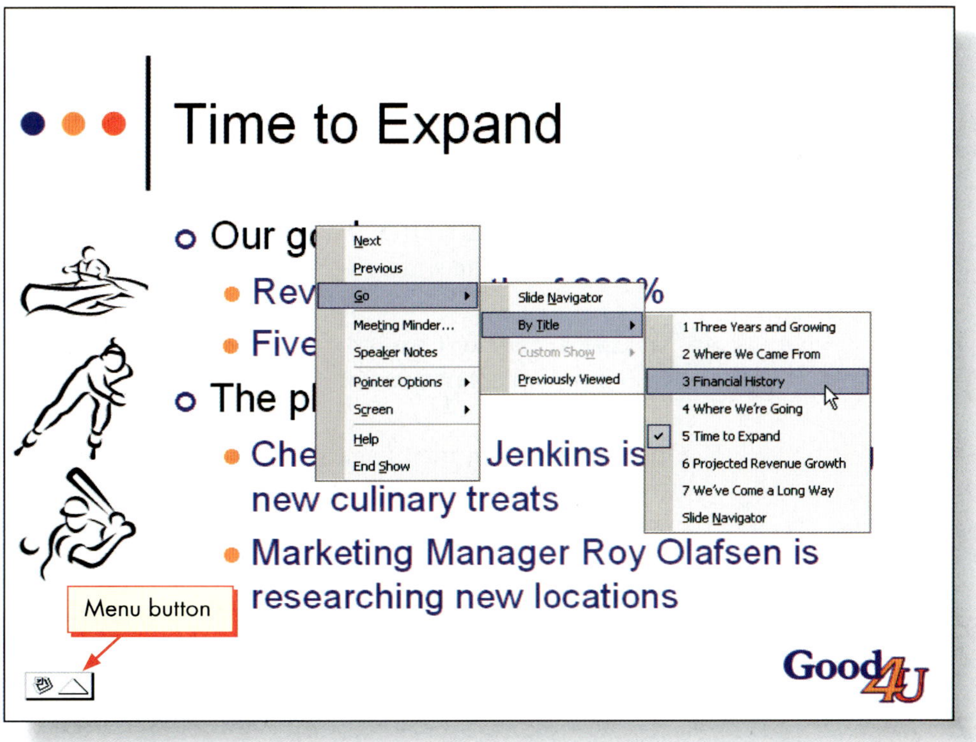

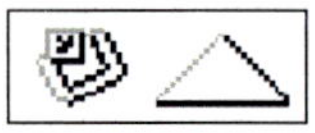

TIP: You can also click the Menu button at the bottom left corner of the slide show screen to open the shortcut menu.

2. Point to Go on the shortcut menu. Notice the additional options for navigating within the slide show. Point to By Title to go to a specific slide in the presentation. Click "3 Financial History" to go to slide 3.
3. Click the left mouse button repeatedly to advance through slide 4 ("Where We're Going"), slide 5 ("Time to Expand"), and slide 6 ("Projected Revenue Growth"), displaying each slide and all the animated slide text and objects. Stop when the four colored columns on slide 6 are displayed.

EXERCISE 1-14 Use the Annotation Pen During a Slide Show

The *annotation pen* is a useful tool with which you can "draw" on your slides during a show. For example, you can use the pen to draw a circle around an important number or underline a word. You can use a special color for the annotation pen to make it stand out on the slide.

1. When all four colored columns on slide 6 are displayed, right-click the screen and then choose Pointer Options from the shortcut menu. In the submenu, choose Pen Color and then choose Red for the pen color. The pointer changes to a pen shape.
2. Using the pen pointer, draw a circle around the "12" at the top left of the chart.
3. Press E on your keyboard to erase the circle.
4. Draw a circle around the "16" and then draw a line under "2004" at the bottom right of the slide. (See Figure 1-16 on the next page.)

TIP: You don't have to draw precisely when using the annotation pen. Pen marks are not permanent—they disappear when you advance the slide.

5. Open the shortcut menu again, choose Pointer Options, and then choose Arrow from the submenu to restore the arrow pointer. (Or press the keyboard shortcut Ctrl+A.)
6. Advance through the last slide. When you reach the end of the presentation, click once more to exit the presentation.

NOTE: If your computer is equipped for sound, you'll hear the audio effects contained on slides 6 and 7.

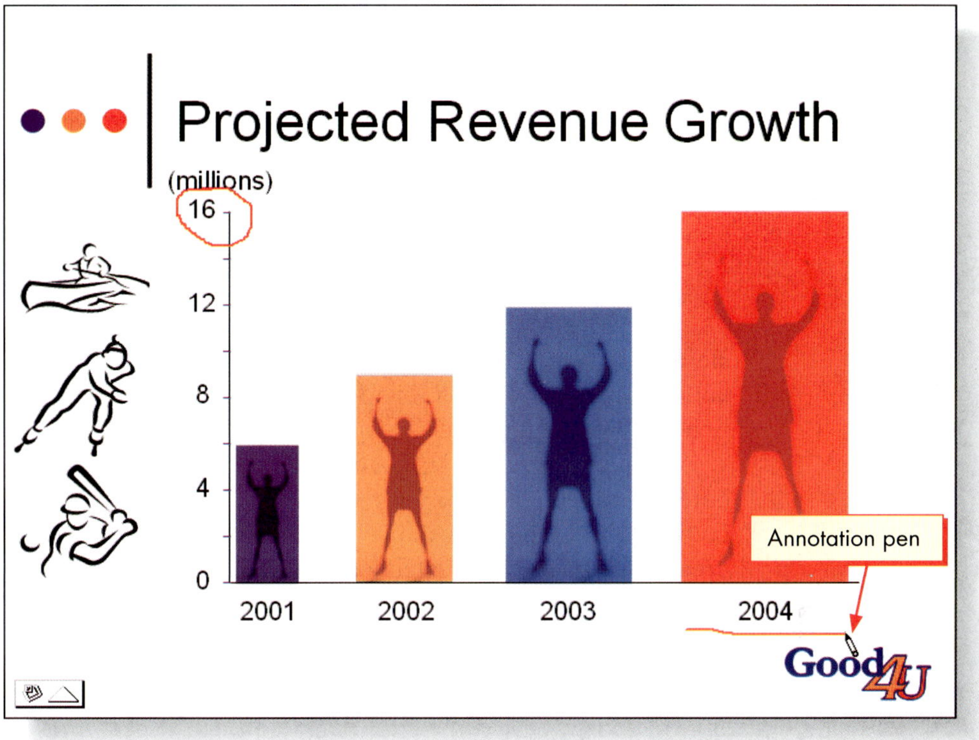

FIGURE 1-16
Using the pen during a slide show

Naming and Saving a Presentation

In PowerPoint, presentations are saved as files. When you create a new presentation or make changes to an existing one, you must save the presentation to make your changes permanent. Until your changes are saved, they can be lost if there's a power failure or a computer problem.

The first step in saving a document is to give it a *filename*. Filenames can be up to 255 characters long.

Throughout the exercises in this book, your document filenames will consist of two parts:

- ***[Your initials]***, which might be your initials or an identifier your instructor asks you to use, such as **rst**
- The number of the exercise, such as **3-1**

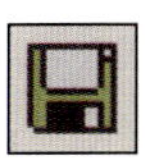

When you're working with an existing file, choosing the Save command (or clicking the Save button on the Standard toolbar) replaces the file on the disk with the file on which you're working. After saving, the old version of the file no longer exists and the new version contains all your changes.

You can give an existing presentation a new name by using the Save As command. The original presentation remains on the disk unchanged and a second presentation with a new name is saved on the disk as well.

TIP: The New Presentation task pane has an option labeled New from existing presentation. When you open a presentation by clicking the link Choose presentation under this option, it automatically becomes a new presentation and you can safely save it by using the Save command without fear of overwriting the presentation on which it is based.

EXERCISE 1-15 Create a Folder for Saving Your Files

Before saving a file, you need to decide where you want to save it: in a folder on your fixed disk drive, on a floppy disk or other removable media, or on a network drive.

When you save a file, it's a good idea to create separate folders for specific categories to help keep your work organized. For example, you might want to create folders for different projects or different customers. In this course, you will create a new folder for each lesson's work.

NOTE: Your instructor will advise you of the proper drive or folder to use when creating your lesson folders.

1. Click File to open the File menu and choose Save As. The Save As dialog box appears.

FIGURE 1-17 Creating a new folder in the Save As dialog box

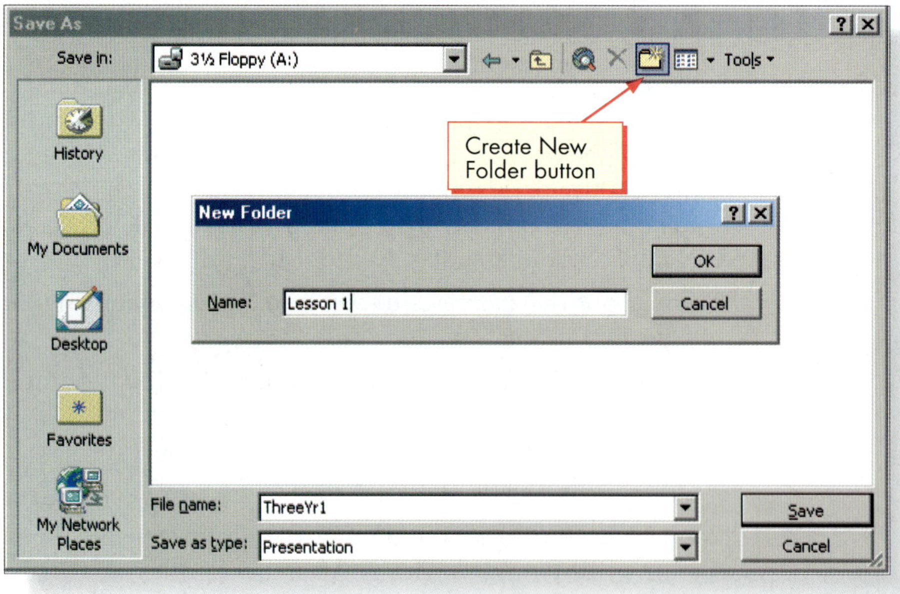

2. Using the Save in list box, follow your instructor's directions to navigate to the location where you should create your folder. If you will be using a diskette, insert a diskette into your floppy drive.

3. Click the Create New Folder button on the dialog box toolbar. The New Folder dialog box opens.
4. In the Name box, key **Lesson 1**. Click OK. A yellow folder icon with the name "Lesson 1" appears in the Save in box.
5. Click Cancel to close the Save As dialog box.

NOTE: Even though you clicked Cancel to close the Save As dialog box, your new folder has been created. You could have saved your presentation before closing the Save As dialog box, but you will do that in the next exercise instead.

EXERCISE 1-16 Name and Save a Presentation

To name files, you can use uppercase letters, lowercase letters, or a combination of both. Filenames can also include spaces. For example, you can use "Good 4 U Sales Report" as a filename.

1. Click File to open the File menu and choose Save As to reopen the Save As dialog box.
2. Navigate to the drive and folder where you created your new Lesson 1 folder.
3. Double-click the Lesson 1 folder to open it.
4. In the File name text box, key ***[your initials]*1-16**.
5. Click Save. Your document is saved and named for future use. Notice that the title bar displays the new filename.

Printing Slides and Handouts

Although the primary way of viewing a presentation is usually as a slide show, you can also print PowerPoint slides, just as you print Word documents or Excel worksheets. PowerPoint provides a variety of print options, including printing each slide on a separate page or printing several slides on the same page.

Throughout this course, to conserve paper and speed up printing, you usually print a *handout* instead of full-size slides. A handout contains several scaled-down slide images on each page (1, 2, 3, 4, 6, or 9 to a page), and is often given to an audience during a presentation.

EXERCISE 1-17 Print a Slide

You can start printing in one of the following ways:

- From the File menu, choose Print.
- Press Ctrl + P.

- From the File menu, choose Print Preview.

- Click the Print button.

The first two methods open the Print dialog box, where you can choose printing options. The third method opens the Print Preview window, which you will use in Exercise 1-18. The Print button prints a presentation with the most recently used print options (or print options as set in the Options dialog box, Print tab).

1. To print the first slide in your presentation, display slide 1, open the File menu and then choose Print. The Print dialog box displays PowerPoint's default settings and indicates the designated printer.

FIGURE 1-18
Print dialog box

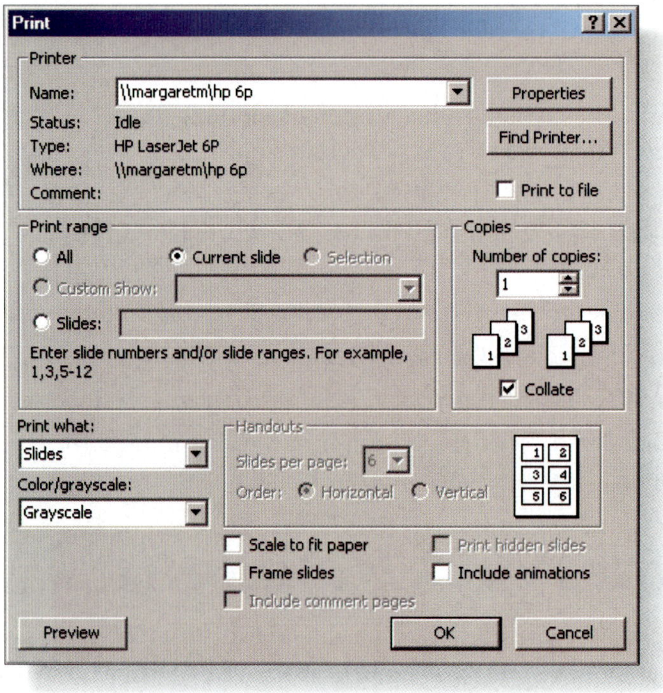

2. In the Print range option box, choose Current Slide.
3. From the Print what drop-down list box, choose Slides.
4. From the Color/grayscale list box, choose Grayscale. This setting optimizes color slides for a black and white printer. (If you have a color printer, you could choose Color instead).
5. Click OK to start printing. As the print job proceeds, you see the animated printer icon on the PowerPoint status bar. You might also see a printer icon on the far right side of the Windows taskbar.

TIP: You can print multiple copies of whatever you are printing by changing the number in the Number of copies box in the middle of the right side of the Print dialog box.

EXERCISE 1-18 Preview a Presentation

The PowerPoint *Print Preview* feature lets you see what your printed pages will look like before you actually print them. You can view preview pages in black and white, grayscale, or color.

1. From the File menu, choose Print.
2. In the Print range option box, choose All.
3. Click Preview in the lower left corner of the dialog box. The Preview Window opens, showing you how the printed slide will appear on paper. The Print Preview toolbar is displayed at the top of the window.

FIGURE 1-19
Print Preview toolbar

TABLE 1-3 Print Preview Toolbar Buttons

TOOLBAR BUTTON	NAME	PURPOSE
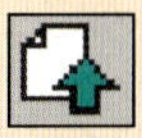	Previous Page	Display the previous page to be printed.
	Next Page	Display the next page to be printed.
	Print	Open the Print dialog box.
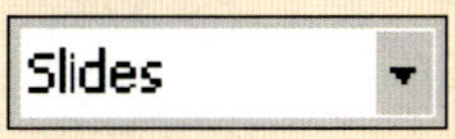	Print What	Choose between printing slides, handouts, notes pages, or an outline.
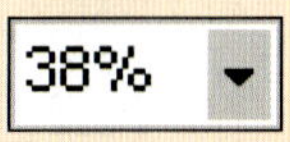	Zoom	Change the magnification in the Preview window.
	Landscape	Set the printed page orientation to landscape.
	Portrait	Set the printed page orientation to portrait.
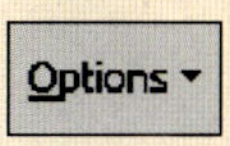	Options	Choose from a variety of options and preview them before printing.
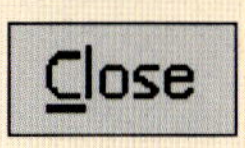	Close Preview	Close the Preview window.

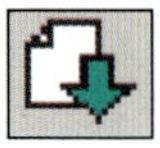

4. On the Print Preview toolbar, click the Next Page button. Page 2 of the printout is displayed.
5. Move your pointer to the m iddle of the slide. Notice that the pointer is in the shape of a magnifying glass.
6. Click the Magnifying glass pointer in the center of the slide. The display is magnified.
7. Click again. The display returns to its regular size.

EXERCISE 1-19 Print a Presentation Handout

Printing several slides on a single page is a handy way to review your work and to create audience handouts. It's also a convenient way to print class assignments. You can create handouts in the Print Preview window or in the Print dialog box.

1. Working in the Print Preview window, click the arrow next to the Print What list box and then choose Handouts (2 slides per page). Two slides are displayed on the preview page.
2. Open the Print What list box again and choose Handouts (9 slides per page). Now the entire presentation is displayed on one page.

3. Click the Landscape button to orient your slides sideways on the page.

4. Click the Options button. Make sure the Frame Slides option is selected.

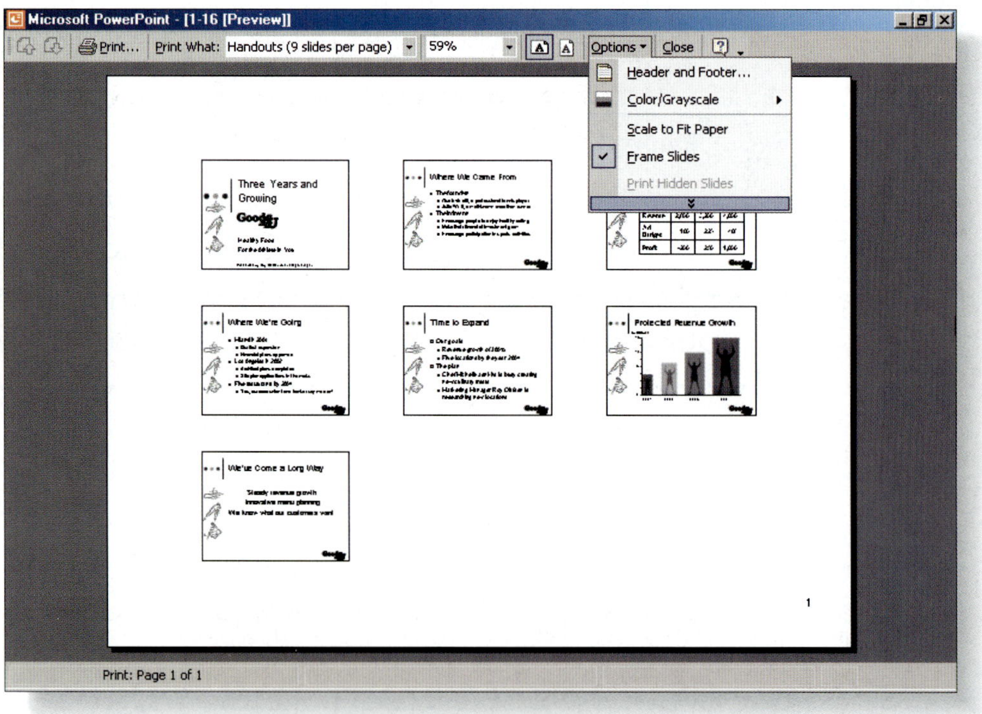

FIGURE 1-20 Choosing printing options

5. Click the Print button. The Print dialog box opens. You can change print settings here as well as in the Print Preview window.
6. Click OK to print your handout page. After printing, the Preview window reappears.
7. Click Close on the Preview toolbar to close the Preview window.

Closing Presentations and Exiting PowerPoint

After you finish working on a presentation and save it, you can close it and open another file or you can exit the program.

To close a presentation and exit PowerPoint, you can:

- Use the File menu.
- Use keyboard shortcuts. Ctrl+W closes a presentation and Alt+F4 exits PowerPoint.
- Use the Close button ☒ in the upper right corner of the window.

EXERCISE 1-20 Close a Presentation and Exit PowerPoint

1. From the File menu, choose Close to close the presentation.
2. Click Yes to save the presentation again. (After printing a presentation, you are usually prompted to save it before closing.)

3. Click the Close button ☒ in the upper right corner of the window to close PowerPoint and display the Windows desktop.

USING HELP

Microsoft PowerPoint Help is an excellent reference tool for reinforcing skills presented in a lesson and for finding more information on any PowerPoint feature.

There are several ways to open the Help window. You can:

- Click Help on the menu bar and then choose Microsoft PowerPoint Help.
- Press F1 on your keyboard.
- Key a question or topic in the Ask a Question box on the right side of the menu bar.

TIP: If you choose one of the first two options, the Microsoft Office Assistant might appear. If you like the Office Assistant, you can key your question in the Office Assistant balloon. If you don't like the Assistant, right-click it and choose Hide from the shortcut menu. To permanently turn off the Assistant, choose Options in the Assistant's balloon; then deselect Use the Office Assistant from the dialog box and click OK.

Get acquainted with PowerPoint Help:

1. Start PowerPoint, if it's not already open.
2. Click the Ask a Question box on the right side of the menu bar.

NOTE: If this is the first time you are using Help, the Ask a Question box contains the text Type a question for help.

3. Key **Views** and then press Enter. A list of Help topics appears.
4. Select About PowerPoint views.

5. Click the Hide button to hide the tabs area of the Help window.

FIGURE 1-21 Using PowerPoint Help

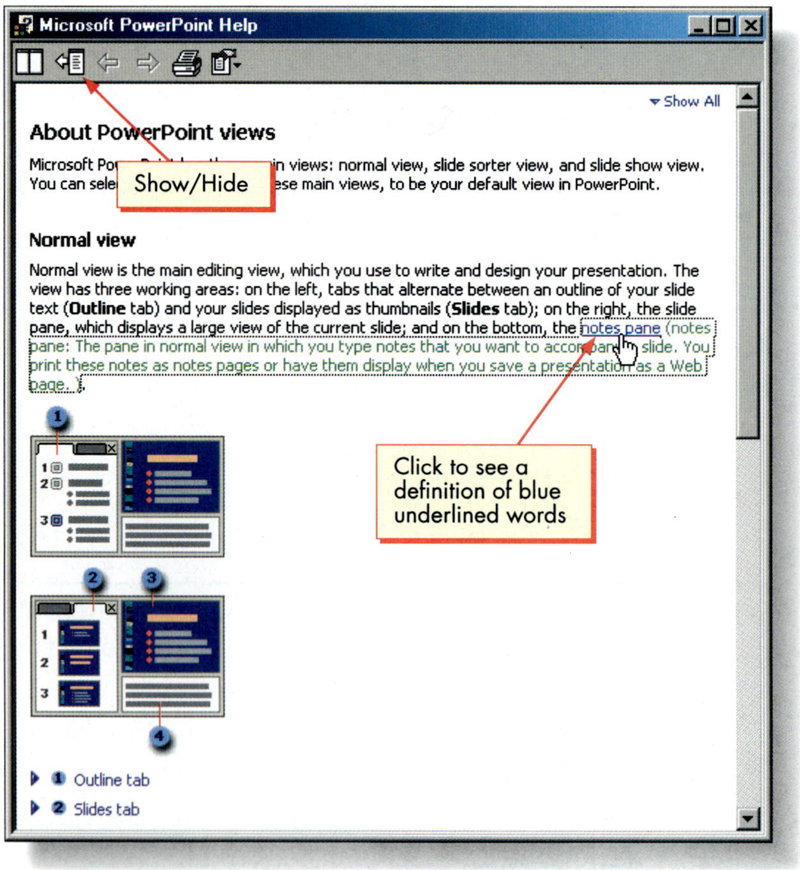

6. Drag the Help window's left border to the left until the Help window fills about half your screen.
7. In the paragraph with the heading "Normal View," point to the blue text notes pane. Notice the hand pointer and the underline that appear. This indicates a link to more information.
8. Click notes pane. A definition of the term appears in green text.
9. Click anywhere in the green text to make it disappear.
10. Scroll down until the blue numbered list of topics appears in the middle of the Help window. Click any topic to expand it. To compress the topic, click it again.
11. Scroll through and read the entire Help window, expanding all topics and defined terms as you go.
12. When you have finished, click the Close button in the upper right corner of the Help window to close it and return to PowerPoint.

LESSON 1 Summary

- Microsoft PowerPoint is a powerful graphics program used to create professional-quality slide presentations.
- To start PowerPoint, click Start on the Windows taskbar, point to Programs, and then select Microsoft PowerPoint from the submenu.
- Identify buttons on the PowerPoint window by pointing to them and waiting for their ScreenTips to appear.
- Menus and toolbars do not always show all the available commands. To see more menu options, point to the menu and wait for it to expand. To see more toolbar buttons, click the Toolbar Options button.
- Toolbars can be docked or floating. To float a docked toolbar, drag its move handle. To dock a floating toolbar, double-click its title bar.
- Key and edit text on a slide in the same way as you would in a word processor.
- When you perform certain tasks, a task pane with related commands appears automatically. Display other task panes by clicking the arrow next to the Other Task Panes button. Hide a task pane by clicking its Close button.
- Use the Slide Show button to run a slide show. A slide show always starts with the slide that is currently selected.
- Use the annotation pen to draw on a slide during a presentation. Marks made with the annotation pen are not permanent and disappear when you move to another slide.

- Choose one of the options in the Print what box in the Print dialog box or in the Print Preview window to print handouts that contain more than one slide per page.

LESSON 1 Command Summary

FEATURE	BUTTON	MENU	KEYBOARD	SPEECH?
Open a presentation		File, Open	Ctrl + O	✓
Display Outline and Slides pane		View, Normal		✓
Display Task pane		View, Task pane		✓
Next Slide			PgDn	✓
Previous Slide			PgUp	✓
Zoom	38%	View, Zoom		✓
Normal view		View, Normal		✓
Slide Sorter view		View, Slide Sorter		✓
Slide Show		View, Slide Show	F5	✓
Annotation pen (Slide Show)		Right-click, Pointer Options, Pen	Ctrl + P	
Next (Slide Show)	Left mouse button	Right-click, Next	N, PgDn	✓
Previous (Slide Show)		Right-click, Previous	P, PgUp	✓
End a slide show		Right-click, End Show	Esc or -	✓
Save		File, Save	Ctrl + S	✓
Save with a different name		File, Save As		✓

continued

LESSON 1 Command Summary *continued*

FEATURE	BUTTON	MENU	KEYBOARD	SPEECH?
Print Preview		File, Print Preview		✓
Print		File, Print	Ctrl + P	✓
Close a presentation		File, Close	Ctrl + W or Ctrl + F4	✓
Exit PowerPoint		File, Exit	Alt + F4	✓

Concepts Review

TRUE/FALSE QUESTIONS

Each of the following statements is either true or false. Indicate your choice by circling T or F.

T F **1.** When you start PowerPoint, it automatically displays a blank presentation.

T F **2.** While in Normal view, you can display either slide thumbnails or outline text, but not both.

T F **3.** You can edit text in Normal view or in the outline pane.

T F **4.** You can display multiple slides as thumbnails in Slide Sorter view.

T F **5.** Editing text in PowerPoint is similar to editing text in a word processor.

T F **6.** When viewing a slide show, pressing the plus sign moves to the next slide.

T F **7.** The annotation pen always draws in black on a light background and white on a dark background.

T F **8.** If you click the Print button , you can choose exactly which items to print.

SHORT ANSWER QUESTIONS

Write the correct answer in the space provided.

1. Where on the PowerPoint window are the view buttons located?

____

2. Name all the ways to use the keyboard for moving to the previous slide during a slide show.

____

3. What are the names of the three view buttons?

____

4. What shape is the mouse pointer when you move it over a text box?

____

5. Which keys can you press to stop a slide show?

____

6. If the Outline and Slides pane is not displayed, what button can you click to make it appear?

____

7. What is the maximum number of slides you can print on a handout page?

____

8. Which menu and menu option would you use to save a copy of your presentation under a different filename?

____

CRITICAL THINKING

Answer these questions on a separate page. There are no right or wrong answers. Support your answers with examples from your own experience, if possible.

1. In this lesson you learned how to display slide thumbnails in the Slides pane and also in Slide Sorter view. Which way do you prefer to view thumbnails and why? What advantages and disadvantages do you think there are for each option?
2. You can produce screen shows, printouts, 35-mm slides, overhead transparencies, and other presentation media with PowerPoint. How might you choose among these options for any particular presentation? Why would you choose one medium over another? What factors would influence your decision?

Lesson Applications

EXERCISE 1-21

Edit text, change presentation views, and save, print, and close a presentation.

1. Open the file **Party1**.
2. Using the Slide pane, make the changes to slides 2 and 3 as shown in Figure 1-22:

FIGURE 1-22

Slide 2

Entertainment

- Audition bands
  - Charlie's Dingbats
  - The Electrolytes
  - ~~Wired Rabbits~~ Pure Power
- Contact Marsha Miles
  - Is she willing to lead dance-style aerobics?
  - Is she available New Year's Eve?

Slide 3

Menu

- Michelle needs suggestions by November 1
- Staff tasting party to be held December ~~2~~ 5
- Menu printing deadline is December 10

3. View each slide in the presentation.
4. Save the presentation as ***[your initials]*****1-21**.
5. Preview the presentation as handouts, 3 slides per page, grayscale, framed, and then print it.
6. Close the presentation.

EXERCISE 1-22

Edit text in Normal view and Slide view, run a slide show, and save, print, and close a presentation.

1. Open the file **JulyFun1**.

2. Move to slide 2. Change "am" in the first and second bullets to **a.m.** Change the date in the last bullet to **June 25th**
3. Click the Outline tab and drag the Outline pane's right border to make it wider.
4. Working on slide 3 in the outline area, change the age in the second bullet from "21" to **18**
5. Save the presentation as ***[your initials]*1-22**.
6. Click the Slides tab and display slide 1. Run a slide show of the presentation, clicking to display each new slide and text animation.
7. Preview and then print the presentation as handouts, 6 slides per page, grayscale, framed.
8. Close the presentation.

EXERCISE 1-23

Edit text, change presentation views, and save, print, and close a presentation.

1. Open the file **DressCd2**.
2. On slide 1, key the word **Personnel** to the left of "Training" so the title reads "Personnel Training Session."
3. Locate the last line of text on slide 2 (which begins "Under no circumstances"). Position the insertion point at the end of that line and key **while on the job**
4. Locate the last line of text on slide 3. Position the insertion point between "Good 4 U" and "test" and key **proficiency** (the phrase should read "Good 4 U proficiency test").
5. Click the Outline tab and make the Outline pane wide enough to work comfortably. Scroll down to display the outline text for slide 4.
6. Working on slide 4 in the Outline pane, delete the periods at the ends of the two sentences that begin "Guests."
7. Below the third bullet, change "Shirts are" to **T-shirts will be**
8. Save the presentation as ***[your initials]*1-23**.
9. Preview and then print the presentation as handouts, 4 slides per page, grayscale, framed.
10. Close the presentation.

EXERCISE 1-24 *Challenge Yourself*

Edit text, print a slide and handouts, and close a presentation.

1. Open the file **RacePrep**.

2. Using whichever view you choose, edit slide 2 and slide 3 as shown in Figure 1-23.

FIGURE 1-23

Slide 2

Entertainment

- The Electrolytes will be here ~~for~~ on marathon eve, ~~injecting mental energy for all~~ charging up the runners
- Julie will again lead her famous pre-marathon "Pump-you-up" chant

Slide 3

Pre-Marathon
Carbo Loading Menu

- Marathon Angel
  - A ~~huge pile~~ mountain of angel hair pasta served with fat-free tomato sauce and ~~sprinkled with~~ tiny bite-sized meatballs
- Bagel Bonanza
  - Bagels brushed with a mixture of olive oil, garlic, and delicate herbs

3. Save the presentation in your Lesson 1 folder as ***[your initials]*1-24**.
4. View the presentation in Slide Sorter view.
5. Run a slide show of the presentation, beginning with slide 1.
6. Preview and then print all slides in grayscale, framed.
7. Print the presentation as handouts, 3 slides per page, grayscale, framed.
8. Close the presentation.

On Your Own

In these exercises you work on your own, as you would in a real-life work environment. Use the skills you've learned to accomplish the task—and be creative.

EXERCISE 1-25

Open the file **SpEvent1**. Change slide 2 so its title is **Fall Events**. Edit the slide's bullets by changing the events to be for September and October, describing activities relating to fall foliage or the outdoors. Save the presentation as ***[your initials]*1-25**. Preview and then print the presentation as handouts, 2 slides per page.

EXERCISE 1-26

Open the file **GoodFood**. On slide 2, replace the text describing the pasta dishes with pasta creations from your imagination. On slide 3, replace the text describing the desserts with your own inventions. Be sure the desserts you describe use healthy ingredients.

Save the presentation as ***[your initials]*1-26**. Preview and then print the presentation as handouts, 3 slides per page.

EXERCISE 1-27

Open the file **DressCd1**. On slides 2 and 3, replace the text under the "Uniform" bullet with a dress code you think would be appropriate for employees at an upscale New York City restaurant. Replace the second main bullet "Skates" with **Jewelry** and change the bullet under it to talk about what kind of jewelry may be worn. On slide 4, upgrade the guest dress code to fit an upscale restaurant scenario. Save the presentation as ***[your initials]*1-27**. Preview and then print the presentation as handouts, 4 slides per page.

LESSON

2

Basic Presentation Tools

OBJECTIVES

MOUS ACTIVITIES

In this lesson:

PP2002 1-1
PP2002 1-2
PP2002 2-2
PP2002 4-2
PP2002 4-3
PP2002 4-8
PP2002 5-1

See Appendix E.

After completing this lesson, you will be able to:

1. Use the AutoContent Wizard.
2. Select, rearrange, and delete slides.
3. Use the spelling checker and style checker.
4. Use the Find and Replace features.
5. Add animation schemes and slide transitions.
6. Add headers and footers.
7. Choose printing options.

Estimated Time: 1¾ hours

This lesson introduces you to basic presentation tools, starting with the AutoContent Wizard. A *wizard* is an online guide that helps you complete a task. The AutoContent Wizard provides step-by-step help for creating a presentation. It creates a complete presentation with sample text on each slide. *Sample text* provides content suggestions for your presentation.

After creating the presentation, you can change the sample text provided by the wizard to suit your needs. Then you can rearrange slides, delete slides, check the presentation for spelling errors, and find and replace text. You can further enhance your presentation by applying headers and footers, text animation, slide transitions, and a variety of print options.

Using the AutoContent Wizard

Using the AutoContent Wizard is a convenient way to create a presentation. The wizard asks a series of questions and uses your answers to develop the framework for your presentation.

EXERCISE 2-1 Use the AutoContent Wizard

1. Start PowerPoint.

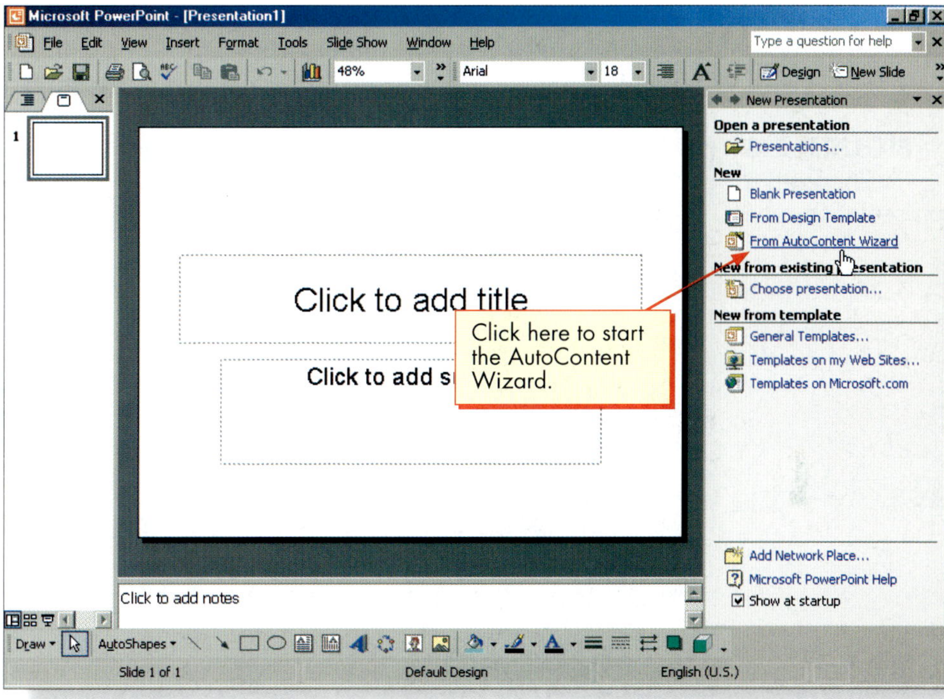

FIGURE 2-1 New Presentation task pane

2. In the New Presentation task pane on the right, choose the From AutoContent Wizard option (the third choice under New).

The AutoContent Wizard opening dialog box appears. The "road map" on the left side of the dialog box uses a green square to indicate where you are in the process. (See Figure 2-2 on the next page.)

NOTE: If you don't see the New Presentation task pane, choose New from the File menu. If the Office Assistant appears, right-click it and choose Hide from the shortcut menu

POWERPOINT

FIGURE 2-2
AutoContent Wizard opening screen

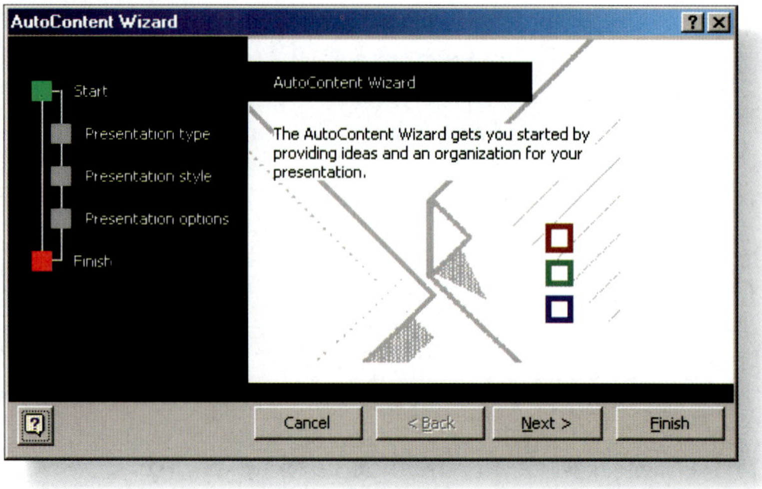

3. In the AutoContent Wizard opening dialog box, click Next. The second window appears. The green square moves to Presentation type.

FIGURE 2-3
Choosing a presentation type

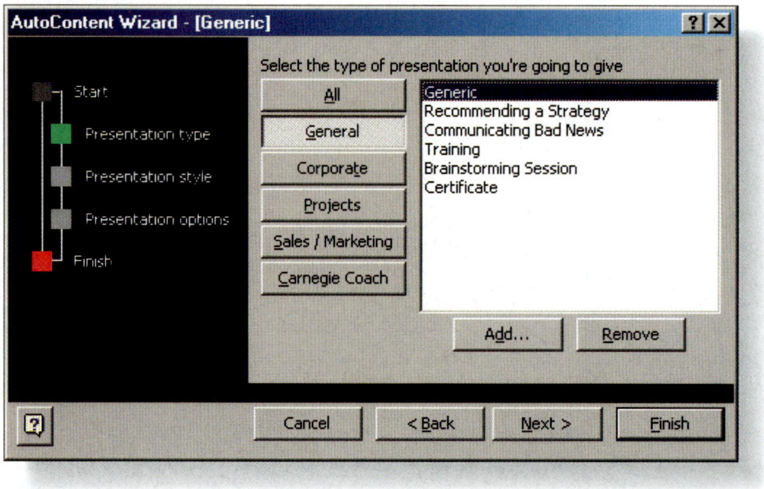

4. Click Sales / Marketing to view the types of presentations available in this category.
5. Click General and choose Recommending a Strategy from the list. Click Next.

   The third window appears. The green square moves to Presentation style. This is where you tell the wizard what format you plan to use when presenting your slide show.
6. Choose On-screen presentation and click Next.
7. In the fourth window, Presentation options, key **Selling to Corporations** in the Presentation title text box. Press Tab to move to the Footer text box

and key your name. Clear the option for Date last updated by clicking its check box.

8. Click Next to move to the last dialog box. Click Finish. PowerPoint creates a seven-slide strategy presentation for you. Notice the presentation design and the sample text.

FIGURE 2-4
Presentation created by using the AutoContent Wizard

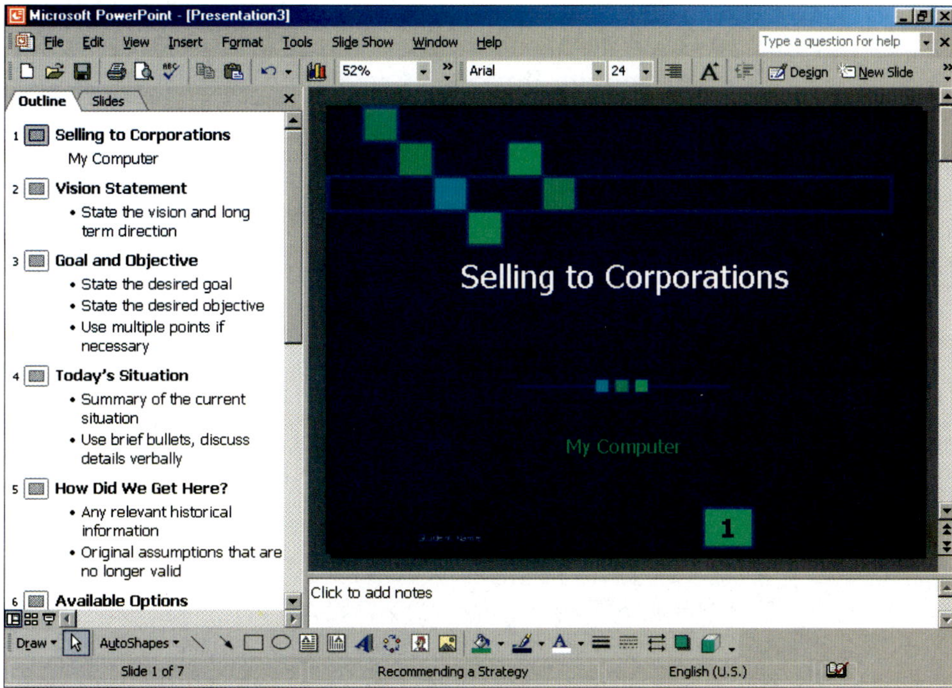

NOTE: The subtitle on slide 1 might have different text than that shown in Figure 2-4. The subtitle text is usually the name that was used to register the PowerPoint software. You change this text in the following exercises.

EXERCISE 2-2 Edit Sample Text in a Title Placeholder

In a wizard-generated presentation, all the slides contain sample text, some in title placeholders and some in body text placeholders. For example, slide 2 is titled "Vision Statement" and slide 3 is named "Goal and Objective." You can select and then edit this sample text.

1. In the Slide pane, click the Next Slide button at the bottom of the vertical scroll bar to view slide 2. Notice the sample text for the title and body text.

2. Display each slide one at a time, examining the sample text as you go. Then move back to slide 2.

REVIEW: To move to other slides, you can drag the scroll box, click the Next Slide button or the Previous Slide button, or press PgDn or PgUp.

3. On slide 2, move the pointer over the title ("Vision Statement") until it becomes an I-beam. Click the I-beam to activate the title placeholder.
4. Drag the I-beam over the sample title text to select it. Key the new title **Corporate Market is Growing** in place of the selected text.
5. Click outside the title placeholder to deactivate it.

REVIEW: After you edit placeholder text, deactivate the placeholder by clicking elsewhere on the screen. Be sure you see the white arrow pointer when you click.

EXERCISE 2-3 Edit Sample Body Text

You can edit the sample bulleted text in a body text placeholder, and you can also add additional bullets.

TABLE 2-1 Selecting Text

METHOD	RESULT
Click and drag	Selects text with the mouse
Double-click a word	Selects the entire word
Ctrl+click text	Selects the sentence
Triple-click text	Selects the paragraph or bulleted item
Click a bullet	Selects all the text for that bullet (in a body text placeholder)

NOTE: When you select bulleted text, the bullet character is not highlighted.

1. Working on slide 2, click the I-beam pointer on the bulleted text beginning with the words "State the vision." The body text placeholder is activated.
2. Position the I-beam to the right of the first bullet and drag to select all the text in the line. Key **Employee events** in place of the selected text.
3. Press Enter to add a new bullet. A dark bullet appears on the new line. It will change to a normal bullet when you key text on the line.

4. Key **Promotional events**
5. Press Enter to add a third bullet and key **Community event sponsorships**
6. Move to the next slide and click the I-beam on any bulleted text to activate the body text placeholder.
7. Move the I-beam onto the first bullet. When you see a four-pointed arrow ✥, click the bullet. The entire line is selected.
8. Key **Increase awareness of our corporate services**
   Notice how the text wraps to a new line.
9. Triple-click the text in the second bullet to select it. Then key **Increase corporate sales by 30%**
10. Press Enter to insert a blank bulleted line after the second bullet. Then key **Increase facility utilization to 85%**
11. Click the last bullet (beginning "Use multiple points") with the four-pointed arrow ✥ and press Delete to remove it.

FIGURE 2-5
Editing sample text on slide 3

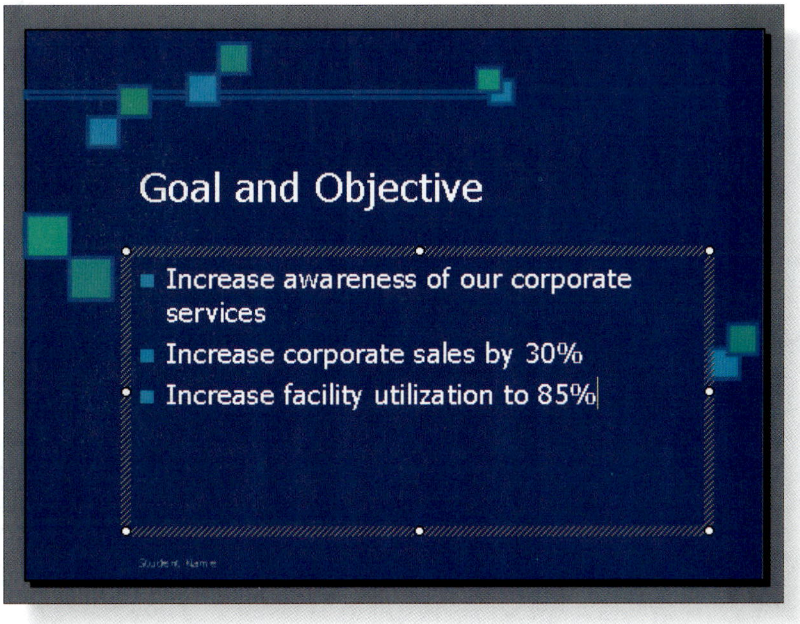

TABLE 2-2 Editing Text

METHOD	RESULT
Arrow key	Moves insertion point right, left, up, or down within the text
Ctrl+Arrow key	Moves insertion point to the next word or paragraph (bulleted item)

continues

TABLE 2-2 Editing Text *continued*

METHOD	RESULT
Backspace	Deletes characters to the left of the insertion point
Ctrl + Backspace	Deletes word to the left of the insertion point
Delete	Deletes characters to the right of the insertion point
Ctrl + Delete	Deletes word to the right of the insertion point

12. Change the title of slide 3 from "Goal and Objective" to **What We Want to Accomplish**

13. Move to slide 4 and change the title to read **Corporate Sales Today**

14. Still working on slide 4, select and delete both bulleted items. Key the following three bulleted lines, pressing Enter to start each new bullet:

- Account for only 1% of revenues
- Only two corporations use our services regularly
- Our facilities are underutilized during mid-week periods

15. Skip slide 5. Edit the text on slides 6 and 7 to match the text shown in Figure 2-6.

FIGURE 2-6

Slide 6

Corporate Business Rewards — Slide title

- Utilize idle facilities
- Increase revenues
- Generate repeat business
- Increase awareness of Good 4 U

Body text

Slide 7

Ways to Get the Business — Slide title

- Host an open house event for corporate officers and managers
- Create an attractive price structure
- Create an attractive brochure with theme party examples

Body text

EXERCISE 2-4 Edit Sample Text by Using the Outline Pane

1. If the Outline and Slides pane is not displayed on the left, click the Normal View button in the lower left corner of the screen.
2. If slide thumbnails are displayed, click the Outline tab to display the Outline pane.
3. In the Outline pane, scroll up until you can see the first slide. The AutoContent Wizard automatically inserted the subtitle text on slide 1. It might contain the name of your computer or some other text.
4. Using the Outline pane, edit the subtitle text on slide 1 to read **Developing a Strategy**

Selecting, Rearranging, and Deleting Slides

Just as you frequently rearrange paragraphs or sentences in a word processing document, you will often need to rearrange or delete slides in a PowerPoint presentation. You can change the arrangement of slides by dragging them to a new position in the Slides pane, in the Outline pane (covered in Lesson 4), or in Slide Sorter view.

You can delete selected slide thumbnails by pressing Delete on your keyboard.

EXERCISE 2-5 Select Multiple Slides

If you select multiple slides, you can move them to a new position all at one time. You can also delete several selected slides at one time. In addition, you can apply transitions, animation schemes, and other effects to a group of selected slides.

There are two ways to select multiple slides:

- To select *contiguous* slides (slides that follow one after another), click the first slide in the selection and then hold down Shift while you click the last slide in the selection.
- To select *noncontiguous* slides (slides that do not follow one after another), click the first slide and then hold down Ctrl while you click each slide you want to add to the selection, one at a time.

1. In the Outline and Slides pane, click the Slides tab to display slide thumbnails.
2. Without clicking, point to each thumbnail one at a time and notice that a ScreenTip appears displaying the title of the slide.

3. Click the thumbnail for slide 2 ("Corporate Market is Growing") to select it.
4. Hold down Shift and click the slide 4 thumbnail ("Corporate Sales Today"). Release Shift.

   Slides 2, 3, and 4 are all selected, as indicated by the heavy borders around their thumbnails. This is a contiguous selection.

FIGURE 2-7 Selecting contiguous slides

NOTE: You can change the number and size of slides displayed in the Slides pane by dragging its border to the right or to the left.

5. With Shift released, click slide 3. Now it is the only slide selected.
6. Hold down Ctrl and click slide 1. Slide 1 and slide 3 are both selected. This is a noncontiguous selection.
7. While holding down Ctrl, click slide 5.

   Now three noncontiguous slides are selected. You can add as many slides as you want to the selection if you hold down Ctrl while clicking a slide thumbnail.

EXERCISE 2-6 Change the Order of Slides by Using the Slides Pane

The Slides pane is a convenient place to rearrange slides. You simply drag selected slide thumbnails to a new position.

1. Click the slide 6 thumbnail to select it. (See Figure 2-8 on the next page.)
2. Position the arrow pointer within the selected slide's border, press the left mouse button, and drag the pointer above the fifth slide.

NOTE: While you are dragging, be sure not to release the left mouse button until it is pointing where you want the selection to go. Otherwise, you might either cancel the selection or drop the slides in the wrong place.

   Notice the horizontal line and the drag-and-drop pointer as you drag. The horizontal line indicates where the slide will go.

FIGURE 2-8
Moving a slide in the Slides pane

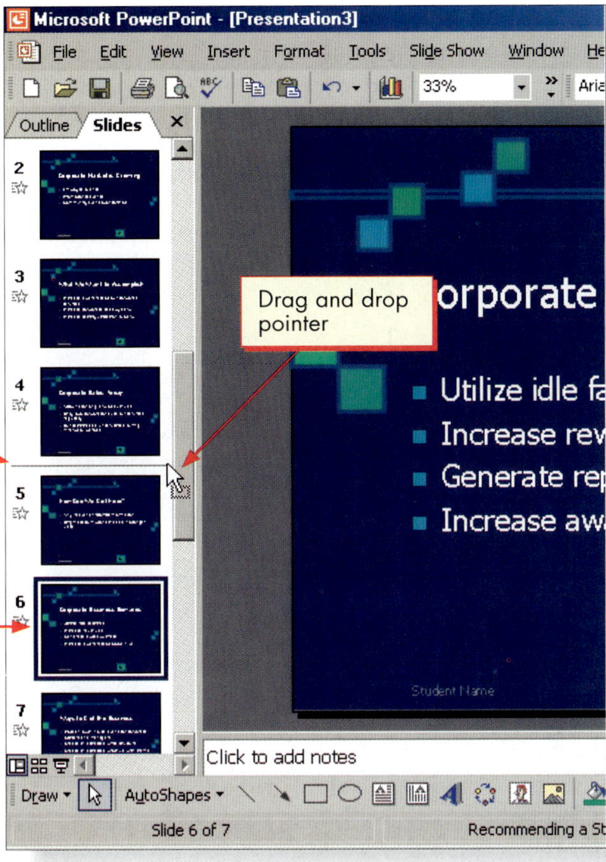

3. Release the mouse button. Slide 6, titled "Corporate Business Rewards," becomes slide 5. Notice the change in the slide number in the Slide pane.

4. Using Shift, make a contiguous selection of slides 2 ("Corporate Market is Growing") through 4 ("Corporate Sales Today").

5. Point to any slide in the selection and drag the selection below the fifth slide. All three slides move to the new position.

EXERCISE 2-7 Change the Order of Slides in Slide Sorter View

Slide Sorter view enables you to see more thumbnails at one time and is convenient if your presentation contains a large number of slides. You select slides in Slide Sorter view in the same way as in the Slides pane.

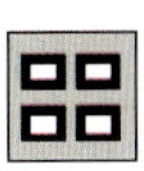

1. Click the Slide Sorter View button in the lower left corner of the window.

2. Click slide 2 ("Corporate Business Rewards") and then hold down Ctrl and click slide 7 ("Ways to Get the Business") to make a noncontiguous selection of the two slides.
3. Release Ctrl and drag the selection until the drag-and-drop pointer rests between slides 5 and 6. A vertical line indicates where the two slides will be inserted.

FIGURE 2-9
Moving a selection of noncontiguous slides in Slide Sorter view

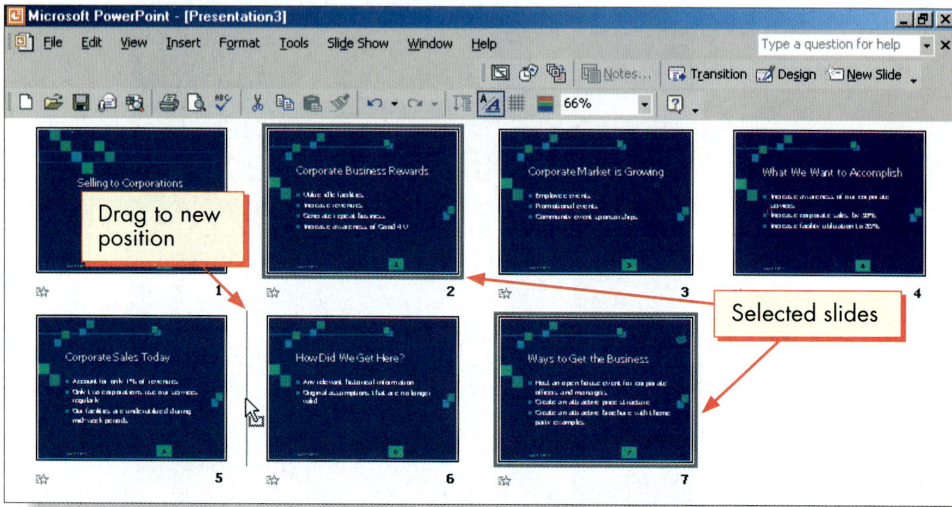

4. Check to make sure your slides are in the following order. If not, rearrange your slides to agree.

   Slide 1: Selling to Corporations
   Slide 2: Corporate Market is Growing
   Slide 3: What We Want to Accomplish
   Slide 4: Corporate Sales Today
   Slide 5: Corporate Business Rewards
   Slide 6: Ways to Get the Business
   Slide 7: How Did We Get Here?
5. Double-click slide 6 ("Ways to Get the Business") to display it in Normal view.

EXERCISE 2-8 Delete Slides

When you want to delete slides, you first select them (in the Slides pane or in Slide Sorter view) the same way you select slides you want to move. You delete them by pressing Delete on your keyboard or by clicking the View menu and selecting the Delete Slide command.

1. Working in Normal view, display the Slides pane if it is not already showing.
2. Click the slide 7 thumbnail to select it. The slide 7 title should be "How Did We Get Here?"
3. Press Delete on your keyboard. Slide 7 is deleted and slide 6 becomes selected.
4. Move to slide 1 and click the Slide Show button to start a slide show.
5. Advance through the slides (using any method), reading the text and observing the built-in animation effects.

REVIEW: To advance through a slide show, click the left mouse button, press PgDn, or press N.

6. Save the presentation as ***[your initials]*2-8** in a new folder for Lesson 2. Do not print the presentation at this point, and do not close it.

Using the Spelling Checker and Style Checker

PowerPoint provides three tools to correct spelling and improve the overall appearance of a presentation:

- Spelling checker, which corrects spelling by comparing words to an internal dictionary file.
- AutoCorrect, which corrects common spelling and capitalization errors automatically as you key text.
- Style checker, which automatically checks a presentation for visual clarity and consistency of case and punctuation.

EXERCISE 2-9 Use the Spelling Checker

The spelling checker in PowerPoint works much the same as it does in other Microsoft Office applications. It flags misspelled words with a red wavy underline as you key text. It can also check an entire presentation at once.

1. Without closing the current presentation, open the file **JulyFun2**. (You'll need to navigate from your Lesson 2 folder to the folder that stores the student files for this course.)

TIP: You can open an existing presentation by clicking More presentations in the New Presentation task pane, if it is displayed. Using this task pane will be explained in more detail in the next lesson.

2. On slide 1, a word in the title has a red wavy underline indicating a spelling error. Right-click the word. Choose the correct spelling ("Celebration") from the shortcut menu.
3. Notice the spelling of "Forth" in the title. This is an example of a word that is correctly spelled but incorrectly used. The spelling checker can't help you with this kind of mistake. Change the spelling to **Fourth**

4. To run the spelling checker for the entire presentation, click the Spelling and Grammar button on the Standard toolbar or press F7.

   PowerPoint highlights "Registraton," the first word it doesn't find in its dictionary. It displays the word in the Spelling and Grammar dialog box and suggests a corrected spelling.

NOTE: You might need to click the Toolbar Options button to find the Spelling button.

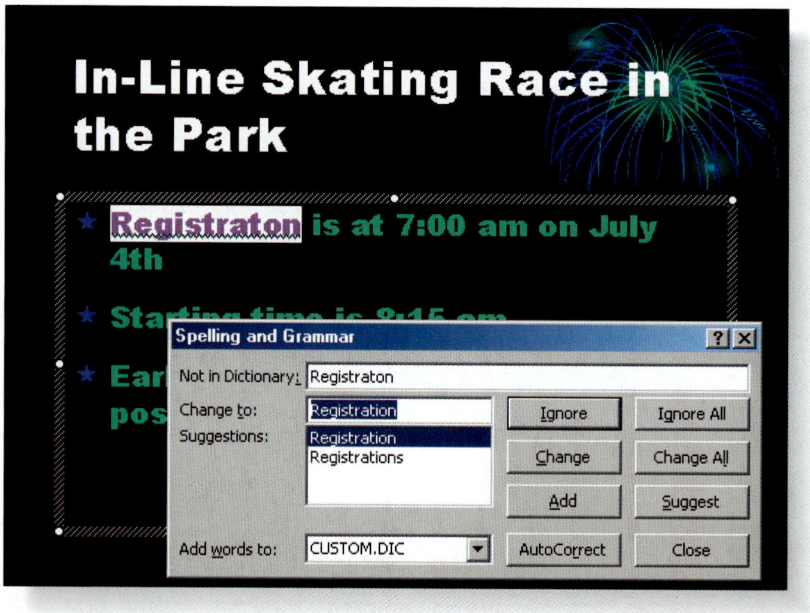

FIGURE 2-10 Using the spelling checker

5. Click Change to apply the correct spelling of "Registration."
6. When the spelling checker locates "slurpee," click Ignore because this word is spelled correctly.

NOTE: If the Spelling dialog box is hiding a misspelled word, move the dialog box to a different position by dragging its title bar.

7. At the next spelling error, click Change to apply the corrected spelling of "raspberries."

8. At the next spelling error, click Change to apply the first suggested spelling, "guardian." Click OK when the spelling check is complete.

EXERCISE 2-10 Use AutoCorrect

If you key "teh" instead of "the" or "can;t" instead of "can't," *AutoCorrect* corrects the word automatically as you key. The correction takes place after you press Spacebar or Enter or enter punctuation, such as a period or comma.

1. Display slide 3 of the active presentation (**JulyFun2**).
2. From the Tools menu, choose AutoCorrect Options, (you might need to expand the menu), and then click the AutoCorrect tab in the AutoCorrect dialog box.
3. If it's not already checked, click the check box for Replace text as you type. This turns on the AutoCorrect feature.

FIGURE 2-11 AutoCorrect dialog box

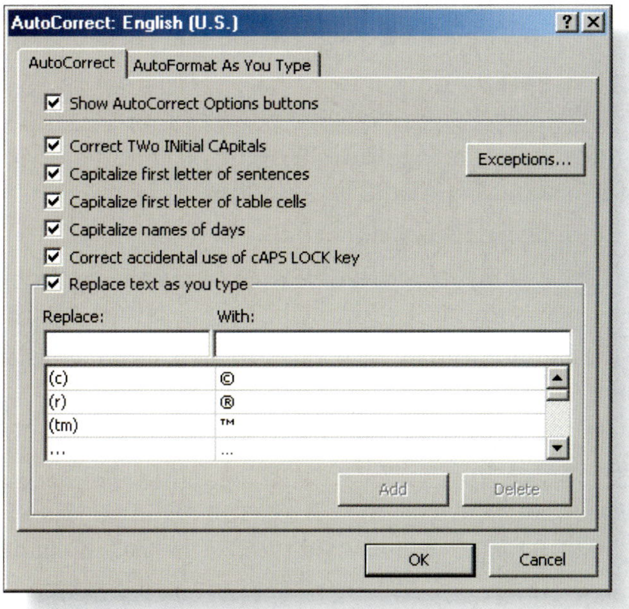

4. Still in the AutoCorrect dialog box, scroll through the list box to see the changes AutoCorrect makes automatically. Click OK to close the AutoCorrect dialog box.
5. Under the first bulleted item on slide 3, select the text "Generously laden with." Key **Amde from** (including the misspelling). "Amde" is automatically corrected to "Made" as soon as you finish keying the word.

TIP: You can add your own common keying mistakes or abbreviations to the AutoCorrect dialog box. For example, you can add "asap" and have it expand to "as soon as possible."

EXERCISE 2-11 Turn On and Use the Style Checker

When the style checker is turned on and the Slide pane is active, the *style checker* automatically looks for consistency, balance, and overall readability of your presentation. For example, if your presentation has a bulleted item that ends with a period or a title that is uppercase when all other titles are in title case, it will mark the problem with a light bulb. You click the light bulb and then choose an appropriate option from the Office Assistant balloon that appears.

Even when the style checker is turned on, the light bulb appears only when the Slide pane is active. For that reason, it is best to use the slide navigation tools, rather than clicking slide thumbnails, to move from slide to slide when checking for style errors.

1. From the Tools menu, choose Options and then click the Spelling and Style tab.
2. Under Style, make sure the Check style option is checked.
3. If an information box appears telling you that the Style Checker uses the Office Assistant, click Enable Assistant.
4. Click OK to close the Options dialog box.
5. In the active presentation (**JulyFun2**), drag the scroll bar in the Slide pane up to display slide 2 ("In-Line Skating Race in the Park").
6. Click the light bulb. The style checker detects a capitalization problem and provides options in an Office Assistant balloon.

FIGURE 2-12 Office Assistant balloon indicating a possible capitalization error

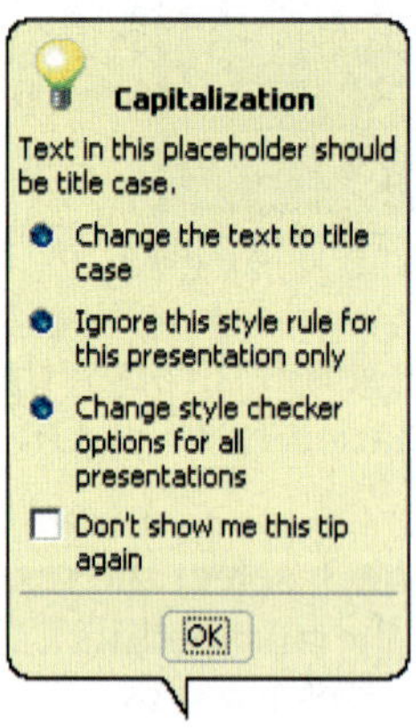

NOTE: The style checker is questioning the uppercase "L" in "In-Line." In a sentence, a hyphenated word such as "in-line" would be lowercase, but in a title, heading or name, it is correct as "In-Line."

7. Click OK because you don't want to change to title case, ignore the rule, or change style checker options.
8. Scroll down to slide 5 and click the light bulb. There's another capitalization problem. This is the only slide in the presentation with an all-uppercase title.

9. Click the first option to change the text to title case. The title text "ENTERTAINMENT" becomes "Entertainment."
10. Check each slide in the presentation. When you see a light bulb, click it, and then click OK. The other items the light bulb finds do not need to be corrected.

TIP: Remember to use the Slide pane's navigation tools and not thumbnails when moving from slide to slide to find light bulbs.

11. Return to slide 1.

EXERCISE 2-12 Turn Off the Style Checker and the Office Assistant

Sometimes the style checker light bulb can be distracting. Fortunately you can turn it off easily and then turn it back on again when you want to use it.

Even when you turn off the style checker, the Office Assistant stays in the background ready to pop up during other tasks. You can turn off the Assistant permanently by displaying it, right-clicking it, choosing Options from its shortcut menu, and deselecting the Use Office Assistant option.

1. From the Tools menu, choose Options and then click the Spelling and Style tab.
2. Under Style, deselect the Check Style check box. Click OK.
3. Click Help to open the Help menu and then choose Show the Office Assistant.
4. Right-click the Office Assistant and choose Options from the shortcut menu.
5. In the Office Assistant dialog box, deselect the Use the Office Assistant check box. Click OK. This action prevents the Office Assistant from popping up as you work.

NOTE: If you choose Hide from the Office Assistant's shortcut menu, it disappears only temporarily and reappears the next time you take an action where it can provide information.

Using Find and Replace

When you create presentations—especially long presentations—you often need to review or change text. In PowerPoint, you can do this quickly by using the Find and Replace commands.

EXERCISE 2-13 Find and Replace Text

The *Find command* locates specified text in a presentation. The *Replace command* finds the text and replaces it with a specified alternative.

1. With slide 1 displayed in the presentation **JulyFun2**, click Edit on the menu bar and choose Find (or press Ctrl+F) to open the Find dialog box.
2. Key **&** in the Find what text box.

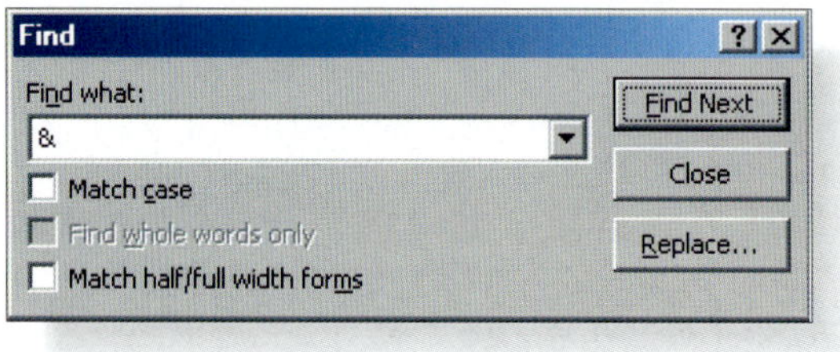

FIGURE 2-13
Find dialog box

3. Click Find Next. PowerPoint locates and selects the text.
4. Close the Find dialog box.
5. Key **and** in place of "&" to be consistent with the first bulleted item on this slide.
6. From the Edit menu, choose Replace (or press Ctrl+H) to open the Replace dialog box.
7. In the Find what text box, key **am**. In the Replace with text box, key **a.m.**
8. Check Match case and Find whole words only to ensure that you find only the lowercase text "am" and not words that contain these letters (such as "America" or "ramp").

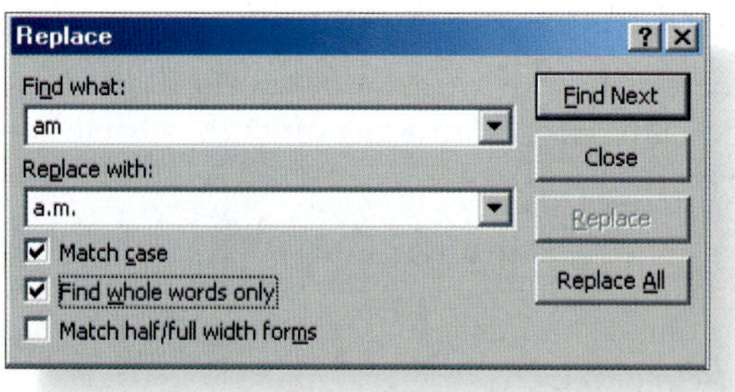

FIGURE 2-14
Replace dialog box

9. Click Find Next. PowerPoint finds the first occurrence of "am." Click Replace. Click Replace again at the next occurrence. A dialog box appears to tell you the search is completed. Click OK.
10. Click Close to close the Replace dialog box.

TIP: If you're certain about what you're looking for, you can use the Replace All command to replace all occurrences of text in one step.

11. Return to slide 1 and save the presentation as ***[your initials]*2-13** in your Lesson 2 folder. Leave the presentation open for the next exercise.

Adding Animation Schemes and Slide Transitions

An *animation scheme* adds visual effects to text during a slide show. For example, you can choose to make text fly onto the screen from the left side, one bullet at a time.

A *slide transition* is an effect that appears between two slides during a slide show. You can choose to make one slide blend into the next in a checkerboard pattern or fade pattern or choose from many other effects. A slide transition is often included as part of an animation scheme.

Transitions and animation schemes can be applied to individual slides, to a group of slides, or to an entire slide show.

EXERCISE 2-14 Apply an Animation Scheme to Selected Slides in a Presentation

Animation schemes are displayed in the Slide Design task pane. The task pane's list box displays a list of recently used schemes (if any), followed by subtle schemes, moderate schemes, and exciting schemes.

When you choose an animation scheme, it is applied to all slides that are currently selected.

1. Working on the presentation ***[your initials]*2-13** in Normal view, move to slide 2.
2. Click Slide Show on the menu bar and choose Animation Schemes. The Slide Design task pane appears on the right side of the screen with a list of animation schemes displayed.

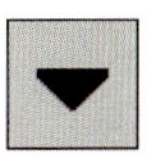

NOTE: If the task pane is already open, you can also display the Slide Design task pane by clicking the Other Task Panes button on the task pane title bar and choosing Slide Design – Animation Schemes from the drop-down list.

3. In the list of animation schemes, under Subtle, choose Faded wipe. A preview of the animated text appears in the Slide pane. (See Figure 2-15 on the next page.)
4. Move to slide 1 and scroll down the list of animations until you see the Exciting heading. Under Exciting, choose Bounce. The Bounce effect is displayed in the Slide pane.

FIGURE 2-15
Choosing the Faded Wipe animation scheme

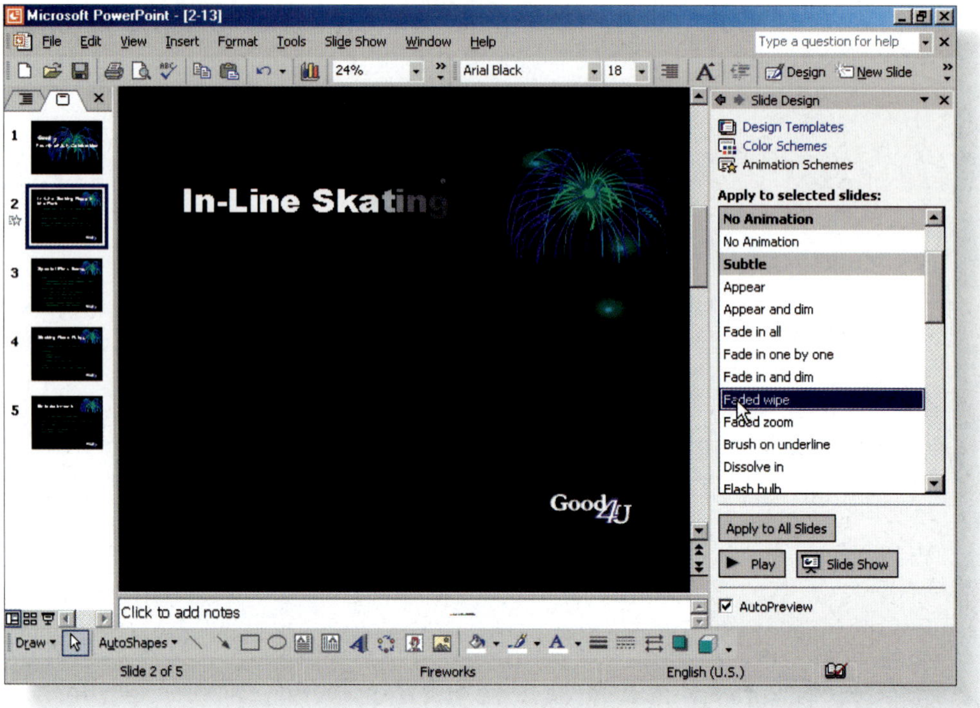

5. Click the slide 3 thumbnail in the Slides pane and then Shift+click slide 5 to select slides 3 through 5.
6. Sample some other animation schemes from the list. Then choose the Elegant scheme, under Moderate. This scheme is applied simultaneously to all the selected slides.
7. Move to slide 1 and click Slide Show (at the bottom of the task pane).

   Notice the Bounce animation effect as slide 1 is displayed.
8. Advance through each slide, observing the Faded Wipe animation on slide 2 and the Elegant animation on slides 3 through 5.
9. Return to Normal view.

EXERCISE 2-15 Apply an Animation Scheme to All Slides in a Presentation

On some occasions you will want to apply different schemes to different slides, but typically you should apply the same scheme to all slides in a presentation.

1. In the list of animation schemes, choose Fade in and dim from the Subtle category.
2. Click Apply to All Slides at the bottom of the Slide Design task pane.

3. View the presentation as a slide show, starting with slide 1. All the slides now have the same animation scheme.
4. Return to Normal view.

EXERCISE 2-16 Add a Slide Transition to a Presentation

In some presentations, you might find you want to use only a transition and not text animation for a slide show. In other cases, you might like a text animation but would prefer a different transition from the one that comes with the animation you selected.

Like animations, slide transitions can be applied to one, several, or all slides in a presentation.

1. Move to slide 1 and choose Slide Transition from the Slide Show menu. (Or, if the task pane is displayed, click the down arrow next to the Other Task Panes button ▼ and choose Slide Transition from the drop-down list.) The Slide Transition task pane appears on the right side of the window.
2. In the list of transitions, choose Checkerboard Across. A preview of the transition effect appears in the Slide pane.

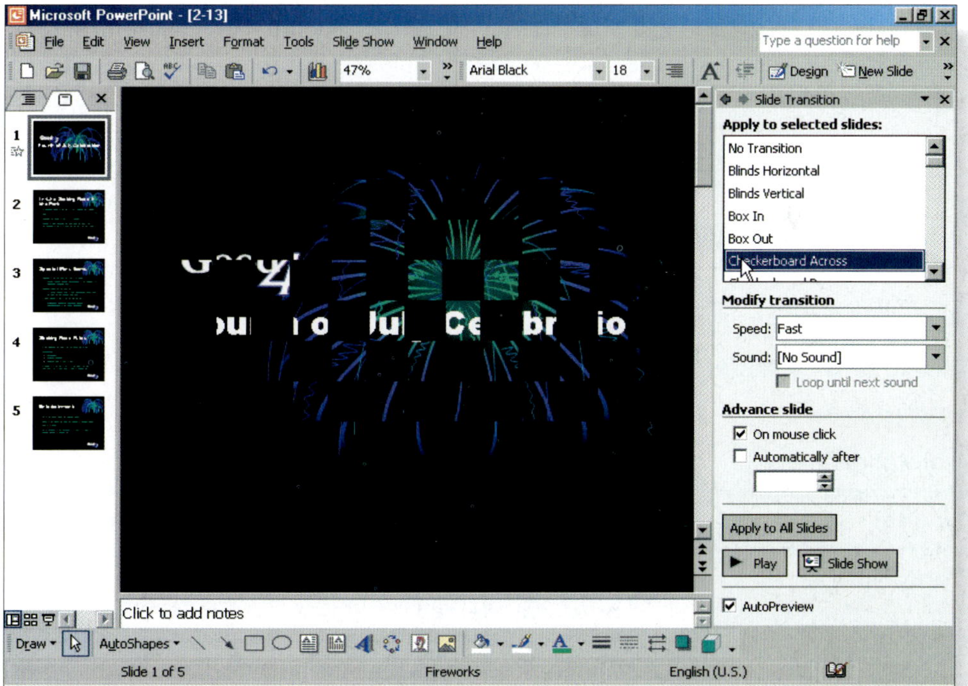

FIGURE 2-16 Choosing the Checkerboard Across transition

3. Under Modify transition, choose Medium for the Speed and Camera for the Sound.

4. Under Advance slide, select On mouse click, if it is not already checked.
5. Click Apply to All Slides near the bottom of the Slide Transition pane.
6. Click Slide Show to run a slide show. Advance through each slide and then return to Normal view.
7. Move to slide 5. Select the Dissolve transition. (Do not click Apply to All Slides). The transition is applied only to the selected slide.
8. Move to slide 1 and apply the Newsflash transition.
9. Save the presentation as ***[your initials]*2-16** in your Lesson 2 folder. Do not print it and do not close it.
10. View the presentation as a slide show, starting with slide 1. Notice that slide 1 and slide 5 have different transitions than the other slides, but all slides have the same animation scheme.
11. When you are finished with the slide show, return to Normal view.

TIP: If you want to apply both an animation scheme and a slide transition, apply the animation scheme first.

Adding Headers and Footers

You can add identifying information to your presentation, such as header or footer text, the date, or a slide or page number. A *header* is text that appears at the top of each notes page or handouts page. A *footer* is text that appears at the bottom of each slide, notes page, or handouts page. Header and footer text appears in special header and footer placeholders.

As is true in Word and Excel, you find the Header and Footer command on the View menu. In PowerPoint, this command opens the Header and Footer dialog box, which has two tabs: the Slide tab and the Notes and Handouts tab.

TABLE 2-3 Adding Identifying Information to Presentations

INFORMATION	DESCRIPTION
Date and Time	Current date and time—can be updated automatically or keyed
Header	Descriptive text on notes and handout pages only
Page Number	Number placed in the lower right corner of notes and handout pages by default
Slide Number	Number you can place on slides, usually in the lower right corner
Footer	Descriptive text on slides, notes pages, and handout pages

EXERCISE 2-17 Add Footers, Dates, and Page Numbers

Using the Slide tab in the Header and Footer dialog box, you can add information to the footer of all slides in a presentation by clicking Apply to All, or you can add footer information to only the current slide by clicking Apply. Using the Notes and Handouts tab, you can insert both header and footer information on handouts and other types of printouts.

1. Working on the presentation ***[your initials]*2-16,** click View on the menu bar and choose Header and Footer. Note the tabs in the Header and Footer dialog box, one for adding information to slides and one for adding information to notes and handouts.

FIGURE 2-17
Header and Footer dialog box, Slide tab

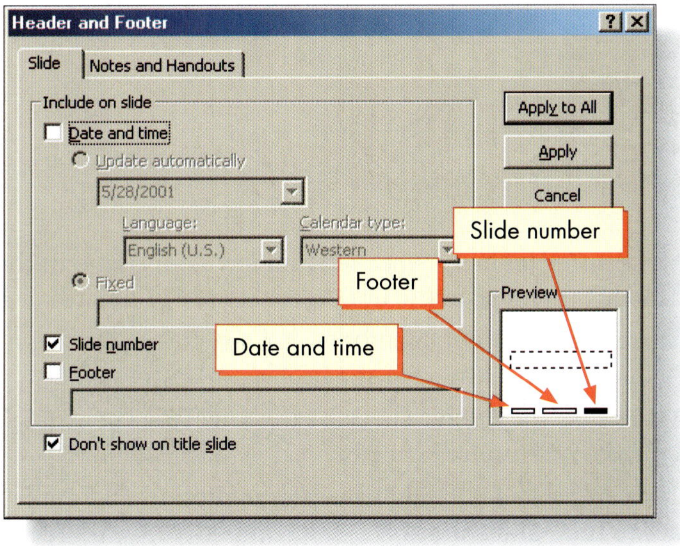

2. In the Preview box, notice the positions for the elements you can place on a slide. As you enable each element by selecting its check box, PowerPoint indicates where the element will print with a bold outline.
3. Click the Slide Number check box to select it.
4. Click the check box labeled Don't show on title slide. When this box is checked, footer and page number information does not appear on the first slide.
5. Clear the Date and Time and Footer check boxes.
6. Click Apply to All. The presentation now has slide numbers at the bottom right of each slide except the title slide.
7. Open the Header and Footer dialog box again and display the Notes and Handouts tab.

8. Under the Date and Time option, click Update Automatically to add today's date. Each time you print the presentation handout, it will include the current date. You can choose different date and time formats from the drop-down list.

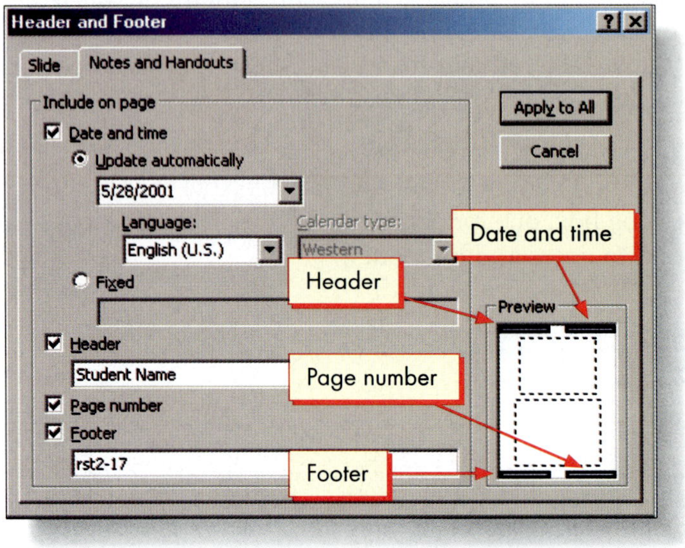

FIGURE 2-18 Header and Footer dialog box, Notes and Handouts tab

9. Make sure Header is checked and key your name in the header text box. The header is printed in the upper left corner of a notes or handouts page.
10. Make sure the Page Number option is checked. Page numbers are printed at the bottom right of the page.
11. Make sure the Footer check box is selected. Then key the filename ***[your initials]*2-17** in its text box.
12. Click Apply to All to add this information to all handout pages you print (but not to individual slides).
13. Save the presentation as ***[your initials]*2-17** in your Lesson 2 folder. Leave the presentation open for printing in the next exercise.

Choosing Print Options

As Lesson 1 demonstrated, PowerPoint provides many ways to print an entire presentation or a portion of a presentation. For example, in the Print dialog box or Print Preview window you can select:

- Individual slides, the current slide, or a range of slides
- Slides, handouts (1, 2, 3, 4, 6 or 9 to a page), notes, or outlines
- Multiple copies and whether or not to collate those copies. (To *collate* means to print all the pages of one copy before printing the first page of the next copy.)

Additionally, there are two options for printing in black and white. The Grayscale option converts the presentation colors to shades of gray. The Pure Black & White option converts all colors to either black or white, eliminating shades of gray. In complex presentation designs, this setting can be useful.

NOTE: Because the Pure Black & White option simplifies your presentation graphics, it can sometimes speed up printing time.

EXERCISE 2-18 Choose Print Options

The Print dialog box is divided into several areas: Printer, Print range, Copies, Print what, and Handouts. Each area presents choices that let you print exactly what you want in a variety of layouts.

1. With the Fourth of July presentation displayed, click File on the menu bar and choose Print to open the Print dialog box.
2. At the top of the Print dialog box, click the down arrow in the Name box. This is where you choose another printer, if one is available.
3. Follow your instructor's directions to choose an appropriate printer from the list.

NOTE: The information below the Name box applies to the selected printer. For example, "Status" indicates if the printer is idle or currently printing other documents.

4. Under Print range, click Slides and key **1,2** in the text box to print only slides 1 and 2.

TIP: To print consecutive slides, you can use a hyphen. For example, enter **2-4** to print slides 2 through 4. To print a combination of slides, you can key the range **1,3,5-9,12** to print slides 1, 3, 5 through 9, and 12.

5. Under Copies, in the Number of copies box, key **2** and click the Collate check box.
6. Choose Slides from the Print what drop-down list box.
7. If you have a black-and-white printer, choose Grayscale from the Color/grayscale list box. If you have a color printer, you can choose Color from the list box.
8. Click OK. In the printouts, notice that only slide 2 is numbered.

TIP: You can create a presentation that uses overhead transparencies by printing your slides on transparency film. Before printing, insert transparency sheets directly into your printer (choosing the correct type for a laser or ink-jet printer).

9. Open the Print dialog box again and set the following options:
- For Print range, choose All to print all slides.
- For Number of copies, key **1**
- In the Print what list box, choose Handouts.
- Under Handouts, set the Slides per page to **3**.
- From the Color/grayscale list box, choose Grayscale.
- Click the Frame slides check box.

10. Click OK to print the presentation handout and close the Print dialog box.

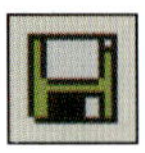

11. Click the Save button to resave the presentation, and then close it. (Your other presentation ***[your initials]*2-8** should still be open.)

EXERCISE 2-19 Choose Print Options in the Print Preview Window

Another way to choose print options is in the Preview window. You can access the Preview window in one of three ways:
- From the File menu, choose Print Preview.
- From the Print dialog box, click Preview.
- Click the Print Preview button on the Standard toolbar.

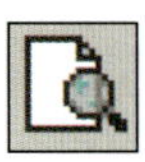

1. Display the presentation ***[your initials]*2-8** ("Selling to Corporations"). Remember that the AutoContent Wizard added a slide footer containing your name.

2. Choose Print Preview from the File menu (or click the Print Preview button on the Standard toolbar).

3. In the Print What drop-down list, choose Handouts (6 slides per page). From the Options menu, choose Color/Grayscale, Grayscale, and then choose Frame slides.

4. Click the down arrow next to Options. At the bottom of the menu, choose Printing Order and then choose Vertical from the submenu. The slides appear in shades of gray and in vertical order on the Preview page.

5. Click the Print button and then click OK to print the handouts.

6. Click Close to close the Preview window.

7. Close the presentation. Click Yes if you are asked to save changes.

USING HELP

PowerPoint's online Help feature is like an interactive teaching tool. One way to explore online Help is to display a list of Help topics. After you choose a topic, PowerPoint displays information or provides a demonstration.

Learn more about getting Help in PowerPoint:

1. Click the Ask a Question box in the upper right corner of your window.
2. Key **print** in the text box and press Enter. A list of related topics appears.
3. Click About printing at the bottom of the list. The About Printing Help window opens.
4. Expand the topic Color, black and white, or grayscale. Review the information.
5. Expand other topics in the window.
6. In the upper left corner of the Help window, click the Show button to display the Help option tabs.
7. Click the Contents tab. If a list of topics does not appear, double-click Microsoft PowerPoint Help to expand the list. Scroll to review the list of Help categories, each of which is represented by a book icon.
8. Double-click the topic Printing Presentations to expand the list of printing topics, each of which is preceded by a question mark page icon.
9. Click the topic Print handouts.
10. Review the information and then click another Printing topic. Close the Help window when you finish.

LESSON 2 Summary

- A wizard is an online guide that helps you complete a task.
- The AutoContent Wizard provides step-by-step guidance to help you create a presentation. It creates a complete presentation with sample text that suggests appropriate content.
- You can edit the sample text in an AutoContent-generated presentation by using any normal editing methods.
- Before keying text in a placeholder, activate it by clicking inside it.
- To change the order of slides in a presentation, use either the Outline pane or Slide Sorter view. Select the slides you want to move; then drag them to a new location. You can also delete selected slides.

- Right-clicking a word flagged with a red wavy line provides a shortcut list of suggested spelling corrections. You can spell-check an entire presentation at one time by using the Spelling and Grammar dialog box.
- When AutoCorrect is activated, common spelling errors are automatically corrected for you as you key text.
- When the Style Checker feature is activated, a light-bulb icon alerts you to possible style errors. To make sure you see all possible light-bulb alerts, navigate through your presentation by using the Slide pane's navigation tools.
- The Find feature and the Replace feature search your entire presentation for specified text. The Replace feature enables you to automatically make changes to matching text it finds.
- Animation schemes and slide transitions add visual interest to slide shows. They can be applied to individual slides, a group of slides, or an entire slide presentation.
- Headers and footers can appear at the top and bottom of notes and handout pages. Footers can also appear at the bottom of slides. They are commonly used to provide page numbers, dates, and other identifying information common to an entire presentation.
- Printing options provide a variety of ways to print your presentation: as slides, handouts, notes pages, and other page formats. Printing options are available in the Print dialog box and in the Print Preview window.

LESSON 2 Command Summary

FEATURE	BUTTON	MENU	KEYBOARD	SPEECH?
Animation scheme		Slide Show, Animation Schemes		✓
AutoContent Wizard		File, New, From AutoContent Wizard (on the task pane)		✓
AutoCorrect		Tools, AutoCorrect Options, AutoCorrect tab, Replace text as you type		✓
Delete selected slides		Edit, Delete Slide	Delete	✓
Delete selected text			Delete	

continues

LESSON 2 Command Summary *continued*

FEATURE	BUTTON	MENU	KEYBOARD	SPEECH?
Find		Edit, Find	Ctrl + F	✓
Headers and footers		View, Headers and Footers		✓
Display Outline and Slides pane		View, Normal		✓
Position an insertion point			Click the I-beam or use arrow keys	✓
Replace		Edit, Replace	Ctrl + H	✓
Select contiguous slides			Shift + click left mouse button	
Select text			Drag the I-beam across the text	
Select a word			Double-click the word	✓
Select a sentence			Ctrl + click left mouse button on the sentence	
Select a paragraph			Triple-click the paragraph	✓
Slide transition		Slide Show, Transition		✓
Turn on or off style checker		Tools, Options, Spelling and Style tab, Check style		✓
Turn on or off spelling checker		Tools, Spelling and Grammar	F7	✓

Concepts Review

TRUE/FALSE QUESTIONS

Each of the following statements is either true or false. Indicate your choice by circling T or F.

T F **1.** The AutoContent Wizard begins a presentation with the title slide.

T F **2.** The title slide in a presentation is limited to one line.

T F **3.** Before editing text in a placeholder, you must click the placeholder to activate it.

T F **4.** You can activate the spelling checker by pressing F1.

T F **5.** The Find command is located on the Edit menu.

T F **6.** You can put headers on slides, but not on handouts.

T F **7.** Slide transitions appear when you move from one slide to the next while presenting a slide show.

T F **8.** The only way to change the order of slides is to drag them to a new position in Slide Sorter view.

SHORT ANSWER QUESTIONS

Write the correct answer in the space provided.

1. When using the mouse, what method other than dragging the I-beam or using Shift+click can you use to select an entire paragraph?

___

2. In the Slide pane, what shape is the pointer when it is placed outside a text box?

___

3. Which feature in PowerPoint, if turned on, replaces typos and commonly misspelled words with the correct spelling as you key?

___

4. How do you select two noncontiguous slides at the same time?

___

5. When the style checker is turned on and you want to find all the light-bulb flags, what method of slide navigation should you avoid using?

___

6. When you use the Header and Footer dialog box to add slide numbers to a presentation, where do the numbers usually appear on the slides?

____

7. How would you use the Print dialog box to print only slides 1, 3, and 5 of a presentation?

____

8. What menu command do you use to display a list of animation schemes in a task pane?

____

CRITICAL THINKING

Answer these questions on a separate page. There are no right or wrong answers. Support your answers with examples from your own experience, if possible.

1. PowerPoint provides tools to help you create a uniform presentation with consistent formatting for each slide. What are the advantages and disadvantages of uniformity for the audience? For the presenter?
2. You can use headers and footers to identify your slides, handouts, and notes. What information is most important to include? Why?

Lesson Applications

EXERCISE 2-20

Create a presentation by using the AutoContent Wizard, edit sample text, move and delete slides, and check spelling.

1. Start the AutoContent Wizard to create a presentation. When choosing a presentation type, click Corporate and choose Company Meeting from the list at the right of the dialog box. Click Next.
2. Complete the rest of the steps in the wizard, choosing On-screen Presentation and keying **Good 4 U Power Bars** as the Presentation title and your name as the Footer. Include the slide number and date. Click Finish when you get to the last step of the wizard.
3. On slide 1, change the subtitle text to **Brainstorming Session**
4. Go to slide 2 and key the following text in the body text placeholder:

   Discuss how Good 4 U can develop and market a power snack (healthy "candy" bar).
5. On slide 4, change the title from "How Did We Do?" to **Product Development**. Replace the current body text with the following four bulleted items:
   - **Features of the product**
   - **Packaging**
   - **Naming**
   - **Promotion**
6. On slide 7, change the title from "Review of Prior Goals" to **Marketing Overview**. Change the bulleted text to:
   - **Customer profile**
   - **Market research**
   - **Advertising budget**
7. Switch to Slide Sorter view and make a noncontiguous selection of slides 3 ("Review of Key Objectives & Critical Success Factors"), 5 ("Organizational Overview"), and 6 ("Top Issues Facing Company").
8. Delete the selected slides.
9. Move slide 10 ("Summary") to the slide 5 position.
10. Make a contiguous selection of slides 6 through 10 and delete them.

    The following slides should remain in the presentation: "Good 4 U Power Bars," "Agenda," "Product Development," "Marketing Overview," and "Summary").
11. Check spelling in the presentation.
12. Move to slide 1 and save the presentation as ***[your initials]*2-20** in your Lesson 2 folder.

POWERPOINT

13. View the presentation as a slide show, clicking the left mouse button to advance through the text and slides.

14. Preview and then print the presentation as handouts, 6 slides per page, grayscale, framed. Close the presentation.

EXERCISE 2-21

Use the AutoContent Wizard, find and replace text, check spelling and style, delete and reorder slides, add a footer, and choose print options.

1. Use the AutoContent Wizard to create a presentation. For the presentation type, choose Training from the General category. The output will be an on-screen presentation. The presentation title is **Customer Relations Training**. Do not include any footer text, the date, or the slide number.
2. On slide 1, change the subtitle text to your name.
3. Delete slide 5 ("Vocabulary") and then delete slide 4 ("Overview"). If an Information box appears, click OK.
4. Change the sample text for existing slides 2 through 5 as shown in Figure 2-19.

FIGURE 2-19

Slide 2
Overview
- How you greet and seat people is critical
- Effective handling of parties guarantees success

Slide 3
Agenda
- Receiving customers
- Handling parties

Slide 4
Parties
- Usher celebrities to their tables
- Direct reporters to their station
- Consult with event planner for details

Slide 5
Receiving Customers
- Be professional, courteous
- Guide skaters and cyclists to equipment storage area
- Practice now by role playing

5. Delete remaining slides 6 and 7.

6. Reverse the positions of slides 4 and 5 so "Receiving Customers" comes before "Parties."
7. Use the Replace command to replace "parties" with "special events" (clear the Match case check box to find both "Parties" and "parties").

TIP: Before using the Replace command, make sure the Match case option is turned off.

8. Turn on the style checker. Correct the style inconsistency in the slide 5 title to change it to title case, consistent with the other slide titles.
9. Turn off the style checker and the Office Assistant.
10. Check spelling in the presentation.
11. Add slide numbers and a slide footer that contains the text **Good 4 U** to each slide except the title slide.
12. Move to slide 1. Save the presentation as ***[your initials]*2-21** in your Lesson 2 folder.
13. View the presentation as a slide show.
14. Preview and then print the presentation as handouts, 6 slides per page, pure black and white, framed.
15. Close the presentation.

EXERCISE 2-22

Change slide text, move a slide, check spelling, add headers and footers, add slide transitions, add text animation schemes, and choose print options.

1. Open the file **SpEvent2**. Change "Student Name" to your name.
2. Using the Find command, find the text "21st century." Close the Find dialog box and key **21st Century** over the selected text. (The "st" should appear as superscript automatically as you key the text.)
3. If the style checker light bulb appears, turn it off.
4. Move slide 2 to the end of the presentation (the slide 6 position).
5. On the new slide 2 ("Objective"), create a line break before the word "Good" by pressing Shift + Enter.

TIP: Pressing Shift + Enter creates a line break within a paragraph. Pressing Enter before the word "Good" would create a new bullet line.

6. Change the title of slide 2 to **Objectives** and add the following bullet point after the existing one:
   - **Increase bookings of special events from entertainment and sports industries**

7. Change the title of slide 3 from "Customer Requirements" to **What Does Everyone Want?**

8. On slide 4 ("Good 4 U Provides"), change the third bulleted item to:
   - **Award-winning service and cuisine**

9. Add a new first bullet to slide 4 that reads:
   - **High-energy, high-profile atmosphere**

10. Change slide 5 ("Next Steps") to read as shown in Figure 2-20.

FIGURE 2-20

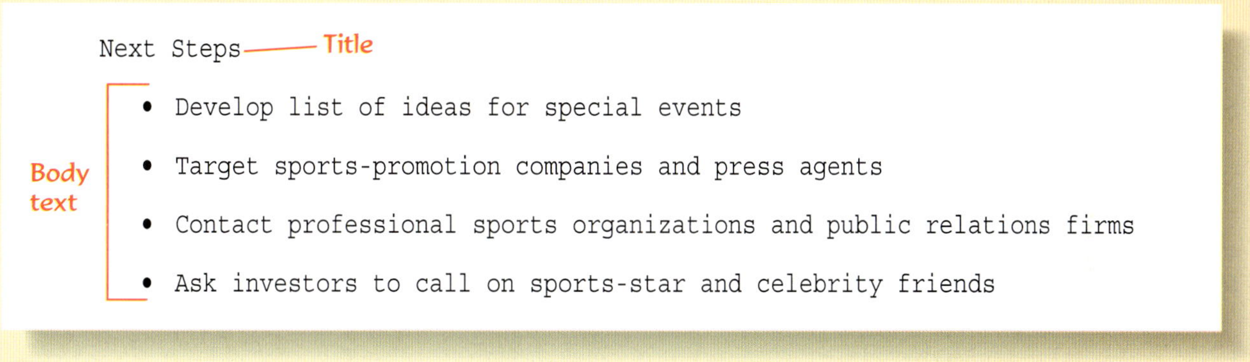

11. Add slide numbers to all slides. Add a handout footer that contains the completed filename, ***[your initials]*2-22**. Add a handout header that contains your name.

12. Apply the Rise up (Moderate) animation scheme to the entire presentation. Then apply the Big title (Exciting) animation scheme to slides 1 and 6 only. View your presentation as a slide show.

13. Move to slide 1 and save the presentation as ***[your initials]*2-22** in your Lesson 2 folder.

14. Preview and then print the presentation as handouts, 6 slides per page in vertical order, grayscale, framed.

15. Close the presentation.

EXERCISE 2-23 Challenge Yourself

Use the AutoContent Wizard, check spelling, find and replace text, add text animation and transitions, and delete and reorder slides.

1. Use the AutoContent Wizard to create a Generic presentation from the General category for output as an on-screen presentation. The presentation title is **Premium Items**. Add the footer **Good 4 U**, and include the slide number, but not the date.

2. On slide 1, change the subtitle text to the following:

   Item 1: Water bottle
   Item 2: Visor
   Item 3: Knee pads

3. Make a noncontiguous selection that includes the thumbnails for slides 2 ("Introduction"), 7 ("Real Life"), and 8 ("What This Means").
4. Delete the selected slides.
5. Use the Replace command to replace each occurrence of the word "Topic" with the word "Item." Use the Match case and Find whole words only options so you replace only "Topic" and not "Topics" or "topic."
6. Edit slides 2 ("Topics of Discussion") through 6 ("Next Steps") so they contain only the text shown in Figure 2-21.

FIGURE 2-21

```
Topics of Discussion

  • Introduce new premium items to give away at special events
  • All premium items will contain the Good 4 U logo

Item 1: Water Bottle

  • Made of durable plastic
  • Excellent for outdoor sports and indoor workouts

Item 2: Knee Pads

  • Made of durable vinyl/foam
  • Essential protection for skaters

Item 3: Visor

  • Made of white cotton blend
  • Adjustable, one size fits all
  • Ideal for tennis, running, walking

Next Steps

  • Create designs
  • Produce prototype items
  • Analyze production costs
```

7. Reverse the order of slide 5 ("Item 3: Visor") and slide 4 ("Item 2: Knee Pads").
8. Edit the titles of slides 4 and 5 so the item numbers are consecutive. The slide 4 title should read **Item 2: Visor** and the slide 5 title should read **Item 3: Knee pads**.
9. Check spelling in the presentation.
10. Add your name to the handout header and the filename ***[your initials]*2-23** to the handout footer, and set the date and time to update automatically.
11. Add an animation scheme and slide transition of your choice. Then view the presentation as a slide show.
12. Move to slide 1 and save the presentation as ***[your initials]*2-23** in your Lesson 2 folder.
13. Preview and then print the presentation as handouts, 6 slides per page, grayscale, framed.
14. Print only slides 1 and 2 as handouts, 2 slides per page, using the pure black and white setting. Close the presentation.

On Your Own

In these exercises you work on your own, as you would in a real-life work environment. Use the skills you've learned to accomplish the task—and be creative.

EXERCISE 2-24

Choose a product or service you enjoy using—for example, a pet grooming service, your favorite snack food, or a new electronic gadget from your imagination. Imagine you are creating a new business to supply that product or service.

Open the file **Selling1**. This presentation contains content suggestions similar to those a wizard would provide. On each of the presentation's slides, substitute information aimed at potential investors promoting your new product or service. Create a handout header and footer that include the date and your name as header and the page number and filename ***[your initials]*2-24** as footer.

Save the presentation as ***[your initials]*2-24**. Preview and then print the presentation as handouts, 6 slides per page, grayscale, framed. Close the presentation.

EXERCISE 2-25

Think of a fund-raising project that would benefit an organization at your school or in your community—for example, a book sale to benefit the local library or a bake sale to raise money for needy families.

Use the AutoContent Wizard's Brainstorming Session from the General category to help you create an on-screen presentation for a planning session for this event. Use 6 or more of the slides the wizard creates. You may rearrange the slides if you think it is appropriate. Create a handout header and footer that include the date and your name as header and the page number and filename ***[your initials]*2-25** as footer.

Save the presentation as ***[your initials]*2-25**. Preview and then print the presentation as handouts, choosing an appropriate number of slides per page, grayscale, framed. Close the presentation.

EXERCISE 2-26

Imagine you are planning to launch a small business—for example, a gourmet restaurant, an antique restoration service, or a computer store. To obtain financing from your local bank, you need to create a simple business plan.

Use the AutoContent Wizard's Business Plan from the Corporate category to help you create your own plan. Use at least 8 slides from the wizard's presentation, substituting information about your imagined business in place of the suggested content text. Create a handout header and footer that include the date and your name as header and the page number and filename ***[your initials]*2-26** as footer.

Save the presentation as ***[your initials]*2-26**. Preview and then print the presentation as handouts, 4 or 6 slides per page, grayscale, framed. Close the presentation.

UNIT 2

Developing a Presentation

LESSON

3

Creating a Presentation from Scratch

OBJECTIVES

MOUS ACTIVITIES

In this lesson:

PP2002 1-1
PP2002 1-2
PP2002 2-2
PP2002 4-1
PP2002 4-4
PP2002 4-8
PP2002 5-1

See Appendix E.

After completing this lesson, you will be able to:

1. Create a new presentation.
2. Add slides to a presentation.
3. Promote and demote text in the Slide pane.
4. Use the Undo and Redo commands.
5. Use design templates.
6. Use the Clipboard task pane.
7. Change the layout of slides.
8. Create and print speaker's notes.

Estimated Time: 1¾ hours

The AutoContent Wizard is a great tool for creating standard presentations, but you will soon find that you want the freedom to design your own slides and layouts. In this lesson you transform a blank presentation into a finished presentation by inserting text and slides, choosing *slide layouts* (arrangements of text and object placeholders for slides), and applying PowerPoint design templates.

You also create *speaker's notes,* which assist a speaker in delivering a presentation or can be included as additional information with presentations published on the Web.

Creating a New Presentation from Scratch

To create a presentation from scratch, you can begin with either:

- A *design template*, which adds a uniform color and design scheme to each slide in the presentation
- A blank presentation (simple text on a plain background), to which you can later apply a design template

You build each slide by choosing a slide layout and keying slide text.

EXERCISE 3-1 Create a New Blank Presentation

One way to create a presentation is to start with a blank slate, focusing first on content, and then adding color and other design elements later.

1. Start PowerPoint. A blank title slide appears, ready for your text input.

NOTE: If PowerPoint is already open and a blank title slide is not displayed, click the New button on the Standard toolbar or choose Blank Presentation in the New Presentation task pane.

FIGURE 3-1 Title slide

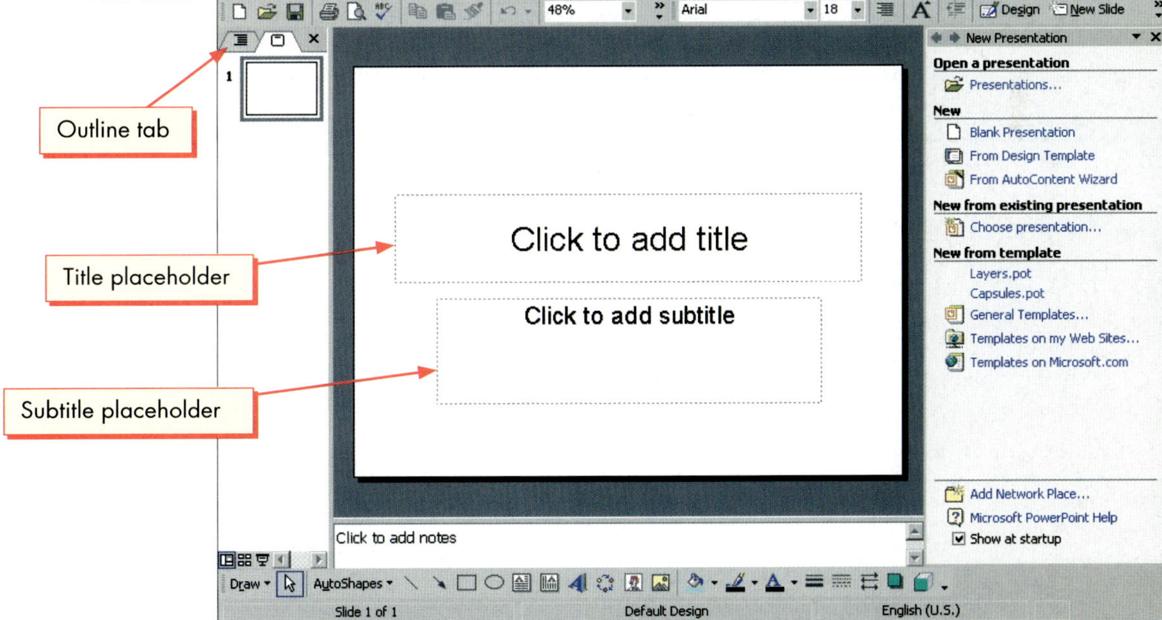

2. Click the title placeholder to activate it and key **For the Pleasure of Your Company**

3. Click the subtitle placeholder and key **Plan Your Next Event with Good 4 U**

NOTE: The documents you create in this course relate to the Case Study about Good 4 U, a fictional restaurant business (see pages 691 through 694).

4. Click the Outline tab on the left side of your screen to display the Outline pane. Notice that both the Slide pane and the Outline pane show the text you key.

REVIEW: If the Outline tab and Slides tab are not displayed on the left side of your screen, click the Normal View button.

5. Position the insertion point after the word "Event" in the subtitle; then press Shift + Enter. The subtitle is now split into two lines. Delete the space before "with" on the second line of the subtitle.

6. Split the title text into two lines so that "Your Company" appears on the second line. Notice that the changes you made are reflected in the Outline pane.

TABLE 3-1 Using the Keyboard to Navigate on a Slide and in a Presentation

KEYSTROKES	RESULT
Ctrl + Enter	Selects and activates the next text placeholder on a slide. If the last placeholder (subtitle or body text) is selected or activated, pressing Ctrl + Enter inserts a new slide after the current slide. Pressing Ctrl + Enter never selects other objects on a slide (including text boxes) that are not placeholders.
Esc	Deactivates the currently activated text placeholder or text box and selects the entire text box instead. If a text box is selected but not activated, pressing Esc deselects the text box.
Tab	If a text placeholder or text box is activated, inserts a tab character at the insertion point; if not activated, selects the next object on the slide. If the insertion point is between a bullet and the first text character on a line, pressing Tab demotes the bulleted text. Pressing Tab repeatedly when no objects are activated cycles through all objects on a slide, but never moves to another slide.
Shift + Tab	If a text box or text placeholder is not activated, selects the previous object on a slide. If the insertion point is between a bullet and the first text character on the line, promotes the bulleted text.

continues

TABLE 3-1 Using the Keyboard to Navigate on a Slide and in a Presentation *continued*

KEYSTROKES	RESULT
Esc, Tab	This key sequence always moves to the next object on a slide, regardless of whether a text box is activated. It never inserts a new slide.
Shift + Enter	If a text box or text placeholder is activated, inserts a new line (but not a new paragraph) at the insertion point.
Enter	If a text box or text placeholder is activated, inserts a new paragraph, including a bullet if in a body text placeholder. If a text box or text placeholder is selected but not activated, selects all the text in the object.
Ctrl + M	Inserts a new slide after the current slide.

Adding New Slides

To insert a new slide after the current slide in a presentation, you can do one of the following:

- Click New Slide on the Formatting toolbar.
- From the Insert menu, choose New Slide or press Ctrl + M.
- Press Ctrl + Enter one or more times until a new slide appears.
- Point to a layout thumbnail on the Slide Layout task pane; then click its down arrow and choose Insert New Slide from the drop-down list.

EXERCISE 3-2 Insert New Slides

When a new slide first appears on your PowerPoint window, you don't need to activate a placeholder to start keying text. When no placeholder is selected, the text you key automatically goes into the title text placeholder. Knowing this can speed up the process of inserting new slides.

1. Click New Slide on the Formatting toolbar. A new slide appears, containing a title text placeholder and a body text placeholder. The Slide Layout task pane appears on the right side of your screen.

NOTE: If the Slide Layout task pane does not appear, open the Format menu and choose Slide Layout. To make sure the Slide Layout task pane appears each time a new slide is inserted, check the Show when inserting new slides box at the bottom of the task pane.

2. Key **Excellent Service**. The text appears automatically in the title placeholder.

FIGURE 3-2
Keying text on a slide

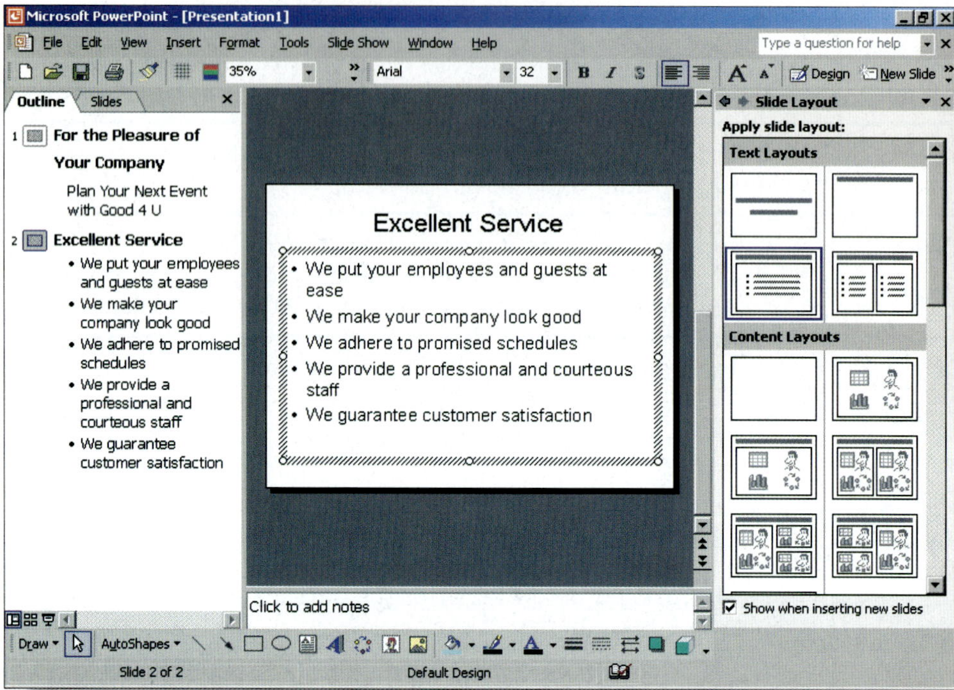

3. Press Ctrl+Enter or click the body text placeholder to activate it and key the following text, pressing Enter at the end of each line:
   - **We put your employees and guests at ease**
   - **We make your company look good**
   - **We adhere to promised schedules**
   - **We provide a professional and courteous staff**
   - **We guarantee customer satisfaction**
4. Press Ctrl+M to create a new text slide.

TIP: When you insert a new slide in a presentation, it uses the same layout as the previous slide (unless the previous slide was the title slide). You learn how to change slide layouts later in this lesson.

5. Key **A Delightful Menu** as the title and then key the following body text:
   - **High-quality, healthy food**
   - **Variety to appeal to a broad range of tastes**
6. In the Slide Layout task pane, point to—but don't click—the first layout thumbnail in the second row. The ScreenTip Title and Text appears below the thumbnail and a down arrow button appears on its right edge.

FIGURE 3-3
Inserting a new slide by using the Slide Layout task pane

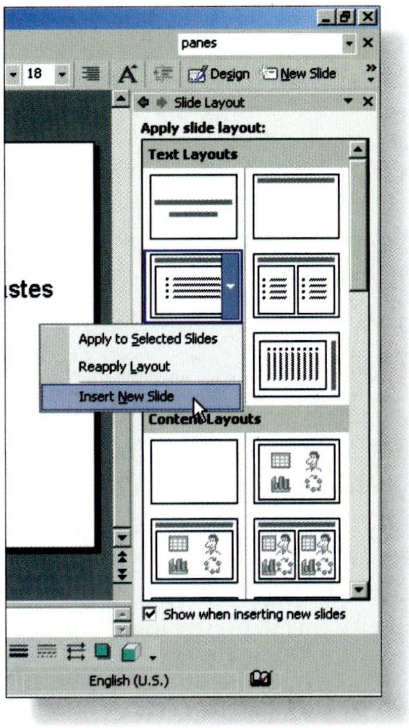

7. Click the down arrow button; then select Insert New Slide from the drop-down list.
8. Key **High-Energy Fun** as the title and then key the following body text:
   - **Athletic decor**
   - **Sports promotions**

   Notice that the AutoCorrect feature automatically adds the accent mark to the word "décor."
9. Press Ctrl+M to insert another slide; then key **A Healthy Atmosphere** as the title and key the following body text:
   - **Smoke-free**
   - **Alcohol optional**
   - **We sell none**
   - **We'll gladly serve your own**

EXERCISE 3-3 Work with the AutoCorrect Options Button

The AutoCorrect Options button appears whenever the AutoCorrect feature changes text that you key. In the previous exercise, AutoCorrect automatically added an accent to the word "décor" and placed a *smart tag* symbol below the word. A smart tag is a button that appears after certain actions to give you a convenient way of making choices related to that action. For example, in the case of the word "décor," the AutoCorrect Options button enables you to undo the change that was automatically made.

Other smart tags will be discussed as they occur in this course.

1. Move to slide 4.
2. Click the word "décor." A small, narrow, blue box appears under its first letter. This is a smart tag.

3. Point to the smart tag. The AutoCorrect Options button appears.
4. Click the AutoCorrect Options button to display its drop-down list. (See Figure 3-4 on the next page.)
5. Choose Change back to "decor" (without the accent).
6. Move to slide 1, check spelling, and then save the presentation as ***[your initials]*3-3** in a new folder for Lesson 3. Leave it open for the next exercise.

FIGURE 3-4
Using the AutoCorrect Options button

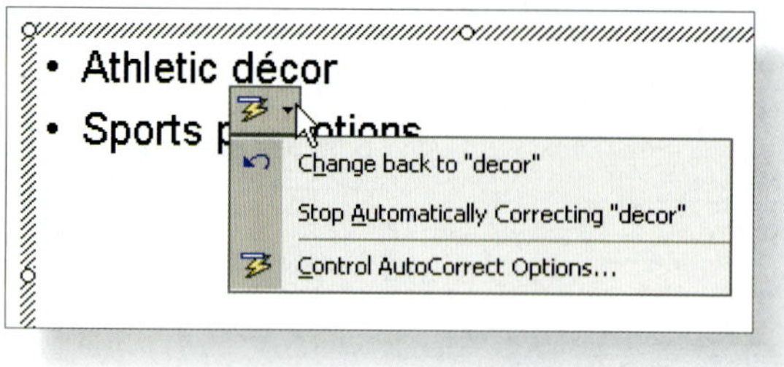

EXERCISE 3-4 Insert Slides from Another Presentation

On occasion you might want to insert a slide from a presentation that you or someone else created previously. You can easily insert slides from other presentations by opening the Insert menu and choosing the Slides from Files command. This action opens the Slide Finder dialog box.

The Slide Finder dialog box enables you to select slides from thumbnails or from a list of slide titles. You can insert all the slides in a presentation by clicking Insert All.

1. Move to slide 1.
2. Open the Insert menu and choose Slides from Files. The Slide Finder dialog box opens.
3. Click Browse to open the Browse dialog box, and then navigate to the drive and folder where your student files are stored.
4. Select the file **SpEvent2** and click Open. Slide thumbnails appear in the lower half of the dialog box.

FIGURE 3-5
Inserting a slide from another presentation

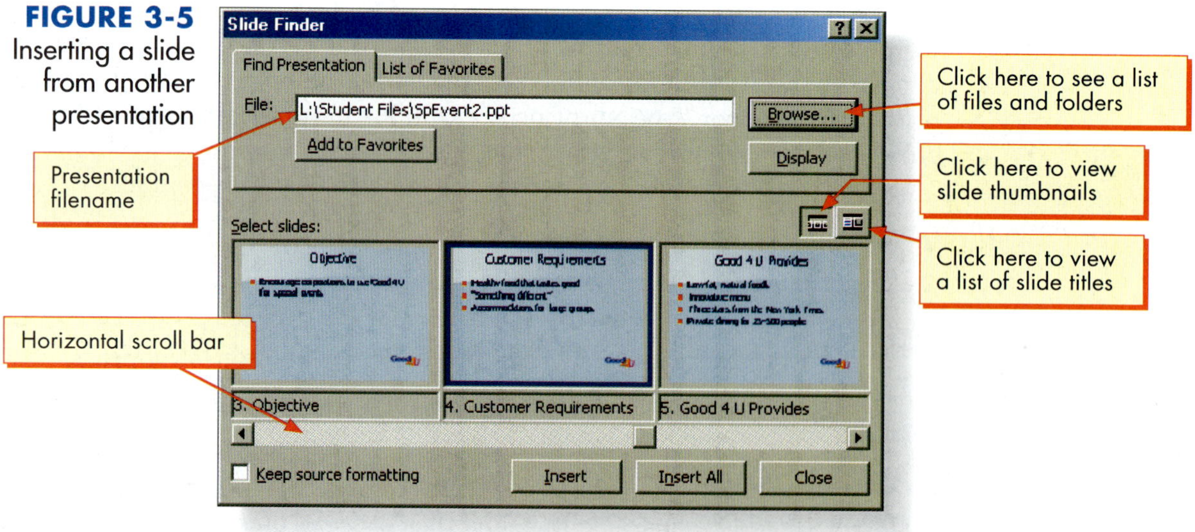

TIP: If you are frequently reusing slides from a particular presentation, navigate to it and then click Add to Favorites. The next time you want to insert a slide from that presentation, click the List of Favorites tab to find it quickly.

5. Locate the two buttons on the right side of the dialog box, just above the slide thumbnails. Click the button farthest to the right. A list of slide titles appears.
6. Select slide 4, "Customer Requirements." Its thumbnail appears on the right.
7. Click the left button just above the thumbnail. The view changes to show three slide thumbnails. You can select slides in either the list view or the thumbnail view.
8. Use the horizontal scroll bar near the bottom of the dialog box to locate slide 4 ("Customer Requirements"). It is already selected.
9. At the lower left corner of the dialog box, make sure that the Keep source formatting check box remains unchecked. If this box is checked, the style and colors as well as the text will be copied to your presentation.
10. Click Insert. The selected slide (slide 4) is inserted after slide 1 in the current presentation.

TIP: If you want to insert all the presentation's slides, you don't have to select them. Instead, click Insert All.

11. Click Close to close the Slide Finder dialog box.

Promoting and Demoting Text on a Slide

When you want to expand on a slide's main points, you can insert indented bulleted text below a main point. This supplemental text is sometimes referred to as a sub-bullet or a level 2 bullet. PowerPoint body text placeholders can have up to five levels of indented text, but you will usually want to limit your slides to two or three levels.

EXERCISE 3-5 Promote and Demote Bulleted Text

Indenting text is very similar to creating an outline in Word. You can *demote* body text by increasing its indent level, or *promote* body text by decreasing its indent level.

1. Move to slide 3 ("Excellent Service") and select the text "We make your company look good."

REVIEW: You can select a bulleted paragraph by clicking its bullet or dragging across its text.

2. Click the Increase Indent button on the Formatting toolbar. The text is reduced in size and indented to the right, and the bullet shape changes.

REVIEW: You might need to click the Toolbar Options button to locate the Increase Indent button and other buttons used in this lesson.

3. Click the Decrease Indent button to return the text to its original size and placement. Notice the change in the Outline pane as you promote and demote text.
4. Position the insertion point anywhere in the next item ("We adhere to promised schedules") and click the Increase Indent button. The item is demoted. Notice that you don't have to select the bulleted text to change its level.
5. In the next item, position the insertion point to the right of the bullet and before the words "We provide a professional." (Do not select the text.) Press Tab. The bullet is demoted.
6. With the insertion point between the bullet and the text, press Shift+Tab. The bullet is promoted to its original level.

NOTE: If you press Tab when the insertion point is within the text, you insert a tab character instead of demoting text.

7. Select the last two items by dragging your I-beam pointer over the text.

NOTE: If you drag the four-pointed arrow instead of the I-beam, you will move the text instead of just selecting it.

8. Press Tab to demote both items. Slide 3 should look like Figure 3-6 (on the next page). If it doesn't, promote or demote text accordingly.
9. Move to slide 6, which is titled "A Healthy Atmosphere."
10. Select and demote the last two bullets, making them subtext under "Alcohol optional."
11. Click the bullet to the left of "Alcohol optional." The bulleted text and the two indented bullets below it are selected.
12. Press Tab or click the Increase Indent button. All three lines are demoted to subtext under "Smoke-free."
13. Promote the selected text to restore the bullet levels.
14. Move to slide 1; then save the presentation as ***[your initials]*3-5** in your Lesson 3 folder but do not print it. Leave the presentation open for the next exercise.

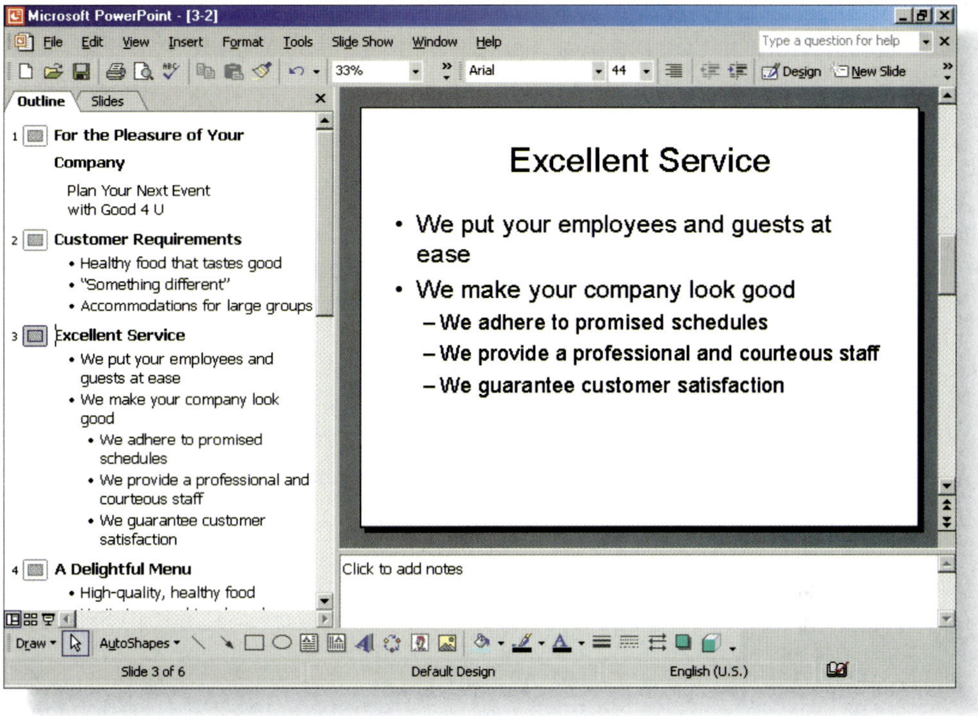

FIGURE 3-6 Demoting bulleted text

Using the Undo and Redo Commands

The Undo button on the Standard toolbar reverses the last action you took. You can undo a series of editing actions, including keying or deleting text, promoting or demoting items, or deleting slides. By using Undo more than once, you can undo multiple actions. The Redo button reapplies editing commands in the order you undid them.

TIP: By default, PowerPoint can undo the last 20 actions. You can increase or decrease this number by choosing Tools, Options, Edit tab, and changing the Maximum number of undos. Increasing the number uses up more RAM memory on your computer.

EXERCISE 3-6 Use the Undo and Redo Commands

In PowerPoint, unlike Word, Undo and Redo are cleared when you save a presentation. In other words, you cannot undo or redo actions performed prior to saving a presentation. Therefore, in PowerPoint, don't save unless you're sure you won't want to undo an action.

1. Move to slide 3 ("Excellent Service"). Select the bulleted text "We make your company look good" and its three sub-bullets.
2. Click the Increase Indent button three times. The items are indented three levels and reduced in size.

FIGURE 3-7
Creating fourth-level and fifth-level bullets

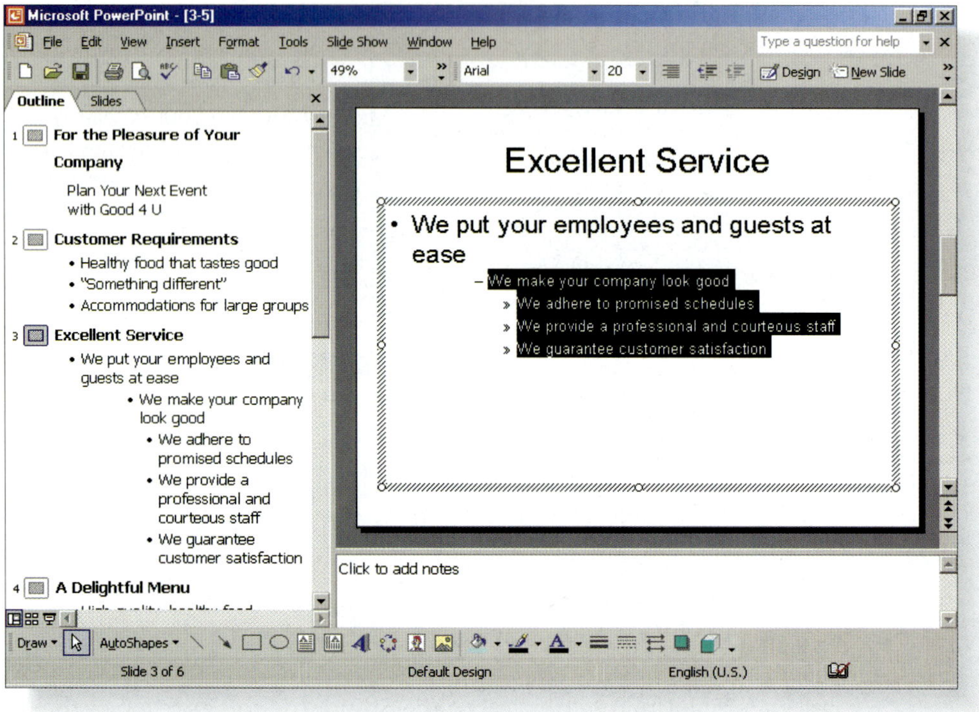

3. From the Edit menu, choose Undo Increase Indent (or Undo Demote). The last indent is undone.
4. Click the Undo button on the Standard toolbar. Another indent level is undone.
5. Press Ctrl+Z, the keyboard shortcut for Undo. The bullets are restored to their original level.
6. Press Ctrl+Y, the keyboard shortcut for Redo. The most recent indent is redone.
7. Click the Redo button. The previous indent is redone.
8. Open the Edit menu and choose Redo Increase Indent. The deepest indent level is redone.
9. Press Delete. The selected text is removed from the slide.
10. Press Ctrl+Z to restore the deleted text.

TIP: It's fairly common to make unintentional deletions and unintentional text moves. The Ctrl+Z key combination is very handy to use when the unexpected happens.

POWERPOINT

11. Press Ctrl + Z three more times to restore the slide to appear as in Figure 3-6 (from the previous exercise). Deselect the selected text.

Working with Design Templates

The presentation you are creating contains no special formatting, colors, or graphics. Sometimes it's convenient to work without design elements so that you can focus all your attention on the presentation's text. Before the presentation is completed, however, you will usually want to apply a design template with visual interest to help capture your audience's attention. You can apply or change a design template before, during, or after you create your presentation.

EXERCISE 3-7 Apply a Design Template

You select a design template from the Slide Design task pane. To display the Slide Design task pane, do one of the following:

- From the Format menu, choose Slide Design.
- Click Design on the Formatting toolbar.
- Double-click the current design template name on the status bar.

1. Click Design on the Formatting toolbar to display the Slide Design task pane.

2. Use the vertical scroll bar in the task pane to view the many design template thumbnails.

3. Point to one of the design template thumbnails. A ScreenTip indicates the template's name. The templates are arranged alphabetically by name.

4. Click any template thumbnail. The design you selected is applied to all the slides in your presentation. Sample several other design templates.

5. Locate the Cascade design in the list of design thumbnails and click it. (If Cascade is not available on your computer, use a different template.)

Notice that each thumbnail on the Slides tab shows the new template design. Note also that the name of the template appears in the center of the status bar below the slide. (See Figure 3-8 on the next page.)

6. Move to slide 1 and view the presentation as a slide show; then return to slide 1 in Normal view.

REVIEW: To view a slide show, move to the slide with which you want to start, then click the Slide Show button. Advance through the show by clicking the left mouse button or pressing PgDn.

FIGURE 3-8
Applying a design template

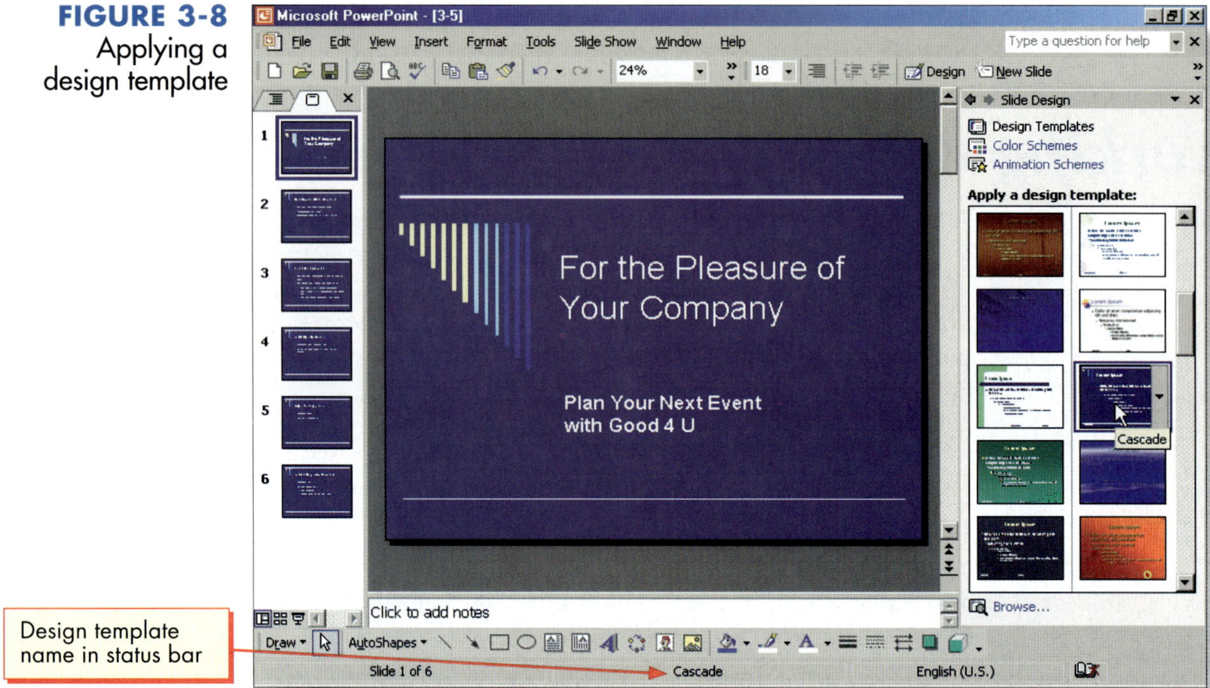

EXERCISE 3-8 Choose a Template Color Scheme

FIGURE 3-9
Slide Design task pane with color schemes displayed

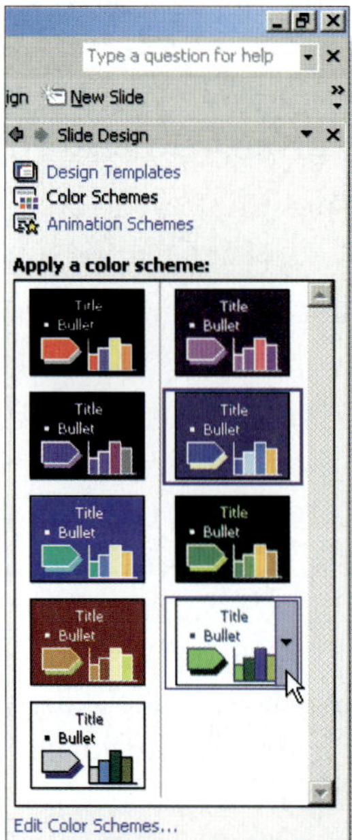

You can apply different colors to the current design template by changing the template's color scheme. To display color schemes for the current design template, display the Slide Design task pane and choose Color Schemes.

You can also customize color schemes, as you'll learn in Lesson 7: "Working with Lines, Fills, and Colors."

1. Near the top of the Slide Design task pane, click Color Schemes. Color scheme samples, appropriate for the current template, are displayed.
2. Click any color scheme to apply it to your presentation and then try some other schemes.
3. Apply the first color scheme (in the upper left corner) with the black background.

NOTE: When referring to color scheme thumbnails, this course assumes that the thumbnails are displayed two across. If your display does not match Figure 3-9, drag the left border of the Slide Design task pane left or right until the thumbnails are displayed two across.

POWERPOINT

4. View the presentation as a slide show; then return to Normal view.

EXERCISE 3-9 Change the Color Scheme for Selected Slides

Sometimes, changing the color of just one or a few selected slides can add emphasis to those slides.

1. With the Slides tab displayed, select the thumbnails for slide 3 ("Excellent Service") and slide 5 (High-Energy Fun") by using the Ctrl+click method.
2. Point to—but do not click—the color scheme with the burgundy background and hot pink accent colors (next to the black background). Notice the gray button with the arrow that appears on the thumbnail's right side.
3. Click the thumbnail's arrow button. A drop-down list of options is displayed.
4. Choose Apply to Selected Slides. The color scheme for slides 3 and 5 changes, but all other slides remain unchanged.
5. View the presentation as a slide show, starting with slide 1.
6. Move to slide 1 and save the presentation as ***[your initials]*****3-9**. Do not close it.

EXERCISE 3-10 Apply a Design Template to Selected Slides

In the same way that you can apply more than one color scheme to a presentation, you can apply more than one template.

1. Select the thumbnails for slides 3 ("Excellent Service") through 6 ("A Healthy Atmosphere") by using Shift+click. (Four slides should be selected.)
2. On the Slide Design task pane, click Design Templates.
3. Point to the Refined slide design thumbnail and click its down arrow.

NOTE: Design template thumbnails are arranged alphabetically by name. You need to scroll down to find the Refined template.

4. Choose Apply to Selected Slides from the drop-down list.
5. View the presentation as a slide show, starting with slide 1.
6. Move to slide 1 and save the presentation as ***[your initials]*****3-10**. Do not close it.

EXERCISE 3-11 Create a New Presentation from a Template

Rather than start a new presentation with a blank white slide, you might prefer to choose a design template first. Some ways to do this are:

FIGURE 3-10
Choosing a task pane

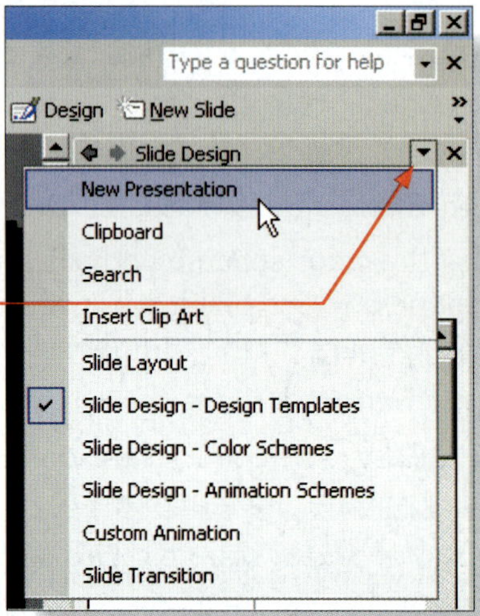

- Display the New Presentation task pane. Under New from template, choose General Templates and then choose a design template from the list.
- If a new blank presentation is already displayed on the screen, click Design on the Formatting toolbar to display the Slide Design task pane; then choose a design template from the thumbnails displayed.

1. With the presentation ***[your initials]*3-10** still open, click the Other Task Panes down arrow on the right side of the task pane title bar; then choose New Presentation.

   The New Presentation task pane is displayed. Notice the New from template heading halfway down in the task pane. (If your task pane is not displayed, choose Task Pane from the View menu.)

2. Under New from template, choose General Templates. The Templates dialog box opens.

FIGURE 3-11
Choosing a template

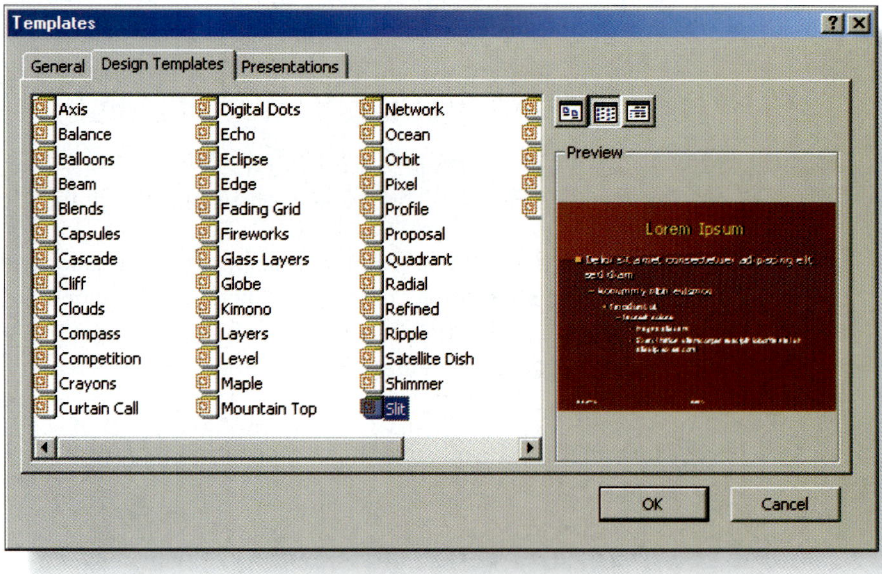

3. Click the Presentations tab to view a list of templates.
4. Click on a template name. A preview is shown on the right side of the screen.
5. Click the Design Templates tab; then click a template name to preview another template.
6. Select the template named Slit (with a red background) and click OK. A new blank presentation opens with the chosen template design applied. There are now two presentations open.
7. Key the title on three lines as shown:

   Introducing
   the Good 4 U
   Sunday Brunch

8. Key the subtitle on two lines:

   Every Sunday
   from 10 a.m. to 2 p.m.

   Notice that AutoCorrect changed the "f" in "from" to uppercase.

9. Click the smart tag under "From" and choose Undo Automatic Capitalization from its drop-down list.
10. Click New Slide on the Formatting toolbar to insert a new slide.
11. On the new slide, key **Sample Menu** as the title with the following as bulleted body text:
    - **Pineapple/grapefruit fizz**
    - **Multigrain pancakes**
    - **Tofu fajitas**
    - **Western omelet**
12. Move to slide 1 and save the presentation as ***[your initials]*3-11**. Keep the presentation open. You will insert more slides later in this lesson.

Using the Clipboard Task Pane

The *Cut, Copy,* and *Paste* commands are almost universally available in computer programs. When you cut selected text or a selected object, it is removed from the presentation and placed on the clipboard. When you copy text or an object, it remains in its original place and a copy is placed on the clipboard. When you paste a clipboard item, a copy of the item is placed at the location of the insertion point and remains on the clipboard to use again if needed.

Each item you cut or copy is stored on the Office *Clipboard*, which can hold up to 24 items at a time. Clipboard items can be viewed and managed by using the Clipboard task pane. When working with the Office Clipboard, it is important to understand that unlike the Cut command, Delete does not save items to the clipboard.

The following cut, copy, and paste keyboard shortcuts are big time-savers when you do extensive editing:

- Ctrl+C Copy
- Ctrl+X Cut
- Ctrl+V Insert (paste) the most recent item stored on the clipboard

If you press Ctrl+C twice, PowerPoint displays the Clipboard task pane.

EXERCISE 3-12 Work with Multiple Open Presentations

You should have two presentations open on your computer at this time (***[your initials]*3-10** and ***[your initials]*3-11**). The names of the open presentations are displayed on the Windows task bar at the bottom of your screen, and they are also listed on PowerPoint's Window menu.

FIGURE 3-12
Switching between open presentations

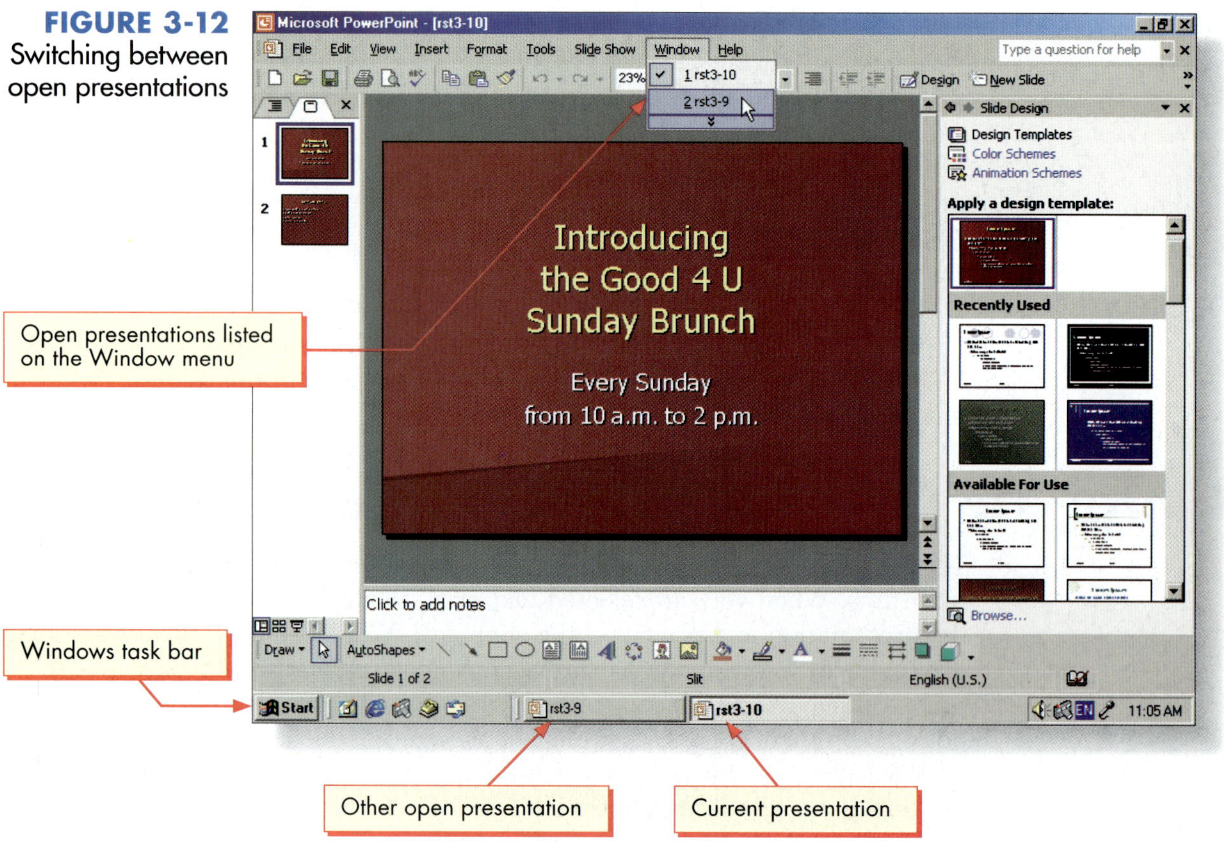

1. Open the Window menu and choose ***[your initials]*3-10**. PowerPoint switches to your other open presentation ("For the Pleasure of Your Company.")
2. On the Windows taskbar at the bottom of your screen, click ***[your initials]*3-11** to switch back to the new presentation (red background).

TIP: Ctrl + F6 cycles through all open presentations.

3. Use either method to switch to ***[your initials]*3-10** (black background).

EXERCISE 3-13 Use Cut, Copy, and Paste to Copy and Rearrange Slides

In Lesson 2 you learned how to rearrange slides by dragging their thumbnails. This exercise presents another way to arrange slides by using the Clipboard task pane. You can open the Clipboard task pane by choosing Office Clipboard from the Edit menu.

1. From the Edit menu, choose Office Clipboard to display the Clipboard task pane.
2. Display the Slides tab, and then click the thumbnail for slide 6 ("A Healthy Atmosphere") to select it.

REVIEW: If the Outline tab and Slides tab are not visible, click the Normal View button.

3. Click the Cut button on the Standard toolbar. This removes the slide and stores it on the clipboard.
4. Select the thumbnail for slide 4 ("A Delightful Menu").

5. Click the Paste button on the Standard toolbar. The cut slide (on the clipboard) is inserted (or pasted) after slide 4. This accomplishes the same thing as if you moved the slide by dragging its thumbnail.

6. Select the slide 1 thumbnail ("For the Pleasure of Your Company"); then click the Copy button on the Standard toolbar. Notice that two slides are stored on the Clipboard task pane.

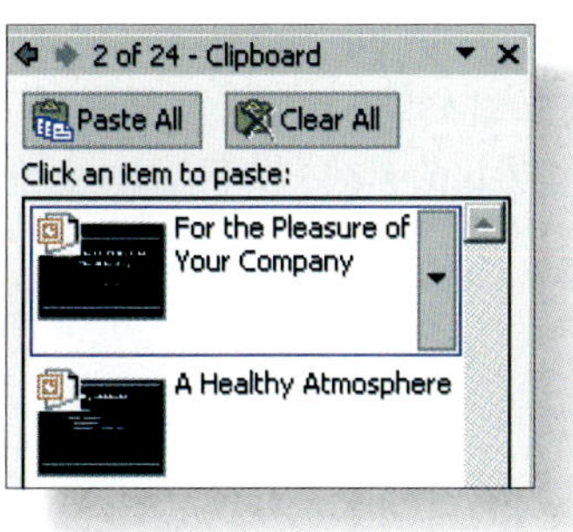

FIGURE 3-13 Using the Clipboard task pane

7. Move to slide 6 ("High-Energy Fun"); then click the first item on the Clipboard task pane ("For the Pleasure of Your Company"). A copy of the slide is inserted at the end of the presentation.
8. Move to slide 7, the copied slide.

9. Delete the subtitle text and key the following text in its place on three lines:

Make Your Next Event Outstanding
Call Good 4 U at
(800) 555-1234

10. Move to slide 1 and save the presentation as ***[your initials]*3-13**. Keep the presentation open for the following exercises.

EXERCISE 3-14 Use Copy and Paste to Rearrange Text

Just as you cut, copy, and paste slides, you can cut, copy, and paste text, and store it on the Office Clipboard.

1. Display slide 2 ("Customer Requirements").
2. Activate the body text placeholder; then click the first bullet to select all its text.
3. Press Ctrl+C to copy the selected text to the clipboard. The selected text appears at the top of the Clipboard task pane. Notice the difference in appearance from the slides on the clipboard.

FIGURE 3-14 Text and slides stored on the Office Clipboard

4. Click the second bullet to select its text; then press Ctrl+X to cut the text from the slide. It too appears on the Clipboard task pane.
5. Move to slide 4 ("A Delightful Menu").
6. Select the first bullet item in the body text placeholder.
7. Click the first item on the Clipboard task pane ("Something Different").

   The clipboard text replaces the selected bullet. The bullet style is different from the other bullet on the slide. Notice the Paste Options button that appears. Paste Options is addressed later in this lesson.
8. Click the second item on the Clipboard task pane ("Healthy food that tastes good"). The text is inserted as a new bullet.
9. Delete slide 2 ("Customer Requirements").

EXERCISE 3-15 Copy Slides to Another Presentation

Earlier in this lesson, you learned how to insert slides from another presentation by using the Slide Finder dialog box. Another way to accomplish the same task is to copy and paste the slides by using the Clipboard task pane.

When beginning a new cut, copy, and paste procedure, it's usually a good idea to clear the Clipboard task pane first by clicking Clear All.

1. At the top of the Clipboard task pane, click Clear All to empty the clipboard.
2. With the Slides tab displayed, copy one at a time slide 3 ("A Delightful Menu") and slide 4 ("A Healthy Atmosphere").
3. Click ***[your initials]*3-11** on the Windows taskbar to switch to your other open presentation.
4. Display slide 1; then click the second slide on the Clipboard task pane ("A Delightful Menu"). The slide is inserted after slide 1, formatted with the current presentation's design template. The Paste Options button appears below the inserted slide's thumbnail.

NOTE: The Paste Options button appears after pasting slides one at a time into a presentation. It does not appear if you use the Paste All button on the Clipboard task pane.

EXERCISE 3-16 Use the Paste Options Button

The Paste Options button appears near a pasted item if the item's *source* formatting is different from the formatting of similar elements in its *destination* presentation. A clipboard item's source is the presentation or other document from which it was cut or copied. Its destination is the presentation or other document in which it is pasted.

1. Click the thumbnail for slide 2 and then click the Paste Options button that appears underneath the thumbnail.
2. Choose Keep Source Formatting from the drop-down list.

   The design template for slide 2 changes to the design of the presentation from which it was copied. This is sometimes desirable, for example, in a very complicated graphic layout.
3. Click the thumbnail and then click the Paste Options button again. This time choose Use Design Template Formatting. The slide design changes to match the other slides in the presentation.
4. Select the slide 1 thumbnail and then click the first item on the Clipboard task pane—the slide "A Healthy Atmosphere." The slide is inserted as slide 2 in the presentation.

5. Add a handout header to the presentation that contains your name. Add a handout footer that contains the text ***[your initials]*3-16**.

REVIEW: To add handout headers and footers, open the View menu and choose Header and Footer.

6. Move to slide 1, spell check the presentation, and then save it as ***[your initials]*3-16a** in your Lesson 3 folder.
7. Preview and then print the presentation as handouts, 4 slides per page, grayscale, framed, landscape orientation, and then close it. The presentation ***[your initials]*3-13** should remain open.
8. To improve the design of ***[your initials]*3-13**, select the thumbnails for slides 3 ("A Delightful Menu") through 5 ("High-Energy Fun") and apply the Refined design template.
9. Save the presentation as ***[your initials]*3-16b** but do not print it. Leave it open for the next exercise.

Changing Slide Layouts

The Slide Layout task pane enables you to choose a layout when you insert a new slide and to change the layout of a slide at a later time if needed. For example, some bulleted text might look better with a two-column layout.

In this lesson you work with *text layouts* that include only text placeholders. In subsequent lessons you work with *content layouts* that include placeholders for pictures, tables, and charts.

EXERCISE 3-17 Insert a New Slide with a Different Layout

1. Move to slide 5 ("High-Energy Fun") and click New Slide on the Formatting toolbar. The Slide Layout task pane appears, and a blank slide is inserted after slide 5. (See Figure 3-15 on the next page.)
2. In the Slide Layout task pane, point to and then click the Title and 2-Column Text layout. The new layout has two body text placeholders.
3. Key the slide title **Events That Are Good 4 U** and then key the following bulleted text in the left body text placeholder:
   - **High-energy meetings**
   - **Productive lunches**
   - **Company celebrations**
   - **Celebrity promotions**

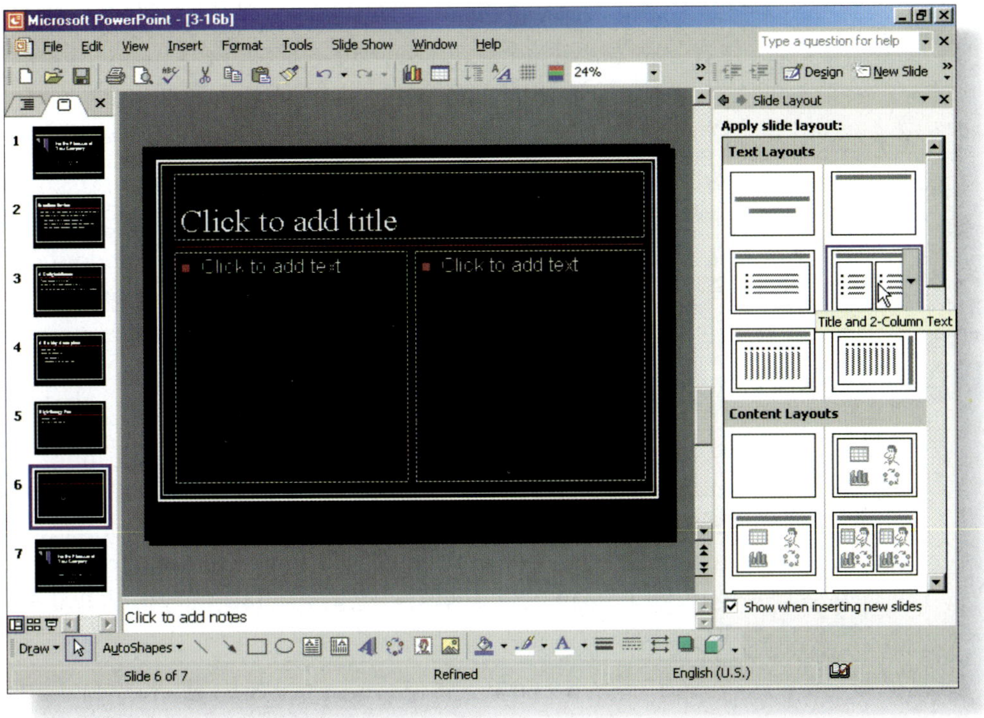

FIGURE 3-15
Choosing a slide layout

4. Key the following bulleted text in the right body text placeholder:
   - **Entertaining customers**
   - **Demonstrating products**
5. Click the Outline tab to display the Outline pane. Notice how each body text placeholder is numbered in the Outline pane.

EXERCISE 3-18 Change the Layout of an Existing Slide

1. Move to slide 5 ("High-Energy Fun") and then click the Title and 2-Column Text layout. The existing body text appears in the left body text placeholder.
2. Select the second bullet ("Sports promotions") and cut it.
3. Click in the right column placeholder (or press Ctrl + Enter) and then paste the bullet. One bullet appears in each column.
4. Add the following item to the left column:
   - **Energetic staff**
5. Add the following item to the right column:
   - **Special event tie-ins**

6. Create headers and footers for notes and handouts: include the date and your name at the top of the page, and the page number and the text ***[your initials]*3-18** at the bottom.
7. Add the footer **Good 4 U Restaurant** on every slide except the title.
8. Move to slide 1, spell-check the presentation, and save it as ***[your initials]*3-18** in your Lesson 3 folder.
9. Preview and then print the presentation as handouts, 9 slides per page, grayscale, landscape, framed. Keep the presentation open for the next exercise.

Working with Speaker's Notes

Speakers often use notes to guide their presentations. In PowerPoint, you can create notes pages for your slides. A printed *notes page* contains a small picture of the slide above text about the slide. The text can include a script, comments, or reminders. Notes pages have additional uses: distribute them as handouts to the audience or include them with presentations published on the Web.

EXERCISE 3-19 Create Speaker's Notes

You key notes directly into the Notes pane, which you can make larger, if needed. Text that is wider than the Notes pane automatically wraps to a new line.

1. Display slide 2 and click the Notes pane to activate it.
2. Key the following text:

   Your choice of a meeting place says a lot about your organization. Good 4 U focuses on service for two reasons:
3. Resize the Notes pane by placing the mouse pointer on the horizontal border between the Slide and Notes panes. The pointer changes to a two-headed arrow ÷. Drag the border up, enlarging the Notes pane until it fills approximately half the window. (See Figure 3-16 on the next page.)
4. Key the following numbered note under the text in the expanded Notes pane:

   1. We want you, your employees, and your guests (friends, clients, investors) to feel at ease.
5. Press Enter. The AutoCorrect Options button appears on the right side of the Notes pane.
6. Click the AutoCorrect Options button and choose Undo Automatic Numbering.

FIGURE 3-16
Resizing the Notes pane

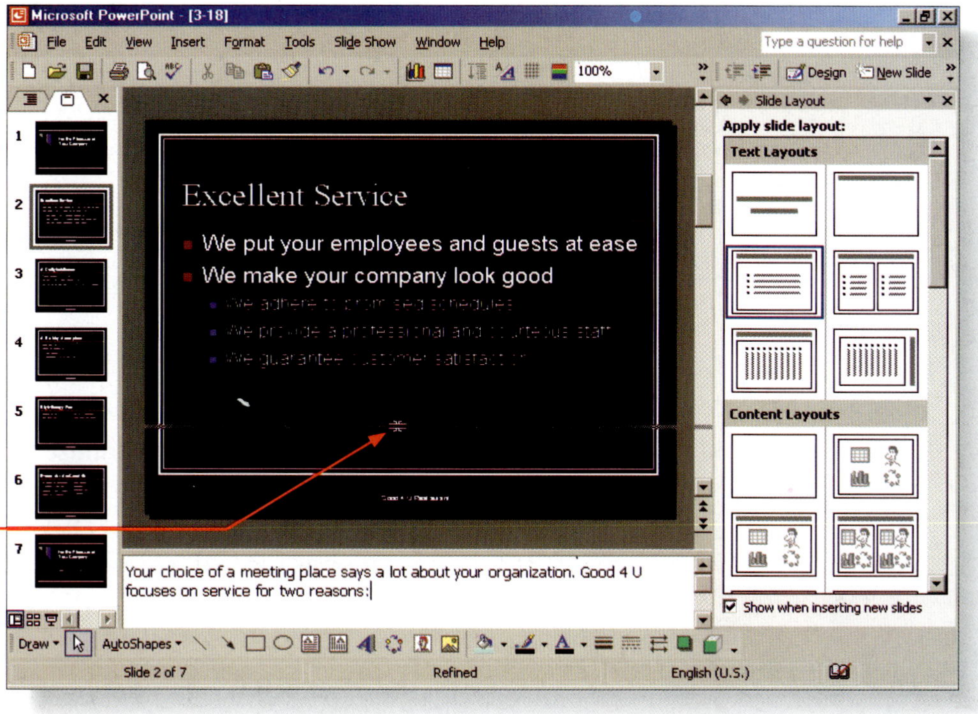

Two-headed arrow pointer

NOTE: You can customize the size of each pane (Slide, Notes, and Outline) by dragging the pane borders.

7. Key the following numbered note under the first one.

   2. We want our professionalism to mirror yours.

8. Move to slide 3 and key the following in the Notes pane on three lines:

   Distribute menus.
   Point out vegetarian and meat dishes.
   Point out healthy beverages.

9. Using the two-headed arrow pointer ÷, drag the upper border of the Notes pane down to make it approximately 1 inch tall.

10. Check spelling in the presentation.

NOTE: The spell-checker checks for errors in note text, header and footer text, and slide text.

11. Change the notes and handouts footer text to ***[your initials]*3-19**.

12. Move to slide 1 and save the presentation as ***[your initials]*3-19** in your Lesson 3 folder.

EXERCISE 3-20 Print Notes Pages

You print notes pages by choosing options in either the Print dialog box or the Print Preview window.

1. Open the Print dialog box. From the Print what drop-down list, choose Notes Pages.
2. Under Print range, select Slides. Key **2-3** in the text box to print notes pages for slides 2 and 3 only.
3. Choose Grayscale.
4. Click Preview.
5. In the Print Preview window, if the display is landscape oriented, click the Portrait button.
6. Click Print to return to the Print dialog box and click OK. Click Close to close the Print Preview window. Close the presentation.

USING HELP

In this lesson you worked with many keyboard shortcuts to help navigate text placeholders and to insert slides. PowerPoint Help has numerous lists of keyboard shortcuts that can speed up your work. It's not necessary to memorize them all, but you should search for shortcuts for operations that you find you are frequently performing.

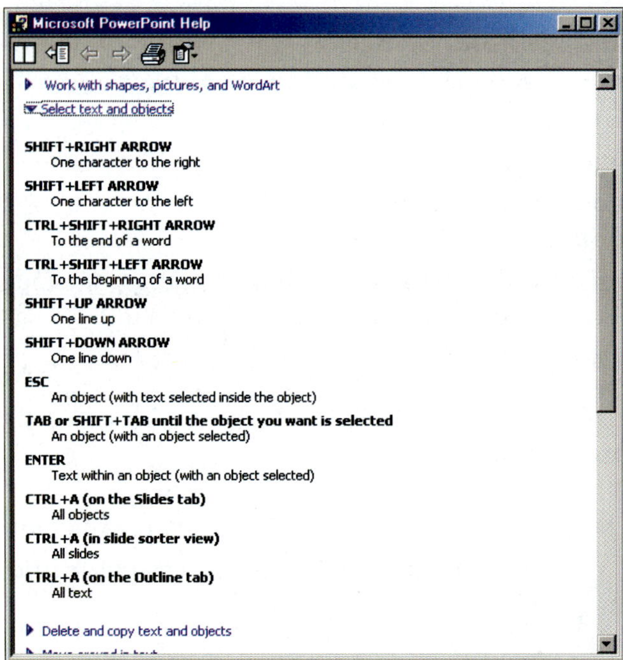

FIGURE 3-17 Using Help to find keyboard shortcuts

Explore keyboard shortcuts:

1. Key **Keyboard** in the Ask a Question box and press Enter.
2. Select Keyboard shortcuts from the drop-down list.
3. Under Common Microsoft PowerPoint tasks, choose the fifth topic, Select text and objects. Maximize the Help window to see the list below the selected topic.

4. Review the list of keyboard shortcuts displayed and then click some other topics.
5. Close the Help window when you finish.

LESSON 3 Summary

- Creating a presentation from scratch lets you concentrate on textual content without the distraction of design elements. Anytime during the process, you can choose a design and color scheme.
- Keyboard shortcuts are a big time-saver when creating a presentation from scratch. For example: Ctrl + Enter moves to the next text placeholder; Ctrl + M inserts a new slide.
- When you insert a new slide, you can choose a slide layout. Slide layouts can be either text layouts or content layouts. They contain various arrangements of text and content placeholders.
- As you key text, PowerPoint's AutoCorrect feature automatically changes common errors that it detects. A smart tag—the AutoCorrect Options button—alerts you of the change and enables you to undo it.
- Slides from another presentation can easily be inserted into your presentation by using the Slide Finder dialog box or by using the Cut, Copy, and Paste commands.
- Promoting and demoting text on a slide is similar to working with an outline in a word processor. When you demote text, you increase its indent. When you promote text, you decrease its indent.
- PowerPoint enables you to undo—and if you change your mind—redo multiple editing actions. The default number of available undos is 20. When you save a presentation, the list of undos is cleared.
- Another way to create a new presentation from scratch is to start with a design template and then insert slides and key text. Choose a design template from the Slide Design task pane.
- Each design template has several predefined color schemes associated with it. You choose color schemes by first clicking Color Schemes on the Slide Design task pane.
- Design templates and color schemes can be applied to individual slides, to a group of selected slides, or to an entire presentation. To apply to a group of slides, first select their slide thumbnails.
- The Clipboard task pane can store up to 24 items that you cut or copy from a presentation. The items can be text, entire slides, or other objects. Insert a

Clipboard task pane item at the current location in your presentation by clicking the item.

- The Clipboard task pane makes it easy to copy items from one presentation to another. Open both presentations; then switch between them by clicking the filename on the Windows task bar or by choosing the file from the Window menu.
- Slides can be rearranged by using drag-and-drop or by using the Cut, Copy, and Paste commands. Text can also be moved or copied by using these commands.
- The Paste Options button enables you to choose between a pasted item's source formatting and its destination formatting. The source is the slide or placeholder from which the item was cut or copied, and the destination is the location where it will be pasted.
- After a slide is inserted, you choose its slide layout from the Slide Layout task pane. If you change your mind later, you can change the layout of the current slide or of a group of selected slide thumbnails.
- Speaker's notes are keyed in the Notes pane, below the Slide pane in Normal view. They can be used as a script for the presenter or as supplemental information for the audience.
- Notes pages contain a small image of a slide at the top of the page and the speaker's notes associated with that slide at the bottom of the page. Notes pages are printed by using the Print dialog box.

LESSON 3 Command Summary

FEATURE	BUTTON	MENU	KEYBOARD	SPEECH?
Insert new slide	New Slide	Insert, New Slide	Ctrl + M	✓
Change slide layout		Format, Slide Layout		✓
Apply design template	Design	Format, Slide Design		✓
Demote			Tab	✓
Promote			Shift + Tab	✓
Undo		Edit, Undo	Ctrl + Z	✓

continues

LESSON 3 Command Summary *continued*

FEATURE	BUTTON	MENU	KEYBOARD	SPEECH?
Redo		Edit, Redo	Ctrl + Y	✓
Create new presentation		File, New	Ctrl + N	✓
Move to next placeholder			Ctrl + Enter	
Choose color scheme		Format, Slide Design, Color Schemes		✓
Cut selected object or text		Edit, Cut	Ctrl + X	✓
Copy selected object or text		Edit, Copy	Ctrl + C	✓
Paste (insert) cut or copied object or text		Edit, Paste	Ctrl + V	✓
Print notes pages		File, Print, Print what		✓
Activate placeholder			Ctrl + Enter	
Deactivate placeholder			Esc	
Insert line break			Shift + Enter	
AutoCorrect options		Tools, AutoCorrect Options		✓
Insert slides from other files		Insert, Slides from Files		✓
Apply color scheme	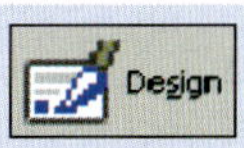	Slide Design task pane, Color Schemes		✓
Switch to another open file		Window, [filename]	Ctrl + F6	✓
Display Clipboard task pane		Edit, Office Clipboard		✓
Clear the Clipboard task pane		Clipboard task pane, Clear All		✓
Paste options				✓

POWERPOINT

Concepts Review

TRUE/FALSE QUESTIONS

Each of the following statements is either true or false. Indicate your choice by circling T or F.

T F 1. You can start a new presentation with a blank template or a design template.

T F 2. You can choose a slide layout in the Slide Layout task pane.

T F 3. You can add a new slide by pressing Ctrl+Y.

T F 4. You can use Ctrl+Tab to demote bullets and Alt+Tab to promote bullets.

T F 5. The keyboard shortcut for undoing a task is Ctrl+Z.

T F 6. You can change a presentation's overall design in the Slide Layout task pane.

T F 7. The only way to insert a slide from another presentation is to use Cut and Paste.

T F 8. You can print notes pages in either grayscale or color.

SHORT ANSWER QUESTIONS

Write the correct answer in the space provided.

1. Which task pane do you use to change a slide from a Title slide to a Title and 2-Column Text slide?

   ____

2. Name three ways to insert a new slide.

   ____

3. You just promoted a bullet. Name at least two ways you can use the mouse to return the bullet to its original size and position.

   ____

4. How do you clear the Office Clipboard of all its contents?

   ____

5. How many items can the Office Clipboard store at one time?

   ____

6. Name two ways to switch from one of several open presentations to another.

____

7. How do you change the color scheme of just one slide in a presentation?

____

8. Which drop-down list in the Print dialog box contains the option to print notes pages?

____

CRITICAL THINKING

Answer these questions on a separate page. There are no right or wrong answers. Support your answers with examples from your own experience, if possible.

1. Review PowerPoint's design templates. In what kinds of presentations might you use the different templates?
2. What are some advantages of starting with a blank presentation instead of using the AutoContent Wizard? Which method do you prefer and why?

Lesson Applications

EXERCISE 3-21

Create a new blank presentation, add slides, change a slide layout, cut and paste text, apply a design template, and change the color scheme.

1. Start a blank presentation.
2. Create a title slide with the text **First in Food Safety** as the title and **Good 4 U Employee Training** as the subtitle
3. Using the Title and Text layout, create three new slides, as shown in Figure 3-18.

FIGURE 3-18

Slide 2

Our Food Safety Programs — Title

- Food handler training
- Management inspections
- Safety supervisors on-site
- Reports to USDA

Slide 3

Safe Food-Handling Practices — Title

- Wear gloves, hair nets, and beard nets
- Wash hands before and after handling food
- Wear clean uniforms
- No smoking

Slide 4

Food Procurement — Title

- Know your suppliers
- Prefer local growers
- Prefer organic food
- Insist on freshness
- Insist on cleanliness
- Test for pesticides

4. Change slide 4 to the Title and 2-Column Text layout.
5. Cut the last three bullets in column 1 and paste them into column 2.

6. Check both body text placeholders for extra blank lines and remove them.
7. Apply the design template Eclipse to the presentation (use ScreenTips to find it).
8. Change the color scheme to the first one in the second row (white background with red, yellow, and blue accents).
9. Change the first slide only to the color scheme with the black background and red, yellow, and green accents.

REVIEW: To change the color scheme for just one slide, select the slide and then point to the color scheme sample, click the down arrow button, and choose Apply to Selected Slides.

10. Check spelling in the presentation.
11. Apply the Comb Horizontal slide transition to slide 1 by using the Slow speed and a sound of your choice. To the other slides, apply the Box Out transition at Slow speed with no sound.
12. View the presentation as a slide show, noting that the first slide is a different color than the others.
13. Create a handout header and footer: include the date and your name as the header, and the page number and text ***[your initials]*3-21** as the footer.
14. Move to slide 1 and save the presentation as ***[your initials]*3-21** in your Lesson 3 folder.
15. Preview and then print the presentation as handouts, 4 slides per page, grayscale, framed, landscape. Close the presentation.

EXERCISE 3-22

Change slide layouts, demote bullets, add slides, cut and paste text, insert a slide from another presentation, and change the color scheme.

1. Open the file **SafeFd1**.
2. Change the color scheme to the last color scheme sample—with the black background. (Use the scroll bar to locate it.)
3. On slide 4, cut the bulleted items in column 2 and paste them at the bottom of column 1. Ignore the Paste Options button that appears; the text is formatted correctly.
4. Change the layout of slide 4 to the Title and Text layout.
5. Edit text in slide 4 and demote bullets as shown in Figure 3-19 (on the next page).

FIGURE 3-19

6. Add a new slide 5, using the text shown in Figure 3-20.

FIGURE 3-20

Inspections

- Training inspections
  - Scheduled
  - Cooperative
- Internal evaluation inspections
- USDA inspections

7. Without closing **SafeFd1**, open the file **SafeFd2**.
8. Display the Clipboard task pane; then copy slide 2 ("Should We Be Safe?").
9. Close **SafeFd2**; then use the Clipboard task pane to insert the copied slide after slide 1 in **SafeFd1**.

10. Click the Paste Options button and choose Keep Source Formatting.
11. Check spelling in the presentation.
12. Apply an animation scheme of your choice to all slides in the presentation.

13. Create a handout header and footer: include the date and your name as the header, and the page number and text ***[your initials]*3-22** as the footer.

14. Move to slide 1 and save the presentation as ***[your initials]*3-22** in your Lesson 3 folder.

15. Preview and then print the presentation as handouts, 6 slides per page, grayscale, framed. Close the presentation.

EXERCISE 3-23

Start a new presentation, add slides, demote bullets, apply a template, and change the color scheme.

1. Create a new presentation, using the text shown in Figure 3-21.

FIGURE 3-21

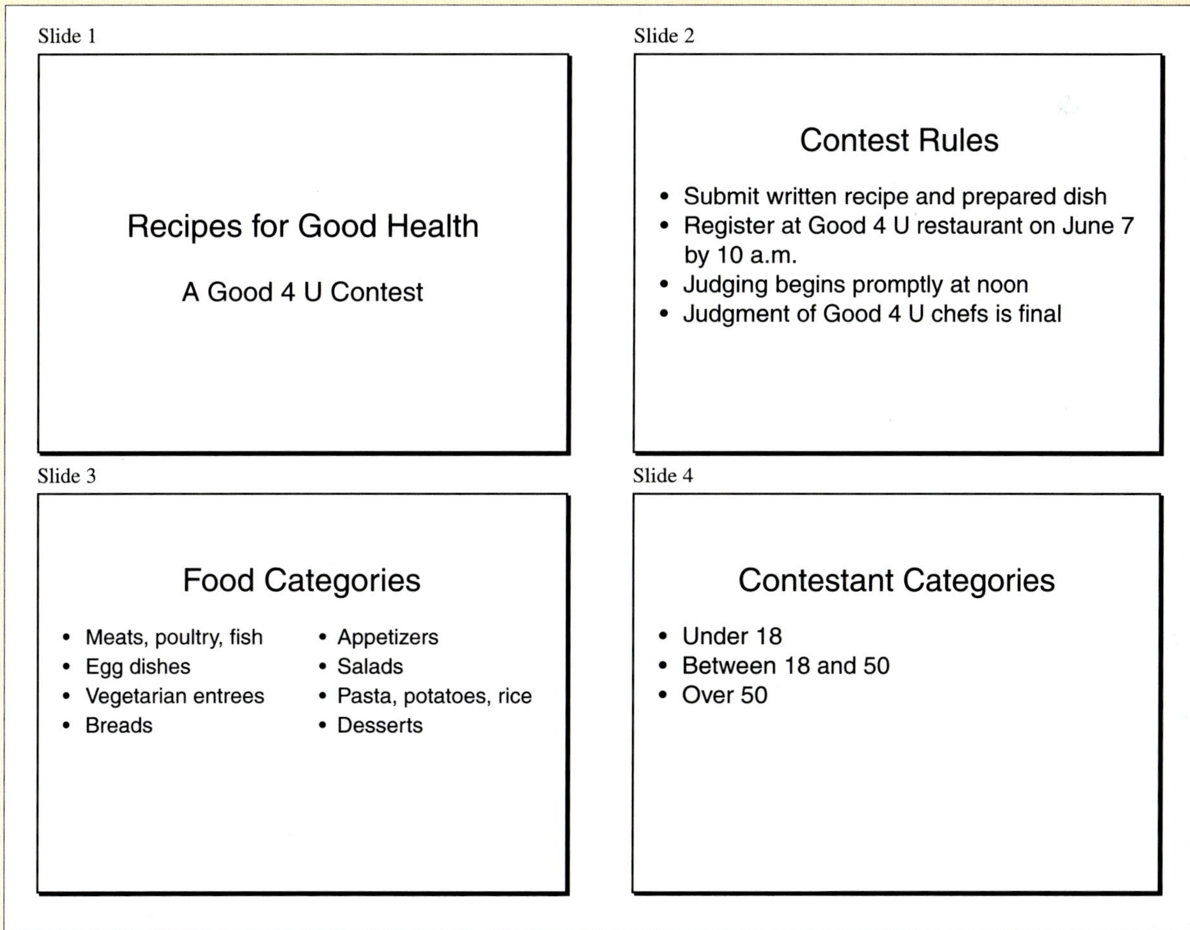

continues

FIGURE 3-21 *continued*

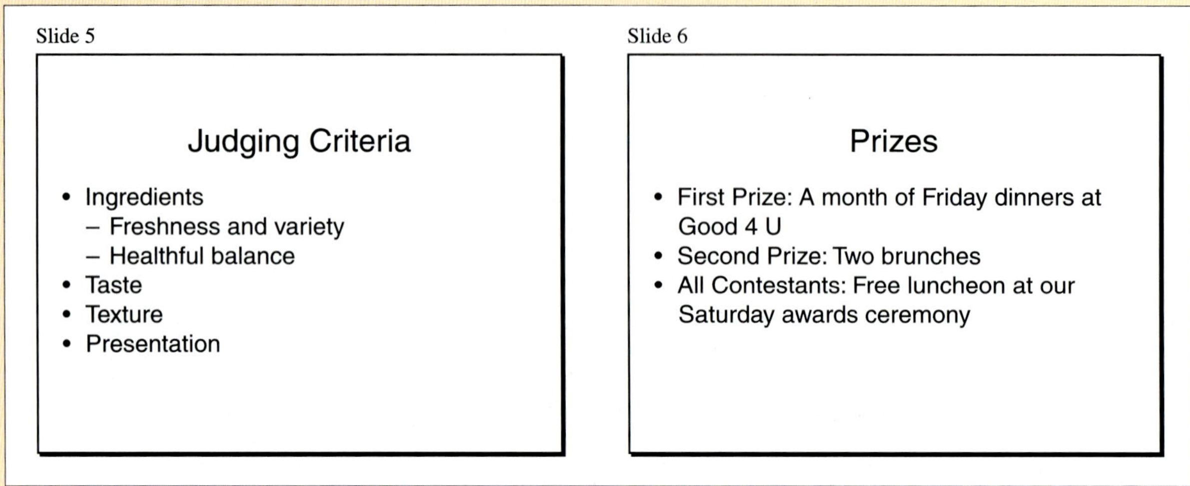

2. Apply a template and color scheme of your choice.
3. Reverse the positions of slides 2 and 3.
4. Check spelling in the presentation.
5. Add an animation scheme to the first slide only and a slide transition to all slides.
6. Add slide numbers to all slides.
7. Create a handout header and footer: include the date and your name as the header, and the page number and text ***[your initials]*3-23** as the footer.
8. Move to slide 1 and save the presentation as ***[your initials]*3-23** in your Lesson 3 folder.
9. Preview and then print slide 3 in full size in grayscale or in color if available.
10. Preview and then print the entire presentation as handouts, 6 slides per page, grayscale, framed. Close the presentation.

EXERCISE 3-24 *Challenge Yourself*

Add a new slide, choose a slide layout, demote bullets, insert slides from another presentation, and add speaker's notes.

1. Open the file **CookCon1**.
2. On slide 1, key the subtitle **Rules, Judging, and Prizes**
3. Add a new slide after the title slide, using the text shown in Figure 3-22 (on the next page).

FIGURE 3-22

```
Contest Rules

•  Submit an original written recipe and dish
   •  Good 4 U Restaurant, Saturday, June 7
   •  10 a.m. to noon
•  Judging is from noon to 2 p.m.
•  Judges' decisions are final
•  Anyone may enter except Good 4 U employees and their families
```

4. Using either the Clipboard task pane or the Slides from Files command, insert slide 2 ("Ingredients to Use") and slide 3 ("Awards") from the presentation **CookCon2** at the end of the presentation.
5. Change slide 5 ("Ingredients to Use") to a Title and 2-Column Text layout; then cut the body text from slide 3 and insert it in the second column of slide 5.
6. Change the title of slide 5 to **Recipe Ingredients**. Insert a new line at the top of the first column. Key **Use** on the new line and demote all the text below it. Insert **Avoid** at the top of the second column and demote all the text below it.
7. Key a speaker's note on slide 1 stating that local businesses are sponsoring this event.
8. Key a speaker's note on slide 2 stating that three volunteer taste testers will be chosen from the entrants.
9. Delete slide 3 ("Ingredients to Avoid"); then rearrange the remaining slides where needed so they appear in the following order:
   - Slide 1 ("Recipe Contest")
   - Slide 2 ("Contest Rules")
   - Slide 3 ("Recipe Ingredients")
   - Slide 4 ("Awards")
   - Slide 5 ("Judging Criteria")
10. Check spelling in the presentation.
11. Review the presentation as a slide show.
12. Create a handout header and footer: include the date and your name as the header, and the page number and text ***[your initials]*3-24** as the footer.
13. Move to slide 1 and save the presentation as ***[your initials]*3-24** in your Lesson 3 folder.

14. Preview and then print slides 1 and 2 as notes pages in grayscale.
15. Preview and then print the presentation as handouts, 6 slides per page, grayscale, framed. Close the presentation.

On Your Own

In these exercises you work on your own, as you would in a real-life work environment. Use the skills you've learned to accomplish the task—and be creative.

EXERCISE 3-25

Imagine that you are organizing a cooking contest for a local gourmet grocery store. Create a presentation describing the contest, including rules, location, and categories. Insert some slides from the student files used in this lesson and edit them to work for your contest. Apply a design template of your choice to the first and last slides in your presentation and apply a different but complementary design template to the other slides. Add an animation scheme of your choice. Save the presentation as ***[your initials]*****3-25**. Preview and then print the presentation as handouts.

EXERCISE 3-26

Create a presentation describing briefly the history of your family, the family of a prominent person in your community, or the family of a national celebrity. Some information that you might include is when the family immigrated to this country, interesting occupations or other facts about individual members of the family, hobbies, and cultural or athletic achievements. Create at least six slides by using design templates, color schemes, and slide transitions. Save the presentation as ***[your initials]*****3-26**. Preview and then print the presentation as handouts.

EXERCISE 3-27

Choose three or more short poems, all by the same author. Create a presentation that includes a title slide with the subject of the poems for the title and the poet's name for the subtitle. For example: "Children's Poems by Mary Moore" or "Romantic Poems by Harry Heartly." After the title slide, insert one slide for each poem, keying its title in the title placeholder and its text in the body text placeholder. Choose a design template and a color scheme that conveys the mood of the poetry. You might want to use a different template or color scheme for each poem. Save the presentation as ***[your initials]*****3-27**. Preview and then print the presentation as handouts.

LESSON 4

Outlines, Hyperlinks, and HTML

OBJECTIVES

MOUS ACTIVITIES

In this lesson:

PP2002 1-1
PP2002 1-2
PP2002 2-1
PP2002 2-2
PP2002 4-4
PP2002 4-8
PP2002 4-10
PP2002 5-1
PP2002 6-4
PP2002 8-4

See Appendix E.

After completing this lesson, you will be able to:

1. **Create a presentation by using the Outline pane.**
2. **Add new slides in the Outline pane.**
3. **Promote and demote outline entries.**
4. **Rearrange text and slides in the Outline pane.**
5. **Import and export outlines.**
6. **Save a presentation as a Web page.**
7. **Work with hyperlinks.**

Estimated Time: 1½ hours

Outlining helps you organize and create a presentation by focusing on content and flow rather than appearance. Working in the Outline pane, you can key text for your slides and then easily rearrange the text. You can also import a Word outline to create a PowerPoint presentation automatically and you can export PowerPoint outline text to Word.

Besides outlining, this lesson also introduces you to hyperlinks and to the HTML file format, which you use to save your PowerPoint presentations as Web pages.

Creating a Presentation by Using the Outline Pane

The Outline pane appears in Normal view. To display the pane, click the **Outline** tab on the upper left side of your PowerPoint window. To give yourself plenty of room for keying text, you can drag the Outline pane's right border to the right.

EXERCISE 4-1 Start a New Presentation in the Outline Pane

When you work in the Outline pane, display the Outlining toolbar, which provides tools to help organize your text.

1. Start a new presentation by using the design template **Crayons**.
2. Click the **Outline** tab to display the Outline pane. In the Outline pane, the blank title slide is represented as a numbered slide icon.

REVIEW: If the Outline tab and Slides tab are not visible, click the Normal View button.

3. To display the Outlining toolbar, open the **View** menu, choose **Toolbars**, and then choose **Outlining** from the submenu. (You can also right-click a toolbar and choose **Outlining**.) The Outlining toolbar appears vertically on the left side of your screen.
4. Enlarge the Outline pane by dragging its right border about 1 inch to the right (by using the +||+ pointer).

5. To gain even more room, close the task pane by clicking its Close button on the right end of the task pane title bar.

FIGURE 4-1
Closing a task pane

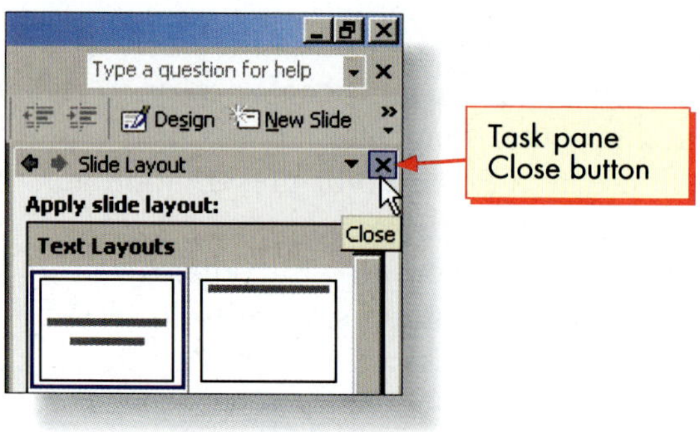

6. To activate the Outline pane, click anywhere inside it. Notice the insertion point to the right of the slide icon.
7. Key **Promotional Posters** as the slide title. The title line appears next to the slide icon. It also appears as red text in the Slide pane. (See Figure 4-2 on the next page.)
8. Press Enter. A new slide icon for slide 2 appears.
9. Press Tab. The new line is now the indented subtitle for slide 1.

FIGURE 4-2
Creating a presentation by using the Outline pane

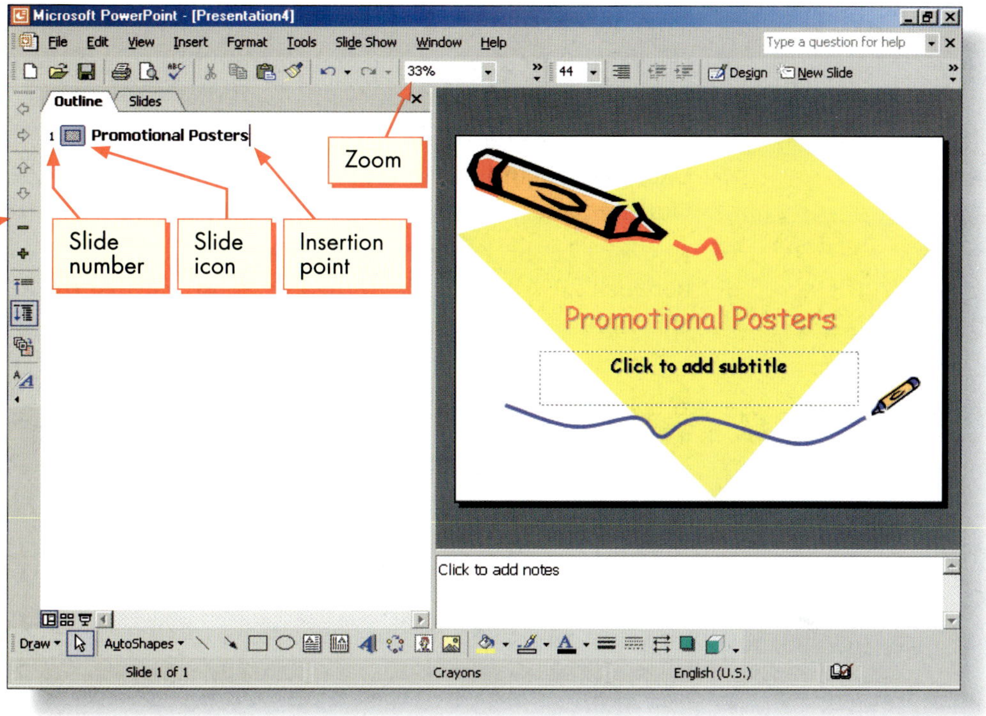

NOTE: Remember from the previous lesson that Tab demotes text, so demoting the title in slide 2 made the line become the subtitle of slide 1.

10. Key **Good 4 U Public Relations Training** as the subtitle text.

EXERCISE 4-2 Use Zoom to Adjust the Size of Outline Text

Lesson 1 introduced you to using *Zoom* in Slide Sorter view. You can also use Zoom to change the magnification of text in the Outline pane, change the size of slide thumbnails, or change the magnification of selected objects on a slide in the Slide pane.

When you use Zoom, first click the pane that you want to magnify. It is important to realize that Zoom does not change the actual size of objects, only the size at which you view them while working.

1. Click anywhere in the Slide pane.

2. On the Standard toolbar, click the arrow next to Zoom and choose 100% from the list box. The objects in the Slide pane are enlarged.

REVIEW: You might need to click the Toolbar Options button to locate the Zoom box and other tools used in this lesson.

3. Click the Zoom arrow again and choose Fit at the bottom of the list box.
4. Click the Slides tab on the Outline and Slides pane to display slide thumbnails. Click the slide thumbnails, and then change the zoom 100%. The slide thumbnail is enlarged.
5. Click the Outline tab to redisplay the Outline pane. Click anywhere in the Outline pane, and then change the zoom to 50%.
6. Key **45%** in the Zoom box and press Enter. You can key any percentage between 20% and 400% in the Zoom box. Adjust the zoom level so that you can comfortably key text.

Adding a New Slide in the Outline Pane

When you insert a slide at any point after the title slide in the Outline pane, it is automatically formatted with the Title and Text layout. As when working in the Slide pane, you can insert a new slide by using the methods shown in the previous lesson:

- Click New Slide on the Formatting toolbar.
- From the Insert menu, choose New Slide or press Ctrl+M.

EXERCISE 4-3 Add New Slides in the Outline Pane

When working in the Outline pane, another way to insert a new slide is to press Enter at the end of a title line. Note that when the insertion point is at the end of a slide title line, pressing Enter inserts a new slide; when the insertion point is at the end of a bulleted text line, pressing Enter inserts a new bulleted line at the same level as the previous line.

1. Working in the Outline pane, place your insertion point anywhere in the slide 1 text and press Ctrl+M. A second slide icon appears. In the Slide pane, a blank slide is displayed using the Title and Text layout. The Slide Layout task pane might also appear.
2. Key **Poster Purpose** as the title and press Enter. A new slide icon appears.
3. Press Tab. The new slide icon changes to a bulleted line for slide 2.
4. Key **Inform customers** and press Enter. A second bullet appears.
5. Key the following bulleted items, pressing Enter to start each new line:
   - **Promote our image**
   - **Design suggestions**
   - **Keep it simple**
   - **Limit the number of text items**

6. Press Ctrl+M. A new slide icon appears. Notice in the Slide pane that the slide has the same layout (Title and Text) as the previous slide.
7. Key the title **Themes** for slide 3.

EXERCISE 4-4 Working with the Title and 2-Column Text Layout

When working in the Outline pane and using a two-column layout, you must use Ctrl+Enter to move to the second column. Lesson 3 showed you how to use Ctrl+Enter in the Slide pane to move from one text placeholder to the next. Pressing Ctrl+Enter does exactly the same thing when you are working in the Outline pane.

1. Click New Slide on the Formatting toolbar. Slide 4 is inserted, both in the Slide pane and in the Outline pane.
2. In the Slide Layout task pane, choose the Title and 2-Column Text layout. Notice the two body text placeholders in the Slide pane.
3. With the insertion point in the Outline pane (next to the slide 4 icon) key the title **Suggested Subjects**
4. Press Ctrl+Enter to insert a bulleted line.
5. Key **Menu items** and press Enter to insert a new bulleted line. Notice the small numbered box to the left of the bullet. This indicates that the bullet is in the first of two body text placeholders on the current slide.
6. Key **Price specials** and press Ctrl+Enter to move to the first bullet in the second column.

NOTE: Notice that Ctrl+Enter, Ctrl+M, Tab, and Shift+Tab work the same way in the Outline pane as in the Slide pane. You may want to review the table "Using the Keyboard to Navigate on a Slide and in a Presentation" in Lesson 3.

7. Key **Holiday events** and press Enter. Key **Sports events** as the second bullet. (See Figure 4-3 on the next page.)
8. Press Ctrl+M and insert a new slide with the Title and Text layout. Key the title **Readability**. You should have five slides listed in the Outline pane.
9. Press Ctrl+Enter and add the following bulleted items on slide 5:
   - **Use large, simple titles**
   - **Use color and graphics**
   - **Limit the number of high-contrast colors**
10. Move to slide 1 and save the presentation as ***[your initials]*4-4** in a new folder for Lesson 4. Do not close the presentation.

FIGURE 4-3
Creating a slide with the Title and 2-Column Text layout

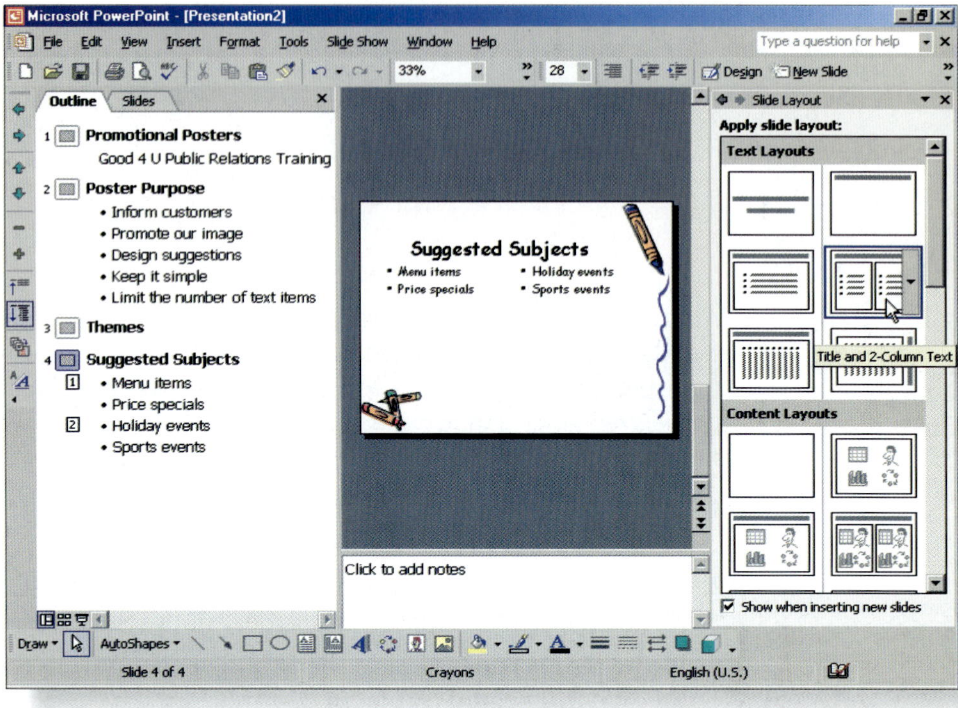

Promoting and Demoting Outline Text

To demote slide titles and promote or demote bulleted items, you can:

- Click the Promote button or the Demote button on the Outlining toolbar.
- Click the Decrease Indent button or the Increase Indent button on the Formatting toolbar.
- Press Tab to demote an entry or Shift + Tab to promote an entry.
- Select an item and drag it to the right to demote it or to the left to promote it.

In the Outline pane, you can also join or split slides by demoting or promoting text. When a title is demoted, it becomes a bulleted item on the previous slide. When a first-level bulleted item is promoted, it becomes the title of a new slide.

EXERCISE 4-5 Promote and Demote Text by Using the Toolbar and Keyboard

To promote or demote a bulleted item in the Outline pane, position the insertion point anywhere on the item and then click the appropriate button on the Outlining toolbar or on the Formatting toolbar. If you prefer using the keyboard, press either Tab or Shift + Tab.

If you click the bullet for an item, the bulleted line and its sub-bullets below it are selected and can be promoted or demoted all at the same time.

1. Working on slide 2 in the Outline pane, position the insertion point anywhere in the line "Design suggestions."
2. Click the Demote button on the Outlining toolbar (or press Tab). The bullet becomes a sub-bullet of the line above it.

NOTE: In Outline view, you can click anywhere in an entry or select the entry before demoting or promoting with Tab or Shift + Tab. When you're working in the Slide pane, if the insertion point is placed inside the text, pressing Tab or Shift + Tab inserts a tab space.

3. Click the Promote button to restore the original position.
4. Select the last two bulleted items on slide 2 by dragging the I-beam across the text.
5. Demote the selected bulleted items by using any method. In outline terminology, slide 2 now has three levels: the title is level 1, "Design suggestions" is at level 2, and "Keep it simple" is at level 3.
6. Position the pointer over the bullet to the left of "Design suggestions." Notice that the pointer changes to a four-pointed arrow ✥.
7. Click the "Design suggestions" bullet. Notice that this bullet and its sub-bullets are selected.
8. Click the Demote button twice. The selected items are demoted two more levels. There are now four indent levels on the slide.
9. Promote the selected bulleted items twice by using any method.

TABLE 4-1 Outlining Toolbar Buttons

BUTTON	PURPOSE
Promote	Raises item one outline level
Demote	Lowers item one outline level
Move Up	Moves selection up one line
Move Down	Moves selection down one line

continues

TABLE 4-1 Outlining Toolbar Buttons *continued*

BUTTON	PURPOSE
Collapse	Displays only titles for selected slides
Expand	Displays details for selected slides
Collapse All	Displays only titles for entire outline
Expand All	Displays detail lines for entire outline
Summary Slide	Creates a new slide from titles of selected slides
Show Formatting	Turns display of character formatting on and off

NOTE: At the end of this lesson, the Command Summary lists keyboard shortcuts for Outlining toolbar buttons.

EXERCISE 4-6 Split and Join Slides

If you have too many bulleted items on one slide, you can divide the items into two slides by promoting a selected item to level 1 (the slide title level). The promoted item becomes the title of a new slide.

You can also join two slides by demoting the title of a slide. The demoted title and its body text are then added to the bottom of the previous slide.

1. Use the vertical scroll bar on the right side of the Outline pane to display slides 4 and 5.
2. Position the pointer over the slide 5 icon. Notice that the pointer changes to a four-pointed arrow.
3. Click the slide 5 icon. The entire slide and all its bullets are selected.
4. Click the Demote button. All of the slide's text is added to the end of slide 4—slide 5 has been joined with slide 4. In the Slide pane, notice that the text is at the bottom of the right column.
5. Click the Promote button. The selected text becomes slide 5 again.
6. Scroll up in the Outline pane so that slide 2 is displayed.

7. On slide 2, click the bullet to the left of "Design suggestions" to select the bullet and the sub-bullets under it.
8. Click the Promote button . The selected text becomes slide 3 with the title "Design suggestions" and two bulleted items, "Keep it simple" and "Limit the number of text items."
9. Capitalize the word "suggestions" in the slide 3 title to make it consistent with other slide titles.
10. Compare the outline text in your presentation with Figure 4-4. If necessary, promote and demote items to match the figure.

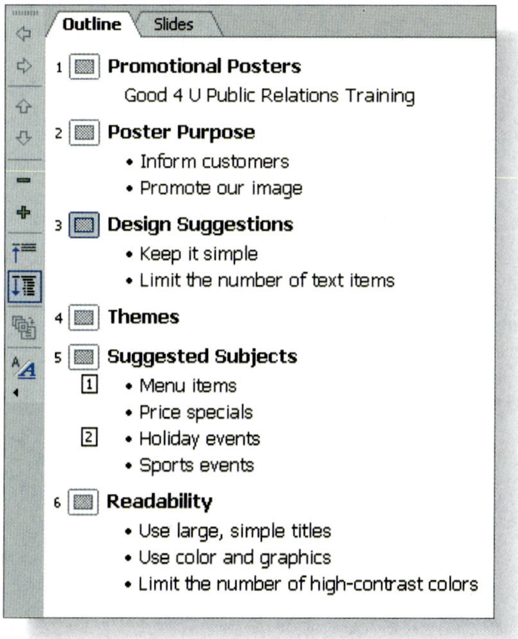

FIGURE 4-4
Joining and splitting slides

11. Move to slide 1 and save the presentation as ***[your initials]*4-6** in your Lesson 4 folder. Do not close the presentation.

EXERCISE 4-7 Promote and Demote by Dragging

Another way to promote and demote an outline item is by dragging. To do this, point to a bullet, and when you see the four-pointed arrow ✥ drag the bullet left or right. As you're dragging, a two-pointed horizontal arrow ↔ should appear, indicating that you can move left or right.

If you drag a selection up or down instead of left or right, the four-pointed arrow ✥ changes to a two-pointed vertical arrow ↕, indicating that you might be changing the order of the lines or dragging the material to a different slide.

If this happens unintentionally, release your mouse button, click Undo [Undo button], and start again.

1. Move the arrow pointer over the slide icon for "Design Suggestions" until it becomes a four-pointed arrow ✥.
2. Click the slide icon. The slide title for slide 3 and its bulleted items are selected.
3. Drag the icon to the right. The pointer becomes a two-pointed arrow ↔, and a vertical line appears.

FIGURE 4-5
Demoting by dragging

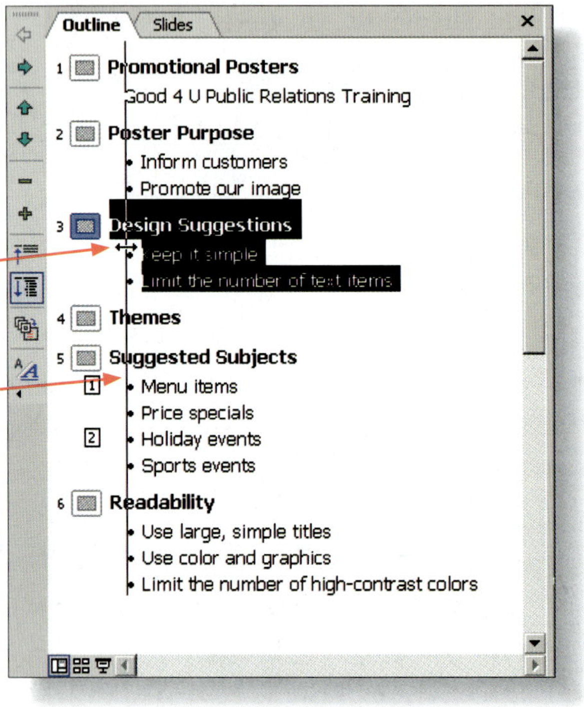

4. Drag until the vertical line aligns with the bullets and then release. The title is demoted to a bullet, and its bullets are demoted to sub-bullets.
5. Position the pointer over the "Design Suggestions" bullet, drag the selected material farther right, and release. The items are demoted another level.
6. Drag the selected material back to the left until the vertical line aligns with the right edge of the slide icons, and release. The material is once again promoted to a separate slide: slide 3.

EXERCISE 4-8 Delete Slides and Slide Text in the Outline Pane

To delete a slide or a bulleted item, you simply click the slide icon or bullet to select it and press Delete. In the Outline pane, you can select multiple contiguous items by using the Shift+click method or dragging the insertion point, but you cannot select noncontiguous items.

1. Point to the bullet in the last line of the outline, "Limit the number of high-contrast colors."
2. Click the bullet to select the line and then press Delete.
3. Assume that this was a mistake and click the Undo button to restore the text.
4. Click the slide icon for slide 4 ("Themes") and press Delete. The slide is deleted, and the remaining slides are renumbered.

Moving Text and Slides in the Outline Pane

In the Outline pane, you can move selected bulleted items or entire slides in several different ways:

- Click the Move Up button or the Move Down button on the Outlining toolbar.
- Drag selected bullets up or down.
- Use Cut and Paste.

If you click the Move Up button or the Move Down button without first selecting an item, only the item that contains the insertion point is moved.

If you want to move entire slides to a new position, first click the Collapse All button to *collapse* the outline. When an outline is collapsed, only the slide icons and the slide titles are displayed. This makes it easier to move an entire slide without accidentally dropping the slide in the middle of another slide. When you want to see the details of the outline, click the Expand All button to *expand* the outline again.

EXERCISE 4-9 Move Bulleted Items

1. On slide 5, select "Use color and graphics" by clicking its bullet.

2. Click the Move Up button on the Outlining toolbar. The selected bullet moves up one line.
3. Click the Move Up button several more times until "Use color and graphics" is the last bullet on the "Design Suggestions" slide.
4. Select the second bullet on the "Design Suggestions" slide ("Limit the number of text items").

5. Click the Move Down button several times until the selected bullet is the first bullet in slide 5 ("Readability").

6. Point to the last bullet on slide 5 ("Limit the number of high-contrast colors").
7. When you see the four-pointed arrow ✥, click the bullet and drag it up. The pointer becomes a two-pointed vertical arrow ↕, and a horizontal line appears.

FIGURE 4-6
Moving an element by dragging

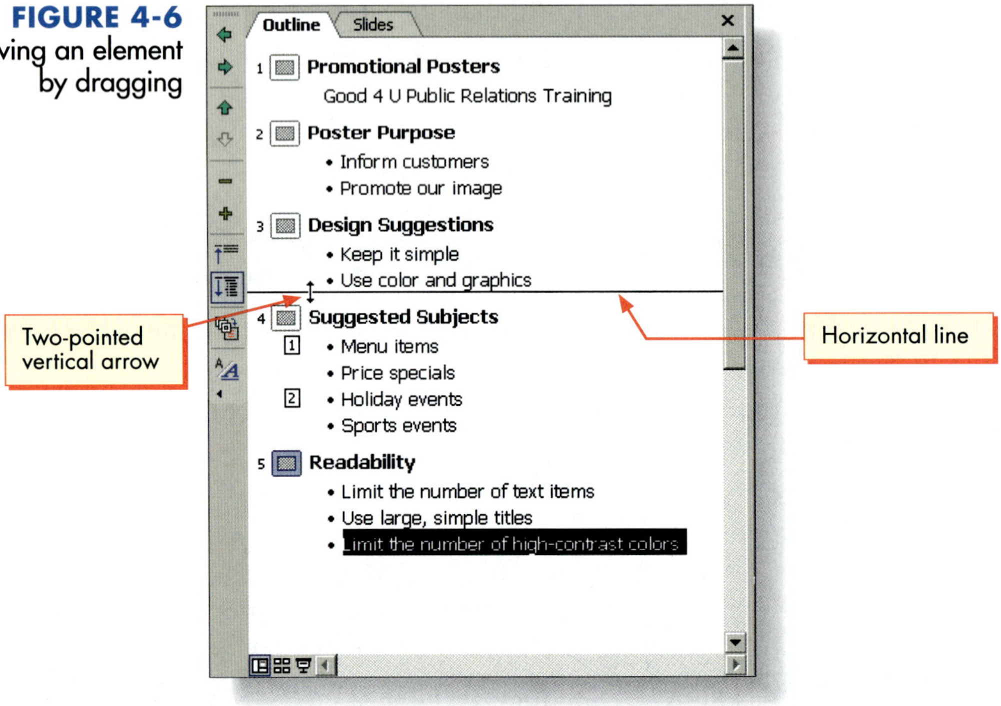

8. Continue to drag up, positioning the horizontal line under "Use color and graphics" on slide 3, and then release.

9. On slide 4, drag the I-beam pointer over the two bulleted items "Holiday events" and "Sports events." Click the Cut button to cut the text.

10. On the same slide, position the insertion point to the left of the "M" in "Menu items" and click the Paste button. All four bulleted items are now in the first column.

NOTE: You can select more than one bullet or slide and drag the selection to a new position. First, drag the I-beam pointer over the text to select it. Next, move the pointer over the selection and use the white drag-and-drop arrow pointer to drag it to a new position. A dotted insertion point guides your placement rather than a horizontal line.

11. Change the layout of slide 4 to the Title and Text layout (one column of bulleted text).
12. On slide 5, move "Use large, simple titles" to the first bullet position on the slide.

EXERCISE 4-10 Change How the Outline Pane Displays Text

By default, the Outline pane displays text in an unformatted style. You can change it to display the text formatting that is used on the actual slides if you prefer. You can also control how much text is displayed by collapsing or expanding the outline.

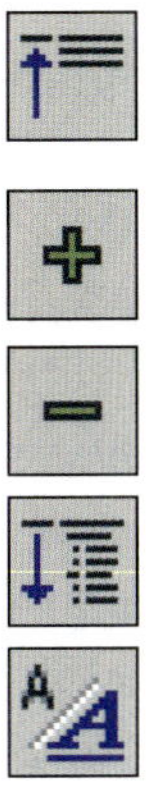

1. Click the Collapse All button on the Outlining toolbar to display only the slide titles in the Outline pane.
2. Click anywhere on the title text for slide 3 ("Design Suggestions").
3. Click the Expand button. The text for slide 3 is expanded, but the other slides remain collapsed.
4. Click the Collapse button. Now all the slides are collapsed.
5. Click the Expand All button to redisplay all the text in the outline.
6. Click the Show Formatting button on the Outlining toolbar. The outline text is now displayed with the same text formatting as in the Slide pane.
7. Click the Show Formatting button again to turn it off.

EXERCISE 4-11 Rearrange Slides in the Outline Pane

When you use the Move Up button or the Move Down button, the selected text moves up or down one line at a time. If you are moving an entire slide, be careful to position the slide between two slides and not in the middle of another slide.

If you collapse an outline before moving slides, all a slide's text will stay together, and there is no danger of dropping a slide in the middle of another slide.

1. Click the "Readability" slide icon to select the entire slide.
2. Click the Move Up button twice. Notice that the last two bullets from slide 4 are now part of slide 5.

FIGURE 4-7 Using the Move Up button

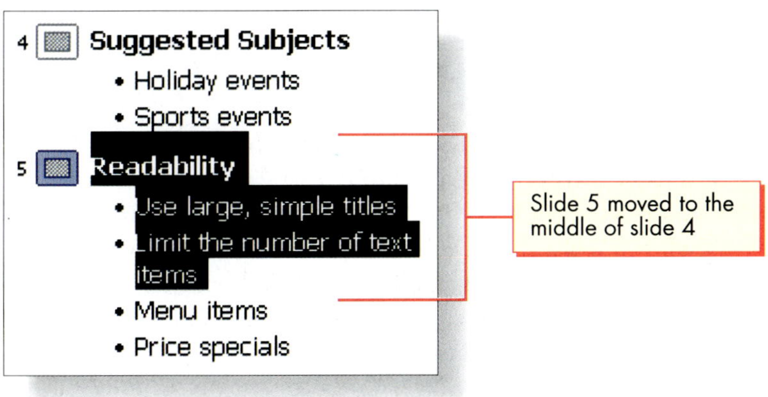

3. Click the Move Down button twice to restore slide 5 to its original position.
4. Click the Collapse All button. Only the slide titles and slide icons are now displayed.
5. Select slide 5 ("Readability"). Drag it up and position it between slides 3 and 4. When you select (or move) a collapsed slide, you select (or move) all its hidden text.

FIGURE 4-8
Dragging in a collapsed outline

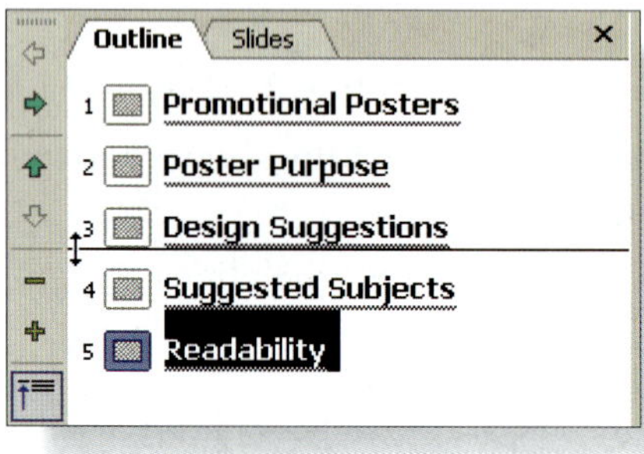

6. Click the Expand All button to display the entire outline.
7. Create a handout header and footer: include the date and your name as the header, and the page number and text ***[your initials]*4-11** as the footer.
8. Move to slide 1 and save the presentation as ***[your initials]*4-11** in your Lesson 4 folder. Leave the presentation open for the next exercise.

EXERCISE 4-12 Print a PowerPoint Outline

In previous lessons you printed either slides or handouts. Using the Print dialog box or the Print Preview window, you can also print a PowerPoint outline.

1. Open the File menu and choose Print.
2. In the Print what list box, choose Outline View.
3. Click Preview. The outline is displayed. Notice that the handout headers and footers are printed on outlines as well as on handouts.
4. Print the outline and close the preview window. Keep the presentation open for the next exercise.

Importing and Exporting Outlines

You can import an outline created in another application (such as Microsoft Word or another word processor) into a new presentation or an existing one. To *import* means to use a file in one application that was created in a different application. PowerPoint uses your outline's structural formatting (tab characters, indents, or heading styles) to create slide titles and bullets.

You can also export a PowerPoint outline in the standardized *rich text format (RTF)* file type (with the file extension .rtf). To *export* is to save a file in a format that can be read by a different application. The rich text format preserves text formatting in a way that can be read by other Microsoft Office programs as well as numerous programs that are not part of the Microsoft Office suite. Note that the rich text format saves a presentation's text only, and not its graphics.

EXERCISE 4-13 Export a Presentation as a Rich Text Format (RTF) Outline

To save a presentation as an outline in the rich text format, use the Save As command and choose the file type Outline/RTF.

1. With the presentation ***[your initials]*4-11** open and displayed, open the File menu and choose Save As.
2. In the Save As dialog box, navigate to your Lesson 4 folder.
3. In the Save as type list box, choose Outline/RTF.

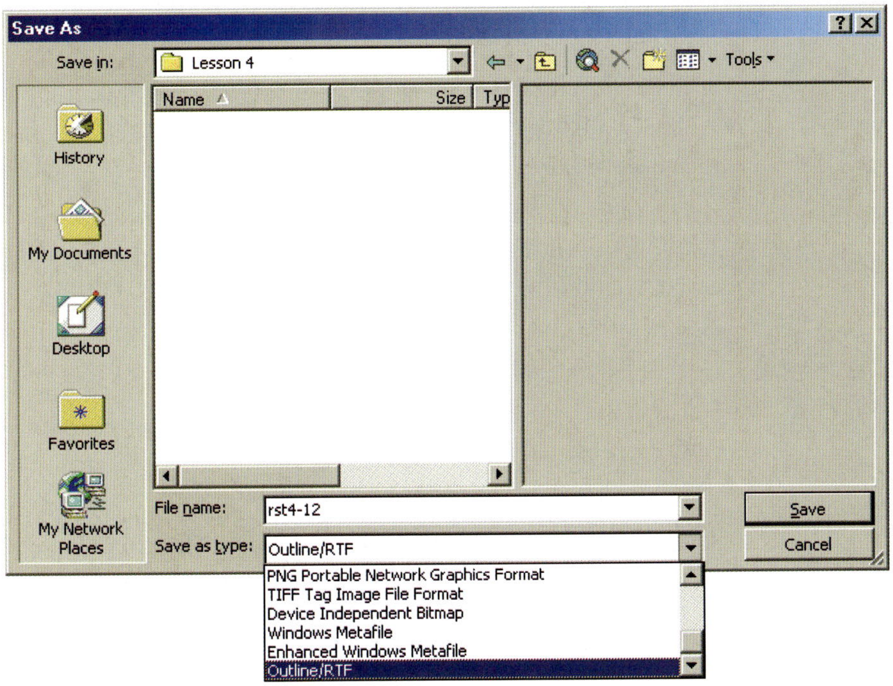

FIGURE 4-9 Saving a presentation as a rich text format outline

4. In the File name box, key ***[your initials]*4-13**. Click Save. The presentation is saved in your Lesson 4 folder as an outline in rich text format.
5. Without closing PowerPoint, start Word.
6. Open the RTF file ***[your initials]*4-13** from your Lesson 4 folder. All the text from your PowerPoint presentation appears in the Word window with the text formatting preserved.

NOTE: You can save a presentation as an outline in Word format by choosing File, Send To, Microsoft Word. The Send To dialog box lets you choose from many options, one of which is Outline only.

7. Print the outline. Close the document but leave Word open for the next exercise.

EXERCISE 4-14 Create an Outline in Word

To create an outline in Word, key the text in Word's Outline view, using the Promote and Demote buttons on Word's Outlining toolbar in much the same way as you key an outline in PowerPoint's Outline pane.

An alternative way to create the Word outline is to assign heading styles to the outline levels. Use the style Heading 1 for the title, Heading 2 for the first level of bulleted text, and so on.

NOTE: If you will be using a word processor other than Microsoft Word, check with your instructor to be sure that the appropriate text converters have been installed on your computer.

1. Working in the Word window, open the File menu and choose New. In the New Document task pane, choose Blank Document.

2. Click the Outline View button in the lower left corner of your Word window to switch to Outline view.

NOTE: Follow your instructor's directions for creating an outline if you're using a different word processor.

3. Key the material shown in Figure 4-10. To create level 2 and level 3 entries, use the Demote and Promote buttons on Word's Outlining toolbar in the same way you would in the PowerPoint Outline pane. Or, use Tab and Shift+Tab.

FIGURE 4-10

```
Poster Ideas
    Good 4 U Public Relations Training
```
Level 2

continues

FIGURE 4-10 *continued*

```
Restaurant Topics
    Menu items                      ┐
    Contests                        │ Level 2
    Ingredient profiles             ┘
        Exotic ingredients          ┐ Level 3
        Organic ingredients         ┘
Vendor Profiles
    Local organic farmers           ┐
    Herb farms                      │ Level 2
    Fisheries                       ┘
Special Event Announcements
    New Health Marathon ——— Level 2
        Pasta party                 ┐ Level 3
        Awards dinner               ┘
    July 4th celebration ——— Level 2
        In-line skating race        ┐ Level 3
        Bike race                   ┘
```

4. Save the outline as ***[your initials]*****4-14** in your Lesson 4 folder.
5. Print the outline and close Word.

EXERCISE 4-15 Create PowerPoint Slides from a Word Outline

There are several ways to create PowerPoint slides from a word processor outline. You can do any one of the following:

- Open the outline file from within PowerPoint.
- Choose Slides from Outline from the Insert menu.
- Open the outline file in Word, choose Send To from the File menu, and then choose Microsoft PowerPoint from the submenu.

1. Working in PowerPoint, click the Open button on the Standard toolbar to display the Open dialog box.
2. In the **Files of type** list box, choose **All Outlines**. Notice that the files in the list box have a Word file icon near the filename.
3. Navigate to your Lesson 4 folder and choose the Word document ***[your initials]*4-14** from the list of files (the outline you created in the previous exercise).
4. Click **Open**. PowerPoint interprets the structure of your outline and creates new slides, creating titles from the level 1 headings and body text from the level 2 and level 3 headings. All the slides use the **Title and Text** layout.
5. Change the layout of the new slide 1 ("Poster Ideas") to **Title Slide**.

REVIEW: To display the Slide Layout task pane, open the Format menu and choose Slide Layout, or click the Other Task Panes button on the task pane's title bar and then choose Slide Layout from the list box.

6. Apply the design template **Layers** and use the color scheme with the black background.
7. Display the Outline pane and enlarge it to see all the text.
8. If necessary, make adjustments to the text in your Outline pane so that it matches Figure 4-11.

FIGURE 4-11
Presentation created from imported outline

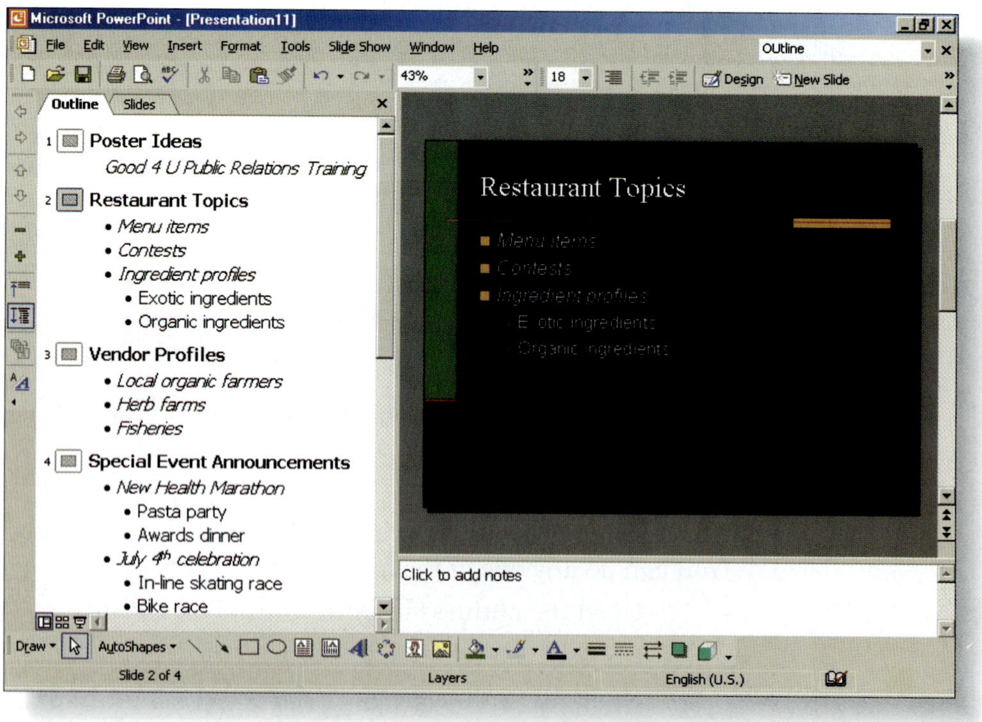

9. Move to slide 1 and save the presentation as ***[your initials]*4-15** in your Lesson 4 folder. Leave the presentation open for the next exercise.

Saving a Presentation as a Web Page

After you save a presentation as a PowerPoint presentation file, you can open it only on a computer that has PowerPoint installed. However, when you save a file by using the *HTML* (*Hypertext Markup Language*) file format, anyone can open and view it by using a *browser* such as Internet Explorer or Netscape Navigator. This means that anyone with a browser can read a PowerPoint presentation saved in the HTML file format, even without PowerPoint installed.

Files saved in the HTML file format are used to create Web pages.

EXERCISE 4-16 Save in HTML File Format

1. Open the File menu and choose Save as Web Page. The Save As dialog box opens. Notice that in the Save as type list box, Web Page has already been chosen.
2. Using the Save In box, navigate to your Lesson 4 folder.
3. In the File name box, notice that the filename of your presentation is already entered for you. Change the filename to ***[your initials]*4-16**.

NOTE: PowerPoint creates a folder of supporting files when you save in HTML format. This folder is saved in the same location as the HTML file and is necessary to display the HTML file in a browser. If you move the HTML file to another location, you need to make sure that the supporting file folder moves along with it.

4. Click Save. The file is saved in HTML format. It can now be read by using the browser Microsoft Internet Explorer 4.0 or a later version.
5. To preview the presentation in your Web browser, open the File menu and choose Web Page Preview. (You might have to expand the menu to locate this command.) The presentation appears in your browser window.
6. Close the browser window by clicking the window's Close button X.

Working with Hyperlinks

Earlier in the lesson you learned how to use a Word outline to create a presentation. Hyperlinks provide another way to get outside information into a presentation.

Hyperlinks are links from a particular place in your presentation to other slides, other PowerPoint presentations, other applications, and the Internet. Hyperlinks can make your presentation more adaptable and more useful.

EXERCISE 4-17 Insert a Hyperlink to Another Presentation

When you want to create a hyperlink to another file (for example, to another PowerPoint presentation), it is a good idea to first copy or save the file to the same directory as the presentation containing the hyperlink. If you move the presentation to another location, be sure to move the hyperlinked file as well. Otherwise, the hyperlink will no longer work after the move.

There are many ways to insert hyperlinks. One convenient way is to select text that relates to the hyperlink; then choose Insert, Hyperlink (or press Ctrl+K) to open the Insert Hyperlink dialog box.

1. Open the file **CookCon2**. Without making any changes, save the file in your Lesson 4 folder with the same filename, **CookCon2**.

2. Close **CookCon2**.

3. Working on ***[your initials]*****4-16,** display slide 2 ("Restaurant Topics") and select the second bulleted item, "Contests."

4. Open the Insert menu and choose Hyperlink (or press Ctrl+K). The Insert Hyperlink dialog box opens.

FIGURE 4-12
Insert Hyperlink dialog box

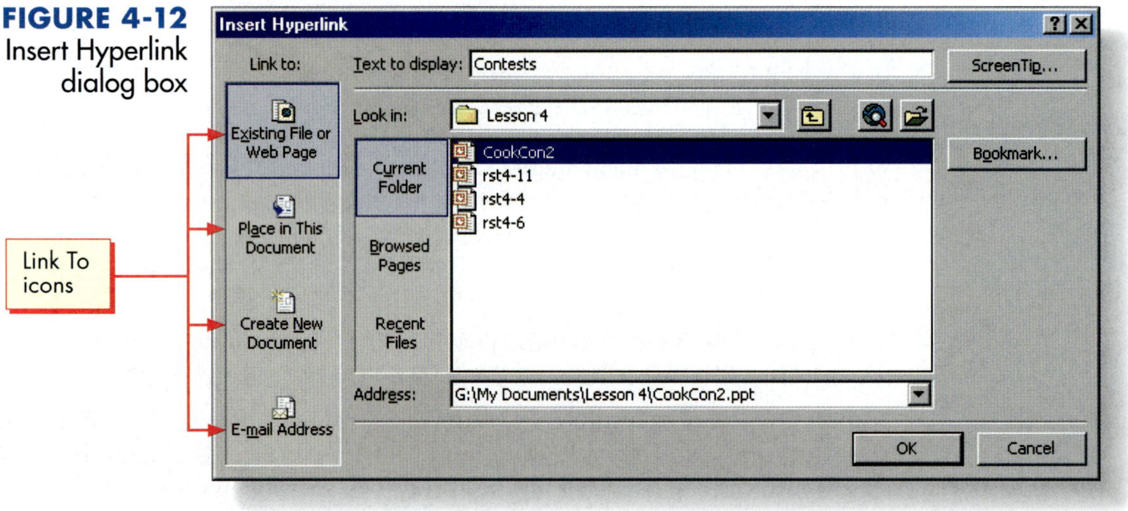

5. In the Link to box on the left side, choose Existing File or Web Page.

6. In the Look in box, navigate to your Lesson 4 folder.

7. From the list of files, select **CookCon2**. Notice the PowerPoint icon to the left of the filename, indicating that the file is a PowerPoint presentation.

8. Click ScreenTip in the upper right corner. The Set Hyperlink ScreenTip dialog box opens.

9. In the ScreenTip text box, key **Recipe contest details**. This is the ScreenTip text that will appear when you point to the hyperlink during a slide show.

FIGURE 4-13
Setting the hyperlink ScreenTip

10. Click OK to close the Set Hyperlink ScreenTip dialog box; then click OK again to close the Insert Hyperlink dialog box.
11. Deselect the text "Contests." The text is now a contrasting color and underlined, indicating that it is a hyperlink.
12. Save the presentation as ***[your initials]*4-17** in your Lesson 4 folder. Leave the presentation open for the next exercise.

EXERCISE 4-18 Using a Hyperlink During a Slide Show

1. Click the Slide Show button to start a slide show on slide 2.
2. In the slide show, point to the hyperlink ("Contests"). The pointer changes to a pointing hand shape. Notice that the ScreenTip displays the text you specified.

FIGURE 4-14
Hyperlink created on a slide

3. Click the hyperlink. The "Cooking Contest" presentation opens.

4. Advance through the "Cooking Contest" slides, pressing Enter when you get to the end. The display returns to slide 2 of the original presentation. Notice that the hyperlink color changed from red to yellow, indicating that the hyperlink location has been visited.
5. Advance through the presentation and return to Normal view.

EXERCISE 4-19 Insert a Hyperlink to an Excel Worksheet

1. Start Excel and open the file **VendExp**.
2. Save the file as **VendExp** in your Lesson 4 folder; then close Excel.
3. Working in PowerPoint, display slide 3 ("Vendor Profiles").
4. Select the title text "Vendor Profiles."
5. Press Ctrl+K to open the Insert Hyperlink dialog box.
6. Under Link to, click Existing File or Web Page.
7. Navigate to your Lesson 4 folder and select **VendExp** from the list of files. Notice the Excel icon to the left of the filename, indicating that this is an Excel file.
8. Click ScreenTip, and then key **Vendor Expenses Chart**. Click OK.
9. Click OK again to close the Insert Hyperlink dialog box.
10. Click the Slide Show button to display slide 3 as a slide show.
11. Click the hyperlink ("Vendor Profiles"). Excel opens, displaying the vendor expense chart.
12. Click the Excel Close button in the upper right corner to close Excel.
13. Press Esc to return to PowerPoint's Normal view.

EXERCISE 4-20 Insert a Hyperlink to a Web Site

NOTE: Internet access is needed to complete this exercise. If you do not have Internet access, you can still do most of the exercise, but you will not be able to test the hyperlink.

1. If you have access to the Internet, make a connection now.
2. Following your instructor's directions, open your browser and search for a Web site related to organic food. Make a note of the Web address (or copy it to the clipboard) and then close your browser. If this is not possible, use the Web address provided in step 5 below or one provided by your instructor.

3. Working on slide 3, select the text "Local organic farmers" and then press Ctrl + K to open the Insert Hyperlink dialog box.
4. Under Link to, click the Existing File or Web Page icon.
5. In the Address box at the bottom of the dialog box, key the address for the Web site you found in step 2 above (or paste it from the clipboard). For example, key **http://www.mofga.org/**

NOTE: Web addresses often change. The Web address provided might not exist at the time that you do this exercise.

6. Click ScreenTip and key descriptive text appropriate to the Web site you are using. For example: **Maine Organic Farmers Association**
7. Click OK to close the Set Hyperlink ScreenTip dialog box. Click OK again to close the Insert Hyperlink dialog box.
8. Create a handout header and footer: include the date and your name as the header, and the page number and text ***[your initials]*****4-20** as the footer.
9. Move to slide 1 and open the Save As dialog box. In the Save as type list box, change the file type to Presentation. Save the presentation as ***[your initials]*****4-20** in your Lesson 4 folder.
10. View the entire presentation as a slide show. Click each hyperlink to test it. When you open the Web site, explore it for a few moments and then close your browser by clicking the Close button in the upper right corner. When the slide show is complete, return to PowerPoint's Normal view.
11. Preview and then print the presentation as handouts, 4 slides per page, grayscale, landscape, framed. Close the presentation.
12. If you made an Internet connection earlier in this exercise, close the connection.

USING HELP

When using the Outline pane, there might be times when the actions you take do not create the results you expected. Help is available to guide you through the process of troubleshooting actions in the Outline pane.

Use Help for information about troubleshooting the Outline pane:

1. Click the Microsoft PowerPoint Help button on the Standard toolbar.
2. If the Office Assistant appears, turn it off permanently: click Options, clear the Use the Office Assistant check box, and click OK.
3. Click the Microsoft PowerPoint Help button again. In the What would you like to do? text box, key **troubleshoot outlines** and click Search.

4. In the list of topics, select Troubleshoot working on the Outline tab.
5. Click Show All in the upper right corner of the Help window to expand the Help topics.

FIGURE 4-15
Help window about the Outline pane

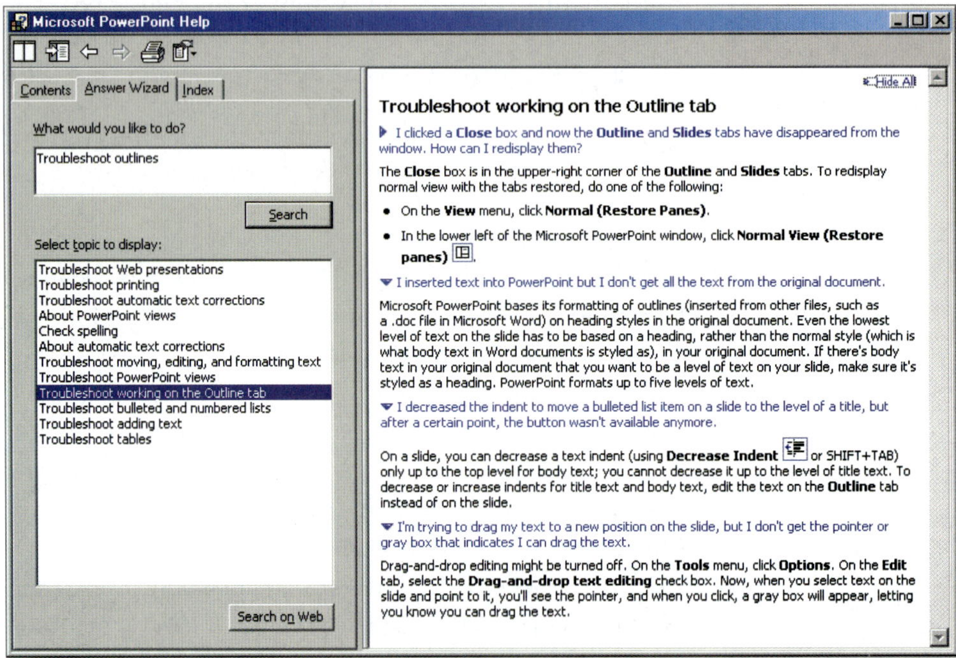

6. Review the information in the Help window. Select another entry from the list of topics if you want.
7. Close the Help window when you finish.

LESSON 4 Summary

- Use the Outline pane to help you organize and create a presentation by focusing on the content and flow rather than the appearance.
- Widen the Outline pane to make a larger work area by dragging its border.
- Use Zoom to enlarge text for easy viewing without affecting its actual size.
- Add new slides and work with slide layouts in the Outline pane by using the same commands as when working in the Slide pane or with slide thumbnails.
- When working in the Outline pane on a new slide with the Title and 2-Column Text layout, press Ctrl + Enter to activate the second column placeholder.

- Use the Outline pane to join two consecutive slides into one by demoting the title of the second slide. Split a slide into two by promoting one of the slide's bullets to the title level.
- An alternative to using the Promote and Demote buttons or keyboard shortcuts is to drag a bullet to the left or right.
- Delete selected slides or text in the Outline pane by pressing Delete.
- Move selected slides or selected bullets up or down in an outline by using the Move Up and Move Down buttons or by dragging the selection up or down.
- Collapse the outline before moving a slide to avoid dropping it in the middle of another slide.
- To move more than one slide or more than one bullet at a time, use the drag-and-drop pointer, or cut and paste. Select multiple items by using the I-beam instead of the four-pointed arrow.
- The Outline pane can display either plain text or text formatted in the same way as it appears on a slide. Turn formatting on and off by using the Show Formatting button.
- PowerPoint outlines can be saved (exported) in the rich text format (RTF) for use with word processors and other programs. Rich text file format preserves text formatting but does not save any associated graphics.
- Word processor outlines can be inserted (imported) into a PowerPoint presentation.
- Creating an outline in Word is very similar to creating an outline in PowerPoint.
- PowerPoint presentations can be saved in Hypertext Markup Language (HTML) format. Using this format, the file can be opened in a browser or used as Web pages.
- Hyperlinks enable you to jump to supplemental material during a slide show presentation. Hyperlinks can link to documents created in other programs, other presentations, and the Internet.
- To use a hyperlink, start a slide show and then click the hyperlinked text. You can distinguish hyperlinked text by its contrasting color and its underline.
- Save the files you plan to use as hyperlinks in the same folder as your presentation before creating the link. If you move your presentation to another location, be sure to move the linked files as well.

LESSON 4 Command Summary

FEATURE	BUTTON	MENU	KEYBOARD	SPEECH?
Display Outline pane	(Outline tab)	View, Normal, click Outline tab		✓
Promote	or		Shift + Tab or Alt + Shift + ←	✓
Demote	or		Tab or Alt + Shift + →	✓
Move Up			Alt + Shift + ↑	✓
Move Down			Alt + Shift + ↓	✓
Collapse All			Alt + Shift + 1	✓
Expand All			Alt + Shift + 1	✓
Expand				✓
Collapse				✓
Show Formatting				✓
Create hyperlink		Insert, Hyperlink	Ctrl + K	✓
Print outline		File, Print, Print what, Outline View		✓
Save as outline		File, Save As, Save as type, Outline/RTF		✓
Insert outline		Insert, Slides from Outline		✓

Concepts Review

TRUE/FALSE QUESTIONS

Each of the following statements is either true or false. Indicate your choice by circling T or F.

T F *1.* To display the Outline pane, you can choose Outline from the Insert menu.

T F *2.* You can display slide thumbnails and the Outline pane at the same time.

T F *3.* You can use Ctrl+Enter both to activate the next slide placeholder and to insert a new slide.

T F *4.* The Demote button on the Outlining toolbar has the same effect as the Decrease Indent button on the Formatting toolbar.

T F *5.* You can drag and drop bulleted items from one slide to another.

T F *6.* You can use the Move Up button to change the positions of slides in your outline.

T F *7.* After you create a slide, you cannot split it into two slides.

T F *8.* You can insert a hyperlink on a slide by pressing Ctrl+M.

SHORT ANSWER QUESTIONS

Write the correct answer in the space provided.

1. Which key do you press to insert another bullet at the same level?

____

2. What happens when you demote the title of slide 3 in a presentation?

____

3. If a slide has five bullets (and no sub-bullets), what happens when you promote the third bullet?

____

4. A slide has several bullets. If you select the title with the four-pointed arrow in Outline view and press Tab, what happens?

____

5. Which toolbar contains the Demote and Promote buttons?

____

6. On what menu do you find a command for saving a presentation as a Web page?

____

7. How can you turn character formatting on and off in Outline view?

____

8. What happens to hyperlink text after you click it during a slide show?

____

CRITICAL THINKING

Answer these questions on a separate page. There are no right or wrong answers. Support your answers with examples from your own experience, if possible.

1. Do you prefer creating slides in the Slide pane or in the Outline pane? Why?
2. When would you want to create your outline in PowerPoint? In Word? What are the advantages of developing an outline in Word?

Lesson Applications

EXERCISE 4-21

Start a new presentation in the Outline pane, add slides, promote and demote text, and move bullets and slides.

1. Start a new presentation.
2. In the Outline pane, create the two slides shown in Figure 4-16.

FIGURE 4-16

3. Make the following changes in the Outline pane:
   - Make “Food services” and its sub-bullets a separate slide. (Don’t forget to change the new slide’s title to title case.)
   - Make “Merchandise” and its sub-bullets a separate slide.
   - Add the following bullets to the “Our Products” slide:
     - **Merchandise**
     - **Food services**
4. Change the order of bullets on the “Merchandise” slide to the following:
   Honeys and confections
   T-shirts
   Caps
5. Collapse the outline and move the “Merchandise” slide before the “Food Services” slide.
6. Expand the outline.
7. Apply the Network design template and use the color scheme with the red background; then change slide 1 to one of the color schemes with the black background.

8. Check spelling in the presentation.
9. Create a handout header and footer: include the date and your name as the header, and the page number and text ***[your initials]*4-21** as the footer.
10. Move to slide 1 and save the presentation as ***[your initials]*4-21** in your Lesson 4 folder.
11. Preview and then print the presentation as handouts, 4 slides per page, grayscale, landscape, framed. Close the presentation.

EXERCISE 4-22

Move bullets in the Outline pane and promote outline items; save a presentation as a Web page.

1. Open the file **Market4** and display the Outline pane.
2. Select and delete slide 2 ("Elements of Marketing").
3. Revise the bullets in the new slide 2 ("Marketing Is About People"), as shown in Figure 4-17.

FIGURE 4-17

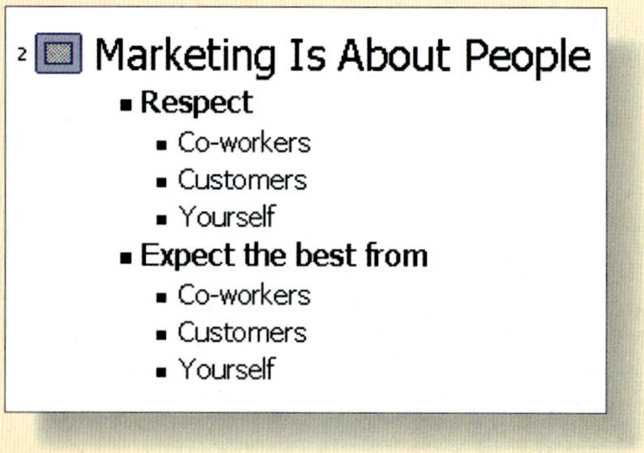

4. Promote each of the bulleted items on slide 3 ("What Are We Marketing?") to three new slides. Correct the capitalization on the new slide titles, and then insert bulleted text on slides 3 through 5 as shown in Figure 4-18.

FIGURE 4-18

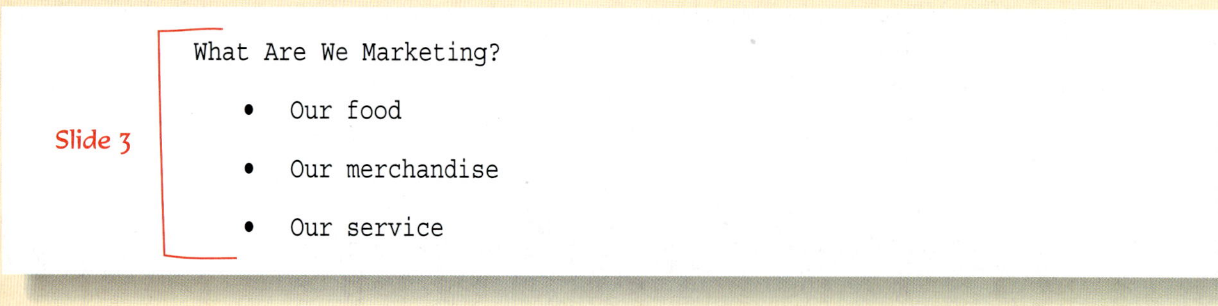

continues

FIGURE 4-18 *continued*

Slide 4

Our Food

- Eat in
- Take out
- Delivered and catered

Slide 5

Our Merchandise

- Food products
- Apparel and accessories

5. Move the three bulleted items under slide 7 ("Marketing Our Staff") and position them under slide 6 ("Our Service").
6. Delete slide 7.
7. View the presentation in the Slide pane and correct the capitalization of titles where necessary.
8. Change the layout of slide 2 to Title and 2-Column Text, moving the second bullet and its sub-bullets to the right column.
9. Check spelling in the presentation.
10. Create a handout header and footer: include the date and your name as the header, and the page number and text ***[your initials]*4-22** as the footer.
11. Move to slide 1 and save the presentation as a Web page in your Lesson 4 folder. Use the filename ***[your initials]*4-22**.
12. Use the Web Page Preview command on the File menu to view the presentation.
13. Preview and then print the presentation as handouts, 6 slides per page, grayscale, framed. Close the presentation.

EXERCISE 4-23

Move, promote, and demote bulleted items in the Outline pane; move slides; and insert a hyperlink to a Word document.

1. Open the file **HonProd1**.

2. Display the Outline pane and adjust it so you can easily read the text. Try clicking the Show Formatting button to see if you like the text formatting on or off.

3. Working in the Outline pane, promote, demote, and move bullets and slides as shown in Figure 4-19. Correct the case of title slides as necessary.

FIGURE 4-19

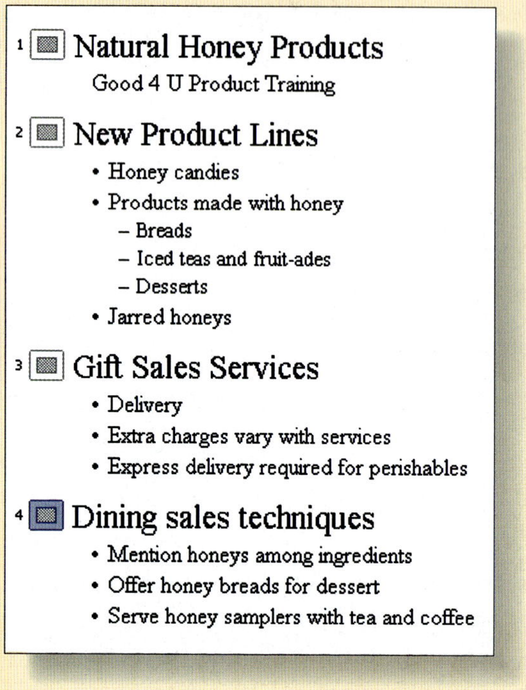

4. On slide 3, move and add text as shown in Figure 4-20:

FIGURE 4-20

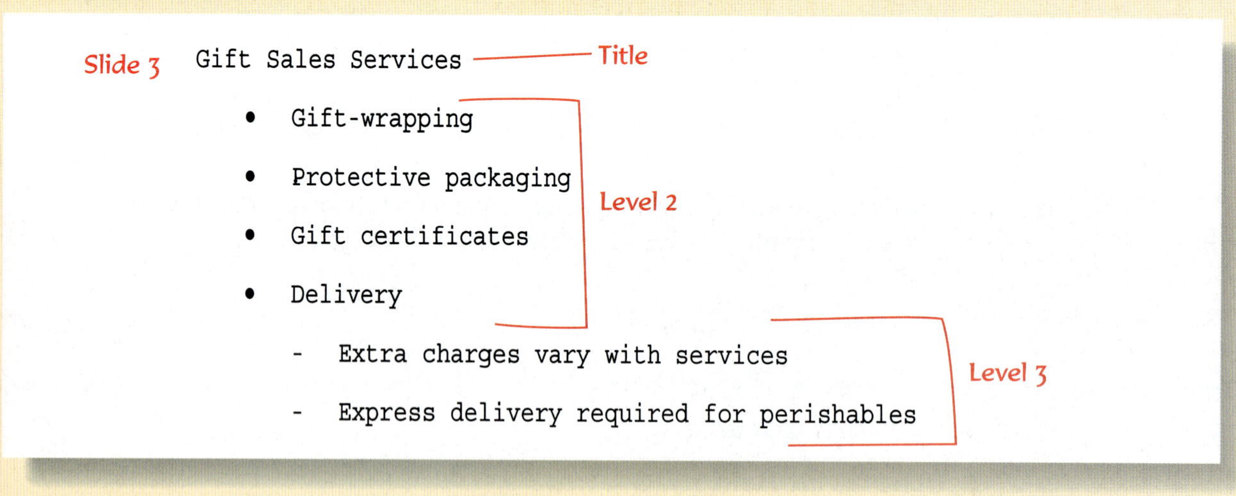

5. Apply the Kimono design template.

6. Open the Word document **Foods1** and save it with the same name in your Lesson 4 folder. Close Word.

7. On slide 2, create a hyperlink that will display the Word file **Foods1** when you click the text "Products made with honey." Give it the ScreenTip **Foods and Beverages Made with Honey**
8. Check spelling in the presentation. (Leave the spelling of "fruit-ades" unchanged.)
9. Apply an animation scheme of your choice to the entire presentation.
10. Create a handout header and footer: include the date and your name as the header, and the page number and text ***[your initials]*4-23** as the footer.
11. Move to slide 1 and save the presentation as ***[your initials]*4-23** in your Lesson 4 folder.
12. View the presentation as a slide show and click the hyperlink on slide 2.
13. Preview and then print the presentation as handouts, 4 slides per page, grayscale, framed. Close the presentation.

EXERCISE 4-24 Challenge Yourself

Insert a word-processed outline into a presentation, move bullets and slides, insert a slide from another presentation, and export an outline to Word.

1. Create a new presentation by opening the outline file **Foods2** in PowerPoint.
2. Using the Slide Finder dialog box, insert all the slides from the presentation **HonProd2** to the end of the presentation.
3. Working in the Outline pane, collapse the outline and then rearrange the slides so that they are in the order shown in Figure 4-21.

FIGURE 4-21

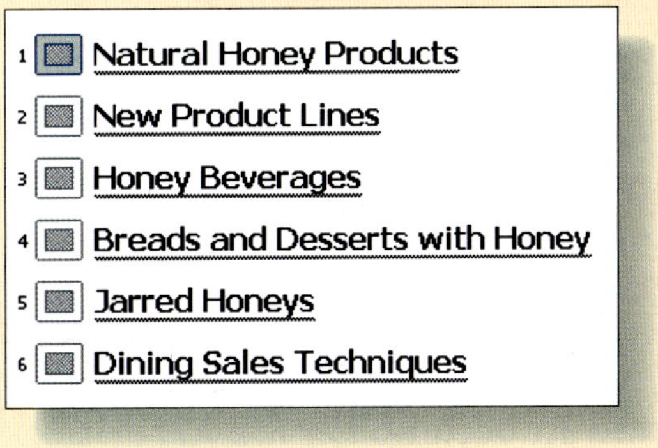

4. Add a new slide after slide 5 with the title **Good 4 U Honey Promotion** and the following bullets:
   - **Honey-tasting contest**
   - **Bread and honey samples at take-out counter**
   - **Complimentary honey candies after meals**

5. Change the slide 3 layout ("Honey Beverages") to Title and 2-Column Text, moving the second main bullet ("Fruit-ades") and its sub-bullets to the second column placeholder. Delete any blank lines in the Outline pane.
6. On slide 7, move "Offer honey breads for dessert" so it is the last bullet on the slide.
7. After slide 7, insert slide 3 ("Gift Sales Services") from the file **HonProd1**.
8. Apply the design template Quadrant and use the color scheme with the black background.

NOTE: If an Internet connection is not available, follow your instructor's directions on how to execute steps 9 and 10 below.

9. If you have a connection to the Internet, search for a Web site that relates to honey products and make a note of its Web address.
10. Using the first bullet on slide 2 ("Products made with honey"), create a hyperlink to the Web site you found in step 9.
11. Check spelling in the presentation.
12. Apply an animation scheme of your choice to the entire presentation.
13. Create a handout header and footer: include the date and your name as the header, and the page number and text ***[your initials]*4-24** as the footer.
14. Move to slide 1 and save the presentation as ***[your initials]*4-24** in your Lesson 4 folder.
15. View the presentation as a slide show. While viewing the show, be sure to click on your hyperlink.
16. Preview and then print the presentation as handouts, 9 slides per page, grayscale, landscape, framed. Close the presentation.

POWERPOINT

On Your Own

In these exercises you work on your own, as you would in a real-life work environment. Use the skills you've learned to accomplish the task—and be creative.

EXERCISE 4-25

Find a newspaper, magazine, or Internet article of interest to you. Pick out the main points in the article and organize them into a three- or four-level outline with at least four main points suitable for slide titles. Create the outline by using any method that is comfortable for you (index cards, Word, PowerPoint, etc.). From the outline, create a PowerPoint presentation. Choose a suitable design template, color scheme, and animation scheme. Save the presentation as ***[your initials]*****4-25**. Preview and then print the presentation as an outline and as handouts.

EXERCISE 4-26

Create an outline describing a familiar process. For example: registration for a course at your school, washing a car, a procedure in your office. Translate the procedure into a PowerPoint presentation. Create at least six slides and use a design template, color schemes, and slide transitions of your choice. Save the presentation as ***[your initials]*****4-26**. Preview and then print the presentation as an outline and as handouts.

EXERCISE 4-27

Imagine that you want to purchase an expensive piece of electronic gear. For example: a scanner for your computer, a high-definition television, a global positioning device for your car. Starting in the Outline pane, create a presentation aimed at your boss, your spouse, your parents, or a friend, justifying this purchase. Create at least six slides and use a design template, color schemes, and slide transitions of your choice. Save the presentation as ***[your initials]*****4-27**. Preview and then print the presentation as an outline and as handouts.

LESSON

5

Working with Text

OBJECTIVES

MOUS ACTIVITIES

In this lesson:

PP2002 2-2
PP2002 3-1
PP2002 4-1
PP2002 4-4
PP2002 4-9

See Appendix E.

After completing this lesson, you will be able to:

1. **Work with fonts and font attributes.**
2. **Use the AutoFit feature.**
3. **Apply text formatting to placeholders.**
4. **Work with bullets and numbered paragraphs.**
5. **Change text alignment.**
6. **Create a PowerPoint table.**
7. **Change the size and position of text placeholders.**
8. **Modify a design template's text placeholders.**

Estimated Time: 1½ hours

You can add interest to a PowerPoint presentation by varying the appearance of text—that includes changing the font, text style, bullet shape, or the position of text. You can change text appearance before or after you key it, or apply changes to the entire text in the presentation at once by applying changes to a master slide.

Working with Fonts

One way to change the appearance of text in your presentation is by changing the font. A *font* is a set of characters with a specific design. You can change the font face (such as Times New Roman or Arial) and the font size. Fonts are measured in *points* (there are 72 points to an inch) indicating how tall a font is.

It is useful to understand that different fonts can take up different amounts of horizontal space, even though they are the same size. For example, a word formatted as 20-point Arial will be wider than a word formatted as 20-point Garamond, as shown in Figure 5-1.

FIGURE 5-1
Comparing fonts

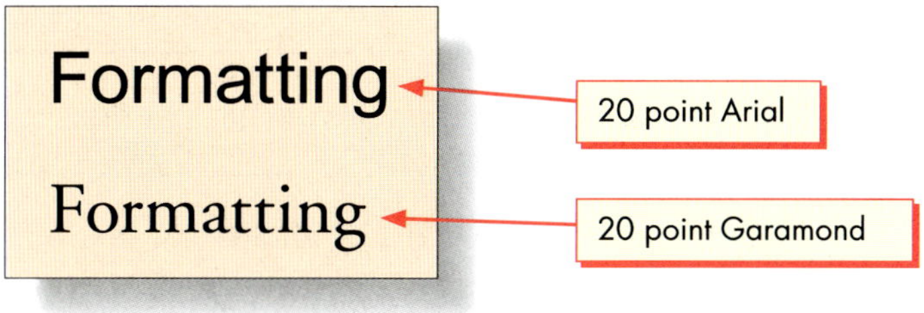

Another way to change the appearance of text is by applying *text attributes*. For example, you can apply a text style (such as bold or italic) and effect (such as underline or shadow). You use the Formatting toolbar or the Font dialog box to change selected text.

FIGURE 5-2
Expanded Formatting toolbar

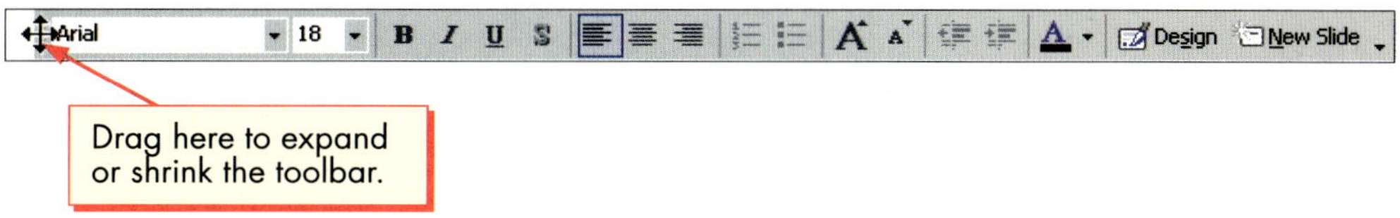

TABLE 5-1 Text Formatting Buttons on the Formatting Toolbar

BUTTON	PURPOSE
Arial ▾ Font	Enables you to choose a font face for selected text or for text to be keyed at the insertion point
18 ▾ Font Size	Enables you to choose a font size for selected text or for text to be keyed at the insertion point
B Bold	Applies the bold attribute to text
I Italic	Applies the italic attribute to text
U Underline	Applies the underline attribute to text

continues

TABLE 5-1 Text Formatting Buttons on the Formatting Toolbar *continued*

BUTTON	PURPOSE
Shadow	Applies a text shadow
Align Left	Left-aligns text in a text placeholder or text box
Center	Centers text in a text placeholder or text box
Align Right	Right-aligns text in a text placeholder or text box
Numbering	Applies numbers in place of bullets
Bullets	Turns bullets on or off
Increase Font Size	Increases the size of selected text by one font size
Decrease Font Size	Decreases the size of selected text by one font size
Decrease Indent	Promotes text; removes one indent level, moving text to the left
Increase Indent	Demotes text; adds one indent level, moving text to the right
Font Color	Changes text color

EXERCISE 5-1 Change the Font Face and Font Size for Selected Text

A convenient way to apply text formatting is to first key the text, focusing on content, and then select the text and apply formatting, such as changing the size or font. When working with fonts, keep in mind that you should limit the number of different fonts used in a presentation to no more than two or three. Also remember that the font size should be at least 18 points if the presentation is going to be viewed on a computer or projected on a screen.

Another thing to be aware of is the type of font you choose. The Font list box on the Formatting toolbar displays all the fonts available for your computer. On the left side of each font is a symbol indicating the font type. TrueType fonts have the following symbol: . Fonts that work specifically with the currently selected printer have the symbol . If you plan to show your presentation on a different computer or print it with a different printer, it is best to choose a TrueType font.

1. Open the file **Health1**.
2. Expand the Formatting toolbar and then locate the toolbar buttons listed in Table 5-1.

NOTE: To expand or shrink a toolbar, place your pointer on the vertical bar at the left end of the toolbar. When you see the four-pointed arrow ✥, drag to the left to expand the toolbar or to the right to shrink the toolbar (the pointer changes to a two-pointed arrow ↔ as you drag).

3. On slide 1, click the title placeholder to activate it and key **Heart**

FIGURE 5-3
Font drop-down list

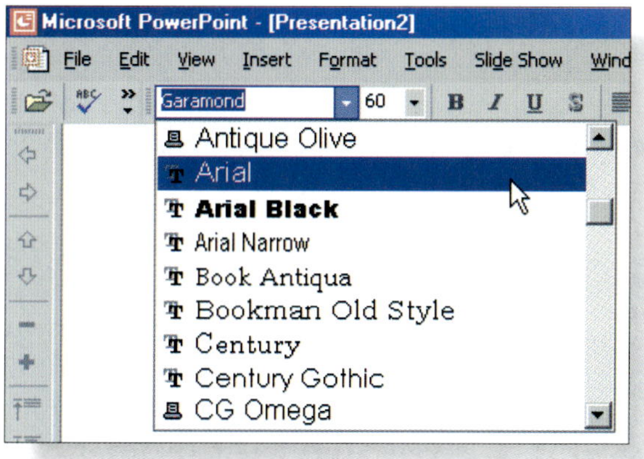

4. Select the word you just keyed.
5. Click the down arrow next to the Font box on the Formatting toolbar.
6. From the drop-down list, choose Arial (scroll up near the top of the list). As you can see, text formatting in PowerPoint is similar to text formatting in a word processor.
7. With "Heart" still selected, click the down arrow next to the Font Size box. Choose 66. The text size increases to 66 points.

FIGURE 5-4
Font Size drop-down list

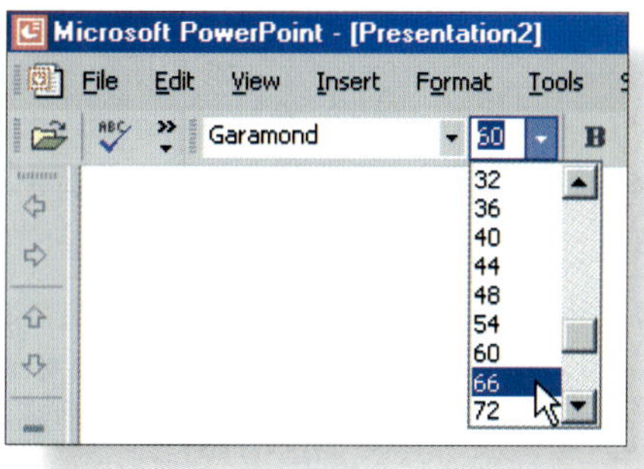

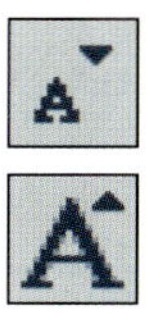

8. Click the Decrease Font Size button . The font size decreases by one size. Notice the number "60" displayed in the Font Size box.
9. Click the Increase Font Size button twice. The font size increases by two sizes, to 72 points (the equivalent of 1 inch tall).

EXERCISE 5-2 Work with Bold, Italic, and Text Color

Sometimes it's convenient to apply text formatting as you key. This is particularly true with bold, italic, and underline if you use the following keyboard shortcuts:

Ctrl+B for bold
Ctrl+I for italic
Ctrl+U for underline

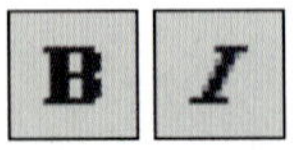

1. Position the insertion point to the right of "Heart" and press Spacebar. Click the Bold button (or press Ctrl+B) and then the Italic button (or press Ctrl+I) to turn these attributes on.
2. Key **Smart!** The word is formatted as bold italic as you key. Notice that this word is also 72-point Arial, like the previous word.
3. Double-click the word "Heart" to select it.

4. Locate the Font Color button on the Formatting toolbar. (You might need to click the Toolbar Options button to find it.) Click its down arrow to open the Font Color menu.

NOTE: If you click the Font Color button and not its down arrow, the color indicated on the button is automatically applied to the selected text. You use the down arrow to choose a different color.

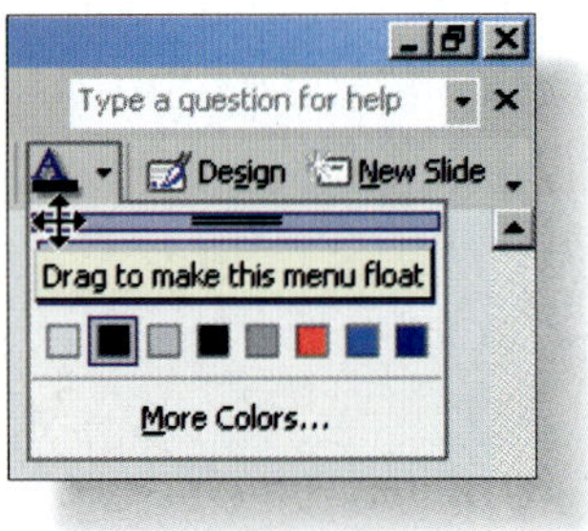

FIGURE 5-5 Font Color menu

5. Position your pointer on the gray bar at the top of the Font Color menu. When you see the four-pointed arrow, drag it down and to the left. Many of PowerPoint's submenus can be converted to floating toolbars in this manner. Unlike menus, floating toolbars stay open and available until you close them.
6. Click the bright red box on the Font Color floating toolbar. The selected text becomes light blue. You don't see the color you applied until you deselect the text.
7. Click in the word "Smart" to deselect "Heart." "Heart" is now red.

8. Close the Font Color toolbar by clicking its Close button. Notice that the color bar on the Font Color button is now red. If you click this button instead of the down arrow, selected text will be changed to red.

EXERCISE 5-3 Use the Font Dialog Box

The Font dialog box is a convenient place to apply several font attributes all at one time. In addition to choosing a font, font style, and font size, this dialog box enables you to choose various effects, such as underline or shadow, and a font color.

1. Select the words "Good 4 U" in the subtitle.
2. Right-click the selected text to display the shortcut menu. Choose Font to open the Font dialog box.
3. Choose the following options in the Font dialog box:
   - From the Font list box, choose Arial.
   - From the Font style list box, choose Bold Italic.
   - From the Size list box, choose 48.
   - Under Effects, check Underline.

   Notice the additional options available in this dialog box.

FIGURE 5-6
Font dialog box

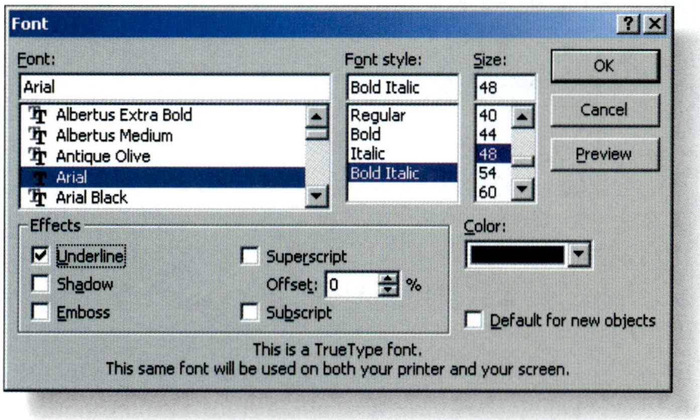

4. Click Preview and drag the Font dialog box to the side so you can see your choices applied to the selected text.
5. Drag the dialog box back to the center of the screen. Click OK to accept the formatting and close the dialog box.

6. With the text still selected, click the Underline button on the Formatting toolbar to turn off underlining. Deselect the text, which is now 48-point bold italic.
7. Position the insertion point after "Good 4 U" and press Enter to create a two-line subtitle. Don't forget to remove the extra space at the beginning of the second line.
8. Create a handout header and footer: include the date and your name as the header, and the page number and text ***[your initials]*5-3** as the footer.
9. Create a slide footer for all slides. Include the date, and in the Footer text box key your name followed by a comma and the text ***[your initials]*5-3**.
10. Save the presentation as ***[your initials]*5-3** in a new folder for Lesson 5.
11. Preview and then print the title slide only, grayscale, framed.

NOTE: You can change text attributes in the Outline pane in the same way as in the Slide pane.

EXERCISE 5-4 Change the Case of Selected Text

If you find that you keyed text in uppercase and want to change it, you don't have to re-key it. By opening the Format menu and choosing the Change Case command, you can change any text to Sentence case, lowercase, UPPERCASE, Title Case, or tOGGLE cASE. You can also cycle through uppercase, lowercase, and either title case or sentence case (depending on what is selected) by selecting text and pressing Shift + F3 one or more times.

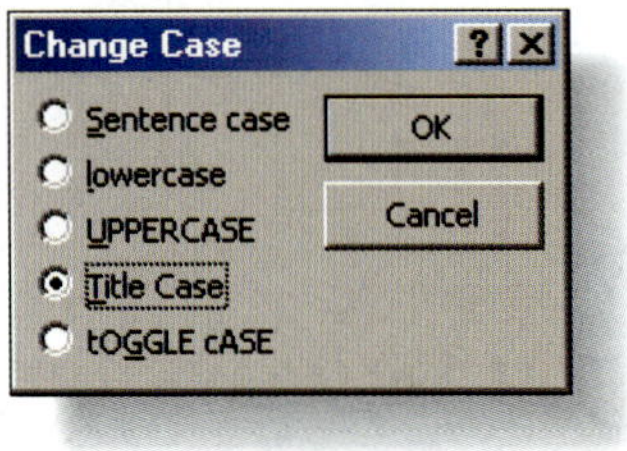

FIGURE 5-7 Change Case dialog box

1. Move to slide 3.
2. Use the I-beam pointer to select the title "Walk to good health," which has only the first word capitalized.
3. Press Shift + F3. The case changes to uppercase. Press Shift + F3 again to change the text to lowercase. Press it a third time to change the text to title case.
4. Select the word "To" in the title. Press Shift + F3 one or more times to change it to lowercase.
5. Select the first item in the body text placeholder by clicking its bullet. This text was keyed with CapsLock accidentally turned on.
6. From the Format menu, choose Change Case. Choose tOGGLE cASE and click OK. This option reverses the current case, changing uppercase letters to lowercase, and lowercase letters to uppercase.
7. Select the two bullets under "Walking" (beginning with "reduces" and "lowers") by dragging your I-beam across all the words. Open the Change Case dialog box, choose Sentence case, and click OK.

EXERCISE 5-5 Change Fonts for an Entire Presentation

After you finish a presentation, you might decide that a different font would look better. You can change the font for the entire presentation easily and quickly with the Replace Fonts command.

1. Display slide 1. The slide contains the fonts Arial and Garamond. The rest of the presentation is in Garamond.
2. From the Format menu, choose Replace Fonts to display the Replace Font dialog box.

3. Drag the dialog box to a corner of the slide so you can see the text.

FIGURE 5-8
Replace Font dialog box

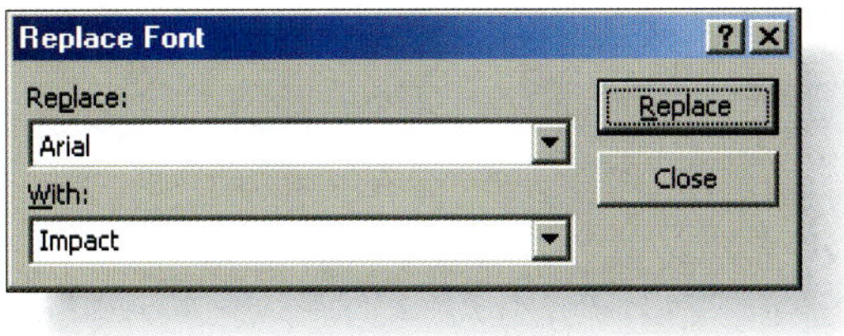

4. Open the Replace drop-down list and choose Arial. (This list contains the fonts currently used in the presentation.)
5. Open the With drop-down list to display the available fonts. Choose Impact and click Replace. The Arial font used in the title and subtitle is replaced with Impact. The dialog box remains open so that you can replace another font.
6. From the Replace list, choose Garamond and from the With list, choose Arial. Click Replace and then click Close. Notice the change in the last line of the subtitle and on the other slides, which are now in Arial instead of Garamond.

Working with the AutoFit Feature

In the previous exercise, changing the font from Garamond to Arial expanded the width of the text. As a result, the text on slide 4 ("Walkers Breakfast with Good 4 U") expands beyond the bottom edge of the text placeholder. If PowerPoint's *AutoFit* option is in effect, the text on slide 4 is automatically adjusted so that it fits the placeholder.

EXERCISE 5-6 Turn On AutoFit

AutoFit can be turned on or off in the AutoCorrect dialog box. To turn the feature on, click the AutoFormat As You Type tab and then check the AutoFit title text to placeholder and the AutoFit body text to placeholder options. To turn the feature off, uncheck these options.

1. From the Tools menu, choose AutoCorrect Options. The AutoCorrect dialog box appears.
2. Click the AutoFormat As You Type tab. (See Figure 5-9 on the next page.)
3. Under Apply as you type, check the AutoFit title text to placeholder and AutoFit body text to placeholder options.
4. Click OK.

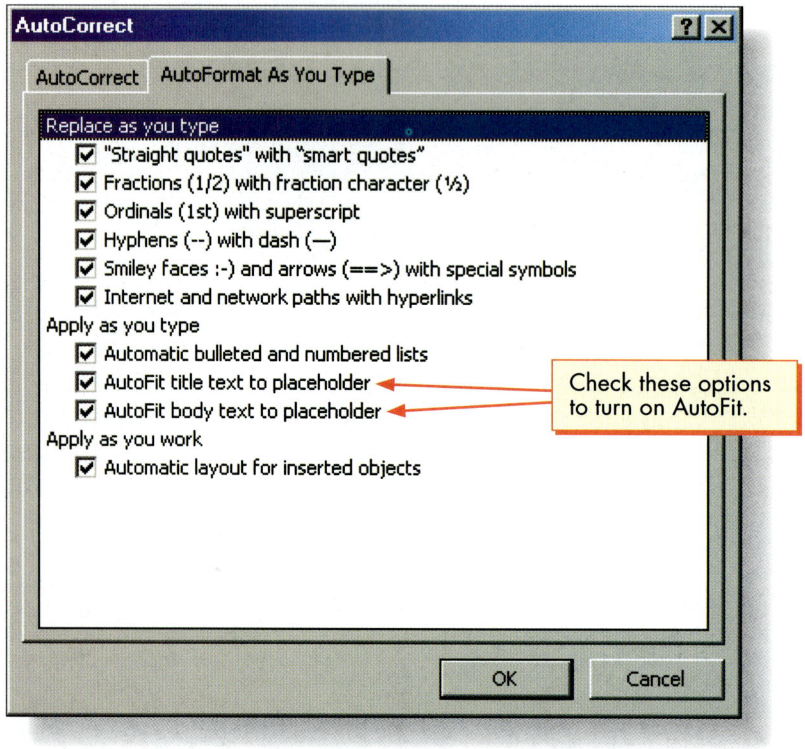

FIGURE 5-9 Turning on AutoFit options

EXERCISE 5-7 Use the AutoFit Options Button

When you activate a placeholder that has a text size problem or has had the text resized by AutoFit, the AutoFit Options button appears near the text, usually in the lower left corner of its text placeholder. You access AutoFit options by clicking the button. This button is similar to the AutoCorrect Options and the Paste Options buttons discussed in Lesson 3: "Creating a Presentation from Scratch."

1. Move to slide 4; then click anywhere in the first bullet beginning "Half-hour." Notice the AutoFit Options button that appears at the lower left corner of the body text placeholder.
2. Click the AutoFit Options button . The AutoFit Options menu appears. (See Figure 5-10 on the next page.)
3. Select Stop Fitting Text to This Placeholder. The text is now too large for the placeholder.
4. Click the AutoFit Options button again and select AutoFit Text to Placeholder. Now the text is reduced to an appropriate size to fit the placeholder.

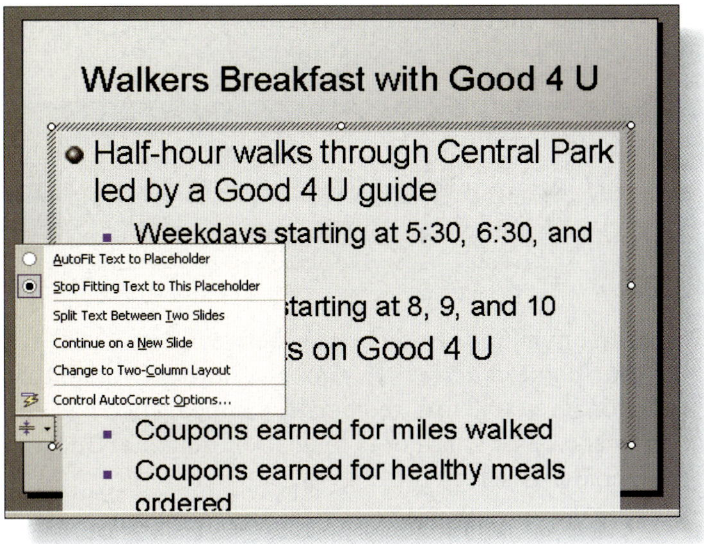

FIGURE 5-10
Working with the AutoFit Options button

Applying Text Formatting to Placeholders

In the previous example you used AutoFit options to change the size of all the text in a placeholder. You can change other formatting features for an entire placeholder by first selecting the placeholder and then choosing the formatting. For example, you can change the text color or font for the entire placeholder, or make all the placeholder text bold.

You can select placeholders several ways:

- Click the border of an active placeholder with the four-pointed arrow ✥.
- Press Esc while a placeholder is active (when the insertion point is in the text).
- Press Tab to select the next placeholder on a slide (only when a text box or text placeholder is not active).

You can deselect placeholders several ways:

- Press Esc to deselect a placeholder or other object. (Press Esc twice if a text placeholder or text box is active.)
- Click an area of the slide where there is no object.

EXERCISE 5-8 Select a Text Placeholder

1. On slide 4, click anywhere in the title text to make the placeholder active. Notice that the border is made of tiny diagonal lines and small white circles.

(Notice also that the AutoFit Options button appears, alerting you that a font size change was made automatically.)

FIGURE 5-11
Selecting a text placeholder

2. Point to any place on the border between two small circles. When you see the four-pointed arrow, click the border. Notice that the insertion point is no longer active and the border's appearance has changed slightly—it is now made up of small dots instead of diagonal lines. This indicates that the placeholder is selected.
3. Press Tab. Now the body text placeholder is selected.

NOTE: Tab cycles through all objects on a slide, not just text placeholders. If a slide contains a graphic object, Tab selects that as well.

4. Press Esc to deselect the body text placeholder. Now nothing on the slide is selected.

EXERCISE 5-9 Apply Formatting to a Selected Text Placeholder

The Increase Font Size and Decrease Font Size buttons change the size of all the text in a selected placeholder by one font size. If there are several sizes of text in the placeholder, each size is changed proportionately. For example, if a text placeholder contains both 24-point text and 20-point text, clicking the Increase Font Size button will change the sizes to 28 points and 24 points at the same time.

Many of the buttons used to format text and text placeholders are toggle buttons. A *toggle button* switches between on and off when you click it. The Shadow button is an example of a toggle button: click it once to apply a shadow, once again to remove it. Other examples of toggle buttons are Bold, Italic, and Underline.

1. Still working on slide 4, click the title placeholder text and then press Esc. This is another way to select an active placeholder.
2. Click the Increase Font Size button on the Formatting toolbar twice. The font size increases, and the font is now too large for the slide.
3. Click the Decrease Font Size button two or more times until the font size is 36 points. (The Font box on the Formatting toolbar indicates the size.)

4. Press [Tab] to select the body text placeholder. Notice the 28+ in the Font Size box. This indicates that there is more than one font size in the placeholder, and the smallest size is 28 points.
5. Click any text in the first bullet. Notice that its font size is 32 points. Notice also that when you click text inside a placeholder, its border is no longer selected. (The diagonal lines return to the border.)
6. Click the first sub-bullet below it, which is 28 points.
7. Press [Esc] to reselect the entire placeholder.
8. Click the Increase Font Size button. The Font Size box now displays 32+, indicating that the smallest text size in the placeholder is 32 points.
9. Click the Decrease Font Size button twice so that 24+ appears in the Font Size box.

TIP: Another way to increase or decrease font size is to press [Ctrl]+[Shift]+[>] or [Ctrl]+[Shift]+[<].

10. Click the down arrow on the Font Color button and choose dark blue (the color sample farthest to the right), making all the body text on this slide dark blue.

11. Click the Shadow button on the Formatting toolbar. Now all the text has a shadow, making it appear darker.
12. Move to slide 1 and save the presentation as ***[your initials]*5-9** but do not print it. Leave the presentation open for the next exercise.

Working with Bullets

When you work with body text placeholders, each line automatically starts with a bullet. You can, however, turn bullets off when the slide would look better without them. You can remove bullets, add new ones, change the shape and color of bullets, and create your own bullets from pictures.

EXERCISE 5-10 Turn Bullets On and Off

Using the Bullets button, you can turn on and off all the bullets in a selected text placeholder or just the bullets for text selected within the placeholder. The Bullets button is another example of a toggle button.

1. Display slide 2. Click within the body text to activate the placeholder. Press [Esc] to select the entire placeholder.

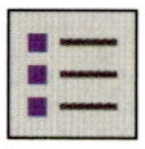

2. Click the Bullets button on the Formatting toolbar. This turns bullets off for the entire placeholder and moves the text to the left.
3. Click the Bullets button again to reapply the bullets.
4. Click within the first bulleted item, "Exercise regularly," and click the Bullets button to turn off the bullet.
5. Click the Bullets button again to reapply the bullet.

EXERCISE 5-11 Change the Color and Shape of a Bullet

You use the Bullets and Numbering dialog box to change the color and shape of a bullet. To change the bullet shape, you can choose a character from another font. Fonts that contain potential bullet characters include Symbol, Wingdings, and Webdings. Another source of bullet characters is the Geometric Shapes subset available for most other fonts.

1. Working on slide 2, select the body text placeholder.
2. Right-click the placeholder border to display the shortcut menu and choose Bullets and Numbering.
3. In the Bullets and Numbering dialog box, click the Bulleted tab.
4. Choose the check mark bullet option.

FIGURE 5-12 Bullets and Numbering dialog box

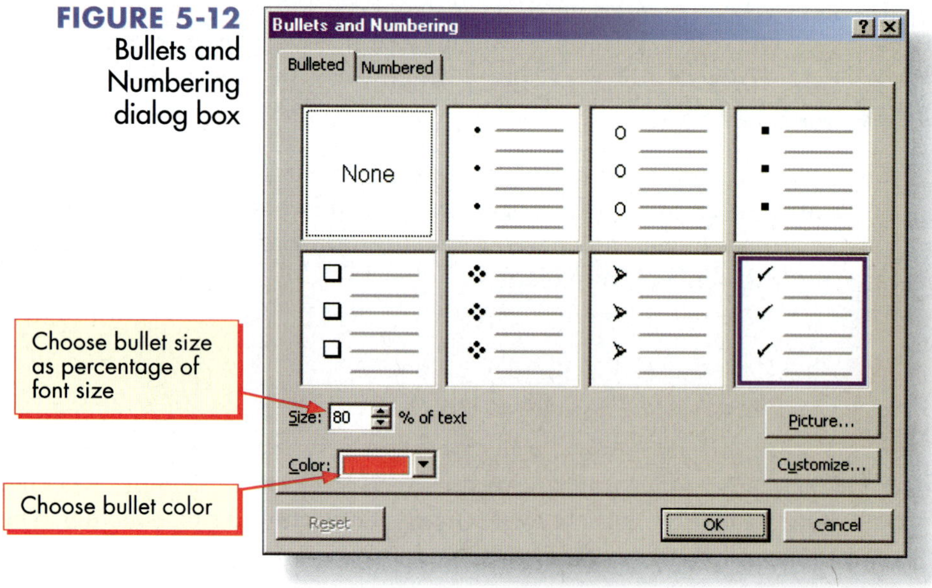

5. In the Color box, choose red.
6. In the Size box, click the down arrow several times until 80 is displayed. Click OK. All bullets on slide 2 are now red check marks, sized at 80% of the font size.

7. Using your I-beam, select the first three lines of bulleted text; then open the Format menu and choose Bullets and Numbering.
8. Click Customize to open the Symbol dialog box.
9. In the Font drop-down list (upper left corner of the dialog box), scroll to the top and choose (normal text).
10. In the Subset drop-down list (upper right corner), choose Miscellaneous Dingbats (near the bottom of the list). Several characters suitable for bullets appear in the dialog box grid.

FIGURE 5-13
Symbol dialog box

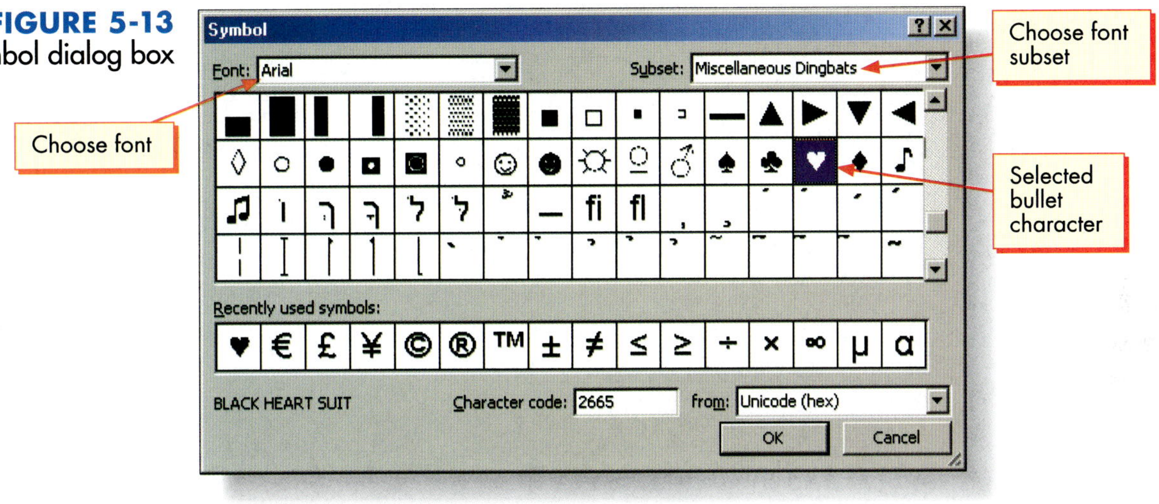

11. Click the heart bullet to select it; then click OK. The Symbol dialog box closes, and the Bullets and Numbering dialog box reappears.
12. Change the Size to 110%. Click OK. The first three bullets on the slide change to red hearts.

EXERCISE 5-12 Create a Bullet from a Picture

Using picture bullets enables you to truly customize a presentation. A picture bullet is created from a graphics file and can be a company logo, a special picture, or anything you create with a graphics program or capture with a scanner or digital camera.

1. Display slide 3 and select the first two bullets (but not the sub-bullets).
2. Open the Bullets and Numbering dialog box, click the Bulleted tab, and then click Picture. The Picture Bullet dialog box displays a variety of colorful bullets. You can choose from one of these bullets or you can import a picture file of your own.

3. Click Import. In the Add Clips to Organizer dialog box, navigate to the location of your student files.
4. Choose the file **Walker** and click Add. The selected picture file is added to the samples shown in the Picture Bullet dialog box.

FIGURE 5-14
Inserting a picture bullet

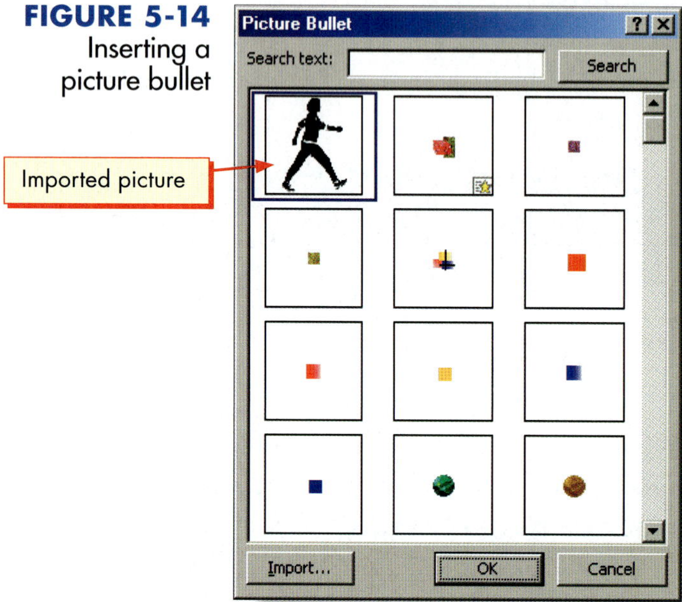

NOTE: You learn more about using pictures and clip art in Lesson 6: "Working with PowerPoint Objects."

5. Click the picture of the person walking to select it and then click OK. The bullets are replaced with picture bullets, but they are too small.
6. With the two bullet items still selected, reopen the Bullets and Numbering dialog box. In the Size box, change the size to 200%. Click OK.
7. Using the steps outlined above, change the bullet for the last bullet item ("Walking is a mood elevator") to the picture of the walker and size it to match the other bullets.
8. If the AutoFit Options button appears near the placeholder, click it and choose AutoFit Text to Placeholder.

EXERCISE 5-13 Create Numbered Paragraphs

Instead of using bullet characters, you can number a list automatically. A numbered list is useful to indicate the order in which steps should be taken or to indicate the importance of the items in a list.

Using the Numbered tab in the Bullets and Numbering dialog box, you can apply a variety of numbering styles, including numbers, letters, and Roman numerals. You can also create a numbered list automatically while you key body text.

1. Display slide 5 and select the body text placeholder.
2. Click the Bullets button to remove the bullets.
3. Select all the text in the placeholder and delete it.
4. With the placeholder activated, key **1.** and press Tab. Key **Walk with us**
5. Press Enter. The second line is automatically numbered "2."

6. Key **Eat with us** and press Enter.
7. Key **Do what's Good 4 U**. The slide now has three items, automatically numbered 1 through 3.
8. Press Esc to select the placeholder; then open the Bullets and Numbering dialog box and click the Numbered tab. Notice that there are several different numbering styles to choose from.
9. In the Color box, choose Black. Click OK.
10. Remove the footer information from the presentation's slides. Then create a handout header and footer: include the date and your name as the header, and the page number and text ***[your initials]*5-13** as the footer.
11. Move to slide 1 and save the presentation as ***[your initials]*5-13** in your Lesson 5 folder.
12. Preview and then print the presentation as handouts, 6 slides per page, grayscale, framed. Leave the presentation open for the next exercise.

TIP: You can control the numbering style that is applied automatically by keying your first item with the style you want, such as **A.** or **i.**

Changing Text Alignment

Bulleted items, titles, and subtitles are all considered paragraphs in PowerPoint. Just as in a word processor, when you press Enter, a new paragraph begins. You can align paragraphs with either the left or right placeholder borders, center them within the placeholder, or justify long paragraphs so both margins are squared off.

EXERCISE 5-14 Change Text Alignment

You can change text alignment for all the text in a placeholder or for just one line, depending on what is selected.

1. Move to slide 5 and select the body text placeholder.

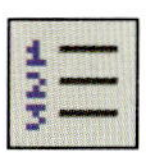

2. Click the Numbering button on the Formatting toolbar to remove the numbering.
3. Position the insertion point in the first line, "Walk with us."
4. From the Format menu, choose Alignment; then choose Align Right from the submenu. The text in the first line aligns to the right.

NOTE: Notice the keyboard shortcuts listed on the Alignment submenu for aligning paragraphs.

5. Click the Align Left button on the Formatting toolbar. The paragraph aligns to the left.
6. Select the placeholder border and click the Center button on the Formatting toolbar. All three lines are centered horizontally within the placeholder.
7. Make the title text bold.

Inserting a PowerPoint Table

A *table* displays information organized in rows and columns. A convenient way to add a table is to insert a new slide and then choose one of the content slide layouts. A *content layout* is a slide layout that contains one or more *content placeholders*. You can insert tables, clip art, pictures, media clips, charts, and diagrams in a content placeholder.

NOTE: There are other ways to insert tables, including drawing them with the pencil tool or using the Insert Table button on the Standard toolbar.

EXERCISE 5-15 Start a Table

When you start a new table, a dialog box asks for the number of rows and columns that the table will contain. It's a good idea to have a general layout planned when you start a table, but it's easy to insert or delete rows and columns later if you change your mind.

1. Move to slide 3 ("Walk to Good Health").
2. Click New Slide on the Formatting toolbar to insert a new slide after slide 3.
3. In the Slide Layout task pane, scroll down so the Content Layouts heading is near the top of the task pane. Notice that there are several layouts, including a blank layout, one with no title placeholder, and some with multiple content placeholders.
4. Point to several different layouts and read their ScreenTips. (See Figure 5-15 on the next page.)
5. Click the layout named Title and Content.
6. In the Title placeholder, key **Executive Walkers Challenge**

FIGURE 5-15 Choosing a content layout

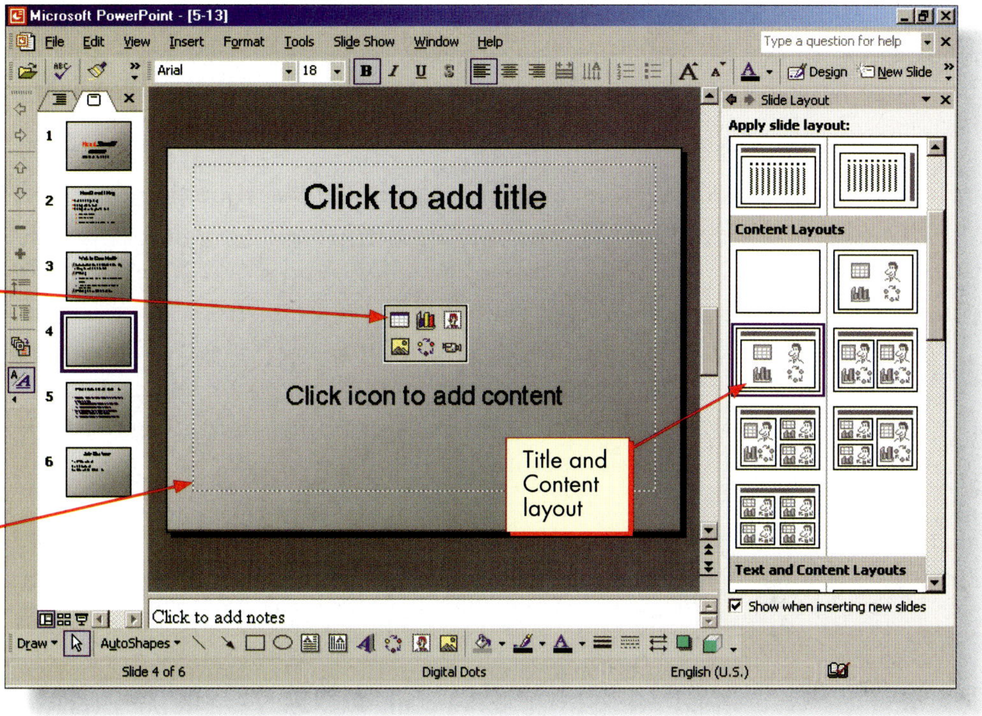

7. In the content placeholder, click the Insert Table icon, the upper left icon in the gray box. The Insert Table dialog box appears.

FIGURE 5-16 Entering number of columns and rows for a table

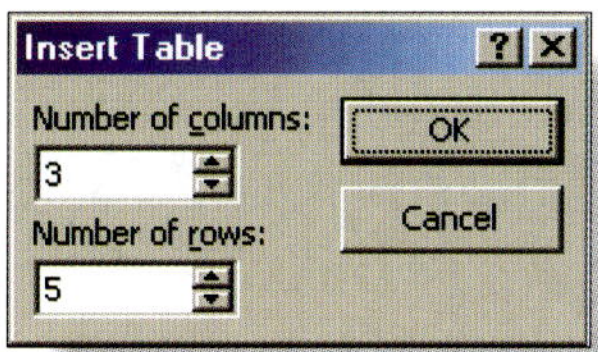

8. Key **3** in the Number of columns box and **5** in the Number of rows box. Click OK. A blank table, sized to fit the placeholder, is inserted. Notice the Tables and Borders floating toolbar that automatically appears.

NOTE: If the Tables and Borders toolbar is not showing, right-click any toolbar and then choose Tables and Borders from the shortcut menu.

EXERCISE 5-16 Practice Navigating in a Table

A table is composed of a series of rows and columns. The rectangle formed by the intersection of a row and a column is called a *cell*. There are many ways that you can move from cell to cell:

- Click the cell.
- Use the Arrow keys ←, →, ↑, or ↓.
- Press Tab to move forward or Shift+Tab to move backward.

NOTE: When a cell is blank, pressing the left arrow key ← or the right arrow key → moves the insertion point left or right one cell. If there is text in a cell, the left and right arrow keys move the insertion point one character to the left or right.

1. Click any table cell. Notice the insertion point in the cell you clicked.
2. Press Tab several times. The insertion point moves through cells from left to right. When you reach the end of a row, pressing Tab moves the insertion point to the beginning of the next row.
3. Press Shift+Tab several times. The insertion point moves through cells from right to left.
4. Press each arrow key several times and observe the movement of the the insertion point.

EXERCISE 5-17 Key Text in a Table

Text that you key appears in the cell containing the insertion point. After text is in a cell, you edit it in the same way as you edit any other text.

1. Click the upper left cell and key **Executive**
2. Press Tab and then key **Gus Irvinelli** in the second cell.
3. Press → to move to the third cell in the first row and key **Roy Olafsen**
4. Press Tab. The insertion point should be in the first cell in the second row.
5. Key the remaining table text as shown in Figure 5-17.

FIGURE 5-17

	Col 1	Col 2	Col 3
Row 1	Executive	Gus Irvinelli	Roy Olafsen
Row 2	Week 1	6 miles	5 miles
Row 3	Week 2	8 miles	9 miles
Row 4	Week 3	4 miles	5 miles
Row 5	Week 4	6 miles	9 miles

EXERCISE 5-18 Insert Rows and Columns in a Table

As you work on your table, you will often find that it needs to be larger than originally planned. If you run out of rows as you key table text, a new row will automatically be inserted at the bottom of the table if you press Tab after keying in the last cell.

If you want to insert rows or columns anywhere else in a table, you can use any of the following commands, which are accessed by clicking Table on the Tables and Borders toolbar:

- Insert Columns to the Left
- Insert Columns to the Right
- Insert Rows Above
- Insert Rows Below

1. With the insertion point in the last cell (containing the text "9 miles"), press Tab. A new blank row is inserted at the bottom of the table. The table is now too big for the slide. This will be fixed later.
2. Key the following text in the new row:

   Total 24 miles 28 miles

3. With the insertion point in the lower right cell (containing "28 miles"), click Table on the Tables and Borders toolbar.

FIGURE 5-18
Inserting a column

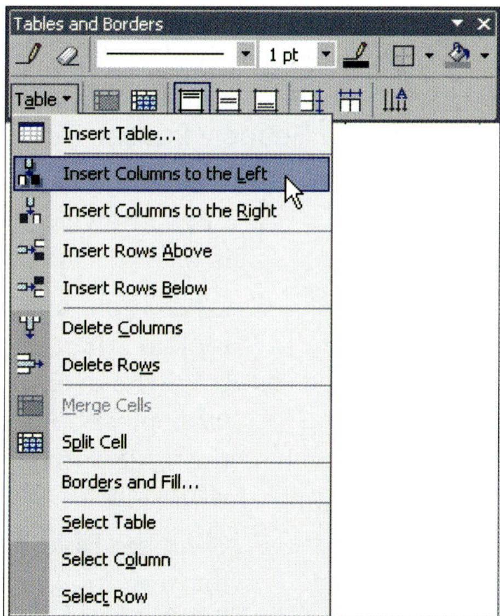

4. From the drop-down menu, choose Insert Columns to the Left. A new column is inserted between "Gus Irvinelli" and "Roy Olafsen." The table is now too wide for the slide, but that will be fixed in a later step.

5. Key the text shown in Figure 5-19 for the new column.

FIGURE 5-19

Row 1	Julie Wolf
Row 2	8 miles
Row 3	5 miles
Row 4	4 miles
Row 5	3 miles
Row 6	20 miles

EXERCISE 5-19 Apply Basic Formatting to a Table

As you can see from the previous exercise, when you insert rows and columns into a table, it can become too large for your slide. An easy way to fix the problem is to reapply the slide layout. Reapplying the slide layout will reduce the size of table cells and table text where necessary to force the table to fit in the content placeholder.

Buttons on the Formatting toolbar and the Tables and Borders toolbar can easily add finishing touches to your table.

1. In the Slide Layout task pane, point to the Title and Content layout icon and click its down arrow.
2. In the drop-down menu, choose Reapply Layout. The table is resized to fit the content placeholder.

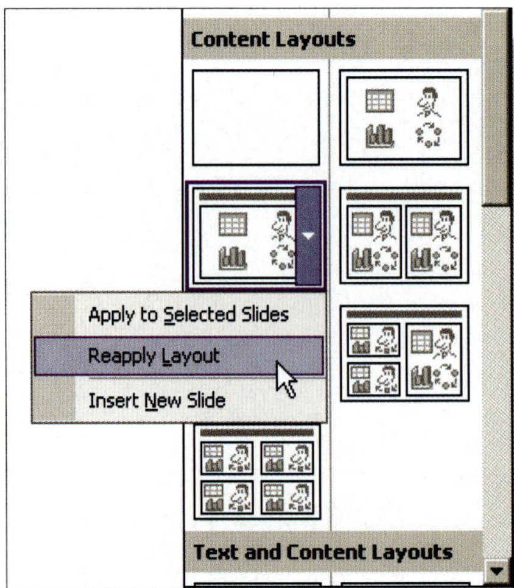

FIGURE 5-20 Reapplying a slide layout

3. Click anywhere in the table to activate it.
4. Click Table on the Tables and Borders toolbar; then choose Select Table from the drop-down menu. The entire table placeholder is selected. (Note the wide dotted border and the small white circles).
5. Click the Bold button **B** on the Formatting toolbar and then click the Decrease Font Size button twice. Now all the text in the table is bold and sized at 24 points.

POWERPOINT

6. Click the Center button on the Formatting toolbar to center all the text horizontally within each cell.

7. Click the Center Vertically button on the Tables and Borders toolbar to center all the text vertically within each cell.
8. Move to slide 1 and save the file as ***[your initials]*****5-19** but do not print it. Keep it open for the next exercise.

Changing Size and Position of Text Placeholders

At times you will want to change the way text is positioned on a slide. For example, you might want to make a text placeholder narrower or wider to control how text wraps to a new line or you might want to move all the text up or down on a slide.

You can change the size and position of text placeholders several ways:

- Drag a *sizing handle* to change the size and shape of a text placeholder. Sizing handles are the eight small circles along the border of a selected text placeholder or other object.
- Drag the placeholder border to move the text to a new position.
- Change placeholder size and position settings by using the Format Placeholder command.

EXERCISE 5-20 Change the Size of a Placeholder by Dragging a Sizing Handle

To change the size or shape of a placeholder, you must first select it, displaying the border made up of tiny dots and sizing handles. It is important to make sure that you're dragging a sizing handle when you want to change a placeholder's size.

Dragging a corner sizing handle changes both the height and width of a placeholder at the same time.

1. Display slide 6 and select the body text placeholder. Notice the small white circles around the border. These are the sizing handles.
2. Position the pointer over the bottom center sizing handle.
3. When the pointer changes to a two-pointed vertical arrow ↕, hold down your left mouse button and drag the bottom border up until it is just below the middle line "Eat with us."

   As you drag, a dotted box shows the changing shape of the placeholder, and the pointer turns into a small cross. When you release the mouse, notice that the position of the text on the slide is unchanged.

FIGURE 5-21
Resizing a placeholder

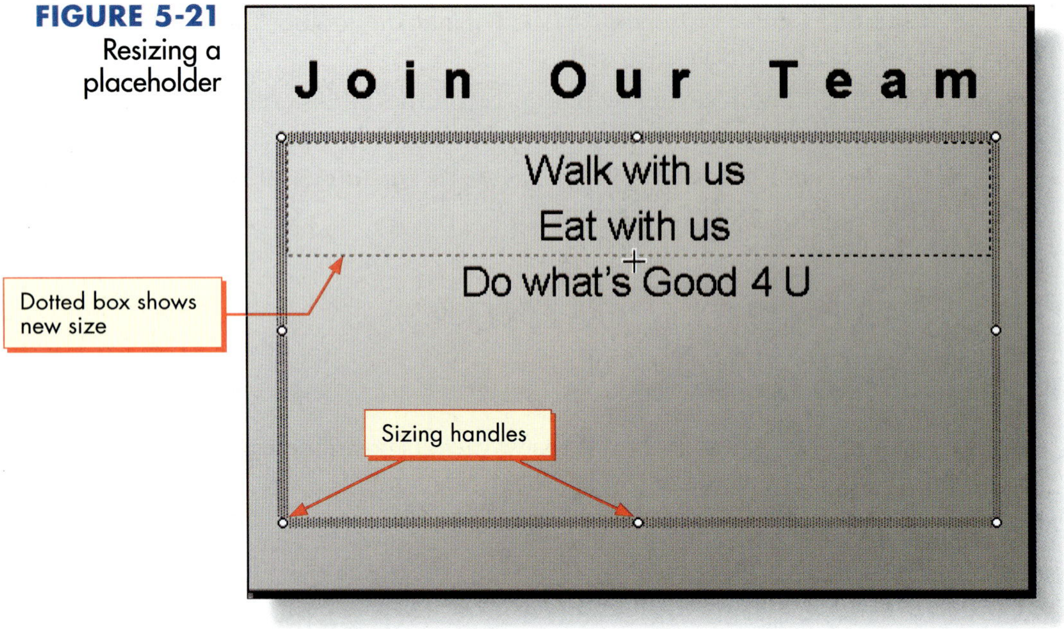

4. Release the mouse button. The text is reduced in size to automatically fit the smaller text placeholder.
5. Click the AutoFit Options button and choose Stop Fitting Text to This Placeholder. The text returns to its original size, but it is too big for the placeholder.
6. Drag the bottom border of the placeholder down just enough so that all the text fits inside the placeholder.
7. Position your pointer over the lower left corner-sizing handle; then drag it toward the center of the text. Both the height and width of the placeholder change.
8. Click the Undo button to restore the placeholder to its previous size.

EXERCISE 5-21 Move a Placeholder by Dragging Its Border

As with changing the size of a placeholder, to change a placeholder's position you must first select it. It is important to make sure that you drag the placeholder border (any part of the border except the sizing handles) when you want to change its position.

1. Select the body text placeholder on slide 6.
2. Position the pointer over the placeholder border anywhere except on a sizing handle. The pointer changes to the four-pointed arrow.

3. Drag the four-pointed arrow ✥ down until the placeholder appears vertically centered on the slide.

FIGURE 5-22
Moving a placeholder

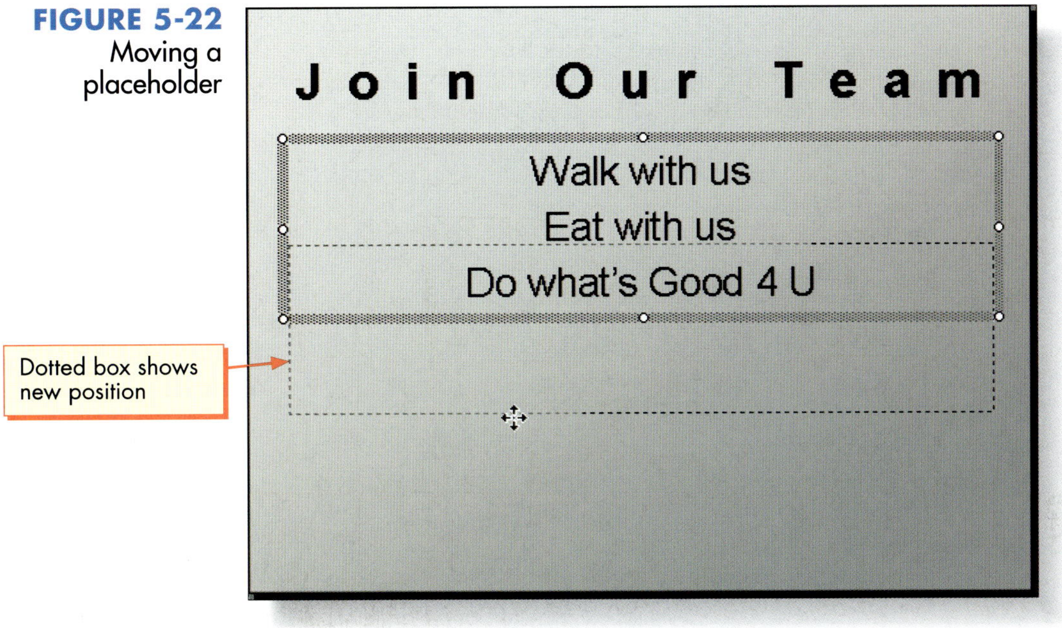

TIP: To fine-tune the position of an object, hold down Alt while dragging. Another way to adjust the position of a selected object is to press the arrow keys.

4. Deselect the placeholder. The text is now attractively placed on the slide.

EXERCISE 5-22 Use the Format Placeholder Command

The Format Placeholder command opens a dialog box, which offers, among other things, a way to change the size and placement of objects by using exact measurements. You'll learn more about other options in this dialog box throughout this course.

1. Move to slide 2.
2. Right-click anywhere in the body text placeholder and choose Format Placeholder from the shortcut menu. The Format AutoShape dialog box appears. Notice the different tabs. (You can also open this dialog box by displaying the Format menu and choosing Placeholder.) (See Figure 5-23 on the next page.)
3. Click the Position tab and key **2** in the Horizontal text box. This places the placeholder 2 inches in from the left edge of the slide.

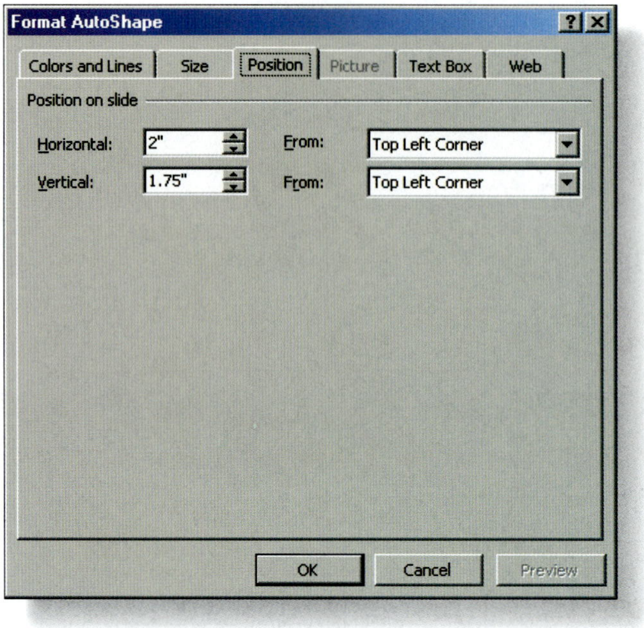

FIGURE 5-23 Format AutoShape dialog box, Position tab

4. Click Preview and drag the dialog box out of the way to see the new position of the text. Notice that the placeholder moved to the right and its border now extends beyond the right edge of the slide.
5. Click the Size tab. Key **4** in the Height box and **6** in the Width box, making the placeholder 4 inches tall and 6 inches wide.
6. Click Preview to see the results and then click OK to close the AutoFormat dialog box. The placeholder is now sized appropriately for the text inside it and is attractively positioned on the slide.
7. Change the handout footer to show the text ***[your initials]*5-22**.
8. Check spelling in the presentation; then move to slide 1 and save the presentation as ***[your initials]*5-22** in your Lesson 5 folder.
9. Preview and then print the presentation as handouts, 6 slides per page, grayscale, framed. Close the presentation.

Modifying a Design Template's Text Placeholders

A *master slide* contains formatted text placeholders and background items that are designed to appear on all slides in a presentation. Changes that you make on a master slide appear on all slides in the presentation that are based on that master. There are two masters you can use for slides:

- Title master, which includes text placeholders for the title and subtitle text on the title slide
- Slide master, which includes text placeholders for the title and body text

In general, the *title master* and the *slide master* contain the same design elements (such as background color, graphic, and text formatting). However, the title master is arranged differently to accommodate title and subtitle text. The slide master is often less elaborate, leaving room for body text and other information. You can change the formatting and design of the masters and thus set the tone for the entire presentation.

EXERCISE 5-23 Change Text Formatting on Master Slides

There are two ways to display the slide and title masters:

- Use the View menu.
- Use Shift + the Normal View button.

1. Display slide 2. Notice that this is the only slide with heart-shaped bullets. You'll use the masters to change all first level-bullets to hearts, to change the text color, and to make some additional changes.

2. To display the slide master, open the View menu, choose Master, Slide Master (or hold down Shift and click the Normal View button). Dotted placeholders indicate the position for title text, body text, and footer information. You can change the size, shape, position, and text attributes for any of these text placeholders.

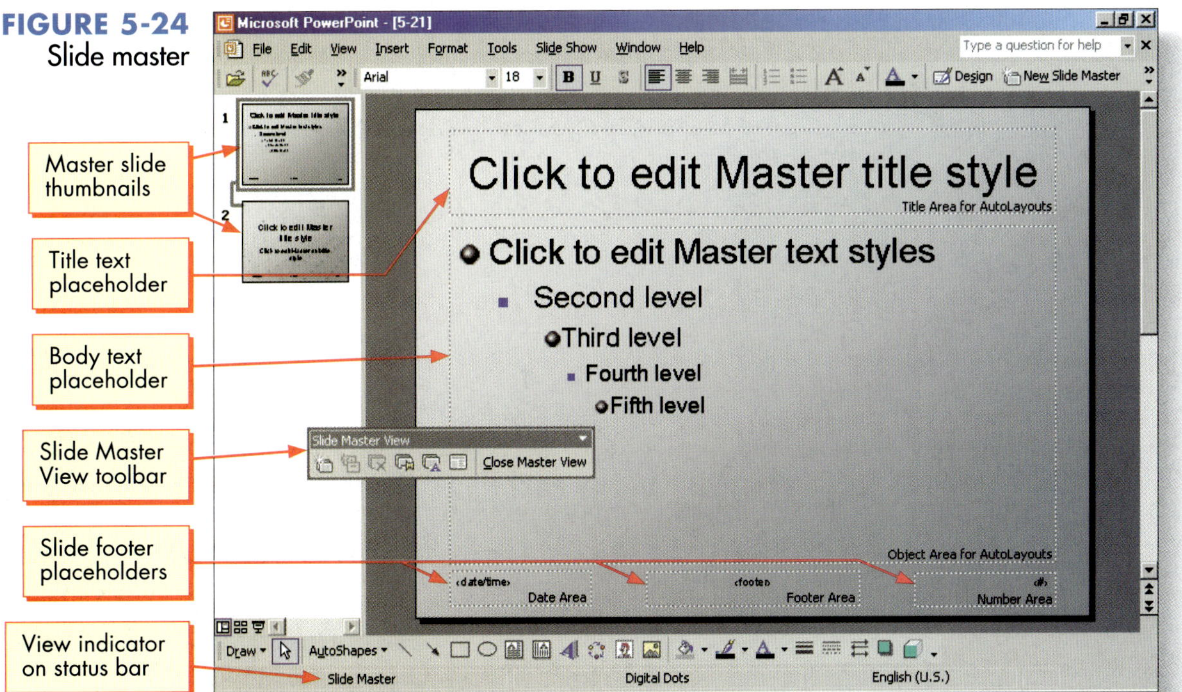

FIGURE 5-24
Slide master

NOTE: An easy way to tell whether you're viewing the slide master or title master is to check the indicator on the left side of the status bar.

3. Select the title placeholder by clicking its dotted border with the four-pointed arrow ✥.
4. Change the font for the title placeholder to Impact by using the Font box on the Standard toolbar.
5. With the title placeholder still selected, change the font size to 44 points and change the font color to red.
6. Click within the first-level bullet on the body text placeholder. Change the bullet character to a red heart from the (normal text), Miscellaneous Dingbats category. Make it 110% of the font size.
7. Format the second-level bullet as a red check mark from the Webdings font sized at 100%.
8. Press PgDn or use the vertical scroll bar to display the title master.

TIP: You can switch between the title and slide masters by pressing PgDn and PgUp, using the vertical scroll bar, or clicking its thumbnail.

9. Review the elements on the title master. Some of the changes you made to the slide master are reflected on the title master (the title text is red, Impact). PowerPoint does this automatically to make sure your presentation is formatted consistently.

FIGURE 5-25
Title master

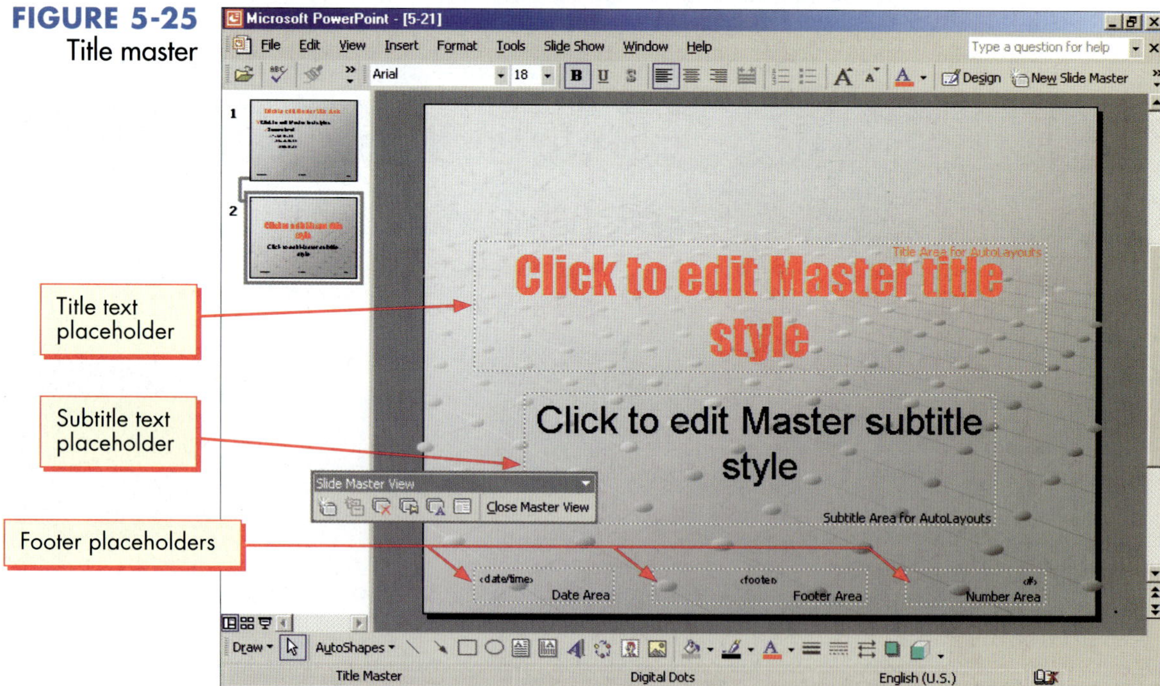

10. Click Close Master View on the Slide Master View toolbar. Slide 2 is displayed.

11. Move to slide 1 and scroll through the presentation. Notice that most (but not all) the changes you made to the masters are reflected in the presentation. You correct this in the next exercise.

EXERCISE 5-24 Reapply a Slide Layout

Changing a master does not override formatting changes you made to individual slides. If you change a slide master after formatting individual slides, you can reapply the slide layout to those slides to make them conform to the new master.

1. From the Format menu, choose Slide Layout to display the Slide Layout task pane.
2. Display slide 1; then right-click the Title Slide layout in the Slide Layout task pane and choose Reapply Layout from the shortcut menu. The title master's formatting replaces the formatting you applied earlier.
3. Display slide 2. You changed the size and position of slide 2's body text placeholder.
4. Reapply the Title and Text layout to slide 2. The placeholder size and position change back to the master's layout.
5. Reapply the Title and Text layout to slides 3 and 5. Leave slides 4 and 6 as is. If the AutoFit Options button appears, click it and choose AutoFit Text to Placeholder.
6. Move to slide 1. Change the notes and handouts footer to show the text ***[your initials]*5-24**
7. Move to slide 1 and save the presentation as ***[your initials]*5-24** in your Lesson 5 folder.
8. View the presentation as a slide show. Preview and then print it as handouts, 6 slides per page, grayscale, framed. Close the presentation.

USING HELP

Working with the slide and title masters helps you create consistent and professional-looking presentations. In later lessons you learn how to place art on a slide master so it appears throughout your presentation.

Use Help to learn more about master slides:

1. Key **slide master** in the Ask a Question box and press Enter.
2. Select the topic About the slide master.

FIGURE 5-26
About the slide master

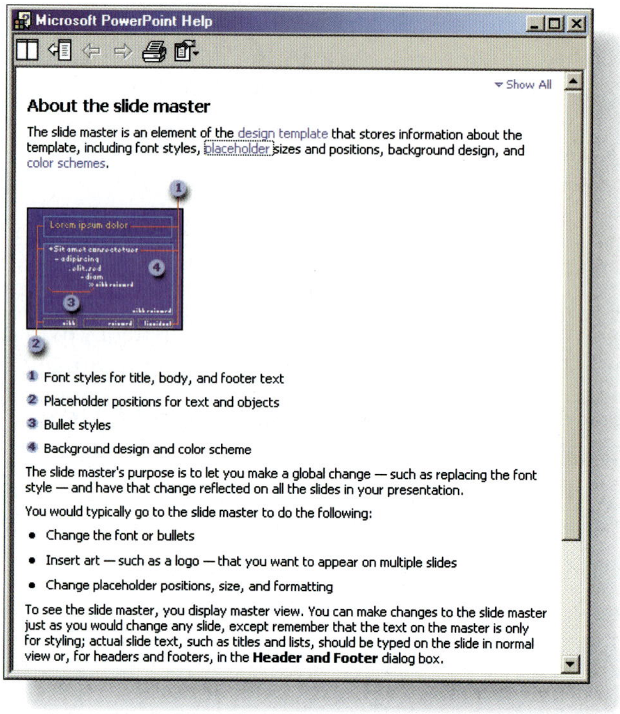

3. Review the information displayed for the topic. Expand each of the subtopics and read them also. Notice that glossary terms appear in blue text. If you encounter a term you are not sure of, click it to see a definition.
4. Close Help when you finish.

LESSON 5 Summary

- A font is a set of characters with a specific design, for example, Arial or Times New Roman.
- Font size (the height of a font) is measured in points, with 72 points to an inch. Fonts of the same size can vary in the width, some taking up more horizontal space than others.
- Change text attributes and effects such as bold, italic, and text color by first selecting the text and then clicking the appropriate buttons on the Formatting toolbar. Or, apply formatting as you key text.
- Many formatting buttons are toggle buttons, meaning that the same button is clicked to turn an effect on and clicked again to turn it off.
- The Font dialog box enables you to apply multiple formatting attributes and effects all at one time. Using the Font dialog box is another way to apply text formatting.

- One or more fonts can be changed for an entire presentation by using the Replace Fonts command.
- When AutoFit is turned on, text is automatically resized to fit its placeholder. You can turn AutoFit features on or off by using the AutoCorrect Options dialog box.
- When a text placeholder with a size problem is selected, the AutoFit button appears near the placeholder. Click the AutoFit button to control how AutoFit affects the text.
- When a text placeholder is selected, formatting that you apply affects all the text in the placeholder.
- Body text placeholders are preformatted to have bulleted paragraphs. Bullets for selected paragraphs or placeholders are turned on or off by clicking the Bullets button.
- Use the Bullets and Numbering dialog box to change the shape, size, and color of bullets or numbers.
- Graphics files can be imported and used as picture bullets.
- Text in placeholders can be aligned with the left or right side of the placeholder, or can be centered or justified.
- A simple table can be easily created by using one of the content slide layouts. Click the Insert Table icon in the content placeholder, and then choose the number of rows and columns needed for the table.
- Move from cell to cell in a table by using Tab, Shift+Tab, arrow keys, or your mouse.
- The Table drop-down list on the Tables and Borders toolbar offers options for inserting rows and columns. If a table becomes too large for the slide, reapply its content slide layout to make it fit.
- Apply basic formatting to a selected table or table cells by using the Formatting toolbar.
- Format text placeholders on master slides in the same way as text placeholders on presentation slides. Making changes to master slides affects all the slides in a presentation.
- Switch between the title master and the slide master by pressing PgUp and PgDn or clicking a thumbnail on the left side of the screen.
- Changes made to master slides do not override formatting changes previously made to individual slides. To update a slide to agree with its master, reapply its slide layout.

LESSON 5 Command Summary

FEATURE	BUTTON	MENU	KEYBOARD	SPEECH?
Increase Font Size	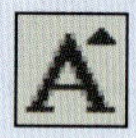	Format, Font, Size	Ctrl + Shift + >	✓
Decrease Font Size		Format, Font, Size	Ctrl + Shift + <	✓
Bold	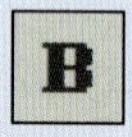	Format, Font, Font style, Bold	Ctrl + B	✓
Italic	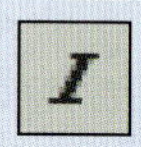	Format, Font, Font style, Italic	Ctrl + I	✓
Underline	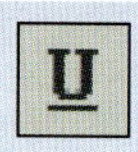	Format, Font, Effects, Underline	Ctrl + U	✓
Text Shadow		Format, Font, Effects, Shadow		✓
Text Color	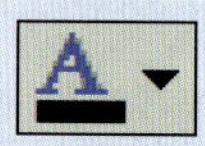	Format, Font, Color		✓
Align Left		Format, Alignment, Align Left	Ctrl + L	✓
Center	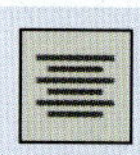	Format, Alignment, Center	Ctrl + E	✓
Align Right		Format, Alignment, Align Right	Ctrl + R	✓
Justify		Format, Alignment, Justify	Ctrl + J	✓
Change case		Format, Change Case	Shift + F3	✓
Apply a font	Font box	Format, Font, Font	Ctrl + Shift + F	✓
Change font size	Font size box	Format, Font, Size	Ctrl + Shift + P	✓
Replace fonts		Format, Replace Fonts		✓

continues

LESSON 5 Command Summary *continued*

FEATURE	BUTTON	MENU	KEYBOARD	SPEECH?
Turn bullets on or off	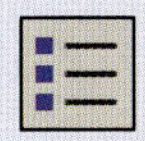	Format, Bullets and Numbering		✓
Turn numbering on or off	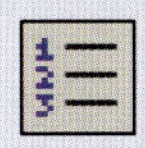	Format, Bullets and Numbering		✓
Select table		Table, Select Table (on the Tables and Borders toolbar)		✓
Insert a table row or column		Table (on the Tables and Borders toolbar)		✓
Display master slide	Shift + 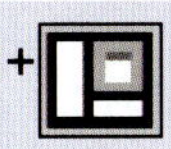	View, Master, Slide Master		✓

Concepts Review

TRUE/FALSE QUESTIONS

Each of the following statements is either true or false. Indicate your choice by circling T or F.

T F **1.** You can change selected text from uppercase to lowercase by using the Shift+F3 keyboard shortcut.

T F **2.** You can apply text attributes before you key text.

T F **3.** Sentence case capitalizes the initial letter of all words in a paragraph.

T F **4.** To search for and replace one font with another throughout a presentation, use the Replace Font dialog box.

T F **5.** Changes on the slide master override changes you make to individual slides.

T F **6.** The button 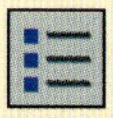 can turn bullets on or off.

T F **7.** The Title Only slide layout has a table wizard to guide you through the creation of a table.

T F **8.** You can drag a sizing handle to reposition a placeholder.

SHORT ANSWER QUESTIONS

Write the correct answer in the space provided.

1. What must you do before you can change an attribute for existing text?

____

2. Which dialog box enables you to change the color of text?

____

3. Which toolbar buttons change font size?

____

4. How can you center text vertically in table cells?

____

5. Which commands do you need to choose to change bullet color?

____

6. How can you display the slide master without using the View menu?

____

7. What is the quickest way to add a row to the bottom of a table?

____

8. What does the button  do to selected text?

____

CRITICAL THINKING

Answer these questions on a separate page. There are no right or wrong answers. Support your answers with examples from your own experience, if possible.

1. Explain how font faces can affect a presentation. Can you use too many fonts in a presentation? Explain your answer.

2. Adding different bullet shapes can add interest and emphasis to a presentation. How do you think a presentation would look if every slide included different bullets? If all the bullets were the same?

Lesson Applications

EXERCISE 5-25

Apply text attributes to selected text and placeholders, work with bullets, make changes to the slide master, resize and reposition placeholders, apply an animation scheme.

1. Open the file **FoodCon**.
2. On the slide master, left-align the text in the title placeholder and make it bold and yellow.
3. Change the first-level bullet to a solid diamond shape from the Wingdings font. Make the bullet yellow and 90% of the text size.
4. On slide 1, change the date in the subtitle placeholder to yellow, 40 points, and bold. Edit the date to the current month and year.
5. Move to slide 4 and change the title to simply "Concession Products" on one line.
6. Change the layout of slide 4 to two columns. Rearrange the text as shown in Figure 5-27.

FIGURE 5-27

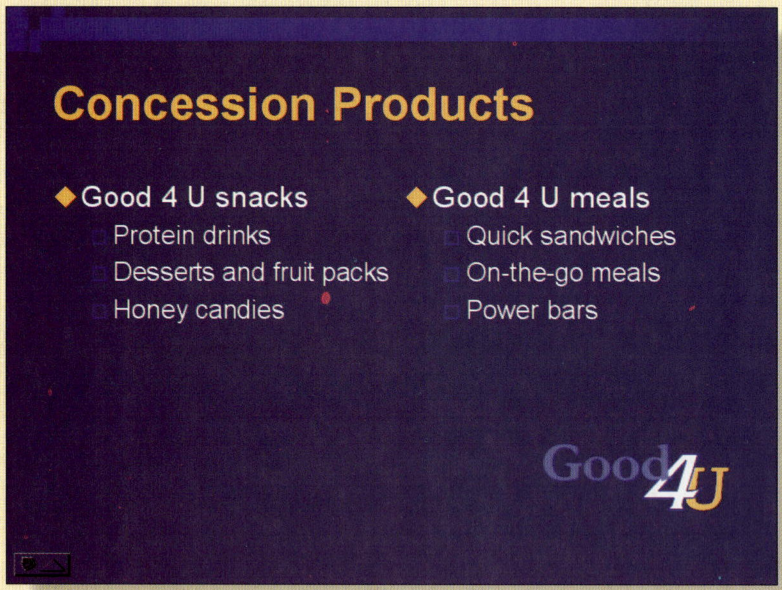

7. After rearranging the text, reapply the slide's layout to automatically adjust the font sizes on the slide.

POWERPOINT

8. Widen the first column placeholder so "Desserts and fruit packs" appears on one line.
9. View the presentation's text in the Outline pane and remove any extra blank lines that you find.
10. Check spelling in the presentation.
11. Apply the Float animation scheme (from the Exciting category) to the entire presentation and then view the presentation as a slide show.
12. Create a handout header and footer: include the date and your name as the header, and the page number and text ***[your initials]*5-25** as the footer.
13. Move to slide 1 and save the presentation as ***[your initials]*5-25** in your Lesson 5 folder.
14. Preview and then print the presentation as handouts, 6 slides per page, grayscale, framed. Close the presentation.

EXERCISE 5-26

Apply text attributes to selected text and text placeholders, work with bullets and the slide master, replace fonts, and create a table.

1. Open the file **WasteMgt**.
2. Make the following changes to the slide master:
   - Remove the text shadow from all placeholders.
   - Make the title text placeholder bold.
   - Change second-level bullets to dark blue check marks (Wingdings 2 font).
   - Italicize the second-level text.
3. Edit slide 1 so the title reads **Recycling Program**, and the subtitle reads **Good 4 U Management Training**. Change the font color of the subtitle to red and make it bold.
4. On slide 2, make the following words bold: "waste," "costs," and "landfill overloads."
5. On slide 3, increase the font size of the title to 54 points.
6. Add the following speaker's notes:

   Slide 2: Discuss how waste reduction is cost-effective.

   Slide 3: Mention our targeted percentages for the coming year.
7. Use the Replace Fonts command to replace the Arial, Arial Black, and Times New Roman fonts with Tahoma.
8. Create a table on a new slide after slide 4, using the text and table arrangement shown in Figure 5-28. Make the text in the first row bold and centered both vertically and horizontally. When all the table text is keyed, select the

entire table and reduce the text size by one increment. Reapply the slide's layout to adjust the overall table size.

FIGURE 5-28

Local Recyclers

Name	Phone	Specialty
Frampton Paper	(800) 555-9876	White office paper, makes recycled paper goods
Andy's Scrap Metal	(800) 555-6565	Aluminum, iron, steel
Marion Mills	(800) 555-1234	Any plastics, must be clean
Cannon Box Co.	(800) 555-5432	Newspaper, cardboard, boxes must be flattened

TIP: To apply formatting to individual cells, just click the cell and then apply the formatting. You can also drag the I-beam across several cells to select them before applying the formatting.

9. Check spelling in the presentation.
10. Apply a slow-speed slide transition of your choice to all slides.
11. Create a handout header and footer: include the date and your name as the header, and the page number and text ***[your initials]*5-26** as the footer.
12. Move to slide 1 and save the presentation as ***[your initials]*5-26** in your Lesson 5 folder.
13. Preview and then print the presentation as handouts, 6 slides per page, grayscale, framed. Print the notes pages for slides 2 and 3. Close the presentation.

EXERCISE 5-27

Apply text attributes to selected text and text placeholders, work with bullets and the slide master, align text, and resize and reposition placeholders.

1. Create a new presentation by opening the Word outline **PwrWalk3** from within PowerPoint.

REVIEW: To open a Word outline in PowerPoint, click the Open button and then choose All Outlines in the Files of type drop-down list.

2. Apply the Eclipse design template to the entire presentation. Change the color scheme to the one with the black background and red, yellow, and green accents.
3. Apply the Title Slide layout to slide 1. Move the second line of the title to the subtitle placeholder and center it.
4. Make the following changes to the slide master (make sure you're not working on the title master):
   - Change all first-level bullets to bicycles (Webdings font, fifth row). Change the bullet size to 100% of text size and change its color to yellow.
   - Change the title text placeholder font to Arial Black.
   - Center the title text.
5. On the title master, center-align the subtitle placeholder.
6. Reapply all slide layouts to make sure the slide master changes are reflected on all slides.
7. Replace "power walking" with **biking** throughout the presentation. Capitalize "Biking" on the title slide.
8. On slide 2, move the text "(fitness and health participants)" to a new line by pressing Shift+Enter before the parentheses.
9. On slide 3, change the case of the body text placeholder to sentence case.
10. On slide 4, resize the body text placeholder to fit the text and drag it so it appears horizontally centered below the title.

NOTE: Don't worry about centering the text box exactly. Just position it so it has an attractive appearance.

11. Check spelling in the presentation.
12. Apply an animation scheme of your choice to all slides; then apply a different animation scheme to the last slide in the presentation.
13. Create a handout header and footer: include the date and your name as the header, and the page number and text ***[your initials]*5-27** as the footer.
14. Move to slide 1 and save the presentation as ***[your initials]*5-27** in your Lesson 5 folder.
15. View the presentation as a slide show. Then preview and print the presentation as handouts, 4 slides per page, grayscale, framed. Close the presentation.

EXERCISE 5-28 Challenge Yourself

Apply text attributes to text and text placeholders, work with bullets and the slide master, change alignment, resize and reposition placeholders.

1. Open the file **Sponsor1**.
2. Scroll through the slides, noticing the inconsistent formatting.
3. Reapply the slide layouts for all the slides; then scroll through the slides again.
4. On the slide master, make the following changes:
   - Increase the font size for the title placeholder by one increment.
   - Change the font for the title placeholder to Arial Black.
   - Decrease the font size for the body text placeholder by one increment.
   - Change the first- and second-level bullets to shapes and colors of your own choice.
5. At the end of the presentation, insert two new slides using the text layout shown in Figure 5-29.

FIGURE 5-29

Slide 7

Annual Event —Title
- Establish volunteer committees
- Schedule year-round support events
  - Training
  - Practice walks
  - Advertising

Slide 8

Paths for Every Pace —Title
- Beginner
- Intermediate
- Experienced

6. Edit the first bullet on slide 2 to read **Increase Good 4 U name recognition**
7. Insert line breaks (Shift+Enter) before the parentheses in the second and third bullets on slide 2. Italicize the text in parentheses.
8. Edit the second bullet on slide 3 to read **Organize training seminars**

9. Edit the bulleted items on slide 5 to read as follows:

FIGURE 5-30

```
•  Lectures in Good 4 U banquet room
     -  Conducted by local marathon winners
•  Training walks in Central Park
     -  Free bananas and Good 4 U sports drinks
```

10. On both slides 4 and 8, make the following changes to the body text placeholders:
    - Increase the text size one increment.
    - Resize the placeholders to fit the text.
    - Reposition the placeholders so that the text appears centered under the titles.
11. Move the first bulleted item on slide 3 ("Advertise Power...") to the last line on the slide. Change this last bullet to sentence case.
12. Move slide 4 ("Advertising") to the end of the presentation so it becomes slide 8.
13. Check spelling in the presentation.
14. Create a handout header and footer: include the date and your name as the header, and the page number and text ***[your initials]*****5-28** as the footer.
15. Move to slide 1 and save the presentation as ***[your initials]*****5-28** in your Lesson 5 folder.
16. Preview and then print the presentation as handouts, 9 slides per page, grayscale, landscape, framed. Close the presentation.

On Your Own

In these exercises you work on your own, as you would in a real-life work environment. Use the skills you've learned to accomplish the task—and be creative.

EXERCISE 5-29

Pick a hobby, sports activity, trade, or profession in which you are interested. Create a PowerPoint presentation to inform others interested in the same activity about the type of equipment they should consider purchasing. Include desirable features, undesirable features, and other information that you think would be helpful. Create at least six slides. Format the presentation by using a design template, color scheme, and text formatting that you think are effective in conveying your information. Choose one or more animation schemes. Save the presentation as ***[your initials]*5-29**. Preview and then print the presentation as an outline and as handouts.

EXERCISE 5-30

Open the file **AdMedia2**. Apply a template and color scheme of your choice; then change the text formatting on the slide master and the title master. Use two different fonts in the presentation; change bullet shapes and colors; and apply bold, underline, or shadow formatting to individual words or entire placeholders where you think it would be effective. Change the size and position of placeholders if you think it improves the look of a slide. Remember to add special effects for emphasis, but don't overdo it. Add a slide transition or animation scheme of your choice. Be prepared to explain your choices. Save the presentation as ***[your initials]*5-30**. Preview and then print the presentation as handouts.

EXERCISE 5-31

Create a summary of your life history or the life of a fictional or historic character. Divide the summary into five chronological age ranges, starting at birth and ending at your present age or some time in the future. Create a suitable title slide and one slide for each of the five age ranges. For each range, create a title with an overall description and three or more bullet points. Using the skills that you have learned up to this point, format the presentation attractively. Include an animation effect or a transition effect. Save the presentation as ***[your initials]*5-31**. Preview and then print the presentation as handouts.

UNIT 3

Customizing a Presentation

LESSON 6

Working with PowerPoint Objects

OBJECTIVES

MOUS ACTIVITIES
In this lesson:
PP2002 2-2
PP2002 3-1
PP2002 3-2
PP2002 3-3

See Appendix E.

After completing this lesson, you will be able to:

1. Work with basic drawing tools.
2. Create basic AutoShapes.
3. Insert clip art.
4. Adjust clip art settings.
5. Use WordArt for special effects.
6. Work with text boxes.
7. Rotate text and other objects.

Estimated Time: 2 hours

An effective slide presentation uses more than text alone. Although text carries most of the information, you can use several types of objects to emphasize your message and draw attention to the presentation. For example, you can add chart objects, free-floating text objects, clip art objects, and scanned photographs to a presentation.

After you add an object to a slide, you can change its size and position. In this lesson, you concentrate on basic changes that can be made to clip art and objects created with PowerPoint's drawing tools. In a later lesson, you learn how to manipulate objects further by applying colors and textured fills, and by rearranging elements within objects.

Working with Basic Drawing Tools

The PowerPoint Drawing toolbar provides you with a variety of tools you can use to create your own drawings. In this lesson, you learn basic drawing skills. In later lessons, you learn how to enhance simple objects and create more complex drawings.

TABLE 6-1 Drawing Toolbar

BUTTON	PURPOSE
Draw	Opens the Draw menu, which contains tools for aligning, grouping, rotating, flipping, and other manipulations of PowerPoint objects.
Select Objects	Selects an object. This tool is automatically in effect when no other tool is in use.
AutoShapes	Opens the AutoShapes menu, which contains predefined shapes you can draw.
Line	Draws a straight line.
Arrow	Draws an arrow.
Rectangle	Draws a rectangle or square.
Oval	Draws an oval or circle.
Text Box	Inserts text anywhere on a slide.
Insert WordArt	Creates a Microsoft WordArt object on a slide.
Insert Diagram or Organization Chart	Creates an Org chart or a diagram on a slide.
Insert Clip Art	Inserts a clip art object.
Insert Picture	Inserts a bitmap or photo image.

continues

TABLE 6-1 Drawing Toolbar *continued*

BUTTON	PURPOSE
Fill Color	Fills an object with colors, patterns, or textures.
Line Color	Changes the color of an object's outline.
Font Color	Changes the color of selected text. The Font Color button also appears on the Formatting toolbar.
Line Style	Chooses a line style and thickness for the outline of a selected object or a straight line that you drew.
Dash Style	Applies dotted or dashed line styles to an object.
Arrow Style	Applies arrowheads to selected lines.
Shadow Style	Applies shadow effects to an object. This is not the same as the Shadow button on the Formatting toolbar, which works only on text.
3-D Style	Applies 3-D effects to an object.

EXERCISE 6-1 Draw Simple Lines and Shapes

In this exercise you practice drawing rectangles, ovals, and straight lines on a blank slide. To draw an object, click the appropriate Drawing toolbar button (Line, Rectangle, or Oval); then drag the cross-shaped mouse pointer + on your slide until the object is the size you want.

You can draw multiple objects by double-clicking a Drawing toolbar button. Double-clicking keeps the button activated so you can draw as many shapes as you want without the need to re-click. When you finish drawing, click the button again to deactivate it.

1. Open the presentation file **Opening1**.

NOTE: Two of the slides in this presentation were created by using the Blank slide layout. The blank layout contains no text placeholders. The text that appears on the slides is placed in text boxes instead of placeholders. You learn to draw text boxes later in this lesson.

2. Insert a new slide after slide 2 and use the **Blank** layout (the first layout under the **Content Layouts** heading). You will use this slide to practice drawing.

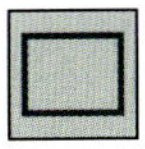

3. Click the Rectangle button on the Drawing toolbar. The mouse pointer changes to a cross +.
4. Move the pointer to the left side of the slide.
5. Click and hold the left mouse button. Drag diagonally down and to the right. Release your mouse button. A white rectangle with a dark blue outline appears. (You learn how to change colors and line styles in the next lesson.) See Figure 6-1 for the approximate size and placement of the completed rectangle.

FIGURE 6-1
Drawing objects on a slide

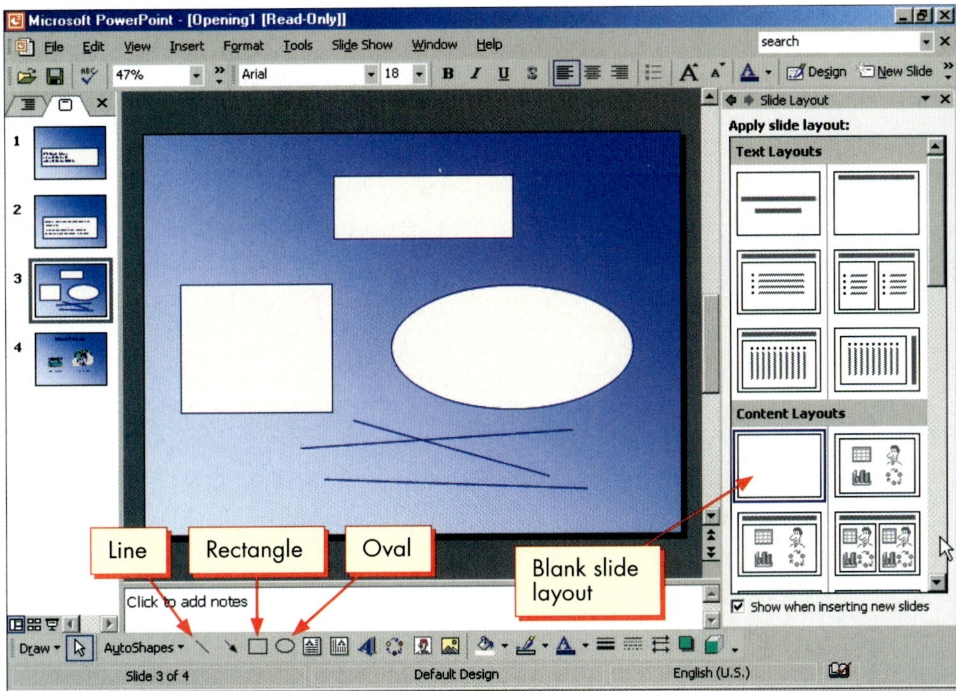

6. Click the Rectangle button again and draw a second rectangle.

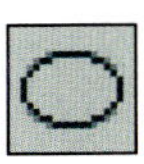

7. Click the Oval button.
8. Draw an oval on the right side of the slide in the same way as you drew a rectangle.

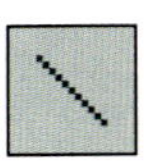

9. Click the Line button; then drag your pointer diagonally to create a line.
10. Double-click the Line button and then draw another line. Notice that the mouse pointer still has the cross shape + and the Line button is still selected.
11. Without clicking the Line button, draw two more lines.
12. Click the Line button again to deactivate it.

EXERCISE 6-2 Delete Objects

If you don't like an object that you created, you can easily remove it from your slide. Simply select the object by clicking it and then press Delete on your keyboard.

1. Click one of the rectangles to select it. Notice the white sizing handles surrounding the rectangle indicating that it is selected.

NOTE: The green handle just above the rectangle is a rotation handle. You rotate objects later in this lesson.

2. Press Delete on your keyboard. The selected rectangle disappears.
3. Press Tab one or more times until one of the lines is selected. (This is another way of selecting an object.)
4. Press Delete to delete the line; then delete the remaining lines. The slide should now contain one rectangle and one oval.

EXERCISE 6-3 Draw Horizontal, Vertical, and Other Constrained Lines

You use Shift to *constrain* an object as you draw it on a slide. You constrain a line to make it perfectly horizontal, vertical, or at a 15-, 30-, 45-or 60-degree angle.

When using Shift to constrain an object, it's important to release your mouse button before releasing Shift. Otherwise, you might accidentally move the mouse when Shift is no longer in effect, resulting in an object that is no longer constrained.

NOTE: Do not be too concerned with the exact placement of objects in these early drawing exercises. The purpose of the exercises is to show you how the drawing tools work; it is not necessary to duplicate the figures exactly.

1. Still working on slide 3, zoom to 100% by using the Zoom box on the Standard toolbar; then scroll to display the lower-left corner of the slide. Zooming in on the area will make it easier to see what you're doing.
2. Double-click the Line button. You're going to draw several constrained lines without needing to re-click the Line button each time you draw.
3. Position the pointer on the left side, near the bottom of the slide.
4. Hold down Shift and drag straight across to the right side of the Slide pane. (As you drag, notice that the line remains straight even if you move the mouse up or down a little.)
5. Release the mouse button first and then release Shift.
6. With the Line button still activated, position the cross pointer + at the left end of the horizontal line. Hold down Shift and drag straight up,

ending near the top of the Slide pane. Release the mouse button and then release Shift.

7. Move the cross pointer to the corner made by the horizontal and vertical lines. While pressing Shift, draw a diagonal line. Without releasing either the mouse or Shift, move your pointer up and then down. Notice how the line "jumps" in 15-degree increments.

FIGURE 6-2
Drawing constrained lines at 15-degree increments

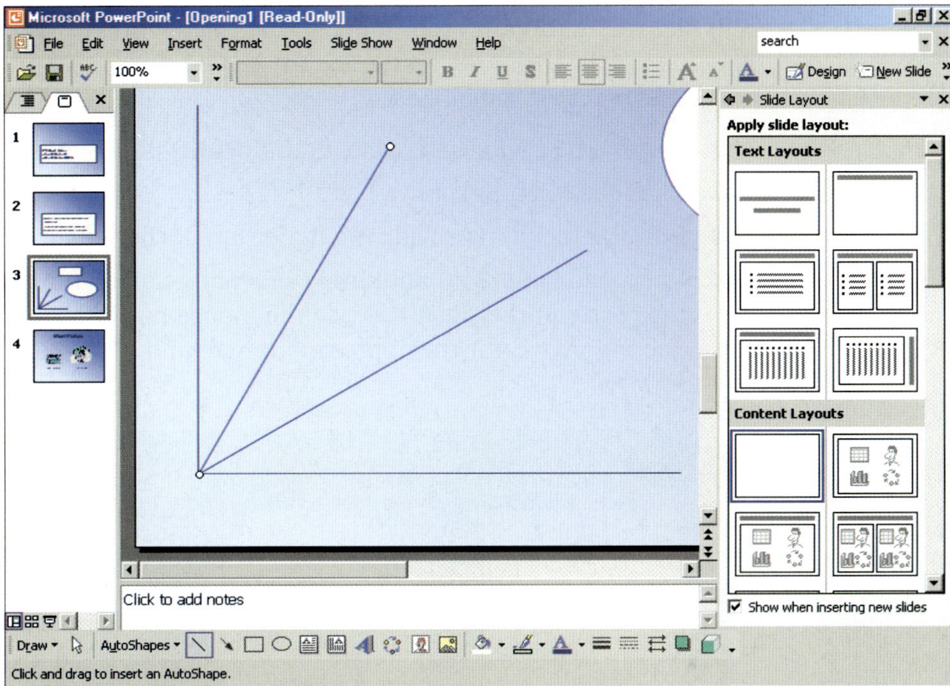

8. When the line is at a 30-degree angle with the horizontal line, release your mouse button and then release Shift. Refer to Figure 6-2 for the approximate line placement and the angle.

9. Starting at the same point, draw another line with a 60-degree angle; then click the Line button to deactivate it.

10. Change the zoom setting to Fit to display the entire slide.

11. Insert a footer only on slide 3 that contains your name, a comma, and the text ***[your initials]*6-3**. (Do not include the date.)

REVIEW: To insert a footer on one slide only, make that the current slide before opening the Header and Footer dialog box; then click Apply instead of Apply to All.

12. Save the presentation as ***[your initials]*6-3** in a new folder for Lesson 6. Print only slide 3, full size, grayscale, and framed. Keep the presentation open for the following exercises.

NOTE: The documents you create in this course relate to the Case Study about Good 4 U, a fictional restaurant business (see pages 809 through 812).

EXERCISE 6-4 Create Squares and Circles

When you constrain other objects, such as rectangles or ovals, they grow at an equal rate horizontally and vertically as you draw, creating symmetrical objects such as squares and circles.

1. Insert a new slide after slide 2 and before slide 3; use the Blank layout.
2. Click the Rectangle button.
3. Position the pointer near the upper-left corner of your slide.
4. Press and hold Shift and drag diagonally down and to the right, ending near the center of the slide. Release the mouse button first and then release Shift. See Figure 6-3 for the approximate size and placement of the completed square.

FIGURE 6-3
Drawing a circle and a square

NOTE: Your square might look more like a rectangle if your monitor's horizontal size and vertical size are not perfectly synchronized. Your square will print correctly even if it is distorted on your screen.

5. Click the Oval button.
6. Position your pointer to the right of the square, near the top of the slide.
7. While pressing Shift, drag diagonally down and to the right to create a circle.

EXERCISE 6-5 Change the Size and Position of Objects You Draw

You resize an object that you draw in the same way that you resize a text placeholder: select it and then drag one of its sizing handles. Holding down Shift and/or Ctrl while dragging a sizing handle has the following effects on an object:

- Shift preserves an object's proportions, meaning that its height grows or shrinks at the same rate as its width, preventing objects from becoming too tall and skinny or too short and wide.
- Ctrl causes an object to grow or shrink from the center of the object rather than from the edge that's being dragged.
- Ctrl+Shift together cause an object to grow or shrink proportionately from its center.

You reposition an object by dragging it with the four-pointed arrow ✥. Simply point anywhere in the object. When you see the four-pointed arrow, drag the object to another place on your slide.

1. Select the circle by clicking anywhere inside it, and then point to its bottom center sizing handle. Your pointer changes to a two-pointed vertical arrow ↕.
2. Drag the handle down. As you drag, the pointer changes to a cross +. The circle has changed into an oval and is now larger.
3. Drag the bottom-left corner handle diagonally up and to the left. The oval is now wider and flattened, taking on an entirely new shape.

4. Click the Undo button twice to restore the circle to its original size and shape.
5. Point to the circle's lower-left corner sizing handle. While holding down Shift, drag diagonally out from the circle's center, making it larger. (Don't worry if the circle overlaps the rectangle.) The circle retains its original shape.
6. While holding down both Ctrl and Shift, drag the lower-left corner sizing handle toward the center of the circle. The circle becomes smaller, shrinking evenly from all edges. (See Figure 6-4 on the next page.)
7. Point to the center of the circle. When you see the four-pointed arrow ✥, drag it down so that the circle's lower edge is about 1 inch from the bottom of your slide.

NOTE: Whenever you drag to move an object or text, make sure you are not dragging a sizing handle by mistake. You must see the four-pointed arrow, and not the two-pointed arrow.

8. Drag the square down on the slide so that it too is about 1 inch from the bottom.

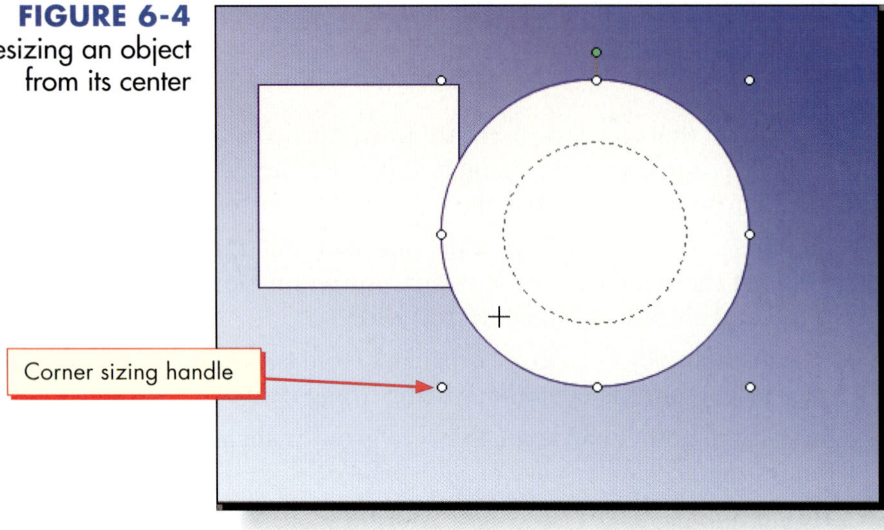

FIGURE 6-4 Resizing an object from its center

9. Save the presentation as ***[your initials]*6-5** in your Lesson 6 folder but do not print it. Leave it open for the next exercise.

EXERCISE 6-6 Resize Objects by Using the Format AutoShape Dialog Box

Just as you can resize text placeholders, you can use the Format AutoShape dialog box to resize objects that you draw. When the selected object is either a circle or a square, both the Height and Width settings on the Size tab will have the same measurement.

1. Still working on slide 3, right-click the square object, choose Format AutoShape from the shortcut menu, and click the Size tab. Notice that the height and width are the same measurement. (See Figure 6-5 on the next page.)
2. Under Scale, check the Lock aspect ratio check box. This will force the height and width of an object to change size at the same rate.
3. In the Size and rotate section, key **3.5** in the Height box; then press Tab to move to the next box. Notice that the measurement in the Width box automatically changes to 3.5. Click OK.

4. Select the circle and then click the Cut button (or press Ctrl+X) to remove the circle from the slide and send it to the clipboard.
5. Insert two new slides after slide 3 that use the Blank slide layout (creating slides 4 and 5.)
6. Paste the circle on the new slide 4.

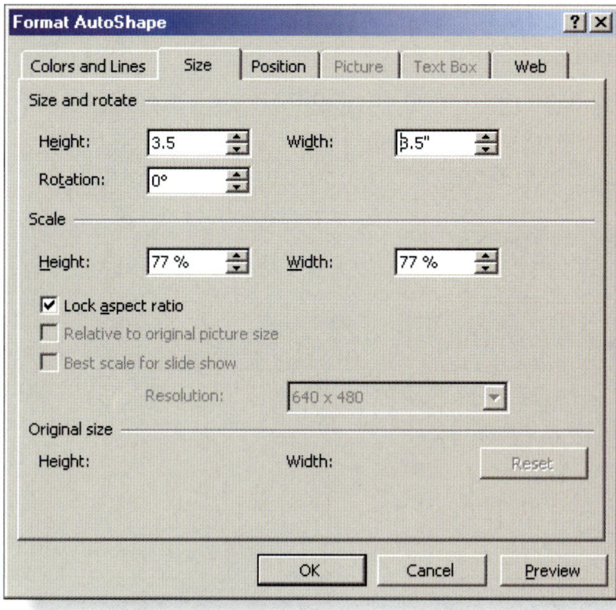

FIGURE 6-5 Resizing an object by using the Format AutoShape dialog box

7. Move to slide 5. You return to slides 3 and 4 later in this lesson to add text and other elements.
8. Draw a 4.5-inch square in the approximate center of slide 5. Using the Format AutoShape dialog box, make the square exactly 4.5 inches wide and 4.5 inches high. Position the square exactly 2.75 inches from the left edge (Horizontal setting) and exactly 1.75 inches down from the top edge (Vertical setting).

Creating Basic AutoShapes

PowerPoint provides an assortment of predefined shapes called *AutoShapes.* You can use AutoShapes to draw perfectly shaped arrows, stars, flowchart objects, callouts, and other shapes with minimal effort.

You resize these shapes the same way you resize other objects. Many shapes include an additional yellow diamond handle, called an *adjustment handle,* which you use to reshape the object after it is drawn.

EXERCISE 6-7 Create AutoShapes

The rectangles, ovals, and lines that you created by using Drawing toolbar buttons are basic AutoShapes. To access a large assortment of basic and specialized AutoShapes, click AutoShapes on the Drawing toolbar and choose from a menu of AutoShape categories. You can change this menu into a floating toolbar as you did with the Font Color menu in Lesson 5. In addition, each AutoShape category has its own menu that can be floated.

1. Working on slide 5, click AutoShapes on the Drawing toolbar to display the AutoShapes menu.
2. Point to each option on the AutoShapes menu to view the shapes on the submenus.
3. Point to Basic Shapes; then position your pointer over the thin gray bar at the top of the Basic Shapes submenu. When you see the four-pointed arrow ✥, drag it to the upper-left corner of your screen. The Basic Shapes submenu is now a floating toolbar.

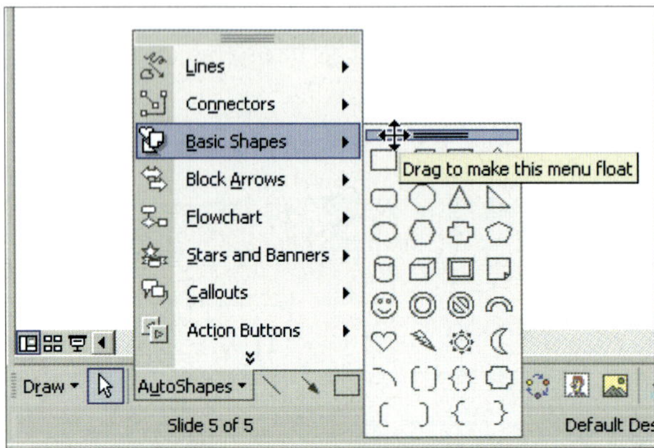

FIGURE 6-6 Making the Basic Shapes menu float

4. Point to the various shapes on the Basic Shapes floating toolbar and read their ScreenTips.

5. Click the Sun shape and then draw a sun, about 1.5 inches in diameter, in the lower right corner of the slide. You draw an AutoShape by dragging the cross pointer, just as when you draw a rectangle or oval.

TIP: You can use Shift to create a symmetrical AutoShape in the same way that you use Shift when you draw a circle or square.

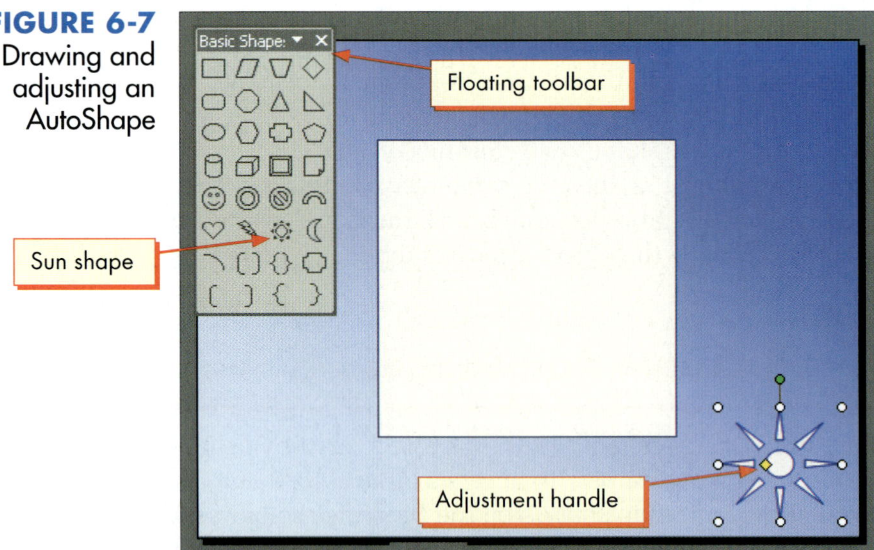

FIGURE 6-7 Drawing and adjusting an AutoShape

POWERPOINT

6. Drag the yellow diamond-shaped adjustment handle ◇ toward the center of the Sun AutoShape to lengthen its points.

7. Click the Close button ☒ on the title bar of the Basic Shapes floating toolbar to close it.

EXERCISE 6-8 Change an AutoShape

If you draw an AutoShape and then decide you want a different shape, you can delete it just as you deleted other objects earlier in this lesson and then draw a new shape.

If you took the time to carefully size and place the AutoShape (and perhaps even key text inside it), you will find that it is more convenient to change the shape instead of deleting and then re-creating it. You change an AutoShape by clicking Draw on the Drawing toolbar and then choosing Change AutoShape from the menu.

1. Select the Sun shape on slide 5.
2. Click Draw on the Drawing toolbar to display the menu.

3. Choose Change AutoShape, and then choose Stars and Banners from the submenu. Choose Change Shape to 16-Point Star.

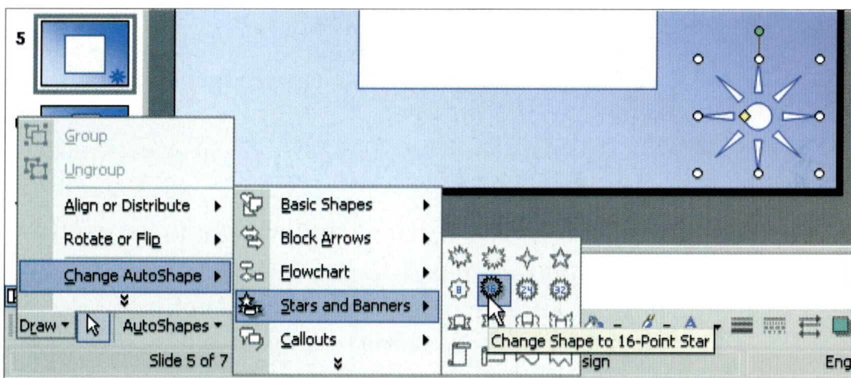

FIGURE 6-8
Changing an AutoShape

EXERCISE 6-9 Place Text in an AutoShape

You can easily transform an AutoShape into an attention-getting background for text. Simply select the AutoShape and key the text (or paste it from the clipboard). You can format and edit the text in the same way as in a text placeholder. The text in an AutoShape is centered by default.

1. Select the 16-Point Star AutoShape.
2. Key **Grand Opening!** The text automatically appears in the center of the star. Notice the diagonal-line border similar to a text placeholder border.
3. Click the AutoShape's border anywhere between two sizing handles to select it.
4. Using the Font Size box on the Formatting toolbar, change the size from 18 points to 28 points. The text becomes too large for the 16-Point Star AutoShape.
5. Drag the center sizing handle on the left side to make the AutoShape wide enough to contain the text. Don't worry if the star shape overlaps the square in the center of the slide.

FIGURE 6-9
Inserting text in an AutoShape

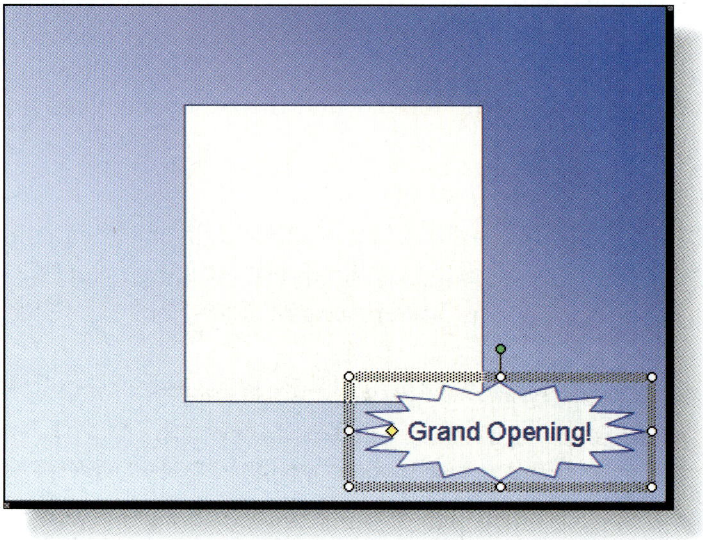

6. Drag the top-center sizing handle down to flatten the AutoShape.
7. Save the presentation as ***[your initials]*6-9** in your Lesson 6 folder but do not print it. Leave the presentation open for the next exercise. You return to slide 5 later in the lesson to complete it.

Inserting Clip Art

Included with Microsoft Office is a collection of ready-to-use pictures known as *clip art* that you can insert on PowerPoint slides. The clip art collection includes *vector drawings*—pictures made up of lines, curves, rectangles, and other objects; *bitmaps*—pictures made up of tiny colored dots; and scanned photographs. These pictures can be accessed from the Insert Clip Art task pane.

You can insert clip art and other pictures into a PowerPoint presentation in several ways:

- Click the Insert Clip Art button on the Drawing toolbar to display the Insert Clip Art task pane.
- Use the Insert menu (Picture, Clip Art) to display the Insert Clip Art task pane.
- Use the Insert Picture button to insert picture files stored on a hard drive, floppy disk, or network drive. This method is useful for pictures that are not part of the Microsoft Clip Organizer collection.

If your slide uses a content layout that includes a content placeholder, double-click the Insert Clip Art icon in the content placeholder to insert clip art.

EXERCISE 6-10 Find and Insert Clip Art

Each clip art picture that Microsoft provides has keywords associated with it. These keywords describe the subject matter of the picture. You search for the keywords to find the art you need for your presentation.

Clip art (and other media such as sound and movie files) is organized into collections and media types. You can choose to search all collections and types or to select a particular type.

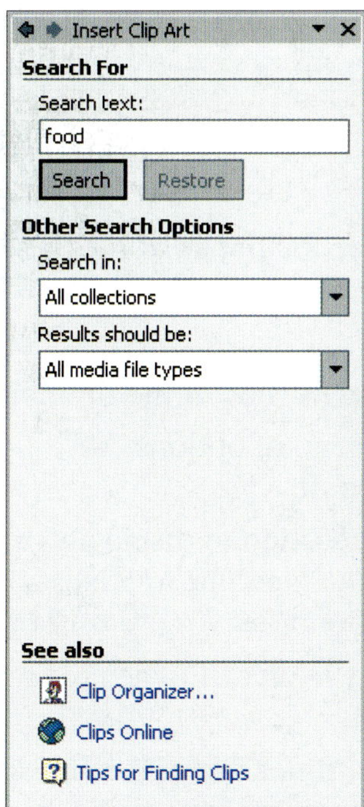

FIGURE 6-10 Insert Clip Art task pane

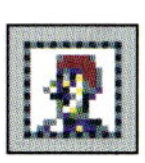

1. If you have Internet access but are not connected, make a connection now (unless your instructor tells you otherwise).
2. Move to slide 1 and then click the Insert Clip Art button on the Drawing toolbar. The Insert Clip Art task pane is displayed.
3. If the Add Clips to Organizer dialog box appears, click Later.
4. In the Insert Clip Art task pane, click the list box arrow for Search in. Notice that Everywhere is checked, meaning that all categories in the Microsoft Clip Organizer will be searched, and if you are connected to the Internet, the Microsoft Office Design Gallery Live will also be searched.
5. Close the list box; then click the list box arrow for Results should be. In this list box you can choose to search all media types or limit your search to specific types. These options are helpful if you have a large

FIGURE 6-11
Search results

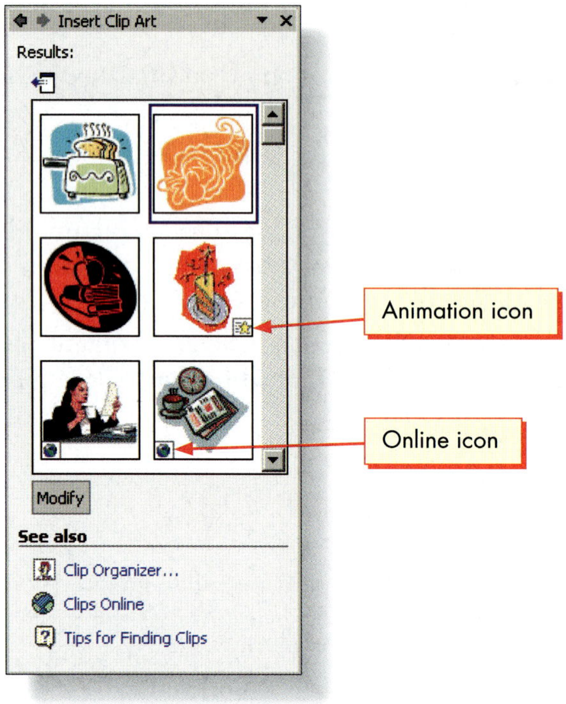

number of media files stored on your computer, or you are searching on the Internet.

6. Key **food** in the Search text box at the top of the Insert Clip Art task pane and then click Search. The Results box shows clips that match the search word.

NOTE: Clips from the Design Gallery Live have an online icon in the lower left corner. Some of these clips also contain a musical note, indicating that they are sound files. Some clips have an animation icon displayed in the lower right corner, indicating that they are movies.

7. Use the scroll bar to review some of the thumbnails.

POWERPOINT

EXERCISE 6-11 Preview Clip Art Images and Insert a Picture

You can preview images in a larger format so you can see more detail before choosing a picture.

1. Without clicking, point to a clip art thumbnail in the task pane. Notice the gray bar with the arrow on the right side of the thumbnail.
2. Click the gray bar to display a menu of options. You can also display this menu by right-clicking a thumbnail.
3. Choose Preview/Properties. In addition to displaying an enlarged picture, this dialog box also shows you the filename and location of the picture, its size, and other helpful information. (See Figure 6-12 on the next page.)

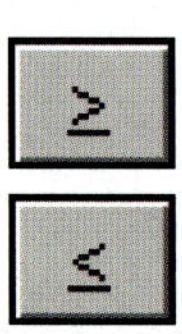

4. Click the Next button below the picture. The next picture in the search results pane is displayed.
5. Click the Next button several times more; then click the Previous button. When you find a picture you like, click Close. Notice that the last picture you previewed has a box around it.
6. With your left mouse button, click the picture you chose. The picture is inserted in the center of the current slide.

FIGURE 6-12
Preview/Properties dialog box

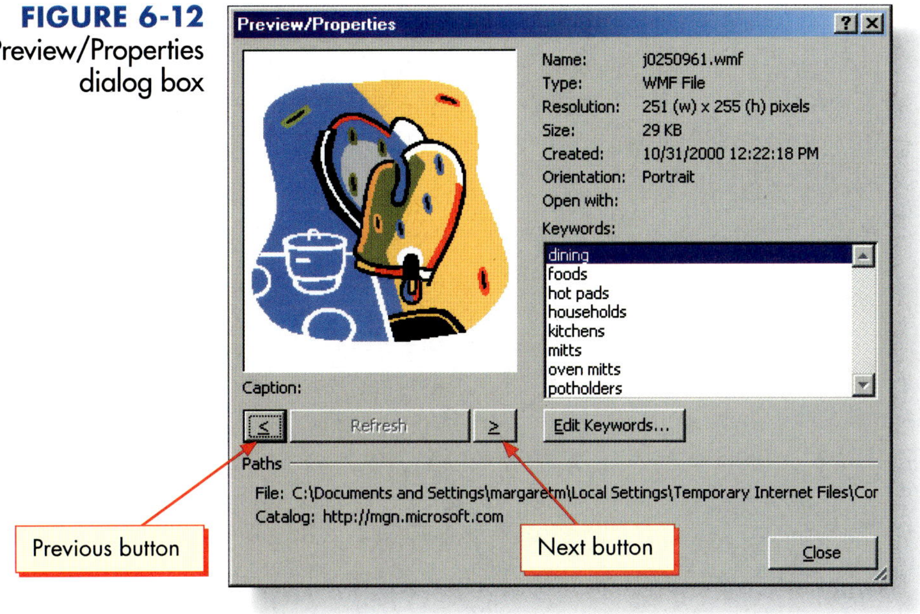

TIP: You can also drag the picture directly from the task pane onto your slide.

EXERCISE 6-12 Modify a Clip Art Search

If you search for a keyword and don't find any pictures, or don't find one you like, you can modify your search and look for something different.

1. Click Modify below the thumbnails. The Search pane reopens.
2. Key **palms** in the Search text box and then click Search. Thumbnails of palm trees and beach scenes should appear. If your Results box is empty, skip step 3 and go to the next exercise.
3. Right-click a simple palm tree image that you like and choose Insert from the shortcut menu. (There should now be two clip art images on your slide. One might be on top of the other.)

EXERCISE 6-13 Copy a Clip Art Image From Another Slide

Sometimes you might insert a picture on a slide and later decide to move it to a different slide. You can cut, copy, and paste pictures in the same way as you cut, copy, and paste text.

1. Move to slide 7. This slide has two clip art images that have been previously inserted.

2. Click the palm tree picture on the right to select it.
3. Click the Copy button to copy the picture to the clipboard.
4. Move to slide 1 and click the Paste button. You now have two or three pictures of various sizes on the slide overlapping one another. Often, when working with clip art, you will want to choose more than one picture and then decide which one to use at a later time.

EXERCISE 6-14 Rearrange and Delete Clip Art Images

You can easily rearrange or delete clip art. Moving clip art is similar to moving a text placeholder or an AutoShape.

1. On slide 1, point to one of the pictures. When you see the four-pointed arrow ✣, drag the picture to the upper right corner of your slide.
2. Drag another picture to the upper left corner, and if you have a third picture on your slide, drag it to the lower left corner.

FIGURE 6-13 Repositioning a picture

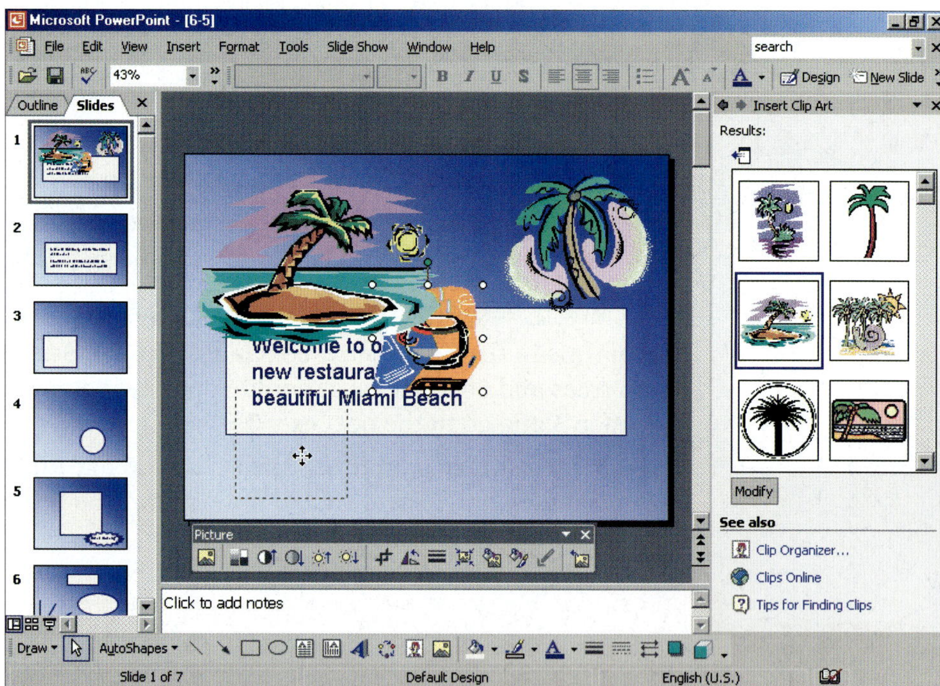

3. Select the food picture and press Delete to remove it from your slide.
4. If there are two palm tree pictures on your slide, delete either one of them. You should have one picture remaining.

5. Drag the remaining picture to the left side of the slide's text, overlapping the blank area of the white box.
6. Save the presentation as ***[your initials]*6-14** but do not print it. Keep the file open for the next exercise.

Adjusting Clip Art Size and Image Settings

You can change the look of clip art images in many ways, including changing the size, contrast, and brightness. The Picture toolbar helps you accomplish this.

EXERCISE 6-15 Resize a Clip Art Image

Resizing a clip art image is similar to resizing a text placeholder or an AutoShape. The one difference is that with a clip art image, you can drag a corner handle without distorting proportions even if you forget to hold down Shift.

1. Select the picture of the palm tree; then place the pointer on the bottom-center sizing handle. The pointer changes to a vertical two-pointed arrow ↕.
2. Drag the handle down. The object becomes taller, distorting the image.
3. Press Ctrl+Z to undo the resizing.
4. With the palm tree still selected, drag a corner handle diagonally away from the center of the picture until the picture is about twice its original size. Dragging the corner handle preserves the image's proportions, without the need to hold down Shift.
5. Right-click the picture and choose Format Picture from the shortcut menu. Click the Size tab.
6. Make sure that Lock aspect ratio is checked. In the Height box, under Size and rotate, key **2.5**. Click OK. The picture is now sized to fit inside the white box.
7. Drag the picture to the blank area on the right side of the white box. You can use the arrow keys or Ctrl+the arrow key to fine-tune the picture's position.
8. Save the presentation as ***[your initials]*6-15** in your Lesson 6 folder but do not print it. Leave it open for the next exercise.

EXERCISE 6-16 Change Clip Art Image Settings

When a picture on a slide is selected, the Picture toolbar usually appears. You can use the Picture toolbar to control various aspects of an image's appearance, such as size, brightness, contrast, and color.

1. Delete slide 6 (your practice slide) and insert a new slide 6 that uses the Blank slide layout.
2. Move to slide 7 and copy the picture labeled "Beach scene" to the clipboard; then paste it on slide 6. This is a clip art image that was previously inserted for you by using the Insert Clip Art task pane.
3. Select the beach scene picture that you copied onto slide 6. If the Picture toolbar is not displayed, right-click the picture and choose Show Picture Toolbar from the shortcut menu.

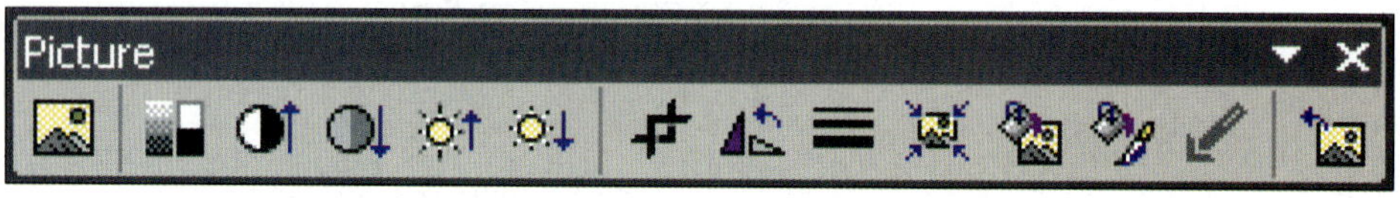

FIGURE 6-14
Picture toolbar

TABLE 6-2 Picture Toolbar

BUTTON	PURPOSE
Insert Picture	Opens the Insert Picture dialog box.
Color	Enables you to change a picture's color to grayscale, black-and-white, or washout.
More Contrast	Increases a picture's contrast.
Less Contrast	Decreases a picture's contrast.
More Brightness	Makes a picture lighter and brighter.
Less Brightness	Makes a picture less bright.
Crop	Enables you to cut away the edges of a picture.
Rotate Left	Turns a picture on its side.
Line Style	Enables you to put a frame around a picture.

continues

TABLE 6-2 Picture Toolbar *continued*

BUTTON	PURPOSE
Compress Pictures	Strips unnecessary information from a picture file to make the file size smaller.
Recolor Picture	Enables you to change individual colors in a vector drawing. This button does not work for bitmaps.
Format Picture	Opens the Format Picture dialog box.
Set Transparent Color	Enables you to select a color on an image to make it disappear. This is best used with a simple vector image when you want to make its background disappear.
Reset Picture	Restores a picture's original attributes if changes were made by using the Picture toolbar buttons.

4. With the picture selected, click the Format Picture button on the Picture toolbar and then click the **Size** tab.
5. Uncheck the **Lock aspect ratio** box (you want to deliberately distort this picture slightly).
6. Under **Size and rotate**, change the **Height** to 7.5 inches and the **Width** to 10 inches. Click **OK**. This makes the picture the same size as the slide.
7. Using the four-pointed arrow ✥, reposition the picture so its edges align with the edges of the slide. The picture now fills the entire slide.
8. With the picture selected, click the More Contrast button on the Picture toolbar five times. The contrast dramatically changes.
9. Click the Less Brightness button six times. Now the picture has changed to a nighttime scene.
10. Click the Color button on the Picture toolbar; then choose **Automatic** from the drop-down menu. The picture's colors are restored to their original state.
11. Click the Color button again, this time choosing **Washout** from the drop-down menu. A very pale image appears. Washout is a good choice if you want to use a picture as a background for text.
12. Click the Less Brightness button three times to fine-tune the color. Compare the brightness and contrast level of your image with the one in Figure 6-15 (on the next page) and adjust it if needed.

FIGURE 6-15
Image-adjusted picture

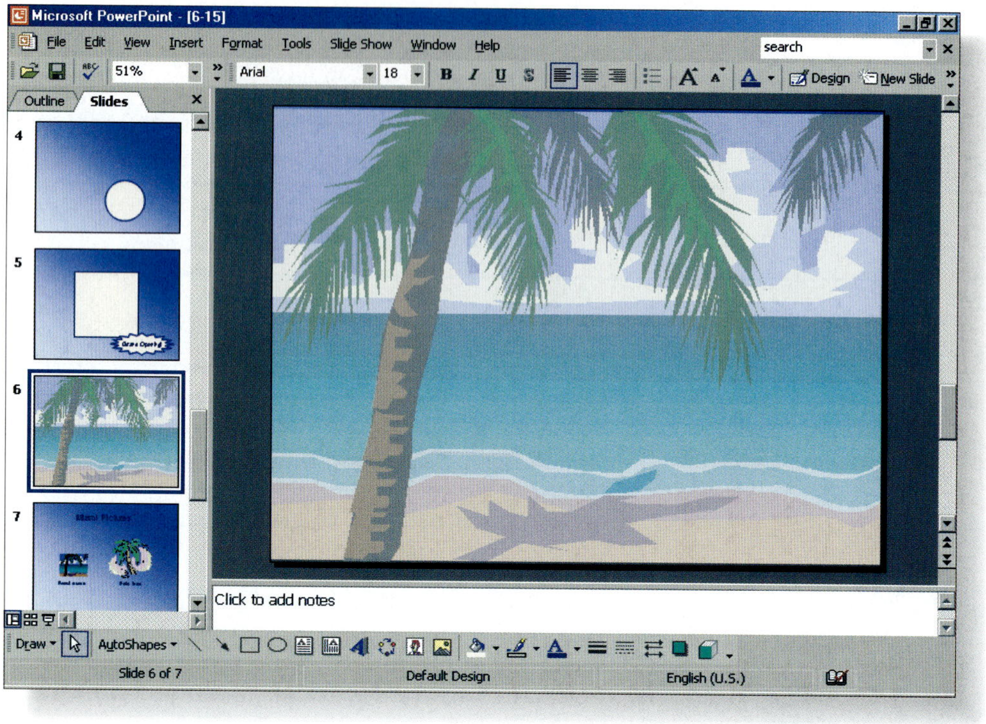

EXERCISE 6-17 Add a Picture to a Master Slide

You can add pictures, AutoShapes, and other objects to a master slide in the same way as you add objects to a presentation slide. Images can be inserted directly, or you can paste them from the clipboard.

1. Select the palm tree image on slide 6 and click the Copy button.
2. Display the slide master.
3. Click the Paste button. The image hides the text placeholders. Because this presentation uses only the Blank slide layout, the hidden placeholders are not a problem.
4. Display the title master and click the Paste button again to copy the image.
5. Close the Master view; then scroll through all the slides to see the effect of the new background.
6. Save the presentation as ***[your initials]*6-17** in your Lesson 6 folder but do not print it. Leave it open for the next exercise.

EXERCISE 6-18 Insert a Bitmap Image

If you have a scanner or a digital camera that connects to your computer, you can insert images directly from those devices onto a slide. There are two ways to work with bitmap (digital) images:

- To insert an image directly onto a slide, set up the picture in the scanner (or set up your camera), open the Insert menu, and choose Picture, From Scanner or Camera. If you have both a camera and a scanner attached to your computer, choose the device from the drop-down list, then choose Web Quality or Print Quality. Click Insert or Custom Insert. You can then use the tools on the Picture toolbar to adjust the image.
- To insert a digital image that is stored on a disk drive, open the Insert menu and choose Picture, From File (or click the Insert Picture button on the Drawing toolbar). In the Insert Picture dialog box, locate the picture file and click Insert.

In this exercise you insert a previously scanned photograph from your student data disk.

1. Display slide 5.
2. Click the Insert Picture button on the Drawing toolbar.
3. In the Insert Picture dialog box, locate the file **Miami2** on your student data disk and click Insert.
4. Use the Size tab on the Format Picture dialog box to lock the picture's aspect ratio and then change its width to 4 inches.

EXERCISE 6-19 Crop a Bitmap Image

The Picture toolbar contains a tool you can use to *crop* (trim) parts of a picture, just as you might do with a page from a magazine by using a pair of scissors.

When you click the cropping tool, a picture's sizing handles change to *cropping handles*—heavy black lines and corners that you drag to trim a picture.

1. Select the Miami picture on slide 5.
2. Click the Crop button on the Picture toolbar. The pointer changes to a cropping tool, and cropping handles appear around the edges of the picture.
3. Position the cropping tool on the bottom center handle and drag the handle up until the dotted cropping line is positioned to cut off the street and most of the first floor (see Figure 6-16 on the next page).

TIP: Try holding down Alt as you crop. This enables you to make very fine adjustments.

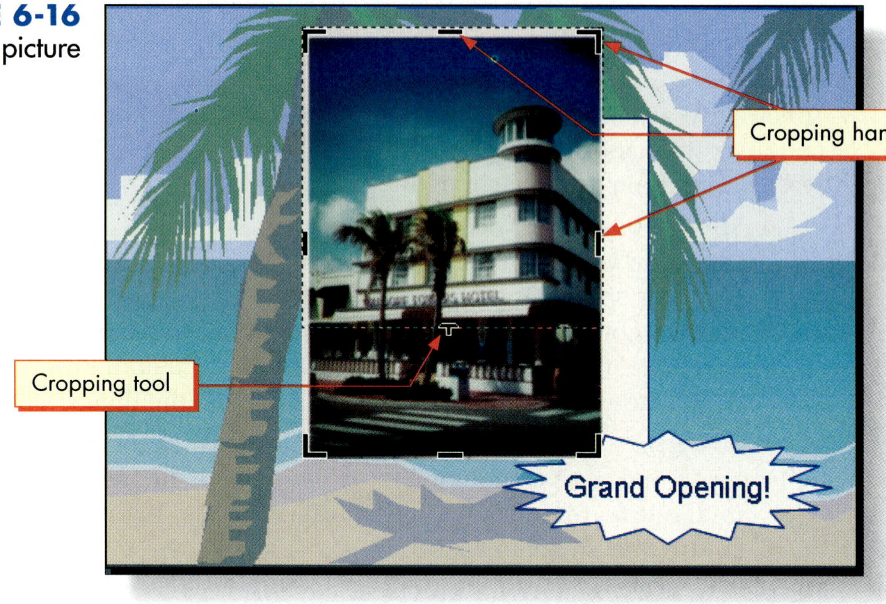

FIGURE 6-16
Cropping a picture

4. Hold down Ctrl and drag the left-center cropping handle to the right about ⅛ inch. Release the mouse button and then release Ctrl. Both the left side and the right side are cropped at the same time. If you hold down Ctrl while dragging a corner cropping handle, all four sides of the picture will be cropped the same amount.
5. Crop the narrow white border from the top of the picture.
6. Click the Crop button on the Picture toolbar to turn it off.
7. Using the four-pointed arrow ✥, drag the picture to position it approximately in the center of the white box. You can hold down Alt while dragging to fine-tune the picture's position.

FIGURE 6-17
Picture after cropping and positioning

TIP: If you crop too far, use the cropping tool to drag the handle in the opposite direction to restore that part of the picture, or click the Undo button.

8. Save the presentation as ***[your initials]*6-19** in your Lesson 6 folder but do not print it. Leave the presentation open for the next exercise.

Using WordArt for Special Effects

WordArt can create special effects with text that are not possible with standard text-formatting tools. You can stretch or curve text and add special shading effects, dramatic 3-D effects, and much more. And because they are drawn objects, you can use drawing tools to modify and enhance WordArt objects.

EXERCISE 6-20 Create and Modify a WordArt Object

In this exercise you create a WordArt object and then modify it by changing its shape and size. It's important to note that WordArt objects are not checked by the spell-checker. PowerPoint treats them as drawing objects, not text. Make sure you key and proofread WordArt objects carefully.

1. Display slide 6 (your practice slide).

2. Click the Insert WordArt button on the Drawing toolbar. The WordArt Gallery dialog box appears.

FIGURE 6-18
WordArt Gallery dialog box

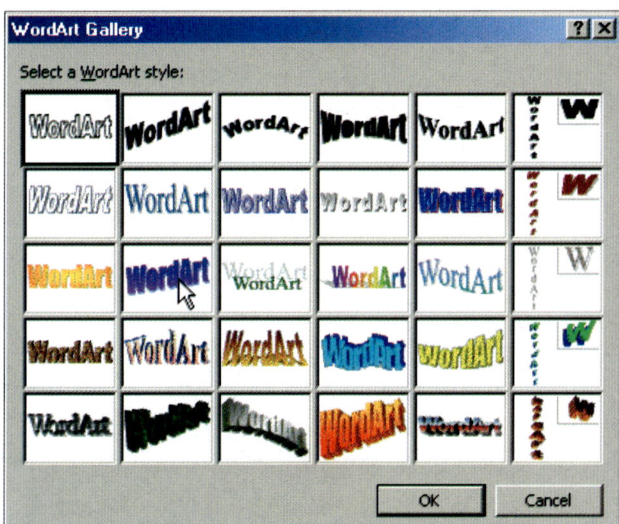

3. Choose the bright purple WordArt style (third row, second column). Click OK. The Edit WordArt Text dialog box appears.

4. Key **Good for You** and click OK. The WordArt text object is added to the slide. Notice that the object is selected and the WordArt toolbar appears.

TABLE 6-3 WordArt Toolbar

BUTTON	PURPOSE
Insert WordArt	Creates a drawing object that uses text effects.
Edit Text	Opens the Edit WordArt Text dialog box, where you can edit the text of the selected WordArt object.
WordArt Gallery	Opens the WordArt Gallery dialog box, where you can change the style for the selected WordArt object.
Format WordArt	Opens the Format WordArt dialog box, where you can work with a variety of WordArt properties.
WordArt Shape	Displays a menu of shapes that you can apply to the selected WordArt object.
WordArt Same Letter Heights	Makes all the letters in the selected WordArt object the same height.
WordArt Vertical Text	Stacks the text in the selected WordArt object vertically so that it reads from top to bottom.
WordArt Alignment	For WordArt that contains multiple lines, aligns the WordArt text.
WordArt Character Spacing	Enables you to adjust the space between characters in the selected WordArt object.

5. Click the WordArt Shape button on the WordArt toolbar.
6. On the WordArt Shape menu, choose Wave 1.

FIGURE 6-19
WordArt Shape menu

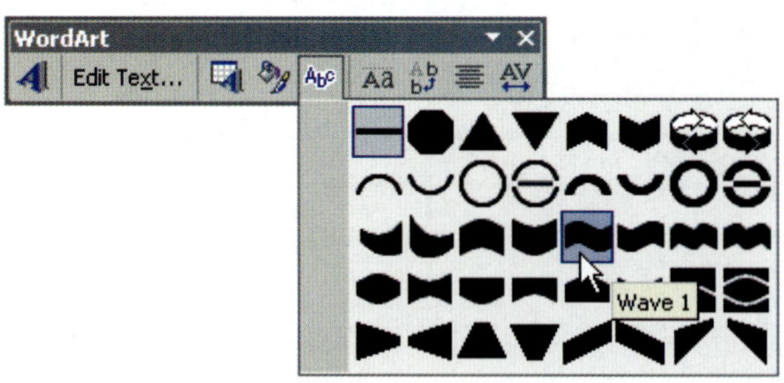

TIP: Many colors and shapes are displayed in the WordArt Gallery. Choose a color that works with your presentation colors, even if you don't like the WordArt shape. Changing the shape of WordArt is sometimes easier than changing the color.

7. While holding down Ctrl, drag the middle-right sizing handle to the right until the WordArt text stretches to within an inch of each side of the slide. Move the WordArt object to the top of the slide.

FIGURE 6-20
Completed WordArt object

EXERCISE 6-21 Edit WordArt Text

WordArt text can be edited only in the Edit WordArt Text dialog box. You open the Edit WordArt Text dialog box by clicking Edit Text on the WordArt toolbar, or by double-clicking the WordArt object.

1. Select the WordArt object.
2. Click Edit Text on the WordArt toolbar.
3. Change the text "Good for You" to **Good 4 U**. Click OK.

EXERCISE 6-22 Customize a Template by Using WordArt

If you want a WordArt object to appear on each slide, you can place it on a master slide, just like you placed a picture on a master previously in this lesson.

1. Right-click the WordArt object and choose Copy from the shortcut menu. The WordArt object is copied onto the clipboard.
2. Display the slide master.
3. Right-click anywhere on the slide master and choose Paste from the shortcut menu. The WordArt object is pasted into the slide master.
4. Close the Master view. Scroll through the presentation to check that the WordArt object appears on every slide in the same location. The AutoShapes on slides 3 and 4 and the text on slide 7 might overlap the WordArt. You fix that in the following exercises.

5. Save the presentation as ***[your initials]*6-22** in your Lesson 6 folder but do not print it. Leave the presentation open for the next exercise.

Working with Text Boxes

Until now, you have worked with text placeholders that automatically appear when you insert a new slide. Sometimes you'll want to put text outside the text placeholders or create free-form text boxes on a blank slide.

You create text boxes by clicking the Text Box button on the Drawing toolbar and then dragging the pointer to define the width of the text box. You can also just click the pointer, and the text box adjusts its width to the size of your text. You can change the size and position of text boxes the same way you change text placeholders.

EXERCISE 6-23 Add Text by Using a Text Box

When you use the Text Box button to create a single line of text, you are free to place that text anywhere on a slide, change its color and font, and rotate it. This type of text is sometimes called *floating text.*

1. Display slide 5.
2. Click the Text Box button on the Drawing toolbar.
3. Place the pointer below the "G" in "Good 4 U" and click. A small text box containing an insertion point appears.

FIGURE 6-21 Creating floating text

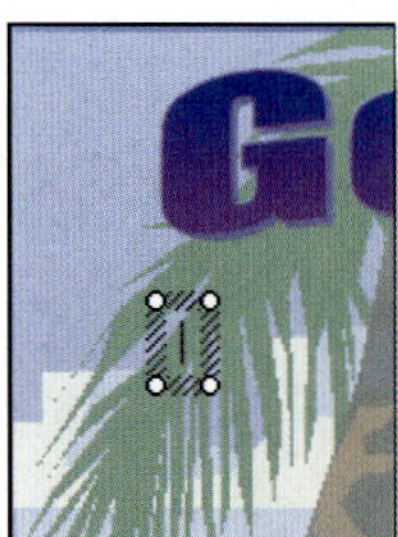

4. Key **Miami!** Notice how the text box widens as you key text.

NOTE: If you accidentally drag as you click the text tool pointer, PowerPoint will think you want to restrict the width of the text box and the text you key will wrap within a tall and narrow text box. If this happens, click Undo and try again.

5. Click the text box border to select it. You select the text box the same way you select a text placeholder. Change the text to 48-point, bold, shadowed, and choose an attractive script font such as Monotype Corsiva or Script MT Bold. Change the text color to turquoise.
6. Using the four-pointed arrow, move the floating text box to the upper-left corner of the photograph. (See Figure 6-22 on the next page.)

FIGURE 6-22
Placement for floating text

EXERCISE 6-24 Wrap Text in a Text Box

When you drag the pointer to define the width of a text box, word wrapping is automatically turned on. As you key, your insertion point automatically jumps to a new line when it gets to the right side of the box. The height of the box automatically adjusts to accommodate additional text lines.

1. Move to slide 3, which contains the white square.
2. Click the Text Box button .
3. Position your pointer in the center of the screen, to the right of the square; then drag to the right to create a rectangle that is about the same width as the white square.
4. In the text box, key **Meet your friends at our outdoor patio for healthy dining in the sun**
5. Click the text box border to select it; then increase the font size to 28 points and center-align the text.
6. Position the white square in the approximate center of the slide; then drag the text box on top until the white box frames it. (If you want to be precise, open the Position tab of the Format AutoShape dialog box, and make the Horizontal setting 3.25 inches and the Vertical setting 2.5 inches.)

TIP: The text appears on top of the square because it was placed on the slide after the square was created. You can force an object to be on top by cutting it and then pasting it after creating the object that you want on the bottom.

7. If necessary, use a sizing handle to adjust the width of the text box so that the text wraps to four lines, as shown in Figure 6-23. Adjust the other elements on the slide to match the picture.

FIGURE 6-23
Text wrapped in a text box

8. Draw a short horizontal line under the text, as shown in Figure 6-23.

9. Move to slide 4. Create a fixed-width text box on the left side of the slide and key the following, pressing Enter or Shift+Enter where indicated and italicizing text where indicated:

Sunday Brunch Specials Enter
Peach Melba Yogurt Shift+Enter
Sunrise Juice Drink Shift+Enter
Asparagus Omelet

10. Increase the font size of "Sunday Brunch Specials" to 28 points and the other text to 24 points. Center-align all the text. (See Figure 6-24 on the next page.)

11. Arrange the text and the circle in the approximate center of the slide as shown in Figure 6-24, and add a horizontal line where shown. Adjust the width of the text box and the diameter of the circle if needed.

TIP: Remember that you can use Alt while dragging or Ctrl when using the arrow keys to fine-tune the position of objects on a slide.

12. Save the presentation as ***[your initials]*****6-24** in your Lesson 6 folder but do not print it. Leave the presentation open for the next exercise.

FIGURE 6-24
Text box arrangement in a circle

Rotating Text and Other Objects

You can rotate almost any PowerPoint object—including text boxes, placeholders, and clip art—by dragging the green *rotation handle* that appears at the top of a selected object. You can also control rotation of text boxes and placeholders by using the Format Text Box and Format AutoShape dialog boxes.

To constrain the rotation of an object to 15-degree increments, hold down Shift while rotating.

EXERCISE 6-25 Rotate a Text Box

FIGURE 6-25
Rotating a text box

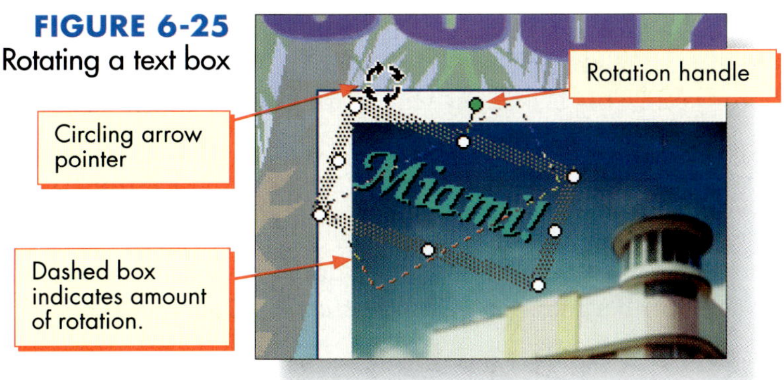

1. On slide 5, click "Miami!"
2. Point to the green rotation handle at the top of the text box and drag it to the right. Notice the circling arrow pointer that appears while you drag.
3. Drag the rotation handle to the left, positioning the text box as shown in Figure 6-26 on the page after next.

TIP: You can key a precise angle of rotation measurement on the Size tab of the Format Text Box dialog box.

EXERCISE 6-26 Edit Text in a Rotated Object

When text is in a rotated position, it can be difficult to edit. Fortunately, when you select a rotated text box for editing, it conveniently returns to a horizontal position while you revise the text.

1. Click anywhere on the text "Miami!" The object and text rotate to a horizontal position for easy text editing.
2. Delete the exclamation point at the end of "Miami!"
3. Click the text box border. The text box returns to its rotated position.
4. With the text box border selected, adjust the rotation angle and the position so that it appears as in Figure 6-26 (on the next page).

EXERCISE 6-27 Rotate an AutoShape

You rotate an AutoShape (or any other object) the same way that you rotate a text box. If the AutoShape contains text, the text also rotates.

1. Still working on slide 5, select the 16-Point Star AutoShape containing the text "Grand Opening!"
2. Hold down Shift and drag the rotation handle two increments to the left. The AutoShape and its text are now rotated 30 degrees.
3. Drag the AutoShape's border diagonally until it overlaps the lower-right corner of the square and photograph. The photograph hides part of the AutoShape. This is because the photograph was placed on the slide after the AutoShape.
4. Cut the AutoShape to the clipboard and then paste it. Now the AutoShape is on top of the photograph. This is an easy way to force an object to appear on the top.
5. Compare slide 5 with Figure 6-26 and make any necessary adjustments.
6. Delete slide 6 (the practice slide) and slide 7 ("Miami Pictures").
7. Create a handout header and footer: include the date and your name as the header, and the page number and text ***[your initials]*6-27** as the footer.

FIGURE 6-26
Edited text in a rotated object

8. Move to slide 1 and save the presentation as ***[your initials]*6-27** in your Lesson 6 folder.
9. Preview and then print the presentation as handouts, 6 slides per page, grayscale, landscape, framed. Close the presentation.

USING HELP

PowerPoint and other Office programs can accept graphics files in many different formats. These formats are for both vector drawings and bitmaps.

Use Help to learn about graphics filters:

1. Key **pictures** in the Ask a Question box on the left side of the menu bar and press Enter.
2. In the drop-down list, choose About pictures.
3. Expand each topic and read about bitmaps and drawn pictures. (See Figure 6-27 on the next page.)
4. Expand any terms that you encounter if you are not familiar with them.
5. Close the Help window when you are finished.

FIGURE 6-27
Help screen about pictures

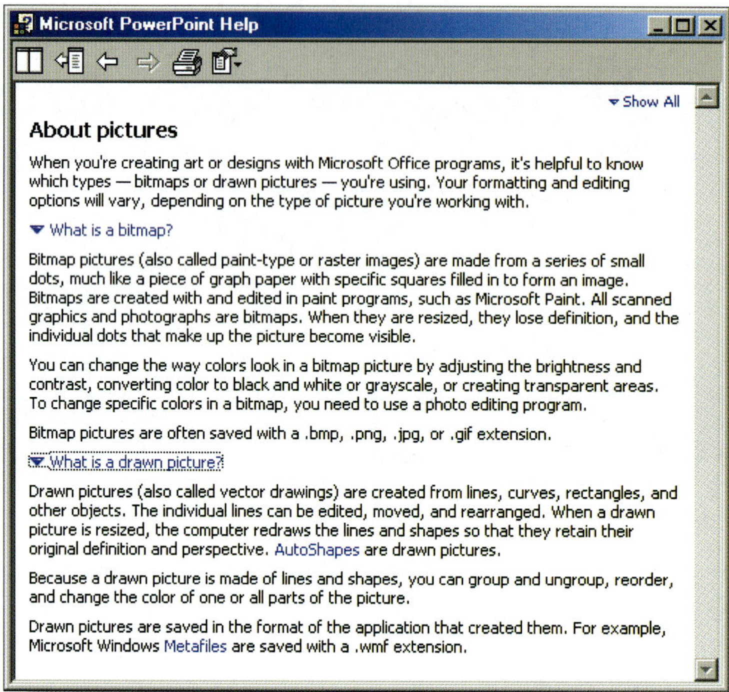

LESSON 6 Summary

- In addition to text placeholders, PowerPoint provides a variety of objects that you can use to enhance the visual appearance of your slides. These include AutoShapes, text boxes, clip art, and scanned photos.
- PowerPoint's basic drawing tools enable you to create squares, circles, rectangles, ovals, and straight lines drawn at any angle.
- You draw a shape by first selecting it on the Drawing toolbar and then dragging diagonally on your slide to define the size of the shape.
- If you don't like a shape you drew, select it and press Delete to remove it from your slide, or click Undo.
- Hold down Shift while drawing a line or other shape to constrain it. Constraining a shape makes it perfectly symmetrical, for example, a circle or a square, or can make a line perfectly horizontal or perfectly vertical.
- Hold down Ctrl while drawing a shape to make it grow from the center instead of from one edge.

- Move a drawn object by pointing to it and dragging the four-pointed arrow ✥ when it appears.
- Change the size of a drawn object by dragging one of its sizing handles (small white circles on its border) with a two-pointed arrow ↕.
- To preserve an object's proportions when resizing it, hold down Shift while dragging a corner sizing handle.
- AutoShapes are predefined shapes that are organized into several categories. To draw an AutoShape, select the shape you want and then drag the cross pointer. After an AutoShape is drawn, you can change it to a different shape.
- When an AutoShape is selected, text that you key appears inside the shape.
- Use the Clip Art task pane to search for clip art. If you are connected to the Internet, the task pane's Search command will automatically search the Microsoft Office Design Gallery Live.
- To see a menu of clip art options, point to a clip art thumbnail in the Clip Art task pane and then click the vertical gray bar that appears on the right side of the thumbnail (or right-click the thumbnail).
- Using the Cut, Copy, and Paste commands, you can easily move or copy clip art from one slide to another or from one presentation to another.
- Resize a clip art image by dragging one of its sizing handles. If you want to preserve proportions, drag a corner handle. If you want to distort the proportions, drag one of the side handles.
- Use the Picture toolbar to adjust a picture's brightness, contrast, color depth, and other picture attributes.
- Pictures and drawn objects can be inserted directly into master slides or can be copied from another location and pasted onto master slides.
- Clip art images (vectors, bitmaps, or scanned images) can be cropped. Cropping is trimming away edges of a picture, much like using scissors to cut out a picture from a newspaper or magazine.
- WordArt enables you to create special effects with text that are not possible with standard text-formatting tools.
- WordArt is modified by using the WordArt Gallery to change its style, by changing its shape, and by editing its text. All these options and many more are available on the WordArt toolbar.
- Text boxes enable you to place text anywhere on a slide. Using the Text Box button, click anywhere on a slide or draw a box and then start keying text.
- Text in a text box can be formatted by using standard text-formatting tools. Change the width of a text box to control how it will word-wrap.

➤ When you select an object on a slide (including text boxes and text placeholders), a green rotation handle appears slightly above the top center sizing handle. Drag the rotation handle left or right to rotate the object.

LESSON 6 Command Summary

FEATURE	BUTTON	MENU	KEYBOARD	SPEECH?
Insert Clip Art		Insert, Picture, Clip Art		✓
Format Picture		Format, Picture		✓
Crop a picture		Format, Picture, Picture tab		✓
Insert WordArt		Insert, Picture, WordArt		✓
Edit WordArt text	Edit Text	Edit Text		✓
Change WordArt shape				✓
Change WordArt style				✓
Format WordArt		Format, WordArt		✓
Text Box		Insert, Text Box		✓
AutoShapes	AutoShapes	Insert, Picture, AutoShapes		✓
Rectangle				✓
Square	Shift +			
Oval				✓
Circle	Shift +			

continues

LESSON 6 Command Summary *continued*

FEATURE	BUTTON	MENU	KEYBOARD	SPEECH?
Line				✓
Constrained line				
Change AutoShape		Draw, Change AutoShape		✓
Search for Clip Art		Search (on the Insert Clip Art task pane)		
Adjust contrast	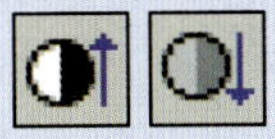	Format, Picture, Picture tab, Contrast		✓
Adjust brightness	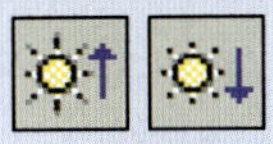	Format, Picture, Picture tab, Brightness		✓
Adjust color		Format, Picture, Picture tab, Color		✓

Concepts Review

TRUE/FALSE QUESTIONS

Each of the following statements is either true or false. Indicate your choice by circling T or F.

T F **1.** Every AutoShape includes an adjustment handle.

T F **2.** When you want to change the height of an object but not the width, press Shift while dragging a corner sizing handle.

T F **3.** Anything placed on a PowerPoint slide is considered an object.

T F **4.** You can type text only in an existing placeholder.

T F **5.** A green handle on a PowerPoint object indicates that the object can be rotated.

T F **6.**  is found on the AutoShapes toolbar.

T F **7.** Use Shift with 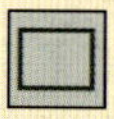 to create a square.

T F **8.** To move a text box, the pointer must remain on the border and not touch a sizing handle.

SHORT ANSWER QUESTIONS

Write the correct answer in the space provided.

1. How do you draw a perfect circle?

____

2. How can you change an object to a different AutoShape without deleting and redrawing it?

____

3. What kind of handle is the yellow diamond?

____

4. How do you create a text box that adjusts its width to the width of the text you key?

____

5. How do you edit the text in a WordArt object?

____

6. What happens when you press Ctrl while you drag a corner sizing handle toward the center of an object?

____

7. Where do you place the pointer when sizing objects?

____

8. If you use the Format Picture dialog box, what option should you check to resize a picture proportionately?

____

CRITICAL THINKING

Answer these questions on a separate page. There are no right or wrong answers. Support your answers with examples from your own experience, if possible.

1. Use the Clip Art task pane to select three pieces of clip art and then explain the type of presentation in which you might use them.
2. In this lesson you placed some text directly in an AutoShape, and you placed some text in a text box that was then placed on top of an AutoShape. Think of reasons why you might place the text in a separate text box instead of directly in an AutoShape.

Lesson Applications

EXERCISE 6-28

Work with lines, AutoShapes, and clip art.

1. Open the file **Market1**.
2. On the slide master, draw a horizontal line at the bottom of the body text placeholder, the same width as the placeholder. Then draw a small Diamond AutoShape overlapping the line and centered approximately on the line, as shown in Figure 6-28. Use Ctrl+arrow keys (or Alt and your mouse) to fine-tune its position.

FIGURE 6-28

3. On slide 1, draw a square, approximately 3 inches wide. Position it attractively on the lower right side of the slide.
4. Use the Insert Clip Art task pane to search for pictures by using the search word **meeting**. Choose a picture that is appropriate in style, content, and color for this slide and insert it.
5. Resize and crop the picture so that it is a little smaller than the square that you drew; then position the picture inside the square. Adjust the size of the picture, if necessary, so the square becomes a frame with a small amount of the green fill showing.
6. On slide 2, draw a 4-inch wide rectangle below the body text placeholder. Find a picture similar to the one you used on slide 1, size and/or crop it to fit the rectangle, and place it on top of the rectangle (just as you did on slide 1 to create a frame around the picture).
7. Move slide 5 before slide 4.
8. Check spelling in the presentation.
9. Create a handout header and footer: include the date and your name as the header, and the page number and text ***[your initials]*6-28** as the footer.
10. Move to slide 1 and save the presentation as ***[your initials]*6-28** in your Lesson 6 folder.
11. Preview and then print the presentation as handouts, 6 slides per page, grayscale, framed. Close the presentation.

POWERPOINT

EXERCISE 6-29

Create a presentation from a Word outline, create and rotate a text box and an AutoShape containing text, and add clip art to the slide master.

1. Create a presentation from the Word document **Cooking1** by opening the Word outline file from within PowerPoint. Change the slide layout of Slide 1 to Title Slide.
2. Apply the design template Level and use the color scheme with the black background.
3. Create a text box in the lower right corner of slide 1 with the text **Good 4 U**. Format the text as 40-point Verdana bold.
4. Rotate the "Good 4 U" text so it slants upward in the lower right corner. Adjust the text position, if necessary.
5. On slide 3, adjust the font size for the title so it fits on one line.
6. Change the layout of slide 4 to Title Only. Below the title, draw a large, 16-Point Star AutoShape, placing it in the center of the slide. Key the following two lines of text in the star:

   The Good 4 U
   Seal of Approval
7. Format the text as 32-point Verdana bold with a text shadow in a color of your choice. Adjust the height and width of the star to suit your taste; then rotate the star so the text slants upward.
8. On the slide master, insert an image of fruit in the lower right corner and adjust its size appropriately.
9. On the title slide, insert the same fruit picture, making it larger and placing it in a prominent position.
10. Apply an exciting animation scheme of your choice to the entire presentation; then apply a different animation scheme to just the first and last slide.
11. Check spelling in the presentation.
12. Create a handout header and footer: include the date and your name as the header, and the page number and text ***[your initials]*6-29** as the footer.
13. Move to slide 1 and save the presentation as ***[your initials]*6-29** in your Lesson 6 folder.
14. View the presentation as a slide show.
15. Preview and then print the presentation as handouts, 4 slides per page, grayscale, landscape, framed. Close the presentation.

EXERCISE 6-30

Insert and rotate a picture from a file, and add clip art to the master slides.

1. Open the file **Recruit1**.
2. On the slide master, increase the title text placeholder font size to 54 points. Change the body text placeholder font to Arial.
3. Insert a picture of an apple on the slide master. Choose a fairly simple image that will work well with the design colors. Size the apple appropriately (no more than 2.25 inches tall) and position it in the lower right corner of the slide.
4. Copy the apple from the slide master and paste it to the title master. Adjust the position of the apple on the title master and make it slightly larger.
5. On slide 1, insert the picture file **Logo1** from your student data disk. Rotate it so that it slants up and place it in the upper-left corner of the slide. Use the Picture toolbar buttons to adjust its contrast and brightness. Use the Set Transparent Color button on the Picture toolbar to make the logo's white background transparent.
6. In the subtitle placeholder, key **New Hires**, a hyphen, and today's date.
7. On slide 2, break the second bulleted item into these two bulleted items:
   - **History of Company**
   - **Company Vision**
8. Still working on slide 2, adjust the size of the body text placeholder to fit its text; then center the placeholder under the slide title.
9. Insert two new slides at the end of the presentation; use the Text slide layout. Key the text in Figure 6-29 on the slides indicated.

FIGURE 6-29

Slide 4

Who's Who

- Julie Wolfe and Gus Irvinelli are the ← Insert line break by using Shift+Enter
  co-owners of the restaurant
- Michele Jenkins is the head chef
- Roy Olafsen is the marketing manager

Slide 5

Summary

- Good 4 U is growing rapidly with our new franchising philosophy
- Our healthy living message has worldwide appeal
- We are relying on you, our new employees, to help us grow

10. Check spelling in the presentation.
11. Scroll through the presentation and check each slide to make sure the apple picture does not interfere with any text. If necessary, readjust the size and/or position of the picture on the slide master and the title master.
12. Create a handout header and footer: include the date and your name as the header, and the page number and text ***[your initials]*6-30** as the footer.
13. Move to slide 1 and save the presentation as ***[your initials]*6-30** in your Lesson 6 folder.
14. Preview and then print the presentation as handouts, 6 slides per page, grayscale, framed. Close the presentation.

EXERCISE 6-31 Challenge Yourself

Use drawing tools, WordArt, and insert pictures.

1. Open the file **Funding1**.
2. Using the Outline pane, insert the body text for each slide as shown in Figure 6-30.

FIGURE 6-30

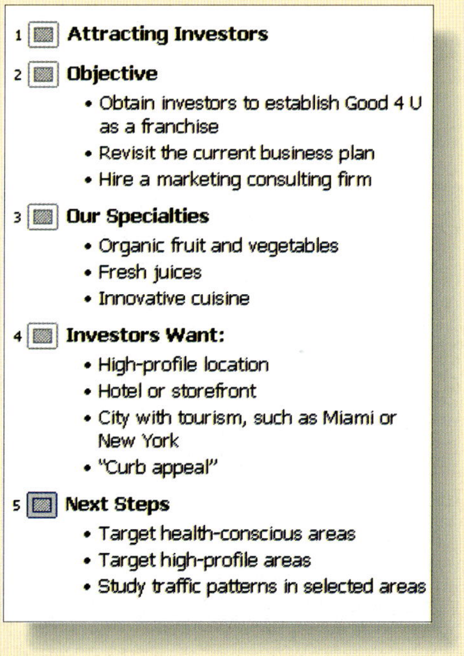

3. Insert the file **Logo1** on the slide master and the title master, placing the logo attractively in the lower right corner of the screen. Use the Set Transparent Color button on the Picture toolbar to remove the logo's white background, and adjust the contrast and brightness so that the logo contrasts the dark background.

4. On slide 1, delete the title text and its placeholder. Use the title text shown in Figure 6-30 to create a WordArt title. Use the WordArt style in the fifth column of the bottom row. Resize the WordArt to stretch across the slide and move it up slightly from the center of the slide.
5. On slides 2 through 5, substitute WordArt titles for the text in the title placeholders. Use the WordArt style on the second row, fourth column (shaded silver color). Position the WordArt where the title placeholders were, and stretch the WordArt titles across the width of the slides.
6. On slide 2, resize the body text placeholder to fit the text; then move the text placeholder to the right so that it appears centered.
7. Still working on slide 2, draw a Cube AutoShape (from the Basic Shapes submenu) under the text placeholder and approximately the same width as the placeholder. Key **Investors are our building blocks** in the AutoShape, format it as 28-point Arial bold, and change the text color to dark blue.
8. On slide 3, remove the bullets from the body text placeholder and center its text. Insert a picture of fruit in one of the content placeholders and a picture of a vegetable in the other. Adjust the size and image settings of the pictures if necessary.
9. On slide 4, insert the picture **Miami1** from your student data disk. Crop and resize the picture so that it fits within the turquoise rectangle and appears to be framed.
10. On slide 5, draw a 15-degree line and three small Block Arrow AutoShapes, rotated to 15 degrees, and arranged as shown in Figure 6-31.

FIGURE 6-31

11. Review each slide and make changes to the size and position of any objects you want to make a pleasing composition.
12. Check spelling in the presentation.
13. Create a handout header and footer: include the date and your name as the header, and the page number and filename ***[your initials]*6-31** as the footer.
14. Move to slide 1 and save the presentation as ***[your initials]*6-31** in your Lesson 6 folder.
15. Preview and then print the presentation as handouts, 6 slides per page, grayscale, framed. Close the presentation.

On Your Own

In these exercises you work on your own, as you would in a real-life work environment. Use the skills you've learned to accomplish the task—and be creative.

EXERCISE 6-32

Open the file **Seminar1**. Choose another design template and color scheme. Create WordArt titles for the title of each slide. Insert a suitable clip art image on the title slide and a complimentary image on the slide master. Change the size, shape, and position of text placeholders and other objects, and change font sizes to create a pleasing composition. Use your own creativity to design a lively presentation, remembering to maintain a clear and unified look throughout. Apply one or more animation schemes. Save the presentation as ***[your initials]*6-32**. Preview and then print the presentation as handouts.

EXERCISE 6-33

Create a presentation entitled "Gift Suggestions for *[choose occasion or person]*." Select five or more suitable items from mail order catalogs and create a separate slide describing each item, including the price and why you selected it. If you have access to a scanner, scan each item's picture from the catalog and insert it on the appropriate slide. If a scanner is not available, insert a suitable clip art image on each slide. Use your own creativity and the tools learned in this and previous lessons to add interest to the slides. Save the presentation as ***[your initials]*6-33**. Preview and then print the presentation as handouts.

EXERCISE 6-34

Imagine that you are about to open a new retail store or restaurant. Using the content and layout of the Miami Beach presentation from this lesson as a general guide, create a presentation with at least five slides announcing the opening of your business. Use clip art, text boxes, AutoShapes, WordArt, and if possible, scanned photos to illustrate your presentation. Include an animation effect or a transition effect. Save the presentation as ***[your initials]*6-34**. Preview and then print the presentation as handouts.

LESSON 7

Working with Lines, Fills, and Colors

OBJECTIVES

MOUS ACTIVITIES
In this lesson:
PP2002 3-3
PP2002 4-1
PP2002 4-4
See Appendix E.

After completing this lesson, you will be able to:

1. Change the line color and line style for PowerPoint objects.
2. Change the fill color of objects.
3. Work with an extended color palette.
4. Work with fill patterns, gradient fills, and textures.
5. Use the Format Painter tool to copy formatting.
6. Work with grayscale settings for better printing.

Estimated Time: 1½ hours

In Lesson 6, you learned how to create shapes and add pictures to your presentation. In that lesson, every shape in a presentation was the same color. This lesson shows you how to enhance your presentation by applying color, patterns, shading, and line styles to shapes you draw, text placeholders, and pictures.

Changing the Line Color and Line Style of Objects

To emphasize or separate text, clip art, or other objects from the rest of your slide, you can create a border by using a variety of color and line options. Borders can be applied to any PowerPoint object, including text boxes, text placeholders, AutoShapes, clip art, and pictures.

EXERCISE 7-1 Apply a Border

The fastest way to add a border to an object is to select the object and then click the Line Style button. *Line style* refers to the type of border or outline that an object has. Options include single, double, and triple lines of varying *line weights*. The weight of a line is its thickness, measured in points.

For more line style options, open the Format AutoShape, Format Text Box, or Format Picture dialog box in one of the following ways:

- Double-click the object.
- Right-click the object; then choose Format AutoShape, Format Text Box, or Format Picture from the shortcut menu.
- From the Format menu, choose Placeholder, AutoShape, Text Box or Picture.

1. Open the file **SanFran1** and move to slide 2.
2. Press Tab one or more times to select the body text placeholder.

3. Click the Line Style button on the Drawing toolbar to display a menu of options.

FIGURE 7-1
Line styles

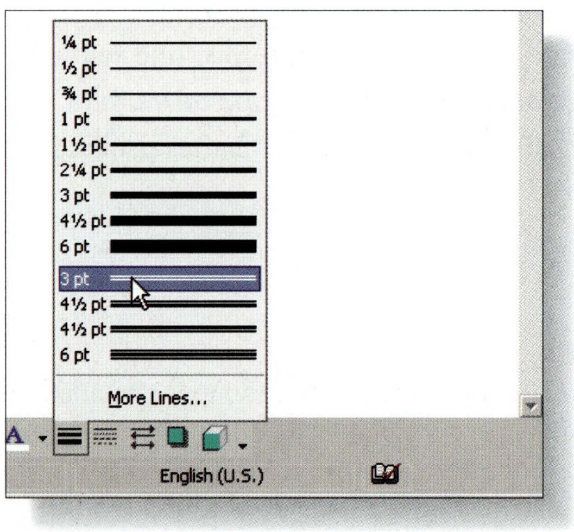

4. Click to select the 3-point double line. A double line now frames the body text.
5. Deselect the text box and change the Zoom to 150% to see the double line clearly. The color of the line is the template's default line color. (You change the line color later in this lesson.)

REVIEW: To change the zoom, you can use the Zoom box on the Standard toolbar or open the View menu and choose Zoom.

6. Select the body text placeholder again and apply the 1-point single-line style to its border.
7. Change the Zoom setting back to Fit.

EXERCISE 7-2 Apply a Dashed Line to an Object

PowerPoint offers a variety of dash styles to apply to lines and borders. A *dash style* is the pattern of dashes and dots that make up a line. Styles include solid line, square dot, dash, and combinations of dashes and dots.

When used sparingly, a dash style can add interest to a presentation. You can apply dash styles to lines, arrows, and object borders. They can be any color and any line weight.

1. Move to slide 3 and select the star object.
2. Apply the 6-point single-line style. A thicker border now surrounds the star.
3. With the star still selected, click the Dash Style button on the Drawing toolbar.

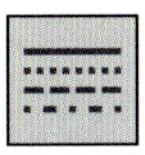

FIGURE 7-2
Dash styles

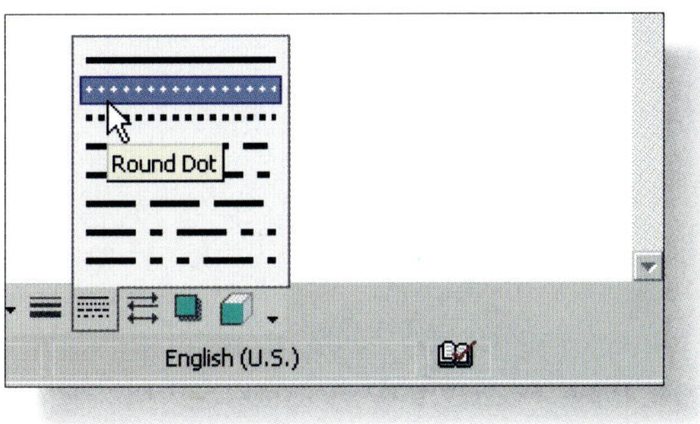

4. Apply the Round Dot style, which is the second style on the menu. A dash-style line or border can produce a dramatic effect.

EXERCISE 7-3 Change the Color of a Border

You can change the color of a border in one of two ways:

- Click the Line Color button on the Drawing toolbar.
- Use the Format AutoShape dialog box (Colors and Lines tab).

The color sample on the Line Color button shows the last color you applied. If you click a color button (such as Line, Fill, or Text) without clicking its arrow, you'll apply the color shown on the button's color bar.

1. Still working on slide 3, select the star shape.

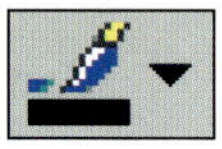

2. Click the arrow for the Line Color button on the Drawing toolbar to display the line color choices. The gray bar at the top of the menu indicates that you can float the menu.
3. Without clicking, move the mouse pointer over each color sample and notice the ScreenTips. These tips identify the automatic colors for the PowerPoint objects that make up a presentation.
4. Click the dark pink color on the right to select it. The ScreenTip indicates that this color is used as an accent color (and as a followed hyperlink if you're creating links to other slides, files, or Web pages).

FIGURE 7-3
Line colors

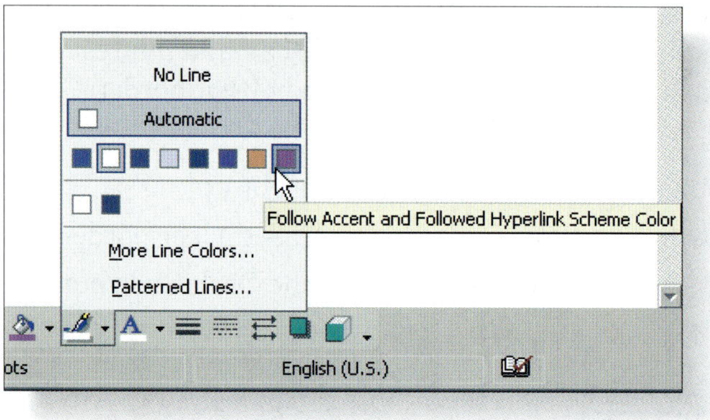

EXERCISE 7-4 Draw and Format Arrows

Besides drawing arrow AutoShapes, you can draw lines with attached arrowheads by using the Arrow button on the Drawing toolbar, or you can add arrowheads to existing lines by using the Arrow Style button or the Format AutoShape dialog box (Colors and Lines tab).

Arrow style options include several varieties of arrowheads, dots, and diamonds. By using the Format AutoShape dialog box, you can control whether to put an arrowhead on either end or on both ends of a line.

1. Move to slide 4.

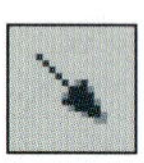

2. Click the Arrow button and draw a diagonal line that slants down from the right, pointing toward the tallest bar on the chart.
3. Deselect the line. Notice the small arrowhead on the end of the line.
4. Select the arrow; then use the Line Style button to change the arrow to a 3-point single-line style. (If you like, you can increase the zoom to see the change more clearly.)

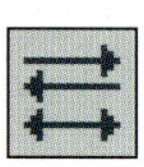

5. Click the Arrow Style button on the Drawing toolbar.

FIGURE 7-4
Arrow styles

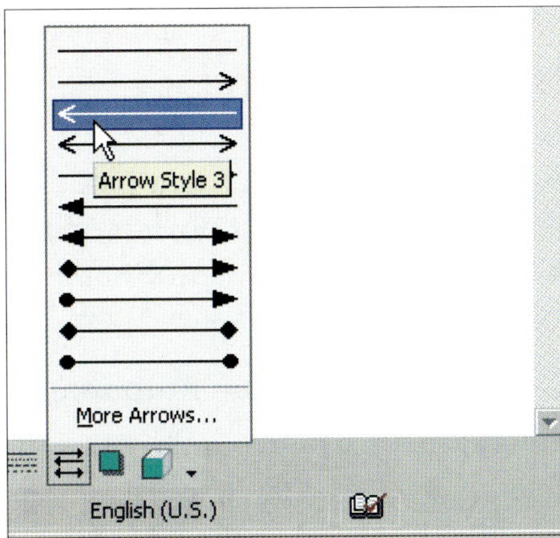

6. Select **Arrow Style 3**, a left-pointing arrow. The arrow points away from the chart.

NOTE: The placement of the arrow is determined by where you started drawing the line. The left arrowhead appears at the beginning of the line, and the right arrowhead appears at the end of the line.

7. Click the Arrow Style button again. Select **Arrow Style 2**, a right-pointing arrow.
8. Adjust the length and angle of the arrow by dragging the sizing handle by its tail, as shown in Figure 7-5.

FIGURE 7-5
Adjusting the arrow

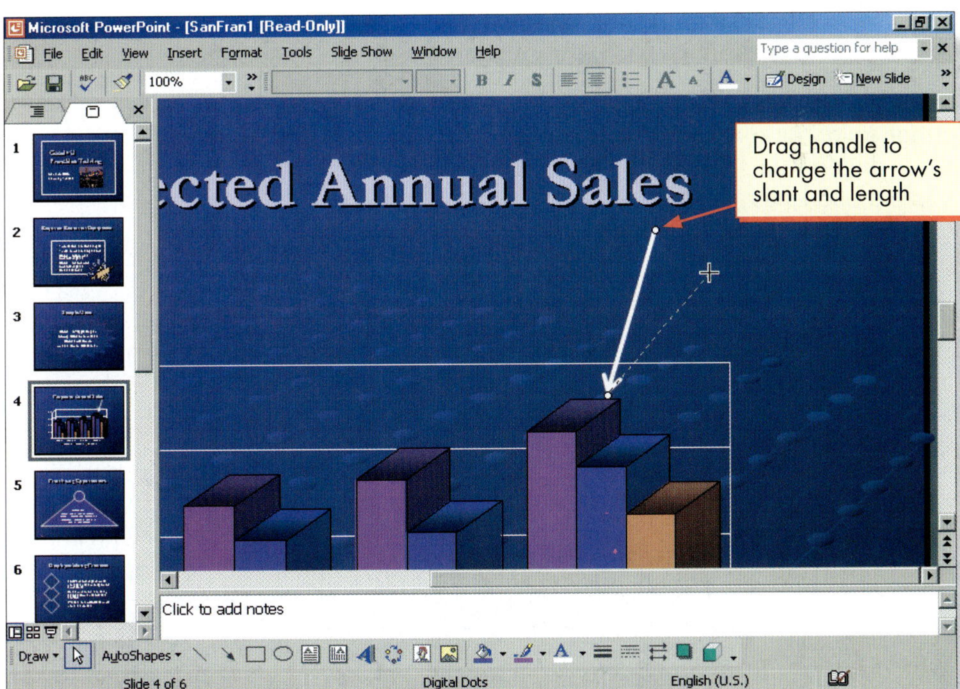

EXERCISE 7-5 Change an Arrow by Using the Format AutoShape Dialog Box

The Format AutoShape dialog box is a convenient place to apply many different types of formatting to all types of PowerPoint objects. Besides letting you change multiple attributes at one time, the Format AutoShape dialog box offers many options that are not available on toolbars.

1. Double-click the arrow to open the Format AutoShape dialog box.
2. Click the Colors and Lines tab.
3. In the Line section, open the Color drop-down list. The first line of color samples represents the colors for the current presentation's color scheme.
4. Point to the first sample on the first line (a blue/gray color). The ScreenTip identifies this sample as the color scheme's background color.
5. Click the blue/gray background color to select it.
6. Click Preview in the lower left corner of the dialog box and then drag the dialog box out of the way to see the new color of the arrow. The arrow fades into the background.
7. Change the color to dark pink, the Accent and Followed Hyperlink Scheme color on the right end of the first line of colors. Preview the change.
8. In the Weight box, click the up arrow several times until 8 pt appears. Click Preview. The arrow is thicker.
9. On the End style drop-down list, choose the first arrow style on the second row (Stealth Arrow).

FIGURE 7-6
Format AutoShape dialog box, Colors and Lines tab

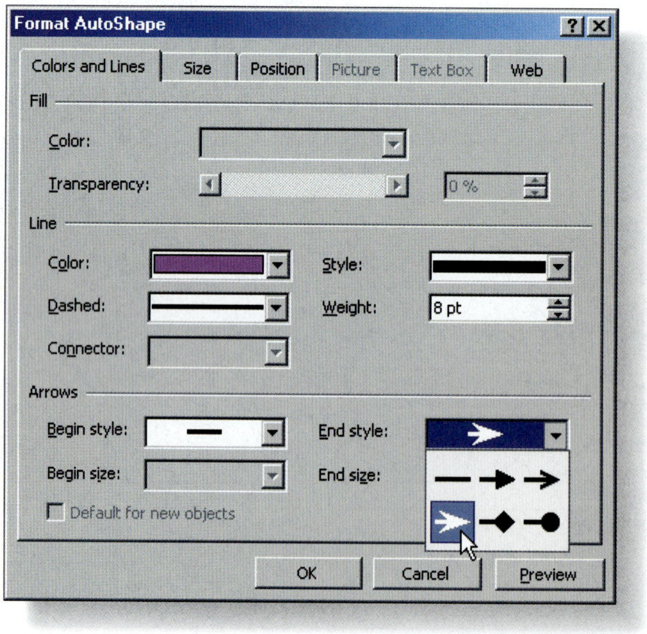

10. On the End size drop-down list, choose the third arrow on the second row (Arrow R Size 6).
11. Click Preview. The arrow is now much wider and has a larger arrowhead.
12. Click OK to accept the changes and close the Format AutoShape dialog box. If you zoomed in on the arrow, change your zoom setting to Fit.

NOTE: You use the same technique to change the color of an object border or a line as you use to change the color of an arrow.

Changing the Fill Color of Objects

When you draw an object on a slide, the color of the object—its *fill color*—is determined by the presentation's color scheme. You can easily change the fill to another color from the presentation's color scheme or to any color you want.

EXERCISE 7-6 Change the Fill Color of an Object

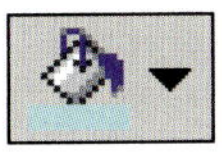

You change the fill color by using one of two options:

- Use the Fill Color button on the Drawing toolbar.
- Use the Format AutoShape dialog box (Colors and Lines tab).

1. Move back to slide 3 and right-click the star. From the shortcut menu, choose Format AutoShape to open the Format AutoShape dialog box.

2. Click the Colors and Lines tab.

FIGURE 7-7
Changing an object's fill color

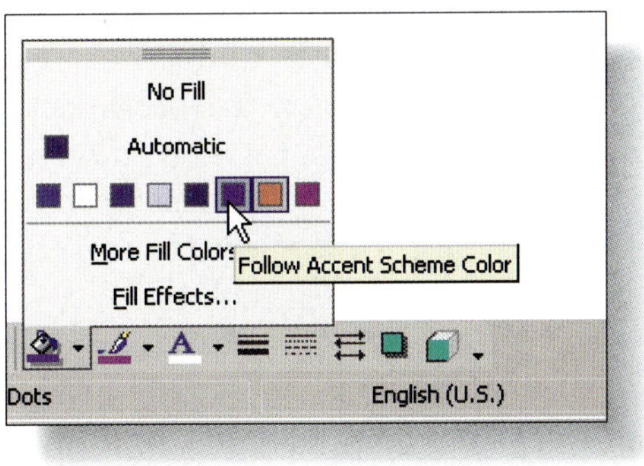

3. In the Fill section of the dialog box, click the arrow next to Color. Choose the gold sample that follows the accent and hyperlink scheme color. Click OK.

4. With the star still selected, click the arrow next to the Fill Color button on the Drawing toolbar. Click the purple sample, the accent scheme color.

EXERCISE 7-7 Remove Fill Colors and Borders from Objects

If you apply a fill or border to an object and later decide you don't want it, it's easy to remove. The first Fill Color option is No Fill, and the first Line Color option is No Line.

1. Move to slide 5 and select the large triangle AutoShape.

2. On the Drawing toolbar, click the arrow for the Fill Color button and choose No Fill. The color disappears, but the line remains.

3. With the triangle still selected, use the Line Color button to choose No Line. The triangle's border disappears. Although it looks like the object disappeared, it is still there.
4. Click the text containing the names of cities and then press Esc to select the object (the invisible triangle).
5. Choose purple (accent scheme color) for the fill. The triangle is once again visible.

Working with an Extended Range of Colors

So far, you have been instructed to choose from only the eight colors that make up the presentation's color scheme. An infinite number of other colors are also available.

It's usually best to stick with the eight colors that make up the color scheme, but at times one or two additional colors can enhance the look of a slide. Be careful when choosing extra colors because too many colors can spoil a presentation.

EXERCISE 7-8 Work with Standard Colors

Extra colors are available from the Colors dialog box. This dialog box has two tabs—Standard and Custom. *Standard colors* are pre-mixed colors that you choose by clicking a sample on the Standard tab. *Custom colors* are colors that you mix yourself on the Custom tab. You can create an infinite variety of custom colors.

You open the Colors dialog box by choosing More Fill Colors from the Fill Color button's drop-down list or by choosing More Line Colors from the Line Color button's drop-down list.

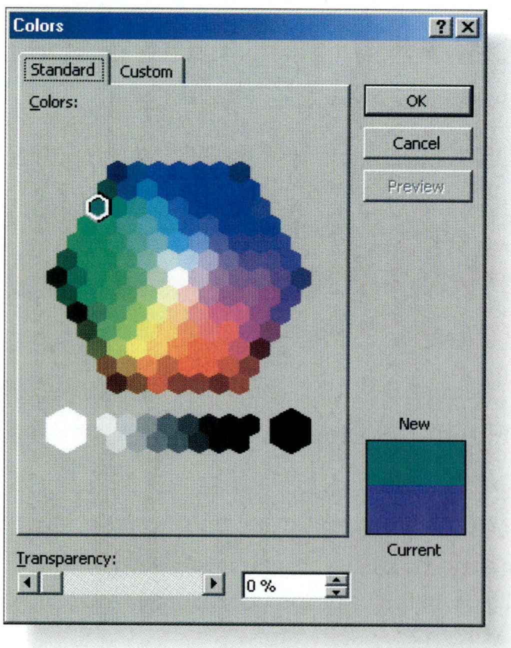

FIGURE 7-8 Working with standard colors

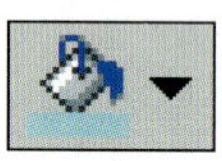

1. With the triangle on slide 5 selected, click the arrow for the Fill Color button.
2. Select More Fill Colors to display the Colors dialog box.
3. Click the Standard tab. A honeycomb of colors is displayed.
4. Click a dark green/blue color in the upper left corner of the

honeycomb. Notice the color sample on the right side of the dialog box, showing you the Current color and the New one you just selected.

5. Click Preview and drag the dialog box out of the way to see the result. Click OK.

EXERCISE 7-9 Work with Custom Colors

The Custom tab on the Colors dialog box enables you to create any color you desire. Drag a crosshair to choose the color you want; then use a scroll bar to choose the brightness level for the color.

After you choose a custom color, it appears on the second line of the Fill Color and Line Color buttons' drop-down lists so you can use it again without having to re-create it.

1. Working on slide 5, select the circle on top of the triangle.
2. Click the arrow for the Fill Color button  and choose More Fill Colors.
3. Click the Custom tab on the Colors dialog box. This dialog box contains a color palette and a vertical bar for choosing brightness.

FIGURE 7-9 Working with custom colors

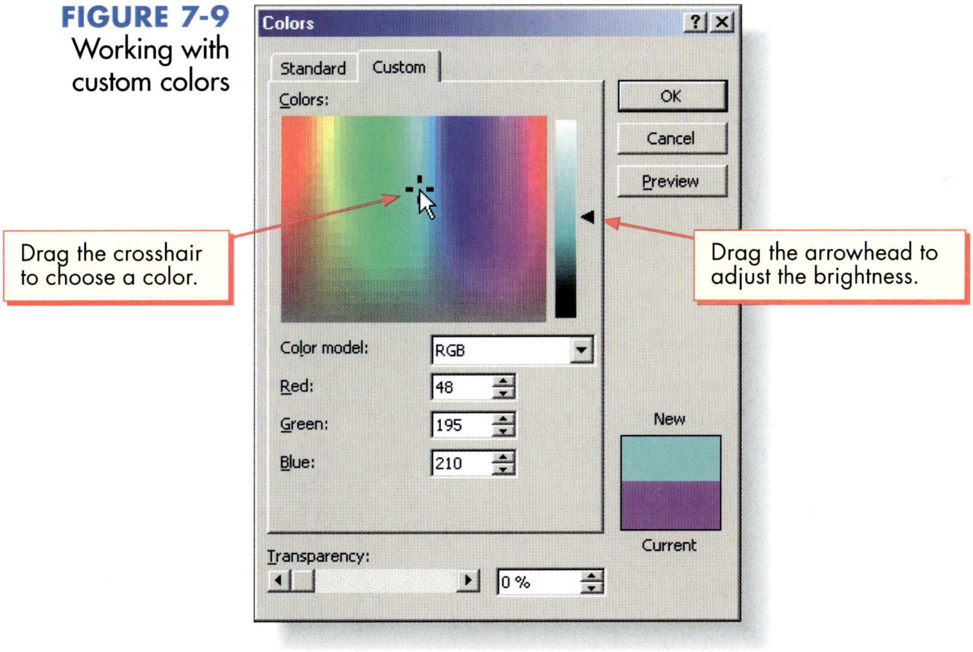

4. Drag the crosshair straight up. Notice in the sample on the lower right corner that the New color is much brighter than the Current color.
5. Drag the crosshair across the top of the palette. All the colors at the top are bright.

6. Drag the crosshair across the bottom of the palette. The colors are subdued.
7. Choose a fairly bright color; then drag the black arrowhead on the vertical bar up and down to see how the color becomes lighter and darker.
8. Experiment with the color palette and the brightness bar until you find a color you like. Click OK.

EXERCISE 7-10 Work with Transparency Settings

Making colors transparent can enhance many PowerPoint color settings. For example, you can make an AutoShape's fill transparent so that a slide's background shows through. Line color can also be made transparent. You can change transparency in the Color dialog box that you used in the previous two exercises.

1. Working on slide 5 with the circle selected, click the arrow for the Fill Color button and choose More Fill Colors. Notice the Transparency slider at the bottom of the dialog box.
2. Drag the Transparency slider to the right, until you see 40% (more or less) in the spin box. Click OK.
3. Using the above steps, change the transparency of the green/blue triangle to 60%. Notice that the slide's background shows through transparent colors.
4. Save the presentation as ***[your initials]*7-10** in a new folder for Lesson 7 but do not print it. Keep it open for the following exercises.

Adding Patterns, Gradient Fills, and Textures

To add more interest to objects on your slides, you can add special effects such as fill patterns, gradient fills, and textures. PowerPoint provides many patterns, including textures that resemble wood and marble surfaces. You can also fill objects with pictures and clip art.

EXERCISE 7-11 Apply a Gradient Fill to an Object

A gradient fill can add interest and dimension to PowerPoint objects. When you apply a *gradient fill*, the object contains colors that blend (or shade) into one another. A gradient fill can use one or two colors, or one of the preset color combinations that are built into PowerPoint.

Besides choosing colors for gradient fills, you can specify the direction of the gradient fill, such as horizontal or diagonal. You can also add transparency effects. When using single-color gradients, you adjust the degree of light and dark by using a slider.

1. Move to slide 3 ("Sample Menu") and select the star AutoShape.
2. Click the arrow for the Fill Color button and choose Fill Effects at the bottom of the menu. The Fill Effects dialog box appears.
3. Click the Gradient tab.
4. In the Colors options box, click Preset. The Preset colors list box appears, containing specially created gradient fills. Select some of these preset colors and then look at the display in the Variants box.

FIGURE 7-10 Fill Effects dialog box

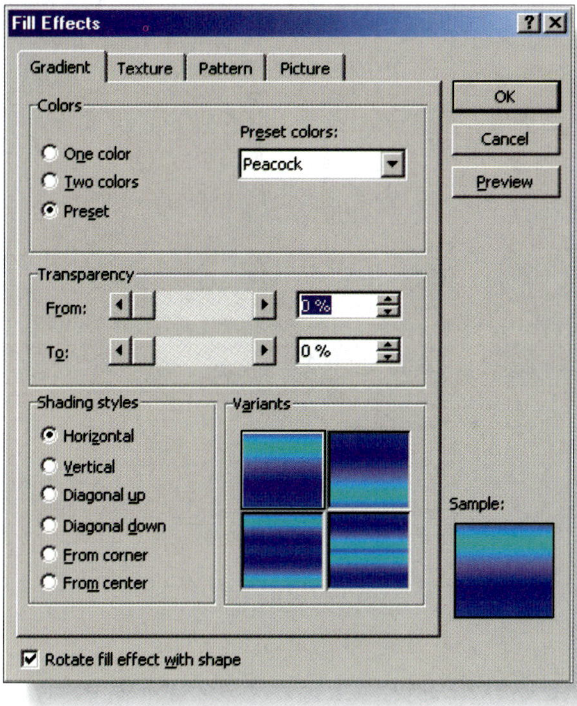

5. Choose Late Sunset from the Preset colors list box.
6. In the Shading Styles options box, choose From corner. Notice that the Sample box changes as you choose different effects.
7. Under Variants, click the option in the upper left corner. Click the Preview button and drag the dialog box out of the way so you can see the effect on the slide.
8. In the Transparency options section, drag the From slider to the right until you see 50% in the spin box. Move the To slider to 50% also.

NOTE: Changing transparency settings does not activate Preview. If you want to preview the results of changing transparency settings, temporarily change one of the other settings in the dialog box.

9. Under Variants, change to the sample in the upper right corner.
10. Click Preview to see the results of the transparency settings. Notice that because of the transparency, the Late Sunset colors are now subdued.

FIGURE 7-11
Setting transparency for a gradient fill

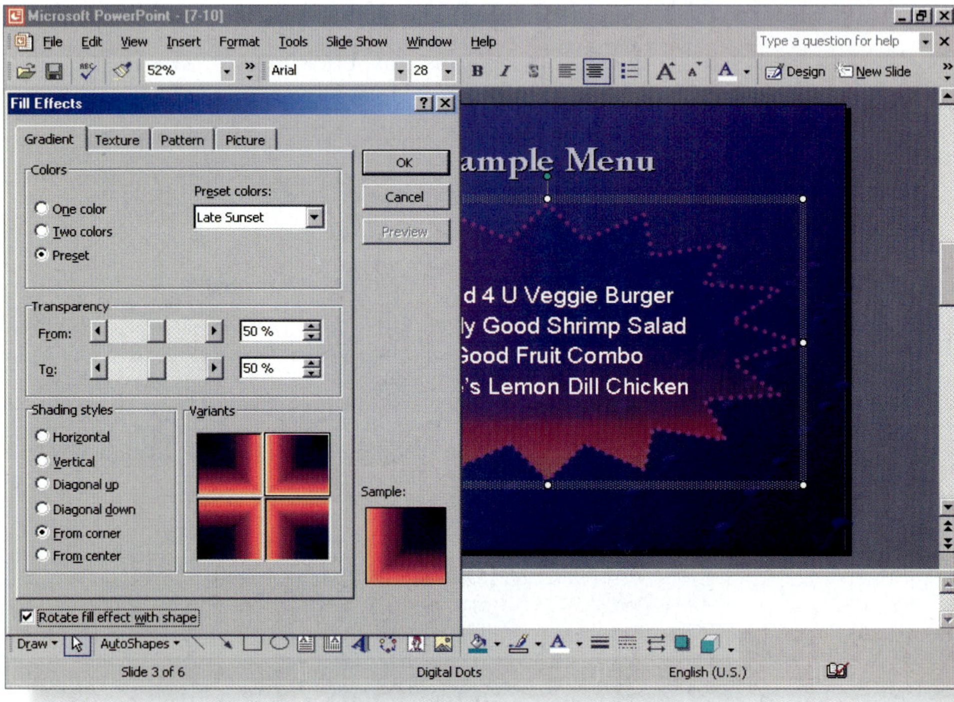

11. Click OK to accept the gradient fill settings and close the dialog box.

EXERCISE 7-12 Shade a Circle to Add Dimension

Applying a one- or two-color gradient fill to a circle can give it the appearance of a sphere.

1. Move to slide 5 and select the circle on top of the triangle.
2. Remove the circle's border.
3. Use the Fill Color button to open the Fill Effects dialog box and display the Gradient tab.
4. Choose the One color option.

5. In the Color 1 list box, choose the dark pink color on the right end of the scheme colors.
6. Move the Dark/Light slider a short distance to the right (still keeping it left of the center) until the Sample shades from very dark gray to dark pink.
7. Move the transparency sliders all the way to the left, for 0% transparency.
8. In the Shading styles options box, choose From center.
9. Choose the left Variants option (the one with the lightest color in the center).
10. Click Preview. The circle now looks like a sphere.
11. If necessary, adjust the circle's shading so that it stands out from the background. Click OK to close the dialog box.
12. Select the triangle; then apply the same gradient fill you used for the star AutoShape in Exercise 7-11 (Late Sunset preset, 50% transparency, shading from corner, upper right variant).

FIGURE 7-12
Using gradient fills

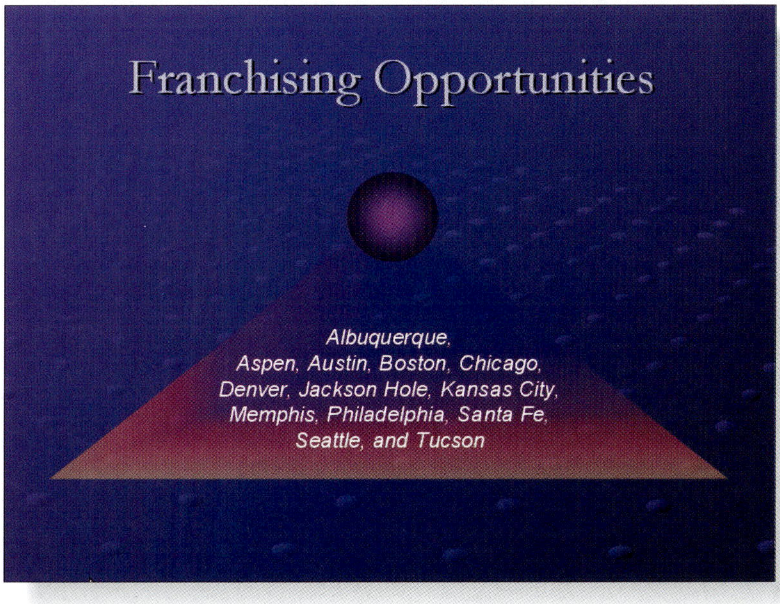

EXERCISE 7-13 Apply a Gradient Fill to a Text Placeholder

You apply fills to text placeholders in the same way that you apply fills to AutoShapes. All the options, including gradient fills and transparency settings, can be used.

When working with gradient transparency settings, you will notice that there are two transparency sliders. The From slider controls Color 1 and the To slider controls Color 2.

1. Move to slide 2 and select the body text placeholder.
2. From the Format menu, choose Placeholder to open the Format AutoShape dialog box.
3. On the Colors and Lines tab, Fill section, click the Color list box arrow and choose Fill Effects.
4. In the Fill Effects dialog box, click the Gradient tab and click the Two colors option.
5. Keep Color 1 as dark blue/gray (fills scheme color), and change Color 2 to the dark pink color on the right end of the color samples.
6. Choose the Horizontal shading style and the upper right variant (which is darkest at the bottom).
7. Under Transparency, drag the From slider right all the way to 100%. Drag the To slider to 20%.
8. Click OK to accept the shading. Click OK again to close the Format AutoShape dialog box.
9. Remove the outline from the text placeholder. Notice how the gradient fill fades into the background.
10. Move to slide 6. Apply the same shading to the text placeholder that you applied on slide 2.
11. Save the presentation as ***[your initials]*7-13** in your Lesson 7 folder but do not print it. Leave the presentation open for the next exercise.

EXERCISE 7-14 Add a Fill Pattern to an Object

When you click the Pattern tab on the Fill Effects dialog box, you can choose from 48 two-color patterns to apply to PowerPoint objects. You can choose any foreground color and any background color to create an endless variety of pattern effects.

1. On slide 6, right-click the top diamond shape and choose Format AutoShape from the shortcut menu.
2. In the Format AutoShape dialog box, open the Color drop-down list in the Line section and choose No Line.
3. From the Color drop-down list box in the Fill section, choose Fill Effects.
4. Click the Pattern tab.
5. Click the Solid Diamond Pattern, which is the last pattern in the last row. Notice that when you click the pattern, its name appears in the box below the pattern samples.

FIGURE 7-13
Adding a pattern fill to an object

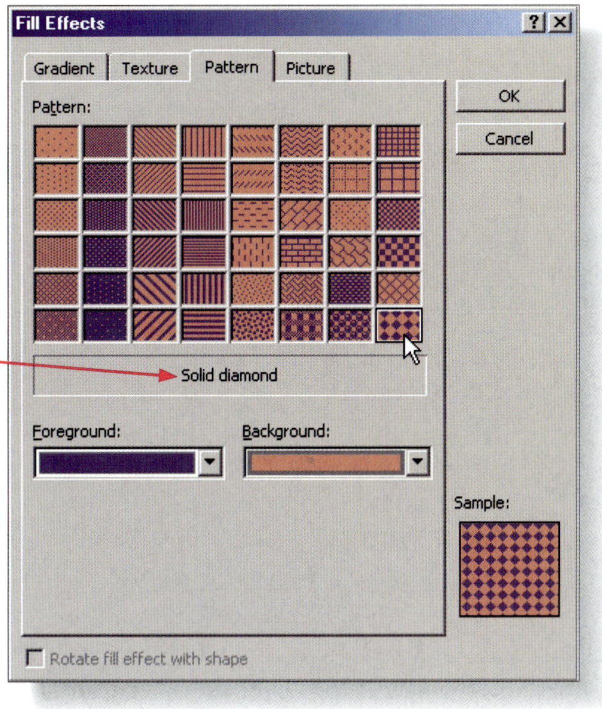

6. Change the Background color to gold and click OK.
7. Click Preview to view the changes.
8. Click OK to close the Format AutoShape dialog box.

EXERCISE 7-15 Add a Textured Fill to an Object

In addition to gradient fills and patterns, you can apply textured fill effects such as marble and wood grain.

1. On slide 6, right-click the middle diamond and open the Format AutoShape dialog box. Click the Colors and Lines tab.
2. In the Fill section, choose Fill Effects from the Color drop-down list and click the Texture tab.
3. Click several different textures, one at a time. Notice the name of the texture and its appearance in the Sample box.

TIP: You are not limited to the textures shown on the Textures tab. If you click Other Texture, you can navigate through your disk drives and network drives to choose graphics files from other sources that you can use as textures.

4. Click Bouquet, the last option in the third row.

FIGURE 7-14
Choosing a textured fill

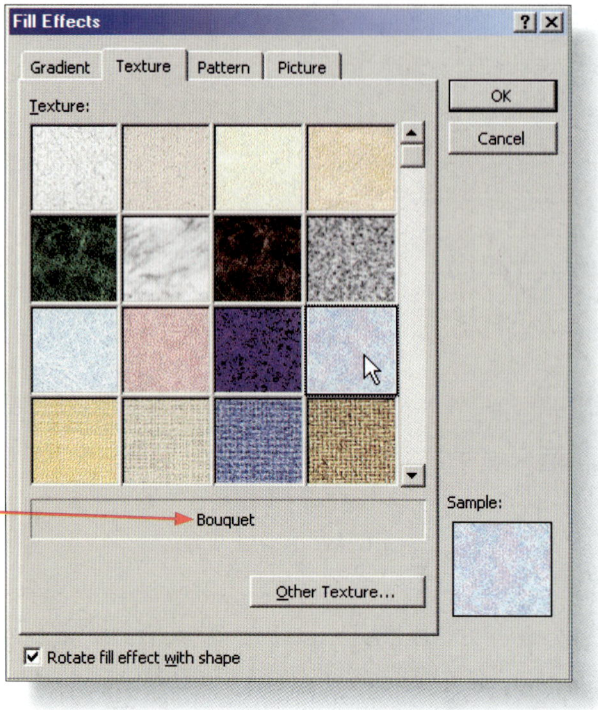

5. Click OK to accept the texture and close the Fill Effects dialog box.
6. Click OK to close the Format AutoShape dialog box.

EXERCISE 7-16 Add a Picture Fill to an Object

You can further customize your slides by using a picture file as an object fill.

1. Select the last diamond on slide 6. Change its border color to black (use More Line Colors).
2. Use the Fill Color button to open the Fill Effects dialog box. Click the Picture tab.
3. Click the Select Picture button. The Select Picture dialog box opens.
4. Navigate to the folder where your student files are stored.
5. Select the file **Emp1** and click Insert.
6. To make sure that the picture's proportions are not distorted, check Lock picture aspect ratio at the bottom of the dialog box. (See Figure 7-15 on the next page.)
7. Click OK. The diamond shape is now filled with an employee picture.
8. Save the file as ***[your initials]*7-16** but do not print it. Leave the presentation open for the next exercise.

FIGURE 7-15
Picture tab on the Fill Effects dialog box

Check here to prevent picture from being distorted

EXERCISE 7-17 Apply a Pattern to an Outline

In the same way that you apply a pattern to fill an object, you can apply one to the border of an object, a line, or an arrow. Depending on the colors you choose, a pattern can soften the effect of a line or accent it.

1. Move to slide 1.
2. Right-click the picture of a San Francisco street and select Format Picture from the shortcut menu.
3. In the Format Picture dialog box, click the Colors and Lines tab.
4. In the Line options section, change the Color to white.
5. Change the line weight to 10 points by keying **10** in the Weight spin box.
6. Click Preview to view the results. (Don't close the dialog box.)
7. Open the Color list in the Line section and choose Patterned Lines.
8. Choose Black for the Foreground color, and the first gray/blue color sample (shadows scheme color) for the Background color.
9. For the pattern, choose the third sample in the third row, named Dark downward diagonal. (See Figure 7-16 on the next page.)

FIGURE 7-16 Picture with diagonal-patterned border

10. Click OK to close the Patterned Lines dialog box. Click OK again to close the Format Picture dialog box.

Using the Format Painter Tool

If you use Word or Excel, you're probably familiar with the *Format Painter* tool. This tool makes it easy to copy the formatting, for example, the fill pattern, from one object to another object.

EXERCISE 7-18 Copy Formatting from One Object to Another Object

When you copy the format of an object, many default settings associated with that object are copied as well. For example, when you copy the formatting of an AutoShape, the default text formatting associated with that AutoShape is copied too (even if there is no text in the AutoShape). If you apply that formatting to a text box, the text formatting might change along with the fill and outline formatting. The Undo command can be handy when using the Format Painter tool.

1. On slide 6, select the checkerboard diamond.

2. Click the Format Painter button on the Standard toolbar. The Format Painter picks up the checkerboard formatting, and the mouse pointer has a paintbrush attached to it.

3. Click within the title text. The text appears in a tiny size with a checkerboard background. Click the Undo button.
4. Select the third diamond (with the picture fill) and double-click the Format Painter button. Double-clicking keeps the Format Painter active so you can copy the formatting to more than one object.
5. Click the top diamond and then click the middle diamond. All diamonds now contain the employee picture fill and are outlined in black. Notice that the Format Painter button is still turned on.
6. Click the Format Painter button again or press Esc to restore the standard mouse pointer.

7. Double-click the top diamond to open the Format AutoShape dialog box and then open the Fill Effects dialog box. The Picture tab is automatically displayed.

8. Click Select Picture. The Select Picture dialog box opens to the folder where you selected the previous picture.

9. Choose **Emp2**; then click Insert and click OK twice.

10. Change the picture in the middle diamond to the file **Emp3**.

EXERCISE 7-19 Copy Object Formatting to a Different Slide

Just as you can copy objects from one slide to another, you can copy formatting from one slide to another by using the Format Painter.

1. Click the body text placeholder on slide 6; then double-click the Format Painter button.

2. Move to slide 1 and click the large rectangle with the white outline. The rectangle takes on the transparent gradient fill of the copied text box format.

3. Move to slide 4 and click the graph. Its background changes to the transparent gradient fill.

4. Click the Format Painter button to turn it off.

5. On slide 4, change the color of the arrow you created earlier to a color that contrasts with its background.

6. Check spelling in the presentation.

7. Create a handout header and footer: include the date and your name as the header, and the page number and text ***[your initials]*7-19** as the footer.

8. Move to slide 1 and save the presentation as ***[your initials]*7-19** in your Lesson 7 folder.

9. View the presentation as a slide show; then preview and print the presentation as handouts, 6 slides per page, grayscale, framed. Leave the presentation open for the next exercise.

Notice in your printout that the slides are dark and some of the detail is lost. You correct that in the following exercises.

Working with Grayscale Settings

In many cases, slides look great in color, but the text becomes difficult or impossible to read when you print in grayscale to a black-and-white printer.

Fortunately, you can display the grayscale view of your presentation in the Slide pane. When the grayscale view is displayed, you can change grayscale settings without affecting the color version of your presentation.

EXERCISE 7-20 Adjust the Grayscale Version of a Presentation

To adjust the grayscale image of a presentation, first display the grayscale version of your presentation in one of the following ways:

- Open the View menu and choose Color/Grayscale, Grayscale.
- Click the Color/Grayscale button and choose Grayscale.

When the grayscale version is in view, select an object on a slide or on a master slide, click Setting on the Grayscale View toolbar, and choose one of the options.

1. Move to slide 1. Click the Color/Grayscale button on the Standard toolbar and choose Grayscale. The slide changes to a grayscale image and the Grayscale View floating toolbar appears.

NOTE: You might need to click the Toolbar Options button to find the Color/Grayscale button.

2. Display the slide master; then click one of the dots in the background picture to select the picture. The sizing handles for this picture extend beyond the slide's border, but you can tell when it is selected by the green rotation handle at the top of the dots.
3. Click Setting on the Grayscale View toolbar.
4. Choose Don't Show from the drop-down list. The dots are no longer visible on the slide master. Although the dots are interesting in the color version, they are too pronounced in the grayscale version, so it's better to hide them.
5. Using the same steps as above, hide the dots on the title master. (See Figure 7-17 on the next page.)
6. Close the Master view. Slide 1 looks better without the dots.
7. Move to slide 2. Slide 2 looks fine, but it will print better if the gradient fill is removed from the body text placeholder.
8. Select the body text placeholder and then click Setting on the Grayscale View toolbar.
9. Choose Black with White Fill from the drop-down list. This setting displays all lines and text in black and eliminates fills.
10. On slides 1, 3, 5, and 6, change the large rectangle, the star shape, the triangle, and the body text box to the Black with White Fill setting in the same way that you changed the text placeholder on slide 2.

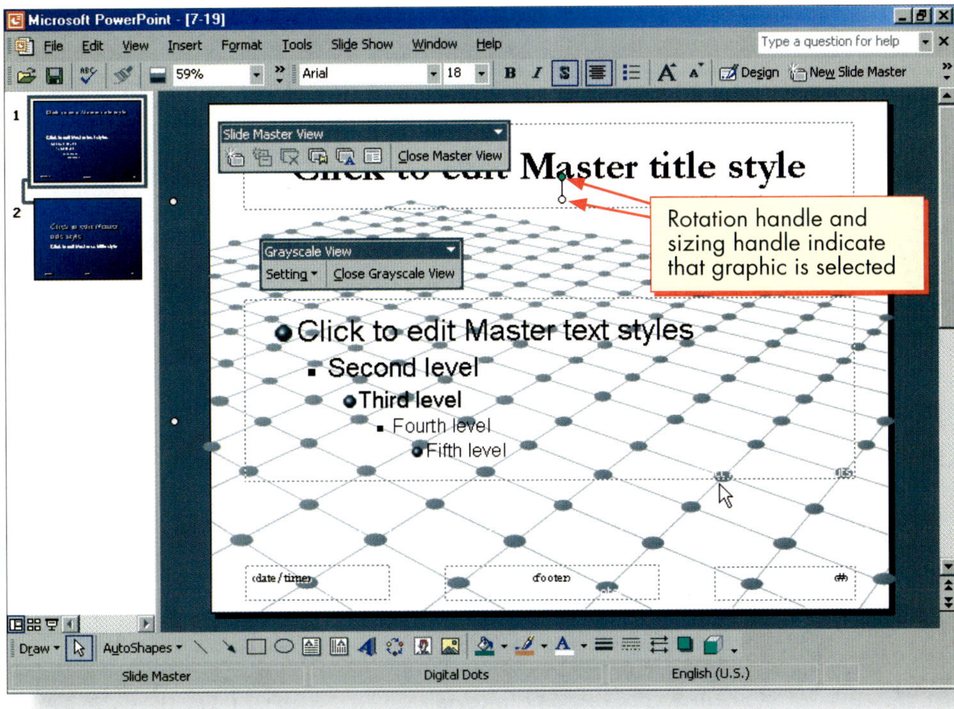

FIGURE 7-17
Changing grayscale settings

11. On slide 4, change the graph setting to Inverse Grayscale.

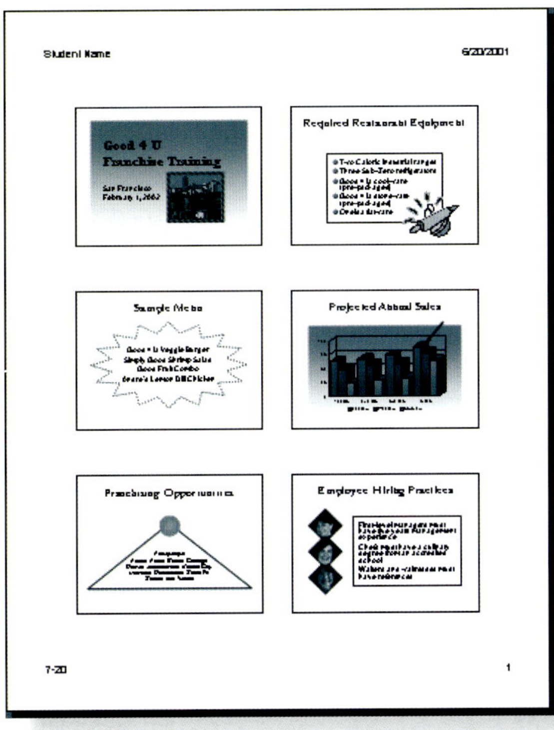

FIGURE 7-18
Presentation after changing grayscale settings

12. On slide 5, change the setting for the sphere on top of the triangle to Light Grayscale.
13. Click Close Grayscale View on the Grayscale View toolbar to view the presentation in color.
14. Update the handout footer to show the text ***[your initials]*7-20**.
15. Move to slide 1 and save the presentation as ***[your initials]*7-20** in your Lesson 7 folder.
16. Preview and then print the presentation as handouts, 6 slides per page, grayscale, framed.

17. Compare your Exercise 7-20 printout to your Exercise 7-19 printout.
18. Close the presentation.

USING HELP

In this lesson you worked with colors that are not part of a presentation's color scheme. Understanding the fine points about scheme colors and non-scheme colors is useful when customizing a presentation.

Use Help to learn more about scheme colors and non-scheme colors:

1. Key **color scheme** in the Ask a Question box and press Enter.
2. Select About color schemes from the drop-down list.

FIGURE 7-19
About color schemes Help topic

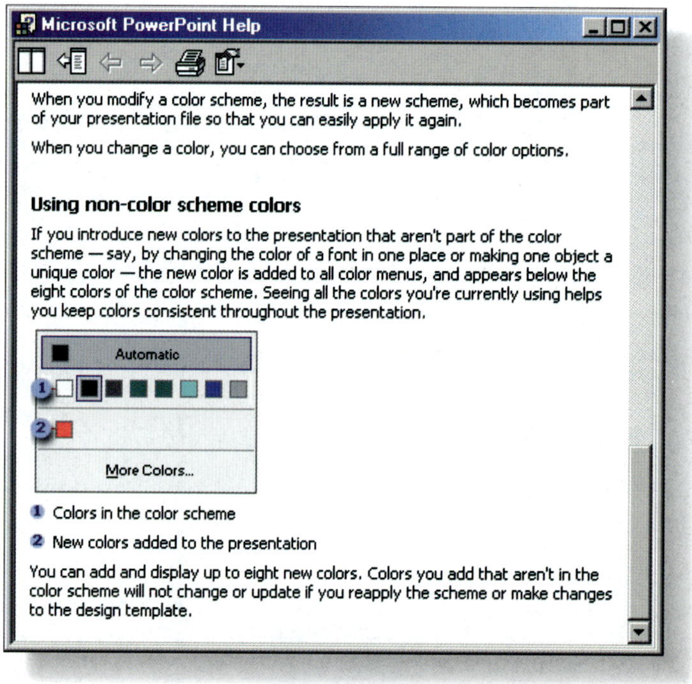

3. Read the information in the Help window, paying special attention to the last topic, Using non-color scheme colors.
4. Close the window when you're finished.

LESSON 7 Summary

- All PowerPoint objects—AutoShapes, text placeholders, text boxes, and WordArt—can be enhanced with the addition of border and fill effects.

- Border effects include solid lines, dashed lines, and patterned lines in any thickness (weight) or color you want.
- Apply border effects by using the Line Color, Line Style, and Dash Style buttons. Or, use the Colors and Lines tab of the Format AutoShape dialog box.
- The Arrow button draws a line with an arrowhead on its end. You can add or remove an arrowhead from any drawn line by using the Arrow Style button.
- The Colors and Lines tab of the Format AutoShape dialog box offers additional ways to format an arrow, enabling you to choose the size and shape of the arrowhead and line formatting options.
- Fill effects include solid colors, patterns, gradients, textures, and pictures. In addition, solid colors and gradients can have varying degrees of transparency, enabling background objects and colors to show through.
- Remove a border from an object by choosing the No Line option from the Line Color button's drop-down list. Remove the fill effect from an object by choosing the No Fill option from the Fill Color button's drop-down list.
- It is usually best to use the eight standard colors that are part of a design template's color scheme, but occasionally an additional color or two can enhance a presentation.
- Additional colors are available by choosing More Fill Colors from the Fill Color button's drop-down list, More Line Colors from the Line Color button's drop-down list, or More Colors from the Font Color button's drop-down list.
- The Colors dialog box enables you to choose from a honeycomb of pre-mixed colors on the Standard tab or to mix your own colors on the Custom tab.
- Gradient fills—the blending of one or more colors into each other—have several options, including the direction and transparency of the effect.
- Pattern fills have 48 varieties, including vertical, horizontal, and diagonal lines; checks; and dots using any two colors that you choose.
- PowerPoint includes several textures that you can use for fill effects. In addition, you can use graphics files containing textures from other sources on your computer or network.
- Any picture—a scanned photograph or other image—can be used to fill an object. When using a picture, you have the choice of distorting the picture to fill the space or preserving its proportions.
- The Format Painter button enables you to copy formatting from one object to another. This is a great time-saver if you applied several effects to an object and want to duplicate it.

- Double-clicking the Format Painter button keeps it active so that multiple objects can receive the copied format. Click the Format Painter button again to turn it off.
- Be careful using the Format Painter because all formatting associated with the object is copied, including default text formatting even if the object does not contain any text.
- The grayscale version of a presentation can be adjusted for clearer printing on black-and-white printers. Adjusting the grayscale settings has no effect on the color version of the presentation.

LESSON 7 Command Summary

FEATURE	BUTTON	MENU	KEYBOARD	SPEECH?
Format line style		Format, AutoShape (or Placeholder, or Text Box), Lines and Colors tab		✓
Change line color		Format, AutoShape (or Placeholder, or Text Box), Lines and Colors tab		✓
Change a line's dash style		Format, AutoShape (or Placeholder, or Text Box), Lines and Colors tab		✓
Format arrowheads		Format, AutoShape (or Placeholder, or Text Box), Lines and Colors tab		✓
Apply fill color, texture, pattern, gradient		Format, AutoShape (or Placeholder, or Text Box), Lines and Colors tab		✓
Draw an arrow				
Switch from Color to Grayscale view		View, Color/Grayscale, Grayscale		✓
Copy formatting of an object				

Concepts Review

TRUE/FALSE QUESTIONS

Each of the following statements is either true or false. Indicate your choice by circling T or F.

T F 1. You can use the Format Painter tool to copy formatting from one slide to another.

T F 2. The Format Painter doesn't copy text formatting.

T F 3. You must be careful when making changes in Grayscale view, because they can affect the colors of your presentation.

T F 4. When you draw an object, it appears in a color that the template chooses.

T F 5. A transparency effect can be applied only to solid fill colors.

T F 6. A gradient fill can have only two colors.

T F 7. A pattern fill can have only two colors.

T F 8. Granite and marble patterns are examples of textured fills.

SHORT ANSWER QUESTIONS

Write the correct answer in the space provided.

1. What dialog box can you use to change line and fill colors for an AutoShape?

____

2. How do you switch the screen display of your presentation from color to grayscale?

____

3. How do you change grayscale settings for PowerPoint objects?

____

4. What gradient fill option should you choose if you want to shade from a color to a very light shade of that same color?

____

5. How do you create a patterned line or border?

____

6. Which toolbar button do you use to add an outline or border to an object?

____

7. How do you remove a fill effect from an object?

____

8. What button can you use to copy fills and colors to another object?

____

CRITICAL THINKING

Answer these questions on a separate page. There are no right or wrong answers. Support your answers with examples from your own experience, if possible.

1. Think of the way you used a gradient fill to add dimension to a simple circle. What other objects could you change by using a gradient fill to add dimension?

2. Which objects in a presentation are most suited to borders? What types of border styles and colors work best against what types of backgrounds?

Lesson Applications

EXERCISE 7-21

Work with gradient fills, create and format an arrow, change grayscale settings, and use the Format Painter.

1. Open the file **Recruit1** and apply the design template Edge. Use the color scheme with the dark brown background (the first sample in the second row if your task pane is wide enough to show two samples across).
2. Insert two new slides after slide 3. Use the text in Figure 7-20.

FIGURE 7-20

Slide 4

```
Who's Who

●  Julie Wolfe, Co-owner
●  Gus Irvinelli, Co-owner
●  Michele Jenkins, Head Chef
●  Roy Olafsen, Marketing Manager
```

Slide 5

```
Summary

●  Six-month probation period
●  Annual salary increases
●  Quarterly stock purchase options
●  Annual profit sharing
```

3. On slide 1, select the title text placeholder and then click the Insert WordArt button on the Drawing toolbar. Create a WordArt title by using the WordArt Gallery sample in the bottom row, fifth column.
4. Delete the title text placeholder and position the WordArt in its place.
5. Using the same WordArt style, substitute WordArt titles for the title text on the remaining slides. Adjust the height of the WordArt titles to make some space between the WordArt and the body text placeholders.

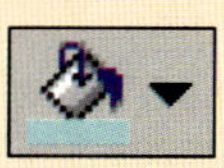

6. Select the WordArt on slide 1. Use the Fill Color button to change the gradient fill to the following:
   - Wheat preset
   - Horizontal shading style
   - Upper left variant

7. Use the Format Painter button to copy the gradient fill from the WordArt on slide 1 to the WordArt on all the other slides.
8. On slide 1, delete the subtitle text placeholder and in its place insert the picture file **Logo1** from your student data disk.
9. Alter the logo by doing the following:
   - Place the logo below the red horizontal line and align it with the left edge of the red line.
   - Make it slightly larger by dragging its lower right corner sizing handle.
   - Use the Set Transparent Color button on the Picture toolbar to remove the logo's white background.
   - Use the Color button on the Picture toolbar to change the color to Washout. Use the More Brightness button to make it white.
10. Insert a suitable clip art picture in the lower right corner of the slide. Position and size it appropriately.
11. Copy the clip art and paste it on the slide master. Resize it if necessary so that it does not conflict with the body text placeholder.
12. On slide 5, draw a 16-point star at the bottom center of the slide. Key the text **Substantial!** inside the star. Format the star as follows:
    - Make it 1.75 inches high and 4 inches wide.
    - Rotate it –10 degrees (+350 degrees)
    - Change the text size to 32 points, change its color to dark brown, and make it bold.
    - Use Format Painter to copy the formatting from the WordArt title and apply it to the star.
    - Adjust the star's position to make a pleasing composition.
13. Using the Arrow button , draw an arrow pointing from the star to the text "Annual profit sharing." Change the arrow's line thickness to 4.5 points.
14. Review all the slides, resizing the WordArt titles if needed to improve the appearance. View the presentation as a slide show.
15. View slide 1 in Grayscale view. Select the now invisible Good 4 U logo and change its grayscale setting to Black.
16. Check spelling in the presentation.
17. Create a handout header and footer: include the date and your name as the header, and the page number and text ***[your initials]*7-21** as the footer.
18. Move to slide 1 and save the presentation as ***[your initials]*7-21** in your Lesson 7 folder.
19. Preview and then print the presentation as handouts, 6 slides per page, grayscale, framed. Close the presentation.

EXERCISE 7-22

Change line colors, line styles, and fill colors of objects; change an AutoShape; add an arrowhead; adjust grayscale settings.

1. Open the file **TrainPt3**. Apply the Blends design template and use the default color scheme (white background, red, yellow, blue accents).
2. On slide 2, delete the dollar sign clip art image. Replace it with an appropriate business image that blends with the color scheme.

3. If the Automatic Layout Options button appears near the picture, click it and choose Undo Automatic Layout. Size and position the new image so it occupies the same position on the slide as the old image.
4. On slide 3, insert a text box near the upper right corner of the graph with the text **Estimating over $89,000** on two lines. Change the font to 20-point Arial bold.
5. Add a 3-point red border to the text box; then change its AutoShape to Line Callout 3.

REVIEW: To change the text box to a callout AutoShape, select the AutoShape and choose Draw, Change AutoShape, Callouts. The Line Callout 3 shape is the third shape in the second row.

6. Use the callout shape's yellow adjustment handles to make the callout line point to the tallest blue column on the graph.
7. With the callout shape selected, apply Arrow Style 6 so that an arrowhead appears on the end of the callout line, pointing to the tallest column.
8. On slide 4, delete the text placeholder. In its place, draw a text box. In the text box, key **10% discount off the lunch menu, Monday through Thursday**
9. Format the text box as follows to give it a blackboard effect:
   - Change the fill color to black.
   - Change the text to white 32-point Tahoma.
   - Apply an 8-point patterned border; use black as the Foreground and white as the Background. Choose the Wide upward diagonal pattern (third from left, last row).
   - Change its AutoShape to a rounded rectangle.
10. Resize and reposition the clip art and the text box if needed to create a pleasing composition.
11. On slide 5, add a 4.5-point square dot border to the text placeholder and change its color to red. Resize the placeholder to fit the text and then reposition the placeholder to make an attractive composition on the slide.

12. On slide 4, change the grayscale setting for the AutoShape to Grayscale. Review all the slides in Grayscale view and make any other necessary adjustments.
13. Check spelling in the presentation.
14. Create a handout header and footer: include the date and your name as the header, and the page number and text ***[your initials]*7-22** as the footer.
15. Move to slide 1 and save the presentation as ***[your initials]*7-22** in your Lesson 7 folder.
16. Preview and then print the presentation as handouts, 6 slides per page, grayscale, framed. Close the presentation.

EXERCISE 7-23

Apply a textured fill, apply patterned lines, and use custom colors.

1. Open the file **Seminar2**. Apply the design template Default Design (the very first design template) and use the color scheme with the dark gray background.
2. On slide 1 below the subtitle, draw a Horizontal Scroll AutoShape (Stars and Banners, second shape on the bottom row). Make the shape slightly wider than the subtitle and about 2 inches high.
3. Key the text **Good 4 U** in the scroll AutoShape and format the text as 40-pt Arial bold shadowed. Change the text color to dark gray (background scheme color)
4. Apply the following formatting to the scroll:
   - Drag the yellow adjustment handle to the right as far as it will go.
   - Change the border to a 3-pt dark gray line (background scheme color); then use the Custom tab of the Colors dialog box to make the line color a noticeably darker shade.
   - Apply a textured fill using the Stationery texture (last selection on the first row)
5. On the slide master, draw a rectangle slightly larger than the body text placeholder and position it on top of the placeholder. Use the Colors and Lines tab of the Format AutoShape dialog box to format the rectangle as follows:
   - Remove the fill color.
   - Under Line, change the Style to a 6-pt triple-line.
   - Change the Weight of the line to 10 points.
   - For the Color of the line choose a Wide downward diagonal pattern using gold as the foreground and a custom darker shade of gold for the background.

P O W E R P O I N T

6. Insert a title master. Remove the gold-outlined rectangle from the title master.

NOTE: If a title master does not exist, insert one by displaying the slide master and then clicking the Insert New Title Master button on the Slide Master View toolbar.

7. On slide 3, delete the clip art image. Insert appropriate images in the content placeholders on slides 2, 3, 4, and 6.
8. On slides 2, 3, 4, and 6, resize and reposition the body text placeholders and the clip art to make pleasing arrangements.
9. On slide 4, edit the text for the first bullet to read **Pentium IV computer (network server)**
10. Delete slide 5 ("Annual Sales Per Division").
11. Apply an animation scheme of your choice to the entire presentation and then view the presentation as a slide show.
12. Check spelling in the presentation.
13. Create a handout header and footer: include the date and your name as the header, and the page number and text ***[your initials]*7-23** as the footer.
14. Move to slide 1 and save the presentation as ***[your initials]*7-23** in your Lesson 7 folder.
15. Preview and then print the presentation as handouts, 6 slides per page, grayscale, framed. Close the presentation.

EXERCISE 7-24 Challenge Yourself

Work with master slides, gradient fills, patterned lines, and grayscale settings.

1. Open the file **Market3**.
2. Change the color scheme to the sample with the dark blue background (the last sample on the bottom row).
3. Working on the title master, click the medium blue area below the subtitle placeholder to select that area. (This is actually a rounded rectangle AutoShape with a dark blue rounded rectangle on top of it).
4. Apply a two-color vertical gradient fill to the selected area with the following properties:
   - Color 1: Medium blue (fills scheme color)
   - Color 2: Light blue (title text scheme color)
   - Shading style: Vertical
   - Variant: Upper-left, with darkest color on the left

5. Select the rounded rectangle that surrounds the subtitle text placeholder and apply a patterned border with the following properties:
   - Foreground: Medium blue (fills scheme color)
   - Background: Medium purple (accent and followed hyperlink scheme color)
   - Pattern: Large checkerboard—last pattern in the fourth row
   - Line weight: 10 points
6. Use Format Painter to copy the patterned border to the large rounded rectangle on the slide master.
7. Apply a two-color gradient fill to the rounded rectangle on the slide master; use dark blue (background scheme color) for Color 1 and medium blue (fills scheme color) for Color 2. Choose the vertical shading style and the variant that has the darkest color on the left.
8. On slide 1, substitute a WordArt title for the title text. Use the upper left sample from the WordArt gallery. Apply a vertical gradient fill by using the Calm Water preset, upper left variant. Resize and position it appropriately.
9. Replace the title text on slides 2 though 5 with WordArt titles that have the same style and formatting as on slide 1. Adjust the size and position appropriately.
10. Review the presentation in Grayscale view and make any necessary adjustments.
11. Apply an animation scheme of your choice and then view the presentation as a slide show.
12. Check spelling in the presentation.
13. Create a handout header and footer: include the date and your name as the header, and the page number and text ***[your initials]*7-24** as the footer.
14. Move to slide 1 and save the presentation as a Web page with the filename ***[your initials]*7-24** in your Lesson 7 folder.
15. Preview and then print the presentation as handouts, 6 slides per page, grayscale, framed. Close the presentation.

POWERPOINT

On Your Own

In these exercises you work on your own, as you would in a real-life work environment. Use the skills you've learned to accomplish the task—and be creative.

EXERCISE 7-25

Plan a menu for a special occasion, such as a birthday dinner, a July 4th barbeque, or a Sunday brunch. Create a title slide, a slide listing all the menu items, and a separate slide for each menu item listing ingredients or a description or both. If you have access to a scanner, include scanned pictures of the menu items. Otherwise, find clip art pictures to illustrate your presentation. Use your own creativity to format an attractive presentation that has some of the fill effects and border effects presented in this lesson. Save the presentation as ***[your initials]*****7-25**. Preview and then print the presentation as handouts.

EXERCISE 7-26

Consult your local newspaper for recreational and cultural events happening next month. Choose at least five events that interest you. Create a presentation with the title "Recommended Events in *[your town]* for the month of *[current month]*" on the first slide. On the second slide, include a list of the events you selected with times and dates. Include a separate slide for each event with a description and picture. Format the presentation by using fill effects and border effects. Save the presentation as ***[your initials]*****7-26**. Preview and then print the presentation as handouts.

EXERCISE 7-27

Open the file **SanFran1** used in this lesson. Change to a different design template and color scheme of your choice. Customize the slide and title masters in some way. Change all the slide titles to WordArt, and apply fill effects and border treatments to all AutoShapes and body text placeholders in the presentation. Be careful to keep the look and style of each slide uniform throughout the presentation, and use good judgment to keep the design from looking too busy. Save the presentation as ***[your initials]*****7-27**. Preview and then print the presentation as handouts.

LESSON

8 Manipulating PowerPoint Objects

OBJECTIVES

After completing this lesson, you will be able to:

1. Select multiple objects.
2. Align, flip, and distribute objects.
3. Group and ungroup objects.
4. Work with layers of objects.
5. Apply object shadows and 3-D effects.
6. Use the Duplicate command.
7. Edit vector-based pictures.

MOUS ACTIVITIES
In this lesson:
PP2002 3-3
See Appendix E.

Estimated Time: 1½ hours

In earlier lessons you learned how to add clip art, scanned images, text objects, and drawings to a presentation. This lesson shows you how to move or change a group of objects, layer objects, and align objects. These techniques help you create more effective presentations.

Selecting Multiple Objects

When you want to treat several objects on a slide the same way, such as making them all the same color, you can select all the objects at the same time by using multiple selection techniques. There are two basic ways to select multiple objects:

- Select one object, hold down Shift, and click another object.
- Draw a selection rectangle around the objects you want to select by dragging the mouse.

You can also select all the objects on a slide by opening the Edit menu and choosing Select All or by pressing Ctrl + A. To deselect all items, simply click a blank area of the slide or press Esc.

EXERCISE 8-1 Select Multiple Objects

To select multiple objects one at a time, first click an object to select it and then add objects to the selection by pressing Shift as you click another object.

1. Open the file **Market2**.
2. With slide 1 displayed, open the Edit menu and choose Select All (or press Ctrl + A). Notice the multiple sets of sizing handles. Every item on slide 1 is selected.
3. Click a blank area on the slide (or press Esc) to deselect the items.
4. Click the long, thin, horizontal arrow at the top of the screen. Notice its sizing handles.
5. Hold down Shift and click the vertical arrow on the right side of the slide. Notice that there are sizing handles around both objects, indicating that they are both selected.

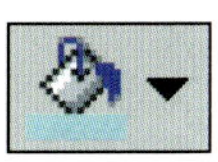

6. With the two arrows selected, use the Fill Color button to change their color to bright green. Both selected arrows change color.
7. With the two bright green arrows selected, press Shift and click the bottom and left arrows. Now all four long thin arrows are selected.

FIGURE 8-1 Multiple selected objects

8. With all the arrows selected, change the fill to a two-color gradient with the following settings:
   - For Color 1, choose white.
   - For Color 2, choose bright green.
   - From Shading styles, choose Vertical.
   - From the Variants, choose the upper-left sample (with white on the left and bright green on the right).
   - At the bottom of the Fill Effects dialog box, deselect Rotate fill effect with shape.

EXERCISE 8-2 Remove an Item from a Group of Selected Objects

You might want to change the composition of a group of selected items as you work. One way is to deselect all the objects by clicking a blank part of the slide. Another way is to hold down Shift and click the selected item to deselect it, leaving the remaining items in the group selected.

1. To deselect the arrow at the top of the slide and leave the other three arrows selected, hold Shift and click the top arrow. The remaining three arrows are still selected.
2. Hold Shift and click the bottom arrow. The bottom arrow is deselected, leaving only the two side arrows selected.
3. Keeping the same colors, change the shading style of the two side arrows to horizontal, using the upper-left variant.
4. Deselect all the arrows by clicking a blank area of the slide; then select the arrow at the bottom of the slide. Change its gradient fill to the one with the bright green on the left side.
5. Save the presentation as ***[your initials]*8-2** in a new folder for Lesson 8 but do not print the presentation. Leave it open for the next exercise.

EXERCISE 8-3 Select Objects by Drawing a Selection Rectangle

To draw a *selection rectangle,* start at a blank area of a slide and drag your mouse pointer diagonally to create a dotted box surrounding the objects that you want to select. Only objects completely enclosed in the selection rectangle are selected.

It takes a little practice to get the knack of where to start a selection rectangle, and it's easy to miss an object. If that happens, try drawing the selection rectangle again, or add a missed object to the selection by using the Shift+click method.

1. Move to slide 2.
2. Position the pointer in the lower-left corner of the slide.
3. Drag the mouse pointer diagonally to the right and up to draw a dotted box—selection rectangle—surrounding all four blue arrows. (It's okay if the box overlaps the slide's text a little.)

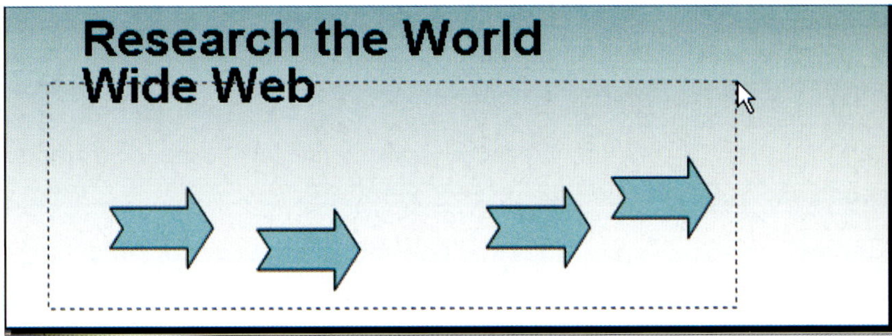

FIGURE 8-2
Selection rectangle

4. Release the mouse button. Notice the sizing handles surrounding each arrow.
5. If one or more of the arrows is not selected, try again, making sure that all arrows are completely inside the selection rectangle.
6. Change the fill of the selected arrows to a vertical two-color gradient, using the same white and bright green as on the arrows on slide 1. Choose the variant that has green on the left side.

Aligning, Flipping, and Distributing Objects

PowerPoint has a number of tools that you can use to reorient objects on a slide. You can rotate and *flip* them, creating mirror images of the original. Selected objects can be aligned with each other, either vertically or horizontally. And you can *distribute* multiple objects, spacing them evenly across the slide either horizontally or vertically.

EXERCISE 8-4 Align Objects Horizontally and Vertically

You access the tools to accomplish alignment and distribution tasks by clicking Draw on the Drawing toolbar, choosing Align or Distribute, and then choosing an appropriate command from the submenu. Note that you can float the submenu.

1. Still working on slide 2, select the four arrows. Notice that the arrows are not positioned evenly on the slide.
2. Display the Align or Distribute floating toolbar by doing the following: Click Draw on the Drawing toolbar and point to Align or Distribute. Point to the

gray title bar on the submenu and drag it to a convenient place on your screen, out of the way of the selected arrows.

NOTE: If the Drawing toolbar is not in view, open the View menu and choose Toolbars, Drawing.

TABLE 8-1 Alignment Options

BUTTON	PURPOSE
Align Left	Vertically aligns the left edges of objects.
Align Center	Vertically aligns the centers of objects.
Align Right	Vertically aligns the right edges of objects.
Align Top	Horizontally aligns the top edges of objects.
Align Middle	Horizontally aligns the center points of objects.
Align Bottom	Horizontally aligns the bottom edges of objects.
Distribute Horizontally	Spaces objects evenly in a horizontal direction.
Distribute Vertically	Spaces objects evenly in a vertical direction.
Relative to Slide	A toggle button. When selected, aligns or spaces objects relative to slide. When not selected, aligns or spaces objects relative to each other.

3. Point to each button on the Align or Distribute toolbar and read their ScreenTips. Notice that the first three buttons on the toolbar control vertical alignment and that the next three buttons control horizontal alignment.
4. Verify that Relative to Slide on the Align and Distribute toolbar is not selected. (A thin black outline indicates when it is turned on.)

NOTE: When working with the Align or Distribute commands, be sure you pay attention to the Relative to Slide button. If it's selected, all alignment actions will be relative to the slide, not the selected objects.

5. Click the Align Top button. The objects line up with the top of the highest arrow.
6. Deselect the arrows; then choose <u>R</u>uler from the <u>V</u>iew menu to display a horizontal and a vertical ruler.
7. Drag the arrow that is farthest to the right up about 1 inch; use the ruler to help you position the object. Drag the arrow that is farthest to the left down to the bottom of the slide.
8. Draw a selection rectangle around all four arrows.

TIP: When drawing a selection rectangle to select objects, start dragging from a blank area on the slide. Don't start dragging from within a text placeholder or you will select text instead of the objects. You know you're inside a text placeholder if the mouse pointer is an I-beam.

9. Click the Align Bottom button. The objects align horizontally again, but this time they align with the bottom object.
10. Click the Undo button to return the arrows to their previous positions.

11. Select the four arrows again and click the Align Left button. The objects align vertically, aligning with the arrow farthest to the left, but one arrow is hidden because it is underneath another arrow.

12. Click the Undo button, reselect the four arrows, and then click the Align Right button. The objects are arranged vertically, aligning with the the arrow farthest to the right. (One arrow is still hidden behind another.)

EXERCISE 8-5 Distribute Objects Horizontally and Vertically

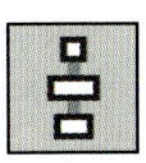

1. Still working on slide 2, with the four arrows selected, click the Distribute Vertically button. The arrows are now evenly spaced but they overlap.
2. Deselect the arrows; then drag the top arrow up about 1.5 inches.
3. Reselect the four arrows and click the Distribute Vertically button again. Now the arrows are spaced farther apart.

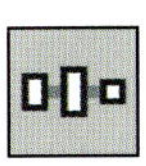

4. With the arrows still selected, click the Distribute Horizontally button. Nothing happens because all the arrows are in the same relative horizontal position.
5. Deselect the arrows; then drag the bottom arrow about 3 inches to the left.
6. Reselect the arrows; then click the Distribute Horizontally button again. Now the arrows are evenly spaced horizontally but they are not aligned.
7. Click the Align Bottom button.

EXERCISE 8-6 Align Objects Relative to the Slide

The **Relative to Slide** option makes it easy to center an object horizontally or vertically on a slide. For example, you can center a placeholder perfectly. You can also use the **Relative to Slide** option to distribute objects evenly across a slide from edge to edge.

1. Still working on slide 2, select the body text placeholder.
2. Click **Relative to Slide** on the Align or Distribute toolbar to select that option.
3. Click the Align Center button. The placeholder is centered horizontally on the slide.
4. Click the Align Middle button. The placeholder is now also centered vertically on the slide.
5. With **Relative to Slide** still selected, select all four arrows at the bottom of the screen.
6. Click the Distribute Horizontally button. Now the arrows are evenly spaced across the entire width of the slide.

FIGURE 8-3 Objects horizontally aligned and distributed

EXERCISE 8-7 Flip and Rotate Objects

Use the Rotate and Flip commands on a single object or a group of objects. You can rotate and flip any PowerPoint object, including text placeholders.

1. To display the Rotate or Flip toolbar, click Draw on the Drawing toolbar, point to Rotate or Flip, and drag the submenu's title bar to float the toolbar.

2. Select the four arrows at the bottom of slide 2. Click the Rotate Right button. The arrows point down.

3. Click the Flip Vertical button. The arrows flip vertically and point up.
4. Check that Relative to Slide is selected and then use the Align Bottom button to align the arrows to the edge of the slide.
5. Select the WordArt title "Objectives."

6. Click the Rotate Left button to place the WordArt on its side.
7. With Relative to Slide selected, click the Align Middle button and then click the Align Left button. The WordArt is now centered vertically and aligned with the left edge of the slide.
8. With the WordArt still selected, use the Right Arrow key on your keyboard to move the WordArt to the right so it's centered between the left edge of the slide and the text placeholder.

FIGURE 8-4
Rotated and flipped objects

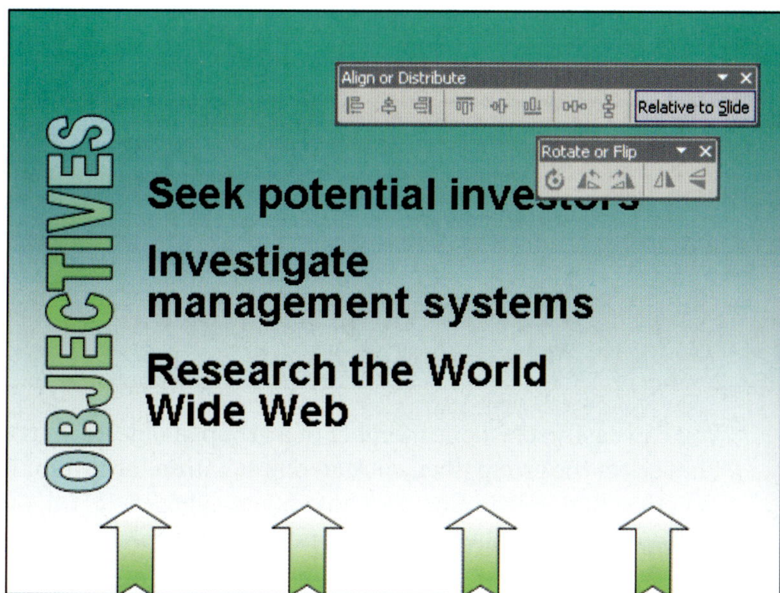

Grouping, Ungrouping, and Regrouping Objects

When you *group* objects, you combine two or more objects so they behave as one. If you then move one member of the group, all the other members move with it.

Grouping assures that objects meant to stay together don't accidentally get moved individually or deleted. When you apply formatting to a group, all the members of the group receive the same formatting.

EXERCISE 8-8 Group Objects

To create a group of objects, first select the objects and then click Draw on the Drawing toolbar and choose Group.

1. Still working on slide 2, select the four arrows at the bottom of the slide. Notice the four sets of sizing handles.
2. From the expanded Draw menu, choose Group. Now there is only one set of sizing handles, indicating that all four arrows are grouped as a single object.

FIGURE 8-5 Objects after grouping

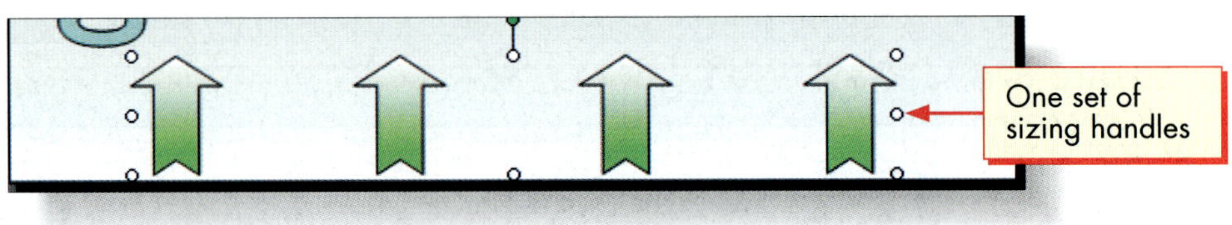

3. Deselect the object. Drag the left arrow up, just below the last text line. All the arrows move up.

EXERCISE 8-9 Format One Member of a Grouped Object

You can easily select one member of a group of objects to make individual changes. First select the group; then click an object within the group. The object displays gray selection handles, indicating that you can change its fill, outline, and orientation without affecting the other objects in the group.

1. Select the grouped arrows. One set of white sizing handles appears.
2. Click the second arrow from the right. Gray handles surround it.

FIGURE 8-6 Selecting a single object in a group

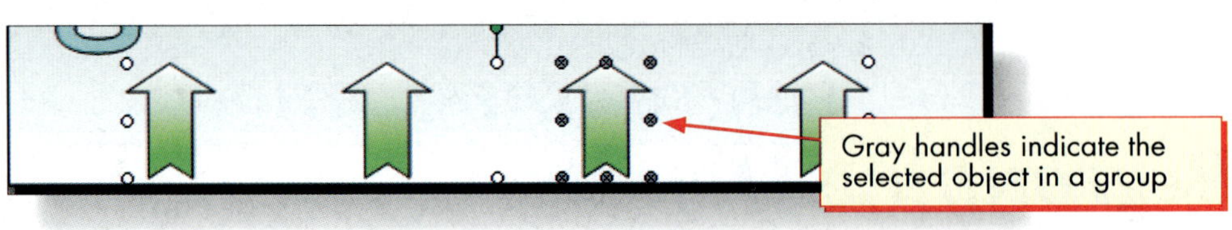

3. Click the Flip Vertical button. The selected arrow points down.

4. Click the Flip Vertical button again to make the arrow point in the same direction as the other arrows in the group.
5. For the selected arrow, change the gradient fill colors as follows: Make Color 1 light blue (fills scheme color) and Color 2 medium green (accent and hyperlink scheme color).

EXERCISE 8-10 Ungroup and Regroup Objects

If you want to delete a member of a group, change its position relative to the other members, or change its size, you must first *ungroup* the objects. When the objects are ungrouped, they once again become individual objects.

After working on individual members of an ungrouped object, you can easily *regroup* the objects by selecting any one of the group's original members. The Regroup command finds all the objects of the original group that remain on the slide and groups them again.

1. Right-click any of the grouped arrows; then choose Grouping from the shortcut menu and Ungroup from the submenu. Each arrow now has its own set of sizing handles.
2. Click a blank area of the slide to deselect all the arrows.
3. Click the left-most arrow to select it (the other arrows should not be selected) and then press Delete. One arrow is deleted from the slide.
4. Select one of the remaining arrows; then open the Draw menu and choose Regroup. The three remaining arrows are grouped again.

5. With the grouped arrows selected, click Rotate Left. The three arrows rotate as one unit.
6. Zoom out (decrease the zoom setting) so that you can see all three arrows.
7. On the Align or Distribute toolbar, select Relative to Slide.

8. With the grouped arrows selected, click the Align Middle button to center the group of arrows vertically (relative to the slide); then click the Align Right Button to right-align the group.
9. With the group still selected, use the Left Arrow key to move the arrows so they are centered between the right edge of the slide and the body text placeholder.
10. Increase the zoom setting to Fit.
11. Right-click the grouped arrows and open the Format Object dialog box. Use the Size tab to change the width of the grouped object to 4.5 inches. Then distribute the group again vertically, relative to the slide. As you can see, grouped objects behave as a single object in many ways. (See Figure 8-7 on the next page.)
12. Close both floating toolbars.

13. Save the presentation as *[your initials]***8-10** in your Lesson 8 folder but do not print it. Leave the presentation open for the next exercise.

FIGURE 8-7
Completed slide 2

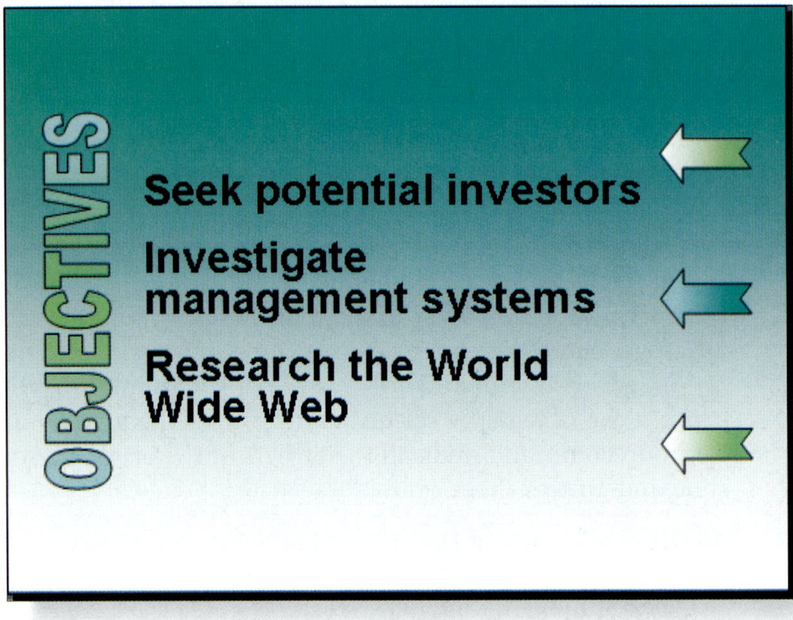

Working with Layers of Objects

Although objects appear to be drawn on one surface, each of a slide's objects actually exists as a separate layer. Imagine that the objects are drawn on individual sheets of transparent plastic stacked on top of one another. When you rearrange the sheets, different objects appear on the top, sometimes hiding parts of the objects beneath them. The most recently drawn object is added to the top of the stack.

Within a stack of objects, you can move an individual object backward and forward by using the buttons on the Order toolbar.

EXERCISE 8-11 Create Overlapping Objects

When you draw a new object on a slide, it automatically becomes the top object on the stack. To change its layer, select it and then click one of the buttons on the Order toolbar. (See Table 8-2 on the next page.)

To manipulate an object that is located behind several other objects, you can send the top objects to the back, one at a time, until the desired object is on top. Or, you can press Tab several times until the desired object is selected and then bring that object to the front.

TABLE 8-2 Order Options

BUTTON	PURPOSE
Bring to Front	Brings an object to the top of the stack
Send to Back	Moves an object to the bottom of the stack
Bring Forward	Brings an object up one layer in the stack
Send Backward	Moves an object down one layer in the stack

1. Move to slide 3. Draw a large rectangle that covers the body text placeholder. The rectangle hides text.
2. Change the rectangle's fill color to 25% transparency. Now you can faintly see the text behind the rectangle.

REVIEW: To change transparency settings, select the object, click the arrow for the Fill Color button, choose More Fill Colors, and then drag the Transparency slider.

3. Click the Undo button to return the rectangle's fill to its original state.
4. Click Draw on the Drawing toolbar, choose Order from the expanded menu, and float the Order submenu.
5. With the rectangle selected, click the Send to Back button on the Order toolbar. The rectangle moves behind the text, and the text is once again visible. Because the text placeholder has no fill, it does not hide the rectangle.
6. Change the rectangle that you drew (not the body text placeholder) to a Notched Right Arrow AutoShape.

REVIEW: To change the AutoShape from a rectangle to a Notched Right Arrow, click Draw, Change AutoShape, Block Arrows, and choose the second shape in the fifth row.

7. Resize the notched arrow and drag its adjustment handle so it looks like the arrow in Figure 8-8 (on the next page).
8. Close the Order floating toolbar.
9. Save the presentation as ***[your initials]*8-11** in your Lesson 8 folder but do not print it. Leave the presentation open for the next exercise.

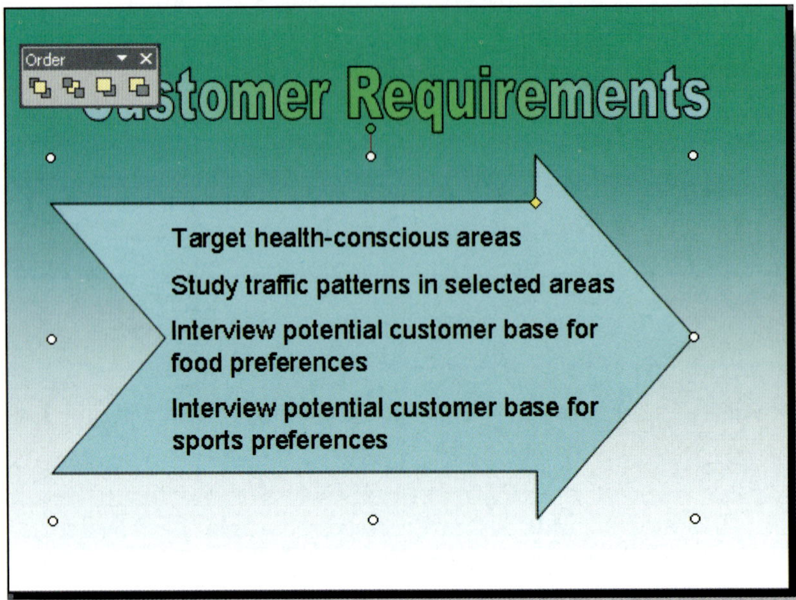

FIGURE 8-8 Overlapping text and AutoShape

Applying Object Shadows and 3-D Effects

You can add interest and depth to an object by applying shadows or 3-D effects. Each of these effects has its own toolbar with buttons that enable you to change the color, depth, and other attributes.

EXERCISE 8-12 Apply a Shadow Effect

To apply a shadow to an object, select the object, click the Shadow Style button on the Drawing toolbar, and choose a style from the drop-down menu.

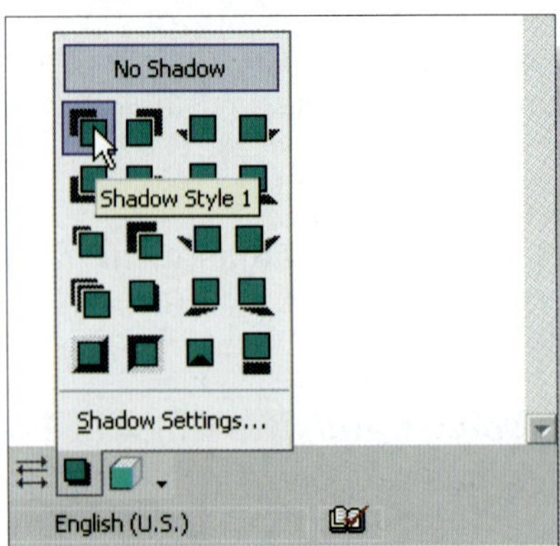

FIGURE 8-9 Shadow Style options

1. Move to slide 1. Select the Explosion AutoShape in the upper-left corner.
2. Click the Shadow Style button on the Drawing toolbar to display a menu of shadow effects.
3. Choose **Shadow Style 1**, which is the first style in the first row. A pale gray shadow appears.

4. Click the Shadow Style button again and choose Shadow Style 3. This shadow style is more dramatic. Each style orients the position and the depth of the shadow in a different way. Try several other shadow styles.
5. Change back to Shadow Style 1.
6. If the object's border is no longer visible, reapply a black border.

NOTE: Some of the shadow styles might change the shadow color or remove the object's border. You learn how to change the shadow color in the next exercise.

EXERCISE 8-13 Customize a Shadow

You can customize an object shadow by displaying the Shadow Settings toolbar and using its buttons. To display the toolbar, click the Shadow Style button on the Drawing toolbar and click Shadow Settings from the drop-down menu.

1. Select the Explosion object.
2. Click the Shadow Style button and choose Shadow Settings. The Shadow Settings toolbar is displayed.

3. Click the Nudge Shadow Up button four times. Notice that each time you click the button, the shadow moves up slightly.

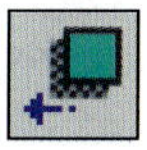

4. Click the Nudge Shadow Left button twice. The shadow gradually moves to the left each time you click the button.

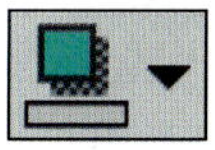

5. Click the arrow on the Shadow Color button and choose dark blue (accent scheme color) for the shadow color. The shadow color is not as dark as the color sample.
6. Click the arrow next to the Shadow Color button again. Notice that Semitransparent Shadow is selected.
7. Click Semitransparent Shadow to deselect this option. The shadow color is now dark blue.
8. Use the Shadow Color button to change the shadow to black, and then make it semitransparent. (See Figure 8-10 on the next page.)

TIP: You can control the degree of transparency for shadows. To do this, click the arrow next to the Shadow Color button, choose More Shadow Colors, and use the Transparency slider in the Colors dialog box.

9. Close the Shadow Settings toolbar.

FIGURE 8-10
AutoShape with shadow effects applied

EXERCISE 8-14 Choose a 3-D Effect

To apply a 3-D effect to an object, select the object, click the 3-D Style button on the Drawing toolbar, and choose a style from the drop-down menu.

1. Still working on slide 1, select the WordArt title "Marketing Strategy."
2. Click the 3-D Style button on the Drawing toolbar to display a menu of 3-D effects.

FIGURE 8-11
3-D menu

3. Choose **3-D Style 2**. A dramatic 3-D effect is applied to the object.
4. Click the 3-D Style button again and choose **3-D Style 18**. Notice that some 3-D styles rotate the object and create depth. Try other styles and note the differences. Like shadows, use these effects sparingly.
5. Reapply **3-D Style 2**.

EXERCISE 8-15 Customize a 3-D Effect

In a manner similar to customizing shadow effects, you can customize a 3-D effect by using buttons on the 3-D Settings toolbar. To display the toolbar, click the 3-D Style button on the Drawing toolbar and select 3-D Settings from the drop-down menu.

You use the 3-D Settings toolbar to change the color, angle of rotation, depth, and other features of the 3-D effect. These tools are fun to use. Try them on all types of objects, not just WordArt.

1. With the WordArt on slide 1 still selected, click the 3-D Style button and choose 3-D Settings.

FIGURE 8-12
3-D Settings toolbar

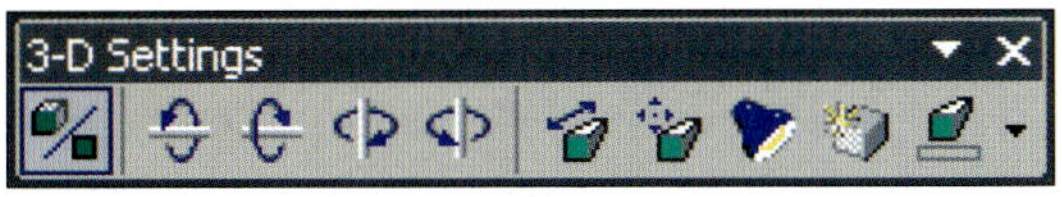

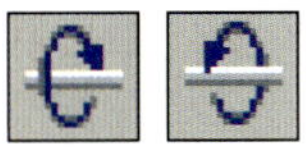

2. On the 3-D Settings toolbar, click the Tilt Up button twice. The angle of the object is shifted up, decreasing its depth.
3. Click the Tilt Down button three times.

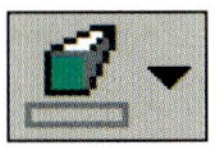

4. Click the arrow on the 3-D Color button. Choose light blue.

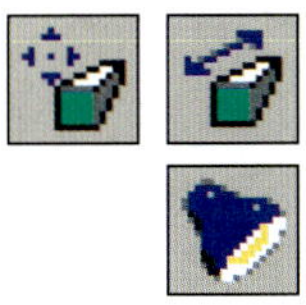

5. Click the Direction button; then choose Perspective from the menu.
6. Click the Depth button and choose Infinity.
7. Click the Lighting button; then choose the center option in the top row (light shining down from the top).
8. Change the 3-D color back to white.
9. Close the 3-D Settings toolbar.
10. Using the Order floating toolbar, bring the Explosion AutoShape (with the text "Good 4 U") to the front and then arrange the Explosion object and the 3-D object to match Figure 8-13.

FIGURE 8-13
3-D and shadow effects on slide 1

11. Change the grayscale setting for the 3-D WordArt title to Grayscale.

12. Save the presentation as ***[your initials]*8-15** in your Lesson 8 folder but do not print it. Leave the presentation open for the next exercise.

Using the Duplicate Command

The Duplicate command is a convenient tool for creating evenly spaced objects, either in a straight row or at an angle. Duplicated objects can overlap one another or be spaced apart. In some ways, the Duplicate command is similar to Copy and Paste, but it does not place a copy on the clipboard. Using the Duplicate command can achieve results similar to the Distribute command that you used earlier in this lesson.

EXERCISE 8-16 Use the Duplicate Command

To duplicate an object, select the object, open the Edit menu, and choose Duplicate or press Ctrl+D. While being careful to keep the duplicated object selected, reposition it if you want, then press Ctrl+D several times until you have the number of duplicates you want.

1. Move to slide 4. Select both the notched arrow and the text box containing the text "Determine methods."

2. Group the selected objects.

3. From the expanded Edit menu, choose Duplicate or press Ctrl+D. A copy appears, slightly offset from the original.

4. Being careful not to deselect the copy, use the arrow keys on your keyboard to move the copy down and to the right. (See Figure 8-14 for approximate positioning of the second arrow and text box.)

NOTE: The Duplicate command works only if the duplicate copy remains selected. As soon as it is deselected, the command is no longer in effect. If that happens, delete the duplicate and start again.

5. Press Ctrl+D. A second copy appears, which is offset the same amount as the first copy.

6. Press Ctrl+D again. You should now have three copies and the original on the slide.

7. Change the text in the duplicated text boxes as shown in Figure 8-14 (on the next page).

8. Select all the text boxes and arrows (everything on the slide except the WordArt title).

FIGURE 8-14
Creating duplicates

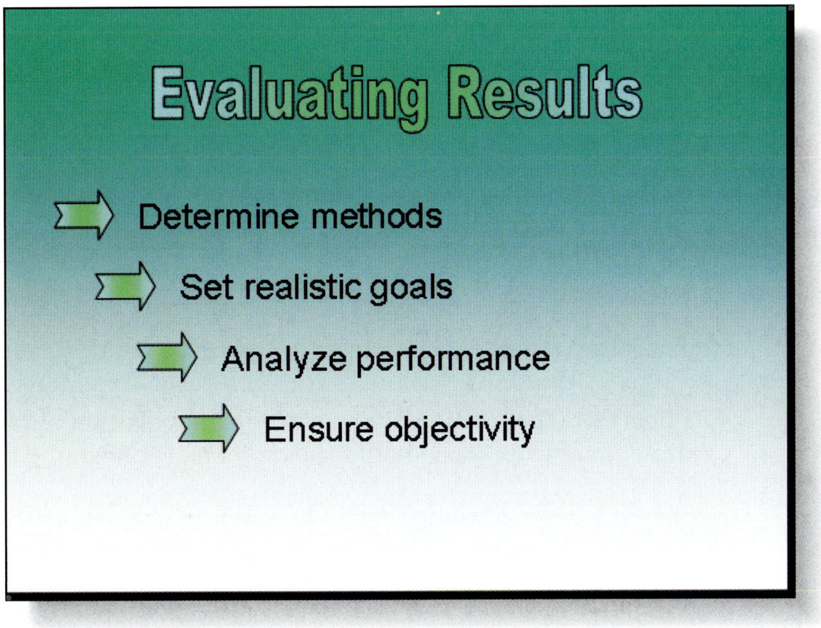

9. Group the selection and center it horizontally relative to the slide.
10. Save the presentation as ***[your initials]*8-16** in your Lesson 8 folder but do not print it. Leave the presentation open for the next exercise.

Advanced Picture Editing

You already learned how to insert, resize, and crop pictures, and how to change image settings such as brightness and contrast.

PowerPoint enables you to perform additional editing on pictures that are vector-based drawings (for example, Windows Metafile drawings with the file extension .wmf). These pictures can be converted (ungrouped) into a collection of ordinary PowerPoint objects.

NOTE: Unlike vector-based drawings, bitmap pictures cannot be ungrouped. To perform extensive editing on bitmap pictures, you need to use a paint-type program such as Imaging for Windows.

EXERCISE 8-17 Edit a Vector-Based Picture

When a vector-based drawing is ungrouped, it is converted into a collection of PowerPoint objects that you can delete, resize, and reposition, just like any objects that you draw. You can also change the fill color and border for parts of a picture that has been converted.

1. Move to slide 5 and select the picture at the bottom of the slide.
2. With the picture selected, change the Zoom setting to 100%.
3. From the Draw menu, choose Ungroup. A dialog box asks whether you want to convert this image to a Microsoft Office drawing object.

FIGURE 8-15
Converting a picture to a Microsoft Office drawing object

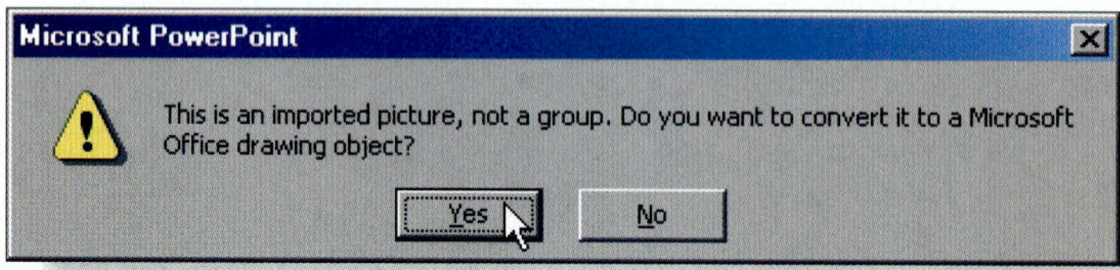

4. Click Yes. The picture is now a grouped collection of Microsoft Office drawing objects. You should see only one set of sizing handles.

NOTE: If you see many sets of sizing handles, you ungrouped the picture more than once. To fix it, regroup the picture or use Undo one or more times until you see just one set of sizing handles.

5. With the picture selected, click the upper-right puzzle piece. It is surrounded with gray selection handles.

FIGURE 8-16
Selecting an object in a converted picture

6. Apply a textured fill of your choice to the selected puzzle piece.
7. Click the lower-right puzzle piece and apply the same textured fill to it.
8. Select the green dress on the figure in the upper right. Change the dress to a fill pattern of your choice using dark green and bright green.

9. Change the brown suit on the figure in the lower-right corner to a fill pattern of your choice using dark blue and gray. (Three separate objects make up the suit.)

EXERCISE 8-18 Delete Parts of a Vector-Based Picture

If you want to delete or move parts of a converted picture, you must first ungroup it one more time.

1. With the picture selected, choose Ungroup from the Draw menu. Now the picture is separated into a large number of small parts.
2. Draw a selection rectangle around the two figures and puzzle pieces on the left. Use Figure 8-17 as a guide to the size and position of the selection rectangle.

FIGURE 8-17 Selecting part of a picture

TIP: Remember that only objects that are completely contained in a selection rectangle are selected. It's okay to allow the selection rectangle to overlap parts of objects that are not to be part of the selection.

3. Press Delete. The two figures on the left are removed from the picture.
4. Compare your picture with Figure 8-18. If too much of the picture was deleted, click the Undo button and try again. If too many parts remain, select the extra parts individually and delete them.
5. Draw a selection rectangle around the remaining parts of the picture and group them. (Do not use the Regroup command.)

6. Use the Align and Distribute toolbar to center the picture horizontally on the slide.

FIGURE 8-18
Completed picture after editing

7. Close any floating toolbars that you opened during this lesson and change the zoom setting to Fit.

8. If the ruler is displayed, hide it by opening the View menu and choosing Ruler.

9. Check spelling in the presentation.

10. Review the grayscale settings for all slides and make any changes that might be necessary.

11. Create a handout header and footer: include the date and your name as the header, and the page number and text ***[your initials]*8-18** as the footer.

12. Move to slide 1 and save the presentation as ***[your initials]* 8-18** in your Lesson 8 folder.

13. Preview and then print the presentation as handouts, 6 slides per page, grayscale, framed. Close the presentation.

LESSON 8 Summary

- Select multiple objects when you want to perform the same operation on all of them, for example, making them all the same color or moving all of them at the same time.

- Select multiple objects one at a time by holding down Shift while clicking each object.
- Select multiple objects all at once by drawing a selection rectangle around them (drag the standard mouse pointer). Be sure to start dragging on a blank area of the slide.
- Add items to the selection by using the Shift+click method. Remove an item from a group of selected items by Shift+clicking it.
- Selected objects can be aligned horizontally or vertically, relative to each other. They can be aligned by their tops, bottoms, middles, right sides, left sides, or centers. They can be aligned relative to the edges of a slide when the Relative to Slide option is selected.
- Selected objects can be distributed (evenly spaced) horizontally or vertically, relative to each other, by using Align or Distribute toolbar buttons. Objects can also be evenly distributed across the width or height of a slide when the Relative to Slide option is turned on.
- Flipping an object creates a mirror image of it. The Rotate Left and Rotate Right buttons rotate objects in 90-degree increments.
- Grouping two or more objects combines them in such a way that they behave as if they were one object.
- An individual member of a group can be selected without ungrouping all the objects. First click the group to select it; then click a member of the group. The gray selection handles indicate which member of the group is selected. The selected group member can have its fill and outline formatted, and can be flipped, but it cannot be deleted, resized, or rotated.
- To delete, resize, or rotate a member of a group, first ungroup it. After you are finished working on individual items of a group, regroup them.
- When objects overlap, use the buttons on the Order toolbar to control which object appears on the top. The most recently drawn object will be on top until you change its order.
- Apply an object shadow or 3-D effect to emphasize an object. There are 20 shadow styles and 20 3-D styles to choose from, and each style can be customized by using the Shadow Settings toolbar or the 3-D Settings toolbar.
- The Duplicate command creates a copy of the selected item, offset by a small amount. Using the Duplicate command multiple times creates an evenly spaced series of duplicated items.
- Vector-based pictures (for example, pictures with the .wmf file extension) can be converted into a group of PowerPoint objects by using the Ungroup command. Once ungrouped, the individual objects can be formatted and manipulated like any PowerPoint object.

LESSON 8 Command Summary

FEATURE	BUTTON	MENU	KEYBOARD	SPEECH?
Select all objects		Edit, Select All	Ctrl + A	✓
Deselect all selected objects			Esc	
Deselect one object from a group of selected objects			Shift +click	
Add to a selection of objects			Shift +click	
Align or distribute objects		Draw, Align or Distribute		✓
Flip or rotate objects		Draw, Rotate or Flip		✓
Group objects		Draw, Group	Ctrl + Shift + G	✓
Ungroup objects		Draw, Ungroup	Ctrl + Shift + H	✓
Regroup objects		Draw, Regroup		✓
Change the order of objects		Draw, Order		✓
Apply an object shadow	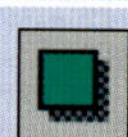			✓
Apply a 3-D effect				✓
Duplicate an object		Edit, Duplicate	Ctrl + D	✓
Display the ruler		View, Ruler		✓

Concepts Review

TRUE/FALSE QUESTIONS

Each of the following statements is either true or false. Indicate your choice by circling T or F.

T F *1.* You cannot use selection rectangles to select multiple objects.

T F *2.* The text in a placeholder always shows even when an object is on top of it.

T F *3.* If you continually click the Rotate Left button, the object eventually returns to its original position.

T F *4.* To select multiple objects, press Shift while clicking each object.

T F *5.* The Duplicate command is available from the Insert menu.

T F *6.* There are 20 different 3-D styles that you can apply to an object.

T F *7.* You cannot change the color of object shadows.

T F *8.* The keyboard command to select all objects on a slide is Ctrl+A.

SHORT ANSWER QUESTIONS

Write the correct answer in the space provided.

1. On what layer does the most recently drawn object appear?

___

2. What appears when you drag the mouse to select multiple objects?

___

3. Which tool do you use to flip an object from left to right?

___

4. To select multiple objects with the mouse, which key do you press while clicking?

___

5. What color are the selection handles when you select an individual object in a grouped object?

___

6. Which Align option do you select to line up objects side-by-side along their bottom edges?

____

7. Which Order option do you use to place an object at the top of all the other objects on a slide?

____

8. What do you need to do to a vector-based picture before you can remove an unwanted element?

____

CRITICAL THINKING

Answer these questions on a separate page. There are no right or wrong answers. Support your answers with examples from your own experience, if possible.

1. In this lesson you learned how to work with layers of objects. Which objects might you place on top of each other? When would you find it useful to overlap them?
2. Think of the way you used the Duplicate command to add evenly spaced objects to your slide. In what other ways could you use this feature? Which objects would you duplicate?

Lesson Applications

EXERCISE 8-19

Select, align, and layer multiple objects; group and ungroup objects; and work with object shadows.

1. Open the file **InfoPak1**.
2. On the title master, select all the tiny diamonds. Align their tops relative to each other. Then distribute them evenly, relative to each other.
3. Select one random diamond and change its color to gold. Group all the diamonds and center the group horizontally, relative to the slide.
4. Copy the group of diamonds and paste them on the slide master. Position the diamonds between the title placeholder and the body text placeholder.
5. Still working on the slide master, change the first-level bullet to the diamond from the Symbol font (sixth row from the bottom). Make it 100% of the font size and change its color to gold.
6. On slide 1, send the large diamond AutoShape behind the subtitle text, align its middle relative to the subtitle text, and center it and the subtitle text horizontally, relative to the slide.
7. On slide 2, adjust the size of the body text placeholder to fit the text; then horizontally center the placeholder on the slide.
8. On slide 3, reduce the width of the body text placeholder to 6.75 inches, reduce the font size to 28 points, and center the placeholder horizontally on the slide. Make the same changes to the placeholder on slide 4.
9. On slide 5, apply an object shadow (by using the Shadow button on the Drawing toolbar) to the text in the diamond. Choose Shadow Style 6, make the shadow color dark red (background scheme color), and adjust the nudge settings to bring the shadow closer to the text. Deselect the semitransparent setting for the object shadow.
10. Group the text box and the diamond, and center them horizontally on the slide. Adjust the vertical position of the group to make a pleasing composition.
11. View the presentation in Grayscale view and make any necessary adjustments to the grayscale settings.
12. Create a handout header and footer: include the date and your name as the header, and the page number and text ***[your initials]*** **8-19** as the footer.
13. Move to slide 1 and save the presentation as ***[your initials]*****8-19** in your Lesson 8 folder.

14. Preview and then print the presentation as handouts, 6 slides per page, grayscale, framed. Close the presentation.

EXERCISE 8-20

Work with shadows and 3-D effects; use the Duplicate command; and align, distribute, and group objects.

1. Open the file **Recruit2**.
2. Delete all graphic elements on the slide master and on the title master. Only the text placeholders should remain.
3. On the title master, draw a 0.25-inch circle, creating a small dot in the center of the slide. Make the dot purple and apply Shadow Style 8. Make the shadow color black and deselect the semitransparent setting.
4. Duplicate the dot you just created 15 times (without repositioning), so you have a total of 16 dots. Select all the dots; then align their tops relative to each other. Distribute the dots horizontally, relative to the slide. You should now have a line of evenly spaced dots across the middle of the title master.
5. Group the dots.
6. Select the title placeholder, the group of dots, and the subtitle placeholder, and distribute them vertically, relative to each other (not to the slide). This spaces the line of dots evenly between the two placeholders.
7. Copy the group of dots and paste it to the slide master, between the title placeholder and the body text placeholder.
8. Move the body text placeholder down 0.5 inch to add some extra space for the dots.
9. Change the bullet shape for all the bullets in the body text placeholder to a solid, thick, right-pointing arrow from the Wingdings3 font. Change their size to 75% and their color to bright green (use More Colors).
10. Change the slide master's title text to Arial Black and apply Shadow Style 6 to the text. Make the shadow slightly more pronounced by nudging it down twice and to the right twice. Change the shadow color to black and deselect the semitransparent setting.
11. On slide 1, replace the title text "New Employee Orientation" with a WordArt title (positioned where the title text would usually be). Use the fifth WordArt style on the second row (the dark blue one). Make the font 54-point Impact.
12. Change the fill color of the WordArt object to purple and the outline color to bright green. Change the WordArt shadow to Shadow Style 8 and change the shadow color to black, with the semitransparent setting not selected. Resize and reposition the WordArt so its shadow does not overlap the purple dots.

13. Draw a rounded rectangle where the subtitle would appear. Make the rectangle 1 inch high and 3.5 inches wide. Apply a black, one-color, horizontal gradient fill with the darkest color at the top. Adjust the shading intensity so the bottom is the same shade as the bottom of the slide's background.
14. Inside the rectangle, key **Good 4 U** in bright green, 44-point Arial bold.
15. Apply the second 3-D style to the rectangle, change its direction to Perspective, change its depth to 72 points, and change its color to purple. Center the rectangle horizontally, relative to the slide.
16. On slide 3, resize the text box to 7 inches wide and center it horizontally on the slide.
17. On slide 4, key the following text in the body text placeholder:
    - Reinforce our message of healthy living
    - Describe our new franchising philosophy
    - Encourage fresh ideas from new employees
18. Make the body text placeholder 5.5 inches wide and center it horizontally on the slide.
19. Adjust the Grayscale view settings in the presentation, as needed.
20. Check spelling in the presentation.
21. Create a handout header and footer: include the date and your name as the header, and the page number and text ***[your initials]*****8-20** as the footer.
22. Move to slide 1 and save the presentation as ***[your initials]*****8-20** in your Lesson 8 folder.
23. Preview and then print the presentation as handouts, 6 slides per page, grayscale, framed. Close the presentation.

EXERCISE 8-21

Group and ungroup objects, align and distribute objects, work with layers, and edit pictures.

1. Open the file **Cooking4**.
2. Apply the Blends design template to the presentation. Change the template's color scheme to one with the black background.
3. On the title master, ungroup the graphic objects and delete the red, blue, and gold rectangles. On the slide master, delete only the red and blue rectangles, allowing the gold one to remain.
4. On slide 1, left-align the subtitle text in its placeholder.
5. Convert the carrot picture to PowerPoint objects. Then select just the orange part and change its fill color to a brighter shade of orange (create a custom color).

6. Increase the carrot's size proportionately, making it 3 inches tall, and rotate it to the right 60 degrees. Position the carrot in the lower-right corner of the slide.
7. Move the apple from the upper-left corner to the middle of the carrot, hiding part of it. (Bring the apple to the front.)
8. Insert a picture of a cluster of grapes (or another fruit or vegetable) that works well with the apple and carrot. Size and rotate the picture appropriately and place it to the left or right of the apple, whichever makes the best grouping.
9. Group the three images and position the group attractively. Copy the group to the slide master. Decrease its size proportionately, making it 75% of the original size, and place it in the lower-right corner.
10. On slide 2, adjust the size of the body text placeholder to fit the text and center it horizontally and vertically relative to the slide.
11. On slide 3, resize and reposition the graph so that it does not overlap the fruit in the lower-right corner. Change the graph's grayscale setting to Inverse Grayscale.
12. On slide 4, reduce the body text by one font size and make the placeholder wide enough so that the bullet text does not wrap to a new line.
13. Reposition the picture and the text box to create an attractive layout. You may change the size of the picture and the text size if you want.
14. Review the presentation in Grayscale view and make adjustments where needed.
15. Create a handout header and footer: include the date and your name as the header, and the page number and text ***[your initials]*8-21** as the footer.
16. Move to slide 1 and save the presentation as ***[your initials]*8-21** in your Lesson 8 folder.
17. Preview and then print the presentation as handouts, 4 slides per page, grayscale, landscape, framed. Close the presentation.

EXERCISE 8-22 *Challenge Yourself*

Align and layer objects, edit pictures, and apply 3-D effects.

1. Open the file **WhoWeAre**.
2. Insert a picture in the lower right corner of slide 1 that is appropriate to the content of the presentation. Size the image appropriately and change its color setting to either grayscale or black-and-white.
3. Insert a different but related picture on the slide master. Choose a simple image and make it approximately 1.5 inches tall. Change its color setting to

grayscale, and move it to the upper-right corner of the slide master. Send it to the back so that it is behind the title text placeholder and other graphics.

4. Change the slide master's title text to 44-point Arial.
5. Rotate or flip the images, if needed, to create better positioning, and adjust the contrast and brightness as you see fit.
6. On slide 1, replace the "Good 4 U" title and its placeholder with a WordArt image by using the first choice in the first row of the WordArt Gallery. Adjust the WordArt width to make it approximately 5.5 inches wide, 1.25 inches high, and position it where the title placeholder usually goes.
7. Apply the 3-D Style 4 (wire frame) to the WordArt. Using the Direction button on the 3-D Settings toolbar, choose the Perspective option, and change the direction to the second choice in the bottom row (which places the perspective vanishing point directly behind and slightly above the WordArt image).
8. On slide 2, resize the body text placeholder to fit the text and center the placeholder horizontally and vertically on the slide.
9. Draw a constrained Diamond AutoShape on slide 2. Make the shape 4.5 inches wide. Change the fill color to a light shade of gray (use More Colors). Remove the outline.
10. Select both the diamond and the body text placeholder and align their middles and centers relative to each other. Send the diamond behind the text.
11. Copy the diamond and paste it to slide 3. Send the diamond to the back and then position it behind the picture of people. Change the picture's color setting to grayscale by using the Color button on the Picture toolbar. Click the More Contrast button three times to sharpen the image slightly. Align the centers and middles of the clip art and diamond relative to each other; then move them slightly to the left.
12. Still working on slide 3, adjust the body text placeholder to fit the text; then adjust its vertical position so it is in balance with the graphic images.
13. Format slide 5 in the same style as slide 3. Format slide 4 in the same style as slide 2.
14. Review the presentation in Grayscale view and make adjustments where needed.
15. Apply an animation scheme of your choice and then view the presentation as a slide show.
16. Create a handout header and footer: include the date and your name as the header, and the page number and text ***[your initials]*****8-22** as the footer.
17. Move to slide 1 and save the presentation as a Web page with the filename ***[your initials]*****8-22** in your Lesson 8 folder.

18. Preview and then print the presentation as handouts, 6 slides per page, grayscale, framed. Close the presentation.

On Your Own

In these exercises you work on your own, as you would in a real-life work environment. Use the skills you've learned to accomplish the task—and be creative.

EXERCISE 8-23

Imagine that you are the marketing manager for a new product: a new ice cream flavor, a new type of breathable waterproof fabric, a new type of golf ball, or whatever else you want. Create a presentation aimed at your company's top management, explaining how you plan to sell this product (for example, advertising strategies, demonstrations, public relations activities). Include at least five slides in your presentation. Use the tools and features presented in this lesson and in previous lessons to create an attractive presentation. Save the presentation as ***[your initials]*8-23**. Preview and then print the presentation as handouts.

EXERCISE 8-24

Create a presentation to recruit volunteers to work for a community event, such as a July 4th celebration, a Memorial Day parade, or a Winter Carnival. In your presentation, describe some of the activities that are part of the event, including dates and times. Also include one or two slides explaining to people why they should become volunteers. Use the tools and features presented in this lesson and in previous lessons to create an attractive presentation. Save the presentation as ***[your initials]*8-24**. Preview and then print the presentation as handouts.

EXERCISE 8-25

Think of an idea for a television show, a radio talk show, a newspaper column, or a community education program. Create a presentation aimed at getting financial backing for your idea. Explain your idea and its benefits. Format your presentation attractively and in keeping with the theme of your idea. Save the presentation as ***[your initials]*8-25**. Preview and then print the presentation as handouts.

Access

Core

2002

Access Core

CASE STUDY

Carolina Critters

UNIT 1

Understanding Access Basics

UNIT 2

Building a Database

CASE STUDY

There's more to learning a database program like Microsoft's Access than keying data in an existing database or running a pre-existing query. You need to know how to use Access in a real-world situation. That's why all these lessons relate to everyday business tasks.

As you work through the lessons, imagine yourself working as an intern for Carolina Critters, a fictional company that manufactures stuffed animals, located in Charlotte, North Carolina.

CAROLINA CRITTERS

Carolina Critters, Inc.

Carolina Critters, Inc. was formed in 1946 by Hector Fuentes, upon his return from serving in the U.S. Navy in World War II. Hector's son, Carlos, took over the company in 1962 and ran it until 1997, when his daughter Lisa assumed the presidency.

Originally producing only stuffed "teddy bears," rabbits, squirrels, and other "cuddly" animals, the company has branched out over the years. It now has 5 product lines and 25 products, producing over $25 million in annual sales. Today, the stuffed animals from Carolina Critters—ranging from traditional teddy bears and cats and dogs, to dinosaurs and endangered species—are sold in department stores and toy stores across the nation. The company also sells products on the Internet.

In your work as an intern at Carolina Critters, you will interact primarily with the 4 key people shown in Figure CS-1. The database that you use will relate to Carolina Critters. As you work, take the time to notice the following things:

- Carolina Critters's unusual method for manufacturing its stuffed animals (see page 997).
- The types of database activities required in a small business to carry on day-to-day activities.

If you are unfamiliar with databases, review the diagram on page 998 for a brief introduction to some important database concepts. These are also covered in the text.

FIGURE CS-1
Key Employees

LISA FUENTES
President

FRANCES FALCIGNO
Sales and Marketing Manager

JAMES MCCLUSKIE
Vice-President, Chief Financial Officer

LUIS GUTIERREZ
Manufacturing Manager

Method of Manufacturing

Carolina Critters, Inc. uses an unusual method of manufacturing. Carolina Critters doesn't buy each individual component for a stuffed animal (such as material for the outer shell, plastic joints for arms and legs, felt pads for paws, specially-made eyes, extruded plastic components for the nose or claws, clothes, stuffing, and so on). Instead, it has approached a small number of suppliers and contracted with them for "kits" containing all the pre-cut, pre-weighed, preformed materials required to manufacture a specific stuffed animal. For example, Robinson Mills, Inc., a supplier in Passaic, New Jersey, provides the kit for "Professor Bear" (pictured here with some of the components included in the kit).

What Is a Database?

A database is a collection of information (or "data") that is organized to make retrieving specific information easy. Access is a software application used to create and manage a computerized database. In Access, a database consists of the following elements (called "objects"): tables, queries, reports, forms, macros, and modules. The following diagram sketches out the relationships between the first four objects.

FIGURE CS-2
Relationships between Database Objects

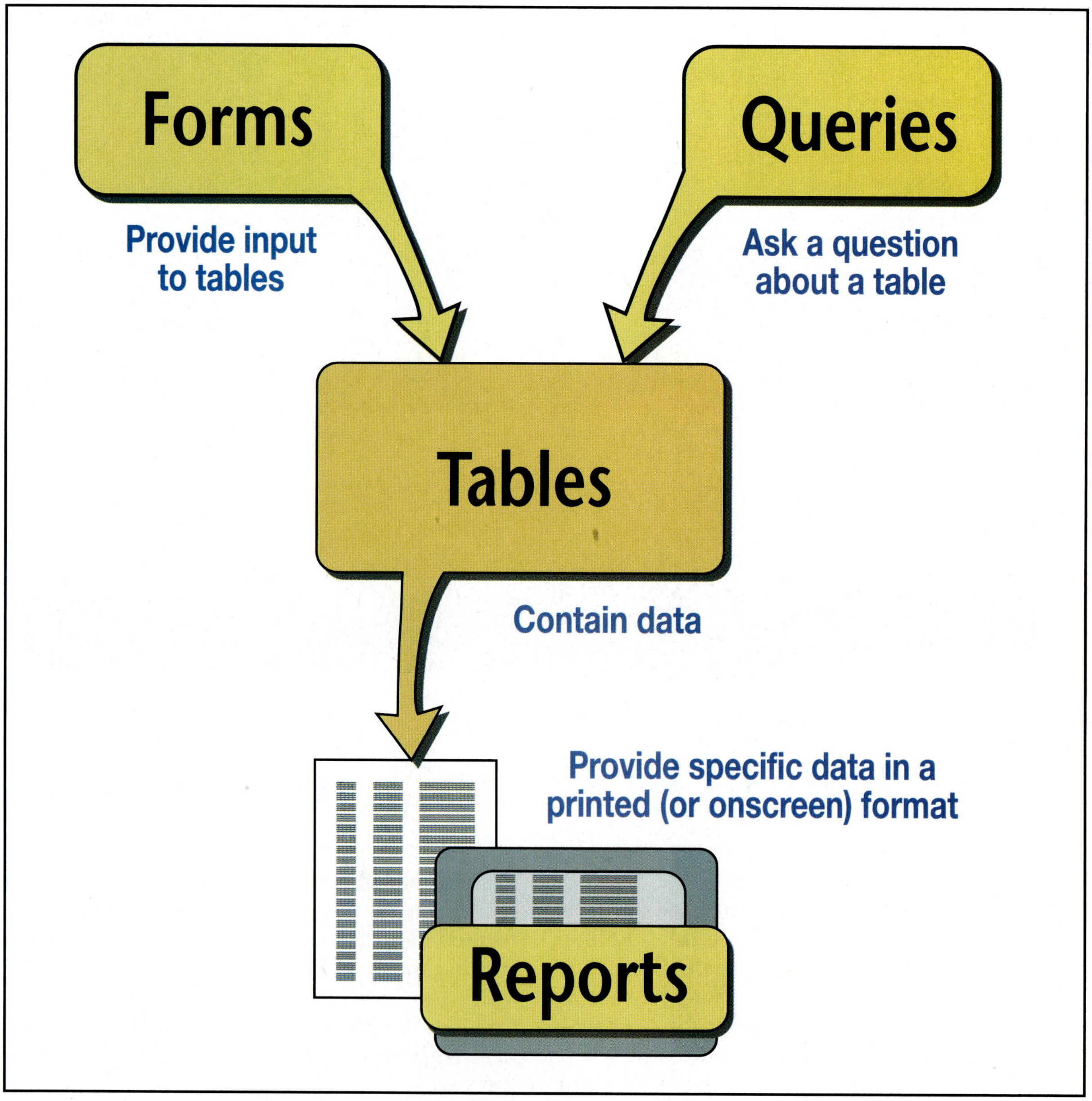

UNIT 1

Understanding Access Basics

LESSON

1

Getting Started with a Database

OBJECTIVES

MOUS ACTIVITIES

In this lesson:

Ac2002 1-1
Ac2002 1-2
Ac2002 1-3
Ac2002 1-4
Ac2002 2-1
Ac2002 3-1

See Appendix E.

After completing this lesson, you will be able to:

1. Copy a database and start Access.
2. Identify parts of the Access screen.
3. Work with objects in the Database window.
4. Work with tables.
5. Work with queries.
6. Open multiple objects.
7. Print a table and a query.
8. Compact and close a database and exit Access.

Estimated Time: 1¾ hours

Microsoft Access is *database software* that tracks information for businesses or individuals. It's included in the Microsoft Office suite and is also available as a stand-alone program.

You use and are part of many databases. The telephone book is a database that displays information about people, companies, associations, and other groups. You are part of your school's database because the school keeps track of when you enrolled, what courses you've taken, what grades you received, where you live, and other important information.

Access is a *relational database management system* (RDBMS). In a relational database, tables can be linked through a common field such as a part number, invoice number, or social security number. You can eliminate duplication of data and enhance data validity by specifying relationships between tables. A relational database is different from a *flat database*. A flat database is a file that stores data that is not linked by common fields. For example, you can use Excel to create a flat database.

Starting Access

An *object* is an element in a database. The main database objects include tables, queries, forms, reports, pages, macros, and modules. You use these objects to store, display, select, or perform an action in your database.

In this lesson, you work with tables and queries. *Tables* are the basic database objects, similar to the tables created in a word processor or spreadsheet program. *Queries* extract data stored in one or more related tables. *Criteria* (required conditions) can be added to select which fields and records will be extracted.

All data is stored in tables. Within each table, data is stored as a record. A *record* contains data about one entity or activity. Examples of records include an individual, an invoice, or a club event. Each data element within a record is a *field*. Fields are shown in columns in a table.

FIGURE 1-1
Sample table

Field

Record

Guernsey	Anna	888-82-2234	8 Darrydowns Dr.	Charlotte	NC	28204-0008
Handigger	Jane	888-89-0987	43 Wilson Place	Dallas	TX	33779-0043
Hayes	Michael	888-78-2390	345 Owen Boulevard	Los Angeles	CA	90052-0345
Hamsa	Sawsan	888-90-4433	1445 West Lane	Kansas City	KC	43909-1445

Your school has a table of students' names, social security numbers, and addresses. A student's name, social security number, and address, collectively, make up a record of information about a single student. A student's address is a field in the record.

Your school probably has another table that lists courses for each semester. Another table might list the students who are enrolled in specific courses. To make the database manageable, the information is not stored in one big table. Your school's database consists of small, manageable tables that are related to each other. One reason for creating a relational database is to be able to manage data efficiently and effectively.

TIP: Data is described as "normalized" when it is broken down into separate, smaller tables with no repetition of data from table to table.

EXERCISE 1-1 Copy a Database and Start Access

There are several ways to start Access, depending on how your system is installed. For example, you can use the Windows taskbar, the Microsoft Office, My Computer, or Windows Explorer. If a shortcut is available to start Access, you can double-click the icon on your desktop.

NOTE: Windows provides many ways to start applications. If you have problems, ask your instructor for help. If you are unfamiliar with Windows, see Appendix A: "Windows Tutorial."

In this course, you cannot work directly from a CD. You need to copy the files you need for a particular lesson to a folder on your hard drive or the network. For example, for Lesson 1, you need the files **CC-01**, **CC-E-01**, and the Images folder. If you need help copying files to your computer, ask your instructor or lab manager for assistance.

NOTE: For more information regarding opening, saving, copying, and moving files, see Appendix B: "File Management." For each lesson, you are required to copy and rename the student database. You should be comfortable managing all aspects of a file in the Windows environment.

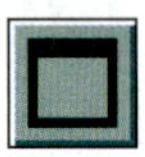

1. Turn on your computer. Windows loads.
2. Right-click the Start button on the Windows taskbar. A shortcut menu opens.
3. Click Explore. When the Windows Explorer opens, click the Maximize button to maximize the window.

NOTE: When you are told to "click" a menu option or a toolbar button, use the left mouse button. Use the left mouse button unless you are told explicitly to "right-click."

4. In the left pane, open the folder Lesson 01. The files contained in the folder appear in the right pane.

NOTE: Your instructor will tell you where the folders and files for this course are located.

5. In the right pane, point at the filename **CC-01** and right-click. Choose Copy from the shortcut menu. (See Figure 1-2 on the next page.)
6. In the left pane, open the My Documents folder.

FIGURE 1-2
Windows Explorer

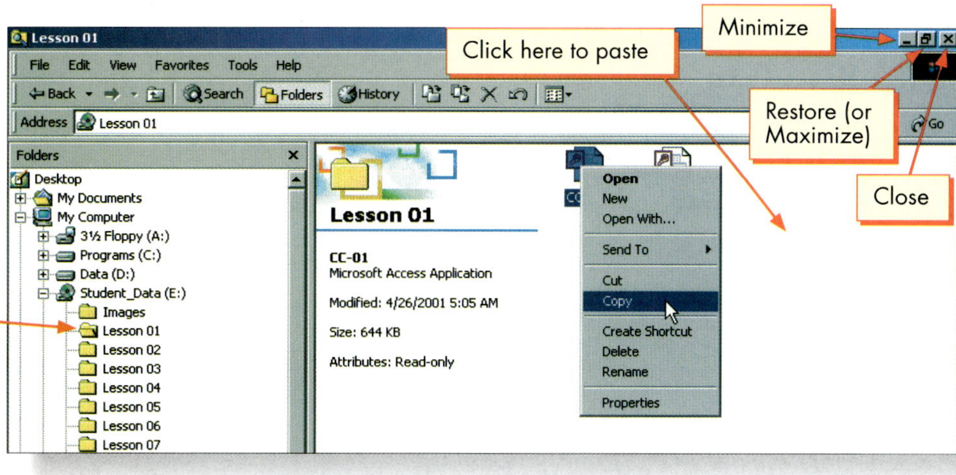

NOTE: Check with your instructor to verify the location where you will store your files. Many times, the My Documents folder is the default folder when you're creating or storing files.

7. In an unused area of the right pane, right-click. Choose Paste from the shortcut menu. A file named **CC-01** appears.
8. Right-click the filename **CC-01** and choose Rename. Press Home and edit the name to ***[your initials]*****CC-01**. Press Enter to accept the new name.
9. Right-click ***[your initials]*****CC-01** and choose Properties. Make certain that the Read-only attribute check box is not checked.

FIGURE 1-3
Properties dialog box

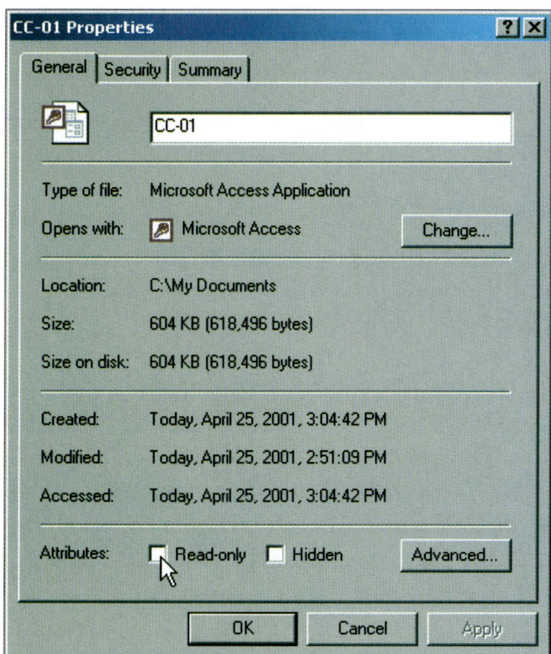

10. Click OK. Close the Explorer.
11. With the left mouse button, click the Start button [Start] on the Windows taskbar and point to Programs.
12. Click Microsoft Access 2002. (You might have to point first to a program group such as Microsoft Office.) After the program is loaded, you will see the New File task pane. You can open an existing database, create a blank database, or create a new database from a template.

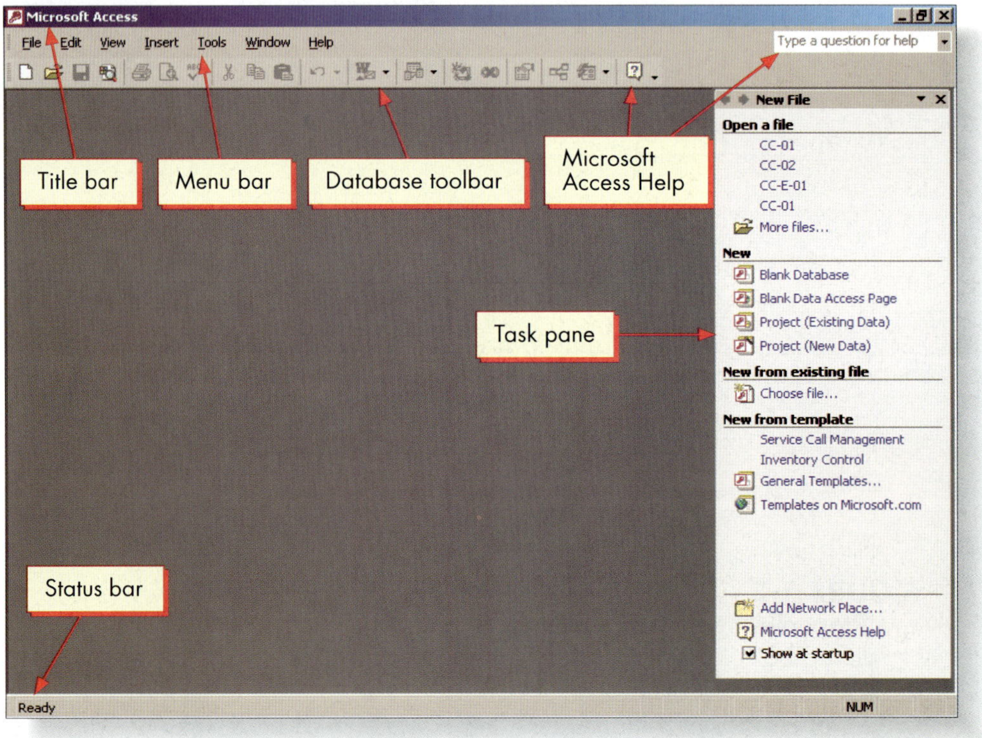

FIGURE 1-4 Initial Access window with New File task pane

13. In the Open a file section, click More files.
14. The Open dialog box opens, showing the files in your default folder. Locate the folder containing ***[your initials]*CC-01** that you pasted and renamed in steps 5 through 8.

NOTE: At the start of each lesson throughout this course, you copy a template database and rename it, using your initials. This distinguishes your database and work from the original and from other students' databases.

15. Double-click ***[your initials]*CC-01** to open the file. Access opens with the Database window. The Database window is the base for operations you perform when working with your database.
16. Maximize the Database window to remove any scroll bars. (See Figure 1-5 on the next page.)

FIGURE 1-5
Access screen with open database

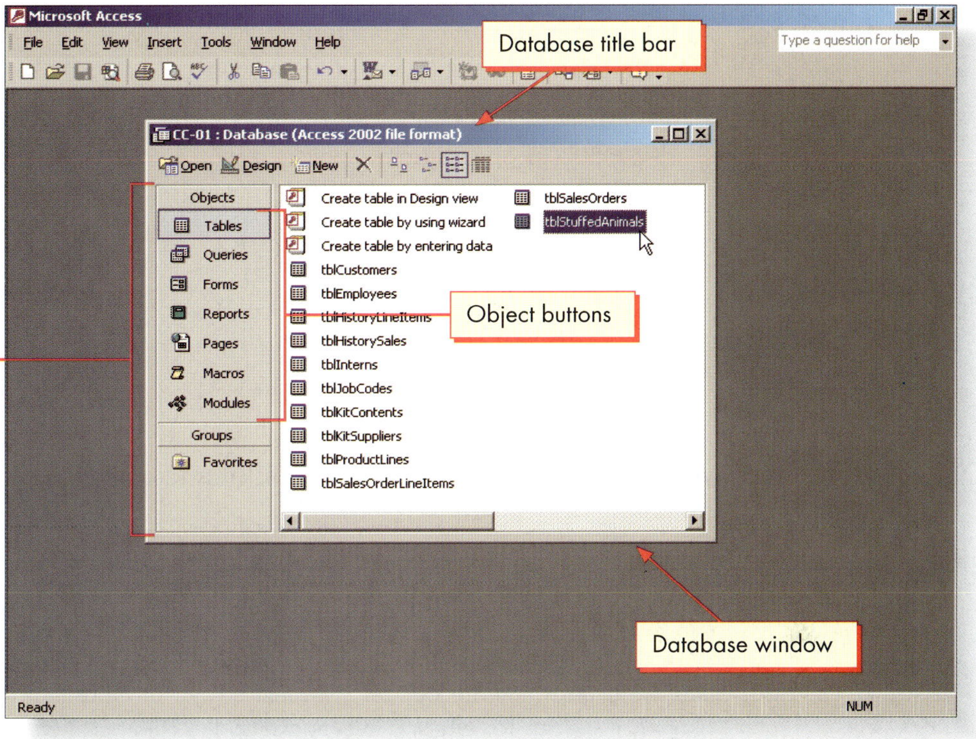

TABLE 1-1 Parts of the Access Screen

PART OF SCREEN	PURPOSE
Title bar	Contains the program name (Microsoft Access).
Database title bar	Contains the name of the database (CC-01).
Menu bar	Displays the names of menus to perform various tasks. You can use the mouse or the keyboard to open menus.
Database toolbar	Displays buttons to execute commands with the mouse. Access opens with the Database toolbar displayed. You learn about other toolbars later.
Database window	Displays a button for each object in the database. Also includes Command buttons to open or design an existing object or create a new one.
Objects bar	Displays buttons for each type of object in the database. By clicking a button, you can work with the database's tables, queries, forms, reports, pages, macros, or modules.

continues

TABLE 1-1 Parts of the Access Screen *continued*

PART OF SCREEN	PURPOSE
Status bar	Displays information about the current task and shows the current mode of operation.
Microsoft Access Help	Provides online Help and tips as you work.

EXERCISE 1-2 Display Database Properties

Database properties are characteristics or attributes that describe and define the database.

1. Move the pointer to File on the menu bar. Click to open the menu.

NOTE: Access 2002 has speech recognition capabilities for menu options. If your computer is set up with a microphone, you can use speech recognition for menu commands, toolbar buttons, and text entry. For more information, see Appendix C. Ask your instructor for information regarding the configuration of your workstation.

2. Move the pointer to Database Properties and click to open the Properties dialog box.

NOTE: If you do not see Database Properties in the menu, click the down-pointing arrows at the bottom of the menu to expand the menu. These arrows indicate more options are available.

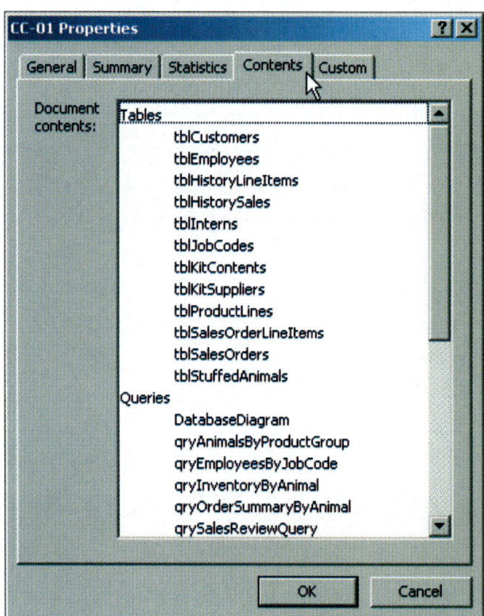

FIGURE 1-6 Properties dialog box, Contents tab

3. Click the Contents tab to see a list of the tables, queries, forms, reports, pages, macros, and modules in the database.

NOTE: There are no macros, modules, or data access pages in your database for Lesson 1.

4. Click OK to close the dialog box.

TABLE 1-2 Properties Dialog Box Tabs

TAB	PURPOSE
General	Contains the date the database was created, last modified, and last opened. Also contains the filename, size, location of the database, and attributes.
Summary	Displays the database title, author, company, category, keywords, and comments.
Statistics	Contains the date the database was created, last modified, printed, and last opened.
Contents	Displays a list of the tables, queries, forms, reports, pages, macros, and modules that the database contains.
Custom	Used to assign a custom property for a file. You can add a name, type, and value for the custom property.

Identifying Parts of the Access Screen

Toolbar buttons are identified by name when you point to them with the mouse.

EXERCISE 1-3 Identify Buttons, Menus, and Menu Items

1. Position the pointer over the New button on the Database toolbar but do not click. A *ScreenTip* (a box with the button name) appears below the button. You choose from a list of sample databases or click the New button to create a blank database.

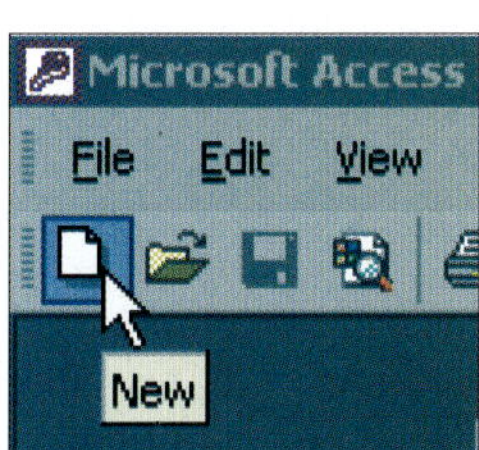

FIGURE 1-7 Identifying toolbar button

2. Move the mouse pointer over the Open button (but don't click). You click this button to open an existing database.

NOTE: Some toolbar buttons are light gray, indicating the command is currently not available. You can still identify the button by positioning the mouse pointer over it.

3. Point to other toolbar buttons to identify them.

TIP: The menu shows which commands have keyboard shortcuts. Keyboard shortcuts appear to the right of the menu command. (Your computer might also show the keyboard shortcut in the ScreenTip.)

4. Move the pointer to Edit on the menu bar and click the left mouse button. This opens the Edit menu. Click Edit to close the menu.

NOTE: If a down-pointing arrow appears at the bottom of the menu, moving the pointer to the bottom of the menu or clicking on the arrow will display all the menu options.

5. Click View to open the View menu. Move the pointer to the Arrange Icons menu option. The right-pointing arrow indicates a submenu. This submenu displays options for arranging the icons in the Database window.

TIP: Office 2002 uses *adaptive menus* to display only the most recently used commands. If you wish to always see all commands available on the menu, select Tools, Customize. In the Options tab of the dialog box, place a checkmark in the box beside Always show full menus and click OK.

FIGURE 1-8 Displaying menu options

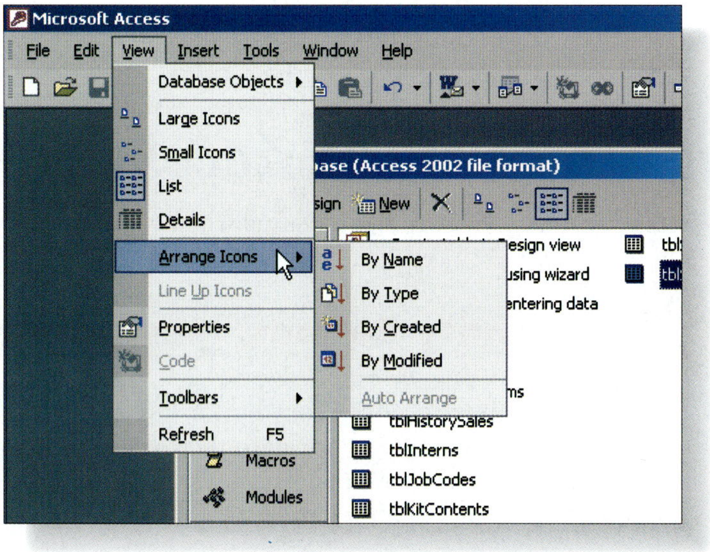

6. Click a blank area of the screen to close the menu. Be careful not to click a menu option or toolbar button.

Looking at Database Objects

At the left of the Database window is an Objects bar showing object buttons. You use these buttons to select the elements with which to work. An object is an item in a database with a specific purpose. It can be a table, a query, or a design element in a form. When you select a button, you see the names of all the objects related to the button that are in the database. For example, if you select the Tables button, the names of all the tables in this database are displayed.

The objects in the databases for this text use *the Leszynski Naming Conventions (LNC)*. These conventions are widely recognized and used by database developers. The object name is preceded by a prefix. Main words are capitalized with no spaces between words.

NOTE: You can read more about this naming convention in the Preface.

TABLE 1-3 Naming Conventions

PREFIX	OBJECT TYPE	EXAMPLE
tbl	Table	tblEmployees
qry	Query	qryKitSuppliers
frm	Form	frmStuffedAnimals
rpt	Report	rptInventoryValue
pge	Page	pgeCustomers
mcr	Macro	mcrPreviewReport
bas	Module	basMyProgram

There are seven types of objects in an Access database:

- Tables store information about a person, place, thing, or event. A table consists of records, which contain fields. The information in a table appears in rows (records) and columns (fields), similar to an Excel worksheet.
- Queries are used to find answers to questions about the data in the database. You can design queries to show fields from one or more tables. You can specify criteria or conditions that must be met for a record to be included. You can use a query to calculate totals or averages from information in the table.
- *Forms* enable you to view, edit, or add records. You can design a form to look like a paper form so people entering the data are familiar with the layout. With most forms, you can see an entire record at one time.
- *Reports* are used to print data. You can group your data, calculate totals, apply different formats, and add graphics to make the report attractive and easy to read.
- *Pages* are HTML documents that are linked to data. They are designed for use in a Web browser and typically require Internet Explorer 5.0 (or later).

- *Macros* run a series of commands. You can write macros for repetitive activities and to automate procedures you use often.
- *Modules* contain Visual Basic for Applications (VBA) functions or procedures.

EXERCISE 1-4 Work in the Database Window

The Table Properties dialog box displays characteristics of a particular table, including the table name, the description, the date the file was created, and the last time the file was updated.

NOTE: The database you work with in this course relates to the Case Study about Carolina Critters, a fictional company that manufactures stuffed animals (see pages 995 through 998).

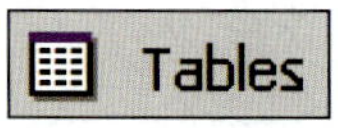

1. Click Tables on the Objects bar. All the tables in the current database are shown. The prefix for a table is *tbl*.
2. Click tblCustomers. Click the Properties button on the right side of the Database toolbar to open the Customers Properties dialog box. Notice the dates when the file was created and modified. Read the description.

FIGURE 1-9 Customers Properties dialog box

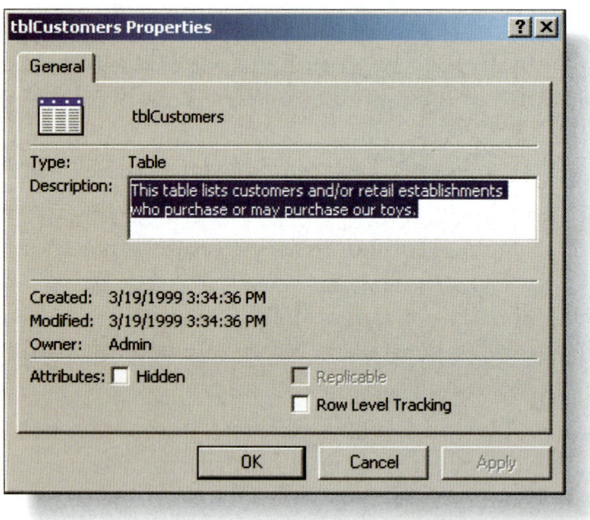

NOTE: An open object can be referred to without its prefix. For example, the tblCustomers Properties box can be referred to as the "Customers Properties dialog box."

3. Click OK to close the dialog box.

4. Point at tblEmployees and right-click. The shortcut menu is a way to quickly access a table's properties. Choose Properties from the shortcut menu to open the Properties dialog box.

5. Click the Close button in the upper right corner of the Employees Properties dialog box to close the dialog box.

6. Click Queries on the Object bar. All the queries in the database are shown. The prefix for a query is *qry*.
7. Click qryInventoryByAnimal. Click the Properties button on the Database toolbar. There is no description for this query.
8. Click OK to close the dialog box.
9. Click Tables on the Objects bar.

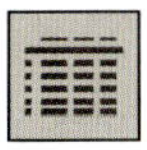

10. Click the Details button in the Database window. Access shows you table descriptions when you set the window to this view.

TIP: Drag the vertical border between column headings to show more of the description.

11. Click Queries on the Objects bar. One of the queries does include a description.

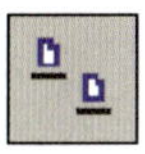
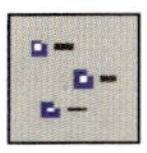

12. Click the Large Icons button and then click the Small Icons button to see what other views are available.

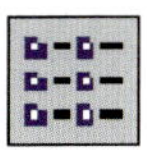

13. Click the List button to return to the original display.
14. Click Tables again. Right-click tblJobCodes. Choose Rename from the shortcut menu.
15. Key **tblMine** and press Enter. The table names are in alphabetical order in List view.
16. Right-click tblMine and choose Rename. Key **tblJobCodes** and press Enter.

TIP: You can rename any database object.

EXERCISE 1-5 Use Datasheet and Design Views

You can look at tables and queries in several views. You can press Ctrl+< to scroll down or Ctrl+> to scroll up through the following table view options.

NOTE: When Keyboard combinations (such as Ctrl+>) are shown in this text, hold down the first key as you press the second key. Release the second key and then release the first key. An example of this entire sequence is: hold down Ctrl, press >, release >, release Ctrl. With practice this sequence becomes easy.

These shortcuts cycle through all four views.

- *Datasheet View.* This view appears when you open a table or query. Datasheet View resembles a worksheet with rows and columns. Each record is displayed in its own row. Each field is shown in its own column. You can enter and edit data, find and sort records, resize rows and columns, and move rows and columns in Datasheet View.
- *Design View.* You use this view to create or modify the layout or structure of a table or query. You do not see the records in this view. In a query, you see a field list and a design grid with sorting directions and criteria. In a table, you see a grid listing field names, the type of data contained in each field (number, text, currency, and so on), and a description of the field. Design View includes field properties with formatting options, default values, validation rules, and other characteristics for each field in the table. (You learn more about data types and field properties in later lessons.)
- *PivotTable View.* You use this view to summarize and analyze data in a table, query, or form. Information is displayed in a table format with columns and rows. You can use different levels of detail or organize data by dragging the fields and items or by showing and hiding items in the drop-down lists for the fields.
- *PivotChart View.* You use this view to summarize and analyze data in a table, query, or form. Information is displayed in a chart form. You can use different levels of detail or organize data by dragging the fields and items or by showing and hiding items in the drop-down lists for the fields.

1. Click tblCustomers. Click the Open command button at the top of the Database window to open the Customers table in Datasheet View. Click the Maximize button to maximize the Table window.

FIGURE 1-10 Customers table datasheet

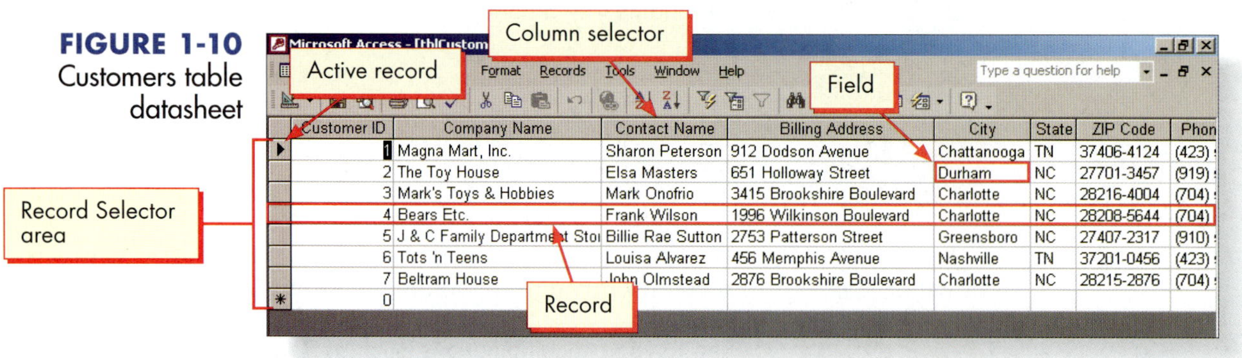

2. With the Customers datasheet displayed, click the down arrow next to the View button on the left side of the Database toolbar. The View shortcut menu appears. (See Figure 1-11 on the next page.)

FIGURE 1-11
Shortcut menu for View button

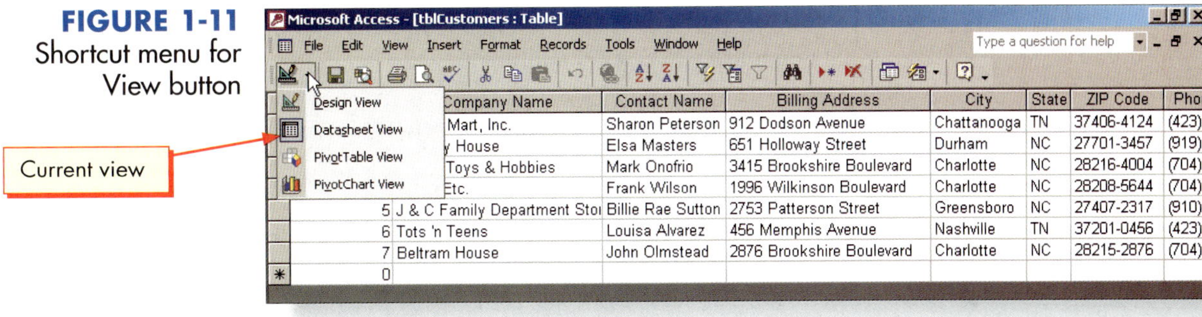

3. Choose Design View from the shortcut menu. This displays the Customers table in Design View. Customer records don't appear in this view. You see the field names, data types, and descriptions.

NOTE: The buttons on the toolbar change, depending on the current view. You can right-click any toolbar to open a shortcut menu to show which toolbars are active.

FIGURE 1-12
Customers table in Design View

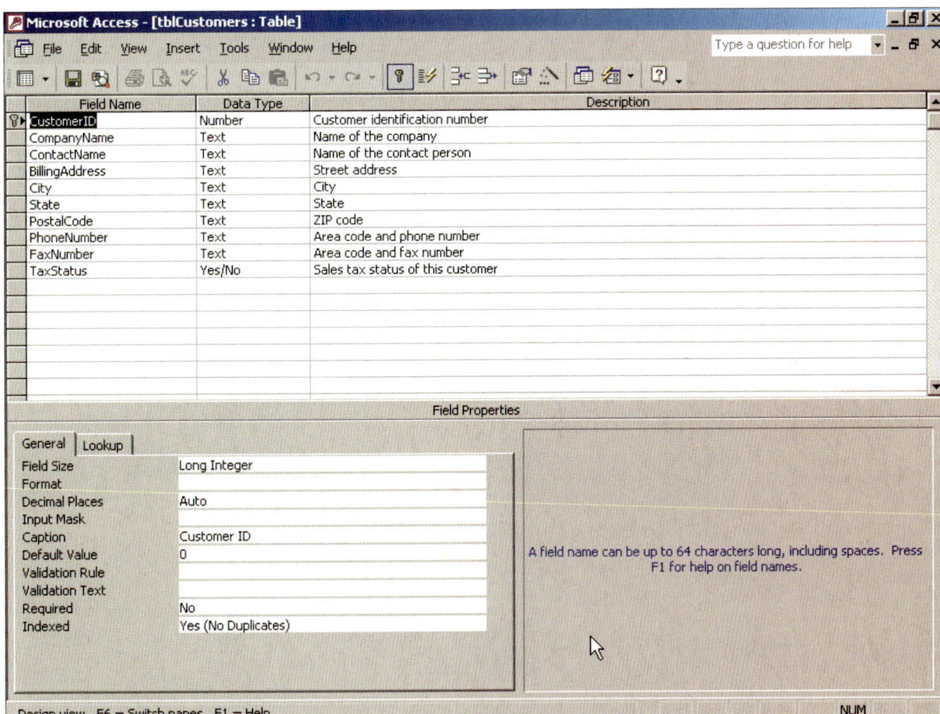

4. Click the Close button [X] to close the Customers table.
5. Double-click the table icon to the left of tblEmployees. The Employees table opens in Datasheet View.

TIP: You can double-click the table icon to the left of the table name, or the table name itself, to open the table.

6. Click the View button (the button, not the down arrow). This displays the Employees table in Design View.

NOTE: The View button is a "toggle" between Design and Datasheet Views. When there are two views for an object, you can click the icon to switch views. The button shows the view that is not currently shown.

7. Click the View button to return to Datasheet View. Close the table.
8. Click **Queries** on the Objects bar. Double-click the query icon to the left of qryInventoryByAnimal. The query opens in Datasheet View.
9. Click the View button to see Design View for a query.

FIGURE 1-13
Inventory query in Design View

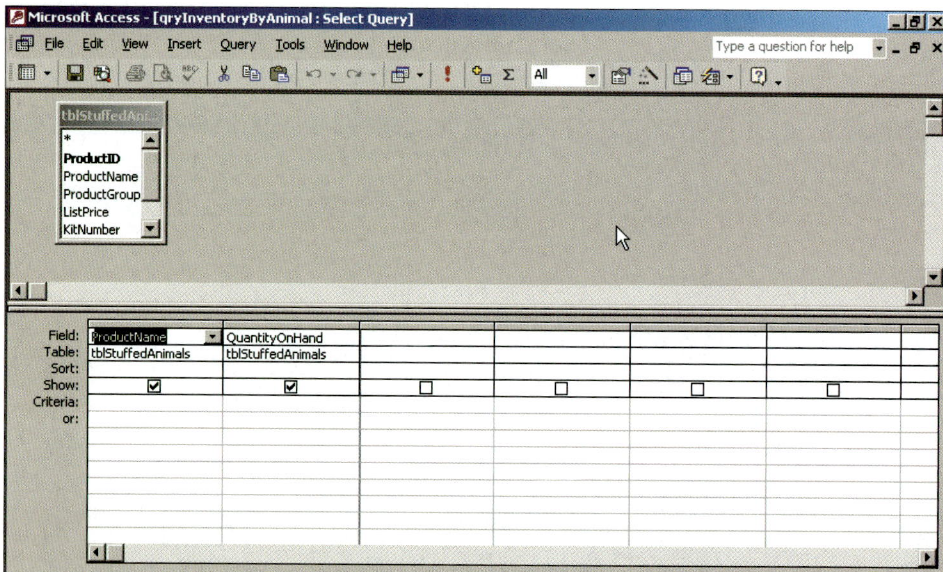

10. Click the Close button.

Working with Tables

The pointer marks the current or active record and where your next action will occur in a table. The pointer appears as a triangle in the narrow empty column to the left of the first field. This column is called the *Record Selector.*

You can use the mouse and the keyboard to move the pointer. You can use navigation buttons to move to a specific record. You can also scroll the records on the screen without moving the pointer.

- Scroll bars frame the right and lower borders of the Table window. You can use the scroll bars to bring different parts of your table into view.

NOTE: When you scroll a window, you change what you see on the screen. You do not move the pointer.

- Navigation buttons are in the lower left corner of the Table window. These buttons include First Record [I◀], Previous Record [◀], Next Record [▶], Last Record [▶I], and New Record [▶*].
- Press [Tab] to move from field to field and [Shift]+[Tab] to move backward.

EXERCISE 1-6 Scroll Through a Table

1. With the ***[your initials]*CC-01** database open, click Tables on the Objects bar. Double-click tblEmployees and click the Maximize button [□] to maximize the Employees table window in Datasheet View.
2. On the vertical scroll bar, click below the scroll box to move down one screen. This is the same as pressing [PgDn].

FIGURE 1-14
Using scroll bars

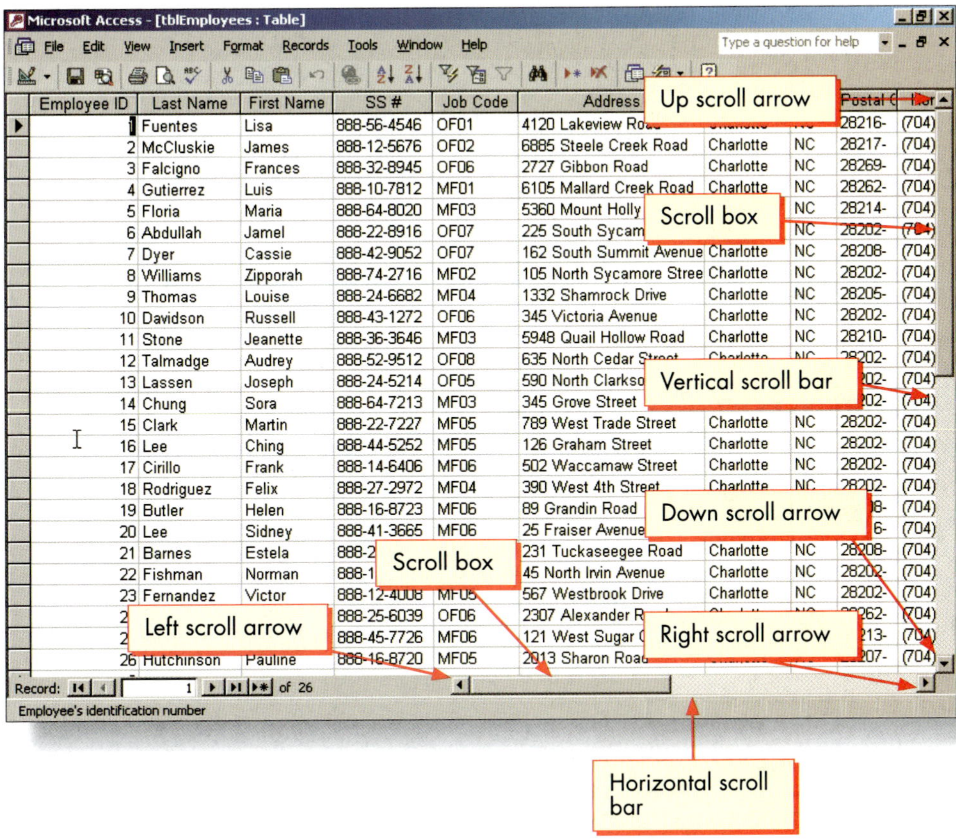

3. Drag the scroll box to the top of the vertical scroll bar.
4. Click the down scroll arrow twice to move down two rows.
5. Click the right scroll arrow on the horizontal scroll bar once; then click the left scroll arrow once to return to the original horizontal position.
6. Click the up scroll arrow on the vertical scroll bar twice. Notice that throughout this scrolling movement, the pointer remains in the first record.

TABLE 1-4 Scrolling Through a Table

TO MOVE THE VIEW	DO THIS
Up one line	Click the up scroll arrow.
Down one line	Click the down scroll arrow.
Up one screen	Click the scroll bar above the scroll box.
Down one screen	Click the scroll bar below the scroll box.
To any relative position	Drag the scroll bar up or down.
To the right	Click the right scroll arrow.
To the left	Click the left scroll arrow.

EXERCISE 1-7 Use Navigation Buttons

The navigation buttons are located in the lower left corner of a table in Datasheet View. You can use these buttons to move the pointer to a specific record or form.

FIGURE 1-15
Navigation buttons

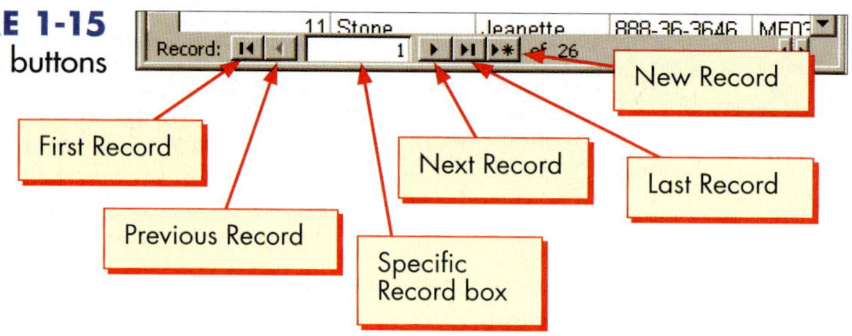

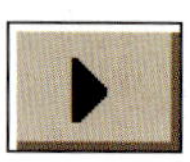

1. With the Employees table open, click the Next Record navigation button once. The next Employee ID is now highlighted. This button moves the pointer one record at a time.

2. Click the Previous Record button once. The pointer moves to the previous record. This button moves one record at a time.

3. Click the Last Record button. The pointer moves to the last record in the table.

4. Click the First Record button. The pointer moves to the first record in the table.

TIP: Press F5 to place the pointer in the Specific Record box (between the navigation buttons). Key the record number, and press Enter to move to that record number.

5. Click the Close button to close tblEmployees.

6. Open tblCustomers as a maximized window. Click the New Record button. This moves the pointer to the end of the table to enter a new record.

TIP: The New Record button also appears on the toolbar.

7. Press PgUp to move to the top of the current screen.
8. Press Tab twice. This moves the pointer to the Contact Name field. Press Shift + Tab once. This moves the pointer back to the Company Name field.

TABLE 1-5

Keyboard Navigation Shortcuts

PRESS	TO DO THIS
Tab	Move to the next field.
Shift + Tab	Move to the previous field.
PgUp	Move up one screen.
PgDn	Move down one screen.
Ctrl + Home	Return to the first record.
Ctrl + End	Move to the last record.

EXERCISE 1-8 Change Column Widths, Row Heights, and Fonts

To make your table easier to view, you can increase or decrease column widths. If a field heading or entry is longer than the text, you can adjust the column to accommodate the heading or entry. You can make the column narrower if there is too much blank space.

You can also make the rows appear to be taller. The default font for Datasheet View is 10-point Arial, but you can change that, too. Changes to the column width, the row height, or the font affect the entire table.

1. In the Customers table, place the pointer on the vertical border between the Company Name and Contact Name column selectors at the tops of the second and third columns. Notice that the pointer changes to a two-headed arrow with a wide vertical bar.

FIGURE 1-16
Resizing columns

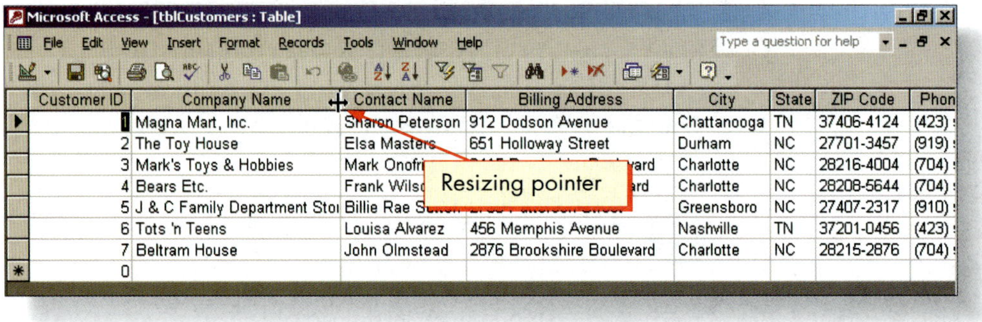

2. Drag the pointer to the right approximately half an inch to allow enough space for the word "Stores" in Record 5. Release the button.

TIP: You can set the width of a column to the widest text by double-clicking its column selector's right vertical border.

3. Place the pointer between the Billing Address and City column selectors. Use the scroll bars to bring the columns into view.
4. When the pointer changes to a two-headed arrow with a wide vertical bar, drag the pointer to the left, making the Address column smaller until it just accommodates the longest billing address.
5. From the Format menu, choose Font. Choose Arial as the font and 12 as the size. Click OK.
6. From the Format menu, choose Font again. Choose 10 as the size. Click OK.
7. Place the pointer on the horizontal line between the first and second row in the Record Selector area to the left of the first field.
8. When the pointer changes to a two-headed arrow, drag the pointer down to make the row approximately twice its current height. (See Figure 1-17 on the next page.)

NOTE: The *layout* of a table is the way it appears on the screen. It includes the size of the columns, the height of the rows, the fonts, the arrangement of the columns, the colors, and other settings.

ACCESS

FIGURE 1-17
Adjusting row height

Resizing pointer

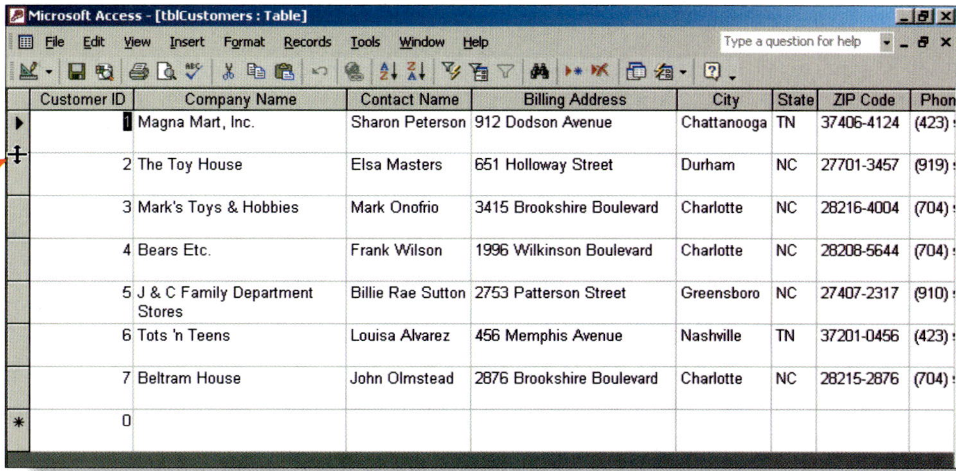

Customer ID	Company Name	Contact Name	Billing Address	City	State	ZIP Code	Phon
1	Magna Mart, Inc.	Sharon Peterson	912 Dodson Avenue	Chattanooga	TN	37406-4124	(423)
2	The Toy House	Elsa Masters	651 Holloway Street	Durham	NC	27701-3457	(919)
3	Mark's Toys & Hobbies	Mark Onofrio	3415 Brookshire Boulevard	Charlotte	NC	28216-4004	(704)
4	Bears Etc.	Frank Wilson	1996 Wilkinson Boulevard	Charlotte	NC	28208-5644	(704)
5	J & C Family Department Stores	Billie Rae Sutton	2753 Patterson Street	Greensboro	NC	27407-2317	(910)
6	Tots 'n Teens	Louisa Alvarez	456 Memphis Avenue	Nashville	TN	37201-0456	(423)
7	Beltram House	John Olmstead	2876 Brookshire Boulevard	Charlotte	NC	28215-2876	(704)
0							

9. Place the pointer on the horizontal line between the first and second rows. Drag the pointer up until the row height accommodates the height of all letters.

10. Right-click the Record Selector for row one. From the shortcut menu, choose Row Height.

11. Make certain that a check appears in the Standard Height check box.

FIGURE 1-18
Row Height dialog box

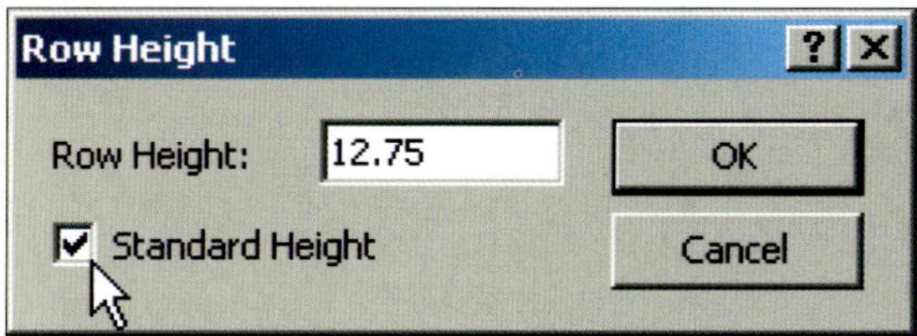

12. Click OK. Close the table. A dialog box appears, prompting you to save the layout of the Customers table. Click Yes to accept the changes.

EXERCISE 1-9 Freeze Fields in a Table

Most tables contain more fields than you can view at one time, so you need to scroll the window. If there is a field you want to see onscreen all the time, you can freeze that field at the left edge of the screen.

1. Open tblEmployees in Datasheet View and maximize the window.

2. Move the pointer to the Employee ID column selector. When the pointer changes to a down-pointing arrow, click. The column is selected.

3. Select Format, Freeze Columns. Then click anywhere in the table to deselect the column. Notice that the right vertical border of the frozen column is slightly heavier than the other vertical lines.

4. Click the right scroll arrow several times to move to the last column. The Employee ID column doesn't scroll.

TIP: To select a block of columns, click the first column selector and then hold down Shift while clicking on the last column in the block.

5. To unfreeze all the columns, choose Unfreeze All Columns from the Format menu.
6. Select the SS# column by clicking the SS# column selector when the pointer is a down-pointing arrow.
7. From the Format menu, choose Freeze Columns. The SS# column moves to the left edge of the table.

TIP: If you freeze a column other than the first column, Access moves that column to be the first column.

8. Click the right scroll arrow several times. The SS# column doesn't scroll.
9. From the Format menu, choose Unfreeze All Columns.
10. Close the Employees table. A dialog box appears, prompting you to save the layout of the Employees table. Click No.

NOTE: If you do not save the layout when you close the table, the columns return to their original positions.

Working with Queries

A query has many of the same characteristics as a table. You can look at all the fields from the table, or you can choose to view only specific fields.

All of the navigation commands in a query are the same as those in a table. You can change the font, the column widths, and the row height as well as freeze columns.

EXERCISE 1-10 Scroll and Navigate in a Query

1. Click the Queries button. Double-click qryItemsByProductID. Make certain that the window is maximized. This query shows two fields from the Stuffed Animals table.
2. Click below the vertical scroll box to move down one screen.
3. Drag the scroll box to the top of the vertical scroll bar.
4. Click the down scroll arrow twice to move down two rows.

NOTE: There is no horizontal scroll bar because the query is not wide enough to need one.

5. Click the up scroll arrow on the vertical scroll bar twice.
6. Click the Next Record button once. The next Animal Name is highlighted.
7. Click the Previous Record button once.
8. Click the Last Record button. The pointer moves to the last record in the query.
9. Click the First Record button.
10. Press F5 to place the pointer in the Specific Record box. Key **8** and press Enter. The pointer moves to the eighth record.
11. Click the Close button to close the query.

EXERCISE 1-11 View a Multiple-Table Query

1. Double-click qryOrderSummaryByAnimal. Make certain the window is maximized. This query shows fields from more than one table.
2. Click the View button. The top half of the screen shows three table field lists with join lines between them. The join lines connect linked fields holding the same data.

FIGURE 1-19 Order Summary query in Design View

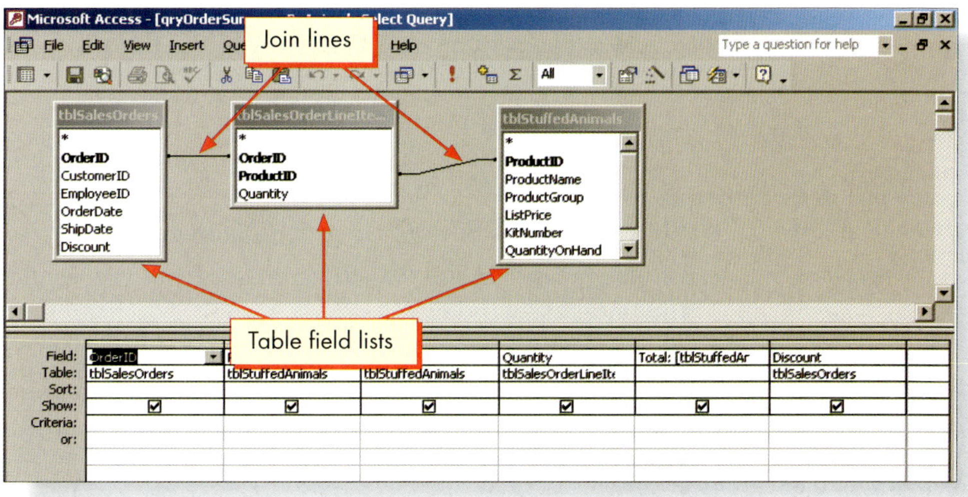

TIP: Join lines are an important concept in a relational database.

3. Click the View button to return to Datasheet View.
4. Place the pointer on the vertical border between the Animal Name and List Price column selectors. The pointer changes to the two-headed arrow with a wide vertical bar.

ACCESS

5. Drag the pointer to the right until there is enough space for the longest animal name.
6. Place the pointer between the Total and Discount field names. When the pointer shows a two-headed arrow, double-click to size the width to the data.
7. Choose Format and then choose Font. Key **t** and choose Times New Roman. Choose 12 as the size. Click OK.
8. Choose Format and then choose Font. Key **a** and choose Arial. Set 10 as the size. Click OK.
9. Place the pointer on the horizontal line between the first and second rows in the Record Selector.
10. When the pointer changes to a two-headed arrow, drag the pointer down to make the row approximately twice its current height.
11. Close the query. A dialog box appears, prompting you to save the layout. Click No to discard the changes.

Working with Multiple Objects

You can open more than one table to compare or contrast data in the tables. You can also open a query and a table at the same time. When you work with multiple objects, you can see the data better if you tile the windows.

EXERCISE 1-12 Open Multiple Tables

1. Click the Tables button. Open tblCustomers.
2. Choose ***[your initials]*CC-01** database from the Window menu to return to the Database window.
3. Open tblEmployees.

4. Click the Database Window button on the toolbar. This also switches you to the Database window. Click the Minimize button in the Database window to minimize it.
5. Select Window, Tile Horizontally. The two tables are tiled. (See Figure 1-20 on the next page.)

NOTE: If you do not minimize the Database window, it is tiled along with the tables.

6. Close both tables.
7. Click the Maximize button in the minimized Database window.

FIGURE 1-20
Horizontally tiled tables

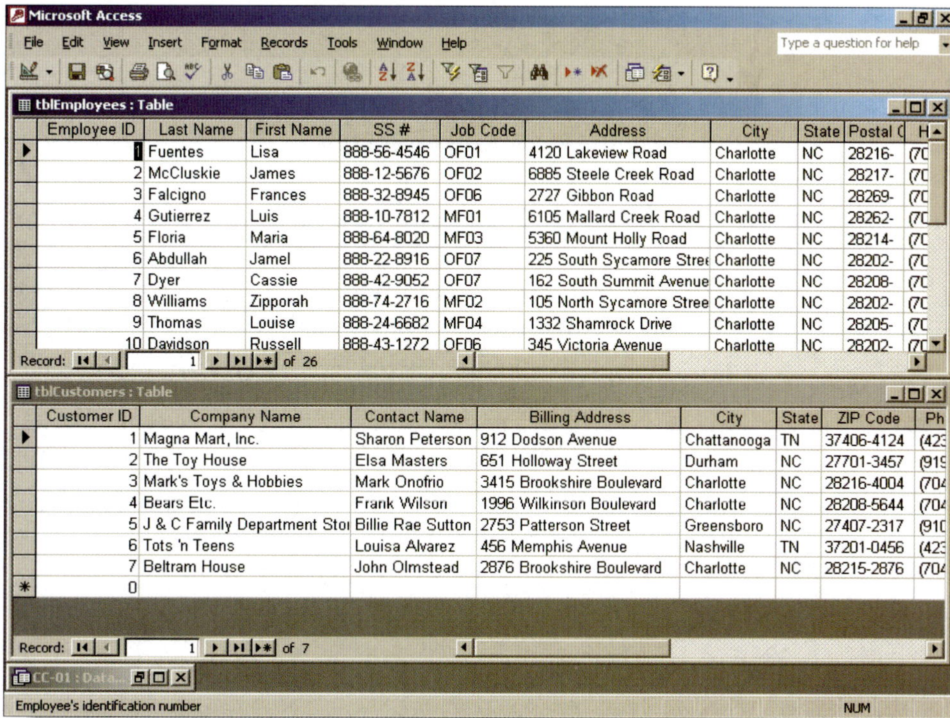

EXERCISE 1-13 Open Multiple Queries

1. Click Queries on the Objects bar. Open qryInventoryByAnimal.
2. Click the Database Window button on the toolbar.
3. Open qryStuffedAnimals.
4. Click the Database Window button. Click the Minimize button in the Database window to minimize it.
5. From the Window menu, choose Tile Vertically. The two queries are tiled.
6. Close both queries.
7. Click the Maximize button in the minimized Database window.

EXERCISE 1-14 Open a Table and a Query

1. Open qryOrderSummaryByAnimal.
2. Click the Database Window button.
3. Click Tables on the Objects bar. Open tblStuffedAnimals.
4. Click the Database Window button. Click the Minimize button.

5. From the Window menu, choose Tile Horizontally. The table and the query are tiled.
6. Close both objects.
7. Click the Maximize button in the minimized Database window.

Printing a Table and a Query

You can print a table or a query as it appears in Datasheet View. You can use any of these methods:

- Click the Print button on the Database toolbar
- Choose File, and then choose Print.
- Press Ctrl + P

The menu and keyboard methods open the Print dialog box, where you choose printing options. Clicking the Print button sends the document directly to the printer, using Access's default settings. It doesn't open the Print dialog box.

EXERCISE 1-15 Change Page Setup

You can set the page orientation to portrait (vertical) or landscape (horizontal). Landscape is better if a table or query contains many fields and you want to fit the data on one printed page.

1. Click Tables on the Objects bar. Open tblCustomers.
2. Choose File and then choose Page Setup to open the Page Setup dialog box. The Margins tab opens by default. This dialog box displays the default margin settings.

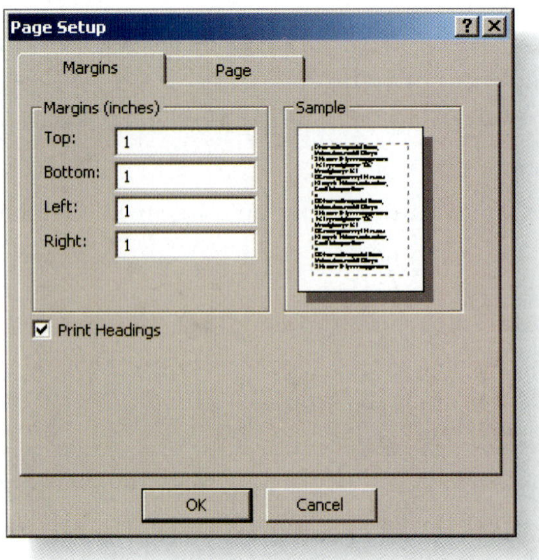

FIGURE 1-21 Page Setup dialog box with default margin settings

3. Click the Page tab. This dialog box displays the orientation, paper, and printer default settings. Click the Landscape option button. (See Figure 1-22 on the next page.)
4. Click OK to close the dialog box.

TIP: Check the orientation for each table or query you print.

FIGURE 1-22
Page Setup dialog box, Page tab

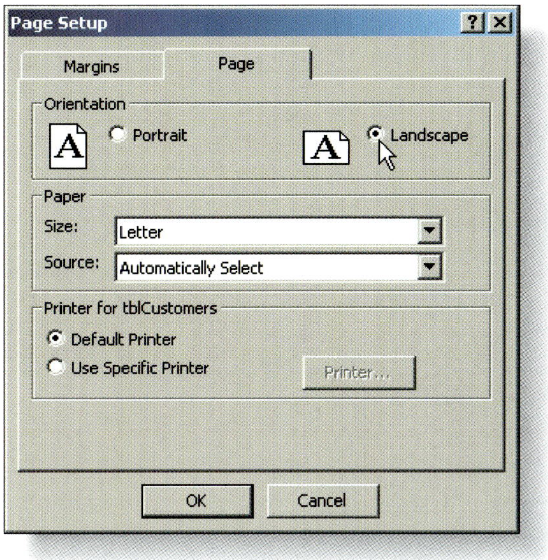

5. Click the Print Preview button to see how your table will print. You can also see how many pages will print.

FIGURE 1-23
Print Preview of Customers table

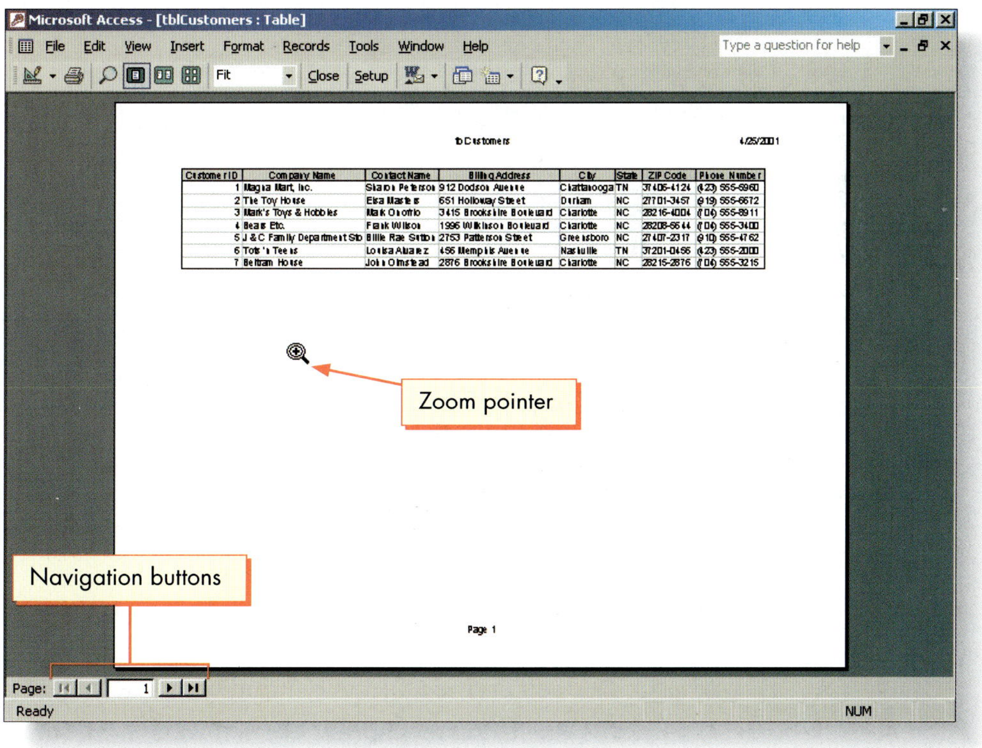

6. Click the Next Page button .

NOTE: Access tiles pages when tables are too wide for the printed page. Only columns that fit on a page print on that page. Columns are not cut in the middle.

7. Click Close to close the preview and return to the Customers table.

Close

TIP: The Close button Close closes the table, not just the preview.

EXERCISE 1-16 Print a Table

1. To print the Customers table, choose File and then choose Print. The Print dialog box opens with your default settings.

FIGURE 1-24
Print dialog box

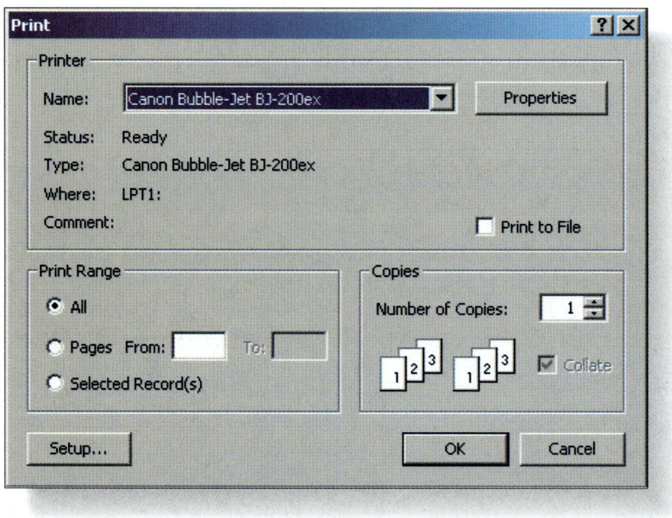

2. Click OK or press Enter to accept the settings. A printer icon appears on the taskbar as the table is sent to the printer.
3. Close the table.

EXERCISE 1-17 Preview and Print a Query

1. Click Queries on the Objects bar and open qryOrderSummaryByAnimal.
2. Click the Print Preview button. This query will fit in portrait orientation on one page.
3. Click the Print button. The query is sent to the printer.

TIP: You can print from the Print Preview window.

4. Click Close to close only the preview.

5. Close qryOrderSummaryByAnimal.

Compacting and Closing a Database and Exiting Access

When you finish working on a database, you should compact it to save disk space. As you work on a database, Access finds and uses space as quickly as it can. The database expands and is usually not as efficiently organized on the disk as it could be. The Compact and Repair Database command reclaims unused space and saves the database efficiently. After you compact the database, you can close it and open another database or you can exit the program.

NOTE: Compacting a database might be compared to running the defragment utility on your hard drive.

There are four ways to close a database and exit Access:

- Use the Close button [X] in the upper right corner of the window when the Database window is maximized.

FIGURE 1-25
Close buttons

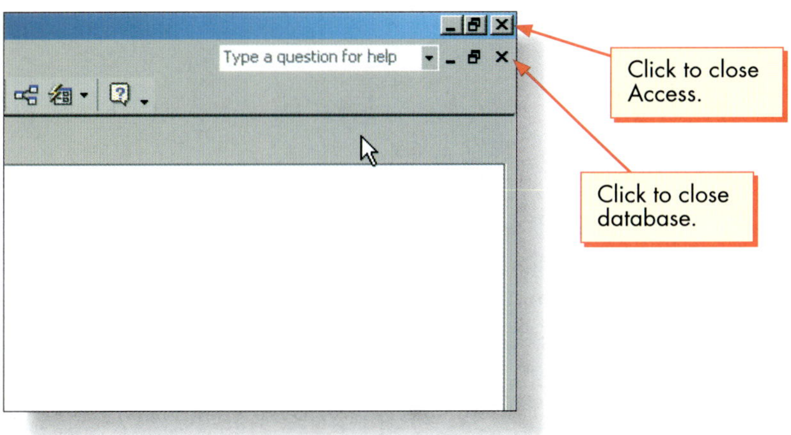

- Use the File menu.
- Use the Database Control icon in the upper left corner of the Database window title bar, next to the database name. Choose Close from the Database Control menu. (See Figure 1-26 on the next page.)

FIGURE 1-26
Control menus

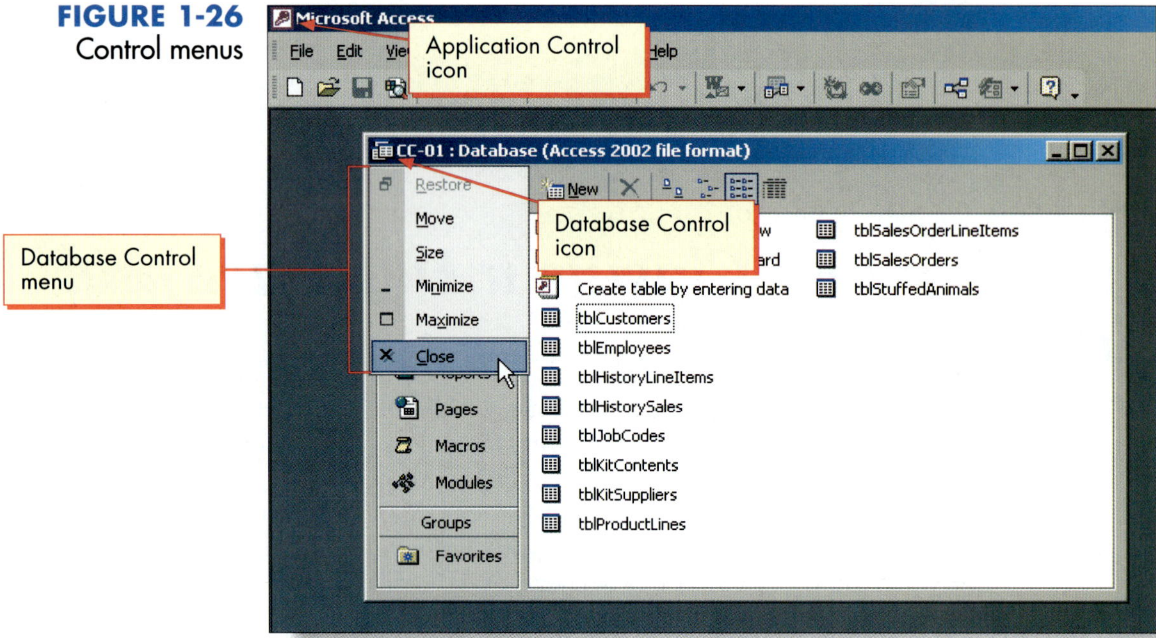

- Use keyboard shortcuts. Ctrl+W or Ctrl+F4 closes a database and Alt+F4 exits Access.

TIP: You can set Access to automatically compact the database each time it is closed by using Tools, Options.

EXERCISE 1-18 Compact and Close a Database and Exit Access

1. Choose Tools and choose Database Utilities. Then choose Compact and Repair Database. The database is compacted and remains open. (See Figure 1-27 on the next page.)
2. Click the Close button [X] to close the database.

NOTE: When no database is open, there is no Database window on the screen.

3. Copy your database file from the directory in which you were working. Paste it to your disk. After verifying that your database was properly copied, delete the copy of your database from the directory in which you were working.

FIGURE 1-27
Tools, Database Utilities menu

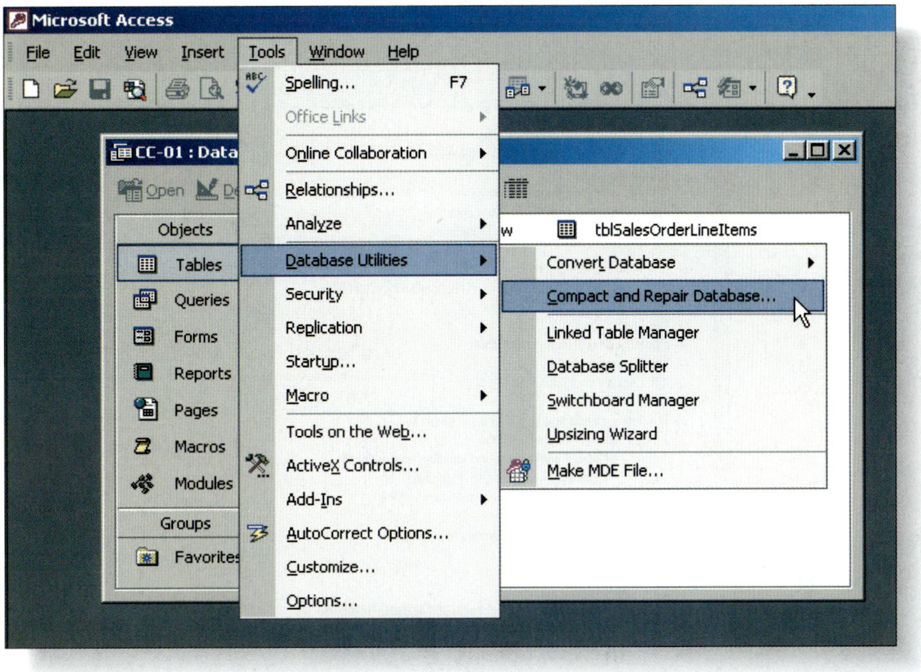

USING HELP

The Microsoft Access Help system is available at all times and is often the quickest and easiest way to determine how to complete a task.

Look up Access commands:

1. From Access, open ***[your initials]*****CC-01**.
2. Open the Help menu and choose Show the Office Assistant. The Office Assistant opens. If you do not see a text box above the Assistant, click the Assistant icon.
3. In the text box for "What would you like to do?" key **backup and restore**. Click Search.
4. In the list of topics, click Backup and restore an Access database.
5. The Microsoft Access window opens. Maximize the window. In the right pane, read the information.
6. In the left pane, click on the topic Compact and repair an Access file. Three topic links appear in the right pane.
7. Click on Compact and repair the current Access file. (See Figure 1-28 on the next page.)

FIGURE 1-28 Microsoft Access Help

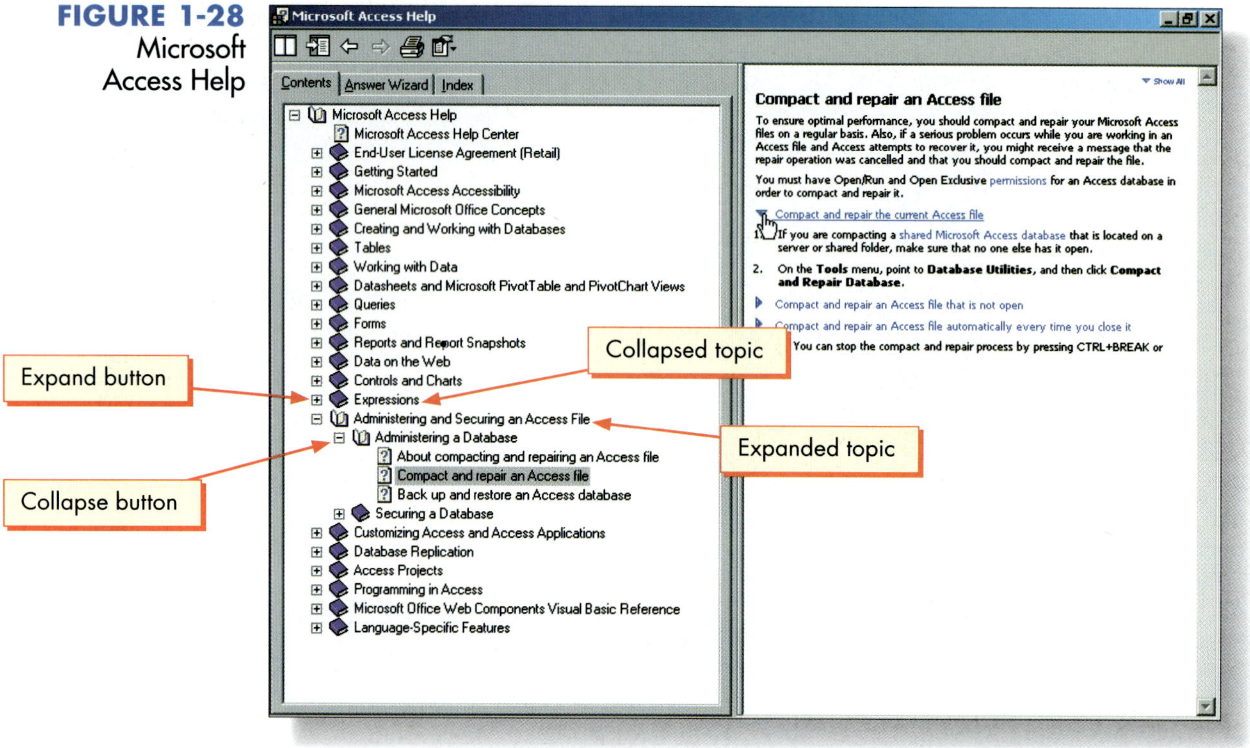

8. Read the Help for the expanded topic. Expand and read the remaining two topics.
9. Close the Help window.
10. Right-click the Office Assistant icon and choose Options. Turn off the option to Use the Office Assistant. The next time you use Help, the Office Assistant will not start unless someone else has turned it on.
11. Close the database.

LESSON 1 Summary

- After copying a file from a CD, you might need to remove the read-only attribute.
- The database properties provide useful information regarding specifications, summary information, statistics, and contents of the file.
- You can perform actions on a database through buttons and menus.
- You can select database objects through the Database window.
- Tables and queries have four different views: Datasheet View, Design View, PivotTable View, and PivotChart View.

- You can view records by scrolling through a Datasheet View.
- Navigation buttons provide efficient means of moving to different records of a Datasheet View.
- You can change column widths, row heights, and fonts in Datasheet View.
- Freeze fields in Datasheet View to lock columns on the far left side of the screen.
- Linked tables create multiple-table queries.
- Multiple tables and queries can be viewed at one time.
- Changing the page setup lets you print a table in landscape format.
- Printing a table displays the data stored in the table.
- You can use Print Preview to look at a table or query prior to actual printing.
- Periodically, you should compact your database.

LESSON 1 Command Summary

FEATURE	BUTTON	MENU	KEYBOARD	SPEECH
Close a document		File, Close	Ctrl + W or Ctrl + F4	✓
Column width		Format, Column Width		✓
Compact		Tools, Database Utilities, Compact and Repair Database		✓
Database Properties		File, Database Properties		✓
Datasheet View		View, Datasheet View		✓
Design View		View, Design View		✓
Exit Access		File, Exit	Alt + F4	✓
Freeze Columns		Format, Freeze Columns		✓
Font		Format, Font		✓
Open		File, Open	Ctrl + O	✓

continues

LESSON 1 Command Summary *continued*

FEATURE	BUTTON	MENU	KEYBOARD	SPEECH
Page Setup		File, Page Setup		✓
Print		File, Print	Ctrl + P	✓
Print Preview		File, Print Preview		✓
Query Properties		View, Properties	Alt + Enter	✓
Row Height		Format, Row Height		✓
Save		File, Save	Ctrl + S	✓
Table Properties		View, Properties	Alt + Enter	✓
Tile Windows Horizontally		Window, Tile Horizontally		✓
Tile Windows Vertically		Window, Tile Vertically		✓
Unfreeze Columns		Format, Unfreeze All Columns		✓

Concepts Review

TRUE/FALSE QUESTIONS

Each of the following statements is either true or false. Indicate your choice by circling T or F.

T F ***1.*** You can have only one object open at a time.

T F ***2.*** An active record can be identified by a triangle in the Record Selector area for that row.

T F ***3.*** A row in a table or query may have a different height than other rows.

T F ***4.*** You can use the navigation buttons to move to a specific record.

T F ***5.*** Records in a table or query do not appear in Datasheet View.

T F ***6.*** A query can use more than one table.

T F ***7.*** You can change the font for individual words in Datasheet View.

T F ***8.*** Freezing fields locks fields to keep them in view.

SHORT ANSWER QUESTIONS

Write the correct answer in the space provided.

1. What is the Leszynski Naming Convention prefix for table names?

____

2. Which buttons do you use to move to different records in a table or query?

____

3. Which view displays the records in columns and rows like an Excel worksheet?

____

4. What command locks a column on the left in a table?

____

5. What command compresses or condenses a database file?

____

6. Which button would move the pointer to Record #2 if it is at Record #3?

____

7. What dialog box contains the description, creation date, and modification date for a table or query?

---

8. Which table view displays the field names, data types, and field properties?

CRITICAL THINKING

Answer these questions on a separate page. There are no right or wrong answers. Support your answers with examples from your own experience, if possible.

1. Why might a person want to open more than one table at a time?

2. How are navigation buttons different from scroll bars? When would you use scroll bars? When would you use navigation buttons?

Lesson Applications

EXERCISE 1-19

Open a database, add a table description, and print a table.

1. Start Access and open ***[your initials]*CC-01**.
2. Rename tblKitSuppliers to show ***[your last name]*** at the end.
3. Open the Properties dialog box for tblKitSuppliers.
4. Key the following description:

   Table contains the supplier name, contact, address, and phone number of companies supplying kits for Carolina Critters.
5. Close the dialog box.
6. Open the table. Change the page orientation to Landscape.
7. Preview the table. Change the font and column size so the table will print on one page.

TIP: You can multiple-select all the columns and double-click one of the borders to AutoFit all columns at once.

8. Print the table. Close it without saving the design changes.
9. Rename tblKitSuppliers to remove ***[your last name]*** and any extra space.

EXERCISE 1-20

Open multiple tables. Switch views.

1. With ***[your initials]*CC-01** open, open tblStuffedAnimals.
2. Open tblProductLines.
3. Minimize the Database window and tile the tables.
4. What is the name of the product group for "Tula Tiger?" What is the product group for "Linda Lamb?" Write your answers on a separate sheet of paper.

TIP: The Stuffed Animals table includes images that do not display in Datasheet View. Line Code and Product Group represent the same data but have different field captions listed in the column heading.

5. Close both tables.
6. Restore the Database window.
7. Open tblKitContents.

8. Change to Design View. What data type is the Cost field? Write your answer on the same piece of paper you used for your answers in step 4.
9. Close the table. Write your name, class information, and today's date on your answer sheet and turn it in to your instructor.

EXERCISE 1-21

Edit the layout and print a query.

1. With ***[your initials]*CC-01** open, rename qryOrderSummaryByAnimal to show ***[your last name]*** at the end.
2. Open the query.
3. Size each column to fit its longest data.
4. Make the row height approximately twice its current height.
5. Print the query.
6. Close and save the layout changes.
7. Rename the query to remove ***[your last name]*** and any spaces.

EXERCISE 1-22 *Challenge Yourself*

Switch views. Change the row height, font, and orientation. Print a table. Compact a database.

1. Rename tblStuffedAnimals to include your last name.
2. Open the table. These are the products sold to retailers by Carolina Critters. Notice what type of information is contained in this table.
3. Switch to Design View for the table. What is the name of the field that contains an image of the product? Write your answer on a separate sheet of paper.
4. In Datasheet View, change the row height so the table shows approximately twice as much space between records.
5. Change the font to 11-point Times New Roman. Size the fields to fit the longest data.
6. Preview the table. While in Print Preview, change to Landscape orientation. Write down the number of pages required to print this table. Write your answer on the same piece of paper you used for your answers in step 3.
7. Print the table. Then close it without saving the layout changes.
8. Rename the table to remove ***[your last name]*** and any spaces.
9. Compact the database, close it, and exit Access. Write your name, class information, and today's date on your answer sheet and turn it in to your instructor.

On Your Own

In these exercises you work on your own, as you would in a real-life work environment. Use the skills you've learned to accomplish the task—and be creative.

NOTE: The "On Your Own" exercises in this text are all related. They form a single project. To complete the project, you must do *all* the "On Your Own" exercises in *each* lesson.

EXERCISE 1-23

You are forming a new club or professional association. Begin by analyzing your needs on paper. Write one or two paragraphs describing the purpose of your club or association and the information you will need to make your organization run efficiently. After you have completed this exercise, continue to the next exercise.

EXERCISE 1-24

Now think specifically about the kind of information your club or association will need to track membership. Write a bulleted list of information you want to collect for each member (ex: first name, email). You should have no fewer than seven items. Continue to the next exercise.

EXERCISE 1-25

Using the list you created in Exercise 1-24, gather information on five potential members. On a single sheet of paper, record the data you collected. Submit your work for Exercises 1-23 through 1-25 to your instructor.

LESSON 2

Adding and Editing Data

OBJECTIVES

MOUS ACTIVITIES

In this lesson:

Ac2002 1-2
Ac2002 1-3
Ac2002 2-1
Ac2002 3-1
Ac2002 4-1
Ac2002 4-2
Ac2002 5-1

See Appendix E.

After completing this lesson, you will be able to:

1. **Add and delete records.**
2. **Edit data in tables and queries.**
3. **Use text editing commands.**
4. **Add records in a form.**
5. **Change views in a form.**
6. **Print a form.**
7. **Edit records in a form.**
8. **Add a picture to a record.**

Estimated Time: 2 hours

In Lesson 1, you were introduced to tables and queries, two types of objects in a database. In this lesson, you continue your work with tables and queries and are introduced to forms. A form is based on a table or query and uses the same underlying data. Forms differ from tables and queries because the data is arranged in a screen format to improve the speed and accuracy of data entry.

In this lesson, you learn how to add and edit data in tables, queries, and forms. You use the duplicate, copy, and paste commands to copy data, which saves time and ensures accuracy. You also learn how to insert images into tables and forms.

A form is used to show data from a table or query. This data is commonly referred to as a *recordset.* A recordset produced from a table is the entire table itself. A recordset produced from a query can be an entire table, a portion of a table, or a combination of one or more tables.

Adding and Deleting Records

It is a simple process to add new records or to delete records that are no longer necessary. When a new student enrolls in your school, for example, a record is added to your school's database. If Carolina Critters discontinues one of their stuffed animals, the company can delete the product information from its database.

TIP: Before you delete a record, you can copy it into an inactive or "history" table so there is always some record of the data.

EXERCISE 2-1 Add Records to a Table

When you are in Datasheet View, you add new records at the end of the table. The row in which the new record will be added is marked by an asterisk in the Record Selector. You move to this new record row by clicking the New Record navigation button ▸* or the New Record button ▸* on the toolbar. The two New Record buttons look the same except that the toolbar button is in color.

REVIEW: The Record Selector is the narrow gray column to the left of the first field in the Datasheet View of a table or query.

You can also enter records by using the Data Entry command. This command hides the existing records while you add new ones.

1. Right-click the Start button Start on the Windows taskbar.
2. Choose Explore and click the Maximize button.
3. In the left pane, open folder Lesson 02 from the location where your Student Files are kept. Point at the filename **CC-02** and right-click.
4. Choose Copy from the shortcut menu.
5. In the left pane, open the My Documents folder. In an unused area of the right pane, right-click. Choose Paste from the shortcut menu.
6. Right-click **CC-02** and choose Rename. Key ***[your initials]*****CC-02** and press Enter.
7. Right-click ***[your initials]*****CC-02** and choose Properties. Make certain that the Read-only attribute check box is not checked. Click OK.

8. Click the Close button ✕ on the Explorer window.
9. Open Access. Locate and open the ***[your initials]*****CC-02** database.

10. Open tblCustomers and click the Maximize button. Click the New Record navigation button ▸*.

TIP: The keyboard shortcut to move to the new record is Ctrl + +.

11. Key the following to create a new record, pressing Tab between field entries. You will see a pencil icon in the Record Selector as you add the record.

TIP: Characters you don't have to key are shown in **blue**. Access automatically formats these fields to include the characters.

FIGURE 2-1 Pencil icon appears in the Record Selector when adding a record

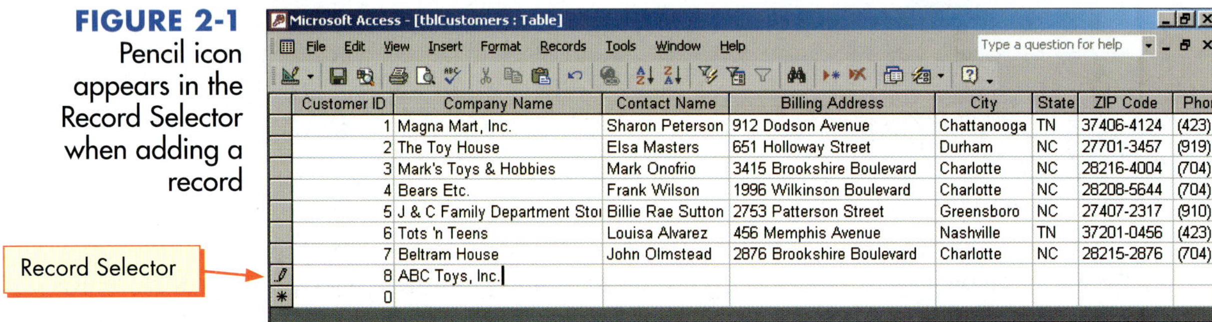

Customer ID	Company Name	Contact Name	Billing Address	City	State	ZIP Code	Phon
1	Magna Mart, Inc.	Sharon Peterson	912 Dodson Avenue	Chattanooga	TN	37406-4124	(423)
2	The Toy House	Elsa Masters	651 Holloway Street	Durham	NC	27701-3457	(919)
3	Mark's Toys & Hobbies	Mark Onofrio	3415 Brookshire Boulevard	Charlotte	NC	28216-4004	(704)
4	Bears Etc.	Frank Wilson	1996 Wilkinson Boulevard	Charlotte	NC	28208-5644	(704)
5	J & C Family Department Sto	Billie Rae Sutton	2753 Patterson Street	Greensboro	NC	27407-2317	(910)
6	Tots 'n Teens	Louisa Alvarez	456 Memphis Avenue	Nashville	TN	37201-0456	(423)
7	Beltram House	John Olmstead	2876 Brookshire Boulevard	Charlotte	NC	28215-2876	(704)
8	ABC Toys, Inc.						
0							

Customer ID:	**8**
Company Name:	**ABC Toys, Inc.**
Contact Name:	**Suzanne Parker**
Billing Address:	**9218 Park West Boulevard**
City:	**Knoxville**
State:	**TN**
ZIP Code:	**39723-9218**
Phone Number:	**(423) 555-1897**
Fax Number:	**(423) 555-1899**

NOTE: Depending on the table design, Access formats fields automatically. For example, you don't have to key the hyphen in the ZIP Code field or the parentheses, space, or hyphen in phone numbers.

12. The Tax Exempt field is a Yes/No field. Leaving it blank means "No." Press Tab to skip it and leave it blank. Access saves the entry and moves the pointer to the next row so you can add another record.

13. Choose Records and then choose Data Entry. Key the following to add another record:

NOTE: In this text, *red italic* indicates specific instructions for that field.

Customer ID:	**9**
Company Name:	**Children's Hospital**
Contact Name:	**Paul Scheider**
Billing Address:	**5274 West First Avenue**
City:	**Durham**
State:	**NC**
ZIP Code:	**27702-5274**
Phone Number:	**(919) 555-1000**
Fax Number:	**(919) 555-1050**
Tax Exempt?:	*Click the box for a check mark to indicate "Yes" and press* Tab.

TIP: You can toggle back and forth from "yes" to "no" in a check box field by pressing the Spacebar.

14. Open the Records menu and choose Remove Filter/Sort to view all records.
15. Click the Close button ☒ to close the table tblCustomers.

EXERCISE 2-2 Add Records in a Query

You can enter new records by using a query. Changes made in the query are simultaneously made to data in the underlying table. As you learn more about queries, you will see that many queries create recordsets that do not include all the fields or records in the table.

1. Click Queries on the Objects bar. Open qryCustomers and click the Maximize button ☐. Press Ctrl + + to move to a new record.
2. Key the following and press Tab between field entries. You will see the pencil icon as you add the record.

Customer ID:	**10**
Company Name:	**New City Circus**
Contact Name:	***[your first and last name]***
Billing Address:	**501 North Canal Street**
City:	**Norfolk**
State:	**VA**
ZIP Code:	**72723-0501**
Phone Number:	**(602) 555-1800**

Fax Number: (602) 555-1801

Tax Exempt?: *Press the* Spacebar *to indicate "Yes" and press* Tab.

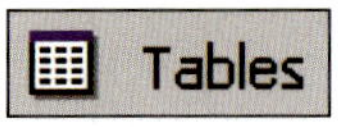

3. Click the Close button to close qryCustomers. Click Tables on the Objects bar.
4. Open tblCustomers and look for the New City Circus record. Because the query has all the same fields as the table, the record is complete.

EXERCISE 2-3 Delete Records from a Table

There are times when records are no longer needed and can be removed from a table. You also might have records that were entered in error and should be deleted.

You can use Delete, the Delete Record button or the Edit menu to delete a record. When you use Delete, you must first select the record(s) to delete.

NOTE: You can delete records from a query the same as in a table.

1. In the Datasheet View of the Customers table, click in the Record Selector to select the row for "Mark's Toys & Hobbies."

FIGURE 2-2
Selecting a record for deletion

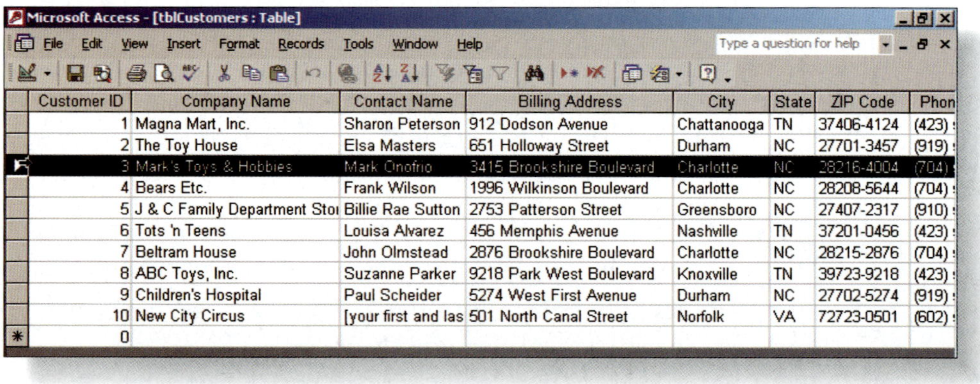

Customer ID	Company Name	Contact Name	Billing Address	City	State	ZIP Code	Phon
1	Magna Mart, Inc.	Sharon Peterson	912 Dodson Avenue	Chattanooga	TN	37406-4124	(423)
2	The Toy House	Elsa Masters	651 Holloway Street	Durham	NC	27701-3457	(919)
3	Mark's Toys & Hobbies	Mark Onofrio	3415 Brookshire Boulevard	Charlotte	NC	28216-4004	(704)
4	Bears Etc.	Frank Wilson	1996 Wilkinson Boulevard	Charlotte	NC	28208-5644	(704)
5	J & C Family Department Sto	Billie Rae Sutton	2753 Patterson Street	Greensboro	NC	27407-2317	(910)
6	Tots 'n Teens	Louisa Alvarez	456 Memphis Avenue	Nashville	TN	37201-0456	(423)
7	Beltram House	John Olmstead	2876 Brookshire Boulevard	Charlotte	NC	28215-2876	(704)
8	ABC Toys, Inc.	Suzanne Parker	9218 Park West Boulevard	Knoxville	TN	39723-9218	(423)
9	Children's Hospital	Paul Scheider	5274 West First Avenue	Durham	NC	27702-5274	(919)
10	New City Circus	[your first and las	501 North Canal Street	Norfolk	VA	72723-0501	(602)
0							

2. Press Delete. The record disappears, and a dialog box opens asking you to confirm the deletion. (See Figure 2-3 on the next page.)

NOTE: You cannot undo a deleted record.

3. Click Yes. Access deletes the record.
4. Click anywhere in the Company Name field for "J & C Family Department Stores" to make it the current record.

FIGURE 2-3
Dialog box confirming deletion

NOTE: When you use the keyboard shortcut or the toolbar button to delete a record, you do not need to select the record. Just click anywhere in the record.

5. Press Ctrl + F11 and then click Yes to confirm the deletion.
6. Click the Close button ☒ to close tblCustomers.

Editing Data in a Table or Query

You might have noticed that you do not need to "save" after you insert or delete a record. Access saves changes to a record as soon as you move the insertion point away from that record. If you move to the next record or a previous record, your changes are saved. You do not need to use the Save command when you edit, delete, or add records. You only use the Save command to save changes to the structure of your object.

TIP: To save your work in a lengthy record while you are editing it, open the Records menu and choose Save Record, or press Shift + Enter.

You can determine if a record was saved by the shape of pointer in the Record Selector. The Record Selector marks the current record and where the insertion point is located. The Record Selector has three shapes:

- A pencil appears when you add or edit text. This indicates the record changes have not been saved.
- A triangle indicates the record has been saved.
- An asterisk marks a new record.

EXERCISE 2-4 Delete Text in a Table

Keyboard shortcuts are available for basic text editing. Table 2-1 summarizes some of the most helpful keyboard shortcuts.

TABLE 2-1 Basic Text Editing

KEY	RESULT
Backspace	Deletes characters to the left of the insertion point.
Ctrl + Backspace	Deletes the word to the left of the insertion point.
Delete	Deletes characters to the right of the insertion point.
Ctrl + Delete	Deletes all the characters to the right of the insertion point to the end of the line.

1. Open tblEmployees in Datasheet View and click the Maximize button to maximize the window.
2. Move the insertion point to the right of the last name for Employee 8 "Williams." (Use the mouse to position the I-beam and click to place the insertion point.)

TIP: To add or insert text, the insertion point must look like an I-beam. A cross-shaped pointer selects the entire field. You cannot edit individual characters when the entire field is selected.

3. Press Backspace five times to delete five characters and key **son**. The Record Selector changes to a pencil symbol as you edit text. "Williams" is changed to "Wilson."

FIGURE 2-4
Editing data

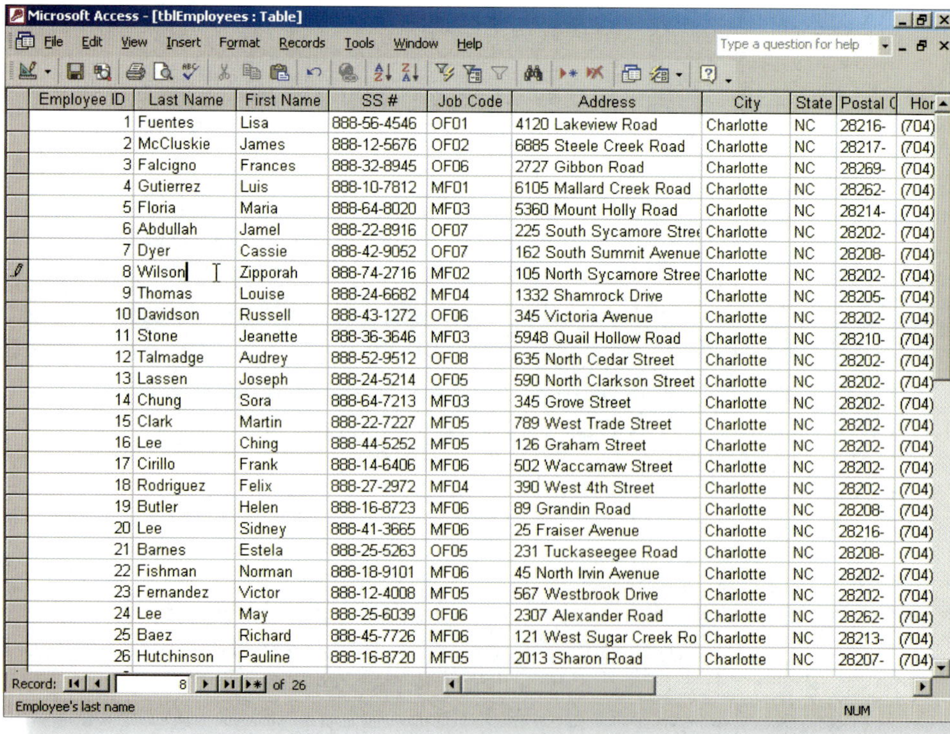

Employee ID	Last Name	First Name	SS #	Job Code	Address	City	State	Postal (	Hor
1	Fuentes	Lisa	888-56-4546	OF01	4120 Lakeview Road	Charlotte	NC	28216-	(704)
2	McCluskie	James	888-12-5676	OF02	6885 Steele Creek Road	Charlotte	NC	28217-	(704)
3	Falcigno	Frances	888-32-8945	OF06	2727 Gibbon Road	Charlotte	NC	28269-	(704)
4	Gutierrez	Luis	888-10-7812	MF01	6105 Mallard Creek Road	Charlotte	NC	28262-	(704)
5	Floria	Maria	888-64-8020	MF03	5360 Mount Holly Road	Charlotte	NC	28214-	(704)
6	Abdullah	Jamel	888-22-8916	OF07	225 South Sycamore Stre	Charlotte	NC	28202-	(704)
7	Dyer	Cassie	888-42-9052	OF07	162 South Summit Avenue	Charlotte	NC	28208-	(704)
8	Wilson	Zipporah	888-74-2716	MF02	105 North Sycamore Stree	Charlotte	NC	28202-	(704)
9	Thomas	Louise	888-24-6682	MF04	1332 Shamrock Drive	Charlotte	NC	28205-	(704)
10	Davidson	Russell	888-43-1272	OF06	345 Victoria Avenue	Charlotte	NC	28202-	(704)
11	Stone	Jeanette	888-36-3646	MF03	5948 Quail Hollow Road	Charlotte	NC	28210-	(704)
12	Talmadge	Audrey	888-52-9512	OF08	635 North Cedar Street	Charlotte	NC	28202-	(704)
13	Lassen	Joseph	888-24-5214	OF05	590 North Clarkson Street	Charlotte	NC	28202-	(704)
14	Chung	Sora	888-64-7213	MF03	345 Grove Street	Charlotte	NC	28202-	(704)
15	Clark	Martin	888-22-7227	MF05	789 West Trade Street	Charlotte	NC	28202-	(704)
16	Lee	Ching	888-44-5252	MF05	126 Graham Street	Charlotte	NC	28202-	(704)
17	Cirillo	Frank	888-14-6406	MF06	502 Waccamaw Street	Charlotte	NC	28202-	(704)
18	Rodriguez	Felix	888-27-2972	MF04	390 West 4th Street	Charlotte	NC	28202-	(704)
19	Butler	Helen	888-16-8723	MF06	89 Grandin Road	Charlotte	NC	28208-	(704)
20	Lee	Sidney	888-41-3665	MF06	25 Fraiser Avenue	Charlotte	NC	28216-	(704)
21	Barnes	Estela	888-25-5263	OF05	231 Tuckaseegee Road	Charlotte	NC	28208-	(704)
22	Fishman	Norman	888-18-9101	MF06	45 North Irvin Avenue	Charlotte	NC	28202-	(704)
23	Fernandez	Victor	888-12-4008	MF05	567 Westbrook Drive	Charlotte	NC	28202-	(704)
24	Lee	May	888-25-6039	OF06	2307 Alexander Road	Charlotte	NC	28262-	(704)
25	Baez	Richard	888-45-7726	MF06	121 West Sugar Creek Ro	Charlotte	NC	28213-	(704)
26	Hutchinson	Pauline	888-16-8720	MF05	2013 Sharon Road	Charlotte	NC	28207-	(704)

Record: 8 of 26
Employee's last name
NUM

ACCESS

4. Use the scroll bar to view the Address field. In Employee #2's record, click between the "6" and the "8" in the Address field.
5. Press Delete once and key **1**. The "6885" changes to "6185."
6. Move to Employee 5's record. In the Address field, click to the left of the word "Holly."
7. Press Ctrl + Backspace. The word "Mount" is deleted.
8. Move to Employee 13's record. In the Address field, click to the right of "Clarkson."
9. Press Ctrl + Delete to delete "Street." Press the spacebar once and key **Road**
10. Click the Close button ☒ to close tblEmployees.

EXERCISE 2-5 Insert Text in a Query

Queries do not store data. When you use a query to make changes to data, you are making changes to the recordset. You are really editing the same records in both the table and the query. When you edit a record in a query, the data in the underlying table is changed because the query's recordset is a subset of the table.

When editing a table or a query, you can insert text or use Overtype mode to key over existing text. Use Insert to switch between Insert and Overtype mode.

1. Click Queries on the Objects bar. Open qryEmployees. Notice that the changes you just made in the Employees table appear in this query.
2. Move to Employee 9's record. In the Last Name field, click to the right of "s" in "Thomas." Key a hyphen and then key **Smith**. As you are keying the name, the beginning of the last name might scroll out of view.
3. Move to Employee 10's record. In the First Name field, click to the left of "Russell."
4. Press Insert to switch to Overtype mode. When you are in Overtype mode, OVR appears on the status bar and the insertion point becomes a block when it is over a character.

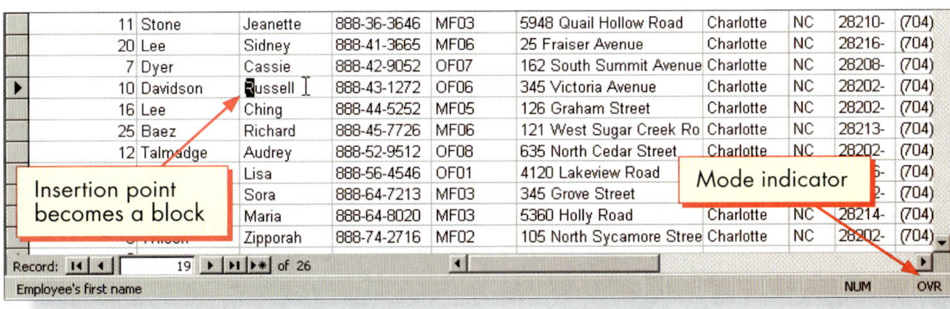

FIGURE 2-5 Overtype mode

5. Key **Raymond**
6. Click the Close button [X] to close qryEmployees.
7. Open qryCustomers in Datasheet View. You are still in Overtype mode.
8. In the "Bears Etc." record, click to the left of "Frank Wilson" in the Contact Name field.
9. Key ***[your first name & last name]*** over the old text. Delete any extra characters.

NOTE: In this text you are often asked to key an identifier such as your name or initials in a field so you can identify your work when you print. The identifier is shown in square brackets, but do not key the brackets.

10. Press Insert to turn off Overtype mode.
11. Click the Close button [X] to close qryCustomers.

Using Editing Commands

Text editing commands are used to make changes to the data within a record. A feature called *AutoCorrect* corrects commonly misspelled words as you key text—for example, correcting "teh" to "the." It also fixes many capitalization errors. There is an Undo command to undo your most recent edits. There are also Duplicate, Cut, Copy, and Paste commands.

EXERCISE 2-6 Correct Errors with AutoCorrect

1. From the Tools menu, choose AutoCorrect and look at the options available.

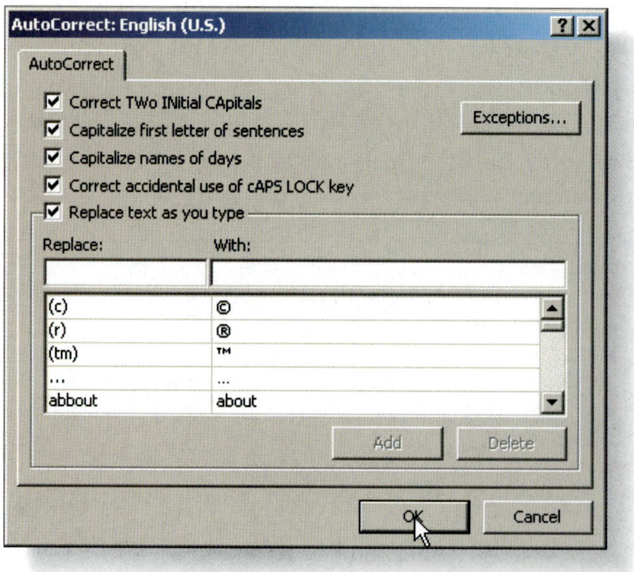

FIGURE 2-6 AutoCorrect dialog box

2. Scroll down the list of entries to see which words are in the AutoCorrect dictionary. Make sure the Replace text as you type option is checked.

NOTE: Microsoft Office products share AutoCorrect, so changes you make in Access affect Word, Excel, and PowerPoint.

TABLE 2-2

AutoCorrect Options

OPTIONS	DESCRIPTION
Correct TWo INitial CApitals	Corrects words keyed with two initial capital letters, such as "THis."
Capitalize first letter of sentence	Capitalizes the first letter in a sentence.
Capitalize names of days	Capitalizes days of the week and months.
Correct accidental use of cAPS LOCK key	Corrects words keyed with Caps Lock on but Shift key pressed, such as cAPS.
Replace text as you type	Makes corrections as you work.

3. Click Cancel to close the dialog box.
4. Click Tables on the Objects bar. Open tblKitContents and maximize the window. Press Ctrl + + to open a new record.
5. Key **Zeb002** in the Kit Number field. Press Tab three times to move to the Kit Contents field.
6. In the Kit Contents field, key **i want teh kit to contain teh follwoing materials** (key a period after the sentence). The field scrolls as you key the sentence, and Access corrects "i," "teh," and "following."

TIP: AutoCorrect makes the correction as soon as you press the spacebar or move the pointer away from the record.

7. Next, key this sentence with the errors (include the period): **TOdya is tuesday.** Access fixes the capitalization.
8. Press CapsLock to lock capitalization. Key **The**, holding down Shift for the "T." Press the spacebar and "tHE" is changed to "The."

9. Delete the record you just keyed by clicking the Delete Record button on the toolbar. Click Yes to confirm the deletion.
10. Press CapsLock to turn off capitalization. Close tblKitContents.

EXERCISE 2-7 Duplicate a Field and Use Undo

You can duplicate the data from a field in the previous record to the same field in the next record by pressing Ctrl + ' (apostrophe). The Duplicate command copies one field at a time.

Access remembers changes to the data and lets you undo most edits. If you accidentally delete text in a field, you can use the Undo command to reverse the action. There are three ways to undo an action:

- Click the Undo button on the toolbar.
- Press Ctrl + Z.
- From the Edit menu, choose Undo.

1. Open tblCustomers and click the maximize button to maximize the window. Click the New Record button on the toolbar.
2. Key **11** as the Customer ID and press Tab.
3. Press Ctrl + ' to duplicate the company name. Press Tab.
4. Press Ctrl + ' to duplicate the Contact Name and press Tab.
5. Complete the record shown here. Press Ctrl + ' for duplicate fields.

Billing Address:	**123 Orchard Lane**
City:	**Norfolk**
State:	**VA**
ZIP Code:	**72723-0123**
Phone Number:	**(602) 555-1023**
Fax Number:	**(602) 555-1051**
Tax Exempt?:	**Yes**

6. Click to the left of your name in this record. Press Ctrl + Delete.

7. Click the Undo button on the toolbar to restore your name.

TIP: The ScreenTip for the Undo button includes the name of the action, such as "Undo Delete" or "Undo Typing."

8. In the Magna Mart record, click to the left of "Avenue." Press Insert to start Overtype mode. Then key **Road** and press the spacebar. Press Insert to turn off Overtype mode. Delete any remaining characters.
9. Press Ctrl + Z twice to restore "Avenue."
10. Click anywhere in Record 11. Press Ctrl + F11 and click Yes. Notice that the Undo button is gray (meaning it is unavailable).

REVIEW: As soon as you move the insertion point away from a record, the record is saved.

11. Close tblCustomers without saving any changes.

EXERCISE 2-8 Use Copy, Paste, the Office Clipboard, and Paste Append

You can copy a block of text from one part of a table to another. There are several ways to copy and paste text:

- Click the Copy and Paste buttons on the toolbar.
- Press Ctrl+C (copy) and Ctrl+V (paste).
- Choose Copy and Paste from the Edit menu.
- Right-click and choose Copy and Paste from the shortcut menu.

You can use the Office Clipboard to paste multiple blocks of text. When you paste the second text block, the Office Clipboard pane opens. From that pane, you can select the item you want to paste.

NOTE: The Windows Clipboard lets you paste one item at a time. Text on the Windows Clipboard can be pasted repeatedly until you place new text on the Clipboard.

You can also paste an entire record from one location to another by using the Paste Append command.

1. Open tblEmployees. Click the New Record button. Key the following, leaving the Job Code field blank.

Employee ID:	**27**
Last Name:	**Kwan**
First Name:	**Sam**
SS#:	**888-11-2222**
Job Code:	*Leave blank.*
Address:	**111 Westbrook Drive**
City:	*Press* Ctrl+'
State:	*Press* Ctrl+'
Postal Code:	**28202-3876**
Home Phone:	**(704) 555-1111**
Emergency Contact:	**John Smith**
Emergency Phone:	**(704) 555-1112**
Photograph:	*Press* Tab *to skip.*

2. Double-click **MF04** in any record to select it.

3. Click the Copy button on the toolbar to place a copy of the text on the Windows Clipboard. Notice that the selected text remains in its original location.
4. Click in the Job Code field in the record you just added.

5. Click the Paste button. A copy of MF04 is pasted into the field.
6. Double-click "Fishman" in Employee ID 22's record. Click the Copy button. The Office Clipboard pane opens with icons for both copied text blocks. If the Office Clipboard is not open, choose Edit and then choose Office Clipboard.

TIP: The first copied text should still be available for pasting and shown on the Office Clipboard pane. The buttons on the Clipboard pane have identifying ScreenTips.

7. Double-click "Helen" in Employee ID 19's record. Click the Copy button on the Clipboard pane.

FIGURE 2-7
Using the Office Clipboard

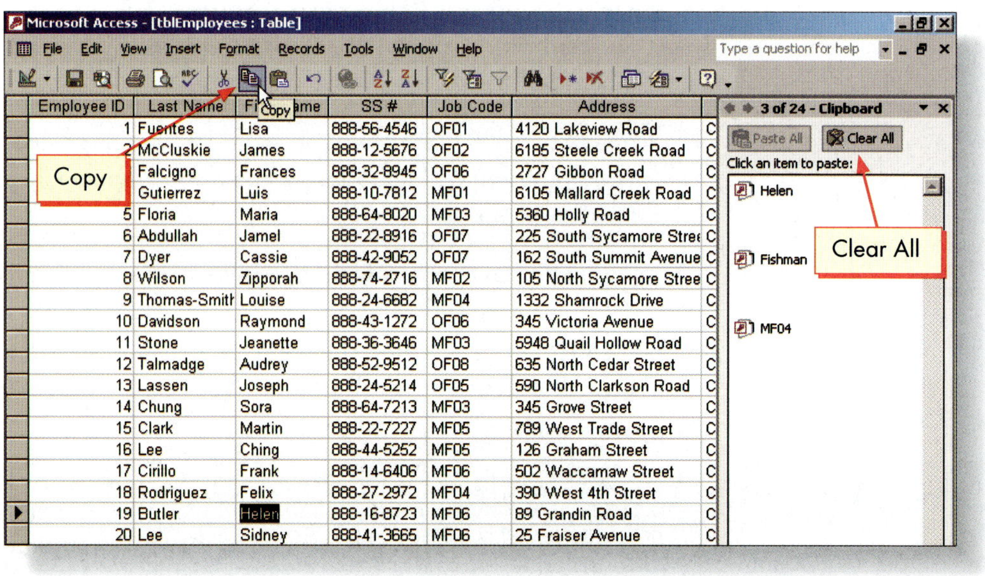

REVIEW: You must use the I-beam pointer to select text.

8. Select "567 Westbrook Drive" in Employee ID 23's record. Click the Copy button. Another icon is added to the Clipboard pane.
9. Click the New Record button. Key the following.

Employee ID:	**28**
Last Name:	***Click the last name icon on the Clipboard pane.***
First Name:	***Click the first name icon on the Clipboard pane.***
SS#:	**888-33-1234**

ACCESS

Job Code:	**OF06**
Address:	*Click the address icon on the Clipboard pane.*
City:	*Press* Ctrl+'
State:	*Press* Ctrl+'
Postal Code:	**28202-3576**
Home Phone:	**(704) 555-1137**
Emergency Contact:	**Michael Fishman**
Emergency Phone:	**(704) 555-1137**
Photograph:	*Press* Tab *to skip.*

10. Click the Clear All button. Click the Close button to close the Clipboard pane.

11. Click in the Record Selector for Employee 28 to select the record. The entire row is highlighted.

12. Click the Copy button. Click the New Record button.

13. Choose Edit and then choose Paste Append. The record is copied.

NOTE: You must change the Social Security number so you do not duplicate it in the table.

14. Change the Employee ID in the pasted record to **29**. Change the SS# to **888-33-0000**

15. Drag in the Record Selector area to select Employee IDs 28 and 29. Both rows are highlighted.

16. Click the Delete Record button and click Yes.

17. Close tblEmployees.

Adding Records in a Form

A form is an Access object in which you can enter, view, sort, edit, and print data, much as you can with a table or a query. A form, however, is designed for screen work, so it is often easier to use than a table. A form has navigation buttons and scroll bars and the same text editing features as a table. A form is linked to a table or query and can show the same fields of a record—it just shows them in a different layout on the screen.

EXERCISE 2-9 Navigate in a Form

You move the insertion point in a form just as you do in a table or query. The navigation buttons are at the bottom of the window. You'll see horizontal and vertical scroll bars when the form is larger than the screen.

1. Click Forms on the Objects bar. The window lists the forms in the current database. Forms should have a *frm* prefix.
2. Double-click frmEmployeeInformation to open it and maximize the window. The navigation buttons are at the bottom left corner of the form.

NOTE: To reduce the size of this database, not all records have images. Images can make databases very large.

FIGURE 2-8
Employee Information Form

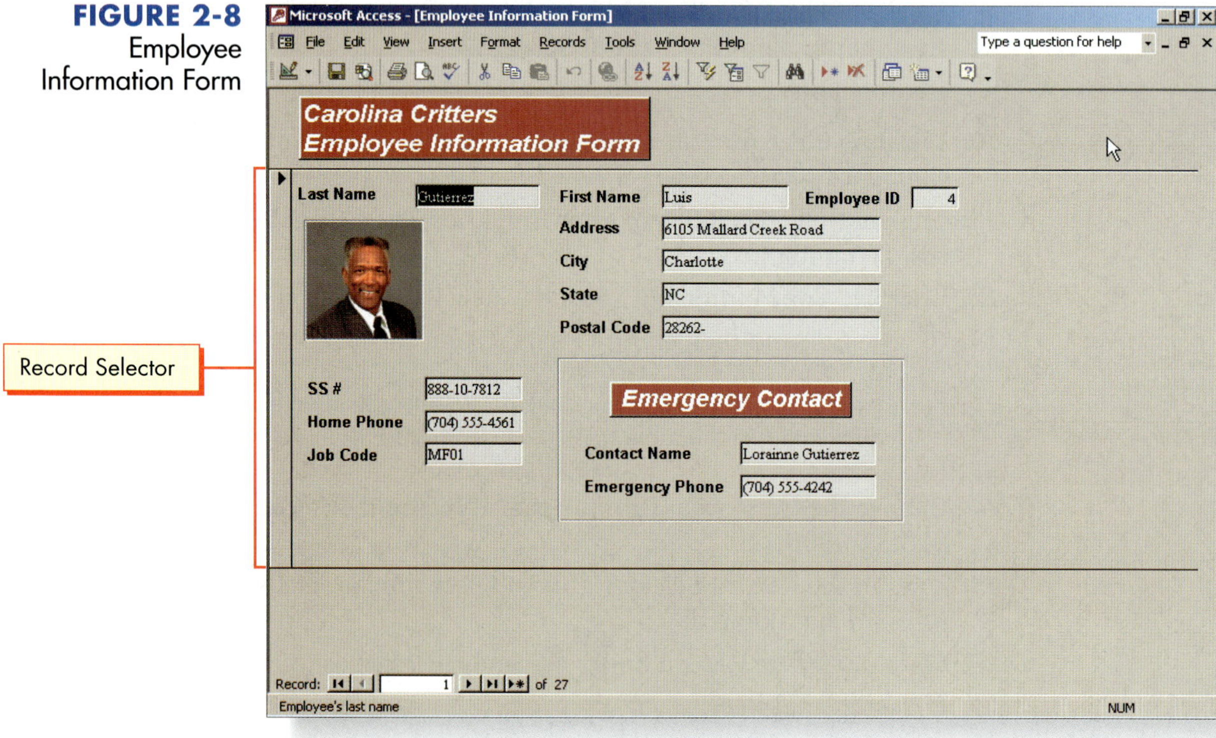

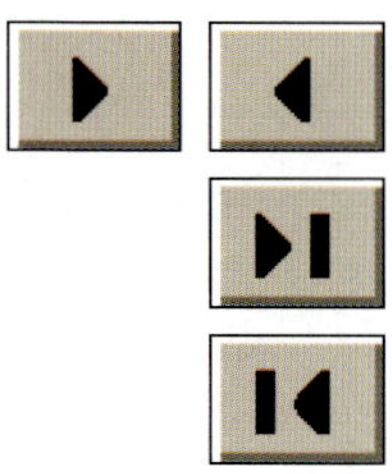

3. Click the Next Record button ▶ until James McCluskie's record appears. If you pass the record, click the Previous Record button ◀.
4. Click the Last Record button ▶|. The pointer moves to the last employee, Zipporah Wilson.
5. Click the First Record button |◀ to move back to the first record, Luis Gutierrez.
6. Press PgDn several times to move forward through the records. Press PgUp to move backward through the records.

EXERCISE 2-10 Add Records with a Form

Forms make it easier to add records, because they can be designed to reproduce the appearance of a paper document. You see one record at a time, often enabling you to see all the fields at once. The fields on the form are from the table but do not have to be in the same order as in the table.

1. With frmEmployeeInformation open, click the New Record button ▶*. A blank form opens.

NOTE: Because you cannot see the previous record when adding a new record, using the Duplicate command Ctrl+' is difficult in a form.

2. Key the following new record, pressing Tab between entries:

Last Name:	**Woodsik**
First Name:	**Sophie**
Employee ID:	**28**
Address:	**456 Victoria Avenue**
City:	**Charlotte**
State:	**NC**
Postal Code:	**28202-7997**
SS#:	**888-55-1111**
Home Phone:	**(704) 555-1601**
Job Code:	**OF06**
Contact Name:	**Howard Woodsik**
Emergency Phone:	**(704) 555-1662**

NOTE: You will insert pictures later in this lesson.

FIGURE 2-9
Pencil icon appears in the Record Selector when entering or editing data in a form

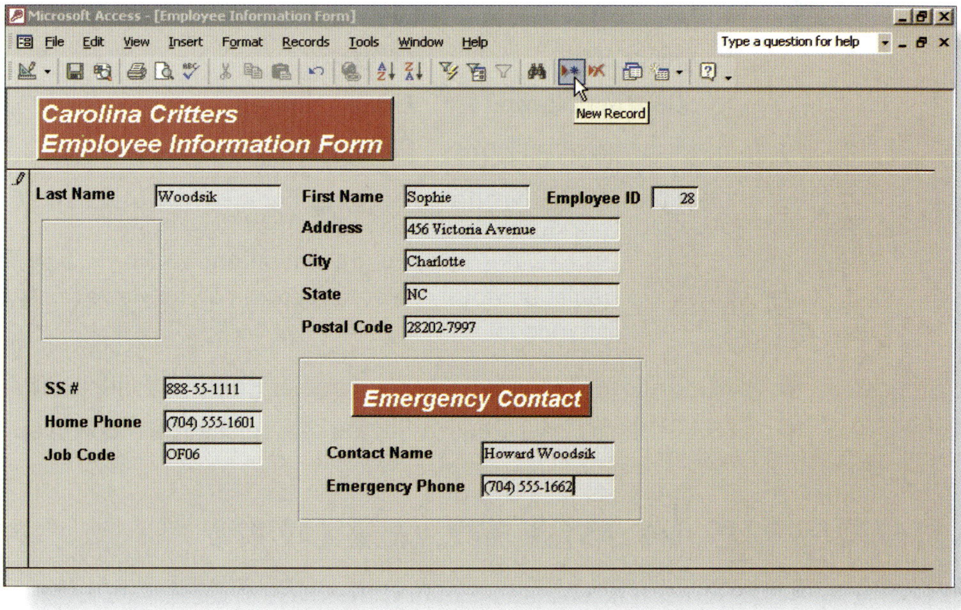

3. Press PgUp several times. The other records are visible, one record per screen.
4. Close the form. Click Tables on the Objects bar and open tblEmployees.
5. Click the Last Record button ▶| to see Sophie's record.
6. Close tblEmployees.

EXERCISE 2-11 Add Records with the Data Entry Command

You can also use the Data Entry command to enter records in a form.

NOTE: When you're using the Data Entry command, existing records are not displayed in the form. You aren't able to navigate through existing records.

1. Open frmEmployeeInformation.
2. Choose Records and then choose Data Entry. Key the following:

Last Name:	**Willis**
First Name:	**Marjorie**
Employee ID:	**29**
Address:	**7737 Derby Avenue**
City:	**Charlotte**
State:	**NC**
Postal Code:	**28202-6443**
SS#:	**888-77-1135**
Home Phone:	**(704) 555-1828**
Job Code:	**MF03**
Contact Name:	**Ellen Gilroy**
Emergency Phone:	**(704) 555-4998**

3. Press PgUp. Nothing happens, because the other records are hidden.

NOTE: When you are entering new records, only the current record is visible. Previously entered records can be viewed only by exiting the Data Entry mode.

4. Choose Records and then choose Remove Filter/Sort.
5. Click the Last Record button ▶| to see the record you entered.

Changing Views in a Form

As with a table and a query, there are several ways to view a form:

TABLE 2-3 Ways to View a Form

VIEW	DESCRIPTION
Form View	Appears when you open a form. You enter data, edit data, and find records in Form View.
Design View	Lets you create or modify the layout of the form. You don't see records in Design View. You see controls, which include labels and text boxes. *Controls* are objects that display information, perform actions, or enhance the appearance of a form or report. *Labels* display text, such as a title, and *text boxes* show data that is stored in fields.
Datasheet View	Displays the records in the default table style.
PivotTable View	Displays summarized data in a table format with columns and rows. Different levels of detail can be viewed.
PivotChart View	Displays data in a chart form. Different levels of detail can be viewed.

In addition to these basic views, you can set a form to show one record at a time, or as many records as will fit on the screen.

EXERCISE 2-12 Use Form and Design Views

1. With frmEmployeeInformation open, click the drop-down arrow next to the View button. The shortcut menu includes Design View, Form View, and Datasheet View. The highlighted icon indicates the current view.

FIGURE 2-10
View menu

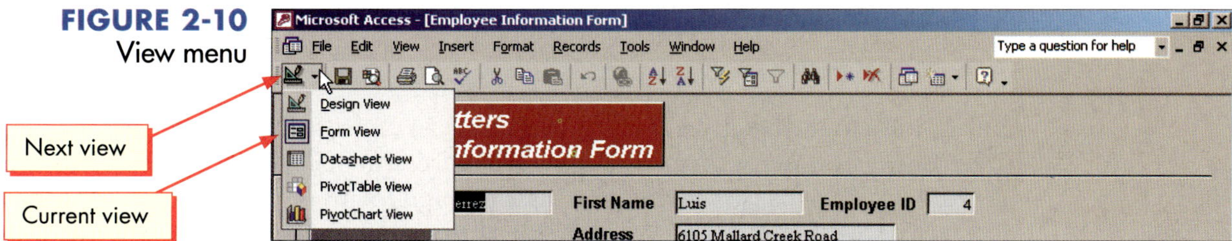

2. Choose Design View from the shortcut menu to display the Employee Information Form in Design View. This view shows controls for the form's labels and text boxes. Notice that records do not appear in this view.

3. Click the View button, not the drop-down arrow. The form now appears in Form View.
4. Click the View button again to return to Design View.

FIGURE 2-11
Employee Information Form in Design View

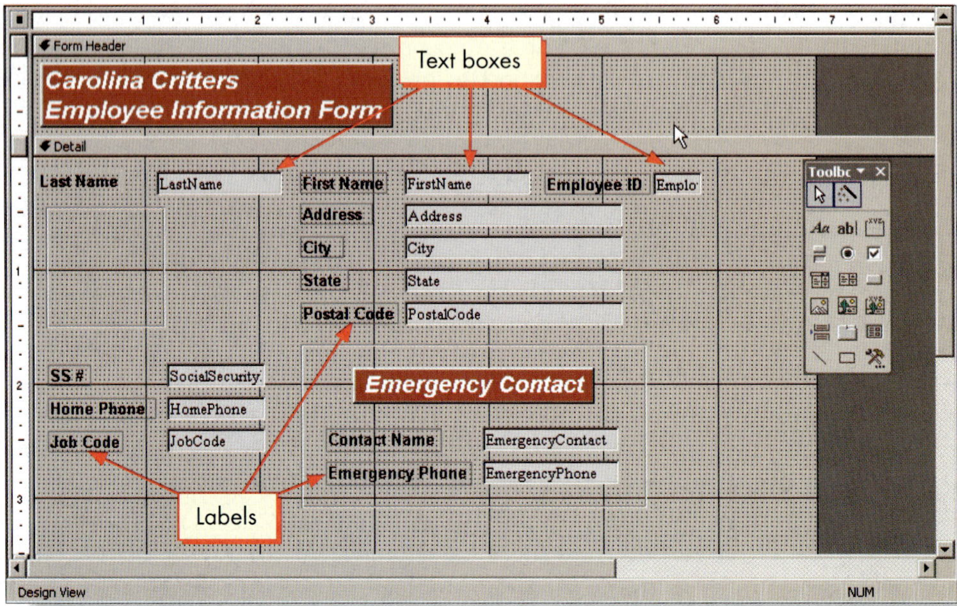

5. Press Ctrl+> to go from Design View to Form View and Ctrl+< to go from Form View to Design View.

NOTE: The View button toggles between Design View and Form View. The button shows the view to which you can switch.

EXERCISE 2-13 Change the Default View for a Form

In addition to the basic ways of looking at a form, Access has another setting that determines how many forms you see on the screen at once. All Access objects have a *property sheet* that lists attributes, settings, and formats for that object. A form's property sheet includes a *Default View* setting that controls how many records are shown onscreen at once.

1. In Design View, click the small etched rectangle at the left edge of the horizontal ruler. This is the Form Selector button. When the form is selected, the rectangle shows a small black square. (See Figure 2-12 on the next page.)

FIGURE 2-12
Selected form

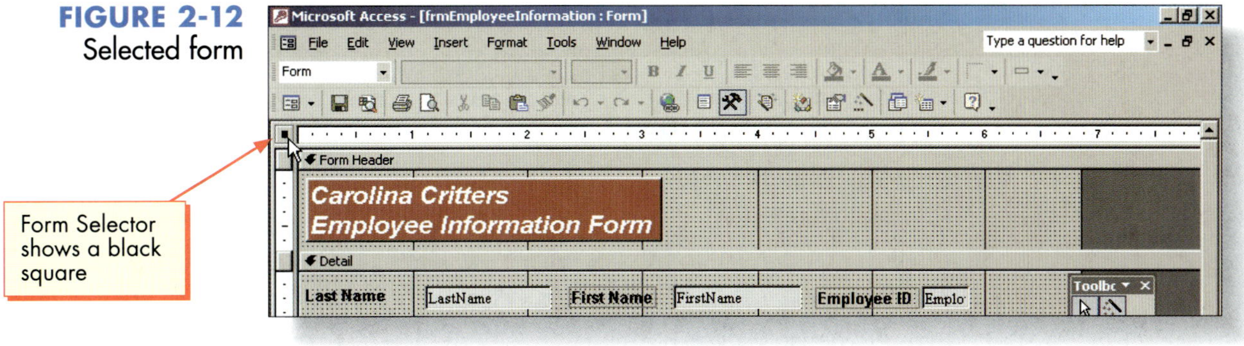

2. Click the Properties button on the toolbar. The Form property sheet opens.

NOTE: A property sheet is a window that can be sized and moved.

3. Click the **Format** tab. The current Default View is Single Form.
4. Click the **Default View** row and then click the drop-down arrow. Choose **Continuous Forms**.

FIGURE 2-13
Form property sheet

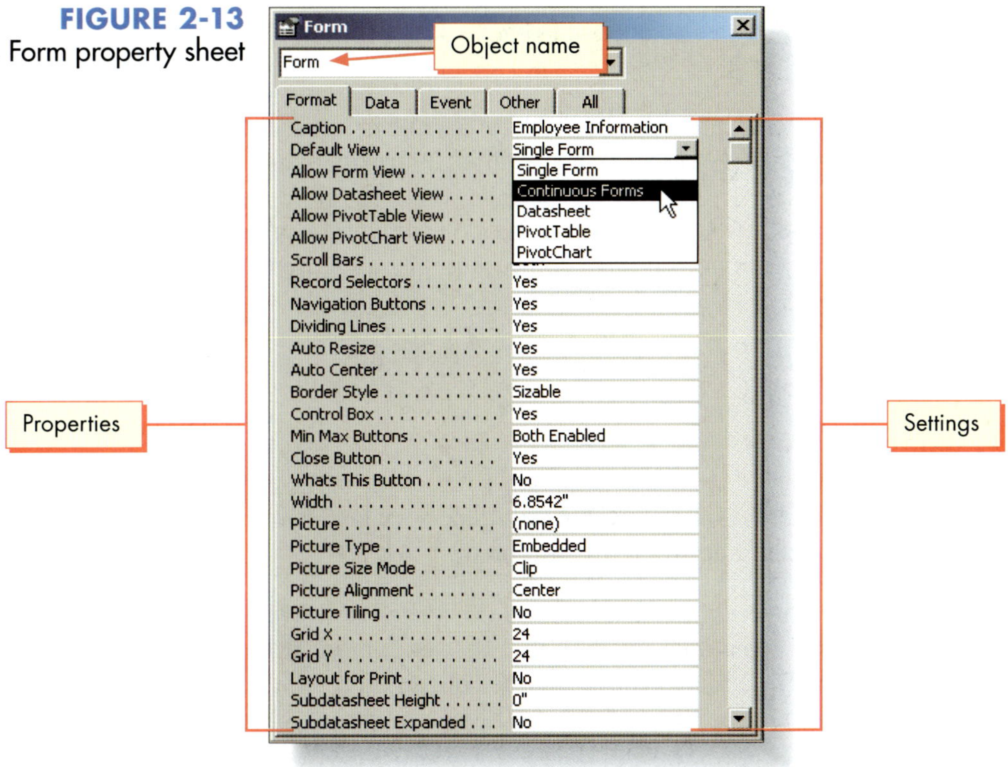

5. Click the View button. The form shows as many forms as can fit on your screen. (This depends on your screen size. You might see only one form.)
6. Use the vertical scroll bar to look at several forms.
7. Click the View button.
8. Click the **Default View** row in the property sheet and its drop-down arrow. Choose **Datasheet**.
9. Click the View button. The form now shows the records like a table.
10. Click the View button. Click the **Default View** row and the drop-down arrow. Choose **Single Form**.
11. Click the Close button to close the Form property sheet.
12. Click the View button.

Printing a Form

The design and layout of a form is optimized for the screen. Although forms are designed for screen work, you can preview and print them. Use any of these methods to print a form:

- Click the Print button on the toolbar.
- From the **File** menu, choose **Print**.
- Press Ctrl+P.

If you click the Print button, all the forms are printed with your default print settings. If there are 29 records in the table, 29 forms print. One form prints for each record.

The menu and keyboard commands open the Print dialog box so you can set a print range or change the page setup. A print range designates certain forms for printing.

EXERCISE 2-14 View a Form in Print Preview

Print Preview shows how your form will look on paper. You might need to change margins or the orientation before you print.

1. Click the Print Preview button to open the Print Preview window. You will probably see a message box that the section width is wider than the page width. This means the form does not fit on the page and requires two or more pages. (See Figure 2-14 on the next page.)

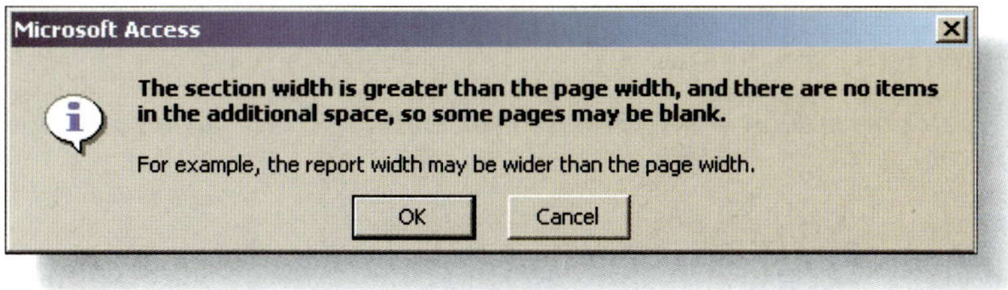

FIGURE 2-14
Page width message box

NOTE: The preview of the Employee Information Form shows two records. The height and width of a form determines the number of records that print per page.

2. Click OK. A preview of the Employee Information Form appears.

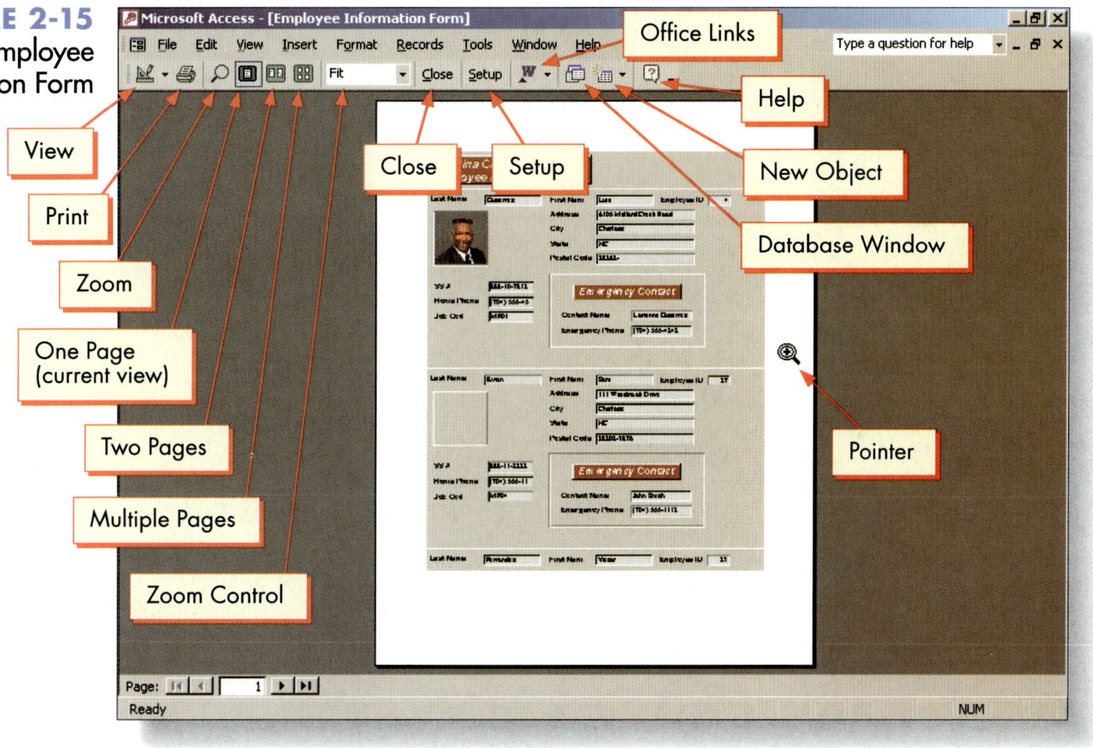

FIGURE 2-15
Preview of Employee Information Form

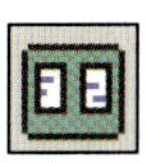

3. Click the Two Pages button. This displays two pages, side by side. The gray vertical bar on the second page is the part of the form that is too wide to fit. It is just part of the form's background. (See Figure 2-16 on the next page.)

4. Click the pointer anywhere on page 1. This enlarges the form, or zooms in. Click the pointer anywhere to reduce the form (zoom out).

NOTE: The pointer is a magnifying glass with a plus (zoom in) or minus sign (zoom out).

FIGURE 2-16
Viewing two pages

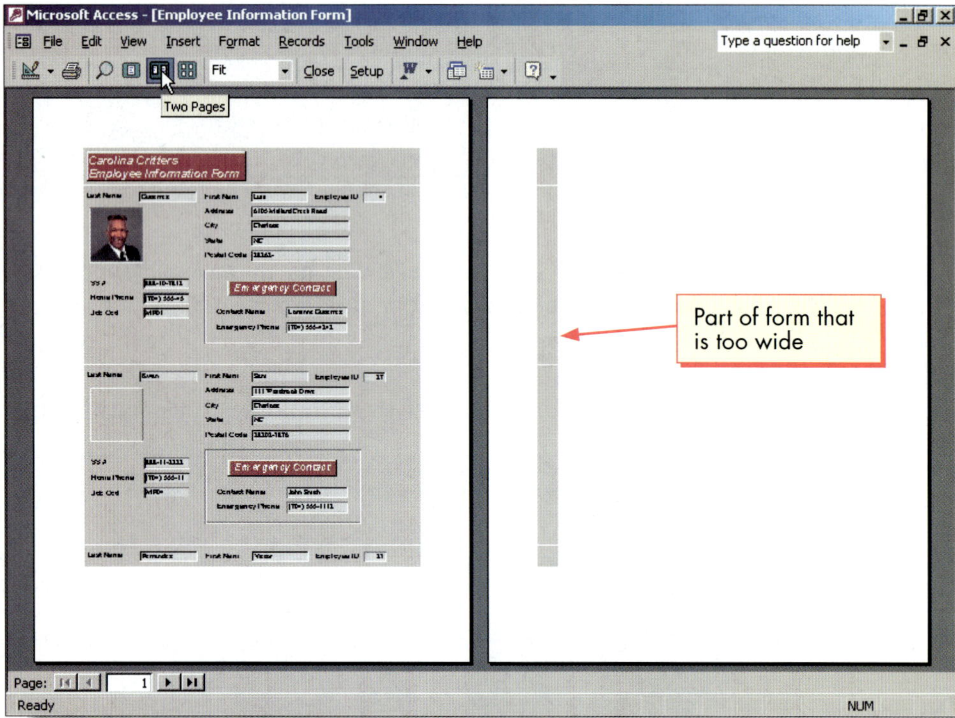

TABLE 2-4 Print Preview Toolbar Buttons

BUTTON/NAME	FUNCTION
View	Switches to Design, Form, Datasheet, PivotTable, or PivotChart View.
Print	Prints the form.
Zoom	Enlarges or reduces the view.
One Page	Displays one page.
Two Pages	Displays two pages.
Multiple Pages	Displays a grid of multiple pages.

continues

TABLE 2-4 Print Preview Toolbar Buttons *continued*

BUTTON/NAME	FUNCTION
Fit Zoom Control Box	Displays a list of view sizes.
Close	Closes Print Preview and returns to Design or Form View.
Office Links	Opens a drop-down list of related Office commands.
Database Window	Opens the Database window.
New Object	Opens a drop-down list of new objects you can create.
Office Help	Opens the Help system.

5. Click the drop-down arrow next to the Zoom Control box and choose 50%.

FIGURE 2-17
Zoom Control menu

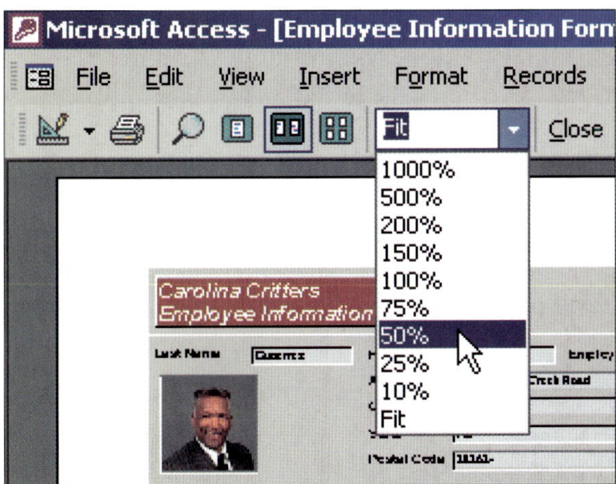

6. Click the One Page button.
7. Close Print Preview by clicking the Close button Close in the middle of the Print Preview toolbar.

TIP: You can use the same Print Preview buttons for a table, query, form, report, or data access pages.

EXERCISE 2-15 Print a Single Form

To print the form for one record (employee), you must select that form in Form View on the screen. You must also choose the Selected Records option in the Print dialog box.

NOTE: The default print range for a form is All records. If you want to print only one record, be very certain you select a record and change the Print Range option in the Print dialog box.

You can set the print orientation to landscape for a form just as for a table or query. This is helpful if the form is wide and doesn't fit on one printed page.

1. With frmEmployeeInformation open, choose File, and then choose Page Setup.
2. Click the Page tab to see the orientation, paper size, and printer.
3. Click the Landscape option button. Click OK to close the dialog box.
4. Click the Print Preview button. After you view the preview, click the Close button Close to close the Preview window.
5. Press PgDn as many times as necessary to move to Record 3 for James McCluskie.
6. Click in the Record Selector area to select the record.

REVIEW: The Record Selector is the narrow bar to the left of the labels and text boxes.

7. Choose File, Print to open the Print dialog box.

TIP: Make sure you don't press the Print button on the toolbar. This will print every record in the table.

8. Click Selected Record(s) as the Print Range. (See Figure 2-18 on the next page.)
9. Click OK to print the form.
10. Click the Close button to close the form without saving changes.

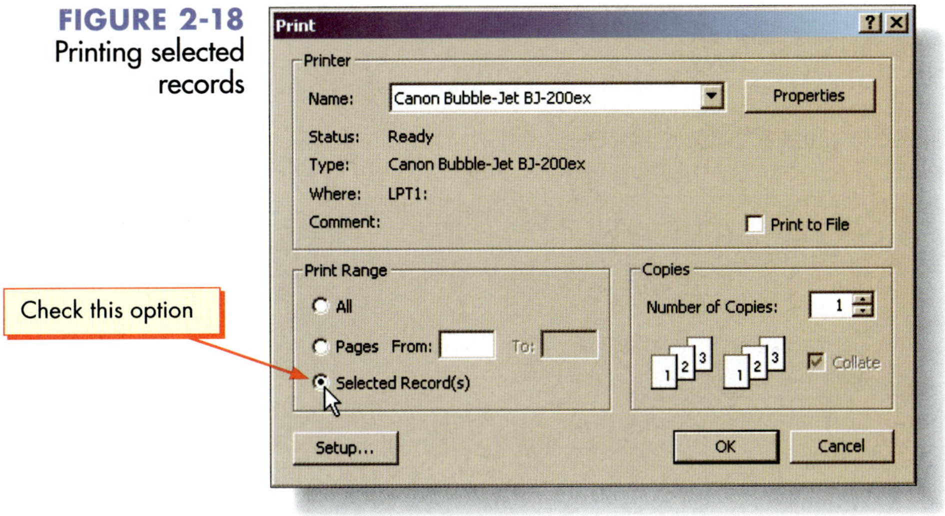

FIGURE 2-18 Printing selected records

Editing Data in a Form

You can edit data in a form with the same shortcuts you use in a table or a query. For example, Backspace deletes a single character and the keyboard combination Ctrl + Delete deletes an entire line.

EXERCISE 2-16 Delete Text in a Form

The data displayed in each field of a form is stored in a table. In the same way that you can delete text from a table by using Datasheet View, you can also delete text from a form.

1. Open frmSalesReviewMain. Click the Next Record button ▶ at the bottom left corner of the screen to move to "The Toy House" record.
2. In the Company Name field, click to the left of "Toy."
3. Press Ctrl + Backspace. Notice that the current record pointer changes to the pencil symbol when you're editing text. "The Toy House" is changed to "Toy House."
4. Click between "0" and "2" in the Order ID field at the top of the form.
5. Press Delete once and key **7**
6. Click to the right of "7" in the Employee ID field. Notice that the Order ID is changed to "20107" in both parts of the form. (See Figure 2-19 on the next page.)

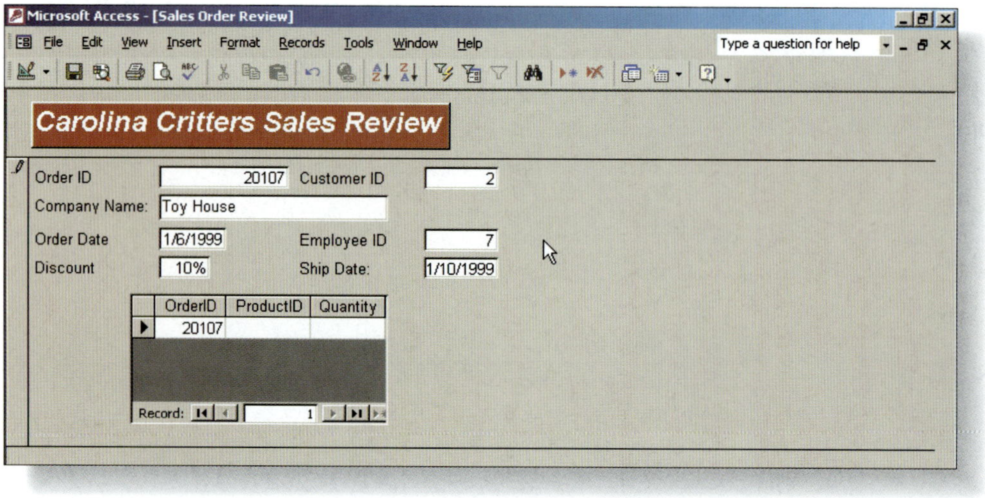

FIGURE 2-19 OrderID changed in both forms

7. Press Backspace and key **6**. The Employee ID is now "6."
8. Click to the left of the first character in the Order Date field.
9. Press Ctrl + Delete. Key ***[your birth date]*** using the mm/dd/yy format.

NOTE: You must key a date in mm/dd/yy format. However, Access might use a different display format.

10. Close the form. Click Tables on the Objects bar and open tblCustomers. Notice the change to "Toy House." (It was "The Toy House."). Close the table.
11. Open tblSalesOrders. Notice OrderID "20107." There is now no Order ID "20102."
12. Change "20107" to "20102." Close the table.

EXERCISE 2-17 Delete Records in a Form

You can delete records when they become inactive. You can delete the current record by using the Edit menu, or you can use the keyboard shortcut, Ctrl + -. You can also select the record and press Delete or use the Delete Record button.

1. Click Forms on the Objects bar. Open frmEmployeeInformation. Move to Martin Clark's record. Click the Record Selector to select the record.
2. Press Delete. Notice the next record is displayed.

NOTE: You cannot use the Undo button to restore a deleted a record. You can re-key the record if your deletion was in error.

3. Click Yes to confirm the deletion.

EXERCISE 2-18 Insert Text in a Form

When editing a form, you can insert text or use Overtype mode to key over existing text. You can also insert text by using the Copy and Paste commands.

1. With frmEmployeeInformation open, move forward to May Lee's record.
2. In the Job Code field, double-click **OF06**. Click the Copy button on the toolbar.

TIP: Double-clicking selects an entire word.

3. Press PgUp to move back to Estela Barnes' record. Double-click the text in the Job Code field, if it is not already selected.
4. Click the Paste button on the toolbar. Estela's job code is changed to "OF06."
5. Move back to Jamel Abdullah's record. In the Job Code field, click to the left of **OF07**.
6. Press Insert to switch to Overtype mode. Key **MF04**
7. Make certain that Overtype mode is on. In the Job Code field, select the 4 and key **5**. The Job Code is now "MF05."
8. Press Insert to turn off Overtype mode.
9. Close the form and open tblEmployees. Notice the changes to Estela Barnes' and Jamel Abdullah's records. Close the table.

Adding a Picture to a Record

The records you have added or edited have had text, number, or date fields. Now you will add images. The Stuffed Animals table has a field to show a picture of the animal. The Employees table has a field to show a photograph of the employee. These images are *OLE (Object Linking and Embedding) objects*. Data that was created in another program, such as an illustration or a drawing program, is an OLE object. You cannot see the picture in Datasheet View, but you can see it in the form.

NOTE: OLE objects include pictures, sound clips, movie clips, spreadsheets, or text documents.

When you add a record with an OLE field such as a picture, you use the Insert Object command. You can insert an image in a table, a query, or a form.

EXERCISE 2-19 Insert a Picture

1. Open tblStuffedAnimals. The **Illustration** field shows **Bitmap Image**, not the picture.
2. Click the View button. The **Product** field is an OLE Object data type.

NOTE: The name of the field is "Product," but it uses a different caption, "Illustration." You will learn about captions in Lesson 4.

3. Click the View button.
4. Click in the **Illustration** field for **Lon Lion**.
5. From the **Insert** menu, choose **Object**. The Insert Object dialog box opens.
6. In the **Object Type** window, select **Paintbrush Picture**.

FIGURE 2-20 Microsoft Access dialog box used to insert objects

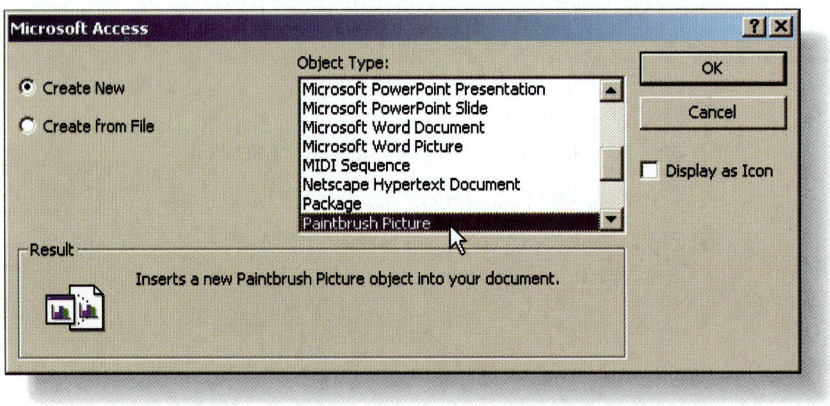

7. Click **OK**. MS-Paint opens. Click **Edit**, and then click **Paste From**.
8. Locate the folder **Images**. Select **Lin003**. (See Figure 2-21 on the next page.)

NOTE: Your instructor will tell you where the Images folder is stored.

9. Click **Open**. Click **Yes** to enlarge the bitmap.

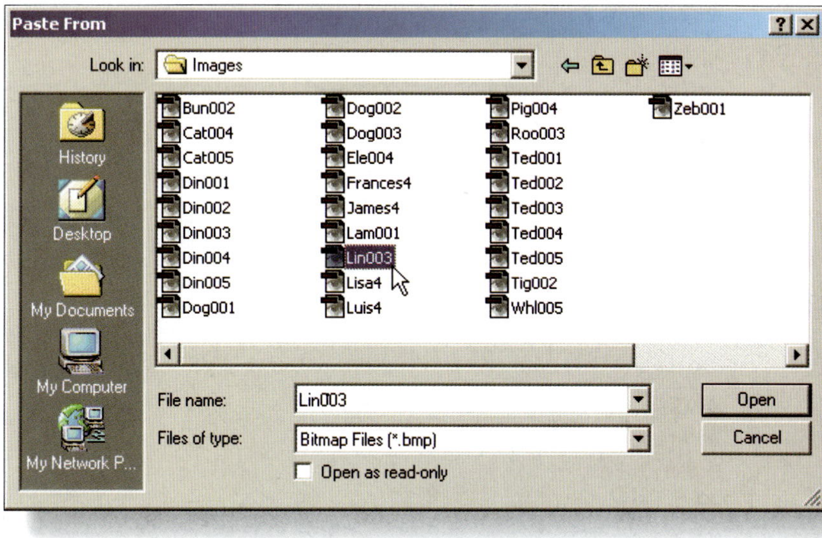

FIGURE 2-21
Using Paintbrush to insert image

10. Click **Image**, and then click **Attributes**. Click the **Black and white** options button. This makes the file smaller.

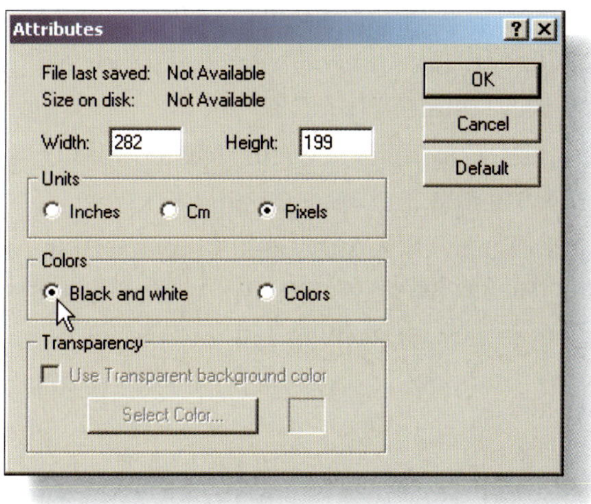

FIGURE 2-22
Setting image attributes

11. Click **OK**. Click **Yes** to convert to black and white. Click **File**, and then click **Exit & Return to tblStuffedAnimals: Table**.
12. Close the table.
13. Click **Forms** on the Objects bar. Open frmStuffedAnimals.
14. Press [PgDn] until you reach the lion's record and see the image.
15. Press [PgDn] to move to Elvira Elephant's record.

TIP: The rectangle that holds the picture is an Access control. You will learn about controls in Lessons 5 and 6.

16. Right-click the empty rectangle where the picture should be. (See Figure 2-23 on the next page.)

FIGURE 2-23
Inserting an Image

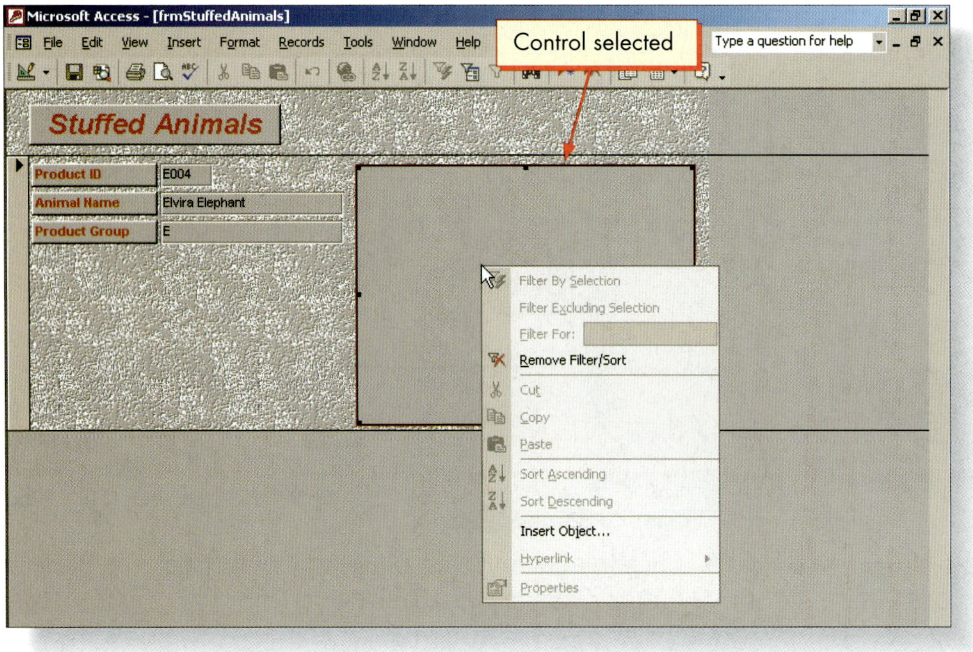

17. Select Insert Object. The Insert Object dialog box opens.

18. Select Paintbrush Picture. Click OK.

19. In MS-Paint, click Edit, and then click Paste From.

20. Find the image **Ele004** and click Open. Click Yes.

21. Click Image, and then click Attributes. Click the Black and white options button. Click OK. Click Yes to convert to black and white.

22. Click anywhere on the form, away from the image.

23. Close the form. Compact and repair the database and then close it.

USING HELP

One way to explore online Help is to display a list of Help topics. You choose a topic and Access displays information or provides a demonstration.

Find Help topics about forms:

1. With ***[your initials]*****CC-02** open, choose Help, and then choose Microsoft Access Help. If the Office Assistant starts, click Options. Clear the check mark from Use the Office Assistant and click OK. Then try again.

2. Click the Contents tab. Scroll the window and size the panes so you can see the names of the topics in the left pane. Each topic is represented by a book icon.

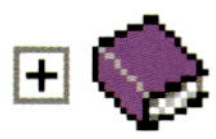

3. Browse through the list of topics to find **Forms**. Click its Expand button.

REVIEW: When a topic is expanded, it shows the Collapse button. When a topic is collapsed, it shows the Expand button.

4. Expand the **Printing and Previewing Forms** topic and then click **Set page setup options for printing**. Microsoft Access Help jumps to the **Printing and Previewing Reports** topic because previewing is the same for Reports and Forms. The Help text appears in the right pane.

FIGURE 2-24
Help Topics window

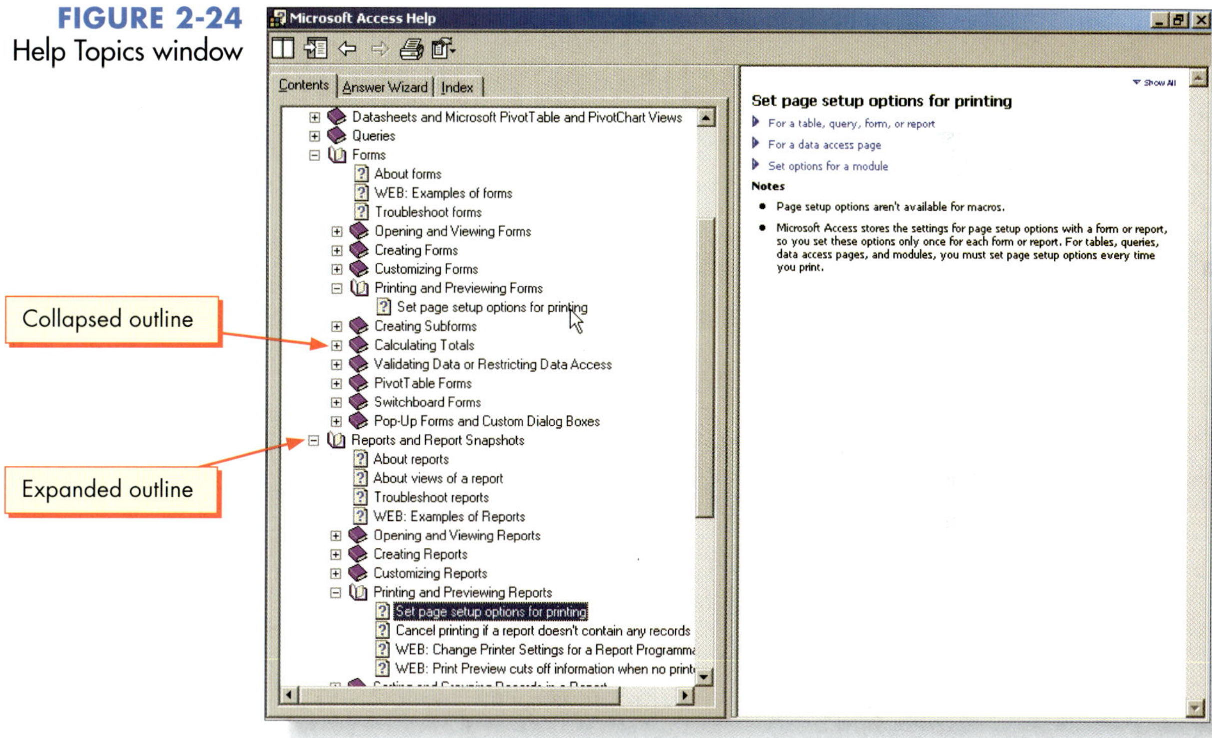

5. Click For a table, query, form or report in the right pane.

6. Read the information, scrolling as necessary.

7. In the left pane, under the topic **Forms**, expand the **Opening and Viewing Forms** topic. Click **About views of a form**.

8. Expand and read Design view and Form view and Datasheet view in the right pane.

9. Click the Close button when you finish.

LESSON 2 Summary

- New records are added and stored in tables.
- Add new records to a table through a query. New records can also be added to a table through a form.
- Delete records from a table by clicking on the Record Selector and pressing the delete key Delete.
- Delete text from individual fields in either a table or a query.
- Add text to individual fields in either a table or a query.
- AutoCorrect corrects commonly misspelled words while text is being added.
- Press Ctrl + ' to duplicate the contents in the field from the previous record .
- Clicking the Undo button will restore the previously deleted text.
- Access allows copying, pasting and paste appending of text in a table or query.
- A form is an Access object that allows entering, viewing, sorting, editing, and printing of records stored in a table.
- When you're using the data entry command in a form, only the current record is visible.
- Modify forms in Design View.
- Change the Default View of a form through Design View.
- Print preview displays on the screen how a form will be printed.
- When printing a single form, you must first select the form.
- Delete text in individual fields through a form.
- You can delete entire records from a table through a form.
- Add text in individual fields through a form.
- You can insert pictures as a field in a table through a form.

LESSON 2 Command Summary

FEATURE	BUTTON	MENU	KEYBOARD	SPEECH
Copy	[Copy button]	Edit, Copy	Ctrl + C	✓
Clipboard		Edit, Office Clipboard	Ctrl + C twice	✓

continues

LESSON 2 Command Summary *continued*

FEATURE	BUTTON	MENU	KEYBOARD	SPEECH
Data Entry		Records, Data Entry		✓
Delete record		Edit, Delete Record	Ctrl + -	✓
Duplicate data			Ctrl + '	
Form Datasheet View		View, Datasheet View		✓
Form Design View		View, Design View		✓
Form View		View, Form View		✓
Insert picture		Insert, Object		✓
Insert current date			Ctrl]+ ;	
New record		Insert, New Record	Ctrl + +	✓
Paste		Edit, Paste	Ctrl + V	✓
Print		File, Print	Ctrl + P	✓
Remove Data Entry		Records, Remove Filter/Sort		✓
Save record		Records, Save Record	Shift + Enter	✓
Undo	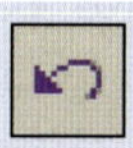	Edit, Undo	Ctrl + Z	✓

Concepts Review

TRUE/FALSE QUESTIONS

Each of the following statements is either true or false. Indicate your choice by circling T or F.

T F 1. The pencil icon appears in the Record Selector after the data is saved.

T F 2. You can use the Undo button to restore a deleted record.

T F 3. When you enter or edit data on a form, you also have to update the underlying table.

T F 4. You can duplicate the data from a field in the previous record to the same field in the next record by pressing Ctrl + D.

T F 5. Forms can be set to show more than one form or record per screen.

T F 6. You can add records in a table, a query, or a form.

T F 7. Access saves changes to the record when you close a form or move to the next record.

T F 8. You can insert various types of objects as data in a table.

SHORT ANSWER QUESTIONS

Write the correct answer in the space provided.

1. What view of a table lets you add records?

____

2. What menu and menu command do you use to place an OLE object in a field?

____

3. What is the keyboard shortcut to delete a record in a table or form?

____

4. What feature do you use to set 50% magnification in Print Preview?

____

5. How do you set the number of forms that can appear on the screen at once?

____

6. How do you print a single form?

____

7. How do you open a form's property sheet?

____

8. Which command is carried out by pressing Ctrl + Z?

____

CRITICAL THINKING

Answer these questions on a separate page. There are no right or wrong answers. Support your answers with examples from your own experience, if possible.

1. You can insert various types of OLE objects in a table or form. Think about different types of businesses (law firms, real estate agencies, music stores, and others) and what types of objects (pictures, sound clips, video clips) each might use.
2. When you delete a record from a table, it cannot be recovered. Discuss business applications in which you should never completely delete or remove records, even though they might be inactive.

Lesson Applications

EXERCISE 2-20

Add records in a table.

1. Open tblKitSuppliers in ***[your initials]*****CC-02** and maximize the window. Add the following new suppliers:

Supplier #:	**5**
Supplier ID:	**EE-05**
Supplier Name:	**Northeast Fabric Supply**
Contact Name:	**[your first and last name]**
Address:	**562 Industrial Parkway**
City:	**Wallingford**
ZIP Code:	**06492-5223**
Phone Number:	**(203) 555-6332**
Fax Number:	**(203) 555-6331**

Supplier #:	**6**
Supplier ID:	**FF-06**
Supplier Name:	**Southern Fabrics, Inc.**
Contact Name:	**Randolph Peterson**
Address:	**2600 Patterson Street**
City:	**Greensboro**
ZIP Code:	**27407-2600**
Phone Number:	**(910) 555-6625**
Fax Number:	**(910) 555-6626**

2. Preview the table. From the Preview window, change to Landscape orientation. Print and close the table.

EXERCISE 2-21

Edit records in a table.

1. Open frmStuffedAnimals and make the corrections shown in Figure 2-25 on the next page. Use navigation commands to find the records to be changed.

TIP: To select a word in a field, double-click it. To select the entire field, press F2.

FIGURE 2-25

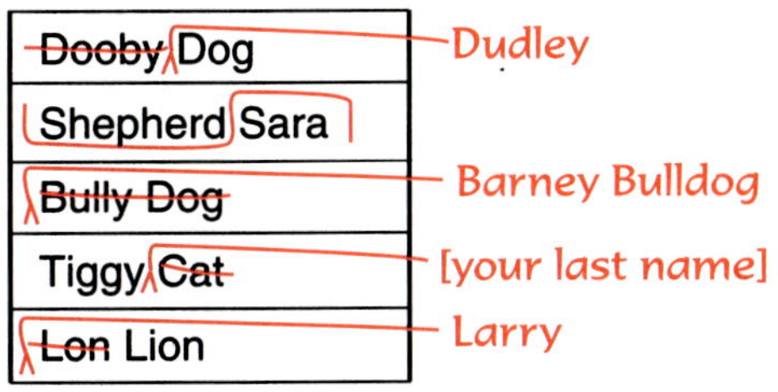

NOTE: Refer to Appendix D to review proofreaders' marks.

2. Close the form and open tblStuffedAnimals. Print the table in portrait orientation.

EXERCISE 2-22

Edit records in a table.

1. Open tblEmployees. Make the Postal Code column wider to display the postal entries in the last few records of the table.
2. Freeze the Employee ID, Last Name, and First Name. Scroll the window to position the Postal Code field next to the names.
3. Using the [↓] and [↑], move from one record to another. Move to the Postal Code field and press [F2] to edit the text. Use the [→] and [←] to position the insertion point. Add the additional postal code numbers to each record. Add text as indicated in Figure 2-26. (Not all the columns appear in the following figure.)

FIGURE 2-26

Employee ID	Last Name	First Name	Postal Code
1	Fuentes	Lisa	28216-1933
2	McCluskie	James	28217-5324
3	Falcigno	Frances	28269-3024
4	Gutierrez	Luis	28262-2202
5	Floria	Maria	28214-1807
6	Abdullah	Jamel	28202-1121
7	Dyer	Cassie	28208-4411

continues

FIGURE 2-26 *continued*

Employee ID	Last Name	First Name	Postal Code
8	Wilson	Zipporah	28202-1141
9	Thomas-Smith	Louise	28205-2546
10	Davidson	Russell	28202-1051
11	Stone	Jeanette	28210-5006
12	Talmadge	Audrey	28202-1212
13	Lassen	Joseph	28202-1216
14	Chung	Sora	28202-1114
15	Clark	Martin	28202-1452
16	Lee	Ching	28202-1330
17	Cirillo	Frank	28202-1133
18	Rodriguez	Felix	28202-1548
20	Lee	Sidney	28216-5572
21	Barnes	Estela	28208-4417
22	Fishman	Norman	28202-1321
23	Fernandez	Victor	28202-1044
24	Lee	May	28262-9712
25	Baez	Richard	28213-6649
26	Hutchinson	Pauline	28207-2642

NOTE: F2 starts Edit mode when the entire field is selected and selects an entire field when there is only an insertion point in the field.

4. Change the name in the last record to your name.
5. Unfreeze all columns.
6. Change the page orientation to landscape. Print the table.
7. Close the table without saving changes to the layout.

ACCESS

EXERCISE 2-23 *Challenge Yourself*

Add pictures to records.

1. Open tblStuffedAnimals.

2. Move to the Professor Bear record and insert the **Ted001** bitmap image. Close the table.
3. Open frmStuffedAnimals. Move to the Professor Bear record and print it.

TIP: Click the rectangle for the picture to insert an image.

4. Insert the **Din004** bitmap image for Triceratops Tony.
5. Select and print this record in landscape format.
6. Compact and repair the database before closing it.

On Your Own

In these exercises you work on your own, as you would in a real-life work environment. Use the skills you've learned to accomplish the task—and be creative.

EXERCISE 2-24

Search the Web for companies that would sell products of interest to members of the club you formed in Lesson 1. If you are unable to locate any companies, search the Web for companies selling clothing that appeals to you. Write down at least five URLs (Web page addresses). Continue to the next exercise.

EXERCISE 2-25

On each of the five Web sites, determine what information the company asks a person when that person places an order or requests a catalog. Write a bulleted list of different information collected by each company on potential customers (for example: first name, email) on the same sheet of paper where you wrote down the five URLs. Continue to the next exercise.

EXERCISE 2-26

On a second sheet of paper, create a new field list by combining the list you created in Exercise 1-24 (in Lesson 1) with the list you created in Exercise 2-25. On a third sheet of paper, organize the items from your new list to sketch a form layout. You might want to refer to Figure 2-8. Submit your work for Exercises 2-24 through 2-26 to your instructor.

LESSON

3

Finding and Sorting Records

OBJECTIVES

MOUS ACTIVITIES

In this lesson:

Ac2002 2-1
Ac2002 3-1
Ac2002 5-2
Ac2002 5-3
Ac2002 5-4

See Appendix E.

After completing this lesson, you will be able to:

1. **Find specific text.**
2. **Use the Replace command.**
3. **Sort records.**
4. **Use filters.**
5. **Create an advanced filter/sort.**
6. **Use AND/OR criteria.**
7. **Build a query.**

Estimated Time: 2 hours

The Find, Replace, Sort, and Filter commands in Access are similar to the Find, Replace, Sort, and Filter commands in other software programs.

- Find and Replace commands search the records for data you specify. To search for a particular employee, for example, you key the employee's name in the dialog box, and Access finds the record.
- Sort commands arrange records in a particular sequence. For instance, you can sort employee records alphabetically by last name or numerically by ID number.
- Filter commands display only records that meet conditions you specify. For example, you can display only customers in Charlotte, North Carolina.

Finding Specific Text

Finding records can be time-consuming if you have to scroll through several thousand of them. You can use the Find command to locate a record quickly.

There are two ways to use Find:

- Choose Edit and then choose Find.
- Press Ctrl + F.

The Find command can search an entire field or part of a field. Searches are not case sensitive, which means Access finds uppercase and lowercase versions of the text.

EXERCISE 3-1 Find Records

1. Copy **CC-03** and rename it ***[your initials]*CC-03**. Make certain it is not a Read-only copy.

REVIEW: If you need help copying and renaming the database, refer to the beginning of Lesson 2.

2. Open tblCustomers and maximize the window.
3. Click Edit and then click Find. Make certain you are on the Find tab.
4. Key **charlotte** in the Find What text box.
5. To search all fields in the table, click the down arrow next to the Look In box and choose "tblCustomers: Table."
6. Click the down arrow next to the Match box and choose Whole Field.
7. Make certain the Search drop-down list is set to All. The All option starts at the current record, continues to the end of the table, and wraps back to records that precede the current record.
8. Make certain that the Match Case option is not selected.

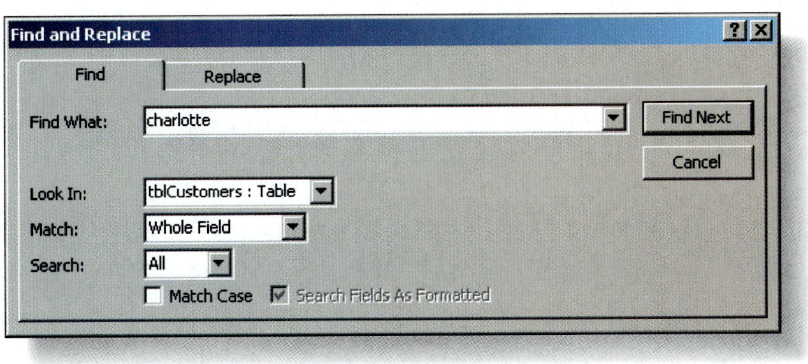

FIGURE 3-1
Find and Replace dialog box

NOTE: To see the results of a search, you can drag the Find and Replace dialog box by its title bar to a location on the screen where it doesn't obscure the results of the search.

TABLE 3-1 Find and Replace Dialog Box Options

OPTION	DESCRIPTION
Look In	Sets the search for the current field or the entire table.
Match: Any Part of Field	Finds records with matching characters anywhere in the field.
Match: Whole Field	Finds records in which an entire field matches the value in the Find What text box.
Match: Start of Field	Finds records in which the beginning of a field matches the Find What entry.
Search: All	Searches forward to the end of the table and wraps back to the beginning.
Search: Up	Searches in the Up (backward) direction only.
Search: Down	Searches in the Down (forward) direction only.
Match Case	Finds exact uppercase and lowercase matches.
Search Fields As Formatted	Enables you to key data in its display format. To find a date that is stored as 1/25/01, you can key 25-Jan-01. This is the slowest search.

9. Click Find Next. Access moves the pointer to the first occurrence of "Charlotte."
10. Click Find Next to move to the next occurrence of "Charlotte."
11. Continue clicking Find Next until Access displays a message that it has finished searching the records.
12. Click OK in the message box. Close the Find and Replace dialog box.

NOTE: The Find and Replace dialog box remains open until you close it.

EXERCISE 3-2 Find Records with Match Case and Match: Any Part of Field

The Find command includes options for fine-tuning how words or phrases are matched. One of these options, Match Case, is used to conduct a case-sensitive search. Another option enables you to look for matches in any part of a field.

1. Move to the end of the table by pressing Ctrl + End.

2. Click the Find button.

NOTE: The text from the prior search Access performed might be in the Find What text box. You can simply key the new search string over it.

3. In the Find What text box, key **durham**

4. Click the Match Case check box. From the Search list box, choose Up to search backward from the current record.

FIGURE 3-2 Choosing options in the Find and Replace dialog box

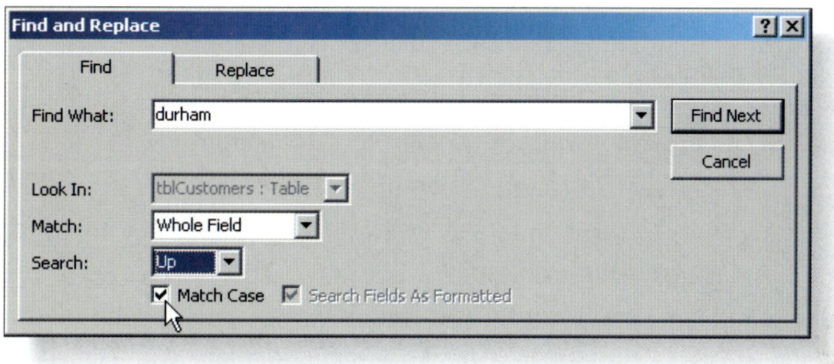

5. Click Find Next to begin the search. There are no matches.

6. Click OK in the message box that says the search is finished.

7. Click anywhere in the Billing Address field of any record.

8. Key **boulevard** in the Find What text box.

9. Choose "Billing Address" for the Look In entry.

TIP: Searches are faster if you use a single field instead of an entire table.

10. In the Match list box, choose Any Part of Field.

11. Deselect the Match Case check box. Set the Search direction to All. Click Find Next. The first match is highlighted.

12. Continue to click Find Next until the message box opens. Click OK.

13. Close the Find and Replace dialog box. Close tblCustomers.

EXERCISE 3-3 Find Records by Using the Asterisk (*)

When you use the Find command, you are actually specifying criteria. *Criteria* are text strings or expressions that Access uses to find matching records. Up to this point, you have used text as criteria (the words "Charlotte" and "Durham").

When you use text as criteria, you can use *wildcards*. These are characters used to represent one or more alphabetical or numerical characters. They are helpful when you are not quite sure of the complete spelling or value.

- A question mark (?) represents a single character. **Mar?** is a criterion that would find "Mary," "Mark," or "Mart"—four-character words that start with "Mar."
- An asterisk (*) represents any number of characters. **Mar*** is a criterion that would find "March," "Martin," "Marigold," or "Marblestone"—words that start with "Mar" regardless of how many letters follow.
- The number sign (#) represents a single numerical character. If you are looking for numbers less than 100, you can key **##** as criteria to eliminate any numbers with three or more digits.

1. Open frmEmployeeInformation.
2. Click the Find button.
3. Key **mf*** in the Find What text box.
4. Set the Look In box to "Employee Information Form." Set the Match criteria to Any Part of Field.
5. From the Search drop-down list box, choose All.
6. Make certain that the Match Case check box is deselected.
7. Click Find Next to find the first occurrence of an "MF" job code.

TIP: Move the Find and Replace dialog box if it is in the way of the Job Code field.

8. Continue clicking Find Next until the message box opens. Notice that records for employees with any "MF" job code are displayed ("MF02," "MF03," and so on).
9. Click OK in the message box.
10. Click anywhere in the Last Name field in the form.
11. In the Find What text box, key **f***. In the Look In box, choose Last Name.
12. Verify that the search will be for All records with no Match Case. Click Find Next.
13. Click Find Next again to see each employee whose last name begins with "F."
14. Close the message box and the Find and Replace dialog box.

15. Close frmEmployeeInformation.

EXERCISE 3-4 Find Records by Using the Question Mark (?)

1. Open frmStuffedAnimals and click in the Animal Name field.

2. Click the Find button. The Look In box shows "Animal Name" because you clicked in that field. Access shows the value of the first field in the first record.

3. Key **T????** in the Find What text box. Each question mark represents one character.

4. Click the down arrow next to the Match list box and choose Start of Field.

5. Click the Match Case check box to select it. In the Search list box, choose All.

6. Click Find Next to begin and continue to click Find Next. Access moves the pointer to each record that begins with a "T" followed by any four characters in the Animal Name field.

TIP: A space is considered a character in Find and Replace activities; therefore, "Tula Tiger" is included in these matches.

7. Click OK to close the message box.

8. In the Find What text box, key **C???**

9. Click in the Product ID field in the form. Click anywhere in the Find and Replace dialog box to update the Look In entry.

10. Click Match Case and choose Search: All. Click Find Next. Access displays the records for animals in the "C" category.

11. Continue clicking Find Next until Access tells you that no additional search items are found.

12. Click OK in the message box and close the Find and Replace dialog box.

13. Close frmStuffedAnimals.

Using the Replace Command

The Replace command finds matching text and substitutes replacement text. You can replace all instances of matching text at once, or you can find and confirm each replacement.

There are two ways to use the Replace command:

- Choose Edit and then choose Replace.
- Press Ctrl+H.

EXERCISE 3-5 Replace Text by Using Find Next

1. Open tblCustomers.
2. Click the Find button. Click the Replace tab. The value in the first field in the first record is shown.
3. In the Find What text box, key **boulevard**. Click in the Billing Address field in the first record.
4. Set the Look In box to Billing Address.
5. Click in the Replace With text box and key **Avenue**
6. In the Match list box, choose Any Part of Field. Use Search: All.
7. Make certain the Match Case check box is not selected.

FIGURE 3-3
Replacing text

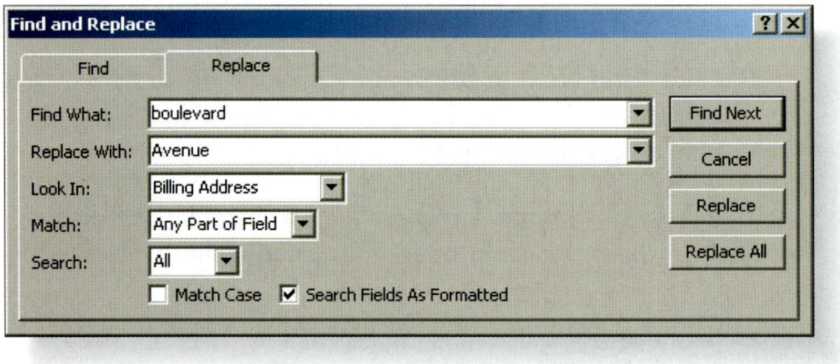

NOTE: If you choose Whole Field in the Match list box, Access matches the entire contents of the field. In this case, the search string "boulevard" would not match "3415 Brookshire Boulevard."

8. Click Find Next to start the search.
9. Click Replace to replace the first occurrence of "Boulevard" with "Avenue" and to find the next occurrence.
10. Click Replace again to replace the next occurrence. Continue clicking Replace until Access indicates that it can't find the text you specified.
11. Click OK in the message box.
12. Close the Find and Replace dialog box and tblCustomers.

EXERCISE 3-6 Replace Text by Using Replace All

The Replace All option in the Replace dialog box replaces all occurrences of text in a table or form without confirmation.

1. Open tblKitSuppliers.
2. Click anywhere in the Address field. Look for the word "Street."
3. Click the Find button and then click the Replace tab.

TIP: Ctrl + H opens the Replace tab on the Find and Replace dialog box.

4. In the Find What text box, key **street** and press Tab. In the Replace With text box, key **Road**. Use Match: Any Part of Field, no Match Case, and Search: All.

NOTE: If you search all fields and all records of the table and use Any Part of Field, you change all occurrences of "street" to "road." An employee named "Mary Ann Street" would become "Mary Ann Road." A town named "Streeter" would become "Roader."

5. Click the Replace All button. Access warns that you cannot undo a Replace activity.

FIGURE 3-4
Access warns that you cannot undo the Replace

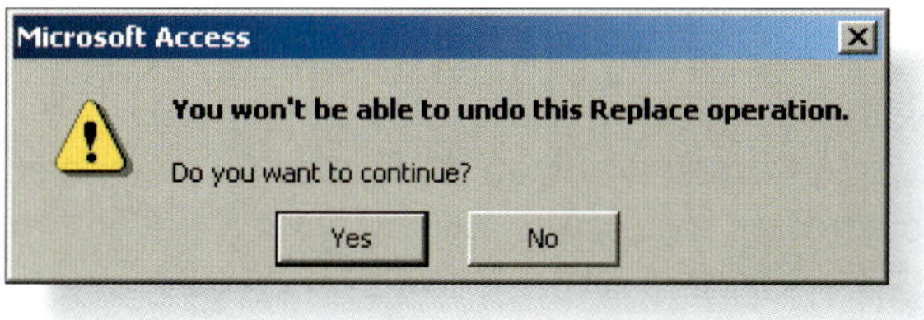

6. Click Yes. All occurrences of "Street" in the Address field are changed to "Road." Close the Find and Replace dialog box.
7. Close tblKitSuppliers.

Sorting Records

Records are displayed in some type of alphabetical or numerical order. By default, Access displays records based on the primary key. The *primary key* is a field in which data is unique for every record. If there is no primary key, Access displays records based on the order in which they were entered.

TIP: A table does not need to have a primary key. However, you do give up database integrity (the stability and soundness of the data) when there is no primary key. You will learn more about this as you continue through the lessons.

You can arrange records in other orders to find information more quickly. For example, records in the Customers table are arranged by CustomerID number, but when you plan sales calls it may be more helpful to see them in order by ZIP code.

The Stuffed Animals table is arranged by ProductID, but you may need to see them in order by price or inventory if you are planning a sales campaign.

You can sort data in three ways:

- Choose Records and then choose Sort.
- Click the Sort Ascending button or Sort Descending button.
- Click the right mouse button and select Sort Ascending or Sort Descending from the shortcut menu.

EXERCISE 3-7 Sort a Single Field

A simple sort uses one field. You can sort records in a table, a query, a form, or a data access page.

1. Open qryEmployees and make certain the window is maximized. Click anywhere in the Last Name field.

TIP: The sort buttons on the toolbar are known as the QuickSort buttons.

2. Click the Sort Ascending button on the toolbar to sort the records by Last Name in ascending order (A to Z).
3. Click the Sort Descending button to sort in descending order (Z to A).
4. Close qryEmployees. Click No when Access asks if you want to save design changes.

NOTE: If you save the design changes after sorting a table or query, the records are saved in the new order.

5. Click Forms on the Objects bar and open frmStuffedAnimals. Click anywhere in the Animal Name field.
6. From the Records menu, choose Sort and then choose Sort Ascending.

FIGURE 3-5 Records menu

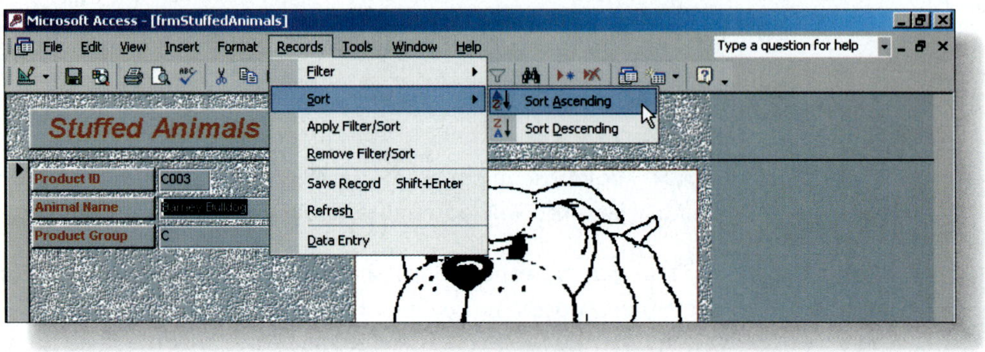

7. Press PgDn to scroll through the records. The records are sorted alphabetically, in ascending order, by animal name.

NOTE: Sorts in a form are not considered design changes, so you are not asked to save the changes.

8. Close frmStuffedAnimals.

EXERCISE 3-8 Sort by Multiple Fields in Datasheet View

You can sort a table or query by more than one field. For example, you might want to view customers by city and alphabetically by customer name within each city. In a datasheet, Access requires that sorted fields be next to each other on the screen. The sorting priority goes from left to right, so the first sort is the leftmost column, the second sort is the next column, and so on.

REVIEW: The top border of a field or column is its column selector.

1. Open tblCustomers. Place the pointer at the top of the State field, on the column selector, and click when the pointer changes to a down-pointing arrow. This selects the column.
2. Click the State field name and drag the column to the left. As you drag, a wide vertical line shows where the column will be dropped. When the vertical line is to the left of the Company Name field, release the mouse button. The State column, still selected, is now to the left of the Company Name column.

FIGURE 3-6 A vertical line shows where the field will be dropped

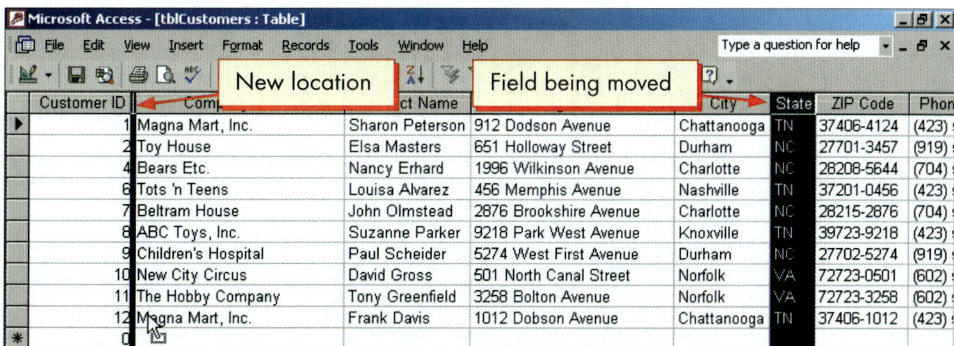

3. Hold down Shift, point to the Company Name column selector, and click when the pointer changes to a down-pointing arrow. This selects both columns.
4. Click the Sort Ascending button. The records are sorted first by state and then by company name within each state.

ACCESS

5. Close tblCustomers without saving changes.

EXERCISE 3-9 Sort a Query in Design View

You can sort a query in Datasheet View by using the QuickSort buttons. This type of sort is part of the layout and is temporary if you do not save the layout changes. You can also sort by one or more fields in Design View. This becomes a permanent sort when you save the query.

To sort a query in Design View, you add the fields to be used in sorting to the design grid. You can add fields to the design grid by double-clicking the field name or by dragging the field name into position.

1. Open qryCustomers. Click the View button . The design grid is on the lower half of the screen. The field list is in the top pane.

FIGURE 3-7 Query Design window

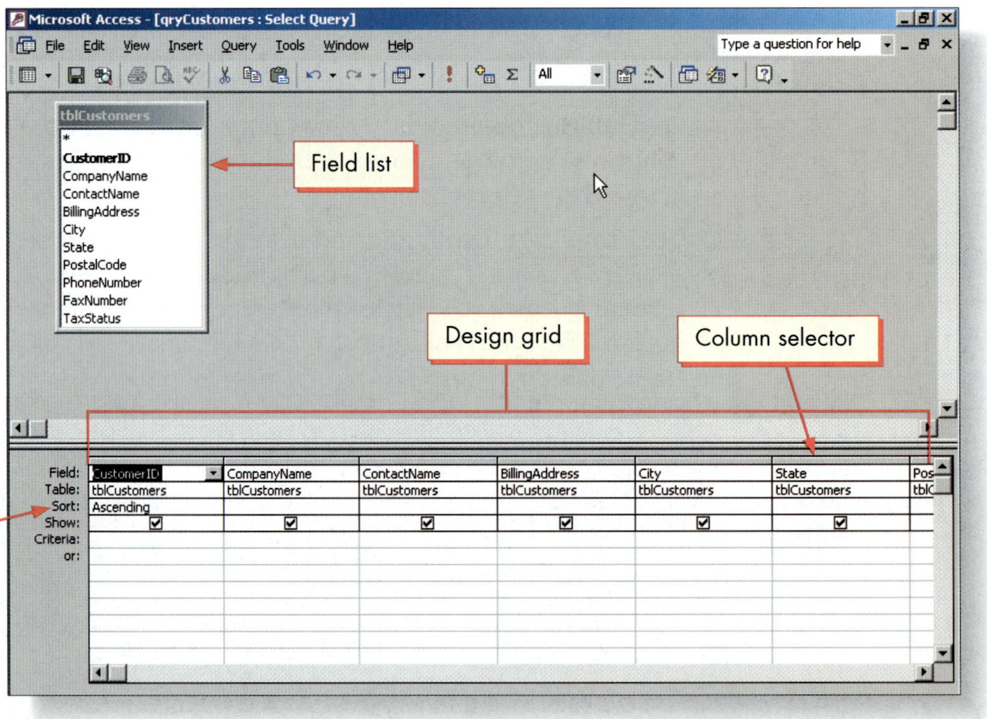

2. Make certain the window is maximized. Notice that the query sorts the records by CustomerID.

3. Click the Sort row for CustomerID. Click the drop-down arrow and choose (not sorted).

4. In the State field column, click the Sort row. Choose Ascending.

5. Click the View button. The records are sorted by state.
6. Click the View button.
7. In the CompanyName column, click the Sort row. Choose Ascending. The design grid now shows two sorts.
8. Click the View button. The records are sorted by the leftmost column in the design grid, the Company Name. The State sort order does not matter in this case.
9. Click the View button.
10. Place the pointer on the column selector for the State field. Click when the pointer changes to a down-pointing arrow.
11. With the column selected, click and drag the column to the left of the Company Name column. Release the mouse button.
12. Click the View button. The records are sorted first by state and then by company name.
13. Close the query and do not save the changes.

Using Filters

A *filter* shows a subset of records (a recordset) matching a criteria you set. You can apply filters in tables, queries, and forms. For example, if you want to find all stuffed animals in the D Product Group, you can create a filter that removes the other records.

There are four types of filters:

- Filter By Selection displays only those records that include selected text. This filter is available as a button, as a menu command, and as an option from a shortcut menu.
- Filter By Form displays records that match criteria on a form. In a blank datasheet or form, you specify a field (or fields), how the field (or fields) are to be sorted, and any additional criteria. Use the Apply Filter/Sort command (or the Apply Filter button) to run the filter. This filter also is available as a button and as a menu command.
- Filter By Input displays records that match a keyed value. It is available only from a shortcut menu. The shortcut menu command is Filter For.
- Filter Excluding Selection excludes all records that match a selected value. This filter is available as a menu command and as an option from a shortcut menu.

NOTE: After you use the Apply Filter button, it turns into the Remove Filter button. Clicking the Remove Filter button displays all records in the table again.

EXERCISE 3-10 Use Filter By Selection

When you create a Filter By Selection, you highlight text to establish it as criteria.

TABLE 3-2 Selecting Text for a Filter By Selection

SELECT	TO DISPLAY
Entire field	Records containing an exact match of the text selected
Start of a field	Records that start with the same character(s) as the selected text
Characters anywhere in the field	Records in which all or part of the field matches the selected text

1. Open tblStuffedAnimals and make certain the window is maximized.
2. Click anywhere in the List Price field for the first record. Press F2 to select the entire field.

3. Click the Filter By Selection button. Access displays only products with list prices of $12.50.

FIGURE 3-8 Products with a list price of $12.50

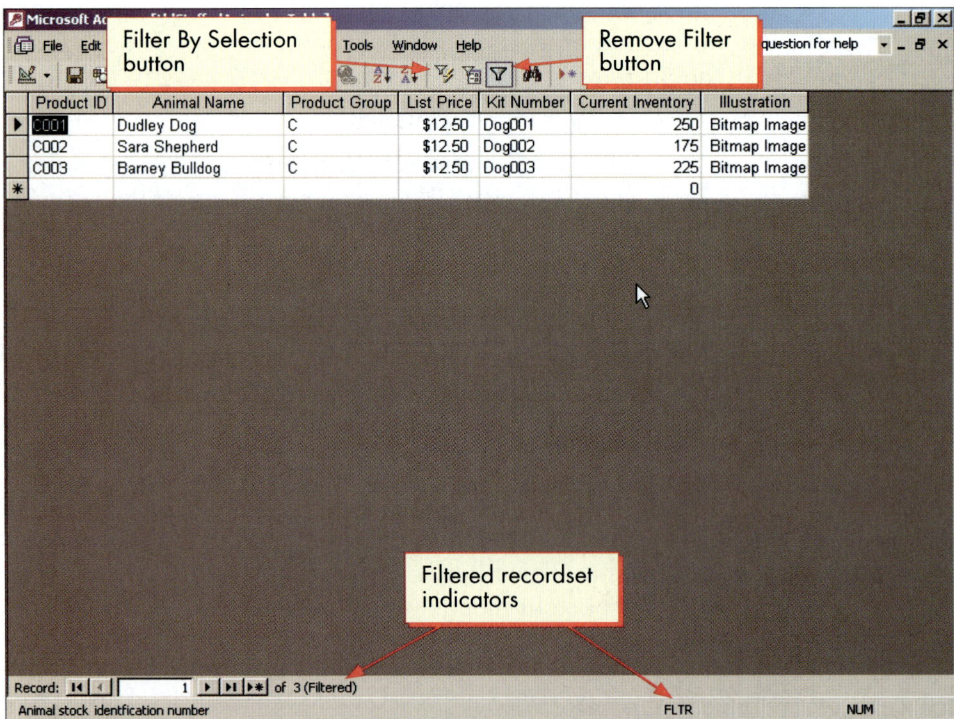

4. Click the Remove Filter button [Remove Filter] to display all the records again.
5. In the Kit Number field, select "Dog" but not the numbers.
6. From the Records menu, choose Filter By Selection. Only the records with Kit Numbers beginning with "Dog" are displayed.
7. From the Records menu, choose Remove Filter/Sort.
8. Close tblStuffedAnimals. Click Yes to save the changes to the table. This saves the last filter you used.

EXERCISE 3-11 Look at the Filter Property

If you save the design changes after applying a filter, that filter is saved as part of the design. You can see it as part of the Table Properties sheet.

1. Open tblStuffedAnimals. Click the Apply Filter button [Apply Filter]. The "Dog" filter is reapplied.
2. Click the View button [View] to switch to the Table Design window.

3. Click the Properties button [Properties]. The Table Properties dialog box shows the filter that has been saved.

NOTE: You can click the Filter row and open the Zoom window Shift + F2.

FIGURE 3-9
Table Properties dialog box

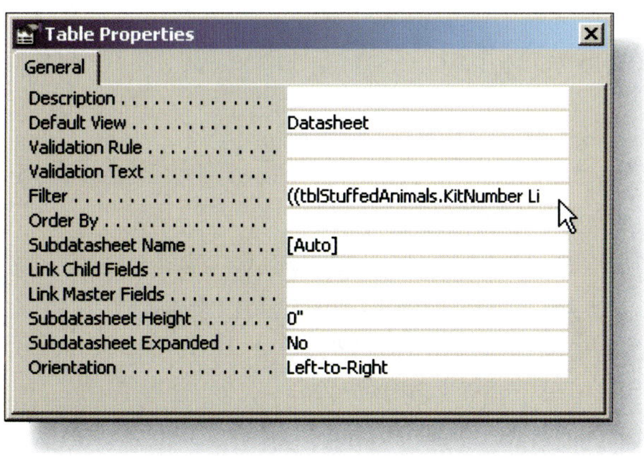

4. Close the Table Properties dialog box and the table.

EXERCISE 3-12 Use an Additive Filter By Selection

After you apply a Filter By Selection, you can apply another Filter By Selection to the filtered records.

1. Open tblEmployees.
2. In the JobCode field, select "MF" (not the number) in any record.
3. Click the Filter By Selection button. The "MF" job code employees are filtered and displayed.
4. In the JobCode field, double-click "MF06" in any record.
5. Click the Filter By Selection button. The records are further filtered.

NOTE: When you click the Filter By Selection button, the filter is automatically applied. You do not need to click the Apply Filter button.

6. Click the Remove Filter button. The filter is no longer applied; however, the filter definition is still stored for later use.
7. Close the table and do not save the design changes.

EXERCISE 3-13 Use Filter By Form

A Filter By Form is more flexible than a Filter By Selection because you can set criteria for more than one field. When you use a Filter By Form, a blank datasheet or form is opened. You key an expression or choose from a drop-down list of values.

TIP: Filter By Form is similar to the AutoFilter command in Microsoft Excel.

1. Open tblEmployees and click the Filter By Form button. A blank Filter By Form datasheet opens.
2. Click in the Job Code field. A drop-down list arrow appears.
3. Press F4 to list the values in the field. Choose "MF05" from the list. Quotation marks appear around "MF05," and the value is entered in the field. (See Figure 3-10 on the next page.)
4. Click the Apply Filter button. The records with job code "MF05" are shown.
5. Click the Remove Filter button.
6. Click the Filter By Form button. Your most recent filter is shown.

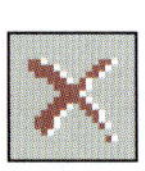

7. Click the Clear Grid button. The filter is cleared.
8. Click in the Job Code field and display the list.
9. Choose "MF05" from the list.

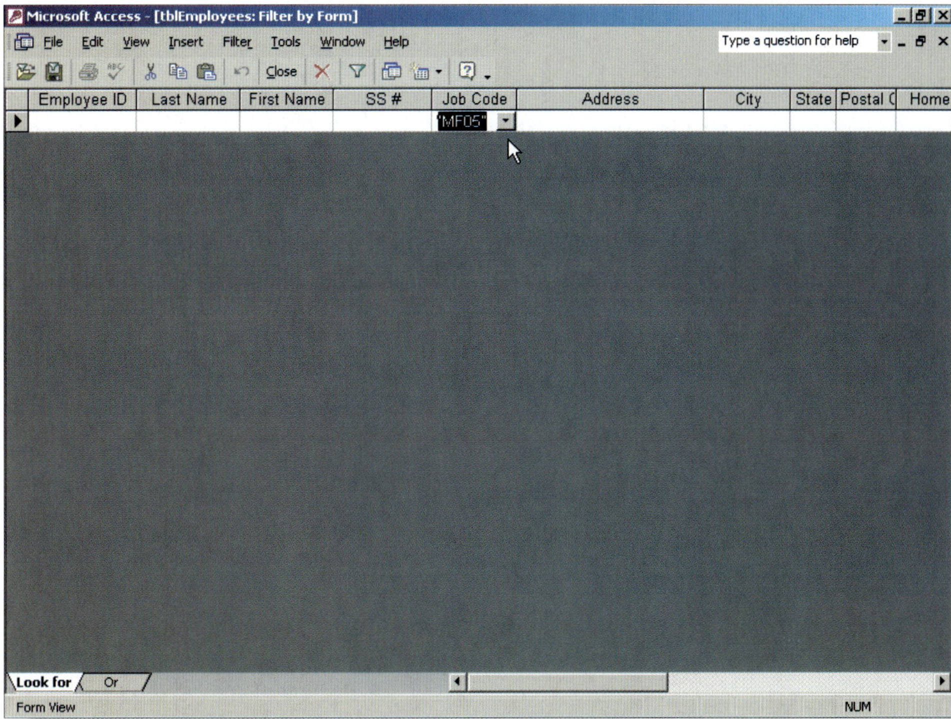

FIGURE 3-10 Criteria in a Filter By Form

10. Click in the Address field, but do not display the list.

11. Key ***street**

TIP: In a Filter By Form, you can use the same wildcards as were used in Find and Replace.

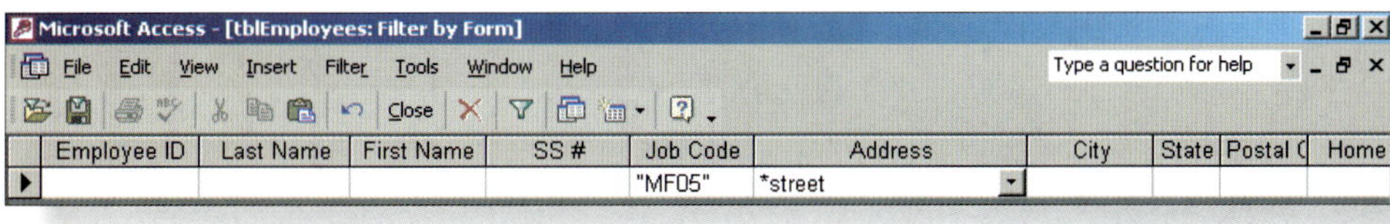

FIGURE 3-11 Two criteria in Filter By Form

NOTE: When you use two criteria on the same Filter By Form, both criteria must exist for each record displayed. You will learn more about this type of criteria in Exercise 3-17.

12. Click the Apply Filter button. The records with job code "MF05" and "street" at the end of the address are shown.

13. Click the Remove Filter button.

14. Close tblEmployees. Do not save the design changes.

EXERCISE 3-14 Use Wildcards and Null Values in Criteria

Wildcards are used to locate records when only part of the information stored in a field is known or to locate a group of records containing common text or numbers.

A *null value* identifies fields that do not contain data. A null value is not the same as the number zero or a space character created by pressing the spacebar. The number zero and a space character are both actual values. Only fields that do not contain any text, numbers, or values are null values.

1. Click Forms on the Object bar. Open frmStuffedAnimals. Make certain the window is maximized.
2. Click the Filter By Form button. A blank form opens.
3. Click in the Animal Name field and key ***dog***
4. Click the Apply Filter button. Two records are filtered, both with the word "Dog" in the name.

NOTE: You can see how many records are filtered by looking at the status bar at the bottom left corner of the screen.

5. Press PgDn to see the other record that fits the criteria.
6. Click the Filter By Form button.
7. Click the Clear Grid button.
8. Click in the Picture field and display the drop-down list. Because this is on OLE data type, your choices are either that the field has something in it (Is Not Null) or does not have anything in it (Is Null).

REVIEW: The picture field is the large rectangle to the right of the three text fields.

9. Choose Is Null.

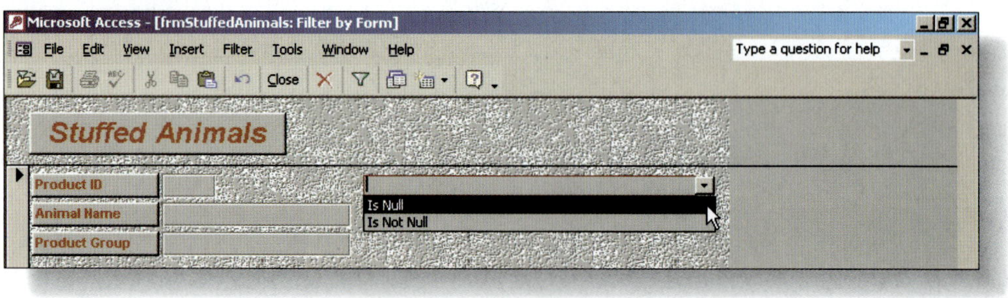

FIGURE 3-12 Using Is Null as a condition

ACCESS

10. Click the Apply Filter button [icon]. The records that do not have pictures are displayed in the recordset. Only the record for Rodney Rooster does not have an image.
11. Close the form.
12. Open frmStuffedAnimals and click the Apply Filter button [icon]. The same filter is applied because it was saved with the form.
13. Click the View button [icon]. Click the Properties button [icon]. The form's property sheet opens.
14. Click the **Data** tab. Notice the **Filter** row and its entry.
15. Close the property sheet and the form.

EXERCISE 3-15 Use Filter By Input and Filter Excluding Selection

The Filter By Input command is available from a shortcut menu displayed by clicking the right mouse button in a field. Although it is called a "Filter By Input," you key your input in the **Filter For** text box in the shortcut menu.

Use **Filter Excluding Selection** to exclude records that match a value. For example, you can filter the records to show all kits except those from a certain supplier.

1. Open tblCustomers.
2. Right-click anywhere in the Company Name field. Choose the **Filter For** text box.
3. Key **children***

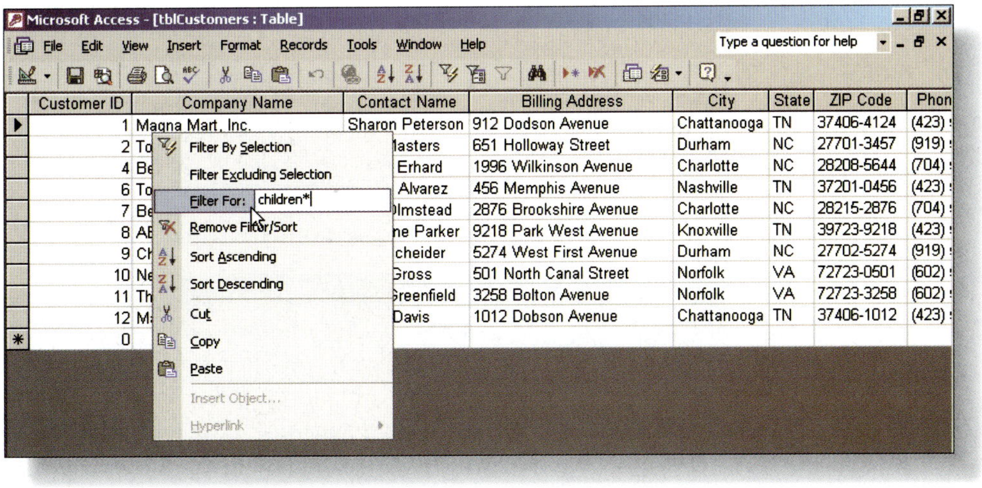

FIGURE 3-13
Use Filter By Input

NOTE: You must key the exact spelling in the Filter For text box, and the insertion point must be in the field used for filtering.

4. Press Enter to apply the filter. The Children's Hospital record is displayed.
5. Click the Remove Filter button and close the table. Do not save the changes.
6. Open tblKitContents.
7. Select "AA-01" in any record and right-click.

REVIEW: Point at the selected text as you right-click.

8. Choose Filter Excluding Selection.

FIGURE 3-14
Use Filter Excluding Selection

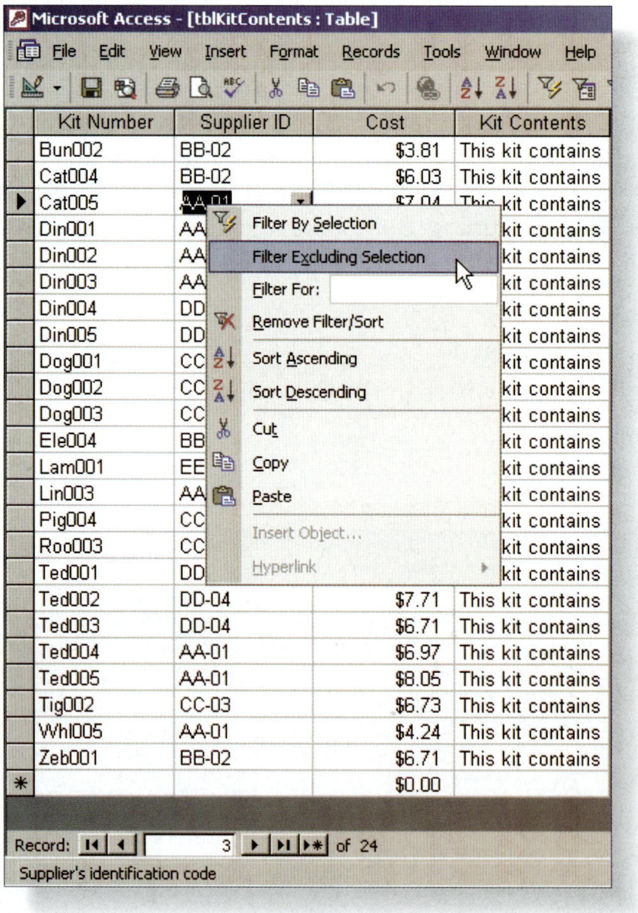

9. All records but those for Supplier AA-01 are shown. Click the Remove Filter button and close the table. Do not save the changes.

Creating an Advanced Filter or Sort

The Filter window enables you to build an Advanced Filter or Sort. You can use several fields and sophisticated expressions by making choices and entering criteria. The top pane in the Filter window displays a list of fields in the table. The bottom pane shows a design grid in which you add field names, sort orders, and criteria expressions. You add only those field names that should be used in the filtering.

TIP: Many of the filters you design in a Filter window can be built in a Filter By Form when you know how to enter the expressions.

EXERCISE 3-16 Create an Advanced Filter

1. Open tblHistorySales and maximize the window.
2. From the Records menu, choose Filter. Then choose Advanced Filter/Sort.
3. If you can't see all the names in the Field Name list box, you can adjust the height of the top pane to provide more space. Place the pointer on the horizontal border between the two panes. It changes to the split pointer.
4. Drag the pointer down to make the top pane taller than the lower pane. Then drag the border of the Field Name list box to make it taller so you can see all the field names.

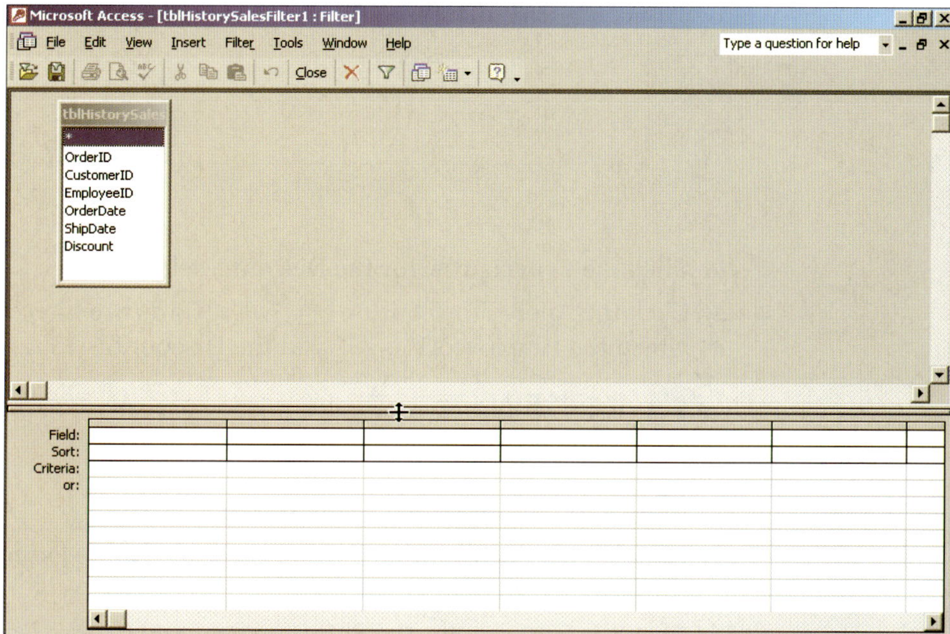

FIGURE 3-15 Resizing the Filter window panes

5. Click the EmployeeID field in the Field Name list box in the top pane. Drag it to the **Field** row of the first column in the lower pane. (When the pointer reaches the lower pane, it shows a field icon.)
6. Click the **Criteria** row under the EmployeeID field in the lower pane. Key **7**. This filter will find records in which the EmployeeID is "7."
7. Click the Apply Filter button. The records are filtered, and the status bar shows the number of records that are displayed.
8. Choose **Records** and then choose **Filter**. Click **Advanced Filter/Sort**.
9. Double-click the Discount field in the Field Name list box. It is added to the design grid in the next available column.

FIGURE 3-16 Adding fields and criteria to the Filter window

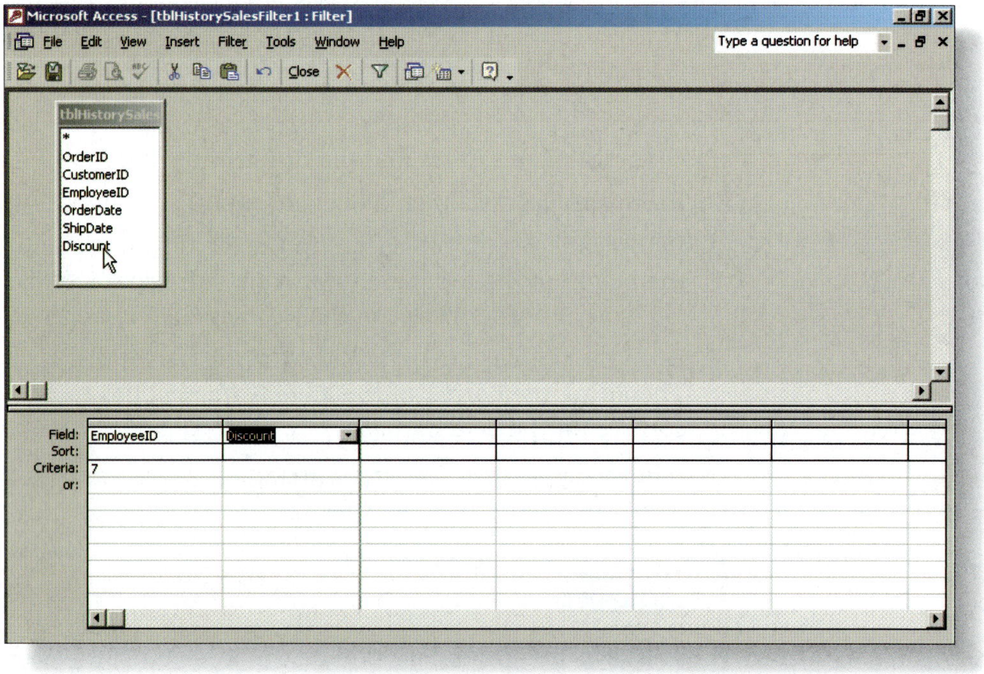

10. Click the Criteria row for the Discount field. Key **.1**
11. Click the Apply Filter button. The records are filtered to show those in which the EmployeeID is "7" and the Discount is 10%.

REVIEW: Ctrl+F6 is a Windows command to toggle between open windows.

12. Press Ctrl+F6 to return to the Design window.
13. Double-click the ShipDate field in the Field Name list box. It is added to the design grid.
14. Click the **Sort** row for the ShipDate field and choose **Descending**.

15. Click the Apply Filter button. The filtered records are sorted with most recent date first.

TIP: You do not need to remove the filter if you do not plan to save the design changes.

16. Close the table. Do not save the design changes.

Using AND/OR Criteria

You have already used more than one condition in some of your filters. Multiple criteria fall into one of two categories—AND or OR. *AND conditions* are database criteria that combine two or more requirements.

An *OR condition* finds records that match any of the criteria you specify. The record needs to match only one of your requirements.

Suppose that you need to list all the stuffed animals in Product Group D and E. Although you might say "D and E," this is actually an OR condition. You want all the products that are in D along with all the products that are in E. This is an OR criteria. It lists products in either Group D or Group E.

Now think about this situation. Suppose you need to list all the stuffed animals in Group D that cost $10.75. A record would have to meet both criteria; this is an AND condition. AND conditions are more restrictive and usually find fewer matching records than OR conditions.

You can use AND/OR conditions in a Filter By Form or in the Filter window.

EXERCISE 3-17 Create an AND/OR Filter By Form

1. Open tblStuffedAnimals and maximize the window.
2. Click the Filter By Form button and click the Clear Grid button.
3. Click in the Product Group field and choose "D" from the list.
4. Click the Apply Filter button.
5. Click the Filter By Form button.
6. Click the **Or** tab at the bottom left of the window. This opens a blank form for the next criteria.

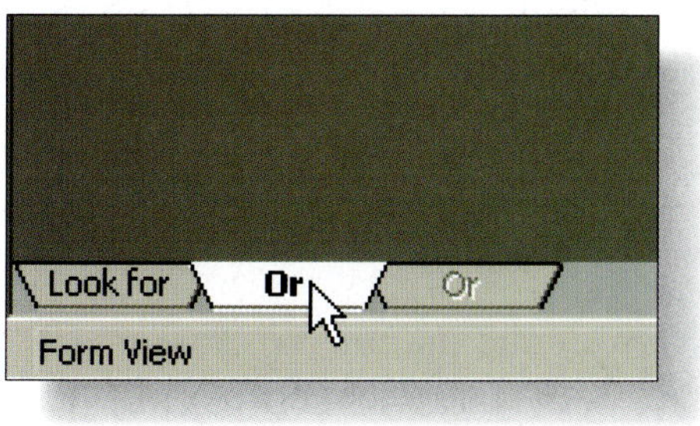

FIGURE 3-17 Click the Or tab to open a new blank form

7. For the Product Group field, choose "E."
8. Click the Apply Filter button. The stuffed animals from either Group D or E are listed.
9. Click the Filter By Form button and click the Clear Grid button.

10. For the Product Group field, choose "E."

11. Click the List Price field and choose 10.75. An AND condition shows all the criteria on the same row.

FIGURE 3-18
An AND condition uses only one form

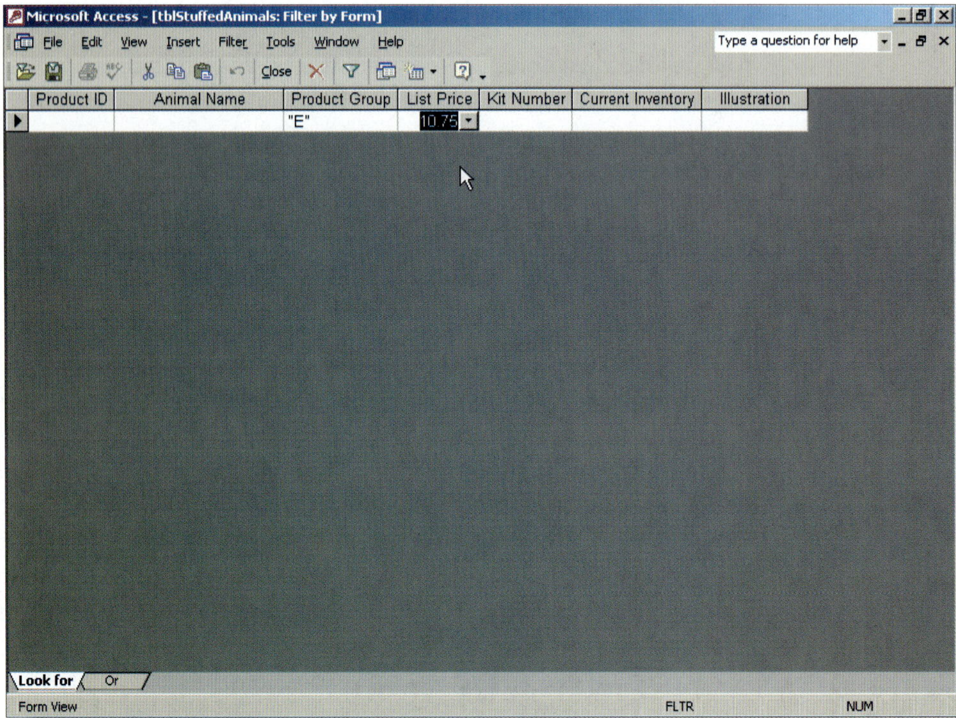

12. Click the Apply Filter button. Stuffed animals from Group E with a list price of $10.75 are listed. Both conditions must be met for the record to be listed.

13. Close the table and do not save the changes.

EXERCISE 3-18 Create an AND/OR Advanced Filter

Filters are very useful for locating and displaying records. When working with large databases, using advanced filters for your searches reduces the time it takes for you to locate important data.

1. Open tblHistorySales and maximize the window.

2. Choose Records and then choose Filter. Click Advanced Filter/Sort.

3. Place the pointer on the horizontal border between the two panes to display the split pointer.

4. Drag the border down to make the top pane taller. Then drag the border for the Field Name list box so you can see more of the field names.

5. Double-click the OrderDate field in the Field Name list box. It is added to the design grid in the first column.
6. Click the **Criteria** row for the Order Date field. Key **>2/1/98**
7. Click the Apply Filter button [Apply Filter icon]. The records are filtered to show those in which the OrderDate is later than 2/1/98.
8. Press Ctrl + F6.

NOTE: When you use a date in a filter or query, Access applies its standard formatting, which encloses the date in # symbols.

9. Double-click the Discount field to add it to the design grid.
10. For the Discount field, click in the **Criteria** row. Key **>0** This is an AND condition; the criteria are entered on the same row.

FIGURE 3-19
An AND condition in the Filter window uses the same row

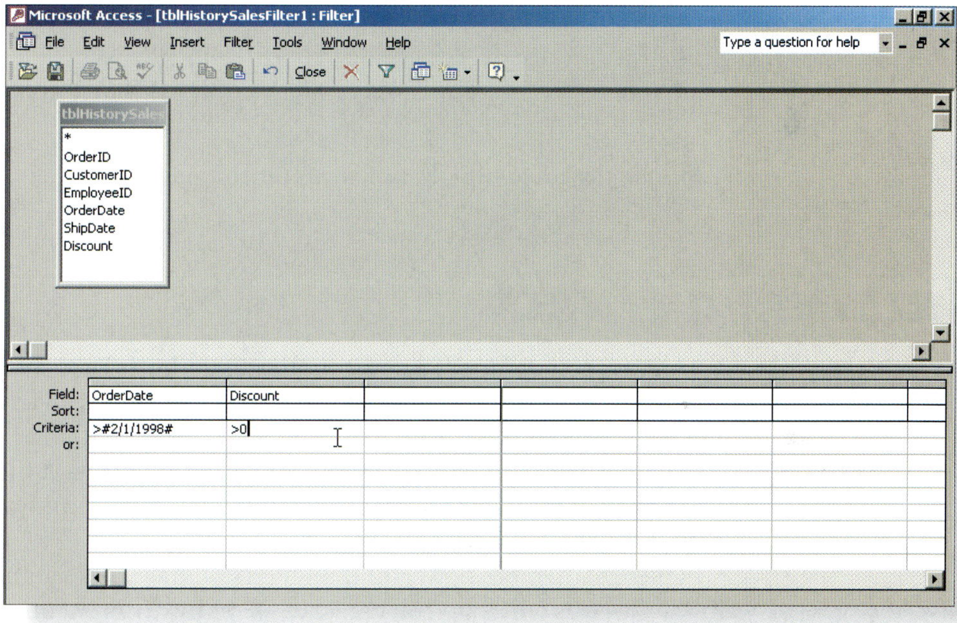

11. Click the Apply Filter button [Apply Filter icon]. The records have an OrderDate after 2/1/98 AND a discount.
12. Press Ctrl + F6. Click the Clear Grid button [Clear Grid icon].
13. Double-click the CustomerID field in the Field Name list box.
14. Click the **Criteria** row for the field and key **1**
15. Click the first **or** row for the field and key **3.** OR conditions are keyed on separate rows. (See Figure 3-20 on the next page.)
16. Click the Apply Filter button [Apply Filter icon]. The filtered records are for Customers 1 OR 3.

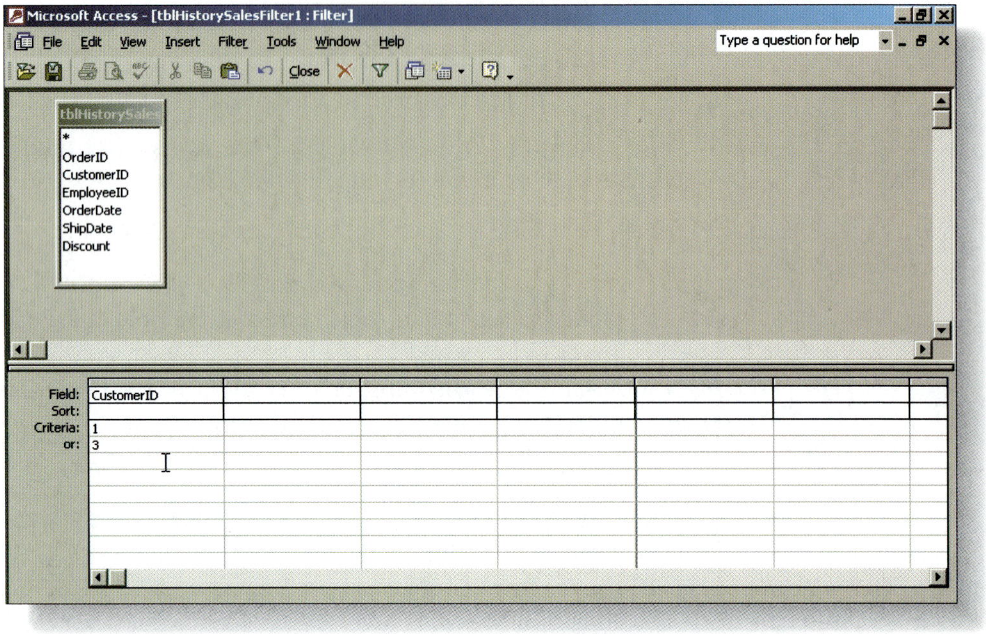

FIGURE 3-20
Using OR criteria in the Filter window

17. Close the table and do not save the changes.

Building a Query

You have already opened several queries in both Datasheet and Design View. A query has many of the same features and properties as an advanced filter, including the field list and the design grid.

With a table, you can save only one filter at a time. A filter is a table property. It is not a database object (like tables, queries, forms, and reports). Only one filter definition can be stored per object.

Queries are more powerful than filters. A query is a database object and appears in the Queries window. You can save as many different queries as necessary, each with a separate name. Unlike a filter, a table can have multiple queries associated to it.

EXERCISE 3-19 Create a Query by Using the Wizard

In Access, the Query Wizard provides simplified steps for designing a query. A *wizard* is a feature that asks questions and uses your answers to create an object automatically. Objects created through a wizard include tables, queries, forms, reports and even databases. Through the wizard, you select the source table, the fields to include, and the order in which the fields appear.

After selecting the fields, you name and run the query. The results of the query you create appear in a Datasheet View. This Datasheet View is a dynaset. A *dynaset* is a dynamic recordset. Changes you make to data in a dynaset are automatically made to the records in the source table.

TABLE 3-3 Wizard Buttons

BUTTON	PURPOSE
>	Adds the selected sample field to the Fields in my new table list.
>>	Adds all the sample fields to the Fields in my new table list.
<	Removes the selected sample field from the Fields in my new table list.
<<	Removes all the sample fields from the Fields in my new table list.

1. Click Query on the Objects bar. Double-click Create query by using wizard.
2. Choose "Table: tblEmployees" from the drop-down list.
3. Double-click on FirstName, LastName, HomePhone, EmergencyContact, and EmergencyPhone.
4. Click Next. Name the query **qryEmergencyContact**

REVIEW: The "qry" prefix is used to identify queries.

5. Click Finish.
6. Move to Sam Kwan's record. Change "Sam" to **Samuel**
7. Close qryEmergencyContact.
8. Open tblEmployees. Move to Samuel Kwan's record. Notice that the changes made in the dynaset were automatically made to the data in the underlying table.
9. Close tblEmployees.

EXERCISE 3-20 Create and Save a Query by Using Design View

You can create a query by using Design View. You have the option of selecting the source table, the fields to include, and the order in which the fields appear, just as you did when using the wizard. Additionally, you can define the criteria used in the query.

1. Click tblHistorySales but do not open it.
2. Click the drop-down arrow next to the New Object button. Choose **Query**.

FIGURE 3-21
New Object shortcut menu

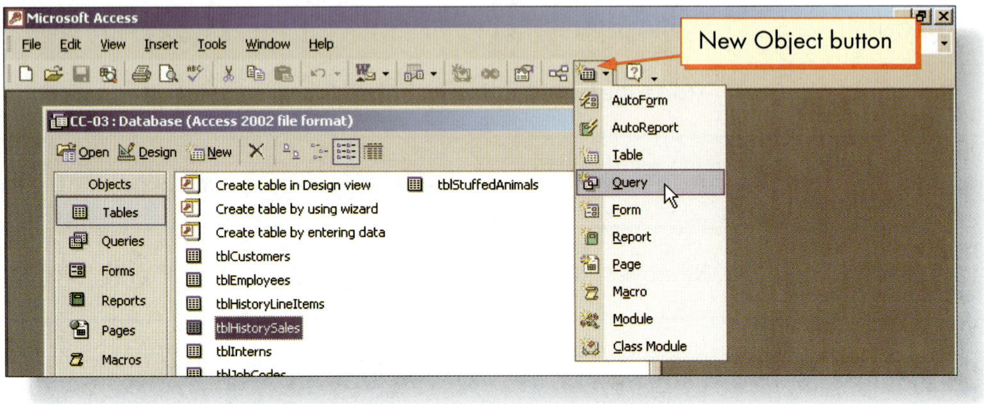

3. The New Query dialog box provides several ways to build a query. Choose **Design View**.

FIGURE 3-22
New Query dialog box

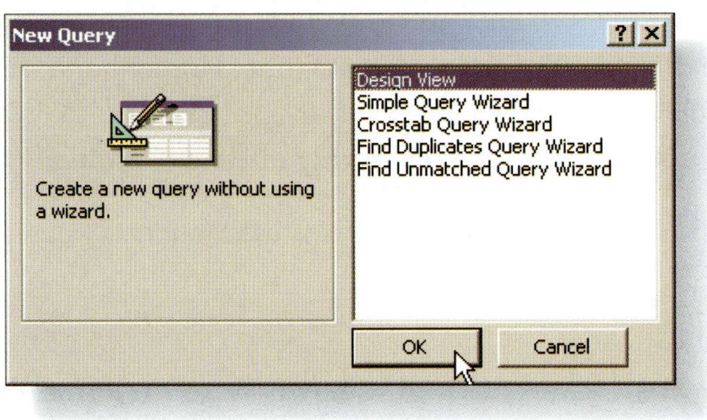

4. Click **OK**. Make certain the window is maximized.
5. Place the pointer on the border between the two panes and make the top pane taller. Then make the Field Name list box taller.
6. In the Field Name list box, double-click the OrderDate field. It is added to the design grid in the first column.
7. Click the **Criteria** row for the OrderDate field. Key **>2/1/98**
8. Click the View button. Only the Order Date field is shown, and only those records in which the OrderDate is after 2/1/98.

REVIEW: You can press Ctrl + > to switch to Datasheet View and then press Ctrl + < to return to Design View.

9. Click the Save button. The Save As dialog box opens.
10. Key **qryHistorySales** as the name and press Enter.

EXERCISE 3-21 Modify a Query

Having created a query either though the wizard or Design View, you can modify the field list, field order, or criteria for the query. You can also add advanced criteria such as AND/OR conditions.

1. Click the View button to return to the design grid.
2. Double-click the Discount field to add it to the design grid.
3. Click on the same **Criteria** row for the Discount field. Key **>0** This is an AND condition; the criteria are entered on the same row.

FIGURE 3-23 An AND condition in the Query Design window uses the same row

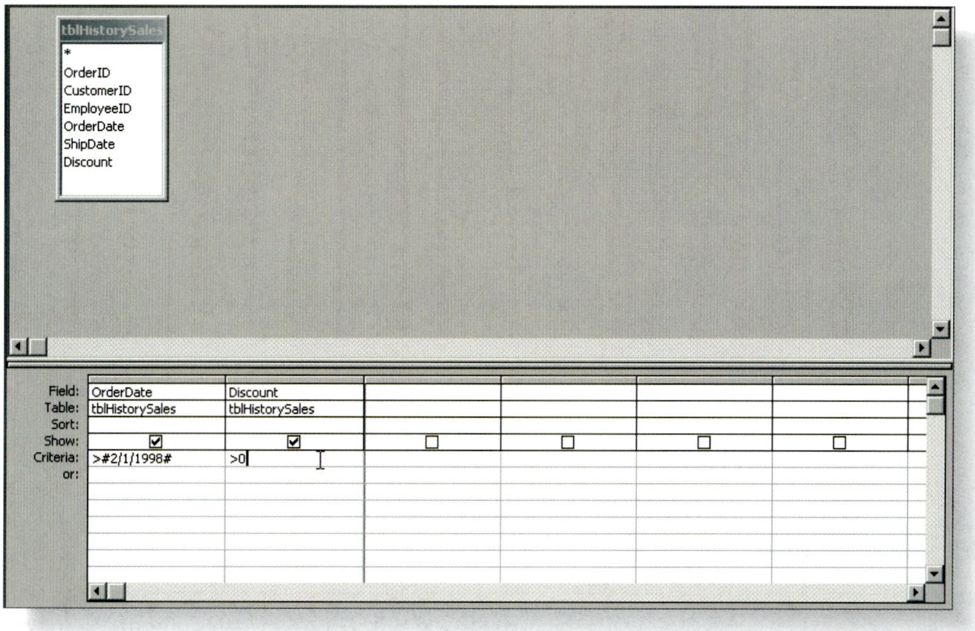

4. Click the View button. Both fields are shown, and the records have an OrderDate after 2/1/98 and a discount.
5. Click the View button. Choose Edit, and then choose Clear Grid.
6. Double-click the OrderID field and the CustomerID field in the field list to add them to the design grid.
7. For the CustomerID field, click the **Criteria** row and key **1**
8. Click the View button. This criteria shows all orders from Customer 1.
9. Return to the design grid.
10. Click the first or row for the CustomerID field and key **3**. (See Figure 3-24 on the next page.)
11. Click the View button. The criteria shows all orders from either Customer 1 or 3.

ACCESS

FIGURE 3-24
OR conditions in a query use different rows

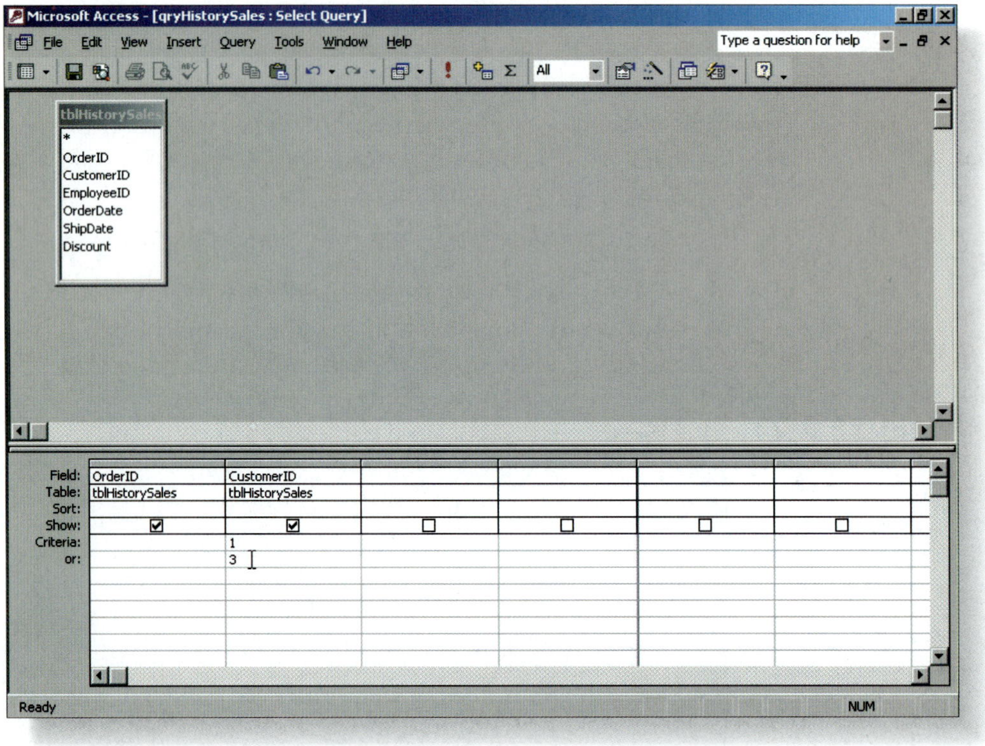

12. Close and save the query.

13. Compact and repair the database; then close it.

USING HELP

A special type of Help called "What's This?" is available for toolbar buttons and many options in a dialog box. When you use "What's This?" the mouse pointer changes to a question mark. You can then point at a button or command name and click to display a ScreenTip. You can also use the Answer Wizard, similar to the Office Assistant, from the Microsoft Access Help window.

Use What's This? and the Answer Wizard:

1. Open tblEmployees in ***[your initials]*CC-03**.

2. Choose Help, and then choose What's This?

3. Point at the Filter By Selection button  and click. A ScreenTip opens with a description of the button.

4. To print the ScreenTip, point at it and click the right mouse button. Choose Print Topic from the shortcut menu. (Click Cancel if you do not want to print the topic.)

5. Click the ScreenTip to close it.

6. Click the What's This? button.
7. Click the File menu and choose Page Setup. A description of the Page Setup feature appears.
8. Click the ScreenTip to remove it.
9. Click the View button. Press Shift+F1 to start the What's This? Help feature.

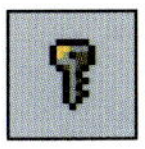

10. Point at the Primary Key button and click. Read the description of "Primary Key" and then click the ScreenTip to close it.
11. Close the table.
12. Choose Help and then choose Microsoft Access Help. If the Office Assistant starts, turn it off.
13. Click the Answer Wizard tab. Triple-click in the What would you like to do? text box.
14. Key **sort records** and press Enter.

FIGURE 3-25
Using the Answer Wizard

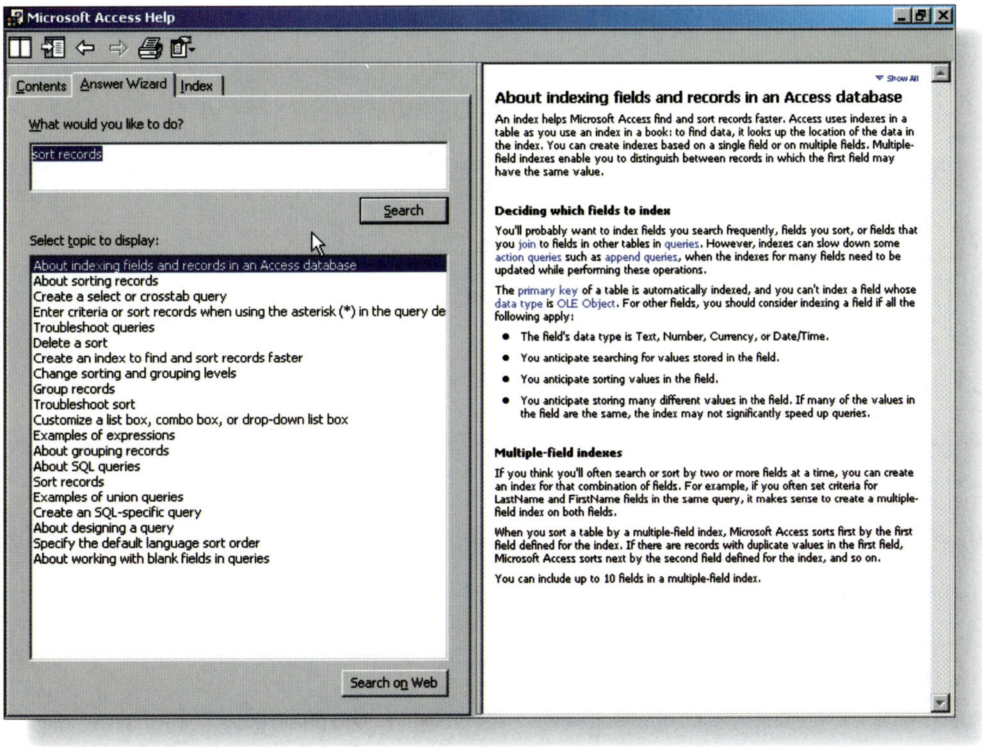

15. Click Delete a sort in the Select a topic to display list box. In the right pane, click Delete a sort order in Form view or Datasheet view. Read the Help window.

16. Triple-click in the What would you like to do? text box.
17. Key **filters and queries** and press Enter.
18. Click About using criteria to retrieve certain records.
19. Click Combining criteria with the And or the Or operator and read all subtopics.
20. Close the Help windows when you have finished.

LESSON 3 Summary

- The Find command helps locate specific records by searching up and down a recordset.
- You can fine-tune searches by matching case and by searching for parts of a field.
- The asterisk (*) wildcard represents any number of characters in a search. The question mark (?) wildcard represents a single character in a search.
- The Replace command matches text and replaces it with other text. The Replace All command replaces text without prompting the user.
- QuickSorts provide easy ways to sort a recordset by a single field in Datasheet View. QuickSorts can sort a recordset by several adjacent fields in Datasheet View.
- You can sort queries in Design View.
- You can use Filter By Selection to sort by an entire field. You can combine Filter By Selections.
- You save filters as a table property.
- A Filter By Form is more flexible than a Filter By Selection.
- You can apply wildcards and Is Null criteria to filters.
- The Filter By Input and Filter Excluding Selection provide flexible methods of creating recordsets.
- You can use several fields and sophisticated expressions in Advanced Filters and Sorts.
- You can use AND conditions and OR conditions in a Filter By Form.
- You can use AND conditions and OR conditions in Advanced Filters.
- The Query Wizard creates simple queries.
- You can create and modify queries by using Design View.

LESSON 3 Command Summary

FEATURE	BUTTON	MENU	KEYBOARD	SPEECH
Apply Filter		Records, Apply Filter/Sort		✓
Display List			F4	
Filter By Selection		Records, Filter, Filter By Selection		✓
Filter By Form		Records, Filter, Filter By Form		✓
Filter Excluding Selection		Records, Filter, Filter Excluding Selection		✓
Find		Edit, Find	Ctrl + F	✓
Next Window			Ctrl + F6	
Remove Filter		Records, Remove Filter/Sort		✓
Replace		Edit, Replace	Ctrl + H	✓
Select Field			F2	
Sort, Ascending		Records, Sort, Ascending		✓
Sort, Descending		Records, Sort, Descending		✓
What's This Help		Help, What's This?	Shift + F1	✓
Zoom Window		View, Properties	Shift + F2	✓

Concepts Review

TRUE/FALSE QUESTIONS

Each of the following statements is either true or false. Indicate your choice by circling T or F.

T F **1.** The results of a Filter By Form created in a table are displayed in a form.

T F **2.** The keyboard command to find text is Ctrl+H.

T F **3.** You can use filters or queries to apply multiple criteria or conditions.

T F **4.** The asterisk (*) wildcard finds exact matches for a single character anywhere in the field.

T F **5.** To narrow your search, you can use the Match Case option to find words with the same capitalization.

T F **6.** When using the Sort command to sort multiple columns in Datasheet View, the columns must be next to each other.

T F **7.** In a query, OR conditions are keyed on separate rows.

T F **8.** A query can be sorted in Datasheet View or Design View.

SHORT ANSWER QUESTIONS

Write the correct answer in the space provided.

1. Why might you need to move the Find and Replace dialog box?

____

2. What command updates all occurrences of data without confirmation?

____

3. What word describes a sort from lowest to highest number or from A to Z?

____

4. How do you add fields to the design grid in the Filter window or Query Design window?

____

5. What is a "dynaset"?

____

6. What criteria is used to find empty records in an OLE field?

___

7. What wildcard character can you use to find a name when you remember only its first three characters?

___

8. What Search option do you select when you want to search an entire table?

___

CRITICAL THINKING

Answer these questions on a separate page. There are no right or wrong answers. Support your answers with examples from your own experience, if possible.

1. The Replace All option can create problems if you haven't thought through a specific Replace All operation. Describe what types of problems or issues might occur and discuss precautions you might take when using Replace All.

2. Filters and queries show only the records that meet your conditions. Give some examples of when and why you might use filters or queries for different tables.

Lesson Applications

EXERCISE 3-22

Sort records. Find and replace data in a table.

1. Start Access and open the file ***[your initials]*****CC-03**. Open tblKitContents.

TIP: Check the options in the Replace dialog box for each activity.

2. Sort the records by Kit Number in descending order.

3. Click in the Kit Number field.

4. Find all occurrences of "pig" within the Kit Number field. Match any part of the word without using a case-sensitive search.

5. Use the Replace command to replace all occurrences of "Ted" with "Bear." Set the Match option to Any Part of Field.

6. Close tblKitContents and do not save the changes.

7. Open tblStuffedAnimals. It includes data related to tblKitContents.

8. Sort by Kit Number in descending order and then use the Replace command to change all occurrences of "Ted" to "Bear."

9. Key your initials in uppercase letters after "Zebra" in the first record.

10. Print the table using landscape orientation.

11. Close the tblStuffedAnimals table and do not save the changes.

REVIEW: Data changes are saved automatically. The design changes were the sort orders.

EXERCISE 3-23

Use filters to display records.

1. Open tblHistoryLineItems.

2. Use Filter By Selection to show all the items for Order 20006. How many product types were ordered? How many total products were ordered? Remove the filter.

NOTE: When you are asked a question in this exercise, write your answers on a piece of paper to hand in. Include your name, class information, and date.

3. Use Filter By Selection to show all the orders that included ProductID F002. How many of this product were sold? Write your answer on your answer sheet. Remove the filter. Notice how many records are in this table.

4. Use Filter Excluding Selection to show orders that did not include ProductID T005. How many records are not this item? Write your answer on your answer sheet. Remove the filter.
5. Close tblHistoryLineItems and do not save the changes.
6. Open frmEmployeeInformation.
7. Right-click in the Last Name field and use Filter For to find Maria Floria's record. Remove the filter.
8. How many records are there? Write your answer on your answer sheet.
9. Create a Filter By Form and clear the grid. Add criteria to find records in which the picture field has a picture. How many records do not have a picture? Write your answer on your answer sheet.
10. Remove the filter and close the form.

EXERCISE 3-24

Use AND and OR conditions in a Filter By Form. Use an Advanced Filter.

1. Open tblKitContents.
2. Use a Filter By Form to find the kits from Suppliers BB-02 or DD-04. How many kits fit the criteria? Remove the filter.

NOTE: When you are asked a question in this exercise, write your answers on a piece of paper to hand in. Include your name, class information, and date.

3. Use a Filter By Form and clear the grid. Find records from Supplier AA-01 that cost more than $5. The cost criteria is >5 with no dollar sign or decimal point. How many kits fit the criteria? Write your answer on your answer sheet.

REVIEW: OR conditions are entered on separate forms. AND conditions are entered on the same form.

4. Close tblKitContents and do not save the changes.
5. Open qryCustomers and create and apply an Advanced Filter. First use the City field to find customers in Chattanooga. Then add the Billing Address field to the filter design so you can find customers in Chattanooga with the word "Dobson" in the address.

TIP: Use wildcards in front of and behind the search string to find matching addresses.

6. Change the Contact name to ***[your first and last name]***.
7. Print the results of the filter; use Landscape orientation.
8. Close the query and do not save changes.

EXERCISE 3-25 Challenge Yourself

Build a query.

1. Choose tblKitSuppliers and use the New Object button to build a query in Design View.
2. Size the panes in the Query Design window.
3. Add the SupplierID, SupplierName, and PhoneNumber fields to the design grid.
4. Add criteria in the SupplierName field to find companies that have any form of the word "fabric" in their names.
5. Save the query as **qrySuppliers*[your last name]***.
6. Print the query.
7. Compact the database and exit Access.

On Your Own

In these exercises you work on your own, as you would in a real-life work environment. Use the skills you've learned to accomplish the task—and be creative.

EXERCISE 3-26

Review the Web sites you located in Exercises 2-24 and 2-25 of the companies that sell products of interest to members of the club you formed. Determine which companies allow products to be sorted or displayed by different conditions. On a sheet of paper, write down the fields that can be sorted or selected. Continue to the next exercise.

EXERCISE 3-27

For one of the Web sites, print three lists of products sorted or filtered by various methods. Write a brief description of the sort or filter being applied on each of the three printouts. Continue to the next exercise.

EXERCISE 3-28

Refer to the form you created in Exercise 2-26. Write down the fields that may be used to sort or filter the information displayed on the form. Sketch two new forms based on your sorting and filtering parameters. Submit your work for Exercises 3-26 through 3-28 to your instructor.

UNIT 2

Building a Database

LESSON

4

Creating Databases and Tables

OBJECTIVES

MOUS ACTIVITIES

In this lesson:

Ac2002 **1-1**
Ac2002 **2-1**
Ac2002 **2-4**
Ac2002 **5-1**
Ac2002 **8-1**

See Appendix E.

After completing this lesson, you will be able to:

1. **Create a new database.**
2. **Create a table by using the Table Wizard.**
3. **Edit field properties.**
4. **Insert and delete fields.**
5. **Create a table in Datasheet View.**
6. **Import data.**

Estimated Time: 1½ hours

In the previous unit, you worked with data in tables, with queries, and with forms in an existing database. You learned how to navigate through records, how to edit data, and how to add records. In this lesson, you learn how to create a new database. Then you learn how to add tables to a database by using:

- The Table Wizard
- Design View
- Datasheet View
- Import

Creating a New Database

In the previous lessons, you worked with two existing databases that included objects and data. Most people work with existing databases rather than creating totally new ones. However, on some occasions you might need to create a new database.

There are two methods for creating databases. One method develops a structure containing major objects (tables, queries, forms, or reports), but no data. The other method creates a blank database without any objects or data.

Prior to creating a new database, you should analyze the needs of the people who will use it. You should plan for the type of data that will be entered, stored, and displayed. Most database designers have had extensive prior experience working with data and databases.

EXERCISE 4-1 Create a Database by Using the Database Wizard

Access provides many database templates that use a wizard to step you through the creation of a new database. A *database template* is a wizard that creates a functional database structure based on user selections. Using the wizard is only valuable when there is a template that closely matches your needs. Each template has a predefined list of fields from which you must select.

When you use a Database Wizard, a main switchboard is created. A *main switchboard* is a form that helps a user navigate around a database. When the database is launched, the main switchboard automatically opens. You then can use the main switchboard to navigate within the database.

NOTE: The databases you create and modify in this course relate to the Case Study (see pages 995 through 998) about Carolina Critters, a fictional company that manufactures stuffed animals.

1. Click the Start button on the Windows taskbar and point to Programs.
2. Click Microsoft Access 2002. (You might have to point first to a program group such as Microsoft Office.) Access loads.

3. After Access is loaded, click the New button. The New File Task Pane appears on the right side of the screen. (See Figure 4-1 on the next page.)
4. In the New from template section, click General Templates.
5. Click the Databases tab.
6. Choose the Asset Tracking wizard and click OK.
7. The File New Database dialog box asks you to name the new database and indicate where to save it. The dialog box shows a default name based on the wizard you specified.

FIGURE 4-1
New File Task Pane

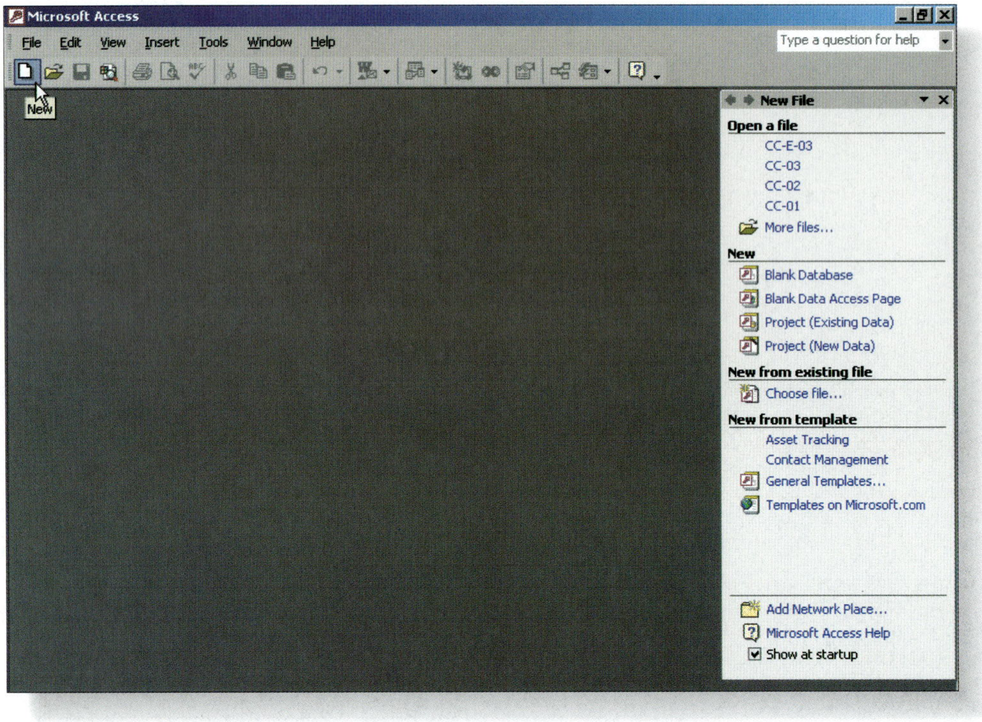

8. Save the new database to your desktop. Click Create to use the default file name, **Asset Tracking1**.

NOTE: At the end of this exercise, you will delete this database. It is used only to demonstrate the Database Wizard. You will not need to keep a copy of the file.

9. The first dialog box explains what this database will store. Click Next.
10. This dialog box lists the tables on the left and the fields for each table on the right. Click each table name on the left and review the field names. A check mark next to the field name indicates that the field will be included in the new database. Access shows optional field names in italic. You can see an optional Home Phone field in the Information about employees table.
11. Click the check box to select the Home Phone field. (See Figure 4-2 on the next page.)
12. Click Next. In the next dialog box, you select the style to be used for all forms. Choose SandStone and click Next.
13. Next you select the report style. Choose Formal and click Next.
14. Title this database **Asset Control** and click Finish. After the database is built, the title appears on the Main Switchboard of the **Asset Tracking1** database. (See Figure 4-3 on the next page.)

FIGURE 4-2
Selecting fields to include in the new database

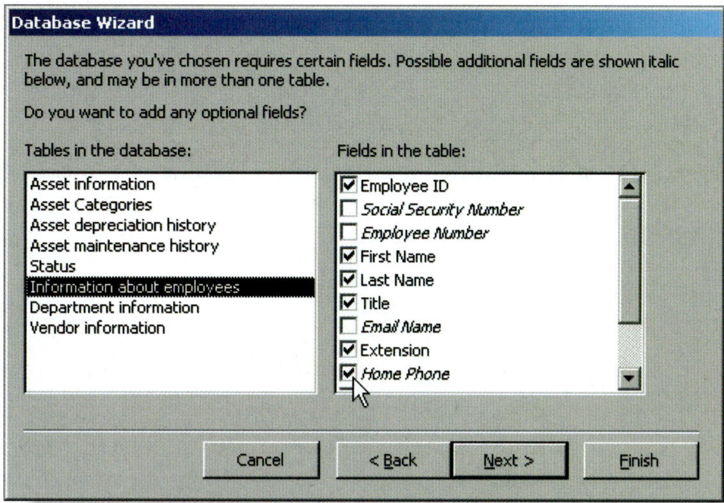

FIGURE 4-3
Main Switchboard and database window

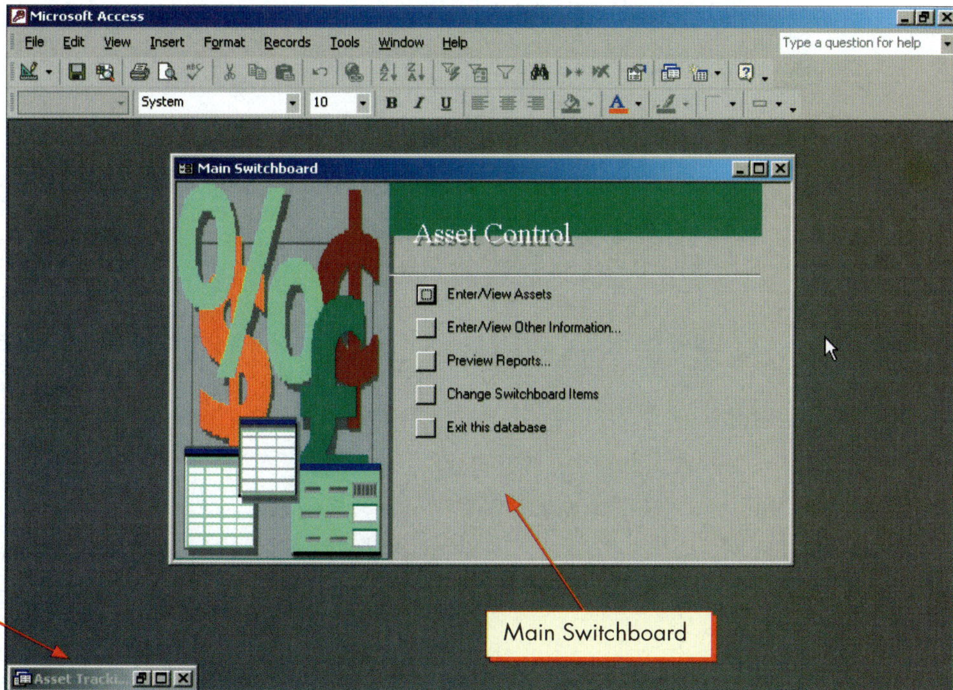

NOTE: Whenever the Main Switchboard is open, the database window is minimized.

15. Close the Main Switchboard Form.

16. Maximize the database window located in the lower left corner of the screen.

17. Notice that the Database Wizard created seven tables, eleven forms, and five reports. However, if you open a table, you will see that it does not contain any data.
18. Close the database.
19. Now that you have seen how the wizard works, delete the Asset Tracking1 database from your desktop.

EXERCISE 4-2 Create a Blank Database

If you cannot find a database template to meet your needs, you must create a blank database from scratch. You only will be required to name the database and specify a location in which to save it. After you have saved the blank database, you must create new tables so you can add data. You will be able to add other major objects such as queries, reports, and forms at a later time.

1. Click the New button. The New File Task Pane appears on the right side of the screen.
2. In the New section, click Blank Database.
3. The File New Database dialog box asks you to name the new database and indicate where it should be saved. It shows a default file name of **db1**.
4. Verify your Save in location.

REVIEW: Your instructor will tell you where to save the database. In this course, do not work on a database from a floppy drive.

5. Triple-click **db1** to select it. Key ***[your first and last name]*** (do not include a space between your names) as the File name.
6. Click Create. A blank database window opens with no objects. Notice the name of the database in the title bar and its file format.

Creating Tables by Using a Wizard

The Table Wizard is a quick and easy way to produce tables containing commonly used fields. In the Table Wizard, you select the type of table (such as customer lists, employee lists, invoices sent, or new projects). The Table Wizard then provides a list of suggested fields. After selecting the fields and naming the table, you can start adding records. Tables created by using the wizard provide a structure you can later modify.

EXERCISE 4-3 Choose Fields in the Table Wizard

The Table Wizard displays predefined table lists in two groups, Personal and Business. Each table has a predefined list of fields. From these lists you select which fields will be used and the order in which they will appear in the new table. After you have finished using the Wizard, you can change the field names and the order in which they appear in the table.

1. With your database window open, click the Tables button. Click the New command button. The New Table dialog box opens.

FIGURE 4-4 New Table dialog box

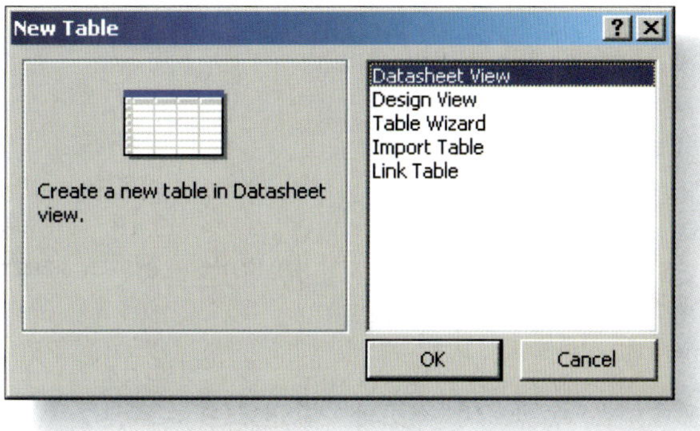

2. Click Table Wizard and OK. The first dialog box of the Table Wizard opens, with sample tables on the left and related sample fields in the middle. The sample tables relate to either business or personal activities.
3. Above the list of Sample Tables, click the Business option button.
4. In the Sample Tables list, select Customers.

FIGURE 4-5 Table Wizard dialog box

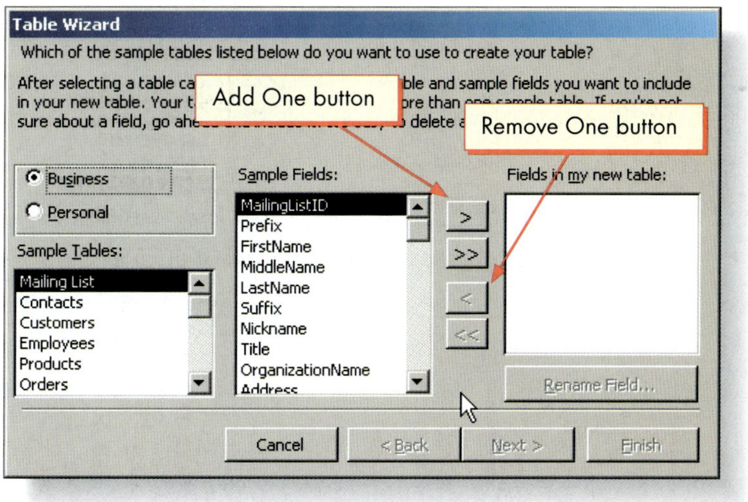

NOTE: The Sample Tables and Sample Fields lists are not in alphabetical order. The field names follow the Leszynski Naming Conventions.

5. Select the CustomerID field and click the Add One button [>]. The CustomerID field is added to the Fields in my new table list.

REVIEW: If you add a sample field to your field list by mistake, select the name and move it back to the Sample Fields list by clicking the Remove One button [<].

6. Add the following sample fields to the **Fields in my new table** list by double-clicking the field in the **Sample Field** list. (You can also select the name and click the Add One button [>].)

   CompanyName
   ContactFirstName
   BillingAddress
   StateOrProvince
   PostalCode
   ContactTitle
   PhoneNumber
   FaxNumber

NOTE: You can create a custom table by choosing sample fields from more than one table.

FIGURE 4-6 Table Wizard dialog box with added fields

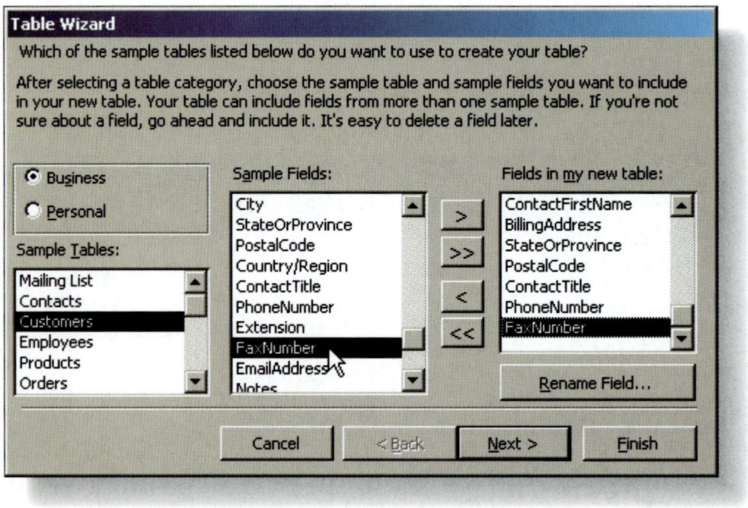

EXERCISE 4-4 Rename Fields in the Table Wizard

While in the Table Wizard, you can rename the selected fields to make the names more descriptive of the data. For example, if your company has customers only in the United States, you might wish to rename the field PostalCode to ZIPCode.

TIP: You can rename a field in Table Design View.

1. Select the CompanyName field in your list.
2. Click the Rename Field command button in the Table Wizard dialog box. The Rename field dialog box opens with the field name highlighted.
3. Key **Customer** in the Rename field text box. Click OK. Customer replaces CompanyName in the Fields in my new table list.

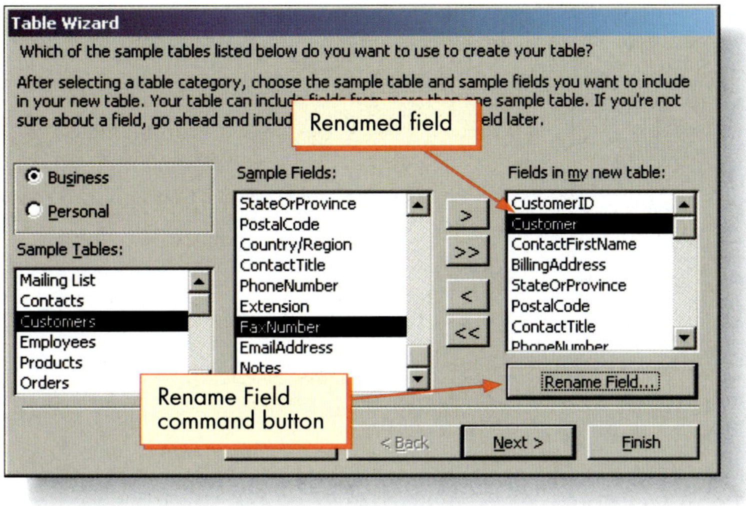

FIGURE 4-7 Renamed field appears in the Fields In My New Table list

4. Select the ContactFirstName field in your list. Click Rename Field.
5. In the Rename field dialog box, edit the name to **ContactName**. Click OK.
6. Rename StateOrProvince to **State** and click OK.
7. Rename ContactTitle to **EmployeeID** and click OK.

EXERCISE 4-5 Name the Table and Enter Records

When using the wizard to create a table, in addition to selecting the fields for the table, you will be asked to define a primary key. Remember that a primary key is a field containing unique data that is used to identify each record in a table. Many business processes use some form of unique identifier such as a check number, an employee social security number, or a customer number.

1. After renaming the fields, click Next. The dialog box asks what you want to name your new table. Access enters a default name based on the sample table you selected.

REVIEW: When creating new tables, you should use the Leszynski Naming Conventions. This means tables are preceded by the prefix "tbl" and the first letter of main words are capitalized with no spaces between words.

ACCESS

2. Key **tblCustomers** in the What do you want to name your table? text box.
3. Read the paragraph about the primary key. Then select No, I'll set the primary key.

FIGURE 4-8 Naming the table

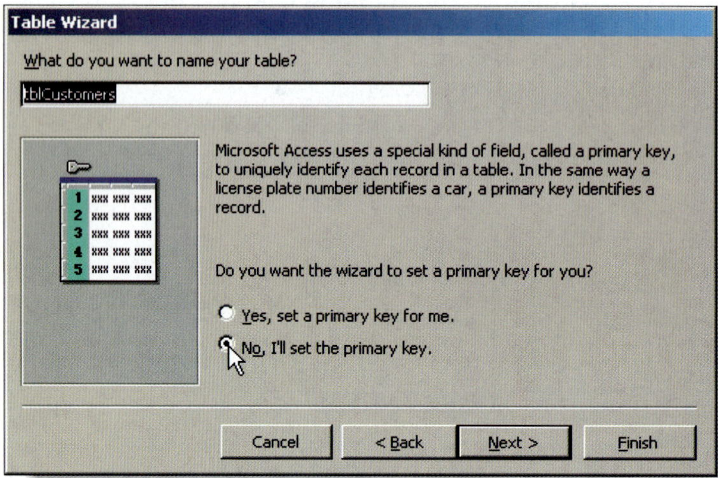

NOTE: When a wizard dialog box has a Back command button, you can use it to return to the previous dialog box to view or change your choices.

4. Click Next. CustomerID will hold unique data for each record, making it the primary key. Select Numbers I enter when I add new records.

FIGURE 4-9 Setting the primary key

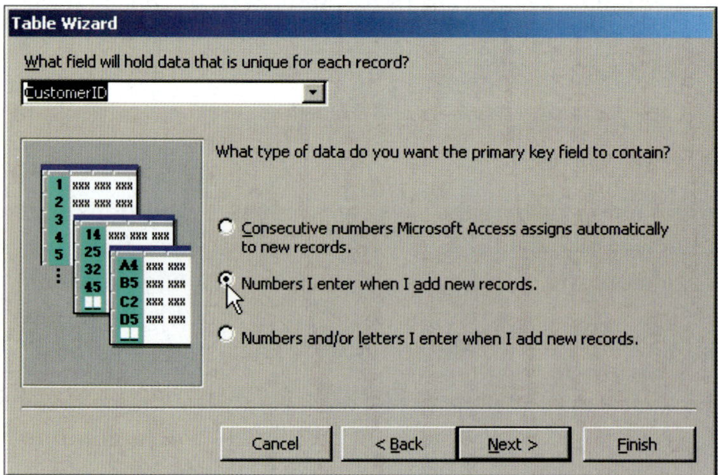

5. Click Next. Access now has the information it needs to create the table. You have the option to modify the table design, enter data directly into the table, or enter data through a form created by a wizard.

6. Select Enter data directly into the table. Click Finish. The table opens, ready for you to enter data. The columns have a default width so you might not see the complete field names.

7. Maximize the window and add the following three records to the table.

REVIEW: Use the Tab key to move from one field to another.

Customer ID:	1
Customer:	Crafts & More
ContactName:	Caroline Morgan
Billing Address:	22651 45th Avenue
State:	WA
Postal Code:	98032-2265
EmployeeID:	6
Phone Number:	(206) 555-1919
Fax Number:	(206) 555-1199

Customer ID:	2
Customer:	Bears & Such
ContactName:	Wayne Fitch
Billing Address:	141 Route 1
State:	VA
Postal Code:	24472-0141
EmployeeID:	7
Phone Number:	(703) 555-2734
Fax Number:	(703) 555-2735

Customer ID:	3
Customer:	The Doll and Bear Barn
ContactName:	Theodora Alexander
Billing Address:	365 Main Street
State:	CT
Postal Code:	06085-0365
EmployeeID:	7
Phone Number:	(860) 555-9116
Fax Number:	(860) 555-9117

8. Close the table.

Editing Field Properties

You use Design View to modify the design or structure of a table. Design View shows the following:

- *Field name* describes the information in the field (a column).
- *Data type* identifies the type of information in the field (such as alphabetic or numeric data.)
- *Field description* is optional and further clarifies the purpose of the field.
- *Field properties* are settings that affect how a field looks and acts. Each data type has a specific list of properties that you can change.

NOTE: Spaces in field names are not recommended in the Access' object naming rules and in the Leszynski Naming Conventions. Spaces create additional requirements for advanced features such as macros and VBA modules.

EXERCISE 4-6 View Table Design

After creating a table by using the Table Wizard, you should check the table design to determine if you need to modify field properties such as Field Size. In Design View, field names are listed on the top half of the screen. The properties for the selected field are displayed on the bottom half of the screen.

You also might need to modify Captions or add field descriptions to make your table more useful. A *Caption* is a field property that controls the column selector in Datasheet View. The field description for a selected field displays in the status bar of objects such as forms or queries.

A key icon to the left of the field indicates which field is the primary key. For each selected property, a short Help message appears in the lower right portion of the screen.

TABLE 4-1 Access Data Types

SETTING	TYPE OF DATA
Text	Alphanumeric data. A text field can be up to 255 characters long. Use Text as the Data Type for numbers that aren't used in calculations (addresses, phone numbers).
Memo	Descriptive text such as sentences and paragraphs. Use a memo field for comments and notes that do not fit other Data Types. A memo field cannot be sorted or used in filters. It can store up to 64,000 characters.

continues

TABLE 4-1 Access Data Types *continued*

SETTING	TYPE OF DATA
Number	Numbers with or without a decimal point. Data in a number field can be used in arithmetic calculations.
Date/Time	Formatted dates or times that can be used in date and time calculations.
Currency	Money values that include the symbol and can be used in arithmetic calculations.
AutoNumber	Consecutive numbers assigned automatically as you add a record. It is also known as a "counter" and often used as the primary key.
Yes/No	Either "Yes" or "No," "True" or "False," or "0" or "–1." Known as a logical field.
OLE Object	Pictures, sound or video clips, or other files created in another application. An OLE field cannot be sorted and is limited in filters.
Hyperlink	Internet site, e-mail address, or file pathname. The data is displayed as hyperlink text. When you click it, Access searches for the Internet site or address or opens the file.

1. Open tblCustomers and maximize the window.

2. Click the View button [icon] to switch to Design View. A window with two panes opens. The top pane lists the field names, Data Types, and descriptions. The wizard does not set descriptions for any field. Notice the small key symbol in the row selector next to the CustomerID field, indicating that this field is the primary key. (See Figure 4-10 on the next page.)
3. Press F6. The insertion point moves to the lower pane. The lower pane displays the field properties of the current field. It includes two tabs, **General** and **Lookup**. In the lower right corner of the screen, a Help window displays definitions and hints related to any field property selected on the left.
4. Press F6 again to move the insertion point to the top pane. Click on the field name Customer. The Customer field properties are now listed in the lower pane.
5. Click the PostalCode row in the top pane and press F6. This field has a Caption that shows a space between the words.
6. Click the PhoneNumber row in the top pane. Notice the Caption for this field in the bottom pane.
7. Click the State row. This text field has no Caption and has a Field Size of 20 spaces.

FIGURE 4-10
Customers table in Design View

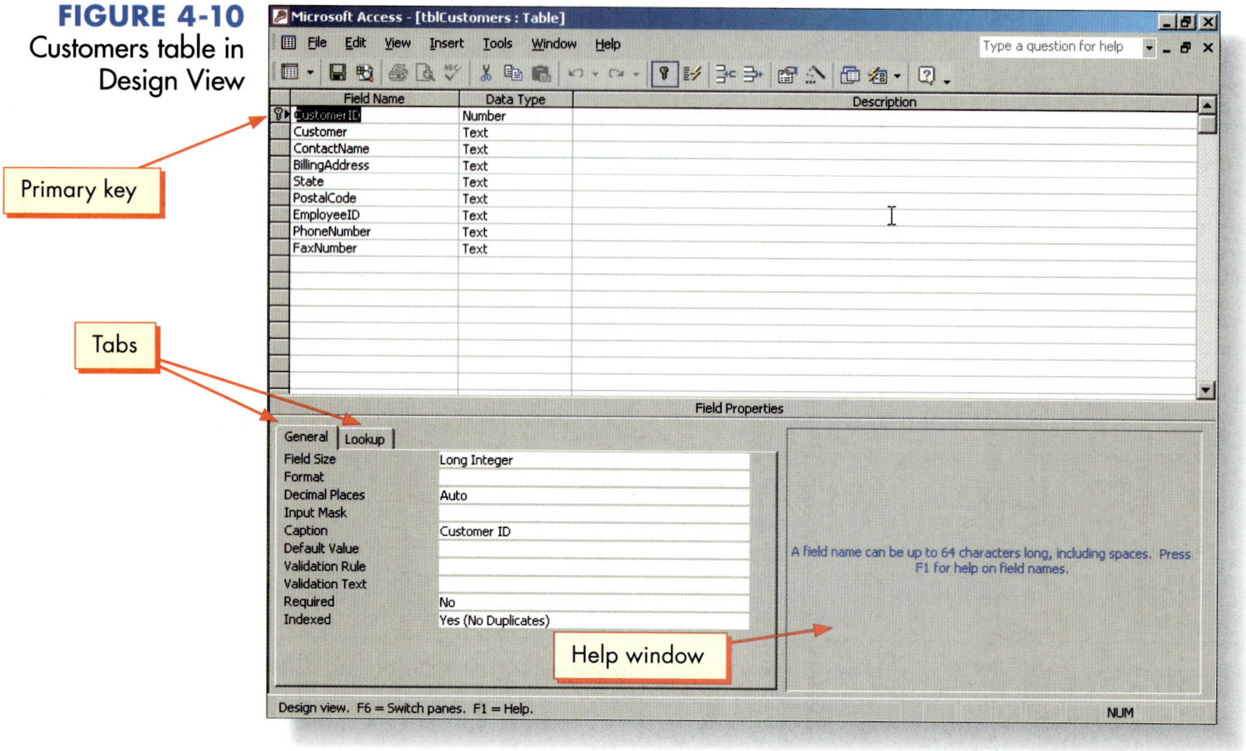

EXERCISE 4-7 Edit Field Properties

At this stage you can use Design View to edit the table structure. Changes to the table design might affect the data already stored in the table. For example, if you have a long title stored as a text field, reducing the size of the field might cut off characters from some records.

TABLE 4-2 Text Field Properties

PROPERTY	PURPOSE
Field Size	Sets the size of a text field and can be up to 255 characters. Access uses only the space it needs for the data when the size is larger than the data. Data that does not fit is cut off.
Format	Defines the appearance of data. You can use a Format to force characters to upper- or lowercase, or you can format dates to appear as "May 5, 2002" even though you key "05/05/02."

continues

TABLE 4-2 Text Field Properties *continued*

PROPERTY	PURPOSE
Input Mask	Displays a model or pattern for entering the data. Examples are the parentheses around an area code or the hyphen in a social security number.
Caption	Sets a label or title for the field other than the field name. The Caption appears as the column title in the table and as the label for the controls in forms and reports.
Default Value	Enters a value for new records. If all employees live in Illinois, you can set "IL" as the Default Value for the State field.
Validation Rule	Expression that specifies criteria or requirements for entering data. The following is an example of a Validation Rule: ">100." This rule would not allow you to enter a number less than 100 in the field.
Validation Text	Text that displays if you violate the Validation Rule. For the rule ">100," you might use the Validation Text "You must enter a value greater than 100."
Required	Requires an entry in the field when set to "Yes."
Allow Zero Length	Used in combination with the Required field to determine if blank text fields can be assigned a zero length string ("") or Null. Blank fields are assigned a "Null" value which is different from zero or no text.
Indexed	Increases the speed of searches and queries, but might slow general operations. Set this to "Yes" for fields that you use to find or sort records.
Unicode Compression	Two-byte character representation for the Jet 4.0 database engine. This format requires more space so this option compresses the data.
IME Mode	Property applies to all East Asian languages.
IME Sentence Mode	Property applies to Japanese only.

1. Select the State field name in the top pane. Press F6. In the Field Size property, key **2** to make the field narrower.
2. Click the BillingAddress field name in the top pane. This text field has a Caption and a Field Size of 255 spaces.
3. In the Field Size property, key **50**

TIP: Text fields should be wide enough to hold most data, but not so wide that they waste space.

4. Click in the Description row for ContactName. Key **Person to call at this location**.
5. Close the table. Because you changed the design of the table, Access reminds you to save it. Click Yes to save the new design.

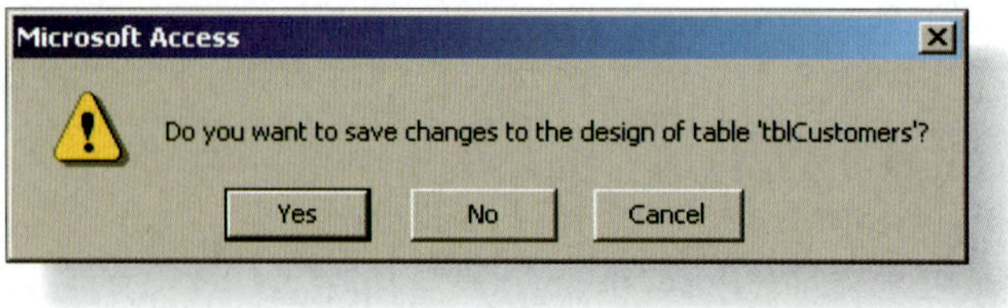

FIGURE 4-11 Save Table dialog box

6. Because you changed the Field Size, Access warns that some data might be lost. It would be cut off or truncated if you make the Field Size too small. That will not happen in this case, so click Yes to continue.

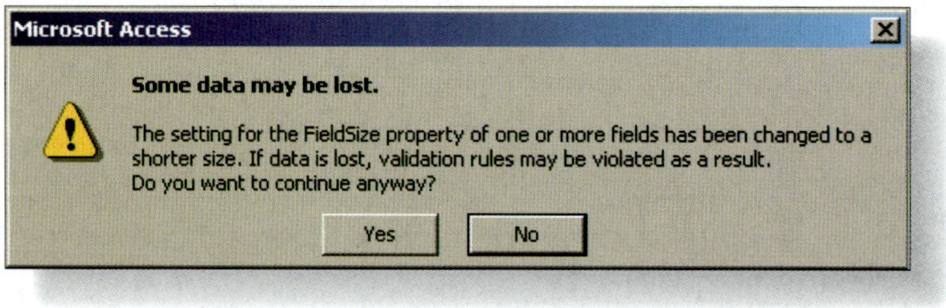

FIGURE 4-12 Access warns that some data might be lost

7. Open tblCustomers and maximize the window.
8. Click anywhere in the ContactName column. Read the description in the status bar in the lower left corner of the screen.
9. Close the table.

NOTE: When you changed the Field Size of the State field, you changed the design size, not the display size. The field requires less space in the database file but can be displayed in any width.

Inserting and Deleting Fields

Maintaining a database requires making periodic adjustments to table structures. As user requirements for company information change, so should your database. You might find that you will need to add or remove fields from one or more tables.

Before adding any field to a table, you should make certain that it does not duplicate an existing field's data. You should never design a database that stores redundant information.

Deleting a field is much more dangerous than adding one. Before deleting a field from a table, make certain that the data contained in the field will never be needed in the future. Good practice is to make a backup copy of the working database prior to modifying any table.

EXERCISE 4-8 Insert a Field in Design View

You can add fields to a table at any time. You might need to do so if you forgot a field while designing a table or discover that you have new data requirements. You can insert new fields in either Design View or Datasheet View.

On occasion, you might create a wide text field or a memo field. It will be difficult to see the entire contents of the field in Datasheet View. You will need to use the Zoom dialog box to display the contents of the field. A *Zoom dialog box* is a text-editing window for lengthy text.

1. Open tblCustomers and click the View button to return to the Design window.

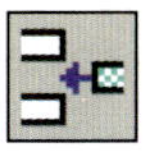

2. Click the State field name. Click the Insert Rows button .

NOTE: When you insert a row, the new row is placed above the selected field.

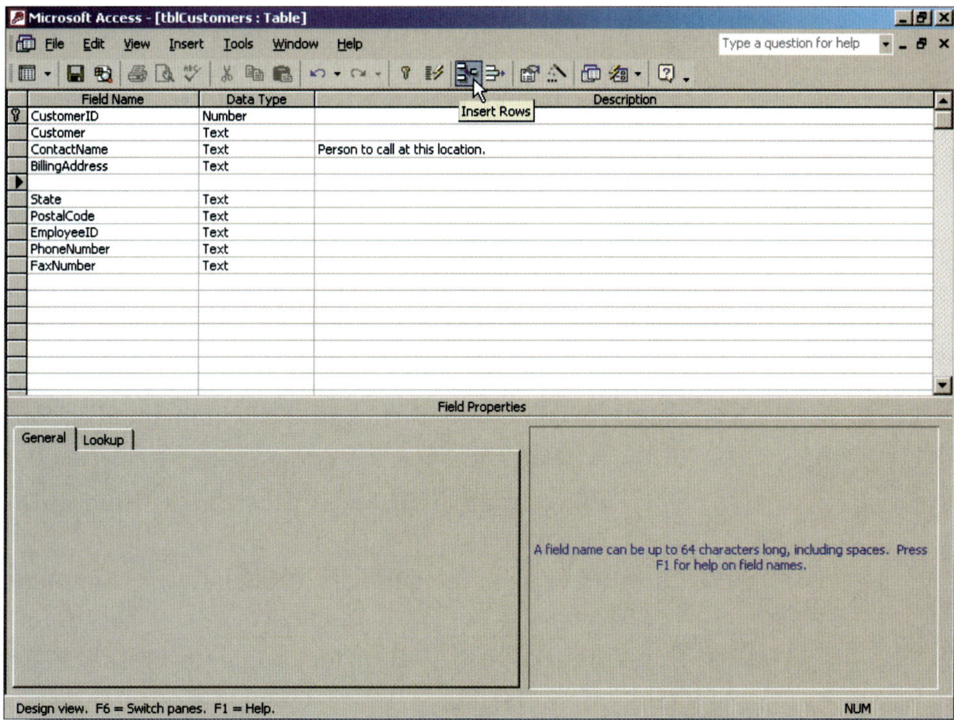

FIGURE 4-13
Inserting a row

3. Key **City** as the Field Name. Press Tab. Text is the default Data Type.
4. Press Tab again. In the Description column, key **City where customer's corporate office is located**.
5. Click the EmployeeID field name. Click Insert, Rows.
6. Key **EMailAddress** as the Field Name. Press Tab. Click the Data Type drop-down arrow and select Hyperlink.
7. Press Tab again. In the Description column, key **Company's E-mail address**
8. For the Caption property of the EMailAddress field, key **E-Mail**
9. In the top pane, click the first blank row after FaxNumber. Key **Comments** as the Field Name.
10. Press Tab. Select Memo as the Data Type.
11. Press Tab. Key **General notes** as the Description.

REVIEW: Changes to the data are saved automatically; however, you must save design changes.

12. Click the View button to return to the datasheet. Access asks you to save the table because you made design changes. Click Yes.

TIP: To edit text in a Hyperlink field, click in the previous field, press Tab to reach the hyperlink field, and then press F2 to display a text cursor.

13. Key the following cities and E-mail addresses in the appropriate columns. Text in a Hyperlink field is formatted as an Internet address. (These addresses are not real, so do not try to access them.)

Crafts & More:	**Seattle**	**mailto:craftsmore@mail.com**
Bears & Such:	**Norfolk**	**mailto:bears@animals.net**
The Doll and Bear Barn:	**Hartford**	**mailto:dollbear@stores.org**

NOTE: The Hyperlink Data Type in Access defaults to a Web address. You must key **mailto:** before the email address to generate an email message rather than launch a Web browser.

14. Scroll the window and click in the Comments field for Record #1.
15. Press Shift+F2 to open the Zoom dialog box.
16. Key **This company will order all small stuffed animals**. (See Figure 4-14 on the next page.)
17. Click OK to close the dialog box. Click in the Comments field for Record #2 and press Shift+F2.
18. Key **This company will order only small teddy bears**. Do not click OK.

NOTE: If you click OK and close the Zoom dialog box before you are ready, press Shift+F2 to open it again.

FIGURE 4-14
Entering text in the Zoom dialog box

19. Select all the text in the Zoom dialog box. Press Ctrl + C to copy the text. Click OK to close the window.
20. Right-click the Comments field of Record #3 and select Paste. You do not have to open the Zoom dialog box for lengthy text.

EXERCISE 4-9 Insert and Delete a Field in Datasheet View

You also can insert fields in Datasheet View. Access inserts text fields with a default width of 50 spaces. Each field will be named Field*n*, where *n* is a sequential number. You can also delete a field in Datasheet View.

1. Click anywhere in the Billing Address column.
2. From the Insert menu, select Column. A new column named Field1 is inserted before the Billing Address column.
3. Click the View button. Field1 is a Text Data Type.
4. Return to Datasheet View.
5. Click anywhere in the Fax Number column.
6. Click Edit, Delete Column.
7. A dialog box asks if you want to delete the field and all the data.

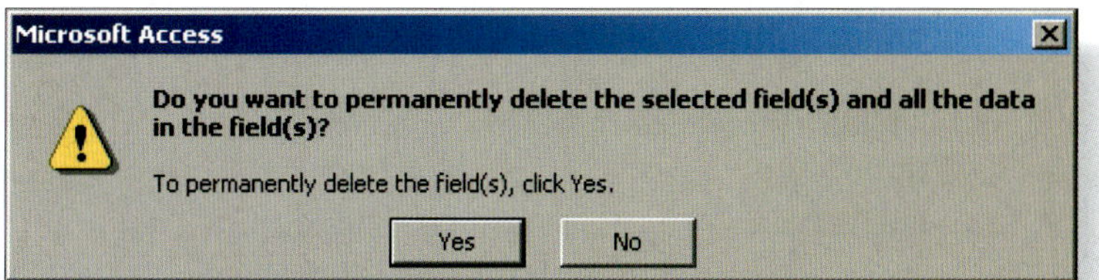

FIGURE 4-15
A message warns that data will be deleted

8. Click Yes to delete the field. Close the table.

Creating Tables in Datasheet View

In addition to using the Table Wizard to create new tables, you can also create new tables in Design View or Datasheet View.

You can create a table by simply entering data into columns and rows. Access evaluates your entries and determines Field Sizes and Data Types. The field names are generic, but you can rename them in Design View. Although it is easy to create a table in Datasheet View, most likely you will need to customize the table in Design View.

EXERCISE 4-10 Create a Table in Datasheet View

If you have the data available to enter into a table, you might choose to create a table by using Datasheet View. Access evaluates the data you key to determine the Data Type for the newly created field.

When you key letters or a combination of letters and numbers, Access defines a text field. When you key only numbers, Access defines a number field. When you key numbers with symbols such as the decimal point (.), the dollar sign ($), or the percent sign (%), Access defines the field as a number field and assigns specific properties to the field. When you key numbers with the forward slash (/) or the colon (:), Access defines the field as a Date/Time field. If your entry is not recognized as a valid number, date, or time, Access defines the field as Text.

1. Click the Tables button. Double-click Create table by entering data. A blank datasheet opens, and the field names are Field1, Field2, and so on.
2. In Field1 for the first row, key **7**
3. Press Tab. Key ***[your last name]*** in Field2.
4. Press Tab. Key **5%** in Field3.
5. Press Tab. Press Ctrl+; to enter today's date in Field4.

NOTE: If you see an error message when you give the current date command, enter the date in this format: *mm/dd/yy*

6. Press Tab. Key **West** in Field5.
7. Key **$6.25** in Field6.

8. Click the Save button. The Save As dialog box opens with a default name.
9. Key **tblReps** as the table name and click OK.
10. A dialog box reminds you that you have not set a primary key. If you choose Yes, Access will create an AutoNumber field. (See Figure 4-16 on the next page.)

FIGURE 4-16
Message box telling you there is no primary key

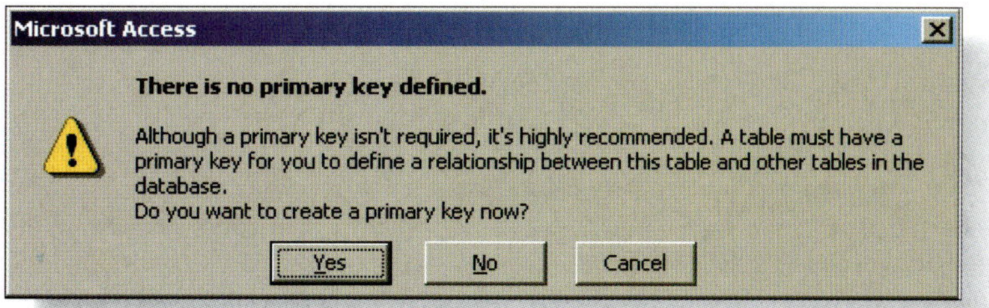

11. Click No. The datasheet displays only the records and fields you entered.

EXERCISE 4-11 Set Captions and Set a Primary Key

You have already viewed how the Table Wizard creates default Captions for fields. Through the Table Design View, you can change existing Captions or add new Captions.

You also learned about the primary key. The primary key is the field that holds unique or different data for each record. When you set a primary key, Access requires that values for this field be unique in each record. For example, if the social security number is the primary key for an employee database, each employee must have a unique social security number. If you attempt to use the same social security number for more than one record, an error will occur.

1. Click the View button. Access analyzed the data you entered and selected an appropriate field type.
2. In the top pane, change the name of Field1 to **EmployeeID**. Click the Caption row in the bottom pane and key **Rep's ID** with a space.
3. Change Field2 to **LastName** and change its Caption to **Last Name**
4. Change Field3 to **CommissionRate** and change its Caption to **Commission Rate**
5. Change Field4 to **HireDate** and set the Caption to **Hire Date**
6. Change Field5 to **Region**. Leave the Caption row blank.
7. Change Field6 to **BasePay** and set the Caption to **Base Pay**

TIP: When a Field Name is one word, you do not need a Caption.

8. Click the EmployeeID row. Click the Primary Key button.
9. Save the table and return to Datasheet View.
10. Enter the following new record. You must enter the date in mm/dd/yy format.

Rep's ID:	**6**
Last Name:	**Gleason**

Commission Rate: .04
Hire Date: 6/6/01
Region: North
Base Pay: $6.50

11. Close the table.

Importing Data

As a database administrator, a goal of yours should be to avoid requiring users to re-enter data already stored in an electronic format. You should transfer the data by importing it into your database. Each time you import data, you make a copy of the original data. The original data is maintained in the source application while you work with a copy of it in your database.

You can import data into an Access database from many different applications, including Excel, Lotus, dBase, Word, or a mainframe database system. After being imported, the table behaves just like any other table.

EXERCISE 4-12 Import Access Data

Data can be imported from other Access databases, including previous versions of Access. In addition to importing tables, Access can import other objects, such as queries, forms, and reports. However, only tables contain data.

1. Right-click the Start button on the Windows taskbar. A shortcut menu opens.

2. Click Explore. When the Explorer opens, click the Maximize button to maximize the window.
3. In the left pane, open folder Lesson 04. The files contained in the folder appear in the right pane.

NOTE: Check with your instructor to verify the location of your student data files and the folder in which you will be working. The folder "My Documents" is often the default folder when you're creating or storing files.

4. In the right pane, point to the filename **CC-E-04** and right-click. Choose Copy from the shortcut menu.
5. In the left pane, open the My Documents folder.
6. Right-click in an unused area of the right pane. Choose Paste from the shortcut menu. A file named **CC-E-04** appears.
7. Close the Explorer.

8. With your ***[your first name and last name]*** database window maximized, click the Tables button.
9. From the File menu, choose Get External Data and then choose Import.
10. In the Import dialog box, find the folder with **CC-E-04** and select the filename. Click Import.
11. In the Import Objects dialog box, click the Tables tab. You can import all major objects (tables, queries, forms, reports, pages, macros, and modules).
12. Select tblSalesReps.

FIGURE 4-17
Importing a table

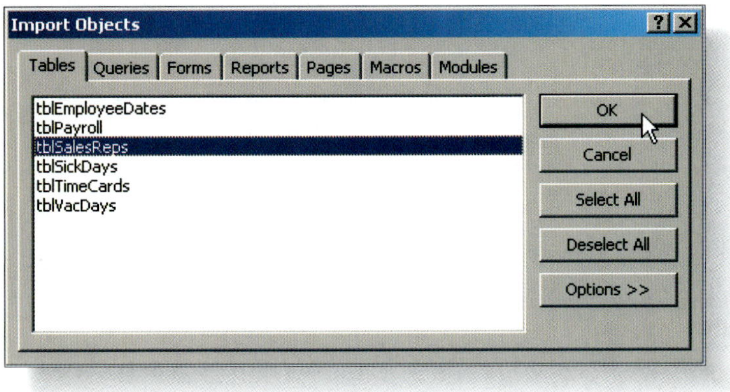

13. Click OK. The table is added to your database. Open tblSalesReps in Design View.
14. Click the first empty Field Name row after Rate and key **Supervisor**. Make the Data Type Text, **25** spaces wide.
15. Save the changes and switch to Datasheet View. The table has a new field. Close the table.

EXERCISE 4-13 Import Excel Data

For most non-Access applications, a wizard steps you through the import process. When importing from a worksheet, you may select all the data from the worksheet or just a range of cells. Your ease in importing data depends greatly on how the information is stored in the application. Use of blank columns and rows in the worksheet adds unnecessary fields and records to your database.

1. In the Tables window, right-click in a white, unused area. Choose Import from the shortcut menu.
2. Click the drop-down arrow for Files of type and choose Microsoft Excel.
3. Set the Look In location to the Lesson 04 folder.
4. Select the **Employees** workbook. (This is a Microsoft Excel worksheet.) Click Import.

5. A wizard starts to help you import the Excel worksheet. Click Show Worksheets.

FIGURE 4-18 Selecting data to import

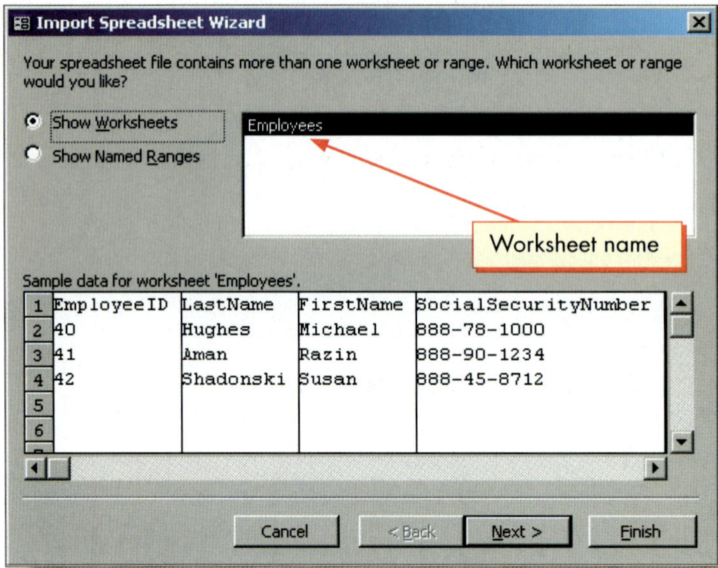

6. Click Next. Click the check box to indicate that the First Row Contains Column Headings.
7. Click Next. You can import the data into a new table, or you can add the records to an existing table.

NOTE: So you can add records, the fields in the imported table must be the same data type and size and in the same order as in the target table.

8. Click the option button for In a New Table. Click Next.
9. For each field in the new table, you can change the Field Name, indicate whether it should be indexed, or skip the field altogether.
10. Click in the SocialSecurityNumber column. Click the drop-down arrow for Indexed and choose Yes (No Duplicates). (See Figure 4-19 on the next page.)
11. Click Next. In the next dialog box, you can set the primary key.
12. Click the option Choose my own primary key. Choose SocialSecurityNumber from the drop-down list. Click Next.
13. In the Import to Table entry box, key **tblNewEmployees**
14. Click Finish. The message box tells you that the table has been imported. Click OK in the message box.
15. Open tblNewEmployees in Datasheet View. Switch to Design View. Text fields are all 255 spaces wide. Close the table.

FIGURE 4-19
Setting a field's options

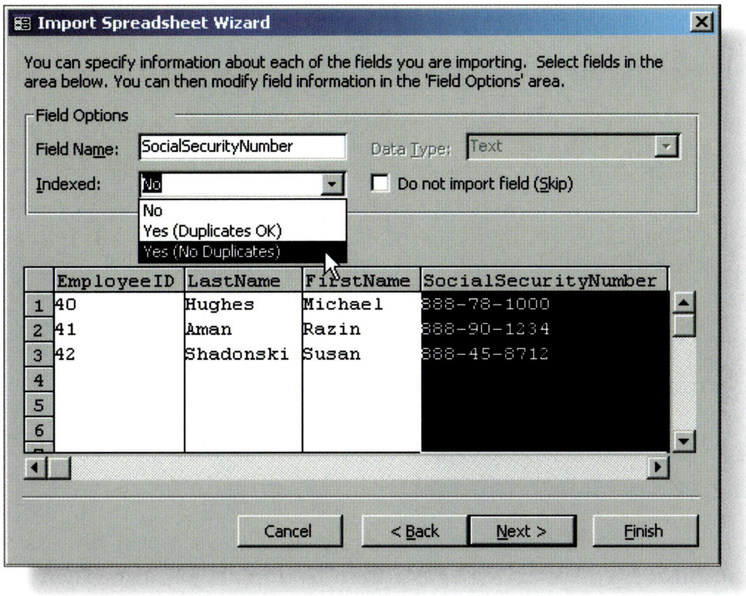

EXERCISE 4-14 Delete Tables

No matter how you created the table, you can delete it from your database. When you delete an imported table, the data is still in the original location from which you imported it. When you delete a table you created from the Wizard or Datasheet View, it is deleted along with any data it contains.

TIP: You can only Undo a deleted table immediately after deleting it.

1. Click tblSalesReps in the Database window. Press Delete.
2. A dialog box verifies that you want to delete this table. Click Yes.
3. Delete tblNewEmployees from the database.
4. Compact and close your database.

LESSON 4 Summary

- The Database Wizard creates a new database from an existing template.
- A new database created through the Database Wizard contains major objects such as tables, forms, and reports, but does not contain data.
- A new database created as a blank database does not contain objects or data.

- The Table Wizard creates a new table based on commonly used fields.
- When using the Table Wizard, you can rename selected fields.
- You can enter data directly into the table after creating and naming a table by using the Table Wizard.
- The properties of any field can be edited after a table is created.
- You can insert fields into and delete them from an existing table through either Design View or Datasheet View.
- When tables are created by using Datasheet View, Access evaluates the data entered to determine the data type for the field to create.
- A Caption is a field property that displays as a column heading in Datasheet View.
- The data contained in a field defined as the primary key of a table must be unique.
- Data imported from another Access database, a non-Access database, or a non-database application can be added to an existing table or used to create a new table.
- Tables can be deleted from an Access database.

LESSON 4 Command Summary

FEATURE	BUTTON	MENU	KEYBOARD	SPEECH
New Database		File, New	Ctrl + N	✓
Insert Row	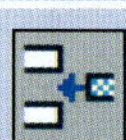	Insert, Rows		✓
Delete Row		Edit, Delete Rows		✓
Primary Key		Edit, Primary Key		✓
Table Properties		View, Properties		✓
Import		File, Get External Data, Import		✓
Delete Table		Edit, Delete	Delete	✓

Concepts Review

TRUE/FALSE QUESTIONS

Each of the following statements is either true or false. Indicate your choice by circling T or F.

T F 1. After you create a table, you can rename fields and change the data type of fields in Design View.

T F 2. When you're creating a table in Datasheet View, all fields are Text data types.

T F 3. The Table Wizard can create a new database.

T F 4. The primary key field of a table must contain unique data.

T F 5. Fields can be deleted only through Datasheet View.

T F 6. Access can import tables, queries, forms, and reports from previous versions of Access.

T F 7. In Datasheet View, the Description property of a field displays at the top of the column instead of the Field Name.

T F 8. The field properties of a table created through a wizard cannot be modified through Design View.

SHORT ANSWER QUESTIONS

Write the correct answer in the space provided.

1. When is it useful to use the Database Wizard to create a database?

____

2. When using the Leszynski Naming Conventions, what would you rename a table called Management Profiles?

____

3. Name the four ways to add a table to a database.

____

4. What kind of data type does the Table Wizard assign to a street address?

____

5. What field data type can store more than 255 characters?

____

6. In what view can you change the data type or description of a field?

7. In Design View, which function key toggles the insertion point between the lower and upper panes?

8. What kind of field must store unique or different data for each record?

CRITICAL THINKING

Answer these questions on a separate page. There are no right or wrong answers. Support your answers with examples from your own experience, if possible.

1. The Access Table Wizard uses field names such as StateOrProvince and PostalCode instead of State or ZIPCode. Why do you think Access does this?
2. Many businesses find it necessary to import tables into Access. Why do you think this is true?

Lesson Applications

EXERCISE 4-15

Create a blank database. Create a table, edit field properties, and enter records.

1. Open a blank database and name it ***[your first, middle, and last initials]***.
2. Using the Table Wizard, add the following fields from the Payments sample table:

   PaymentID

   CustomerID

   OrderID

   PaymentAmount

   PaymentDate
3. Name the table **tblPayments*[your last name]***.
4. Choose the option to set the primary key yourself and use the PaymentID field with consecutive numbers assigned by Access.
5. Select the option to enter records directly in the table.
6. Enter the following record:

Payment ID:	***Press*** Tab
Customer ID:	**1**
Order ID:	**20101**
Payment Amount:	**500**
Payment Date:	**1/1/02**

7. In Design View, change the Field Size of the OrderID field to Double.
8. Change to Datasheet View and save the table. Add the following records:

Payment ID:	***Press*** Tab
Customer ID:	**2**
Order ID:	**20102**
Payment Amount:	**750**
Payment Date:	**10/1/02**

Payment ID:	***Press*** Tab
Customer ID:	**5**
Order ID:	**20103**
Payment Amount:	**1000**
Payment Date:	**2/7/02**

TIP: If you key the diagonals in a date, you do not need to key leading zeros for the date or month.

9. Size the columns to the widest text or title.
10. Print the table in portrait orientation.

EXERCISE 4-16

Delete a field in Datasheet View. Change field properties. Rename a table.

1. Change to Datasheet View.
2. Delete the CustomerID field.
3. Change to Design View.
4. Change the Caption for Order ID to **Order Number**
5. Change the Caption for Payment Amount to **Amount Paid**
6. Change the Caption for Payment Date to **Date Paid**
7. Resize the columns appropriately.
8. Rename the table as **tblNewPayments**
9. Print the table in portrait orientation.
10. Close the table.

EXERCISE 4-17

Create a table in Datasheet View. Set Captions and Field Sizes. Set a primary key.

1. Create a new table by entering data.
2. Add the following record:

Field1:	**464-23-4824**
Field2:	**Supplies**
Field3:	**10/15/02**
Field4:	**$14.85**
Field5:	**Cleaning Supplies**
Field6:	**Trash Bags, Soap, and Paper Towels**

3. Save the table as **tblEmployeeExpenses***[your first and last name]*.
4. Set EmployeeID as the primary key.
5. Rename the field names to the following:

Field1:	**EmployeeID**
Field2:	**ExpenseType**

Field3:	**DatePurchased**
Field4:	**AmountSpent**
Field5:	**Purpose**
Field6:	**Description**

6. Change the Caption for EmployeeID to Employee SSN
7. Add appropriate Captions to the other fields.
8. Enter the following record:

EmployeeID:	**234-45-7890**
ExpenseType:	**Supplies**
DatePurchased:	**10/22/02**
AmountSpent:	**$25.34**
PurposeOfExpense:	**Office Supplies**
Description:	**Pens, Staples, Memo Pads**

9. Based on the data you have just entered; resize the four text fields to an appropriate width.
10. Resize columns so all data is visible.
11. Print the table in landscape orientation.
12. Save and close the table.

EXERCISE 4-18 *Challenge Yourself*

Create a new database. Import data. Enter data.

1. Use the Database Wizard to create a database that will keep track of expenses for a company. Name it **Expenses*[your initials]***
2. Make sure you include a field to store the date an employee is hired.
3. The company is only concerned with domestic expenses, so there is no need to store what country an employee is from.
4. Change the names of fields StateOrProvince and PostalCode to better fit a company located in the United States.
5. Import payroll information from **CC-E-04** into the new database.
6. Add one new record in the table Employees. Use your real name in the record, but make up the rest of the data.
7. Print the new record in landscape orientation.
8. Compact and close your database.

On Your Own

In these exercises you work on your own, as you would in a real-life work environment. Use the skills you've learned to accomplish the task—and be creative.

EXERCISE 4-19

Using the Database Wizard, select a template that will assist you in creating a database to store the member information you collected and organized for the On Your Own exercises of Lessons 1 through 3. Enter the member information. Print the table. On the first sheet of your printout, write the name of the template you selected. Continue to Exercise 4-20.

EXERCISE 4-20

Review the structure of the main table in the database you created in the Exercise 4-19. On a blank sheet of paper, list the fields, data types, and field sizes from the table that are most appropriate for your organization's needs. Add any additional fields that would improve the usability of the table. Without using the Database Wizard, create a blank database. Create a table to store the data. Enter the member information. Print the table. Continue to Exercise 4-21.

EXERCISE 4-21

Search the Web for Microsoft Access Templates. Locate a template that will enhance the database you created in the previous exercise. Using the template you located on the Internet, create a new database. Enter appropriate data for at least five records. Print the table. Submit to your instructor the printouts from Exercises 4-19 through 4-21 along with your field list from 4-20. Make sure your name, the date, and the class are written on the printouts. Keep a copy of the three databases you created in Exercises 4-19 through 4-21. They will be used in subsequent lessons.

LESSON 5

Managing Data Integrity

OBJECTIVES

After completing this lesson, you will be able to:

1. **Create relationships between tables.**
2. **Work with referential integrity.**
3. **Work with subdatasheets.**
4. **Use default values, formats, and input masks.**
5. **Use the Lookup Wizard.**

Estimated Time: 1 hour

MOUS ACTIVITIES

In this lesson:

Ac2002 2-1
Ac2002 2-2
Ac2002 2-3
Ac2002 2-4
Ac2002 6-1
Ac2002 6-2

See Appendix E.

A *relationship* is a link or connection between two tables sharing a common field. Relationships are critical for properly designed databases. They change a flat database, containing isolated data, into a relational database, containing linked data. For tables to relate to each other, they must share common data. In an integrated database, tables can link to one or more other tables.

Relationships must be planned; they do not just happen. Understanding them—and how to set them—takes time and practice. As you work more extensively with databases, you will learn more about their subtleties.

Creating Relationships Between Tables

Relationships between tables can be graphically viewed in the Relationships window. Tables display as field lists. Related fields from each table are connected by a join line. A *join line* graphically represents the relationship between two tables. Each end of the join line connects to the related fields of two tables.

The related field between the two tables must be of the same data type and the same size. The related fields do not need to use the same name. However, you will find it much easier to create and recognize relationships when the common fields use the same field name in both tables.

EXERCISE 5-1 Look at an Existing Relationship

The Relationships window shows existing relationships in the current database. One or more relationships can be displayed at a time. When more than two tables are displayed, it is advantageous to arrange the tables to allow optimum viewing of all join lines.

1. Find the **Asset Tracking** database located in the folder Lesson 05. This is a copy of the database you created in Lesson 4.

NOTE: Ask your instructor where files for this Lesson are saved. They might be located on your computer, on the network, or on a student disk.

2. Make a copy of this file on your hard drive and name it **Asset Tracking*[your initials]***. Open **Asset Tracking*[your initials]***.

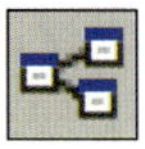

3. Close the Main Switchboard. Click the Relationships button and maximize the Relationships window.

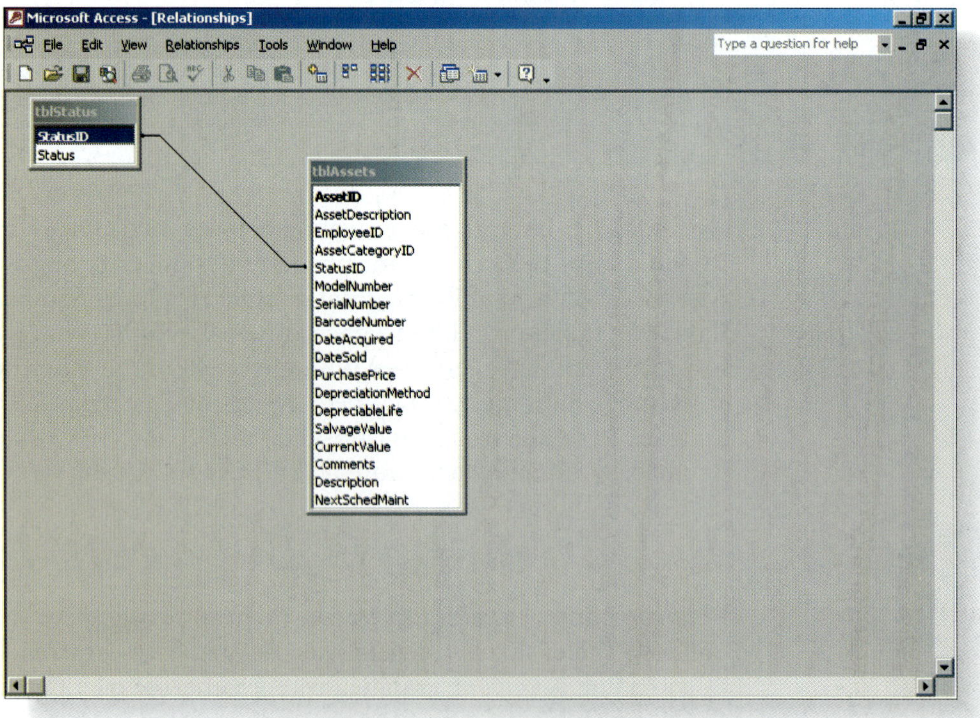

FIGURE 5-1 Relationships window

ACCESS

REVIEW: In a field list, the key field for a table is bold.

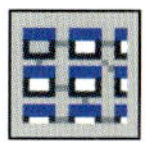

4. Click the Show All Relationships button. All tables that have a relationship with other tables will open. The line connecting two tables represents the relationship between the tables.
5. Resize the field lists so all field names are visible.

REVIEW: Click and drag the bottom or right edge of a list box to resize it.

6. Click and drag the title bar of each field list and rearrange them to appear as shown in Figure 5-2.

FIGURE 5-2
Relationships window with field lists rearranged

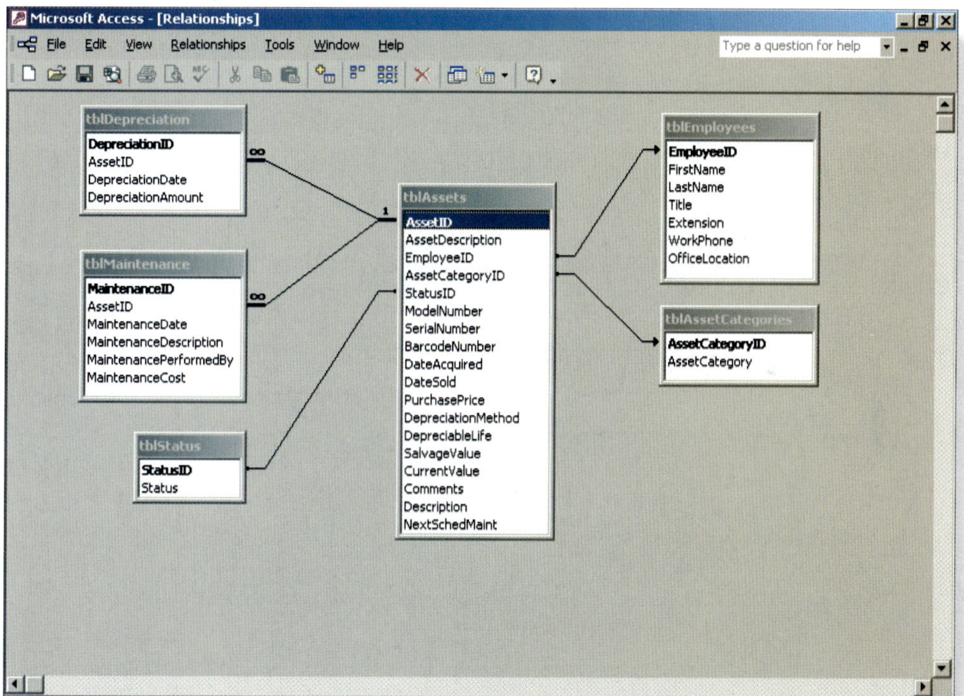

7. Right-click the sloping part of the join line between tblAssets and tblStatus to open the shortcut menu for a join line. (See Figure 5-3 on the next page.)

NOTE: Make sure you open the shortcut menu for a join line. It will enable you to edit relationships or to delete the join line. You might accidentally open the shortcut menu for the Relationships window or for a field list. Neither of these menus offers you the option to edit relationships or to delete the join line.

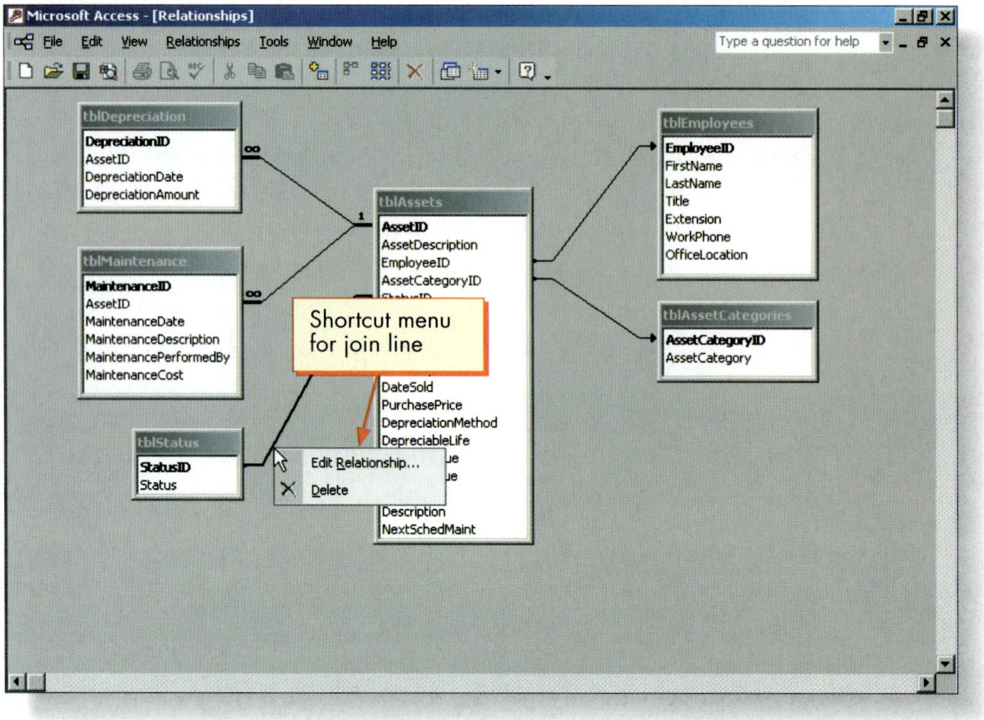

FIGURE 5-3
Shortcut menu

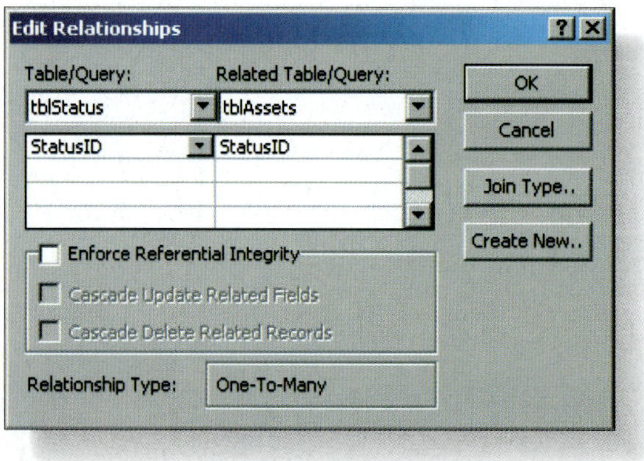

FIGURE 5-4
Edit Relationships dialog box

8. Choose Edit Relationship.

NOTE: You will learn more about the types of relationships later in this lesson.

9. Click Cancel to close the dialog box.

ACCESS

EXERCISE 5-2 Print Relationships

Printing relationships helps a database administrator document and troubleshoot database integrity. Access creates a graphical report showing field lists and join lines. (You will learn more about reports in the next lesson.)

1. Choose File, Print Relationships. Access generates a report and opens it in Print Preview.

2. Click the Print button.
3. Click the Close button Close without saving the report.
4. Close the Relationships window. A message box might ask if you want to save the new layout. Click **Yes.**
5. Close the database without closing Access.

EXERCISE 5-3 Create a Relationship in the Relationships Window

You have just looked at a relational database with integrated tables. You will now build a relationship between isolated tables by creating a relationship directly in the Relationships window. You create relationships by dragging or drawing a line between the two common field names.

Different relationships can be produced depending on whether the common fields are primary key fields or foreign key fields. A *foreign key field* is the field that refers to the primary key field in a related table.

Access provides various types of relationships between two tables. If the common field is a primary key in the first table and not a primary key in the second table, the relationship is a *One-To-Many relationship*. This means one record in the first table can connect to one or more records in the second table.

If the common fields in both the first and the second tables are primary keys, the relationship is a *One-To-One relationship*. This means one record in the first table can connect to only one record in the second table.

If the common fields in the first or the second table are not primary keys, an *Indeterminate relationship* is created. Access does not have enough information to determine the relationship between the two tables.

1. Make a copy of CC-05 and rename it ***[your initials]*CC-05**. Open ***[your initials]*CC-05**.
2. Click the Relationships button. This window shows no relationships.
3. Click the Show All Relationships button. Nothing happens. This proves that the entire database has no relationships set up.

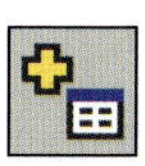

4. Click the Show Table button. The Show Table dialog box lists the tables and queries that are in the database.

NOTE: The Show Table dialog box sometimes opens automatically when no relationships are present in the database.

5. Click the **Tables** tab. Double-click **tblCustomers** to add its field list to the window.

TIP: If you cannot see the field lists, move the Show Table dialog box.

6. Double-click tblHistorySales.

FIGURE 5-5 Show Table dialog box

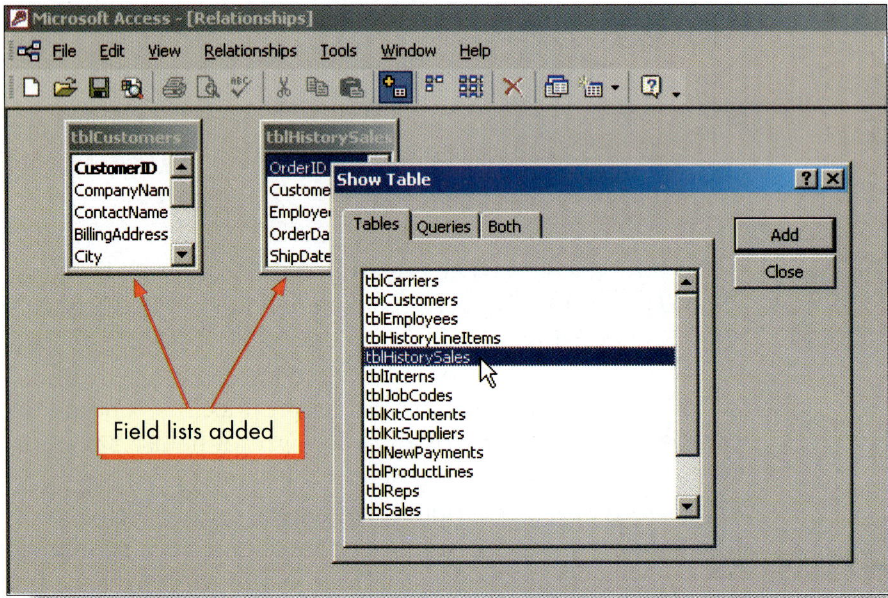

NOTE: If a field list is added more than once, the title bar of the duplicate field list shows a number after the table name. You can delete duplicates by clicking in the field list and pressing Delete.

7. Close the Show Table dialog box. Maximize the Relationships window.
8. Size and position the field lists so you can see all the field names.
9. In the tblCustomers list, click the CustomerID field. The field name is bold because it is the primary key in this table.
10. Click and drag the CustomerID field from the tblCustomers field list to the CustomerID field in the tblHistorySales field list.
11. The Edit Relationships dialog box opens. The Relationship Type is one-to-many because the CustomerID (primary key) appears only once in the table tblCustomers but can appear many times in the table tblHistorySales.
12. Click Create. A join line links the common field names.

13. Click the Clear Layout button.
14. Click Yes to clear the layout.
15. Click the Show All Relationships button.

NOTE: The Clear Layout button clears the way tables are arranged but does not delete the relationships between them.

16. Resize each field list so all field names are visible.

17. Click the Save button. Close the Relationships window.

Working with Referential Integrity

When a relationship is one-to-many and the tables are in the same database, you can use additional database rules known as *referential integrity*. These rules keep track of changes in related tables and help eliminate mistakes, accidental deletions, and other common errors. Referential integrity cannot be set for Indeterminate relationships.

EXERCISE 5-4 Enforce Referential Integrity

1. Open tblHistorySales. Change the Customer ID in the first record to **15**. Close the table.

2. Open tblCustomers. Notice that there is no Customer ID 15. Referential integrity would prevent this type of error from being made. Close the table.

3. Open tblHistorySales. Change the Customer ID 15 back to **1**. Close the table.

4. Click the Relationships button.

5. Right-click the sloping join line between the two field lists. Select Edit Relationship. The Relationship Type is One-To-Many.

6. Click the check box to select Enforce Referential Integrity.

FIGURE 5-6 Enforcing referential integrity

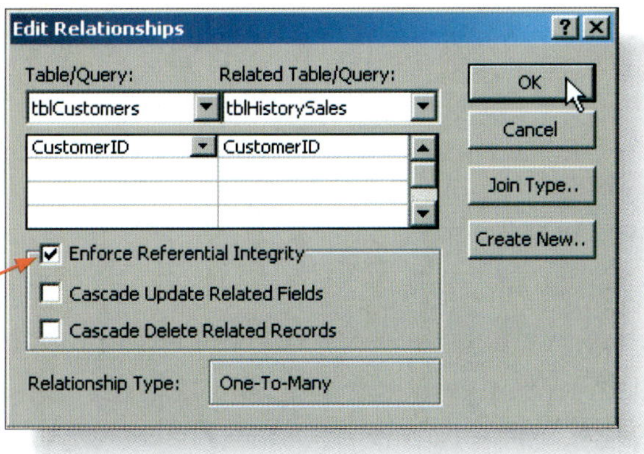

Enforcing referential integrity

7. The Relationship Type remains a One-To-Many relationship. Click OK. The join line represents referential integrity because it now displays a 1 for the "one" side of the relationship and an infinity symbol (∞) for the "many" side.

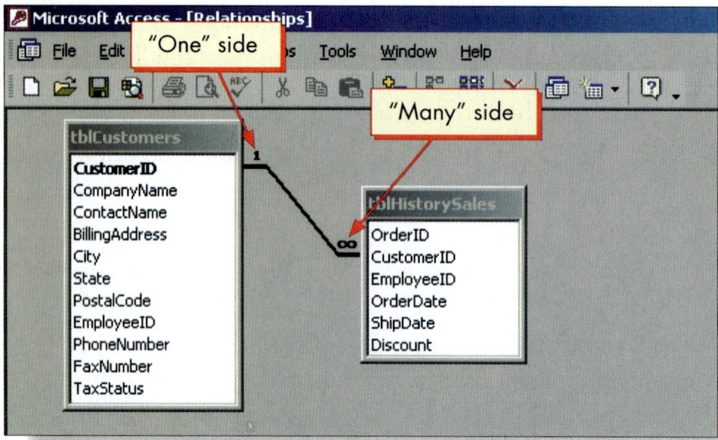

FIGURE 5-7 One-To-Many relationship

8. Save and close the Relationships window.
9. Open tblHistorySales. Change the Customer ID in the first record to **15**. Press ↓ to save the record.
10. A message box alerts you to a problem. Click OK.

FIGURE 5-8 Referential Integrity finds an error

11. Change the Customer ID back to **1**. Close the table.

EXERCISE 5-5 Remove Referential Integrity

Removing referential integrity can be relatively easy. When you delete the join line between two field lists in the Relationships window, you delete the relationship between the two corresponding tables.

1. Click the Relationships button.
2. Right-click the join line between tblCustomers and tblHistorySales.
3. Choose Delete from the shortcut menu. Click Yes in the warning dialog box. The One-To-Many relationship and the rules for Referential Integrity have been deleted.
4. Save the changes to the layout and close the Relationships window.

Working with Subdatasheets

When a table viewed in Datasheet View is on the "one" side of a One-To-Many relationship, a subdatasheet is generated. A *subdatasheet* is a datasheet nested inside another datasheet. You can see records from the related table while in Datasheet View of the primary table. The common field will be the primary key field in the main table and a foreign key field in the related table.

EXERCISE 5-6 Insert a Subdatasheet

1. Open tblCustomers and maximize the window.
2. From the Insert menu, choose Subdatasheet. The Insert Subdatasheet dialog box lists the tables in the database.
3. Click the Tables tab and choose tblHistorySales.
4. In the Link Child Fields box, Access displays a common field of CustomerID in the table tblHistorySales. In the Link Master Fields box, Access has found a common field of CustomerID in the main table tblCustomers. Click OK.

FIGURE 5-9
Inserting a subdatasheet

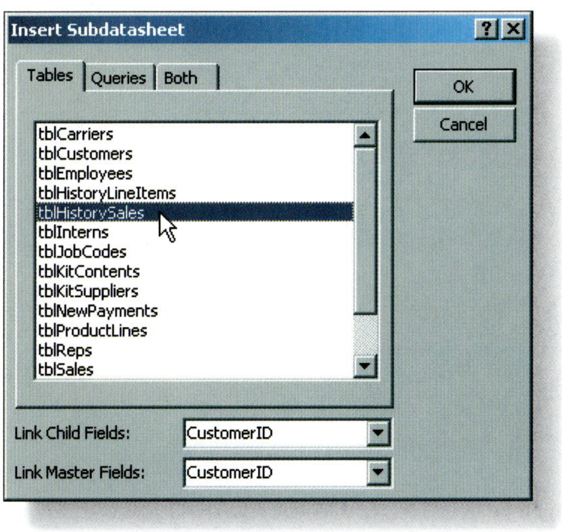

5. The message box alerts you that there are no relationships between these two tables. Click Yes. Access creates the relationship for you and a subdatasheet appears.

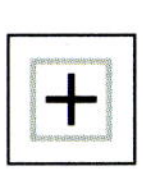

6. The subdatasheet shows an Expand icon in the first column. Click the Expand icon in the fourth record to expand the subdatasheet. It displays information about the customer's purchases.

FIGURE 5-10
Expanded subdatasheets

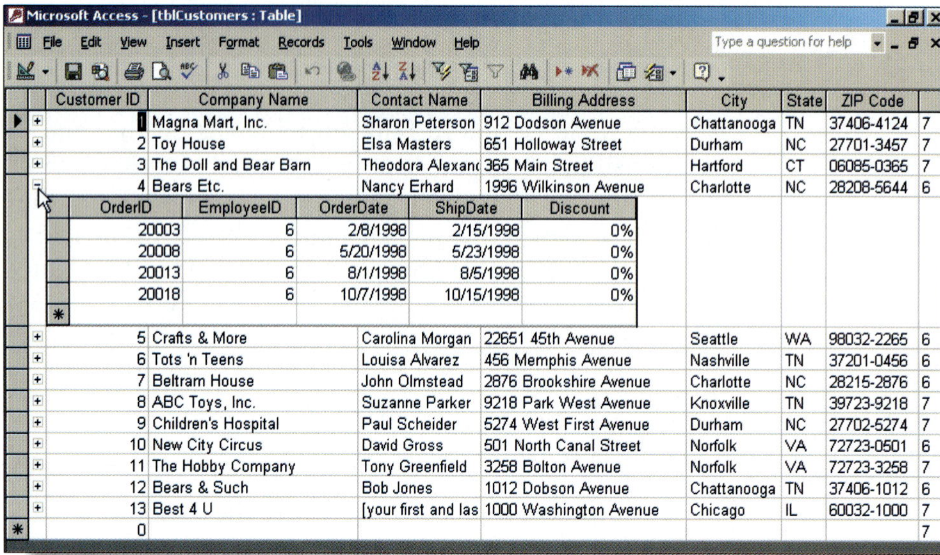

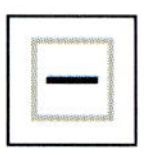

7. Click the Collapse icon [−] to collapse the subdatasheet.
8. Expand and collapse the subdatasheet for another customer.

NOTE: You can expand or collapse all subdatasheets in a table by choosing Format, Subdatasheet, Expand All or Collapse All.

9. Save and close the table.

EXERCISE 5-7 Remove a Subdatasheet

If the database users will not need to see the subdatasheet, you might decide to remove it from the main datasheet. You can remove the displayed subdatasheet in Design View. Although the subdatasheet no longer displays, the relationship between the two tables remains.

1. Open tblCustomers.
2. Click Format, Subdatasheet, and Remove.
3. Save and close the table.

Using Default Values, Formats, and Input Masks

As you improve the design of your database, you will want to add features to improve the speed at which users can enter data. The field properties that can speed data entry are default values, formats, and input masks. In addition to enabling users to work faster, these properties also increase accuracy and consistency.

EXERCISE 5-8 Set Default Values

A *default value* sets the same field value for all new records. For example, if the majority of your employees live in the same state, you can set the default value of the state field to appear automatically in each new record.

Previously entered records will not be changed. The default value displays only when a user is entering new records. If the data being entered is not the same as the default value, the user can key over the default value.

1. Select tblCustomers. Click the Design button to open the table in Design View. Maximize the window.
2. Click on the Field Name EmployeeID.
3. Click in the Default Value row and key **7**

FIGURE 5-11 Setting default values

Default value

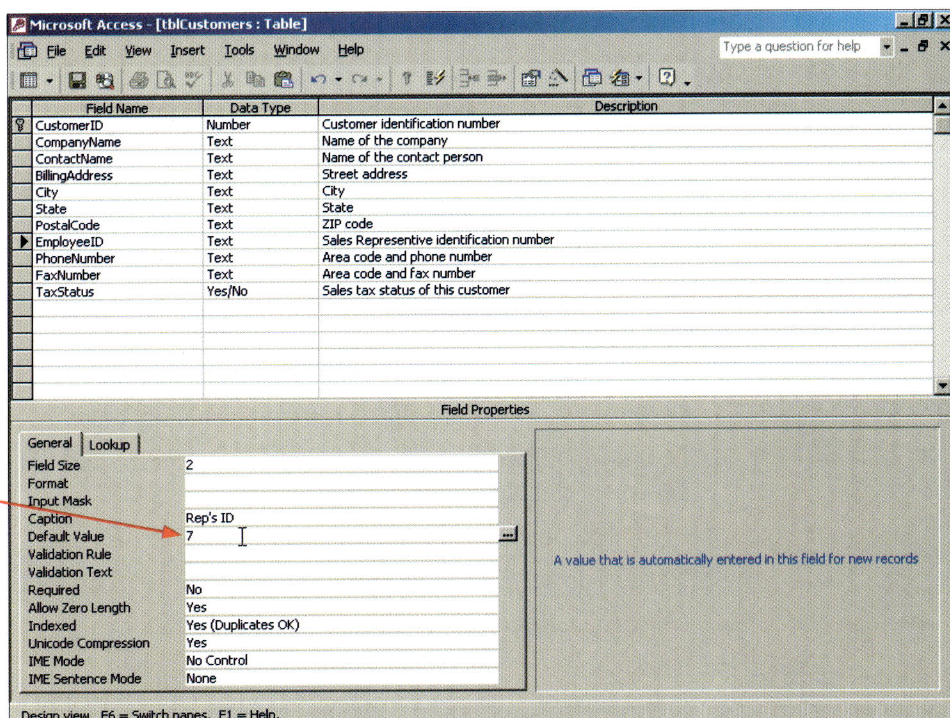

4. Click the View button to return to Datasheet View. Click **Yes** to save the design changes.
5. Add the following record. The EmployeeID is entered for you.

Customer ID:	**13**
Company Name:	**Best 4 U**
Contact Name:	***[your first and last name]***
Billing Address:	**1000 Washington Avenue**
City:	**Chicago**
State:	**il**
ZIP Code:	**60032-1000**
Rep's ID:	*Press* Tab
EmployeeID:	*Press* Tab
Phone Number:	**(312) 555-1000**
Fax Number:	**(312) 555-1199**
Tax Exempt?:	*Press* Tab

EXERCISE 5-9 Add a Field, Set Formats, and Change the Data Type

You can assist database users when entering data by specifying formats. A *format* determines the way data is displayed. For example, you can set the format for a date to show the month spelled out. You can set the format for currency amounts to show dollar signs. You can set the format for text to show only uppercase letters. For some data types, you can select from predefined formats. For others, you enter a custom format.

NOTE: You should not key formatting symbols such as the dollar sign. They can be misinterpreted as text data by Access.

1. Click the View button to return to Design View.
2. In the top pane, click in the blank row after TaxStatus. Key **InitialOrder-Date** as the field name.
3. Press Tab and key **d** to choose Date/Time. Press F6.
4. In the Format row, click the drop-down arrow and select Long Date.
5. Click the Caption row and key **Initial Order**.

6. Click the View button and save the changes.
7. Click on the Customer ID column selector to select the first column.
8. Hold down Shift and click the Company Name column selector to select the second column.
9. Choose Format, Freeze Columns. Scroll right to see the customer name and the Initial Order column.

10. Add the following dates to the existing records:

Doll and Bear Barn:	**7/7/02**
Crafts & More:	**5/1/01**
Bears & Such:	**6/1/01**
Best 4 U:	**12/01/02**

TIP: Size the column so you can see the formatted date.

11. Choose Format, Unfreeze All Columns.

12. Return to Design View and click in the State row in the top pane.

13. Click the Format row in the bottom panel. Click the drop-down arrow. There are no predefined formats for a text field.

14. Press F1 to open a Help window regarding formats.

15. Read about the Format property. Click Text and Memo Data Types.

16. Read the explanation of the greater-than symbol (>). Close the Help window.

17. In the Format row for the State field, key **>**

FIGURE 5-12
Setting a format for a text field

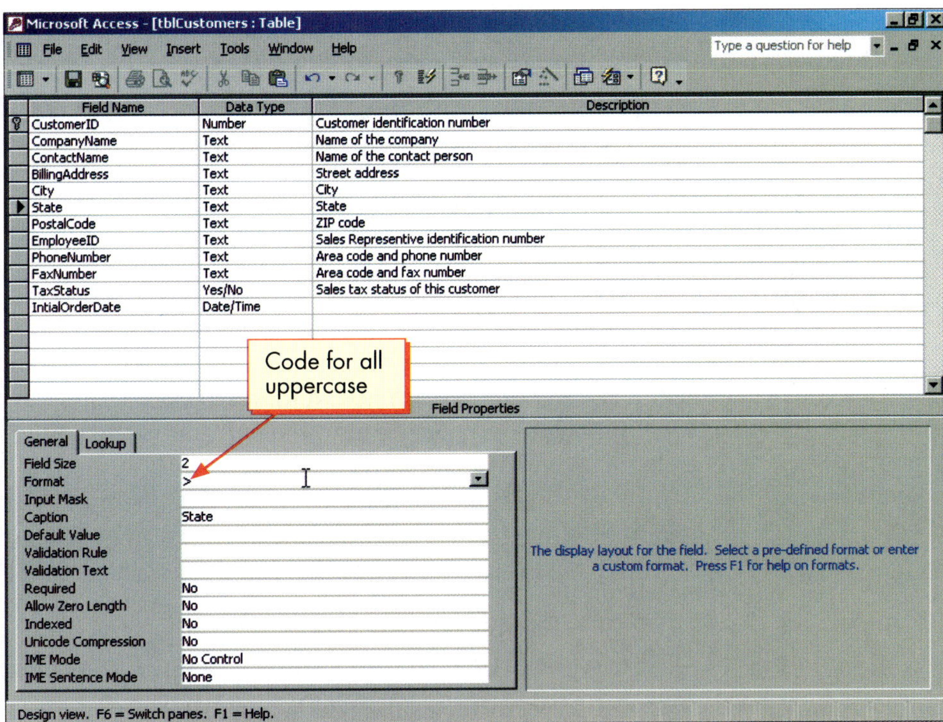

18. In the top pane, click on EmployeeID.

19. Press Tab and key **n** to change the Data Type to Number.

NOTE: Text fields are left-aligned; numbers are right-aligned.

20. Press F6 and set the Default Value to **7**
21. Click the Save button and switch to Datasheet View.
22. Enter the following new record. The EmployeeID is again entered for you. The state will be capitalized when you move to the next field. The date also will be formatted when you move to the next record.

Customer ID:	**14**
Company Name:	**Caroline's Crib**
Contact Name:	**Laurie Roberts**
Billing Address:	**20200 West Governors Drive**
City:	*Press* Ctrl + '
State:	**il**
ZIP Code:	**60682-0200**
Rep's ID:	*Press* Tab
EmployeeID:	*Press* Tab
Phone Number:	**(312) 555-2234**
Fax Number:	**(312) 555-2232**
Tax Exempt?:	*Press* Tab
Initial Order:	**12/15/02**

EXERCISE 5-10 Insert a Field with an Input Mask

An *input mask* is a field property that displays a pattern for entering data. In Datasheet View, the input mask would display as (__) __-__ where the underlines are placeholders for entering numbers. An Input Mask Wizard exists for telephone numbers, social security numbers, and other common fields.

In Design View, an input mask for a telephone number is !\(999") "000\-0000. The number nine (9) is used as a placeholder for optional numbers and the number zero (0) is used as a placeholder for required numbers.

1. Switch to Design View for tblCustomers.
2. Click on the Field Name TaxStatus. Click the Insert Rows button.
3. Key **NightNumber** as the Field Name. Press Tab. This is a Text data type.
4. Press Tab. Key **After hours phone number** as the Description.
5. In the Field Size row, double-click 50. Key **14**
6. In the Caption row, key **After Hours**

7. Click the Input Mask row.
8. Click the Build button.
9. Before the Input Mask Wizard starts, you must save the table design. Click Yes.
10. The Input Mask Wizard lists several common masks and shows how the data is displayed. Select the Phone Number mask.

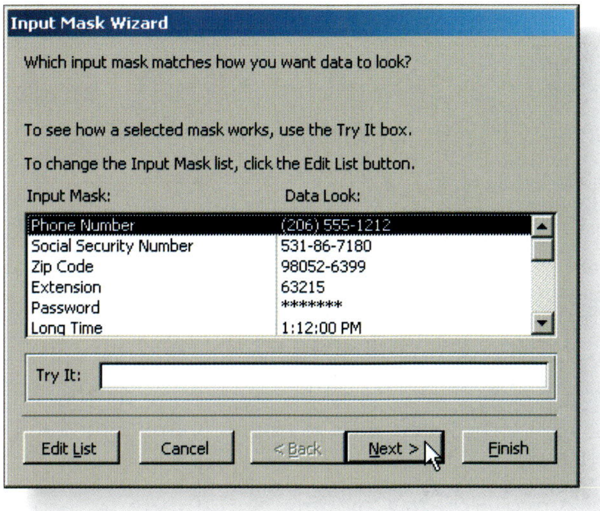

FIGURE 5-13
Input Mask Wizard dialog box

11. Click Next. The wizard asks if you want to change the input mask. Click in the Try It entry box.
12. Click at the beginning of the mask and key your phone number.

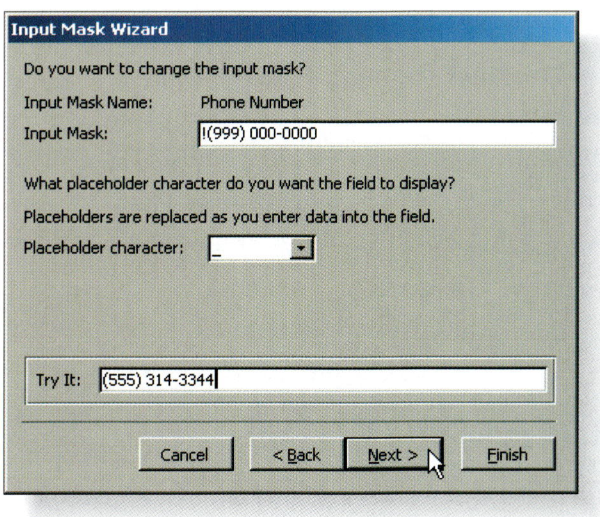

FIGURE 5-14
Change Input Mask dialog box

13. Click Next. The wizard asks how you want to store the data. Select With the symbols in the mask, like this.

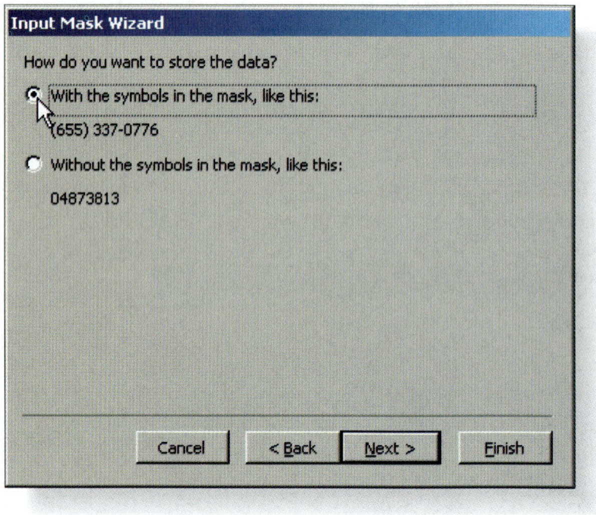

FIGURE 5-15 Storage option dialog box

14. Click Next. Read the final message and click Finish.
15. Change to Datasheet View and save the table.
16. Click on the Customer ID column selector to select the first column.
17. Hold the Shift and click the Company Name column selector to select the second column.
18. Choose Format, Freeze Columns. Scroll right to see the Customer Name and the After Hours column.
19. Add the following phone numbers to the existing records:

TIP: If the input mask does not appear, press F2.

The Doll and Bear Barn:	**(860) 555-6576**
Crafts & More:	**(206) 555-3130**
Bears & Such:	**(703) 555-1470**
Best 4 U:	**(312) 555-9523**
Caroline's Crib:	**(312) 555-8281**

20. Choose Format, Unfreeze All Columns.
21. Close the table and save the changes.

Using the Lookup Wizard

Relationships let you use lookup fields. A *lookup field* displays input choices from another table so you can enter data by choosing from a list. Instead of keying a product group in tblStuffedAnimals, for example, you can "look it up" from tblProductLines.

Companies often use codes within their databases. For the casual observer, the codes might appear meaningless. However, data entry operators quickly become familiar with the codes and their associated meanings. Codes are used because they use less space than lengthy text describing the record.

You can create a lookup field for the ProductGroup field in tblStuffedAnimals. The Lookup Wizard, listed as a Data Type, guides you step-by-step through the process of creating the lookup field.

EXERCISE 5-11 Modify Field Size and Data Type

TblStuffedAnimals and tblProductLines share the common field ProductGroup. For a lookup field to work as expected, the fields should be the same size and must be of the same Data Type.

1. Open tblProductLines. The ProductGroup field lists a one-character code for each product category.

NOTE: The Caption for ProductGroup is "Line Code."

2. Click the View button. Click the field named ProductGroup. It is a Text data type, one space wide, and is the primary key. Close the table.
3. Open tblStuffedAnimals. This table also has a field named ProductGroup. Maximize the window.
4. Click the View button. Click the ProductGroup row. It is Text, 30 spaces wide, and is not the primary key.
5. Press F6 and change the field size to **1** to match tblProductLines.
6. Click the Save button. Click Yes. No data will be lost.
7. Switch to Datasheet View to verify that the data is still there.
8. Return to Design View. Click in the Data Type column for the ProductGroup row. Click the drop-down arrow and select Lookup Wizard.

NOTE: You can use Insert, Lookup Column to start the Lookup Wizard.

9. In the first dialog box, choose I want the lookup column to look up the values in a table or query. Click Next.
10. In the next dialog box, select the related table. Choose tblProductLines and click Next.
11. Double-click ProductGroup to transfer it to the Selected Fields list. Click Next.

12. The next dialog box shows the ProductGroup field with all its values from the tblProductLines. Double-click the right border of the column selector. Click Next.

13. Insert a space in the label for your lookup column. Click Finish.

14. A message box tells you that the table must be saved before relationships can be created. Click Yes.

15. Click the Lookup tab in the Field Properties section. The Display Control for this field should now show a combo box. The Row Source Type is Table/Query. The Row Source row shows the complex code that the wizard created to link these two tables.

NOTE: A combo box control has a drop-down arrow and expands to show a list when you click the arrow.

FIGURE 5-16 Lookup tab for ProductGroup field

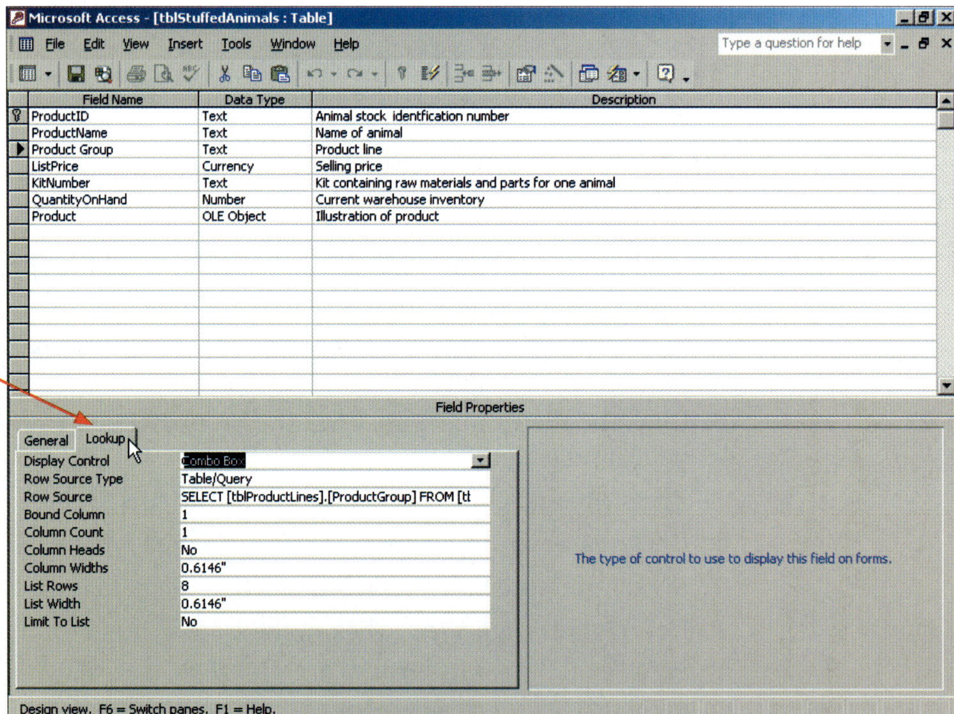

16. Save the table and switch to Datasheet View.

EXERCISE 5-12 Add Data with a Lookup Field

A lookup field ensures accuracy and consistency because the user can only select a value from a predefined list. Users enter data in a lookup field by clicking the drop-down arrow and selecting a value from the list.

1. Click the New Record button.
2. Add the following record:

Product ID:	**T006**
Animal Name:	**Easter Bear**
Product Group:	***From the drop-down list, select T.***
List Price:	**14.5**
Kit Number:	**Bear006**
Inventory:	**200**
Illustration:	***Leave blank.***

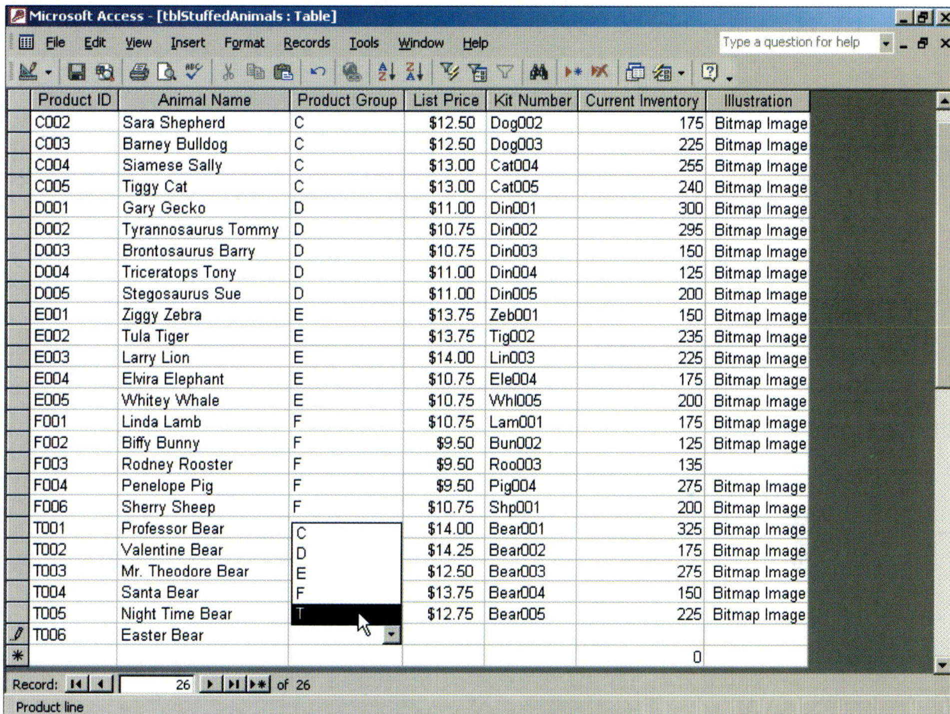

Product ID	Animal Name	Product Group	List Price	Kit Number	Current Inventory	Illustration
C002	Sara Shepherd	C	$12.50	Dog002	175	Bitmap Image
C003	Barney Bulldog	C	$12.50	Dog003	225	Bitmap Image
C004	Siamese Sally	C	$13.00	Cat004	255	Bitmap Image
C005	Tiggy Cat	C	$13.00	Cat005	240	Bitmap Image
D001	Gary Gecko	D	$11.00	Din001	300	Bitmap Image
D002	Tyrannosaurus Tommy	D	$10.75	Din002	295	Bitmap Image
D003	Brontosaurus Barry	D	$10.75	Din003	150	Bitmap Image
D004	Triceratops Tony	D	$11.00	Din004	125	Bitmap Image
D005	Stegosaurus Sue	D	$11.00	Din005	200	Bitmap Image
E001	Ziggy Zebra	E	$13.75	Zeb001	150	Bitmap Image
E002	Tula Tiger	E	$13.75	Tig002	235	Bitmap Image
E003	Larry Lion	E	$14.00	Lin003	225	Bitmap Image
E004	Elvira Elephant	E	$10.75	Ele004	175	Bitmap Image
E005	Whitey Whale	E	$10.75	Whl005	200	Bitmap Image
F001	Linda Lamb	F	$10.75	Lam001	175	Bitmap Image
F002	Biffy Bunny	F	$9.50	Bun002	125	Bitmap Image
F003	Rodney Rooster	F	$9.50	Roo003	135	
F004	Penelope Pig	F	$9.50	Pig004	275	Bitmap Image
F006	Sherry Sheep	F	$10.75	Shp001	200	Bitmap Image
T001	Professor Bear	C	$14.00	Bear001	325	Bitmap Image
T002	Valentine Bear	D	$14.25	Bear002	175	Bitmap Image
T003	Mr. Theodore Bear	E	$12.50	Bear003	275	Bitmap Image
T004	Santa Bear	F	$13.75	Bear004	150	Bitmap Image
T005	Night Time Bear	T	$12.75	Bear005	225	Bitmap Image
T006	Easter Bear					
					0	

FIGURE 5-17 Choose the value from the lookup column

3. Close the table.

EXERCISE 5-13 View the Created Relationship

When you created the lookup field, Access identified a relationship between tbl-ProductLines and tblStuffedAnimals based on the common field ProductGroup. You can now view that relationship in the Relationships window.

1. Click the Relationships button.

2. The Relationships window shows the last layout you saved. Click the Clear Layout button and click **Yes**.
3. Click the Show Table button.
4. Double-click tblProductLines and tblStuffedAnimals. Close the **Show Table** dialog box. Resize and rearrange the field lists so all field names and the join line are visible.
5. Double-click the join line to open the **Edit Relationships** dialog box. This is a One-To-Many relationship. The main table is tblProductLines; it has the primary key. Click **OK**.
6. Close the Relationships window. A message box asks if you want to save the changes to the layout. Click **Yes**.
7. Compact and close the database.

LESSON 5 Summary

- The current relationship layout displays in the Relationships window.
- Clicking the Show All Relationships button shows the currently viewed relationship and all other relationships in the database.
- Print relationships to troubleshoot and document portions of your database structure.
- Clicking and dragging from one common field in a field list to the other common field in another field list creates a relationship.
- Referential integrity can be enforced in a One-To-Many relationship or a One-To-One relationship, but not in an Indeterminate relationship.
- Deleting the line between two field lists in the Relationships window will remove the relationship between the two tables.
- Records from the related table can display as a subdatasheet within the datasheet of the primary table.
- When you add a default value to a field, values in previously entered records do not change.
- Formats help standardize how data will be displayed in Datasheet View.
- Input masks help standardize how data is entered.
- Lookup fields help standardize data entry by displaying input choices from another table.

LESSON 5 Command Summary

FEATURE	BUTTON	MENU	KEYBOARD	SPEECH
Insert Row	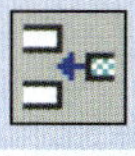	Insert, Rows		✓
Delete Row		Edit, Delete Rows		✓
Insert Subdatasheet		Insert, Subdatasheet		✓
Expand Subdatasheet	+	Format, Subdatasheet, Expand All		✓
Collapse Subdatasheet	−	Format, Subdatasheet, Collapse All		✓
Show Table		Relationships, Show Table		✓
View Relationships	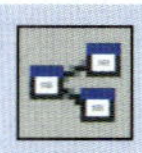	Tools, Relationships		✓
Print Relationships		File, Print Relationships		✓

Concepts Review

TRUE/FALSE QUESTIONS

Each of the following statements is either true or false. Indicate your choice by circling T or F.

T F **1.** A lookup field lets you select a value from a list instead of keying the value.

T F **2.** When you clear the Relationships window, you also delete the relationships.

T F **3.** The set of database rules for relationships is known as validation norms.

T F **4.** A subdatasheet is a nested datasheet inside a main datasheet and shows records from a related table.

T F **5.** Using a default value can improve the speed, accuracy, and consistency of data entry.

T F **6.** Deleting the join line between two field lists in the Relationships window deletes the corresponding tables.

T F **7.** The Relationships window can display more than one relationship at a time.

T F **8.** You must use an input mask for data entry when a field has a Date/Time data type.

SHORT ANSWER QUESTIONS

Write the correct answer in the space provided.

1. What field property can you use to display data in a particular style?

___

2. What graphic represents the relationship between two tables in the Relationships window?

___

3. In a One-To-Many relationship with referential integrity, how can you identify the table on the "many" side of the relationship?

___

4. How do you delete a relationship in the Relationships window?

___

5. What button do you click to start the Input Mask Wizard?

____

6. In the Format property, what symbol is used to capitalize all data in a field?

____

7. How do you start the Lookup Wizard?

____

8. What field property automatically enters a value for each new record?

____

CRITICAL THINKING

Answer these questions on a separate page. There are no right or wrong answers. Support your answers with examples from your own experience, if possible.

1. The One-To-Many relationship is the most commonly used relationship in business databases. Why do you think this is true?

2. Input masks and default values are very useful when controlling data entry. When would it not be appropriate to use an input mask or default value?

Lesson Applications

EXERCISE 5-14

Create a relationship between tables. Set referential integrity. Print relationships.

1. Open the Relationships window and clear the layout.
2. Add tblNewPayments and tblSalesOrders to the window. Size the field lists to see the field names. Determine which is the common field.
3. Create a One-To-Many relationship with referential integrity between the tables. Save and close the layout.

TIP: The fields used for a relationship must be the same size and data type.

4. Open tblNewPayments and enter another payment from Customer #4. Use OrderID **20500** and key an amount and date. Press Enter after the last field to see the error message.
5. Click OK in the message box.
6. Close the table and click OK in the message box again. Then click Yes. The record is not added to tblNewPayments, because there is no Order #20500 in tblSalesOrders.
7. From the Relationships window, print the relationship between these two tables.
8. Close the report without saving.
9. Save and close the Relationships window.

EXERCISE 5-15

Add a field. Set a format. Add data.

1. Open ***[your initials]*****CC-05**, if it is not already open.
2. Open the tblKitSuppliers table in Design View.
3. Insert a field between the City and PostalCode fields. Name the field **State** and choose Text as the data type. Set the Field Size at **2**. Set the Format to uppercase characters.
4. Change to Datasheet View and save the table.
5. Key the following states in the appropriate rows:

Mills Fabric & Notion Supply:	**il**
Laramie Fabric Works:	**co**
Colby Manufacturing Company:	**nc**
Northeast Fabric Supply:	**ct**
Southern Fabrics, Inc:	**nc**
Robinson Mills, Inc.:	**nj**

6. Change the contact name in the first record to ***[your first and last name]***.
7. Print the table in landscape orientation. Close the table.

EXERCISE 5-16

Insert a subdatasheet. View the relationship. Print and then delete the relationship.

1. Open tblEmployees in Datasheet View.
2. Insert a subdatasheet that shows the job title of each employee. Use the table tblJobCodes with the common field JobCode.
3. Allow Access to create the relationship.
4. Print only the relationship between tblEmployees and tblJobCodes.
5. Delete the relationship between tblEmployees and tblJobCodes.
6. Save and close the Relationships window.

EXERCISE 5-17 *Challenge Yourself*

Create a new table. Add fields, input masks, and a lookup field. Create relationships. Enforce referential integrity. Add data. Print tables and relationships.

1. Create a new table named tblImportantDates. Create a field that acts as a foreign key field and links to the table tblEmployees.
2. In the new table, add a date field and a comment field.
3. Add an input mask for the date field and make the foreign key field a lookup field.
4. Modify the relationship between the two tables to enforce referential integrity.
5. Add at least five records to tblImportantDates to test your structure.
6. Print each table in a landscape orientation.
7. Print the relationship.
8. Compact and close your database.

On Your Own

In these exercises you work on your own, as you would in a real-life work environment. Use the skills you've learned to accomplish the task—and be creative.

EXERCISE 5-18

Review the designs for the three databases you created in Exercises 4-19 through 4-21. Select one of the three databases to continue developing. Identify two additional tables you might need to make your database designs more useful. The relationships between the main table and the two additional tables should be One-To-Many. On a blank sheet of paper, list the field names, data types, field sizes, and attributes for the two new tables. Identify the common fields among the three tables. Continue to Exercise 5-19.

EXERCISE 5-19

Create the two tables you designed in Exercise 5-18. Add appropriate field properties to each table to make your design more useful. Create One-To-Many relationships with referential integrity between the tables. Test the referential integrity of the tables. Add at least five records to each empty table. Print each table and its relationships. Continue to Exercise 5-20.

EXERCISE 5-20

Search the Internet for images or graphics you might wish to use in your database. Design and create a new table to store the images. Create an appropriate relationship between this new table and the main table. Insert the images into the new table. Print the relationship. Keep a copy of the database you modified in Exercises 5-18 through 5-20. It might be used in subsequent lessons. Submit to your instructor the printouts from Exercises 5-18 through 5-20, along with your field list from 5-18.

LESSON 6

Adding Forms to a Database

OBJECTIVES

MOUS ACTIVITIES

In this lesson:

Ac2002 3-1
Ac2002 3-2
Ac2002 4-1
Ac2002 4-2
Ac2002 8-2
Ac2002 8-3

See Appendix E.

After completing this lesson, you will be able to:

1. Create AutoForms.
2. Create a form using the Form Wizard.
3. Work with form sections.
4. Work with controls on a form.
5. Add a calculated control to a form.
6. Modify format properties.
7. Use the Web to display data.

Estimated Time: 2 hours

You have already used tables, queries, and forms to enter and edit data. When you use a table or a query, the records are displayed in rows. If a table or query has many fields, you cannot see the entire record at once and need to scroll. Instead of scrolling, it's often better to view one record at a time by using a form.

There are other advantages to using forms:

- You can arrange data in an attractive format that may include special fonts, colors, shading, and images.
- You can design a form to match a paper source document.
- You can determine totals and make other calculations.
- You can display data from more than one table.

Creating AutoForms

The quickest way to create a form for any table or query is to use an *AutoForm*, a form layout that includes all fields in a specified arrangement. After you specify a recordset, Access creates an AutoForm that includes all the fields. You can create an AutoForm from the Tables or the Queries window by selecting the table or query and clicking the New Object button. From the Forms window and the New Form dialog box, you can choose between a columnar and a tabular AutoForm. A columnar AutoForm shows one record at a time with the fields in columns or lists. A tabular AutoForm displays each record in a row with fields in separate columns.

NOTE: When you use the New Object button, the AutoForm style is the same as the last AutoForm used at your computer.

EXERCISE 6-1 Create an AutoForm by Using the New Object Button

The New Object button is available on the Tables and Queries toolbars. You click the table or query you want to use and then choose what object you want to create from the New Object drop-down list.

1. Make a copy of **CC-06** and **CC-E-06**. Rename them to ***[your initials]*CC-06** and ***[your initials]*CC-E-06**. Make sure neither new file is Read-only. Open ***[your initials]*CC-06**.
2. Click the Tables button. Click tblStuffedAnimals to highlight the name.
3. Click the drop-down arrow for the New Object button.

FIGURE 6-1 New Object drop-down menu

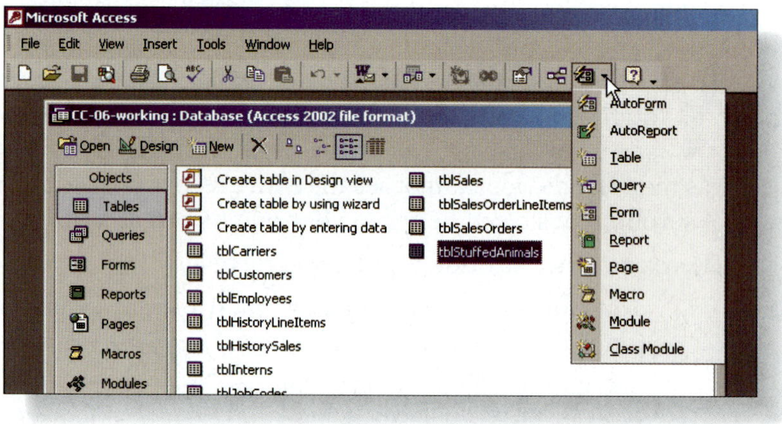

4. Choose AutoForm. A simple form opens, showing the first record from tblStuffedAnimals. The navigation buttons are at the bottom left corner of the form.

FIGURE 6-2
AutoForm with fields displayed in a single column

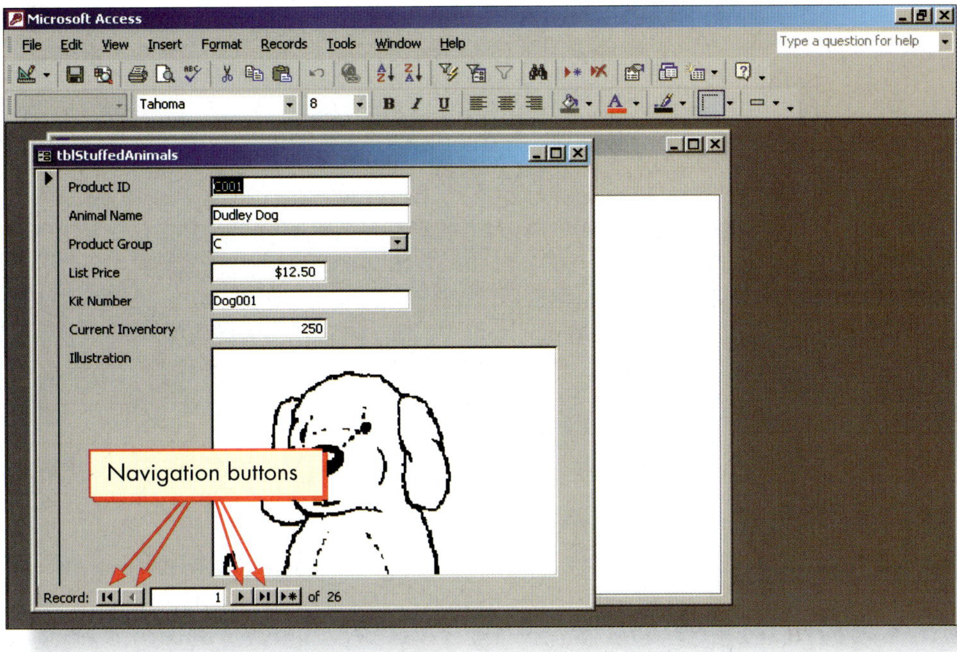

5. Click the Next Record button. Click the Last Record button. Click the Previous Record button. Click the First Record button.
6. Close the form without saving it.

EXERCISE 6-2 Create a Multiple-Table Query

Forms are based on recordsets (tables or queries). If two tables are linked by a common field, you can build a query that uses fields from both tables.

REVIEW: A query is a database object that extracts information from the table or from other queries.

1. Click tblStuffedAnimals to highlight the name.
2. Click the drop-down arrow for the New Object button.
3. Choose Query. The New Query dialog box opens so you can choose how to build your query.

TIP: The face of the New Object button shows the most recently used choice.

4. Choose Design View and click **OK**. Maximize the window. The window shows one field list.

5. Place the pointer on the border between the top and bottom panes. Size the panes and the field list so you can see the field names.

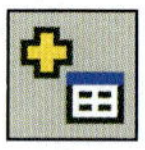

6. Click the Show Table button . You can add tables to the query design.
7. Double-click tblProductLines. The field list appears in the top pane with an automatic join line for the common field.

FIGURE 6-3
Show Table dialog box in Query Design window

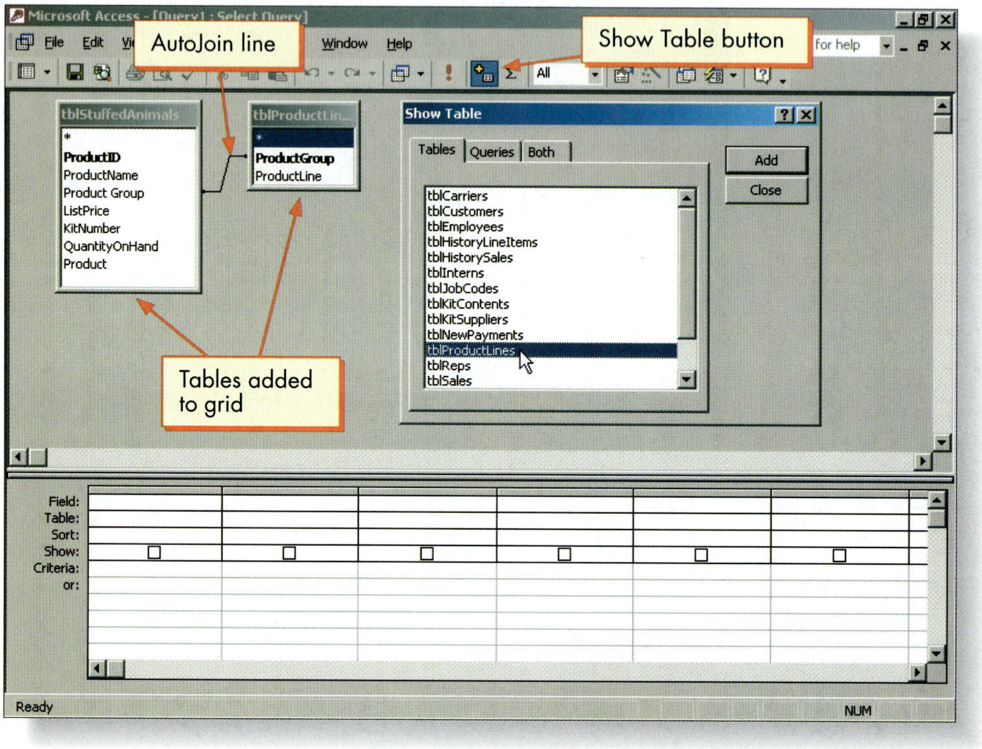

NOTE: When two tables are placed in a query and no relationships have been defined, Access creates an AutoJoin if each table has a field with the same name and data type and one of these fields is a primary key.

8. Close the Show Table dialog box. Adjust the size of the field lists so you can see them both.
9. In the tblStuffedAnimals field list, double-click these field names:

   ProductID

   ProductName

   ProductGroup

   KitNumber

   Product
10. In the tblProductLines list, double-click ProductLine.

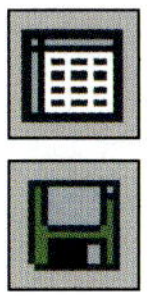

11. Click the View button to see the results.

12. Click the Save button. Name the query **qryProductLines**.

13. Close the query.

EXERCISE 6-3 Create an AutoForm from the Forms Window

When you create a form from the Forms window, you need to choose the query or table in the drop-down list in the New Form dialog box.

1. Click the Forms button and the New button. The New Form dialog box opens.

2. Click AutoForm: Columnar in the list.

3. Click the drop-down arrow for Choose the table or query where the object's data comes from. The list displays the names of tables and queries in the database. Choose qryProductLines.

REVIEW: Press F4 to display a drop-down list when the cursor is in the field.

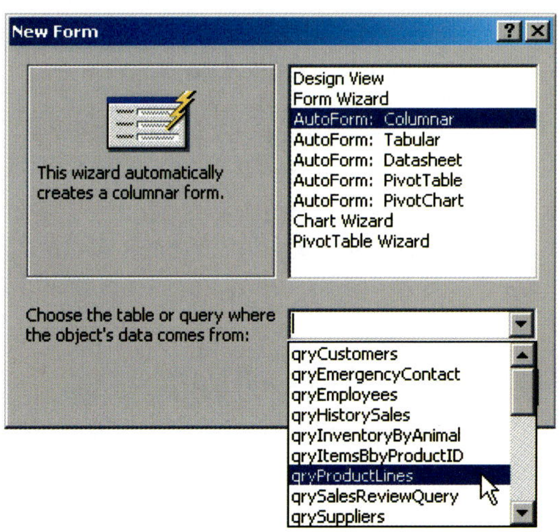

FIGURE 6-4 Drop-down list displaying existing tables and queries

4. Click OK. Access creates a form with the fields in columns. Access displays the first record from the Product Lines query. (See Figure 6-5 on the next page.)

NOTE: The appearance of your form might differ slightly from that of the form shown in Figure 6-5 if it has a different style applied to it.

5. Press PgDn several times to navigate through the records, and then press PgUp. Press Ctrl+End to move to the last record. Press Ctrl+Home to return to the first record.

6. Click the Save button. Change the name to **frmProductLines** and click OK. Close the form.

FIGURE 6-5
AutoForm with fields in columns

Using the Form Wizard

You can create a similar form by using the Form Wizard. The Form Wizard lets you select fields, a layout, and a style. The layout determines if the records are arranged in columns or rows. A style selects colors, backgrounds, and fonts automatically.

NOTE: A form is created from a recordset and does not have to include all the fields from the query or table.

EXERCISE 6-4 Create a Form by Using the Form Wizard

Most business databases contain commonly used fields such as social security numbers and phone numbers. Database designers often use the Form Wizard to create a template they can modify to enhance the speed and accuracy of data entry.

1. Click the Forms button and then click New.
2. In the New Form dialog box, select Form Wizard.
3. Display the drop-down list of tables and queries. Select tblStuffedAnimals and click OK.

NOTE: If you make a mistake selecting the table or query, you can select it in the first Form Wizard dialog box.

4. The dialog box asks which fields to use on the form. Click the Add All button >> to choose all fields.

5. Click KitNumber in the <u>S</u>elected Fields list. Click the Remove One button [<] to move it back to the list on the left.

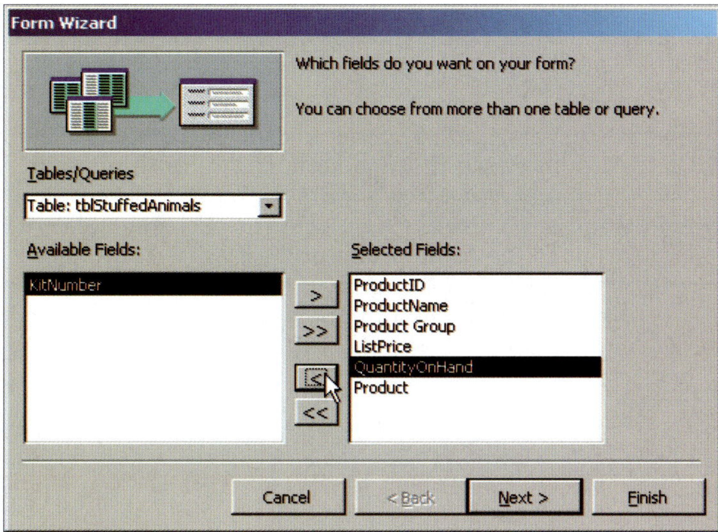

FIGURE 6-6 Selected fields to be included on the form

6. Click <u>N</u>ext. The dialog box asks you to choose a layout. Select <u>C</u>olumnar.

7. Click <u>N</u>ext. The next dialog box lists several styles. Click each style to see a preview.

8. Click Standard as the style for your form. Then click <u>N</u>ext.

9. The dialog box asks for a title for the form. This is the name used to save the form; it does not appear anywhere on the form. Key **frmAnimals**

10. Select <u>O</u>pen the form to view or enter information and then click <u>F</u>inish.

Working with Form Sections

Forms are designed to be viewed on a screen, but they can be printed. A form is divided into sections; some are visible on the screen and others on the printed page. You see the sections when you change to Design View.

NOTE: The sections that initially appear in a form depend on how you created it.

Almost all forms have a *Detail section* to display one record. The *Form Header* appears once at the top of a form and is used to display such things as titles, images, and photographs. The *Form Footer* is similar to the Form Header, but appears at the bottom of a form. The *Page Header* is a section that prints at the top of each printed page. The *Page Footer* prints at the bottom of each page. A Page Header or Page Footer is often used for page numbers or dates.

TABLE 6-1 Sections of a Form

NAME OF SECTION	PURPOSE
Detail	Displays each record in a separate form.
Form Header	Appears once at the top of the form; typically includes a title, logo, date, or other similar data.
Form Footer	Appears once at the bottom of the form; typically includes a company name, logo, date, or other similar data.
Page Header	Prints at the top of each page.
Page Footer	Prints at the bottom of each page.

EXERCISE 6-5 Open and Size the Form Header

When you scroll through a form, the Form Header always displays at the top of the Form window. If the information in the Detail section is too large to display on one screen, it is good practice to place relevant information such as the title of the form in the Form Header.

1. Click the View button. Design View shows the sections and the objects in those sections. You also see a Standard toolbar, a Formatting toolbar, and the Toolbox.

NOTE: The Toolbox might be floating; you can anchor it with the other toolbars by double-clicking its title bar.

FIGURE 6-7
Form Design View

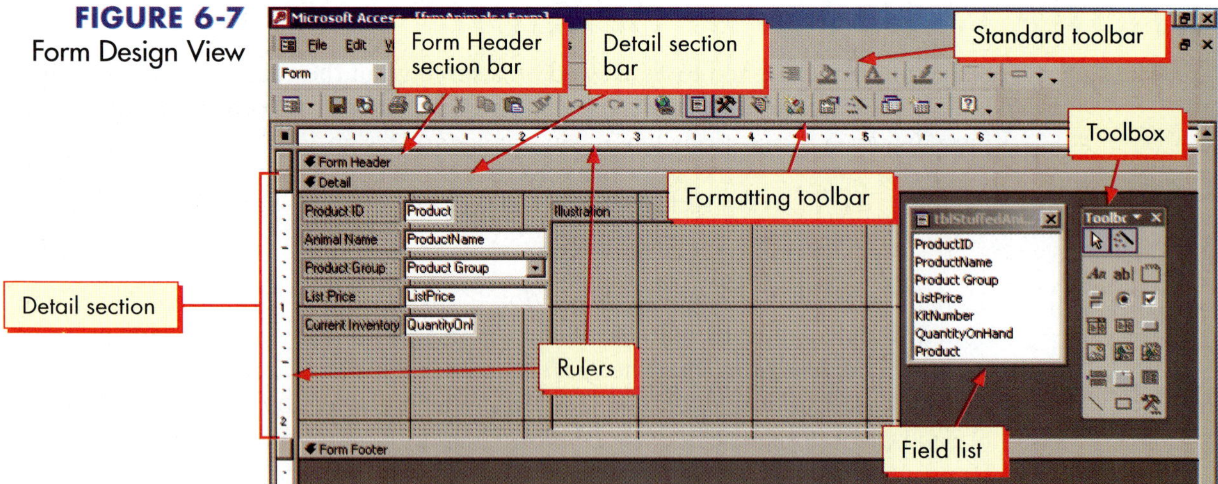

2. Place the pointer on the border between the **Form Header** and **Detail** section bars. The pointer changes to a two-headed arrow.
3. Drag the pointer down below the CurrentInventory field. This makes the **Form Header** section about 1.5 inches tall.

FIGURE 6-8
Opening the Form Header

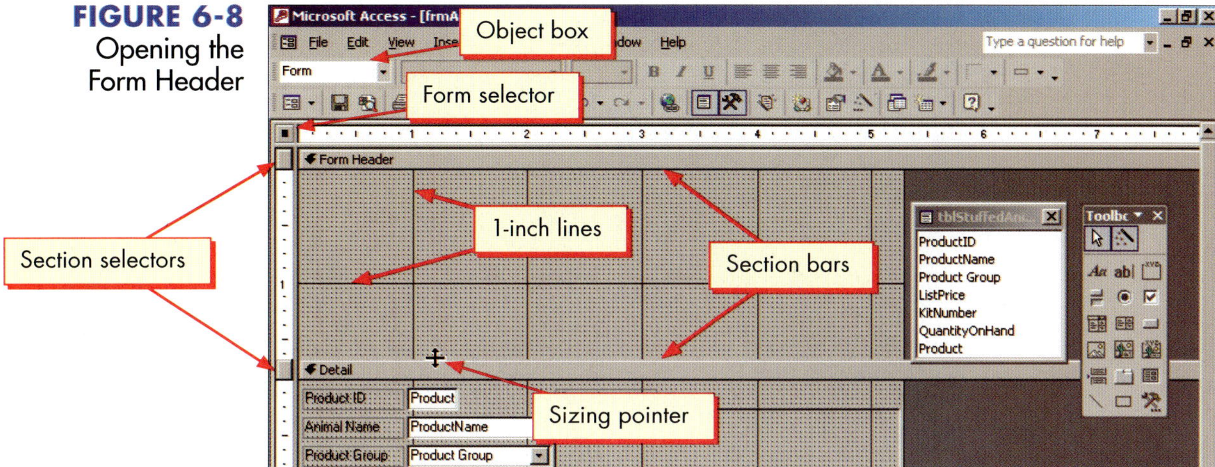

4. Drag the **Detail** border up to the 1-inch mark on the vertical ruler. (Notice the line that extends vertically and horizontally on the design grid. You should drag the border until it meets the line extending horizontally in the design grid from the 1-inch mark on the vertical ruler.)

TIP: Each square of the design grid is 1 inch by 1 inch.

5. Double-click the **Form Header** section bar. The Form Header property sheet opens, listing the settings for this section. Click the **Format** tab. Change the **Height** to **.75**. (See Figure 6-9 on the next page.)

6. Click the Close button. The **Form Header** section is now precisely sized.
7. Move the pointer to the right edge of the form (the gray area with dots.) When the pointer changes to a two-headed arrow, drag to the right until the edge of the form reaches the 6-inch mark on the horizontal ruler.

8. Click the Form Selector to the left of the horizontal ruler. A small black rectangle means the entire form is selected. The Object box on the Formatting toolbar shows that the Form is selected.

NOTE: All objects in a form, as well as all parts of the form, have a property sheet. Select an object and press F4 to open its property sheet.

FIGURE 6-9
Form Header property sheet

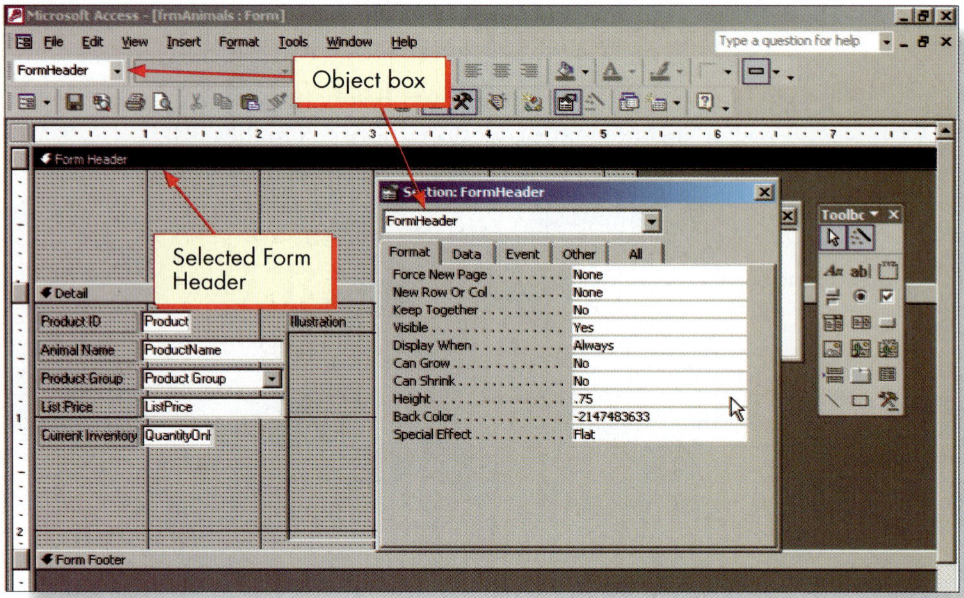

EXERCISE 6-6 Add a Label to the Form Header

The Label tool in the Toolbox is used to enter text or titles in a form. It appears on all forms and does not change from record to record.

You can format a label much as you format text in a word processor. You can select the font, color, weight, and size of type. The Formatting toolbar includes buttons for most of these settings. Changes you make from the toolbar automatically are recorded in the label's property sheet. Changes to the position or size of an object are also recorded automatically in the label's property sheet.

When you select a label or any other object eight small black squares known as *selection handles* appear around the object. Selecting the top left selection handle moves the object. The other seven selection handles are also known as *sizing handles*. You can use them to adjust the size of the object.

1. Click the Label button in the toolbox. The pointer changes to a crosshair cursor with the letter A.
2. Place the pointer in the Form Header section at the left edge. Click and then drag down and to the right to draw a box about 2 inches wide and .5 inch tall. When you release the mouse button, you see the box and a text insertion point.
3. Key **Stuffed Animals** and press Enter. The label box is selected and displays the eight selection handles around its edges.

NOTE: Pressing Enter does not move the cursor to the next line in a label. It finishes the label and selects it.

FIGURE 6-10
Adding a label to the Form Header

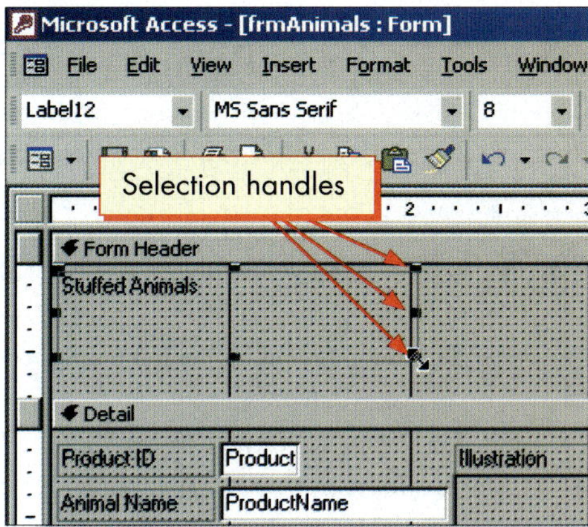

4. The Formatting toolbar displays the font name and size. Click the drop-down arrow next to the Font list box. Key **t** to move to the first font name that begins with "T." Select Times New Roman.
5. Click the drop-down arrow next to the Font Size list box. Click **18**.
6. Place the pointer on any selection handle except the top left one to display a two-headed arrow. Double-click. This sizes the label box to fit the text.
7. Place the pointer on the middle right selection handle to display a two-headed arrow. Drag to the right about 1 inch. This resizes the label box to a custom size.

FIGURE 6-11
Sizing the label box

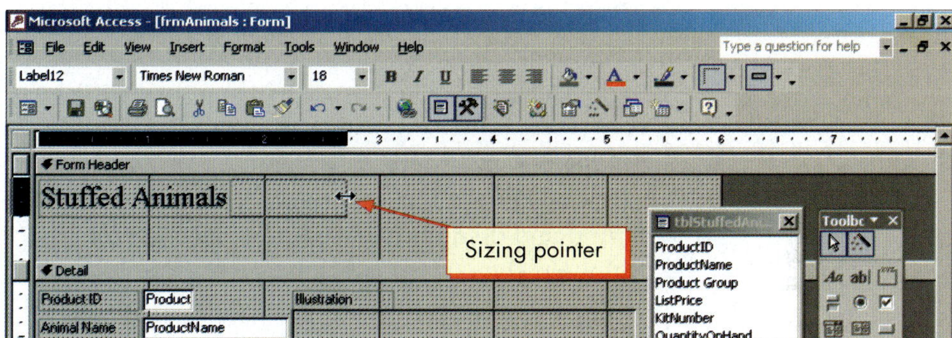

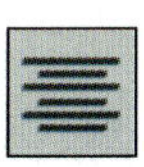

8. Click the Center button on the Formatting toolbar. This centers the text within the box.
9. Double-click any sizing handle again.

10. Click the drop-down arrow next to the Font/Fore Color button on the Formatting toolbar to open a palette.
11. Click a medium blue color tile to change the text. (See Figure 6-12 on the next page.)

12. Click the drop-down arrow next to the Fill/Back Color button. Select white from the color palette.

13. Click the View button to see the changes. Close and save the form.

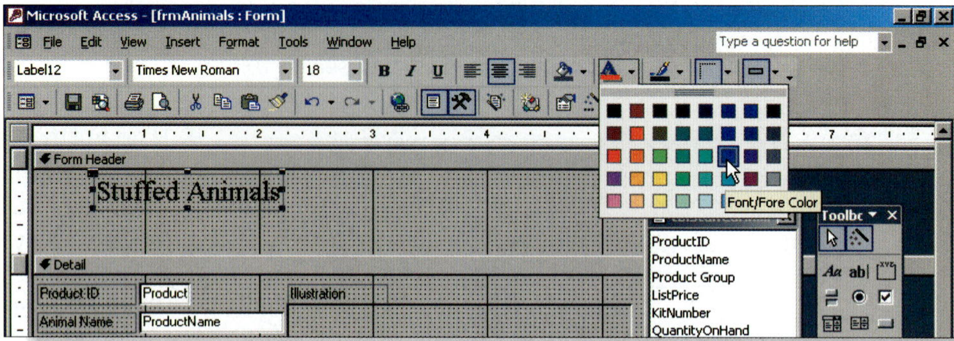

FIGURE 6-12 Changing the font color

Working with Controls on a Form

When you view a form in Design View, you see its controls. A *control* displays data, performs an action, or adds a design element. A control can be bound, unbound, or calculated.

- A *bound control* is linked to a recordset; it has a data source. Use bound controls to enter or change data. The data in a bound control changes from record to record.
- An *unbound control* displays labels, titles, lines, rectangles, or other design elements. It has no data source and isn't linked to a recordset.
- A *calculated control* uses an expression as its source of data. A calculated control can use field names, arithmetic operators, constant numbers, or functions. It is not a field in a recordset.

To change any control, you first select it. Many controls initially include a text box and an attached label. To select the control as a whole, click the text box. Labels are unbound and do not affect the information in a recordset.

As you move the pointer over the top or bottom borders of a selected control, the Move pointer (an open-hand pointer) appears. The Move pointer moves the text box and its label.

When you place the pointer on the top left selection handle of a control, a hand with a pointing finger appears. This pointer moves the individual bound part of a control (a text box) or unbound part of a control (a label). You can size either part of a control by placing the pointer on a handle other than the top left one and displaying a two-headed arrow.

TABLE 6-2 Special Pointers

NAME	POINTER	USED TO
Open-hand	✋	Move a control and its label.
Upward-pointing hand	☝	Move a label or text box separately.
Two-headed arrow	↕ ↗ ↔	Resize a control vertically, diagonally, or horizontally.

EXERCISE 6-7 Select and Move Controls

Text boxes have a white background. Labels have black text and a background matching the rest of the form.

1. In the Forms window, select frmAnimals and click Design.

NOTE: An attached label shows the caption from the field as a default.

2. Click the ProductName text box; its label shows "Animal Name." Handles appear around the borders of the text box. The name of the selected object appears in the Object box at the left edge of the Formatting toolbar.

3. Click the QuantityOnHand text box; its label is "Current Inventory." Its name appears in the Object box.

4. Click the List Price label, not the text box. The Object box indicates this is a label.

5. Click the large box for the picture. The Object name box shows "Product," the name of the field. The label "Illustration" displays above the box.

6. Double-click the **Detail** section bar to open its property sheet.

TIP: You do not need to type the quotation mark (") to show inches when entering a size in a property sheet.

7. Click the **Format** tab and set the **Height** to **4** inches. Close the property sheet.

8. Click the large picture box. This is the Product control.

9. Place the pointer on either the top or bottom edge of the box (but not on a handle). The pointer changes to an open-hand pointer.

10. Drag the control below the other controls and to the left to align under the Current Inventory label. (See Figure 6-13 on the next page.)

REVIEW: If you make an error sizing or moving a control, click the Undo button and try again.

11. Click the ProductName text box. Place the pointer on the top or bottom edge of the text box (but not on a handle). The pointer changes to an open-hand pointer.

12. Drag the control to the right and up to align with the ProductID control. Place the left edge of the Animal Name label at the 2-inch mark on the horizontal ruler.

NOTE: When you select a text box, the label is included in the selection.

FIGURE 6-13
Moving a control

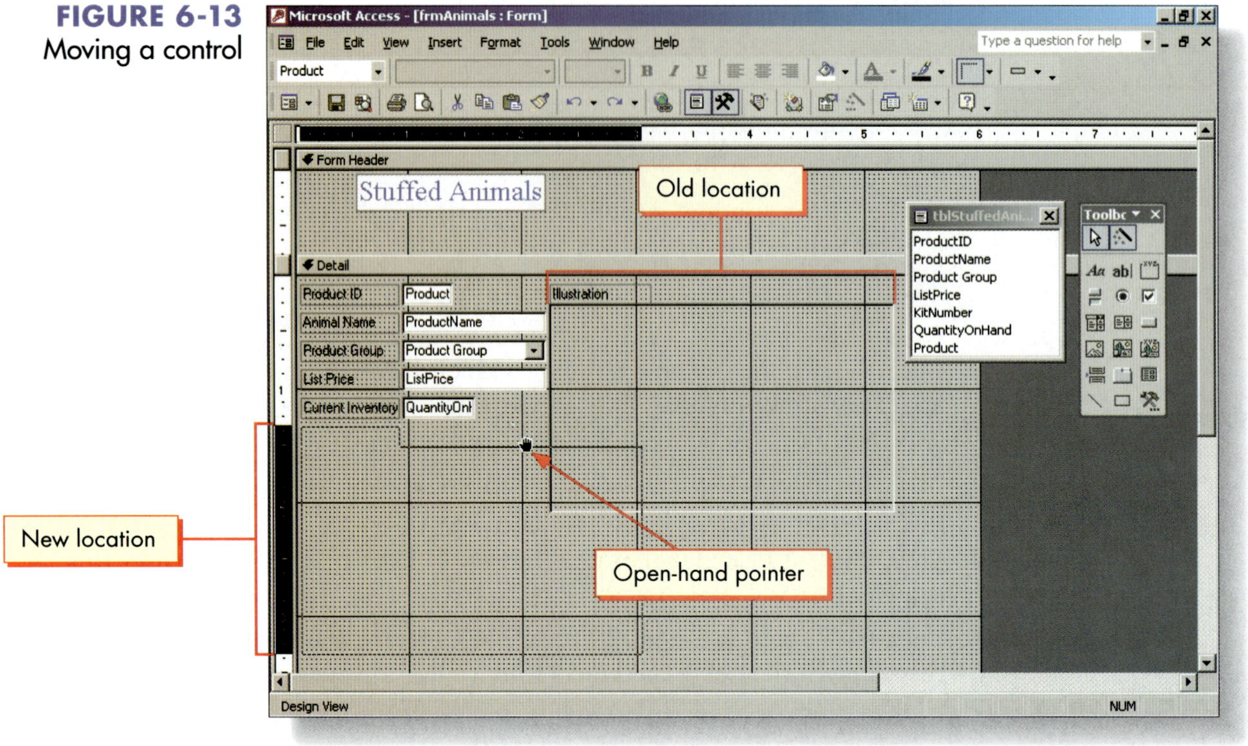

13. Select the ProductGroup text box. Hold down Ctrl and press → to nudge the control to the right. Repeat this step several times.

14. Hold down Ctrl and press ↑ to nudge the control up. Nudging moves the control one pixel at a time.

15. Drag the ProductGroup control beneath the ProductName control. Nudge it until one row of grid dots shows between it and the ProductName text box.

16. Select the ListPrice text box. Press Shift and select the QuantityOnHand text box. Both controls are selected.

17. Point at the top or bottom edge of either control until you see the open-hand pointer. Drag both controls below the ProductGroup control, leaving a space of one row of grid dots.

18. Click an unused part of the form to deselect all controls.

19. Click the View button to see your changes.

EXERCISE 6-8 Adjust the Size of Controls

You can adjust the width and height of the text box or the label box. You can select multiple controls and change them all at once.

1. Click the View button to return to Design View.
2. Select the QuantityOnHand text box. Point at the middle sizing handle on the right edge. The pointer changes to a horizontal two-headed arrow.
3. Drag the pointer to the right to make the box the same width as the ListPrice text box.
4. Press Shift and click the ListPrice text box to add it to the selection. Repeat the steps to add the ProductGroup, ProductName, and ProductID text boxes to the selection. All the text boxes show handles.

5. Click the Properties button on the Standard toolbar. The property sheet shows that this is a multiple selection.
6. Click the **Format** tab. Set the **Width** to **1** inch. Press ↑ to see your changes.

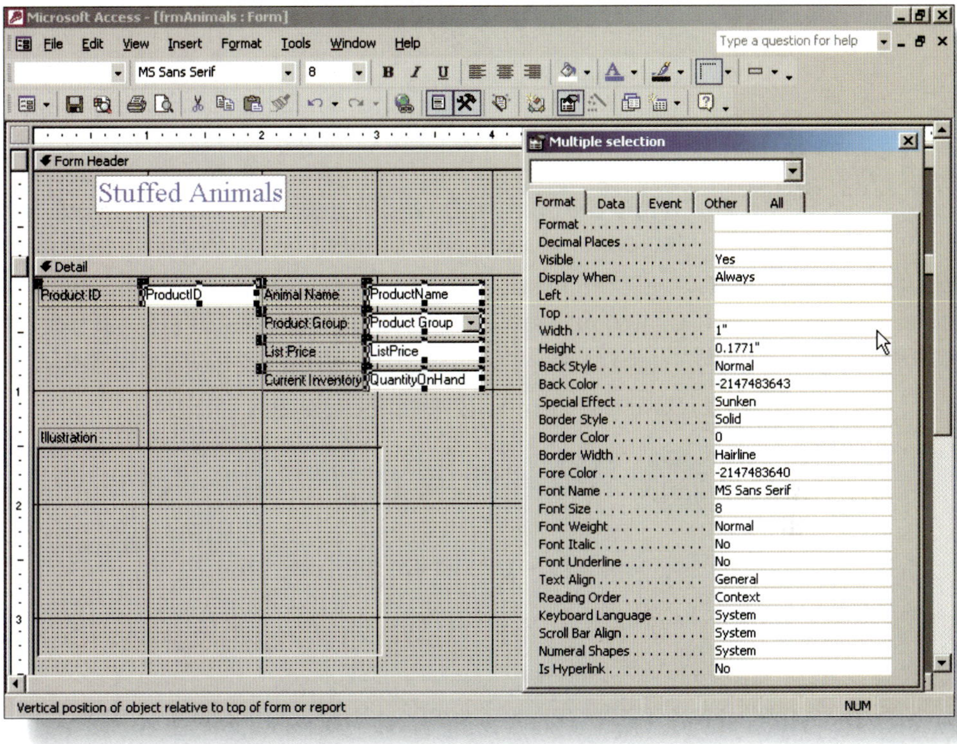

FIGURE 6-14
Multiple selections of controls

7. Close the property sheet and deselect the controls. Switch to Form View to see your changes. Then return to Design View.
8. Point at the bottom edge of the horizontal ruler, close to the 3.5-inch mark, directly above the text boxes in the **Detail** section. When the pointer is a solid black arrow, click to select the controls in a column. (See figure 6-15 on the next page.)
9. From the **Format** menu, choose **Vertical Spacing**, **Make Equal**. Access evens the spacing between the controls.

ACCESS

FIGURE 6-15 Selecting multiple controls in a column

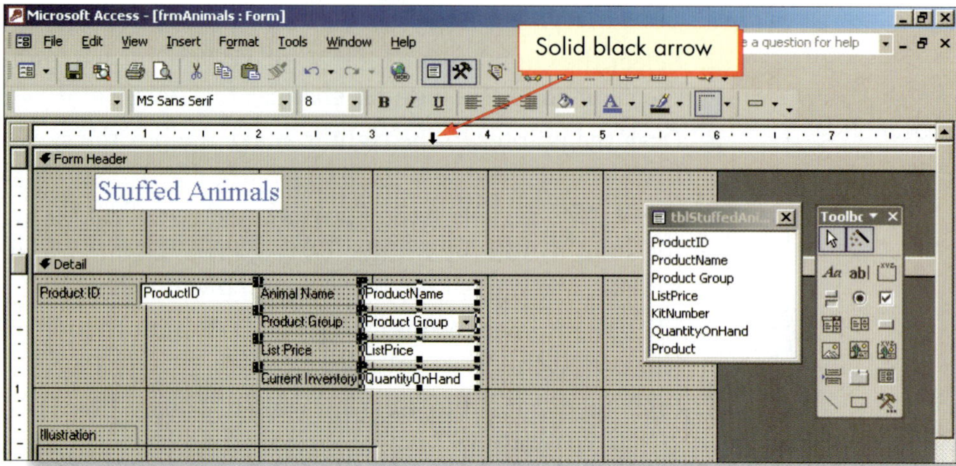

NOTE: The Vertical Spacing command uses the space between the first two controls as a guide for the others.

10. While the controls are still selected, choose Format, Vertical Spacing, and Increase. More space is added between each set of controls.
11. Click the ProductID text box. Hold down Shift and press ← to size the control in small increments. Repeat this several times.
12. Click the View button to see the changes.
13. Save the form and return to Design View.

TIP: You can save a form in either Design or Form View.

EXERCISE 6-9 Align and Move Controls

As you move and size controls, you might place them so they are no longer vertically or horizontally aligned. The Align command lines up controls at the top, bottom, left, or right. You can align both text boxes and labels.

1. Select the ProductID text box. Press Shift and select the Product ID label, the ProductName text box, and the Animal Name label.
2. Choose Format, Align, Top to align the top borders of the controls. Deselect the controls.
3. Select the labels Animal Name, Product Group, List Price, and Current Inventory. Choose Format, Align, Left. Deselect the labels.

4. Select the ProductName text box. Point at the move handle (top left). The pointer changes to an upward pointing hand.
5. Drag the text box to the right until its left edge is about at the 3-inch mark, moving it away from its label.
6. Select the ProductGroup text box and display the upward pointing hand pointer. Drag the box to the 3-inch mark. Repeat for the ListPrice and QuantityOnHand text boxes.

NOTE: You cannot move multiple controls with the move handle (upward pointing hand pointer).

TABLE 6-3 Alignment Options

CHOOSE	TO DO THIS
Left	Vertically align the left edges of the controls with the control that is the farthest to the left.
Right	Vertically align the right edges of the controls with the control that is the farthest to the right.
Top	Horizontally align the top edges of the controls with the control that is the highest.
Bottom	Horizontally align the bottom edges of the controls with the control that is the lowest.
To Grid	Align the uppermost corner of the selected control to the design grid.

7. Click anywhere in the unused portion of the form to deselect the controls.
8. Save the changes. Switch to Form View to see your form.

EXERCISE 6-10 Use the Property Sheet

Each control, object, and section on a form has its own *property sheet.* A property sheet lists all the characteristics or attributes for that object.

Properties depend on the type of object. Properties for a label, for example, include such things as font size, font name, and font color. Properties for a text box include a format setting, a data source, and whether the data is visible. When you're selecting a property, a short description of what the property will control appears in the status bar.

For a bound control, many properties are inherited from the table. For example, if you used the Yes/No check box for a field in the table, that control is a Yes/No check box in the form. If you set the Currency format in the table, the control inherits the Currency format in the form.

NOTE: A form inherits the field properties of the table. Changes to the form's properties do not affect the table's properties.

1. Click the View button to return to Design View.
2. Right-click the ProductName text box (not the label). Choose Properties from the shortcut menu. The **Text Box** property sheet for ProductName opens. It has five tabs and shows the name of the control in the title bar and the drop-down list box.
3. Click the **All** tab. The property sheet is a window that you can size and move. Drag the border of the window to make it taller. Scroll to view the list of properties for the text box.

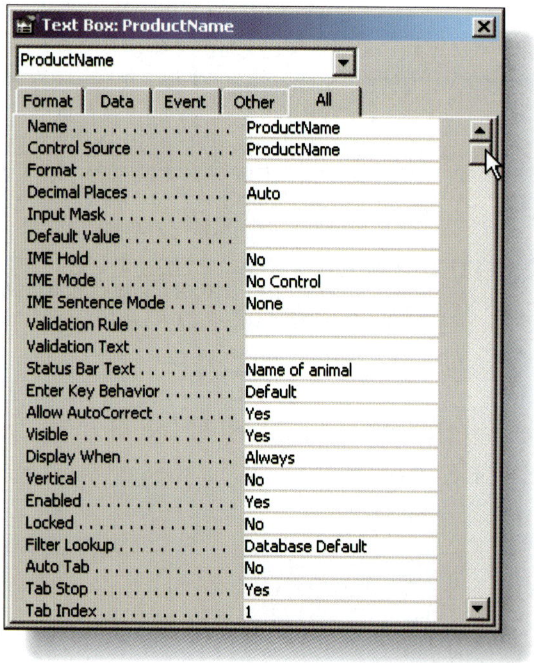

FIGURE 6-16 Text Box property sheet for ProductName

4. Select ListPrice from the drop-down list box. The title bar shows the name and type of property sheet.
5. Scroll through the properties on the **All** tab. Notice that the properties for a label are different from the properties for a text box.

TIP: You can double-click an unselected control to open its property sheet.

6. Click the **Format** tab. Change the Width to **3**. This makes the label 3 inches wide. Close the property sheet.
7. Because the label is too wide, click the Undo button.
8. Double-click the box for the picture to open its property sheet. The title bar shows that this control is a Bound Object Frame.
9. Pictures have a property called **Size Mode** (on the **Format** tab) that specifies how the picture fits in the box.
10. Click the **Size Mode** row and its drop-down arrow. Choose **Stretch**. (See Figure 6-17 on the next page.)

FIGURE 6-17
Bound Object Frame property sheet

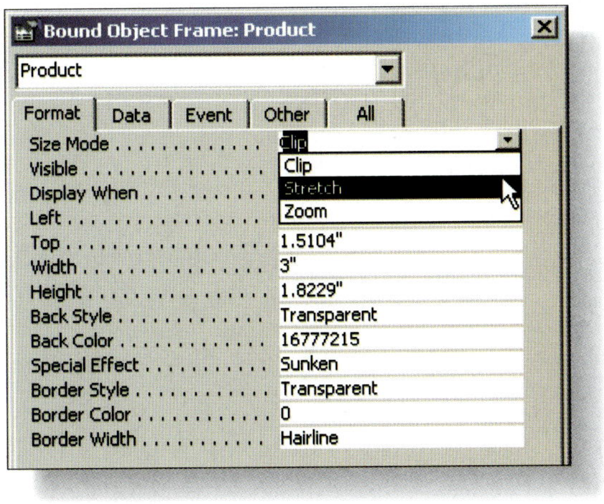

11. Close the property sheet.

12. Switch to Form View. The picture is resized to fit the box.

13. Save your form.

EXERCISE 6-11 Set Tab Order

Tab order determines where the insertion point goes when you press Tab in Form View. The usual order is left-to-right, top-to-bottom. When you move controls in Design View, the tab order might be changed and might not be what you expect.

1. Press Tab to move from field to field. The order is left-to-right, top-to-bottom. Finish so the pointer is in the Product ID field on any record.

NOTE: If your tab order is not left-to-right, top-to-bottom, you might have already made a change that adjusted the tab order.

2. Switch to Design View.

3. Drag the ProductID control to the right of the QuantityOnHand control.

4. Select the ProductName control and drag it where the ProductID control was.

5. Switch to Form View.

6. Press Tab to move from field to field. With the controls rearranged, the tab order is no longer left-to-right, top-to-bottom.

7. Switch to Design View.

8. Click the **Detail** section bar to select the section. Choose **View**, **Tab Order**. The **Tab Order** dialog box opens.

9. Click **Auto Order** to set the tab order left-to-right, top-to-bottom. (See Figure 6-18 on the next page.)

10. Click **OK**. Return to Form View.

11. Check the tab order. Close the form without saving the changes.

FIGURE 6-18 Tab Order dialog box

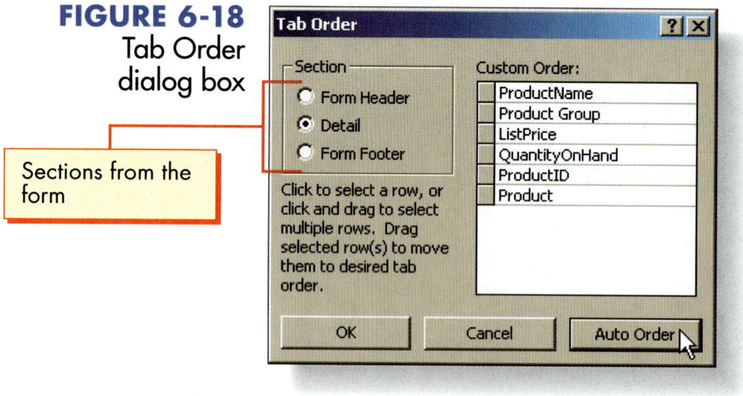

Adding a Calculated Control to a Form

A calculated control uses an expression instead of a field. An expression might combine arithmetic operators (+ – * /), constants, field names, or functions.

EXERCISE 6-12 Create a Form from the Query Window

Your next form includes the name of a stuffed animal product and the number of units in inventory. After creating and saving the form, you use an unbound control to calculate a new cost.

1. Click the Queries button. Click **qryInventorybyAnimal** to select it.
2. Click the New Object drop-down arrow. Select Form.
3. The New Form dialog box opens with the query name.
4. Click Form Wizard and click OK.
5. The dialog box asks which fields to use on the form. Click the Add All button >>.
6. Click Next. Select Columnar for the layout.
7. Click Next. Click Stone as the style, and then click Next.
8. Edit the title to show **frmNewInventory**. Select Open the form to view or enter information and then click Finish.
9. Maximize the window.

EXERCISE 6-13 Add a Calculated Control

You add calculated controls by using the Text Box button ab in the toolbox. You can add expressions to the control Source row by using the Expression Builder. An *expression* is any legal combination of text, numbers, or symbols that represents a value. The *Expression Builder* lets you build an expression by selecting field names, operators, functions, constants, and other elements. Because a calculated control has no inherited format, you will need to specify the format after you create the control.

1. Click the View button.
2. Click the Field List button. This turns the field list on and off. Finish with the Field List displayed.
3. Place the pointer on the right edge of the form and drag to the 5-inch mark.
4. Click the Text Box button ab in the toolbox. The pointer shows a crosshair and the text box icon.
5. Click at the 4-inch mark on the design grid on the same row as the QuantityOnHand text box. A new unbound text box with a label appears on the form.

FIGURE 6-19
Adding a text box

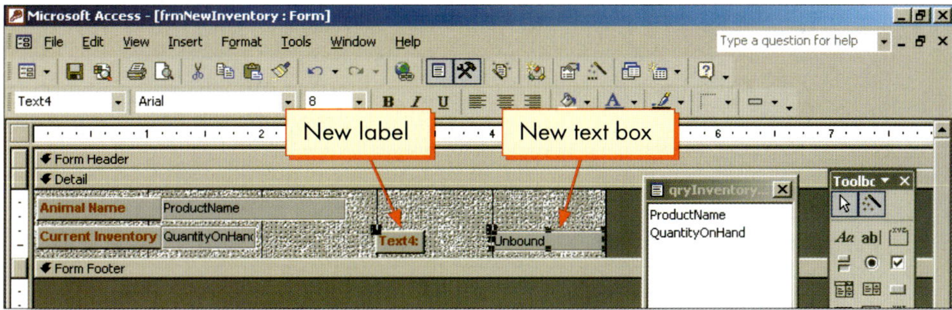

NOTE: The default label for new text boxes is "Text" followed by a number and a colon.

6. Click the new label. Click again within its text to display an I-beam.
7. Click and drag to select the whole default label "Text##:" (Access uses ## to indicate that this could be any number.) Key **New Quantity** as the new label and delete the colon.

TIP: When you click twice to display an I-beam, you might accidentally open the property sheet if you click too fast. If you do, close the property sheet and try again.

8. Double-click the unbound text box. Click the Data tab.
9. Click the Control Source row; read the status bar. There is a drop-down list and a Build button. The drop-down arrow displays a list of the fields in the underlying query. (See Figure 6-20 on the next page.)

FIGURE 6-20
Control Source row

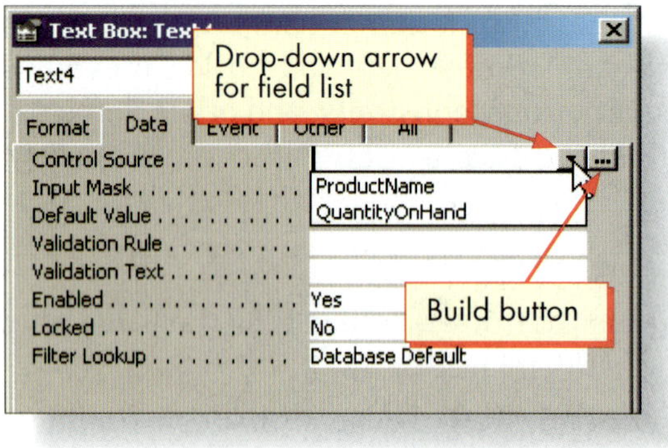

TIP: Press Esc to close the field list if you open it.

10. Click the Build button ... to open the Expression Builder. In the left panel, your frmNew-Inventory form is shown as the current object at the top of the list.

TABLE 6-4

Parts of the Expression Builder

PART	PURPOSE
Expression box	White area at the top of the window that shows the formula as you build it. (Also called the preview area.)
Operator row	Set of buttons with common arithmetic and logical symbols below the preview area.
Left panel	List of folders with objects available for use.
Middle panel	Contents of the folder selected in the left panel.
Right panel	Details or properties of the object selected in the middle panel.
Paste button	Copies selected object or command into the preview area.

11. In the middle panel, click <Field List>. The right panel shows the fields in the form.

12. Double-click QuantityOnHand in the middle panel. It is pasted into the preview area with square brackets. Access applies its standard formatting for expressions you build in the Expression Builder.

NOTE: You can double-click the field names or select them and click the Paste button.

13. Click the multiplication button * in the operator row. It appears in the Preview window after [QuantityOnHand].

14. Key **1.1**

FIGURE 6-21
Expression Builder with an expression

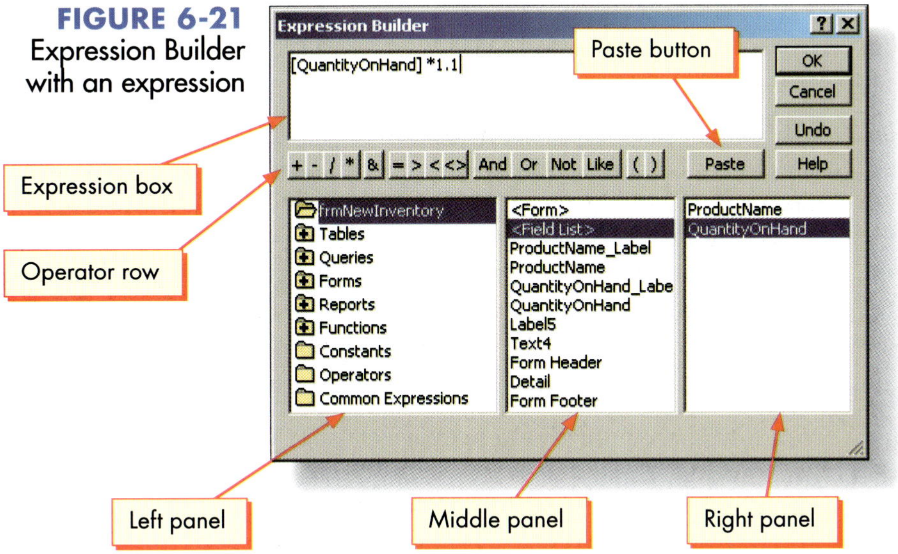

15. Click OK to close the Expression Builder. The expression is entered in standard Access format in the Control Source row of the property sheet.

TIP: You must click the OK button to accept the changes in the Expression Builder.

16. Click the Format tab in the property sheet. Click the Format row and its drop-down arrow. Choose Fixed.

17. Click the Decimal Places row and choose **0**.

18. Click the Other tab. Key **NewQuantity** in the Name property; this is the name of the control.

19. Click on another property; notice that the title bar has changed to show the new name of the control.

20. Close the property sheet. The calculated control appears on the form.

21. Change to Form View. Press PgDn to view a few records.

22. Close and save the form. You are returned to the Queries window where you started when you began creating this form.

Modifying Format Properties

No matter how you create a form, you can apply styles, colors, and fonts to give the form an attractive and professional look. You can change border styles and background colors for controls. You can even change the background color for an entire section. In addition to your own formatting, you can use a predefined style template for the form.

EXERCISE 6-14 Create a Multiple-Table Query with a Calculated Field

Multiple table queries are created when two or more tables are combined to create a unique recordset. Each table must relate to another table through a common field.

You can create a multiple-table query that uses a calculated field. The calculated field will display as a new column in the recordset. Using calculated fields saves storage space by displaying numerical results only at the time that you need the information. For example, it would not be necessary to store the total cost of items ordered if you had already stored the quantity ordered and the price of each item.

1. In the Tables window, click tblKitContents to highlight the name.
2. Click the drop-down arrow for the New Object button. Choose Query.
3. Choose Design View and click OK. Maximize the window. Adjust the size of the panes and the field list.
4. Click the Show Table button. Double-click tblKitSuppliers and then double-click tblStuffedAnimals. Notice the join lines for the common fields. Adjust the size of the new field lists.

TIP: You can arrange field lists in the Queries window to eliminate criss-crossed join lines just as in the Relationships window.

5. Close the Show Table dialog box.
6. In the tblStuffedAnimals list, double-click ProductName.
7. In the tblKitContents list, double-click these field names:

   KitNumber

   Cost
8. In the tblKitSuppliers list, double-click SupplierName. (See Figure 6-22 on the next page.)
9. Click the Save button. Name the query **qryKitCosts**

10. Click the Field row for the first empty column (the fifth column). Then click the Build button to open the Expression Builder.
11. Double-click Cost in the middle panel. Key **+.75** to increase the cost by 75 cents. Click OK to close the Expression Builder.
12. Click the View button to see the results. Return to Design View.
13. In the new calculated field, drag across Expr1 and key **NewCost**. Leave the colon.

NOTE: The colon separates the caption from the actual expression.

14. Click the Properties button. Set the Format to Currency.
15. Set the Caption to **New Cost**. Close the property sheet.

FIGURE 6-22
Multiple-table query in Design View

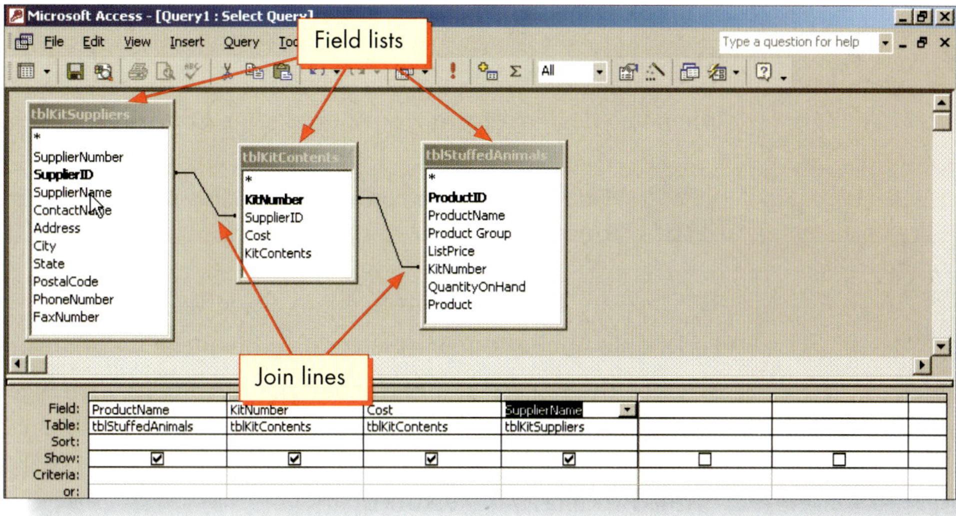

16. View the results. Then save and close the query.

17. Click the Queries tab. Click qryKitCosts. Click the drop-down arrow for New Object. Select AutoForm.

18. Click the Save button and name the form **frmKitCosts**

EXERCISE 6-15 Open the Form Header/Footer

When you create an AutoForm, the Form Header is not open. You need to turn it on from the View menu. When you turn on the Form Header/Footer option, both the header and footer sections open.

1. In form frmKitCosts, switch to Design View.

2. Choose View, Form Header/Footer. The Form Header and Form Footer sections open.

3. Drag the bottom border of the Form Header to make the section about 1 inch tall.

4. Click the Label button. Draw a label about 1.5 inches wide and .5 inch tall near the left edge of the Form Header.

5. Key **Increased Kit Costs** and press Enter.

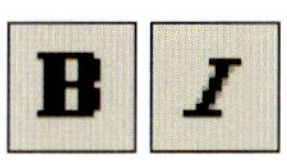

6. Change the font and size to 20-point Arial. Click the Bold button **B** and the Italic button *I*.

7. Double-click a sizing handle to adjust the size of the label to show the title. The Form Header resizes to fit the new label.

8. Place the pointer on the bottom edge of the form. Drag the edge up to the bottom of the Form Footer section bar. This closes the Form Footer.

9. Save the form.

EXERCISE 6-16 Move, Align, and Space Controls

When you design a form, you should align controls and space them appropriately.

REVIEW: The Form Selector is the etched rectangle to the left of the horizontal ruler.

1. Click the Field List button to close the field list.
2. Double-click the Form Selector to open the form's property sheet.
3. Click the Format tab and make the form **6.25** inches wide. Close the property sheet.
4. Select the SupplierName text box and drag it and its label to the right of the ProductName text box.
5. Select the NewCost text box and drag it up, closer to the Cost text box.
6. Select the ProductName text box. Place the pointer on the move handle (the top left selection handle) to display the upward-pointing hand pointer. Drag the text box closer to its label. Leave about four columns of dots between the text box and the label.
7. Repeat these steps for the KitNumber text box.

TIP: You cannot nudge a single label or text box by using Ctrl and an arrow key. You must drag the label or text box.

8. Select the ProductName, KitNumber, Cost, and NewCost text boxes.
9. Click the Properties button. Click the Format tab.
10. Click the Left row and set the left position for all the selected controls at **1** inch. Then set the Width at **1.25** inches. Close the property sheet.

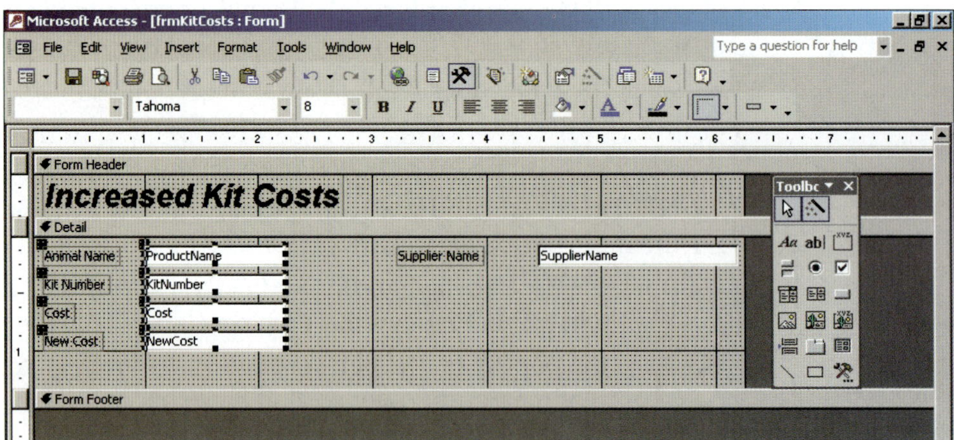

FIGURE 6-23 Labels positioned closer to text boxes and resized

11. Select the SupplierName text box and drag it until the label starts at the 3-inch mark. Then drag the text box closer to its label, showing about four columns of dots.

12. Set the width of the SupplierName text box at **2** inches.

13. Position the pointer at the left edge of the form, on the right border of the vertical ruler, on the row for the Name controls. The pointer displays a solid black arrow. Click to select all the controls in the row.

FIGURE 6-24
Selecting a row of controls

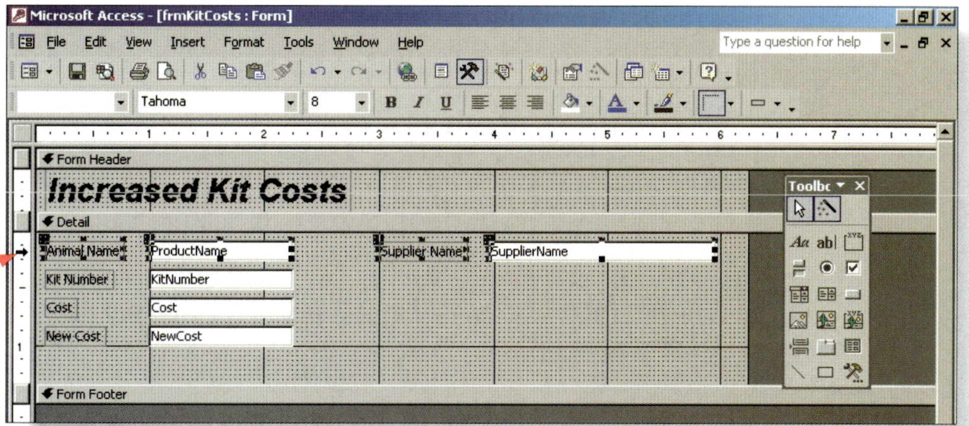

TIP: You can also click the bottom edge of the horizontal ruler to select a column of controls.

14. Choose Format, Align, Top to align the controls on their top edges.

15. Position the pointer on the bottom border of the horizontal ruler, above the Animal Name and other labels. Click to select all the controls in the column, including the main title.

16. Point at the label in the Form Header and press Shift and click to deselect the control.

17. Choose Format, Align, and Left to align the labels in the Detail section on their left edges. Leave the labels selected.

18. Position the pointer on the bottom border of the horizontal ruler, above the ProductName and other text boxes. Press Shift and click to add the text boxes to the selection. The main title is included again.

19. Point at the label in the Form Header and press Shift and click.

20. Choose Format, Vertical Spacing, and Make Equal. While the controls are selected, choose Format, Vertical Spacing, and Increase.

21. Save the form and switch to Form View.

22. Press Tab to determine how the insertion point moves through the form.

23. Return to Design View.

24. Click the **Detail** section bar. Choose **View** and then **Tab Order**. Click **AutoOrder**. Click **OK**.
25. Return to Form View and check the tab order.
26. Return to Design View and save the form.

EXERCISE 6-17 Change the Font and Set a Special Effect

You can quickly change the font and font size to make the text easier to read. You can also apply special effects to a control. Special effects change the appearance of the border around the control.

1. With frmKitCosts open in Design View, position the pointer at the left edge of the form, on the first row of name controls in the **Detail** section. With the solid black arrow, drag down to select all controls in the **Detail** section.

TIP: You can select one row of controls and add others by pressing Shift and clicking.

2. Click the **Font** arrow and choose **Arial**. Click the **Font Size** arrow and choose **11**.
3. While the controls are selected, choose **Format**, **Size**, and **To Fit**. The controls are sized to fit the font.

TIP: The Size, To Fit command is helpful but might not make the controls wide enough for all the text. Always preview your form.

4. Deselect the controls and switch to Form View. Several controls are now not wide enough, because the font is larger.
5. Return to Design View and select the ProductName text box.
6. Place the pointer on the top left handle and drag the text box to the right until you see the complete Animal Name label.
7. Make the ProductName text box slightly wider.
8. Preview the form to see if the text box is wide enough. Return to Design View. Adjust the size of the text box and move it until you can see all the animal names.
9. Open the property sheet for the ProductName text box. Check the **Width** property.
10. Click the KitNumber text box and make it the same width as the ProductName text box. Repeat these steps for the Cost and New Cost text boxes.
11. Select the KitNumber, Cost, New Cost, and ProductName text boxes. Choose **Format**, **Align**, **Right**.

12. Select the Supplier Name label (not the text box).
13. Drag the label by itself to the left until you see all of it.
14. Press Shift and click to add the Animal Name label to the selection. Repeat these steps to add the other labels in the Detail section.
15. Click the drop-down arrow for the Special Effect button in the toolbar. Place the pointer on each button in the palette to see its name.

NOTE: If you click a button that has a drop-down arrow, you apply the current color or style. You must click the drop-down arrow to see the choices.

16. Select Etched for the labels. Save the form.

EXERCISE 6-18 Change Colors

Controls have a fill or background color and a border or outline color. The font can also have a color. Each section on a form has a fill or background color, too.

1. With frmKitCosts open in Design View, select the label in the Form Header.
2. Click the drop-down arrow for the Fill/Back Color button. Choose red.
3. While the label is selected, click the drop-down arrow for the Font/Fore Color button. Choose white.

TIP: Some special effects cannot have Fill/Back colors.

4. While the label is selected, click the drop-down arrow for the Special Effects button. Select Raised.
5. Click the Detail section bar to select the section.
6. Because red is the current Fill/Back color, you do not need to display the palette. Click the Fill/Back Color button.
7. Change to Form View. As you might guess, red is not a good background color for a form. It would be tiresome to look at it all day. Return to Design View.
8. Click the Undo button.
9. Select all the text boxes, not the labels.
10. Click the drop-down arrow for the Line/Border Color button. Select red.
11. Change to Form View. The border color overrides the special effect. Return to Design View.
12. With the text boxes selected, apply a Sunken special effect. The Sunken effect cannot have a border color.
13. View and save the form. Return to Design View. Click anywhere in an unused part of the form to deselect all controls.

EXERCISE 6-19 Apply an AutoFormat

An *AutoFormat* is a style template or preformatted design. A template applies font sizes and colors, border colors, and background colors to the entire form or to parts of the form.

1. With frmKitCosts open in Design View, click the Form Selector. The Object box shows Form.
2. Choose Format, AutoFormat.
3. The AutoFormat dialog box lists the names of the style templates. As you click each name, the preview appears. Click each AutoFormat name. Choose Blends.

NOTE: You can apply your own local formatting after using an AutoFormat.

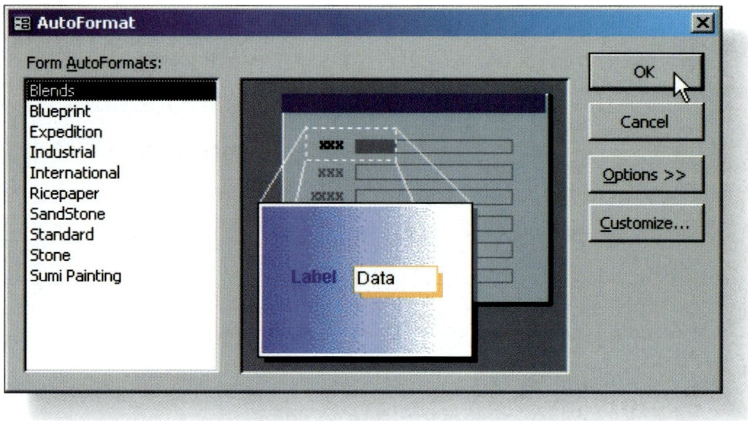

FIGURE 6-25 AutoFormat dialog box

4. Click OK. The form is reformatted. Change to Form View to see the changes.
5. Return to Design View. Click the Form Header section bar to select only that section.

6. Click the AutoFormat button. Click Industrial and click OK. Only the label in the Form Header is reformatted.
7. Use the AutoFormat to change the Form Header back to Blend.
8. Click the Form Selector.
9. Click the AutoFormat button. Click International.
10. Click the Option button.
11. Turn off the Font and the Color so only the Border is changed. Click OK. (See Figure 6-26 on the next page.)
12. Close the form without saving the changes.

FIGURE 6-26
AutoFormat options

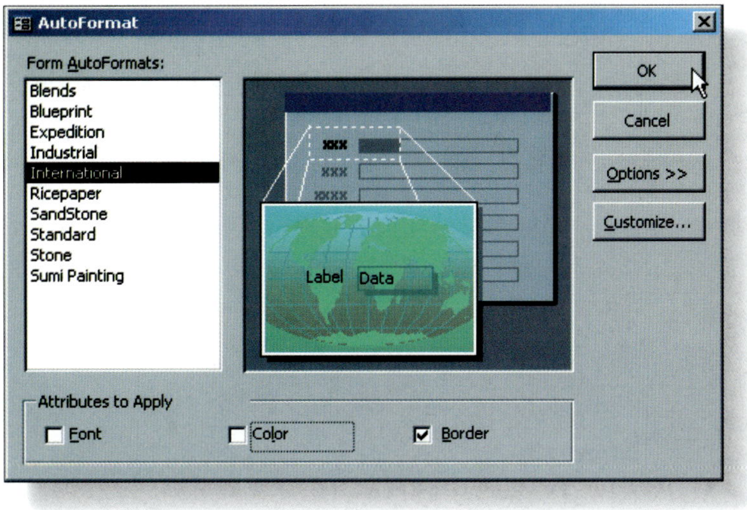

Using the Web to Display Data

You can save tables, queries, forms, or reports as Web pages. This allows you or others to look at your work by using a browser that can display the HTML format. *HTML* (Hypertext Markup Language) is the standard formatting language for Web documents. HTML documents are stored separately from the database.

You can share data through the Internet with Data Access Pages. To users, the Data Access Pages appear similar to forms. However, instead of viewing and changing data directly through the database, the user connects through an Internet browser.

EXERCISE 6-20 Save a Form as a Web Page

When you save a form as a Web page, the Web document shows the data in a tabular arrangement, like the table or query. However, it does not show any of the formatting or arrangement of controls from your form.

1. Click the Forms button. Click frmKitCosts to highlight it.
2. Choose File, Export. The Export Form To dialog box opens.
3. Set the Save in folder to your usual working folder.
4. Click the Save as type drop-down arrow. Choose HTML Documents. The default file name is the same as your form.
5. Click Export. (See Figure 6-27 on the next page.)
6. The HTML Template dialog box lets you choose a style sheet for Web pages. Leave the entry box empty and click OK.

NOTE: You can preview your Web document in Word or in your browser. You can choose File, Web Page Preview in Word to launch your browser.

FIGURE 6-27
Exporting a form as a Web document

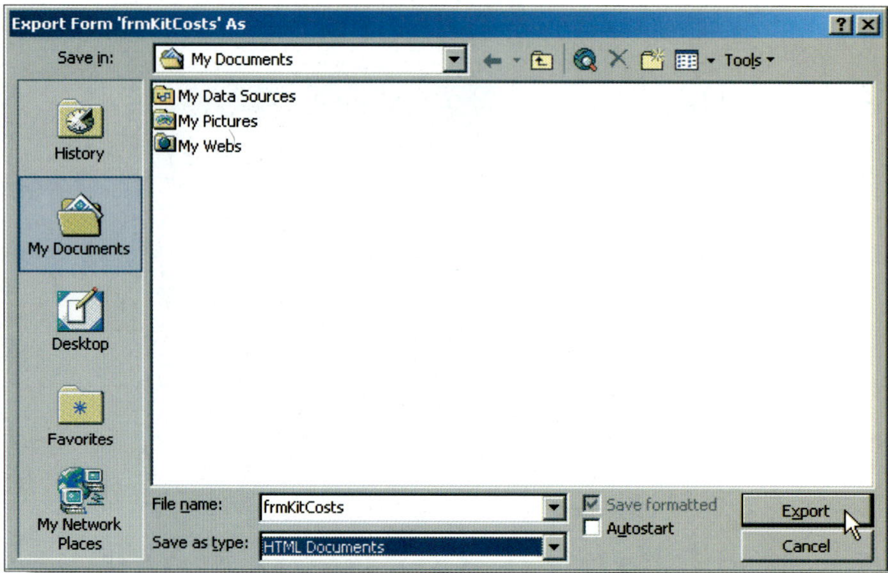

7. Start Word and open the HTML file **frmKitCosts**. Although the data displayed as a form in your database, the HTML document displays the raw data as a table.

FIGURE 6-28
Viewing the Web document in Word

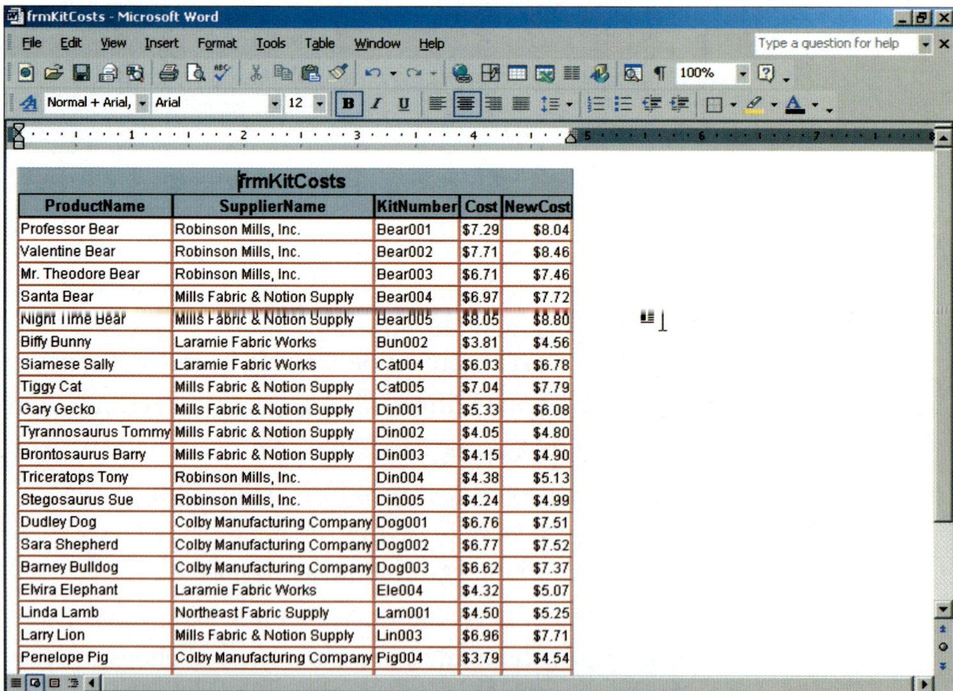

ProductName	SupplierName	KitNumber	Cost	NewCost
Professor Bear	Robinson Mills, Inc.	Bear001	$7.29	$8.04
Valentine Bear	Robinson Mills, Inc.	Bear002	$7.71	$8.46
Mr. Theodore Bear	Robinson Mills, Inc.	Bear003	$6.71	$7.46
Santa Bear	Mills Fabric & Notion Supply	Bear004	$6.97	$7.72
Night Time Bear	Mills Fabric & Notion Supply	Bear005	$8.05	$8.80
Biffy Bunny	Laramie Fabric Works	Bun002	$3.81	$4.56
Siamese Sally	Laramie Fabric Works	Cat004	$6.03	$6.78
Tiggy Cat	Mills Fabric & Notion Supply	Cat005	$7.04	$7.79
Gary Gecko	Mills Fabric & Notion Supply	Din001	$5.33	$6.08
Tyrannosaurus Tommy	Mills Fabric & Notion Supply	Din002	$4.05	$4.80
Brontosaurus Barry	Mills Fabric & Notion Supply	Din003	$4.15	$4.90
Triceratops Tony	Robinson Mills, Inc.	Din004	$4.38	$5.13
Stegosaurus Sue	Robinson Mills, Inc.	Din005	$4.24	$4.99
Dudley Dog	Colby Manufacturing Company	Dog001	$6.76	$7.51
Sara Shepherd	Colby Manufacturing Company	Dog002	$6.77	$7.52
Barney Bulldog	Colby Manufacturing Company	Dog003	$6.62	$7.37
Elvira Elephant	Laramie Fabric Works	Ele004	$4.32	$5.07
Linda Lamb	Northeast Fabric Supply	Lam001	$4.50	$5.25
Larry Lion	Mills Fabric & Notion Supply	Lin003	$6.96	$7.71
Penelope Pig	Colby Manufacturing Company	Pig004	$3.79	$4.54

8. Exit Word without saving and return to Access.

EXERCISE 6-21 Create a Data Access Page

When a company wants to share Access information with customers or employees through the Internet, the company needs to create a Data Access Page and place it on the Web server. A *Data Access Page* is an object that acts like a form but whose controls are Internet compatible. A direct link is established between the Data Access Page and the source recordset.

1. Click the Pages button. Double-click Create data access page by using wizard.
2. Click the drop-down arrow for Tables/Queries and choose tblSalesOrders.
3. Click the Add All button >>. Click Next.
4. Do not use any grouping. Click Next.
5. Sort by OrderID in ascending order. Click Next.
6. Edit the name of the page to **pgeSalesOrders**. This will be the name of the page inside Access.
7. Choose the option to Open the page. Click Finish. The page opens in Page View, similar to Form View.

FIGURE 6-29
Data Access Page in Page View

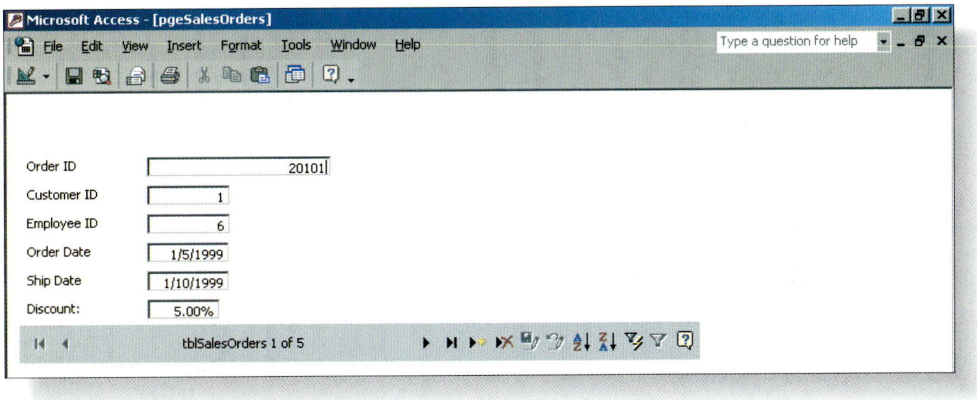

8. Click the Save button. Save the page using the same name.
9. Close the page. Notice that the page icon is a shortcut. The main page is located outside the database.
10. Compact and repair the database and exit Access.
11. Start Internet Explorer.

NOTE: So you can view data in Access 2002 Data Access Pages, your workstation must have an active Internet connection.

12. Choose File, Open. Click the Browse button. Set the Look in folder to the location where your files are stored.

13. Choose **pgeSalesOrders**. Click Open.
14. Click OK. This is a current view of the table. The Data Access Page has a row of navigation buttons.
15. Close Internet Explorer.

LESSON 6 Summary

- You can create simple forms by using the New Object button and selecting AutoForm.
- Tables in a multiple-table query are linked by common fields.
- The Form Wizard guides you through the process of creating a form.
- Form Headers display at the top of each form window and Form Footers display at the bottom of each form window.
- You can resize labels in a Form Header or Form Footer by repositioning the selection handles.
- Text boxes are distinct from labels in appearance and purpose.
- The width and height of text boxes and label boxes can be changed individually or as a group.
- You can reposition multiple objects in a form by using the Align command.
- The property sheet for each object in a form lists all the characteristics or attributes for that object.
- The tab order determines the sequence of the insertion point.
- Calculated fields are arithmetic expressions based on one or more fields in a recordset.
- The Expression Builder guides you in the creation of a calculated field.
- Calculated fields can be created in any type of query, including multiple table queries.
- Well-designed forms have controls that are aligned and spaced properly.
- The font type, font size, special effects, background color, border color, and outline color change the appearance of objects.
- AutoFormat applies font sizes, font colors, border colors, and background colors of an entire form or parts of a form.

- Web pages allow Access forms to be displayed as HTML pages. The data can be viewed using the Internet, but cannot be modified.
- Data Access Pages enable records to be viewed, entered, and modified through the Internet.

LESSON 6 Command Summary

FEATURE	BUTTON	MENU	KEYBOARD	SPEECH
View Properties		View, Properties	F4	✓
AutoFormat		Format, AutoFormat		✓
Field List		View, Field List		✓
Fill/Back Color				
Font/Fore Color				
Line/Border Color				
Special Effect				
Tab Order		View, Tab Order		✓
Label				
Text Box				
Align		Format, Align		✓
Web Page		File, Export		✓

Concepts Review

TRUE/FALSE QUESTIONS

Each of the following statements is either true or false. Indicate your choice by circling T or F.

T F 1. As you move controls on a form, the tab order adjusts so controls are always in left-to-right and top-to-bottom order.

T F 2. Every form contains a main section and a subsection.

T F 3. You can export a form to the World Wide Web.

T F 4. An AutoForm creates a form that includes all the fields in a selected table.

T F 5. The pointer changes to an open hand when you place it on the top left selection handle.

T F 6. You can use AutoFormat to select a style template for a form.

T F 7. You can change the background color of a Form Header section in Form View.

T F 8. Field properties from the table are inherited when a form is created.

SHORT ANSWER QUESTIONS

Write the correct answer in the space provided.

1. What section on a form shows different data for each record?

____

2. What type of information might be displayed in the Form Header section?

____

3. Which button do you use when adding a calculated control to a form?

____

4. What opens when you click the Build button [...] in a query?

____

5. What is the name of the list of characteristics or settings for every object in a form?

____

6. What determines where the insertion pointer moves when you press Tab or Enter in a form?

____

7. What button changes the text color in a label or a text box?

____

8. What does your pointer look like while you are moving a label or text box separately?

____

CRITICAL THINKING

Answer these questions on a separate page. There are no right or wrong answers. Support your answers with examples from your own experience, if possible.

1. You have edited, added, and searched records in a table and in a form. What commands are the same? What commands are different? Describe differences or similarities between a table and a form.
2. In this lesson you were introduced to some ideas about designing forms. What design principles might be effective for forms? How would the design ideas be different from printed reports?

Lesson Applications

EXERCISE 6-22

Create an AutoForm. Modify controls and properties. Open the Form Header and add a label.

1. Open ***[your initials]*****CC-06**.

REVIEW: Use the New Form dialog box to create a columnar AutoForm.

2. Create a columnar AutoForm for tblKitSuppliers. Save the form as **frmSuppliers**.

REVIEW: Ctrl+A is a Windows shortcut to select all.

3. Press Ctrl+A to select all the controls and change them to 10 points. Size them to fit.
4. Make the form 6 inches wide and apply the SandStone AutoFormat.
5. Select the State label and press Delete. Move the State text box to the 3.25-inch mark on the same line as the City text box.

REVIEW: If you delete a text box by mistake, drag it back to the Detail section from the Field List.

6. Delete the ZIP Code label. Move the PostalCode text box next to the State text box. Delete the City label.
7. Select all the text boxes except the State and PostalCode. Open the property sheet and make the text boxes 2 inches wide. Deselect the controls.

REVIEW: You can select all controls in a "column" from the horizontal ruler or you can press Shift and click.

8. Move the Phone and Fax Number controls closer to the address so everything is consistently spaced.
9. View your form and return to Design View. Make any adjustments you feel would help visibility.
10. Open the Form Header property sheet and make it **.75** inches high.
11. Draw a label in the Form Header about 3 inches wide. Key **Carolina Critters** on the first line. Press Shift+Enter for a line break, and key **Approved Suppliers**. Press Enter.

12. Make the label 18-point Arial bold italic, and adjust the size to fit the text on two lines as you keyed it.

13. Change the label text color to white. Change the Fill/Back color to black and apply the raised special effect.

14. Position the header label to align on the left with the controls in the Detail section. Move the label and size the section so there is a row of dots above and below the label.

15. Size the Detail section to show one row of grid dots below the last control.

16. Select all the text boxes and apply the Etched effect. Save the form.

17. Add a new record:

REVIEW: The current field might change background color as you are adding/editing data.

Supplier #:	**7**
Supplier ID:	**HH-08**
Supplier Name:	***Key your last name and then key*** **& Associates**
Contact Name:	***Key your first and last name***
Address:	***Key your address***
City:	***Key your city***
State:	***Key your state, using two characters***
Postal Code:	***Key your ZIP code***
Phone Number:	**(123)-555-0000**
Fax Number:	**(123)-555-0001**

REVIEW: To print a single form, choose File, Print.

18. Click the Print Preview button. Make sure no text is cut off. Close the preview.

19. Select your record and print it.

20. Save and close the form. Compact and close the database.

EXERCISE 6-23

Create a form by using the wizard. Filter the records in a form. Replace data in a form. Save the form as an HTML file.

1. Open ***[your initials]*****CC-E-06**.

2. Create a form for tblSickDays by using the Form Wizard. Use all fields and make it a justified layout. Use the Industrial style and name the form **frmSickDays**

NOTE: A justified layout places controls left to right, stacked in rows, with no spacing between rows.

3. Open the Form Header and add a label for **Employee Sick Days**. Make it 14-point Arial bold italic. Size the box to fit the label. Save the form.
4. Create a Filter By Form to determine how many employees took 2/5/01 as a sick day. Apply and remove the filter. Write your answer on a piece of paper.
5. Create an Advanced Filter that shows how many employees took 2/5/01 or 2/14/01 as a sick day. Remove the filter. Write your answer.
6. Create a Filter By Form to determine how many employees took 9/1/01 as a sick day. Write your answer.
7. While the records are filtered, replace all occurrences of 9/1/01 with your 0birthday in 2002. Use the *mm/dd/yy* format for both dates. Remove the filter.

REVIEW: You can click the drop-down arrow for the View button and switch to Datasheet View to see all records in a table layout.

8. Close and save the form.
9. Export the form frmSickDays as an HTML file.
10. Open the HTML file **frmSickDays** in Internet Explorer and print.

EXERCISE 6-24

Create a form with the Form Wizard. Modify form controls. Add a form header with a label.

1. Import tblEmployees from ***[your initials]*CC-06** into ***[your initials]*CC-E-06**.
2. Create a new form for tblEmployees by using the Form Wizard. Use these fields:
   - EmployeeID
   - LastName
   - FirstName
   - EmergencyContact
   - EmergencyPhone
3. Use a columnar layout and the Standard style. Name the form **frmEmerInfo**

4. Maximize the window. Make the form 6 inches wide.
5. Change all the controls (labels and text boxes) to 10-point Arial. Size them to fit.
6. Select all the controls except the EmployeeID and drag them to the right side of the form to get them out of the way as you reposition them.
7. Position the FirstName control two rows of dots below the EmployeeID control. Position the LastName control to the right of the FirstName control, with the label aligned left at the 3.25-inch mark.
8. Position the EmergencyContact control below the FirstName control. Position the EmergencyPhone control to the right of the EmergencyContact control and aligned with the LastName control. Use consistent spacing.
9. Select the EmployeeID text box and open its property sheet. Set its Left position and its Width at **1.5** inches. Leave the property sheet open.
10. Click the FirstName text box and change its Left position and Width to **1.5**. Do the same for the EmergencyContact text box.
11. Align the labels for Employee ID, First Name, and Emergency Contact on the left.
12. Use the Move handle to position the EmergencyPhone text box at the 4.5-inch mark. Do the same for the LastName text box. Align the labels on the left.
13. Make both of these text boxes **1.5** inches wide to match the others. Then make the form slightly wider.
14. Set the tab order. Close the Field List window.

TIP: A form is easy to use when the controls are the same size and aligned well.

15. Open the Form Header and make it 1 inch tall. Add a label with **Emergency Information**. Make it 24-point Arial bold italic. Show the label on a single line. Select colors and a special effect for this label.
16. Save the form.
17. Find the record for Joseph Lassen. Change the first and last names to yours.
18. Print your record and close the form.

EXERCISE 6-25 Challenge Yourself

Create a multiple-table query. Create an AutoForm. Add a calculated control.

1. Create a new query in Design View for tblEmployees and tblPayroll.

REVIEW: The join line is on the SocialSecurityNumber field.

2. Add the fields FirstName and LastName from tblEmployees. From tblPayroll, add SocialSecurityNumber and HourlyRate.
3. In the Criteria row for HourlyRate, key **is not null**
4. Save the query as **qryHrWages**. View the dynaset and close the query.
5. Create a columnar AutoForm for qryHrWages.
6. Make all controls 10-point Arial. Size them to fit.
7. Increase the vertical spacing between controls twice.
8. Change the form width to **6** inches.
9. Set all text box widths to **1.5** inches.

TIP: You can click to place a text box instead of drawing the control.

10. Add a Text box at the 4-inch mark on the same row as HourlyRate. Edit the new label to show **Monthly Pay** with no colon. Format it as 10-point Arial and size it to fit.
11. Use the Build button [...] to set the control source for the unbound text box to **HourlyRate*140**.

NOTE: The number "140" is a constant that you must key in the preview area.

12. Set the format for Monthly Pay text box to Currency and its width to **1.5** inches.
13. Change its Name property to **Pay**
14. Format the font for this control to match the others.
15. Save the form as **frmHrWages**

TIP: Press Shift + Enter or Ctrl + Enter to create a line break in a label.

16. In the Form Header, add a label. Key **Carolina Critters** on the first line. Key **Hourly Employee Wages** on the second line. Key **Confidential *[your last name]*** on the third line.
17. Format the label as 16-point Arial bold italic. Size the label and the form header as needed, and keep the label as a three-line title. Save the form.
18. Click the Print Preview button. Several forms will print per page, depending on your printer. Size the Detail section so all the records fit on two pages.

NOTE: You often need to check a printed form to verify the sizes of controls.

19. Print the records. Save the form and close it.
20. Compact and close your database. Exit Access.

On Your Own

In these exercises you work on your own, as you would in a real-life work environment. Use the skills you've learned to accomplish the task—and be creative.

EXERCISE 6-26

Using the Form Wizard, create a form for the main table of the database you modified in Exercise 5-20. Include all fields from the table in your form. On the form printout, sketch changes that will improve each form. Using the Form Wizard, create forms for each additional table in your database. Print a copy of each form. On each form printout, sketch changes that will improve each form. On each form, write your name and "Exercise 6-26." Continue to Exercise 6-27.

EXERCISE 6-27

Modify your forms to incorporate the improvements you sketched. In the Form Footer of each form, include your name and **Exercise 6-27**. In the Form Header, include the name of the form and the current date. Print the data contained in each of your tables. Print a copy of each form. Test your redesigned forms by having another person enter the data. On each form printout, sketch changes that will improve your form. Continue to Exercise 6-28.

EXERCISE 6-28

Modify your forms appropriately. Analyze your database design. Determine if any additional forms might be required for queries or recordsets. Create any additional forms you might need. On each form, include your name and **Exercise 6-28** in the Form Footer. Print a copy of each form. Submit the copies of the forms you printed in Exercises 6-26 through 6-28 to your instructor. Keep a copy of the database you modified in Exercise 6-28. It will be used in subsequent lessons.

LESSON 7

Adding Reports to a Database

OBJECTIVES

MOUS ACTIVITIES

In this lesson:

Ac2002 7-1
Ac2002 7-2
Ac2002 7-3
Ac2002 8-2

See Appendix E.

After completing this lesson, you will be able to:

1. Create a report by using a wizard.
2. Work with report sections.
3. Work with controls in a report.
4. Create and modify AutoReports.
5. Add a calculation to a report.
6. Use Format Painter and conditional formatting.
7. Create a multicolumn report and mailing labels.
8. Export data to Excel and Word.

Estimated Time: 2 hours

Forms are the best way to view data on your screen. If you want a well-designed printed page, however, you should use a report. Although you can print a table or form, reports are best suited for a printed format. In a report you can:

- Show data in an attractive format that may include variations in fonts, colors, shading, and borders.
- Show certain fields or records rather than the entire table.
- Group and sort records with summaries and totals.
- Add images.
- Display fields from more than one table.

In this lesson you learn how to create reports by using the Report Wizard and AutoReports. You will work with Design View for a report (which has the same types of controls as Design View for a form). Working with controls will also be very similar to working with controls in a form. However, the design considerations for a report are different, because reports are usually printed to a black-and-white printer.

Creating a Report by Using the Report Wizard

The Report Wizard lets you choose the fields, the layout, and the style for a report. The style selects fonts, lines, and colors automatically. You can also choose whether to group records and how to sort them.

EXERCISE 7-1 Create a Report with the Wizard

1. Make a copy of **CC-07** and **CC-E-07**. Rename them as ***[your initials]*CC-07** and ***[your initials]*CC-E-07**. Make sure neither new file is Read-Only. Open ***[your initials]*CC-07**.
2. Click the Tables button and select tblEmployees.
3. Click the New Object drop-down arrow and choose Report.
4. In the New Report dialog box, select Report Wizard.

FIGURE 7-1 New Report dialog box

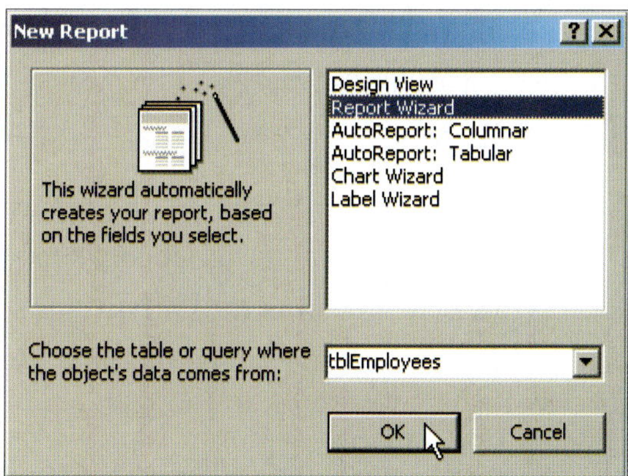

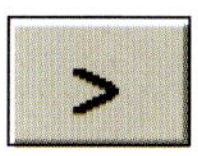

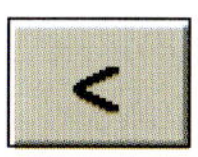

5. Click OK. The first Report Wizard dialog box asks which fields to use in the report. Click the EmployeeID field and then click the Add One button > to move the field to the Selected Fields list.

REVIEW: If you move a field to the right by mistake, click the Remove One button < to move it back.

6. Double-click the following field names to move them to the Selected Fields list:

   LastName

   FirstName

   SocialSecurityNumber

   JobCode

7. Click Next. The dialog box asks if you want to group the records. You will add the groups later. Click Next.
8. The next dialog box asks if you want to sort the records. You can use up to four fields for sorting in ascending or descending order.

NOTE: The Ascending/Descending button switches between ascending and descending order.

9. Click the drop-down arrow for the first sort field and choose LastName.
10. Click the drop-down arrow for the second sort field and choose JobCode.

FIGURE 7-2
Sorting in the Report Wizard

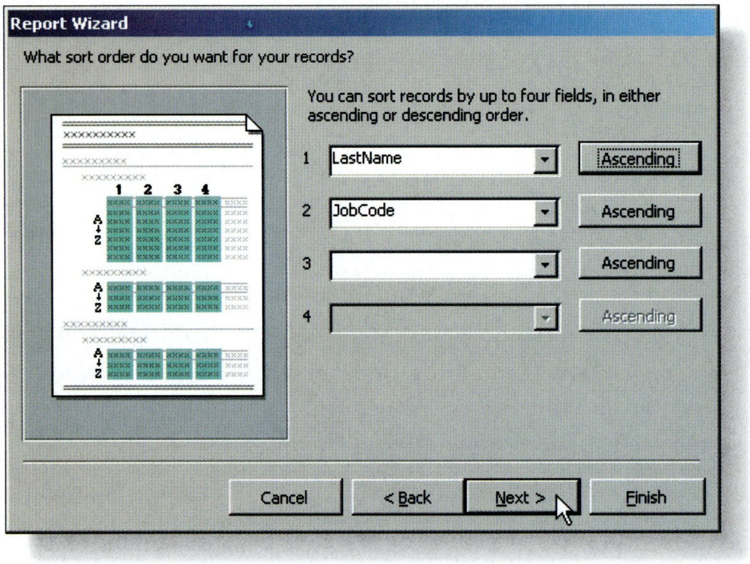

11. Click Next. The dialog box asks which layout and orientation you want. Select Tabular. (A tabular report prints the records in rows.)
12. Select Portrait. (Portrait orientation is taller than it is wide.)
13. Make sure there is a check mark for Adjust the field width so all fields fit on a page. This forces all the fields to fit on the page, but it can make them too small to show all the data.
14. Click Next to see the available styles. The Preview window simulates the appearance of each style. Click each style name to preview it.
15. Choose Formal. (See Figure 7-3 on the next page.)
16. Click Next. The dialog box asks for a title. This becomes the name of the report and appears as a title on the printed page. Key **rptEmpByCode*[your initials]***
17. You can choose here to preview the report or modify the design. Select Preview the report and click Finish.

FIGURE 7-3
Selecting the report style

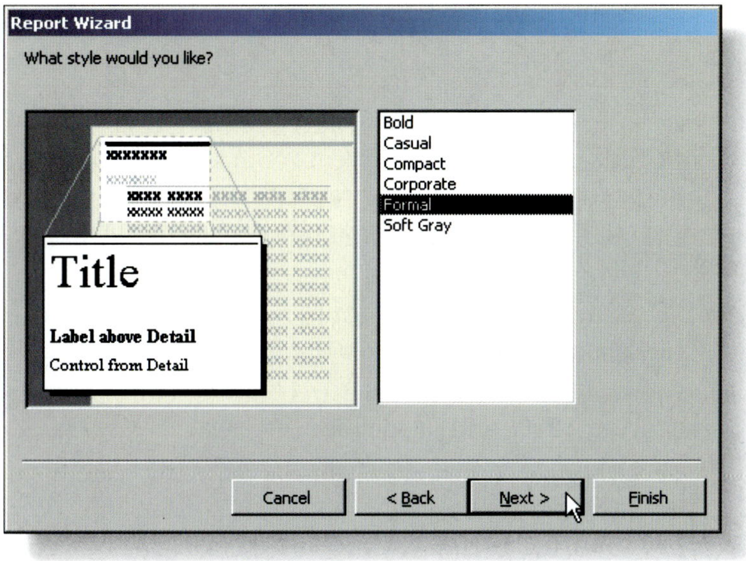

NOTE: Report names are preceded by **rpt** in the Leszynski Naming Conventions.

18. The report opens in Print Preview. Maximize the window.

FIGURE 7-4
Report maximized in Print Preview

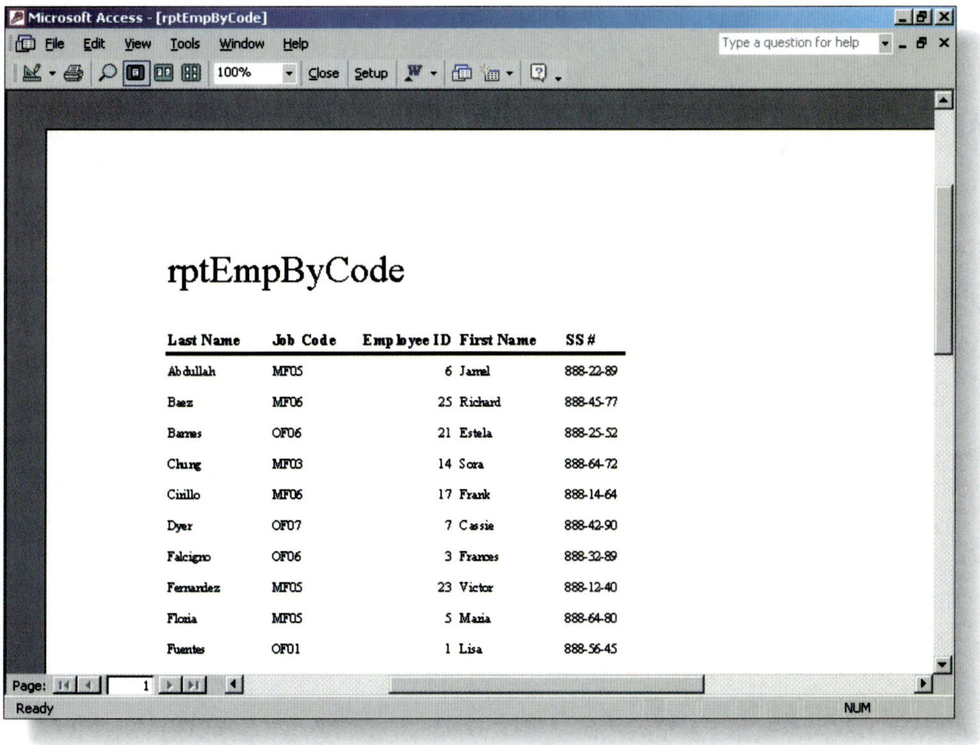

EXERCISE 7-2 Use Print Preview

Reports open in a 100% size, which attempts to show the report at the size it will print. You can change to different zoom sizes to get an overall impression of the layout or to zoom in and enlarge the data. The Zoom box in the toolbar shows the current size. The pointer displays a magnifying glass with a minus sign when you are in 100% view.

1. Click anywhere in the report to zoom out and view the entire page. The viewing size is Fit, and the pointer shows a plus sign.
2. Point anywhere on the page and click to zoom in. The pointer switches between 100% and Fit views.
3. Click the drop-down arrow for the Zoom box and try other sizes. Finish with the Zoom size at 100%.

TIP: The pointer switches between the two most recently used sizes.

Close

4. Click the Close button on the toolbar Close to switch to Design View. The wizard arranges the fields left to right based on your sorting choices, and order fields are selected.

Working with Report Sections

In Design View, you can see the Standard toolbar, the Formatting toolbar, the Toolbox, and the report sections. A report has a Detail section that shows a row or column for each record, depending on the layout. The *Report Header* section prints once at the beginning of the report (on the first page) and the *Report Footer* section prints once at the end of the report (on the last page). Headers and footers can contain main titles, summary calculations, design lines, and even images. The *Report Page Header* section, which prints at the top of every page, and the *Report Page Footer* section, which prints at the bottom of every page, are often used for page numbers and the date. Reports may also have one or more *Group Header* or *Group Footer* sections. These sections are used for group titles and summaries.

NOTE: Your toolbars might be in a different order. You can anchor the Toolbox with the other toolbars by double-clicking its title bar.

FIGURE 7-5
Design View for the report

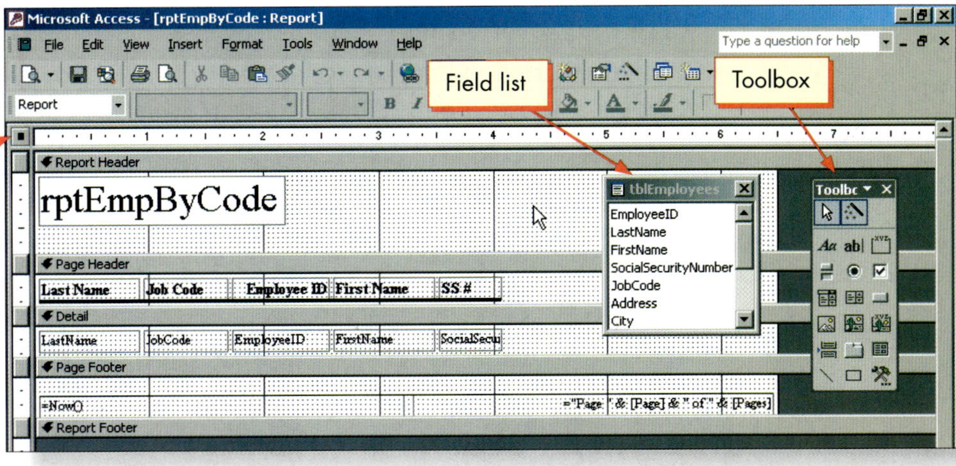

TABLE 7-1 Sections of a Report

NAME OF SECTION	PURPOSE
Report Header	Prints once at the top of the report (first page). It might include a title, logo, or image.
Page Header	Prints once at the top of every page. It might include column headings, page numbers, or a date.
Group Header	Prints once at the start of each group. It might display a group title.
Detail Section	Prints each record from the table or query.
Report Header	Prints once at the bottom of the report (last page). It might include summaries or totals.
Page Footer	Prints once at the bottom of every page. It might include page numbers or a date.
Group Footer	Prints once at the end of each group. It might include a total or other calculation for the group.

EXERCISE 7-3 Change Section and Report Properties

You can change section properties from the property sheet or from the Formatting toolbar.

1. Click the Report Header section bar. The Object box shows that the "Report-Header" is selected.

2. Click the Properties button. The Report Header property sheet opens.
3. Click the **Format** tab. Change the **Height** to **.75** and press Enter. The **Back Color** row shows a numeric code to represent the current color.

FIGURE 7-6
Report Header property sheet

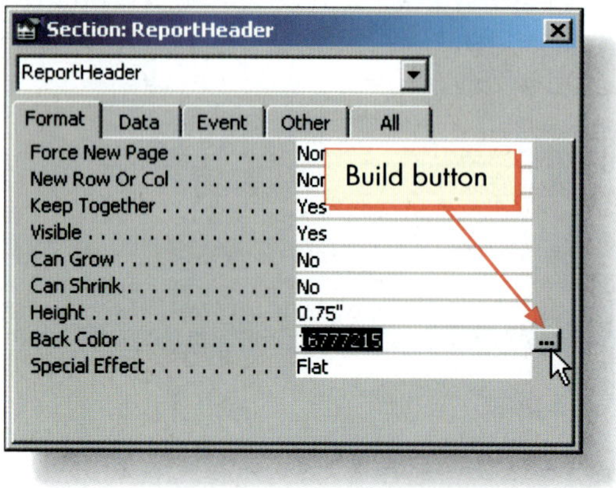

4. Click the Build button. A color palette opens.

NOTE: The Build button opens different dialog boxes for the different rows in the property sheet.

5. Choose any light color and click **OK**. The new code is shown. Close the property sheet.

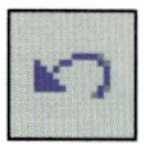

6. Click the Undo button to remove the background color.
7. Double-click the **Page Header** section bar to open its property sheet.
8. Click the **Format** tab. Change the Height to **.75** and press Enter. Leave the property sheet open.
9. Click the **Detail** section bar. The property sheet updates to show the current section.
10. Click the **Format** tab and choose a different back color. Close the property sheet.

11. While the **Detail** section is selected, click the Fill/Back Color button. The current color is applied to the section.

REVIEW: The current Fill/Back color appears beneath the bucket on the icon.

12. Click the drop-down arrow for the Fill/Back Color button. Select white.

13. Click the Report Selector button to display a solid black square. Click the Properties button. This property sheet lists settings for the report.
14. Click the **All** tab. Review the report properties and then close the property sheet.
15. Position the pointer on the top edge of the **Detail** section bar to display a double-ended arrow. Drag upward to size the **Page Header** section to show one row of dots below the horizontal line.
16. Save the report.

EXERCISE 7-4 Add a Group Section

A *group* organizes or categorizes the records by a particular field. For example, you can group the records by job code in rptEmpByCode. All the employees who are tailors would be listed together, all the assemblers/finishers would be listed together, and so on. As you establish groups, you can also indicate how the records should be sorted.

To use groups, you add a Group Header/Footer to the report, creating Group sections.

TABLE 7-2 Group Section Properties

GROUP SECTION	OPTION	PURPOSE
Group Header	Yes or No	Display or hide a Group Header section.
Group Footer	Yes or No	Display or hide a Group Footer section.
Group On	(Depends on data type)	Identifies what value, or range of values, makes a group.
Group Interval	(Enter a number)	Interval or number of characters to use in identifying the group.
Keep Together	Yes or No	Keeps group together on one page.

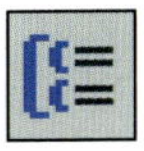

1. With rptEmpByCode open in Design View, click the Sorting and Grouping button. The Sorting and Grouping dialog box shows the sorting choices you made in the Report Wizard.
2. Click in the Field/Expression column for the LastName row. The Group Properties show that no Group Header or Group Footer is used.
3. Click in the Field/Expression column for the JobCode row. No Group Header or Group Footer is used here, either.

4. Click the Group Header box for the JobCode field. Click the arrow and select Yes. The Group icon appears to the left of the field name. (See Figure 7-7 on the next page.)
5. Close the dialog box. The report now has a JobCode Header section.

6. Click the Print Preview button. The records are not grouped by job code. Close the preview.
7. Click the Sorting and Grouping button.
8. Point at the row selector for the JobCode row to display a black arrow. Click to select the row.

FIGURE 7-7 Sorting and Grouping dialog box

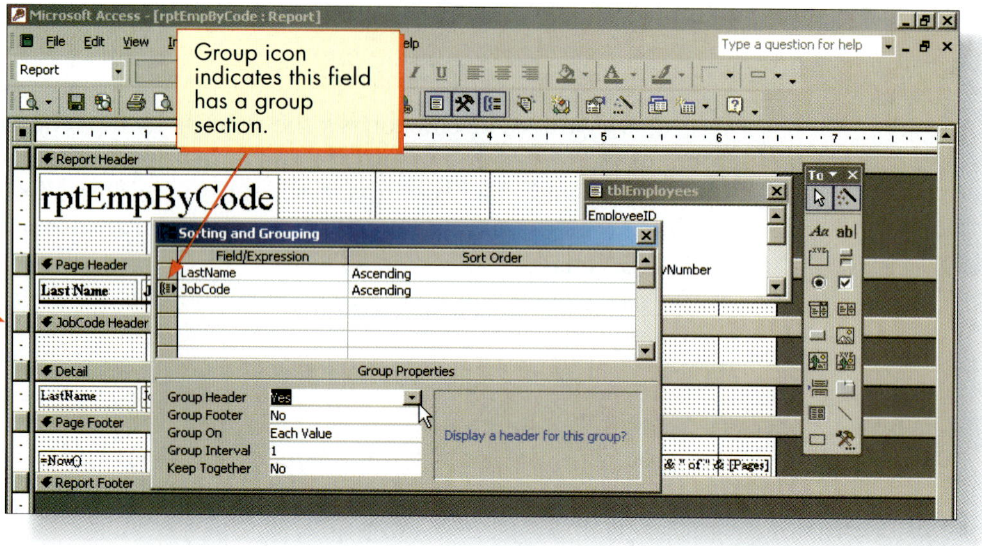

9. Point at the row selector to display a white arrow, and then drag the row to be first. Close the dialog box.

NOTE: The field used for grouping must be first in the Sorting and Grouping dialog box.

10. Preview the report. Notice that the records are now grouped by Job Code.

11. Close the preview and save the report.

EXERCISE 7-5 Create a Non-Breaking Group

The default page break for a report occurs when the text reaches the bottom margin. You can control how groups are kept together so they are not split between pages. Of course, some groups are too large to print on a single page.

1. Drag the top of the **Page Footer** bar down to show three rows of dots below the controls in the **Detail** section. Preview the report. Notice if any groups split between pages.

2. Return to Design View.

3. Click the Sorting and Grouping button. Click the JobCode row in the top part of the dialog box.

4. Click the **Keep Together** row in the bottom part of the dialog box. Display the list and choose **Whole Group**.

5. Close the dialog box.

6. Preview the report. Click the Two Pages button. Then click the One Page button.

Working with Controls on a Report

Just as with forms, reports have bound controls (such as text boxes), unbound controls (such as labels), and calculated controls. You can move, size, align, and format controls in a report just as you do in a form.

EXERCISE 7-6 Move and Delete Controls

Depending on the number of changes you need to make to a report, you might find that it is faster for you to delete controls and reinsert them instead of moving them.

1. With rptEmpByCode open in Design View, select the Job Code label in the Page Header section. Drag the control into the JobCode Header at the left edge.

FIGURE 7-8 Moving controls into the Group Header

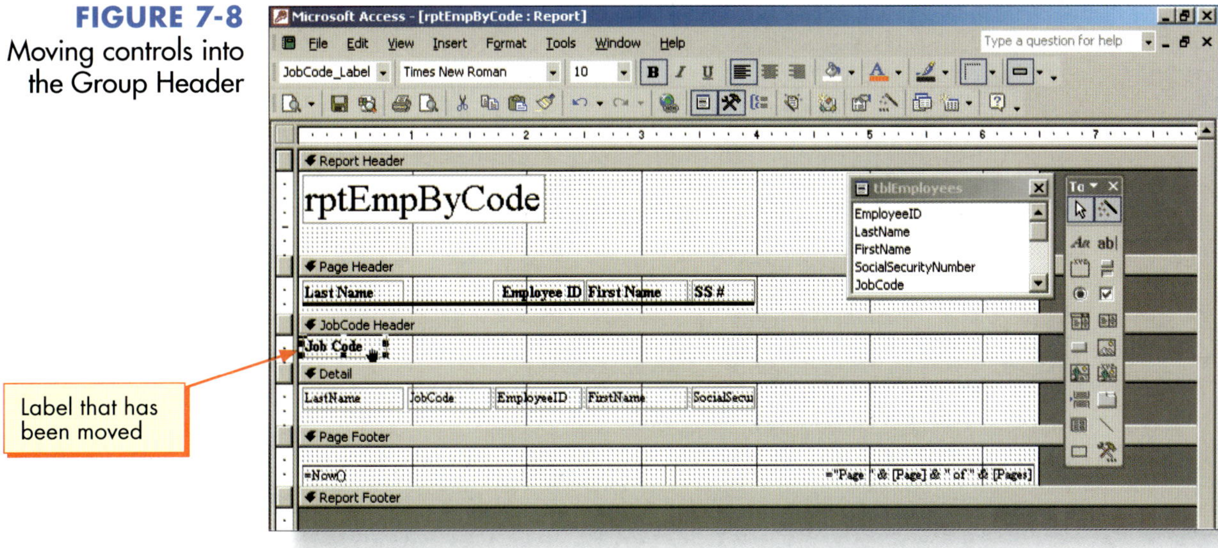

2. Select the JobCode text box in the Detail section and drag it into the JobCode Header, next to the label.

TIP: When you move controls from one section to another, move one control at a time.

3. Select the SS# label in the Page Header section and the SocialSecurityNumber text box in the Detail section. Press Delete.

4. Select the Employee ID label in the Page Header section and the Employee ID text box in the Detail section.

5. Drag both controls to the right, across the First Name controls to the 3.5-inch mark.
6. Hold down Shift and add the First Name label and the First Name text box to the selection so four controls are selected.
7. Move all four controls left to the 1.25-inch mark.

TIP: You can click the View button or the Print Preview button to view a report.

8. Preview the report to see if all the data is visible.

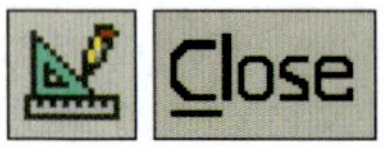

TIP: You can click the View button or the Close button Close to return to Design View.

9. To return to Design View, click the View button.
10. Save your changes.

EXERCISE 7-7 Add a Field to a Report

When you add a field to a report, the field label and field text box are inserted as a unit. Each control can then be sized and moved individually or together.

1. Click the Field List button to open the Field List window, if it is not visible.
2. Size or scroll the window until you see the City field.
3. Drag the City field to the **Detail** section at the 4.5-inch mark.

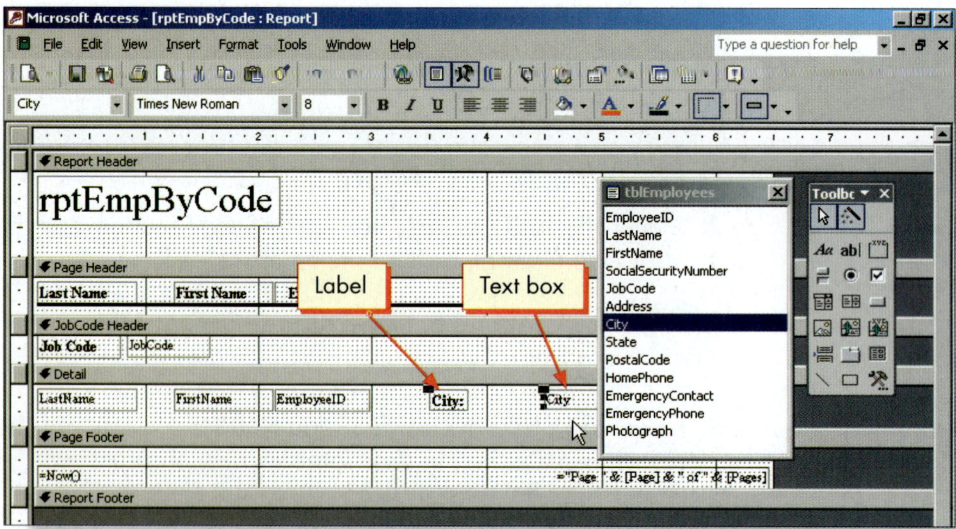

FIGURE 7-9 Adding a field to the report

4. Select the City label (not the text box). Press Delete.
5. Drag the City text box to the 3.5-inch mark.

REVIEW: Use the grid dots as an aid when you size and align controls.

6. Close the Field List window and save the report.

EXERCISE 7-8 Copy a Label, Size a Line, and Size a Section

You now need a new label for the city field. One way to enter the label so it uses the same format as the other labels is to copy and edit an existing label. You also need to resize the horizontal line in the Page Header section to match your new field.

1. Select the Employee ID label in the Page Header section.
2. Click Ctrl+C to copy. Then click Ctrl+V to paste. The copy is placed below the original, and the section expands.

FIGURE 7-10 Copying a control

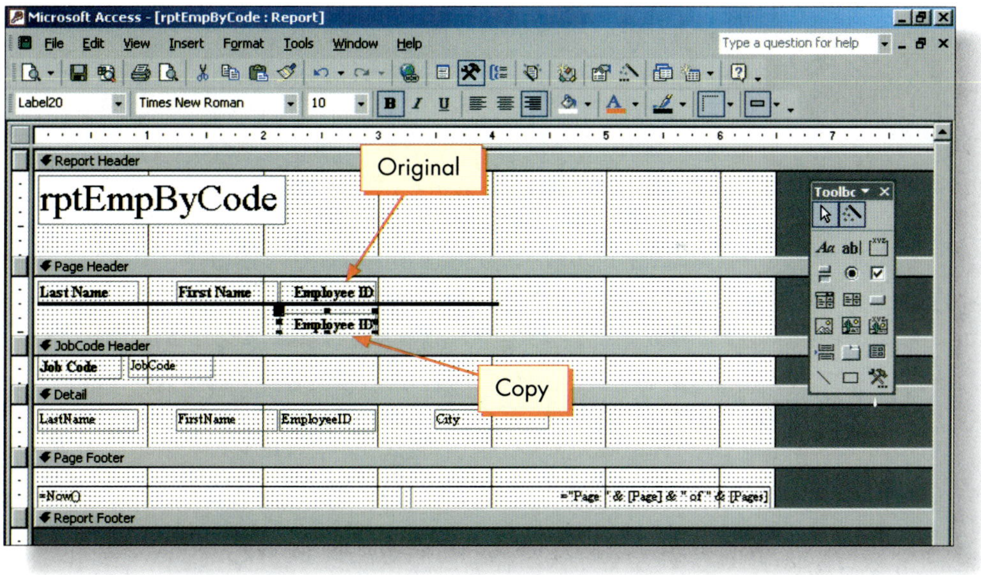

3. Drag the copied label to the 3.5-inch mark above the horizontal line, in the same section.

NOTE: The wizard added horizontal lines to the Page Header and Page Footer. These design elements make the report more attractive.

4. Click in the copied label to display an I-beam. Delete the text. Then key **City** and press Enter.

5. Double-click a sizing handle to size the label. Press Ctrl + ← to nudge the control close to the 3.75-inch mark.
6. Click the horizontal line below the controls in the Page Header. The Object box shows that a line is selected.
7. Position the pointer on the far right selection handle to display an angled two-headed arrow.
8. Hold down Shift and drag the end of the line to the 6.5-inch mark.

TIP: Holding down Shift keeps the line straight.

9. Place the pointer on the top edge of the JobCode Header bar. Drag the bar up to show two rows of dots below the horizontal line.
10. Size the Detail section to show one row of dots below the controls.

NOTE: Designing a report is a matter of trial and error. Switch back and forth between Print Preview and Design View often.

11. Preview the report. Then return to Design View and save it.

EXERCISE 7-9 Change Font Size and Align Controls

Most printed reports use a 10-, 11-, or 12-point font size for the body of the report. This is easier to read than the default 8-point font size.

After making various edits to the controls, you should align them. To align controls, you must have at least two controls selected.

1. Place the pointer to the right of the vertical ruler, next to the row of controls in the Page Header. The pointer changes to a black arrow.

NOTE: A Group Header can be identified by the field name in the section bar. The records are grouped by this field.

2. Drag down to select all the controls in the Page Header, the JobCode Header, and the Detail sections. (See Figure 7-11 on the next page.)
3. Click the drop-down arrow next to Font Size and choose **11**.
4. While the controls are selected, choose Format, Size, and To Fit.
5. Click in a blank area of any section to deselect the controls.
6. Select the First Name label in the Page Header and the FirstName text box in the Detail section.
7. Press Ctrl + ← to nudge them to the 1-inch mark.

FIGURE 7-11
Selecting several rows of controls

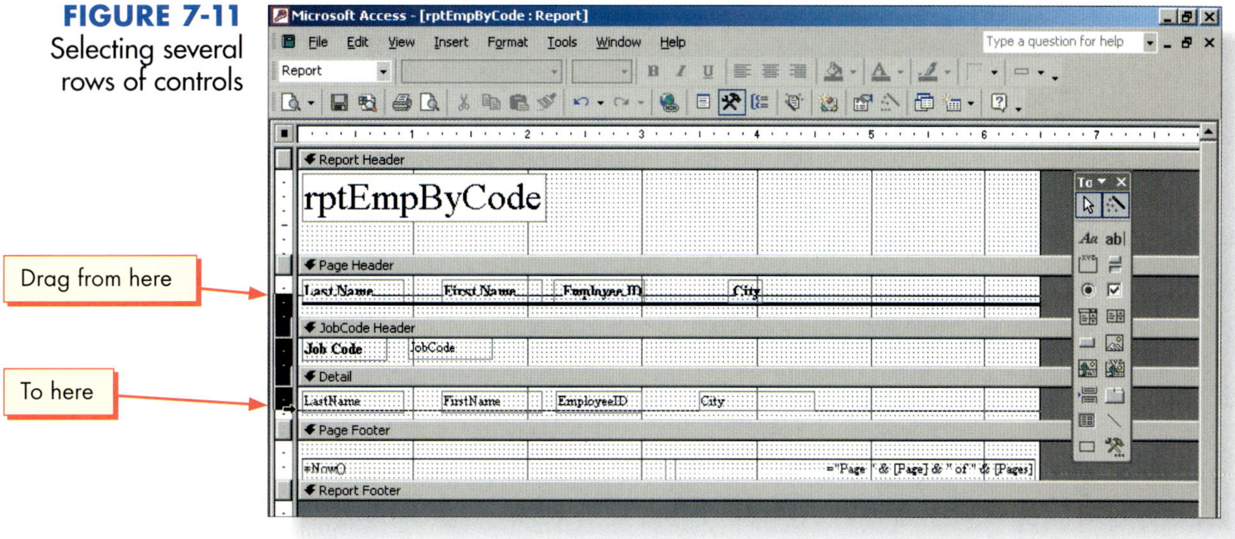

8. Place the pointer to the right of the vertical ruler for the JobCode Header section to display the black arrow. Click to select the controls.
9. Choose Format, Align, and Bottom.
10. Select the row of controls in the Detail section and align them on the top.
11. Show one row of dots below the controls in the JobCode Header. Do the same for the Detail section.
12. Preview both pages of the report and return to Design View.
13. Save the report and then return to Print Preview.

EXERCISE 7-10 Edit Common Expression Controls

The wizard added two controls to the Page Footer. Both controls use common expressions to display the date and the page number. A *common expression* is a predefined control with built-in commands. Common expressions display frequently-used controls such as current date, current time, current page number, or total pages.

1. In Print Preview for rptEmpByCode, zoom until you can see the entire page.
2. Point at the Footer text at the left and click. This zooms in on that part of the page. The Footer displays the current date.
3. Scroll to the right to see the page number.
4. Zoom out and return to Design View.
5. Right-click the =Now() control in the Page Footer and select Properties. The property sheet title bar shows that this is a text box.

NOTE: If the property sheet shows that this is a line, you selected the horizontal line above the controls. Click again to select the text box.

6. Click the Data tab. The Control Source for this control is an Access common expression that displays the current date.

FIGURE 7-12
Current date expression

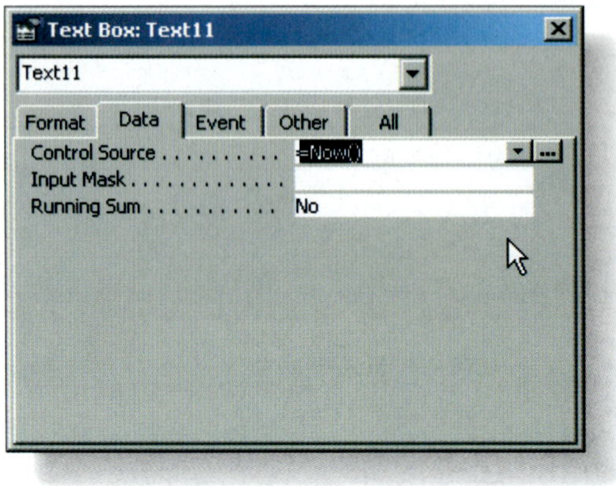

7. Click the Format tab. Click the Format row and choose Medium Date.
8. Change the Width to **1.5**. Close the property sheet.
9. Right-click the page number control and open its property sheet.
10. Click the Data tab. Click the Control Source row and the Build button [...]. The Expression Builder shows the Access code for this control.

TIP: You can select common expressions in the Expression Builder.

11. Close the Expression Builder and click the Format tab. Change the Width to **1.5**. Close the property sheet.
12. Drag the page number control to the right edge of the report.
13. Preview both pages. Close and save the report.

Creating and Modifying AutoReports

An *AutoReport* is a default, standard report that includes all the fields and a style. Your only decision is to select the query or table used as the basis for the report. An AutoReport that you create from the New Report dialog box usually has Report, Detail, and Page sections. It does not include Group sections. An AutoReport can be either columnar or tabular.

TIP: You can print a tabular report one record to a page.

EXERCISE 7-11 Create a Columnar AutoReport

A columnar AutoReport prints each field on a separate line in one or more columns. The field may have a label to its left or perhaps above it. The columnar style is also known as a vertical report. Columnar style can be used when the report has many fields that would not fit across the page in a tabular arrangement. You might use a columnar report when you want each record to print on a separate page. You can print a columnar report in portrait or landscape orientation.

1. Click the Queries button and open **qryStuffedAnimals** in Design View. The query uses one table and has no criteria.
2. Add the ProductGroup field, and add the criteria **d** to show only records from the D (Dinosaur) category. Save and close the query.
3. Click the New Object drop-down arrow and choose Report. Choose AutoReport: Columnar.
4. Click OK. View the report in Fit and 100% sizes. The records might be separated by horizontal lines, depending on the last style used on your computer.

5. Click the Last Page button to determine the page length of the report.

TIP: When the report is in a Fit view, you can press PgUp and PgDn to navigate through the pages.

6. Click the First Page button to return to page 1.
7. Click Close to switch to Design View.
8. Save the report as **rptColAnimals**.

EXERCISE 7-12 Apply an AutoFormat

An AutoReport might not use the style you prefer. Generally, Access uses the last style that was selected on your computer. You can apply an AutoFormat instead of using the style Access uses.

1. With **rptColAnimals** open in Design View, click the Report Selector button, the square to the left of the horizontal ruler. A black rectangle appears in the box to show that the entire report is selected.

REVIEW: The Object box in the Standard toolbar says "Report" when the entire report is selected.

2. Click the AutoFormat button and choose Bold. Click OK and preview the report.
3. Return to Design View.

NOTE: An AutoReport created directly from the New Object list includes a Detail section and empty Page Footers and Page Headers.

EXERCISE 7-13 Modify Control Properties

You can edit controls in any report section, as well as add group sections. Each section can include bound controls (such as text boxes), unbound controls (such as labels), and calculated controls. A field control consists of its unbound label, if any, and its bound control.

This report has a bound object frame for the picture. A *bound object frame* is a control that displays an OLE data type field from the table. Its properties are similar to those for a text box.

The Text Align property determines how a label is positioned within its box. It is similar to the Alignment commands in Word and Excel.

1. In Design View for rptColAnimals, select the large Illustration frame and drag it with its label to the 3.5-inch mark, aligned at the top with the ProductID controls.
2. Right-click the Illustration frame and open its property sheet. Notice that the control is a bound object frame. Make it **2** inches wide and **1.5** inches high. Set the Size Mode to Zoom.
3. Drag the top edge of the Page Footer bar up to show two rows of dots below the bound object frame.
4. Place the pointer on the right edge of the vertical ruler to display a black arrow. Drag to select the controls in the Detail section, but not the horizontal line.

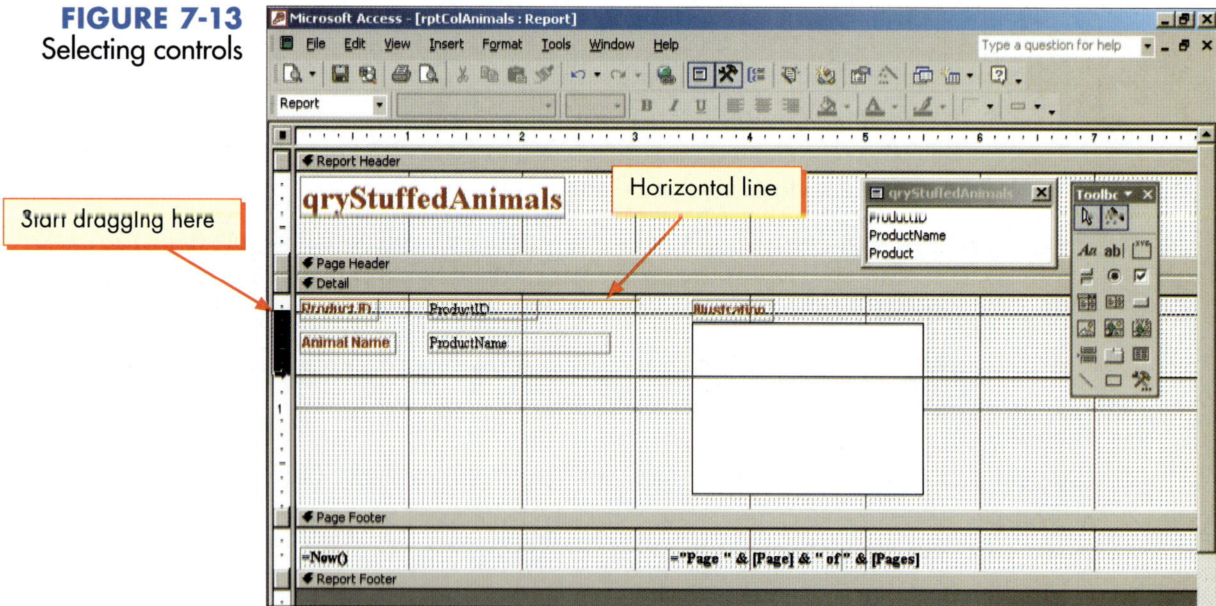

FIGURE 7-13 Selecting controls

5. Press Ctrl+↓ three times to nudge all the controls lower in the section.

6. While the controls are selected, change them to 10-point Arial. Choose Format, Size, and To Fit. Deselect the controls.

REVIEW: The solid lines in the design layout grid are at 1-inch intervals.

7. Delete the Illustration label and drag the frame to align at the top with the ProductID controls.
8. Drag the Page Footer bar to show two rows of dots below the frame.

TIP: You can edit a label from the property sheet by changing the Caption. You can also change a label, using the label box in Design View.

9. Change the Main Title to **Stuffed Animals**
10. Attempt to drag the right edge of the report to the 6-inch mark. Notice that you cannot do this because the Page Number control in the Page Footer extends past that mark.
11. Select the Page Number text box and drag the right middle handle to the 5.5-inch mark.
12. Drag the right edge of the report to the 6-inch mark.
13. Preview the report to see the date and page numbers. You might see a message box telling you that the section width is greater than the page width. Click OK if the message box appears. The Page Number control might be too close or even overlap the Date control. Return to Design View.

NOTE: The right middle handle for the Date control is close to or possibly inside the Page Number control.

14. Select the Date control. Drag its right middle handle to the 3-inch mark.

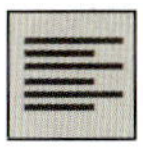

15. Click the Align Left button.

TIP: The Text Align command is listed near the bottom of the Format tab in the property sheet.

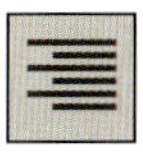

16. Select the Page Number control and click the Align Right button. Align this control on the right with the bound object frame. (See Figure 7-14 on the next page.)
17. Preview the report. Return to Design View and save it.
18. Select the bound object frame.

19. Click the drop-down arrow for the Line/Border Color button. Choose the color that matches the title and the labels.

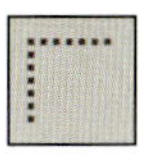

20. Click the drop-down arrow for the Line/Border Width button. Select **4** pt.

FIGURE 7-14
Report (in Design View)

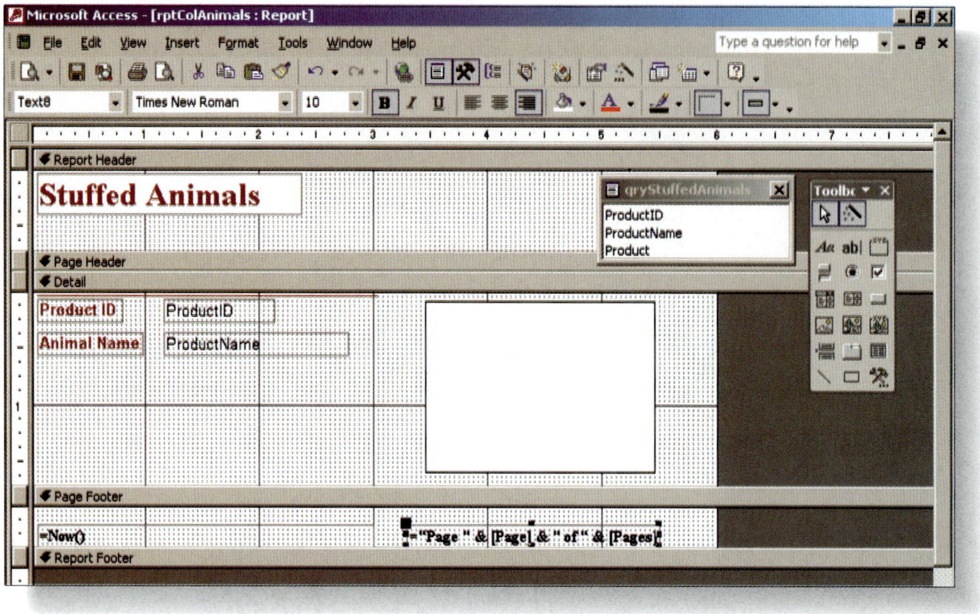

21. View the report in 100% and Fit sizes. Return to Design View.
22. Select the label in the Report Header. Apply a Shadowed special effect.
23. Open the property sheet for the label. Click the Border Color row and the Build button [...]. Choose the color that matches the label text.
24. Click OK and close the property sheet.
25. Preview the report. Return to Design View and save.

EXERCISE 7-14 Modify a Horizontal Line Control

This AutoReport displays a horizontal line near the top of the Detail section. Anything in the Detail section prints with each record, so the line repeats with each record. You can delete this line and add a new vertical dotted line.

You can adjust the setting of the *selection marquee* (the dotted line indicating that an object is selected). If the setting is full, you must click and drag over the entire object to select it. However, the default setting for the selection marquee is partial. You only need to click and drag over a portion of an object to select it.

1. Select the horizontal line at the top of the Detail section in Design View. Press Delete.
2. Click in an unused area of the window to deselect all controls. Point to the intersection of the 3-inch horizontal line and 1-inch vertical line in the Detail Section. Click and drag up and to the left until you have part of the ProductID label in the selection marquee.

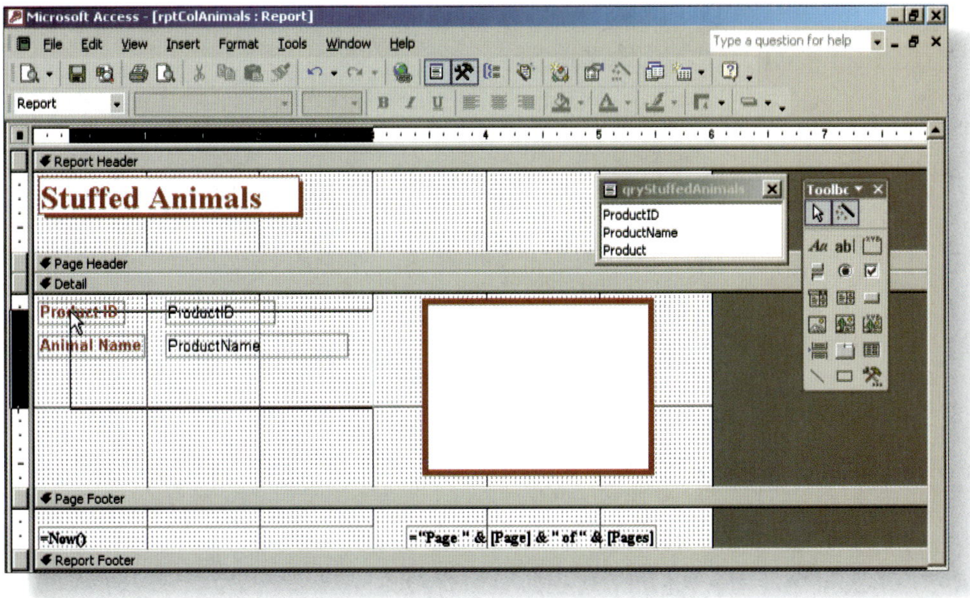

FIGURE 7-15 Drawing a selection marquee

TIP: You can start the selection marquee from any corner of your planned selection; start where you have the most room.

3. Drag the selected controls to the left until the labels start at the .25-inch mark on the horizontal ruler.

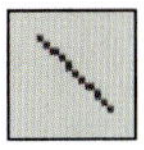

4. Click the Line button in the Toolbox.
5. Point midway between the Product ID label and the left edge of the report. Hold down Shift and draw a vertical line that is the same height as the bound object frame.

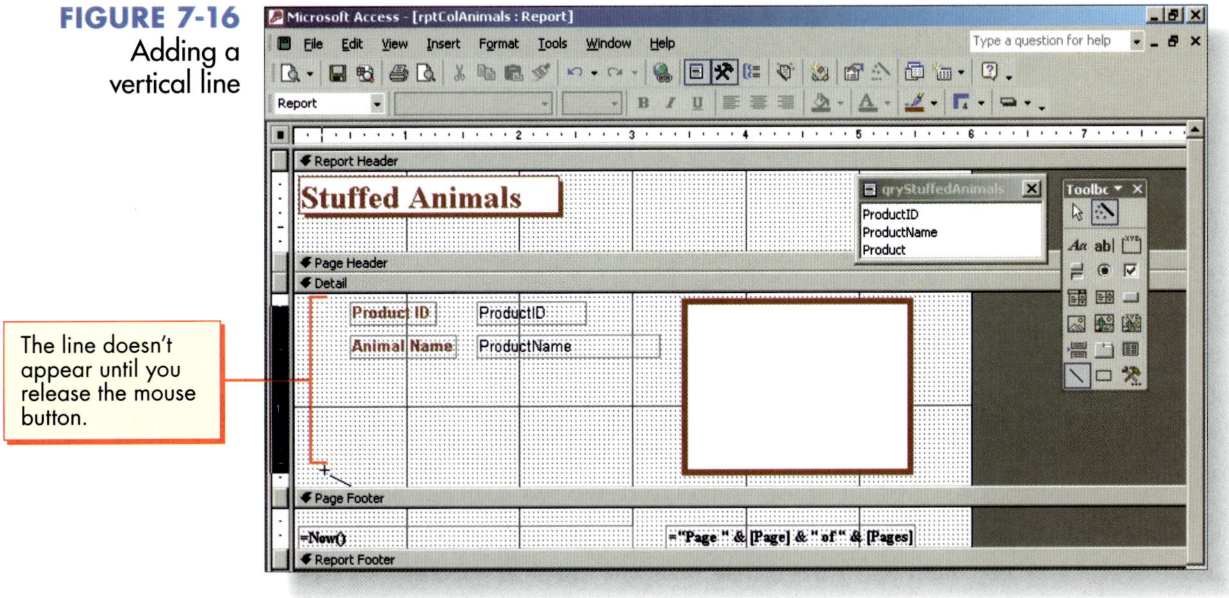

FIGURE 7-16 Adding a vertical line

6. Double-click the line to open its property sheet. Click the Format tab and the Border Style row.
7. Choose Dots. Click the Border Width row and choose **4 pt**.
8. Set the Height at **1.5**. Close the property sheet.
9. Align this line at the top with the bound object frame.

REVIEW: Hold down Shift and drag an end handle to shorten or lengthen a line.

10. Preview the report. Save and close it.

EXERCISE 7-15 Create a Tabular AutoReport

A tabular AutoReport shows each record on a separate line, usually with labels at the top of the column. Tabular reports are best for printing many records on the same page. You can print a tabular report in portrait or landscape orientation.

1. Create a query using tblCustomers and tblSalesOrders. The join line appears for the CustomerID field.
2. From tblCustomers, add CompanyName to the grid. From tblSalesOrders, add OrderID and OrderDate. Sort by OrderID in ascending order.
3. Save the query as **qryReminder**
4. Click the Field row for the fourth column and click the Build button.
5. Double-click OrderDate in the middle panel. Key **+365** and click OK.
6. View the query and return to Design View.
7. Change Expr1 to **OneYear**, leaving the colon.
8. Set the caption to **One Year Later**.
9. Save and close the query.
10. Select qryReminder in the Queries window, click the New Object drop-down arrow, and choose Report. Choose AutoReport: Tabular and click OK.
11. Maximize the window and view the report in a Fit size. (See Figure 7-17 on the next page.)
12. Return to Design View.
13. Double-click the Page Number control and set the Left property at **4**. Make the control **1.5** inches wide. Do not close the property sheet.
14. Click the Date control and make it **2** inches wide. Close the property sheet.
15. Click the Line button in the Toolbox. Position the pointer at the left edge in the Page Footer, on the second row of dots.

FIGURE 7-17
Tabular AutoReport in Print Preview

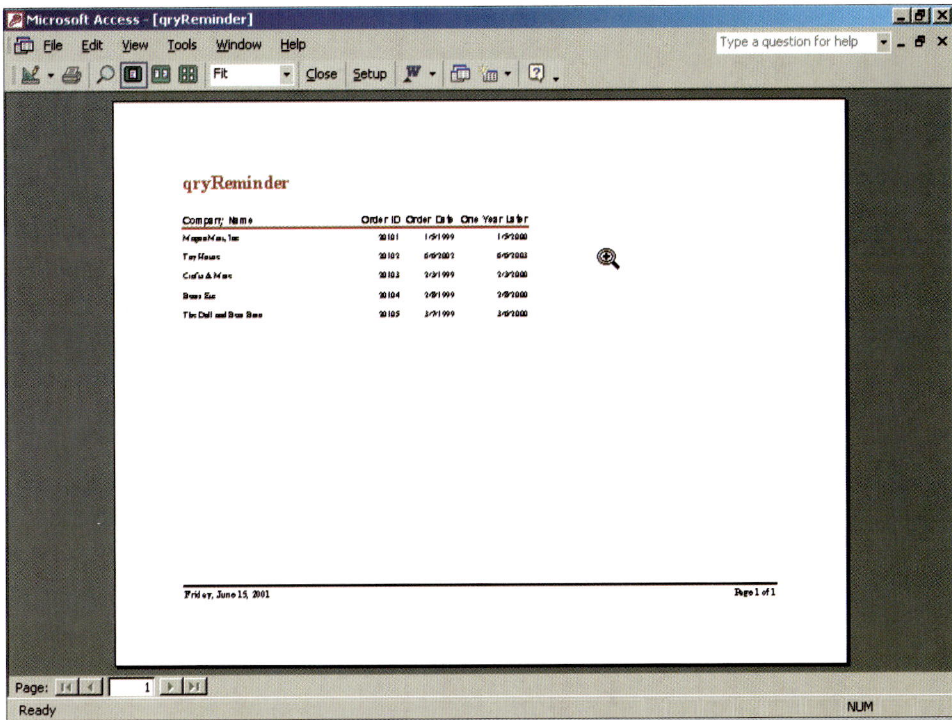

16. Hold down Shift and drag to draw a line that ends at the 6.5-inch mark on the horizontal ruler.

TIP: If you aren't satisfied with the line, select it, press Delete, and try again.

17. Preview the report. You might see the section-width error message box. Click OK if you do.

FIGURE 7-18
Section-width error message box

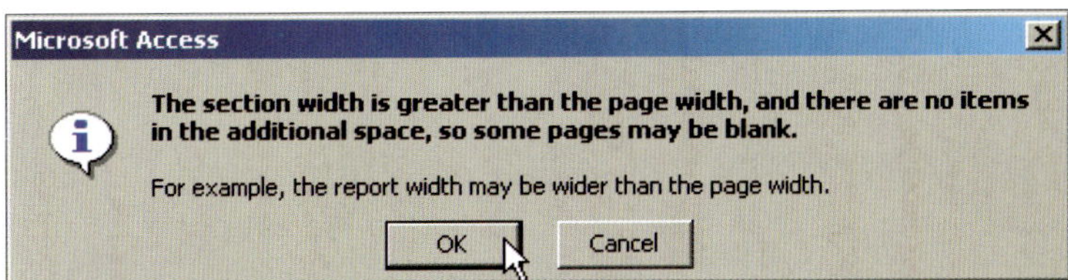

18. Click the Two Pages button. Blank pages mean that the report is too wide. Return to Design View.

19. In the Page Footer, the solid line is too wide; resize it so the right margin ends at the 6.5-inch mark.

20. Drag the right edge of the report to the 6.5-inch mark. Drag the page number control to align on the right with the horizontal line.

21. Select the Date and Page controls in the Page Footer and choose Format, Align, and Top.

22. Save the report as **rptRemDates**. Preview and close the report.

Adding a Calculated Control

Calculated fields should not be keyed into a table. Instead, they should be calculated when they are needed in a query, form, or a report. In the Stuffed Animals report, for example, you can compute the total inventory value for each product by multiplying the list price by the quantity on hand.

EXERCISE 7-16 Add a Calculated Control in a Report

You will now modify an existing report to calculate the inventory value of the stuffed animals based on the number of units in inventory and on the list price. You will use an unbound control to calculate a new cost.

1. Open **rptStuffedAnimals** in Design View.

2. Click the Text Box button ab. Click at the 5.5-inch mark in the Detail section.

REVIEW: You can click to place a text box or label at a default size.

3. Select and delete the label, not the unbound control.
4. Open the property sheet for the unbound control.
5. Click the Other tab. Change the Name to **CurrentValue**.
6. Click the Data tab. In the Control Source row, click the Build button ....
7. In the middle panel, click <Field List> to show only the table fields in the right panel.

REVIEW: The middle panel in the Expression Builder lists all objects in the folder or in the object selected in the left panel.

8. Double-click ListPrice in the right panel.

9. Click * symbol once for multiplication.
10. Double-click QuantityOnHand in the right panel. (See Figure 7-19 on the next page.)
11. Click OK. Click the Format tab and the Format row. Choose Currency and close the property sheet.
12. Position the control so that its left edge aligns at the 5-inch mark.

FIGURE 7-19
Expression Builder with an expression

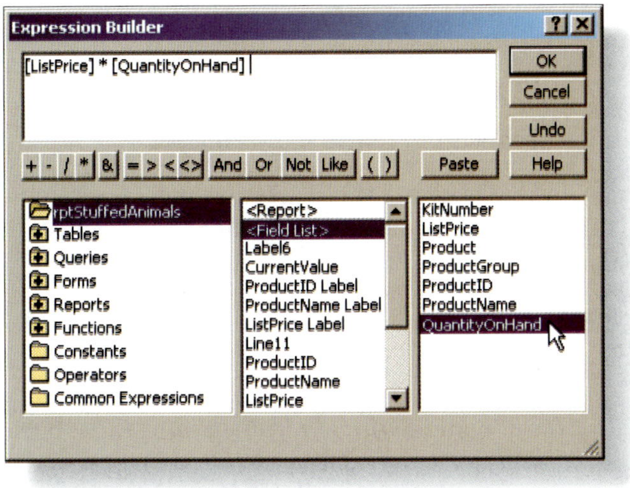

13. Click the List Price label in the Page Header. Press Ctrl + C and then press Ctrl + V.

14. Drag the copied label to be the title for the calculated control. Change the label to **Value**

15. Align the Value label and the calculated control on the right.

16. Align the labels in the Page Header on the top.

17. Drag the top edge of the Detail bar up to show two rows of dots below the line in the Page Header.

18. Select and extend the horizontal line.

19. Save the report.

Using Format Painter and Conditional Formatting

The *Format Painter* is a tool that copies the font, size, color, and alignment from one control to another. It saves you from having to set the individual properties for each control. To use the Format Painter, you select the control that has the formatting, click the Format Painter button, and then click the control to be changed.

You can also apply *conditional formatting*. Conditional formatting is a style, color, or other setting that displays under certain conditions. For example, you can set conditional formatting to show values over $15,000 in a different color, in bold, or underlined.

EXERCISE 7-17 Use the Format Painter

You use the Format Painter to give the calculated control the same format as the other controls in the Detail section of the report.

1. With rptStuffedAnimals open in Design View, select the ListPrice text box.

2. Click the Format Painter button. The pointer changes to an arrow with a paintbrush.

3. Click the calculated control. The font and size are copied.
4. Double-click each text box in the **Detail** section to autofit its height. Align the controls on the top.
5. Select one of the labels in the **Page Header**.
6. Click the Format Painter button.
7. Click the Date control in the **Page Footer**. Double-click a handle to autofit the height.

REVIEW: Double-clicking a sizing handle for a text box autofits only the height, not the width.

8. Move the Date to align with the Value controls at the right.
9. Preview the report and size the Date control so you can see the entire Date.
10. Size the **Detail** section so there are two rows of grid dots below the controls.

EXERCISE 7-18 Use Conditional Formatting

Many database designers use conditional formatting to call attention to records that are outside a specified parameter. Often managers use reports to track sales, production, and inventory levels. Conditional formatting helps to quickly identify action that might need to be taken.

1. Click the calculated control in the **Detail** section.
2. Choose **Format**, **Conditional Formatting**. The top half of the dialog box shows the current formatting.
3. Click the first drop-down arrow for **Condition 1**. Select **Field Value Is**.
4. Click the second drop-down arrow and select **between** as the operator.
5. Click in the third box and key **3000**
6. Click in the last box and key **3500**. The condition is that the value in the calculated control is between 3000 and 3500.
7. In the **Condition 1** area, set the Fill/Back Color to a dark blue and the Font/Fore Color to white. This sets the color for the value if it is between 3000 and 3500. (See Figure 7-20 on the next page.)

NOTE: You can choose a different color by clicking the drop-down arrow to display the palette.

8. Click **OK**.
9. Preview, save, and close the report.

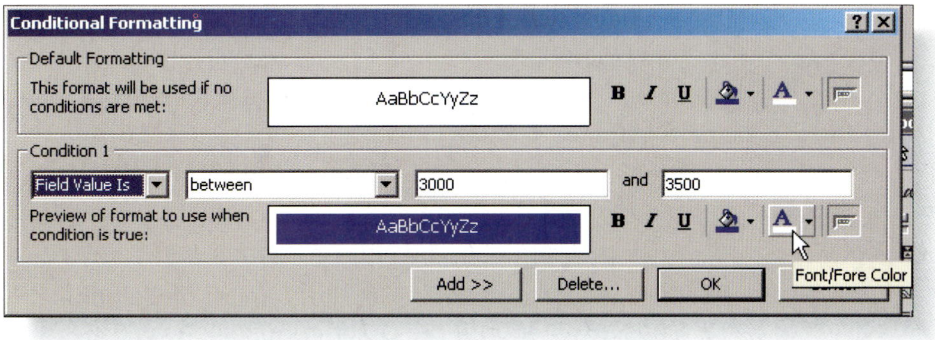

FIGURE 7-20 Conditional Formatting dialog box

Creating a Multicolumn Report and Labels

In addition to columnar and tabular reports, you can format a report to show the data in more than one column. You can use either a wizard or Design View to lay out the fields, usually in a single column. Then use the Page Setup command to set the number and width of the printed columns.

You can also create labels by using the Label Wizard, an option in the New Report dialog box. The wizard lists common label brands and sizes, including mailing labels, package labels, CD and cassette labels, and more.

EXERCISE 7-19 Create a Multicolumn Report for a Query

In addition to creating reports by selecting predefined labels, you can create custom multicolumn reports to fit nonstandard labels.

1. Open qryStuffedAnimals in Design View. Delete the criteria, save, and close the query.
2. With qryStuffedAnimals highlighted, click the New Object drop-down arrow. Select Report.
3. Choose AutoReport: Columnar and click OK. The AutoReport shows all the fields in a single column.
4. Return to Design View.

NOTE: The AutoFormats for reports are different from the AutoFormats for forms because the report AutoFormats are designed for printing.

5. Click the AutoFormat button. Choose Formal and click OK.

6. Select all the controls in the Detail section. Choose Format, Vertical Spacing, and Decrease.
7. Select the controls in the Page Footer and delete them. Close the Page Footer.
8. Preview the report in a Fit size. While in Print Preview, choose File, Page Setup.
9. Click the Page tab and choose Landscape.
10. Click the Columns tab. Set the Number of Columns to **2**. Set the Row Spacing to **.15** and the Column Spacing to **.25**.
11. Set the Column Size Width to **3.5** inches.
12. Choose Across, then Down for the Column Layout.

FIGURE 7-21 Setting up a multicolumn report

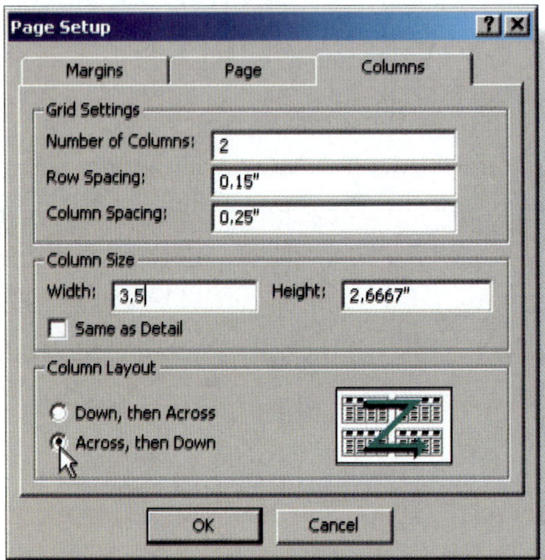

13. Click OK. The records are shown in two columns across the page.
14. Preview several pages of the report. Return to Design View.

NOTE: You do not see two columns in Design View. The first page might also show fewer records because of the space the title requires.

15. Save the report as **rptMultiCol** and close it.

EXERCISE 7-20 Create Package Labels

The Label Wizard assists you in creating package labels. After you select a label type and size, the Label Wizard asks which fields to place on the label, which font to use, and how to sort the labels.

1. In the Reports window, click New. Choose Label Wizard and tblStuffedAnimals. Click OK.
2. In the first wizard dialog box, choose Avery as the manufacturer. Choose English as the Unit of Measure and Sheet Feed as the Label Type. Choose 5388 as the product number for labels that measure 3 inches by 5 inches, 1 label across the page. Click Next.
3. Set the font as 18-point Times New Roman, Normal weight, with a black text color. Click Next.
4. Press Enter once to insert a blank line in the prototype.
5. Key **Product ID:** and press the spacebar twice.
6. Double-click ProductID to place it in the prototype.
7. Press Enter twice to leave a blank line in the prototype.
8. Key **Product Name:** and press the spacebar twice. Double-click ProductName to place it in the prototype. Press Enter twice.
9. Key **Kit Number:** and press the spacebar twice. Double-click KitNumber to place it in the prototype.

FIGURE 7-22
Prototype for large labels

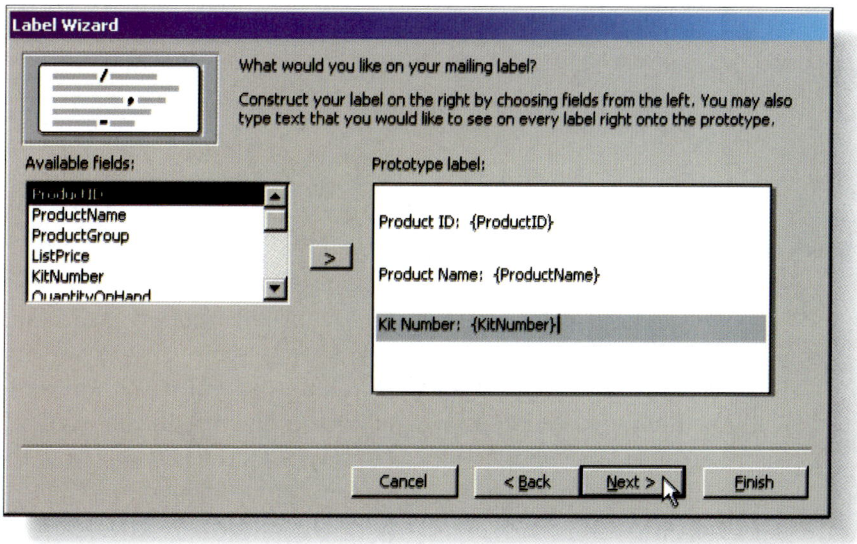

10. Click Next. In the next dialog box, choose ProductID for the Sort Order and click Next.
11. In the last wizard dialog box, change the name to **rptAnimalLabels**. Select the option See the labels as they will look printed. Click Finish.
12. The labels are one across. The report is eight pages long. Maximize the window and view several pages in a Fit size.

13. Return to Design View. The "&" joins the text you keyed to the data on the same line. The blank lines show an equal sign and two quotation marks surrounding a blank space.

FIGURE 7-23
Design View for large labels

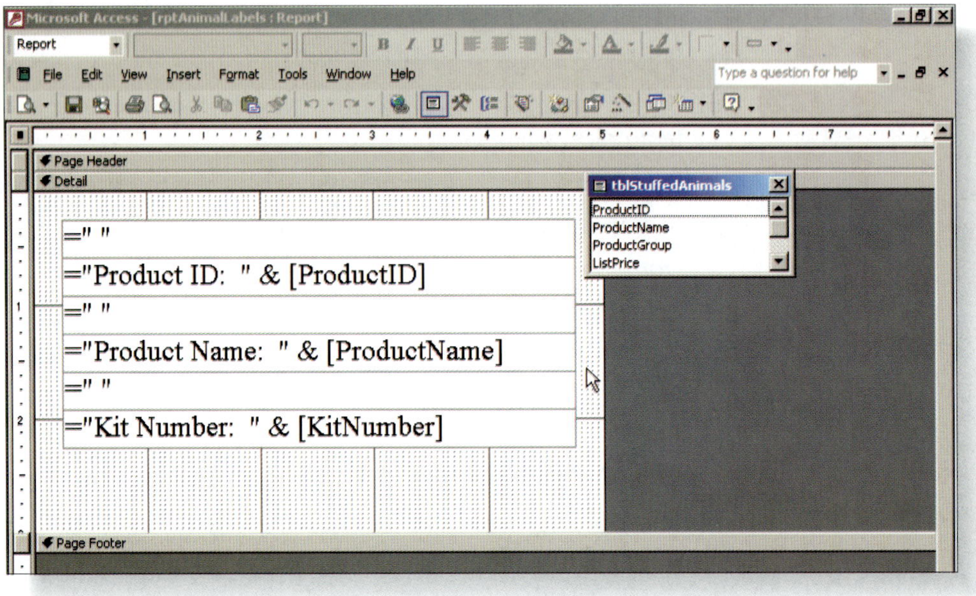

14. Close and save the report.

Exporting Data to Excel or Word

A recordset can be exported to a spreadsheet program (such as Excel) or a word processing program (such as Word). You can also export to several other formats. When you export a table, you create an unformatted file for the other program. You can, of course, then format the new file in the other application.

When you export a form or a report, the results show the underlying data and not the design of the form or report.

EXERCISE 7-21 Export a Table to Excel

When you export a table to Excel, Access attempts to match the table's field type and properties to create a similar worksheet. Field types such as currency are directly converted.

1. Right-click tblCustomers and choose Export.

2. Click the drop-down arrow for Save as type and choose Microsoft Excel 97-2002.
3. The default filename is the name of the table. The file extension for an Excel workbook is automatically entered. Click Export.
4. Start Excel and open the spreadsheet **tblCustomers**.
5. Maximize Excel and the workbook. The fields are set to default Excel screen width. Notice the Yes/No field shows true or false rather than a check mark. This is how Excel interprets that data.

FIGURE 7-24
Exported table in Excel

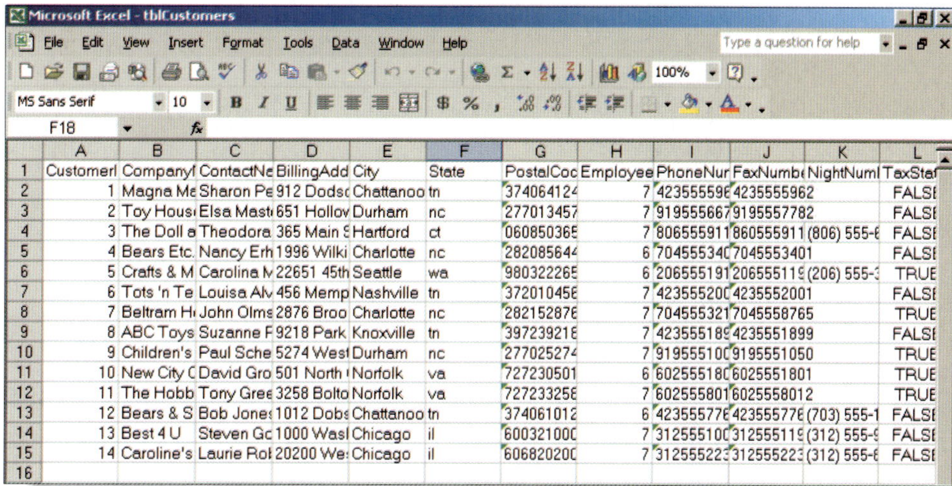

	A	B	C	D	E	F	G	H	I	J	K	L
1	CustomerI	CompanyN	ContactNa	BillingAdd	City	State	PostalCoc	Employee	PhoneNur	FaxNumbe	NightNuml	TaxStat
2	1	Magna Ma	Sharon Pe	912 Dodsc	Chattanoo	tn	374064124	7	423555596	4235555962		FALSE
3	2	Toy Hous	Elsa Mast	651 Hollov	Durham	nc	277013457	7	919555667	9195557782		FALSE
4	3	The Doll a	Theodora	365 Main S	Hartford	ct	060850365	7	806555911	860555911	(806) 555-6	FALSE
5	4	Bears Etc.	Nancy Erh	1996 Wilki	Charlotte	nc	282085644	6	704555340	7045553401		FALSE
6	5	Crafts & M	Carolina M	22651 45th	Seattle	wa	980322265	6	206555191	206555119	(206) 555-3	TRUE
7	6	Tots 'n Te	Louisa Alv	456 Memp	Nashville	tn	372010456	7	423555200	4235552001		FALSE
8	7	Beltram H	John Olms	2876 Broo	Charlotte	nc	282152876	7	704555321	7045558765		TRUE
9	8	ABC Toys	Suzanne F	9218 Park	Knoxville	tn	397239218	7	423555189	4235551899		FALSE
10	9	Children's	Paul Sche	5274 West	Durham	nc	277025274	7	919555100	9195551050		TRUE
11	10	New City C	David Gro	501 North	Norfolk	va	727230501	6	602555180	6025551801		TRUE
12	11	The Hobb	Tony Gree	3258 Bolto	Norfolk	va	727233258	7	602555801	6025558012		TRUE
13	12	Bears & S	Bob Jones	1012 Dobs	Chattanoo	tn	374061012	6	423555776	423555776	(703) 555-1	FALSE
14	13	Best 4 U	Steven Gc	1000 Wasl	Chicago	il	600321000	7	312555100	312555119	(312) 555-9	FALSE
15	14	Caroline's	Laurie Rol	20200 We	Chicago	il	606820200	7	312555223	312555223	(312) 555-6	FALSE
16												

6. Close the workbook, but not Excel.

EXERCISE 7-22 Drag and Drop a Table to Excel

By opening both Excel and Access, you can drag and drop a table from Access to a blank worksheet in Excel. A new worksheet is automatically created, showing the table's data.

TIP: If you drag and drop a query to Excel, you see the dynaset in Excel.

1. Close all applications other than Access and Excel.
2. Right-click on an open area of the taskbar.
3. Choose Tile Window Vertically from the shortcut menu. Excel and Access are tiled side-by-side on the desktop.

4. Arrange the application windows so you can see tblCustomers in the Access window and Cell A1 in the Excel window.
5. Click and drag tblCustomers from the Access window to Cell A1 in the Excel window. Release the mouse button when it shows the plus sign with the pointer.

FIGURE 7-25
Dragging and dropping the table

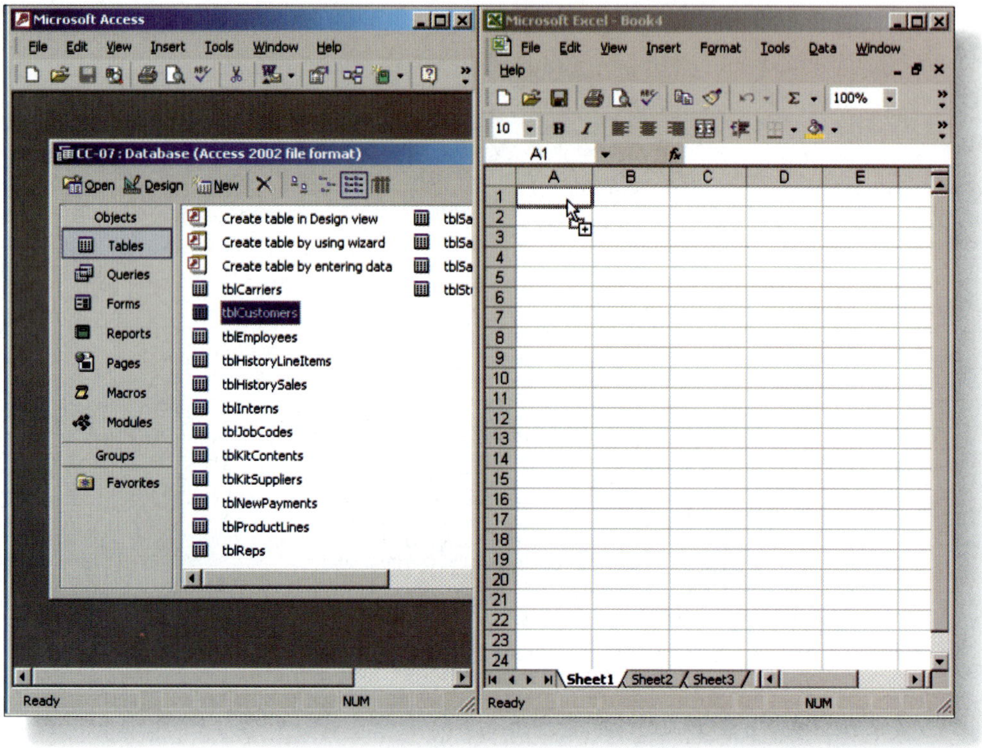

6. Maximize the Excel application window and the workbook. Review the table. You can widen columns and change the colors in Excel.
7. Exit Excel without saving the table.
8. Maximize the Access window.

EXERCISE 7-23 Export a Query to Word

Word does not have a database-type structure like Excel. To create a file that is recognized by Word, Access converts the query's dynaset to a comma-delimited file. This means the raw data is exported with commas separating ("delimiting") each field in a record. When you export a query, you create a file that includes the records displayed in the query's Datasheet View.

TIP: You cannot export a parameter query because it requires an entry from the keyboard to display a dynaset.

1. Click the Queries button. Right-click qryKitCosts and choose Export.
2. Click the drop-down arrow for Save as type and choose Text Files.
3. The default filename is the name of the query. Click Export.
4. The Export Text Wizard guides you through exporting the file. The wizard has determined that the fields are delimited. In this case, the delimiter is a comma.

FIGURE 7-26
Delimiter is a comma for the query

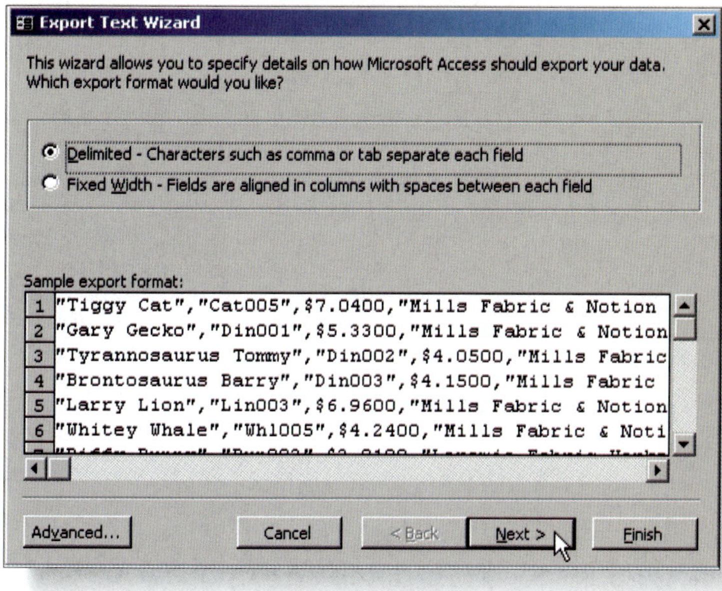

5. Click Next. Click the Comma button to mark the character used to separate the fields. Click Include Field Names on First Row. Click Next.
6. In the Export to File name box, verify the folder and filename. Click Finish. Click OK in the message box that confirms the export is completed and indicates the file location.

TIP: To find the document in Word, set the Files of Type in the Open dialog box to show All Files.

7. Start Word and open the text file **qryKitCosts**.
8. Click OK.

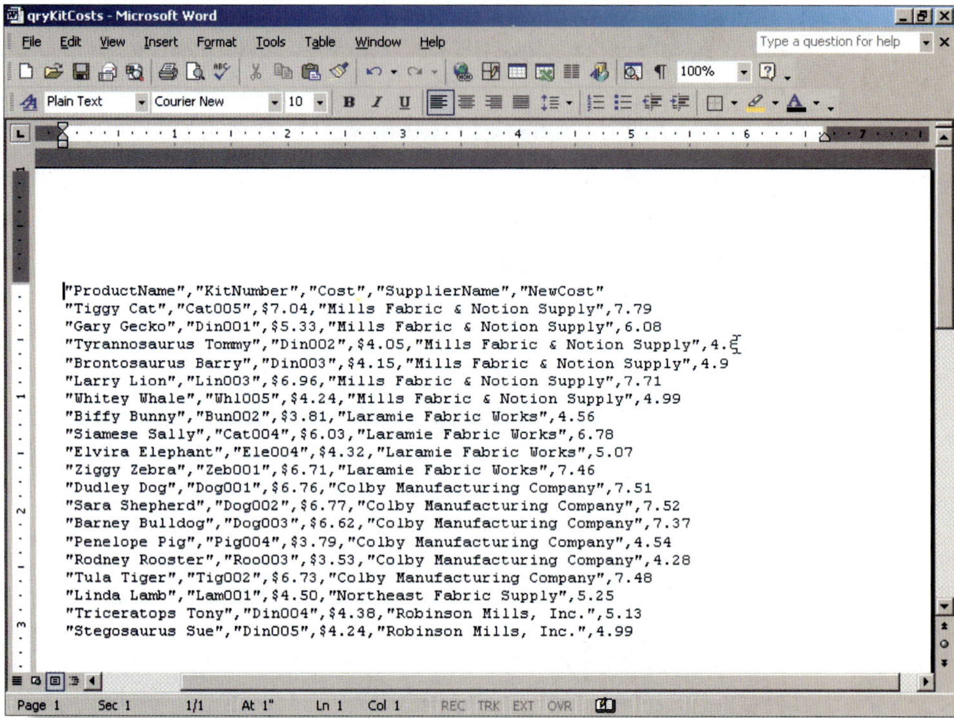

FIGURE 7-27 Exported data in Word

9. Exit Word. Compact your database and close it. Exit Access.

USING HELP

Use Help Contents to view information about sections in a report.

Find out more about using Help:

1. Turn off the Office Assistant. Choose Help and Microsoft Access Help. Click the Contents tab.
2. Find and click Reports and Report Snapshots.
3. Expand Customizing Reports.
4. Expand Report Sections.
5. Click and read the topic About sections of a report.
6. In the left panel, click Resize a section. In the right panel, click and read Resize a form or report section.
7. Close the Help window.

LESSON 7 Summary

- You can create simple reports by using the Report Wizard.
- Before printing a report, a good practice is to view the report in Print Preview.
- You can view and modify section properties in the property sheet.
- You can use group sections to organize and summarize information based on categories.
- Page breaks can be forced to occur before and after group sections.
- You can move, size, align, and format controls in reports in much the same way as in forms.
- You can add fields to a report by using the Field List window.
- When adding fields to a report, take care to align other controls in the Report Header or Report Footer to match the Detail section.
- Controls should be sized and aligned to make the report easier to read.
- The Date and Page Number are common controls created by the Report Wizard.
- Columnar-style reports are most commonly used when the length of the data is too wide to properly display in tabular format.
- AutoFormat applies font sizes, font colors, border styles, and border colors to an entire report or parts of a report.
- The property sheet for each object in a report lists all the characteristics or attributes for that object.
- Horizontal lines in a report can be move or resized just as any other object.
- In a tabular report, each record displays on a separate line.
- Calculated controls display the results of a numeric expression based on one or more fields in a record.
- You can set the properties of multiple objects simultaneously by using the Format Painter.
- Conditional formatting applies a property only when certain conditions are met.
- Records in a multicolumn report or label display in two or more columns.
- The Label Wizard can create nonstandard package labels.
- You can easily export an Access table to Excel by dragging and dropping the table from Access into Excel.
- Comma-delimited files can be created to transfer data from Access to Word.

LESSON 7 Command Summary

FEATURE	BUTTON	MENU	KEYBOARD	SPEECH
AutoFormat		Format, AutoFormat		✓
Conditional Formatting		Format, Conditional Formatting		✓
Field List		View, Field List		✓
Format Painter				
Multicolumn Report		File, Page Setup		
One Page		View, Pages, One Page		✓
Print Preview		View, Print Preview		✓
Sorting and Grouping		View, Sorting and Grouping		✓
Two Pages		View, Pages, Two Pages		✓
Zoom		View, Zoom		✓

Concepts Review

TRUE/FALSE QUESTIONS

Each of the following statements is either true or false. Indicate your choice by circling T or F.

T F *1.* A tabular report displays data in rows with column headings, similar to a worksheet.

T F *2.* Use the Text Box button to add a calculated control to a report.

T F *3.* Conditional formatting depends on criteria you enter in the dialog box.

T F *4.* You can move controls from one section to another in a report.

T F *5.* A Report Header prints at the top of every page.

T F *6.* You cannot change the name of a control.

T F *7.* Common expressions include calculations such as [HourlyRate]+[Bonus].

T F *8.* You add a new section to a report when you group records.

SHORT ANSWER QUESTIONS

Write the correct answer in the space provided.

1. What section of a report includes the data from the records?

___

2. How do you create a multicolumn report?

___

3. In what menu are the Page Header and Report Header options listed?

___

4. What is the name of the dialog box you use to select fields, common expressions, or arithmetic operators?

___

5. What does the expression =Now() do?

___

6. What tool should you use to add a calculated control to a report?

___

7. Is a label a bound or an unbound control?

---

8. What button on the toolbar copies the font and colors from one control to another?

CRITICAL THINKING

Answer these questions on a separate page. There are no right or wrong answers. Support your answers with examples from your own experience, if possible.

1. You used the Line tool in this lesson to add a design element to a report. What other tools might be good design ideas for a printed report?

2. In this lesson you learned how to change the size, position, and color of labels and text boxes by using the property sheet. What are the advantages of using the property sheet instead of the mouse and toolbars?

Lesson Applications

EXERCISE 7-24

Create a multicolumn report by using the Report Wizard. Size controls. Add a label. Export a query.

1. Open *[your initials]*CC-07.
2. Use the Report Wizard to create a report for qryInventoryByAnimal.
3. In the wizard, choose both fields, but do not add grouping. Sort by ProductName in ascending order.
4. Use justified layout, portrait orientation, and Bold style.
5. Title the report **rptCurrInv**. Preview each page in Fit and 100% sizes.
6. Select the Current Inventory label and the QuantityOnHand text box. Drag either right middle handle until the right edges align at the 2.75-inches mark.

NOTE: The rectangle gives the appearance of a border. Click any edge of the rectangle to select it.

7. Select the black rectangle. Size it to match the QuantityOnHand controls.
8. Change the report to use two columns that are 3 inches wide. Determine your own row and column spacing so all the records fit on one page. The columns should run across and then down.
9. Delete the Page Number control. Add a label in its place and key ***[your first and last name]***.
10. Use the Format Painter to copy the format from the Date text box to the new label.
11. Edit the label in the Report Header to read **Current Inventory**
12. Save and print the report. Close the report.
13. Export the data used to create rptCurrInv to a text file.
14. Using Microsoft Word, print the text file.

EXERCISE 7-25

Create an AutoReport. Modify controls. Add labels and common expressions.

1. Create a tabular AutoReport for qryCustomers.
2. Apply the Compact AutoFormat to the entire report.

REVIEW: Controls must be selected to adjust the horizontal or vertical spacing.

3. Delete the FaxNumber text box and its label.
4. Select all the labels in the Page Header. Make the horizontal spacing equal.
5. Select all the text boxes in the Detail section and make the horizontal spacing equal.
6. Preview the report and then move individual labels or text boxes so each label is positioned well over its column.
7. Select and position the controls in the Detail section so there is one row of dots above and below the controls in the section. You might need to resize the section.
8. Preview the report; it might be too wide. Check for blank pages.
9. Change the left and right margins to **.75** inch.
10. Preview again. Check all text boxes to see if they are wide enough, and make adjustments. Move and resize to make the report attractive.
11. Save the report as **rptCustomers**
12. Edit the label in the Report Header to show **Carolina Critters Customers.** Align it on the left with the labels in the Page Header section.
13. Add a label with your name in the Page Footer. Move and position the Date and Page Number controls to make the report attractive.
14. Preview, print, and save the report. Close the report.

EXERCISE 7-26

Sort and group records in a report. Add a calculated control for the group.

1. Open **rptCustomers** in Design View. Maximize the window.
2. Open the Sorting and Grouping dialog box and place State in the Field/Expression list. Turn on the Group Header and the Group Footer for State. Set the Keep Together property to Whole Group. Show CompanyName as the second Field/Expression, but do not turn on its Group Header or Group Footer.
3. Drag the State label from the Page Header into the State Header at the left edge. Drag the State text box from the Detail section into the State Header next to the State label.
4. Use the Format Painter to copy the format from the label in the Page Header to the State text box.
5. Size, move, and align the labels and text boxes so nothing is cut off.
6. Add a new text box so its label starts at the 1-inch mark in the State Footer.

7. Change the label to **# of Customers**
8. Open the property sheet for the unbound text box. Open the Expression Builder.
9. Click in the preview area and key **count(** to start the expression.
10. Click <Field List> and double-click CustomerID. Then key a closing parenthesis to finish the expression. Your expression should show:
    =count([CustomerID])

REVIEW: Name a control on the Other tab of the property sheet.

11. Change the name of this control to **StateTotal**
12. Copy the format from the label in the Page Header to the calculated control.
13. Size, move, and align the controls if you feel it is needed. Size the sections so there is space between groups of customers.
14. Save, print, and close the report.

EXERCISE 7-27 Challenge Yourself

Create a report based on a query.

1. Double-click **qryEmployeesByJobCode** to open it. The Enter Parameter Value dialog box asks for a job code.
2. Key **of06** and press Enter. The query shows only those people in the OF06 job category. Close the query.
3. Use the Report Wizard to create a report for qryEmployeesByJobCode.
4. Use all the fields, do no grouping, and sort by last name. Use a tabular layout and portrait orientation. Use the Casual style. Title the report **rptCodeGroup**
5. In the Enter Parameter Value dialog box, key **mf06** and press Enter. The report is filtered to show employees in the MF06 category.
6. In Design View, add a label for your name in the Report Header.
7. Change the title of the report to **Employee Code Group**
8. Print the report and close it.
9. Compact the database and close it.

On Your Own

In these exercises you work on your own, as you would in a real-life work environment. Use the skills you've learned to accomplish the task—and be creative.

EXERCISE 7-28

Review the design of the database you modified in Exercise 6-28. On a sheet of paper, sketch three reports that will enhance the usability of this database. On each sketched report, describe who would use the report, the reason the information on the report is valuable, and the frequency at which the report will be printed. Name each report and give it a title that best describes the purpose for the report. Write your name and "Exercise 7-28" on each sketch. Continue to Exercise 7-29.

EXERCISE 7-29

Based on the sketches you created in Exercise 7-28, create three reports. Select the style and layout most appropriate for each report. Arrange the controls in a way that you feel is appropriate. In the Page Footer, include your name and "Exercise 7-29." In the Report Header, include the title of the report. Print a copy of each report. Continue to Exercise 7-30.

EXERCISE 7-30

Create a Group for your report. Depending on your design, you might need to add a field to a table and enter appropriate data. Select a name, title, style, and layout appropriate for the report. Arrange the controls appropriately. In the Page Footer, include your name and "Exercise 7-30." Test your report in Print Preview. You might need to sort the records for the grouping to work correctly. Print the report. Submit the copies, the sketches, and the reports you printed in Exercises 7-28 through 7-30 to your instructor. Keep a copy of the database you modified in Exercise 7-30. It will be used in subsequent lessons.

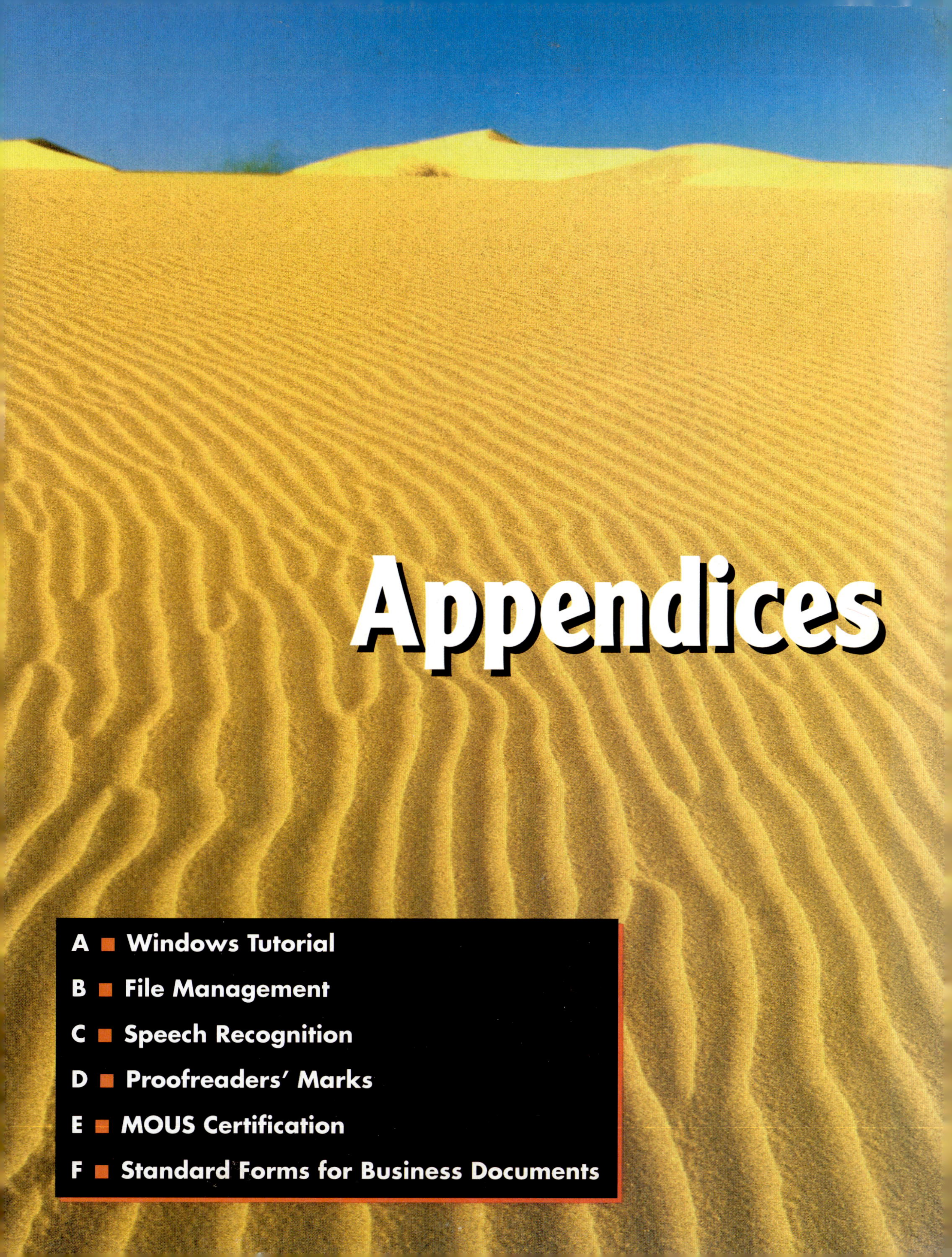

Appendices

APPENDIX A

Windows Tutorial

If you're unfamiliar with Windows, review this Windows Tutorial carefully. You'll learn how to use a mouse; how to start Windows; how to use the taskbar, menus, and dialog boxes; and other important aspects of Windows.

If you're familiar with Windows but need help navigating Windows files and folders, refer to Appendix B: "File Management." There you'll find information on how Windows stores information and how to use Windows Explorer.

NOTE: All examples from this Tutorial refer specifically to Windows 2000. If you are using any other version of Windows, your screen might differ slightly from the images shown in this Tutorial. However, because most basic features are common to all versions of Windows, this Tutorial should be helpful to you no matter what version of Windows you use.

Using the Mouse

Although you can use the keyboard with Windows, you'll probably find yourself using the mouse most of the time. A *mouse* is a pointing device that is typically attached to your computer. You roll the mouse on any flat surface, or on a *mouse pad*, typically a smooth pad on which the mouse rests. The mouse is used to move a pointer on the computer screen. A *pointer* is typically a small arrow that you move on the computer screen to accomplish specific tasks.

As you roll the mouse (typically on a mouse pad), the pointer on the computer screen moves in the direction you move the mouse. Thus, when you roll the mouse to the left, the pointer on the screen moves to the left. When you roll the mouse to the right, the pointer on the screen moves to the right. By using the mouse you can position the pointer on objects on the computer screen.

TIP: When moving the mouse on the mouse pad, if you reach the edge of the pad, just pick up the mouse and place it in the center of the pad. This won't change the position of the pointer on the screen.

A mouse typically has two buttons at the front (the edge of the mouse where the cord attaches)—one on the left and one on the right. (A mouse might also have a center button or a wheel, but these are not typical; therefore, a center button or wheel isn't discussed in this Tutorial.)

To choose an item on the computer screen by using the mouse, roll the mouse until the pointer on the screen is over the desired item. Then press and release the left mouse button once. Pressing and releasing the mouse button is referred to as a *click*. Doing this twice is referred to as a *double-click*. Whenever you're told to "click" or "double-click" an item on the computer screen, use the left mouse button.

The right mouse button is used less frequently. Pressing and quickly releasing the right mouse button is referred to as a *right-click*.

You can use the mouse to *drag* an object to another location on-screen. To do this you position the pointer on the object you want to drag, hold down the left mouse button, and roll the mouse until the pointer is at the position where you want to drop the object. Then release the mouse button and the object is dropped at the specified location. (You can see why this type of mouse action is also referred to as *drag-and-drop*.)

You can also select an object by using the mouse. To do this you position the pointer on one side of the object, hold down the left mouse button, and roll the mouse until the pointer reaches the other side of the object. Then release the mouse button. The selected object is highlighted in some way. In Windows, you often need to select an object before you can perform some action on it. For example, you often need to select an object before you can copy it.

As you progress in this Tutorial you will become familiar with the terms in Table A-1 describing the actions you can take with a mouse.

TABLE A-1 Mouse Terms

TERM	DESCRIPTION
Point	Roll the mouse until the tip of the pointer is touching the desired item on the computer screen.
Click	Quickly press and release the left mouse button.
Double-click	Quickly press and release the left mouse button twice.
Drag (or drag-and-drop)	Point to an object on-screen, hold down the left mouse button, and roll the mouse until the pointer is in position. Then release the mouse button.
Right-click	Quickly press and release the right mouse button.
Select	Hold down the left mouse button; roll the mouse so the pointer moves from one side of an object to another. Then release the mouse button.

As you perform actions on-screen using the mouse, the on-screen pointer changes its appearance, depending on where it's located and what operation you are performing. Table A-2 shows the most common types of pointers.

TABLE A-2 Frequently Used Mouse Pointers

POINTER	DESCRIPTION
Pointer	Used to point to objects.
I-Beam	Used in keying, inserting, and selecting text.

continues

TABLE A-2 Frequently Used Mouse Pointers *continued*

POINTER	DESCRIPTION
2-Headed Arrow	Used to change the size of objects or windows.
4-Headed Arrow	Used to move objects.
Hourglass	Indicates the computer is processing a command. While the hourglass is displayed, it is best to wait rather than try to continue working.
Hand	Used in Window's Help system to display additional information.

Starting Windows

All computers are not set up the same way. In most cases, however, when you turn on your computer, Windows loads automatically and the Windows desktop appears. The *desktop* is the area that first appears on the computer screen after you start Windows. The desktop is your on-screen work area. All the elements you need to start working with Windows appear on the desktop.

1. Turn on the computer. Windows begins loading, and a Windows log-on screen displays.

NOTE: On some computers, the log-on screen does not appear automatically. You might have to press the following keys, all at once, and then quickly release them: Ctrl, Alt and Delete. If your computer is on a network, your instructor might need to provide you with special start-up instructions.

2. You now need to log on to Windows, using your user name and password. To start this process, move the pointer to the User name box. The pointer turns into an I-beam. If someone else's name appears in the User name box, use Delete or Backspace to delete the name before keying yours. Key your user name. If you make a mistake, press Backspace to delete your mistakes and then key correctly.

NOTE: If you don't know your Windows user name and password, ask your instructor for help. If your computer is attached to a network, you also might be prompted to log on to the network before you log on to Windows.

3. When you finish keying your user name, move the pointer to the Password box and key your password.
4. When your user name and password are correctly keyed, click OK. The Windows desktop appears.

The Windows Desktop

The left side of the Windows desktop contains *icons,* small pictures that represent programs, files, or folders. If you double-click an icon, the program, file, or folder represented by that icon opens. (Appendix B: "File Management" contains a complete discussion of files and folders.)

FIGURE A-1
Windows desktop

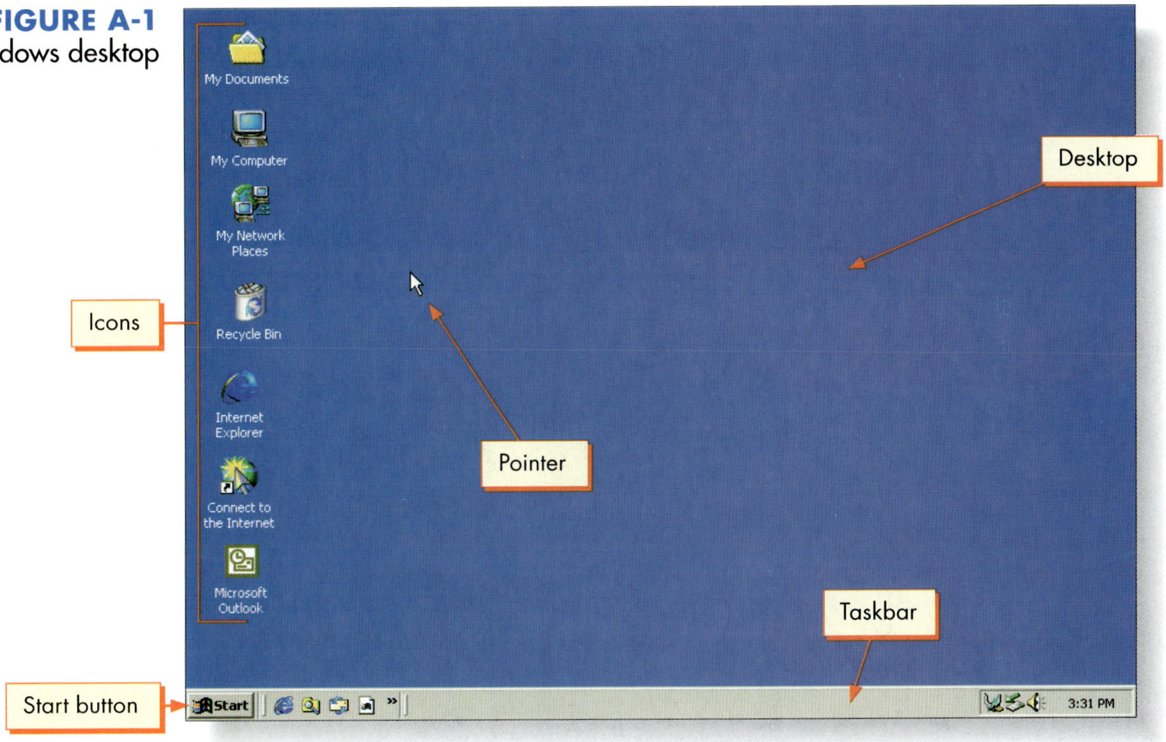

NOTE: Depending on how your computer is set up, your icons might be different from those shown in Figure A-1.

Two important icons are found on virtually all Windows desktops:

- My Computer
  When you double-click this icon, a new window opens showing icons representing the disk drives available on your computer (and on your network, if you are on one). Use My Computer when you want to view the contents of a hard disk or a floppy disk.

- Recycle Bin
  When you double-click this icon, a new window opens listing files you have deleted. Until you empty the Recycle bin, these files can be undeleted and used.

Another important component of the desktop is the *taskbar.* This bar usually appears at the bottom of the desktop. Buttons on the taskbar show which programs and windows are currently open.

Using the Start Menu

The taskbar contains the Start button Start, which is the most important button in Windows. Clicking the Start button causes the Start menu to appear. This menu provides a list of commands and shortcuts to files. From the Start menu you can perform many Windows tasks. Table A-3 describes the components of the Start menu.

FIGURE A-2
Start menu

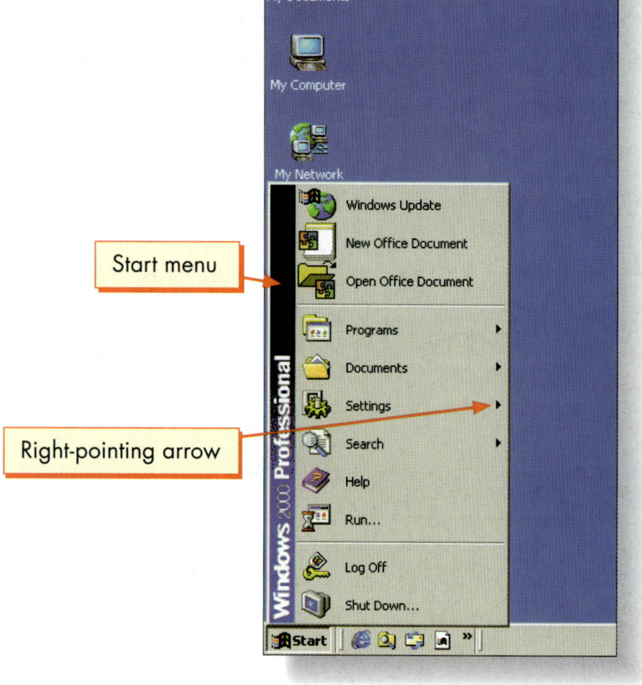

Some items on the Start menu also show a right-pointing arrow. This means additional choices are available on a secondary menu, called a *submenu*. When you point to a menu item with a right-pointing arrow, the submenu appears.

1. Click the Start button Start on the Windows taskbar.
2. The Start menu appears.

NOTE: The Start menu can be customized. It might not show the Log Off command. It might show the Favorites command, which displays a list of favorite Internet addresses. It might also show the commands with individual letters underlined. You can use the underlined letters as an alternate method of executing a command. Instead of clicking the command, you key the letter that is underlined.

TABLE A-3 Start Menu

COMMAND	USE
Windows Update	Connects to the Microsoft Web site for Windows updates.
New Office Document	Starts a new Microsoft Office document of any type.
Open Office Document	Opens an existing Microsoft Office document.
Programs	Displays a submenu listing the programs on your computer. Clicking a program instructs Windows to start the program.
Documents	Displays a submenu listing recently opened documents.
Settings	Displays a submenu listing system components for which you can change settings.

continues

TABLE A-3 Start Menu *continued*

COMMAND	USE
Search	Displays a submenu listing commands that enable you to locate a file, folder, Internet address, or people.
Help	Starts the Windows Help function. Windows Help instructs you how to perform tasks in Windows.
Run	Allows you to type a command to start a program.
Log Off	Closes all programs, disconnects your computer from the network and Internet, and prepares your computer for someone else to use.
Shut Down	Shuts down, restarts, or places your computer in a stand-by mode.

Using the Programs Command

Most programs on your computer can be started from the **Programs** command on the **Start** menu. This is the easiest way to open a program.

The **Programs** menu normally uses the *Personalized Menus* feature in Windows. This feature keeps the menus relatively uncluttered by hiding items that have not been used recently. You expand the menu to its full size, showing all its options, by clicking the down arrow at the bottom of the menu.

1. With the Start menu open on your screen, point to **Programs**. (Or, you can click **Programs.**) The Programs submenu appears, listing the programs installed on your computer. Every computer has a different list of programs.
2. Point to the down arrow at the bottom of the **Programs** submenu (or click it). The Programs menu is expanded to its full size.

FIGURE A-3
Programs submenu

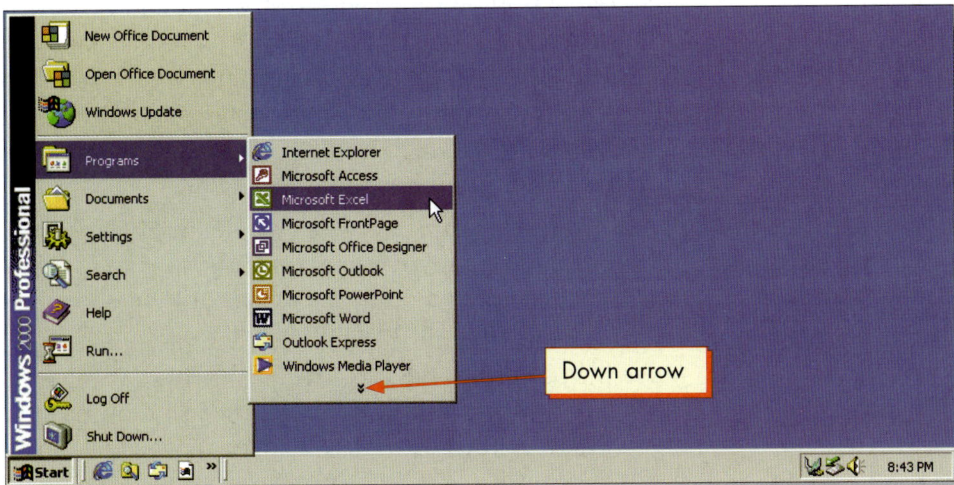

3. Point to the program you want to open and click. (For the purposes of this Tutorial, you can open Excel, a spreadsheet program in Microsoft Office.) In a few seconds, the program you selected loads and its first screen appears. Notice that a button for the program appears on the taskbar.

Using the Taskbar

Using the taskbar, you can switch between open programs and between open documents within a program. Windows displays a button on the taskbar for each program and document that is currently open.

The window in which you are working is called the *active* window. The title bar for the active window is highlighted, and its taskbar button is also highlighted.

1. The program window you opened in the previous procedure should still be open. To open a second program, click the Start button, choose Programs from the Start menu, and then choose an option from the Programs submenu. (For the purpose of this Tutorial, you can open Word, a word-processing program in Microsoft Office.) Notice how the second program covers the first. The window containing the second program is now active. Its title bar is highlighted, as is its button on the taskbar.
2. Click the button on the taskbar for the first program you opened. The first program (Excel) appears again.
3. Click the button on the taskbar for the second program (Word) to switch back to it.

4. Start a new blank document in Word by clicking the New Blank Document button on the Word toolbar. (Toolbars are usually located near the top of the screen. See Figure A-4 on the next page.) Notice that each open document has its own taskbar button so you can easily switch between documents.
5. Click the button on the taskbar for the first program you opened (Excel). Now practice using the taskbar to switch between program windows and between document windows until you feel comfortable.
6. Move the pointer to the top edge of the taskbar until it changes from a pointer to a two-headed arrow. Using the two-headed arrow, you can move the taskbar or change its size.
7. With the pointer displayed as a two-headed arrow, hold down the left mouse button and move the arrow up until the task bar moves up, changing position with the status bar at the bottom of the program window. (See Figure A-4 for the location of the status bar.)
8. Move the pointer to the top edge of the taskbar once again until the two-headed arrow displays. Hold down the left mouse button and move the arrow down to the bottom of the screen. The taskbar is restored to its original position.

FIGURE A-4 Excel is the active window.

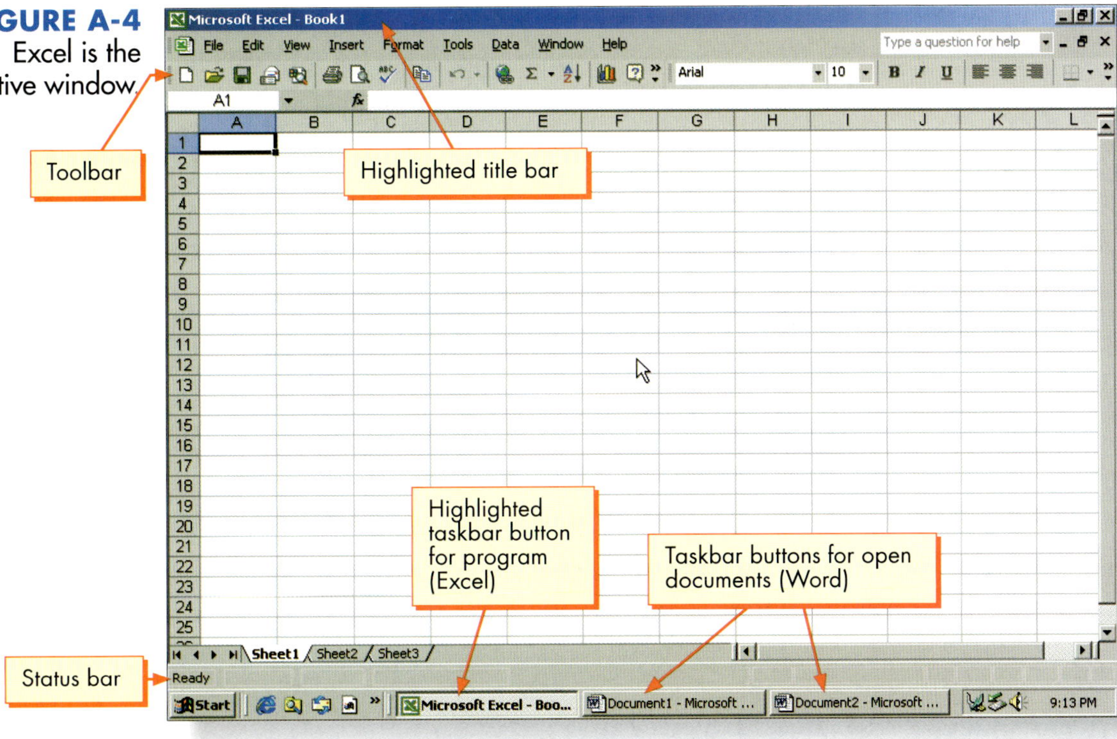

NOTE: You might sometimes see the taskbar displayed along the sides or the top of the desktop. You can change the position of the taskbar on the desktop by dragging it. You do this by placing the pointer over the taskbar, holding down the left mouse button, moving the pointer to the new location, and then releasing the mouse button.

Using Menus

Most Windows applications use a similar menu structure. You use the mouse to open a menu containing various menu options (these are often called commands). You can open a menu by clicking the name of a menu from the *menu bar,* a row of menu names just below the title bar. Then you can click a menu option from the menu to execute that menu option.

Alternatively, you can use the keyboard to open menus and choose menu options. To open a menu, you press Alt and the underlined letter of the menu name at the same time. For example, to open the File menu, you hold down Alt and press F. You can use the keyboard again to choose a menu option. For example, with the File menu open, you use Alt+S (the underlined character from the Save command) to choose the Save command. Using a combination of Alt and a key underlined in the command you want to choose is a type of *keyboard shortcut.*

1. Make the Excel window the active window (if it is not already) by clicking its button on the taskbar.

2. Click Edit on the menu bar. The Edit menu appears.

Three dots following a menu option indicate that a dialog box is displayed when that menu option is chosen. (The next section of this Tutorial discusses dialog boxes.) Some commands also show toolbar buttons or keyboard shortcuts next to the command name. These are alternative ways to execute the command.

Notice that each of the menu names has an underlined character.

FIGURE A-5
Edit menu from Excel

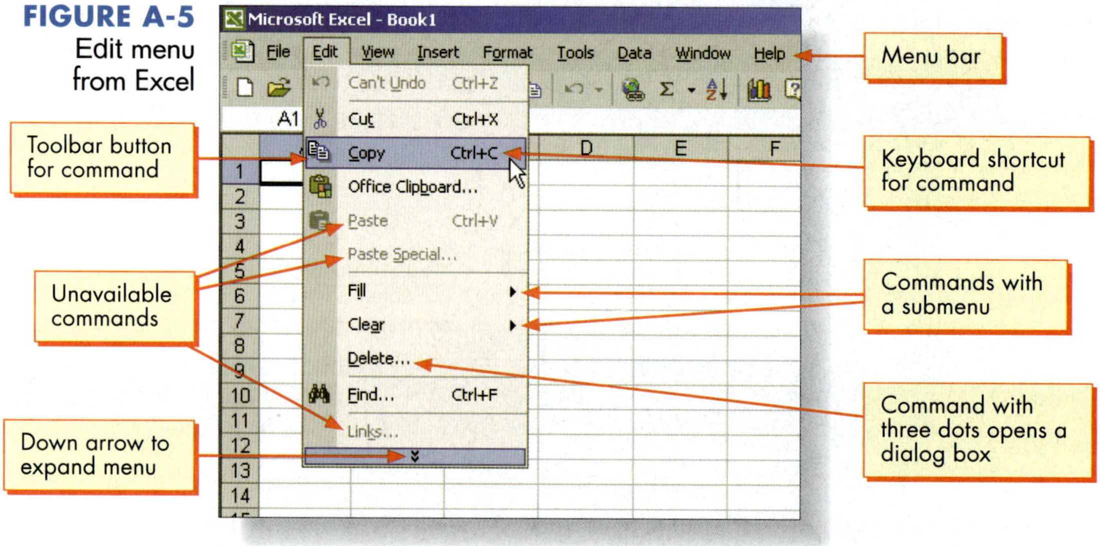

3. Click Edit on the menu bar again. The menu closes.
4. Press Alt + E, the keyboard shortcut for the Edit menu. The Edit menu appears again.
5. Click Edit on the menu bar again to close the Edit menu.
6. Press Alt + V, the keyboard shortcut for the View menu. The View menu appears.

FIGURE A-6
View menu expanded from Excel

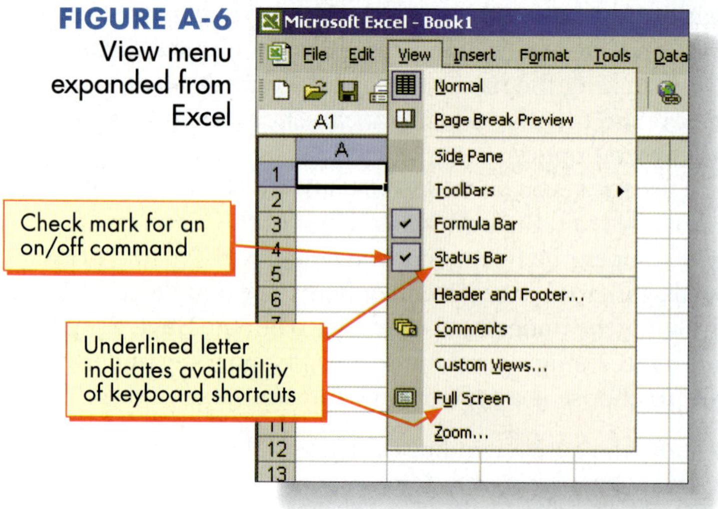

7. Click the down arrow at the bottom of the menu to display the entire View menu. Some commands have check marks next to them. This means the command can be turned on or off.

   Notice also that all the commands in the menu have an underlined letter, indicating that they, too, have keyboard shortcuts.
8. Click View to close the View menu.

Using Dialog Boxes

Windows applications make frequent use of dialog boxes. A *dialog box* is a window that requests input from you related to a command you have chosen. All Windows applications use a common dialog box structure.

1. Make the Word program the active window.
2. Choose File on the menu bar. The File menu appears.
3. Click the down arrow at the bottom of the menu to display the entire File menu. The three dots following the Print command indicate that when you choose Print, a dialog box will be displayed.
4. Choose Print. The Print dialog box appears. It contains some of the most common types of dialog box options.

FIGURE A-7
Print dialog box in Word

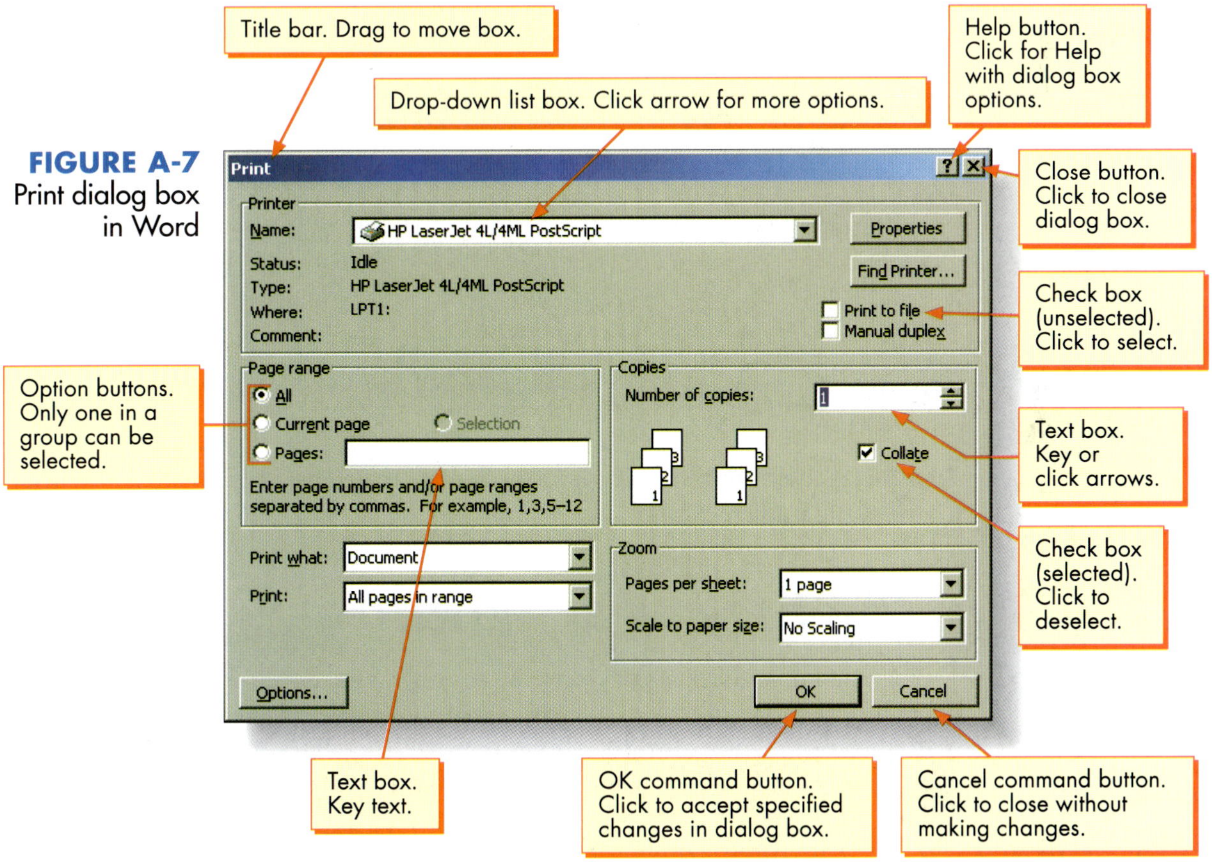

NOTE: The underlined letters indicate the options that have keyboard shortcuts. For example, to choose All as the print range, you would key Alt + A.

5. Click Cancel, which is located in the lower right corner of the dialog box. The Print dialog box closes without making any changes.
6. Make Excel the active window.

7. Click Format on the menu bar. The Format menu appears.
8. Choose Cells. The Format Cells dialog box displays.

   The tabs under the title bar are the most significant feature of this type of dialog box. (See Figure A-8.)
9. Click the Font tab, if it is not already displayed.

   To use the scroll bar in the Font, Font style, or Size list boxes, you can click the vertical scroll arrows to scroll through the options. You can also drag the scroll box up or down to scroll through the options.

FIGURE A-8
Format Cells dialog box, Font tab, in Excel

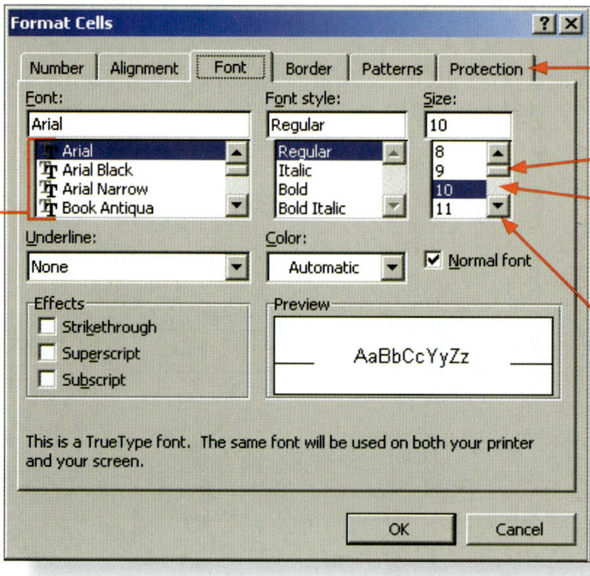

10. Click Cancel in the lower right corner of the dialog box to close it without making any changes.

Changing the Size of a Window

You can change the sizes of your windows by using either the mouse or the sizing buttons. *Sizing buttons* are the small buttons on the right side of the title bar that allow you to resize, minimize, or maximize the window. (See Figure A-9.) This can be especially useful when you'd like to display several open windows on your desktop and see them simultaneously.

There are three sizing buttons that can appear on the title bar of every window: the Minimize button, the Maximize button, and the Restore Down button. Table A-4 (on the next page) describes each of these buttons.

1. Make Excel the active window, if it is not already. Click the Maximize button on the Excel title bar if the Excel window does not fill the entire desktop.
2. Click the Restore Down button on the Excel title bar. The Excel window reduces in size, and the Word window appears behind it. Notice that the highlighted title bar of the Excel window indicates it is the active window.

TABLE A-4 **Sizing Buttons**

BUTTON	USE
Minimize	Reduces the window to a button on the taskbar
Maximize	Enlarges the window to fill the entire desktop (appears only when a window is reduced)
Restore Down	Returns the window to its previous size and desktop position (appears only when a window is maximized)

3. Move the pointer to the border of the Excel window. The pointer changes to a two-headed arrow ↔.

TIP: Sometimes the borders of a window can move off the computer screen. If you're having trouble with one border of a window, try another border or drag the entire window onto the screen by using the title bar.

4. With the two-headed arrow displayed, drag the border to make the window smaller.
5. Click the title bar of one of the Word windows behind the Excel window. The Word window becomes the active window. The Excel window is still open, but it is now behind the Word window.
6. Click the Maximize button if the Word window does not fill the entire desktop.
7. Click the Minimize button on the title bar of the Word window. The Excel window becomes the active window. The second Word window appears behind the Excel window.

8. Click the Close button on the title bar of the second Word window. The Excel window is still the active window. Notice there are only two program buttons on the taskbar now.
9. Make the Word window the active window by clicking the Word button on the taskbar.
10. Click the Restore Down button on the Word window. The Word window reduces in size. The Excel window might be partially visible behind the Word window. You can drag the two reduced windows so parts of both can be seen simultaneously.
11. Drag the title bar of the Word window until you can see more of the Excel window. Use both title bars to reposition the windows.

    Some program windows, such as those for Excel and Word, contain two sets of sizing buttons. The upper set (on the title bar) controls the program window. The lower set controls the sizing of the document within the program window. See Figure A-9 (on the next page) for the location of the lower set in Word and Excel.

FIGURE A-9
Displaying two program windows simultaneously

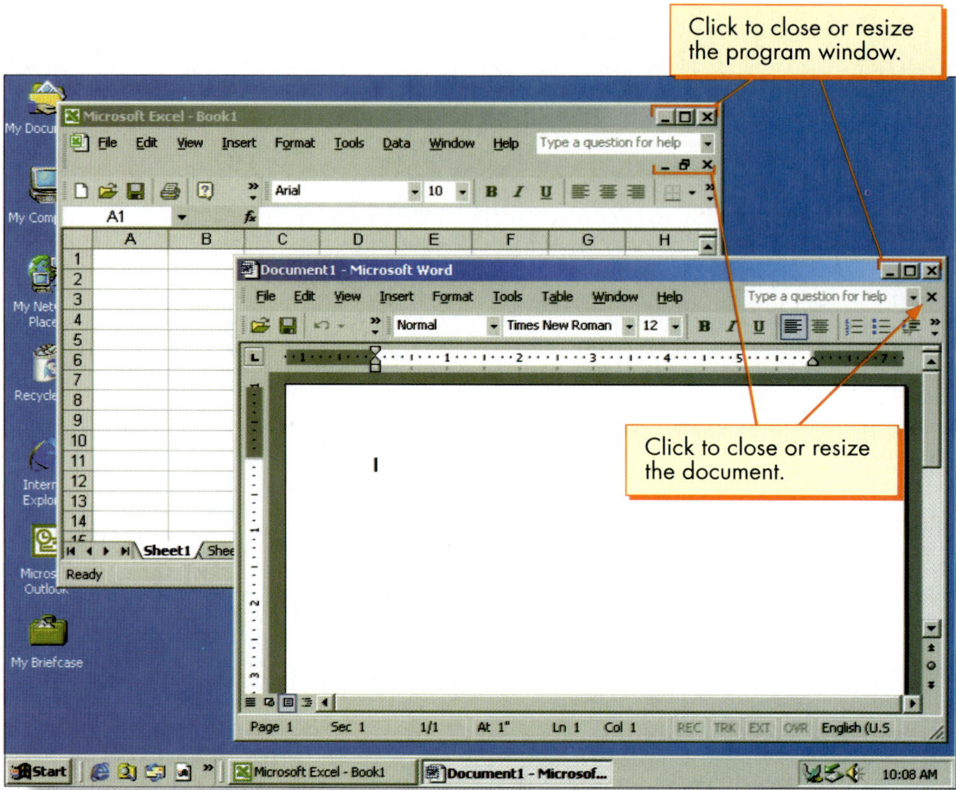

12. Click the Close button on the title bars of each of the two program windows to close them. You have a clean desktop again.

Using the Documents Command

Windows lets you open an existing document by using the Documents command on the Start menu. This command allows you to open one of the last 15 documents previously opened on your computer.

1. Click the Start button on the taskbar to display the Start menu.

2. Choose Documents. The Documents submenu appears, showing you the last 15 documents that were opened.

3. Click a document. The program in which the document was created opens and the document displays. For example, if the document you chose is a Word document, Word opens and the document appears in a Word program window.

4. Click the program window's Close button (remember, it is the Close button on the title bar). The program window closes and the desktop is clear once again.

Using the Settings Command

The **Settings** command on the **Start** menu lets you change the way Windows looks and works. Because your computer in school is used by other students, you should be very careful when changing settings. Others might expect Windows to look and work the standard way. Having Windows look or work in a nonstandard way could easily confuse them.

FIGURE A-10
Settings submenu

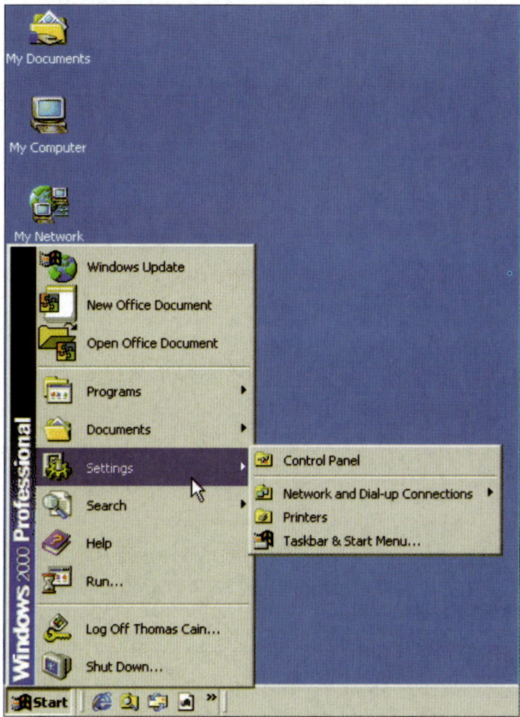

NOTE: Talk to your instructor before changing any settings on your computer.

1. Click the Start button **Start** on the taskbar.
2. Choose **Settings**. The **Settings** submenu displays.
3. Click anywhere on the desktop to close the **Settings** submenu without making any changes.

TABLE A-5 Settings Options

OPTION	USE
Control Panel	Displays the Control Panel window, which lets you change screen colors, add or remove programs, change the date and time, and change other settings for your hardware and software.
Network and Dial-up Connections	Displays a submenu that lets you make connections with other computers or a private network.
Printers	Displays the Printers window, which lets you add and remove printers, as well as modify your printer settings.
Taskbar & Start Menu	Displays the Taskbar and Start Menu Properties dialog box, which you use to customize the taskbar and add and remove programs on the Start menu.

Using the Search Command

If you don't know where a file or folder is located, you can use the Search command on the Start menu to help you find and open it.

1. Click the Start button on the taskbar.
2. Choose Search. The Search submenu appears.
3. Choose For Files or Folders. The Search Results dialog box appears.

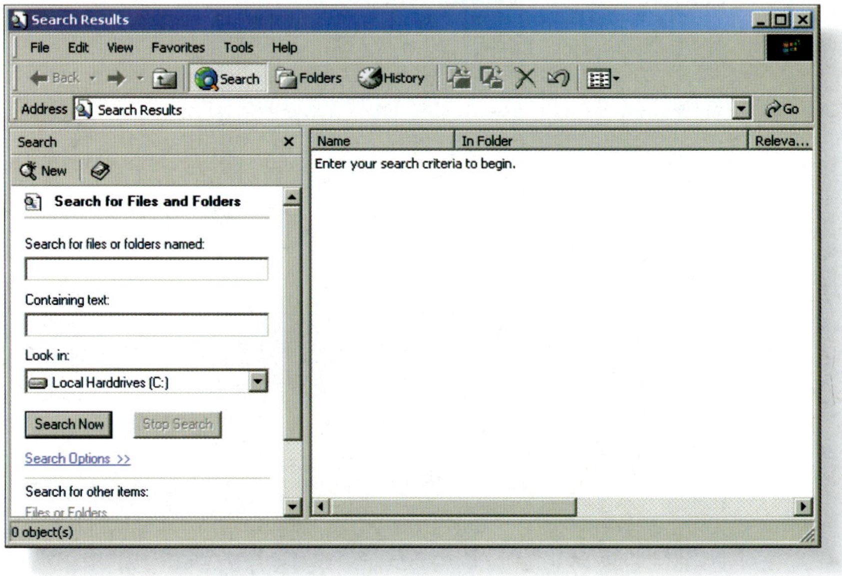

FIGURE A-11 Search Results dialog box

4. In the Search for files or folders named text box, key the name of the file or folder you want to find. Remember, you can use Backspace or Delete to delete any keying errors you make.

TIP: To search files for specific text, use the Containing text text box. To search for files by date, size, type, or other attributes, click Search Options.

5. Click the down arrow next to the Look in text box to specify where you want Windows to search. The default location is the C drive.
6. Click Search Now to start the search. Any matches for the file are shown on the right side of the dialog box.
7. Double-click on any found item to open the program and view the file or folder Windows has located.
8. When you are finished with your search, close all open windows and clear your desktop.

Using the Run Command

Windows allows you to start a program by using the Run command and keying the program name. This command is often employed to run a "setup" or "install" program that installs a new program on your computer.

1. Click the Start button Start on the taskbar.
2. Choose Run. The Run dialog box appears.

FIGURE A-12
Run dialog box

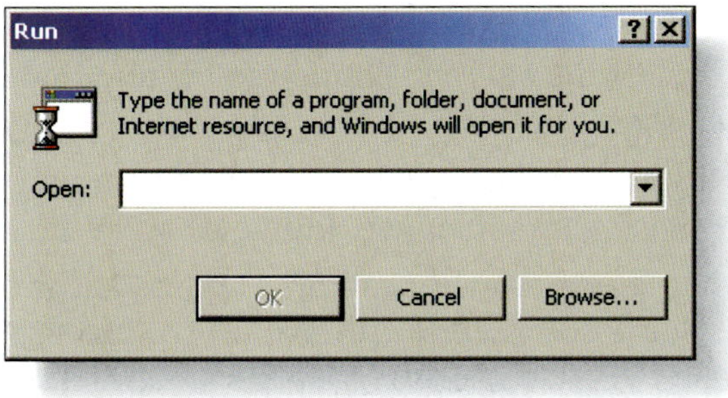

3. If you know the name of a program you want to run, key the name in the Open text box. Often you will need to click Browse to open a drop-down list of the disk drives, folders, and files available to you.
4. Click Cancel to close the Run dialog box.

Displaying a Shortcut Menu

When the mouse pointer is on an object or an area of the Windows desktop and you right-click, a shortcut menu appears. A *shortcut menu* typically contains commands that are useful in working with the object or area of the desktop to which you are currently pointing.

FIGURE A-13
Shortcut menu for the desktop

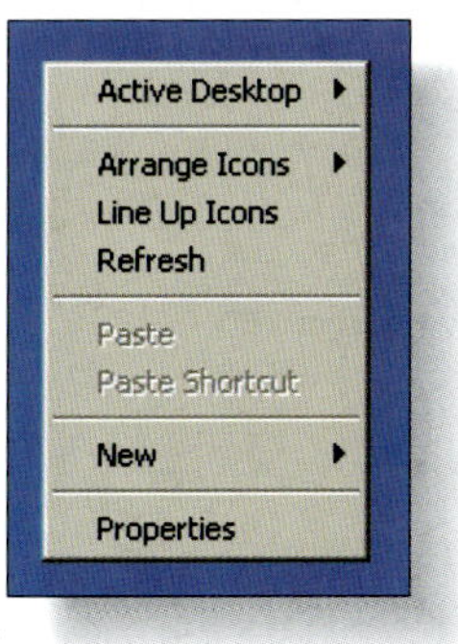

1. Position the mouse pointer on a blank area of the desktop and right-click. A shortcut menu appears with commands that relate to the desktop, including arranging icons and displaying properties.
2. Click outside the shortcut menu to close it.
3. Right-click the time in the bottom right corner of the taskbar. A shortcut menu appears with a command that relates to adjusting the time.
4. Click Adjust Date/Time. The Date/Time Properties dialog box appears. You can use this dialog box to adjust your computer's date and time.
5. Click Cancel.
6. Click outside the shortcut menu to close it.
7. Right-click an icon to display its shortcut menu, and then close the menu.

Exiting Windows

You should always exit any open applications and Windows before turning off the computer. This is the best way to be sure your work is saved. Windows also performs other "housekeeping" routines that ensure everything is ready for you when you next turn on your computer. Failure to shut down properly will often force Windows to perform time-consuming system checks the next time it is loaded.

To exit Windows, use the Shut Down command on the Start menu. This command has several shut-down options:

- Log off. Logs off the current Windows user and makes Windows available for another user to log on.
- Restart. Restarts the computer without shutting off the power. This is sometimes necessary when you add new software.
- Shut down. Closes all open programs and makes it safe to turn off the computer. Some computers will turn off the power automatically.
- Stand by. Places the computer in stand-by mode, which generally turns off the screen display and puts the computer in "hibernation." (This option is not available on all computers.)

1. Click the Start button Start on the taskbar.
2. Choose Shut Down from the Start menu. The Shut Down Windows dialog box appears.

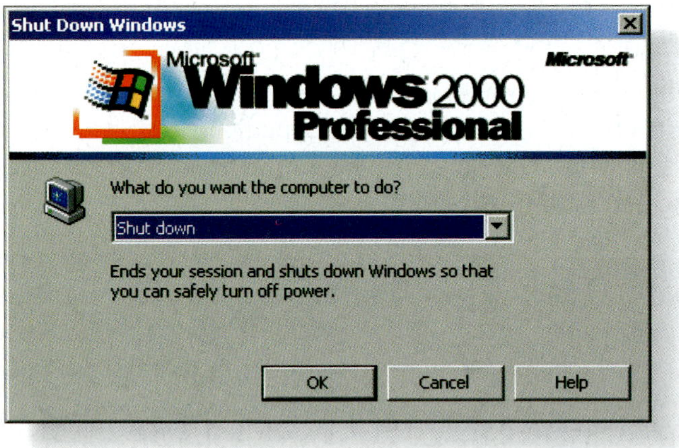

FIGURE A-14 Shut Down Windows dialog box

3. Click the down arrow next to the text box and select Shut Down if it is not already selected.
4. Click OK. Windows prompts you to save changes in any open documents. It then prepares the computer to be shut down. Windows will tell you when it is safe to turn off your computer.
5. When Windows tells you it is safe to turn off your computer, turn off your computer and your monitor.

APPENDIX B

File Management

Most of your tasks in Windows 2000 will involve working with information stored on your computer. This Appendix briefly explains how information is stored in Windows 2000.

It also introduces you to one of the most useful programs for managing information in Windows—the Windows Explorer. This program shows you how information is organized on your computer and provides you with the tools to manage it.

Files and Folders

The basic unit of storage in Windows is a *file*. The documents you create and use, as well as the programs you use, are all files. These files are stored in *folders*, which can contain other folders as well as files.

Filenames in Windows may be up to 255 characters, including spaces. A filename also has a three-letter extension, which identifies the type of file. For example, the extension "doc" identifies a file as a Word document. The extension is separated from the filename by a period (often called a "dot"), as in "Birthday.doc."

NOTE: By default, file extensions are not displayed. To display them in Windows Explorer, open the Tools menu, choose Folder Options, diplay the View tab, and then clear the Hide file extensions for known file types check box.

Opening Windows Explorer

One of the most useful tools in Windows 2000 for managing folders and files on your computer is *Windows Explorer*. This program displays folders and files in a hierarchical structure, similar to a family tree. It allows you to browse through all your computer's drives and folders in a single window. You can also use it to see the contents of other computers on your network.

To open Windows Explorer:

1. Click the Start button on the taskbar.
2. Choose Programs.
3. From the Programs submenu, choose Accessories.
4. From the Accessories submenu, choose Windows Explorer. (If Windows Explorer does not appear on the Accessories menu, click the down arrow at the bottom of the menu to display the entire Accessories menu.). (See Figure B-1 on the next page.)

FIGURE B-1
Starting Windows Explorer

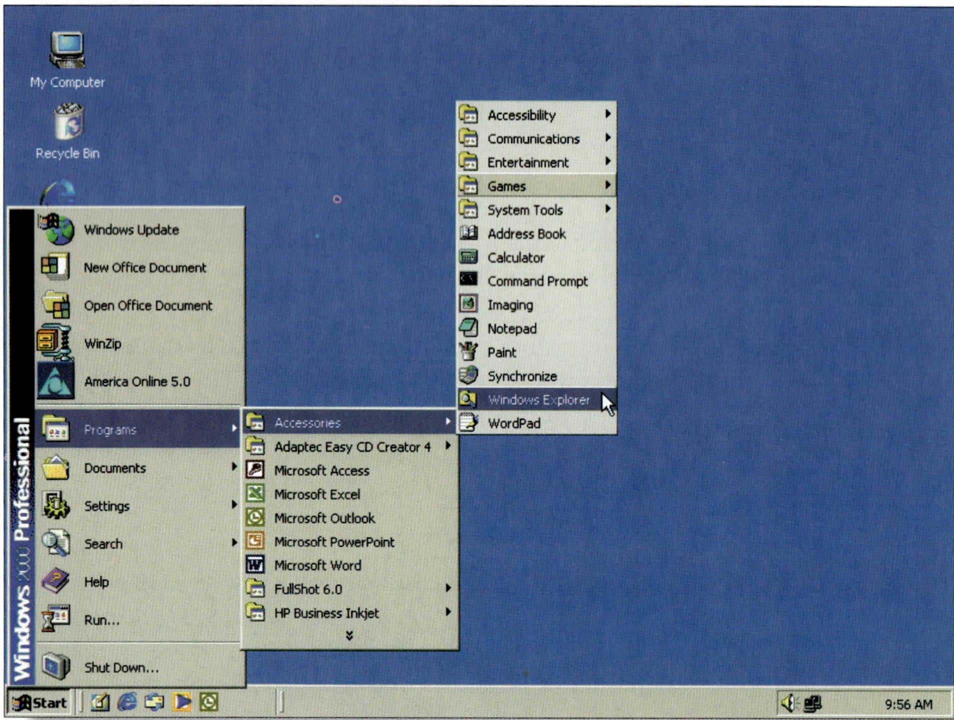

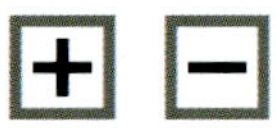

Windows Explorer appears. The window is divided into two panes: The left pane shows the network (if any) and the hierarchy of computers, drives, and folders. The right pane shows the contents of the item you click on the left pane. Various icons are used to represent folders, computers, drives, and networks. Notice the Plus symbols ⊞ and Minus symbols ⊟. These are used to navigate among the drives and folders on your computer.

FIGURE B-2
Windows Explorer

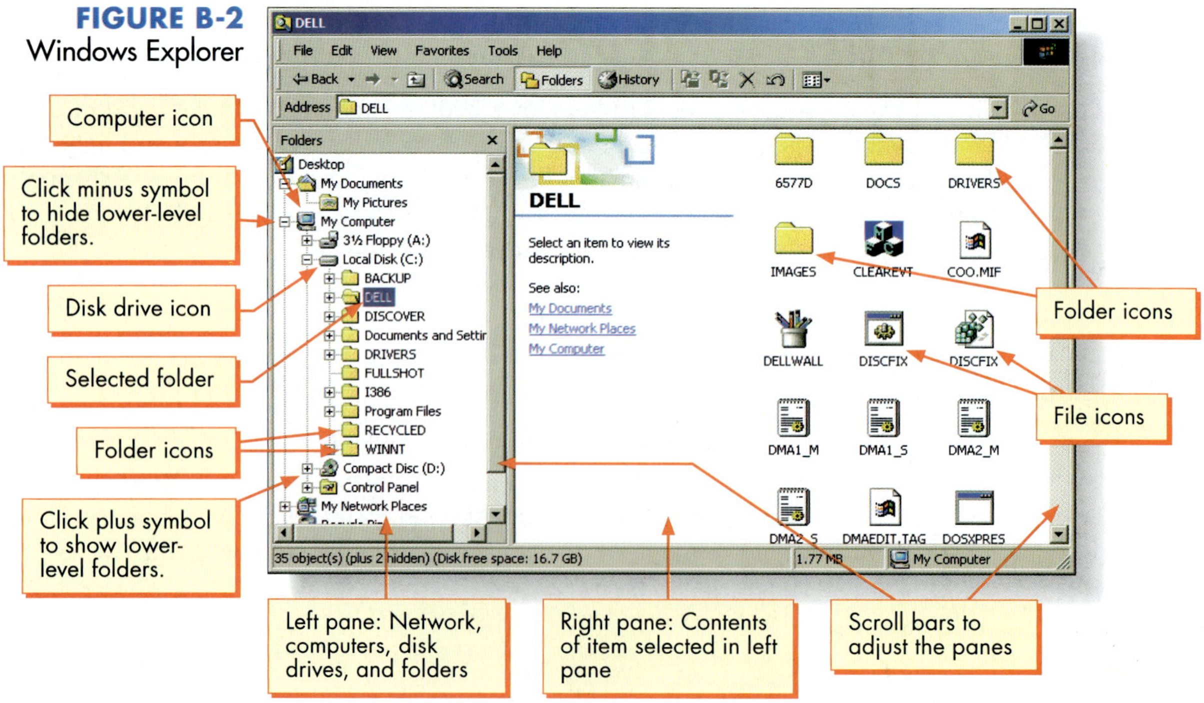

NOTE: The right pane of your Windows Explorer window might look different than the one shown in Figure B-2. Windows Explorer enables you to control the way in which files and folders are displayed in the right pane. The icons might be sized differently, or the contents of the folder might be arranged in a column format, showing details such as file type, date, and size.

Navigating Using Windows Explorer

Practice navigating through your computer's files and folders using the Windows Explorer:

1. Click the Plus symbol ⊞ next to a folder or disk drive icon. The lower-level branches under that folder or drive display.

TIP: Any folder displaying a Plus symbol ⊞ contains one or more folders within that folder.

2. Click the Plus symbol ⊞ next to other folder icons.

   Notice that as you display the branches of the hierarchy, the symbol next to the folder icon changes to a Minus symbol ⊟.

3. Click a Minus symbol ⊟ next to a folder icon. The hierarchy under the folder collapses and the lower-level branches under it are hidden.
4. Click a folder icon. The contents of the folder display.

   Folders selected in the left pane are displayed in the right pane.

5. Use the scroll bars on the right sides of the two panes if the contents of either pane extend beyond the viewing area.

Copying Files and Folders

You can use Windows Explorer to manage files and folders on you computer. Common management tasks include copying files or folders, moving files or folders to new locations, renaming files or folders, deleting unneeded files or folder, and creating new file folders.

To copy a file or folder from one location to another:

1. In the left pane, click the folder icon containing the file you wish to copy. The files within that folder appear in the right pane.

NOTE: You might have to click several folders in the hierarchy to finally display the folder containing the file you wish to copy.

2. Locate the file in the right pane and right-click it. A shortcut menu appears.

TIP: You can select multiple files to copy. When files are adjacent to one another, select the first file, press and hold Shift, and click the last file. All files between the first and last files will be selected for copying. To select nonadjacent files, select the first file, press and hold Ctrl, select the remaining files, and then click.

3. Select Copy from the shortcut menu.
4. In the left pane, locate the folder to which you will copy the file. Right-click the folder icon. A shortcut menu appears.

TIP: Use the Plus symbols ⊞ and the scroll bar to adjust the viewing area if the folder isn't displayed.

5. Choose Paste from the shortcut menu. The file is copied to the new folder. The file is now located in both the original location and the new location.

Copying Files on to Floppy Disks

To transport a file from your school to your home, you will typically need to copy the file onto a floppy disk. To copy a file from your computer to a floppy disk:

1. Insert a floppy disk in your floppy disk drive (typically this is Drive A).
2. In the left pane, click the folder icon containing the file you wish to copy. The files within that folder appear in the right pane.

NOTE: You might have to click several folders in the hierarchy to finally display the folder containing the file you wish to copy.

3. Locate the file in the right pane and right-click it. A shortcut menu appears.

TIP: You can select multiple files to copy to a floppy disk. When files are adjacent to one another, select the first file, press and hold Shift, and click the last file. All files between the first and last files will be selected for copying. To select nonadjacent files, select the first file, press and hold Ctrl, select the remaining files, and then click.

4. Choose Send To from the shortcut menu.
5. Choose 3½ Floppy (A) from the submenu. The file is copied to the disk.

Moving Files and Folders

You can also move file or folders from one location to another. This process is very similar to copying a file to another location. However, rather than choosing Copy from the shortcut menu when you right-click the file, you choose the Cut command.

To move a file or folder from one location to another:

1. In the left pane, click the folder icon containing the file you wish to move. The files within that folder appear in the right pane.

NOTE: You might have to click several folders in the hierarchy to finally display the folder containing the file you wish to move.

2. Locate the file in the right pane and right-click it. A shortcut menu appears.

TIP: You can select multiple files to copy. When files are adjacent to one another, select the first file, press and hold Shift, and click the last file. All files between the first and last files will be selected for copying. To select nonadjacent files, select the first file, press and hold Ctrl, select the remaining files, and then click.

3. Select Cut from the shortcut menu.
4. In the left pane, locate the folder to which you will move the file. Right-click the folder icon. A shortcut menu appears.

TIP: Use the Plus symbols ⊞ and the scroll bar to adjust the viewing area if the folder isn't displayed.

5. Choose Paste from the shortcut menu. The file is moved to the new folder. The file is located in only the new location. It has been moved from the original location.

Files can also be moved using the drag-and-drop method:

1. In the left pane, click the folder icon containing the file you wish to move. The files within that folder appear in the right pane.

NOTE: You might have to click several folders in the hierarchy to finally display the folder containing the file you wish to move.

2. Locate the file in the right pane and select it.
3. Hold down the left mouse button and drag the file to the left pane. Position the pointer over the desired folder. The folder icon is highlighted.

TIP: If the folder contains lower-level branches and your target location is within a lower level, the lower level will automatically display after a few moments. You can move the pointer near the top or bottom edge of the pane to scroll if the desired folder doesn't appear on-screen.

4. Release the mouse button when the desired folder is highlighted. The file is moved from the original location into the highlighted folder.

NOTE: You can only move a file from one location to another on the same disk when using the drag-and-drop method. If the target location is a different disk, a copy is made. You can also use the drag-and-drop method to copy a file by pressing Ctrl and holding down the left mouse button when selecting the file to copy.

Deleting Files and Folders

When you delete a file or folder, it is placed in the Recycle Bin. To delete a file or folder:

1. Locate the file or folder. A folder can be located in the left or right pane. A file will always be in the right pane.
2. Right-click the file or folder.
3. Choose Delete from the shortcut menu.

TIP: If you mistakenly delete a file or folder (and you haven't emptied the Recycle Bin), you can restore it by clicking the Recycle Bin to open it, right-clicking the item you want to restore, and choosing Restore from the shortcut menu.

Renaming Files and Folders

A common file management task is renaming files and folder. Often companies develop a unique naming structure for their files.

1. Locate the file or folder and right-click it. A shortcut menu appears.
2. Choose Rename from the shortcut menu.
3. Key the new name. Delete the old filename.
4. Press Enter to complete the process.

Creating New Folders

Creating folders is a necessary part of file management. They are like folders in a file cabinet. Some people like to use many folders, with a few items in each one. Others use fewer folders with many files in each. You will develop your own system, but try to be consistent in your folder structure. Consistency makes it easier to locate files easily.

To create a new folder:

1. Select (highlight) the disk or folder in the left pane where you want to locate the new folder.
2. Choose File from the menu bar.
3. Choose New from the File menu.
4. Choose Folder from the submenu. The folder is created in the folder or disk you selected. You can now rename the folder.

APPENDIX C

Speech Recognition

The *speech recognition* feature in Microsoft Office enables you to dictate text into any Office program. You also can use your voice to select menu commands, toolbar buttons, dialog box selections, and task pane items. The speech recognition feature is not intended for completely hands-free operation. It is best used in combination with the mouse or keyboard.

To use speech recognition, your computer must be equipped with the following:

- A high-quality close-talk (headset) microphone with gain adjustment. (You use gain adjustment to make your input louder for use by the system.)
- A 400 megahertz or faster computer.
- 128 MB or more of memory.
- Windows 98 or later or Windows NT 4.0 or later.
- Microsoft Internet Explorer 5 or later.

Installing the Speech Recognition Feature

The speech recognition feature is installed in Word (typically by performing a custom installation). To install the speech recognition in Word:

1. Start Word.
2. Choose Tools from the menu, and then choose Speech. (You might need to click the down arrow at the bottom of the Tools menu to display the entire menu.) You'll be asked if you wish to install the feature.
3. Click Yes. After the feature is installed, it is available in the Tools menu in all Office programs.

NOTE: Installation requires the Office XP CD-ROM.

Speech Training

You increase speech recognition accuracy by training the computer to recognize how you speak. You are offered training when the speech recognition feature is first installed. You also can train the computer at any time after installation.

Speech training helps the computer learn to recognize how you speak. You train the computer by reading text out loud. Microsoft Office listens to your voice and creates a speech recognition user profile. A *user profile* is information created and stored by the speech recognition training program that the computer uses in recognizing your unique voice. After you've created the profile and have completed the initial training, you can improve the computer's accuracy by completing additional voice training sessions. There are eight different voice training sessions. The more training sessions you complete, the more accurate the computer will be in recognizing your voice.

Microsoft Office lets you create multiple speech recognition user profiles. This is particularly useful when more than one individual uses the speech recognition feature on a single computer.

To create your user profile and begin speech recognition training, complete the following steps:

1. Press the Start button.
2. On the Start menu, choose Settings, and then choose Control Panel. The Control Panel appears.

3. Double-click the Speech icon. The Speech Properties dialog box appears. One or more Recognition Profiles might already be listed. You now will create your own profile.

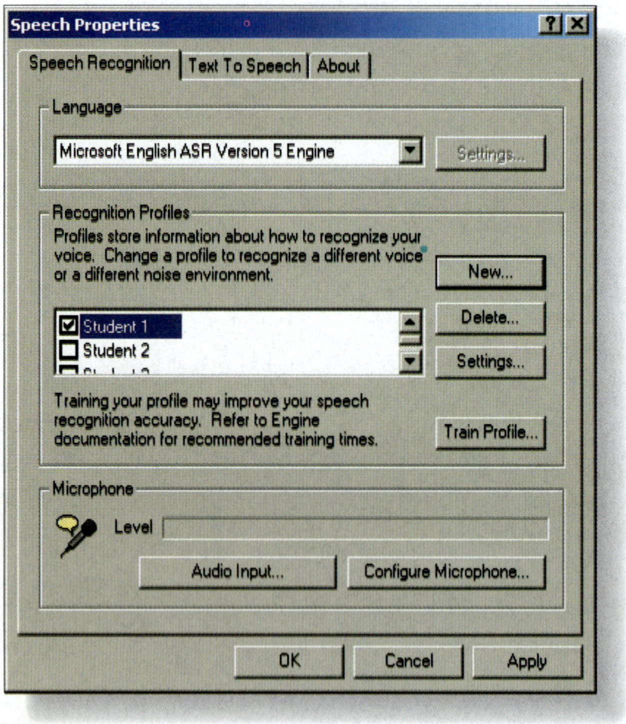

FIGURE C-1 Speech Properties dialog box

NOTE: You can also access the Speech Properties dialog box by clicking the Tools button on the Language toolbar and then choosing Options from the menu.

4. Click New. The Profile Wizard dialog box appears.

5. In the **Profile** text box, key ***[your name]*** and then click **Finish**. The Speech Properties dialog box reappears. Your profile is added to the list of available profiles.
6. Make sure your profile is the currently selected profile shown under **Recognition Profiles**. This means your profile is the profile the computer will use when speech recognition is activated in any Microsoft Office program.

NOTE: To begin voice training, you could have clicked Next instead of Finish in the Profile Wizard dialog box. However, Office requires users with new profiles to complete voice training the first time they activate speech recognition, even if they have already completed training in the Profile Wizard dialog box. You will be prompted to begin voice training the first time you use the speech recognition feature in any Office program.

7. Click **OK** to close the Speech Properties dialog box, and then close the Control Panel.
8. Click the Start button on the Windows taskbar. Choose **Programs** on the Start menu, and then choose **Microsoft Word**. (You can open any Office program in which you want to use speech recognition; in this exercise, you will use Word.) When Word opens, the Language bar is displayed automatically.

TIP: If the speech recognition feature has been installed and the Language bar does not appear in the Office programs, its display has been turned off. To redisplay the Language bar, click the Start button on the Windows taskbar, choose Settings from the Start menu, and then choose Control Panel. On the Control Panel, double-click the Text Services icon, and then click Language Bar. Select Show the Language bar on the desktop.

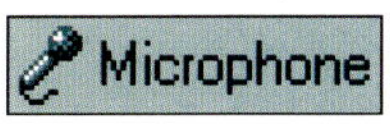

9. Click the Microphone button on the Language toolbar to activate speech recognition training. The Welcome to Office Speech Recognition dialog box appears.

NOTE: If the Welcome to Office Speech Recognition dialog box does not appear when you click the Microphone button, you need to make sure Office considers you the current user and is using your profile. Click the Tools button on the Language toolbar, choose Current User, and then select your profile. Now when you click the Microphone button, you will activate the speech recognition training.

10. Click **Next** to begin the Office Speech Recognition training. There are two parts to the training: microphone training and voice training. The Microphone Wizard dialog box appears first. This wizard helps you adjust your microphone for the best results in speech recognition.

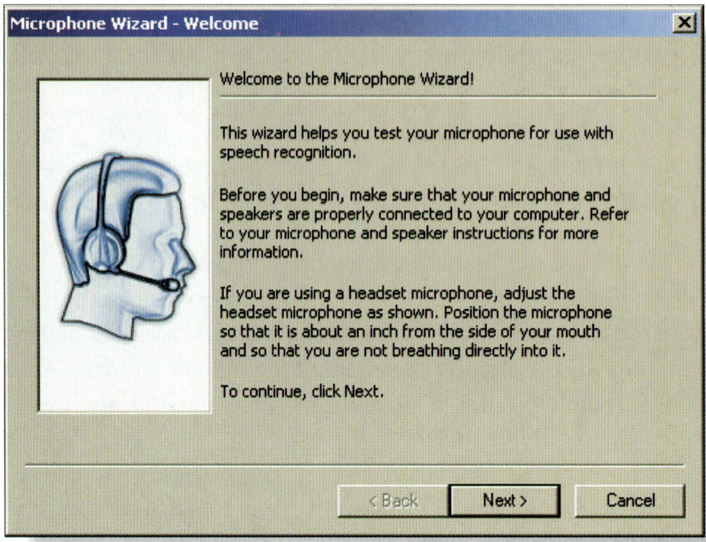

FIGURE C-2
Microphone Wizard

11. Click **Next** and complete the Microphone Wizard. When you click **Finish** at the last Microphone Wizard screen, the Voice Training dialog box for the Microsoft Speech Recognition Training Wizard appears. This wizard trains the computer to recognize your voice.

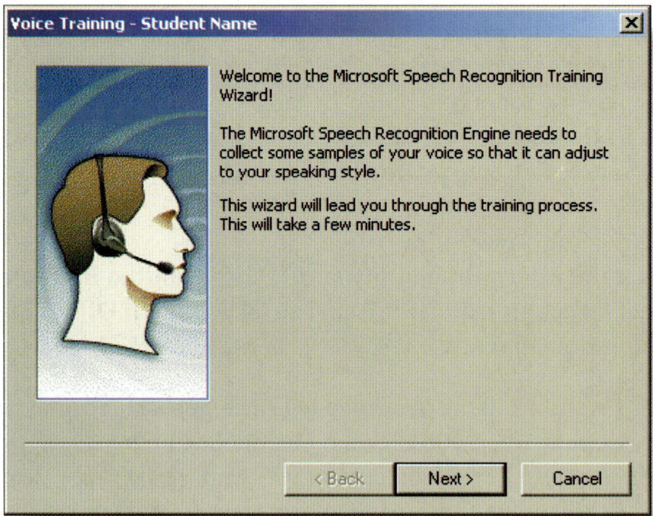

FIGURE C-3
Voice Training

12. Click **Next** to begin the voice training. You'll first be asked some questions about your gender and age, and then you'll read some text out loud.
13. When you complete the voice training, click **Finish**. A short video follows that demonstrates the use of the speech recognition feature. To improve the computer's accuracy in recognizing your speech, it is recommended that you conduct additional training sessions.

NOTE: The video that follows the voice training requires the Flash Player plug-in to run. This is a free program by Macromedia that is used to play movies. If this program is not already installed on your computer, your browser might automatically connect you to the Macromedia Web site. You'll be prompted to begin downloading the plug-in. The video appears only once, after you complete your first speech recognition voice training session.

14. To conduct additional training sessions, click the Tools button on the Language bar, and then choose Training. The Voice Training dialog box appears. Notice that there are eight different sessions. Each contains different material for you to read aloud. You can perform sessions more than once. After you have used speech recognition, you might wish to do more training.

FIGURE C-4
Voice Training, additional sessions

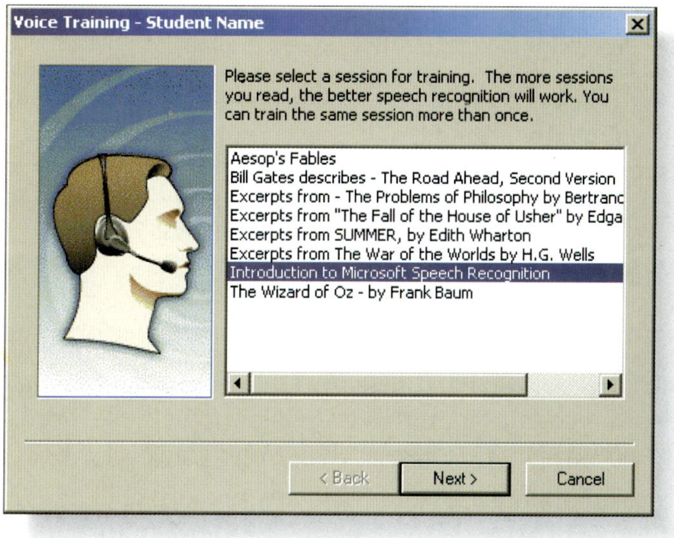

15. Click Cancel to close the Voice Training dialog box, and close Word.

Beginning Speech Recognition: Dictation Mode

After the speech recognition feature is installed and you have completed your initial training, you can use it in any Microsoft Office program. There are two modes of speech recognition:

- *Dictation mode* lets you dictate text into any Office program. For example, you can use the Dictation mode to dictate a Word document or an Outlook e-mail message.
- The *Voice Command mode* lets you select menu commands, toolbar buttons, dialog box options, and task pane items by using your voice.

Speech recognition commands are activated by using the buttons on the Language toolbar. The Language toolbar is displayed automatically in all Office programs if the speech recognition feature has been installed. Table C-1 describes each of the buttons on the Language toolbar.

TABLE C-1 Language Toolbar

BUTTON	PURPOSE
Correction	Presents correction options for selected text. (Not present in applications where there is no text entry.)
Microphone	Turns the microphone on and off.
Dictation	Turns on the Dictation mode so the words you speak are turned into text.
Voice Command	Turns on the Voice Command mode so you can select menu, toolbar, dialog box, and task pane items using your voice.
Tools	Displays a drop-down menu for various options, including selecting the current user profile and performing additional voice training.

To begin using the speech recognition feature, perform the following steps:

1. Start Word. (You can open any Office program in which you want to use speech recognition; in this exercise, you will use Word.) When Word opens, the Language bar is displayed automatically.
2. If the microphone is not already turned off, click the Microphone button Microphone on the Language toolbar to turn it off.
3. Click the Tools button Tools on the Language toolbar, and then choose Current User. Select your profile if it is not already selected.

NOTE: Make sure the computer is using your voice profile before you begin using speech recognition.

4. Position your microphone.
5. Click the Microphone button Microphone. The microphone is activated, and the Language toolbar expands.
6. Click the Dictation button Dictation on the Language toolbar or say *"Dictation."* You are now in the Dictation mode.
7. Say *"I am now using Microsoft Office speech recognition."* As you speak, the computer displays a blue bar for text it is processing. The words appear when processing is completed.

FIGURE C-5
Speech recognition processing spoken text in Dictation mode

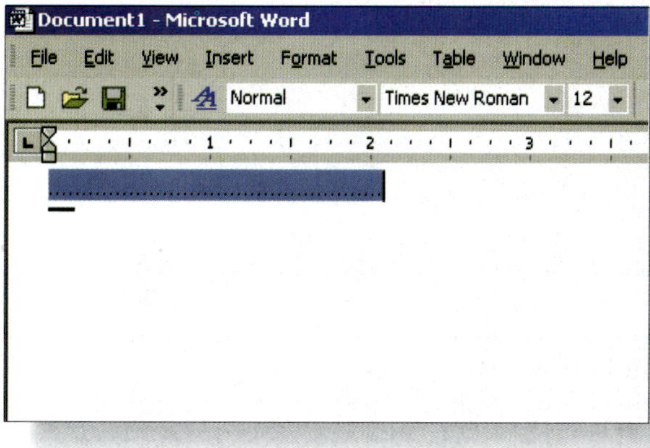

8. Say *"Period."* The computer places a period at the end of the sentence and adds a space for the next sentence.

Correcting Mistakes

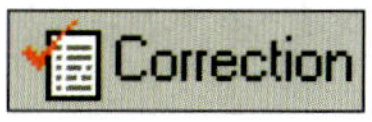

Mistakes can be corrected in several ways:

- You can place the insertion point on the incorrect word and click the Correction button 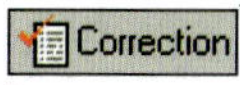 on the Language toolbar. You'll be shown a list of correction alternatives.
- You can select the incorrect word or phrase and dictate the correct text.
- You can key over errors by using the mouse or keyboard. In Dictation mode, you can select the text, say *"Spelling mode,"* pause slightly, and then spell the correction.

The computer recognizes many common punctuation and keyboard symbols. For example, "semicolon," "question mark," and "open parenthesis" all generate the appropriate characters in Dictation mode.

1. Say *"As I speak, comma, the words I speak appear on the screen. Period."* The computer places a comma after the first phrase and a period at the end of the sentence, and the first letter in the sentence is capitalized.

2. If the computer has made any mistakes in the text you dictated in the previous step, try using some of the techniques just described to correct them.

Using Voice Command Mode

In Voice Command mode, you can activate menus, toolbar buttons, dialog box and task pane items, and certain keystrokes. Table C-2 provides some other useful voice commands.

TABLE C-2 **Useful Voice Commands**

COMMAND	RESULT
Say *"spelling mode"*	In Dictation mode, lets you spell a word.
Say *"new line"*	In Dictation mode, inserts a line break and places the insertion point at the beginning of the new line.
Say *"force num"*	In Dictation mode, lets you dictate all numbers as digits.
Say *"new paragraph"*	In Dictation mode, inserts a new paragraph and places the insertion point at the beginning of the new paragraph.
Say *"expand"*	In Voice Command mode, displays an entire menu when all commands on a menu are not visible.
Say *"escape"*	In Voice Command mode, cancels a menu.

1. Say "*Voice Command.*" The computer is now in Voice Command mode.

NOTE: You can switch between Dictation mode and Voice Command mode by saying *"Dictation"* or *"Voice Command."*

2. Say "*Return.*" The computer places a Return (Enter) after the sentence. The insertion point is now on the next line.
3. Say "*Backspace.*" The computer backspaces to the end of the sentence.
4. Use the mouse to select "speech recognition" in the first sentence.
5. Say "*Italic.*" The selected text is italicized. In Voice Command mode, you can activate toolbar buttons.
6. Move the insertion point to the end of the second sentence.
7. Say "*Return.*" The computer places a Return after the sentence.
8. Say "*Return.*" The computer moves the insertion point down another line.
9. Click the Dictation button [Dictation] or say "*Dictation.*" The computer switches back to Dictation mode.
10. Say "*Speech recognition is a powerful tool. Period.*"

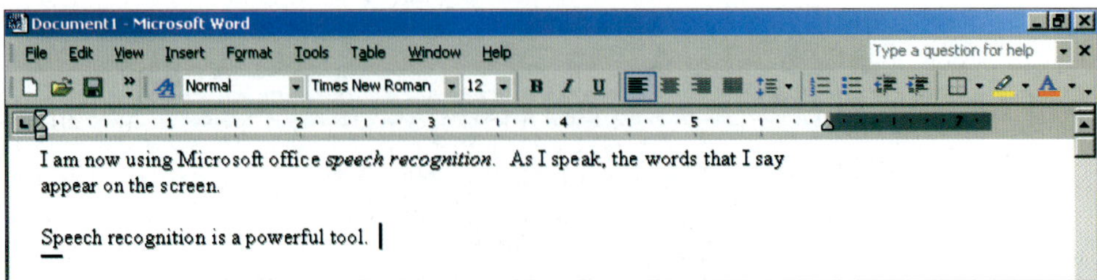

FIGURE C-6 Text dictated into a Word document

11. Click the Voice Command button [Voice Command] or say "*Voice Command.*"

12. Say *"File."* The File menu displays. You can activate menu commands in Voice Command mode.
13. Say *"Print."* The Print command on the File menu is selected, and the Print dialog box displays.
14. Say *"OK."* The document prints. You can make dialog box selections by using your voice in the Voice Command mode.
15. Click the Microphone button Microphone or say *"Microphone"* to turn off the microphone. It is good practice to turn off the microphone when it's not in use.
16. Close Word without saving the document.

NOTE: If you find the computer making a significant number of mistakes, make sure your microphone is adjusted correctly. You can also improve the computer's accuracy by completing more training sessions.

APPENDIX D

Proofreaders' Marks

PROOFREADERS' MARK		DRAFT	FINAL COPY
¶	Start a new paragraph	ridiculous! ¶If that is so	ridiculous! If that is so
⁀‿	Delete space	to gether	together
# ^	Insert space	Itmay be	It may not be
	Move as shown	it is not true	it is true
∿	Transpose	beleivable	believable
		is it so	it is so
○	Spell out	2 years ago	two years ago
		16 Elm St.	16 Elm Street
^	Insert a word	How much it? (is)	How much is it?
OR	Delete a word	it may not be true	it may be true
^ OR	Insert a letter	temperture (a)	temperature
OR	Delete a letter and close up	committment to buny	commitment to buy
OR	Change a word	and if you won't (but, can't)	but if you can't
Stet	Stet (don't delete)	I was very glad (Stet)	I was very glad
/	Make letter lowercase	Federal Government	federal government
≡	Capitalize	Janet L. greyston	Janet L. Greyston
˅	Raise above the line	in her new book*	in her new book*
^	Drop below the line	H2SO4	H_2SO_4

PROOFREADERS' MARK		DRAFT	FINAL COPY
⊙	Insert a period	Mr⊙Henry Grenada	Mr. Henry Grenada
^	Insert a comma	a large,old house	a large, old house
∨	Insert an apostrophe	my childrens car	my children's car
∨∨	Insert quotation marks	he wants a loan	he wants a "loan"
= OR =^	Insert a hyphen	a first=rate job	a first-rate job
		ask the coowner	ask the co-owner
M	Insert an em-dash	Here it is cash!	Here it is—cash!
N	Insert an en-dash	Pages 1 5	Pages 1–5
___	Insert underscore	an issue of Time	an issue of Time
(ital) ___	Set in italic	(ital) The New York Times	*The New York Times*
(bf) ~~~	Set in boldface	(bf) the Enter key	the **Enter** key
(rom) ___	Set in roman	(rom) the *most* likely	the most likely
{ }	Insert parentheses	left today May 3	left today (May 3)
⊐	Move to the right	$38,367,000 ⊐	$38,367,000
⊏	Move to the left	⊏ Anyone can win!	Anyone can win!
ss [	Single-space	ss [I have heard he is leaving	I have heard he is leaving
ds [	Double-space	ds [When will you have a decision?	When will you have a decision?
(+ 1 line)	Insert 1 line space	Percent of Change 16.25 (+ 1 line)	Percent of Change 16.25
(– 1 line)	Delete (remove) 1 line space	Northeastern (– 1 line) regional sales	Northeastern regional sales

APPENDIX E

MOUS Certification

Part 1: MOUS Activities Related to Lessons

TABLE E-1

Word 2002: Core MOUS Activities Related to Lessons

CODE	ACTIVITY	LESSON
W2002-1	**Inserting and Modifying Text**	
W2002 1-1	Insert, modify and move text and symbols	1, 2, 4, 6
W2002 1-2	Apply and modify text formats	3
W2002 1-3	Correct spelling and grammar usage	1, 6
W2002 1-4	Apply font and text effects	3
W2002 1-5	Enter and format Date and Time	7
W2002 1-6	Apply character styles	3
W2002 2	**Creating and Modifying Paragraphs**	
W2002 2-1	Modify paragraph formats	4
W2002 2-2	Set and modify tabs	5
W2002 2-3	Apply bullet, outline, and numbering format to paragraphs	4
W2002 2-4	Apply paragraph styles	4
W2002 3	**Formatting Documents**	
W2002 3-1	Create and modify a header and footer	8
W2002 3-2	Apply and modify column settings	10
W2002 3-3	Modify document layout and Page Setup options	7, 8
W2002 3-4	Create and modify tables	9
W2002 3-5	Preview and Print documents, envelopes, and labels	7
W2002 4	**Managing Documents**	
W2002 4-1	Manage files and folders for documents	2
W2002 4-2	Create documents using templates	7
W2002 4-3	Save documents using different names and file formats	1, 2
W2002 5	**Working with Graphics**	
W2002 5-1	Insert images and graphics	11
W2002 5-2	Create and modify diagrams and charts	11
W2002 6	**Workgroup Collaboration**	
W2002 6-1	Compare and Merge documents	12
W2002 6-2	Insert, view and edit comments	12
W2002 6-3	Convert documents into Web pages	12

TABLE E-2

Excel 2002: Core MOUS Activities Related to Lessons

CODE	ACTIVITY	LESSON
Ex2002 1	**Working with Cells and Cell Data**	
Ex2002 1-1	Insert, delete and move cells	4
Ex2002 1-2	Enter and edit cell data including text, numbers, and formulas	1, 2, 3, 4, 5, 7, 10
Ex2002 1-3	Check spelling	3
Ex2002 1-4	Find and replace cell data and formats	1, 3
Ex2002 1-5	Work with a subset of data by filtering lists	10
Ex2002 2	**Managing Workbooks**	
Ex2002 2-1	Manage workbook files and folders	1
Ex2002 2-2	Create workbooks using templates	5
Ex2002 2-3	Save workbooks using different names and file formats	1, 7
Ex2002 3	**Formatting and Printing Worksheets**	
Ex2002 3-1	Apply and modify cell formats	2, 4, 5, 6, 7, 10
Ex2002 3-2	Modify row and column settings	4
Ex2002 3-3	Modify row and column formats	2, 4
Ex2002 3-4	Apply styles	6
Ex2002 3-5	Use automated tools to format worksheets	3
Ex2002 3-6	Modify Page Setup options for worksheets	3, 5, 6, 9
Ex2002 3-7	Preview and print worksheets and workbooks	1, 3, 5, 8, 10
Ex2002 4	**Modifying Workbooks**	
Ex2002 4-1	Insert and delete worksheets	4, 10
Ex2002 4-2	Modify worksheet names and positions	1, 2, 10
Ex2002 4-3	Use 3-D references	10
Ex2002 5	**Creating and Revising Formulas**	
Ex2002 5-1	Create and revise formulas	2, 5
Ex2002 5-2	Use statistical, date and time, financial, and logical functions in formulas	2, 5, 6, 7
Ex2002 6	**Creating and Modifying Graphics**	
Ex2002 6-1	Create, modify, position and print charts	8
Ex2002 6-2	Create, modify and position graphics	9
Ex2002 7	**Workgroup Collaboration**	
Ex2002 7-1	Convert worksheets into web pages	9
Ex2002 7-2	Create hyperlinks	7
Ex2002 7-3	View and edit comments	9

TABLE E-3

PowerPoint 2002: Comprehensive MOUS Activities Related to Lessons

CODE	ACTIVITY	LESSON
PP2002 1	**Creating Presentations**	
PP2002 1-1	Create presentations (manually and using automated tools)	1, 2, 3, 4
PP2002 1-2	Add slides to and delete slides from presentations	2, 3, 4
PP2002 1-3	Modify headers and footers in the slide master	2
PP2002 2	**Inserting and Modifying Text**	
PP2002 2-1	Import text from Word	4
PP2002 2-2	Insert, format, and modify text	1, 2, 3, 4, 5, 6
PP2002 3	**Inserting and Modifying Visual Elements**	
PP2002 3-1	Add tables, charts, clip art, and bitmap images to slides	5, 6
PP2002 3-2	Customize slide backgrounds	6
PP2002 3-3	Add Office art elements to slides	6, 7, 8
PP2002 3-4	Apply custom formats to tables	➡
PP2002 4	**Modifying Presentation Formats**	
PP2002 4-1	Apply formats to presentations	3, 5, 7
PP2002 4-2	Apply animation schemes	2
PP2002 4-3	Apply slide transitions	2
PP2002 4-4	Customize slide formats	3, 4, 5, 7
PP2002 4-5	Customize slide templates	➡
PP2002 4-6	Manage a slide master	➡
PP2002 4-7	Rehearse timing	➡
PP2002 4-8	Rearrange slides	2, 3, 4
PP2002 4-9	Modify slide layout	5
PP2002 4-10	Add links to a presentation	4
PP2002 5	**Printing Presentations**	
PP2002 5-1	Preview and print slides, outlines, handouts, and speaker notes	1, 2, 3, 4
PP2002 6	**Working with Data from Other Sources**	
PP2002 6-1	Import Excel charts to slides	➡
PP2002 6-2	Add sound and video to slides	➡
PP2002 6-3	Insert Word tables on slides	➡
PP2002 6-4	Export a presentation as an outline	4
PP2002 7	**Managing and Delivering Presentations**	
PP2002 7-1	Set up slide shows	➡
PP2002 7-2	Deliver presentations	1

➡ This activity is covered in the companion Office 2002 Expert text.

continues

TABLE E-3 *continued*

PowerPoint 2002: Comprehensive MOUS Activities Related to Lessons

CODE	ACTIVITY	LESSON
PP2002 7	**Managing and Delivering Presentations** ***continued***	
PP2002 7-3	Manage files and folders for presentations	1
PP2002 7-4	Work with embedded fonts	➡
PP2002 7-5	Publish presentations to the Web	➡
PP2002 7-6	Use Pack and Go	➡
PP2002 8	**Workgroup Collaboration**	
PP2002 8-1	Set up a review cycle	➡
PP2002 8-2	Review presentation comments	➡
PP2002 8-3	Schedule and deliver presentation broadcasts	➡
PP2002 8-4	Publish presentations to the Web	4

➡ This activity is covered in the companion Office 2002 Expert text.

TABLE E-4

Access 2002: Core MOUS Activities Related to Lessons

CODE	ACTIVITY	LESSON
Ac2002 1	**Creating and Using Databases**	**Lessons**
Ac2002 1-1	Create Access databases	1, 4
Ac2002 1-2	Open database objects in multiple views	1, 2
Ac2002 1-3	Move among records	1, 2
Ac2002 1-4	Format datasheets	1
Ac2002 2	**Creating and Modifying Tables**	
Ac2002 2-1	Create and modify tables	1, 2, 3, 4, 5
Ac2002 2-2	Add a pre-defined input mask to a field	5
Ac2002 2-3	Create Lookup fields	5
Ac2002 2-4	Modify field properties	4, 5
Ac2002 3	**Creating and Modifying Queries**	
Ac2002 3-1	Create and modify Select queries	1, 2, 3, 6
Ac2002 3-2	Add calculated fields to Select queries	6
Ac2002 4	**Creating and Modifying Forms**	
Ac2002 4-1	Create and display forms	2, 6
Ac2002 4-2	Modify form properties	6
Ac2002 5	**Viewing and Organizing Information**	
Ac2002 5-1	Enter, edit, and delete records	2, 4
Ac2002 5-2	Create queries	3

continues

TABLE E-4

Access 2002: Core MOUS Activities Related to Lessons *continued*

CODE	ACTIVITY	LESSON
Ac2002 5	**Viewing and Organizing Information** ***continued***	
Ac2002 5-3	Sort records	3
Ac2002 5-4	Filter records	3
Ac2002 6	**Defining Relationships**	
Ac2002 6-1	Create one-to-many relationships	5
Ac2002 6-2	Enforce referential integrity	5
Ac2002 7	**Producing Reports**	
Ac2002 7-1	Create and format reports	7
Ac2002 7-2	Add calculated controls to reports	7
Ac2002 7-3	Preview and print reports	7
Ac2002 8	**Integrating with Other Applications**	
Ac2002 8-1	Import data to Access	4
Ac2002 8-2	Export data from Access	7
Ac2002 8-3	Create a simple data access page	6

Part 2: Lessons Related to MOUS Activities*

TABLE E-5

Word 2002: Lessons Related to Core MOUS Activities

LESSON	CODES
1 Creating a Document	1-1, 1-3, 4-3
2 Selecting and Editing Text	1-1, 4-1, 4-3
3 Formatting Characters	1-2, 1-4, 1-6
4 Formatting Paragraphs	1-1, 2-1, 2-3, 2-4
5 Tabs and Tabbed Columns	2-2
6 Writing and Editing Tools	1-1, 1-3
7 Margins, Templates, and Printing Options	1-5, 3-3, 3-5, 4-2
8 Page and Section Breaks, Headers and Footers	3-1, 3-3
9 Tables	3-4
10 Columns	3-2
11 Graphics and Charts	5-1, 5-2
12 Sharing Your Work	6-1, 6-2, 6-3

*MOUS Activity codes are abbreviated in the tables in this part.

For more information about the Microsoft Office User Specialist (MOUS) program, go to www.mous.net.

TABLE E-6

Excel 2002: Lessons Related to Core MOUS Activities

LESSON	CODES
1 Getting Started with Excel	1-2, 1-4, 2-1, 2-3, 3-7, 4-2
2 Creating a Workbook	1-2, 3-1, 3-3, 4-2, 5-1, 5-2
3 Using Editing and Formatting Tools	1-2, 1-3, 1-4, 3-5, 3-6, 3-7
4 Working with Cells, Columns, Rows, and Sheets	1-1, 1-2, 3-1, 3-2, 3-3, 4-1
5 Using Simple Formulas and Functions	1-2, 2-2, 3-1, 3-6, 3-7, 5-1, 5-2
6 Using Logical and Financial Functions	3-1, 3-4, 3-6, 5-2
7 Using Advanced Functions and Hyperlinks	1-2, 2-3, 3-1, 5-2, 7-2
8 Building Charts	3-7, 6-1
9 Adding Design Elements	3-6, 6-2, 7-1, 7-3
10 Working with Multiple Worksheets and Lists	1-2, 1-5, 3-1, 3-7, 4-1, 4-2, 4-3

TABLE E-7

PowerPoint 2002: Lessons Related to Comprehensive MOUS Activities

LESSON	CODES
1 What is PowerPoint?	1-1, 2-2, 5-1, 7-2, 7-3
2 Basic Presentation Tools	1-1, 1-2, 1-3, 2-2, 4-2, 4-3, 4-8, 5-1
3 Creating a Presentation from Scratch	1-1, 1-2, 2-2, 4-1, 4-4, 4-8, 5-1
4 Outlines, Hyperlinks, and HTML	1-1, 1-2, 2-1, 2-2, 4-4, 4-8, 4-10, 5-1, 6-4, 8-4
5 Working with Text	2-2, 3-1, 4-1, 4-4, 4-9
6 Working with PowerPoint Objects	2-2, 3-1, 3-2, 3-3
7 Working with Lines, Fills, and Colors	3-3, 4-1, 4-4
8 Manipulating PowerPoint Objects	3-3

TABLE E-8

Access 2002: Lessons Related to Core MOUS Activities

LESSON	CODES
1 Getting Started with a Database	1-1, 1-2, 1-3, 1-4, 2-1, 3-1
2 Adding and Editing Data	1-2, 1-3, 2-1, 3-1, 4-1, 5-1
3 Finding and Sorting Records	2-1, 3-1, 3-19, 3-21, 5-3, 5-4
4 Creating Databases and Tables	1-1, 2-1, 2-4, 5-1, 8-1
5 Managing Data Integrity	2-1, 2-2, 2-3, 2-4, 6-1, 6-2
6 Adding Forms to a Database	3-1, 4-1, 4-2, 6-14, 6-21
7 Adding Reports to a Database	7-1, 7-2, 7-3, 8-2

APPENDIX F

Standard Forms for Business Documents

Reference manuals, such as *The Gregg Reference Manual,* provide a variety of letter and memorandum styles, as well as styles for reports and other documents. Many businesses also have their own styles for documents. This Appendix includes two basic styles—for a business letter and a memorandum. It also shows the most common format for a continuation page (used for either letters or memos).

TABLE F-1 Parts of a Letter

PART OF LETTER	LOCATION/DESCRIPTION
Heading	
Letterhead or return address	Often appears on pre-printed stationery; can also be created in Word. Includes the company name, address, and other contact information.
Date line	Two inches from the top of the page on letterhead stationery or on the third line below a Word letterhead. Use date format shown in Figure F-1.
Opening	
Inside address	Starts on the fourth line below the date; consists of name and address (and possibly company name and job title) of person to whom you are writing.
Salutation	On the second line below the inside address; typically includes a courtesy title (Mr., Mrs., Ms., Miss) and ends with a colon.
Body	
Message	Content of the letter, single-spaced with one blank line between paragraphs.
Closing	
Complimentary closing	On the second line below the last line of the body of the letter. Common closings are "Sincerely" or "Sincerely yours" followed by a comma.
Writer's identification	On the fourth line below the closing, to leave space for a signature; includes the writer's name and job title (and sometimes the department).
Reference initials	On the second line below the writer's name and title; consists of the typist's initials in small letters.
Enclosure notation	On new line below the reference initials if letter has an enclosure. Specify the number of enclosures. Can also use "Attachment" if enclosure is attached.
Optional features	*Filename notation*—indicates document name for reference purposes; *delivery notation*—method of delivery (other than regular mail); *copy notation*—people who will receive copies of the letter (usually begins with "c:" or "cc:")

FIGURE F-1
Business letter style

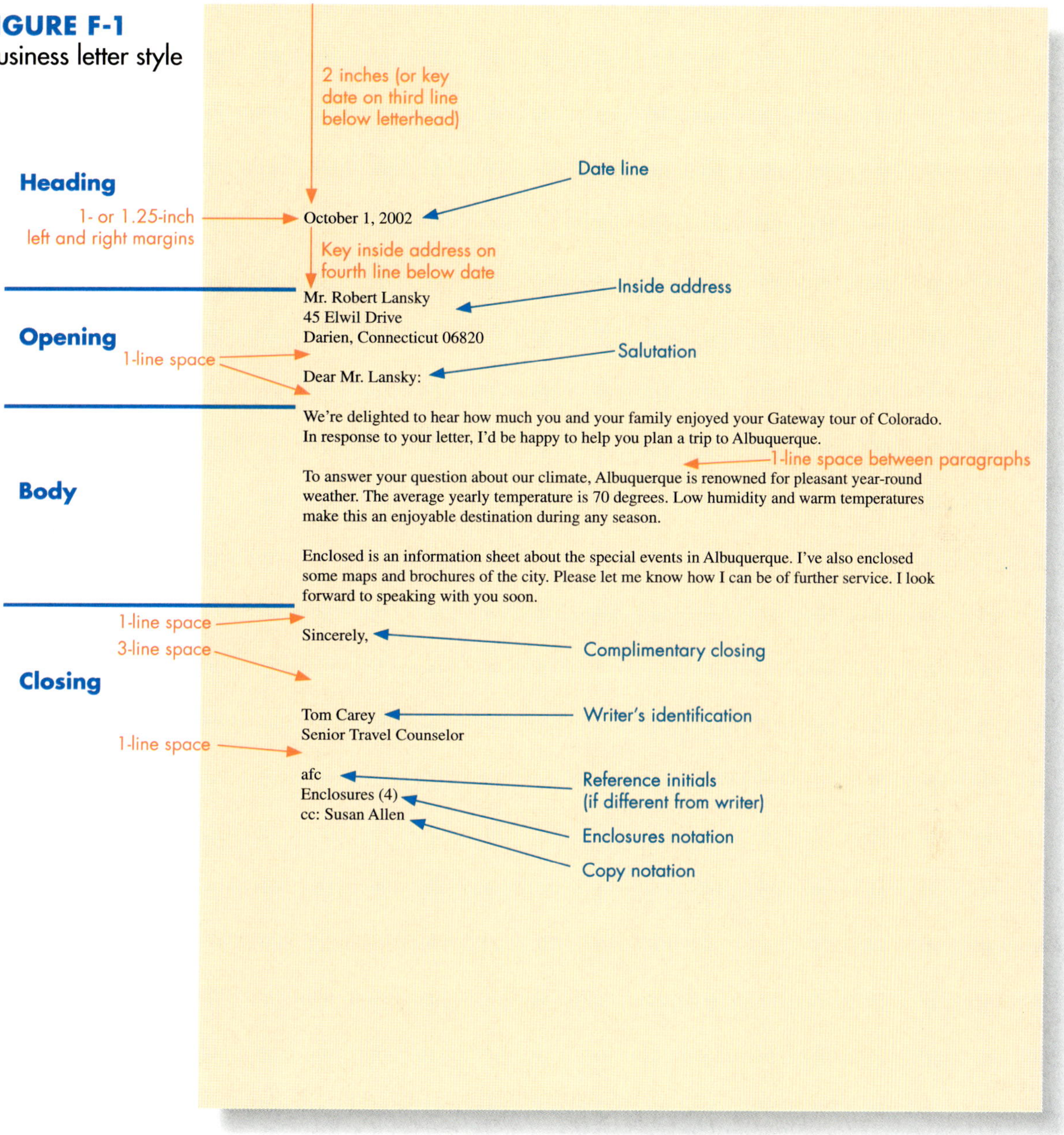

FIGURE F-2
Continuation page header for 2-page (or longer) letter or memo

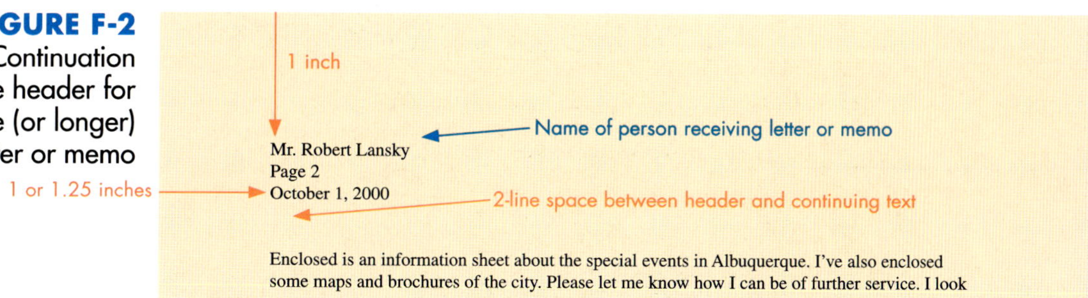

TABLE F-2 Parts of a Memo

PART OF MEMO	LOCATION/DESCRIPTION
Heading	Starts two inches from top of page using plain paper or letterhead stationery or on third line below Word letterhead. Consists of guide words ("MEMO TO," "FROM," "DATE," and "SUBJECT") in capital letters followed by a colon. Entries after guide words align at a 1-inch left tab setting. Use date format shown in Figure F-3.
Body	Starts on the third line below the memo heading; contains the message, single-spaced with one blank line between paragraphs.
Closing	On the second line below the last paragraph; includes reference initials (the typist's initials in small letters). Might also include an enclosure notation, a file name notation, and a copy notation or distribution list.

FIGURE F-3
Memorandum style

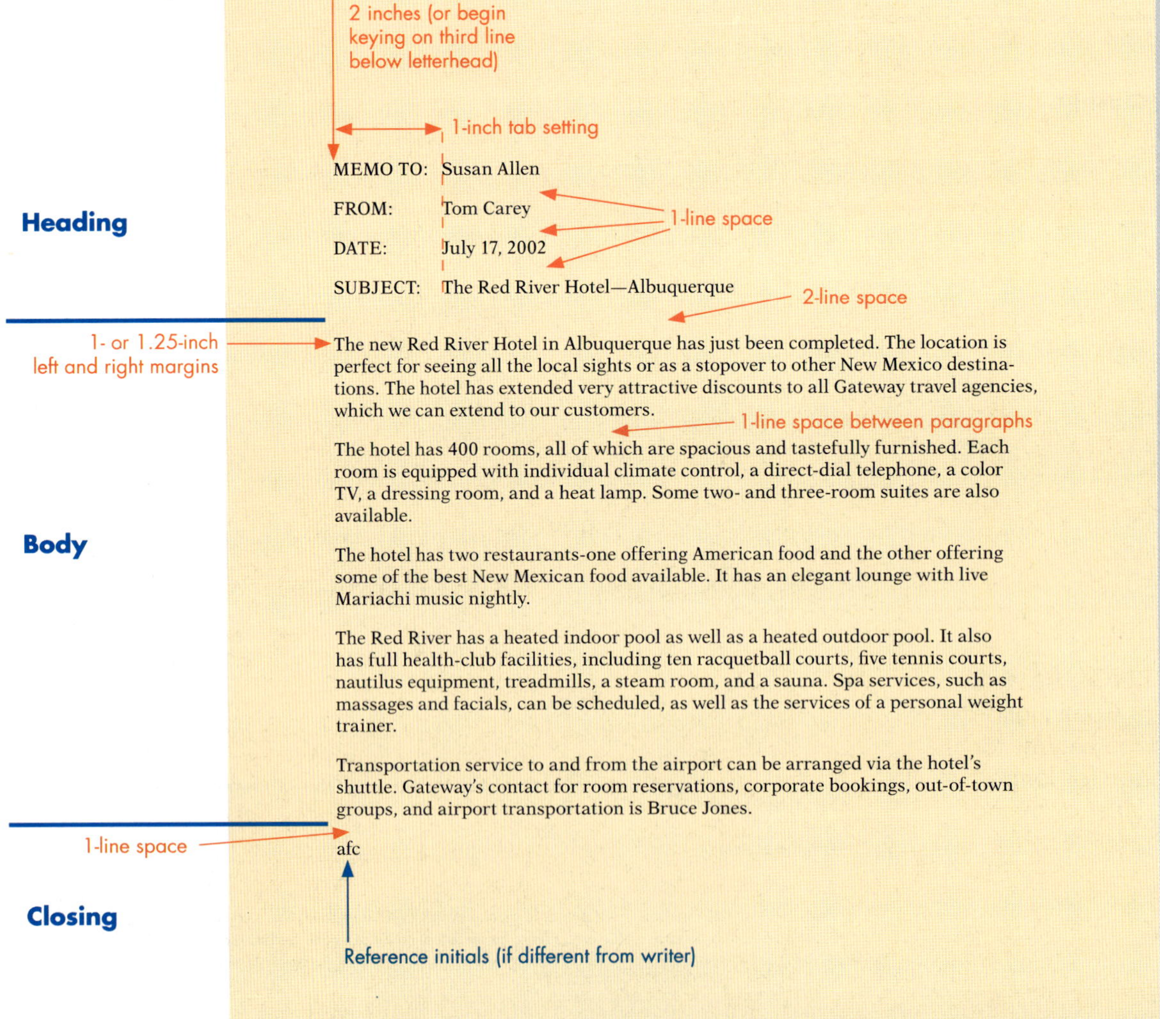
MEMO TO: Susan Allen

FROM: Tom Carey

DATE: July 17, 2002

SUBJECT: The Red River Hotel—Albuquerque

The new Red River Hotel in Albuquerque has just been completed. The location is perfect for seeing all the local sights or as a stopover to other New Mexico destinations. The hotel has extended very attractive discounts to all Gateway travel agencies, which we can extend to our customers.

The hotel has 400 rooms, all of which are spacious and tastefully furnished. Each room is equipped with individual climate control, a direct-dial telephone, a color TV, a dressing room, and a heat lamp. Some two- and three-room suites are also available.

The hotel has two restaurants-one offering American food and the other offering some of the best New Mexican food available. It has an elegant lounge with live Mariachi music nightly.

The Red River has a heated indoor pool as well as a heated outdoor pool. It also has full health-club facilities, including ten racquetball courts, five tennis courts, nautilus equipment, treadmills, a steam room, and a sauna. Spa services, such as massages and facials, can be scheduled, as well as the services of a personal weight trainer.

Transportation service to and from the airport can be arranged via the hotel's shuttle. Gateway's contact for room reservations, corporate bookings, out-of-town groups, and airport transportation is Bruce Jones.

afc

Word Glossary

Antonym Word that is opposite in meaning to another word. (6)

AutoComplete Automatic feature that suggests the completed word when you key the first four or more letters of a day, month, date, or AutoText entry. (6)

AutoCorrect Automatic feature that corrects commonly misspelled words as you key text. You can create AutoCorrect entries for text you frequently misspell. (6)

AutoRecover Word feature that automatically saves an open document in the background. This backup version of the document can then be recovered in case the original is lost or damaged in a power failure or because of a system problem. (2)

AutoText Automatic feature that can insert over 40 commonly used entries, including letter salutations and closings. You can also create AutoText entries for text you frequently use. (6)

Border Accent line or box added to text or to a page. (4)

Bulleted list List of text in which each item is preceded by a symbol, such as a bullet character. (4)

Cell Portion of a table that is formed by the intersection of rows and columns. (9)

Character style Named format that uses specific font and character formatting options. (3)

Clip art Ready-to-use drawings that can be inserted into a document. (11)

Clipboard Temporary storage area in the computer's memory used to hold text or other information that is cut or copied. (6)

Clips Multimedia files that can be clip art, photographs, movies, or sound files. (11)

Comment reference mark Vertical line that appears where a reviewer has inserted a comment; mark is color-coded to reviewer. (12)

Comments Electronic notes that you add to a document. (12)

Contiguous text Any group of characters, words, sentences, or paragraphs that follow one another. (2)

Continuation page header Header text that appears beginning on page 2 of a multi-page letter or memo, consisting of the addressee name, page number, and date. (8)

Continuous section break Section break that continues from the text preceding it and does not start on a new page. (8)

Crop Trim a picture so only a portion of the original shows. (11)

Cut and paste Method for moving text or other information by removing it from a document, storing it on the Clipboard, and then placing it in a new location. (6)

Cycle diagram Diagram that illustrates a process that has a continuous cycle. (11)

Data series Collections of related data points plotted in a chart. (11)

Datasheet Table in Microsoft Graph from which data is charted. (11)

Drag and drop Method for moving or copying text or other objects short distances by dragging them. (6)

Em dash Special character that produces a dash that is twice as wide as an en dash; used in sentences where you would normally insert two hyphens. (4)

En dash Special character that produces a dash slightly wider than a hyphen. (4)

End mark Short horizontal bar on the Word screen that indicates the end of the document. (1)

End-of-cell marker Character that indicates the end of the content of a cell in a table. (9)

End-of-row marker Character to the right of the gridline of a row in a table; indicates the end of the row. (9)

Filename Unique name given to a document saved in Word. (1)

First-line indent Indents only the first line of a paragraph. (4)

Floating graphic Graphic inserted in the drawing layer of a document so it can be positioned freely on the page, in front of or behind text and other objects. (11)

Font Type design applied to an entire set of characters, including all letters of the alphabet, numerals, punctuation marks, and other keyboard symbols. (3)

Footer Text that appears in the bottom margin of a page throughout a section or document. (8)

Gridlines Lines that mark the boundaries of cells in a table. (9)

Hanging indent Indents the second and subsequent lines of a paragraph. (4)

Hard page break Page break that you insert manually at a specific point in a document. (8)

Header row First row (or second if the table has a title row) of a table, in which each cell contains a heading for the column of text beneath it. (9)

Header Text that appears in the top margin of a page throughout a section or document. (8)

HTML (Hypertext Markup Language) File format used to make a document readable in a browser, on an intranet, or on the World Wide Web. (12)

Hyperlink Usually formatted as blue underlined text that you click to open a software feature (such as a dialog box or Help topic) or to go to an E-mail address or Web page. (3)

I-beam Shape of the mouse pointer when it's positioned in the text area. (1)

Indent markers On Word's ruler, rectangular or triangular objects that you can drag to control a paragraph's indents. (4)

Indent Setting that increases the distance between the side of a paragraph and the left or right margin. (4)

Inline graphic Graphic inserted in a line of text, on the same layer as the text. (11)

Insert mode Mode of text entry that lets you insert text without overwriting existing text. The Insert key on the keyboard is a toggle key, used to switch between Insert mode and Overtype mode. (1)

Insertion point Vertical blinking bar on the Word screen that indicates where an action will begin. (1)

Justify Paragraph alignment option that aligns text evenly along the left and right margins. (4)

Landscape Page orientation setting in which the page is wider than it is tall. Envelopes are printed Landscape. (7)

Leader tab Pattern of dots, dashes, or solid underlines used to fill the empty space to the left of a tab stop. (5)

Left indent Indents the left side of a paragraph. (4)

Legal blackline Word feature that lets you compare and merge two documents. The differences between the two documents appear in a new document as revision marks. (12)

Line space Amount of vertical space between lines of text in a paragraph; line spacing is measured in points and is generally one, one and a half, or two times the height of each line. (4)

Line-break character Symbol entered to start a new line within a paragraph. Inserted by pressing Shift + Enter. (2)

Margin Space at the top, bottom, left, and right of the document, from the edge of text to the edge of the paper. (4)

Markup balloon Contains comments or tracked changes in the margin of a document in Print Layout view. (12)

Markup Comments and tracked changes, such as insertions, deletions, and formatting changes. (12)

Menu bar Row of text items (menu names) that appears below the title bar. Each item, when clicked, displays a list of commands. (1)

Negative indent Text that extends into the left margin. (4)

Nonbreaking hyphen Hyphen that prevents Word from breaking hyphenated words at the end of a line. Inserted by pressing Ctrl + Shift + hyphen. (2)

Nonbreaking space Space between two words, defined by a special character, that prevents Word from breaking the two words at the end of a line. Inserted by pressing Ctrl + Shift + Spacebar. (2)

Noncontiguous text Text items (characters, words, sentences, or paragraphs) that do not follow one another but appear in different parts of a document. (2)

Nonprinting character Symbol for a tab, paragraph, space, or another special character that appears on the screen but not in the printed document. (2)

Numbered list List of text in which each item is numbered, using one of many numbering styles. (4)

Organizational chart Diagram that illustrates the top-down relationship of members of an organization. (11)

Orientation The direction (horizontal or vertical) in which a document is printed. (7)

Orphan First line of a paragraph, separated from the rest of the paragraph by a page break and displayed at the bottom of a page. (8)

Outline numbered list Text organized as a numbered outline. (4)

Overtype mode Mode of text entry that lets you key over existing text. The Insert key on the keyboard is a toggle key, used to switch between Insert mode and Overtype mode. (1)

Pagination Process of flowing text from line to line and from page to page. The process of determining when and where a new page should begin in a document. (8)

Paragraph alignment Position of a paragraph between its left and right margins. (4)

Paragraph mark On-screen symbol (¶) that marks the end of a paragraph. (1)

Paragraph space Amount of space (measured in points) before and after a paragraph. (4)

Paragraph style Formatting instructions applied to a paragraph. May include alignment, line spacing, paragraph spacing, indents, and character formatting. (4)

Placeholder text Formatted text in a template or other file that you replace with your own information. (7)

Point Measure of type size; 72 points equals one inch. (3)

Portrait Page orientation setting in which the page is taller than it is wide. Letters are printed Portrait. (7)

Positive indent Any indent that occurs between the left and right margins. (4)

Property Any information, such as the filename, date created, or file size, that describes a document. (2)

Proportional sizing Resizing an image while maintaining its relative height and width. (11)

Pyramid diagram Diagram that illustrates foundation-based relationships. (11)

Radial diagram Diagram that illustrates relationships of objects to a main object. (11)

Reviewer Person who adds a comment or tracked change to a document. (12)

Reviewing pane Narrow horizontal pane that opens at the bottom of the screen to display revisions and comments. (12)

Revision bars Black vertical lines that appear to the left of each line with a revision. (12)

Revision mark Mark Word applies to text that has been changed while the Track Changes feature is turned on. (12)

Right indent Indents the right side of a paragraph. (4)

Ruler Part of the Word screen that shows placement of indents, margins, and tabs. (1)

Sans serif Font characteristic in which the font (Arial, for example) has no decorative lines, or serifs, projecting from its characters. (3)

Scale Change the size of an image as a percentage of its original size. (11)

ScreenTip Brief explanation or identification of an on-screen item, such as a menu command, dialog box option, or toolbar button. (1)

Scroll bars Used with the mouse to move right or left and up or down within a document to view text not currently visible on-screen. (1)

Section break Double-dotted lines that appear on-screen to indicate the beginning and end of a section. (7)

Section Portion of a document that has its own formatting. (7)

Selection rectangle Box formed by the sizing handles of a selected object. (11)

Selection Selected portion of a document (or an entire document) that appears highlighted on the screen. (2)

Serif Font characteristic in which the font (Times New Roman, for example) has decorative lines projecting from its characters. (3)

Shading Various grades of color applied to the background of text. (4)

Shortcut menu Menu showing a list of commands relevant to a particular item. To display a shortcut menu, point to the item and right-click the mouse. (3)

Sizing handles Squares or circles that appear around the border of a selected object, used for resizing the object. (11)

Smart tags Document text—such as a date or address—that appears with a purple dotted underline and is recognized as data with which you can perform actions. For example, a name labeled with a smart tag can be added to a Microsoft Outlook contact list, without opening Outlook. (6)

Soft page break Page break that is inserted automatically by Word and continually adjusted to reflect changes in the document. (8)

Special characters Characters that do not appear on the keyboard, such as ¢, £, and §. (4)

Speech recognition Feature in Microsoft Office XP that lets you dictate text and commands into any Office program by using a microphone. (1)

Status bar Located at the bottom of the Word screen, it displays information about the task you are performing, shows the position of the insertion point, and shows the current mode of operation. (1)

Synonym Word that is similar in meaning to another word. (6)

Tab character Nonprinting character used to indent text. (2)

Tab marker Symbol used to indicate the type and location of a tab on the ruler. (5)

Tab stop Position of a tab setting. (5)

Table Grid of rows and columns that intersect to form cells. (9)

Target diagram Diagram that illustrates steps toward a goal. (11)

Task pane Pane to the right of the text area that gives easy access to a variety of functions. (1)

Template File that contains formatting information, styles, and text for a particular type of document. (7)

Text wrapping Graphic option that lets text flow around a floating graphic or that positions the object behind or in front of text. (11)

Thesaurus Tool used to look up synonyms for a selected word. (6)

Title bar Displays the name of the current document at the top of the Word screen. (1)

Toolbars Contain buttons you click to initiate a wide range of commands. Each button is represented by an icon. (1)

Tracked changes Revision marks that show where an insertion, deletion, or other editing change occurred. (12)

Venn diagram Diagram that illustrates where areas overlap between objects. (11)

Web theme Design elements (including color, background, and bullets) that provide an attractive look to a document or Web page. (12)

Widow Last line of a paragraph, separated from the rest of the paragraph by a page break and displayed at the top of a page. (8)

Wizard Automated and interactive template that walks you through the creation of a particular type of document. (7)

Excel Glossary

3-D effect Command that applies a three-dimensional look to an object so it appears to have a depth, as well as a height and width. (9)

3-D reference Cell address in a formula that refers to cells in another worksheet. (10)

Absolute reference Cell address that does not change when copied in a formula. (5)

Active cell Cell that appears outlined with a thick border on the worksheet. It is ready to accept data or a formula or, if it already contains data or a formula, it is ready to be modified. (1)

Adjustment handle Yellow diamond handle on an object used to change the shape and design of the object. (9)

Annuity Series of equal payments made at regular intervals for a set period of time. (6)

Argument Values or cell ranges between parentheses in a function, or what a function needs to complete its calculation. (5)

Arithmetic mean Average of values calculated by adding the values and then dividing the total by the number of values. (5)

Arithmetic operators Math symbols for calculations (+, -, /, and *). (2)

Ascending Sort order that arranges rows alphabetically (A to Z) or from low value to high value. (10)

AutoCalculate Feature that displays sums, averages, counts, maximum, or minimums in the status bar. (2)

AutoComplete Feature that displays a suggested label after you key the first character in a cell in the column. (4)

AutoCorrect Excel feature that corrects common spelling errors as you type. (3)

AutoFill command Command that copies or extends data from a cell or range of cells to adjacent cells. (3)

Autofit To size a column to its longest entry or size a row to the font. (2)

AutoFormat Built-in set of formatting instructions that applies fonts, colors, borders, and other formats to a range. (3)

AutoShape Common, recognized figure, shape, or outline on the Drawing toolbar. (9)

Border Line drawn around a cell or range of cells. (4)

Bounding box Rectangular outline around an object. (9)

Callout Descriptive text enclosed in a shape. Callouts typically include a line or arrow that points to data or an object on the worksheet. (9)

Category axis What is shown in a chart, created from row or column headings. (8)

Category title Optional label for the category axis. (8)

Cell Intersection of a column and row in a worksheet with an address or reference such as Cell B5. (1)

Cell address Column letter and row number that identifies a location in the worksheet. Example: B2 is the cell at the intersection of column B and row 2. In cell addresses, the column letter always is shown first. Also referred to as "cell reference." (1)

Cell alignment Excel feature that establishes how the contents of a cell are positioned within the cell. (4)

Cell reference See "cell address." (1)

Character space Average width of a numeric character in the current font. (2)

Character string Sequence of letters, numbers, or other symbols. (3)

Chart Visual display of worksheet data. (8)

Chart area Background of a chart. (8)

Chart title Optional title or name for the chart. (8)

Column Vertical group of cells in a worksheet, identified by an alphabetic letter or letters. (1)

Combination chart Single chart with multiple series using different chart types or number scales. (8)

Comment Cell attachment with descriptive or explanatory text. (9)

Data label Optional title shown for a value in a chart. (8)

Data marker Object that displays individual values, such as a bar or column. (8)

Data point One value from a data series. (8)

Data series Collection of related values in the worksheet. (8)

Descending Sort order that arranges rows in reverse alphabetical order (Z to A) or from high value to low value. (10)

Discussion comment Worksheet attachment that is visible in a browser for online collaboration. (9)

Drag-and-drop pointer Four-headed arrow that appears when the pointer rests on the edge of a cell. It is used to copy or cut a cell or range by dragging. (4)

Draw layer Invisible layer, separate from and on top of the worksheet, that holds drawing objects and images. (9)

Electronic spreadsheet software Computer software that produces reports with business and personal calculations, database management, or charts. (1)

Embedded chart Chart that appears on the same sheet as the worksheet data. (8)

Exponentiation Arithmetic operator that raises a number to a power. For example, 3^2 represents "3 to the second power" or 32, which means 3 x 3 or 9. (2)

Filename File identifier; name of a workbook. (2)

Fill handle Small rectangle at the lower right corner of a cell or range used for extending a series or copying data. (3)

Filter Specification or criteria applied to data in a list to display or hide certain rows. (10)

Financial function Function that performs a common business calculation involving money. (6)

Folder Storage location for work files on a disk, CD, or disk drive. (1)

Footer Data that prints at the bottom of each page in a worksheet. (3)

Formula Series of calculations, expressions, numbers, and operators to carry out an arithmetic command. (1)

Function Built-in mathematical formula included in Excel. (2)

Function Arguments dialog box Dialog box that displays Help and entry areas for completing a function. (5)

Fv Financial function argument that specifies the value of an amount at the end of the total time period. (6)

Gradient Blend of colors used to fill charts and other objects. (8)

Gridline Horizontal or vertical line in the plot area to mark values. (8)

Header Data that prints at the top of each page in a worksheet. (3)

Home Cell A1, the top left cell in the worksheet. This is the active cell when you open a new workbook. (1)

HTML Hypertext Markup Language, a widely used format for Web pages. (9)

Hyperlink Clickable text or object that, when clicked, displays another file, another program, or an Internet site/address. (7)

Integer Whole number, a number with no decimal or fractional parts. (7)

Interval Number of steps between values or labels in a series. (3)

Label Entry in a cell that begins with a letter. Labels are aligned at the left edge of the cell and are not used in calculations. (2)

Landscape Print orientation that prints a page that is wider than it is tall. (5)

Leading zero Zero shown as the first digit in a value. (4)

Legend Chart object that explains the colors, patterns, or symbols used in the chart. (8)

List Table of information with a row of headings and rows of data. (10)

Live link Formula that refers to another cell. (10)

Logical function Function involved in determining whether something is true. (6)

Marker Small black rectangle at the location for margin and column edges in Print Preview. (3)

Math hierarchy Alternative term for order of precedence. (5)

Mixed reference Cell address that adjusts either the row or the column when the formula is copied. (5)

Name box Text box with a drop-down arrow at the left edge of the formula bar. You can use it to view the address of the cell that is currently active or to move the pointer to another cell. (1)

Nested function Function inside another function. The second or third functions are used as arguments in the first function. (7)

Nper Financial function argument that specifies the total number of time periods or payments. (6)

Numeric keypad Set of number and symbol keys at the right of the keyboard. (4)

Object Separate element or part of a worksheet. (8)

Office Clipboard Temporary memory area that can hold up to 24 copied elements. (4)

Order of operation Alternative term for order of precedence. (5)

Order of precedence Mathematical rules that determine which part of a formula is calculated first. (5)

Page break Code that tells the printer to start a new page. On-screen it is shown as a solid or dashed line. (6)

Page orientation Print setting that determines landscape or portrait orientation. (5)

Pattern Cross-hatched, dotted, or other pattern used to fill charts and other objects. (8)

Pick from List Feature that displays a list of all labels already in a column. (4)

Pixel Single screen dot. (2)

Plot area Rectangular area bounded by the category and value axes. (8)

Portrait Print orientation that prints a page that is taller than it is wide. (5)

Print area Range of cells to be printed. (10)

Pv Financial function argument that specifies the current cash value of the money transaction. (6)

Range Group of cells that forms a rectangle. (2)

Range address Address for a range, showing the upper left cell address and the lower right cell address separated by a colon. (2)

Rate Financial function argument that specifies the interest rate for the time period. (6)

Relative reference Cell address that adjusts to the row or column where a copied formula is located. (5)

Replacement string Sequence of characters that is exchanged for existing data in the Replace command. (3)

Rotation handle Green circle that acts as a handle to rotate an object. (9)

Rounding To make a value larger or smaller depending on a specified digit to the left or right of the decimal point. (7)

Row Horizontal group of cells identified by a number in a worksheet. (1)

Scale Range of values on the value axis of a chart. The scaled is based on the data. (8)

ScreenTip Box on the screen with the name of a button. It appears when you rest the mouse pointer on the button. (1)

Secondary axis Separate set of values for a data series. (8)

Secondary scale Set of axis values that is different from the primary set. (8)

Selection handles Small black rectangles that surround an object, indicating it is selected or active. (8)

Selection pointer White cross-shaped pointer used to select or activate cells. (1)

Serial number Value assigned to a date in Excel. (7)

Series Sequence of numbers, dates, or times that follows a pattern. (2)

Shading Background pattern or color for a cell or range of cells. (4)

SmartTag Screen icon that flags or points out a problem or other issue to be checked. (1)

Style Set of formatting specifications for labels and values. (6)

Syntax Defines the necessary parts for a function, and the order of those parts. (5)

Template Model or sample workbook that can include font types, styles, alignment settings, borders, labels, values, and formulas. It is saved with an **.xlt** extension. (5)

Texture Grainy or non-smooth surface appearance used to fill charts and other objects. (8)

Tick mark Line or marker on an axis to display values. (8)

TIF Tagged Image Format, a popular file format for printed images. (9)

Tiled Object that repeats at a default size across the worksheet. (9)

Type Financial function argument that specifies whether the payment/deposit is made at the beginning or end of the period. (6)

Value Entry in a cell that begins with a number or an arithmetic symbol. A value is right-aligned in the cell and is included in calculations. Arithmetic symbols include =, -, and +. (2)

Value axis Horizontal or vertical grouping of values from the worksheet. (8)

View Set of display and print settings for a workbook. Includes column widths, hidden columns/rows, filters, window layout, and more. (10)

Volatile Formula results that change depending on the day/time. (7)

Whole number Value without a fraction or decimal. (5)

Wildcard Character that represents one or more letters or numbers (3). Keyboard character (* or ?) used in filters to represent unknown characters. (10)

Windows Clipboard Temporary memory area that holds cut or copied data. (4)

Wizard Series of dialog boxes that lead you step-by-step through the process of creating an object or using a complex feature. (8)

WordArt Application included in Microsoft Office that inserts shaped and colored text as an object. (9)

Workbook Excel file that holds worksheets with data. A workbook has an **.xls** filename extension. (1)

Worksheet Individual page or sheet in a workbook, shown by a tab at the bottom of the screen. (1)

Zoom size Setting that controls how much of the worksheet appears at once on the screen. (1)

PowerPoint Glossary

Activate To click a placeholder with the I-beam pointer. An activated placeholder can accept text that you key. (1)

Adjustment handle Yellow diamond-shaped handle found on many AutoShapes that is used to change a prominent feature of a shape. For example, you can change the size of an arrowhead relative to the body of the arrow, or you can change the tilt of a triangle. (6)

Animation scheme Preset visual effects that control how text appears on the screen during a slide show. For example, the title might fly into place in a spiral fashion, and the body text might fly up from the bottom one bullet point at a time. (2)

Annotation pen Pointer that you can use to "draw" on the screen during a slide show presentation. Annotation pen marks are not permanent. They disappear when the slide is no longer displayed. (1)

Arrow style Shape of an arrowhead on the end of a line. Arrowheads come in several varieties, including dots and diamonds. They can be placed on either end of a line or on both ends. (7)

AutoCorrect Feature that automatically corrects common spelling errors and typos as you key text. It can be turned on or off, and you can customize it by adding errors that you frequently make. (2)

AutoFit Feature that automatically adjusts the size of text when needed so that it fits in its text placeholder. (5)

AutoShape One of a group of predefined shapes that are easy to draw. Available shapes include rectangles, circles, and other basic shapes, arrows, flowchart symbols, stars, banners, callouts, lines, and connectors. (6)

Bitmap Picture made up of tiny colored dots. The more you enlarge a bitmap, the more blurred it becomes. You can crop bitmaps and easily change the contrast and brightness. Other changes can be made only by using a paint-type graphics program. Examples of bitmaps are pictures created in a paint program, photographs and other images that come from a scanner, and images that come from a digital camera. (6)

Body text Text in the body of a slide or other document. On a PowerPoint slide, body text is usually placed in a body text placeholder. (1)

Browser Software program, such as Microsoft Internet Explorer or Netscape Navigator, which interprets HTML files and formats them into Web pages for viewing on an intranet or on the Internet. (4)

Bullet A small dot, square, or other symbol placed to the left of each item in a list or series of paragraphs to add emphasis and readability. Bullets are often used in presentations and outlines. (1)

Clip art Ready-to-use graphic images that you can insert in a presentation. (6)

Clipboard Temporary storage place for cut and copied items. (3)

Collapse In the Outline pane, to hide the body text so that only the slide titles are displayed. (4)

Collate To print all the pages of one copy before starting to print the first page of the next copy. When pages are not collated, all the copies of page 1 are printed first, then all the copies of page 2, etc. (2)

Constrain To control moving or drawing an object in precise increments or proportions. When you constrain a rectangle as you draw it, it becomes a square; a constrained oval becomes a circle. (6)

Content layout Slide layout that includes placeholders for pictures, charts, clip art, and diagrams. (3)

Content placeholder Placeholder designed to hold tables, clip art, pictures, media clips, charts, or diagrams. (5)

Contiguous slides Slides that follow one after another. For example, slides numbered 2, 3, and 4 are contiguous. See "Noncontiguous slides." (2)

Copy To copy a selected object or text from a presentation and store it on the clipboard without removing the selection from its original place. (3)

Crop To trim the vertical or horizontal edges of a picture. (6)

Cropping handles Four heavy black dashes on the sides and the four heavy black corners of a picture selected for cropping. When you drag one of these handles with the cropping tool, an edge of the picture is cut away (trimmed). (6)

Custom color Color that you mix on the Custom tab of the Colors dialog box. You can create an infinite variety of custom colors. (7)

Cut To remove a selected object or text from a presentation and store it on the clipboard. (3)

Dash style Pattern of dashes and dots that make up a line. Styles include solid line, square dot, dash, and combinations of dashes and dots. Dash styles can be applied to object borders, lines, and arrows. (7)

Demote To move selected text to the next-lower outline or heading level. (3)

Design template Custom design that you apply to a presentation to give it a uniform color scheme and a particular "look." (3)

Destination When working with clipboard objects, the presentation or other document in which the objects are pasted. (3)

Distribute To evenly space selected objects, either in relation to one another or across the length or width of a slide. Objects can be distributed either horizontally or vertically. (8)

Docked toolbar Toolbar that is attached to one of the edges of the program window. (1)

Drag To move an object by pointing to it or selecting it, and then holding down the left mouse button while moving the mouse to a different location. (1)

Expand In the Outline pane, to display all the text contained in placeholders for each slide. (4)

Export To save a file in a format that can be read by a different application from the one in which it was created. For example, saving a PowerPoint presentation outline in a format that can be used by a word processor. (4)

Filename Unique name given to a PowerPoint presentation file, a Word document file, or files created by other applications. (1)

Fill color Color of an object. Objects can be filled with a solid color, a patterned, a gradient, a textured, a picture, or have no fill at all. (7)

Find command Locates specified text in a presentation. (2)

Flip To reverse an object either horizontally or vertically, creating a mirror image of the original object. (8)

Floating text Text contained in a text box (as differentiated from a text placeholder). Floating text can be formatted by using the tools on the Formatting toolbar, can be easily placed anywhere on a slide, and can be rotated. (6)

Floating toolbar Toolbar that is not attached to the edge of the program window. It can be moved freely by dragging its title bar. (1)

Font Set of text characters with a specific design, for example, Arial or Times New Roman. (5)

Footer Text that appears at the bottom of each slide, notes page, or handouts page. (2)

Format Painter Button on the Standard toolbar used to copy formatting from one object to another. (7)

Gradient fill Object fill effect in which one color blends or fades into another color. (7)

Grayscale Rendering of slides in shades of gray for printing on a black-and-white printer. (2)

Group To combine selected objects so that they behave as one object. (8)

Handout Printout that contains 1, 2, 3, 4, 6, or 9 PowerPoint slides per page. (1)

Header Text that appears at the top of each slide, notes page, or handouts page. (2)

HTML Acronym for Hypertext Markup Language. See "Hypertext Markup Language." (4)

Hyperlink Text or graphic object you click to move to another slide, another application, or a location on the Internet. Hyperlinks are often displayed as contrasting underlined text. (4)

Hypertext Markup Language File format used to make a file readable when using a browser on the Internet or on an intranet. (4).

I-beam Mouse pointer that has the shape of an uppercase "I." The I-beam pointer indicates a location where you can insert text. (1)

Import To use a file in an application that was created with a different application. For example, opening a word-processed outline in PowerPoint. (4)

Insertion point Vertical flashing bar indicating the position where text that you key will be inserted. Clicking an I-beam mouse pointer is one way to place an insertion point. (1)

Line style Type of border or outline that an object has. Options include single, double, and triple lines of varying line weights. (7)

Line weight Thickness of a line measured in points. (7)

Master slide Slide that stores a design template's arrangement for slides, including the size and position of placeholders, text formatting, and graphic elements. There are two types of master slides: the slide master and the title master. (5)

Menu bar Displays the names of menus you use to perform various tasks. You can open menus by using the mouse or the keyboard. (1)

Noncontiguous slides Slides that do not follow one after another. For example, slides numbered 1, 4, 5, and 7 are noncontiguous. See "Contiguous slides." (2)

Notes page Printout containing a slide image at the top of the page and speaker's notes that were entered in the Notes pane underneath. Notes pages are often used by speakers as cue cards during a presentation. (3)

Notes pane Area where you can add presentation notes for either the presenter or the audience. The Notes pane is located below the Slide pane. (1)

Outline and Slides pane Area that can display either an outline of the presentation's text or thumbnails of the presentation's slides. You choose either Outline or Slides by clicking the appropriate tab. (1)

Paste To insert an item stored on the clipboard at the current location. (3)

Placeholder Box that can contain title text, body text, pictures, or other objects. Most slide layouts contain placeholders. A placeholder's formatting, size, and position is set on a master slide. (1)

Point Unit of measure for the height of the tallest character in a font set. There are 72 points to an inch. (5)

Print preview Feature that enables you to see what your printed pages will look like before you actually print them. You can view preview pages in black-and-white, grayscale, or color. (1)

Promote To move selected text to the next-higher outline or heading level. (3)

Proofreaders' marks Special notation used to mark up a printed draft with changes to be made before final printing. Some proofreaders' marks might be confusing if you are unfamiliar with them. For example, a hand-written "=" indicates that a hyphen is to be inserted. (1)

Proportion Relationship between the height and width of an object. When an object is resized, its proportions will be preserved if both the height and width of the object change at the same rate or percentage. An object that is out of proportion is either too tall and skinny, or too short and wide. (6)

Regroup Recombine objects that were at one time part of the same group. (8)

Replace command Locates specified text in a presentation and replaces it with different text that you specify. (2)

Rich text format Standard file type that converts document formatting into instructions that Microsoft programs and many other programs can read and interpret. (4)

Rotation handle Green handle that appears above a selected object. You change the rotation of an object by dragging the rotation handle. You constrain the rotation to 15-degree increments by holding down s while rotating the object. (6)

RTF Acronym for rich text format. See "Rich text format." (4)

Sample text Text provided by the AutoContent Wizard that suggests content for your presentation. You change the sample text to suit the needs of your presentation. (2)

ScreenTip Box that identifies the name of an on-screen object when you point to the object. (1)

Scroll bars Used with the mouse to move a slide view or outline text right or left, and up or down. You can also use the vertical scroll bar to move from slide to slide. (1)

Selection rectangle Dotted box that you draw by dragging the mouse pointer to select objects on a slide. All objects contained inside the rectangle are selected. (8)

Sizing handle One of eight small circles along the border of a selected text placeholder or other object. It is used to change the size and shape of the placeholder or object. (5)

Slide layout Arrangement of text and/or object placeholders that can be applied to a new or existing slide. (3)

Slide master Master slide that includes a title text placeholder and a body text placeholder. The slide master controls how all slides except title slides are arranged. (5)

Slide pane Area where you create, edit, and display presentation slides. (1)

Slide transition Visual effect that you can apply to enhance the way the screen changes during a slide show as you move from one slide to another. For example, the current slide could fade to a black screen before the next slide appears. (2)

Source When working with clipboard objects, the presentation or other document from which the objects were cut or copied. (3)

Speaker's notes Notes that can be entered for each slide in a presentation. Speaker's notes can be printed and then used to assist the speaker during a presentation, or they can add supplemental information to include with presentations published on the Web. (3)

Spelling checker Feature that corrects spelling by comparing words to an internal dictionary file. (2)

Standard color Premixed color that you choose by clicking a sample on the Standard tab of the Colors dialog box. (7)

Status bar Displays information about the presentation you're working on. It is located at the bottom of the PowerPoint window. (1)

Style checker Feature that checks your presentation for consistency in punctuation and capitalization, as well as the number of fonts and text sizes used. (2)

Table Organized arrangement of information in rows and columns, generally used for reference purposes. (5)

Task pane Area that appears at appropriate times on the right side of the PowerPoint window, displaying a list of commands that are relevant to the task on which you are currently working. (1)

Text attributes Styles and effects applied to text. For example, bold, italic, underline, shadow. (5)

Text layout Slide layout that includes only text placeholders.(3)

Thumbnail Miniature version of a graphic image. In PowerPoint, a miniature version of a slide is often referred to as a "thumbnail." (1)

Title bar Colored bar (usually blue) at the top of most windows that contains identifying information. In the case of the PowerPoint main window, the title bar contains the name of the presentation. (1)

Title master Master slide that includes text placeholders for the title and subtitle of a title slide. (5)

Title text Text that usually appears at the top of a PowerPoint slide. Title text is usually placed in a title text placeholder. (1)

Toggle button Toolbar button that turns a feature on or off by clicking it. (5)

Toolbar Row of buttons that give instant access to a wide range of commands. Each button is represented by an icon and accessed by using the mouse. PowerPoint opens with the Standard and Formatting toolbars displayed in abbreviated form on one line at the top of the screen and the

Drawing toolbar at the bottom of the screen. (1)

Transition, Slide See "Slide transition." (2)

Ungroup To separate a group of objects into its components. When an object is ungrouped, each of its elements behaves as an individual object. (8)

Vector drawing Picture made up of an arrangement of line segments and shapes that can be scaled to any size or aspect ratio without blurring. Vector drawings can be modified in PowerPoint by recoloring and by adding, removing, and rearranging individual elements. An AutoShape is an example of a simple vector drawing. (6)

View buttons Three buttons located on the lower-left corner of the PowerPoint window. You use these buttons to switch between Normal view (the default), Slide Sorter view, and Slide Show view. (1)

Wizard Online guide that leads you through the steps to complete a task. (2)

Zoom To change the magnification of either the Outline and Slides pane or the Slide pane, whichever one is active. Zoom changes the size at which you view objects, but not their actual size. (4)

Access Glossary

AND condition Used when two or more parameters must be true. (3)

AutoCorrect Feature that corrects spelling and capitalization errors as you type. (2)

AutoForm Form layout that includes all fields in a specified arrangement. (6)

AutoFormat Predefined style template for forms and reports. (6)

AutoReport Default report that includes a style and all fields for the query or table; can be either columnar or tabular. (7)

Bound control Control that is linked to a field in a recordset. (6)

Bound object frame Control in a form or report that displays OLE data. (7)

Calculated control Control that uses an expression or formula as its data source. (6)

Caption The field property that controls the column selector in Datasheet View. (4)

Common expression Control with built-in commands to display dates, times, and page numbers. (7)

Conditional formatting Formatting that displays under certain conditions. (7)

Control Object that displays information, performs an action, or enhances appearance in a form, report, or data access page. (2)

Control Object appearing on a form in Design View that displays data, performs an action, or adds a design element. A control can be bound, unbound, or calculated. (6)

Criteria Requirements or specifications data must meet. (1)

Criteria Text strings or expressions used to find matching records. (3)

Data Access Page Object that acts like a form but whose controls are Internet compatible. A direct link is established between the Data Access Page and the source recordset. (6)

Data type Type of information in a field (such as alphabetic, numeric, or OLE object). Set in Design View. (4)

Database integrity Stability and soundness of the data. (3)

Database properties Dialog box that provides descriptive information about the database, such as filenames, most recent editing date, author, size of database, and others. (1)

Database software Collection of data that tracks information for a business or individual. (1)

Database template A wizard that creates a functional database structure based on user selections. (4)

Datasheet View Way of looking at a table that displays the records in rows and columns, similar to a spreadsheet. (1)

Default value Field property that sets the same value for all new records. (5)

Default View Form property that determines how many forms appear onscreen at once. (2)

Design View Screen used for determining, formatting, and editing the structure or layout of a table, a form, a query, or a report. (1)

Detail section Form or report part that shows data for one record. (6)

Dynaset Results of a query. If data is edited or changed in the dynaset, the source table's data will be changed also. (1)

Dynaset Recordset created by a query allowing dynamic changes to the data in the source table. (3)

Expression Any legal combination of text, numbers, or symbols that represents a value. (6)

Expression Builder Dialog box that enables you to build a formula or calculation by selecting field names, constants, functions, or other elements. (6)

Field Individual piece of information in a record, represented by a column in a table. (1)

Field description Optional clarification of purpose of a field in a table. Set in Design View. (4)

Field name A description of the information in a field (a column). (4)

Field properties Formats, settings, and other attributes set in Design View for a table. (4)

Filter Used to create a subset of records that match criteria. (3)

Flat Database Database that contains all data in a single table. (1)

Foreign key field Field that refers to the primary key field in the related table. (5)

Form Database object that displays information from the table or query in an attractive, easy-to-read screen format. Forms can be used to edit and add records. (1)

Form Footer Section that appears once at the bottom of a form. (6)

Form Header Section that appears once at the top of a form. (6)

Form View Screen layout for a record that is designed to be easy to read and to improve the speed and accuracy of data entry. (2)

Format Field property that determines how data is displayed. (5)

Format Painter Tool that copies the font, size, color, and alignment from one control to another. (7)

Group Section of a report that organizes or categorizes the records by a particular field. (7)

Group Footer Section of a report that prints once at the bottom of each group. (7)

Group Header Section of a report that prints once at the top of each group. (7)

HTML Hypertext Markup Language, a standard formatting language for Web documents. (6)

Indeterminate relationship Relationship that occurs when Access does not have enough information to determine the relationship between the two tables. (5)

Input mask Field property that displays a pattern for entering data. (5)

Join line Graphical representation of a relationship between two tables. Each end of the join line connects to a related field in a table.(5)

Label Control that shows text such as a title. (2)

Layout Design of a table, report, or form. (1)

Leszynski Naming Conventions Object-naming standard widely recognized and used by database designers. Object names are preceded with standardized prefixes signifying their object type. (LNC) (1)

Lookup field Field property that displays input choices from another table, enabling you to enter data by choosing from a list. (5)

Macro Database object used to run routine tasks with a series of commands. (1)

Main Switchboard A form that helps a user navigate around a database. (4)

Module Database object used to run Visual Basic for Applications (VBA) functions and procedures. (1)

Null value Value that is nothing. Blank field that does not contain either numbers or spaces. (3)

Object Element or part of a database. Main objects include tables, queries, forms, reports, pages, macros, and modules. (1)

OLE object Object linking and embedding for a data type created in another program. Examples include picture, sound, and movie files. (2)

One-To-Many relationship Relationship that occurs when the common field is a primary key in the first table and not a primary key in the second table. (5)

One-To-One relationship Relationship that occurs when the common fields in both the first and second tables are primary keys. (5)

OR condition Used when only one of two or more parameters must be true. (3)

Page Database object used to post a table or query as a Web page. (1)

Page Footer Section that prints at the bottom of each printed page. (6)

Page Header Section that prints at the top of each printed page. (6)

Pivot Chart View Screen with data displayed in a chart form. (1)

Pivot Table View Screen with data displayed in a table format with columns and rows. (1)

Primary Key Field whose data is different for each record. Used to identify record. (3)

Property sheet Dialog box that lists format, data, and other settings for an object. (2)

Property sheet List of settings for an object. (6)

Query Database object that extracts information from the table or other queries. (1)

Record One entity (person, place, thing, or event) in a table holding related data, shown as a row. (1)

Record selector Icon that marks the current or active record. It changes shape depending on the status of the record. (1)

Recordset Collection of data from a table or query. (2)

Referential integrity Database rules for checking and validating data entry; keeps track of changes in related tables. (5)

Relational database management system Database software that uses relationships between data to eliminate duplication of data. (1)

Relationship Link or connection between two tables sharing a common field. (5)

Report Database object that displays information from a table or query in a printable page format. (1)

Report Footer Section of a report that prints once at the bottom (last page) of the report. (7)

Report Header Section of a report that prints once at the top (first page) of the report. (7)

Report Page Footer Section of a report that prints at the bottom of every page. (7)

Report Page Header Section of a report that prints at the top of every page. (7)

ScreenTip Name or function of an object. It appears when you rest the mouse pointer on the object. (1)

Selection handles Small black rectangles around an active object in a form or report. (6)

Selection marquee The dotted line indicating that an object is selected. The settings for the selection marquee can be adjusted, requiring objects to be selected by clicking and dragging over the entire object or only over a portion of an object. (7)

Sizing handle Any selection handle on a control except the top left one. Sizing handles are used to adjust the width or height of the control. (6)

Subdatasheet A related table nested within a primary table. The subdatasheet shows records from the related table while user is in the primary table. (5)

Tab order Form setting that determines insertion point movement through a form. (6)

Table Database object that stores related data in records with fields. (1)

Text box Object that shows data from a field in a form, report, or data access page. (2)

Unbound control Control that is not linked to a recordset; includes titles, lines or images. (6)

Wildcards Search characters (* # ?) used to represent one or more alphabetical or numerical positions. (3)

Zoom dialog box A text-editing window for lengthy text.

Word Index

D

E

F

G

U

V

W

Excel Index

C

PowerPoint Index

R

S

Access Index

D

M

N

O

P

Q

R

S

Photo Credits

Page 3: PhotoDisc, Inc.; Page 6: Clark/FPG; Rogers/FPG; Keller/FPG; Krasowitz/FPG; Wilson/FPG; Krasowitz/FPG; Scott/FPG; Reggie Parker Images Unlimited/FPG; Luria/FPG; Luria/FPG; Chapple/FPG; Krasowitz/FPG; Page 7: PhotoDisc, Inc.;Page 89: PhotoDisc, Inc.; Page 181: PhotoDisc, Inc.; Page 249: PhotoDisc, Inc.; Page 299: PhotoDisc, Inc.; Page 359: PhotoDisc, Inc.; PhotoDisc, Inc.; PhotoDisc, Inc.; PhotoDisc, Inc.; Page 360: PhotoDisc, Inc.; Page 361: PhotoDisc, Inc.; Page 495: PhotoDisc, Inc.; Page 583: PhotoDisc, Inc.; Page 692: PhotoDisc, Inc.; Page 693: Balterman/FPG; Page 694: Lang/FPG; Luria/FPG; TaylorFPG; Gage/FPG; Page 695: PhotoDisk, Inc.; Page 769: PhotoDisc, Inc.; Page 883: PhotoDisc, Inc.; Page 995: Laubacher/FPG; Chris/FPG; Telegraph Color Library/FPG; Losh/FPG; Rathe/FPG; Page 996: Leo Images Photography; Leo Images Photography; Leo Images Photography; Leo Images Photography; Page 999: PhotoDisc, Inc.; Page 1115: PhotoDisc, Inc.; Page A-1: PhotoDisc, Inc.;